W9-BCO-189

Principles of
Risk Management and Insurance

The Addison-Wesley Series in Finance

Principles of
RISK MANAGEMENT
AND INSURANCE

GEORGE E. REJDA

NINTH EDITION

Addison
Wesley

Boston San Francisco New York
London Toronto Sydney Tokyo Singapore Madrid
Mexico City Munich Paris Cape Town Hong Kong Montreal

Editor-In-Chief: Denise Clinton
Aquisitions Editor: Donna Battista
Director of Development: Sylvia Mallory
Managing Editor: Jim Rigney
Editorial Assistant: Deb Tokars
Senior Production Supervisor: Nancy Fenton
Marketing Manager: Deborah Meredith
Senior Manufacturing Buyer: Hugh Crawford
Cover Design: Regina Hagen Kolenda
Media Producer: Bethany Tidd
Supplements Coordinator: Diana Theriault
Rights and Permissions Advisor: Dana Weightman
Project Coordination, Text Design, Art Studio,
    and Electronic Page Makeup: Thompson Steele, Inc.
Cover photos: PictureQuest

Library of Congress Cataloging-in-Publication Data

Rejda, George E., 1931-
    Principles of risk management and insurance / George E. Rejda.—9th ed.
        p.   cm. (Addison-Wesley series in finance)
    Includes bibliographical references and index.
    ISBN 0-321-23687-4 (alk. paper)
    1. Insurance.   3. Risk (Insurance).   3. Risk management.   I. Title. II. Series

HG8051.R44   2004
368—dc22

                                        2004047606

1 2 3 4 5 6 7 8 9 10—CRW—08 07 06 05 04

CONTENTS

PREFACE

The eighth edition of *Principles of Risk Management and Insurance* appeared two years ago. Since that time, a number of significant events have roused the nation. The United States has waged a pre-emptive and controversial war on Iraq with the hope of finding weapons of mass destruction; the federal Department of Homeland Security was created to protect the country against terrorism; the mutual fund industry became the target of a federal investigation because of major scandals involving late trading and market timing; key executives of major corporations have received lengthy prison terms because of securities fraud and illegal accounting practices; and the breathtaking pictures and spacecraft exploration of Mars by the National Aeronautics and Space Administration (NASA) reveal signs of water on that planet.

Fast-forward to the present. The search for weapons of mass destruction in Iraq continues with little success; talk-show hosts endlessly debate the merits of the war in Iraq; Saddam Hussein, the cruel and brutal former dictator of Iraq, is in custody and faces charges as a war criminal; and Al-Qaida terrorists and suicide bombers continue to kill and maim innocent people. The Securities and Exchange Commission (SEC) is proceeding with its investigation of the mutual funds industry; and hurricanes, tornadoes, floods, and earthquakes continue their awesome destruction. To say that we live in a risky and dangerous world is an enormous understatement.

Likewise, the insurance industry has experienced rapid changes in the last two years. The property and casualty industry incurred severe underwriting losses from the September 11, 2001, terrorist attacks. After raising premiums sharply in response to the attacks, the industry is slowly returning to profitability with a significant reduction in the combined loss and expense ratio. Other noteworthy changes include passage of the Terrorism Risk Insurance Act of 2002, which provides a fed-

eral backup against future terrorist attacks; increased emphasis on enterprise risk management in commercial risk management programs; continuing medical malpractice insurance problems; and the increased use of credit-based insurance scores for purposes of underwriting and rating. In addition, the Insurance Services Office (ISO) has drafted a new 2005 Personal Auto Policy (PAP); new commercial lines coverages have been introduced; and a new Medicare prescription law has been passed that covers prescription drugs for beneficiaries beginning in 2006. The latest Board of Trustees reports show that the financial position of Medicare has deteriorated rapidly, and the date of exhaustion of the Hospital Insurance (HI) trust fund has been moved forward by seven years, to 2019. Finally, mergers and consolidation of insurers continue, but at a slower pace, and congressional hearings have been held to examine the quality of state regulation of the insurance industry.

The ninth edition of *Principles of Risk Management and Insurance* discusses these and other significant changes. As in earlier editions, the text is designed for a beginning undergraduate course in risk management and insurance with no prerequisites. Thoroughly revised and updated, the ninth edition provides a complete and current treatment of major areas in risk management and insurance. Coverage includes basic concepts of risk and insurance, introductory and advanced topics in risk management, legal principles, property and liability insurance, life and health insurance, employee benefits, social insurance, and functional and financial operations of insurers. The ninth edition once again places primary emphasis on the consumers of insurance and blends basic risk management and insurance principles with consumer considerations. In addition, the text addresses personal risk management and financial planning, so that students can apply basic concepts immediately to their own lives.

CONTENT CHANGES IN THE NINTH EDITION

Thoroughly updated, the ninth edition provides an in-depth analysis of current issues, which readers have come to expect from *Principles of Risk Management and Insurance*. Timely changes include the following:

1. **Increased emphasis on enterprise risk management.** Chapters 1 and 3 introduce students to the emerging concept of enterprise risk management in commercial risk management programs. Chapter 4 discusses enterprise risk management in greater detail and provides new application problems for students to solve.

2. **Updated discussion of the medical malpractice problem.** Chapter 7 includes a timely and updated discussion of the current medical malpractice insurance problem and new approaches for dealing with the problem.

3. **Credit-Based Insurance Scores.** Credit-based insurance scores are becoming more important in the underwriting and rating of homeowners insurance and personal auto insurance. Chapters 9, 11, and 28 provide in-depth discussions of this controversial topic.

4. **New 2005 Personal Auto Policy (PAP).** The Insurance Service Office (ISO) is introducing a revised PAP that will become effective in most jurisdictions in 2005. Chapter 10 summarizes the important changes in the revised PAP.

5. **New approaches for dealing with uninsured drivers.** Chapter 11 discusses two novel approaches for dealing with the problem of uninsured drivers—low-cost auto insurance for low-income drivers, and "no pay, no play" laws that prohibit uninsured motorists from suing negligent drivers for noneconomic damages in the event of an auto accident.

6. **Deletion of material on federal crop insurance.** Because few instructors discuss federal crop insurance in the introductory course, the material on federal crop insurance discussed in Chapter 12 has been deleted.

7. **Updated discussion of commercial lines coverages.** Many instructors use the text in an advanced course in property and liability insurance. Chapters 13–15 provide an updated discussion of major commercial property, liability, and crime insurance coverages.

8. **New material on life insurance.** Chapter 16 discusses the use of interactive calculators for determining the amount of life insurance to own and the opportunity cost of owning life insurance. Chapter 17 provides an expanded discussion of variable universal life insurance and the risks involved in purchasing this type of life insurance. The desirability of cash-value life insurance is re-examined in light of recent research studies by the Consumer Federation of America.

9. **Annuities and individual retirement accounts (IRAs).** Chapter 20 provides an updated discussion of annuities and individual retirement accounts (IRAs); identifies the risks associated with variable annuities; and points out factors to consider in the selection of a traditional IRA or Roth IRA.

10. **Updated discussion of managed care plans.** Chapter 22 gives readers an updated discussion of managed care health insurance plans, examines new developments in managed care plans, and discusses new cost containment techniques.

11. **Updated discussion of qualified retirement plans.** Chapter 23 features an updated discussion of major employer-sponsored retirement plans and funding problems in defined benefit retirement plans.

12. **New Medicare prescription drug program.** Chapter 24 provides a detailed discussion of the controversial Medicare Prescription Drug, Improvement, and Modernization Act of 2003. The new Medicare law provides coverage for prescription drugs for beneficiaries beginning in 2006 and contains several controversial provisions to modernize Medicare.

13. **Medicare financial crisis.** Chapter 24 also discusses the rapid deterioration in the financial condition of Medicare. The 2004 Board of

Trustees report showed that the Hospital Insurance (HI) trust fund will have a negative cash flow for 2004, and the projected date of exhaustion of the trust fund has been moved forward seven years to 2019, down from 2026 in last year's report.

14. **Role of insurance companies in the financial services industry.** Chapter 25 provides new material on the current role of insurance companies in the financial services industry.

15. **Terrorism Risk Insurance Act of 2002.** Chapter 26 outlines the major characteristics of the Terrorism Risk Insurance Act of 2002, which provides a federal backup for insurers in the event of future terrorist attacks.

16. **State regulation of insurance.** Chapter 28 discusses several approaches by the National Association of Insurance Commissioners to update and modernize state regulation of the insurance industry.

KEY FEATURES OF THE NINTH EDITION

1. **New *Insight* boxes.** Instructors and students have enthusiastically endorsed the *Insight* boxes in previous editions. *Insights* are powerful learning tools that provide real-world applications of key principles or concepts discussed in the chapter. The majority of *Insights* in the previous edition have been replaced by compelling new ones. Readers should look for these attention grabbers and others throughout the text:

- Study: Surgeons Leave Tools Inside 1500 Patients a Year
- How Many Complaints Have Been Filed Against Your Insurance Company?
- Skyrocketing Premiums Force Doctors to Seek Other Options for Coverage
- Variable Universal Life Insurance: Is It Worth It?
- Another Look at Cash Value Life Insurance as an Investment

- Credit Insurance Overcharges Cost Consumers Billions of Dollars Annually
- How to Increase the Odds of Being Killed or Injured While Driving
- The Ten Top Reasons to Purchase the Rental Car Collision Damage Waiver (CDW)
- Using a Cell Phone While Driving Can Be Dangerous to Your Health
- More Drivers Are on the Roads; Who Are You Most Likely to Run Into? A Student? A Politician? A Librarian?
- Which States Give Defendants the Best Legal Deal?
- Medical Errors Rank with Highway Accidents and Breast Cancer as a Major Killer in the United States
- Mold Claims Remain a Critical Problem in Homeowners Insurance
- What Is Covered under a Homeowners Policy if a Storm Occurs?
- Who Let the Dogs Out?—Avoid Being Bitten by a Lawsuit
- Identity Theft Insurance Can Protect Your Good Name
- Warning: Internet Shopping May Not Produce the Best Prices for Life Insurance
- Annuity Death Benefit Starts Paying Its Way
- Ten Questions to Answer Before You Buy a Variable Annuity
- Traditional vs. Roth: Which Is Right for You?
- Study Shows U.S. Doctors Are Not Following Guidelines
- How to Get Health Insurance If You Are Uninsurable

- Nearly Two-Thirds of Corporate Pension Plans Underfunded, Watson Wyatt Research Finds

- Ten Common 401(k) Mistakes

2. Updated Internet resources. The ninth edition provides updated Web sites that students can easily access. The ninth edition also has an Internet site (available at www.aw-bc.com/rejda). After studying each chapter, students can take a self-administered test online and get instant feedback on how well they have mastered the material.

3. New review and application questions. Most chapters contain new review and application questions and problems to help students understand the material discussed in the chapter.

4. Technical accuracy. As in past editions, numerous risk management and insurance experts have reviewed the text for technical accuracy, especially in areas where changes have occurred rapidly. The ninth edition offers technically accurate and up-to-date material.

5. Clarity in writing. Risk management and insurance topics can intimidate students if presented in a disjointed or abstract manner. Because readability is critical, the text presents principles and concepts clearly and directly, and strives to be the most user-friendly of texts.

SUPPLEMENTS

The ninth edition contains a number of supplementary materials to help busy instructors save time and teach more effectively. The following supplements are available to qualified domestic adopters, but in some cases may not be available to international adopters.

Companion Web Site. As stated earlier, the ninth edition is accompanied by an Internet site at www.aw-bc.com/rejda that allows students to work through a variety of exercises and to take a self-assessment quiz after studying the chapter material. The Web site also provides an online syllabus builder that allows instructors to create a calendar of assignments for each class and to track student activity with an electronic grade book.

Instructor's Manual with Transparency Masters. Designed to reduce start-up costs and class preparation time, this comprehensive manual contains teaching notes; lecture outlines; answers to all end-of-chapter review, application, and case questions; and transparency masters that illustrate key points.

Revised Test Bank. Prepared by Professor Michael J. McNamara of Washington State University, this revised test bank enables instructors to construct objective exams quickly and easily. The test bank contains numerous mini-case objective questions that test the critical thinking and analytical skills of students.

Study Guide. Also prepared by Michael J. McNamara, this study tool is an improvement over traditional study guides. Its many exercises enable students to apply basic concepts to their own personal risk management program. Each chapter contains objective questions similar to the test bank questions, worksheets (where appropriate) for solving end-of-chapter cases, and answers to all questions at the end of each chapter for quick reference and self-testing.

Instructor's Resource CD-ROM. Fully compatible with Windows and Macintosh computers, this CD-ROM provides a number of resources. First, PowerPoint lecture slides are available that enhance classroom performance. Second, the CD-ROM contains Microsoft Word files for the entire contents of the instructor's manual. Finally, the CD-ROM includes computerized test bank files. The easy-to-use software is a valuable test preparation tool that allows busy professors to view, edit, and add questions.

ACKNOWLEDGMENTS

A market-leading textbook is never written alone. I owe an enormous intellectual debt to many people for their kind and gracious assistance. Numerous educators, risk management experts, and industry personnel have taken time out of their busy schedules to review part or all of the ninth edition, to provide supplementary materials, to make valuable comments, or to provide other assistance. They include the following:

Patricia Arnold, The University of Texas at Austin

Steve Avila, Ball State University

Burton T. Beam, Jr., The American College

Joseph M. Belth, Professor Emeritus, Indiana University

Wayne Biddle, Grove City College

John Bishop, East Carolina University

James Carson, Florida State University

Louis Cheng, Hong Kong Polytechnic

Pat Cheshier, California State University, Sacramento

Mark Cross, Miami University of Ohio

Jeff DeTurris, Insurance Services Office (ISO)

Michael Finke, University of Missouri, Columbia

George Flanigan, Illinois State University

Arthur L. Flitner, American Institute for Chartered Property Casualty Underwriters

Edward Graves, The American College

Daniel Klein, Bowling Green State University

Gene C. Lai, Washington State University

Michael J. McNamara, Washington State University

Robert J. Myers, former chief actuary, Social Security Administration

Rob Olson, International Risk Management Institute (IRMI)

Mark Power, Iowa State University

William H. Rabel, Life Office Management Association (LOMA)

Clarence Rose, Radford University

Philip Swicegood, Gardner-Webb University

Kenn B. Tacchino, Widener University

Eric Wiening, Insurance and Risk Management/Author-Educator-Consultant

Millicent W. Workman, Director of Risk Financing, Baptist Memorial Health Care Corporation

Special thanks are due Professor Michael J. McNamara of Washington State University. Professor McNamara revised Chapter 4 on advanced topics in risk management, and the study guide as well. He also designed new risk management application problems for students to solve in Chapter 4, revised the test bank, and reviewed each chapter for technical accuracy. As a result, the ninth edition is a substantially improved product.

I would also like to thank Sylvia Mallory and Donna Battista at Addison-Wesley for their substantive editorial comments, marketing insights, and technical suggestions. Dana Weightman at Addison-Wesley resolved many difficult and delicate problems in obtaining permission to use copyrighted material.

Finally, the fundamental objective underlying the ninth edition remains the same as in earlier editions—I have attempted to write an intellectually stimulating and visually attractive textbook from which students can learn and professors can teach.

George E. Rejda, Ph.D., CLU
V.J. Skutt University Professor of Insurance
University of Nebraska—Lincoln

PART ONE

BASIC CONCEPTS IN RISK MANAGEMENT AND INSURANCE

CHAPTER 1

RISK IN OUR SOCIETY

"When we take a risk, we are betting on an outcome that will result from a decision we have made, though we do not know for certain what the outcome will be."

Peter L. Bernstein
Against the Gods, The Remarkable Story of Risk

LEARNING OBJECTIVES

After studying this chapter, you should be able to

◆ Explain the meaning of risk.

◆ Distinguish between pure risk and speculative risk.

◆ Identify the major pure risks that are associated with financial insecurity.

◆ Understand how risk is a burden to society.

◆ Explain the major methods of handling risk.

*A*shley, age 15, heard the doorbell ring at 11:00 PM. When she opened the door, a male intruder forced his way into the house and brutally assaulted her at knifepoint in the privacy of her home. The police caught the assailant who posted bail and later pleaded guilty to the assault. On the date of sentencing, he failed to appear and forfeited the bond. As a result of the assault, Ashley is experiencing severe physical and emotional problems and fears the assailant may return.

The shocking attack that Ashley experienced shows clearly that we live in a risky world. Other tragedies occur daily. Foreign terrorists and suicide bombers periodically kill or maim thousands of bystanders throughout the world. Innocent children die as a result of gang drive-by shootings. Motorists are killed or severely injured by drunk drivers. Home owners lose their homes and personal property because of fires, floods, hurricanes, earthquakes, and other natural disasters. Others incur catastrophic medical bills and the loss of earnings because of heart attacks, cancer, AIDS, or other diseases. Still others face financial ruin because they negligently injure someone and cannot pay a liability judgment and other legal expenses.

This chapter discusses the nature and treatment of risk in our society. Topics discussed include the meaning of risk, the major types of risk that threaten our financial security, and the basic methods for handling risk.

MEANING OF RISK

There is no single definition of risk. Economists, behavioral scientists, risk theorists, statisticians, and actuaries each have their own concept of risk. However, risk traditionally has been defined in terms of uncertainty. Based on this concept, **risk** *is defined here as uncertainty concerning the occurrence of a loss.*[1] For example, the risk of being killed in an auto accident is present because uncertainty is present. The risk of lung cancer for smokers is present because uncertainty is present. The risk of flunking a college course is present because uncertainty is present.

Although risk is defined as uncertainty in this text, employees in the insurance industry often use the term *risk* to identify the property or life being insured. Thus, in the insurance industry, it is common to hear statements such as "that driver is a poor risk" or "that building is an unacceptable risk."

Finally, when risk is defined as uncertainty, some authors make a careful distinction between objective risk and subjective risk.

Objective Risk

Objective risk (also called degree of risk) *is defined as the relative variation of actual loss from expected loss.* For example, assume that a property insurer has 10,000 houses insured over a long period and, on average, 1 percent, or 100 houses, burn each year. However, it would be rare for exactly 100 houses to burn each year. In some years, as few as 90 houses may burn; in other years, as many as 110 houses may burn. Thus, there is a variation of 10 houses from the expected number of 100, or a variation of 10 percent. This relative variation of actual loss from expected loss is known as objective risk.

Objective risk declines as the number of exposures increases. More specifically, *objective risk varies inversely with the square root of the number of cases under observation.* In our previous example, 10,000 houses were insured, and objective risk was 10/100, or 10 percent. Now assume that 1 million houses are insured. The expected number of houses that will burn is now 10,000, but the variation of actual loss from expected loss is only 100. Objective risk is now 100/10,000, or 1 percent. Thus, as the square root of the number of houses increased from 100 in the first example to 1000 in the second example (10 times), objective risk declined to one-tenth of its former level.

Objective risk can be statistically calculated by some measure of dispersion, such as the standard deviation or the coefficient of variation. Because objective risk can be measured, it is an extremely useful concept for an insurer or a corporate risk manager. As the number of exposures increases, an insurer can predict its future loss experience more accurately because it can rely on the law of large numbers. The **law of large numbers** states that as the number of exposure units increases, the more closely the actual loss experience will approach the expected loss experience. For example, as the number of homes under observation increases, the greater is the degree of accuracy in predicting the proportion of homes that will burn. The law of large numbers is discussed in greater detail in Chapter 2.

Subjective Risk

Subjective risk *is defined as uncertainty based on a person's mental condition or state of mind.* For example, a customer who was drinking heavily in a bar may foolishly attempt to drive home. The driver may be uncertain whether he will arrive home safely without being arrested by the police for drunk driving. This mental uncertainty is called subjective risk.

The impact of subjective risk varies depending on the individual. Two persons in the same situation can have a different perception of risk, and their behavior may be altered accordingly. If an individual experiences great mental uncertainty concerning the occurrence of a loss, that person's behavior may be affected. High subjective risk often results in conservative and prudent behavior, while low subjective risk may result in less conservative behavior. For example, a motorist previously arrested for drunk driving is aware that he has consumed too much alcohol. The driver may then compensate for the mental uncertainty by getting someone else to drive the car home or by taking a cab. Another driver in the same situation may perceive the risk of being arrested as slight. This second driver may drive in a more careless and reckless manner; a low subjective risk results in less conservative driving behavior.

CHANCE OF LOSS

Chance of loss is closely related to the concept of risk. **Chance of loss** *is defined as the probability that an event will occur.* Like risk, "probability" has both objective and subjective aspects.

Objective Probability

Objective probability *refers to the long-run relative frequency of an event based on the assumptions of an infinite number of observations and of no change in the underlying conditions.* Objective probabilities can be determined in two ways. First, they can be determined by deductive reasoning. These probabilities are called *a priori probabilities.* For example, the probability of getting a head from the toss of a perfectly balanced coin is 1/2 because there are two sides, and only one is a head. Likewise, the probability of rolling a 6 with a single die is 1/6, since there are six sides and only one side has six dots on it.

Second, objective probabilities can be determined by inductive reasoning, rather than by deduction. For example, the probability that a person age 21 will die before age 26 cannot be logically deduced. However, by a careful analysis of past mortality experience, life insurers can estimate the probability of death and sell a five-year term life insurance policy issued at age 21.

Subjective Probability

Subjective probability *is the individual's personal estimate of the chance of loss.* Subjective probability need not coincide with objective probability. For example, people who buy a lottery ticket on their birthday may believe it is their lucky day and overestimate the small chance of winning. A wide variety of factors can influence subjective probability, including a person's age, gender, intelligence, education, and the use of alcohol.

In addition, a person's estimate of a loss may differ from objective probability because there may be ambiguity in the way in which the probability is perceived. For example, assume that a slot machine in a gambling casino requires a display of three lemons to win. The person playing the machine may perceive the probability of winning to be quite high. But if there are 10 symbols on each reel and only one is a lemon, the objective probability of hitting the jackpot with three lemons is quite small. Assuming that each reel spins independently of the others, the probability that all three will simultaneously show a lemon is the product of their individual probabilities ($1/10 \times 1/10 \times 1/10 = 1/1000$). This knowledge is advantageous to casino owners, who know that most gamblers are not trained statisticians and are therefore likely to overestimate the objective probabilities of winning.

Chance of Loss Distinguished from Risk

Chance of loss can be distinguished from objective risk. Chance of loss is the probability that an event that causes a loss will occur. Objective risk is the relative variation of actual loss from expected loss. *The chance of loss may be identical for two different groups, but objective risk may be quite different.* For example, assume that a property insurer has 10,000 homes insured in Los Angeles and 10,000 homes insured in Philadelphia and that the chance of loss in each city is 1 percent. Thus, on average, 100 homes should burn annually in each city. However, if the annual variation in losses ranges from 75 to 125 in Philadelphia, but only from 90 to 110 in Los Angeles, objective risk is greater in Philadelphia even though the chance of loss in both cities is the same.

PERIL AND HAZARD

The terms *peril* and *hazard* should not be confused with the concept of risk discussed earlier.

Peril

Peril *is defined as the cause of loss.* If your house burns because of a fire, the peril, or cause of loss, is the fire. If your car is damaged in a collision with another car, collision is the peril, or cause of loss. Common perils that cause property damage include fire, lightning, windstorm, hail, tornadoes, earthquakes, theft, and burglary.

Hazard

A **hazard** *is a condition that creates or increases the chance of loss.* There are four major types of hazards:

- Physical hazard
- Moral hazard
- Morale hazard
- Legal hazard

Physical Hazard   A **physical hazard** *is a physical condition that increases the chance of loss.* Examples of physical hazards include icy roads that increase the chance of an auto accident, defective wiring in a building that increases the chance of fire, and a defective lock on a door that increases the chance of theft.

Moral Hazard   **Moral hazard** *is dishonesty or character defects in an individual that increase the frequency or severity of loss.* Examples of moral hazard include faking an accident to collect from an insurer, submitting a fraudulent claim, inflating the amount of a claim, and intentionally burning unsold merchandise that is insured.

Moral hazard is present in all forms of insurance, and it is difficult to control. Dishonest individuals often rationalize their actions on the grounds that "the insurer has plenty of money." This view is incorrect because the insurer can pay claims only by collecting premiums from other insureds. Because of moral hazard, premiums are higher for everyone.

Insurers attempt to control moral hazard by careful underwriting of applicants for insurance and by various policy provisions, such as deductibles, waiting periods, exclusions, and riders. These provisions are examined in Chapter 6.

Morale Hazard   Some insurance authors draw a subtle distinction between moral hazard and morale hazard. Moral hazard refers to dishonesty by an insured that increases the frequency or severity of loss. **Morale hazard** *is carelessness or indifference to a loss because of the existence of insurance.* Some insureds are careless or indifferent to a loss because they have insurance. Examples of morale hazard include leaving car keys in an unlocked car, which increases the chance of theft; leaving a door unlocked that allows a burglar to enter; and changing lanes suddenly on a congested interstate highway without signaling. Careless acts like these increase the chance of loss.

Legal Hazard   Legal hazard *refers to characteristics of the legal system or regulatory environment that increase the frequency or severity of losses.* Examples include adverse jury verdicts or large damage awards in liability lawsuits, statutes that require insurers to include coverage for certain benefits in health insurance plans, such as coverage for alcoholism; and regulatory action by state insurance departments that restrict the ability of insurers to withdraw from the state because of poor underwriting results.

BASIC CATEGORIES OF RISK

Risk can be classified into several distinct categories. The most important categories are the following:

- Pure and speculative risk
- Fundamental risk and particular risk
- Enterprise risk

Pure Risk and Speculative Risk

Pure risk *is defined as a situation in which there are only the possibilities of loss or no loss.* The only possible outcomes are adverse (loss) and neutral (no loss). Examples of pure risks include premature death, job-related accidents, catastrophic medical expenses, and damage to property from fire, lightning, flood, or earthquake.

Speculative risk *is defined as a situation in which either profit or loss is possible.* For example, if you purchase 100 shares of common stock, you would profit if the price of the stock increases but would lose if the price declines. Other examples of speculative risks include betting on a horse race, investing in real estate, and going into business for yourself. In these situations, both profit and loss are possible.

It is important to distinguish between pure and speculative risks for three reasons. First, private insurers typically insure only pure risks. With certain exceptions, private insurers generally do not insure speculative risks, and other techniques for dealing with speculative risk must be used. (One exception is that some insurers will insure institutional portfolio investments and municipal bonds against loss.)

Second, the law of large numbers can be applied more easily to pure risks than to speculative risks.

The law of large numbers is important because it enables insurers to predict future loss experience. In contrast, it is generally more difficult to apply the law of large numbers to speculative risks to predict future loss experience. An exception is the speculative risk of gambling, where casino operators can apply the law of large numbers in a most efficient manner.

Finally, society may benefit from a speculative risk even though a loss occurs, but it is harmed if a pure risk is present and a loss occurs. For example, a firm may develop new technology for producing inexpensive computers. As a result, some competitors may be forced into bankruptcy. Despite the bankruptcy, society benefits because the computers are produced at a lower cost. However, society normally does not benefit when a loss from a pure risk occurs, such as a flood or earthquake that devastates an area.

Fundamental Risk and Particular Risk

A **fundamental risk** *is a risk that affects the entire economy or large numbers of persons or groups within the economy.* Examples include rapid inflation, cyclical unemployment, and war because large numbers of individuals are affected.

The risk of a natural disaster is another important risk. Hurricanes, tornadoes, earthquakes, floods, and forest and grass fires can result in billions of dollars of property damage and numerous deaths. In 1999, Hurricane Floyd caused about $2 billion of insured losses. In 1994, a major earthquake in Northridge, California, caused about $13 billion of insured losses and the loss of numerous lives. In 1992, Hurricane Andrew caused insured losses of about $16 billion and the failure of a number of property insurers.

More recently, the risk of a terrorist attack is rapidly emerging as a fundamental risk. Many countries have experienced a substantial increase in terrorism in recent years, resulting in substantial property damage and the loss of human lives. The terrorist attack in the United States on September 11, 2001, resulted in the loss of four commercial jets, destruction of the World Trade Center towers in New York City, substantial damage to the Pentagon, and thousands of dead or missing persons. Estimated insured

EXHIBIT 1.1
The Ten Most Costly Catastrophes, United States

			Insured loss ($ millions)	
Rank	Date	Peril	Dollars when occurred	in 2002 dollars[1]
1.	Sep. 11, 2001	World Trade Center, Pentagon terrorist attacks[2]	$20,300.0	$20,620.9 (estimate)
2.	Aug 1992	Hurricane Andrew	15,500.0	19,874.9
3.	Jan. 1994	Northridge, California earthquake	12,500.0	15,173.8
4.	Sep. 1989	Hurricane Hugo	4,195.0	6,086.1
5.	Sep. 1998	Hurricane Georges	2,900.0	3,200.7
6.	Jun. 2001	Tropical Storm Alison	2,500.0	2,539.5
7.	Oct. 1995	Hurricane Opal	2,100.0	2,478.9
8.	Sep. 1999	Hurricane Floyd	1,960.0	2,116.5
9.	Mar. 1993	20-state winter storm	1,750.0	2,178.7
10.	Oct. 1991	Oakland, California fire	1,700.0	2,245.4

[1]Adjusted to 2002 dollars by the Insurance Information Institute.
[2]Property coverage only.
NOTE: Data are from Insurance Services Office, Inc. (ISO) and Insurance Information Institute.

SOURCE: Hartwig, Robert P., "The Terrorist Attacks of September 11, 2001: Impacts and Implications for the Insurance Industry." November 2001.

losses are about $40 billion. Property losses at the World Trade Center alone exceeded $20 billion. The terrorist attack is the largest single catastrophic loss in the United States to date (see Exhibit 1.1).

In contrast to a fundamental risk, a **particular risk** *is a risk that affects only individuals and not the entire community.* Examples include car thefts, bank robberies, and dwelling fires. Only individuals experiencing such losses are affected, not the entire economy.

The distinction between a fundamental and a particular risk is important because government assistance may be necessary to insure a fundamental risk. Social insurance and government insurance programs, as well as government guarantees and subsidies, may be necessary to insure certain fundamental risks in the United States. For example, the risk of unemployment generally is not insurable by private insurers but can be insured publicly by state unemployment compensation programs. In addition, flood insurance subsidized by the federal government is available to business firms and individuals in flood-prone areas.

Enterprise Risk

Enterprise risk *is a relatively new term that encompasses all major risks faced by a business firm. Such risks include pure risk, speculative risk, strategic risk, operational risk, and financial risk.* We have already explained the meaning of pure and speculative risk. *Strategic risk* refers to uncertainty regarding the firm's financial goals and objectives; for example, if a firm enters a new line of business, the line may be unprofitable. *Operational risk* results from the firm's business operations; for example, a bank that offers new online banking services may incur losses if "hackers" break into the bank's computer.

Enterprise risk also includes financial risk, which is becoming more important in a commercial risk management program. **Financial risk** *refers to the uncertainty of loss because of adverse changes in commodity prices, interest rates, foreign exchange rates, and the value of money.* For example, a food company that agrees to deliver cereal at a fixed price to a supermarket in six months may lose money if grain prices rise. A bank with a large portfolio of Treasury bonds may incur losses if interest rates rise. Likewise, an American corporation doing business in Japan may lose money when Japanese yen is exchanged for American dollars.

Enterprise risk is becoming more important in commercial risk management, which is a process that organizations use to identify and treat major and minor risks. In the evolution of commercial risk management, some risk managers are now considering all types of risk in one program. **Enterprise risk management** *combines into a single unified treatment program all major risks faced by the firm.* As explained earlier, these risks include pure risk, speculative risk, strategic risk, operational risk, and financial risk. By packaging major risks into a single program, the firm can offset one risk against another. As a result, overall risk can be reduced. As long as all risks are not perfectly correlated, the combination of risks can reduce the firm's overall risk. In particular, if some risks are negatively correlated, overall risk can be significantly reduced. Chapter 4 discusses enterprise risk management in greater detail.

Treatment of financial risks typically requires the use of complex hedging techniques, financial derivatives, futures contracts, options, and other financial instruments. Some firms appoint a chief risk officer (CRO), such as the treasurer, to manage the firm's financial risks. Chapter 4 discusses financial risk management in greater detail.

TYPES OF PURE RISK

The preceding discussion shows several ways of classifying risk. However, in this text, we emphasize primarily the identification and treatment of pure risk. Major types of pure risk that can create great financial insecurity include (1) personal risks, (2) property risks, and (3) liability risks.

Personal Risks

Personal risks *are risks that directly affect an individual.* They involve the possibility of the complete loss or reduction of earned income, extra expenses, and the depletion of financial assets. There are four major personal risks:[2]

- Risk of premature death
- Risk of insufficient income during retirement
- Risk of poor health
- Risk of unemployment

Risk of Premature Death **Premature death** *is defined as the death of a family head with unfulfilled financial obligations.* These obligations can include dependents to support, a mortgage to be paid off, or children to educate. If the surviving family members receive an insufficient amount of replacement income from other sources or have insufficient financial assets to replace the lost income, they may be financially insecure.

Premature death can cause financial problems only if the deceased has dependents to support or dies with unsatisfied financial obligations. Thus, the death of a child age seven is not "premature" in the economic sense.

There are at least four costs that result from the premature death of a family head. First, the human life value of the family head is lost forever. The **human life value** *is defined as the present value of the family's share of the deceased breadwinner's future earnings.* This loss can be substantial; the actual or potential human life value of most college graduates can easily exceed $500,000. Second, additional expenses may be incurred because of funeral expenses, uninsured medical bills, probate and estate settlement costs, and estate and inheritance taxes for larger estates. Third, because of insufficient income, some families may have trouble making ends meet or covering expenses. Finally, certain noneconomic costs are also incurred, including emotional grief, loss of a role model, and counseling and guidance for the children.

Risk of Insufficient Income During Retirement The major risk associated with old age is insufficient income during retirement. The vast majority of workers in the United States retire before age 65. When they retire, they lose their earned income. Unless they have sufficient financial assets on which to draw, or have access to other sources of retirement income, such as Social Security or a private pension, they will be exposed to financial insecurity during retirement.

The majority of workers experience a substantial reduction in their money incomes when they retire, which can result in a reduced standard of living. *For example, the median income for all households in the United States in 2001 was $42,228. In contrast, the median income for households with an aged householder age 65 and over was only $23,118 in 2001, or 45 percent less.*[3] This amount is generally insufficient for retired workers who have substantial additional expenses, such as high uninsured medical bills, or high property taxes, or are paying for the cost of long-term care in a nursing home.

Most workers are not saving enough for a comfortable retirement. During the next 15 years, more than 70 million American workers will retire from their jobs. However, an alarming number of them will be financially unprepared for a comfortable retirement. According to a 2002 survey by the Employee Benefit Research Institute, the amounts saved for retirement by all workers are generally small. *Fifteen percent of the workers reported saving nothing for retirement; another 32 percent have saved less than $50,000; only 18 percent reported saving $100,000 or more for retirement (see Exhibit 1.2).* In general, these amounts are relatively small for a comfortable retirement.

Risk of Poor Health   Poor health is another important personal risk. The risk of poor health includes both the payment of catastrophic medical bills and the loss of earned income. The costs of major surgery have increased substantially in recent years. For example, an open heart operation can cost more than $300,000, a kidney or heart transplant can cost more than $500,000, and the costs of a crippling accident requiring several major operations, plastic surgery, and rehabilitation can exceed $600,000. In addition, long-term care in a nursing home can cost $60,000 or more each year. Unless these persons have adequate health insurance, private savings and financial assets, or other sources of income to meet these expenditures, they will be financially insecure. In particular, the inability of some people to pay catastrophic medical bills is a leading cause of personal bankruptcy (see Insight 1.1).

The loss of earned income is another major cause of financial insecurity if the disability is severe. In cases of long-term disability, there is a substantial loss of earned income, medical bills are incurred, employee benefits may be lost or reduced, savings are often depleted, and someone must take care of the disabled person.

Most workers seldom think about the financial consequences of long-term disability. The probability of becoming disabled before age 65 is much higher than is commonly believed, especially at the younger ages. *For individuals age 25, the 1985 Commissioners*

EXHIBIT 1.2
Total Accumulated for Retirement, by Age Group

	All Workers	Workers 20–39 Years	Workers 40–59 Years	Retirees (age 60+)
Nothing	15%	22%	13%	11%
$1–$9,999	12	21	9	16
$10,000–$24,999	11	15	8	9
$25,000–$49,999	9	9	9	4
$50,000–$74,999	8	7	7	4
$75,000–$99,999	5	3	7	5
$100,000–$149,999	6	3	6	3
$150,000–$249,999	6	2	8	5
$250,000 or more	6	2	9	9
Don't know/refused	23	16	24	36

SOURCE: Excerpted from *The 2002 Retirement Confidence Survey Summary of Findings* (Washington, DC: Employee Benefit Research Institute, 2002).

INSIGHT 1.1

Medical Bills Account for 40 Percent of Bankruptcies

Exorbitant medical bills in the United States play a huge part in personal bankruptcies, accounting for about 40 percent of the filings in 1999, according to a recent study.

About 500,000 Americans filed for bankruptcy protection in 1999 largely because of heavy medical expenses, according to the study, which was published in a finance journal, *Norton's Bankruptcy Adviser.*

"Very little attention has been paid to the number of people who are in bankruptcy because of serious medical problems," said the study's lead author, Harvard law professor Elizabeth Warren. "It's a reminder that many of the families in bankruptcy have been pressed to the edge by expenses stemming from illness or injury."

Professor Warren and colleagues found that elderly people and women, as well as families headed by single women, were the groups in bankruptcy that were hardest hit by medical expenses. The findings illustrate how fragile middle-class status is for many American families, Professor

Warren said. These families are "just one serious illness away from financial collapse," she said. "What a scary way to think about America."

Professor Warren and her colleagues, Teresa Sullivan, dean of graduate studies at the University of Texas, and lawyer Melissa Jacoby, surveyed people who filed for bankruptcy in 1999 in eight judicial circuits nationwide, accounting for about 18 percent of all filers.

If the results are projected nationwide, 326,441 bankruptcies in 1999 were related to an illness or injury to the filer or a family member, and 267,575 other filers had substantial medical bills though they also listed other reasons—or gave no reason—for their bankruptcies. In addition to serious illness or injury, experts have also cited job loss or divorce as frequent causes of bankruptcy.

SOURCE: Adapted from Scott Gottlieb "Medical Bills Account for 40% of Bankruptcies," at www.bmj.com, May 30, 2003. Reprinted with permission from the BMJ Publishing Group.

Disability Table shows that the probability of being totally disabled for 90 or more days prior to age 65 is 54 percent.[4] The loss of earned income during an extended disability can be financially very painful.

Risk of Unemployment   The risk of unemployment is another major threat to financial security. Unemployment can result from business cycle downswings, technological and structural changes in the economy, seasonal factors, and imperfections in the labor market.

Several important trends have aggravated the problem of unemployment. To hold down labor costs, large corporations have downsized, and their workforce has been permanently reduced; employers are increasingly hiring temporary or part-time workers to reduce labor costs; millions of jobs have been lost to foreign nations because of global competition; and increases in worker productivity have reduced the rate of growth in new jobs.

Regardless of the reason, unemployment can cause financial insecurity in at least three ways. First, workers lose their earned income and employee benefits. Unless there is adequate replacement income or past savings on which to draw, the unemployed worker will be financially insecure.

Second, because of economic conditions, the worker may be able to work only part-time. The reduced income may be insufficient in terms of the worker's needs. Finally, if the duration of unemployment is extended over a long period, past savings and unemployment benefits may be exhausted.

Property Risks

Persons owning property are exposed to **property risks**—the risk of having property damaged or lost from numerous causes. Real estate and personal property can be damaged or destroyed because of fire, lightning, tornadoes, windstorms, and numerous other causes. There are two major types of loss associated with the destruction or theft of property: direct loss and indirect or consequential loss.

Direct Loss   A **direct loss** *is defined as a financial loss that results from the physical damage, destruction, or theft of the property.* For example, if you own a restaurant that is damaged by a fire, the physical damage to the restaurant is known as a direct loss.

Indirect or Consequential Loss   An **indirect loss** *is a financial loss that results indirectly from the occurrence of a direct physical damage or theft loss.* Thus,

INSIGHT 1.2

Study: Surgeons Leave Tools Inside 1500 Patients a Year

Surgical teams accidentally leave clamps, sponges and other tools inside about 1500 patients nationwide each year, according to the biggest study of the problem yet.

The mistakes largely result not from surgeon fatigue but from the stress arising from emergencies or complications discovered on the operating table, the researchers reported.

It also happens more often to fat patients, simply because there is more room inside them to lose equipment, according to the study.

Both the researchers and several other experts agreed that the number of such mistakes is small compared with the roughly 28 million operations a year in the United States. "But no one in any role would say it's acceptable," said Dr. Donald Berwick, president of the Boston-based nonprofit Institute for Healthcare Improvement.

The study was done by researchers at Brigham and Women's Hospital and Harvard School of Public Health, both in Boston. It was published in the *New England Journal of Medicine.*

The researchers checked insurance records from about 800,000 operations in Massachusetts for 16 years ending in 2001. They counted 61 forgotten pieces of surgical equipment in 54 patients.

From that, they calculated a national estimate of 1500 cases yearly. A total of $3 million was paid out in the Massachusetts cases, mostly in settlements.

Two-thirds of the mistakes happened even though the equipment was counted before and after the procedure, in keeping with the standard practice.

Most lost objects were sponges, but also included were metal clamps and electrodes. In two cases, 11-inch retractors—metal strips used to hold back tissue—were forgotten inside patients. In another operation, four sponges were left inside someone.

The lost objects were usually lodged around the abdomen or hips but sometimes in the chest, vagina or other cavities. They often caused tears, obstructions or infections. One patient died of complications, but the researchers withheld details for reasons of privacy.

Most patients needed additional surgery to remove the object, but sometimes it came out by itself or in a doctor's office.

In other cases, patients were not even aware of the object, and it turned up in later surgery for other problems.

The study found that emergency operations were nine times more likely to lead to such mistakes, and operating-room complications requiring a change in procedure were four times more likely.

SOURCE: *Lincoln Journal Star,* January 16, 2003, p. 3A. Reprinted with permission of the Associated Press.

in addition to the physical damage loss, the restaurant would lose profits for several months while the restaurant is being rebuilt. The loss of profits would be a **consequential loss.** Other examples of a consequential loss would be the loss of rents, the loss of the use of the building, and the loss of a local market.

Extra expenses are another type of indirect, or consequential, loss. For example, suppose you own a newspaper, bank, or dairy. If a loss occurs, you must continue to operate regardless of cost; otherwise, you will lose customers to your competitors. It may be necessary to set up a temporary operation at some alternative location, and substantial extra expenses would then be incurred.

Liability Risks

Liability risks are another important type of pure risk that most persons face. Under our legal sys-

tem, you can be held legally liable if you do something that results in bodily injury or property damage to someone else. A court of law may order you to pay substantial damages to the person you have injured.

The United States is a litigious society, and lawsuits are common. Motorists can be held legally liable for the negligent operation of their vehicles. Operators of boats and lake owners can also be held legally liable because of bodily injury to boat occupants, swimmers, and water skiers. Business firms can be held legally liable for defective products that harm or injure customers; physicians, attorneys, accountants, engineers, and other professionals can be sued by patients and clients because of alleged acts of malpractice. The liability exposure of surgeons who commit negligent acts is especially high (see Insight 1.2). In addition, new types of lawsuits are constantly emerging. For example, some ministers have faced lawsuits brought by church members because of improper counseling.

Liability risks are of great importance for several reasons. *First, there is no maximum upper limit with respect to the amount of the loss.* You can be sued for any amount. In contrast, if you own property, there is a maximum limit on the loss. For example, if your car has an actual cash value of $15,000, the maximum physical damage loss is $15,000. But if you are negligent and cause an accident that results in serious bodily injury to the other driver, you can be sued for any amount—$50,000, $500,000, or $1 million or more—by the person you have injured.

Second, a lien can be placed on your income and financial assets to satisfy a legal judgment. For example, assume that you injure someone, and a court of law orders you to pay damages to the injured party. If you cannot pay the judgment, a lien may be placed on your income and financial assets to satisfy the judgment. If you declare bankruptcy to avoid payment of the judgment, your credit rating will be impaired.

Finally, legal defense costs can be enormous. If you have no liability insurance, the cost of hiring an attorney to defend you can be staggering. If the suit goes to trial, attorney fees and other legal expenses can be substantial.

BURDEN OF RISK ON SOCIETY

The presence of risk results in certain undesirable social and economic effects. Risk entails three major burdens on society:

- The size of an emergency fund must be increased.
- Society is deprived of certain goods and services.
- Worry and fear are present.

Larger Emergency Fund

It is prudent to set aside funds for an emergency. However, in the absence of insurance, individuals and business firms would have to increase the size of their emergency fund to pay for unexpected losses. For example, assume you have purchased a $200,000 home and want to accumulate a fund for repairs if the home is damaged by fire, hail, windstorm, or some other peril. Without insurance, you would have to save at least $25,000 annually to build up an adequate fund within a relatively short period of time. Even then, an early loss could occur, and your emergency fund may be insufficient to pay the loss. If you are a middle-income wage earner, you would find such saving difficult. In any event, the higher the amount that must be saved, the more current consumption spending must be reduced, which results in a lower standard of living.

Loss of Certain Goods and Services

A second burden of risk is that society is deprived of certain goods and services. For example, because of the risk of a liability lawsuit, many corporations have discontinued manufacturing certain products. Numerous examples can be given. Some 250 companies in the world once manufactured childhood vaccines; today, only a small number of firms manufacture vaccines, due in part to the threat of liability suits. Other firms have discontinued the manufacture of certain products, including asbestos products, football helmets, silicone-gel breast implants, and certain birth-control devices because of fear of legal liability.

Worry and Fear

A final burden of risk is that worry and fear are present. Numerous examples can illustrate the mental unrest and fear caused by risk. Parents may be fearful if a teenage son or daughter departs on a skiing trip during a blinding snowstorm because the risk of being killed on an icy road is present. Some passengers in a commercial jet may become extremely nervous and fearful if the jet encounters severe turbulence during the flight. A college student who needs a grade of C in a course to graduate may enter the final examination room with a feeling of apprehension and fear.

METHODS OF HANDLING RISK

As we stressed earlier, risk is a burden not only to the individual but to society as well. Thus, it is important to examine some techniques for meeting the problem of risk. There are five major methods of handling risk:

- Avoidance
- Loss control
- Retention
- Noninsurance transfers
- Insurance

Avoidance

Avoidance is one method of handling risk. For example, you can avoid the risk of being mugged in a high-crime rate area by staying out of the area; you can avoid the risk of divorce by not marrying; and a business firm can avoid the risk of being sued for a defective product by not producing the product.

Not all risks should be avoided, however. For example, you can avoid the risk of death or disability in a plane crash by refusing to fly. But is this choice practical or desirable? The alternatives—driving or taking a bus or train—often are not appealing. Although the risk of a plane crash is present, the safety record of commercial airlines is excellent, and flying is a reasonable risk to assume.

Loss Control

Loss control is another important method for handling risk. Loss control consists of certain activities that reduce both the frequency and severity of losses. Thus, loss control has two major objectives: loss prevention and loss reduction.

Loss Prevention   Loss prevention aims at reducing the probability of loss so that the frequency of losses is reduced. Several examples of personal loss prevention can be given. Auto accidents can be reduced if motorists take a safe-driving course and drive defensively. The number of heart attacks can be reduced if individuals control their weight, give up smoking, and eat healthy diets.

Loss prevention is also important for business firms. For example, strict security measures at airports and aboard commercial flights can reduce hijacking by terrorists. Boiler explosions can be prevented by periodic inspections by safety engineers; occupational accidents can be reduced by the elimination of unsafe working conditions and by strong enforcement of

safety rules; and fires can be prevented by forbidding workers to smoke in a building where highly flammable materials are used. In short, the goal of loss prevention is to prevent the loss from occurring.

Loss Reduction   Strict loss-prevention efforts can reduce the frequency of losses, yet some losses will inevitably occur. Thus, the second objective of loss control is to reduce the severity of a loss after it occurs. For example, a department store can install a sprinkler system so that a fire will be promptly extinguished, thereby reducing the severity of loss; a plant can be constructed with fire-resistant materials to minimize fire damage; fire doors and fire walls can be used to prevent a fire from spreading; and a community warning system can reduce the number of injuries and deaths from an approaching tornado.

From the viewpoint of society, loss control is highly desirable for two reasons. *First, the indirect costs of losses may be large, and in some instances can easily exceed the direct costs*. For example, a worker may be injured on the job. In addition to being responsible for the worker's medical expenses and a certain percentage of earnings (direct costs), the firm may incur sizable indirect costs: a machine may be damaged and must be repaired; the assembly line may have to be shut down; costs are incurred in training a new worker to replace the injured worker; and a contract may be canceled because goods are not shipped on time. By preventing the loss from occurring, both indirect costs and direct costs are reduced.

Second, the social costs of losses are reduced. For example, assume that the worker in the preceding example dies from the accident. Society is deprived forever of the goods and services the deceased worker could have produced. The worker's family loses its share of the worker's earnings and may experience considerable grief and financial insecurity. And the worker may personally experience great pain and suffering before dying. In short, these social costs can be reduced through an effective loss-control program.

Retention

Retention is a third method of handling risk. Retention means that an individual or a business firm retains all or part of a given risk. Risk retention can be either active or passive.

Active Retention   Active risk retention means that an individual is consciously aware of the risk and deliberately plans to retain all or part of it. For example, a motorist may wish to retain the risk of a small collision loss by purchasing an auto insurance policy with a $250 or higher deductible. A home-owner may retain a small part of the risk of damage to the home by purchasing a homeowners policy with a substantial deductible. A business firm may deliberately retain the risk of petty thefts by employees, shoplifting, or the spoilage of perishable goods. In these cases, a conscious decision is made to retain part or all of a given risk.

Active risk retention is used for two major rea-sons. First, it can save money. Insurance may not be purchased at all, or it may be purchased with a deductible; either way, there is often a substantial saving in the cost of insurance. Second, the risk may be deliberately retained because commercial insur-ance is either unavailable or unaffordable.

Passive Retention   Risk can also be retained pas-sively. Certain risks may be unknowingly retained because of ignorance, indifference, or laziness. Pas-sive retention is very dangerous if the risk retained has the potential for destroying you financially. For example, many workers with earned incomes are not insured against the risk of total and permanent disability under either an individual or group dis-ability income plan. However, the adverse financial consequences of total and permanent disability gen-erally are more severe than the financial conse-quences of premature death. Therefore, people who are not insured against this risk are using the tech-nique of risk retention in a most dangerous and in-appropriate manner.

In summary, risk retention is an important tech-nique for handling risk, especially in a modern cor-porate risk management program, which will be discussed in Chapters 3 and 4. Risk retention, how-ever, is appropriate primarily for high-frequency, low-severity risks where potential losses are rela-tively small. Except under unusual circumstances, risk retention should not be used to retain low-frequency, high-severity risks, such as the risk of cat-astrophic medical expenses, long-term disability, or legal liability.

Noninsurance Transfers

Noninsurance transfers are another technique for handling risk. The risk is transferred to a party other than an insurance company. A risk can be transferred by several methods, among which are the following:

- Transfer of risk by contracts
- Hedging price risks
- Incorporation of a business firm

Transfer of Risk by Contracts   Unwanted risks can be transferred by contracts. For example, the risk of a defective television or stereo set can be transferred to the retailer by purchasing a service contract, which makes the retailer responsible for all repairs after the warranty expires. The risk of a rent increase can be transferred to the landlord by a long-term lease. The risk of a price increase in construc-tion costs can be transferred to the builder by having a fixed price in the contract.

Finally, a risk can be transferred by a **hold-harmless clause**. For example, if a manufacturer of scaffolds inserts a hold-harmless clause in a contract with a retailer, the retailer agrees to hold the manu-facturer harmless in case a scaffold collapses and someone is injured.

Hedging Price Risks   Hedging price risks is another example of risk transfer. **Hedging** is a technique for transferring the risk of unfavorable price fluctua-tions to a speculator by purchasing and selling futures contracts on an organized exchange, such as the Chicago Board of Trade or New York Stock Exchange.

For example, the portfolio manager of a pension fund may hold a substantial position in long-term U.S. Treasury bonds. If interest rates rise, the value of the Treasury bonds will decline. To hedge that risk, the portfolio manager can sell U.S. Treasury bond futures. Assume that interest rates rise as expected, and bond prices decline. The value of the futures contract will also decline, which will enable the portfolio manager to make an offsetting pur-chase at a lower price. The profit obtained from closing out the futures position will partly or com-pletely offset the decline in the market value of the Treasury bonds. Of course, markets do not always move as expected, so the hedge may not be perfect. Transaction costs also are incurred. However, by hedging, the portfolio manager has reduced the potential loss in bond prices if interest rates rise.

Incorporation of a Business Firm Incorporation is another example of risk transfer. If a firm is a sole proprietorship, the owner's personal assets can be attached by creditors for satisfaction of debts. If a firm incorporates, personal assets cannot be attached by creditors for payment of the firm's debts. In essence, by incorporation, the liability of the stockholders is limited, and the risk of the firm having insufficient assets to pay business debts is shifted to the creditors.

Insurance

For most people, insurance is the most practical method for handling a major risk. Although private insurance has several characteristics, three major characteristics should be emphasized. First, *risk transfer* is used because a pure risk is transferred to the insurer. Second, the *pooling technique* is used to spread the losses of the few over the entire group so that average loss is substituted for actual loss. Finally, the risk may be reduced by application of the *law of large numbers* by which an insurer can predict future loss experience with greater accuracy. Each of these characteristics is treated in greater detail in Chapter 2.

CASE APPLICATION

Michael is a college senior who is majoring in marketing. He owns a high-mileage 1992 Ford that has a current market value of $2500. The current replacement value of his clothes, television set, stereo set, cell phone, and other personal property in a rented apartment totals $10,000. He wears disposable contact lenses, which cost $300 for a six-month supply. He also has a waterbed in his rented apartment that has leaked water in the past. An avid runner, Michael runs five miles daily in a nearby public park that has the reputation of being extremely dangerous because of drug dealers, numerous assaults and muggings, and drive-by shootings. Michael's parents both work to help him pay his tuition.

For each of the following risks or loss exposures, identify an appropriate risk management technique that could have been used to deal with the exposure. Explain your answer.

a. Physical damage to the 1992 Ford because of a collision with another motorist
b. Liability lawsuit against Michael arising out of the negligent operation of his car
c. Total loss of clothes, television, stereo, and personal property because of a grease fire in the kitchen of his rented apartment
d. Disappearance of one contact lens
e. Waterbed leak that causes property damage to the apartment
f. Physical assault on Michael by gang members who are dealing drugs in the park where he runs
g. Loss of tuition assistance from Michael's father who is killed by a drunk driver in an auto accident

SUMMARY

■ There is no single definition of risk. Risk traditionally has been defined as uncertainty concerning the occurrence of a loss.

■ Objective risk is the relative variation of actual loss from expected loss. Subjective risk is uncertainty based on an individual's mental condition or state of mind.

■ Chance of loss is defined as the probability that an event will occur; it is not the same thing as risk.

■ Peril is defined as the cause of loss. Hazard is any condition that creates or increases the chance of loss.

■ There are four major types of hazards. Physical hazard is a physical condition present that increases the chance of loss. Moral hazard is dishonesty or character defects in an individual that increase the chance of loss. Morale hazard is carelessness or indifference to a loss because of the existence of insurance. Legal hazard refers to characteristics of the legal system or regulatory environment that increase the frequency or severity of losses.

- A pure risk is a risk where there are only the possibilities of loss or no loss. A speculative risk is a risk where either profit or loss is possible.

- A fundamental risk is a risk that affects the entire economy or large numbers of persons or groups within the economy, such as inflation, war, or recession. A particular risk is a risk that affects only the individual and not the entire community or country.

- Enterprise risk is a relatively new term that encompasses all major risks faced by a business firm. Enterprise risk management combines into a single unified treatment program all major risks faced by the firm. Such risks include pure risk, speculative risk, strategic risk, operational risk, and financial risk.

- Financial risk refers to the uncertainty of loss because of adverse changes in commodity prices, interest rates, foreign exchange rates, and the value of money.

- The following types of pure risk can threaten an individual's financial security:

    Personal risks

    Property risks

    Liability risks

- Personal risks are those risks that directly affect an individual. Major personal risks include the following:

    Risk of premature death

    Risk of insufficient income during retirement

    Risk of poor health

    Risk of unemployment

- A direct loss to property is a financial loss that results from the physical damage, destruction, or theft of the property.

- An indirect, or consequential, loss is a financial loss that results indirectly from the occurrence of a direct physical damage or theft loss. Examples of indirect losses are the loss of use of the property, loss of profits, loss of rents, and extra expenses.

- Liability risks are extremely important because there is no maximum upper limit on the amount of the loss; a lien can be placed on income and assets to satisfy a legal judgment; substantial legal defense costs and attorney fees may also be incurred.

- Risk entails three major burdens on society:

    The size of an emergency fund must be increased.

    Society is deprived of needed goods and services.

    Worry and fear are present.

- There are five major methods of handling risk:

    Avoidance

    Loss control

    Retention

    Noninsurance transfers

    Insurance

KEY CONCEPTS AND TERMS

Avoidance
Chance of loss
Direct loss
Enterprise risk
Enterprise risk
  management
Financial risk
Fundamental risk
Hazard
Hedging
Hold-harmless clause
Human life value
Incorporation
Indirect, or consequential
  loss
Law of large numbers
Legal hazard
Liability risks
Loss control
Moral hazard
Morale hazard
Noninsurance transfers
Objective probability
Objective risk
Particular risk
Peril
Personal risks
Physical hazard
Premature death
Property risks
Pure risk
Retention
Risk
Speculative risk
Subjective probability
Subjective risk

REVIEW QUESTIONS

1. a. Explain the meaning of risk.
   b. How does objective risk differ from subjective risk?

2. a. Define chance of loss.
   b. What is the difference between objective probability and subjective probability?

3. a. What is the difference between *peril* and *hazard?*
   b. Define *physical hazard, moral hazard, morale hazard,* and *legal hazard.*

4. a. Explain the difference between pure risk and speculative risk.
   b. How does fundamental risk differ from particular risk?

5. a. Explain the meaning of enterprise risk.
   b. What is financial risk?

6. a. What is enterprise risk management?
   b. How does enterprise risk management differ from traditional risk management?

7. List the major types of pure risk that are associated with great financial insecurity.

8. Describe the major social and economic burdens of risk on society.

9. Explain the difference between a direct loss and an indirect or consequential loss.

10. Briefly explain each of the following methods of handling risk. Give an example of each.
    a. Avoidance
    b. Loss control
    c. Retention
    d. Noninsurance transfers
    e. Insurance

APPLICATION QUESTIONS

1. Assume that the chance of loss is 3 percent for two different fleets of trucks. Explain how it is possible that objective risk for both fleets can be different even though the chance of loss is identical.

2. Several types of risk are present in the American economy. For each of the following, identify the type of risk that is present. Explain your answer.
   a. The Department of Homeland Security alerts the nation of a possible attack by terrorists or suicide bombers.
   b. A house may be severely damaged in a fire.
   c. A family head may be totally disabled in a plant explosion.
   d. An investor purchases 100 shares of Microsoft stock.
   e. A river that periodically overflows may cause substantial property damage to thousands of homes in the floodplain.
   f. Home buyers may be faced with higher mortgage payments if the Federal Reserve raises interest rates at its next meeting.
   g. A worker on vacation plays the slot machines in a casino.

3. There are several techniques available for handling risk. For each of the following risks, identify an appropriate technique, or combination of techniques, that would be appropriate for dealing with the risk.
   a. A family head may die prematurely because of a heart attack.
   b. An individual's home could be totally destroyed in a hurricane.
   c. A new car could be severely damaged in an auto accident.
   d. A negligent motorist may be ordered to pay a substantial liability judgment to someone who is injured in an auto accident.
   e. A surgeon could be sued for medical malpractice.
   f. An individual may be forced to declare bankruptcy because he or she cannot pay catastrophic medical bills.

4. Andrew owns a gun shop in a high crime rate area. The store does not have a camera surveillance system. The high cost of burglary and theft insurance has substantially reduced his profits. A risk management consultant points out that several methods other than insurance can be used to handle the burglary and theft exposure. Identify and explain two noninsurance methods that could be used to deal with the burglary and theft exposure.

5. Risk managers use a number of methods for handling risk. For each of the following, what method for handling risk is used? Explain your answer.
   a. The decision not to carry earthquake insurance on a firm's main manufacturing plant
   b. The installation of an automatic sprinkler system in a hotel
   c. The decision not to produce a product that might result in a product liability lawsuit
   d. Requiring retailers who sell the firm's product to sign an agreement releasing the firm from liability if the product injures someone.

INTERNET RESOURCES

- The **American Risk and Insurance Association (ARIA)** is the premier professional association of risk management and insurance educators and professionals. ARIA is the publisher of *The Journal of Risk and Insurance* and *Risk Management and Insurance Review*. Links are provided to research, teaching, and other risk and insurance sites. Visit the site at

  http://www.aria.org

- The **Risk Theory Society** is an organization within the American Risk and Insurance Association that promotes research in risk theory and risk management. Papers are distributed in advance to the members and are discussed critically at its annual meeting. Visit the site at

http://www.aria.org/rts

- The **Huebner Foundation and Geneva Association** act as an international clearinghouse for researchers and educators in insurance economics and risk management. The Huebner foundation at the University of Pennsylvania provides graduate fellowships to promising scholars in the areas of risk management and insurance education. The Geneva Association is an international organization that promotes research dealing with worldwide insurance activities. Visit the site at

  http://www.huebnergeneva.org

- The **Insurance Information Institute** is a trade association that provides consumers with insurance information and the filing of claims from terrorist attacks, hurricanes, floods, earthquakes, and other natural disasters. Visit the site at

  http://www.iii.org

- **Society for Risk Analysis (SRA)** provides an open forum for all persons interested in risk analysis, including risk assessment, risk management, and policies related to risk. SRA considers threats from physical, chemical, and biological agents and from a variety of human activities and natural events. SRA is multidisciplinary and international. Visit the site at

  http://www.sra.org

SELECTED REFERENCES

Bernstein, Peter L. *Against the Gods, The Remarkable Story of Risk*. New York: Wiley, 1996.

Rejda, George E. "Causes of Economic Insecurity." In *Social Insurance and Economic Security*, 6th ed. Upper Saddle River, NJ: Prentice-Hall, 1999, pp. 4–9.

The 2003 Retirement Confidence Survey, Summary of Findings. Washington: Employee Benefit Research Institute, 2003.

U.S. Census Bureau, *Money Income in the United States, 2001*, Current Population Reports, P60-218. Washington, DC: Government Printing Office, 2002.

Wiening, Eric A. *Foundations of Risk Management and Insurance*, First Edition. Malvern, PA: American Institute for Chartered Property Casualty Underwriters/Insurance Institute of America, 2002, Ch. 1.

NOTES

1. Risk has also been defined as (1) variability in future outcomes, (2) chance of loss, (3) possibility of an adverse deviation from a desired outcome that is expected or hoped for, (4) variation in possible outcomes that exist in a given situation, and (5) possibility that a sentient entity can incur a loss.
2. This section is based on George E. Rejda, *Social Insurance and Economic Security*, 6th ed. Upper Saddle River, NJ: Prentice-Hall, 1999, pp. 4–9.
3. U.S. Census Bureau, Current Population Reports, P60-218, *Money Income in the United States, 2001* (Washington, DC: Government Printing Office, 2002), table 1.
4. Data based on the 1985 Commissioners Disability Table as cited in Edward E. Graves, ed., *McGill's Life Insurance*, 3rd ed. (Bryn Mawr, PA: The American College, 2000), table 7.2, p. 168.

Students may take a self-administered test on this chapter at
www.aw-bc.com/rejda

CHAPTER 2

INSURANCE AND RISK

"Insurance: An ingenious modern game of chance in which the player is permitted to enjoy the comfortable conviction that he is beating the man who keeps the table."

Ambrose Bierce

LEARNING OBJECTIVES

After studying this chapter, you should be able to

◆ Explain the basic characteristics of insurance.

◆ Explain the law of large numbers.

◆ Describe the requirements of an insurable risk from the viewpoint of a private insurer.

◆ Identify the major insurable and uninsurable risks in our society.

◆ Describe the major types of insurance.

◆ Explain the social benefits and social costs of insurance.

Matthew, age 28, is a self-employed carpenter who experienced severe headaches and blurred vision. A medical exam revealed a large brain tumor that required immediate surgery. The surgeon's fee, hospital bills, and other expenses totaled $200,000. In addition, he could not work for almost one year. Like many small business owners, Matthew did not have any health insurance or disability income insurance. Because of the lack of insurance, Matthew experienced great financial insecurity and eventually had to declare bankruptcy.

Matthew's unexpected surgery shows that poor health can cause serious financial problems. In Chapter 1, we identified other major risks that can create financial insecurity. For most people, insurance is the most important technique for handling risk. Consequently, you should understand how insurance works. This chapter discusses the basic characteristics of insurance, requirements of an insurable risk, major lines of insurance, and social benefits and social costs of insurance.

DEFINITION OF INSURANCE

There is no single definition of insurance. Insurance can be defined from the viewpoint of several disciplines, including law, economics, history, actuarial science, risk theory, and sociology. But each possible definition will not be examined at this point. Instead, we will examine those common elements that are typically present in any insurance plan. However, before proceeding, a working definition of insurance—one that captures the essential characteristics of a true insurance plan—must be established.

After careful study, the Commission on Insurance Terminology of the American Risk and Insurance Association has defined insurance as follows.[1] **Insurance** *is the pooling of fortuitous losses by transfer of such risks to insurers, who agree to indemnify insureds for such losses, to provide other pecuniary benefits on their occurrence, or to render services connected with the risk.* Although this definition may not be acceptable to all insurance scholars, it is useful for analyzing the common elements of a true insurance plan.

BASIC CHARACTERISTICS OF INSURANCE

Based on the preceding definition, an insurance plan or arrangement typically includes the following characteristics:

- Pooling of losses
- Payment of fortuitous losses
- Risk transfer
- Indemnification

Pooling of Losses

Pooling or the sharing of losses is the heart of insurance. **Pooling** *is the spreading of losses incurred by the few over the entire group, so that in the process, average loss is substituted for actual loss.* In addition, pooling involves the grouping of a large number of exposure units so that the law of large numbers can operate to provide a substantially accurate prediction of future losses. Ideally, there should be a large number of similar, but not necessarily identical, exposure units that are subject to the same perils. Thus, pooling implies (1) the sharing of losses by the entire group, and (2) prediction of future losses with some accuracy based on the law of large numbers.

With respect to the first concept—loss sharing—consider this simple example. Assume that 1000 farmers in southeastern Nebraska agree that if any farmer's home is damaged or destroyed by a fire, the other members of the group will indemnify, or cover, the actual costs of the unlucky farmer who has a loss. Assume also that each home is worth $200,000, and, on average, one home burns each year. In the absence of insurance, the maximum loss to each farmer is $200,000 if the home should burn. However, by pooling the loss, it can be spread over the entire group, and if one farmer has a total loss, the maximum amount that each farmer must pay is only $200 ($200,000/1000). In effect, the pooling technique results in the substitution of an average loss of $200 for the actual loss of $200,000.

In addition, by pooling or combining the loss experience of a large number of exposure units, an insurer may be able to predict future losses with greater accuracy. From the viewpoint of the insurer, if future losses can be predicted, objective risk is reduced. Thus, another characteristic often found in many lines of insurance is risk reduction based on the law of large numbers.

The **law of large numbers** *states that the greater the number of exposures, the more closely will the actual results approach the probable results that are expected from an infinite number of exposures.*[2] For example, if you flip a balanced coin into the air, the *a priori* probability of getting a head is 0.5. If you flip the coin only ten times, you may get a head eight times. Although the observed probability of getting a head is 0.8, the true probability is still 0.5. If the coin were flipped 1 million times, however, the actual number of heads would be approximately 500,000. Thus, as the number of random tosses increases, the actual results approach the expected results.

A practical illustration of the law of large numbers is the National Safety Council's prediction of the number of motor vehicle deaths during a typical holiday weekend. Because millions of vehicles are on the road, the National Safety Council has been able to predict with some accuracy the number of motorists who will die during a typical Fourth of July weekend. For example, assume that 500 to 700 motorists are expected to die during a typical July 4 weekend.

Although individual motorists cannot be identified, the actual number of deaths for the group of motorists as a whole can be predicted with some accuracy.

However, for most insurance lines, the actuary seldom knows the true probability and severity of loss. Therefore, estimates of both the average frequency and the average severity of loss must be based on previous loss experience. If there are a large number of exposure units, the actual loss experience of the past may be a good approximation of future losses. As noted in Chapter 1, objective risk varies inversely with the square root of the number of cases under observation: as the number of exposures increases, the relative variation of actual loss from expected loss will decline. Thus, the insurer can predict future losses with a greater degree of accuracy as the number of exposures increases. This concept is important because an insurer must charge a premium that will be adequate for paying all losses and expenses during the policy period. The lower the degree of objective risk, the more confidence an insurer has that the actual premium charged will be sufficient to pay all claims and expenses and provide a margin for profit.

A more rigorous statement of the law of large numbers can be found in the appendix at the end of this chapter.

Payment of Fortuitous Losses

A second characteristic of private insurance is the payment of fortuitous losses. A **fortuitous loss** *is one that is unforeseen and unexpected and occurs as a result of chance.* In other words, the loss must be accidental. The law of large numbers is based on the assumption that losses are accidental and occur randomly. For example, a person may slip on an icy sidewalk and break a leg. The loss would be fortuitous. Insurance policies do not cover intentional losses.

Risk Transfer

Risk transfer is another essential element of insurance. With the exception of self-insurance,[3] a true insurance plan always involves risk transfer. **Risk transfer** *means that a pure risk is transferred from the insured to the insurer, who typically is in a* *stronger financial position to pay the loss than the insured.* From the viewpoint of the individual, pure risks that are typically transferred to insurers include the risk of premature death, poor health, disability, destruction and theft of property, and personal liability lawsuits.

Indemnification

A final characteristic of insurance is indemnification for losses. **Indemnification** *means that the insured is restored to his or her approximate financial position prior to the occurrence of the loss.* Thus, if your home burns in a fire, a homeowners policy will indemnify you or restore you to your previous position. If you are sued because of the negligent operation of an automobile, your auto liability insurance policy will pay those sums that you are legally obligated to pay. Similarly, if you become seriously disabled, a disability-income insurance policy will restore at least part of the lost wages.

REQUIREMENTS OF AN INSURABLE RISK

Insurers normally insure only pure risks. However, not all pure risks are insurable. Certain requirements usually must be fulfilled before a pure risk can be privately insured. From the viewpoint of the insurer, there are ideally six requirements of an **insurable risk.**

- There must be a large number of exposure units.
- The loss must be accidental and unintentional.
- The loss must be determinable and measurable.
- The loss should not be catastrophic.
- The chance of loss must be calculable.
- The premium must be economically feasible.

Large Number of Exposure Units

The first requirement of an insurable risk is a large number of exposure units. Ideally, there should be a large group of roughly similar, but not necessarily identical, exposure units that are subject to the same peril or group of perils. For example, a large number of frame dwellings in a city can be grouped together for purposes of providing property insurance on the dwellings.

The purpose of this first requirement is to enable the insurer to predict loss based on the law of large numbers. Loss data can be compiled over time, and losses for the group as a whole can be predicted with some accuracy. The loss costs can then be spread over all insureds in the underwriting class.

Accidental and Unintentional Loss

A second requirement is that the loss should be accidental and unintentional; ideally, the loss should be fortuitous and outside the insured's control. Thus, if an individual deliberately causes a loss, he or she should not be indemnified for the loss.

The requirement of an accidental and unintentional loss is necessary for two reasons. First, if intentional losses were paid, moral hazard would be substantially increased, and premiums would rise as a result. The substantial increase in premiums could result in relatively fewer persons purchasing the insurance, and the insurer might not have a sufficient number of exposure units to predict future losses.

Second, the loss should be accidental because the law of large numbers is based on the random occurrence of events. A deliberately caused loss is not a random event because the insured knows when the loss will occur. Thus, prediction of future experience may be highly inaccurate if a large number of intentional or nonrandom losses occur.

Determinable and Measurable Loss

A third requirement is that the loss should be both determinable and measurable. This means the loss should be definite as to cause, time, place, and amount. Life insurance in most cases meets this requirement easily. The cause and time of death can be readily determined in most cases, and if the person is insured, the face amount of the life insurance policy is the amount paid.

Some losses, however, are difficult to determine and measure. For example, under a disability-income policy, the insurer promises to pay a monthly benefit to the disabled person if the definition of disability stated in the policy is satisfied. Some dishonest claimants may deliberately fake sickness or injury to collect from the insurer. Even if the claim is legitimate, the insurer must still determine whether the insured satisfies the definition of disability stated in the policy. Sickness and disability are highly subjective, and the same event can affect two persons quite differently. For example, two accountants who are insured under separate disability-income contracts may be injured in an auto accident, and both may be classified as totally disabled. One accountant, however, may be stronger willed and more determined to return to work. If that accountant undergoes rehabilitation and returns to work, the disability-income benefits will terminate. Meanwhile, the other accountant would still continue to receive disability-income benefits according to the terms of the policy. In short, it is difficult to determine when a person is actually disabled. However, all losses ideally should be both determinable and measurable.

The basic purpose of this requirement is to enable an insurer to determine if the loss is covered under the policy, and if it is covered, how much should be paid. For example, Shannon has an expensive fur coat that is insured under a homeowners policy. It makes a great deal of difference to the insurer if a thief breaks into her home and steals the coat, or the coat is missing because her husband stored it in a dry-cleaning establishment but forgot to tell her. The loss is covered in the first example but not in the second.

No Catastrophic Loss

The fourth requirement is that ideally the loss should not be catastrophic. This means that a large proportion of exposure units should not incur losses at the same time. As we stated earlier, pooling is the essence of insurance. If most or all of the exposure units in a certain class simultaneously incur a loss, then the pooling technique breaks down and becomes unworkable. Premiums must be increased to prohibitive levels, and the insurance technique is no longer a viable arrangement by which losses of the few are spread over the entire group.

Insurers ideally wish to avoid all catastrophic losses. In reality, however, this is impossible, because catastrophic losses periodically result from floods, hurricanes, tornadoes, earthquakes, forest fires, and other natural disasters. Catastrophic losses can also result from acts of terrorism.

Several approaches are available for meeting the problem of a catastrophic loss. First, reinsurance can be used by which insurance companies are indemnified by reinsurers for catastrophic losses. **Reinsurance** *is the shifting of part or all of the insurance originally written by one insurer to another*. The reinsurer is then responsible for the payment of its share of the loss. Reinsurance is discussed in greater detail in Chapter 26.

Second, insurers can avoid the concentration of risk by *dispersing their coverage over a large geographical area*. The concentration of loss exposures in a geographical area exposed to frequent floods, earthquakes, hurricanes, or other natural disasters can result in periodic catastrophic losses. If the loss exposures are geographically dispersed, the possibility of a catastrophic loss is reduced.

Finally, financial instruments are now available for dealing with catastrophic losses. These instruments include catastrophe bonds, which are designed to pay for a catastrophic loss. Catastrophe bonds are discussed in Chapter 26.

Calculable Chance of Loss

A fifth requirement is that the chance of loss should be calculable. The insurer must be able to calculate both the average frequency and the average severity of future losses with some accuracy. This requirement is necessary so that a proper premium can be charged that is sufficient to pay all claims and expenses and yield a profit during the policy period.

Certain losses, however, are difficult to insure because the chance of loss cannot be accurately estimated, and the potential for a catastrophic loss is present. For example, floods, wars, and cyclical unemployment occur on an irregular basis, and prediction of the average frequency and the severity of losses is difficult. Thus, without government assistance, these losses are difficult for private carriers to insure.

Economically Feasible Premium

A final requirement is that the premium should be economically feasible. The insured must be able to pay the premium. In addition, for the insurance to be an attractive purchase, the premiums paid must be substantially less than the face value, or amount, of the policy.

To have an economically feasible premium, the chance of loss must be relatively low. One view is that if the chance of loss exceeds 40 percent, the cost of the policy will exceed the amount that the insurer must pay under the contract. For example, an insurer could issue a $1000 life insurance policy on a man age 99, but the pure premium would be about $980, and an additional amount for expenses would have to be added. The total premium would exceed the face amount of the insurance.[4]

Based on the preceding requirements, most personal risks, property risks, and liability risks can be privately insured, because the requirements of an insurable risk generally can be met. In contrast, *most market risks, financial risks, production risks, and political risks are difficult to insure by private insurers.*[5] These risks are speculative, and the requirements of an insurable risk discussed earlier are not easily met. In addition, the potential of each risk to produce a catastrophe loss is great; this is especially true for political risks, such as the risk of war. Finally, calculation of a proper premium may be difficult because the chance of loss cannot be accurately estimated. For example, insurance that protects a retailer against loss because of a change in consumer tastes, such as a style change, generally is not available. Accurate loss data are not available, and there is no accurate way to calculate a premium. The premium charged may or may not be adequate to pay all losses and expenses. Since private insurers are in business to make a profit, certain risks are difficult to insure because of the possibility of substantial losses.

TWO APPLICATIONS: THE RISKS OF FIRE AND UNEMPLOYMENT

You will understand more clearly the requirements of an insurable risk if you can apply these requirements to a specific risk. For example, consider the risk of fire to a private dwelling. This risk can be privately insured because the requirements of an insurable risk are generally fulfilled (see Exhibit 2.1).

Consider next the risk of unemployment, which generally is not privately insurable at the present time. How well does the risk of unemployment meet the requirements of an insurable risk? As is evident in Exhibit 2.2, the risk of unemployment does not completely meet the requirements.

First, predicting unemployment is difficult because of the different types of unemployment and labor. There are professional, highly skilled, semi-skilled, unskilled, blue-collar, and white-collar workers. Moreover, unemployment rates vary significantly by occupation, age, gender, education, marital status, city, state, and by a host of other factors, including government programs and economic policies that frequently change. Also, the duration of unemployment varies widely among the different groups. In addition, because a large number of workers can become unemployed at the same time, a potential catastrophic loss is present. And because the different types of unemployment occur irregularly, it is difficult to calculate the chance of loss

EXHIBIT 2.1
Risk of Fire as an Insurable Risk

Requirements	*Does the risk of fire satisfy the requirements?*
1. Large number of exposure units	Yes. Numerous exposure units are present.
2. Accidental and unintentional loss	Yes. With the exception of arson, most fire losses are accidental and unintentional.
3. Determinable and measurable loss	Yes. If there is disagreement over the amount paid, a property insurance policy has provisions for resolving disputes.
4. No catastrophic loss	Yes. Although catastrophic fires have occurred, all exposure units normally do not burn at the same time.
5. Calculable chance of loss	Yes. Chance of fire can be calculated, and the average severity of a fire loss can be estimated in advance.
6. Economically feasible premium	Yes. Premium rate per $100 of fire insurance is relatively low.

Exhibit 2.2
Risk of Unemployment as an Insurable Risk

Requirements	Does the risk of unemployment satisfy the requirements?
1. Large number of exposure units	Not completely. Although there are a large number of employees, predicting unemployment is difficult because of the different types of unemployment and labor.
2. Accidental and unintentional loss	No. A large proportion of unemployment is due to individuals who voluntarily quit their jobs.
3. Determinable and measurable loss	Not completely. The level of unemployment can be determined, but the measurement of loss is difficult. Some unemployment is involuntary; however, some unemployment is voluntary.
4. No catastrophic loss	No. A severe national recession or depressed local business conditions could result in a catastrophic loss.
5. Calculable chance of loss	No. The different types of unemployment generally are too irregular to estimate the chance of loss accurately.
6. Economically feasible premium	No. Adverse selection, moral hazard, and the potential for a catastrophic loss could make the premium unaffordable.

accurately. For these reasons, the risk of unemployment generally is not privately insurable, but it can be insured by social insurance programs. Social insurance programs are discussed later in the chapter.

ADVERSE SELECTION AND INSURANCE

When insurance is sold, insurers must deal with the problem of adverse selection. **Adverse selection** *is the tendency of persons with a higher-than-average chance of loss to seek insurance at standard (average) rates, which if not controlled by underwriting, results in higher-than-expected loss levels.* For example, adverse selection can result from high-risk drivers who seek auto insurance at standard rates, from persons with serious health problems who seek life or health insurance at standard rates, and from business firms that have been repeatedly robbed or burglarized and that seek crime insurance at standard rates. If the applicants for insurance with a higher-than-average chance of loss succeed in obtaining the coverage at standard rates, we say that the insurer is "adversely selected against." If not controlled by underwriting, adverse selection can result in higher-than-expected loss levels.

Although adverse selection can never be completely eliminated, it can be controlled by careful underwriting. **Underwriting** *refers to the process of selecting and classifying applicants for insurance.* Applicants who meet the underwriting standards are insured at standard or preferred rates. If the underwriting standards are not met, the insurance is denied or an extra premium must be paid. Insurers frequently sell insurance to applicants who have a higher-than-average chance of loss, but such applicants must pay higher premiums. The problem of adverse selection arises when applicants with a higher-than-average chance of loss succeed in obtaining the coverage at standard or average rates.

Policy provisions are also used to control adverse selection. Examples are the suicide clause in life insurance and the preexisting conditions clause in health insurance. These policy provisions are discussed in greater detail later in the text when specific insurance contracts are analyzed.

INSURANCE AND GAMBLING COMPARED

Insurance is often erroneously confused with gambling. There are two important differences between them. *First, gambling creates a new speculative risk, while insurance is a technique for handling an already existing pure risk.* Thus, if you bet $300 on a horse race, a new speculative risk is created, but if you pay $300 to an insurer for fire insurance, the risk of fire is already present and is transferred to the insurer by a contract. No new risk is created by the transaction.

The second difference between insurance and gambling is that gambling is socially unproductive, because the winner's gain comes at the expense of the loser. In contrast, insurance is always socially productive, because neither the insurer nor the insured is placed in a position where the gain of the winner comes at the expense of the loser. The insurer and the insured both have a common interest in the prevention of a loss. Both parties win if the loss does not occur. Moreover, frequent gambling transactions generally never restore the losers to their former financial position. In contrast, insurance contracts restore the insureds financially in whole or in part if a loss occurs.

INSURANCE AND HEDGING COMPARED

In Chapter 1, we discussed the concept of hedging, by which risk can be transferred to a speculator through purchase of a futures contract. An insurance contract, however, is not the same thing as hedging. Although both techniques are similar in that risk is transferred by a contract, and no new risk is created, there are some important differences between them. *First, an insurance transaction involves the transfer of insurable risks, because the requirements of an insurable risk generally can be met.* However, hedging is a technique for handling risks that are typically uninsurable, such as protection against a decline in the price of agricultural products and raw materials.

A second difference between insurance and hedging is that insurance can reduce the objective risk of an insurer by application of the law of large numbers. As the number of exposure units increases, the insurer's prediction of future losses improves, because the relative variation of actual loss from expected loss will decline. Thus, many insurance transactions reduce objective risk. In contrast, hedging typically involves only risk transfer, not risk reduction. The risk of adverse price fluctuations is transferred to speculators who believe they can make a profit because of superior knowledge of market conditions. The risk is transferred, not reduced, and prediction of loss generally is not based on the law of large numbers.

TYPES OF INSURANCE

Insurance can be classified as either private or government insurance. Private insurance includes life and health insurance and property and liability insurance. Government insurance includes social insurance programs and all other government insurance plans. Thus, the major types of insurance, both private and public, can be classified as follows:

- Private insurance
    Life and health insurance
    Property and liability insurance
- Government insurance
    Social insurance
    Other government insurance

Private Insurance

Life and Health Insurance   At the end of 2002, 1171 life and health insurers were doing business in the United States.[6] **Life insurance** pays death benefits to designated beneficiaries when the insured dies. The benefits pay for funeral expenses, uninsured medical bills, estate taxes, and other expenses. The death proceeds can also provide periodic income payments to the deceased's beneficiary. In addition, life insurers sell group and individual retirement plans that pay retirement benefits. Life and health insurers also sell individual and group health insurance plans that cover medical expenses because of sickness or injury. Finally, both life and health insurers sell disability income plans that pay income benefits during a period of disability.

Property and Liability Insurance   In 2002, there were 3330 property and liability insurers in the United States.[7] **Property insurance** indemnifies property owners against the loss or damage of real or personal property caused by various perils, such as fire, lightning, windstorm, or tornado. **Liability insurance** covers the insured's legal liability arising out of property damage or bodily injury to others.

Property and liability insurance is also called property and casualty insurance. In practice, nonlife insurers typically use the term **property and casualty insurance** (rather than property and liability insurance) to describe the various coverages and operating results. **Casualty insurance** *is a broad field of insurance that covers whatever is not covered by fire, marine, and life insurance; casualty lines include*

Exhibit 2.3
Property and Casualty Insurance Coverages

1. Personal lines
   - Private passenger auto insurance
   - Homeowners insurance
   - Personal umbrella liability insurance
   - Boat owners insurance
2. Commercial lines
   - Fire and allied lines insurance
   - Commercial multiple peril insurance
   - General liability insurance
   - Workers compensation insurance
   - Commercial auto insurance
   - Accident and health insurance
   - Inland marine and ocean marine insurance
   - Professional liability insurance
   - Equipment breakdown insurance (also called boiler and machinery insurance)
   - Fidelity and surety bonds
   - Crime insurance
   - Other miscellaneous lines

auto, liability, burglary and theft, workers compensation, and health insurance.

Exhibit 2.3 identifies the major property and casualty coverages sold today. The various coverages can be grouped into two major categories—personal lines and commercial lines. This division, however, is not completely precise and accurate because of the overlap of certain coverages. For example, although inland marine insurance is a commercial line, it also covers certain personal property, such as expensive jewelry and furs.

1. *Personal Lines.* **Personal lines** *refer to coverages that insure the real estate and personal property of individuals and families or provide protection against legal liability.* Major personal lines include the following:
   - **Private passenger auto insurance** protects the insured against legal liability arising out of auto accidents that cause property damage or bodily injury to others. Auto insurance also includes physical damage insurance on a covered auto for damage or loss resulting from a collision, theft, or other perils.

- **Homeowners insurance** covers the dwelling, other structures, and personal property against loss or damage from numerous perils, including fire, lightning, windstorm, or tornado. The policy also includes theft coverage and personal liability insurance. A homeowners policy is a **multiple-line policy,** which refers to state legislation that allow insurers to write fire and casualty lines in one policy.
- **Personal umbrella liability insurance** provides protection against a catastrophic lawsuit or judgment. Coverage applies on an excess basis after any underlying insurance coverages are exhausted. Policy limits typically range from $1 million to $10 million.
- **Boat owners insurance** covers the boats and watercraft of individuals and families. A boat owners package policy combines into one policy physical damage insurance on the boat, liability insurance, medical expense insurance, and other coverages.

2. *Commercial Lines.* **Commercial lines** *refer to property and casualty coverages for business firms, nonprofit organizations, and government agencies.* Major commercial lines include the following:
   - **Fire insurance** covers losses caused by fire and lightning; it is usually sold as part of a package policy, such as a commercial multiple peril policy. **Allied lines** refer to coverages that are usually purchased with fire insurance, such as coverage for windstorm, hail, and vandalism. Indirect losses can also be covered, including the loss of business income, rents, and extra expenses.
   - **Commercial multiple peril insurance** is a package policy, which can be written to include property insurance, general liability insurance, business income insurance, equipment breakdown insurance, and crime insurance.
   - **General liability insurance** covers the legal liability of business firms and other organizations that arise out of property damage or bodily injury to others. Legal liability can arise out of the ownership of business property, sale or distribution of products, and manufacturing or contracting operations.
   - **Workers compensation insurance** covers workers for a job-related accident or disease. The

insurance pays for medical bills, disability income benefits, rehabilitation benefits, and death benefits to the dependents of an employee whose death is job related.

- **Commercial auto insurance** covers the legal liability of business firms arising out of the ownership or operation of business vehicles. It also includes physical damage insurance on covered business vehicles for damage or loss resulting from a collision, theft, or other perils.
- **Accident and health insurance** is also sold by property and casualty insurers. This line is similar to the health insurance coverages sold by life and health insurers.
- **Inland marine insurance** covers goods being shipped on land, which include imports, exports, domestic shipments, and means of transportation (for example, bridges, tunnels, and pipelines). Inland marine insurance also covers personal property such as fine art, jewelry, and furs.
- **Ocean marine insurance** covers ocean-going vessels and their cargo from loss or damage because of perils of the sea; contracts are also written to cover the legal liability of shippers and owners.
- **Professional liability insurance** provides protection against malpractice lawsuits or lawsuits that result from a substantial error or omission. Professional liability insurance covers the professional acts or omissions of physicians, surgeons, attorneys, accountants, and other professionals. For example, **medical malpractice insurance** covers physicians and other health-care providers for liability claims arising out of harm or injury to patients.
- **Equipment breakdown insurance** (also called **boiler and machinery insurance**) is a highly specialized line that covers losses due to the accidental breakdown of covered equipment. Such equipment includes steam boilers, air conditioning and refrigeration equipment, and electrical generating equipment.
- **Fidelity bonds** cover loss caused by the dishonest or fraudulent acts of employees, such as embezzlement and the theft of money. **Surety bonds** provide for monetary compensation in the case of failure by bonded persons to per-

form certain acts, such as failure of a contractor to construct a building on time.
- **Crime insurance** covers the loss of property, money, and securities because of burglary, robbery, theft, and other crime perils.
- Other lines include **aircraft insurance,** which provides physical damage insurance on covered aircraft and liability coverage for legal liability arising out of the ownership or operation of aircraft. **Credit insurance** covers manufacturers and wholesalers against loss because an account receivable is uncollectible. **Financial guaranty insurance** guarantees the payment of principal and interest on debt instruments issued by the insured.

Government Insurance

Numerous government insurance programs are in operation at the present time. Government insurance can be divided into social insurance programs and other government insurance programs.

Social Insurance Social insurance programs are government insurance programs with certain characteristics that distinguish them from other government insurance plans. These programs are financed entirely or in large part by mandatory contributions from employers, employees, or both, and not primarily by the general revenues of government. The contributions are usually earmarked for special trust funds; the benefits, in turn, are paid from these funds. In addition, the right to receive benefits is ordinarily derived from or linked to the recipient's past contributions or coverage under the program; the benefits and contributions generally vary among the beneficiaries according to their prior earnings, but the benefits are heavily weighted in favor of low-income groups. Moreover, most social insurance programs are compulsory. Covered workers and employers are required by law to pay contributions and participate in the programs. Finally, eligibility requirements and benefit rights are usually prescribed exactly by statute, leaving little room for administrative discretion in the award of benefits.[8]

Major social insurance programs in the United States include the following:

- Old-Age, Survivors, and Disability Insurance (Social Security)

- Medicare
- Unemployment insurance
- Workers compensation
- Compulsory temporary disability insurance
- Railroad Retirement Act
- Railroad Unemployment Insurance Act

Old-Age, Survivors, and Disability Insurance, commonly known as Social Security, is a massive income-maintenance program that provides retirement, survivor, and disability benefits to eligible individuals and families.

Medicare is part of the total Social Security program and covers the medical expenses of most people age 65 and older and certain disabled people younger than age 65.

Unemployment insurance programs provide weekly cash benefits to eligible workers who experience short-term involuntary unemployment. Regular state unemployment benefits are typically paid up to 26 weeks after certain eligibility requirements are met. Extended benefits also may be available to unemployed workers who exhaust their regular benefits.

As noted earlier, *workers compensation insurance* covers workers against a job-related accident or disease. Although workers compensation is a casualty line sold by private insurers, it is also an important form of social insurance. The social insurance aspects of workers compensation are discussed in Chapter 24.

In addition, *compulsory temporary disability insurance,* which exists in five states, Puerto Rico, and the railroad industry, provides for the partial replacement of wages that may be lost because of a temporary nonoccupational disability.[9] The *Railroad Retirement Act* provides retirement benefits, survivor benefits, and disability income benefits to railroad workers who meet certain eligibility requirements. Finally, the *Railroad Unemployment Insurance Act* provides unemployment and sickness benefits to railroad employees.

Other Government Insurance Programs Other government insurance programs exist at both the federal and state level. However, these programs do not have the distinguishing characteristics of social insurance programs. Important federal insurance programs include the Federal Employees Retirement System, the Civil Service Retirement System, various life insurance programs for veterans, pension termination insurance, insurance on checking and savings accounts in commercial banks and saving and loan associations (Federal Deposit Insurance Corporation), federal flood insurance, federal crop insurance, and numerous other programs.

Government insurance programs also exist at the state level. These programs include the Wisconsin State Life Fund, title insurance programs in a few states, and the Maryland Automobile Insurance Fund. In addition, competitive and monopoly workers compensation funds are in operation in many states. Finally, the majority of states have special health insurance pools that make health insurance available to persons who are uninsurable or substandard in health.

BENEFITS OF INSURANCE TO SOCIETY

The major social and economic benefits of insurance include the following:

- Indemnification for loss
- Reduction of worry and fear
- Source of investment funds
- Loss prevention
- Enhancement of credit

Indemnification for Loss

Indemnification permits individuals and families to be restored to their former financial position after a loss occurs. As a result, they can maintain their financial security. Because insureds are restored either in part or in whole after a loss occurs, they are less likely to apply for public assistance or welfare benefits, or to seek financial assistance from relatives and friends.

Indemnification to business firms also permits firms to remain in business and employees to keep their jobs. Suppliers continue to receive orders, and customers can still receive the goods and services they desire. The community also benefits because its tax base is not eroded. In short, the indemnification function contributes greatly to family and business stability and therefore is one of the most important social and economic benefits of insurance.

Reduction of Worry and Fear

A second benefit of insurance is that worry and fear are reduced. This is true both before and after a loss. For example, if family heads have adequate amounts of life insurance, they are less likely to worry about the financial security of their dependents in the event of premature death; persons insured for long-term disability do not have to worry about the loss of earnings if a serious illness or accident occurs; and property owners who are insured enjoy greater peace of mind because they know they are covered if a loss occurs. Worry and fear are also reduced after a loss occurs, because the insureds know that they have insurance that will pay for the loss.

Source of Investment Funds

The insurance industry is an important source of funds for capital investment and accumulation. Premiums are collected in advance of the loss, and funds not needed to pay immediate losses and expenses can be loaned to business firms. These funds typically are invested in shopping centers, hospitals, factories, housing developments, and new machinery and equipment. The investments increase society's stock of capital goods, and promote economic growth and full employment. Insurers also invest in social investments, such as housing, nursing homes, and economic development projects. In addition, because the total supply of loanable funds is increased by the advance payment of insurance premiums, the cost of capital to business firms that borrow is lower than it would be in the absence of insurance.

Loss Prevention

Insurance companies are actively involved in numerous loss-prevention programs and also employ a wide variety of loss-prevention personnel, including safety engineers and specialists in fire prevention, occupational safety and health, and products liability. Some important loss-prevention activities that property and liability insurers strongly support include the following:

- Highway safety and reduction of automobile deaths

- Fire prevention
- Reduction of work-related disabilities
- Prevention of auto thefts
- Prevention and detection of arson losses
- Prevention of defective products that could injure the user
- Prevention of boiler explosions
- Educational programs on loss prevention

The loss-prevention activities reduce both direct and indirect, or consequential, losses. Society benefits, since both types of losses are reduced.

Enhancement of Credit

A final benefit is that insurance enhances a person's credit. Insurance makes a borrower a better credit risk because it guarantees the value of the borrower's collateral or gives greater assurance that the loan will be repaid. For example, when a house is purchased, the lending institution normally requires property insurance on the house before the mortgage loan is granted. The property insurance protects the lender's financial interest if the property is damaged or destroyed. Similarly, a business firm seeking a temporary loan for Christmas or seasonal business may be required to insure its inventories before the loan is made. If a new car is purchased and financed by a bank or other lending institution, physical damage insurance on the car may be required before the loan is made. Thus, insurance can enhance a person's credit.

COSTS OF INSURANCE TO SOCIETY

Although the insurance industry provides enormous social and economic benefits to society, the social costs of insurance must also be recognized. The major social costs of insurance include the following:

- Cost of doing business
- Fraudulent claims
- Inflated claims

Cost of Doing Business

One important cost is the cost of doing business. Insurers consume scarce economic resources—land, labor, capital, and business enterprise—in providing insurance to society. In financial terms, an expense loading must be added to the pure premium to cover the expenses incurred by insurance companies in their daily operations. An **expense loading** *is the amount needed to pay all expenses, including commissions, general administrative expenses, state premium taxes, acquisition expenses, and an allowance for contingencies and profit.* Sales and administrative expenses of property and liability insurers consume 22 cents of each premium dollar, whereas operating expenses of life insurers account for 13 percent of total expenditures.[10] As a result, total costs to society are increased. For example, assume that a small country with no property insurance has an average of $100 million of fire losses each year. Also assume that property insurance later becomes available, and the expense loading is 35 percent of losses. Thus, total costs to this country are increased to $135 million.

However, these additional costs can be justified for several reasons. First, from the insured's viewpoint, uncertainty concerning the payment of a covered loss is reduced because of insurance. Second, the costs of doing business are not necessarily wasteful, because insurers engage in a wide variety of loss-prevention activities. Finally, the insurance industry provides jobs to millions of workers in the United States. However, because economic resources are used up in providing insurance to society, a real economic cost is incurred.

Fraudulent Claims

A second cost of insurance comes from the submission of fraudulent claims. Examples of fraudulent claims include the following:

- Auto accidents are faked or staged to collect benefits.
- Dishonest claimants fake slip-and-fall accidents.
- Phony burglaries, thefts, or acts of vandalism are reported to insurers.
- False health insurance claims are submitted to collect benefits.
- Dishonest policyowners take out life insurance policies on insureds who are later reported as having died.

The payment of such fraudulent claims results in higher premiums to all insureds. The existence of insurance also prompts some insureds to deliberately cause a loss so as to profit from insurance. These social costs fall directly on society.

Some types of insurance fraud are especially outrageous. The Coalition Against Insurance Fraud has established a "hall of shame" for insurance scams that are strikingly large, brazen, vicious, and in some cases, stupid (see Insight 2.1).

Inflated Claims

Another cost of insurance relates to the submission of inflated or "padded" claims. Although the loss is not intentionally caused by the insured, the dollar amount of the claim may exceed the actual financial loss. Examples of inflated claims include the following:

- Attorneys for plaintiffs sue for high-liability judgments that exceed the true economic loss of the victim.
- Insureds inflate the amount of damage in automobile collision claims so that the insurance payments will cover the collision deductible.
- Disabled persons often malinger to collect disability-income benefits for a longer duration.
- Insureds exaggerate the amount and value of property stolen from a home or business.

Inflated claims must be recognized as an important social cost of insurance. Premiums must be increased to pay the additional losses. As a result, disposable income and the consumption of other goods and services are reduced.

Cost of Fraudulent and Inflated Claims

According to the Insurance Information Institute, property and casualty insurance fraud totaled $31 billion in 2002. When insurance fraud of all types is considered, including life and health insurance, the total cost of insurance fraud is estimated to be between $85 billion and $120 billion annually. *To put these figures in proper perspective, the National Insurance Crime Bureau estimates that an average household pays an additional $200 to $300 in insurance premiums each year because of fraud.*[11]

INSIGHT 2.1

Insurance Fraud Hall of Shame (cases closed in 2002)

The Coalition Against Insurance Fraud has compiled a list of insurance fraud cases that are especially shocking. The following is a sampling of the cases.

- World Trade Center fraud. Charles and Cynthia Gavett turned one of America's worst tragedies into a scam to steal nearly $628,000 from life insurers. Charles told seven insurers that his wife Cynthia died in the September 11, 2002 attack. The couple collected $273,000 from insurers before the swindle fell apart. Each received 10 years in state prison in May 2002.

- Giving addicts free booze and drugs so they would die faster. Jimmie and Isom Turquitt lured alcoholics and drug addicts off the streets of Birmingham, AL by promising them jobs and rooms at the brothers' rural property. The Turquitts took out more than 100 life insurance policies worth $8.6 million on the addicts. The brothers gave free booze and drugs to the addicts so they would die faster and actually collected more than $1.6 million before the scam was broken up. Isom hung himself in prison. Jimmie received life without parole in federal prison in March 2002.

- Burying an eight ton cotton picker. Georgia farmer Curtis Donald Keene fell behind in payments on his eight-ton cotton picker—the size of two garbage trucks. He dug a pit and buried the John Deere behemoth and told his insurer that thieves had stolen it. Cotton States Insurance paid $102,300. However a neighbor noticed a patch of distinctive John Deere poking from the soil. Once word spread, neighbors set up lawn chairs to watch two backhoes and workers churn the soil to uncover the cotton picker. Keene was convicted in state superior court in August 2001. He was ordered to repay the money when the case was closed in 2002.

- Auto insurance scam inside a police station. Belinda Lovander was an employee with the New York Police Department. Using a computer, she wrote 22 fake police reports of car crashes that were staged by a car ring or never happened at all. The crime ring collected $900,000 in insurance claims for bogus injuries. At least 115 people were busted for the massive fraud—the largest bust of its kind in New York state history. Lovander was sentenced to six years in state prison in March 2002.

- Staging faked auto accidents. Quentin "Flint" Hawkins stole $10 million from insurers over a 20-year fraud rampage by staging fake auto accidents. Hawkins paid $500 or more to drivers and passengers in cars they maneuvered into low speed accidents. "Injured" passengers submitted bogus injury claims to insurers for up to $50,000 each. Hawkins recruited police officers, his sons, bowling alley buddies, and others to participate. Incredibly, one woman sent Hawkins a resume for work as a fake accident victim; she got the job. Hawkins received five years in federal prison in September 2002.

- Performing unnecessary and painful heart operations. Dr. Andrew Cubria performed more than 750 mostly worthless and painful heart operations, such as angioplasties, inserting catheters and stents, and even pacemakers to bilk the Medicaid program out of millions of dollars. Cubria preyed on Chicago's impoverished seniors, homeless people, and addicts and lured them from inner city shelters with promises of cash, cigarettes, and food. At least two died from the operations. Cubria received 12 1/2 years in federal prison in June 2002.

- Scuttling a luxury yacht. Rex DeGeorge, a wealthy Beverly Hills lawyer, tried to scuttle his 76-foot luxury yacht off the coast of Italy to bilk insurers out of $3.5 million. DeGeorge and a crony spent all night drilling holes in the hull, but the yacht would not sink. DeGeorge received 7 1/2 years in federal prison in June 2002. However, he did get away with 32 other suspicious claims worth millions, including three other yachts he insisted had sunk.

- Torching her car for insurance. Jaelynn Sealey's burned-out car seemed like a vicious hate crime against a peaceful black woman but actually was an insurance swindle by Sealey herself. The black former Hunterville, NC woman said hate mongers had torched her Chevy Cavalier and crudely scrawled a racial slur on her garage door. More than 400 local residents raised money to help her. However, investigators soon realized the arson was a ruse. Sealey received six months in federal prison in September 2002. The neighbors want an apology and their money back.

- Workers compensation fraud. Richard Martinez accidentally blew up an illegal meth lab above his mother's bakery in Santa Ana, CA. He somehow convinced the bakery's insurer to pay him $40,000 in workers compensation benefits after he was burned over 60 percent of his body. Kemper Insurance exposed the scam. Martinez received almost four years in state prison in September 2002 and must pay his own hospital bills. His mother's bakery never reopened.

- Bashing holes in the roof to inflate a small insurance claim. Public adjustor Steven Budge used a huge log to bash gaping holes in the roof of his uncle's home to inflate a small insurance claim into a $70,000 whopper. However, a neighbor secretly videotaped the bashing. Liberty Mutual saw the tape and sued. The jury denied the claim.

SOURCE: Adaptation of *Insurance Fraud Hall of Shame*, Coalition Against Insurance Fraud at www.insurancefraud.org.

There are numerous definitions of insurance. Based on the definition of insurance stated in the text, indicate whether each of the following guarantees is considered insurance.

a. A television set is guaranteed by the manufacturer against defects for 90 days.

b. A new set of radial tires is guaranteed by the manufacturer against road defects for 50,000 miles.

c. A builder of new homes gives a 10-year guarantee against structural defects in the home.

d. A cosigner of a note agrees to pay the loan balance if the original debtor defaults on the payments.

e. A large group of homeowners agrees to pay for losses to homes that burn during the year because of fire.

Lax Public Attitude toward Fraud

A relatively high percentage of Americans have a lax attitude toward fraud. *According to a recent survey by the Insurance Research Council (IRC), one in three Americans say it is acceptable to inflate insurance claims.* However, on the positive side, the IRC survey also showed that public acceptance of insurance fraud is declining (see Insight 2.2).

The Coalition against Insurance Fraud conducted a study to gain insight on why Americans tolerate insurance fraud. Respondents offered the following possible reasons for committing insurance fraud: (1) to save money or reduce costs, (2) to get expensive work done they would not otherwise be able to afford, and (3) to "get back" at insurance companies because they believe insurers do not conduct business fairly. [12]

Although fraudulent and inflated claims must be recognized as a social cost of insurance, the economic benefits of insurance generally outweigh these costs. Insurance reduces worry and fear; the indemnification function contributes greatly to social and economic stability; financial security of individuals and firms is preserved; and from the perspective of insurers, objective risk in the economy is reduced. The social costs of insurance can be viewed as the sacrifice that society must make to obtain these benefits.

INSIGHT 2.2

One in Three Americans Say It's Acceptable to Inflate Insurance Claims, But Public Acceptance of Insurance Fraud Is Declining

One in three U.S. adults—33 percent—say that it is all right to exaggerate insurance claims under certain circumstances, according to a recent Insurance Research Council (IRC) survey. These respondents agreed that it is acceptable to increase the amount of an insurance claim by a small amount to make up for a deductible. Just over one in five respondents (22 percent) agreed that it is acceptable to increase the amount of a claim to make up for insurance premiums paid when no claims were made. In contrast, fewer respondents tolerated dishonesty in areas other than insurance, such as exaggerating income or experience in a job interview or withholding information on a loan application or from the IRS.

The IRC has been monitoring public attitudes toward claim padding and other forms of insurance fraud for more than a decade. The 2002 results show that acceptance of claim padding and buildup has been declining steadily since 1997, when acceptance levels peaked. In addition, the 2002 study found that tolerance for specific examples of application and claim fraud dropped considerably since they were last measured in 1991.

"Despite the fact that many Americans continue to tolerate opportunistic fraud such as claim padding, the survey results are encouraging. They suggest that, compared to previous years, the public is becoming less tolerant of all forms of insurance fraud. In addition, the data suggest that Americans are becoming increasingly concerned about he impact of insurance fraud on the cost and availability of insurance. They are also more willing to support strict measures to prevent and prosecute fraud," said Elizabeth A. Sprinkel, senior vice president, who heads the IRC.

SOURCE: Excerpted from Insurance Research Council, "One in Three Americans Say It's Acceptable to Inflate Insurance Claims, But Public Acceptance of Insurance Fraud is Declining," *News Release*, July 24, 2003.

SUMMARY

- There is no single definition of insurance. However, a typical insurance plan contains four elements:

  Pooling of losses

  Payment of fortuitous losses

  Risk transfer

  Indemnification

  Pooling means that the losses of the few are spread over the group, and average loss is substituted for actual loss. Fortuitous losses are unforeseen and unexpected and occur as a result of chance. Risk transfer involves the transfer of a pure risk to an insurer. Indemnification means that the victim of a loss is restored in whole or in part by payment, repair, or replacement by the insurer.

- The law of large numbers states that the greater the number of exposures, the more likely the actual results will approach the expected results. The law of large numbers permits an insurer to estimate future losses with some accuracy.

- There are several ideal requirements of an insurable risk.

  There must be a large number of exposure units.

  The loss must be accidental and unintentional.

  The loss must be determinable and measurable.

  The loss should not be catastrophic.

  The chance of loss must be calculable.

  The premium must be economically feasible.

- Most personal risks, property risks, and liability risks can be privately insured, because the requirements of an insurable risk generally can be met. However, most market risks, financial risks, production risks, and political risks generally are difficult to insure by private insurers.

- Adverse selection is the tendency of persons with a higher-than-average chance of loss to seek insurance at average rates, which, if not controlled by underwriting, results in higher-than-expected loss levels.

- Insurance is not the same as gambling. Gambling creates a new speculative risk, whereas insurance deals with an existing pure risk. Also, gambling is socially unproductive, because the winner's gain comes at the expense of the loser. Insurance is always socially productive because both the insured and insurer benefit if the loss does not occur.

- Insurance is not the same as hedging. Insurance involves the transfer of a pure risk, whereas hedging involves the transfer of a speculative risk. Also, insurance may reduce objective risk because of the law of large numbers. Hedging typically involves only risk transfer and not risk reduction.

- Insurance can be classified into private and government insurance. Private insurance consists of life and health insurance and property and liability insurance. Government insurance consists of social insurance and other government insurance programs.

- The major benefits of insurance to society are as follows:

  Indemnification for loss

  Reduction of worry and fear

  Source of investment funds

  Loss prevention

  Enhancement of credit

- Insurance entails certain social costs to society, which include the following:

  Cost of doing business

  Fraudulent claims

  Inflated claims

KEY CONCEPTS AND TERMS

Adverse selection

Casualty insurance

Commercial lines

Expense loading

Fidelity bonds

Fortuitous loss

Indemnification

Inland marine insurance

Insurance

Law of large numbers

Life and health insurance

Multiple-line insurance

Ocean marine insurance

Personal lines

Pooling

Property and liability insurance

Reinsurance

Requirements of an insurable risk

Risk transfer

Social insurance

Surety bonds

Underwriting

REVIEW QUESTIONS

1. Explain each of the following characteristics of a typical insurance plan.
   a. Pooling of losses
   b. Payment of fortuitous losses
   c. Risk transfer
   d. Indemnification

2. Explain the law of large numbers.

3. Certain requirements ideally should be fulfilled before a pure risk can be privately insured. Explain the six requirements of an insurable risk.

4. Identify the approaches that insurers can use to deal with the problem of a catastrophic loss.

5. Why are most market risks, financial risks, production risks, and political risks considered difficult to insure by private insurers?

6. a. What is the meaning of *adverse selection?*
   b. Identify some methods that insurers use to control for adverse selection.

7. What are the two major differences between insurance and gambling?

8. What are the two major differences between insurance and hedging?

9. a. Identify the major fields of private insurance.
   b. Identify several property and casualty insurance coverages.

10. a. Explain the basic characteristics of social insurance programs.
    b. List the major social insurance programs in the United States.

APPLICATION QUESTIONS

1. No risk completely meets all of the ideal requirements of an insurable risk, but some risks come much closer to meeting them than others. Compare the risks of (i) fire with (ii) war in terms of how well they meet the requirements of an insurable risk.

2. a. Private insurers provide social and economic benefits to society. Explain the following benefits of insurance to society.
   (1) Indemnification for loss
   (2) Enhancement of credit
   (3) Source of funds for capital investment and accumulation
   b. Explain the major social and economic costs of insurance in the American economy.

3. Buildings in flood zones are difficult to insure by private insurers because the ideal requirements of an insurable risk are difficult to meet.
   a. Identify the ideal requirements of an insurable risk.

   b. Which of the requirements of an insurable risk are not met by the flood peril?

4. Private insurance provides numerous coverages that can be used to meet specific loss situations. For each of the following situations, identify a private insurance coverage that would provide the desired protection.
   a. Emily, age 28, is a single parent with two dependent children. She wants to make certain that funds are available for her children's education if she dies before her youngest child finishes college.
   b. Danielle, age 16, recently obtained her driver's license. Her parents want to make certain they are protected if Danielle negligently injures another motorist while driving a family car.
   c. Jacob, age 30, is married with two dependents. He wants his income to continue if he should become totally disabled and unable to work.
   d. Tyler, age 35, recently purchased a house for $200,000 that is located in an area where tornadoes frequently touch down. He wants to make certain that funds are available if the house is damaged or destroyed in a tornado.
   e. Nathan, age 40, owns an upscale furniture store. He wants to be protected if a customer is injured while shopping in the store and sues Nathan for the bodily injury.

5. Fraudulent claims and inflated claims are serious problems for insurers today. Surveys show that a relatively high percentage of Americans have a lax attitude toward insurance fraud.
   a. What are some possible reasons why some insureds believe it is acceptable to defraud insurers?
   b. What is the financial impact of fraudulent and inflated claims on insurance premiums?

INTERNET RESOURCES

- The **American Insurance Association (AIA)** is an important trade and service organization for more than 400 property and casualty insurers. The site lists available publications, position papers on important issues in property and casualty insurance, press releases, insurance-related links, and names of state insurance commissioners. Visit the site at

  http://www.aiadc.org

- The **Coalition Against Insurance Fraud** is an alliance of consumer, law enforcement, and insurance industry groups that attempt to reduce insurance fraud through public education and action. Numerous examples of fraudulent claims are listed. Visit this interesting site at

  http://www.insurancefraud.org

- The **Insurance Information Institute (III)** is an excellent site for obtaining information on property and liability insurance. III provides timely consumer information on auto, homeowners, and business insurance, submission of claims and rebuilding after catastrophes, and ways to save money. The site contains background material and information for the news media, including television, newspapers, and radio. Visit this important site at

  http://www.iii.org

- **Insure.com** provides timely consumer information on new developments in auto, home, life, and health insurance. The site provides information on annuities, insurance company ratings, and state insurance regulations. The site also has a complaint finder, lawsuit library, links to other sites, and reader forums. It is an excellent source for background material. Visit the site at

  http://www.insure.com

- The **Insurance Journal** is a definitive online source of timely information on the property/casualty industry. A free online newletter is available that provides breaking news on important developments in property and casualty insurance. Visit the site at:

  http://www.insurancejournal.com

- **InsWeb** operates an online insurance marketplace that enables consumers to get quotes for numerous insurance products, including auto, homeowners, and renters insurance, term insurance, and individual health insurance. Overall, it is an excellent source of information for consumers. Visit the site at

  http://www.insweb.com

- The **National Association of Mutual Insurance Companies** is a trade association that represents mutual insurance companies involved in property and casualty insurance. Visit the site at

  http://www.namic.org

SELECTED REFERENCES

Life Insurers Fact Book 2003. Washington, DC: American Council of Life Insurers, 2003.

The I. I. I. Insurance Fact Book 2004. New York, NY: Insurance Information Institute, 2004.

Wiening, Eric A. *Foundations of Risk Management and Insurance,* First Edition. Malvern, PA: American Institute for Chartered Property Casualty Underwriters/Insurance Institute of America, 2002.

Wiening, Eric A., George E. Rejda, Constance M. Luthardt, and Cheryl L. Ferguson. *Personal Insurance,* First Edition, 2002. Malvern, PA: American Institute for Chartered Property Casualty Underwriters/Insurance Institute of America, 2002.

NOTES

1. *Bulletin of the Commission on Insurance Terminology of the American Risk and Insurance Association,* (October 1965).
2. Robert I. Mehr and Sandra G. Gustavson, *Life Insurance: Theory and Practice,* 4th ed. (Plano, TX: Business Publications, 1987), p. 31.
3. Self-insurance is discussed in Chapter 3.
4. Robert I. Mehr, Emerson Cammack, and Terry Rose, *Principles of Insurance,* 8th ed. (Homewood, IL: Richard D. Irwin, 1985), pp. 36–37.
5. Market risks include the risks of adverse price changes in raw materials, general price level changes (inflation), changes in consumer tastes, new technology, and increased competition from competitors. Financial risks include the risks of adverse price changes in the price of securities, adverse changes in interest rates, and the inability to borrow on favorable terms. Production risks include shortages of raw materials, depletion of natural resources, and technical problems in production. Political risks include the risks of war, acts of terrorists, overthrow of government, adverse government regulations, and the nationalization of foreign plants by a hostile government.
6. *Life Insurers Fact Book 2003* (Washington, DC: American Council of Life Insurers, 2003), p. 9.
7. *The I. I. I. Insurance Fact Book 2004* (New York: Insurance Information Institute, 2004), p. v.

8. George E. Rejda, *Social Insurance and Economic Security,* 6th ed. (Upper Saddle River, NJ: Prentice-Hall, 1999), p. 11.

9. The five states are California, Hawaii, New Jersey, New York, and Rhode Island.

10. *The I. I. I. Fact Book 2004,* p. 14; *Life Insurers Fact Book 2003,* Figure 5.1, p. 71.

11. *The I. I. I. Fact Book 2004,* p. 120.

12. Coalition Against Insurance Fraud, Site Index, "Four Faces: Why Americans Do-and-Don't-Tolerate Insurance Fraud," at http://insurancefraud.org/site_index_set.html

Students may take a self-administered test on this chapter at
www.aw-bc.com/rejda

APPENDIX

Basic Statistics and the Law of Large Numbers*

In no industry is the application of probability and statistics more important than in the insurance industry. Insurance actuaries constantly face a tradeoff when determining the premium to charge for coverage: the premium must be high enough to cover expected losses and expenses, but low enough to remain competitive with premiums charged by other insurers. Actuaries apply statistical analysis to determine expected loss levels and expected deviations from these loss levels. Through the application of the law of large numbers, insurers reduce their risk of adverse outcomes.

In this appendix, we review some statistical concepts that are important to insurers, including probability, central tendency, and dispersion. Next, we examine the law of large numbers and how insurance companies apply it to reduce risk.

PROBABILITY AND STATISTICS

To determine expected losses, insurance actuaries apply probability and statistical analysis to given loss situations. The probability of an event is simply the long-run relative frequency of the event, given an infinite number of trials with no changes in the underlying conditions. The probability of some events can be determined without experimentation. For example, if a "fair" coin is flipped in the air, the probability the coin will come up "heads" is 50 percent, and the probability it will come up "tails" is also 50 percent. Other probabilities, such as the probability of dying during a specified year or the probability of being involved in an auto accident, can be estimated from past loss data.

A convenient way of summarizing events and probabilities is through a probability distribution. A probability distribution lists events that could occur and the corresponding probability of each event's occurrence. Probability distributions may be discrete, meaning that only distinct outcomes are possible, or continuous, meaning that any outcome over a range of outcomes could occur.[1]

Probability distributions are characterized by two important measures: central tendency and dispersion. Although there are several measures of central tendency, the measure most often employed is the mean (μ) or expected value (EV) of the distribution.[2] *The mean or expected value is found by multiplying each outcome by the probability of occurrence, and then summing the resulting products:*

$$\mu \text{ or } EV = \Sigma\, X_i\, P_i$$

*Prepared by Michael J. McNamara, Washington State University.

For example, assume that an actuary estimates the following probabilities of various losses for a certain risk:

Amount of Loss (X_i)		Probability of Loss (P_i)		$X_i P_i$
$ 0	×	.30	=	$ 0
$360	×	.50	=	$180
$600	×	.20	=	$120
		$\Sigma X_i P_i$	=	$300

Thus, we could say that the mean or expected loss given the probability distribution is $300.

Although the mean value indicates central tendency, it does not tell us anything about the riskiness or dispersion of the distribution. Consider a second probability-of-loss distribution:

Amount of Loss (X_i)		Probability of Loss (P_i)		$X_i P_i$
$225	×	.40	=	$ 90
$350	×	.60	=	$210
		$\Sigma X_i P_i$	=	$300

This distribution also has a mean loss value of $300. However, the first distribution is riskier because the range of possible outcomes is from $0 to $600. With the second distribution, the range of possible outcomes is only $125 ($350 − $225), so we are more certain about the outcome with the second distribution.

Two standard measures of dispersion are employed to characterize the variability or dispersion about the mean value. These measures are the variance (σ^2) and the standard deviation (σ). The variance of a probability distribution is the sum of the squared differences between the possible outcomes and the expected value, weighted by the probability of the outcomes:

$$\sigma^2 = \Sigma P_i (X_i - EV)^2$$

So the variance is the average squared deviation between the possible outcomes and the mean. Because the variance is in "squared units," it is necessary to take the square root of the variance so that the central tendency and dispersion measures are in the same units. The square root of the variance is the

standard deviation. The variance and standard deviation of the first distribution are as follows:

$$\sigma^2 = .30(0 - 300)^2 + .50(360 - 300)^2$$
$$+ .20(600 - 300)^2$$
$$= 27,000 + 1,800 + 18,000$$
$$= 46,800$$
$$\sigma = \sqrt{46,800} = 216.33$$

For the second distribution, the variance and standard deviation are:

$$\sigma^2 = .40(225 - 300)^2 + .60(350 - 300)^2$$
$$= 2,250 + 1,500$$
$$= 3,750$$
$$\sigma = \sqrt{3,750} = 61.24$$

Thus, while the means of the two distributions are the same, the standard deviations are significantly different. *Higher standard deviations, relative to the mean, are associated with greater uncertainty of loss; therefore, risk is higher. Lower standard deviations, relative to the mean, are associated with less uncertainty of loss; therefore, risk is lower.*

The two probability distributions used in the discussion of central tendency and dispersion are "odd" in that only three and two possible outcomes, respectively, could occur. In addition, specific loss levels corresponding to the probabilities are assigned. In practice, estimating the frequency and severity of loss is difficult. Insurers can employ both actual loss data and theoretical loss distributions in estimating losses.[3]

LAW OF LARGE NUMBERS

Even if the characteristics of the population were known with certainty, insurers do not insure populations. Rather, they select a sample from the population and insure the sample. Obviously, the relationship between population parameters and the characteristics of the sample (mean and standard deviation) is important for insurers, since actual experience may vary significantly from the population parameters. The characteristics of the sampling distribution help to illustrate the law of large numbers, the mathematical foundation of insurance.

EXHIBIT A2.1
Sampling Distribution Versus Sample Size

EXHIBIT A2.2
Standard Error of the Sampling Distribution Versus Sample Size

It can be shown that the average losses for a random sample of n exposure units will follow a normal distribution because of the Central Limit Theorem, which states:

> If you draw random samples of n observations from any population with mean μ_x and standard deviation σ_x, and n is sufficiently large, the distribution of sample means will be approximately normal, with the mean of the distribution equal to the mean of the population ($\mu_{\bar{x}} = \mu_x$), and the standard error of the sample mean ($\sigma_{\bar{x}}$) equal to the standard deviation of the population (σ_x) divided by the square root of n ($\sigma_{\bar{x}} = \sigma_x / \sqrt{n}$). This approximation becomes increasingly accurate as the sample size, n, increases.

The Central Limit Theorem has two important implications for insurers. First, it is clear that the sample distribution of means does not depend on the population distribution, provided n is sufficiently large. *In other words, regardless of the population distribution (bimodal, unimodal, symmetric, skewed right, skewed left, and so on), the distribution of sample means will approach the normal distribution as the sample size increases.* This result is shown in Exhibit A2.1.

The normal distribution is a symmetric, bell-shaped curve. It is defined by the mean and standard deviation of the distribution. About 68 percent of the distribution lies within one standard deviation of the mean, and about 95 percent of the distribution lies within two standard deviations of the mean. The normal curve has many statistical applications (hypothesis testing, confidence intervals, and so on), and is easy to use.

The second important implication of the Central Limit Theorem for insurers is that the standard error of the sample mean distribution declines as the sample size increases. Recall that the standard error is defined as

$$\sigma_{\bar{x}} = \sigma_x / \sqrt{n}$$

In other words, the standard error of the sample mean loss distribution is equal to the standard deviation of the population divided by the square root of the sample size. Because the population standard deviation is independent of the sample size, *the standard error of the sampling distribution, $\sigma_{\bar{x}}$, can be reduced by simply increasing the sample size.*

This result has important implications for insurers. For example, assume that an insurer would like to select a sample to insure from a population where the mean loss is \$500 and the standard deviation is \$350. As the insurer increases the number of units insured (n), the standard error of the sampling distribution ($\sigma_{\bar{x}}$) will decline. The standard error for various sample sizes is summarized here:

n	$\sigma_{\bar{x}}$
10	110.68
100	35.00
1,000	11.07
10,000	3.50
100,000	1.11

Thus as the sample size increases, the difference between actual results and expected results decreases. This result is shown graphically in Exhibit A2.2.

Obviously, when an insurer increases the size of the sample insured, underwriting risk (maximum insured losses) increases because more insured units could suffer a loss. The underwriting risk for an insurer is equal to the number of units insured multiplied by standard error of the average loss distribution, $\sigma_{\bar{x}}$. Recalling that $\sigma_{\bar{x}}$ is equal to $\sigma_x / \sqrt{n}$, we can rewrite the expression for underwriting risk as:

$$n \times \sigma_{\bar{x}} = n \times \sigma_x / \sqrt{n} = \sqrt{n} \times \sigma_x$$

Thus, while underwriting risk increases with an increase in the sample size, it does not increase proportionately. Rather, it increases by the square root of the increase in the sample size.

Insurance companies are in the loss business—they expect some losses to occur. It is the deviation between actual losses and expected losses that is the major concern. By insuring large samples, insurers reduce their objective risk. There truly is "safety in numbers" for insurers.

NOTES

1. The number of runs scored in a baseball game is a discrete measure as partial runs cannot be scored. Speed and temperature are continuous measures as all values over the range of values can occur.
2. Other measures of central tendency are the median, which is the middle observation in a probability distribution, and the mode, which is the observation that occurs most often.
3. Introductory statistics texts discuss several popular theoretical distributions, such as the binomial and Poisson distributions, that can be used to estimate losses. Another popular distribution, the normal distribution, is discussed in the following section.

CHAPTER 3

INTRODUCTION TO RISK MANAGEMENT

"The essence of risk management lies in maximizing the areas where we have some control over the outcome while minimizing the areas where we have absolutely no control over the outcome . . ."

Peter L. Bernstein
Against the Gods: The Remarkable Story of Risk

LEARNING OBJECTIVES

After studying this chapter, you should be able to

◆ Define risk management and explain the objectives of risk management.

◆ Describe the steps in the risk management process.

◆ Explain the major risk control techniques, including
  Avoidance
  Loss prevention
  Loss reduction

◆ Explain the major risk financing techniques, including
  Retention
  Noninsurance transfers
  Insurance

◆ Apply the principles of risk management to a personal risk management program.

astovica Construction is a large construction company in Omaha, Nebraska. In the past year, the number of workers injured on the job has increased, which has substantially increased the company's workers compensation costs. Theft of materials and supplies from job sites has also increased. A management consultant has recommended that the company establish a risk management program to deal with these problems. Risk management is a process that identifies the loss exposures faced by a firm and uses a number of methods, including insurance, to handle those exposures. After implementing the program, the firm saw dramatic results. Job-related injuries declined, employee theft decreased, and workers compensation premiums were reduced. The firm's profitability also increased.

Clearly, Lastovica Construction benefited from its risk management program. Other organizations have also recognized the merits of risk management. Today, risk management is widely used by corporations, small employers, nonprofit organizations, and state and local governments. Even students can benefit from a personal risk management program.

This chapter—the first of two dealing with risk management—discusses the fundamentals of traditional risk management. The following chapter discusses the newer forms of risk management that are rapidly emerging, including enterprise risk management and financial risk management. In this chapter, we discuss the meaning of risk management, objectives of risk management, steps in the risk management process, and the various techniques for treating loss exposures. The chapter concludes with a discussion of personal risk management.

MEANING OF RISK MANAGEMENT

Risk management *is a process that identifies loss exposures faced by an organization and selects the most appropriate techniques for treating such exposures.* Because the term "risk" is ambiguous and has different meanings, many risk managers use the term "loss exposure" to identify potential losses. A **loss exposure** *is any situation or circumstance in which a loss is possible, regardless of whether a loss occurs.* Examples of loss exposures include manufacturing plants that may be damaged in an earthquake or flood, defective products that may result in lawsuits against the company, and the possible theft of company property because of inadequate security. In the past, risk managers generally considered only pure loss exposures faced by the firm. However, newer forms of risk management are emerging that consider both pure and speculative loss exposures faced

by the firm. This chapter discusses only the traditional treatment of pure loss exposures. The newer forms of risk management—such as enterprise risk management—are discussed in Chapter 4.

OBJECTIVES OF RISK MANAGEMENT

Risk management has important objectives. These objectives can be classified as follows:[1]

- Preloss objectives
- Postloss objectives

Preloss Objectives

Important objectives before a loss occurs include economy, reduction of anxiety, and meeting legal obligations.

The first objective means that the firm should prepare for potential losses in the most economical way. This preparation involves an analysis of the cost of safety programs, insurance premiums paid, and the costs associated with the different techniques for handling losses.

The second objective is the reduction of anxiety. Certain loss exposures can cause greater worry and fear for the risk manager and key executives. For example, the threat of a catastrophic lawsuit from a defective product can cause greater anxiety than a small loss from a minor fire.

The final objective is to meet any legal obligations. For example, government regulations may require a firm to install safety devices to protect workers from harm, to dispose of hazardous waste materials properly, and to label consumer products appropriately. The risk manager must see that these legal obligations are met.

Postloss Objectives

Risk management also has certain objectives after a loss occurs. These objectives include survival, continued operation, stability of earnings, continued growth, and social responsibility.

The most important postloss objective is survival of the firm. Survival means that after a loss occurs, the firm can resume at least partial operations within some reasonable time period.

The second postloss objective is to continue operating. For some firms, the ability to operate after a loss is extremely important. For example, a public utility firm must continue to provide service. Banks, bakeries, dairies, and other competitive firms must continue to operate after a loss. Otherwise, business will be lost to competitors.

The third postloss objective is stability of earnings. Earnings per share can be maintained if the firm continues to operate. However, a firm may incur substantial additional expenses to achieve this goal (such as operating at another location), and perfect stability of earnings may not be attained.

The fourth postloss objective is continued growth of the firm. A company can grow by developing new products and markets or by acquiring or merging with other companies. The risk manager must therefore consider the effect that a loss will have on the firm's ability to grow.

Finally, the objective of social responsibility is to minimize the effects that a loss will have on other per-

EXHIBIT 3.1
Steps in the Risk Management Process

Identify loss exposures.

Analyze the loss exposures.

Select the appropriate techniques for treating the loss exposures
1. Risk control
   • Avoidance
   • Loss prevention
   • Loss reduction
2. Risk financing
   • Retention
   • Noninsurance transfers
   • Commercial insurance

Implement and monitor the risk management program.

sons and on society. A severe loss can adversely affect employees, suppliers, creditors, and the community in general. For example, a severe loss that shuts down a plant in a small town for an extended period can cause considerable economic distress in the town.

STEPS IN THE RISK MANAGEMENT PROCESS

There are four steps in the risk management process (see Exhibit 3.1):

- Identify loss exposures
- Analyze the loss exposures
- Select appropriate techniques for treating the loss exposures
- Implement and monitor the risk management program

Each of these steps is discussed in some detail in the sections that follow.

IDENTIFYING LOSS EXPOSURES

The first step in the risk management process is to identify all major and minor loss exposures. This step involves a painstaking analysis of all potential losses. Important loss exposures relate to the following:

1. Property loss exposures
   - Building, plants, other structures
   - Furniture, equipment, supplies
   - Computers, computer software, and data
   - Inventory
   - Accounts receivable, valuable papers and records
   - Company planes, boats, mobile equipment
2. Liability loss exposures
   - Defective products
   - Environmental pollution (land, water, air, noise)
   - Sexual harassment of employees, discrimination against employees, wrongful termination
   - Premises and general liability loss exposures
   - Liability arising from company vehicles
   - Misuse of the Internet and e-mail transmissions, transmission of pornographic material
   - Directors' and officers' liability suits
3. Business income loss exposures
   - Loss of income from a covered loss
   - Continuing expenses after a loss
   - Extra expenses
   - Contingent business income losses
4. Human resources loss exposures
   - Death or disability of key employees
   - Retirement or unemployment
   - Job-related injuries or disease experienced by workers
5. Crime loss exposures
   - Holdups, robberies, burglaries
   - Employee theft and dishonesty
   - Fraud and embezzlement
   - Internet and computer crime exposures
   - Theft of intellectual property
6. Employee benefit loss exposures
   - Failure to comply with government regulations
   - Violation of fiduciary responsibilities
   - Group life and health and retirement plan exposures
   - Failure to pay promised benefits
7. Foreign loss exposures
   - Acts of terrorism
   - Plants, business property, inventory
   - Foreign currency risks
   - Kidnapping of key personnel
   - Political risks
8. Reputation and public image of the company

A risk manager has several sources of information that he or she can use to identify the preceding loss exposures. They include the following:

- *Risk analysis questionnaires.* Questionnaires require the risk manager to answer numerous questions that identify major and minor loss exposures.
- *Physical inspection.* A physical inspection of company plants and operations can identify major loss exposures.
- *Flowcharts.* Flowcharts that show the flow of production and delivery can reveal production bottlenecks where a loss can have severe financial consequences for the firm.
- *Financial statements.* Analysis of financial statements can identify the major assets that must be protected, loss of income exposures, and key customers and suppliers.
- *Historical loss data.* Historical and departmental loss data over time can be invaluable in identifying major loss exposures.

In addition, risk managers must keep abreast of industry trends and market changes that can create new loss exposures and cause concern. Major risk management issues include rising workers compensation costs, effects of mergers and consolidations by insurers and brokers, increasing litigation costs, financing risk through the capital markets, and repetitive motion injury claims. Protection of company assets and personnel against acts of terrorism is another important issue.

ANALYZE THE LOSS EXPOSURES

The second step in the risk management process is to analyze the loss exposures. This step involves an estimation of the frequency and severity of loss. **Loss frequency** *refers to the probable number of losses that may occur during some given time period.* **Loss severity** *refers to the probable size of the losses that may occur.*

Once the risk manager estimates the frequency and severity of loss for each type of loss exposure, the various loss exposures can be ranked according to their relative importance. For example, a loss exposure with the potential for bankrupting the firm is much more important in a risk management program than an exposure with a small loss potential.

In addition, the relative frequency and severity of each loss exposure must be estimated so that the risk manager can select the most appropriate technique, or combination of techniques, for handling each exposure. For example, if certain losses occur regularly and are fairly predictable, they can be budgeted out of a firm's income and treated as a normal operating expense. If the annual loss experience of a certain type of exposure fluctuates widely, however, an entirely different approach is required.

Although the risk manager must consider both loss frequency and loss severity, severity is more important, because a single catastrophic loss could wipe out the firm. Therefore, the risk manager must also consider all losses that can result from a single event. Both the maximum possible loss and maximum probable loss must be estimated. The **maximum possible loss** *is the worst loss that could happen to the firm during its lifetime.* The **maximum probable loss** *is the worst loss that is likely to happen.* For example, if a plant is totally destroyed in a flood, the risk manager estimates that replacement cost, debris removal, demolition costs, and other costs will total $10 million. Thus, the maximum possible loss is $10 million. The risk manager also estimates that a flood causing more than $8 million of damage to the plant is so unlikely that such a flood would not occur more than once in 50 years. The risk manager may choose to ignore events that occur so infrequently. Thus, for this risk manager, the maximum probable loss is $8 million.

Catastrophic losses are difficult to predict because they occur infrequently. However, their potential impact on the firm must be given high priority. In contrast, certain losses, such as physical damage losses to cars and trucks, occur with greater frequency, are usually relatively small, and can be predicted with greater accuracy.

SELECT THE APPROPRIATE TECHNIQUES FOR TREATING THE LOSS EXPOSURES

The third step in the risk management process is to select the most appropriate technique, or combination of techniques, for treating the loss exposures. These techniques can be classified broadly as either risk control or risk financing.[2] **Risk control** *refers to techniques that reduce the frequency and severity of losses.* **Risk financing** *refers to techniques that provide for the funding of losses.* Many risk managers use a combination of techniques for treating each loss exposure.

Risk Control

As noted above, risk control is a generic term to describe techniques for reducing the frequency or severity of losses. Major risk-control techniques include the following:

- Avoidance
- Loss prevention
- Loss reduction

Avoidance Avoidance *means a certain loss exposure is never acquired, or an existing loss exposure is abandoned.* For example, flood losses can be avoided by not building a new plant in a floodplain. A pharmaceutical firm that markets a drug with dangerous side effects can withdraw the drug from the market.

The major advantage of avoidance is that the chance of loss is reduced to zero if the loss exposure is never acquired. In addition, if an existing loss exposure is abandoned, the chance of loss is reduced or eliminated because the activity or product that could produce a loss has been abandoned. Abandonment, however, may still leave the firm with a residual liability exposure from the sale of previous products.

Avoidance, however, has two major disadvantages. First, the firm may not be able to avoid all losses. For example, a company may not be able to avoid the premature death of a key executive. Second, it may not be feasible or practical to avoid the exposure. For example, a paint factory can avoid losses arising from the production of paint. Without paint production, however, the firm will not be in business.

Loss Prevention Loss prevention *refers to measures that reduce the frequency of a particular loss.* For example, measures that reduce truck accidents include driver examinations, zero tolerance for alcohol or drug abuse, and strict enforcement of safety rules. Measures that reduce lawsuits from defective products include installation of safety features on hazardous products, placement of warning labels on dangerous products, and institution of quality-control checks.

INSIGHT 3.1

Loss Control Pays Big Benefits in Risk Management Programs

Loss control pays, as sixty-one percent of risk management executives claim a savings of $3 or more for every $1 invested in workplace safety, a survey by Liberty Mutual has found.

Ninety-five percent of 200 risk management executives surveyed said workplace safety has a positive impact on a company's financial performance, according to the findings of the "Executive Survey of Workplace Safety" announced by Boston-based Liberty Mutual Group.

The survey reveals that risk management executives believe that the benefits of workplace safety go beyond a company's bottom line. Indeed, 70 percent report that protecting employees is a leading benefit of workplace safety.

The survey helps shed light on the impact that two types of costs associated with workplace accidents are having on U.S. businesses—direct costs (payments to injured employees and their medical care providers), and indirect costs (such as lost productivity and overtime).

Of those surveyed, 70 percent see a relationship between these costs. *Forty percent reported that $1 of direct costs generates between $3 and $5 of indirect costs.*

By comparing the findings on indirect costs with its own research on the direct costs of workplace accidents and illness, Liberty Mutual estimates that U.S. businesses are paying between $155 billion and $232 billion annually for workers' compensation losses.

SOURCE: Adapted from Caroline McDonald, "Workplace Safety Pays, Survey Shows," *National Underwriter,* Property & Casualty/Risk & Benefits Management Edition, September 17, 2001, p. 26.

Loss Reduction Loss reduction *refers to measures that reduce the severity of a loss after it occurs.* Examples include installation of an automatic sprinkler system that promptly extinguishes a fire; segregation of exposure units so that a single loss cannot simultaneously damage all exposure units, such as having warehouses with inventories at different locations; rehabilitation of workers with job-related injuries; and limiting the amount of cash on the premises.

In conclusion, effective risk control techniques can reduce significantly the frequency and severity of claims. *A study by one insurer shows that for every $1 invested in workplace safety, savings of $3 or more are possible.* Effective safety programs reduce both direct costs (payments to injured workers and health care providers) and indirect costs (such as overtime and lost productivity). Insight 3.1 discusses this study in greater detail.

Risk Financing

As stated earlier, risk financing refers to techniques that provide for the funding of losses after they occur. Major risk-financing techniques include the following:

- Retention
- Noninsurance transfers
- Commercial insurance

Retention Retention *means that the firm retains part or all of the losses that can result from a given loss.* Retention can be either active or passive. Active risk retention means that the firm is aware of the loss exposure and plans to retain part or all of it, such as collision losses to a fleet of company cars. Passive retention, however, is the failure to identify a loss exposure, failure to act, or forgetting to act. For example, a risk manager may fail to identify all company assets that could be damaged in an earthquake.

Retention can be effectively used in a risk management program under the following conditions:[3]

- *No other method of treatment is available.* Insurers may be unwilling to write a certain type of coverage, or the coverage may be too expensive. Also, noninsurance transfers may not be available. In addition, although loss prevention can reduce the frequency of loss, all losses cannot be eliminated. In these cases, retention is a residual method. If the exposure cannot be insured or transferred, then it must be retained.
- *The worst possible loss is not serious.* For example, physical damage losses to cars in a large firm's fleet will not bankrupt the firm if the cars are separated by wide distances and are not likely to be simultaneously damaged.
- *Losses are highly predictable.* Retention can be effectively used for workers compensation claims, physical damage losses to cars, and

shoplifting losses. Based on past experience, the risk manager can estimate a probable range of frequency and severity of actual losses. If most losses fall within that range, they can be budgeted out of the firm's income.

Determining Retention Levels   If retention is used, the risk manager must determine the firm's **retention level,** *which is the dollar amount of losses that the firm will retain.* A financially strong firm can have a higher retention level than one whose financial position is weak.

Although a number of methods can be used to determine the retention level, only two methods are summarized here. First, a corporation can determine the maximum uninsured loss it can absorb without adversely affecting the company's earnings. One rough rule is that the maximum retention can be set at 5 percent of the company's annual earnings before taxes from current operations.

Second, a company can determine the maximum retention as a percentage of the firm's net working capital—for example, between 1 and 5 percent. Although this method does not reflect the firm's overall financial position for absorbing a loss, it does measure the firm's ability to fund a loss.

Paying Losses   If retention is used, the risk manager must have some method for paying losses. The following methods are typically used:[4]

- *Current net income.* The firm can pay losses out of its current net income and treat losses as expenses for that year. A large number of losses could exceed current income, however, and other assets may then have to be liquidated to pay losses.
- *Unfunded reserve.* An unfunded reserve is a bookkeeping account that is charged with actual or expected losses from a given exposure.
- *Funded reserve.* A funded reserve is the setting aside of liquid funds to pay losses. Funded reserves are not widely used by private employers, because the funds may yield a much higher rate of return by being used in the business. Also, contributions to a funded reserve are not income-tax deductible. Losses, however, are tax deductible when paid.
- *Credit line.* A credit line can be established with a bank, and borrowed funds may be used to pay losses as they occur. Interest must be paid on the loan, however, and loan repayments can aggravate any cash-flow problems a firm may have.

Captive Insurer   Losses can also be paid by a captive insurer. A **captive insurer** *is an insurer owned by a parent firm for the purpose of insuring the parent firm's loss exposures.* There are different types of captive insurers. A **pure captive** is an insurer owned by only one parent, such as a corporation. An **association or group captive** is an insurer owned by several parents. For example, corporations that belong to a trade association may own a captive insurer. Many captive insurers are located in the Caribbean because of a favorable regulatory climate, relatively low capital requirements, and low taxes. Some captive insurers are domiciled in the United States. In particular, because of a favorable regulatory and legislative environment, the number of new captives licensed in Vermont has increased in recent years (see Exhibit 3.2).

Captive insurers are formed for several reasons, including the following:

- *Difficulty in obtaining insurance.* The parent firm may have difficulty obtaining certain types of insurance from commercial insurers, so it forms a captive insurer to obtain the coverage. This pattern is especially true for global firms that often cannot purchase certain coverages at reasonable rates from commercial insurers, including liability insurance, political risk insurance, and insurance against terrorist attacks.
- *Lower costs.* Forming a captive may reduce insurance costs because of lower operating expenses, avoidance of an agent's or broker's commission, and retention of interest earned on invested premiums and reserves that commercial insurers would otherwise receive. Also, the problem of wide fluctuations in commercial insurance premiums is avoided.
- *Easier access to a reinsurer.* A captive insurer has easier access to reinsurance, because reinsurers generally deal only with insurance companies, not with insureds.
- *Formation of a profit center.* A captive insurer can become a source of profit if it insures other parties as well as the parent firm and its subsidiaries.

Tax Treatment of Captives   As a general rule, premiums paid to a single-parent captive are not

Exhibit 3.2
Vermont Captives Licensed Per Year (as of December 31, 2002)

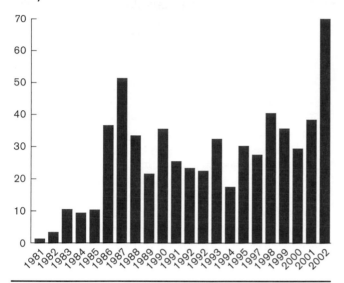

income-tax deductible. The Internal Revenue Service (IRS) argues that there is no substantial transfer of risk to an insurer, and the premiums paid are similar to the contributions to a self-insurance reserve, which are not income-tax deductible.

There are numerous exceptions, however, to the above general rule. In a number of cases in 1991, the courts ruled that premiums paid to a captive are income-tax deductible if the captive also does a significant amount of business with unaffiliated companies or unrelated third-parties. In 1992, a federal appeals court ruled that a corporation could deduct premiums paid to a captive insurer if the captive insurer obtains at least 30 percent of its business from unrelated third parties. In 1997, a series of rulings allowed deductions for taxpayers in certain situations involving holding companies; the rulings permitted deductions for unpaid claims to be taken in the year in which the loss occurred.

In June 2001, the IRS issued a ruling that will have an important impact on captive insurers. In the ruling, the IRS abandoned the "economic family theory," which served as the basis for denying insurance status and the deduction of premiums paid to single-parent captives. According to experts, this ruling will have the following implications for captive insurers:[5]

- *A single-parent captive that covers only the risks of its parent will continue to be challenged by the IRS because of the lack of risk shifting and risk distribution.* The captive will also remain in tax jeopardy if the parent directly or indirectly guarantees the obligations of the captive insurer, or the captive is undercapitalized.
- *It appears that the IRS will no longer pursue pure captives that write a significant level of brother-sister risks (other affiliates of the parent corporation).* The IRS may accept brother-sister risks because a "balance sheet test" will be substituted for the now defunct "economic family theory."
- *Because the ruling did not address how much unrelated business a captive must write to have a true "insurance" plan, existing case law will continue to govern (at least 30 percent of the net premiums must be derived from unrelated loss exposures).* However, it appears that the IRS has abandoned its former extreme position that, no matter how much unrelated business a pure captive insures, the parent corporation can never deduct the premiums.

The tax treatment of captives is not completely settled at the present time and continues to be an ongoing issue.

Self-Insurance   Our discussion of retention would not be complete without a brief discussion of self-insurance. The term self-insurance is commonly used by risk managers to describe aspects of their risk management programs. **Self-insurance** *is a special form of planned retention by which part or all of a given loss exposure is retained by the firm.* A better name for self-insurance is self-funding, which expresses more clearly the idea that losses are funded and paid for by the firm.

Self-insurance is widely used in workers compensation insurance. Self-insurance is also used by employers to provide group health, dental, vision, and prescription drug benefits to employees. Firms often self-insure their group health insurance benefits because they can save money and control healthcare costs. There are other benefits of self-insurance as well (see Insight 3.2).

INSIGHT 3.2

Benefits of Self-Insurance in Group Health Plans

According to a 2000 report by the Employee Benefit Research Institute (EBRI), approximately 50 million workers and their dependents receive benefits from group health plans sponsored by their employers. This figure represents 33 percent of the 150 million total participants in private employment-based group health plans nationally.

There are several reasons why employers choose the self-insurance option, which include the following:

- The employer can customize the plan to meet the specific health care needs of the employees, as opposed to purchasing a "one size fits all" insurance policy.
- The employer maintains control over the health plan reserves, which allows interest income to be maximized. The employer retains the income from the investment of premiums that would otherwise go to insurers.

- Cash flow is improved. The employer does not have to prepay for coverage.
- The employer is not subject to conflicting state health insurance laws and regulations, such as state-mandated health insurance benefits. Self-insured plans are regulated under the Employee Retirement Income Security Act (ERISA), which preempts state law.
- The employer is not subject to state health insurance premium taxes. These taxes generally are 2 to 3 percent of the premiums.
- The employer is free to contract with health-care providers or network providers that best meet the needs of the employees.

SOURCE: Adapted from Self-Insured Health Plans: Questions and Answers, Self-Insurance Institute of America, 2001.

Finally, self-insured plans are typically protected by some type of stop-loss insurance that limits the employer's out-of-pocket costs once losses exceed certain limits.

Risk Retention Groups Federal legislation allows employers, trade groups, governmental units, and other parties to form risk retention groups. A **risk retention group** *is a group captive that can write any type of liability coverage except employer liability, workers compensation, and personal lines.* For example, a group of physicians may find medical malpractice liability insurance difficult to obtain or too expensive to purchase. The physicians can form a risk retention group to insure their medical malpractice loss exposures (See Insight 3.3).

Risk retention groups are exempt from many state insurance laws that apply to other insurers. Nevertheless, they must be licensed as a liability insurer in at least one state.

Advantages and Disadvantages of Retention The retention technique has both advantages and disadvantages in a risk management program.[6] The major advantages are as follows:

- *Save money.* The firm can save money in the long run if its actual losses are less than the loss component in the insurer's premium.

- *Lower expenses.* The services provided by the insurer may be provided by the firm at a lower cost. Some expenses may be reduced, including loss-adjustment expenses, general administrative expenses, commissions and brokerage fees, loss-control expenses, taxes and fees, and the insurer's profit.
- *Encourage loss prevention.* Because the exposure is retained, there may be a greater incentive for loss prevention.
- *Increase cash flow.* Cash flow may be increased, because the firm can use the funds that normally would be paid to the insurer at the beginning of the policy period.

The retention technique, however, has several disadvantages:

- *Possible higher losses.* The losses retained by the firm may be greater than the loss allowance in the insurance premium that is saved by not purchasing the insurance. Also, in the short run, there may be great volatility in the firm's loss experience.
- *Possible higher expenses.* Expenses may actually be higher. Outside experts such as safety engineers may have to be hired. Insurers may be able to provide loss control and claim services less expensively.
- *Possible higher taxes.* Income taxes may also be higher. The premiums paid to an insurer are

---

INSIGHT 3.3

Skyrocketing Premiums Force Doctors to Seek Other Options for Coverage

The last straw for ear, nose, and throat specialist Dr. Tom Boran and his partner came when their annual malpractice insurance premiums rose from $54,000 to $92,000 this year.

Neither has lost a lawsuit, and while treating more patients helped them pay the cost, that left them mentally and physically exhausted at day's end, Boran said.

"You get to the point where a lot of physicians say, 'Life has to be better than this,'" said Boran, who practices in Pottsville, Pa.

So like many other doctors, they have looked beyond commercial malpractice underwriters and discovered self-insuring policies offered by newly forming physician-run mutual companies or so-called risk retention groups. With some doctors shut out of the malpractice marketplace by rising premiums or a dearth of policy writers, the groups are increasingly appealing.

In many cases, the mutuals simply offer an option to doctors who were stuck with an underwriter of last resort after their previous commercial insurers pulled their policies or went under. Although mutuals emphasize profits less than commercial insurers that answer to shareholders, they don't always deliver lower premiums.

Risk retention groups can offer lower premiums by targeting physicians in lower-risk specialties or geographic areas.

While Boran and his partner haven't decided yet, many other doctors have. Risk retention groups for physicians have more than doubled in the past 18 months, and with older physician-owned mutual insurance companies stretched too thin to write new policies, new ones are popping up.

Should a mutual insurance company go under, its outstanding claims are typically covered at least in part by an industry-financed guaranty fund. Risk retention groups are another story: Doctors largely are left holding the bag for any claims that arise from the period in which the group covered them.

"Across the nation, we see entrepreneurs coming into the marketplace, and that's fine as long as they're well-capitalized," said Lawrence Smarr, president of the Physician Insurers Association of America.

Smarr said 36 domestic physician-run insurers, most of which are mutuals, are members of his organization, which began 25 years ago as the groups began to form during a previous malpractice crunch.

Risk retention groups were authorized by federal law in 1986 to underwrite malpractice liability. Today, there are 17 existing physicians' risk retention groups, 10 of which formed since January 2002, according to the Risk Retention Reporter, an industry publication.

Policyholders make contributions to finance the group's initial capitalization and generally are responsible for the operation's expenses.

Mutual insurance companies are largely run the same way, but in general have stricter regulatory requirements, including the amount of initial capitalization.

Examples of startups in recent months include: a risk retention group for physicians in central Pennsylvania and another for emergency room physicians in New Jersey; two physician-run mutual insurance companies in Missouri and another in Kentucky.

All four states are on the list of 18 that the American Medical Association identifies as those with a malpractice liability crisis.

SOURCE: The Associated Press, "Alternative Rx for Malpractice," *Journal Star*, July 1, 2003, p. 4A. Reprinted with permission of the Associated Press.

---

immediately income-tax deductible. However, if retention is used, only the amounts paid out for losses are deductible, and the deduction cannot be taken until the losses are actually paid. Contributions to a funded reserve are not income-tax deductible.

Noninsurance Transfers Noninsurance transfers are another risk-financing technique. **Noninsurance transfers** *are methods other than insurance by which a pure risk and its potential financial consequences are transferred to another party*. Examples of noninsurance transfers include contracts, leases, and hold-harmless agreements. For example, a com-

pany's contract with a construction firm to build a new plant can specify that the construction firm is responsible for any damage to the plant while it is being built. A firm's computer lease can specify that maintenance, repairs, and any physical damage loss to the computer are the responsibility of the computer firm. A firm may insert a hold-harmless clause in a contract, by which one party assumes legal liability on behalf of another party. Thus, a publishing firm may insert a hold-harmless clause in a contract, by which the author, not the publisher, is held legally liable if the publisher is sued for plagiarism.

In a risk management program, noninsurance transfers have several advantages:[7]

- The risk manager can transfer some potential losses that are not commercially insurable.
- Noninsurance transfers often cost less than insurance.
- The potential loss may be shifted to someone who is in a better position to exercise loss control.

However, noninsurance transfers have several disadvantages:

- The transfer of potential loss may fail because the contract language is ambiguous. Also, there may be no court precedents for the interpretation of a contract that is tailor-made to fit the situation.
- If the party to whom the potential loss is transferred is unable to pay the loss, the firm is still responsible for the claim.
- An insurer may not give credit for the transfers, and insurance costs may not always be reduced.

Insurance   Commercial insurance is also used in a risk management program. Insurance is appropriate for loss exposures that have a low probability of loss but for which the severity of loss is high.

If the risk manager uses insurance to treat certain loss exposures, five key areas must be emphasized:[8]

- Selection of insurance coverages
- Selection of an insurer
- Negotiation of terms
- Dissemination of information concerning insurance coverages
- Periodic review of the program

First, the risk manager must select the insurance coverages needed. The coverages selected must be appropriate for insuring the major loss exposures identified in step one. To determine the coverages needed, the risk manager must have specialized knowledge of commercial property and liability insurance contracts. Commercial insurance is discussed in Chapters 13–15.

The risk manager must also determine if a deductible is needed and the size of the deductible. A **deductible** *is a provision by which a specified amount is subtracted from the loss payment otherwise payable to the insured.* A deductible is used to eliminate small claims and the administrative expense of adjusting these claims. As a result, sub-

stantial premium savings are possible. In essence, a deductible is a form of risk retention.

Most risk management programs combine the retention technique discussed earlier with commercial insurance. In determining the size of the deductible, the firm may decide to retain only a relatively small part of the maximum possible loss. The insurer normally adjusts any claims, and only losses in excess of the deductible are paid.

Another approach is to purchase **excess insurance**—*a plan in which the insurer does not participate in the loss until the actual loss exceeds the amount a firm has decided to retain.* A firm may be financially strong and may wish to retain a relatively larger proportion of the maximum possible loss. The retention limit may be set at the maximum probable loss (not maximum possible loss). For example, a retention limit of $1 million may be established for a single fire loss to a plant valued at $25 million. The $1 million would be viewed as the maximum probable loss. In the unlikely event of a total loss, the firm would absorb the first $1 million of loss, and the commercial insurer would pay the remaining $24 million.

Second, the risk manager must select an insurer or several insurers. Several important factors come into play here, including the financial strength of the insurer, risk management services provided by the insurer, and the cost and terms of protection. The insurer's financial strength is determined by the size of policyowners' surplus, underwriting and investment results, adequacy of reserves for outstanding liabilities, types of insurance written, and the quality of management. Several trade publications are available to the risk manager for determining the financial strength of a particular insurer. One of the most important rating agencies is the A. M. Best Company, which rates insurers based on their relative financial strength.

The risk manager must also consider the availability of risk management services in selecting a particular insurer. An insurance agent or broker can provide the desired information concerning the risk management services available from different insurers. These services include loss-control services, assistance in identifying loss exposures, and claim adjustment services.

The cost and terms of insurance protection must be considered as well. All other factors being equal, the risk manager would prefer to purchase insurance at the lowest possible price. Many risk managers will solicit competitive premium bids from several insurers to get the necessary protection and services at the lowest price.

Third, after the insurer or insurers are selected, the terms of the insurance contract must be negotiated. If printed policies, endorsements, and forms are used, the risk manager and insurer must agree on the documents that will form the basis of the contract. If a specially tailored **manuscript policy**[9] is written for the firm, the language and meaning of the contractual provisions must be clear to both parties. In any case, the various risk management services the insurer will provide must be clearly stated in the contract. Finally, if the firm is large, the premiums may be negotiable between the firm and insurer. In many cases, an agent or broker will be involved in the negotiations.

In addition, information concerning insurance coverages must be disseminated to others in the firm. The firm's employees and managers must be informed about the insurance coverages, the various records that must be kept, and the risk management services that the insurer will provide. Those persons responsible for reporting a loss must also be informed. The firm must comply with policy provisions concerning how notice of a claim is to be given and how the necessary proofs of loss are to be presented.

Finally, the insurance program must be periodically reviewed. This review is especially important when the firm has a change in business operations or is involved in a merger or acquisition of another firm. The review includes an analysis of agent and broker relationships, coverages needed, quality of loss control services provided, whether claims are paid promptly, and numerous other factors. Even the basic decision—whether to purchase insurance or retain the risk—must be reviewed periodically.

Advantages of Insurance The use of commercial insurance in a risk management program has certain advantages:[10]

- The firm will be indemnified after a loss occurs. The firm can continue to operate and may experience little or no fluctuation in earnings.
- Uncertainty is reduced, which permits the firm to lengthen its planning horizon. Worry and fear are reduced for managers and employees, which

should improve their performance and productivity.
- Insurers can provide valuable risk management services, such as loss-control services, exposure analysis to identify loss exposures, and claims adjusting.
- Insurance premiums are income-tax deductible as a business expense.

Disadvantages of Insurance The use of insurance also entails certain disadvantages and costs:

- The payment of premiums is a major cost, because the premium consists of a component to pay losses, an amount for expenses, and an allowance for profit and contingencies. There is also an opportunity cost. Under the retention technique discussed earlier, the premium could be invested or used in the business until needed to pay claims. If insurance is used, premiums must be paid in advance, and the opportunity to use the funds is foregone.
- Considerable time and effort must be spent in negotiating the insurance coverages. An insurer or insurers must be selected, policy terms and premiums must be negotiated, the firm must cooperate with the loss-control activities of the insurer, and proof of loss must be filed with the insurer following a loss.
- The risk manager may have less incentive to follow a loss-control program, because the insurer will pay the claim if a loss occurs. Such a lax attitude toward loss control could increase the number of noninsured losses as well.

Which Method Should Be Used?

In determining the appropriate method or methods for handling losses, a matrix can be used that classifies the various loss exposures according to frequency and severity. This matrix can be useful in determining which risk management method should be used (see Exhibit 3.3).

The first loss exposure is characterized by both low frequency and low severity of loss. One example of this type of exposure would be the potential theft of office supplies. This type of exposure can be handled by retention, because the loss occurs infrequently and, when it does occur, it seldom causes financial harm.

The second type of exposure is more serious. Losses occur frequently, but severity is relatively low. Examples of this type of exposure include physical damage losses to automobiles, workers compensation claims, shoplifting, and food spoilage. Loss prevention should be used here to reduce the frequency of losses. In addition, because losses occur regularly and are predictable, the retention technique can also be used. However, because small losses in the aggregate can reach sizable levels over a one-year period, excess insurance could also be purchased.

The third type of exposure can be met by insurance. As stated earlier, insurance is best suited for low-frequency, high-severity losses. High severity means that a catastrophic potential is present, while a low probability of loss indicates that the purchase of insurance is economically feasible. Examples of this type of exposure include fires, explosions, natural disasters, and liability lawsuits. The risk manager could also use a combination of retention and commercial insurance to deal with these exposures.

The fourth and most serious type of exposure is one characterized by both high frequency and high severity. This type of exposure is best handled by avoidance. For example, a truck driver with several convictions for drunk driving may apply for a job with a trucking company. If the driver is hired and injures or kills someone while under the influence of alcohol, the company would be faced with a catastrophic lawsuit. This exposure can be handled by avoidance. The driver should not be hired.

IMPLEMENT AND MONITOR THE RISK MANAGEMENT PROGRAM

At this point, we have discussed three of the four steps in the risk management process. The fourth step is to implement and monitor the risk management program. This step begins with a policy statement.

Risk Management Policy Statement

A **risk management policy statement** is necessary to have an effective risk management program. This statement outlines the risk management objectives of the firm, as well as company policy with respect to treatment of loss exposures. It also educates top-level executives in regard to the risk management process, gives the risk manager greater authority in

the firm, and provides standards for judging the risk manager's performance.

In addition, a **risk management manual** may be developed and used in the program. The manual describes in some detail the risk management program of the firm and can be a very useful tool for training new employees who will be participating in the program. Writing the manual also forces the risk manager to state precisely his or her responsibilities, objectives, and available techniques. The manual also includes important information, such as procedures to follow in an emergency.

Cooperation with Other Departments

The risk manager does not work alone. Other functional departments within the firm are extremely important in identifying pure loss exposures and methods for treating these exposures. These departments can cooperate in the risk management process in the following ways:

- *Accounting.* Internal accounting controls can reduce employee fraud and theft of cash.
- *Finance.* Information can be provided showing how losses can disrupt profits and cash flow, and the effect that losses will have on the firm's balance sheet and profit and loss statement.
- *Marketing.* Accurate packaging can prevent liability lawsuits. Safe distribution procedures can prevent accidents.
- *Production.* Quality control can prevent the production of defective goods and liability lawsuits. Effective safety programs in the plant can reduce injuries and accidents.
- *Human resources.* This department may be responsible for employee benefit programs, pen-

EXHIBIT 3.3
Risk Management Matrix

Type of Loss	Loss Frequency	Loss Severity	Appropriate Risk Management Technique
1	Low	Low	Retention
2	High	Low	Loss prevention and retention
3	Low	High	Insurance
4	High	High	Avoidance

sion programs, safety programs, and the company's hiring, promotion, and dismissal policies.

This list indicates how the risk management process involves the entire firm. Indeed, without the active cooperation of the other departments, the risk management program will be a failure.

Periodic Review and Evaluation

To be effective, the risk management program must be periodically reviewed and evaluated to determine whether the objectives are being attained. In particular, risk management costs, safety programs, and loss-prevention programs must be carefully monitored. Loss records must also be examined to detect any changes in frequency and severity. Finally, the risk manager must determine whether the firm's overall risk management policies are being carried out, and whether the risk manager is receiving the cooperation of the other departments in carrying out the risk management functions.

BENEFITS OF RISK MANAGEMENT

The previous discussion shows that the risk management process involves a complex and detailed analysis. Despite their complexities, however, an effective risk management program yields substantial benefits to the firm or organization. Major benefits include the following:

- The preloss and postloss risk management objectives are more easily attainable.
- The cost of risk is reduced, which may increase the company's profits. The **cost of risk** is a risk management tool that measures certain costs. These costs include premiums paid, retained losses, outside risk management services, financial guarantees, internal administrative costs, and taxes, fees, and certain other expenses.
- Because the adverse financial impact of pure loss exposures is reduced, a firm may be able to enact an enterprise risk management program that treats both pure and speculative loss exposures.
- Society also benefits since both direct and indirect (consequential) losses are reduced. As a result, pain and suffering are reduced.

In conclusion, it is clear that risk managers are extremely important to the financial success of business firms in today's economy. In view of their importance, risk managers are paid relatively high salaries (see Insight 3.4).

PERSONAL RISK MANAGEMENT

The principles of corporate risk management are also applicable to a personal risk management program. **Personal risk management** *refers to the identification of pure risks faced by an individual or family, and to the selection of the most appropriate technique for treating such risks.* Personal risk management considers other methods for handling risk in addition to insurance.

Steps in Personal Risk Management

A personal risk management program involves four steps: (1) identify loss exposures, (2) analyze the loss exposures, (3) select appropriate techniques for treating the loss exposures, and (4) implement and review the program periodically.

Identify Loss Exposures The first step is to identify all loss exposures that can cause serious financial problems. Catastrophic financial losses can result from the following:

1. Personal loss exposures
   - Loss of earned income to the family because of the premature death of the family head
   - Insufficient income and financial assets during retirement
   - Catastrophic medical bills and the loss of earnings during an extended period of disability
   - Loss of earned income from unemployment
   - Identity theft
2. Property loss exposures
   - Direct physical damage to a home and personal property because of fire, lightning, windstorm, flood, earthquake, or other causes
   - Indirect losses resulting from a direct physical damage loss, including extra expenses, moving to another apartment or home during the period of reconstruction, loss of rents, and loss of use of the building or property

INSIGHT 3.4

How Much Do Risk Managers Earn?

A survey of 1484 risk managers by Logic Associates shows that the average risk manager received a salary of $145,000 in 2002. Risk managers typically receive a bonus as well. Almost all employers provide pensions. In addition, many risk managers drive company cars and receive stock options. The actual salaries, however, vary by the annual dollar sales volume of the firm. In general, the largest firms pay the highest salaries as shown in the following table.

Dollar Sales Volume	Average Salary	Average Bonus	Total
$0–$200 million	$ 81,423	$ 2,426	$ 83,849
$201 mil.–$500 million	96,399	3,736	100,135
$500 mil.–$1 billion	109,903	5,810	115,713
$1billion–$2 billion	126,477	8,795	135,272
$2 billion–$4 billion	144,330	13,287	157,617
$4 billion–$7 billion	173,227	19,883	193,110
$7 billion–15 billion	198,258	25,131	223,389
Over $15 billion	234,011	31,942	265,953

SOURCE: Adapted from Sam Friedman, "Risk Manager Salaries Rise, But So Do Employer Demands," *National Underwriter*, Property & Casualty/Risk & Benefits Management Edition, April 7, 2003, p. 10.

- Theft of valuable personal property, including money and securities, jewelry and furs, paintings and fine art, cameras, computer equipment, coin and stamp collections, and antiques
- Direct physical damage losses to cars, motorcycles, and other vehicles from a collision and other-than-collision losses
- Theft of cars, motorcycles, or other vehicles

3. Liability loss exposures
- Legal liability arising out of personal acts that cause bodily injury or property damage to others
- Legal liability arising out of libel, slander, defamation of character, and similar exposures
- Legal liability arising out of the negligent operation of a car, motorcycle, boat, or recreational vehicle
- Legal liability arising out of business or professional activities
- Payment of attorney fees and other legal defense costs

Analyze the Loss Exposures The second step is to analyze the loss exposures. The frequency and severity of potential losses should be estimated so that the most appropriate technique can be used to deal with the exposure. For example, the chance that your home will be totally destroyed by a fire, tornado, or hurricane is relatively small, but the severity of the loss can be catastrophic. Such losses should be insured because of their catastrophic potential. On the other hand, if loss frequency is high, but loss severity is low, such losses should not be insured (such as minor scratches and dents to your car). Other techniques such as retention are more appropriate for handling these types of small losses. For example, minor physical damage losses to your car can be retained by purchasing collision insurance with a deductible.

Select Appropriate Techniques for Treating the Loss Exposures The third step is to select the most appropriate technique for treating each loss exposure. The major methods are avoidance, risk control, retention, noninsurance transfers, and insurance.

1. *Avoidance.* Avoidance is one method for treating a loss exposure. For example, you can avoid being mugged in a high-crime rate area by staying out of the area. You can avoid the loss from the sale of a home in a depressed real estate market by renting instead of buying.
2. *Risk control.* Risk control refers to activities that reduce both the frequency and severity of loss. For example, you can reduce the chance of an auto accident by driving within the speed limit, taking a safe driving course, and driving defensively. Car theft can be prevented by locking the car, removing the keys from the ignition, and installing anti-theft devices.

Risk control can also reduce the severity of a loss. For example, wearing a helmet reduces the severity of a head injury in a motorcycle accident. Wearing a seat belt reduces the severity of an injury in an auto accident. Having a fire extinguisher on the premises reduces the severity of a fire.

3. *Retention.* Retention means that you retain part or all of a loss if it should occur. As noted earlier, risk retention can be active or passive. Active risk retention means you are aware of the risk and plan to retain part or all of it. For example, you can retain small collision losses to your car by buying a collision insurance policy with a deductible. Likewise, you can retain part of a loss to your home or to personal property by buying a homeowners policy with a deductible.

Risk can also be retained passively because of ignorance, indifference, or laziness. This practice can be dangerous if the retained risk could result in a catastrophic loss. For example, many workers are not insured against the risk of long-term disability, even though the adverse financial consequences from a long-term permanent disability generally are more severe than the financial consequences of premature death. Thus, workers who are not insured against this risk are using risk retention in a most dangerous and inappropriate manner.

4. *Noninsurance transfers.* Noninsurance transfers are methods other than insurance by which a pure risk is transferred to a party other than an insurer. For example, the risk of damage to rental property can be transferred to the tenant by requiring a damage deposit and by inserting a provision in the lease holding the tenant responsible for damages. Likewise, the risk of a defective television set can be transferred to the retailer by purchasing an extended-warranty contract that makes the retailer responsible for labor and repairs after the warranty expires.

5. *Insurance.* In a personal risk management program, most people rely heavily on insurance as the major method for dealing with risk. The use of insurance in a personal risk management program is discussed in greater detail later in the text when specific insurance contracts are analyzed.

Implement and Monitor the Program Periodically
The final step is to implement the personal risk management program and review the program periodically. At least every two or three years, you should determine whether all major loss exposures are adequately covered. You should also review your program at major events in your life, such as a divorce, birth of a child, purchase of a home, change of jobs, or death of a spouse or family member.

CASE APPLICATION

City Bus Corporation provides school bus transportation to private and public schools in Lancaster County. City Bus owns 50 buses that are garaged in three different cities within the county. The firm faces competition from two larger bus companies that operate in the same area. Public school boards and private schools generally award contracts to the lowest bidder, but the level of service and overall performance are also considered.

a. Briefly describe the steps in the risk management process that should be followed by the risk manager of City Bus.
b. Identify the major loss exposures faced by City Bus.

c. For each of the loss exposures identified in (b), identify a risk management technique or combination of techniques that could be used to handle the exposure.
d. Describe several sources of funds for paying losses if retention is used in the risk management program.
e. Identify other departments in City Bus that would also be involved in the risk management program.

SUMMARY

- Risk management is a process to identify loss exposures faced by an organization or individual and to select the most appropriate techniques for treating such exposures.

- Risk management has several important objectives. Preloss objectives include the goals of economy, reduction of anxiety, and meeting legal obligations. Postloss objectives include survival of the firm, continued operation, stability of earnings, continued growth, and social responsibility.

- There are four steps in the risk management process.

    Identify loss exposures.

    Analyze the loss exposures.

    Select appropriate techniques for treating the loss exposures.

    Implement and monitor the risk management program.

- Risk control refers to techniques that reduce the frequency and severity of accidental losses. Major risk-control techniques include avoidance, loss prevention, and loss reduction.

- Risk financing refers to techniques that provide for the funding of losses after they occur. Major risk-financing techniques include retention, noninsurance transfers, and commercial insurance.

- Avoidance means that a loss exposure is never acquired or an existing loss exposure is abandoned. Loss prevention refers to measures that reduce the frequency of a particular loss. Loss reduction refers to measures that reduce the severity of a loss after it occurs.

- Retention means that the firm retains part or all of the losses that result from a given loss exposure. This technique can be used if no other method of treatment is available, the worst possible loss is not serious, and losses are highly predictable. Losses can be paid out of the firm's current net income; an unfunded or funded reserve can be established to pay losses; a credit line with a bank can provide funds to pay losses; or the firm can form a captive insurer.

- The advantages of retention are the saving of money on insurance premiums, lower expenses, greater incentive for loss prevention, and increased cash flow. Major disadvantages are possible higher losses that exceed the loss component in insurance premiums, possible higher expenses if loss-control and claims personnel must be hired, and possible higher taxes.

- A captive insurer is an insurer that is owned and established by a parent firm for the purpose of insuring the parent firm's loss exposures. Captive insurers are often formed because of difficulty in obtaining insurance. They can also provide for lower costs; easier access to a reinsurer; and the formation of a profit center.

- Self-insurance or self-funding is a special form of planned retention by which part or all of a given loss exposure is retained by the firm.

- Noninsurance transfers are methods other than insurance by which a pure risk and its financial consequences are transferred to another party.

- Noninsurance transfers offer several advantages. The risk manager may be able to transfer some uninsurable exposures; noninsurance transfers may cost less than insurance; and the potential loss may be shifted to someone who is in a better position to exercise loss control.

- Noninsurance transfers also have several disadvantages. The transfer of a potential loss may fail because the contract language is ambiguous; the firm is still responsible for the loss if the party to whom the potential loss is transferred is unable to pay the loss; and an insurer may not give sufficient premium credit for the transfers.

- Commercial insurance can also be used in a risk management program. Use of insurance involves a selection of insurance coverages, selection of an insurer, negotiation of contract terms with the insurer, dissemination of information concerning the insurance coverages, and periodic review of the insurance program.

- The major advantages of insurance include indemnification after a loss occurs, reduction in uncertainty, availability of valuable risk management services, and the income-tax deductibility of the premiums. The major disadvantages of insurance include the cost of insurance, time and effort that must be spent in negotiating for insurance, and a possible lax attitude toward loss control because of the existence of insurance.

- A risk management program must be properly implemented and administered. This effort involves preparation of a risk management policy statement, close cooperation with other individuals and departments, and periodic review of the entire risk management program.

■ The principles of corporate risk management can also be applied to a personal risk management program.

KEY CONCEPTS AND TERMS

Association or group captive	Maximum probable loss
Avoidance	Noninsurance transfers
Captive insurer	Personal risk management
Cost of risk	Pure captive
Deductible	Retention
Excess insurance	Retention level
Loss exposure	Risk control
Loss frequency	Risk financing
Loss prevention	Risk management
Loss reduction	Risk management manual
Loss severity	Risk management policy statement
Manuscript policy	Risk retention group
Maximum possible loss	Self-insurance

REVIEW QUESTIONS

1. What is the meaning of risk management?

2. Explain the objectives of risk management both before and after a loss occurs.

3. Describe the steps in the risk management process.

4. a. Identify the sources of information that a risk manager can use to identify loss exposures.
   b. What is the difference between the maximum possible loss and maximum probable loss?

5. a. Explain the meaning of risk control.
   b. Explain the following risk control techniques.
      1. Avoidance
      2. Loss prevention
      3. Loss reduction

6. a. Explain the meaning of risk financing.
   b. Explain the following risk financing techniques.
      1. Retention
      2. Noninsurance transfers
      3. Insurance

7. What conditions should be fulfilled before retention is used in a risk management program?

8. a. Define a captive insurer.
   b. Explain the advantages of a captive insurer in a risk management program.

9. a. What is self insurance?
   b. What is a risk retention group?

10. a. Explain the advantages of using insurance in a risk management program.
    b. Explain the disadvantages of using insurance in a risk management program.

APPLICATION QUESTIONS

1. S & L Equipment manufactures and sells scaffolds and ladders that are used by construction firms. The products are sold directly to independent retailers in the United States. The company's risk manager knows that the company could be sued if a scaffold or ladder is defective, and someone is injured. Because the cost of products liability insurance has increased, the risk manager is considering other techniques to treat the company's loss exposures.
   a. Describe the steps in the risk management process.
   b. For each of the following risk management techniques, describe a specific action using that technique that may be helpful in dealing with the company's products liability exposure.
      (1) Avoidance
      (2) Loss prevention
      (3) Loss reduction
      (4) Noninsurance transfers

2. The Swift Corporation has 5000 sales representatives and employees in the United States who drive company cars. The company's risk manager has recommended to the firm's management that the company should implement a partial retention program for collision losses to company cars.
   a. Explain the advantages and disadvantages of a partial retention program to the Swift Corporation.
   b. Identify the factors that the Swift Corporation should consider before it adopts a partial retention program for collision losses to company cars.
   c. If a partial retention program is adopted, what are the various methods the Swift Corporation can use to pay for collision losses to company cars?
   d. Identify two *risk control* measures that could be used in the company's partial retention program for collision losses.

3. Avoidance is a risk control technique that can be used effectively in a risk management program.

a. What is the major advantage of using the technique of avoidance in a risk management program?

b. Is it possible or practical for a firm to avoid all potential losses? Explain your answer.

4. A risk management program must be implemented and periodically monitored to be effective. This step requires the preparation of a *risk management policy statement* and a *risk management manual*. The cooperation of other departments is also necessary.

a. What benefits can the firm expect to receive from a well-prepared risk management policy statement?

b. Identify several departments within a firm that are especially important in a risk management program.

5. Chris and Karen are married and own a three-bedroom home in a large Midwestern city. Their son, Christian, attends college away from home and lives in a fraternity house. Their daughter, Kelly, is a senior in high school. Chris is an accountant who works for a local accounting firm. Karen is a marketing analyst and is often away from home several days at a time. Kelly earns extra cash by babysitting on a regular basis.

The family's home contains household furniture, personal property, a computer that Chris uses to prepare business tax returns on weekends, and a laptop computer that Karen uses while traveling. The Swifts also own three cars. Christian drives a 1995 Ford; Chris drives a 2002 Pontiac for both business and personal use; and Karen drives a 2004 Toyota and a rental car when she is traveling. Although the Swifts have owned their home for several years, they are considering moving because of the recent increase in violent crime in their neighborhood.

a. Describe briefly the steps in the personal risk management process.

b. Identify the major pure risks or pure loss exposures to which Chris and Karen are exposed with respect to each of the following:
(1) Personal loss exposures
(2) Property loss exposures
(3) Liability loss exposures

c. With respect to each of the loss exposures mentioned above, identify an appropriate personal risk management technique that could be used to treat the exposure.

INTERNET RESOURCES

- **Captive.com** disseminates information about captive insurers. The organization claims that its Web site enables risk managers, owners of captives, and anyone who has an interest in alternative risk transfer techniques to meet with colleagues, ask questions, and find needed resources. Visit the site at

  http://www.captive.com

- The **International Financial Risk Institute** provides a comprehensive introduction to financial risk management. This site educates readers on the most valuable official documents on this subject. Along with a risk management checklist, this site also includes a regulatory documents library, a collection of risk management case studies, and a risk management glossary. Visit the site at

  http://riskinstitute.ch

- The **Nonprofit Risk Management Center** conducts research and education on risk management and insurance issues that are of special concern to nonprofit organizations. The organization provides technical assistance, a newsletter, easy-to-read publications, and workshops and conferences related to risk management and insurance. The organization also offers risk management consulting services. Visit the site at

  http://www.nonprofitrisk.org

- The **Public Risk Management Association** represents risk managers of state and local governmental units. The organization provides practical training and education for risk managers in the public sector; publishes a magazine, newsletter, and detailed issue-specific publications. Visit the site at

  http://www.primacentral.org

- The **Risk and Insurance Management Society (RIMS)** is the premier professional association in the United States for risk managers and corporate buyers of insurance. RIMS provides a forum for the discussion of common risk management issues, supports loss-prevention activities, and makes known to insurers the insurance needs of its members. RIMS has local chapters in major cities and publishes *Risk Management* magazine. Visit the site at

  http://www.rims.org

■ The **Self-Insurance Institute of America** is a national association that promotes self-insurance as an alternative method for financing losses. The organization publishes technical articles on self-insurance, holds educational conferences, and promotes the legislative and regulatory interests of the self-insurance industry at both the federal and state levels. Visit the site at

http://www.siia.org

SELECTED REFERENCES

Barton, Thomas, William G. Shenkir, and Paul L. Walker. *Making Enterprise Risk Management Pay Off: How Leading Companies Implement Risk Management.* Upper Saddle River, NJ: Financial Times Prentice Hall, 2002.

Elliott, Michael W. *Fundamentals of Risk Financing,* First Edition. Malvern, PA: American Institute for Chartered Property Casualty Underwriters/Insurance Institute of America, 2002.

Harrington, Scott. E. and Gregory R. Niehaus. *Risk Management and Insurance,* 2nd ed. Boston, MA: Irwin/McGraw-Hill, 2004.

Head, George L., ed. *Essentials of Risk Control,* 3rd ed., vols. 1 and 2. Malvern, PA: Insurance Institute of America, 1995.

Head, George L., and Stephen Horn II. *Essentials of Risk Management,* 3rd ed., vols. 1 and 2. Malvern, PA: Insurance Institute of America, 1997.

Wiening, Eric A. *Foundations of Risk Management and Insurance.* Malvern, PA: American Institute for Chartered Property Casualty Underwriters/Insurance Institute of America, 2002.

Williams, C. Arthur, Jr., Michael L. Smith, and Peter C. Young. *Risk Management and Insurance,* 8th ed. Boston, MA: Irwin/McGraw-Hill, 1998.

NOTES

1. Robert I. Mehr and Bob A. Hedges, *Risk Management: Concepts and Applications* (Homewood, IL: Richard D. Irwin, 1974), chs. 1–2; see also Eric A. Wiening, *Foundations of Risk Management and Insurance* (Malvern, PA: American Society for Chartered Casualty Property Underwriters/Insurance Institute of America, 2002), ch. 3, and George L. Head and Stephen Horn II, *Essentials of Risk Management,* 3rd ed., vol. 1 (Malvern, PA: Insurance Institute of America, 1997), pp. 70–79.

2. This section is based on Head and Horn, pp. 36–44, and C. Arthur Williams, Jr., et al., *Principles of Risk Management and Insurance,* 2nd ed., vol. 1 (Malvern, PA: American Institute for Property and Liability Underwriters, 1981), chs. 2–3.

3. Williams et al., pp. 125–126.

4. Head and Horn, pp. 40–42.

5. Memorandum on IRS ruling 2001-31 issued by Tom Jones at McDermott, Will, and Emery, Chicago, June 7, 2001, to Captive Insurance Companies Association at http://www.captive.com/IRS2001_31.html

6. Williams et al., pp. 126–133.

7. Ibid., pp. 103–104.

8. Ibid., pp. 107–123, 146–151.

9. A manuscript policy is one specifically designed for a firm to meet its specific needs and requirements.

10. Williams et al., pp. 108–116.

CHAPTER 4

ADVANCED TOPICS IN RISK MANAGEMENT*

"The field of risk management is undergoing monumental change. Risk managers must understand financial markets and be able to effectively incorporate quantitative analysis and technology in their risk management programs"

Millicent W. Workman, CPCU,
Director of Risk Financing,
Baptist Memorial Health Care Corporation

LEARNING OBJECTIVES

After studying this chapter, you should be able to

◆ Explain the meaning of financial risk management and enterprise risk management.

◆ Describe the impact of the underwriting cycle and consolidation in the insurance industry on the practice of risk management.

◆ Explain the securitization of risk, including catastrophe bonds and weather options.

◆ Explain the methods that a risk manager employs to forecast losses.

◆ Show how financial analysis can be applied to risk management decision making.

◆ Describe other risk management tools that may be of assistance to risk managers.

*Prepared by Michael J. McNamara, Washington State University.

Susan Carley had experience in both insurance claims and underwriting when she accepted a staff position in the Risk Management Department of Northeast Petroleum Products (NPP) in 1999. NPP owns and operates a petroleum refinery and 72 service stations. The company also sells heating oil to more than 90,000 business and residential customers in the New England region and in two Canadian provinces.

Susan quickly became frustrated as NPP's risk manager was "old school," equating risk management with insurance management. Often risk management decisions were based on the whims of the risk manager rather than on sound financial analysis. Susan stayed with the company and began to work on her MBA, taking courses two nights a week. In addition to general business courses, Susan concentrated her efforts in statistics and finance. When NPP's risk manager retired earlier this year, Susan was offered the job as risk manager. Susan agreed to accept the position, provided she was given the latitude to make some major changes in the risk management program. She is interested, for example, in expanding the program beyond the traditional risks addressed by a risk management program. The chief financial officer is supportive, and has encouraged Susan to make greater use of financial analysis in her decision making.

As discussed in Chapter 3, Susan's job as risk manager will involve more than simply purchasing insurance. She must identify the loss exposures faced by the company, analyze those exposures, select and implement a combination of risk treatment measures, and monitor the success of the risk management program.

This chapter builds on the discussion of risk management in Chapter 3 and discusses some advanced topics in risk management. Topics discussed include the changing scope of risk management, insurance market dynamics, loss forecasting, financial analysis in risk management decision making, and application of several risk management tools.

THE CHANGING SCOPE OF RISK MANAGEMENT

Traditionally, risk management was limited in scope to pure loss exposures, including property risks, liability risks, and personnel risks. An interesting trend emerged in the 1990s, however, as many businesses began to expand the scope of risk management to include speculative financial risks. Recently, some businesses have gone a step further, expanding their risk management programs to consider all risks faced by the organization.

Financial Risk Management

Business firms face a number of speculative financial risks. **Financial risk management** *refers to the* *identification, analysis, and treatment of speculative financial risks.* These risks include the following:

- Commodity price risk
- Interest rate risk
- Currency exchange rate risk

Commodity Price Risk Commodity price risk *is the risk of losing money if the price of a commodity changes.* Producers and users of commodities face commodity price risks. For example, consider an agricultural operation that will have thousands of bushels of grain at harvest time. At harvest, the price of the commodity may have increased or decreased, depending on the supply and demand for grain. Because little storage is available for the crop, the grain must be sold at the current market price, even if that price is low. In a similar fashion, users and distributors of commodities face commodity price risks. Consider a cereal company that has promised to deliver 500,000 boxes of cereal at an agreed-upon price in six months. In the meantime, the price of grain—a commodity needed to produce the cereal—may increase or decrease, altering the profitability of the transaction. The first part of Exhibit 4.1 shows how futures contracts can be used to hedge a commodity price risk.

Interest Rate Risk Financial institutions are especially susceptible to interest rate risk. **Interest rate risk** *is the risk of loss caused by adverse interest rate movements.* For example, consider a bank that has loaned money at fixed interest rates to home purchasers under 15- and 30-year mortgages. If interest rates increase, the bank must pay higher interest rates on deposits while the mortgages are locked-in at lower interest rates. Similarly, a corporation might issue bonds at a time when interest rates are high. For the bonds to sell at their face value when issued, the coupon interest rate must equal the investor-required rate of return. If interest rates later decline, the company must still pay the higher coupon interest rate on the bonds.

Currency Exchange Rate Risk The currency exchange rate is the value for which one nation's currency may be converted to another nation's currency. For example, one Canadian dollar might

be worth the equivalent of two-thirds of one U.S. dollar. At this currency exchange rate, one U.S. dollar may be converted to one and one-half Canadian dollars.

U.S. companies that have international operations (such as NPP's Canadian operations) are susceptible to currency exchange rate risk. **Currency exchange rate risk** *is the risk of loss of value caused by changes in the rate at which one nation's currency may be converted to another nation's currency.* For example, a U.S. company faces currency exchange rate risk when it agrees to accept a specified amount of foreign currency in the future as payment for goods sold or work performed. Likewise, U.S. companies with significant foreign operations face an earnings risk because of fluctuating exchange rates. When a U.S. company generates profits abroad, those gains must be translated back into U.S. dollars. When the U.S. dollar is strong (that is, when it has a high value relative to a foreign currency), the foreign currency purchases fewer U.S. dollars and the company's earnings therefore are lower. A weak U.S. dollar (that is, when it has a low value relative to a foreign currency) means that foreign profits can be exchanged for a larger number of U.S. dollars, and consequently the firm's earnings are higher.

Managing Financial Risks The traditional separation of pure and speculative risks meant that different business departments addressed these risks. Pure risks were handled by the risk manager through risk retention, risk transfer, and loss control. Speculative risks were handled by the finance division through contractual provisions and capital market instruments. Examples of contractual provisions that address financial risks include call features on bonds that permit bonds with high coupon rates to be retired early and adjustable interest rate provisions on mortgages through which the interest rate varies with interest rates in the general economy. A variety of capital market approaches are also employed, including options contracts, forward contracts, futures contracts, and interest rate swaps.[1] The second part of Exhibit 4.1 shows how options can help to manage the risk of a decrease in the price of common stock.

During the 1990s, some businesses began taking a more holistic view of the pure and speculative risks

Exhibit 4.1
Managing Financial Risk—Two Examples

---

1. Hedging a Commodity Price Risk Using Futures Contracts

A corn grower estimates in May that his production will total 20,000 bushels of corn, with the harvest completed by December. Checking the price of futures contracts, he notices that the price of December corn is $2.90 per bushel. He would like to hedge the risk that the price of corn will be lower at harvest time and can do so by the appropriate use of futures contracts. Because corn futures contracts are traded in 5000 bushel units, he would sell four contracts in May totaling 20,000 bushels in the futures market. In December, he would buy back four contracts to offset his futures position. As demonstrated below, it doesn't matter whether the price of corn has increased or decreased by December. By using futures contracts and ignoring transaction expenses, he has locked in total revenue of $58,000.

If the market price of corn drops to $2.50 per bushel in December:

Revenue from sale of corn	20,000 × $2.50	=	$50,000
Sale of four contracts at $2.90 in May	58,000		
Purchase of four contracts at $2.50 in December	50,000		
Gain on futures transaction			8,000
Total revenue			$58,000

If the market price of corn increases to $3.00 per bushel in December:

Revenue from sale of corn	20,000 × $3.00	=	$60,000
Sale of four contracts at $2.90 in May	58,000		
Purchase of four contracts at $3.00 in December	60,000		
Loss on futures transaction			(2,000)
Total revenue			$58,000

2. Using Options to Protect against Adverse Stock Price Movements

Options on stocks can be used to protect against adverse stock price movements. A call option gives the owner the right to buy 100 shares of stock at a given price during a specified period. A put option gives the owner the right to sell 100 shares of stock at a given price during a specified period. While there are many options strategies used to reduce risk, one simple alternative is discussed here: buying put options to protect against a decline in the price of stock that is already owned.

Consider someone who owns 100 shares of a stock priced at $43 per share. The owner may be concerned that the price of the stock will fall. At the same time, however, the owner may not wish to sell the stock as the sale would trigger taxation of a capital gain. In addition, the owner may believe that the price of the stock could increase. The stockholder could purchase a put option to offset a price decline.

Assume there is a put option available with a strike (exercise) price of $40. The owner of the stock could purchase the option. If the price of the stock increases, the stock owner has lost the purchase price of the option (called the premium), but the stock price has increased. But what if the price of the stock declines, say to $33 per share? In the absence of the put option, the stock owner has lost $10 ($43–$33) per share on paper. As owner of the put option, however, the stock holder has the right to sell 100 shares at $40 per share. Thus the option is "in the money" by $7 per share ($40–$33) ignoring the option premium. The put option could be sold to offset the paper loss. Using put options in this way protects against losing money if the price of the stock declines.

---

faced by the organization, hoping to achieve cost savings and better risk treatment solutions by combining coverage for both types of risk. In 1997, Honeywell became the first company to enter into an "integrated risk program" with American International Group (AIG).[2] An **integrated risk program** *is a risk treatment technique that combines coverage for pure and* *speculative risks in the same contract.* At the time, Honeywell was generating more than one-third of its profits abroad. Its integrated risk program provided traditional property and liability insurance, as well as coverage for currency exchange rate risk.

In recognition of the fact that they are treating these risks jointly, some organizations have created a new position. The **chief risk officer (CRO)** *is responsible for treatment of risks (pure, speculative, and others) faced by the organization.*[3] Combining responsibilities in one area permits treatment of the risks in a unified, and often more economical way. For example, the risk manager may be concerned about a large self-insured property claim. The financial manager may be concerned about losses caused by adverse changes in the exchange rate. Either loss, by itself, may not harm the organization if the company has a strong balance sheet. The occurrence of both losses, however, may damage the business more severely. An integrated risk management program can be designed to consider both contingencies by including a double-trigger option. A **double-trigger option** is *a provision that provides for payment only if two specified losses occur.* Thus payments would be made only if a large property claim and a large exchange rate loss occurred. The cost of such coverage is less than the cost of treating each risk separately.

Enterprise Risk Management

Encouraged by the success of financial risk management, some organizations are taking the next logical step. **Enterprise risk management** *is a comprehensive risk management program that addresses an organization's pure risks, speculative risks, strategic risks, and operational risks.* Pure and speculative risks were defined previously. *Strategic risk* refers to uncertainty regarding the organization's goals and objectives, and the organization's strengths, weaknesses, opportunities, and threats. *Operational risks* are risks that develop out of business operations, including such things as manufacturing products and providing services to customers. By packaging all of these risks in a single program, the corporation offsets one risk against another, and in the process reduces its overall risk. As long as the risks combined in the program do not exhibit perfect positive correlation, the combination of exposures reduces risk. Indeed, if some of the risks are negatively correlated, risk can be reduced significantly.

Consider NPP's operations, for example. During the summer, the company agrees to deliver heating oil in the fall at a specified price. Between summer and the delivery date, the price of heating oil may increase. Considering this risk only, Susan Carley may decide to use heating oil futures contracts to hedge the company's price risk. NPP's other business operations, which include 72 service stations, provide a natural hedge position, however. If the price of fuel increases during the summer months, NPP will make money through its service station operations but lose money covering the promised heating oil delivery. Likewise, if the price of heating oil and gasoline falls between the summer and the fall, NPP will make money delivering heating oil at a price higher than the current market price of heating oil at a time when gasoline sales may not be as profitable.

To what extent have enterprise risk management (ERM) programs actually been adopted? Early studies estimated that 30 to 35 percent of U.S. and North American companies had adopted ERM.[4] Recently, Tillinghast-Towers Perrin conducted a number of studies of ERM adoption and practices across a wide spectrum of industries.[5] They found that 49 percent of the companies surveyed had fully (11 percent) or partially (38 percent) adopted ERM programs. Usage of ERM was most prominent in the financial services sector (the largest adopters being global insurers), followed by energy and mining, manufacturing, and telecommunications companies.

Organizations adopting ERM programs did so for several reasons. Among the reasons cited were: holistic treatment of risks facing the organization, advantage over competing businesses, positive impact upon revenues, reduction in earnings volatility, and compliance with corporate governance guidelines. Some barriers cited by survey respondents included: organization culture, turf battles, management's perception that ERM is not a priority, lack of a formal process, and deficiencies in intellectual capital and technology.

INSURANCE MARKET DYNAMICS

Chapter 3 discussed the various methods of dealing with risk. When property and liability loss exposures are not eliminated through risk avoidance, losses that occur must be financed in some other way. The risk manager must choose between two methods of funding losses: *risk retention* and *risk transfer*. Retained losses can be paid out of current earnings, from loss reserves, by borrowing, or by a captive

EXHIBIT 4.2
Combined Ratio for All Lines of Property and Liability Insurance, 1956–2002*

Combined ratio

SOURCE: Data from 1998–2002 include state funds. *Best's Aggregates & Averages—Property/Casualty* (Oldwick, NJ: A.M. Best Company, 2003), p. 350.

insurance company. Risk transfer shifts the burden of paying for losses to another party, most often a property and liability insurance company. Decisions about whether to retain risks or to transfer them are influenced by conditions in the insurance marketplace. Three important factors influencing the insurance market are:

- The underwriting cycle
- Consolidation in the insurance industry
- Securitization of risk

The Underwriting Cycle

For many years, a cyclical pattern has been observed in a number of underwriting results and profitability measures in the property and liability insurance industry. *This cyclical pattern in underwriting stringency, premium levels, and profitability is referred to as the* **underwriting cycle.** *Property and liability insurance markets fluctuate between periods of tight underwriting standards and high premiums, called a*

"hard" insurance market, *and periods of loose underwriting standards and low premiums, called a* "soft" insurance market.

A number of measures can be used to ascertain the status of the underwriting cycle. Exhibit 4.2 shows the combined ratio for the property and liability insurance industry over time. The **combined ratio** *is the ratio of paid losses and loss adjustment expenses plus underwriting expenses to premiums.* If the combined ratio is greater than 1 (or 100 percent), underwriting operations are unprofitable. For example, the combined ratio of 107 for 2002 indicates that for every $1 that insurers collected in premiums, they paid out $1.07 in claims and expenses. If the combined ratio is less than 1 (or 100 percent), insurance companies are making money on underwriting operations.

Risk managers must consider current premium rates and underwriting standards when making their retention and transfer decisions. When the market is "soft," insurance can be purchased at favorable terms (for example, lower premiums, broader coverage, removal of exclusions). In a "hard" market, more retention is used because some insurance coverages are limited in availability or may not be affordable. The continued soft market of the late 1990s, for example, led some risk managers to purchase multiple-year insurance contracts in an effort to lock-in favorable terms.

What causes these price fluctuations in property and liability insurance markets? Although a number of explanations have been offered,[6] two obvious factors affect property and liability insurance pricing and underwriting decisions:

- Insurance industry capacity
- Investment returns

Insurance Industry Capacity In the insurance industry, **capacity** *refers to the relative level of surplus.* **Surplus** *is the difference between an insurer's assets and its liabilities.* When the property and liability insurance industry is in a strong surplus position, insurers can reduce premiums and loosen underwriting standards, because they have a cushion to draw on if underwriting results prove unfavorable. Given the flexibility of financial capital and the competitive nature of the insurance industry, other insurers often follow suit if one insurer takes this step. As competition intensifies, premiums are reduced further, and underwriting standards are applied less stringently. Underwriting losses begin to mount for insurers, because inadequate premiums have been charged. Underwriting losses reduce insurers' surplus, and at some point, premiums must be raised and underwriting standards tightened to restore the depleted surplus. These actions will lead to a return to profitable underwriting, which helps to replenish the surplus. When adequate surplus is restored, insurers once again become able to reduce premiums and loosen underwriting standards, causing the cycle to repeat.

External factors (such as earthquakes, hurricanes, and large liability awards) may increase the level of claims, thereby reducing surplus. The insurance market was already hardening when the World Trade Center (WTC) was attacked in September 2001. It is estimated that the insured claims stemming from this disaster will be in the $40 billion range. While much of the WTC losses will be paid by reinsurance companies, the reinsurers will pass these large losses back to primary insurers in the form of higher premiums. Primary insurers in turn will increase insurance premiums paid by insurance purchasers.

While some disasters are limited to certain coverage lines (e.g., Hurricane Andrew primarily caused large claims under personal lines property insurance), the WTC disaster produced what in the insurance industry is called a "clash loss." A **clash loss** *occurs when several insurance lines simultaneously experience huge losses.* The WTC disaster was unique in that it created large losses for workers compensation insurers, property insurers, aircraft liability insurers, business income insurers, life and health insurers, and several others.

It is important to note that insurance price volatility and underwriting results vary across lines of insurance. Liability insurance tends to exhibit greater price volatility with occasional insurance availability problems for certain lines. For example, during the mid- to late-1990s, employment-related practices liability insurance (EPLI) was expensive and in some cases difficult to obtain. This coverage protects an employer against liability arising out of wrongful termination, sexual harassment, employment and advancement discrimination, and similar claims.[7] At the present time, a problem insurance line is Director's and Officer's liability insurance (D&O). This coverage protects organizational leaders against the claims of stockholders, employees, retirees, customers, suppliers, and others. Recent cases in which corporate leaders were alleged to have caused harm to others through their malfeasance (e.g. Enron, WorldCom, Tyco, and Adelphia) help to explain the present market condition.[8]

Investment Returns Would you sell insurance if, for every dollar you collected in premiums, you expected to pay 78 cents in losses and 30 cents in expenses? That payout rate would lead to a loss of 8 cents per dollar of premiums collected. Property and liability insurance companies can, and often do, sell coverages at an expected loss, hoping to offset underwriting losses with investment income. In reality, insurance companies are in two businesses: underwriting risks and investing premiums. If insurers expect favorable investment results, they can sell their insurance coverages at lower premium rates, hoping to offset underwriting losses with investment income. This practice is known as cash flow underwriting.

During the period from 1980 through 2002, the combined ratio for the property and casualty insurance industry exceeded 100.0 in every year except one (1997). Insurers routinely lost money underwriting risks during this period and relied on investment income to offset these losses. Many people cite the high rate of return on the equity portion of insurers' investment portfolios as a major factor contributing to the prolonged soft market in the early and mid-1990s. Toward the end of the decade and in the first part of the new decade, however, equity returns dipped and interest rates plunged, reducing the rate of return on invested assets.[9] Indeed, while total assets in the property and casualty industry increased from 1998 to 2002, net investment income fell during the same period.[10] If insurers cannot rely on investment income to offset underwriting losses, steps must be taken to produce more profitable underwriting results. Such steps include premium increases, more restrictive coverage, and tightened underwriting standards.

Consolidation in the Insurance Industry

While changes were occurring in insurance product markets, changes were also occurring among the organizations operating in this sector of the economy. In the financial services industry, the 1990s constituted a period of great **consolidation**. **Consolidation** *means the combining of business organizations through mergers and acquisitions.* A number of consolidation trends have changed the insurance marketplace for risk managers:

- Insurance company mergers and acquisitions
- Insurance brokerage mergers and acquisitions
- Cross-industry consolidations

Insurance Company Mergers and Acquisitions Given the market structure of the property and liability insurance industry (numerous companies, relatively low barriers to entry given the flexibility of financial capital, and relatively homogenous products), the greater number of insurance company consolidations in the 1990s may not have severe effects on the operations of risk managers.[11] Risk managers may notice, however, that the marketplace is popu-

lated by fewer but larger, independent insurance organizations as a result of consolidation. Mergers and acquisitions are discussed in greater detail in Chapter 25.

Insurance Brokerage Mergers and Acquisitions Consolidation of insurance brokerages has had profound consequences for risk managers. **Insurance brokers** *are intermediaries who represent insurance purchasers. Insurance brokers offer an array of services to their clients, including attempting to place their clients' business with insurers.* Clearly, a risk manager wants to obtain insurance coverages and related services under the most favorable financial terms available. Periodically, risk managers contact several insurance agents and insurance brokers in an effort to obtain competitive insurance coverage bids. The number of large, national insurance brokerages has declined significantly in recent years because of consolidation. For example, before the consolidation of recent years, a risk manager could obtain coverage bids through Sedgwick Group, Johnson & Higgins, and Marsh & McLennan. As a result of consolidation, these three large, independent brokerages are now a single entity—Marsh and McLennan Companies, Inc. Other large insurance brokerages have merged with or been acquired by other insurance brokerages as well.[12]

Cross-Industry Consolidation Consolidation in the financial services arena is not limited to mergers between insurance companies or between insurance brokerages. Boundaries separating institutions with depository functions, institutions that underwrite risk, and securities businesses were enacted in Depression-era legislation. The divisions between banks, insurance companies, and securities firms began to blur in the 1990s. The U.S. Congress formally struck down the barriers with passage of the Financial Services Modernization Act of 1999 (also known by the names of the bill's sponsors, Gramm-Leach-Bliley). The 1998 merger between Citibank and Travelers, which created Citigroup, provides an excellent example of an integrated financial services company. The consolidated company included Citibank, Travelers Insurance Group, Smith Barney, and several other financial services operations. In 2002, Citigroup decided to spin-off Travelers Insurance. A second example is the announcement in

2001 by Wells Fargo that it would acquire ACO Brokerage, parent firm of Acordia Inc., a large insurance brokerage. In addition to mergers and acquisitions between different types of financial institutions, some financial services companies are simply diversifying their operations by expanding into new sectors. State Farm Insurance, for example, has its own bank, offers mortgages, and sells mutual funds.[13]

Securitization of Risk

Another important development in insurance and risk management is the accelerating use of securitization of risk. **Securitization of risk** *means that insurable risk is transferred to the capital markets through creation of a financial instrument, such as a catastrophe bond, futures contract, options contract, or other financial instrument.* The impact of risk securitization upon the insurance marketplace is an immediate increase in capacity for insurers and reinsurers. Rather than relying upon the capacity of insurers only, securitization provides access to the capital of many investors.

Insurers were among the first organizations to experiment with securitization. USAA Insurance Company, through a subsidiary, issued a catastrophe bond in 1997 to protect the company against catastrophic hurricane losses. **Catastrophe bonds** *are corporate bonds that permit the issuer to skip or defer scheduled payments if a catastrophic loss occurs.* Under the terms of the USAA bond, investors were paid principal and interest provided that hurricane losses during a time period did not exceed a specified level. Principal and interest would be lost, however, if hurricane claims exceeded a trigger point. In the largest catastrophe bond transaction in 2002, Hanover Reinsurance securitized $230 million in earthquake, hurricane and wind risk in the U.S., Japan, and Europe by issuing catastrophe bonds through a subsidiary. Swiss Re, Lloyd's, USAA, and Nissay Dowa also issued cat bonds during 2002.[14]

Catastrophe bonds are not the only way in which risk can be securitized. The profitability of many businesses is determined, in large part, by weather conditions. Utility companies, agricultural enterprises, resorts, and other businesses face weather-related risk and uncertainty. More and more of these businesses are turning to the weather derivatives market, the fastest growing segment of the derivatives market, for assistance in managing this risk. *A* **weather option** *provides a payment if a specified weather contingency (e.g. temperatures higher or lower than normal) occurs.* For an update on the weather derivatives market, see Insight 4.1.

LOSS FORECASTING

The risk manager must also identify the risks the organization faces, and then analyze the potential frequency and severity of these loss exposures. Although loss history provides valuable information, there is no guarantee that future losses will follow past loss trends. Risk managers can employ a number of techniques to assist in predicting loss levels, including the following:

- Probability analysis
- Regression analysis
- Forecasting based on loss distributions

Probability Analysis

Chance of loss is the probability that an adverse event will occur. The probability (P) of such an event is equal to the number of events likely to occur (X) divided by the number of exposure units (N). Thus, if a vehicle fleet has 500 vehicles and on average 100 vehicles suffer physical damage each year, the probability that a fleet vehicle will be damaged in any given year is:

$$P(\text{physical damage}) = 100/500 = .20 \text{ or } 20\%$$

Some probabilities of events can be easily deduced (for example, the probability that a fair coin will come up "heads" or "tails"). Other probabilities (for example, the probability that a male age 50 will die before reaching age 60) may be estimated from prior loss data.

The risk manager must also be concerned with the characteristics of the event being analyzed. Some events are **independent events**—*the occurrence does not affect the occurrence of another event.* For example, assume that a business has production facilities in Louisiana and Virginia, and that the probability of a fire at the Louisiana plant is 5 percent and that the probability of a fire at the Virginia plant is 4 percent. Obviously, the occurrence of one of these events does not influence the occurrence of the other event. If events are independent, the probability that

INSIGHT 4.1

The Weather (Derivatives) Report

Weather derivatives have come a long way since 1997 when a handful of American energy companies developed several dozen over-the-counter (OTC) contracts. Weather derivatives are traded on the Chicago Mercantile Exchange (CME), The London International Financial Futures Exchange, and the Helsinki Exchange, with futures and options exchanges in other countries also seriously considering this innovation.

Although the notional value of contracts written in the past year was down $1 million from the previous year, from April 2002 through March 2003, the number of contracts transacted worldwide nearly tripled according to the Weather Risk Management Association. This amounts to 11,756 contracts with a value of nearly $4.2 billion.

Originally targeted toward utilities to enable them to hedge against unseasonable weather, these derivatives are now used by farmers, resorts, casinos, the travel industry, manufacturers of seasonal equipment, underwriters, reinsurers, and any other sector with revenues subject to the vagaries of the weather.

Prior to the development of weather derivatives, businesses were unable to hedge against overall weather conditions. Some micro hedges existed, such as weather insurance (event insurance) and agricultural futures, but these are narrowly focused. Weather insurance hedges a *narrow window of time,* often one day. Agricultural futures hedge a tiny sector of the economy, such as soybeans. These micro hedges, even when aggregated, do not allow businesses to hedge against the risk of pervasively adverse weather conditions.

The impetus for the development of weather derivatives was the extreme warm winter of 1997 through 1998, when El Niño depressed the revenues of many utilities. An OTC market for weather options quickly emerged, but it proved ineffective due to lack of liquidity, an absence of price transparency, and the ever-present risk of counter-party default.

The embryonic OTC market for weather derivatives languished until 2001 when the Chicago Mercantile Exchange introduced exchange-traded weather derivatives (both futures and options) which created the liquidity, price transparency and counterparty certainty that the market needed to be viable. Later in the same year, the London International Financial Futures Exchange introduced weather futures that now allow Europeans to hedge against their respective weather conditions. In 2002, the Helsinki Exchange began trading weather futures to allow Scandinavian countries to hedge against their adverse weather conditions.

Currently, the weather derivatives market—which includes exchange-traded futures and options, as well as OTC contracts—is the fastest growing derivatives market in the world. In 2002, the CME alone traded $4.3 billion of weather derivatives contracts. Although this amount is just a fraction of the multitrillion-dollar derivatives market, it represents remarkable growth considering that 2002 was the first full year that CME offered such contracts.

What has caused such impressive growth? First, economists estimate that nearly 20 percent of the U.S. economy is directly or inversely affected by the weather. Such a percentage most likely applies to other developed economies, too, explaining the subsequent adoption of this contract by exchanges in England and Scandinavia.

Second, the exchanges are doing a good job of tooting their own horn. They heavily advertise this contract in applicable sectors so more and more firms are learning about and using this innovation. So far, ski lodges in the United States, pubs in the United Kingdom, restaurants and retail shops in Europe and golf courses in Japan have all used weather derivatives to hedge their revenue against the risk of adverse weather.

Finally, this growth is being fueled by new corporate governance codes, especially in the United States, which require companies to identify and hedge against foreseeable risks. Such regulation is especially applicable for utilities, which are publicly regulated.

Weather derivatives will continue to expand in Asia and Australia, as well as in the strongholds of Europe and the United States. This growth will likely develop from the latest movement toward smaller contracts, a broader spectrum of users, and a diversification in the types of weather protection acquired.

SOURCE: Russ Ray, "The Weather (Derivatives) Report," *Risk Management Magazine* (August 2003), p. 56. Reprinted with permission from *Risk Management Magazine.* © 2003 Risk and Insurance Management Society, Inc. All Rights Reserved.

they will occur together is the product of the individual probabilities. Thus, the probability that both production facilities will be damaged by fire is

P(fire at Louisiana plant)
$\times\ P$(fire at Virginia plant) $= P$(fire at both plants)
$.04 \times .05 = .002$ or $.2\%$

Other events can be classified as **dependent events**—*the occurrence of one event affects the occurrence of the other.* If two buildings are located close together, and one building catches on fire, the probability that the other building will burn is increased. For example, suppose that the individual probability of a fire loss at each building is 3 percent. The probability that the second building will have a fire given that the first building has a fire, however, may be 40 percent. Then what is the probability of two fires? This probability is a conditional probability that is equal to the probability of the first event multiplied by the probability of the second event given that the first event has occurred:

$$P(\text{fire at one bldg}) \times P\left(\begin{array}{c}\text{fire at second bldg} \\ \text{given fire at first bldg}\end{array}\right)$$
$$= P(\text{both burn})$$
$$.03 \times .40 = .012 \text{ or } 1.20\%$$

Events may also be mutually exclusive. *Events are* **mutually exclusive** *if the occurrence of one event precludes the occurrence of the second event.* For example, if a building is destroyed by fire, it cannot also be destroyed by flood. Mutually exclusive probabilities are additive. If the probability that a building will be destroyed by fire is 2 percent and the probability that the building will be destroyed by flood is 1 percent, then the probability the building will be destroyed by either fire or flood is

$$P(\text{fire destroys bldg}) + P(\text{flood destroys bldg})$$
$$= P(\text{fire or flood destroys bldg})$$
$$.02 + .01 = .03 \text{ or } 3\%$$

If the independent events are not mutually exclusive, then more than one event could occur. Care must be taken not to "double-count" when determining the probability that at least one event will occur. For example, if the probability of minor fire damage is 4 percent and the probability of minor flood damage is 3 percent, then the probability of at least one of these events occurring is

$$P(\text{minor fire}) + P(\text{minor flood})$$
$$- P(\text{minor fire and flood}) = P(\text{at least one event})$$
$$.04 + .03 - (.04) \times (.03) = .0688 \text{ or } 6.88\%$$

Assigning probabilities to individual and joint events and analyzing the probabilities can assist the risk manager in formulating a risk treatment plan.

Regression Analysis

Regression analysis is another method for forecasting losses. **Regression analysis** *characterizes the rela-*

tionship between two or more variables and then uses this characterization to predict values of a variable. One variable—the dependent variable—is hypothesized to be a function of one or more independent variables. It is not difficult to envision relationships that would be of interest to risk managers in which one variable is dependent upon another variable. For example, consider workers compensation claims. It is logical to hypothesize that the number of workers compensation claims should be positively related to some variable representing employment (for example, the number of employees, payroll, or hours worked). Likewise, we would expect the number of physical damage claims for a fleet of vehicles to increase as the size of the fleet increases or as the number of miles driven each year by fleet vehicles increases.

The first panel in Exhibit 4.3 provides data for a company's annual payroll in thousands of dollars and the corresponding number of workers compensation claims during the year. In the second panel of Exhibit 4.3, the number of claims is plotted against payroll. Regression analysis provides the coordinates of the line that best fits the points in the chart.[15] This line will minimize the sum of the squared deviations of the points from the line. Our hypothesized relationship is as follows:

$$\text{Number of workers compensation claims}$$
$$= B_0 + (B_1 \times \text{Payroll [in thousands]})$$

where B_0 is a constant and B_1 is the coefficient of the independent variable.

The regression results provided at the bottom of Exhibit 4.3 were obtained using spreadsheet software. The coefficient of determination, R-square, ranges from 0 to 1 and measures the model fit. An R-square value close to 1 indicates that the model does a good job of predicting Y values. By substituting the estimated payroll for next year (in thousands), the risk manager estimates that 509 workers compensation claims will occur in the next year.

Forecasting Based on Loss Distributions

Another useful tool for the risk manager is loss forecasting based on loss distributions. A **loss distribution** *is a probability distribution of losses that could occur.* Forecasting by using loss distributions works

EXHIBIT 4.3
Relationship Between Payroll and Number of Workers Compensation Claims

Year	Payroll in thousands	Workers compensation claims
1993	$ 400	18
1994	520	26
1995	710	48
1996	840	96
1997	1200	110
1998	1500	150
1999	1630	228
2000	1980	250
2001	2300	260
2002	2900	300
2003	3400	325
2004	4000	412

Regression results: $Y = -6.1413 + .1074\ X,\ R^2 = .9519$

Predicted number of claims next year, if the payroll is $4.8 million:

$Y = -6.1413 + (.1074 \times 4800)$

$Y = 509.38$

well if the history of losses tends to follow a specified distribution and the sample size is large. Knowing the parameters that specify the loss distribution (for example, mean, standard deviation, and frequency of occurrence) enables the risk manager to estimate the number of events, severity, and confidence intervals. Many loss distributions can be employed, depending on the pattern of losses. The first section of the appendix at the end of this chapter discusses loss forecasting based on the normal distribution, a widely used distribution.

FINANCIAL ANALYSIS IN RISK MANAGEMENT DECISION MAKING

Risk managers must make a number of important decisions, including whether to retain or transfer loss exposures, which insurance coverage bid is best, and whether to invest in loss control projects. The risk manager's decisions are based on economics—weighing the costs and benefits of a course of action to see whether it is in the economic interests of the company and its claimholders. Financial analysis

can be applied to assist in risk management decision making. To make decisions involving cash flows in different time periods, the risk manager must employ time value of money analysis.

The Time Value of Money

Because risk management decisions will likely involve cash flows in different time periods, the time value of money must be considered. The **time value of money** *means that when valuing cash flows in different time periods, the interest-earning capacity of money must be taken into consideration.* A dollar received today is worth more than a dollar received one year from today, because the dollar received today can be invested immediately to earn interest. Therefore, when evaluating cash flows in different time periods, it is important to adjust dollar values to reflect the earning of interest.

A lengthy discourse on the time value of money is beyond the scope of this text.[16] Instead, we will limit our treatment to the valuation of single cash flows.

Suppose you open a bank account today and deposit $100. The value of the account today—the present value—is $100. Further assume that the bank is willing to pay 4 percent interest, compounded annually, on your account. What is the account balance one year from today? At that time, you would have your original $100, plus an additional 4 percent of $100, or $4 in interest:

$$\$100 + (\$100 \times .04) = \$104$$

Factoring, you would have

$$\$100 \times (1 + .04) = \$104$$

Thus, if you multiply the starting amount (the present value, or *PV*) by 1 plus the interest rate (*i*), it will give you the amount one year from today (the future value, or *FV*):

$$PV \times (1 + i) = FV$$

If you want to know the account balance after two years, simply multiply the balance at the end of the first year by 1 plus the interest rate. In this way, we arrive at the simple formula for the future value of a present amount:

$$PV (1 + i)^n = FV, \text{ where "} n \text{" is the number of time periods}$$

In the second year, not only will you earn interest on the original deposit, but you will also earn interest on the $4 in interest you earned in the first period. *Because you are earning interest on interest (compound interest), the operation through which a present value is converted to a future value is called* **compounding.**

Compounding also works in reverse. Assume that you know the value of a future cash flow, but you want to know what the cash flow is worth today, adjusting for the time value of money. Dividing both sides of our compounding equation by $(1 + i)^n$ yields the following expression:

$$PV = \frac{FV}{(1 + i)^n}$$

Thus, if you want to know the present value of any future amount, divide the future amount by 1 plus the interest rate, raised to the number of periods. *This operation—bringing a future value back to present value—is called* **discounting.**

Financial Analysis Applications

In many instances, the time value of money can be applied in risk management decision making. We will consider two applications:

- Analyzing insurance coverage bids
- Loss-control investment decisions

Analyzing Insurance Coverage Bids   Assume that Susan Carley would like to purchase property insurance on a building. She is analyzing two insurance coverage bids. The bids are from comparable insurance companies, and the coverage amounts are the same. The premiums and deductibles, however, differ. Insurer A's coverage requires an annual premium of $90,000 with a $5000 per-claim deductible. Insurer B's coverage requires an annual premium of $35,000 with a $10,000 per-claim deductible. Susan is wondering whether the additional $55,000 in premiums is warranted to obtain the lower deductible. Using some of the loss forecasting methods just described, Susan predicts the following losses will occur:

Expected Number of Losses	Expected Size of Losses
12	$ 5000
6	$10,000
2	over $10,000
$n = 20$	

Which coverage bid should Susan select, based on the number of expected claims and the magnitude of these claims? For simplicity, assume that premiums are paid at the start of the year, losses and deductibles are paid at the end of the year, and 5 percent is the appropriate interest (discount) rate.

With Insurer A's bid, Susan's expected cash outflows in one year would be the first $5000 of 20 losses that are each $5000 or more, for a total of $100,000 in deductibles. The present value of these payments is

$$PV = \frac{100,000}{(1 + .05)^1} = \$95,238$$

The present value of the total expected payments ($90,000 insurance premium at the start of the year plus the present value of the deductibles) would be $185,238.

With Insurer B's bid, Susan's expected cash outflows for deductibles at the end of the year would be

$$(\$5000 \times 12) + (\$10,000 \times 6) \\ + (\$10,000 \times 2) = \$140,000$$

The present value of these deductible payments is

$$PV = \frac{140,000}{(1 + .05)^1} = \$133,333$$

The present value of the total expected payments ($35,000 insurance premium at the start of the year plus the present value of the deductibles) would be $168,333. Because the present values calculated represent the present values of cash outflows, Susan should select the bid from Insurer B, because it minimizes the present value of the cash outflows.

Loss-Control Investment Decisions Loss-control investments are undertaken in an effort to reduce the frequency and severity of losses. Such investments can be analyzed from a capital budgeting perspective by employing time value of money analysis. **Capital budgeting** *is a method of determining which capital investment projects a company should undertake.* Only those projects that benefit the organization financially should be accepted. If not enough capital is available to undertake all of the acceptable projects, then capital budgeting can assist the risk manager in determining the optimal set of projects to consider.

A number of capital budgeting techniques are available.[17] Methods that take into account time value of money, such as net present value (*NPV*), should be employed. The **net present value** *of a project is the sum of the present values of the future cash flows minus the cost of the project.*[18] Cash flows are generated by increased revenues and reduced expenses. The cash flows are discounted at an interest rate that considers the rate of return required by the organization's capital suppliers and the riskiness of the project. A positive net present value represents an increase in value for the firm; a negative net present value would decrease the value of the firm if the investment were made.

For example, Susan Carley has noticed a distressing trend in premises-related liability claims from several of NPP's service stations. Patrons claim to have been injured on the premises (for example,

slip-and-fall injuries near gas pumps), and they have sued NPP for their injuries. Susan has decided to install camera surveillance systems at several of the "problem" service stations at a cost of $85,000 per system. She expects each surveillance system to generate an after-tax net cash flow of $40,000 per year for three years. The present value of $40,000 per year for three years discounted at the appropriate interest rate (we assume 8 percent) is $103,084. Therefore, the *NPV* of this project is

$$NPV = PV \text{ of future cash flows} - \text{cost of project} \\ = \$103,084 - \$85,000 \\ = \$18,084$$

As the project has a positive net present value, the investment is acceptable.

Although the cost of a project is usually known with some certainty, the future cash flows are merely estimates of the benefits that will be obtained by investing in the project. These benefits may come in the form of increased revenues, decreased expenses, or a combination of the two. Although some revenues and expenses associated with the project are easy to quantify, other values—such as employee morale, reduced pain and suffering, public perceptions of the company, and lost productivity when a new worker is hired to replace an injured experienced worker—can prove difficult to measure.

OTHER RISK MANAGEMENT TOOLS

Our discussion of advanced risk management topics would not be complete without a brief discussion of some other risk management tools. We will divide our discussion into four parts:

- Risk management information systems (RMIS)
- Risk management intranets and Web sites
- Risk maps
- Value at risk (VAR) analysis

Risk Management Information Systems (RMIS)

A key concern for risk managers is accurate and accessible risk management data. A **risk management information system (RMIS)** *is a computerized* *database that permits the risk manager to store and analyze risk management data and to use such data to predict and attempt to control future loss levels.* Risk management information systems may be of great assistance to risk managers in decision making. Such systems are marketed by a number of vendors, or they may be developed in-house.[19]

Risk management information systems have multiple uses. With regard to property exposures, the database may include a listing of a corporation's properties and the characteristics of those properties (construction, occupancy, protection, and exposure), property insurance policies, coverage terms, loss records, a log of fleet vehicles (including purchase dates, claims history, and maintenance records), and other data. On the liability side, the database may contain a listing of claims, the status of individual claims (pending, filed, in litigation, being appealed, or closed), historic claims, exposure bases (payroll, number of fleet vehicles, number of employees, and so on), and liability insurance coverages and coverage terms.

Organizations with many employees often find risk management information systems of great assistance in tracking employees, especially in the area of workers compensation claims. For example, a business with production facilities across the country may self-insure its workers compensation program but hire a third party to administer the program. In addition to settling claims, the third party administrator (TPA) may provide detailed claims records to the company that become part of the company's database. Armed with these data, the risk manager can perform a number of analyses, such as examining the number of injuries incurred by geographic region, by type of injury or body part (for example, laceration or lower back injury), by job classification, and by employee identification number. Such an analysis may reveal, for example, that the injury rate is greater in the Southwest region or that a small number of employees account for a disproportionately high number of claims. In turn, the risk manager may use the results in measuring the effectiveness of loss-control investments and in targeting additional loss control efforts. Accurate workers compensation records are also important if the business decides to purchase private insurance, because past performance must be documented to obtain lower premiums from insurers.

Risk Management Intranets and Web Sites

Some risk management departments have established their own Web sites, which include answers to "frequently asked questions" (FAQs) and a wealth of other information. In addition, some organizations have expanded the traditional risk management Web site into a risk management intranet. An **intranet** *is a Web site with search capabilities designed for a limited, internal audience.*[20] For example, a software company that sponsors trade shows at numerous venues each year might use a risk management intranet to make information available to interested parties within the company. Through the intranet, employees can obtain a list of procedures to follow (formulated by the risk management department) along with a set of forms that must be signed and filed before the event can be held (such as hold-harmless agreements).

Risk Maps

Some organizations have developed or are developing sophisticated "risk maps." **Risk maps** *are grids detailing the potential frequency and severity of risks faced by the organization.* Construction of these maps requires risk managers to analyze each risk that the organization faces before plotting it on the map. Use of risk maps varies from simply graphing the exposures to employing simulation analysis to estimate likely loss scenarios. In addition to property, liability, and personnel exposures, financial risks and other risks that fall under the broad umbrella of "enterprise risk" may be included on the risk map.[21]

Value at Risk (VAR) Analysis

A popular risk assessment technique in financial risk management is value at risk (VAR) analysis. **Value at risk (VAR)** *is the worst probable loss likely to occur in a given time period under regular market conditions at some level of confidence.* The concept is often applied to a portfolio of assets, such as a mutual fund or a pension fund, and is similar to the concept of "maximum probable loss" in traditional property and liability risk management.[22] For example, a mutual fund may have the following VAR characteristics: there is a 5 percent probability that the value of the portfolio may decline by $50,000 in any single trading day. In this case, the worst probable loss is $50,000, the time period is one trading day, and the level of confidence is 95 percent. Based on a VAR estimate, the risk level could be increased or decreased, depending on risk tolerance. Value at risk can also be employed to examine the risk of insolvency for insurers. VAR can be determined in a number of ways, including using historical data and running a computer simulation. While VAR is used in financial risk management, a growing number of organizations are considering financial risk under the broadened scope of risk management.

CASE APPLICATION

Great West States (GWS) is a railroad company operating in the Western United States. Juanita Salazar is risk manager of GWS. At the direction of the company's chief executive officer, she is searching for ways to handle the company's risks in a more economical way. The CEO stressed that Juanita should consider not only pure risks but also financial risks. Juanita discovered that a significant financial risk facing the organization is a commodity price risk—the risk of a significant increase in the price of fuel oil for the company's locomotives. A review of the company's income and expense statement showed that last year about 18 percent of its expenses were related to fuel oil.

Juanita was also asked to determine whether the installation of a new sprinkler system at the corporate headquarters building would be justified. The cost of the project would be $40,000. She estimates the project would provide an after-tax net cash flow of $25,000 per year for three years, with the first of these cash flows coming one year from today.

GWS is considering expanding its routes to include Colorado, New Mexico, Texas, and Oklahoma. The company is concerned about the number of derailments that might occur. Juanita ran a regression with "thousands of miles GWS locomotives traveled" as the independent variable and "number of derailments" as the dependent variable. Results of the regression are as follows:

$$Y = 2.31 + .022X$$

With the expansion, GWS trains will travel an estimated 640,000 miles next year.

a. With regard to the fuel oil price risk:
   (1) Discuss how Juanita could use futures contracts to hedge the price risk.
   (2) Discuss how a double-trigger, integrated risk management plan could be employed.
b. What is the net present value (NPV) of the sprinkler system project, assuming the rate of return required by GWS investors is 10 percent?
c. How many derailments should Juanita expect next year, assuming the regression results are reliable and GWS goes ahead with the expansion plan? (*Hint:* Be careful of scale factors when considering the independent variable.)

SUMMARY

- Financial risk management is the identification, analysis, and treatment of speculative financial risks. Such risks include commodity price risk, interest rate risk, and currency exchange rate risk.

- An integrated risk program is a risk treatment technique that combines coverage for pure and speculative risks within the same contract.

- Enterprise risk management is a comprehensive risk management program that addresses an organization's pure, speculative, strategic, and operational risks.

- A cyclical pattern—called the underwriting cycle—has been observed in underwriting stringency, premium levels, and profitability in the property and liability insurance industry. In a "hard" insurance market, premiums are high and underwriting standards are tight. In a "soft" insurance market, premiums are low and underwriting standards are loose.

- Two important factors that affect property and liability insurance company pricing and underwriting decisions are the level of capacity in the insurance industry and investment returns.

- The insurance industry has been experiencing consolidation through insurance company mergers and acquisitions, insurance brokerage mergers and acquisitions, and cross-industry consolidation.

- Insurers, reinsurers, and others are using securitization of risk to transfer risk to the capital markets through creation of a financial instrument, such as catastrophe bond or a derivative.

- Risk managers can use a number of techniques to predict losses. These techniques include probability analysis, regression analysis, and forecasting by using loss distributions.

- When analyzing events, the characteristics of the events must be considered. Events may be independent, dependent, or mutually exclusive.

- Regression analysis is a method of characterizing the relationship that exists between two or more variables and then using the characterization as a predictor.

- In analyzing cash flows in different periods, the risk manager must consider the time value of money.

- Changing a present value into a future value is called compounding; determining the present value of a future amount is called discounting.

- Risk managers can apply time value of money analysis in many situations, including insurance coverage bid analysis and loss control investment analysis.

- A risk management information system (RMIS) is a computerized database that permits risk managers to store and analyze risk management data and to use such data to predict future losses.

- Risk managers may use Web sites, intranets, risk maps, and value at risk (VAR) analysis in their risk management programs.

KEY CONCEPTS AND TERMS

Capacity
Capital budgeting
Catastrophe bond
Chief risk officer (CRO)
Clash loss
Combined ratio
Commodity price risk
Compounding
Consolidation
Currency exchange
  rate risk
Dependent events

Discounting
Double-trigger option
Enterprise risk
  management
Financial risk
  management
"Hard" insurance market
Independent events
Insurance brokers
Integrated risk program
Interest rate risk
Intranet

Loss distribution
Mutually exclusive
  events
Net present value (NPV)
Regression analysis
Risk management
  information system
  (RMIS)
Risk maps

Securitization of risk
"Soft" insurance market
Surplus
Time value of money
Underwriting cycle
Value at risk (VAR)
  analysis
Weather option

REVIEW QUESTIONS

1. Name three speculative financial risks that may be considered by a risk manager.

2. How does enterprise risk management differ from traditional risk management?

3. What is the underwriting cycle? Differentiate between a "hard" and a "soft" insurance market.

4. What is meant by "consolidation" in the insurance industry?

5. How does securitization of risk increase capacity in the property and liability insurance industry?

6. a. Why is loss forecasting necessary when making a decision about whether to retain or transfer loss exposures?
   b. What techniques can a risk manager use to predict future losses?

7. What is the danger of simply using past losses to estimate future losses?

8. Why is time value of money analysis used in risk management decision making?

9. What variables are difficult to quantify when analyzing investments in loss-control projects?

10. a. What is a risk management information system (RMIS)?
    b. How does a risk management Web site differ from a risk management intranet?

APPLICATION QUESTIONS

1. Integrated risk management programs are new to many risk managers and the insurance companies that offer such programs. What additional expertise, aside from knowledge of property and liability insurance, must an insurance company possess to offer integrated risk management products?

2. A risk manager self-insured a property risk for one year. The following year, even though no losses had occurred, the risk manager purchased property insurance to address the risk. What is the best explanation for the change in how the risk was handled, even though no losses had occurred?

3. Why do insurance brokerage mergers and acquisitions have a greater influence on corporate risk managers than do property and liability insurance company mergers and acquisitions?

4. a. What would be the effect of ignoring the time value of money when making risk management decisions?
   b. What does the net present value of a loss control investment really represent to the owners of the organization?

5. During a "hard" insurance market, a manufacturing company decided to self-insure its workers compensation loss exposure. The company hired a third party to administer the workers compensation claims. Even though the risk was being self-insured, the risk manager insisted that the third-party administrator maintain meticulous records. When asked why such detailed records were necessary, the risk manager replied, "For story time with an insurance company next year." What did the risk manager mean?

INTERNET RESOURCES

■ The **International Financial Risk Institute** provides a comprehensive introduction to financial risk management. This site educates readers on the most valuable official documents on this subject. Along with a risk management checklist, this site also includes a regulatory documents library, a collection of risk management case studies, and a risk management glossary. Visit the site at

http://www.riskinstitute.ch

■ The **Nonprofit Risk Management Center** conducts research and education on risk management and insurance issues that are of special concern to nonprofit organizations. The organization publishes a newsletter, easy-to-read publications, and informative briefs on frequently asked questions related to risk management and insurance. The organization also offers consulting services and risk audits. Visit the site at

http://www.nonprofitrisk.org

■ The **Public Risk Management Association** represents risk managers of state and local governmental units. The organization provides practical training and education for risk managers in the public sector; publishes a magazine, newsletter, and detailed issue-specific publications; and provides cutting-edge updates on federal regulations and legislation. Visit the site at

http://www.primacentral.org

■ The **Risk and Insurance Management Society (RIMS)** is the premier professional association in the United States for risk managers and corporate buyers of insurance. RIMS provides a forum for the discussion of common risk management issues, supports loss-prevention activities, and makes known to insurers the insurance needs of its members. RIMS has local chapters in major cities and publishes *Risk Management* magazine. Visit the site at

http://www.rims.org

■ The **Self-Insurance Institute of America** is a national association that promotes self-insurance as an alternative method for financing losses. The organization publishes technical articles on self-insurance, holds educational conferences, and promotes the legislative and regulatory interests of self-insurance at both the federal and state levels. Visit the site at

http://www.siia.org

■ The **Casualty Actuarial Society (CAS)** promotes the application of actuarial science to property, casualty, and similar loss exposures. To learn more about the CAS, its research, and its publications, access the Web site at

http://www.casact.org

■ The Insurance Information Institute's *Financial Services Fact Book* is available on-line. The *Fact Book* includes information on insurance company and insurance broker consolidation, securitization of insurance risk, and related topics. Visit the site at

http://www.financialservicesfacts.org

■ Two industry education organizations provide professional designation programs in risk management. The **American Institute for CPCU** offers the "Associate in Risk Management" (ARM) designation. The **National Alliance for Insurance Education and Research** offers the "Certified Risk Manager" (CRM) designation. For information about these professional designations, visit the Web sites at

http://aicpcu.org and http://scic.com

SELECTED REFERENCES

Barton, Thomas L., William G. Shenkir, and Paul L. Walken. *Making Enterprise Risk Management Pay Off,* Prentice Hall, 2002.

Enterprise Risk Management in the Insurance Industry— 2002 Benchmarking Survey Report, Tillinghast-Towers Perrin, 30 pages.

Harrington, Scott E., and Gregory R. Niehaus. *Risk Management and Insurance,* 2nd ed., Irwin/McGraw Hill, 2004.

Leimberg, Stephan R., Donald J. Riggin, Albert J. Howard, James W. Kallman, and Donald L. Schmidt. *The Tools & Techniques of Risk Management & Insurance,* The National Underwriter Company, 2002.

Williams, C. Arthur, Michael L. Smith, and Peter C. Young. *Risk Management and Insurance,* 8th ed., 1998. Irwin/McGraw Hill.

NOTES

1. See an investments text for a detailed explanation of these capital market instruments.
2. As reported in "Who Needs Derivatives?" by Caroyln T. Geer, *Forbes Magazine,* April 21, 1997.
3. To learn more about the positioning, role and job of a Chief Risk Officer (CRO), see: "The CRO is Here to Stay," by James Lam, *Risk Management,* April 2001, pp. 16–22; "Implementing Enterprise Risk Management: The Emerging Role of the Chief Risk Officer," International Risk Management Institute (IRMI), Inc., Web site January 2002; and "Rising Power of the Chief Risk Officer," by Des Dearlove, *Times on Line,* April 30, 2003.
4. Data reported by KPMG at the Third Annual Global Risk Management Summit and quoted in "ERM Advice for Pioneers," *Risk Management,* October 2001, p. 64; and "Enterprise Risk Management: Implementing New Solutions," The Economist Intelligence Unit (written in cooperation with MMC Enterprise Risk), 2001.
5. As discussed in "ERM Lessons Across Industries," by Jerry Miccolis of Tillinghast-Towers Perrin, March 2003. Miccolis draws upon data from three recent ERM surveys, including Tillinghast-Towers Perrin's "Enterprise Risk Management in the Insurance Industry, 2002 Benchmarking Survey Report."
6. For a review of the literature on the causes of underwriting cycles, see Renbao Chen, Kie Ann Wong, and Hong Chew Lee, "Underwriting Cycles in Asia," *Journal of Risk and Insurance,* 1999, Vol. 66, No. 1, pp. 29–47.
7. The Equal Employment Opportunity Commission reports that more than $1 billion was awarded in employment practices liability claims between 1992 and 1998 (reported in "Businesses Face Minefield in Employment Practices Liability," by Robert Bregman, *San Antonio Business Journal,* October 25, 1999. Several settlements are illustrative. A Michigan jury awarded $5.5 million to a former truck driver with epilepsy in an Americans with Disabilities Act case. A jury in Philadelphia awarded over half a million dollars in a case in which an employee was subjected to slurs about the plaintiff's national origin. Mitsubishi settled two sexual harassment cases for over $45 million.
8. A study by Tillinghast-Towers Perrin showed that D&O premiums rose by nearly 30 percent on average in 2002, on the heels of sharp increases in 2001. Some companies faced triple-digit premium increases. Insurers employed tougher underwriting guidelines and limited coverage limits for some purchasers. See "Study Finds D&O Liability Premiums Soar, Shareholder Claims Increase," *Insurance Journal,* May 5, 2003, West Issue, for other findings of the Tillinghast-Towers Perrin survey.
9. The rate of return on invested assets in the U.S. property and casualty insurance industry for the late 1990s and early 2000s, by year, was:

1998	9.0%
1999	6.9%
2000	4.9%
2001	3.5%
2002	2.3%

    These values were taken from *Best's Aggregates & Averages,* Property/Casualty Edition, 2003, page 311.
10. Total assets of the U.S. property and casualty insurance industry were $830.1 billion in 1998 and $1.04 trillion in 2002. Net investment income in the industry was $41.1 billion in 1998 and $40.1 billion in 2002. These values were taken from *Best's Aggregates & Averages,* Property/Casualty Edition, 2003, pp. 311 and 349.

11. Although the number of property and casualty insurers is decreasing due to consolidation, a study by the Insurance Information Institute (III) showed the industry is still highly competitive. In 2002, the top four insurers wrote 28.3 percent of premiums. The next 45 insurers wrote 49.6 percent of premiums. In other words, 50 different insurers were responsible for approximately 78 percent of the premiums written. This statistics were take from "Property/Casualty Insurance Industry Concentration," http://www.finincialservicesfacts.org.

12. For a listing of insurance broker mergers and acquisitions, see "Broker Consolidation—Where Is It Heading," by Peter Godfrey, *Risk Management*, August 1998, pp. 10–22. Also see the Insurance Information Institute's (III's) *Financial Services Fact Book* referenced in the preceding note.

13. See the "Consolidation" link in the III's *Financial Services Fact Book* referenced in the previous note at the Web site referenced in endnote 11 for a discussion of cross-industry consolidation.

14. See the "Securitization" link in the III's *Financial Services Fact Book*.

15. The line that best fits the data minimizes the sum of the squared deviations of the points from the line. Business statistics and econometrics textbooks provided a more detailed discussion of regression analysis.

16. Introductory business finance textbooks discuss the time value of money in greater detail. The time value of money calculations displayed here may also be performed using a financial calculator. Such calculators ease financial computations as the time value of money functions are preprogrammed in the calculator.

17. Other methods include the internal rate of return, accounting rate of return, and the payback method. Net present value is preferred by many people because it employs the time value money, uses the appropriate cash flow, and provides a dollars and cents answer that is easy to interpret.

18. The relevant cash flow measure captures increased revenues and decreased expenses. Depreciation is not subtracted directly as it is a noncash expense. Depreciation is considered, however, when determining the tax liability.

19. For a discussion of some criteria when selecting a Risk Management Information System (RMIS) see "Shopping for a New RMIS," by Ritza Vaughn, *Risk Management*, October 2003, pp. 12–16.

20. For a discussion of risk management intranets, see "Net Working," by Mark Dorn, *Risk Management*, June 1999, pp. 41–44.

21. For a discussion of risk mapping, see "Enhanced Risk Mapping," by Howard Kesternbaum, *Risk Management*, October 2001, pp. 40–46.

22. Value-at-Risk is discussed in many contexts by many authors. For a representative discussion, see "Value-at-Risk: An Overview," by David M. Rowe and Arnold Miyamoto, *The Journal of Lending & Credit Risk Management*, February 1999, pp. 70–72; Chapter 2 of *Making Enterprise Risk Management Pay Off*, Thomas L. Barton, William G. Shenkir, and Paul L. Walker, 2002, Prentice Hall; and "Value at Risk (VAR): The New Benchmark for Managing Market Risk," Giuseppe Tardivo, *Journal of Financial Management and Analysis*, Jan. 2002, pp. 16–26.

APPENDIX

RISK MANAGEMENT APPLICATION PROBLEMS

Risk managers need a number of skills to be successful. The ability to forecast losses, to apply time value of money analysis, and to use a variety of risk management tools is important. This appendix provides additional information on some quantitative aspects of risk management and some application problems. Solutions to the numbered application problems appear at the end of the appendix.

LOSS FORECASTING

Risk managers may employ probability distributions to assist in loss forecasting. Several distributions are available, including the normal, binomial, exponential, Poisson, and others. Selection of the distribution is often based upon loss history, especially when the number of losses is large. We will examine application of the normal distribution, which is used in many situations.

The normal distribution is a symmetric bell curve summarized by two parameters: the expected value and the standard deviation (m and s, respectively, in the discussion that follows). The area under the curve is equal to one, with 50 percent of the distribution on either side of the expected value. Based on the values of m and s, and an "Areas Under a Normal Curve" table (see Exhibit A4.1), the proba-

bility of any event (x) can be estimated based on the standard variate, z:

$$z = \frac{x - m}{s}$$

For example, assume that the number of weather-related property losses is normally distributed with a mean (m) equal to 16 and standard deviation (s) equal to 3. What is the probability that the number of weather-related property losses will be between 16 and 22? Substituting values into the formula, we can solve for the standard variate, z, which equals 2.00. The area corresponding to a standard variate of 2.00, according to Exhibit A4.1, is 0.4772. Therefore, the probability that between 16 and 22 weather-related losses will occur is almost 48 percent.

1. Assume the number of physical damage losses for a large fleet of vehicles is normally distributed with a mean of 400 and a standard deviation of 80. What is the probability that:

    a. More than 440 losses will occur?
    b. Between 320 and 480 losses will occur?
    c. Between 460 and 520 losses will occur?

The standard variate can also be used to determine "x values" corresponding to a given probability. Based on the previous information (normally-distributed losses, mean of 400, standard deviation of

EXHIBIT A4.1
Areas Under the Normal Curve (One Tail)

z	.00	.01	.02	.03	.04	.05	.06	.07	.08	.09
0.0	.0000	.0040	.0080	.0120	.0160	.0199	.0239	.0279	.0319	.0359
0.1	.0398	.0438	.0478	.0517	.0557	.0596	.0636	.0675	.0714	.0753
0.2	.0793	.0832	.0871	.0910	.0948	.0987	.1026	.1064	.1103	.1141
0.3	.1179	.1217	.1255	.1293	.1331	.1368	.1406	.1443	.1480	.1517
0.4	.1554	.1591	.1628	.1664	.1700	.1736	.1772	.1808	.1844	.1879
0.5	.1915	.1950	.1985	.2019	.2054	.2088	.2123	.2157	.2190	.2224
0.6	.2257	.2291	.2324	.2357	.2389	.2422	.2454	.2486	.2517	.2549
0.7	.2580	.2611	.2642	.2673	.2704	.2734	.2764	.2794	.2823	.2852
0.8	.2881	.2910	.2939	.2967	.2995	.3023	.3051	.3078	.3106	.3133
0.9	.3159	.3186	.3212	.3238	.3264	.3289	.3315	.3340	.3365	.3389
1.0	.3413	.3438	.3461	.3485	.3508	.3531	.3554	.3577	.3599	.3621
1.1	.3643	.3665	.3686	.3708	.3729	.3749	.3770	.3790	.3810	.3830
1.2	.3849	.3869	.3888	.3907	.3925	.3944	.3962	.3980	.3997	.4015
1.3	.4032	.4049	.4066	.4082	.4099	.4115	.4131	.4147	.4162	.4177
1.4	.4192	.4207	.4222	.4236	.4251	.4265	.4279	.4292	.4306	.4319
1.5	.4332	.4345	.4357	.4370	.4382	.4394	.4406	.4418	.4429	.4441
1.6	.4452	.4463	.4474	.4484	.4495	.4505	.4515	.4525	.4535	.4545
1.7	.4554	.4564	.4573	.4582	.4591	.4599	.4608	.4616	.4625	.4633
1.8	.4641	.4649	.4656	.4664	.4671	.4678	.4686	.4693	.4699	.4706
1.9	.4713	.4719	.4726	.4732	.4738	.4744	.4750	.4756	.4761	.4767
2.0	.4772	.4778	.4783	.4788	.4793	.4798	.4803	.4808	.4812	.4817
2.1	.4821	.4826	.4830	.4834	.4838	.4842	.4846	.4850	.4854	.4857
2.2	.4861	.4864	.4868	.4871	.4875	.4878	.4881	.4884	.4887	.4890
2.3	.4893	.4896	.4898	.4901	.4904	.4906	.4909	.4911	.4913	.4916
2.4	.4918	.4920	.4922	.4925	.4927	.4929	.4931	.4932	.4934	.4936
2.5	.4938	.4940	.4941	.4943	.4945	.4946	.4948	.4949	.4951	.4952
2.6	.4953	.4955	.4956	.4957	.4959	.4960	.4961	.4962	.4963	.4964
2.7	.4965	.4966	.4967	.4968	.4969	.4970	.4971	.4972	.4973	.4974
2.8	.4974	.4975	.4976	.4977	.4977	.4978	.4979	.4979	.4980	.4981
2.9	.4981	.4982	.4982	.4983	.4984	.4984	.4985	.4985	.4986	.4986
3.0	.4987	.4987	.4987	.4988	.4988	.4989	.4989	.4989	.4990	.4990

80), above what number of physical damage claims do the highest 10 percent of x values fall? We know that the area to the right of the value of x is 10 percent. As the table shows probabilities between the expected value and x, we need to look in the table for a z value corresponding to .40. This z value is approximately 1.28. By substituting all of the known values back into our expression for z, we can solve for x:

$$1.28 = \frac{x - 400}{80}, x = (80 \times 1.28) + 400, x = 502.4$$

So 10 percent of all claims are above 502 claims.

TIME VALUE OF MONEY

The importance of the timing of cash flows and the interest-earning capacity of money was discussed in Chapter 4. Several additional time value of money/risk management examples are provided below for your consideration:

2. A sprinkler system for XYZ Company's production facility will cost $175,000. The project will provide net after-tax cash flows of $50,000 per year for five years. Assuming an interest (discount) rate of 6 percent, what is the net present value (NPV) of this project? Does the NPV indicate this project is acceptable?

3. Under the terms of an out-of-court settlement in a class-action case, a pharmaceutical company must pay plaintiffs $500,000 per year for the next seven years, with the first payment one year from today. The company plans to create a funded claims reserve, and reserve assets can earn a 6 percent annual rate of return. What amount is needed to fully-fund the reserve today, assuming the first disbursement to the plaintiffs is made one year from today?

4. Good-As-Gold (GAG), a canine obedience school, is being sued by the parents of a child who was injured by a dog in the custody of GAG. Two out-of-court settlements are under consideration. Under the first, GAG would pay the injured party $50,000 per year for 10 years, with the first payment one year from today. Under the second alternative, GAG would pay the injured party $50,000 today and $500,000 ten years from today. Which of these offers is best from GAG's perspective, assuming a 6 percent interest rate?

OTHER RISK MANAGEMENT APPLICATIONS

When losses are retained, an accurate forecast of the timing and magnitude of payments is needed to assure adequate financial resources will be on-hand to pay claims. Consider the following example:

5. Harris Company began operations this year. The company retains property losses and estimates that property losses will be $100,000 this year. Property losses are expected to increase at a rate of 30 percent per year for the next two years. Harris expects to pay for 80 percent of property losses in the year the loss occurs, with the other 20 percent paid in the following year. How much in retained losses will Harris have to pay this year and in each of the next two years?

Property losses are easier to adjust and settle than are liability claims. In the case of liability, claims attributable to a specific year may not be reported until several years in the future. Once a claim is reported, there may be a lengthy process to determine whether the claim is valid and if damages should be awarded. And, of course, court decisions and damage awards may be appealed. The ability to forecast ultimate claims for various liability lines is an important skill for a risk manager. Consider the following two examples:

6. The Risk Manager of GBB Company has noted that GBB pays 40 percent (dollar value) of its general liability claims during the policy year. For the year just concluded, GBB paid $180,000 in new general liability claims. What total value of general liability claims should GBB expect for the year just concluded?

7. GBB Company has also noted that 30 percent of the product liability claims attributable to a policy year are actually filed during the policy year. For the year that just ended, a total of 24 product liability claims were filed. How many product liability claims should GBB expect, ultimately, to be attributable to the year that just ended?

Liability exposures often are described as having a "long tail," meaning that significant time can pass before all claims are reported, investigated, and settled. Loss development factors are multipliers that can be applied to claims settled to date to estimate what the ultimate claims for a period will equal.

8. Based on past workers compensation claims data, GBB's risk manager estimated loss develop-

ment factors of 4.2 for year-end values one year ago, 3.4 for year-end values two years ago, 2.3 for year-end values three years ago, 1.5 for year-end values four years ago, and 1.10 for year-end values five years ago. Workers compensation losses settled to date for the previous five years are:

5 Years Ago	4 Years Ago	3 Years Ago	2 Years Ago	Last Year
$450,000	$430,000	$400,000	$340,000	$300,000

Based on the loss development factors and claims settled to date, what are the ultimate workers compensation claims expected for each of the last five years?

SOLUTIONS

1. a. The z-value is: $(440 - 400)/80 = .50$. A z-value of .50 corresponds to an area of .1915. This value represents the area between 400 and 440. As the question asks for the probability of more than 440, the answer is the balance in the remainder of the tail: $.50 - .1915 = .3085$. So there is about a 31 percent probability that more than 440 losses will occur.

   b. The question asks for the area one standard deviation above and one standard deviation below the mean. As the curve is symmetric, we can calculate one area, and multiply the value by two to get the total area. The z-value is: $(480 - 400)/80 = 1.00$. A z-value of 1.00 corresponds to an area of .3413. Multiplying this value by two, we get .6826. With a normal distribution, about 68 percent of the observations fall within one standard deviation of the mean.

   c. We need to determine the area between 460 and 520. We can calculate the area between 400 and 520 first, and then subtract from this value the area between 400 and 460. The difference in areas should be the area between 460 and 520. The z-value for the first area is: $(520 - 400)/80 = 1.50$. This value corresponds to an area of .4332. The z-value for the second area is: $(460 - 400)/80 = .75$. This value corresponds to an area of .2734. The difference between these areas is .1598, so the probability of between 460 and 520 losses occurring is about 16 percent.

2. The present value of $50,000 per year for five years, assuming a 6 percent interest rate, is $210,618. Netting the present value of the future cash flows against the cost of the project, $175,000, produces a net present value (NPV) of $35,618. As the NPV is positive, the project is acceptable.

3. The question is how much money would have to be placed in a claims reserve today so that at the end of the year for the next seven years, $500,000 could be withdrawn from the account. The answer is simply the present value of $500,000 per year for seven years, assuming an interest rate of 6 percent. That value is $2,791,191.

4. The present value of $50,000 per year for 10 years is $368,004. The present value of the second alternative is $50,000 today plus the present value of $500,000 to be paid 10 years from today. This total is $329,197. As GAG would like to minimize the present value of its cash outflows, the second alternative is preferred. Note that the first alternative involves a lower cash outflow ($500,000 total dollars) than the second alternative ($550,000 total dollars). However, when adjusted for the timing of the cash flows, the second alternative is better.

5. Losses in year one are expected to be $100,000. Assuming a 30 percent growth rate, losses will be $130,000 in year two. Applying a 30 percent growth rate again, Harris Company should expect losses of $169,000 in year three. The loss payout pattern is 80 percent in the year of occurrence, with the balance paid out the following year. So:

   Year 1 = $100,000 × .80 = $80,000
   Year 2 = $130,000 × .80 + $100,000 × .20
                 = $124,000
   Year 3 = $169,000 × .80 + $130,000 × .20
                 = $161,200

(Note that these figures have not been adjusted for the time value of money.)

6. GBB pays out 40 percent of the total ("x") during the policy year. If 40 percent of x is $180,000; then x must be $450,000.

7. Based on past experience, 30 percent of ultimate claims for policy year ("*x*") are filed during the policy year. If 30 percent of *x* is 24, then x must be 80 claims.

8. The earliest data are "seasoned"—in other words, as we get further away from the current year, there should be less adjustment needed. The more recent years have had less time to develop. Thus, additional claims are more likely to be reported for the recent years and the value of existing claims is likely to be understated. Applying the loss development factors provided to the current data, we have:

$450,000 × 1.10 = $495,000
for the year five years ago
$430,000 × 1.50 = $645,000
for the year four years ago
$400,000 × 2.30 = $920,000
for the year three years ago
$340,000 × 3.40 = $1,156,000
for the year two years ago
$300,000 × 4.20 = $1,260,000 for last year

PART TWO

LEGAL PRINCIPLES IN RISK AND INSURANCE

Chapter 5
Fundamental Legal Principles

Chapter 6
Analysis of Insurance Contracts

CHAPTER 5

FUNDAMENTAL LEGAL PRINCIPLES

*"It is unfair to believe everything we hear about lawyers—
some of it may not be true."*

Gerald F. Lieberman

LEARNING OBJECTIVES

After studying this chapter, you should be able to

◆ Explain the fundamental legal principles that are reflected in insurance contracts, including
  principle of indemnity
  principle of insurable interest
  principle of subrogation
  principle of utmost good faith

◆ Explain how the legal concepts of representations, concealment, and warranty support the principle of utmost good faith.

◆ Describe the basic requirements for the formation of a valid insurance contract.

◆ Show how insurance contracts differ from other contracts.

◆ Explain the law of agency and how it affects the actions of insurance agents.

*P*aul, age 28, is dually addicted to drugs and alcohol. He recently moved to another state and applied for auto insurance in that state. Paul stated in the application that he had never been fined for a moving vehicle violation and had no offenses other than traffic tickets. In fact, Paul had three convictions for driving under the influence of alcohol and drugs and had been involved in several auto accidents. The insurer issued the policy. Shortly thereafter, Paul had another accident in which the other driver was seriously injured. The driver sued Paul for her injury. After investigating the claim, the insurer denied liability because Paul lied on the application and made several material misrepresentations. Paul's introduction to insurance law was costly and financially painful.

As Paul discovered, insurance law can have substantial legal consequences for you after a loss occurs. When you buy insurance, you expect to be paid for a covered loss. Insurance law and contractual provisions determine whether you can collect and how much will be paid. Insurance contracts are complex legal documents that reflect both general rules of law and insurance law. Thus, you should have a clear understanding of the basic legal principles that underlie insurance contracts.

This chapter discusses the fundamental legal principles on which insurance contracts are based, legal requirements for a valid insurance contract, and legal characteristics of insurance contracts that distinguish them from other types of contracts. The chapter concludes with a discussion of the law of agency and its application to insurance agents.

PRINCIPLE OF INDEMNITY

The principle of indemnity is one of the most important legal principles in insurance. The **principle of indemnity** *states that the insurer agrees to pay no more than the actual amount of the loss; stated differently, the insured should not profit from a loss.* Most property and liability insurance contracts are contracts of indemnity. If a covered loss occurs, the insurer should not pay more than the actual amount of the loss. Nevertheless, a contract of indemnity does not mean that all covered losses are always paid in full. Because of deductibles, dollar limits on the amount paid, and other contractual provisions, the amount paid may be less than the actual loss.

The principle of indemnity has two fundamental purposes. *The first purpose is to prevent the insured*

from profiting from a loss. For example, if Kristin's home is insured for $200,000, and a partial loss of $50,000 occurs, the principle of indemnity would be violated if $200,000 were paid to her. She would be profiting from insurance.

The second purpose is to reduce moral hazard. If dishonest insureds could profit from a loss, they might deliberately cause losses with the intention of collecting the insurance. If the loss payment does not exceed the actual amount of the loss, the temptation to be dishonest is reduced.

Actual Cash Value

The concept of *actual cash value* underlies the principle of indemnity. In property insurance, the basic method for indemnifying the insured is based on the actual cash value of the damaged property at the time of loss. The courts have used three major methods to determine actual cash value:

- Replacement cost less depreciation
- Fair market value
- Broad evidence rule

Replacement Cost Less Depreciation Under this rule, **actual cash value** *is defined as replacement cost less depreciation.* This rule has been used traditionally to determine the actual cash value of property in property insurance. It takes into consideration both inflation and depreciation of property values over time. Replacement cost is the current cost of restoring the damaged property with new materials of like kind and quality. Depreciation is a deduction for physical wear and tear, age, and economic obsolescence.

For example, Sarah has a favorite couch that burns in a fire. Assume she bought the couch five years ago, the couch is 50 percent depreciated, and a similar couch today would cost $1000. Under the actual cash value rule, Sarah will collect $500 for the loss because the replacement cost is $1000, and depreciation is $500, or 50 percent. If she were paid the full replacement value of $1000, the principle of indemnity would be violated. She would be receiving the value of a new couch instead of one that was five years old. In short, the $500 payment represents indemnification for the loss of a five-year-old couch. This calculation can be summarized as follows:

$$Replacement\ cost = \$1000$$
$$Depreciation = \$500\ (couch\ is\ 50\ percent\ depreciated)$$
$$Actual\ cash\ value = Replacement\ cost - Depreciation$$
$$\$500 = \$1000 - \$500$$

Fair Market Value Some courts have ruled that fair market value should be used to determine actual cash value of a loss. **Fair market value** *is the price a willing buyer would pay a willing seller in a free market.*

The fair market value of a building may be below its actual cash value based on replacement cost less depreciation. This difference is due to several reasons, including a poor location, deteriorating neighborhood, or economic obsolescence of the building. For example, in major cities, large homes in older residential areas often have a market value well below replacement cost less depreciation. If a loss occurs, the fair market value may reflect more accurately the value of the loss. In one case, a building valued at $170,000 based on the actual cash value rule had a market value of only $65,000 when a loss occurred. The court ruled that the actual cash value of the property should be based on the fair market value of $65,000 rather than on $170,000.[1]

Broad Evidence Rule Many states now use the broad evidence rule to determine the actual cash value of a loss. The **broad evidence rule** *means that the determination of actual cash value should include all relevant factors an expert would use to determine the value of the property.* Relevant factors include replacement cost less depreciation, fair market value, present value of expected income from the property, comparison sales of similar property, opinions of appraisers, and numerous other factors.

Although the actual cash value rule is used in property insurance, different methods are employed in other types of insurance. In liability insurance, the insurer pays up to the policy limit the amount of damages that the insured is legally obligated to pay because of bodily injury or property damage to another. In life insurance, the amount paid when the insured dies is the face value of the policy. In business income insurance, the amount paid is usually based on the loss of profits plus continuing expenses when the business is shut down because of a loss from a covered peril.

Exceptions to the Principle of Indemnity

There are several important exceptions to the principle of indemnity. They include the following:

- Valued policy
- Valued policy laws
- Replacement cost insurance
- Life insurance

Valued Policy A **valued policy** *is a policy that pays the face amount of insurance if a total loss occurs.* Valued policies typically are used to insure antiques, fine arts, rare paintings, and family heirlooms. Because of the difficulty of determining the actual value of the property at the time of loss, the insured and insurer both agree on the value of the property when the policy is first issued. For example, you may have a valuable antique clock that was owned by your great-grandmother. Assume that the clock is worth $10,000 today and is insured for that amount. If the clock is totally destroyed in a fire, you would be paid $10,000—not the actual cash value. Because the amount paid may exceed the actual cash value, the principle of indemnity is violated.

Valued Policy Laws Valued policy laws are another exception to the principle of indemnity.[2] A **valued policy law** *is a law that exists in some states that requires payment of the face amount of insurance to the insured if a total loss to real property occurs from a peril specified in the law.* The specified perils to which a valued policy law applies vary among the states. Laws in some states cover only fire; other states cover fire, lightning, windstorm, and tornado; and some states include all insured perils. In addition, the laws generally apply only to real property, and the loss must be total. For example, a building insured for $200,000 may have an actual cash value of $175,000. If a total loss from a fire occurs, the face amount of $200,000 would be paid. Because the insured would be paid more than the actual cash value, the principle of indemnity would be violated.

The original purpose of a valued policy law was to protect the insured from an argument with the insurer if an agent had deliberately overinsured property so as to receive a higher commission. After a total loss, the insurer might offer less than the face amount for which the policyowner had paid premiums on the grounds that the building was overinsured. However, the importance of a valued policy law has declined over time because inflation in property values has made overinsurance less of a problem. Underinsurance is now the greater problem, because it results in both inadequate premiums for the insurer and inadequate protection for the insured.

Despite their reduced importance, valued policy laws can lead to overinsurance and an increase in moral hazard. Most buildings are not physically inspected before they are insured. If an insurer fails to inspect a building for valuation purposes, overinsurance and possible moral hazard may result. The insured may not be concerned about loss prevention, or may even deliberately cause a loss to collect the insurance proceeds. Although valued

policy laws provide a defense for the insurer when fraud is suspected, the burden of proof is on the insurer to prove fraudulent intent. Proving fraud is often difficult. For example, in an older case, a house advertised for sale at $1800 was insured for $10,000 under a fire insurance policy. About six months later, the house was totally destroyed by a fire. The insurer denied liability on the grounds of misrepresentation and fraud. An appeals court ordered the face amount of insurance to be paid, holding that nothing prevented the company from inspecting the property to determine its value. The insured's statement concerning the value of the house was an expression of opinion, not a representation of fact.[3]

Replacement Cost Insurance Replacement cost insurance is a third exception to the principle of indemnity. **Replacement cost insurance** *means there is no deduction for depreciation in determining the amount paid for a loss.* For example, assume that the roof on your home is 5 years old and has a useful life of 20 years. The roof is damaged by a tornado, and the current cost of replacement is $10,000. Under the actual cash value rule, you would receive only $7500 ($10,000 − $2500 = $7500). Under a replacement cost policy, you would receive the full $10,000 (less any applicable deductible). Because you receive the value of a brand new roof instead of one that is 5 years old, the principle of indemnity is violated.

Replacement cost insurance is based on the recognition that payment of the actual cash value can still result in a substantial loss to the insured, because few persons budget for depreciation. In our example, you would have had to pay $2500 to restore the damaged roof, since it was one-fourth depreciated. To deal with this problem, replacement cost insurance can be purchased to insure homes, buildings, and business and personal property.

Life Insurance Life insurance is another exception to the principle of indemnity. A life insurance contract is not a contract of indemnity but is a valued policy that pays a stated sum to the beneficiary upon the insured's death. The indemnity principle is difficult to apply to life insurance for the obvious reason that the actual cash value rule (replacement cost less depreciation) is meaningless in determining the value of a human life. Moreover, to plan for personal and business purposes, such as the need to provide a specific amount of monthly income to the deceased's dependents, a certain amount of life insurance must be purchased before death occurs. For these reasons, a life insurance policy is another exception to the principle of indemnity.

PRINCIPLE OF INSURABLE INTEREST

The principle of insurable interest is another important legal principle. The **principle of insurable interest** *states that the insured must be in a position to lose financially if a loss occurs.* For example, you have an insurable interest in your car because you may lose financially if the car is damaged or stolen. You have an insurable interest in your personal property, such as a television set or computer, because you may lose financially if the property is damaged or destroyed.

Purposes of an Insurable Interest

To be legally enforceable, all insurance contracts must be supported by an insurable interest. Insurance contracts must be supported by an insurable interest for the following reasons.[4]

- To prevent gambling
- To reduce moral hazard
- To measure the amount of the insured's loss in property insurance

First, an insurable interest is necessary to prevent gambling. If an insurable interest were not required, the contract would be a gambling contract and would be against the public interest. For example, you could insure the property of another and hope for a loss to occur. You could similarly insure the life of another person and hope for an early death. These contracts clearly would be gambling contracts and would be against the public interest.

Second, an insurable interest reduces moral hazard. If an insurable interest were not required, a dishonest person could purchase a property insurance contract on someone else's property and then deliberately cause a loss to receive the proceeds. But if the insured stands to lose financially, nothing is gained by causing the loss. Thus, moral hazard is reduced.

In life insurance, an insurable interest requirement reduces the incentive to murder the insured for the purpose of collecting the proceeds.

Finally, in property insurance, an insurable interest measures the amount of the insured's loss. Most property contracts are contracts of indemnity, and one measure of recovery is the insurable interest of the insured. If the loss payment cannot exceed the amount of one's insurable interest, the principle of indemnity is supported.

Examples of an Insurable Interest

Several examples of an insurable interest are discussed in this section. However, it is helpful at this point to distinguish between an insurable interest in property and liability insurance and in life insurance.

Property and Liability Insurance *Ownership of property* can support an insurable interest because owners of property will lose financially if their property is damaged or destroyed.

Potential legal liability can also support an insurable interest. For example, a dry-cleaning firm has an insurable interest in the property of the customers. The firm may be legally liable for damage to the customers' goods caused by the firm's negligence.

Secured creditors have an insurable interest as well. A commercial bank or savings and loan institution that lends money to buy a house has an insurable interest in the property. The property serves as collateral for the mortgage, so if the building is damaged, the collateral behind the loan is impaired. A bank that makes an inventory loan to a business firm has an insurable interest in the stock of goods, because the goods are collateral for the loan. However, the courts have ruled that unsecured or general creditors normally do not have an insurable interest in the debtor's property.[5]

Finally, a *contractual right* can support an insurable interest. Thus, a business firm that contracts to purchase goods from abroad on the condition that they arrive safely in the United States has an insurable interest in the goods because of the loss of profits if the merchandise does not arrive.

Life Insurance The question of an insurable interest does not arise when you purchase life insurance on your own life. The law considers the insurable interest requirement to be met whenever a person voluntarily purchases life insurance on his or her life. Thus, you can purchase as much life insurance as you can afford, subject of course to the insurer's underwriting rules concerning the maximum amount of insurance that can be written on any single life. Also, when you apply for life insurance on your own life, you can name anyone as beneficiary. The beneficiary is not required to have an insurable interest in your life.[6]

If you wish to purchase a life insurance policy on the life of another person, however, you must have an insurable interest in that person's life. Close family ties or marriage will satisfy the insurable interest requirement in life insurance. For example, a husband can purchase a life insurance policy on his wife and be named as beneficiary. Likewise, a wife can insure her husband and be named as beneficiary. A grandparent can purchase a life insurance policy on the life of a grandchild. However, remote family relationships will not support an insurable interest. For example, cousins cannot insure each other unless a pecuniary relationship is present.

If there is a **pecuniary interest**, the insurable interest requirement in life insurance can be met. Even when there is no relationship by blood or marriage, one person may be financially harmed by the death of another. For example, a corporation can insure the life of an outstanding salesperson, because the firm's profit may decline if the salesperson dies. One business partner can insure the life of the other partner and use the life insurance proceeds to purchase the deceased partner's interest if he or she dies.

When Must an Insurable Interest Exist?

In property insurance, the insurable interest must exist at the time of the loss. There are two reasons for this requirement. First, most property insurance contracts are contracts of indemnity. If an insurable interest did not exist at the time of loss, a financial loss would not occur. Hence, the principle of indemnity would be violated if payment were made. For example, if Mark sells his home to Susan, and a fire occurs before the insurance on the home is canceled, Mark cannot collect because he no longer has an insurable interest in the property. Susan cannot collect either because she is not named as an insured under the policy.

Second, you may not have an insurable interest in the property when the contract is first written but may expect to have an insurable interest in the future, at the time of possible loss. For example, in ocean marine insurance, it is common to insure a return cargo by a contract entered into prior to the ship's departure. However, the policy may not cover the goods until they are on board the ship as the insured's property. Although an insurable interest does not exist when the contract is first written, you can still collect if you have an insurable interest in the goods at the time of loss.

In contrast, in life insurance, the insurable interest requirement must be met only at the inception of the policy, not at the time of death. Life insurance is not a contract of indemnity but is a valued policy that pays a stated sum upon the insured's death. Because the beneficiary has only a legal claim to receive the policy proceeds, the beneficiary does not have to show that a loss has been incurred by the insured's death. For example, if Michelle takes out a policy on her husband's life and later gets a divorce, she is entitled to the policy proceeds upon the death of her former husband if she has kept the insurance in force. The insurable interest requirement must be met only at the inception of the contract (see Insight 5.1).

PRINCIPLE OF SUBROGATION

The principle of subrogation strongly supports the principle of indemnity. **Subrogation** *means substitution of the insurer in place of the insured for the purpose of claiming indemnity from a third person for a loss covered by insurance.*[7] The insurer is therefore entitled to recover from a negligent third party any loss payments made to the insured. For example, assume that a negligent motorist fails to stop at a red light and smashes into Megan's car, causing damage in the amount of $5000. If she has collision insurance on her car, her company will pay the physical damage loss to the car (less any deductible) and then attempt to collect from the negligent motorist who caused the accident. Alternatively, Megan could attempt to collect directly from the negligent motorist for the damage to her car. Subrogation does not apply if a loss payment is not made. However, to the extent that a loss payment is made, the insured gives

INSIGHT 5.1

No Insurable Interest at the Time of Death: Is a Corporation Entitled to the Life Insurance Proceeds?

Legal Facts

A corporation purchased a $1 million life insurance policy on an officer who was a 20 percent stockholder in the company. Shortly thereafter, the officer sold his stock and resigned. Two years later he died. The insurer paid the death proceeds to the corporation. The personal representative of the deceased insured's estate claimed the insurable interest was only temporary and must continue until death. Is the corporation entitled to the policy proceeds even though it had no insurable interest at the time of death?

Court Decision

The court rejected the argument that the corporation's insurable interest must continue until death.[a] Its decision reflects the principle that termination of an insurable interest before the policy matures does not affect the policyholder's right of recovery under a policy valid at its inception. The insurable interest requirement must be met only at the inception of the policy.

[a]*In re Al Zuni Trading*, 947 F.2d 1402 (1991).
SOURCE: Adapted from Buist M. Anderson, *Anderson on Life Insurance, 1992 Supplement* (Boston, MA: Little, Brown, 1992), p. 29. ©1992, Little, Brown and Company.

to the insurer legal rights to collect damages from the negligent third party.

Purposes of Subrogation

Subrogation has three basic purposes. *First, subrogation prevents the insured from collecting twice for the same loss.* In the absence of subrogation, the insured could collect from the insurer and from the person who caused the loss. The principle of indemnity would be violated because the insured would be profiting from a loss.

Second, subrogation is used to hold the guilty person responsible for the loss. By exercising its subrogation rights, the insurer can collect from the negligent person who caused the loss.

Finally, subrogation helps to hold down insurance rates. Subrogation recoveries can be reflected in the rate-making process, which tends to hold rates below where they would be in the absence of subrogation.

Importance of Subrogation

You should keep in mind five important corollaries of the principle of subrogation.

1. *The general rule is that by exercising its subrogation rights, the insurer is entitled only to the amount it has paid under the policy.*[8] Some insureds may not

be fully indemnified after a loss because of insufficient insurance, satisfaction of a deductible, or legal expenses in trying to recover from a negligent third party. Many policies currently have a provision stating how a subrogation recovery is to be shared between the insured and insurer.

In the absence of any policy provision, the courts have used different rules in determining how a subrogation recovery is to be shared. *One view is that the insured must be reimbursed in full for the loss; the insurer is then entitled to any remaining balance up to the insurer's interest, with any remainder going to the insured.*[9] For example, Andrew has a $200,000 home insured for only $160,000 under a homeowners policy. Assume that the house is totally destroyed in a fire because of faulty wiring by an electrician. The insurer would pay $160,000 to Andrew and then attempt to collect from the negligent electrician. After exercising its subrogation rights against the negligent electrician, assume that the insurer has a net recovery of $100,000 (after deduction of legal expenses). Andrew would receive $40,000, and the insurer can retain the balance of $60,000.

2. *The insured cannot impair the insurer's subrogation rights.* The insured cannot do anything after a loss that interferes with the insurer's right to proceed against a negligent third party. For example, if the insured waives the right to sue the negligent party, the

right to collect from the insurer for the loss is also waived. This case could happen if the insured admits fault in an auto accident or attempts to settle a collision loss with the negligent driver without the insurer's consent. If the insurer's right to subrogate against the negligent motorist is adversely affected, the insured's right to collect from the insurer is forfeited.[10]

3. *The insurer can waive its subrogation rights in the contract.* To meet the special needs of some insureds, the insurance company may waive its subrogation rights by a contractual provision for losses that have not yet occurred. For example, to rent an apartment house, a landlord may agree to release the tenants from potential liability if the building is damaged. If the landlord's insurer waives its subrogation rights, and if a tenant negligently starts a fire, the insurer would have to reimburse the landlord for the loss, but could not recover from the tenant because the subrogation rights were waived.

The insurer may decide not to exercise its subrogation rights after a loss occurs. The legal expenses may exceed the possible recovery; a counterclaim against the insured or insurer may be filed by the alleged wrongdoer; the insurer may wish to avoid embarrassment of the insured; or the insurer company may wish to maintain good public relations.[11]

4. *Subrogation does not apply to life insurance and to most individual health insurance contracts.* Life insurance is not a contract of indemnity, and subrogation has relevance only for contracts of indemnity. Individual health insurance contracts usually do not contain subrogation clauses.[12]

5. *The insurer cannot subrogate against its own insureds.* If the insurer could recover a loss payment for a covered loss from an insured, the basic purpose of purchasing the insurance would be defeated.

PRINCIPLE OF UTMOST GOOD FAITH

An insurance contract is based on the **principle of utmost good faith**—*that is, a higher degree of honesty is imposed on both parties to an insurance contract than is imposed on parties to other contracts.* This principle has its historical roots in ocean marine insurance. An ocean marine underwriter had to place great faith in statements made by the applicant for insurance concerning the cargo to be shipped. The property to be insured may not have been visually inspected, and the contract may have been formed in a location far removed from the cargo and ship. Thus, the principle of utmost good faith imposed a high degree of honesty on the applicant for insurance.

The principle of utmost good faith is supported by three important legal doctrines: representations, concealment, and warranty.

Representations

Representations *are statements made by the applicant for insurance.* For example, if you apply for life insurance, you may be asked questions concerning your age, weight, height, occupation, state of health, family history, and other relevant questions. Your answers to these questions are called representations.

The legal significance of a representation is that the insurance contract is voidable at the insurer's option if the representation is (1) material, (2) false, and (3) relied on by the insurer.[13] **Material** *means that if the insurer knew the true facts, the policy would not have been issued, or it would have been issued on different terms. False* means that the statement is not true or is misleading. *Reliance* means that the insurer relies on the misrepresentation in issuing the policy at a specified premium.

For example, Joseph applies for life insurance and states in the application that he has not visited a doctor within the last five years. However, six months earlier, he had surgery for lung cancer. In this case, he has made a statement that is false, material, and relied on by the insurer. Therefore, the policy is voidable at the insurer's option. If Joseph dies shortly after the policy is issued, say three months, the company could contest the death claim on the basis of a material misrepresentation. Insight 5.2 provides an additional application of this legal principle.

If an applicant for insurance states an opinion or belief that later turns out to be wrong, the insurer must prove that the applicant spoke fraudulently and intended to deceive the company before it can deny payment of a claim. For example, assume that you are asked if you have high blood pressure when

INSIGHT 5.2

Misrepresentation in Application for Auto Insurance

Legal Facts

The insured misrepresented that she had no traffic violations in the prior three-year period. After an accident, a check of her record revealed that she had two speeding tickets in that period. The insurer denied coverage.

Court Decision

State law regarding the voiding of insurance requires that the misrepresentation must be material and made with the intent to deceive. The insured claimed that she had forgotten about the two tickets, and therefore had no intent to deceive. The court ruled that it is unlikely she would forget both events. Decision is for the insurer.[a]

[a]*Benton v. Shelter Mutual Ins. Co.*, 550 So.2d 832 (La.App.2 Cir. 1989).

SOURCE: Adapted from "Misrepresentations in Auto Coverage Applications," *FC & S Bulletins*, Miscellaneous Property section, Fire and Marine volume, October 1997, p. M.35.5.

you apply for health insurance, and you answer "no" to the question. If the insurer later discovers you have high blood pressure, to deny payment of a claim, it must prove that you intended to deceive the company. Thus, a statement of opinion or belief must also be fraudulent before the insurer can refuse to pay a claim.

An **innocent misrepresentation** of a material fact, if relied on by the insurer, also makes the contract voidable. An innocent misrepresentation is one that is unintentional. A majority of court opinions have ruled that an innocent misrepresentation of a material fact makes the contract voidable.

Finally, the doctrine of material misrepresentations also applies to statements made by the insured after a loss occurs. If the insured submits a fraudulent proof of loss or misrepresents the value of the items damaged, the insurer has the right to void the coverage (see Insight 5.3).

Concealment

The doctrine of concealment also supports the principle of utmost good faith. A **concealment** *is intentional failure of the applicant for insurance to reveal a material fact to the insurer.* Concealment is the same thing as nondisclosure; that is, the applicant for insurance deliberately withholds material information from the insurer. The legal effect of a material concealment is the same as a misrepresentation—the contract is voidable at the insurer's option.

To deny a claim based on concealment, a nonmarine insurer must prove two things: (1) the con-

cealed fact was known by the insured to be material, and (2) the insured intended to defraud the insurer.[14] For example, Joseph DeBellis applied for a life insurance policy on his life. Five months after the policy was issued, he was murdered. The death certificate named the deceased as Joseph DeLuca, his true name. The insurer denied payment on the grounds that Joseph had concealed a material fact by not revealing his true identity and that he had an extensive criminal record. In finding for the insurer, the court held that intentional concealment of his true identity was material and breached the obligation of good faith.[15]

The doctrine of concealment is applied in a harsher manner in ocean marine insurance. An ocean marine insurer is not required to prove that the concealment is intentional. Applicants are required to reveal all material facts that pertain to the property to be insured. The applicant's lack of awareness of the materiality of the fact is of no consequence. Thus, an ocean marine insurer can successfully deny payment of a claim if it can show that the concealed fact is material.

Warranty

The doctrine of warranty also reflects the principle of utmost good faith. A **warranty** *is a statement that becomes part of the insurance contract and is guaranteed by the maker to be true in all respects.*[16] For example, in exchange for a reduced premium, a liquor store owner may warrant that an approved burglary and robbery alarm system will be opera-

INSIGHT 5.3

Misrepresentation in Proof of Loss

Legal Facts

The insured experienced a burglary loss of $9000 and misrepresented the value of the items stolen. The insured provided receipts that showed a purchase price of $900 for a stereo set and $1500 for video equipment. The insurer proved that the stereo set cost only $400, and that the insured had not purchased the video equipment.

Court Decision

The court allowed the insurer to void coverage in its entirety. The court ruled that (1) insureds have an obligation to pro-

vide the insurer with true receipts, submit to an examination under oath, and provide a sworn proof of loss, and (2) the misrepresentations were material because they were made to mislead, discourage, or deflect the insurer's investigation of the claim.[a]

[a]*Passero v. Allstate Ins. Co.* 554 N.E.2d 384 (Ill. App. lst Dist. 1990).

SOURCE: Adapted from "Misrepresentation in Proofs of Loss," *FC & S Bulletins,* Miscellaneous Property section, Fire and Marine volume, October 1997, p. M.35.5.

---

tional at all times. A bank may warrant that a guard will be on the premises twenty-four hours a day. Likewise, a business firm may warrant that an automatic sprinkler system will be in working order throughout the term of the policy. A clause describing the warranty becomes part of the contract.

Based on the common law, in its strictest form, a warranty is a harsh legal doctrine. Any breach of the warranty, even if minor or not material, allowed the insurer to deny payment of a claim. During the early days of insurance, statements made by the applicant for insurance were considered to be warranties. If the statement were untrue in any respect, even if not material, the insurer could deny payment of a claim based on a breach of warranty.

Because strict application of the warranty doctrine harmed many insureds, state legislatures and the courts have softened and modified the harsh common law doctrine of warranty over time. Some modifications of the warranty doctrine are summarized as follows:

- Statements made by applicants for insurance are considered to be representations and not warranties. For example, statements made by applicants for life and health insurance are considered to be representations and not warranties. Thus, the insurer cannot deny liability for a claim if a misrepresentation is not material.
- Most courts will interpret a breach of warranty liberally in those cases where a minor breach

affects the risk only temporarily or insignificantly.

- "Increase in hazard" statutes have been passed that state that the insurer cannot deny a claim unless the breach of warranty increases the hazard.
- Statutes have been passed that allow the insured to recover for a loss unless the breach of warranty actually contributed to the loss.

REQUIREMENTS OF AN INSURANCE CONTRACT

An insurance policy is based on the law of contracts. To be legally enforceable, an insurance contract must meet four basic requirements: offer and acceptance, consideration, competent parties, and legal purpose.

Offer and Acceptance

The first requirement of a binding insurance contract is that there must be an **offer and an acceptance** of its terms. In most cases, the applicant for insurance makes the offer, and the company accepts or rejects the offer. An agent merely solicits or invites the prospective insured to make an offer. The requirement of offer and acceptance can be examined in greater detail by making a careful distinction between property and liability insurance, and life insurance.

In property and liability insurance, the offer and acceptance can be oral or written. In the absence of specific legislation to the contrary, oral insurance contracts are valid. As a practical matter, most property and liability insurance contracts are in written form. The applicant for insurance fills out the application and pays the first premium (or promises to pay the first premium). This step constitutes the offer. The agent then accepts the offer on behalf of the insurance company. In property and liability insurance, agents typically have the power to bind their companies through use of a binder. A **binder** *is a temporary contract for insurance and can be either written or oral.* The binder obligates the company immediately prior to receipt of the application and issuance of the policy. Thus, the insurance contract can be effective immediately, because the agent accepts the offer on behalf of the company. This procedure is usually followed in personal lines of property and liability insurance, including homeowners policies and auto insurance. However, in some cases, the agent is not authorized to bind the company, and the application must be sent to the company for approval. The company may then accept the offer and issue the policy or reject the application.

In life insurance, the procedures followed are different. A life insurance agent does not have the power to bind the insurer. Therefore, the application for life insurance is always in writing, and the applicant must be approved by the insurer before the life insurance is in force. The usual procedure is for the applicant to fill out the application and pay the first premium. A **conditional premium receipt** is then given to the applicant. The most common conditional receipt is the "insurability premium receipt." If the applicant is found insurable according to the insurer's normal underwriting standards, the life insurance becomes effective as of the date of the application. Some insurability receipts make the life insurance effective on the date of the application or the date of the medical exam, whichever is later.

For example, assume that Aaron applies for a $100,000 life insurance policy on Monday. He fills out the application, pays the first premium, and receives a conditional premium receipt from the agent. On Tuesday morning, he takes a physical examination, and on Tuesday afternoon, he is killed in a boating accident. The application and premium will still be forwarded to the insurer, as if he were still alive. If he is found insurable according to the insurer's underwriting rules, the life insurance is in force, and $100,000 will be paid to his beneficiary.

However, if the applicant for life insurance does not pay the first premium when the application is filled out, a different set of rules applies. Before the life insurance is in force, the policy must be issued and delivered to the applicant, the first premium must be paid, and the applicant must be in good health when the policy is delivered. Some insurers also require that there must be no interim medical treatment between submission of the application and delivery of the policy. These requirements are considered to be "conditions precedent"—in other words, they must be fulfilled before the life insurance is in force.[17]

Consideration

The second requirement of a valid insurance contract is **consideration**—the value that each party gives to the other. The insured's consideration is payment of the first premium (or a promise to pay the first premium) plus an agreement to abide by the conditions specified in the policy. The insurer's consideration is the promise to do certain things as specified in the contract. This promise can include paying for a loss from an insured peril, providing certain services, such as loss prevention and safety services, or defending the insured in a liability lawsuit.

Competent Parties

The third requirement of a valid insurance contract is that each party must be **legally competent.** *This means the parties must have legal capacity to enter into a binding contract.* Most adults are legally competent to enter into insurance contracts, but there are some exceptions. Insane persons, intoxicated persons, and corporations that act outside the scope of their authority cannot enter into enforceable insurance contracts. Minors normally are not legally competent to enter into binding insurance contracts; but most states have enacted laws that permit minors to enter into a valid life insurance contract.

The insurer must also be legally competent. Insurers generally must be licensed to sell insurance in the state, and the insurance sold must be within the scope of its charter or certificate of incorporation.

Legal Purpose

A final requirement is that the contract must be for a **legal purpose.** An insurance contract that encourages or promotes something illegal or immoral is contrary to the public interest and cannot be enforced. For example, a street pusher of heroin and other illegal drugs cannot purchase a property insurance policy that would cover seizure of the drugs by the police. This type of contract obviously is not enforceable because it would promote illegal activities that are contrary to the public interest.

DISTINCT LEGAL CHARACTERISTICS OF INSURANCE CONTRACTS

Insurance contracts have distinct legal characteristics that make them different from other legal contracts. Several distinctive legal characteristics have already been discussed. As we noted earlier, most property and liability insurance contracts are contracts of indemnity; all insurance contracts must be supported by an insurable interest; and insurance contracts are based on utmost good faith. Other distinct legal characteristics are as follows:

- Aleatory contract
- Unilateral contract
- Conditional contract
- Personal contract
- Contract of adhesion

Aleatory Contract

An insurance contract is aleatory rather than commutative. An **aleatory contract** *is a contract where the values exchanged may not be equal but depend on an uncertain event.* Depending on chance, one party may receive a value out of proportion to the value that is given. For example, assume that Jessica pays a premium of $600 for $200,000 of homeowners insurance on her home. If the home were totally destroyed by fire shortly thereafter, she would collect an amount that greatly exceeds the premium paid. On the other hand, a homeowner may faithfully pay premiums for many years and never have a loss.

In contrast, other commercial contracts are commutative. A **commutative contract** *is one in which the values exchanged by both parties are theoretically equal.* For example, the purchaser of real estate normally pays a price that is viewed to be equal to the value of the property.

Although the essence of an aleatory contract is chance, or the occurrence of some fortuitous event, an insurance contract is not a gambling contract. Gambling creates a new speculative risk that did not exist before the transaction. Insurance, however, is a technique for handling an already existing pure risk. Thus, although both gambling and insurance are aleatory in nature, an insurance contract is not a gambling contract because no new risk is created.

Unilateral Contract

An insurance contract is a unilateral contract. A **unilateral contract** *means that only one party makes a legally enforceable promise.* In this case, only the insurer makes a legally enforceable promise to pay a claim or provide other services to the insured. After the first premium is paid, and the insurance is in force, the insured cannot be legally forced to pay the premiums or to comply with the policy provisions. Although the insured must continue to pay the premiums to receive payment for a loss, he or she cannot be legally forced to do so. However, if the premiums are paid, the insurer must accept them and must continue to provide the protection promised under the contract.

In contrast, most commercial contracts are *bilateral* in nature. Each party makes a legally enforceable promise to the other party. If one party fails to perform, the other party can insist on performance or can sue for damages because of the breach of contract.

Conditional Contract

An insurance contract is a **conditional contract.** That is, the insurer's obligation to pay a claim depends on whether the insured or the beneficiary has complied with all policy conditions. **Conditions** *are provisions inserted in the policy that qualify or place limitations* *on the insurer's promise to perform.* The conditions section imposes certain duties on the insured if he or she wishes to collect for a loss. Although the insured is not compelled to abide by the policy conditions, he or she must do so to collect for an insured loss. The insurer is not obligated to pay a claim if the policy conditions are not met. For example, under a homeowners policy, the insured must give immediate notice of a loss. If the insured delays for an unreasonable period in reporting the loss, the insurer can refuse to pay the claim on the grounds that a policy condition has been violated.

Personal Contract

In property insurance, insurance is a **personal contract,** *which means the contract is between the insured and the insurer.* Strictly speaking, a property insurance contract does not insure property, but insures the owner of property against loss. The owner of the insured property is indemnified if the property is damaged or destroyed. Because the contract is personal, the applicant for insurance must be acceptable to the insurer and must meet certain underwriting standards regarding character, morals, and credit.

A property insurance contract normally cannot be assigned to another party without the insurer's consent. If property is sold to another person, the new owner may not be acceptable to the insurer. *Thus, the insurer's consent is normally required before a property insurance policy can be validly assigned to another party.* In contrast, a life insurance policy can be freely assigned to anyone without the insurer's consent because the assignment does not usually alter the risk or increase the probability of death.

Conversely, a loss payment for a property loss can be assigned to another party without the insurer's consent. Although the insurer's consent is not required, the contract may require that the insurer be notified of the assignment of the proceeds to another party.

Contract of Adhesion

A **contract of adhesion** *means the insured must accept the entire contract, with all of its terms and conditions.* The insurer drafts and prints the policy, and the insured generally must accept the entire document and cannot insist that certain provisions be added or deleted or the contract rewritten to suit the insured. Although the contract can be altered by the addition of endorsements and riders or other forms, the contract is drafted by the insurer. To redress the imbalance that exists in such a situation, *the courts have ruled that any ambiguities or uncertainties in the contract are construed against the insurer.* If the policy is ambiguous, the insured gets the benefit of the doubt.

The general rule that ambiguities in insurance contracts are construed against the insurer is reinforced by the principle of reasonable expectations. The **principle of reasonable expectations** *states that an insured is entitled to coverage under a policy that he or she reasonably expects it to provide, and that to be effective, exclusions or qualifications must be conspicuous, plain, and clear.*[18] Some courts have ruled that insureds are entitled to the protection that they reasonably expect to have, and that technical restrictions in the contract should be clear and conspicuous. For example, in one case, a liability insurer refused to defend the insured on the grounds that the policy excluded intentional acts. The court ruled that the insurer was responsible for the defense costs. The insured had a reasonable expectation that defense costs were covered under the policy because the policy covered other types of intentional acts.[19]

LAW AND THE INSURANCE AGENT

An insurance contract normally is sold by an agent who represents the principal (the insurer). An agent is someone who has the authority to act on behalf of someone else. The principal (insurer) is the party for whom action is to be taken. Thus, if Patrick has the authority to solicit, create, or terminate an insurance contract on behalf of Apex Insurance, he would be the agent and Apex Insurance would be the principal.

General Rules of Agency

Important rules of law govern the actions of agents and their relationship to insureds. They include the following:[20]

- There is no presumption of an agency relationship.

- An agent must have authority to represent the principal.
- A principal is responsible for the acts of agents acting within the scope of their authority.

No Presumption of an Agency Relationship   There is no presumption that one person legally can act as an agent for another. Some visible evidence of an agency relationship must exist. For example, a person who claims to be an agent for an auto insurer may collect premiums and then abscond with the funds. The auto insurer is not legally responsible for the person's actions if it has done nothing to create the impression that an agency relationship is in existence. However, if the person has a business card, rate book, and application blanks supplied by the insurer, then it can be presumed that a legitimate agent is acting on behalf of that insurer.

Authority to Represent the Principal   An agent must be authorized to represent the principal. An agent's authority is derived from three sources: (1) express powers, (2) implied powers, and (3) apparent authority.

Express powers are powers specifically conferred on the agent. These powers are normally stated in the **agency agreement** between the agent and the principal. The agency agreement may also withhold certain powers. For example, a life insurance agent may be given the power to solicit applicants and arrange for physical examinations. Certain powers, however, such as the right to extend the time for payment of premiums or the right to alter contractual provisions in the policy, may be denied.

Agents also have **implied powers.** Implied powers refer to the authority of the agent to perform all incidental acts necessary to fulfill the purposes of the agency agreement. For example, an agent may have the express authority to deliver a life insurance policy to the client. It follows that the agent also has the implied power to collect the first premium.

Finally, an agent may bind the principal by **apparent authority.** If an agent acts with apparent authority to do certain things, and a third party is led to believe that the agent is acting within the scope of reasonable and appropriate authority, the principal can be bound by the agent's actions. Third parties have to show only that they have exercised

due diligence in determining the agent's authority based on the agent's actual authority or conduct of the principal. For example, an agent for an auto insurer may frequently grant his or her clients an extension of time to pay overdue premiums. If the insurer has not expressly granted this right to the agent and has not taken any action to deal with the violation of company policy, it could not later deny liability for a loss on the grounds that the agent lacked authority to grant the time extension. The insurer first would have to notify all policyowners of the limitations on the agent's powers.

Principal Responsible for Acts of Agents   A final rule of agency law is that the principal is responsible for all acts of agents when they are acting within the scope of their authority. This responsibility also includes fraudulent acts, omissions, and misrepresentations.

In addition, knowledge of the agent is presumed to be knowledge of the principal with respect to matters within the scope of the agency relationship. For example, if a life insurance agent knows that an applicant for life insurance is addicted to alcohol, this knowledge is imputed to the insurer even though the agent deliberately omits this information from the application. Thus, if the insurer issues the policy, it cannot later attack the validity of the policy on the grounds of alcohol addiction and the concealment of a material fact.

Waiver and Estoppel

The doctrines of waiver and estoppel have direct relevance to the law of agency and to the powers of insurance agents. The practical significance of these concepts is that an insurer legally may be required to pay a claim that it ordinarily would not have to pay.

Waiver *is defined as the voluntary relinquishment of a known legal right.* If the insurer voluntarily waives a legal right under the contract, it cannot later deny payment of a claim by the insured on the grounds that such a legal right was violated. For example, assume that an insurer receives an application for insurance at its home office, and that the application contains an incomplete or missing answer. Assume that the insurer does not contact the applicant for additional information, and the policy is issued. The insurer later could not deny payment of a claim on the basis of an incomplete application. In effect, the insurer has waived its requirement that the application be complete by issuing the policy.

The legal term *estoppel* was derived centuries ago from the English common law. **Estoppel** *occurs when a representation of fact made by one person to another person is reasonably relied on by that person to such an extent that it would be inequitable to allow the first person to deny the truth of the representation.*[21] Stated simply, if one person makes a statement to another person who then reasonably relies on the statement to his or her detriment, the first person cannot later deny the statement

was made. The law of estoppel is designed to prevent persons from changing their minds to the detriment of another party. For example, assume that Richard's auto insurance premium is due. He calls his agent and asks for an extension of time. The agent states, "Don't worry. There is a 10-day grace period for overdue premiums." If Richard has an accident during the so-called grace period, the insurer cannot deny liability for the loss on the grounds that the premium was not paid on time. In effect, the insurer would be stopped, or prevented, from denying payment of the claim. Richard has reasonably relied on the statement by his agent, and the insurer cannot later change its mind to Richard's detriment.

CASE APPLICATION

Carmine purchased an automobile service station from Ben. The purchase price included the building, equipment, and other assets. The business was financed by a loan from National Bank, which held a mortgage on the building. Carmine also converted a one-car repair bay into a short-order restaurant. When Carmine applied for property insurance on the business, he did not tell the insurance company about the restaurant because his premiums would have been substantially increased. Six months after the business opened, a car caught fire and damaged the roof over a bay in the service station area.

a. Do any of the following parties have an insurable interest in the business at the time of the fire?
Ben
Carmine
National Bank

b. Ben told Carmine he could save money by taking over Ben's insurance instead of buying a new policy. Would it be appropriate for Carmine to take over Ben's insurance without notifying Ben's insurer? Explain.

c. Investigation of the fire revealed that the car owner knew the gas tank had a leak, but this information was not disclosed to Carmine when the car was brought in for service. Explain how subrogation might apply in this case.

d. Did Carmine show utmost good faith when he applied for property insurance on the business? Explain.

e. Could Carmine's insurer deny coverage for the fire on the basis of a material concealment? Explain.

SUMMARY

- The principle of indemnity states that the insurer should not pay more than the actual amount of the loss; in other words, the insured should not profit from a covered loss.

- There are several exceptions to the principle of indemnity. These exceptions include a valued policy, valued policy laws, replacement cost insurance, and life insurance.

- The principle of insurable interest means that the insured must stand to lose financially if a loss occurs. All insurance contracts must be supported by an insurable interest to be legally enforceable. There are three purposes of the insurable interest requirement:

  To prevent gambling

  To reduce moral hazard

  To measure the amount of loss in property insurance

- In property and liability insurance, the ownership of property, potential legal liability, secured creditors, and contractual rights can support the insurable interest requirement.

- In life insurance, the question of an insurable interest does not arise when a person purchases life insurance on his or her own life. If life insurance is purchased on the life of another person, there must be an insurable interest in that person's life. Close family ties, blood, marriage, or a pecuniary interest will satisfy the insurable interest requirement in life insurance.

- In property insurance, the insurable interest requirement must be met at the time of loss. In life insurance, the insurable interest requirement must be met only at the inception of the policy.

- The principle of subrogation means that the insurer is entitled to recover from a negligent third party any loss payments made to the insured. The purposes of subrogation are to prevent the insured from collecting twice for the same loss, to hold the negligent person responsible for the loss, and to hold down insurance rates.

- If the insurer exercises its subrogation rights, the insured generally must be fully restored before the insurer can retain any sums collected from the negligent third party. Also, the insured cannot do anything that might impair the insurer's subrogation rights. However, the insurer can waive its subrogation rights in the contract either before or after the loss. Finally, subrogation does not apply to life insurance contracts and to most individual health insurance contracts.

- The principle of utmost good faith means that a higher degree of honesty is imposed on both parties to an insurance contract than is imposed on parties to other contracts.

- The legal doctrines of representations, concealment, and warranty support the principle of utmost good faith. Representations are statements made by the applicant for insurance. The insurer can deny payment for a claim if the representation is material and false, and is relied on by the insurer in issuing the policy at a specified premium. In the case of statements of belief or opinion, the misrepresentation must also be fraudulent before the insurer can deny a claim. Concealment of a material fact has the same legal effect as a misrepresentation: the contract is voidable at the insurer's option.

- A warranty is a statement of fact or a promise made by the insured, which is part of the insurance contract and must be true if the insurer is to be liable under the contract. Based on common law, any breach of the warranty, even if slight, allows the insurer to deny payment of a claim. The harsh, common law doctrine of a warranty, however, has been modified and softened by court decisions and statutes.

- To have a valid insurance contract, four requirements must be met:
  There must be an offer and acceptance.
  Consideration must be exchanged.
  The parties to the contract must be legally competent.
  The contract must be for a legal purpose.

- Insurance contracts have distinct legal characteristics. An insurance contract is an *aleatory contract* where the values exchanged may not be equal and depend on the occurrence of an uncertain event. An insurance contract is *unilateral* because only the insurer makes a legally enforceable promise. An insurance contract is *conditional* because the insurer's obligation to pay a claim depends on whether the insured or beneficiary has complied with all policy provisions. A property insurance contract is a *personal contract* between the insured and insurer and cannot be validly assigned to another party without the insurer's consent. A life insurance policy is freely assignable without the insurer's consent. Finally, insurance is a *contract of adhesion*, which means the insured must accept the entire contract, with all of its terms and conditions; if there is an ambiguity in the contract, it will be construed against the insurer.

- Three general rules of agency govern the actions of agents and their relationship to insureds:
  There is no presumption of an agency relationship.
  An agent must have the authority to represent the principal.
  A principal is responsible for the actions of agents acting within the scope of their authority.

- An agent can bind the principal based on express powers, implied powers, and apparent authority.

- Based on the legal doctrines of waiver and estoppel, an insurer may be required to pay a claim that it ordinarily would not have to pay.

KEY CONCEPTS AND TERMS

Actual cash value
Agency agreement
Aleatory contract
Apparent authority
Binder
Broad evidence rule
Commutative contract
Concealment
Conditional contract
Conditions
Conditional premium
 receipt
Consideration
Contract of adhesion
Estoppel
Express powers
Fair market value
Implied powers
Innocent misrepresentation
Legal purpose
Legally competent parties

Material fact
Offer and acceptance
Pecuniary interest
Personal contract
Principle of indemnity
Principle of insurable
 interest
Principle of reasonable
 expectations
Principle of utmost
 good faith
Replacement cost
 insurance
Representations
Subrogation
Unilateral contract
Valued policy
Valued policy law
Waiver
Warranty

REVIEW QUESTIONS

1. a. Explain the principle of indemnity.
    b. How is actual cash value calculated?
    c. How does the concept of actual cash value support the principle of indemnity?

2. a. What is a valued policy? Why is it used?
    b. What is a valued policy law?
    c. What is a replacement cost policy?

3. a. Explain the meaning of an insurable interest.
    b. Why is an insurable interest required in every insurance contract?

4. a. Explain the principle of subrogation.
    b. Why is subrogation used?

5. Explain the following legal doctrines:
    a. misrepresentation
    b. concealment
    c. warranty

6. List the four requirements that must be met to have a valid insurance contract.

7. Insurance contracts have certain legal characteristics that distinguish them from other contracts. Explain

the following legal characteristics of insurance contracts.
    a. Aleatory contract
    b. Unilateral contract
    c. Conditional contract
    d. Personal contract
    e. Contract of adhesion

8. Explain the general rules of agency that govern the actions of agents and their relationship to insureds.

9. Identify three sources of authority that enable an agent to bind the principal.

10. Explain the meaning of:
    a. Waiver
    b. Estoppel

APPLICATION QUESTIONS

1. Scott borrowed $500,000 from the Gateway Bank to purchase a fishing boat. He keeps the boat at a dock owned by the Marina Company. He uses the boat to earn income by fishing. Scott also has a contract with the Blue Fin Fishing Company to transport shrimp from one port to another.
    a. Do any of the following parties have an insurable interest in Scott or his property? If an insurable interest exists, explain the extent of the interest.
       (1) Gateway Bank
       (2) Marina Company
       (3) Blue Fin Fishing Company
    b. If Scott did not own the boat but operated it on behalf of the Blue Fin Fishing Company, would he have an insurable interest in the boat? Explain.

2. Ashley purchased a dining room set for $5000 and insured the furniture on an actual cash value basis. Three years later, the set was destroyed in a fire. At the time of loss, the property had depreciated in value by 50 percent. The replacement cost of a new dining room set at the time of loss was $6000. Ignoring any deductible, how much will Ashley collect from her insurer? Explain your answer.

3. Taylor purchased a 20-year-old house for $200,000. The house has an estimated useful life of 80 years. Taylor insured the house for $200,000. The replacement cost of a similar house with materials of like kind and quality is $240,000. The house is totally destroyed in a tornado.

a. Based on the actual cash value rule, how much will Taylor collect from her insurer (ignore any deductible)?

b. If the loss occurs in a state with a valued policy law, how much will Taylor collect from her insurer (ignore any deductible)?

4. Nicholas owns a laptop computer that was stolen. The laptop cost $2000 when it was purchased two years ago. A similar laptop computer today can be purchased for $1800. Assuming that the laptop was 50 percent depreciated at the time the theft occurred, what is the actual cash value of the loss?

5. Megan owns an antique table that has a current market value of $12,000. The table is specifically insured for $12,000 under a valued policy. The table is totally destroyed when a tornado touched down and damaged Megan's home. At the time of loss, the table had an estimated market value of $10,000. How much will Megan collect for the loss? Explain your answer.

6. A drunk driver ran a red light and smashed into Kristen's car. The cost to repair the car is $8000. She has collision insurance on her car with a $500 deductible.

a. Can Kristen collect from both the negligent driver's insurer and her own insurer? Explain your answer.

b. Explain how subrogation supports the principle of indemnity.

7. One requirement for the formation of a valid insurance contract is that the contract must be for a legal purpose.

a. Identify three factors, other than the legal purpose requirement, that are essential to the formation of a binding insurance contract.

b. Explain how each of the three requirements in part (a) is fulfilled when the applicant applies for an auto insurance policy.

8. Nicole is applying for a health insurance policy. She has a chronic liver ailment and other health problems. She honestly disclosed the true facts concerning her medical history to the insurance agent. However, the agent did not include all the facts in the application. Instead, the agent stated that he was going to cover the material facts in a separate letter to the insurance company's underwriting department. However, the agent did not furnish the material facts to the insurer,

and the contract was issued as standard. A claim occurred shortly thereafter. After investigating the claim, the insurer denied payment. Nicole contends that the company should pay the claim because she answered honestly all questions that the agent asked.

a. On what basis can the insurance company deny payment of the claim?

b. What legal doctrines can Nicole use to support her argument that the claim should be paid?

INTERNET RESOURCES

■ **InsWeb** offers insurance quotes from the nation's strongest insurers. You can get quotes for auto insurance, homeowners insurance, term life insurance, individual health insurance, and other insurance lines as well. Visit the site at

http://www.insweb.com

■ **Law Links** is a comprehensive legal resource guide for both attorneys and consumers. The site has a "Legal Subjects Index." Click on "Insurance Law" for a variety of legal topics relevant to insurance consumers. Visit the site at

http://www.lawlinks.com

■ The **Legal Information Institute** of Cornell Law School provides detailed information on legal topics, including insurance law. Legal topics are listed alphabetically under "Law About . . ." Click on to "Insurance" for federal and state insurance statutes, recent court decisions on insurance, and related links. Visit the site at

http://www.law.cornell.edu

■ **Nolo.com** is a leading source of self-help legal information for consumers, including topics on insurance law. The "Legal Encyclopedia" section contains several articles on insurance for consumers. Visit the site at

http://www.nolo.com

SELECTED REFERENCES

Anderson, Buist M. *Anderson on Life Insurance*. Boston: Little, Brown, 1991. See also *Anderson on Life Insurance, 1996 Supplement.*

Crawford, Muriel L. *Life and Health Insurance Law*, 8th ed. Boston, MA: Irwin/McGraw-Hill, 1998.

Fire, Casualty & Surety Bulletins. Fire and Marine volume. Erlanger, KY: National Underwriter Company. These bulletins contain interesting cases concerning the meaning of actual cash value, insurable interest, and other legal concepts.

Graves, Edward E., and Burke A. Christensen, eds. *McGill's Legal Aspects of Life Insurance*, 3rd ed. Bryn Mawr, PA: The American College, 2002.

Keeton, Robert E., and Alan I. Widiss. *Insurance Law: A Guide to Fundamental Principles, Legal Doctrines, and Commercial Practices.* Student edition. St. Paul, MN: West Publishing, 1988.

Lorimer, James J., et al. *The Legal Environment of Insurance,* 4th ed., vols. 1 and 2. Malvern, PA: American Institute for Chartered Property and Liability Underwriters, 1993.

Wiening, Eric A. *Foundations of Risk Management and Insurance*, First Edition. Malvern, PA: American Institute for CPCU/Insurance Institute of America, 2002, chs. 11–19.

Wiening, Eric A., and Donald S. Malecki. *Insurance Contract Analysis.* Malvern, PA: American Institute for Chartered Property Casualty Underwriters, 1992.

NOTES

1. *Jefferson Insurance Company of New York v. Superior Court of Alameda County,* 475 P. 2d 880 (1970).
2. Valued policy laws are in force in Arkansas, Florida, Georgia, Kansas, Louisiana, Minnesota, Mississippi, Missouri, Montana, Nebraska, New Hampshire, North Dakota, Ohio, South Carolina, South Dakota, Tennessee, Texas, West Virginia, and Wisconsin. California also has a law that allows insureds to request a valued policy by paying for the insurance company's cost of inspection and property valuation. Iowa's law provides that the amount of insurance stated in a building insurance policy is *prima facie* evidence of the insurable value of the property on the date of the policy. Although Iowa's law is not a true valued policy law, it has the effect of shifting the burden of proof as to value of the building from the insured to the insurer in the settlement of claims.
3. *Gamel v. Continental Ins. Co.,* 463 S.W. 2d 590 (1971). For additional information concerning valued policy laws, the interested student should consult the

Fire, Casualty & Surety Bulletins, Fire and Marine volume, Misc. Property section (Erlanger, KY: National Underwriter Company).
4. Edwin W. Patterson, *Essentials of Insurance Law,* 2nd ed. (New York: McGraw-Hill, 1957), pp. 109–111, 154–159.
5. Patterson, p. 114.
6. Buist M. Anderson, *Anderson on Life Insurance* (Boston: Little, Brown, 1991), p. 361.
7. Patterson, pp. 147–148.
8. James J. Lorimer et al., *The Legal Environment of Insurance,* 3rd ed., vol. 1 (Malvern, PA: American Institute for Property and Liability Underwriters, 1987), p. 376.
9. Lorimer et al., p. 377.
10. Patterson, p. 149.
11. C. Arthur Williams, Jr., George L. Head, Ronald C. Horn, and G. William Glendenning, *Principles of Risk Management and Insurance,* 2nd ed., vol. 2 (Malvern, PA: American Institute for Property and Liability Underwriters, 1981), p. 228.
12. Group health insurance contracts may contain subrogation clauses.
13. James J. Lorimer et al., *The Legal Environment of Insurance,* 4th ed., vol. 1 (Malvern, PA: American Institute for Chartered Property Casualty Underwriters, 1993), pp. 202–205.
14. Ibid., pp. 112–114.
15. Ibid., pp. 115–116.
16. Edward E. Graves and Burke A. Christensen, eds., *McGill's Legal Aspects of Life Insurance,* 2nd ed. (Bryn Mawr, PA: The American College, 1997), p. 62.
17. Ibid., p. 30.
18. James J. Lorimer et al., *The Legal Environment of Insurance,* 3rd ed., vol. 1 (Malvern, PA: American Institute for Property and Liability Underwriters, 1987), pp. 402–403.
19. Ibid., p. 403.
20. Graves and Christensen, pp. 82–85.
21. Patterson, pp. 495–496.

Students may take a self-administered test on this chapter at

www.aw-bc.com/rejda

CHAPTER 6

ANALYSIS OF INSURANCE CONTRACTS

"Let's kill all the lawyers."

William Shakespeare

LEARNING OBJECTIVES

After studying this chapter, you should be able to

◆ Identify the basic parts of any insurance contract.

◆ Explain the meaning of an "insured" in an insurance contract.

◆ Describe the common types of deductibles that appear in insurance contracts, including
  Straight deductible
  Calendar year deductible

◆ Explain how coinsurance works in a property insurance contract.

◆ Show how coinsurance works in a health insurance contract.

◆ Explain how losses are paid when more than one insurance contract covers the same loss.

*B*randon, age 32, is an electrical engineer who lives in San Francisco, CA. He purchased a home for $450,000. Shortly after he moved in, an earthquake occurred that caused about $100,000 in damages to the home. Brandon was upset when his agent told him that the homeowners policy would not cover the loss. He made the common mistake of not reading his homeowners policy. As a result, he was not aware of the major policy exclusions, including the exclusion of earthquakes.

Brandon is not alone. Most people do not read or understand the contractual provisions that appear in their insurance policies. Individuals typically own several insurance policies, including auto and homeowners insurance as well as life and health insurance. These policies are complex legal documents that reflect the legal principles discussed in Chapter 5.

Although insurance contracts are not identical, they contain similar contractual provisions. This chapter discusses the basic parts of an insurance policy, the meaning of an "insured," endorsements and riders, deductibles, coinsurance, and other-insurance provisions. Grasping these topics will provide you with a foundation for a better understanding of specific insurance contracts discussed later in the text.

BASIC PARTS OF AN INSURANCE CONTRACT

Despite their complexities, insurance contracts generally can be divided into the following parts:

- Declarations
- Definitions
- Insuring agreement
- Exclusions
- Conditions
- Miscellaneous provisions

Although all insurance contracts do not necessarily contain all six parts in the order given here, such a classification provides a simple and convenient framework for analyzing most insurance contracts.

Declarations

The declarations section is the first part of an insurance contract. **Declarations** *are statements that provide information about the property or activity to be insured.* Information contained in the declarations section is used for underwriting and rating purposes and for identification of the property or activity to be insured. The declarations section usually can be found on the first page of the policy or on a policy insert.

In property insurance, the declarations page typically contains information concerning the identification of the insurer, name of the insured, location of the property, period of protection, amount of insurance, amount of the premium, size of the deductible (if any), and other relevant information. In life insurance, although the first page of the policy technically is not called a declarations page, it contains the insured's name, age, premium amount, issue date, and policy number.

Definitions

Insurance contracts typically contain a page or section of definitions. Key words or phrases have quotation marks ("...") around them or are in **boldface** type. For example, the insurer is frequently referred to as "we," "our," or "us." The insured is referred to as "you" and "your." The purpose of the various definitions is to define clearly the meaning of key words or phrases so that coverage under the policy can be determined more easily.

Insuring Agreement

The insuring agreement is the heart of an insurance contract. The **insuring agreement** *summarizes the major promises of the insurer*. The insurer, in other words, agrees to do certain things, such as paying losses from covered perils, providing certain services (such as loss-prevention services), or agreeing to defend the insured in a liability lawsuit. The promises of the insurer and the conditions under which losses are paid are described in the insuring agreement.

There are two basic forms of an insuring agreement in property and liability insurance: (1) named-perils coverage and (2) "all-risks" coverage. *Under a* **named-perils policy,** *only those perils specifically named in the policy are covered.* If the peril is not named, it is not covered. For example, in the homeowners policy, personal property is covered for fire, lightning, windstorm, and certain other named perils. Only losses caused by these perils are covered. Flood damage is not covered because flood is not a listed peril.

Under an "all-risks" policy, all losses are covered except those losses specifically excluded. "All-risks" policies are also called an **open-perils policy** and a **special coverage policy.** If the loss is not excluded, then it is covered. For example, the physical damage section of the personal auto policy covers losses to a covered auto. Thus, if a smoker burns a hole in the upholstery, or a bear in a national park damages the vinyl top of a covered auto, the losses would be covered because they are not excluded.

"All-risks" coverage is generally preferable to named-perils coverage, because the protection is broader with fewer gaps in coverage. If the loss is not excluded, then it is covered. In addition, a greater burden of proof is placed on the insurer to deny a claim. *To deny payment, the insurer must prove that the loss is excluded. In contrast, under a named-perils contract, the burden of proof is on the insured to show that the loss was caused by a named peril.*

Insurers and rating organizations generally have deleted the word *all* in their "all-risks" policy forms or are using special terminology. In the homeowners

policy drafted by the Insurance Services Office, the phrase *"risk of direct loss to property"* is now used instead of the term *"all-risks."* However, this term is interpreted to mean that all losses are covered except those losses specifically excluded. Likewise, the Insurance Services Office has drafted a *special-causes-of-loss form* that is used in commercial property insurance. Once again, this terminology is interpreted to mean that all losses are covered except those losses excluded. The deletion of any reference to "all-risks" is intended to avoid creating unreasonable expectations among policyowners that the policy covers all losses, even those losses that are specifically excluded.

Life insurance is another example of an "all-risks" policy. Most life insurance contracts cover all causes of death whether by accident or by disease. The major exclusions are suicide during the first two years of the contract; certain aviation hazard exclusions, such as military flying, crop dusting, or sports piloting; and in some contracts, death caused by war.

Exclusions

Exclusions are another basic part of any insurance contract. There are three major types of exclusions: excluded perils, excluded losses, and excluded property.

Excluded Perils   The contract may exclude certain perils, or causes of loss. In a homeowners policy, the perils of flood, earth movement, and nuclear radiation or radioactive contamination are specifically excluded. In the physical damage section of the personal auto policy, collision is specifically excluded if the car is used as a public taxicab. In property and liability insurance, most insurance contracts exclude coverage for acts of war. The war exclusion clause is important today because of the terrorist attack on the United States on September 11, 2001, which raised questions whether insurers would pay such claims (see Insight 6.1).

Excluded Losses   Certain types of losses may be excluded. For example, in a homeowners policy, failure of an insured to protect the property from further damage after a loss occurs is excluded. In the personal liability section of a homeowners policy, a liability lawsuit arising out of the operation of an

INSIGHT 6.1

Does the War Clause Exclude Acts of Terrorism?

Most property and liability contracts exclude coverage for acts of war, whether declared or undeclared, but does the war clause apply to acts of terrorism? On September 11, 2001, foreign terrorists hijacked four commercial jets; two jets crashed into the World Trade Center towers in New York City; the third crashed into the Pentagon in Arlington, Virginia, and the fourth crashed in a field in Pennsylvania. The terrorist acts produced the largest single catastrophic loss in the history of the United States, caused billions of dollars in property damage, and a devastating loss of human lives. President George W. Bush and members of Congress declared that the terrorist acts were "acts of war." Questions were initially raised whether insurers would use the war exclusion clause to deny payment of claims. The insurance industry, however, generally took the position that the war exclusion clause did not apply to acts of terrorism, and claims were paid.

Most U.S. courts in the past have generally ruled that the war exclusion clause applies only to hostilities between sovereign nations and not by terrorist or guerilla groups. Past court decisions generally support this view. For example, in 1974, a federal appeals court ruled that the hijacking and destruction of a Pan American World Airways jet by the Palestine Liberation Organization in 1970 was not an act of war but an act committed by a terrorist group. The court reasoned that the hijackers were agents of a radical political group and were not a sovereign nation.[a]

[a] *Pan American World Airways, Inc. v. Aetna Casualty & Surety Company*, 505 F.2d 989 (2d Circuit 1974).

automobile is excluded. Professional liability losses are also excluded; a specific professional liability policy is needed to cover this exposure.

Excluded Property   The contract may exclude or place limitations on the coverage of certain property. For example, in a homeowners policy, certain types of personal property are excluded, such as cars, planes, animals, birds, and fish. In a liability insurance policy, property of others in the care, control, and custody of the insured is usually excluded.

Reasons for Exclusions   Exclusions are necessary for the following reasons:[1]

- Some perils considered uninsurable
- Presence of extraordinary hazards
- Coverage provided by other contracts
- Moral hazard problems
- Coverage not needed by typical insureds

Exclusions are necessary because the peril may be considered uninsurable by commercial insurers. A given peril may depart substantially from the requirements of an insurable risk, as discussed in Chapter 2. For example, most property and liability insurance contracts exclude losses for potential catastrophic events such as war or exposure to nuclear radiation. A health insurance contract may exclude losses within the direct control of the insured, such as an intentional, self-inflicted injury. Finally, predictable declines in the value of property, such as wear and tear and inherent vice, are not insurable. "Inherent vice" refers to the destruction or damage of property without any tangible external force, such as the tendency of fruit to rot and the tendency of diamonds to crack.

Exclusions are also used because extraordinary hazards are present. A hazard is a condition that increases the chance of loss or severity of loss. Because of an extraordinary increase in hazard, a loss may be excluded. For example, the premium for liability insurance under a personal auto policy is based on the assumption that the car is normally used for personal and recreational use and not as a taxicab. The chance of an accident, and a resulting liability lawsuit, is much higher if the car is used as a taxicab for hire. Therefore, to provide coverage for a taxicab at the same premium rate for a family car could result in inadequate premiums for the insurer and unfair rate discrimination against other insureds who are not using their vehicles as taxicabs.

Exclusions are also necessary because coverage can be better provided by other contracts. Exclusions are used to avoid duplication of coverage and to limit coverage to the policy best designed to provide it. For example, a car is excluded under a homeowners policy because it is covered under the personal auto policy and other auto insurance contracts. If both policies covered the loss, there would be unnecessary duplication.

In addition, certain property is excluded because of moral hazard or difficulty in determining and measuring the amount of loss. For example, homeowner contracts typically limit the coverage of money to $200. If unlimited amounts of money were covered, fraudulent claims would increase. Also, loss-adjustment problems in determining the exact amount of the loss would also increase. Thus, because of moral hazard, exclusions are used.

Finally, exclusions are used because the coverage is not needed by the typical insured. For example, most homeowners do not own private planes. To cover aircraft as personal property under the homeowners policy would be grossly unfair to the vast majority of insureds who do not own planes because premiums would be substantially higher.

Conditions

The conditions section is another important part of an insurance contract. **Conditions** *are provisions in the policy that qualify or place limitations on the insurer's promise to perform.* In effect, the conditions section imposes certain duties on the insured. If the policy conditions are not met, the insurer can refuse to pay the claim. Common policy conditions include notifying the insurer if a loss occurs, protecting the property after a loss, preparing an inventory of damaged personal property, and cooperating with the insurer in the event of a liability suit.

Miscellaneous Provisions

Insurance contracts also contain a number of miscellaneous provisions. In property and liability insurance, miscellaneous provisions include cancellation, subrogation, requirements if a loss occurs, assignment of the policy, and other-insurance provisions. In life and health insurance, typical miscellaneous provisions include the grace period, reinstatement of a lapsed policy, and misstatement of age. Details of these provisions are discussed later in the text when specific insurance contracts are analyzed.

DEFINITION OF THE "INSURED"

Insurance contracts typically contain a definition of the "insured" under the policy. The contract must indicate the person or persons for whom the protection is provided. Several possibilities exist concerning the persons who are insured under the policy. First, some policies insure only *one person*. For example, in most life insurance contracts, only one person is specifically named as insured under the policy.

Second, the policy may contain a formal definition of the named insured. The **named insured** *is the person or persons named in the declarations section of the policy.* For example, in a homeowners policy, the named insured includes the person named in the declarations page and his or her spouse if a resident of the same household. Thus, Emily may be the named insured under a homeowners policy. Her husband is also included in the definition of the named insured as long as he resides in the same household.

The policy may also cover other parties even though they are not specifically named in the policy. For example, in addition to the named insured, a homeowners policy covers resident relatives of the named insured or spouse and any person under age 21 who is in the care of an insured, such as a foreign exchange student. The homeowners policy also covers resident relatives under age 24 who are full-time students and away from home. The personal auto policy covers the named insured and spouse, resident relatives, and any other person using the auto with the permission of the named insured (see Insight 6.2). In short, a contract may provide broad coverage with respect to the number of persons who are insured under the policy.

ENDORSEMENTS AND RIDERS

Insurance contracts frequently contain **endorsements and riders.** The terms *endorsements* and *riders* are often used interchangeably and mean the same thing. *In property and liability insurance, an endorsement is a written provision that adds to, deletes from, or modifies the provisions in the original contract. In life and health insurance, a rider is a provision that amends or changes the original policy.*

INSIGHT 6.2

Are You Covered When You Drive Another Person's Car?

College students frequently drive cars that are owned by roommates or friends. Will your auto insurance policy cover you when you drive another person's car? Likewise, you may give permission to your roommate or friend to drive your car. Is your roommate or friend covered under your policy? To answer that question, we must first examine the definition of an insured that appears in the personal auto policy.

"Insured" as used in this Part means:[a]

1. *You or any "family member for the ownership, maintenance or use of any auto or trailer."*

2. *Any person using "your covered auto."*

3. *For "your covered auto," any person or organization but only with respect to legal responsibility for acts or omissions of a person for whom coverage is afforded under this Part.*

4. *For any auto or "trailer," other than "your covered auto," any other person or organization but only with respect to legal responsibility for acts or omissions of you or any "family member" for whom coverage is afforded under this Part. This provision applies only if the person or organization does not own or hire the auto or "trailer."*

For example, Chris and Karen Swift are the named insured under the personal auto policy that contains the above provision. Their son, Patrick, lives in a college dormi-

tory during the school year while away from home. Although he does not live at home presently, he qualifies as a family member since the college stay is temporary, and he regards his parents' home as his permanent residence address.

Patrick drives a Honda titled in his parents' names. Because he is a family member, he clearly is an insured under the policy. What happens if Patrick allows his girlfriend to drive the Honda? Although she is not a family member, she nevertheless qualifies as "any person using your covered auto." Thus, the girlfriend is an insured.

What if Patrick occasionally drives his roommate's car? Assuming Patrick is a family member under his parents' policy, Patrick is insured while driving any car, including the roommate's car.

Finally, assume that Patrick is involved in an auto accident while delivering Thanksgiving food baskets for a local charity. The injured party sues both Patrick and the charitable organization. Patrick clearly is an insured and is covered. Is the charity also an "insured" under Patrick's policy? The answer is yes. The definition of an insured extends coverage to any person or organization who is legally responsible for any acts or omissions by an insured. Thus, the charitable organization is considered an insured. Patrick's insurer must defend the charity in the suit.

[a]Insurance Services Office, 1998 Personal Auto Policy.

There are numerous endorsements in property and liability insurance that modify, extend, or delete provisions found in the original policy. For example, a homeowners policy excludes coverage for earthquakes. However, an earthquake endorsement can be added that covers damage from an earthquake or from earth movement.

In life and health insurance, numerous riders can be added that increase or decrease benefits, waive a condition of coverage present in the original policy, or amend the basic policy. For example, a waiver-of-premium rider can be added to a life insurance policy. If the insured becomes disabled, all future premiums are waived after an elimination period of six months, as long as the insured remains disabled according to the terms of the rider.

An endorsement attached to a contract generally takes precedence over any conflicting terms in the contract, unless a law or regulation requires that a

standard policy be used or that a policy contain certain provisions. An endorsement cannot be used to circumvent the purpose of legislation by modifying the terms of a standard policy or by changing the wording of a required provision. If an endorsement is contrary to a law or regulation, the policy is read and applied as if that endorsement did not exist.[2]

DEDUCTIBLES

A deductible is a common policy provision that requires the insured to pay part of the loss. A **deductible** *is a provision by which a specified amount is subtracted from the total loss payment that otherwise would be payable.* Deductibles typically are found in property, health, and auto insurance contracts. A deductible is not used in life insurance because the insured's death is always a total loss, and a deductible would simply reduce the face amount of insurance. Also, a deductible generally is not used in personal liability insurance because the insurer must provide a legal defense, even for a small claim. The insurer wants to be involved from the first dollar of loss so as to minimize its ultimate liability for a claim. Also, the premium reduction that would result from a small deductible in personal types of third-party liability coverages would be relatively small.[3]

Purposes of Deductibles

Deductibles have several important purposes. They include the following:

- To eliminate small claims
- To reduce premiums
- To reduce moral and morale hazard

A deductible eliminates small claims that are expensive to handle and process. For example, an insurer can easily incur expenses of $500 or more in processing a $100 claim. Because a deductible eliminates small claims, the insurer's loss-adjustment expenses are reduced.

Deductibles are also used to reduce premiums paid by the insured. Because deductibles eliminate small claims, premiums can be substantially reduced. Insurance is not an appropriate technique for paying small losses that can be better budgeted out of personal or business income. Insurance should be used to cover large catastrophic events, such as medical expenses of $500,000 or more from an extended terminal illness. Insurance that protects against a catastrophic loss can be purchased more economically if deductibles are used. This concept of using insurance premiums to pay for large losses rather than for small losses is often called the **large-loss principle.** The objective is to cover large losses that can financially ruin an individual and exclude small losses that can be budgeted out of the person's income.

Other factors being equal, a large deductible is preferable to a small one. For example, many motorists with auto insurance have policies that contain a $250 deductible for collision losses instead of a $500 or larger deductible. They may not be aware of how expensive the extra insurance really is. For example, assume you can purchase collision insurance on your car with a $250 deductible at an annual premium of $600, while a policy with a $500

deductible has an annual premium of $525. If you select the $250 deductible over the $500 deductible, you have an additional $250 of collision insurance, but you must pay an additional $75 in annual premiums. Using a simple benefit-cost analysis, you are paying an additional $75 for an additional $250 of insurance, which is a relatively expensive increment of insurance. When analyzed in this manner, larger deductibles are preferable to smaller deductibles.

Finally, deductibles are used by insurers to reduce both moral and morale hazard. Some dishonest insureds may deliberately cause a loss in order to profit from insurance. Deductibles reduce moral hazard because the insured may not profit if a loss occurs.

Deductibles are also used to reduce morale hazard. Morale hazard is carelessness or indifference to a loss because of insurance, which increases the chance of loss. Deductibles encourage people to be more careful with respect to the protection of their property and prevention of a loss.

Deductibles in Property Insurance

The following deductibles are commonly found in property insurance contracts:

- Straight deductible
- Aggregate deductible

Straight Deductible   With a **straight deductible,** *the insured must pay a certain number of dollars of loss before the insurer is required to make a payment.* Such a deductible typically applies to each loss. An example can be found in automobile collision insurance. For instance, assume that Ashley has collision insurance on her new Toyota, with a $500 deductible. If a collision loss is $7000, she would receive only $6500 and would have to pay the remaining $500 herself.

Aggregate Deductible   Commercial insurance contracts sometimes contain an aggregate deductible. An **aggregate deductible** means that all losses that occur during a specified time period, usually a policy year, are accumulated to satisfy the deductible amount. Once the deductible is satisfied, the insurer pays losses in excess of the deductible. For example, assume that the policy contains an aggregate deductible of $10,000. Also assume that losses of $1000 and $2000 occur, respectively, during the policy year. The insurer pays nothing because the deductible is not met. However, if a third loss of $8000 occurs during the same time period, the insurer would pay $1000. Any other losses occurring during the policy year would be paid in full.

Deductibles in Health Insurance

In health insurance, the deductible can be stated in terms of dollars or time. Deductibles in health insurance include the following:

- Calendar-year deductible
- Corridor deductible
- Elimination (waiting) period

Calendar-year Deductible   A calendar-year deduct-ible *is a type of aggregate deductible that is found in basic medical expense and major medical insurance contracts.* Eligible medical expenses are accumulated during the calendar year, and once they exceed the deductible amount, the insurer must then pay the benefits promised under the contract. Once the deductible is satisfied during the calendar year, no additional deductibles are imposed on the insured.

Corridor Deductible   Employers with basic medical expense plans often wish to supplement the basic benefits with major medical benefits. A **corridor deductible** *is a deductible that can be used to inte-grate a basic medical expense plan with a supple-mental major medical expense plan.* The corridor deductible must be satisfied before the major med-ical plan pays any benefits.

The corridor deductible applies only to eligible medical expenses that are not covered by the basic medical expense plan. For example, assume that Janet has $20,000 of covered medical expenses, of which $16,000 is paid by the basic medical expense plan. If the supplemental major medical plan has a $300 cor-ridor deductible, Janet must pay $300. The supple-mental plan will cover the remaining $3700 of expenses, subject to any limitations or coinsurance provisions that may apply.

Elimination (Waiting) Period   A deductible can also be expressed as an elimination period. An **elimina-tion waiting period** *is a stated period of time at the beginning of a loss during which no insurance bene-*

fits are paid. An elimination period is appropriate for a single loss that occurs over some time period, such as the loss of work earnings. Elimination periods are commonly used in disability-income contracts. For example, disability-income insurance contracts that replace part of a disabled worker's earnings typically have elimination periods of 30, 60, or 90 days, or even longer periods.

COINSURANCE

Coinsurance is a contractual provision that often appears in property insurance contracts. This is especially true of commercial property insurance contracts.

Nature of Coinsurance

A **coinsurance clause** *in a property insurance contract requires the insured to insure the property for a stated percentage of its insurable value. If the coinsurance requirement is not met at the time of loss, the insured must share in the loss as a coinsurer.* The insurable value of the property is the actual cash value, replace-ment cost, or some other value described in the val-uation clause of the policy. If the insured wants to collect in full for a partial loss, the coinsurance requirement must be satisfied. Otherwise, the insured will be penalized if a partial loss occurs.

A coinsurance formula is used to determine the amount paid for a covered loss. The coinsurance formula is as follows:

$$\frac{\text{Amount of insurance carried}}{\text{Amount of insurance required}} \times \text{Loss} = \frac{\text{Amount}}{\text{of recovery}}$$

For example, assume that a commercial building has an actual cash value of $500,000 and that the owner has insured it for only $300,000. If an 80 per-cent coinsurance clause is present in the policy, the required amount of insurance based on actual cash value is $400,000 (80% × $500,000). If a replace-ment cost policy is used, the required amount of insur-ance would be based on replacement cost. Thus, if a $10,000 loss occurs, only $7500 will be paid by the insurer. This calculation can be illustrated as follows:

$$\frac{\$300,000}{\$400,000} \times \$10,000 = \$7500$$

Since the insured has only three-fourths of the required amount of insurance in force at the time of loss, only three-fourths of the loss, or $7500, will be paid. Because the coinsurance requirement is not met, the insured must absorb the remaining amount of the loss.

Finally, in applying the coinsurance formula, two additional points should be kept in mind. First, the amount paid can never exceed the amount of the actual loss even though the coinsurance formula produces such a result. This case could happen if the amount of insurance carried is greater than the required amount of insurance. Second, the maximum amount paid for any loss is limited to the face amount of insurance.

Purpose of Coinsurance

The fundamental purpose of coinsurance is to achieve **equity in rating.** Most property insurance losses are partial rather than total losses. But if everyone insures only for the partial loss rather than for the total loss, the premium rate for each $100 of insurance would be higher. This rate would be inequitable to insureds who wish to insure their property to full value. For example, if everyone insures to full value, assume that the pure premium rate for fire insurance is 25 cents for each $100 of insurance, ignoring expenses and the profit allowance of the insurer (see Exhibit 6.1).

However, if each property owner insures only for a partial loss, the pure premium rate will increase from 25 cents per $100 of fire insurance to 40 cents per $100 (see Exhibit 6.2). This rate would be inequitable to property owners who want to insure their buildings to full value. If full coverage is desired, the insured would have to pay a higher rate of 40 cents, which we calculated earlier to be worth only 25 cents. This rate would be inequitable. *So, if the coinsurance requirement is met, the insured receives a rate discount, and the policyowner who is underinsured is penalized through application of the coinsurance formula.*

As an alternative to coinsurance, *graded rates* can be used, by which rate discounts are given as the amount of insurance to value is increased. However, this system requires an accurate appraisal of each property to determine the required amount of insurance, which would be extremely expensive for the insurer. In addition, the appraisal method is unsatisfactory if property values fluctuate widely during the

EXHIBIT 6.1
Insurance to Full Value

Assume that 2000 buildings are valued at $200,000 each and are insured to full value for a total of $400 million of fire insurance. The following fire losses occur:

2 total losses	=	$400,000
30 partial losses at $20,000 each	=	$600,000
Total fire losses paid by insurer	=	$1,000,000
Pure premium rate	=	$\dfrac{\$1,000,000}{\$400,000,000}$
	=	25 cents per $100 of insurance

EXHIBIT 6.2
Insurance to Half Value

Assume that 2000 buildings are valued at $200,000 each and are insured to half value for a total of $200 million of fire insurance. The following fire losses occur:

2 total losses ($400,000)

Insurer pays only	=	$200,000
30 partial losses at $20,000 each	=	$600,000
Total fire losses paid by insurer	=	$800,000
Pure premium rate	=	$\dfrac{\$800,000}{\$200,000,000}$
	=	40 cents per $100 of insurance

policy period. For these reasons, the coinsurance formula, rather than a table of graded rates, is used to achieve equity in rating.

Coinsurance Problems

Some practical problems arise when a coinsurance clause is present in a contract. First, inflation can result in a serious coinsurance penalty if the amount of insurance is not periodically increased for inflation. The insured may be in compliance with the coinsurance clause when the policy first goes into effect; however, price inflation could increase the replacement cost of the property. The result is that the insured may not be carrying the required amount of insurance at the time of loss, and he or she will then be penalized if a loss occurs. Thus, if a coinsurance clause is present, the amount of insurance carried should be periodically evaluated to determine whether the coinsurance requirement is being met.

Second, the insured may incur a coinsurance penalty if property values fluctuate widely during the policy period. For example, there may be a substantial increase in inventory values because of an unexpected arrival of a shipment of goods. If a loss occurs, the insured may not be carrying sufficient insurance to avoid a coinsurance penalty. One solution to this problem is an *agreed value optional coverage,* by which the insurer agrees in advance that the amount of insurance carried meets the coinsurance requirement. Another solution is a *reporting form,* by which property values are periodically reported to the insurer.

Finally, if a small loss occurs, the insured may incur a financial hardship if he or she is required to take a physical inventory of the undamaged and damaged goods for purposes of determining whether the coinsurance requirement has been met. Under a *waiver of inventory clause,* the insured is relieved of the obligation of taking a physical inventory of the undamaged goods if the loss is less than 2 percent of the amount of insurance.

COINSURANCE IN HEALTH INSURANCE

Health insurance contracts frequently contain a coinsurance clause, which is technically called a **percentage participation clause.** In particular, major medical policies typically have a coinsurance provision that requires the insured to pay a certain percentage of covered medical expenses in excess of the deductible. A typical plan requires the insured to pay 20 or 25 percent of covered expenses in excess of the deductible. For example, assume that Megan has covered medical expenses in the amount of $50,500, and that she has a major medical policy with a $500 deductible and an 80–20 coinsurance clause. The insurer pays 80 percent of the bill in excess of the deductible, or $40,000, and Megan pays 20 percent, or $10,000 (plus the deductible).

The purposes of coinsurance in health insurance are (1) to reduce premiums and (2) to prevent over-utilization of policy benefits. Because the insured pays part of the cost, premiums are reduced. In addition, the patient will not demand the most expensive medical services if he or she pays part of the cost.

OTHER-INSURANCE PROVISIONS

Other-insurance provisions typically are present in property and liability insurance and health insurance contracts. These provisions apply when more than one contract covers the same loss. *The purpose of these provisions is to prevent profiting from insurance and violation of the principle of indemnity.* If the insured could collect the full amount of the loss from each insurer, there would be profiting from insurance and a substantial increase in moral hazard. Some dishonest insureds would deliberately cause a loss to collect multiple benefits.

Some important other-insurance provisions in property and liability insurance include (1) the pro rata liability clause, (2) contribution by equal shares, and (3) primary and excess insurance.

Pro Rata Liability

Pro rata liability is a generic term for a provision that applies when two or more policies of the same type cover the same insurable interest in the property. *Each insurer's share of the loss is based on the proportion that its insurance bears to the total amount of insurance on the property.* For example, assume that Jacob owns a building and wishes to insure it for $500,000. For underwriting reasons, insurers may limit the amount of insurance they will write on a given property. Assume that an agent places $300,000 of insurance with Company A, $100,000 with Company B, and $100,000 with Company C, for a total of $500,000. If a $100,000 loss occurs, each company will pay only its pro rata share of the loss (see Exhibit 6.3). Thus, Jacob would collect $100,000 for the loss, not $300,000.

The basic purpose of the pro rata liability clause is to preserve the principle of indemnity and to prevent profiting from insurance. In the preceding example, if the pro rata liability clause were not present, the insured would collect $100,000 from each insurer, or a total of $300,000 for a $100,000 loss.

EXHIBIT 6.3
Pro Rata Liability Example

Company A	$\frac{\$300,000}{\$500,000}$ or .60 $\times$ \$100,000	= \$60,000
Company B	$\frac{\$100,000}{\$500,000}$ or .20 $\times$ \$100,000	= \$20,000
Company C	$\frac{\$100,000}{\$500,000}$ or .20 $\times$ \$100,000	= \$20,000
	Total loss payment	= \$100,000

Contribution by Equal Shares

Contribution by equal shares is another type of other-insurance provision that is frequently found in liability insurance contracts. Each insurer shares equally in the loss until the share paid by each insurer equals the lowest limit of liability under any policy, or until the full amount of the loss is paid. For example, assume that the amount of insurance provided by Companies A, B, and C is $100,000, $200,000, and $300,000, respectively. If the loss is $150,000 each insurer pays an equal share, or $50,000 (see Exhibit 6.4).

However, if the loss were $500,000, how much would each insurer pay? In this case, each insurer would pay equal amounts until its policy limits are exhausted. The remaining insurers then continue to share equally in the remaining amount of the loss until each insurer has paid its policy limit in full, or until the full amount of the loss is paid. Thus, Company A would pay $100,000, Company B would pay $200,000, and Company C would pay $200,000 (see Exhibit 6.5). If the loss were $600,000, Company C would pay the remaining $100,000.

Primary and Excess Insurance

Primary and excess insurance is another type of other-insurance provision. The primary insurer pays first, and the excess insurer pays only after the policy limits under the primary policy are exhausted.

Auto insurance is an excellent example of primary and excess insurance. For example, assume that Bob occasionally drives Jill's car. Bob's policy

EXHIBIT 6.4
Contribution by Equal Shares (Example 1)

Amount of Loss = $150,000			
	Amount of Insurance	*Contribution by Equal Shares*	*Total Paid*
Company A	$100,000	$50,000	$50,000
Company B	$200,000	$50,000	$50,000
Company C	$300,000	$50,000	$50,000

EXHIBIT 6.5
Contribution by Equal Shares (Example 2)

Amount of Loss = $500,000			
	Amount of Insurance	*Contribution by Equal Shares*	*Total Paid*
Company A	$100,000	$100,000	$100,000
Company B	$200,000	$100,000 + $100,000	$200,000
Company C	$300,000	$100,000 + $100,000	$200,000

has a liability insurance limit of $100,000 per person for bodily injury liability. Jill's policy has a limit of $50,000 per person for bodily injury liability. If Bob negligently injures another motorist while driving Jill's car, both policies will cover the loss. *The normal rule is that liability insurance on the borrowed car is primary and any other insurance is considered excess.* Thus, if a court orders Bob to pay damages of $75,000, Jill's policy is primary and pays the first $50,000. Bob's policy is excess and pays the remaining $25,000.

The **coordination-of-benefits provision** in group health insurance is another example of primary and excess coverage. This provision is designed to prevent overinsurance and the duplication of benefits if one person is covered under more than one group health insurance plan.

The majority of states have adopted part or all of the coordination-of-benefits provisions developed by the National Association of Insurance Commissioners (NAIC). The rules are complex, and only two of them are discussed here. *First, coverage as an employee is usually primary to coverage as a dependent.* For example, assume that Jack and Kelly McVay both work, and that each is insured as a dependent under the other's group health insurance

CASE APPLICATION

Joseph owns a motorboat that struck and damaged another boat anchored at a marina. When the accident occurred, Joseph's friend, Jennifer, was operating the motorboat. The owner of the damaged boat has asked Jennifer to pay for the damage. Joseph is listed as the named insured on the declarations page of a boat-owners liability policy. Joseph's policy included the following provisions:

What Is Covered

"We" will pay all sums which an "insured" becomes legally obligated to pay as damages due to bodily injury or property damage arising out of the ownership, maintenance, or use of the described vessel.

What Is Not Covered

"We" do not cover liability arising from the ownership, maintenance, or use of the described vessel:
1. that results from an intentional act of an insured . . .
2. to persons while they are being towed by the described vessel as water skiers, aquaplaners, or similar water sports.

Definitions

1. The words "you" and "your" mean the persons named on the Declarations.
2. The words "we," "us," and "our" mean the company providing this insurance.

3. "Bodily Injury" means bodily harm, sickness, or disease to a person.
4. "Insured" means "you" and
   • "your" spouse;
   • "your" relatives if residents of your household;
   • persons under the age of 21 in "your" care;
   • a person who operates a covered vessel with "your" permission.
5. "Property damage" means an injury to or the destruction of property. This includes the loss of use.

   a. The above provisions refer to a *described vessel.* Identify the section of the policy that would identify and describe Joseph's motorboat.
   b. Explain whether Joseph's policy would provide coverage for the claim against Jennifer. Identify the policy provisions that would be relevant in this situation.
   c. The owner of the damaged boat uses the boat to transport customers for deep-sea fishing. The owner is also holding Jennifer responsible for the loss of revenues while the boat is being repaired. Explain whether Joseph's policy would pay for the lost revenues.
   d. Assume that a skier towed by Joseph's motorboat is injured because of Joseph's negligence. If the injured skier sued Joseph for the injury, would he be covered under the policy? Explain.

plan. If Jack incurs covered medical expenses, his policy pays first as primary coverage. He then submits his unreimbursed expenses (such as the deductible and coinsurance payments) to Kelly's insurer. Kelly's coverage then applies as excess insurance. No more than 100 percent of the eligible medical expenses are paid under both plans.

Second, the birthday rule applies to dependents in families where the parents are married or are not separated. Under this rule, *the plan of the parent whose birthday occurs first during the year is primary.* For example, assume that Kelly's birthday is in January, and Jack's birthday is in July. If their daughter is hospitalized, Kelly's plan is primary. Jack's plan would be excess. The purpose of the birthday rule is to eliminate gender discrimination with respect to coverage of dependents.

SUMMARY

- Insurance contracts generally can be divided into the following parts:

  Declarations

  Definitions

  Insuring agreement

  Exclusions

  Conditions

  Miscellaneous provisions

- Declarations are statements concerning the property or activity to be insured.

- The definitions page or section defines the key words or phrases so that coverage under the policy can be determined more easily.

- The insuring agreement summarizes the promises of the insurer. There are two basic types of insuring agreements:

  Named-perils coverage

  "All-risks" coverage

- All policies contain one or more exclusions. There are three major types of exclusions:

  Excluded perils

  Excluded losses

  Excluded property

- Exclusions are necessary for several reasons. Certain perils are considered uninsurable by private insurers; extraordinary hazards may be present; coverage is provided by other contracts; moral hazard is present to a high degree; and coverage is not needed by the typical insured.

- Conditions are provisions that qualify or place limitations on the insurer's promise to perform. The conditions section imposes certain duties on the insured if he or she wishes to collect for a loss.

- Miscellaneous provisions in property and liability insurance include cancellation, subrogation, requirements if a loss occurs, assignment of the policy, and other insurance provisions.

- The contract also contains a definition of the "insured." The contract may cover only one person, or it may cover other persons as well even though they are not specifically named in the policy.

- An endorsement, or rider, is a written provision that adds to, deletes from, or modifies the provisions in the original contract. An endorsement or rider normally has precedence over any conflicting terms in the contract to which the endorsement is attached.

- A deductible requires the insured to pay part of the loss. A specified amount is subtracted from the total loss payment that otherwise would be payable. Deductibles are used to eliminate small claims, to reduce premiums, and to reduce moral and morale hazard. Examples of deductibles include a straight deductible, aggregate deductible, calendar-year deductible, corridor deductible, and elimination (waiting) period.

- A coinsurance clause in property insurance requires the insured to insure the property for a stated percentage of its insurable value at the time of loss. If the coinsurance requirement is not met at the time of loss, the insured must share in the loss as a coinsurer. The fundamental purpose of coinsurance is to achieve equity in rating.

- A coinsurance clause (percentage participation clause) is typically found in major medical policies. A typical provision requires the insurer to pay 80 percent of covered expenses in excess of the deductible and the insured to pay 20 percent.

- Other-insurance provisions are present in many insurance contracts. These provisions apply when more than one policy covers the same loss. The purpose of these provisions is to prevent profiting from insurance and violation of the principle of indemnity. Some important other-insurance provisions include the pro rata liability clause, contribution by equal shares, and primary and excess insurance.

KEY CONCEPTS AND TERMS

Aggregate deductible
"All-risks" policy
Calendar-year deductible
Coinsurance clause
Conditions
Contribution by equal
 shares
Coordination-of-benefits
 provision
Corridor deductible
Declarations
Deductible
Elimination (waiting)
 period
Endorsements and
 riders
Equity in rating
Exclusions
Insuring agreement
Large-loss principle
Named insured
Named-perils policy
Open-perils policy
Other-insurance
 provisions
Percentage participation
 clause (coinsurance)
Primary and excess
 insurance
Pro rata liability
Special coverage policy
Straight deductible

REVIEW QUESTIONS

1. Identify the basic parts of an insurance contract.

2. a. Describe the major types of exclusions typically found in insurance contracts.
   b. Why are exclusions used by insurers?

3. a. Define the term *conditions*.
   b. Does the insurer have to pay an otherwise covered loss if the insured fails to comply with the policy conditions? Explain your answer.

4. a. What is the meaning of "named insured"?
   b. Can other parties be insured under a policy even though they are not specifically named? Explain your answer.

5. a. What is an endorsement or rider?
   b. If an endorsement conflicts with a policy provision, how is the problem resolved?

6. a. Describe the following types of deductibles:
    (i) straight deductible
    (ii) calendar-year deductible
    (iii) aggregate deductible
   b. Explain the purposes of deductibles in property insurance contracts.

7. a. Explain how a coinsurance clause in property insurance works.
   b. What is the fundamental purpose of a coinsurance clause?

8. Describe a typical coinsurance clause (percentage participation clause) in a major medical policy.

9. a. What is the purpose of other-insurance provisions?
   b. Give an example of the pro-rata liability clause.

10. Explain the meaning of *primary insurance* and *excess insurance?*

APPLICATION QUESTIONS

1. Michael owns a small plane that he flies on weekends. His agent informs him that aircraft are excluded as personal property under the homeowners policy. As an insured, he feels that his plane should be covered just like any other personal property he owns.
   a. Explain to Michael the rationale for excluding certain types of property, such as aircraft, under the homeowners policy.
   b. Explain some additional reasons why exclusions are present in insurance contracts.

2. a. A manufacturing firm incurred the following insured losses, in the order given, during the current policy year.

Loss	Amount of Loss
A	$ 2500
B	3500
C	10,000

   How much would the company's insurer pay for each loss if the policy contained the following type of deductible?
   (1) $1000 straight deductible
   (2) $15,000 annual aggregate deductible
   b. Explain the coordination-of-benefits provision that is typically found in group medical expense plans.

3. Stephanie owns a small warehouse that is insured for $200,000 under a commercial property insurance policy. The policy contains an 80 percent coinsurance clause. The warehouse is damaged by fire to the extent of $50,000. The replacement cost of the warehouse at the time of loss is $500,000.

   a. What is the insurer's liability, if any, for this loss? Show your calculations.

   b. Assume that Stephanie carried $500,000 of property insurance on the warehouse at the time of loss. If the amount of loss is $10,000, how much will she collect?

   c. Explain the theory or rationale of coinsurance in a property insurance contract.

4. Andrew owns a commercial office building that is insured under three property insurance contracts. He has $100,000 of insurance from Company A, $200,000 from Company B, and $200,000 from Company C.

   a. Assume that the pro-rata liability provision appears in each contract. If a $100,000 loss occurs, how much will Andrew collect from each insurer? Explain your answer.

   b. What is the purpose of the other-insurance provisions that are frequently found in insurance contracts?

5. Assume that a $300,000 liability claim is covered under two liability insurance contracts. Policy A has a $500,000 limit of liability for the claim, while Policy B has a $125,000 limit of liability. Both contracts provide for *contribution by equal shares*.

   a. How much will each insurer contribute toward this claim? Explain your answer.

   b. If the claim were only $50,000, how much would each insurer pay?

6. Assume that Mike drives Donna's car with her permission and negligently injures another person while driving her car. Mike has an auto insurance contract with a liability insurance limit of $100,000 per person for bodily injury liability. Donna has a similar policy with a liability limit of $50,000 per person.

   (1) If a court awards a liability judgment of $75,000 against Mike, how much will each insurer pay?

   (2) If the liability judgment is $200,000, how much will each insurer pay?

7. Ashley has a major medical health insurance policy with a $2 million lifetime limit. The policy has a $500 calendar year deductible and an 80-20 coinsurance clause (percentage participation clause). Ashley had outpatient surgery to remove a bunion on her foot and incurred medical bills of $10,000. How much will Ashley's insurer pay? How much will Ashley have to pay?

8. The Lincoln Saltdogs is a professional minor league baseball team in the Northern League. The clubhouse is insured for $300,000 under a commercial property insurance policy with an 80 percent coinsurance clause. The current replacement cost of the clubhouse is $500,000. After a playoff game for the league championship, a whirlpool tub for injured players shorted out, and a fire ensued. The clubhouse sustained a $40,000 fire loss. Ignoring any deductible, how much will the team's insurer pay for the loss?

INTERNET RESOURCES

■ The **New York State Insurance Department** publishes a number of consumer publications on basic insurance contracts that can be ordered online. The publications are helpful in understanding the various contractual provisions and coverages that appear in homeowners and auto insurance and other insurance contracts. Visit the site at

   http://www.ins.state.ny.us

■ The **Office of the Commissioner of Insurance, State of Wisconsin** also makes available consumer publications on specific insurance contracts. These publications are helpful in understanding the contractual provisions and coverages that appear in life, health, auto, and homeowners insurance. Visit the site at

   http://oci.wi.gov

■ The **Insurance Information Institute** publishes consumer materials dealing with property and liability insurance. The publications can help you understand the contractual provisions and coverages that appear in homeowners, auto, personal liability, and flood insurance, and other property and liability insurance coverages. Visit the site at

   http://www.iii.org

■ The **Texas Department of Insurance** provides a considerable amount of consumer information on auto, homeowners, life and health, and other types of insurance. Information on how to file a complaint is also provided. Visit the site at

http://www.tdi.state.tx.us/index.html

SELECTED REFERENCES

Anderson, Buist M. *Anderson on Life Insurance.* Boston: Little, Brown, 1991. See also *Anderson on Life Insurance—1996 Supplement.*

Crawford, Muriel L. *Life and Health Insurance Law,* 8th ed. Boston: Irwin/McGraw-Hill, 1998.

Keeton, Robert E., and Alan I. Widiss. *Insurance Law: A Guide to Fundamental Principles, Legal Doctrines, and Commercial Practices,* student edition. St. Paul, MN: West Publishing, 1988.

Lorimer, James J., et al. *The Legal Environment of Insurance,* 4th ed., vols. 1 and 2. Malvern, PA: American Institute for Property and Liability Underwriters, 1993.

Wiening, Eric A. *Foundations of Risk Management and Insurance.* Malvern, PA: American Society for CPCU/ Insurance Institute of America, 2002, chs. 11–19.

Wiening, Eric A., and Donald S. Malecki. *Insurance Contract Analysis.* Malvern, PA: American Institute for Chartered Property Casualty Underwriters, 1992.

NOTES

1. C. Arthur Williams, Jr., George L. Head, Ronald C. Horn, and G. William Glendenning, *Principles of Risk Management and Insurance,* 2nd ed., vol. 2 (Malvern, PA: American Institute for Property Casualty Underwriters, 1981), pp. 52–56.

2. Williams et al., pp. 60–61.

3. Ibid., pp. 200–201.

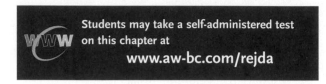

Students may take a self-administered test on this chapter at
www.aw-bc.com/rejda

PART THREE
PERSONAL PROPERTY AND LIABILITY RISKS

CHAPTER 7

THE LIABILITY RISK

"I was never ruined but twice, once when I lost a lawsuit and once when I won one."

Voltaire

*R*ichard, age 45, lives in an upscale suburb in San Diego, CA. He owns a large German shepherd dog that he often allows to run unattended and without a leash. One morning, the dog suddenly attacked a female jogger who was viciously bitten on the face, arms, and legs. She required 80 stitches to close the wounds and also needed plastic surgery to restore her face. She was unable to work for almost one year because of severe nerve damage in one leg. The injured jogger sued Richard for her bodily injuries and was awarded damages of $200,000. Richard could not pay the entire judgment, and his credit was severely impaired.

Richard experienced the legal effects of being negligent in a financially painful manner. Like Richard, other people often face similar liability situations. Motorists are sued because of the negligent operation of their vehicles, and someone is killed or injured. Corporations are sued because of defective products that injure others, aggressive accounting practices and accounting fraud that result in investor losses, insider trading, violation of security laws, and inadequate oversight of management by boards of directors. Physicians, attorneys, accountants, engineers, and other professionals are sued for malpractice, negligence, and incompetence. Even governmental and charitable institutions are sued today because they no longer enjoy complete immunity from lawsuits. Thus, the liability risk is extremely important to people who wish to avoid or minimize potential losses.

This chapter discusses the law of negligence and the tort liability system in the United States. This knowledge forms the foundation for an understanding of liability insurance discussed later in the text. Specific topics discussed include the law of negligence, elements of a negligent act, application of the law of negligence to specific liability situations, and current tort liability problems.

BASIS OF LEGAL LIABILITY

Each person has certain legal rights. A **legal wrong** *is a violation of a person's legal rights, or a failure to perform a legal duty owed to a certain person or to society as a whole.*

There are three broad classes of legal wrongs. A *crime* is a legal wrong against society that is punishable by fines, imprisonment, or death. A *breach of contract* is another class of legal wrongs. Finally, a **tort** is a legal wrong for which the law allows a remedy in the form of money damages. The person who is injured or harmed (called the **plaintiff** or *claimant*) by the actions of another person (called the *defendant* or **tortfeasor**) can sue for damages.

Torts generally can be classified into three categories:

- Intentional torts
- Absolute or strict liability
- Negligence

Intentional Torts

Legal liability can arise from an intentional act or omission that results in harm or injury to another person or damage to the person's property. Examples of intentional torts include assault, battery, trespass, false imprisonment, fraud, libel, slander, and patent or copyright infringement.

Absolute Liability

Because the potential harm to an individual or society is so great, some people may be held liable for the harm or injury done to others even though negligence cannot be proven. **Absolute liability** *means that liability is imposed regardless of negligence or fault.* Absolute liability is also referred to as **strict liability.** Some common situations of absolute liability include the following:

- Blasting operations that injure another person
- Manufacturing of explosives
- Owning wild or dangerous animals
- Crop spraying by airplanes
- Occupational injury and disease of employees under a workers compensation law

Negligence

Negligence is another type of tort that can result in substantial liability. Because negligence is so important in liability insurance, it merits special attention.

LAW OF NEGLIGENCE

Negligence *typically is defined as the failure to exercise the standard of care required by law to protect others from an unreasonable risk of harm.* The meaning of the term standard of care is based on the care required of a reasonably prudent person. In other words, your actions are compared with the actions of a reasonably prudent person under the same circumstances. If your conduct and behavior are below the standard of care required of a reasonably prudent person, you may be found negligent.

The standard of care required by law is not the same for each wrongful act. Its meaning is complex and depends on the age and knowledge of the parties involved; court interpretations over time; skill, knowledge, and judgment of the claimant and tortfeasor; seriousness of the harm; and a host of additional factors.

Elements of a Negligent Act

To collect damages, the injured person must show that the tortfeasor is guilty of negligence. There are four essential **elements of a negligent act:**

- Existence of a legal duty
- Failure to perform that duty
- Damage or injury to the claimant
- Proximate cause relationship between the negligent act and the infliction of damages

Existence of a Legal Duty   *The first requirement is the existence of a legal duty to protect others from harm.* For example, a motorist has a legal duty to stop at a red light and to drive an automobile safely within the speed limits. A manufacturer has a legal duty to produce a safe product. A physician has a legal duty to inquire about allergies before prescribing a drug.

If there is no legal duty imposed by law, you cannot be held liable. For example, you may be a champion swimmer, but you have no legal obligation to dive into a swimming pool to save a two-year-old child from drowning. Nor do you have a legal obligation to stop and pick up a hitchhiker at night when the temperature is 30 degrees below zero. To be guilty of negligence, there must first be a legal duty or obligation to protect others from harm.

Failure to Perform That Duty   *The second requirement is the failure to perform the legal duty required by law:* that is, you fail to comply with the standard of care to protect others from harm. Your actions would be compared with the actions of a reasonably prudent person under similar circumstances. If your conduct falls short of this standard, the second requirement would be satisfied.

The defendant's conduct can be either a positive or negative act. A driver who drives at high speeds in a residential area or runs a red light is an example of a positive act that a reasonably prudent person would not do. A negative act is simply the failure to act: you fail to do something that a reasonably prudent person would have done. For example, if you injure someone because you failed to repair the faulty brakes on your car, you could be found guilty of negligence.

Damage or Injury   *The third requirement is damage or injury to the claimant.* The injured person must show damage or injury as a result of the actions of the alleged tortfeasor. For example, a speeding motorist may run a red light, smash into your car, and seriously injure you. Because you are injured and your car is damaged, the third requirement of a negligent act has been satisfied.

The dollar amount of damages awarded in a judgment depends on several factors. There are three types of damage awards:

- Special damages
- General damages
- Punitive damages

Special damages are awarded for losses that can be determined and documented, such as medical expenses, loss of earnings, or property damage.

General damages are awarded for losses that cannot be specifically measured or itemized, such as compensation for pain and suffering, disfigurement, or loss of companionship of a spouse.

Finally, **punitive damages** are designed to punish people and organizations so that others are deterred from committing the same wrongful act.

Proximate Cause Relationship The final requirement of a negligent act is that a proximate cause relationship must exist. A **proximate cause** *is a cause unbroken by any new and independent cause, which produces an event that otherwise would not have occurred.* That is, there must be an unbroken chain of events between the negligent act and the infliction of damages. For example, a drunk driver who runs a red light and kills another motorist would meet the proximate cause requirement.

Defenses Against Negligence

Certain legal defenses can defeat a claim for damages. Some important legal defenses include the following:

- Contributory negligence
- Comparative negligence
- Last clear chance rule
- Assumption of risk

Contributory Negligence A few states have **contributory negligence laws.**[1] Contributory negligence *means that if the injured person's conduct falls below the standard of care required for his or her protection, and such conduct contributed to the injury, the injured person cannot collect damages.*

Thus, under the strict common law, if you contributed in any way to your own injury, you cannot collect damages. For example, if a motorist on an expressway suddenly slows down without signaling and is rear-ended by another driver, the failure to signal could constitute contributory negligence. The first motorist cannot collect damages for injuries if contributory negligence is established.

Comparative Negligence Because of the harshness of contributory negligence laws if strictly applied, most states have enacted some type of comparative negligence law. Such laws allow an injured person to recover damages even though he or she has contributed to the injury. Under a **comparative negligence law,** if both the plaintiff (injured person) and the defendant contribute to the plaintiff's injury, the financial burden of the injury is shared by both parties according to their respective degrees of fault.

Comparative negligence laws are not uniform among the states. The major types of comparative negligence laws can be classified as follows:[2]

- Pure rule
- 49 percent rule
- 50 percent rule

Under the *pure rule,* you can collect damages for your injury even if you are negligent, but your damage award is reduced proportionately. For example, if you are 60 percent responsible for an auto accident and your actual damages are $10,000, your damage award is reduced by 60 percent to $4000.

Under the *49 percent rule,* you can recover reduced damages only if your negligence is less than the negligence of the other party. This rule means you can recover from the other party only if you are 49 percent or less at fault.

Under the *50 percent rule,* you can recover reduced damages only if your negligence is not greater than the negligence of the other party. This rule means you can recover only if you are not more than 50 percent at fault. You should not confuse the 50 percent rule with the 49 percent rule discussed earlier. Unlike the 49 percent rule, the 50 percent rule allows both parties to recover damages when both parties are equally at fault. However, each party's recovery would be limited to 50 percent of the actual damages.

Last Clear Chance Rule   Another statutory modification of the contributory negligence doctrine is known as the **last clear chance rule,** *which states that a plaintiff who is endangered by his or her own negligence can still recover damages from the defendant if the defendant has a last clear chance to avoid the accident but fails to do so.* For example, a jaywalker who walks against a red light is breaking the law. But if a motorist has a last clear chance to avoid hitting the jaywalker and fails to do so, the injured jaywalker can recover damages for the injury.

Assumption of Risk   The **assumption of risk** doctrine is another defense that can be used to defeat a claim for damages. *Under this doctrine, a person who understands and recognizes the danger inherent in a particular activity cannot recover damages in the event of an injury.* In effect, the assumption of risk bars recovery for damages even though another person's negligence causes the injury. For example, assume you are teaching a friend with a severe vision impairment to drive a car, and he negligently crashes into a telephone post and injures you. He could use the assumption of risk doctrine as a legal defense if you sue for damages.

IMPUTED NEGLIGENCE

Imputed negligence *means that under certain conditions, the negligence of one person can be attributed to another.* Several examples can illustrate this principle. First, an *employer–employee relationship* may exist where the employee is acting on behalf of the employer. The negligent act of an employee can be imputed to the employer. Therefore, if you are driving a car to deliver a package for your employer and negligently injure another motorist, your employer could be held liable for your actions.

Second, many states have some type of **vicarious liability law,** by which a motorist's negligence is imputed to the vehicle's owner. For example, if the driver is acting as an agent for the owner of the vehicle, the owner can be held legally liable. Thus, if Jeff drives Lisa's car to a dry cleaner to pick up a garment, Lisa could be held legally liable if Jeff should injure someone while driving the car.

Third, under the **family purpose doctrine,** the owner of an automobile can be held liable for the negligent acts committed by immediate family members while they are operating the family car. Thus, if Shannon, age 16, negligently injures another motorist while driving her father's car and is sued for $100,000, her father could be held liable.

In addition, imputed negligence may arise out of a *joint business venture.* For example, two brothers may be partners in a business. One brother may negligently injure a customer with a company car, and the injured person sues for damages. Both partners could be held liable for the injury.

A **dram shop law** is a final example of imputed negligence. Under such a law, a business that sells liquor can be held liable for damages that may result from the sale of liquor. For example, assume that a bar owner continues to serve a customer who is drunk, and that after the bar closes, the customer injures three people while driving home. The bar owner could be held legally liable for the injuries.

RES IPSA LOQUITUR

An important modification of the law of negligence is the doctrine of **res ipsa loquitur,** meaning "the thing speaks for itself." *Under this doctrine, the very fact that the injury or damage occurs establishes a presumption of negligence on behalf of the defendant. It is then up to the defendant to refute the presumption of negligence.* That is, the accident or injury normally would not have occurred if the defendant had not been careless. Examples of the doctrine of *res ipsa loquitur* include the following:

- A dentist extracts the wrong tooth.
- A surgeon leaves a surgical sponge in the patient's abdomen.
- A surgical operation is performed on the wrong patient.

To apply the doctrine of *res ipsa loquitur,* the following requirements must be met:

- The event is one that normally does not occur in the absence of negligence.
- The defendant has exclusive control over the instrumentality causing the accident.
- The injured party has not contributed to the accident in any way.

SPECIFIC APPLICATIONS OF THE LAW OF NEGLIGENCE

Property Owners

Property owners have a legal obligation to protect others from harm. However, the standard of care owed to others depends upon the situation. Three groups traditionally have been recognized: (1) trespasser, (2) licensee, and (3) invitee.[3] However, as will be discussed later, a number of jurisdictions have abolished or modified these common law classifications.

Trespasser   A **trespasser** *is a person who enters or remains on the owner's property without the owner's consent*. In general, the trespasser takes the property as he or she finds it. The property owner does not have any obligation to the trespasser to keep the land in reasonably safe condition. However, the property owner cannot deliberately injure the trespasser or set a trap that would injure the trespasser. The duty to refrain from injuring the trespasser or from setting a trap to injure that person is sometimes referred to as the *duty of slight care*.

Licensee   A **licensee** *is a person who enters or remains on the premises with the occupant's expressed or implied permission*. Examples of licensees include door-to-door salespersons, solicitors for charitable or religious organizations, police officers and firefighters when they are on the property to perform their duties, and social guests in almost all jurisdictions. A licensee takes the premises as he or she finds them. However, the property owner or occupant is required to warn the licensee of any unsafe condition or activity on the premises, which is not apparent or open, but there is no obligation to inspect the premises for the benefit of the licensee.

Invitee   An **invitee** *is a person who is invited onto the premises for the benefit of the occupant*. Examples of invitees include business customers in a store, mail carriers, and garbage collectors. In addition to warning the invitee of any dangerous condition, the occupant has an obligation to inspect the premises and to eliminate any dangerous condition revealed by the inspection. For example, a store escalator may be faulty. The customers must be warned about the unsafe escalator (perhaps by a sign) and prevented from using it. The faulty escalator must be repaired; otherwise, customers in the store could be injured, and the owner would be liable.

Many jurisdictions have abolished either partly or completely the preceding common law classifications with respect to the degree of care owed to visitors. According to the Nebraska Supreme Court, the majority of states and the District of Columbia have either reconsidered the traditional common law classification scheme or have abolished some or all of the categories.[4]

Attractive Nuisance Doctrine

An **attractive nuisance** *is a condition that can attract and injure children*. Under the attractive nuisance doctrine, the occupants of land are liable for the injuries of children who may be attracted by some dangerous condition, feature, or article. This doctrine is based on the principles that children may not be able to recognize the danger involved and may be injured, and that it is in the best interest of society to protect them rather than protect the owner's right to the land. Thus, the possessor of the land must keep the premises in a safe condition and use ordinary care to protect the trespassing children from harm.[5]

Several examples can illustrate the attractive nuisance doctrine, by which the occupant or owner can be held liable:

- A homeowner carelessly leaves a ladder standing on the side of the house. A small child climbs the ladder and falls off the roof breaking both legs.
- A homeowner has a miniature house for the children. A neighbor's child attempts to enter through an unlocked window, which falls on her neck and strangles her.
- A building contractor carelessly leaves the keys in a tractor. While driving the tractor, two small boys are seriously injured when the tractor overturns.

Owners and Operators of Automobiles

The owner of an automobile who drives in a careless and irresponsible manner can be held liable for property damage or bodily injury sustained by another person. There is no single rule of law that can be applied in this situation. The legal liability of the owner who is also the operator has been modified over time by court decisions, comparative negligence laws, the last clear chance rule, no-fault auto insurance laws (see Chapter 11), and a host of additional factors. However, the laws in all states clearly require the owner of an automobile to exercise reasonable care while operating the automobile.

With respect to the liability of the owner who is not the operator, the general rule is that the owner is not liable for the negligent acts of operators. But there are exceptions to this general principle. In all states the owner can be held liable for an operator's negligence if an *agency relationship* exists. As stated earlier, if your friend drives your car on a business errand for you and injures someone, you can be held liable. In addition, under the *family purpose doctrine* discussed earlier, the owner of an automobile can be held liable for the negligent operation of the vehicle by an immediate family member.

Governmental Liability

Based on the common law, federal, state, and local governments could not be sued unless the government gave its consent. The immunity from lawsuits was based on the doctrine of **sovereign immunity,** meaning that the king or queen can do no wrong. This doctrine, however, has been significantly modified over time by both statutory law and court decisions.

A governmental unit can be held liable if it is negligent in the performance of a **proprietary function.** Proprietary functions of government typically include the operation of water plants; electrical, transportation, and telephone systems; municipal auditoriums; and similar money-making activities. Thus, if some seats collapse at a rock concert in a city auditorium, the city can be sued and held liable for injuries to spectators. With respect to **governmental functions**—for example, the planning of a sewer system—immunity from lawsuits has also been eroded. Today, governmental entities can be sued in almost every aspect of governmental activity, including false arrest, failure to meet certain standards of care, and failure to arrest.

Charitable Institutions

At one time, charitable institutions were generally immune from lawsuits. This immunity has gradually been eliminated by state law and court decisions. The trend today is to hold charities responsible for acts of negligence. This is particularly true with respect to commercial activities. For example, a hospital operated by a religious order can be sued for malpractice, and a church sponsoring a dance, carnival, or bingo game can be held liable for injuries to participants.

Employer and Employee Relationships

Under the doctrine of **respondeat superior,** an employer can be held liable for the negligent acts of employees while they are acting on the employer's behalf. Thus, if a sales clerk in a sporting goods store carelessly drops a barbell set on a customer's toe, the owner of the store can be held liable.

For an employer to be held liable for the negligent acts of the employees, two requirements must be fulfilled. *First, the worker's legal status must be that of an employee.* A person typically is considered an employee if he or she is given detailed instructions on how to do a job, is furnished tools or supplies by the employer, and is paid a wage or salary at regular intervals. *Second, the employee must be acting within the scope of employment when the negligent act occurred.* That is, the employee must be engaged in the type of work that he or she is employed to perform. There is no simple test to determine whether the tort is committed within the scope of employment. Numerous factors are considered, including whether the act is authorized by the employer, whether the act is one commonly performed by the employee, and whether the act is intended to advance the employer's interests.[6]

Parents and Children

Under the common law, parents usually are not responsible for their children's torts. Children who reach the age of reason are responsible for their own wrongful acts. However, there are several exceptions to this general principle. *First, a parent can be held liable if a child uses a dangerous weapon, such as a gun or knife, to injure someone.* For example, if a 10-year-old child is permitted to play with a loaded revolver, and someone is thereby injured or killed, the parents can be held responsible. *Second, the parent can be legally liable if the child is acting as an agent for the parent.* For example, if a son or daughter is employed in the family business, the parents can be held liable for any injury to a customer caused by the child's actions. *Third, if a family car is operated by a minor child, the parents can be held liable under the family purpose doctrine discussed earlier.* In addition, property damage and vandalism by children have increased over time, especially by teenagers. *Most states have passed laws that hold the parents liable for the willful and malicious acts of children that result in property damage to others.* For example, Nebraska has a parental liability law that holds the parents liable for the willful and intentional destruction of property by minor children.

Animals

Owners of wild animals are held absolutely liable (strict liability) for the injuries of others even if the animals are domesticated. For example, an owner of an exotic pet such as a tiger is absolutely liable if the pet escapes and injures someone even if the owner uses due care in keeping the animal restrained.

In addition, depending on the state, strict liability may also be imposed on the owners of ordinary house dogs. Until recently, dog owners were liable for dog bites and other injuries only if the injured person could prove that the owner knew the dog was dangerous. If the dog had never bitten anyone previously, the dog owner usually was not liable. *However, in about 30 states and the District of Columbia, the injured person has to show only that the dog caused the injury; in such cases, the dog owner is liable based on the doctrine of strict liability.*[7]

CURRENT TORT LIABILITY PROBLEMS

Certain tort liability problems have emerged that create serious problems for risk managers, business firms, physicians, and liability insurers. Timely lia-

bility problems that merit discussion include the following:

- Defective tort liability system
- Medical malpractice crisis
- Corporate fraud and lax corporate governance
- Increase in asbestos law suits

Defective Tort Liability System

Critics charge that the present tort liability system in the United States has numerous defects that reduce its effectiveness in compensating injured victims. Major defects include the following:

- Rising tort liability costs
- Inefficiency in compensating injured victims
- Uncertainty of legal outcomes
- Higher liability awards
- Long delays in settling lawsuits

Rising Tort Liability Costs Critics claim that the present system is costly and that tort costs are rising rapidly. The number of lawsuits has increased over time, and the legal costs of settling these lawsuits are enormous. The tort system in the United States cost $205 billion in 2001, which is equivalent to a tax of $721 per citizen or a 5 percent wage tax. *In 2005, estimated tort costs are expected to rise to $298 billion, or 2.4 percent of the nation's gross domestic product* (see Exhibit 7.1). These costs are substantially higher in the United States than in other industrialized countries, which makes it more difficult for American companies to compete in the global marketplace (see Exhibit 7.2).

Several factors help explain the substantial increase in tort costs over time. These factors include (1) social inflation that results in juries and judges being desensitized to the value of the dollar when damages are awarded, (2) aggressive and creative litigation strategies by plaintiffs' attorneys to maximize awards, (3) rising medical costs that increase the costs of personal injury claims, (4) abuses in class action lawsuits and the definition of a "class," (5) actions by the states and courts in striking down portions of state tort reform legislation, (6) an increase in the number and size of stockholder lawsuits against boards of directors and

EXHIBIT 7.1
Cost of U.S. Tort System (Billions of Dollars)

Billions of dollars

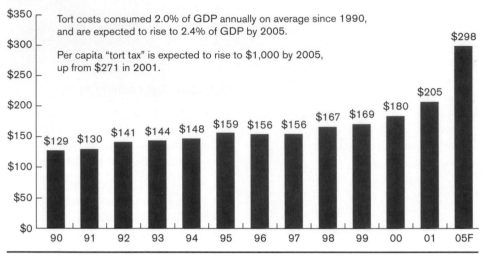

NOTE: Data are from Tillinghast-Towers Perrin. 2005 forecast from Tillinghast.
SOURCE: From Robert P. Hartwig, *Liability Trends, Issues and Jury Verdicts: Impact on Insurance Liability and Excess Casualty Markets,* Insurance Information Institute, October 2003.

EXHIBIT 7.2
Tort Costs as a Percent of GDP*

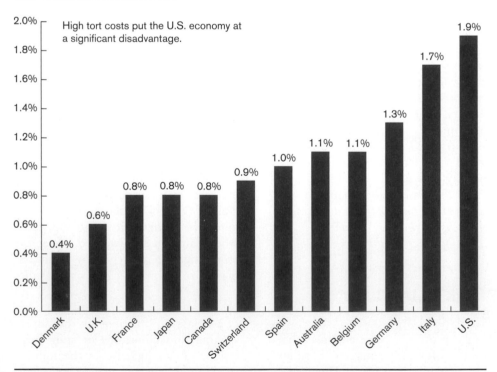

* 1998 (latest available)
NOTE: Data are from Tillinghast-Towers Perrin.
SOURCE: From Robert P. Hartwig, *Liability Trends, Issues and Jury Verdicts: Impact on Insurance Liability and Excess Casualty Markets,* Insurance Information Institute, October 2003.

company officers because of corporate fraud, greed, illegal manipulation of earnings, and accounting scandals, (7) a deep pocket syndrome in which some plaintiffs' attorneys deliberately go after defendants who can pay large settlements, and (8) exploitation of high verdict cases by the media.[8] In addition, tort costs have increased because of an upward adjustment of liabilities tied to asbestos claims (discussed later).

Inefficiency in Compensating Injured Victims

Critics argue that the present system is inefficient in compensating injured victims. The number of class action lawsuits has increased over time. However, critics charge that plaintiffs often receive relatively small amounts for their injuries or doubtful benefits (such as coupons to buy the defendant's product), while attorneys receive a disproportionate share of the settlement.

In addition, *critics argue the present system is inefficient because injured victims receive less than half of each tort dollar paid.* A Tillinghast study found that out of each dollar spent on liability claims, injured victims received only 22 cents for their actual economic loss (such as medical bills and loss of earnings) and another 24 cents for noneconomic loss (such as pain and suffering). The remaining 54 cents paid for claimants' attorneys, defense costs, and administrative costs (see Exhibit 7.3).

Uncertainty of Legal Outcomes

Critics also argue that because of changing legal doctrines, there is considerable uncertainty in predicting legal outcomes. The result is considerable confusion for insurers, employers, risk managers, government officials, and taxpayers.

For example, an injured party at one time had to prove that the other party was at fault to collect damages. Today, emphasis is on providing the injured party with some form of legal redress, regardless of blame. Thus, critics argue that the ability to pay is more important today than determining who is at fault, and that the burden of paying injured persons falls heavily on insurers, wealthy people, corporations, and others with "deep pockets."

As a result of the uncertainty in legal outcomes, property and liability insurers often must pay tort liability claims that they did not envision paying when the coverage was first written.

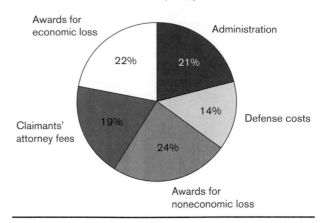

EXHIBIT 7.3
Where the Tort Dollar Goes (2001)

- Awards for economic loss 22%
- Administration 21%
- Defense costs 14%
- Awards for noneconomic loss 24%
- Claimants' attorney fees 19%

SOURCE: Excerpted from *U.S. Tort Costs: 2002 Update, Trends and Findings on the Costs of the U.S. Tort System*, Tillinghast-Towers Perrin, p. 17.

Higher Liability Awards Critics also argue that liability awards for certain types of lawsuits continue to grow. According to Jury Verdict Research, the *median* medical malpractice jury award was $1 million in 2001, up 43 percent from the 1999 figure of $700,000 (see Exhibit 7.4). The frequency of multi-million dollar awards in recent years for most types of defendants has also increased. These cases include motor vehicle liability, personal negligence, premises liability, business and government negligence, medical malpractice, and products liability (see Exhibit 7.5).

Higher liability awards increase the liability costs of business firms and result in premium increases for liability insurance. In addition, many firms, especially those that have been sued, are now purchasing higher liability insurance limits, which also increase the cost of goods and services to consumers.

Finally, the likelihood of a catastrophic award varies drastically by venue. Some states are perceived to treat defendants fairly and equitably, while certain other states are perceived to have expensive legal systems. Moreover, at the county level, tort reform advocates view certain counties as "judicial hellholes" because the counties are perceived to be drastically unfair to corporate defendants and insurers (see Insight 7.1).

Long Delays in Settling Lawsuits The tort system is also marred by long delays in settling lawsuits.

EXHIBIT 7.4
National Compensatory Median Jury Award in Medical Malpractice Cases

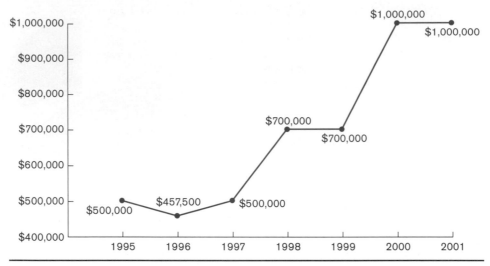

Cases take months or even years to settle. In 1950, only 20 civil trials in the federal courts lasted longer than 20 days. By 1981, the number of comparable lengthy trials had increased ninefold. More recent studies show that lengthy delays are still a problem. The National Center for State Courts found that the median processing time in 1989 for all tort cases in 25 urban trial courts studied was 441 days. Data

EXHIBIT 7.5
Trends in Million Dollar Verdicts*

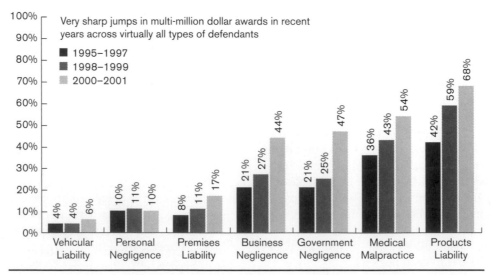

* Verdicts of $1 million or more.
NOTE: Data are from Jury Verdict Research and the Insurance Information Institute.
SOURCE: From Robert P. Hartwig, *Liability Trends, Issues and Jury Verdicts: Impact on Insurance Liability and Excess Casualty Markets,* Insurance Information Institute, October 2003.

INSIGHT 7.1

Which States Give Defendants the Best Legal Deal?

Some plaintiff attorneys are notorious for "forum shopping." That is, they prefer to file suits in those jurisdictions where legal outcomes are favorable to injured clients. Conversely, defendants in civil cases prefer jurisdictions where the legal outcomes are likely to favor them.

The likelihood that a defendant will have to pay a catastrophic award varies drastically by venue. Some states are kinder to defendants than others. The U.S. Chamber of Commerce ranked the liability systems in 50 states perceived to be the most equitable based on several factors, including fairness, jury predictability, treatment of class action suits, and punitive damages. The top ten states in 2003 perceived to be the most equitable were:

1. Delaware
2. Nebraska
3. Iowa
4. South Dakota
5. Indiana
6. North Dakota
7. Utah
8. Virginia
9. Minnesota
10. New Hampshire

The bottom states ranked 41–50 with the most expensive legal systems were:

41. New Mexico
42. South Carolina
43. Hawaii
44. California
45. Arkansas
46. Texas
47. Louisiana
48. Alabama
49. West Virginia
50. Mississippi

At the city and county level, some jurisdictions are perceived to be so drastically unfair to corporate defendants and liability insurers that they are called "judicial hellholes" by tort reform advocates. Given the history of damages awarded to plaintiffs in these jurisdictions, they are probably the last place on earth in which a corporation would want to defend a liability suit. These include:

- Alameda County, California
- Los Angeles County, California
- Jefferson County, Texas
- Hidalgo County, Texas
- Starr County, Texas
- City of St. Louis, Missouri
- 22nd Judicial District, Mississippi
- Madison County, Illinois
- Orleans Parish, Louisiana

In some of the above counties, there are more plaintiffs in asbestos-related lawsuits than there are residents.

SOURCE: Adapted from David Dial, et al., "Tort Excess: The Necessity for Reform from a Policy, Legal and Risk Management Perspective," *Hot Topics & Insurance Issues,* Insurance Information Institute.

from Jury Verdict Research show that for 2001, it still took about 39 months from the time of the incident for a trial to begin in motor vehicle accidents and 51 months in medical malpractice cases.[9]

A considerable amount of time involves a pretrial examination of the facts, such as interviews, depositions, and requests for documents. Repeated requests for documents can be time-consuming and expensive during the discovery stage of a suit. Moreover, attorneys frequently use delaying tactics during the discovery stage as an economic weapon against opponents. The overall result is a substantial increase in delay and cost.

Tort Reform Most states have enacted or are considering some type of tort-reform legislation to deal

with the preceding defects. Some important tort reforms include the following:

- *Capping noneconomic damages, such as pain and suffering.* Many states have enacted or are considering legislation that would place a maximum limit on noneconomic damages, such as compensation for pain and suffering. Reform measures would apply to all types of tort suits or only to specific suits, such as medical malpractice.
- *Reinstating the state-of-the art defense.* This proposal has relevance with respect to products liability suits. If the product conformed to the prevailing state of the art at the time it was manufactured, it would not be considered a defective product today.

- *Restricting punitive damage awards.* Punitive damages were originally intended to punish defendants for egregious conduct and to deter others from engaging in the same behavior. However, in many cases, awards for punitive damages are so large that they bear little relationship to the compensatory damages awarded by the courts. Many states have already passed laws that limit the imposition of punitive damages. Other states are considering legislation that would limit the maximum amount that could be paid for punitive damages or restrict the imposition of punitive damages to certain types of cases.

- *Modifying the collateral source rule.* Under the **collateral source rule**, *the defendant cannot introduce any evidence that shows the injured party has received compensation from other collateral sources.* For example, a delivery driver who is injured in a rear-end collision may be able to collect medical expenses from the negligent driver. However, job-related medical expenses are also covered under a state's workers compensation law. Therefore, the injured driver might "double dip" and receive a total amount that exceeds the medical bills. The collateral source rule would be modified so that recovery from other sources could be considered in determining the amount of damages. The effect would be to reduce the size of the damages awarded.

- *Modifying the **joint and several liability rule**.* Under this rule, *several people may be responsible for the injury, but a defendant who is only slightly responsible may be required to pay the full amount of damages.* This could happen if one defendant had substantial financial assets ("deep pockets"), and the other defendants had few or no assets. Under tort reform, the joint and several liability rule would be modified. For example, many states now prohibit application of the joint and several liability rule to noneconomic damages, such as pain and suffering.

- *Alternative dispute resolution (ADR) techniques.* Another proposal is to use alternative disputes resolution (ADR) techniques to resolve legal disputes. *An ADR is a technique for resolving a legal dispute without litigation.* For example, **arbitration** is a technique by which parties in a dispute agree to be bound by the decision of an independent third party. **Mediation** is a technique by which a neutral third party tries to arrange a settlement without resorting to litigation. To reduce lawsuits between insurers and consumers over claims, many states now use binding arbitration or formal mediation to resolve disputes.

Obstacles to Tort Reform by State Courts   Although the states have enacted hundreds of tort reforms since the mid-1980s, state courts frequently nullify such reforms. Dozens of court decisions have nullified tort reform laws to curb excessive awards and frivolous suits. In 1996, the South Dakota Supreme Court declared unconstitutional a cap on total compensatory damages of $1 million in medical malpractice lawsuits. In 1997, the Illinois Supreme Court struck down the Omnibus Tort Reform Act enacted in 1995. In addition, a circuit court judge in Florida ruled that the entire 1999 tort reform measure was unconstitutional. Finally, a number of states have thrown out statutes that place caps on pain and suffering. As a result of court decisions, the liability laws now vary widely among the states.

Medical Malpractice Crisis

Medical malpractice is one of the most important liability issues today. Medical malpractice occurs when a negligent act or omission by a physician or other health-care professional results in injury or harm to the patient. For example, a physician who prescribes the wrong drug that causes a patient's death could be guilty of medical negligence. Likewise, an orthopedic surgeon who amputates the wrong leg is another example of medical malpractice.

An unfavorable medical outcome alone does not necessarily mean the physician is negligent. To determine liability, the patient must show that the doctor deviated from the generally accepted standards of practice in this particular case. In addition, if the standard of care was not followed, the patient must show that this failure caused the injury. The physician's negligence must cause injury or harm to the patient. Even if the physician makes the wrong diagnosis, fails to treat the illness or injury properly, or prescribes the wrong drug, there is no case unless the

EXHIBIT 7.6
**Medical Malpractice: Tort Cost Growth Is Skyrocketing
(Billions of Dollars)**

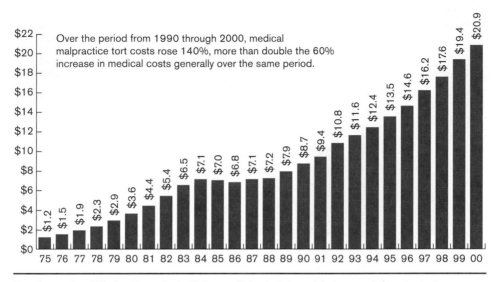

Over the period from 1990 through 2000, medical malpractice tort costs rose 140%, more than double the 60% increase in medical costs generally over the same period.

NOTE: Data are from Tillinghast-Towers Perrin, US Bureau of Labor Statistics, and the Insurance Information Institute.
SOURCE: From Robert P. Hartwig, *Liability Trends, Issues and Jury Verdicts: Impact on Insurance Liability and Excess Casualty Markets,* Insurance Information Institute, April 8, 2003.

negligence actually caused the injury or worsened the condition.

Medical malpractice tort costs have soared in recent years. From 1990 through 2000, medical malpractice tort costs increased 140 percent, more than double the 60 percent increase in medical costs generally over the same period (see Exhibit 7.6). The *average* jury award in medical malpractice cases more than tripled between 1994 and 2001 (see Exhibit 7.7).

The medical malpractice crisis has had a severe financial impact on health care providers and insurers. Malpractice insurance premiums have soared; some physicians pay $50,000 or more annually for coverage. Many physicians have abandoned high-risk areas, such as obstetrics, gynecology, and neurosurgery. Groups of physicians have staged protests and walkouts in certain parts of the country. Malpractice insurers have incurred heavy underwriting losses, and several malpractice insurers have withdrawn from the medical malpractice market. Finally, some physicians have formed physician-owned insurance companies because malpractice insurance is too costly or not available.

Reasons for Medical Malpractice Crisis   There is no single reason that explains the medical malpractice crisis in the United States. Two major factors, however, are the following:

- *Many malpractice suits undoubtedly are due to medical errors by health care providers, especially errors that result in the death of patients.* One study concluded that medical errors rank with highway accidents and breast cancer as a major killer in the United States (see Insight 7.2).
- As stated earlier, *many insurers have experienced significant underwriting losses,* which have resulted in substantial increases in medical malpractice premiums for certain medical specialties. Also, legal defense costs incurred by insurers to defend malpractice suits are relatively high even when the health care provider wins. One measure of underwriting profit or loss is the **combined ratio,** which is the percentage of each premium dollar an insurer spends on claims and expenses. When the

EXHIBIT 7.7
Average Jury Award in Medical Malpractice Cases
(Millions of Dollars)

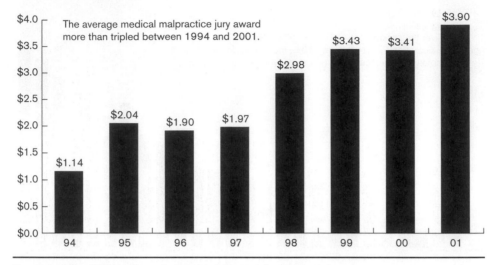

NOTE: Data are from Tillinghast-Towers Perrin and the Insurance Information Institute.
SOURCE: From Robert P. Hartwig, *Liability Trends, Issues and Jury Verdicts: Impact on Insurance Liability and Excess Casualty Markets,* Insurance Information Institute, April 8, 2003.

combined ratio is over 100, the insurer has an underwriting loss. *In 2001, the combined ratio was 153.3. This means that malpractice insurers paid out $153 in losses and expenses for each* *$100 of premiums taken in as a result of their underwriting operations* (see Exhibit 7.8). Estimates for 2002 indicate that the combined ratio continues to worsen and may reach 165.

INSIGHT 7.2

Medical Errors Rank with Highway Accidents and Breast Cancer as a Major Killer in the United States

Many malpractice suits are due to medical errors that result in the death of patients. The Institute of Medicine estimates that medical errors may cause 44,000 to 98,000 deaths each year. Even using the lower estimate, the Institute of Medicine claims that more people die in a given year as a result of medical errors than from motor vehicle accidents, breast cancer, or AIDS.[a]

Opportunities for mistakes and errors result from a number of factors, including the following:[b]

- Medication errors in prescribing and dispensing drugs, both in and out of the hospital
- More care and increasingly complex care that is provided in ambulatory settings, such as outpatient surgical centers, clinics, and physician offices

- Decentralized and fragmented health care delivery system, such as frequent referral of patients to multiple health-care providers, none of whom has access to complete information about the patient
- Few demands for improvements in patient safety by group purchasers of health care

The Institute of Medicine believes that a large percentage of adverse effects from medical errors can be prevented by a greater emphasis on patient safety.

[a] Linda T. Kohn, Janet M. Corrigan, and Molla S. Donaldson, eds., "Executive Summary," *To Err Is Human, Building a Safer Health System* (Washington, DC: National Academy Press, 2000).
[b] Ibid.

Exhibit 7.8
Medical Malpractice Combined Ratio

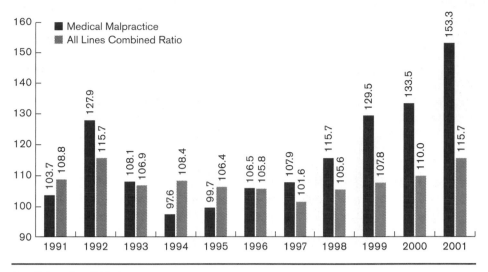

Note: Data are from AM Best.
Source: From Robert P. Hartwig, *Liability Trends, Issues and Jury Verdicts: Impact on Insurance Liability and Excess Casualty Markets*, Insurance Information Institute, April 8, 2003.

In addition, according to the Insurance Information Institute, the following factors may contribute to the medical malpractice problem.[10]

- *People are more litigious than in the past.*
- *The media has made more people aware of the vulnerability of physicians to malpractice suits.*
- *The intimate relationship between patients and physicians that existed in the past has been lost.*
- *Physicians and other medical experts will now testify against physicians in malpractice cases.*
- *Physicians accuse attorneys of filing malpractice suits because of the high fees that attorneys can collect if they win.*
- *Some state medical boards are reluctant to discipline their own members.*
- *There is growing resentment against large for profit health-care firms and managed care plans.*

Regardless of the reason, the majority of medical malpractice plaintiffs appear to lose if the case goes to a jury. According to Jury Verdict Research, *the medical malpractice plaintiff recovery rate overall in 2001 was only 39 percent.*[11]

Approaches to Medical Malpractice Crisis Several approaches have been taken to solve the medical malpractice problem. They include the following:

- *Place caps on noneconomic damages.* Many states have enacted laws that place caps on the amount paid for noneconomic damages. How effective are these laws? The empirical studies conflict and the results differ. One study of 15 large states from 1990 to early 2001 showed that states with caps on noneconomic damages have below-average medical malpractice loss costs for physicians, and that states without caps have the highest medical malpractice costs.[12] In contrast, a study by Weiss Ratings showed that while caps have lowered the amount of claim payments, caps on noneconomic damages have failed to prevent sharp increases in medical malpractice insurance premiums.[13]
- *Arbitration panels.* Some states have formed arbitration panels to resolve disputes between physicians and patients.
- *Attorney fees.* Limitations would be placed on contingent fees charged by attorneys.

- *Shorter period for filing suits.* The period for filing suits against physicians would be shortened, such as within three years of the injury.
- *More effective medical review boards.* State review boards would be upgraded so that problem physicians could be identified more easily. Physicians cited by review boards would have to undergo retraining.
- *Training programs to reduce medical errors.* Training programs to reduce medical errors would be intensified, especially in the use of new technology.
- *Proposed federal legislation.* In early 2003, the U.S. House of Representatives approved a reform bill that would limit noneconomic damages to $250,000; place restrictions on attorney fees by a sliding scale; limit the statute of limitations to the filing of a claim to three years from the date of the injury; and assign proportional liability for the injury according to responsibility.

Corporate Fraud and Lax Corporate Governance

One of the most important liability issues today is the problem of corporate fraud and lax corporate governance. In recent years, many large corporations have used dishonest or aggressive accounting practices to inflate stated earnings and profits; other companies have concealed or misstated certain accounting transactions. When these practices were discovered, earnings were revised downward, and shareholders lost millions of dollars. Because of class action suits by angry stockholders, employees, and investors, several large corporations have been forced into bankruptcy, including Enron, WorldCom, and Global Crossing. Thousands of employees have lost their jobs and a large part of their retirement savings as well. In addition, the Securities and Exchange Commission has indicted numerous company officials in different industries for securities fraud, illegal accounting practices, destruction of company records, and obstruction of justice. Some company officials pleaded guilty and are now serving lengthy federal prison sentences.

Some accounting firms are also in trouble because of accounting fraud, illegal manipulation of earnings, laxity in detecting corporate fraud in their audits, and aggressive accounting practices. A federal jury found the Arthur Andersen accounting firm guilty of obstructing justice and shredding Enron-related documents; the firm was fined $500,000 and placed on probation for five years; and thousands of employees lost their jobs.

Boards of directors are under heavy attack for lax corporate governance and inadequate oversight of management. Boards are criticized because of the disconnect between the boards and audit committees, poor internal controls and accountability, excessive executive salaries and loans, undisclosed CEO and director financial arrangements, compromising of auditors and lawyers, and unclear disclosure of complex financial transactions (such as off-balance-sheet transactions and the use of derivatives). Critics claim that many board members are mere figureheads who are on the board because of their prominent name or national visibility; that board members may not understand complex financial transactions that often involve mathematical formulas, derivatives, and hedging techniques; and that board members often serve on multiple boards and cannot devote the time necessary to understand and scrutinize the actions of management.

To deal with the problem, in 2002 Congress enacted the bipartisan *Sarbanes-Oxley Act* corporate accountability law. The new law is designed to expose and punish acts of corruption, restore confidence in corporate America, and protect small investors. The new law requires the company's CEO and CFO to swear to the accuracy of the quarterly and annual financial reports; makes it generally unlawful for an accounting firm to provide major nonaudit services to a company while auditing the company's books; prohibits companies from retaliating against stock market analysts who criticize them; requires companies to disclose whether the board of directors' audit committee has at least one member who is a financial expert; and makes tampering with company records a crime with increased criminal penalties for mail and wire fraud. In addition, the legislation created a new nonprofit entity, the Public Company Accounting Oversight Board, to review and discipline accountants.

Corporate fraud and greed also have had a significant financial impact on *directors and officers lia-*

bility insurance (D&O). D&O insurance covers directors and company officers for their negligent acts and for deceptive statements that result in lawsuits against the company. Losses and premiums have substantially increased, and underwriting has tightened. Chapter 14 discusses D&O insurance in greater detail.

Increase in Asbestos Lawsuits

A critical liability problem is the significant increase in the number and cost of asbestos suits over time. Exposure to materials containing asbestos can cause lung cancer and other respiratory diseases. Because the disease has a long latency period, it can take as long as 40 years for someone exposed to asbestos to be diagnosed with an asbestos-related disease.

The first asbestos suit was filed in 1966. By the end of 2000, more than 600,000 people had filed claims for asbestos-related personal injuries, and more than 6000 companies were named as defendants.[14] Many of these companies are no longer in business, and bankruptcies continue to increase (see Exhibit 7.9). One reason for the surge in suits is the

increased number of claimants who file claims against more than one company. Many claimants who have signs of exposure but not a debilitating disease file multiple claims because they fear if they later develop an asbestos disease, the company responsible may be bankrupt because of asbestos claims. The claims are not confined to a single industry, but include both traditional industries and new industries (see Exhibit 7.10).

Another part of the problem is the sharp escalation in asbestos costs over time. Insured losses for asbestos lawsuits are enormous and are at least $122 billion. Future costs are expected to reach $200 billion. *To put these figures in proper perspective, insured losses for asbestos claims substantially exceed the losses incurred by insurers as a result of the September 11, 2001 terrorist attacks, and are also greater than the world's ten largest catastrophes* (see Exhibit 7.11).

Solving the asbestos problem is not easy. Some proposals to resolve the problem include the following:[15]

■ *Establish a national trust fund to pay claimants.* At the time of this writing, Congress is

EXHIBIT 7.9
Asbestos Bankruptcies Are Rising Sharply

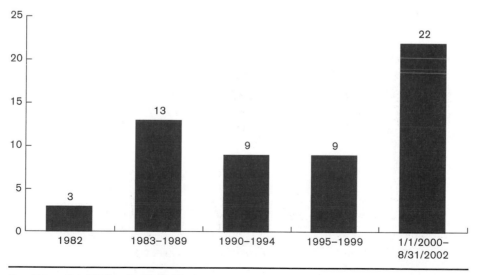

NOTE: Data are from RAND Institute for Civil Justice.
SOURCE: From Robert P. Hartwig, *Liability Trends, Issues and Jury Verdicts: Impact on Insurance Liability and Excess Casualty Markets,* Insurance Information Institute, April 8, 2003.

EXHIBIT 7.10
Asbestos Claims: Killing Corporate America

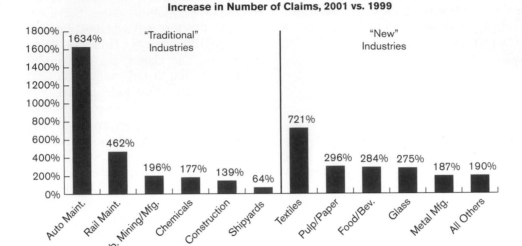

Increase in Number of Claims, 2001 vs. 1999

NOTE: Data are from Claims Resolution Management Corporation and Insurance Information Institute.
SOURCE: From Robert P. Hartwig, *Liability Trends, Issues and Jury Verdicts: Impact on Insurance Liability and Excess Casualty Markets,* Insurance Information Institute, April 8, 2003.

EXHIBIT 7.11
World's Top 10 Biggest Catastrophes vs. Asbestos (by insured loss)

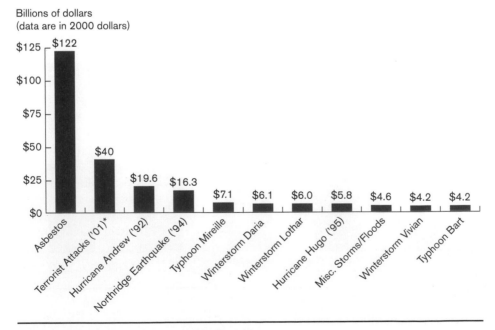

Billions of dollars
(data are in 2000 dollars)

NOTE: Data are from Swiss Re and Insurance Information Institute.
SOURCE: From Robert P. Hartwig, *Liability Trends, Issues and Jury Verdicts: Impact on Insurance Liability and Excess Casualty Markets,* Insurance Information Institute, April 8, 2003.

considering legislation that would establish a national trust fund to pay claimants. Defendant companies and their insurers would contribute to the fund, which would compensate asbestos victims over several decades based on clearly defined medical criteria. A trust fund would ensure finality to the problem.

- *Establish clear medical criteria for determining loss.* The criteria would include requiring the manifestation of an asbestos-related disease before a claim is filed.

- *Create a single venue for asbestos litigation.* The objective here is to eliminate "forum shopping" by plaintiff's attorneys who seek the most favorable jurisdiction to try the case.

- *Cap legal fees.* Legal fees would be capped in asbestos cases, such as a sliding scale of attorney fees.

CASE APPLICATION

Michael went deer hunting with Ed. After seeing bushes move, Michael quickly fired his rifle at what he thought to be a deer. However, Ed caused the movement in the bushes and was seriously injured by the bullet. Ed survived and later sued Michael on the grounds that "Michael 's negligence was the proximate cause of the injury."

a. Based on the above facts, is Michael guilty of negligence? Your answer must include a definition of negligence and the essential elements of a negligent act.

b. Michael 's attorney believes that if contributory negligence could be established, it would greatly influence the outcome of the case. Do you agree with Michael's attorney? Your answer must include a definition of contributory negligence.

c. If Michael can establish comparative negligence on the part of Ed, would the outcome of the case be changed? Explain your answer.

d. Assume that Michael and Ed are hunting on farmland without obtaining permission from the owner. If Michael fell into a marshy pond covered by weeds and injured his back, would the property owner be liable for damages? Explain your answer.

SUMMARY

- A tort is a legal wrong for which the law allows a remedy in the form of money damages. There are three categories of torts: intentional torts, absolute or strict liability, and negligence.

- Negligence is defined as the failure to exercise the standard of care required by law to protect others from an unreasonable risk of harm. There are four elements of a negligent act:

> Existence of a legal duty
> Failure to perform that duty
> Damages or injury to the claimant
> Proximate cause relationship

- *Contributory negligence* means that if the injured person's conduct falls below the standard of care required for his or her protection, and such conduct contributed to the injury, the injured person cannot collect damages. Under a *comparative negligence law,* the injured person can collect, but the award for damages is reduced. Under the *last clear chance rule,* the plaintiff who is endangered by his or her own negligence can still recover damages from the defendant if the defendant has a last clear chance to avoid the accident but fails to do so. Under the *assumption of risk doctrine,* a person who understands and recognizes the danger inherent in a particular activity cannot recover damages in the event of injury.

- Under certain conditions, the negligence of one person can be imputed to another. Imputed negligence may arise from an employer–employee relationship, vicarious liability law, family purpose doctrine, joint business venture, or a dram shop law.

- Under the doctrine of *res ipsa loquitur* (the thing speaks for itself), the very fact that the injury or damage occurs establishes a presumption of negligence on behalf of the defendant.

- The standard of care required by law varies with the situation. Specific liability situations can involve property owners, attractive nuisances, owners and operators of automobiles, governmental units and charitable institutions, employers and employees, parents and children, and the owners of animals.

- Tort reform advocates claim that the present tort liability system in the United States has the following defects:

  Rising tort liability costs

  Inefficiency in compensating injured victims

  Uncertainty of legal outcomes

  Higher liability awards

  Long delays in settling lawsuits

- Some tort reform proposals include the following:

  Capping noneconomic damages, such as pain and suffering

  Reinstating the state-of-the art defense

  Restricting punitive damage awards

  Modifying the collateral source rule

  Modifying the joint and several liability rule

  Alternative dispute resolution (ADR) techniques

- The medical malpractice crisis is due to several factors. These causes include medical errors by health care providers, large underwriting losses by insurers that result in substantial premium increases for malpractice insurance, increased willingness of patients to sue physicians, exploitation of malpractice suits by the media, loss of the intimate relationship between physicians and patients that existed in the past, increased willingness of physicians and medical experts to testify against other physicians, increased tendency for attorneys to file malpractice suits because of potentially high fees, and the ineffectiveness or reluctance of some state medical boards to discipline physicians.

- Corporate fraud and lax corporate governance are important tort liability issues. Many corporations have been sued because of dishonest or aggressive accounting practices that inflate stated earnings and profits, concealment or misstatement of certain accounting transactions that have resulted in enormous investor losses, violation of security laws, destruction of company records, and obstruction of justice.

- Boards of directors have been sued because of lax corporate governance and inadequate oversight of management.

- The number of asbestos lawsuits has increased substantially over time. Some proposals to deal with asbestos claims include the establishment of a national trust fund to pay claimants over several decades, requiring evidence of an asbestos-related disease before a claim can be filed, creation of a single venue for asbestos litigation to eliminate "forum shopping," and placing a cap on legal fees.

KEY CONCEPTS AND TERMS

Absolute (strict) liability	Joint and several liability rule
Alternative dispute resolution (ADR) techniques	Joint underwriting association (JUA)
Arbitration	Last clear chance rule
Assumption of risk	Legal wrong
Attractive nuisance	Licensee
Collateral source rule	Mediation
Combined ratio	Negligence
Comparative negligence law	Plaintiff
Contributory negligence law	Proprietary function
Dram shop law	Proximate cause
Elements of a negligent act	Punitive damages
Family purpose doctrine	*Res ipsa loquitur*
General damages	*Respondeat superior*
Governmental function	Sovereign immunity
Imputed negligence	Special damages
Invitee	Tort
	Tortfeasor
	Trespasser
	Vicarious liability law

REVIEW QUESTIONS

1. a. Define the meaning of negligence.
    b. Explain the four elements of a negligent act.

2. What is the meaning of absolute (strict) liability?

3. Explain the following types of damages:
    a. Special damages
    b. General damages
    c. Punitive damages

4. Describe the following legal defenses that can be used by defendants who are accused of negligence:
    a. Contributory negligence
    b. Comparative negligence
    c. Last clear chance rule
    d. Assumption of risk doctrine

5. Explain the meaning of imputed negligence.

6. Explain the meaning of *res ipsa loquitur.*

7. Briefly describe the standard of care to protect others from harm for each of the following liability situations:
   a. Property owners
   b. An attractive nuisance
   c. Owners and operators of automobiles
   d. Governmental units and charitable institutions
   e. Employers and employees
   f. Parents and children
   g. Owners of animals

8. a. Explain the major defects in the tort liability system in the United States.
   b. Identify several proposals for tort reform in the United States.

9. a. Explain the reasons for the medical malpractice crisis in the United States.
   b. Identify several proposals for dealing with the medical malpractice problem in the United States.

10. Briefly explain the following tort liability problems:
    a. Corporate fraud and lax corporate governance
    b. Increase in asbestos suits

APPLICATION QUESTIONS

1. Smith Construction is building a warehouse for Raymond. The construction firm routinely leaves certain construction machinery at the building site overnight and on weekends. Late one night, Fred, age 10, began playing on some of Smith's construction equipment. Fred accidentally released the brakes of a tractor on which he was playing, and the tractor rolled down a hill and smashed into the building under construction. Fred was severely injured in the accident. Fred's parents sue both Smith Construction and Raymond for the injury.
   a. Based on the elements of a negligent act, describe the requirements that must be met for Smith Construction to be held liable for negligence.
   b. Describe the various classes of persons that are recognized by the law with respect to entering upon the property of another. In which class of persons would Fred belong?
   c. What other legal doctrine is applicable in this case because of Fred's age? Explain your answer.

2. a. Parkway Distributors is a wholesale firm that employs several outside salespersons. Emily, a salesperson employed by Parkway Distributors, was involved in an accident with another motorist while she was using her car to make regular sales calls for Parkway Distributors. Emily and the motorist are seriously injured in the accident. The motorist sues both Emily and Parkway Distributors for the injury based on negligence.
      (1) Describe the requirements that the motorist must establish to show that Emily is guilty of negligence.
      (2) On what legal basis might Parkway Distributors be held legally liable for the injury to the motorist? Explain your answer.
   b. Tom asks his girlfriend, Shania, to go to a supermarket and purchase some steaks for dinner. While driving Tom's car to the supermarket, Shania runs a stop sign and seriously injures a pedestrian. Does Tom have any legal liability for the injury? Explain your answer.

3. Whirlwind Mowers manufactures and sells power lawn mowers to the public and distributes the products through its own dealers. Andrew is a homeowner who has purchased a power mower from an authorized dealer on the basis of the dealer's recommendation that "the mower is the best one available to do the job." Andrew was cutting his lawn when the mower blade flew off and seriously injured his leg.
   a. Andrew sues Whirlwind Mowers and asks damages based on negligence in producing the power mower. Is Whirlwind Mowers guilty of negligence? Explain your answer.
   b. The doctrine of *res ipsa loquitur* can often be applied to cases of this type. Show how this doctrine can be applied to this case. Your answer must include a definition of *res ipsa loquitur*.
   c. Explain the various types of damage awards that Andrew might receive if Whirlwind Mowers is found guilty of negligence.

4. Mathew was involved in an auto accident. He was judged to be 40 percent at fault in the accident, and the other party was judged to be 60 percent at fault. Mathew's actual damages were $50,000. Under a pure comparative negligence law, how much, if any, will Mathew receive for his injury?

5. Dr. Jones is an orthopedic surgeon. One patient required arthroscopic surgery on his right knee because of cartilage damage. When the patient awoke from surgery, he was surprised to see bandages on both knees. He was told that Dr. Jones made an incision on the wrong knee, realized his mistake, and

then proceeded with the surgery on the correct knee. In this case, Dr. Jones is presumed to be negligent under which legal doctrine?

6. Sarah is a college student who was late for class. She tried to cross the street in the middle of the block instead of at the intersection corner where a traffic light was in operation. A motorist hit her. Although Sarah placed herself in danger, she may be able to collect for her injuries if she can show that the motorist had an opportunity to avoid hitting her but failed to do so. Identify the legal rule that might apply in Sarah's case.

7. Elizabeth was injured in a work-related auto accident. She sued the other driver for her injuries, and the case went to court. While questioning Elizabeth, the defendant's attorney asked her if her injuries were paid under the company's group health insurance plan. Elizabeth's attorney immediately objected to the question. The judge ruled that the question was improper and instructed the jury to disregard the question. Based on the judge's reaction to the question, identify the legal rule that is in force in the jurisdiction where the trial took place.

8. Daniel believes that a chemical company is responsible for contaminating some land that he owns. He files suit against the chemical company. Rather than have the case go to court, the chemical company's attorney suggests arbitration to resolve the legal dispute. Explain how arbitration would work in this case.

INTERNET RESOURCES

- **Law Links** is a comprehensive legal resource guide for both attorneys and consumers. The site has a "Legal Subjects Index." Click on "Accident and Personal Injury Law" for introductory articles on accidents and personal injury. See also "Insurance Law." Visit the site at

  http://www.lawlinks.com

- **FreeAdvice.com** is a leading legal site for consumers and small businesses. The site provides general legal information to help people understand their legal rights on numerous legal topics but is not a substitute for an attorney. Check out "Accident & Personal Injury Law" and "Insurance Law." Visit the site at

  http://www.freeadvice.com

- **Nolo.com** is a leading source of self-help legal information for consumers, including topics dealing with personal injury law. Visit the site at

  http://www.nolo.com

- The **Legal Information Institute** of Cornell Law School provides detailed information on torts, personal injury, and products liability law. Legal topics are listed alphabetically under "Law About . . ." Click on Insurance for various topics and statutes dealing with insurance law. Related links are also given. Visit the site at

  http://www.law.cornell.edu

- The **RAND Institute for Civil Justice** publishes numerous high quality research studies that make recommendations for improving the civil justice system in the United States. Several studies examine many of the liability issues discussed in this chapter. Visit the site at

  http://www.rand.org/icj/

SELECTED REFERENCES

Dial, David, et al. "Tort Excess: The Necessity for Reform from a Policy, Legal and Risk Management Perspective," *Hot Topics & Insurance Issues,* Insurance Information Institute at http://www.iii.org/media/hottopics/

Hartwig, Robert P. *Liability Trends, Issues and Jury Verdicts: Impact on Insurance Liability and Excess Casualty Markets,* Insurance Information Institute, October 2003.

Lorimer, James J., et al. *The Legal Environment of Insurance,* 4th ed., vol. 2. Malvern, PA: American Institute for Chartered Property Casualty Underwriters, 1993.

"Medical Malpractice," *Hot Topics & Insurance Issues,* Insurance Information Institute, February 2004.

The I.I.I. Insurance Fact Book 2004. New York: Insurance Information Institute, 2004.

"Liability System," *Hot Topics & Insurance Issues,* Insurance Information Institute, February 2004.

Mallor, Jane P., et al. *The Legal Environment, First CPCU Edition.* New York: McGraw-Hill, 2000.

U.S. Tort Costs: 2002 Update, Trends and Findings on the Costs of the U.S. Tort System, Tillinghast-Towers Perrin, 2003.

"Verdict and Settlement Study Released: No Change in Median Medical Malpractice Jury Award, Plaintiff

Recovery Rate Up a Fraction," JVR *News Release,* March 20, 2003.

Walter, Michael A., and Russel L. Sutter. "A Fresh Look at the Tort System," Tillinghast-Towers Perrin, *Emphasis* (2003/1).

NOTES

1. According to the American Tort Reform Association, the District of Columbia, Alabama, Maryland, North Carolina, and Virginia still have contributory negligence doctrines in effect. See "The Liability System," *Hot Topics & Insurance Issues,* Insurance Information Institute, February 2004.

2. James J. Lorimer et al. *The Legal Environment of Insurance,* 4th ed., vol. 2 (Malvern, PA: America Institute for Property and Liability Underwriters, 1993), pp. 18–19.

3. This section is based on Donald J. Hirsch, *Casualty Claim Practice,* 6th ed. (Burr Ridge, IL: Irwin, 1996), pp. 58–62.

4. *Opinion of the Supreme Court of Nebraska, Case Title, Roger W. Heins, Appellant, v. Webster County, Nebraska, doing business as Webster County Hospital, Appellee.* Filed August 23, 1996, No. S-94-713.

5. Lorimer et al., p. 30.

6. Lorimer et al., p. 132.

7. Northeast Louisiana Chapter of the Society of CPCU, "Liability Concerns of Dog Owners and Their Insurers," *CPCU Journal,* vol. 45, no. 3 (September 1992), p. 184.

8. David Dial et al., "Tort Excess: The Necessity for Reform from a Policy, Legal and Risk Management Perspective," *Hot Topics & Insurance Issues,* Insurance Information Institute at http://www .iii.org/ media/hottopics.

9. "Liability System," *Hot Topics & Insurance Issues,* Insurance Information Institute, February 2004.

10. "Medical Malpractice," *Hot Topics & Insurance Issues,* Insurance Information Institute, February 2004.

11. "Verdict and Settlement Study Released: No Change in Median Medical Malpractice Jury Award, Plaintiff Recovery Rate Up a Fraction," JVR *News Release,* March 20, 2003.

12. "Latest Studies," *Insurance Digest,* Insurance Information Institute, June 2003.

13. Ibid.

14. *The I.I.I. Insurance Fact Book 2003* (New York: Insurance Information Institute, 2003), p. 114.

15. David Dial et al., "Tort Excess: The Necessity for Reform from a Policy, Legal and Risk Management Perspective," *Hot Topics & Insurance Issues,* Insurance Information Institute at http://www.iii.org/ media/hottopics/insurance/liability/tort/.

CHAPTER 8

HOMEOWNERS INSURANCE, SECTION I

"There's no place like home, after the other places close."

English Proverb

Vicki, age 38, is a single parent with a son, age 10. She recently purchased a small house in Red Oak, Iowa. Although money is tight, she feels that she can make the mortgage payments by following a strict budget. Shortly after moving in, a tornado touched down on her block. Although Vicki and her son were not injured, her house was badly damaged. It will cost $50,000 to repair the house. In addition, Vicki had to rent a furnished apartment for five months while the house was being repaired. Fortunately, she owned a homeowners policy, which covered most of the loss. Instead of being financially ruined, Vicki recovered from the disaster and moved on with her life.

Insurers pay similar homeowners claims daily. As a result, homeowners and renters are protected against the financial devastation that can result from a loss. This chapter discusses the popular homeowner policies that are used today to insure homes, condominiums, and personal property.

Each homeowners policy is divided into two major sections. Section I covers the property of the insured, which can include a home or condominium, other structures, and personal property. Section II provides personal liability insurance and covers medical payments to others. This chapter discusses only the Section I provisions. The Section II provisions are discussed in Chapter 9.

HOMEOWNERS 2000 PROGRAM

Homeowners insurance contracts were first introduced in the 1950s. Since that time, they have been revised several times. The following discussion is based on the Homeowners 2000 Program developed by the Insurance Services Office (ISO).[1]

ISO forms are widely used throughout the United States. Some insurers, however, use the homeowners forms designed by the American Association of Insurance Services (AAIS), which is an advisory organization similar to ISO. Other insurers use their own forms, which differ slightly from the ISO forms.

Eligible Dwellings

A homeowners policy on a private dwelling is designed for the owner-occupants of a one-, two-, three-, or four-family dwelling used exclusively for private residential purposes (although certain business occupancies are permitted, such as a home day care business and offices for business or profes-

sional purposes). A one-family dwelling may not be occupied by more than one additional family or two roomers or boarders. Separate homeowners forms are written for renters and condominium owners.

Overview of Homeowners Policies

The following forms are now used in the current ISO homeowners program:

- HO-2 (broad form)
- HO-3 (special form)
- HO-4 (contents broad form)
- HO-5 (comprehensive form)
- HO-6 (unit-owners form)
- HO-8 (modified coverage form)

Homeowners 2 (Broad Form) Homeowners 2 *is a named-perils policy that insures the dwelling, other structures, and personal property against loss from certain listed perils.* Covered perils include fire,

INSIGHT 8.1

Don't Ignore a Homeowners Policy if You Rent

A recent survey conducted for the Independent Insurance Agents & Brokers of America found that nearly two-thirds of the renters living in U.S. rental properties have no renters insurance.[a] However, replacing your property may cost more than you think if a loss occurs. An average two-bedroom apartment can easily contain personal property that may cost more than $20,000 to replace. For example, Bob and Jill graduated from college, married, and moved to Minneapolis, MN. Like most married couples, they wanted to save money for a down payment on a home. Unfortunately, a burglar broke into their apartment and stole a new big-screen television set, camcorder, stereo, diamond ring, camera, silverware, and cash hidden in a jewelry box. The loss totaled $9000. The couple had no insurance. When the couple sued the landlord on the grounds of inadequate security, a judge ruled the landlord was not liable. In short, the couple had to eat the loss.

Thousands of renters experience similar uninsured losses each year. HO-4 (contents broad form) is designed for renters and covers furniture, clothes, and most other personal property. The policy also provides a limited amount of insurance for building additions and alterations, such as wallpaper in the kitchen. Personal property is covered both on and off the premises for numerous perils, including fire and lightning, windstorm or hail, explosion, vandalism or malicious mischief, and theft. HO-4 does not cover the building, however, because the owner is responsible for insurance on the building.

If the tenant cannot live in the apartment because of a covered loss, such as a fire, the policy pays the additional living expenses of temporarily living in another apartment or house. It also provides at least $100,000 of personal liability insurance that covers the tenant and spouse if either is sued because of property damage or bodily injury to another person. Even fire legal liability is covered. For example, if a malfunctioning barbecue set on the patio causes a fire and damages the apartment, legal liability arising out of the fire would be covered.

[a] "Survey Says Two-Thirds of U.S. Renters Live Without Insurance," insurancejournal.com, National News, August 18, 2003.

lightning, windstorm, hail, explosion, and other perils. A complete list of covered perils can be found in Exhibit 8.1. HO-2 also covers the additional living expenses or fair rental value in the event a covered loss makes the dwelling uninhabitable.

Homeowners 3 (Special Form)   Homeowners 3 *insures the dwelling and other structures against risk of direct physical loss to property*. This means that all direct physical losses to the dwelling and other structures are covered, except those losses specifically excluded. Losses to the dwelling and other structures are paid on the basis of full replacement cost with no deduction for depreciation if certain conditions (discussed later) are met.

Personal property is covered for the same broad form perils listed in HO-2. Homeowners 3 is a popular and widely used form that is discussed in greater detail later in this chapter.

Homeowners 4 (Contents Broad Form)   Homeowners 4 *is designed for tenants who rent apart-*

ments, houses, or rooms. Homeowners 4 covers the tenant's personal property against loss or damage and also provides personal liability insurance. Personal property is covered for the same named perils listed in Homeowners 2. In addition, 10 percent of the insurance on personal property can be applied to cover any additions or alterations to the building made by the insured. Most renters need a homeowners policy (see Insight 8.1).

Homeowners 5 (Comprehensive Form)   The Homeowners 2000 Program reintroduced Homeowners 5, a policy form that provides open perils coverage ("all risks coverage") on both the buildings and personal property. HO-5 was withdrawn from use when the 1984 homeowners program was introduced. After that time, similar coverage was available by endorsing the HO-3 policy.

The HO-5 form insures the dwelling, other structures, and personal property against the risk of direct physical loss to property. This provision means that all direct physical losses are covered except those losses specifically excluded. Unlike the other home-owners forms that cover personal property only for certain named perils, HO-5 insures personal property for all direct physical losses except those losses specifically excluded.

Homeowners 6 (Unit-Owners Form)   Homeowners 6 *is designed for the owners of condominium units and cooperative apartments.* The condominium association carries insurance on the building and other property owned in common by the owners of the different units. Homeowners 6 covers the personal property of the unit owner for the same named perils listed in Homeowners 2. In addition, there is a minimum of $5000 of insurance on the condominium unit that covers certain property, such as built-in appliances, carpets, additional kitchen cabinets, and wallpaper. Finally, the policy pays a loss assessment charge of up to $1000 if the insured is assessed for a loss not covered by the condominium association's insurance.

Homeowners 8 (Modified Coverage Form)   Homeowners 8 *is a modified coverage form that covers loss to the dwelling and other structures on the basis of repair cost, which is the amount required to repair or replace damaged property using common construction materials and methods.* Payment is not based on replacement cost. In some states, actual cash value is used to determine the amount payable.

The HO-8 policy is designed for an older home whose replacement cost exceeds its market value. For example, an older home with a replacement cost of $250,000 may have a market value of only $150,000. Insurers will not insure a home for replacement cost when its current market value is substantially lower. Thus, to make homeowners coverage available for older homes and to reduce moral hazard, the HO-8 form has been developed.

The HO-8 policy provides only limited coverage for the theft of personal property. Theft coverage is limited to a maximum of $1000 per occurrence and applies only to losses that occur on the residence premises.

Exhibit 8.1 compares the various homeowners forms, basic coverages, and insured perils.

ANALYSIS OF HOMEOWNERS 3 POLICY (SPECIAL FORM)

In the remainder of this chapter, we examine the major provisions that appear in Section I in the Homeowners 3 policy (special form). As you study this section, you may find it helpful to refer to the Homeowners 3 policy in Appendix A at the end of the text.

Persons Insured

The definitions page in the homeowners policy defines the meaning of an "insured." The following persons are insured under the Section I coverages:

- *Named insured and spouse.* The named insured and spouse if a resident of the named insured's household are both covered.
- *Family members.* Relatives residing in the named insured's household are also covered.
- *Other persons under age 21.* Other persons under age 21 who are in the care of an insured are covered. This definition can include a foster child, a ward of the court, or a foreign exchange student.
- *Full-time student away from home.* A full-time student who was a resident of the named insured's household before moving out to attend school is also covered, provided the student is under age 24 and a relative of the named insured, or is under age 21 and in the care of an insured.

In addition to these people, the following persons are insured under the Section II coverages:

- *Any person legally responsible for covered animals or watercraft.* For example, if you leave your dog with a neighbor, the neighbor is covered if the dog bites someone. However, the policy excludes coverage for a person or organization having custody of animals or watercraft for business purposes, such as an operator of a dog kennel or a boat marina.
- *With respect to a motor vehicle to which the insurance applies, employees of the insured while working for the insured.* For example, if an employee injures someone while mowing the insured's lawn with a riding mower owned by the insured, the employee is covered under the insured's policy.

Exhibit 8.1
Comparison of ISO Homeowners Coverages

Coverage	HO-2 (broad form)	HO-3 (special form)	HO-4 (contents broad form)
	Section I Coverages		
A. Dwelling	Minimum varies by company.	Minimum varies by company.	Not applicable
B. Other structures	10% of A	10% of A	Not applicable
C. Personal property	50% of A	50% of A	Minimum amount varies.
D. Loss of use	30% of A	30% of A	30% of C
Covered perils	Fire or lightning Windstorm or hail Explosion Riot or civil commotion Aircraft Vehicles Smoke Vandalism or malicious mischief Theft Falling objects Weight of ice, snow, or sleet Accidental discharge or overflow of water or steam Sudden and accidental tearing apart, cracking, burning, or bulging of a steam, hot water, air conditioning, or automatic fire protective sprinkler system, or from within a household appliance Freezing of a plumbing, heating, air conditioning, or automatic fire sprinkler system, or of a household appliance Sudden and accidental damage from artificially generated electrical current Volcanic eruption	Dwelling and other structures are covered against risk of direct physical loss to property. All losses are covered except those losses specifically excluded. Personal property is covered for the same perils as HO-2.	Same perils as HO-2 for personal property
	Section II Coverages[a]		
E. Personal liability	$100,000	$100,000	$100,000
F. Medical payments to others	$1000 per person	$1000 per person	$1000 per person

[a] Minimum amounts can be increased.

Exhibit 8.1 (continued)
Comparison of ISO Homeowners Coverages

HO-5 (comprehensive form)	HO-6 (unit-owners form)	HO-8 (modified coverage form)
Section I Coverages		
Minimum varies by company.	$5000 minimum.	Minimum varies by company.
10% of A	Included in Coverage A.	10% of A
50% of A	Minimum amount varies.	50% of A
30% of A	50% of C	10% of A
Dwelling and other structures are covered against risk of direct physical loss to property. All direct physical losses are covered except those losses specifically excluded.	Same perils as HO-2 for personal property	Fire or lightning
		Windstorm or hail
		Explosion
		Riot or civil commotion
		Aircraft
		Vehicles
		Smoke
Personal property is covered against risk of direct physical loss to property. All direct physical losses are covered except those losses specifically excluded.		Vandalism or malicious mischief
		Theft (applies only to loss on the residence premises up to a maximum of $1000)
		Volcanic eruption
Section II Coverages[a]		
$100,000	$100,000	$100,000
$1000 per person	$1000 per person	$1000 per person

SECTION I COVERAGES

There are four basic coverages and several additional coverages in Section I of the Homeowners 3 policy:

- Coverage A: Dwelling
- Coverage B: Other structures
- Coverage C: Personal property
- Coverage D: Loss of use
- Additional coverages

Coverage A: Dwelling

Coverage A covers the dwelling on the residence premises as well as any structure attached to the dwelling. Thus, the home and an attached garage or carport would be insured under this section. Materials and supplies intended for construction or repair of the dwelling or other structures are also covered here.

Coverage A specifically excludes land. Thus, if the land on which the dwelling is located is damaged from an insured peril—such as an airplane crash—the land is not covered.

Coverage B: Other Structures

Coverage B insures other structures on the residence premises that are separated from the dwelling by clear space. This coverage includes a detached garage, tool shed, or horse stable. Structures connected to the dwelling only by a fence, utility line, or other similar connection are considered to be other structures.

The amount of insurance under Coverage B is based on the amount of insurance on the dwelling (Coverage A). Under the HO-3 policy, 10 percent of the insurance on the dwelling applies as additional insurance to the other structures. For example, if the home is insured for $200,000, the other structures are covered for $20,000.

Coverage B has several important exclusions. First, with the exception of a private garage, there is no coverage if the other structure is rented to someone who is not a tenant of the dwelling. For example, assume that Todd owns and occupies a home that has a horse stable on the premises. If Todd rents the horse stable to another person, he would have no coverage if the stable burns in a fire.

Second, other structures from which a business is conducted are not covered. Thus, if Charles operates an auto repair business in a detached garage, the garage is not covered if it is damaged in a tornado.

Third, other structures used to store business property are excluded. However, the current form will cover a structure that contains business property owned by the insured or tenant of the dwelling, provided such property does not include gaseous or liquid fuel, other than fuel in a permanently installed fuel tank in a vehicle parked in the structure. For example, if a professional painter stores ladders in a storage shed on the premises, the shed would be covered as long as it does not contain gaseous or liquid fuel (other than fuel in a parked vehicle).

Coverage C: Personal Property

Personal property owned or used by an insured is covered anywhere in the world. This provision also includes borrowed property. In addition, after a loss and at the named insured's request, the insurance can be extended to cover the personal property of a guest or resident employee while the property is in any residence occupied by an insured. For example, if you invite a guest to dinner in your home and the guest's coat burns in a fire, the loss can be covered under your policy.

The amount of insurance on personal property is equal to 50 percent of the insurance on the dwelling. That amount can be increased. For example, if Eric's home is insured for $200,000, an additional $100,000 of insurance applies to personal property. The full amount of insurance on personal property applies both on and off the premises anywhere in the world. *One exception is that if personal property is usually located at another residence, such as a cabin or vacation home, the off-premises coverage is limited to 10 percent of Coverage C, or $1000, whichever is greater.* For example, assume that Eric has $100,000 of insurance on his personal property. He could take that property on an extended trip to Europe and have coverage up to a maximum of $100,000 while it is off the premises. Assume by contrast that Eric owns a cabin or summer home on a river, and that furniture and fishing gear are normally kept there the entire year. In this case, a maximum of $10,000 (10% × $100,000) would apply to the loss of personal property at that location.

Exhibit 8.2
Special Limits of Liability

Type of Property	Amount
1. Money, bank notes, bullion, gold, silver, platinum, coins, medals, stored value cards, and smart cards	$200
2. Securities, valuable papers, manuscripts, personal records, passports, tickets, and stamps	$1500
3. Watercraft of all types	$1500
4. Trailers not used with watercraft of all types	$1500
5. Theft of jewelry, watches, furs, and precious and semiprecious stones	$1500
6. Theft of firearms and related equipment	$2500
7. Theft of silverware, goldware, platinumware, and pewterware	$2500
8. Property on the residence premises used primarily for business purposes	$2500
9. Property away from the residence premises used primarily for business purposes (except adaptable electronic equipment described in 10 and 11 below)	$500
10. Electronic apparatus, while in or upon a motor vehicle, but only if the apparatus is equipped to be operated by power from the motor vehicle's electrical system while still capable of being operated by other power sources	$1500
11. Electronic apparatus used primarily for business *while away from the premises and not in or upon a motor vehicle.* The apparatus must be equipped to be operated by power from the motor vehicle's electrical system while still capable of being operated by other power sources.	$1500

The 10 percent limitation does not apply to personal property that is moved from the residence premises because the residence premises is being repaired or remodeled and is not a fit place in which to live or store property. For example, the limitation does not apply to personal property located at a residence temporarily occupied by an insured while the residence premises is undergoing repair or remodeling and is not a fit place in which to live.

The limitation also does not apply to personal property in a newly acquired principal residence for 30 days from the time the named insured begins to move the property there. The amount of insurance under Coverage C applies in full to such personal property during the 30-day period. However, the insurer must be notified within 30 days for full protection to continue.

Special Limits of Liability Because of moral hazard and loss-adjustment problems, and a desire by the insurer to limit its liability, certain types of property have maximum dollar limits on the amount paid for any loss (see Exhibit 8.2).

The $200 limit on money includes coin collections. If you have a valuable coin collection, it should be scheduled and insured for a specific amount of insurance. A **schedule** is a list of covered property with specific amounts of insurance. A valuable stamp collection should also be insured separately because there is a $1500 limit on stamps.

Coverage on watercraft of all types is limited to $1500, including trailers, furnishings, equipment, and outboard motors. A boat with a value in excess of this limit should be insured separately.

The theft of jewelry and furs is limited to a maximum of $1500. Expensive jewelry and furs should be scheduled and specifically insured. In addition, there is a $2500 limit on the theft of firearms and a $2500 limit on the theft of silverware, goldware, platinumware, and pewterware. Thus, a valuable silverware collection should be specifically insured based on the current value of the collection. Note that the limits on jewelry and furs, guns, silverware, and goldware apply only to the theft peril. The full amount of insurance applies to losses from other covered perils.

Property used primarily for business purposes is limited to $2500 on the premises and $500 away from the premises. However, the $500 limit does not apply to adaptable electronic apparatus.

The homeowners policy provides $1500 of coverage on portable electronic apparatus used in motor vehicles that can also be operated independently from other power sources, such as certain portable television sets, cellular phones, fax machines, and CD players. *The limitation applies to electronic apparatus while in or upon a motor vehicle but only if the apparatus is equipped to be operated by power from the motor vehicle's electrical system while still capable of being operated by other power sources.* The limit applies to electronic equipment used either for personal or business use while in or upon a motor vehicle.

Finally, there is a $1500 limit on electronic apparatus used primarily for business while away from the residence premises and not in or upon a motor vehicle. The apparatus must be equipped to be operated by power from the motor vehicle's electrical system while still capable of being operated by other power sources. For example, a laptop computer used primarily for business purposes is covered up to $1500 if it is stolen while you are on a business trip.

Property Not Covered   Certain types of property are excluded under Coverage C. The following property is not covered.

1. *Articles separately described and specifically insured.* Coverage C does not cover articles separately described and specifically insured under either the homeowners policy or some other policy. The intent here is to avoid duplicate coverage. Thus, if jewelry or furs are specifically insured, Coverage C of the homeowners policy will not contribute toward the loss.

2. *Animals, birds, and fish.* Pets are excluded because they are difficult to value. Specialized coverages can be used to cover valuable animals, such as thoroughbred horses and pedigreed dogs.

3. *Motor vehicles.* Motor vehicles and their accessories and equipment are specifically excluded. Thus, cars, motorcycles, and motorscooters are excluded under the policy. Likewise, the theft of a car battery or hubcaps from the car would not be covered.

The exclusion also applies to electronic equipment and accessories designed to be operated solely by power from the electrical system of a motor vehicle, but only while the property is in or upon the motor vehicle. Accessories include antennas, tapes, wires, records, discs, and similar property that can be used with the electronic equipment while in or upon the vehicle. Thus, the theft of stereo tapes, CD decks, and similar property is excluded from coverage. You should remember that the exclusion of electronic equipment and accessories applies only while the property is in or upon the vehicle. A stereo tape or CB radio that is removed from the vehicle and taken into the house would be covered under the homeowners policy.

Finally, motor vehicles not required to be registered for use on public roads that are used solely to service the insured residence or designed to assist the handicapped are exempt from the exclusion. Thus, a garden tractor, riding lawn mower, or electric wheelchair would normally be covered under the policy.

4. *Aircraft and parts.* Aircraft and parts are specifically excluded. However, the policy does cover hobby or model aircraft not used or designed to carry people or cargo.

5. *Hovercraft and parts.* The Homeowners 2000 Program added a new exclusion of hovercraft and parts. A hovercraft is a self-propelled vehicle that generates a cushion of air on which to move.

6. *Property of roomers, boarders, and other tenants.* Property of roomers and boarders who are not

related to an insured is excluded. Thus, if the insured rents a room to a student, the student's property is not covered under the insured's homeowners policy. However, the property of roomers, boarders, and tenants related to an insured is covered.

7. *Property in a regularly rented apartment.* Property in an apartment regularly rented or being held for rental to others by an insured is specifically excluded. However, as discussed later, the homeowners policy provides some coverage for landlord's furnishings in an apartment on the residence premises that is regularly rented or held for rental.

8. *Property rented or held for rental to others off the residence premises.* Property away from the residence premises that is rented to others is specifically excluded. For example, if Jennifer owns a bike rental business, the bicycles are not covered under Jennifer's homeowners policy.

9. *Business records.* The homeowners policy excludes business data stored in books of account, drawings or other paper records, or in computers and related equipment. The overall effect of this exclusion is to eliminate coverage for the expense of reproducing business records.

10. *Credit cards, electronic fund transfer cards, or access devices.* Coverage of personal property does not include credit cards, electronic fund transfer cards, or access devices. There is some coverage for the unauthorized use of such cards under Additional Coverages (discussed later).

11. *Water or steam.* The Homeowners 2000 Program excludes coverage of water or steam as personal property. Thus, water or steam delivered through a public water main or from the insured's own well is now excluded. Also, water in a swimming pool is not covered either.

Coverage D: Loss of Use

Coverage D provides protection when the residence premises cannot be used because of a covered loss. The amount of additional insurance under this coverage is 30 percent of the amount of insurance on the dwelling (Coverage A). Three benefits are provided: *additional living expense, fair rental value, and prohibited use.*

Additional Living Expense If a covered loss makes the residence premises not fit to live in, the company pays the additional living expenses that the insured may incur as a result of the loss. **Additional living expense** *is the increase in living expenses actually incurred by the insured to maintain the family's normal standard of living.* For example, assume that the home Heather owns is damaged by a fire. If she rents a furnished apartment for three months at $800 per month, the additional living expense of $2400 would be covered.

Fair Rental Value The fair rental value is also paid when part of the premises is rented to others. **Fair rental value** *means the rental value of that part of the residence premises rented to others or held for rental less any expenses that do not continue while the premises are not fit to live in.* For example, Heather may rent a room to a student for a monthly rent of $200. If the home is uninhabitable after a fire, and it takes three months to rebuild, Heather would receive $600 for the loss of rents (less any expenses that do not continue). This payment would be in addition to the payment under the additional living expense coverage described earlier.

Prohibited Use Loss-of-use coverage also includes prohibited use losses. Even if the covered home is not damaged, a civil authority may prohibit the insured from using the premises because of direct damage to neighboring premises from an insured peril. The additional living expenses and fair rental value can be paid for up to two weeks. For example, Heather may be ordered out of her home by a fire marshal because the house next door is unstable after an explosion occurred. Her additional living expenses and fair rental value loss would be covered for up to two weeks.

Additional Coverages

In addition to basic Coverages A, B, C, and D, the HO-3 policy provides several additional coverages.

Debris Removal   The homeowners policy pays the reasonable expense of removing the debris of covered property damaged by an insured peril. Debris removal also pays the cost of removing volcanic ash or dust from a volcanic eruption that causes a direct loss to a building or property inside a building.

The cost of removing debris is included in the policy limit that applies to the damaged property. However, if the actual damage plus the cost of removal exceed the policy limit, an additional 5 percent of the amount of insurance is available for debris removal. For example, assume that a detached garage is covered for $30,000, and a total loss from a fire occurs. If the entire $30,000 is needed to rebuild the garage, up to $1500 is available for debris removal.

In addition, the Homeowners 2000 Program broadens the coverage for the removal of fallen trees from the premises. The policy covers the removal of trees owned by the named insured felled by windstorm or hail, or by the weight of ice, snow, or sleet. Coverage also applies to the removal of a neighbor's tree felled by a Coverage C peril. Coverage applies provided the tree (1) damages a covered structure, or (2) blocks a driveway and prevents a motor vehicle required to be registered for road use from entering or leaving the residence premises, or (3) blocks and prevents use of a ramp or access fixture designed to assist a handicapped person to enter and leave the dwelling. The maximum paid is limited to $1000 regardless of the number of fallen trees. No more than $500 of that limit is paid for the removal of any one tree.

Reasonable Repairs   The policy pays the reasonable cost of necessary repairs incurred by the insured to protect the property from further damage after a covered loss occurs. For example, a broken picture window may have to be temporarily boarded up immediately after a severe windstorm to protect personal property from further damage.

Trees, Shrubs, and Other Plants   The homeowners policy covers trees, shrubs, plants, or lawns on the residence premises against loss from a limited number of perils. *Coverage is provided only for fire, lightning, explosion, riot, civil commotion, aircraft, vehicles not owned or operated by a resident of the premises, vandalism, malicious mischief, or theft.* Note that *windstorm* is not listed. If an expensive

tree is blown over in a severe windstorm, the cost of replacing the tree is not covered.

The maximum limit for a loss under this coverage is 5 percent of the insurance that covers the dwelling. However, no more than $500 of that limit can be applied to any single tree, plant, or shrub (but not lawns).

Fire Department Service Charge   The policy pays up to $500 if the named insured is liable by a contract or agreement for a fire department charge when firefighters from another municipality are called to protect covered property from an insured peril. A deductible does not apply to this coverage.

Property Removal   If property is removed from the premises because it is endangered by an insured peril, direct loss from any cause is covered for a maximum of 30 days while the property is removed. Thus, furniture being moved and stored in a public warehouse because of a fire in the home is covered for a direct loss from any cause for a maximum of 30 days. For example, if an earthquake occurred and damaged the furniture stored in a warehouse after the fire, the loss caused by the otherwise excluded earthquake would be covered.

Credit Card, Electronic Fund Transfer Card or Access Device, Forgery and Counterfeit Money   If credit cards are stolen or lost and used in an unauthorized manner, any loss to the insured is covered up to a maximum of $500. Likewise, loss that results from the theft or unauthorized use of an insured's electronic fund transfer card is covered. If a forged or altered check results in a loss to the insured, it is also covered. If the insured accepts counterfeit money in good faith, that loss is covered, too. A deductible does not apply to this coverage.

Loss Assessment   The insurer pays up to $1000 for any loss assessment charged against the named insured by a corporation or association of property owners because of the direct loss to property collectively owned by all members. For example, property owners in a subdivision may belong to a homeowners association that collectively owns a neighborhood swimming pool with a small storage shed. Assume that lightning destroys the storage shed. If the homeowners association subsequently assesses each property owner his or her share of the loss, the insurer will pay the loss assessment charge that otherwise the property owner would have to pay.

Collapse   Collapse of a building is covered as an additional coverage. The policy defines collapse as an abrupt falling down or caving in of a building or any part of a building with the result that the building or part of the building cannot be occupied for its intended use.

Collapse of a building (or any part of a building) is covered only if the loss is caused by any of the following:

- Perils insured against in Coverage C
- Hidden decay, unless known to the insured prior to collapse
- Hidden insects or vermin damage, unless known to the insured prior to collapse
- Weight of contents, equipment, animals, or people
- Weight of rain that collects on a roof
- Use of defective materials or methods in construction, remodeling, or renovation if the collapse occurs during the course of construction, remodeling, or renovation

Glass or Safety Glazing Material   The policy covers the breakage of glass or safety glazing material that is part of a covered building, storm door, or storm window. Damage to covered property from the glass or safety glazing material is also covered. For example, if a baseball breaks a storm window, the glass damage is covered. If the shattering of glass also causes damage to a lamp near the window, the lamp damage would be covered.

Landlord's Furnishings   The homeowners policy will pay up to $2500 for loss to the named insured's appliances, carpets, and other household furnishings in each apartment on the residence premises that is regularly rented out or held for rental by an insured. The coverage applies to all losses caused by the perils insured against (Coverage C perils), with the exception of theft. For example, Susan has a furnished apartment on the second floor of her house that is rented to students. The appliances, carpets, and furniture inside the apartment are covered up to $2500.

Ordinance or Law   Many communities have building codes that may increase the cost of repairing or reconstructing a damaged building. For example, a new ordinance may require the use of copper pipes rather than galvanized or plastic pipes when the pipes must be replaced after a loss.

The named insured can now apply up to 10 percent of the amount of insurance under Coverage A to cover the increased costs of construction or repair because of some ordinance or law. If higher amounts of insurance are desired, an endorsement can be added to the policy. The coverage provided is additional insurance.

Grave Markers   The Homeowners 2000 Program added a new additional coverage for grave markers. Grave markers, including mausoleums, are covered for up to $5000 for loss caused by a peril insured against under Coverage C.

Deductible   A deductible of $250 applies to each covered loss. The deductible can be increased to reduce premiums. Increasing the deductible to $500 can reduce premiums by up to 12 percent; a $1000 deductible can reduce premiums by up to 25 percent. The deductible does not apply to a fire department service charge or to losses involving credit cards, ATM cards, forgery, or counterfeit money.

In 17 states that are vulnerable to catastrophes, insurers can use *percentage deductibles* rather than dollar deductibles to limit their exposure to catastrophe losses from natural disasters, such as hurricanes, windstorms, or hail. *Depending on the state and insurer, percentage deductibles for windstorm and hail losses, which may be mandatory in some coastal areas of a state, vary from 1 percent to 15 percent of the home's insured value:*[2] Depending on the state, policyholders may be given a "buy back option," which requires payment of a higher premium to have a traditional dollar deductible.

SECTION I PERILS INSURED AGAINST

In this section, we discuss the various perils, or causes of loss, to covered property.

Dwelling and Other Structures

The dwelling and other structures are insured against "risk of direct physical loss to property." *This means that all direct physical losses are covered except certain losses specifically excluded.* If a loss to the dwelling or other structure is not excluded, the loss is covered under the policy.

Excluded Losses Certain types of losses to the dwelling and other structures, however, are specifically excluded. They include the following:

1. *Collapse.* Losses involving collapse are specifically excluded, except those collapse losses covered under "additional coverages" discussed earlier.
2. *Freezing.* Freezing of a plumbing, heating, air conditioning, or automatic fire protection sprinkler system, or household appliance is not covered unless heat is maintained in the building, or the water supply is shut off and drained.

   However, if the building has an automatic sprinkler system, the insured is required to use reasonable care to continue the water supply and maintain heat in the building for the coverage to apply.
3. *Fences, pavement, patio, and similar structures.* Damage to a fence, pavement, patio, swimming pool, foundation, and similar structures is not covered if the damage is caused by freezing and thawing, or from the pressure or weight of water or ice.
4. *Dwelling under construction.* Theft to a dwelling under construction, or of materials and supplies used in construction, is not covered until the dwelling is both completed and occupied.
5. *Vandalism and malicious mischief.* Damage from vandalism, malicious mischief, or the breakage of glass and safety-glazing materials is not covered if the dwelling is vacant for more than 60 consecutive days immediately before the loss.
6. *Mold, fungus, or dry rot.* Loss to the dwelling or other structures from mold, fungus, or dry rot is excluded. However, an undetected loss—mold, fungus, or dry rot within the walls, ceilings, or beneath the floor caused by the accidental discharge of water or steam from a plumbing, heating, air conditioning, household appliance, or fire sprinkler system—is covered under the policy. In addition, loss from the discharge or overflow of water from a storm drain, water, or sewer pipe off the residence premises is covered as well.

   Payment of claims involving contamination from mold is a critical issue that has serious financial implications for insurers. It is one of the most important issues in homeowners insurance today (see Insight 8.2).
7. *Other exclusions.* The following losses are also excluded:
   - Wear and tear, marring, deterioration
   - Mechanical breakdown, latent defect, inherent vice (tendency of property to decompose)
   - Smog, rust or other corrosion, or dry rot
   - Smoke from agricultural smudging or industrial operations
   - Discharge, seepage, or release or escape of pollutants unless the discharge or release is caused by a Coverage C peril
   - Settling, cracking, shrinking, bulging, or expansion of pavements, patios, foundations, walls, floors, roofs, or ceilings
   - Birds, vermin, rodents, or insects
   - Animals owned or kept by an insured

Personal Property

Personal property (Coverage C) is covered on a named-perils basis. The policy pays for a direct physical loss to personal property from the perils discussed in the following section.

Fire or Lightning The homeowners policy covers a direct physical loss to property from fire or lightning. Direct physical loss means that fire or lightning is the proximate cause of the loss. **Proximate cause** *means there is an unbroken chain of events between the occurrence of a covered peril and damage or destruction of the property.* For example, assume a fire starts in the bedroom of your home. Firefighters spray the other rooms to keep the fire from spreading, and the water causes considerable damage to your books, furniture, and drapes. The entire loss is covered, including the water damage, because fire is the proximate cause of loss.

What is a fire? The homeowners policy does not define a fire; however, various court decisions have clarified its meaning. Two requirements must be met. *First, there must be combustion or rapid oxidation that causes a flame or at least a glow.* Thus, scorching, heating, and charring that occur without

INSIGHT 8.2

Mold Claims Remain a Critical Problem in Homeowners Insurance

A standard homeowners policy excludes damage from mold, rust, rot, and mildew. A homeowners policy covers mold contamination only if it results from a covered peril. For example, mold damage from a water pipe that bursts would be covered because water damage from a water pipe that bursts is a covered peril. However, mold damage caused by excessive humidity, water leaks, condensation, or flooding is considered a maintenance issue for the homeowner and is not covered.

The number of mold claims submitted to insurers has increased significantly in recent years. Possible reasons include construction defects in houses and lack of uniform inspection standards in some areas, which allow bacteria to grow; intense media coverage; considerable misinformation about health defects from mold; near hysteria by homeowners in some areas; exploitation of mold claims by trial attorneys; and erosion of the mold exclusion by juries or judicial interpretation.

Texas and California account for the majority of mold claims. Mold claims are also a serious problem in Florida, Arizona, and Nevada. *In Texas alone, mold claims increased*

1306 percent between the first quarter of 2000 and the fourth quarter of 2001 (see box). An average mold claim today costs about $35,000 and can easily exceed $100,000.

Homeowner insurers have experienced substantial underwriting losses in recent years. Mold claims and related water damage claims are major factors in these losses. Insurers are responding to the mold crisis by raising premiums substantially, by inserting clarifying language in their policies as to what is covered, or by excluding mold losses altogether. Some insurers may exclude mold losses but provide coverage by an endorsement with a higher premium.

In addition, many insurers will not renew a homeowners policy if the homeowner files a claim for water damage. Also, a property owner who purchases a home that has a history of water problems and previous claims may find it difficult to obtain a homeowners policy.

SOURCE: Adapted from Robert P. Hartwig, Insurance Information Institute, *Mold and Insurance: Is the Worst Behind Us?*, Casualty Actuarial Society, Seminar on Ratemaking, San Antonio, TX, March 27, 2003.

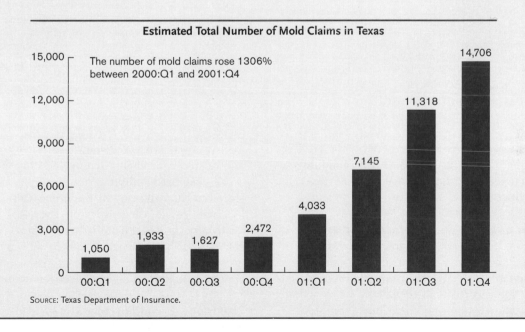

Estimated Total Number of Mold Claims in Texas

The number of mold claims rose 1306% between 2000:Q1 and 2001:Q4

00:Q1	1,050
00:Q2	1,933
00:Q3	1,627
00:Q4	2,472
01:Q1	4,033
01:Q2	7,145
01:Q3	11,318
01:Q4	14,706

SOURCE: Texas Department of Insurance.

a flame or glow are not covered. For example, a garment accidentally scorched by an iron is not covered because there is no flame or glow.

Second, the fire must be hostile or unfriendly. A hostile fire is outside its normal confines. A friendly

fire is intentionally started and is exactly where it is supposed to be. For example, the glow at the end of a lit cigar would be a friendly fire. However, if the burning ashes fell on a couch causing a fire, the fire would be hostile, and the loss would be covered.

INSIGHT 8.3

What Is Covered Under a Homeowners Policy if a Storm Occurs?

You probably know that ordinary homeowners policies don't cover flood damage. You need special insurance for that, available only through the National Flood Insurance Program. But your homeowners insurance may cover more storm and water damage than you think. "If you do have damage, don't make assumptions about what is covered and what is not," warns Jeanne Salvatore, spokeswoman for the Insurance Information Institute. "Call your agent immediately."

Here's how storm damage is usually handled, according to the Institute and officials at State Farm, the nation's largest homeowners insurer:

- A tree falls on your house. Your homeowners policy covers damage to the house and up to $500 to remove the tree.
- Your roof is damaged and rain ruins your floors and furniture. Your policy covers the roof, floor, and furniture.
- Flying debris breaks windows and rain damages the indoors. Again, your homeowners policy will pay for the windows and the rain damage.
- Flying debris lands in your pool, breaking tiles or the filter. The homeowners policy covers the damage.
- Pressure from waterlogged soil cracks the walls of your pool. The loss is not covered under your homeowners policy. Pools aren't covered by flood insurance, either.

- Your car is flooded inside your garage. Look to your auto insurance's comprehensive coverage for help.
- High winds knock out your electricity for days, ruining hundreds of dollars worth of food in your freezer. Your homeowners policy may cover it.
- Rising water floods your first floor. You're covered only if you have flood insurance.
- Sewers or drains back up into your house. Usually, you're covered under a homeowners policy only if you have a separate endorsement for sewer or drain backup. Flood insurance will cover the damage if there has been flooding locally.
- Your house is flooded, and then a broken gas line starts a fire. The fire triggers coverage under your homeowners policy.
- Part of your yard is washed away. Neither your homeowners nor a flood policy will pay.
- Soil is washed away from around your home's foundation, causing it to crack or shift. There is no coverage under your homeowners policy. A flood insurance policy would pay only if there was local flooding and the problem occurred within 72 hours of the water receding from your home.

SOURCE: Adapted from Elizabeth Razzi, "Water, Water Everywhere. (Brief Article)," *Kiplinger's Personal Finance Magazine,* May 2000.

The homeowners policy also covers the peril of lightning. For example, the cost of rebuilding a chimney damaged by lightning would be covered, even if no fire occurs.

Windstorm or Hail Windstorm or hail damage is also covered. However, damage to the interior of the building and its contents because of rain, snow, sand, or dust is not covered unless there is an opening in the roof or wall caused by wind or hail that allows the elements to enter. For example, if a window is left open, rain damage to a sofa is not covered under the HO-3 policy. But if the wind or hail should break the window, allowing rain to enter through the opening, the water damage to personal property inside the room would be covered.

An important exclusion applies to boats. Boats and related equipment are covered only while inside a fully enclosed building. For example, if a boat is stored in the driveway of the home and is damaged by a windstorm, the loss is not covered.

Many homeowners submit claims for windstorm and hail damage. Insight 8.3 discusses in greater detail the types of storm losses that are covered and excluded under a homeowners policy.

Explosion Broad coverage is provided for damage caused by an explosion. Any type of explosion loss is covered, such as a furnace explosion that damages personal property.

Riot or Civil Commotion Damage to personal property from a riot or civil commotion is covered.

Each state defines the meaning of a riot. It is usually defined as an assembly of three or more persons who commit a lawful or unlawful act in a violent or tumultuous manner, to the terror or disturbance of others. Civil commotion is a large or sustained riot that involves an uprising of the citizens.

Aircraft   Aircraft damage, including damage from self-propelled missiles and spacecraft, is covered. For example, if a commercial jet crashes into your residence, damage to your personal property is covered. Likewise, if a self-propelled missile from a nearby military base goes astray, the property is covered against loss.

Vehicles   Property damage from vehicles is covered. For example, if your suitcase, clothes, and camera are damaged in an auto accident, the loss is covered. Likewise, if you carelessly back out of the garage and run over your bicycle, the loss is covered.

Smoke   Sudden and accidental damage from smoke is covered, including emissions of smoke or fumes from a furnace or related equipment. For example, if the fireplace malfunctions and smoke pours into the family room, any smoke damage to the furniture, rugs, or drapes is covered. However, smoke damage from agricultural smudging or industrial operations is specifically excluded.

Vandalism or Malicious Mischief   If someone enters your home and intentionally damages your personal property, the loss is covered.

Theft   Theft losses are covered, including the attempted theft and the loss of property when it is likely that the property has been stolen.

Although coverage of theft is fairly broad, there are several exclusions. They include the following:

1. *Theft by an insured is excluded.* For example, if Danielle, age 16, steals $100 from her mother's purse before running away from home, the theft is not covered.
2. *Theft in or to a dwelling under construction,* or of materials and supplies used in the construction of a dwelling, is not covered until the dwelling is completed and occupied.

3. *Theft from any part of the premises rented to someone other than an insured is not covered.* For example, if the insured rents a room to a student, the theft of a radio owned by the insured and located inside the room would not be covered.

Several important exclusions also apply when the theft occurs away from the residence premises. They include the following:

1. *Temporary residence.* If property is located at any other residence owned, rented to, or occupied by an insured, the loss is not covered unless an insured is temporarily residing there. For example, Brian owns a cabin on the river. Theft of property inside the cabin is not covered unless Brian is temporarily residing there. He is not required to be physically present in the residence at the time of loss, but he must be temporarily living or residing there. For example, if he is fishing at the river when the theft occurs, the loss would be covered.

   In addition, *theft of personal property of an insured student while at a residence away from home is covered if the student has been there any time during the 60 days immediately preceding the loss.* For example, assume you are attending college and are temporarily living away from home. If your television set is stolen from your college residence, the loss is covered by your parent's HO-3 policy if you have been there any time during the 60-day period preceding the loss.
2. *Watercraft.* Theft of a boat, its furnishings, equipment, and outboard motor is excluded if the theft occurs away from the premises.
3. *Trailers and campers.* Theft of trailers or campers away from the premises is not covered. Trailers and campers can be covered under the personal auto policy, which is discussed in Chapter 10.

Falling Objects   Damage to personal property from falling objects is covered. However, loss to property inside the building is not covered unless the roof or outside wall of the building is first damaged by the falling object. For example, if a hand mirror on a stand falls and breaks, the loss is not covered. But if the mirror falls and breaks because the exterior of the dwelling is first damaged by a falling tree, the loss would be covered.

Weight of Ice, Snow, or Sleet Damage to indoor personal property resulting from the weight of ice, snow, or sleet is covered. For example, if the weight of snow causes the roof to sag, any damage to the personal property inside the dwelling would be covered.

Accidental Discharge or Overflow of Water or Steam If loss results from an accidental discharge or overflow of water or steam from a plumbing, heating, air conditioning, or automatic fire protective sprinkler system, or from a household appliance, the property damage is covered. For example, if an automatic dishwasher malfunctions and floods the kitchen, water damage to personal property, such as an area rug, would be covered. However, the cost of repairing the system or appliance from which the water or steam escapes is not covered.

Sudden and Accidental Tearing Apart, Cracking, Burning, or Bulging of a Steam, Hot Water, Air Conditioning, or Automatic Fire Protective Sprinkler System, or Appliance for Heating Water If any of these perils causes damage to personal property, the loss is covered. For example, damage to personal property from a hot water heater that suddenly cracks is covered.

Freezing of a Plumbing, Heating, Air Conditioning, or Automatic Fire Protective Sprinkler System, or Household Appliance Freezing is not covered unless the insured used reasonable care to maintain heat in the building, or shuts off the water supply and drains the system.

However, if there is an automatic sprinkler system in the building, the insured must use reasonable care to continue the water supply and maintain heat for coverage to apply.

Sudden and Accidental Damage from an Artificially Generated Electrical Current For example, an electrical power surge that causes an electric clothes dryer to burn out would be covered. However, loss to tubes, transistors, or electronic components that are part of appliances, computers, or home entertainment units is specifically excluded. Thus, a television picture tube that burns out is not covered.

Volcanic Eruption Loss resulting from a volcanic eruption is also covered. However, losses caused by earthquakes, land shock waves, or tremors are excluded.

SECTION I EXCLUSIONS

In addition to the specific exclusions previously discussed, several general exclusions appear in the policy.

Ordinance or Law

With the exception of the ordinance or law coverage described earlier under the additional coverages section, and glass replacement as required by law, the policy excludes loss due to any ordinance or law. However, as we noted earlier, if the amount of insurance provided under the additional coverages section is inadequate, higher amounts can be obtained by an endorsement to the policy.

Earth Movement

Property damage from earth movement is excluded. This includes damage from an earthquake, shock waves from a volcanic eruption, landslide, mudslide or mudflow, subsidence or sinkholes, or earth sinking or shifting. However, an ensuing loss caused by fire or explosion is covered. An earthquake endorsement can be added to the policy.

Water Damage

Property damage from certain water losses is specifically excluded. The following types of water damage losses are not covered:

- Floods, surface water, waves, tidal water, and overflow or spray from a body of water
- Water or water-borne material that backs up through sewers or drains or overflows from a sump
- Water or water-borne material below the surface of the ground that exerts pressure on or seeps through a building, sidewalk, driveway, foundation, swimming pool, or other structure

Power Failure

There is no coverage for loss caused by the failure of power or other utility service if the failure takes place off the residence premises. For example, if the contents of a freezer thaw and spoil because of the failure of an electrical power plant 10 miles away, the loss is not covered. However, if the power failure is caused by an insured peril on the residence premises, any resulting loss is covered. Thus, if lightning strikes the home and power is interrupted on the premises, the spoilage of food in a freezer is covered.

Neglect

If the insured neglects to use all reasonable means to save and preserve the property at or after the time of loss, the loss is not covered. For example, a broken picture window may have to be boarded up after a windstorm to protect personal property in the room from further damage.

War

Property damage from war is specifically excluded. War is commonly excluded in property insurance contracts.

Nuclear Hazard

Nuclear hazard losses are excluded, including nuclear reaction, radiation, or radioactive contamination. For example, if a radiation leak from a nuclear power plant contaminates your property, the loss is not covered.

Intentional Loss

An intentional loss is excluded. An intentional loss is a loss arising out of any act the insured commits or conspires to commit with the intent to cause a loss. For example, if the insured arranges to have his home burned to collect the claim payment, the loss is not covered.

Governmental Action

Loss due to governmental action is also excluded. Governmental action refers to the destruction, con-fiscation, or seizure of property by any governmental or public authority. For example, the house and cash of a drug dealer that are seized by drug enforcement officials would not be covered. However, the exclusion does not apply to acts ordered by a government or public authority to prevent the spread of a fire.

Weather Conditions

This exclusion applies only to weather conditions that contribute to a loss that would otherwise be excluded. For example, landslide damage caused by excessive rain and heavy winds is excluded under this provision. Likewise, flooding or earth movement caused by excessive rain is excluded. However, damage to a house caused solely by windstorm or hail would be covered.

Acts or Decisions

This exclusion applies to losses that result from the failure to act by any person, group, organization, or government body. For example, if a governmental unit fails to develop a plan to control flood losses, property damage from a flood that resulted from failure to develop a plan would not be covered.

Faulty, Inadequate, or Defective Planning and Design

Also excluded are losses that result from faulty or defective planning, zoning, design, workmanship, materials, or maintenance. For example, a completed house that pulls away from the foundation because of faulty design or poor construction would not be covered.

SECTION I CONDITIONS

Section I in the homeowners policy contains numerous conditions. The most important are discussed here.

Insurable Interest and Limit of Liability

If more than one party has an insurable interest in the property, the insurer's liability for any one loss is limited to each insured's insurable interest at the time of loss but not to exceed the maximum amount of insurance.

Duties After a Loss

The insured must perform certain duties after a loss occurs. The insurer has the right to deny coverage for a loss if the insured does not comply with his or her duties and such failure is prejudicial to the insurer. The following duties are required:

- *Give prompt notice.* The insured must give prompt notice to the insurer or an agent of the insurer. In case of a theft, the police must be notified as well. The card company must also be notified in case of loss or theft of a credit or ATM card.
- *Protect the property.* The insured must protect the property from further damage, make reasonable and necessary repairs to protect the property, and keep an accurate record of the repair expenses.
- *Prepare an inventory of damaged personal property.* The inventory must show in detail the quantity, description, actual cash value, and the amount of loss. Taking an inventory of your property before a loss occurs is highly advisable.
- *Exhibit the damaged property.* The insured may be required to show the damaged property to the insurer as often as is reasonably required. The insured may also be required to submit to questions under oath without any other insured being present and sign a sworn statement.
- *File a proof of loss within 60 days after the insurer's request.* The proof of loss must include the time and cause of loss, interest of the insured and all others in the property, all liens on the property, other insurance covering the loss, and other relevant information.

Loss Settlement

This section of the homeowners policy deals with the payment of losses. You should know how losses are paid under a homeowners policy.

Personal Property   Covered losses to personal property are paid on the basis of *actual cash value* at the time of loss but not to exceed the amount neces-sary to repair or replace the property. Losses to carpets, domestic appliances, awnings, and outdoor antennas and outdoor equipment are also paid on an actual cash value basis. In addition, loses to structures that are not buildings, as well as grave markers, are paid on an actual cash value basis.

Personal property can be insured for replacement cost by adding a replacement cost endorsement to the policy. Under this endorsement, there is no deduction for depreciation in determining the amount paid for a loss to personal property. You should consider insuring your personal property on the basis of replacement cost. Otherwise, if a loss occurs, you could pay a substantial amount of money out of pocket (see Insight 8.4).

Dwelling and Other Structures   Covered losses to the dwelling and other structures are paid on the basis of replacement cost with no deduction for depreciation. Replacement cost insurance on the dwelling is one of the most valuable features in a homeowners policy. If the amount of insurance carried is equal to at least 80 percent of the replacement cost of the damaged building at the time of loss, full replacement cost is paid with no deduction for depreciation up to the limits of the policy. **Replacement cost** *is the amount necessary to repair or replace the dwelling with material of like kind and quality at current prices.* For example, assume that a home has a current replacement value of $200,000 and is insured for $160,000. If the home is damaged by a tornado, and repairs cost $40,000, the full $40,000 is paid with no deduction for depreciation. If the home is totally destroyed, however, the maximum amount paid for the damage to the building is the face amount of the policy—in this case, $160,000.

A different set of rules applies if the amount of insurance is less than 80 percent of the replacement cost at the time of loss. Stated simply, if the insurance carried is less than 80 percent of the replacement cost, the insured receives the *larger* of the following two amounts:

(1) Actual cash value of that part of the building damaged

or

INSIGHT 8.4

The Big Gap Between Replacement Cost and Actual Cash Value Can Empty Your Wallet

If you own personal property, you should consider the big gap between replacement cost and actual cash value. *You stand to pay a large amount out of pocket because of depreciation if the loss payment is based on actual cash value.* The table below, based on the depreciation schedule of a large property and liability insurer, shows that the insured would receive $7790 (less the deductible) based on *replacement cost* compared with only $3967 based on *actual cash value.* Actual cash value is replacement cost less depreciation.

Item	Age	Replacement Cost	Depreciation	Actual Cash Value
Television set	5 years	$ 900	$ 450	$ 450
Sofa	4 years	1500	600	900
Draperies	2 years	2000	400	1600
5 women's dresses	4 years	500	400	100
3 men's shoes	2 years	200	133	67
3 end tables	15 years	1200	900	300
Refrigerator	10 years	800	560	240
Area rug	New	200	0	200
Cosmetics	6 months	200	180	20
Kitchen dishes	4 years	250	200	50
30 cans food	New	40	0	40
Total		$7790	$3823	$3967

NOTE: The above hypothetical losses show the effect of depreciation, which is based on age and condition of the property; the older the item, the greater is the amount of depreciation.

$$(2) \quad \frac{\text{Amount of insurance carried}}{80\% \times \text{Replacement cost}} \times \text{Loss}$$

For example, assume that a dwelling has a replacement cost of $200,000, but is insured for only $120,000. The roof of the house is 10 years old and has a useful life of 20 years, so it is 50 percent depreciated. Assume that the roof is severely damaged by a tornado, and the replacement cost of a new roof is $20,000. Ignoring the deductible, the insured receives the larger of the following two amounts:

(1) Actual cash value = $20,000 − $10,000
  = $10,000

$$(2) \quad \frac{\$120,000}{80\% \times \$200,000} \times \$20,000 = \$15,000$$

The insured receives $15,000 for the loss. The entire loss would have been paid if the insured had carried at least $160,000 of insurance.

With the exception of losses that are both less than 5 percent of the amount of insurance and less than $2500, the insured must actually repair or replace the property to receive full replacement cost. Otherwise, the loss is paid on the basis of actual cash value. However, the insured can submit a claim for the actual cash value and then collect an additional amount when the actual repair or replacement is completed, provided the additional claim is made within 180 days after the loss.

Extended and Guaranteed Replacement Cost A home may be damaged beyond repair in a major catastrophe, such as a hurricane or tornado. Also, there may be a shortage of lumber and other building materials after a catastrophe occurs, which can substantially increase the cost of rebuilding. Insuring your home for only 80 percent of replacement cost will not provide complete protection. Some insurers make available an **extended replacement cost endorsement,** which pays an extra 20 percent or more above the policy limits, depending on the insurer. The insured agrees to insure the dwelling for full replacement cost and must also notify the insurer if alterations increase the value of the dwelling.

A few insurers offer a **guaranteed replacement cost** policy. The insured agrees to insure the home to 100 percent of its estimated replacement cost rather than 80 percent. *If a total loss occurs, the insurer agrees to replace the home exactly as it was before the loss even if the replacement cost exceeds the amount of insurance stated in the policy.* For example, if the home is insured for $200,000 and it costs $250,000 to restore the home to its previous condition, the insurer will pay $250,000. Because of underappraising the value of the home by some insurance agents, price gouging by some contractors because of a shortage of building materials, inflation, and fraud in some cases, guaranteed replacement cost policies are rapidly disappearing.

Loss to a Pair or Set

In the event of **loss to a pair or set,** *the insurer can elect either to repair or replace any part of the pair or set or to pay the difference between the actual cash value of the property before and after the loss.* For example, assume that Kathy has a set of three matching wall decorations hanging on the wall in her living room, and one of the decorations is badly damaged in a fire. The insurer can elect either to replace or repair the damaged wall decoration or to pay the difference in the actual cash value of the set before and after the loss.

Appraisal Clause

The **appraisal clause** *is used when the insured and insurer agree that the loss is covered, but the amount of the loss is in dispute.* Either party can demand that the dispute be resolved by an appraisal. Each

party selects a competent and impartial appraiser. The appraisers then select an umpire. If they cannot agree on an umpire after 15 days, a judge in a court of record will appoint one. If the appraisers fail to agree on the amount of the loss, only their differences are submitted to the umpire. An agreement in writing by any two of the three is then binding on both parties. Each party pays the fee of his or her appraiser, and the umpire's fee is shared equally by both parties.

Other Insurance and Service Agreement

If other insurance covers a Section I loss, the insurer will pay only the proportion of the loss that its limit of liability bears to the total amount of insurance covering the loss. The pro rata liability clause was explained in Chapter 6.

The Homeowners 2000 Program added a new provision when a home warranty or service agreement covers the loss. Many homeowners purchase home warranty contracts or appliance service agreements that guarantee the repair or replacement of defective parts if certain conditions are met. The homeowners policy is excess over any amount payable under a home warranty or service agreement.

Suit Against the Insurer

No legal action can be brought against the insurer unless all policy provisions have been complied with, and legal action is started within two years after the loss occurs.

Insurer's Option

After giving written notice to the insured, the insurer has the right to repair or replace any part of the damaged property with like property. For example, assume that a television set is stolen. By giving written notice, the insurer can replace the stolen TV with a similar item rather than paying cash. Insurers often can purchase television sets, stereos, and other types of property from wholesale distributors at a lower cost than the insured would pay in the retail market. By exercising the replacement option, an insurer can meet its contractual obligation for a covered loss, but its loss settlement costs can be reduced.

Loss Payment

The insurer is required to make a loss payment directly to the insured unless some other person is named in the policy or is legally entitled to receive the loss payment. In many homeowners contracts, a mortgagee (lender) is named in the policy, which allows the mortgagee to receive a loss payment to the extent of its insurable interest. A legal representative of the insured is also entitled to receive a loss payment. For example, if Angela dies before receiving payment for a covered loss, the loss payment is made to the executor of her estate.

Abandonment of Property

The insurer is not obligated to accept any property abandoned by the insured after a loss occurs. The insurer has the option of paying for the damaged property in full and then taking the damaged property as salvage, or the insurer can elect to have the property repaired. However, the decision to exercise these options belongs to the insurer. For example, assume your personal property is insured for $50,000. A fire occurs, and the salvage value of the property after the loss is $10,000. The insurer can pay you $40,000, or it can take the damaged property and pay you $50,000. However, you cannot abandon the property to the insurer and demand payment of $50,000.

Mortgage Clause

The **mortgage clause** is designed to protect the mortgagee's insurable interest. The mortgagee usually is a savings and loan institution, commercial bank, or other lending institution that makes a loan to the mortgagor (home buyer) so that the property can be purchased. The property serves as collateral for the mortgage loan. If the property is damaged or destroyed, the collateral securing the loan is impaired, and the loan might not be repaid.

The mortgagee's insurable interest in the property can be protected by the mortgage clause that is part of the homeowner policy. *Under this provision, if the mortgagee is named in the policy, the mortgagee is entitled to receive a loss payment from the insurer to the extent of its interest, regardless of any policy violation by the insured.* For example, if Troy intentionally sets fire to his house, his loss is not covered because the fire is intentional. However, the mortgagee's insurable interest in the property is still protected. The loss payment would be paid to the mortgagee to the extent of the mortgagee's interest. The mortgagee is also entitled to a 10-day cancellation notice if the insurer decides to cancel.

In exchange for the guarantee of payment, the mortgage clause imposes certain obligations on the mortgagee. They are as follows:

- To notify the insurer of any change in ownership, occupancy, or substantial change in risk of which the mortgagee is aware
- To pay any premium due if the insured neglects to pay the premium
- To provide a proof-of-loss form if the insured fails to do so
- To give subrogation rights to the insurer in those cases where the insurer denies liability to the insured but must make a loss payment to the mortgagee

Policy Period

The policy period begins and ends at 12:01 A.M. standard time on the dates specified in the policy period. Only losses that occur during the policy period are covered.

Concealment or Fraud

There is no coverage for all insureds if any insured intentionally conceals or misrepresents any material fact, engages in fraudulent conduct, or makes false statements relating to the insurance. The provision applies both before and after a loss.

SECTION I AND II CONDITIONS

The homeowners policy contains several common conditions that apply to both Sections I and II. They are summarized as follows:

- *Liberalization Clause.* If the insurer broadens the coverage it offers without charging a higher premium within 60 days before inception of the policy or during the policy period, the broadened coverage applies immediately to the present policy. However, the liberalization clause does not apply to changes that are implemented with a general program revision that includes both a broadening and restriction of coverage.

- *Waiver or Change of Policy Provisions.* A waiver or change in any policy provision must be approved in writing by the insurer to be valid.

- *Cancellation.* The insured can cancel at any time by returning the policy or by notifying the insurer in writing when the cancellation is to become effective.

  The insurer can cancel under the following conditions:

  1. The premium is not paid. The insured must be given at least 10 days' written notice of cancellation.

  2. A new policy can be canceled for any reason if it has been in force for less than 60 days and is not a renewal policy. The insured must be given at least 10 days' notice of cancellation.

  3. If the policy has been in force for 60 or more days or is a renewal policy, the insurer can cancel if there is a material misrepresentation of fact that would have caused the insurer not to issue the policy, or if the risk has increased substantially after the policy was issued.

  4. If the policy is written for a period longer than one year, it can be canceled for any reason on the anniversary date by giving the insured at least 30 days' notice of cancellation.

- *Nonrenewal of the Policy.* The insurer has the right not to renew the policy when it expires. The insured must be given at least 30 days' notice before the expiration date if the policy is not renewed.

- *Assignment of the Policy.* The homeowners policy cannot be assigned to another party without the insurer's written consent. Thus, if Richard sells his home to Michelle, he cannot validly assign his homeowners policy to Michelle unless the insurer agrees to the assignment. The homeowners policy is a personal contract between the insured and insurer. The assignment provision allows the insurer to select its own insureds and provides some protection against moral hazard and adverse selection. However, after a loss occurs, the loss payment can be freely assigned to another party without the insurer's consent. The party who receives the payment does not become a new insured, and the risk to the insurer is not increased.

- *Subrogation.* A general principle is that an insured cannot unilaterally waive the insurer's right of subrogation against a third party who caused the loss without jeopardizing coverage under the policy. However, the homeowners policy contains an important exception to this general principle. The subrogation clause allows the insured to waive in writing, before a loss occurs, all rights of recovery against any person. For example, assume that Jerome lives in one unit of a duplex and rents out the other unit. The lease may state that Jerome as landlord waives his right of recovery against the tenant if the tenant should negligently cause a loss (such as a fire). The waiver would protect the tenant against a subrogation recovery by Jerome's insurer if the tenant should cause a loss. To be effective, however, the waiver must be in writing before a loss occurs.

  If the right of recovery is not waived, the insurer may require the insured to assign all rights of recovery against a third party to the extent of the loss payment. This provision allows the insurer to exercise its subrogation rights against a negligent third party who caused the loss.

- *Death of Named Insured or Spouse.* If the named insured or resident spouse dies, coverage is extended to the legal representative of the deceased but only with respect to the premises and property of the deceased. Coverage also continues for resident relatives who are insured under the policy at the time of the named insured or spouse's death.

CASE APPLICATION

Jack and Jane are married and own a home insured for $150,000 under an unendorsed HO-3 policy. The replacement cost of the home is $250,000. Personal property is insured for $75,000. Jane has jewelry valued at $10,000. Jack has a coin collection valued at $15,000 and a high-speed motorboat valued at $20,000.

a. Assume you are a financial planner who is asked to evaluate the couple's HO-3 policy. Based on the above facts, do you believe that their present coverages are adequate? If not, make several recommendations for improving the coverage.

b. A fire damaged one bedroom. The actual cash value of the loss is $10,000. The cost of repairs is $16,000. How much will the insurer pay for the loss?

c. A burglar broke into the home and stole a new television set, jewelry, and several paintings. The actual cash value of the stolen property is $4000. The cost of replacing the property is $9000. In addition, the coin collection was also taken. Indicate the extent, if any, to which an unendorsed HO-3 policy will cover the preceding losses.

d. Assume that Jack and Jane have a disagreement with their insurer concerning the value of the above losses. How would the dispute be resolved under their HO-3 policy?

e. Assume that Jane operates an accounting business from her home. Her home business office contains a computer used solely for business, office furniture, file cabinets, and other business personal property. Explain whether her HO-3 policy would cover business personal property used in a home business.

SUMMARY

- The homeowners policy can be used to cover the dwelling, other structures, personal property, additional living expenses, personal liability claims, and medical payments to others.

- Section I provides coverage on the dwelling, other structures, personal property, loss-of-use benefits, and additional coverages. Section II provides personal liability insurance to the insured and also covers the medical expenses of others who may be injured while on the insured premises or by some act of the insured or by an animal owned by the insured.

- The HO-2 policy (broad form) covers the dwelling, other structures, and personal property against loss on a named-perils basis.

- The HO-3 policy (special form) covers the dwelling and other structures against risk of direct physical loss to the described property. All losses to the dwelling and other structures are covered except those losses specifically excluded. Personal property is covered only on a named-perils basis.

- The HO-4 policy (contents broad form) is designed for renters. HO-4 covers the personal property of tenants on a named-perils basis and also provides personal liability insurance.

- The HO-5 policy (comprehensive form) insures the dwelling, other structures, and personal property against the risk of direct physical loss to property. All direct physical losses are covered except those losses specifically excluded.

- The HO-6 policy (unit-owners form) is designed for condominium owners. HO-6 covers the personal property of the insured on a named-perils basis. There is also a minimum of $5000 of insurance on the condominium unit that covers certain property, such as alterations, fixtures, and improvements.

- The HO-8 policy (modified coverage form) is designed for older homes. Losses to the dwelling and other structures are paid on the basis of repair cost, which is the amount required to repair or replace the property using common construction materials and methods. Losses are not paid based on replacement cost.

- The conditions section imposes certain duties on the insured after a loss to covered property occurs. The insured must give immediate notice of the loss; the property must be protected from further damage;

the insured must prepare an inventory of the damaged personal property and may be required to show the damaged property to the insurer as often as is reasonably required; and proof of loss must be filed within 60 days after the insurer's request.

- The replacement cost provision is one of the most valuable features of the homeowners policy. Losses to the dwelling and other structures are paid on the basis of replacement cost if the insured carries insurance at least equal to 80 percent of the replacement cost at the time of loss. Losses to personal property are paid on the basis of actual cash value. However, an endorsement can be added that covers personal property on a replacement cost basis.

- The mortgage clause provides protection to the mortgagee. The mortgagee is entitled to receive a loss payment from the insurer regardless of any policy violation by the insured.

KEY CONCEPTS AND TERMS

Additional living expense
Appraisal clause
Extended replacement cost endorsement
Fair rental value
Guaranteed replacement cost
Homeowners 2 (broad form)
Homeowners 3 (special form)
Homeowners 4 (contents broad form)
Homeowners 5 (comprehensive form)
Homeowners 6 (unit-owners form)
Homeowners 8 (modified coverage form)
Liberalization clause
Loss to a pair or set
Mortgage clause
Proximate cause
Replacement cost
Schedule

REVIEW QUESTIONS

1. Identify the basic types of homeowner policies that are used today.

2. Identify the persons who are an "insured" under a homeowners policy.

3. The Section I property coverages provide different types of coverages to an insured. For each of the fol-

lowing coverages, briefly describe the type of coverage provided, and give an example of a loss that would be covered.
   a. Coverage A—Dwelling
   b. Coverage B—Other Structures
   c. Coverage C—Personal Property
   d. Coverage D—Loss of Use
   e. Additional Coverages

4. a. Briefly describe the special limits of liability that apply to certain types of personal property.
   b. Why are these special limits used?

5. a. Coverage A and Coverage B under a Homeowners 3 policy insure the dwelling and other structures against "risk of direct physical loss." Explain the meaning of this term.
   b. Coverage C under a Homeowners 3 policy covers personal property on a named perils basis. List the various perils that are covered.

6. List the major exclusions that are found in Section I of the Homeowners 3 policy.

7. Briefly describe the duties imposed on the insured after a property loss occurs.

8. The Section I Conditions section of the Homeowners 3 policy deals with the payment of losses to an insured.
   a. How is the amount paid for a covered loss to personal property determined?
   b. How is the amount paid for a covered loss to the dwelling and other structures determined?

9. a. Describe the extended replacement cost endorsement that can be added to a Homeowners 3 policy.
   b. What is a guaranteed replacement cost policy?

10. A property owner typically gets a mortgage loan to purchase a house. Explain briefly how the mortgage clause protects the insurable interest of the lending institution (mortgagee).

APPLICATION QUESTIONS

1. Heather owns a home with a replacement cost of $400,000 that is insured under a Homeowners 3 policy for $280,000. The roof was badly damaged in a severe windstorm, and it will cost $20,000 to repair the roof. The actual cash value of the loss is $10,000.

Ignoring any deductible, how much will Heather collect for the loss?

2. Michelle purchased a Homeowners 3 policy with no special endorsements to cover her home and personal property. A fire occurred and destroyed a wide screen television set. Heather paid $4000 for the set new, and it was 25 percent depreciated when the fire occurred. The replacement cost of a similar television set is $5000. Ignoring any deductible, how much will Michelle collect for the loss?

3. Tom and Cindy Jones insured their home and personal property under an unendorsed Homeowners 3 policy. The home has a current replacement cost of $300,000. The policy contains the following limits:

    Coverage A $240,000
    Coverage B   24,000
    Coverage C   120,000
    Coverage D   72,000

   The home was badly damaged in a fire, and the family was forced to live in a motel for 60 days while their home was being rebuilt. Undamaged personal property was stored in a rental unit during the period of reconstruction. What dollar amount, if any, is payable under their Homeowners 3 policy for the following (ignore any deductible)?
   a. Three bedrooms were totally destroyed in the fire. The replacement cost of restoring the bedrooms is $80,000. The actual cash value of the loss is $50,000.
   b. Monthly mortgage payment of $1500 on their home
   c. Rental of motel room at $100 daily for 60 days
   d. Meals eaten in the motel restaurant for 60 days at an average cost of $60 daily (food costs at home average $20 daily)
   e. Rent for storing undamaged furniture in a rental unit while the home is being rebuilt, $200 monthly

4. Megan has her home and personal property insured under an unendorsed Homeowners 3 (special form) policy. Indicate whether each of the following losses is covered. If the loss is not covered, explain why it is not covered.
   a. Megan carelessly spills a can of paint while painting a bedroom. A wall-to-wall carpet that is part of the bedroom is badly damaged and must be replaced.
   b. Water backs up from a clogged drainpipe, floods the basement, and damages some books stored in a box.
   c. Megan's house is totally destroyed in a tornado. Her valuable Doberman pinscher dog is killed in the tornado.
   d. Smoke from a nearby industrial plant damages Megan's freshly painted house.
   e. Megan is on vacation, and a thief breaks into her hotel and steals a suitcase containing jewelry, money, clothes, and an airline ticket.
   f. Megan's son is playing baseball in the yard. A line drive breaks the living room window.
   g. A garbage truck accidentally backs into the garage door and shatters it.
   h. Defective wiring causes a fire in the attic. Damage to the house is extensive. Megan is forced to move into a furnished apartment for three months while the house is being rebuilt.
   i. Megan's son, age 20, is attending college but is home for Christmas. A stereo set is stolen from his dormitory room during his absence.
   j. During the winter, heavy snow damages part of the front lawn, and the sod must be replaced.
   k. During a windstorm, an elm tree is blown over.
   l. Carpeting is damaged from the overflow of water from a bathtub because Megan left the water running while answering the telephone.
   m. The home is badly damaged in a severe earthquake. As a result of the earthquake, the front lawn has a three-foot crack and is now uneven.
   n. An icemaker in the refrigerator breaks and water seeps into the flooring and carpets, causing considerable damage to the dwelling.

5. James has his home and personal property insured under a Homeowners 3 (special form) policy. The dwelling is insured for $120,000. The replacement cost of the home is $200,000. Indicate the extent to which each of the following losses would be covered under James's Homeowners 3 policy. (Ignore the deductible.)
   a. Lightning strikes the roof of the house and severely damages it. The actual cash value of the damaged roof is $10,000, and it will cost $16,000 to replace the damaged portion.
   b. A living room window is broken in a hailstorm. The drapes are water stained and must be replaced.

The actual cash value of the damaged drapes is $400. Replacement cost is $600.

c. The hot water heater explodes and damages some household contents. The actual cash value of the damaged property is $2000, and the cost of replacing the property is $3200.

6. Sarah owns a valuable diamond ring that has been in her family for generations. She is told by an appraiser that the ring has a current market value of $50,000. She feels that the ring is adequately insured because she owns a Homeowners 3 (special form) policy. Is Sarah correct in her thinking? If not, how would you advise her concerning proper protection of the ring?

7. Paul has his home and its contents insured under a Homeowners 3 (special form) policy. He carries $160,000 of insurance on the home, which has a replacement cost of $200,000. Explain the extent to which each of the following losses is covered. (Ignore the deductible.) If Paul's policy does not cover the loss or inadequately covers any of these losses, show how full coverage can be obtained.

a. Paul's stamp collection, which is valued at $5000, is stolen from his home.

b. Teenage vandals break into Paul's home and destroy a painting that has a market value of $1000.

c. A motorboat stored in the driveway of Paul's home is badly damaged during a hailstorm. The actual cash value of the damaged portion is $8000, and its replacement cost is $20,000.

8. Craig owns a home with a replacement cost of $200,000 that is subject to a $100,000 mortgage held by First Federal as the mortgagee. Craig has the home insured for $160,000 under the HO-3 policy, and First Federal is named as mortgagee under the Mortgage Clause. Assume there is a covered fire loss to the dwelling in the amount of $50,000. To whom would the loss be paid? Explain your answer.

INTERNET RESOURCES

- The **Insurance Information Institute** provides timely information on homeowners insurance and other personal property insurance coverages. Articles on homeowners insurance and other property and liability coverages can be accessed directly online. Visit the site at

  http://www.iii.org

- **Insure.com** provides up-to-date information, premium quotes, and other consumer information on homeowners insurance. In addition, the site includes timely information and news releases about events that affect the insurance industry. Visit the site at

  http://www.insure.com

- **Insurance.com** provides premium quotes on a variety of insurance products, including homeowners and renters insurance, auto insurance, life insurance, and health insurance. You can even get quotes on pet insurance. Visit the site at

  http://www.insurance.com

- **INSWEB** provides premium quotes on homeowners, auto, and other insurance products. You can comparison shop with ease from your computer. The site also provides articles from industry, consumer, and regulatory groups. Visit the site at

  http://www.insweb.com

- **Quicken.com** provides timely information on homeowners, condominium, renters, and auto insurance. The site also provides premium quotes for homeowners, auto, and life insurance, as well as other personal insurance lines. Visit the site at

  http://www.quicken.com/insurance

- The **National Association of Insurance Commissioners (NAIC)** has a link to all state insurance departments, which provide a considerable amount of consumer information on homeowners insurance. Click on State Insurance Web Sites. For starters, check out New York, Wisconsin, and California. Visit the site at

  http://www.naic.org

SELECTED REFERENCES

"Automated Underwriting Tools: Credit & CLUE," *Hot Topics & Insurance Issues,* Insurance Information Institute, March 2004.

"Catastrophes: Insurance Issues," *Hot Topics & Insurance Issues,* Insurance Information Institute, February 2004.

Fair, Isaac and Company, Inc. *Predictiveness of Credit History for Insurance Loss Relativities,* A Fair, Isaac Paper, October 1999.

Fire, Casualty & Surety Bulletins, Personal Lines volume, Dwelling section. Erlanger, KY: National Underwriter Company. The bulletins are updated monthly.

Hamilton, Karen L., and Cheryl L. Ferguson. *Personal Risk Management and Property-Liability Insurance,* First Edition. Malvern, PA: American Institute for Chartered Property Casualty Underwriters/Insurance Institute of America, 2002.

Hartwig, Robert P. "White Paper: The Use of Credit Information in Personal Lines Insurance Underwriting," *Hot Topics & Insurance Issues,* Insurance Information Institute, Insurance Issues Series, Vol. 1, No. 2, June 2003.

Wiening, Eric A., George E. Rejda, Constance M. Luthardt, and Cheryl L. Ferguson. *Personal Insurance,* First Edition. Malvern, PA: American Institute for Chartered Property Casualty Underwriters/Insurance Institute of America, 2002.

NOTES

1. The discussion of homeowners insurance in this chapter is based on the *Fire, Casualty & Surety Bulletins,* Personal Lines volume, Dwelling section (Erlanger, KY: National Underwriter Company); and the copyrighted homeowners forms drafted by the Insurance Services Office (ISO). The ISO forms and various policy provisions are used with the permission of ISO.
2. "Catastrophes: Insurance Issues," *Hot Topics & Insurance Issues.* (New York: Insurance Information Institute, February 2004).

Students may take a self-administered test on this chapter at
www.aw-bc.com/rejda

CHAPTER 9

HOMEOWNERS INSURANCE, SECTION II

"How to win in court: If the law is on your side, pound on the law; if the facts are on your side, pound on the facts; if neither is on your side, pound on the table."

Unknown

LEARNING OBJECTIVES

After studying this chapter, you should be able to

◆ Explain the personal liability coverage found in Section II of the homeowners policy.

◆ Explain the medical payments to others coverage found in Section II of the homeowners policy.

◆ Identify the major exclusions that apply to the Section II coverages in the homeowners policy.

◆ Explain the following endorsements that can be added to a homeowners policy:
  Inflation guard endorsement
  Personal property replacement cost endorsement

◆ Explain the important rules that consumers should follow when shopping for a homeowners policy.

Megan, age 25, graduated from a small Midwestern liberal arts college and accepted a job with a public relations firm in Atlanta, GA. She was anxious to start work so that she could pay off her student loans. She rented an apartment and carelessly started a grease fire when she was grilling steaks on the deck to her apartment. Her apartment and two adjacent apartments were severely damaged. The management company sued Megan for the fire loss and was awarded damages of $125,000. Megan did not own a homeowners policy, which would have paid a large part of the loss. Her goal of early repayment of her student loans received a serious setback.

Megan learned in a painful way the value of personal liability insurance. This chapter discusses the important provisions that appear in Section II of a homeowners policy. Section II provides personal liability insurance to the name insured and his or her family members and also covers the medical expenses of others who are injured by personal acts of an insured or by an animal owned by an insured.

The chapter also discusses several endorsements that can be added to a homeowners policy to broaden the coverages. It concludes with a discussion of important rules to follow when you shop for a homeowners policy.

PERSONAL LIABILITY INSURANCE

Personal liability insurance protects the named insured and family members against legal liability arising out of their personal acts. The insurer will provide a legal defense and pay those sums that an insured is legally obligated to pay up to the policy limit.[1] With the major exceptions of legal liability arising out of the negligent operation of an automobile, and business and professional liability, most personal acts are covered.

The Homeowners 2000 Program by the Insurance Services Office (ISO) made several changes to the Section II coverages. The following section discusses the latest edition of the Section II coverages in the homeowners policy.

Insuring Agreements

The Section II liability coverages in the homeowners policy provide the following two coverages:

- Coverage E: Personal liability, $100,000 per occurrence

- Coverage F: Medical payments to others, $1000 per person

Higher limits are available for a small additional premium.

Coverage E: Personal Liability Personal liability *insurance protects an insured when a claim or suit for damages is brought because of bodily injury or property damage caused by an insured's negligence.* If you are liable for damages, the insurer will pay up to the policy limits those sums that you are legally obligated to pay. Damages also include any prejudgment interest awarded against you.

The minimum amount of liability insurance is $100,000 for each occurrence. The insurance amount is a single limit that applies to both bodily injury and property damage liability on a per-occurrence basis. **Occurrence** *is defined as an accident, including continuous or repeated exposure to substantially the same general harmful conditions, which results in bodily injury or property damage during the policy period.* An occurrence can be a sudden accident, or it can be a gradual series of incidents that occur over time.

INSIGHT 9.1

Who Let the Dogs Out?—Avoid Being Bitten by a Lawsuit

Man's best friend is sinking its teeth into your homeowners insurance policy. *Dog bites now account for one-third of all homeowner's insurance liability claims, costing roughly $310 million, according to the Insurance Information Institute (I.I.I.).*

Approximately 4.7 million people are bitten by dogs annually, resulting in an estimated 800,000 injuries, fifty percent of which are to children under the age of 18. During 1979–1998, (the most recent numbers available), dog attacks killed more than 300 Americans. With 70 percent of the bites occurring on the dog owner's property, there clearly is a greater need for training.

Dog Owner's Liability

Any dog can hurt someone. Even normally docile dogs may bite when they are frightened or when protecting their puppies, owners, or food.

Under most state laws, if your dog bites someone, you are responsible for the expenses and damages. Homeowners and renters insurance policies typically cover dog bite liability, according to the I.I.I. Most policies provide $100,000 to $300,000 in liability coverage. If the claim is under your limit, your policy will pay. If it exceeds your limit, you are responsible for all damages above that amount, including legal expenses.

Most insurance companies insure homeowners with dogs. However, once your dog has bitten someone, the insurance company my suggest the homeowner find the dog a new home, charge a higher premium, nonrenew the homeowner's insurance policy, or exclude the dog from the coverage.

SOURCE: Adapted from "Who Let The Dogs Out?—Avoid Being Bitten With a Lawsuit, Warns the I.I.I.," Insurance Information Institute, *Press Releases*, May 6, 2002.

The insurer also agrees to provide a legal defense even if the suit is groundless, false, or fraudulent. The insurer has the right to investigate and settle the claim or suit either by defending you in a court of law or by settling out of court. As a practical matter, most personal liability suits are settled out of court. The insurer must defend you and cannot offer or tender its policy limits to be relieved of its duty to defend. Unless the claim is settled for a lessor amount, defense coverage continues until the policy limits are exhausted by payment of a judgment or settlement.

Personal liability coverage is broad. The following examples illustrate the types of losses covered:

- Your dog bites a small child; dog bites account for one-third of all homeowners liability claims (see Insight 9.1).
- While burning leaves in the yard, you accidentally set fire to your neighbor's house.
- A guest in your home trips on a torn carpet and sues you for bodily injury.
- You are shopping and carelessly break an expensive Chinese vase.

Personal liability insurance is based on legal liability. Before the insurer will pay any sums for damages, you must be legally liable. In contrast, medical payments to others, discussed next, is not based on negligence or legal liability.

Coverage F: Medical Payments to Others This coverage is a mini-accident policy that is part of a homeowners policy. Medical payments to others is not based on legal liability. The insured is not required to be legally liable for coverage to apply. In contrast, personal liability coverage discussed earlier requires the insured to be legally liable for the coverage to apply.

Medical payments to others *pays the reasonable medical expenses of another person who is accidentally injured either on an insured location, or by the activities of an insured, resident employee, or animal owned by or in the care of an insured.* This coverage can be illustrated by the following examples:

- A guest slips in your home and breaks an arm. Reasonable medical expenses are paid up to the policy limits.
- A neighbor's child falls off a swing in your backyard and is injured. The child's medical expenses are covered up to the policy limits.
- You are playing golf and accidentally injure another golfer.
- Your dog bites a neighbor. The neighbor's medical expenses are paid up to the policy limits.

The insurer will pay all necessary medical expenses incurred or medically ascertained within three years from the date of the accident. The medical expenses covered are the reasonable charges for medical and surgical procedures, X-rays, dental care, ambulances, hospital stays, professional nursing, prosthetic devices, and funeral services.

Medical payments coverage does not apply to you or to regular residents of your household, other than a residence employee. For example, a swing set in your backyard may collapse, and your daughter and a neighbor's child are injured. Only the medical expenses of the neighbor's child are covered. An exception is a residence employee who is injured on the premises. For example, a baby-sitter may burn her hand while cooking lunch for your children. Her medical expenses would be covered under the policy, unless the state's workers compensation law applies to the loss.

With respect to the medical expenses of others, the policy states the situations under which coverage applies. Medical payments to others applies only to the following persons and situations:

- To a person on the insured location (discussed later) with the insured's permission
- To a person off the insured location, if the bodily injury
  - Arises out of a condition on the insured location or the ways immediately adjoining
  - Is caused by activities of an insured
  - Is caused by a residence employee in the course of employment by an insured
  - Is caused by an animal owned by or in the care of an insured

Medical payments to others cover the medical expenses of a person who is accidentally injured while on an insured location with the permission of an insured. *Insured locations* include the following:

- Residence premises shown in the declarations
- Any other residence acquired during the policy period, such as a summer home
- Rented garage or storage unit
- Nonowned premises where the insured is temporarily residing, such as a motel room
- Vacant land other than farmland
- Land owned or rented to an insured on which a residence is being built for an insured

- Cemetery plots or burial plots
- Part of a premises occasionally rented to an insured for nonbusiness purposes, such as a hall rented for a wedding reception

Medical payments to others also covers injuries away from an insured location if the injury arises out of a condition on the insured location or ways immediately adjoining, or is caused by activities of the insured, by a resident employee in the course of employment by an insured, or by an animal owned or in the care of an insured. For example, coverage applies to a pedestrian who trips or falls on an icy sidewalk or street adjacent to the premises. Coverage also applies if an insured accidentally injures another player while playing basketball. Likewise, if a baby-sitter takes your children to a public park and accidentally injures another child, coverage applies. In a similar manner, if your dog escapes from a fenced yard and bites someone, coverage applies.

SECTION II EXCLUSIONS

The Section II coverages contain numerous exclusions. The Homeowners 2000 program revised the definitions, exclusions, and related exceptions for motor vehicles, watercraft, and aircraft, and it added a new exclusion for hovercraft liability (discussed later).

There are three sets of exclusions that apply to personal liability (Coverage E) and medical payments to others (Coverage F). One set of exclusions applies to both coverages; one set applies only to Coverage E; and one set applies only to Coverage F.

Motor Vehicle Liability Coverages E and F exclude liability arising out of motor vehicles if the involved vehicle is

- Registered for use on public roads or property
- Not registered for use on public roads or property but such registration is required by law or government regulation
- Used in an organized race or speed contest
- Rented to others
- Used to carry persons or cargo for a charge
- Used for any business purpose, except for a motorized golf cart while on a golfing facility

Thus, liability arising out of cars, trucks, motorcycles, mopeds, and motorbikes is not covered. In addition, if you are towing a boat trailer, horse trailer, or rental trailer, coverage does not apply. Coverage can be obtained by purchasing an auto insurance policy.

Certain vehicles, however, are exceptions to the preceding exclusion, and therefore, coverage applies. The preceding exclusion of motor vehicles does not apply to the following:

- *The vehicle is in dead storage on a insured location.* For example, a car may be on blocks in the insured's garage. A liability claim arising out of dead storage of the car is covered if the car is not subject to motor vehicle registration.
- *The vehicle is used solely to service an insured's residence.* For example, if a lawn mower is used solely at the insured's residence, coverage applies if an insured injures someone while using the mower.
- *The vehicle is designed to assist the handicapped.* For example, if a handicapped person injures someone while operating a motorized wheelchair, coverage applies.
- *The vehicle is designed for recreational use off public roads and is not owned by the insured, or it is owned by the insured, and the occurrence takes place on an insured location.* For example, property damage caused by the insured while operating a rented snowmobile would be covered. Also, an owned snowmobile used on an insured location would be covered.
- *A motorized golf cart owned by an insured is also covered.* The cart must be designed to carry no more than four people and must have a maximum speed of no more than 25 miles per hour. Coverage applies if the cart is on a golfing facility and is used to play golf or some other recreational activity allowed by the facility. Coverage also applies if the cart is used to travel to and from an area where motor vehicles or golf carts are parked or stored, or is used to cross public roads at designated points to access the facility. Finally, coverage applies at a private residential community, including its roads upon which a motorized golf cart can legally travel, which is subject to the authority of property owner's association and contains the insured's residence. Thus, if the insured has a home in a

private residential community that has a golf course and injures someone while driving the golf cart to the facility, coverage would apply.

Watercraft Liability   The Section II coverages exclude watercraft liability if the boat is used in an organized race or speed contest (except sailboats or a predicted log cruise), rented to others, used to carry people or cargo for a fee, or used for any business purpose.

Certain watercraft are exceptions to the preceding exclusion, and therefore coverage applies. Exhibit 9.1 indicates the types of watercraft covered under a homeowners policy and an example of each type.

Aircraft Liability   The Section II coverages exclude aircraft liability. An aircraft is any device used or designed to carry people or cargo in flight, such as an airplane, helicopter, glider, or hot air balloon. However, the exclusion does not apply to model or hobby aircraft not used or designed to carry people or cargo.

Hovercraft Liability   The Homeowners 2000 Program added a new exclusion for hovercraft liability. A hovercraft is defined as a self-propelled motorized ground effect vehicle and includes flarecraft and air cushion vehicles.

Expected or Intentional Injury   The Section II coverages do not apply to bodily injury or property damage that is expected or intended by an insured. For example, suppose a softball player intentionally hits the umpire with a bat, and it is clear that the player intended to injure the umpire. Any claim or suit for damages would not be covered.

The exclusion does not apply to bodily injury that results from the use of reasonable force by an insured to protect persons or property. Thus, if Mark injures a mugger who is trying to rob him, any resulting suit for damages would be covered.

Business Activities   Liability arising out of a business activity is excluded. A business is defined as a trade, profession, or occupation that the insured engages in on a full-time, part-time, or occasional basis. It also includes any other activity engaged in

Exhibit 9.1
Watercraft Exposures Covered by Section II of the HO-3 Policy

Covered Watercraft Liability Exposures	Examples
1. Watercraft that are stored	A 30-foot sailboat stored out of the water at a marina for the winter
2. Sailboats (with or without auxiliary power) shorter than 26 feet	A 17-foot catamaran owned by the insured
3. Sailboats (with or without auxiliary power) longer than 26 feet *not owned by or rented to* an insured	A 32-foot sailboat the insured borrowed from her brother for a vacation
4. Inboard or inboard-outdrive watercraft with engines of 50 horsepower or less that are *not owned by* an insured	A 50-horsepower inboard motor boat borrowed from a neighbor
5. Inboard or inboard-outdrive watercraft of more than 50 horsepower *not owned by or rented to* an insured	A 150-horsepower inboard motor boat borrowed from a neighbor
6. Watercraft with one or more outboard engines or motors with 25 total horsepower or less	A fishing boat with 15-horsepower motor, owned by the insured
7. Watercraft with one or more outboard engines or motors with more than 25 total horsepower that are *not owned* by an insured	A boat with 75-horsepower outboard motor, borrowed from a friend
8. Watercraft with outboard engines or motors of more than 25 total horsepower owned by an insured if acquired during the policy period. If the insured acquires such watercraft before policy period, they are covered only if the insured: • declares them at the policy inception, or • reports the intention to insure them within 45 days of acquiring them	A new boat with 100-horsepower outboard motor purchased by the insured after the effective date of the policy

Source: Eric A. Wiening, George E. Rejda, Constance M. Luthardt, and Cheryl L. Ferguson, *Personal Insurance,* First Edition. Malvern, PA.: American Institute for Chartered Property Casualty Underwriters/Insurance Institute of America, 2002, Exhibit 6-3, p. 6.10.

for money or other compensation. For example, if you operate a beauty shop in your home and carelessly burn a customer with a hair dryer, a lawsuit by the customer is not covered.

Certain activities, however, are not subject to the business exclusion:

- Activities for which no insured received more than $2000 in total compensation for the 12 months prior to the policy period
- Volunteer activities for which no money is received except for expenses
- Providing home care services without compensation, other than the mutual exchange of such services

- Providing home day care services to a relative

For example, a garage sale not conducted as a regular business, volunteer work for a local church, and baby-sitting by a grandmother for her grandchildren would be covered.

In addition, legal liability arising out of the rental of any part of the premises is excluded. For example, if you own a twelveplex apartment house that is rented to students, liability claims arising out of ownership of the apartment building are not covered.

There are several exceptions to the rental exclusion. First, if a house is occasionally rented and used only as a residence, coverage applies. For example, if a professor rents out his or her home while on sabbatical leave, coverage will still apply.

Coverage also applies if part of the residence is rented to others. For example, assume that you live in a duplex and rent the other unit to a single family. Liability coverage still applies if the renting family does not take in more than two roomers or boarders.

Coverage also applies if part of the insured residence is rented and used as an office, school, studio, or private garage. For example, if a room above a garage is rented to an artist who uses the room as a studio, the insured still has coverage for claims arising out of the rental.

Finally, coverage also applies to an insured under age 21 who is involved in a part-time or occasional self-employed business with no employees. For example, teenagers are covered while delivering newspapers, washing cars, cutting lawns, or babysitting.

Professional Services Legal liability arising out of professional services is excluded. Physicians and dentists are not covered for malpractice claims under the homeowners policy. Also, attorneys, accountants, nurses, architects, engineers, and other professionals are not covered for legal liability for rendering or failing to render professional services. The loss exposures involving professional activities are substantially different from those faced by the typical homeowner. For this reason, a professional liability policy is necessary to cover professional activities. Professional liability insurance is examined in greater detail in Chapter 14.

Uninsured Locations Liability arising out of the ownership or rental of a premises that is not an "insured location" is also excluded. The meaning of "insured location" has already been explained. Examples of uninsured locations would be farmland owned or rented by an insured, a principal or secondary residence owned by an insured other than the named insured or spouse, and land owned by the insured on which a 12-unit apartment is being built.

War Section II coverages exclude war, undeclared war, civil war, insurrection, rebellion, and other hostile military acts. The homeowners contracts also exclude liability arising out of the discharge of a nuclear weapon even if accidental.

Communicable Disease Exclusion Liability arising out of the transmission of a communicable disease by an insured is excluded under both personal liability insurance and medical payments to others. The exclusion applies to all communicable diseases and is not limited only to sexually transmitted diseases.

Sexual Molestation, Corporal Punishment, or Physical or Mental Abuse The homeowners policy excludes bodily injury or property damage liability arising out of sexual molestation, corporal punishment, or physical or mental abuse.

Controlled Substance Exclusion Liability arising out of the use, sale, manufacture, delivery, transfer, or possession of a controlled substance is specifically excluded. Controlled substances include methamphetamine, cocaine, LSD, marijuana, and all narcotic drugs. The exclusion does not apply to the legitimate use of prescription drugs by a person who is following the orders of a licensed physician.

Personal Liability Exclusions

Another set of exclusions applies only to personal liability (Coverage E).

Contractual Liability Contractual liability *means that an insured agrees to assume the legal liability of another party by a written or oral contract.* The policy excludes the following contractual liability exposures:

- *Liability of an insured for any loss assessment* charged against the insured as a member of any association, corporation, or community of property owners. However, an additional coverage (discussed later) provides $1000 of coverage for a loss assessment if certain conditions are met.
- *Liability under any contract or agreement is excluded.* However, the exclusion does not apply to written contracts that (1) directly relate to the ownership, maintenance, or use of an insured location, or (2) where the liability of others is assumed by the insured prior to an occurrence. Thus, there would be coverage for liability assumed under a written lease, an equipment rental agreement if the equipment is used to maintain the residence premises, or other written contracts

where legal liability of a nonbusiness nature is assumed by an insured prior to an occurrence.

Property Owned by the Insured *Property damage to property owned by the insured is also excluded.* Thus, if a teenage son accidentally breaks some furniture, the parents' claim for damages against their son would not be covered.

Property in the Care of the Insured *Damage to property rented to, occupied or used by, or in the care of the insured is not covered.* For example, if you damage an apartment that you are renting, a lawsuit by the landlord for the damage would not be covered.

The exclusion does not apply to property damage caused by fire, smoke, or explosion. For example, if you rent an apartment and carelessly start a fire, you can be held liable for the damage. In such a case, the homeowners policy would cover the property damage to the apartment up to the policy's liability limit.

Workers Compensation *There is no coverage for bodily injury to any person who is eligible to receive benefits provided by the named insured under a workers compensation, nonoccupational disability, or occupational disease law.* This is true if the workers compensation benefits are either mandatory or voluntary. In some states, domestic workers must be covered for workers compensation benefits by their employers; in other states, the coverage is voluntary.

Nuclear Energy *The homeowners policy excludes liability arising out of nuclear energy.* If any insured is involved in a nuclear incident, any resulting liability is not covered by the homeowners policy.

Bodily Injury to an Insured *There is no coverage for bodily injury to the named insured or to any insured as defined in the policy.* For example, if one spouse accidentally trips and injures the other spouse, the injured spouse cannot collect damages.

Medical Payments Exclusions

Another set of exclusions under Section II applies only to medical payments to others (Coverage F).

Injury to a Resident Employee Off an Insured Location *If an injury to a resident employee occurs off an insured location and does not arise out of or in the course of employment by an insured, medical payments coverage does not apply.* For example, if Tanya is employed by the insured as a cook and is injured in a car accident on her way home, her medical expenses are not covered.

Workers Compensation This exclusion is similar to the workers compensation exclusion discussed earlier under personal liability insurance. *Medical payments coverage does not apply to any person who is eligible to receive benefits provided by the named insured under a workers compensation, nonoccupational disability, or occupational disease law.* The injured employee's medical expenses should be covered by workers compensation insurance.

Nuclear Energy *Medical payments coverage does not cover any person for bodily injury that results from nuclear reaction, radiation, or radioactive contamination.*

Persons Regularly Residing on the Insured Location *Medical payments coverage does not cover injury to any person (other than a residence employee of an insured) who regularly resides on any part of the insured location.* Thus, a tenant injured in a household accident cannot receive payment for medical expenses. The intent here is to minimize collusion among household members.

SECTION II ADDITIONAL COVERAGES

A homeowners policy provides several additional coverages, including coverage for claim expenses, first-aid expenses, damage to property of others, and loss-assessment charges.

Claim Expenses

Claim expenses are paid as an additional coverage. The insurer pays the court costs, attorney fees, and other legal expenses incurred in providing a legal defense. The claim expenses are paid in addition to the policy limits for liability damages.

The insurer also pays the premiums on bonds required in a suit defended by the insurer. For example, a judgment may be appealed, and if an appeal bond is required, the insurer pays the premium.

Reasonable expenses incurred by the insured at the insurer's request to assist in the investigation and defense of a claim or suit are also paid. This obligation includes payment for the actual loss of earnings up to $250 per day. Finally, interest on a judgment that accrues after the judgment is awarded, but before payment is made, is also paid by the insurer.

First-Aid Expenses

The insurer pays any **first-aid expenses** incurred by the insured for bodily injury covered under the policy. For example, a guest may slip in your home and break a leg. If you call an ambulance to take the injured person to the hospital and are later billed for $400 by the ambulance company, this amount would be paid as a first-aid expense.

Damage to Property of Others

Damage to property of others *pays up to $1000 per occurrence for property damage caused by an insured*. The damaged property is valued on the basis of replacement cost. This coverage can be illustrated by the following examples:

- A son, age 10, accidentally breaks a neighbor's window while playing softball.
- At a party, you carelessly burn a hole in the owner's carpet with your cigarette.
- You borrow your neighbor's lawn mower and accidentally damage the blade by striking a rock.

The insured is not required to be legally liable for coverage to apply. The loss is paid even when there is no legal obligation to do so.

The purpose of this coverage is to preserve personal friendships and keep peace in the neighborhood. Also, in many states, the parents are held responsible for the property damage caused by a young child. If this coverage were not provided, the person whose property is damaged would have to file a claim for damages against the insured who caused the damage.

A maximum of $1000 is paid under this coverage. Amounts in excess of this limit are paid only by proving negligence and legal liability by the person who caused the damage.

Damage to property of others also contains a unique set of exclusions. The major ones are summarized as follows:

- *Property Covered Under Section I.* Property damage is excluded to the extent of any amount recoverable under Section I of the policy.
- *Intentional Property Damage by an Insured Age 13 or Older.* If the property damage is intentionally caused by an insured, age 13 or older, coverage does not apply. This exclusion is relevant to teenage vandalism, which is a serious national problem. Thus, if a teenager damages a plate-glass window with a slingshot, deliberately knocks over a mailbox, or maliciously damages a tree, the parents' policy will not cover the property damage.
- *Property Owned by an Insured.* Property damage to property owned by an insured is also excluded. For example, if a son damages some power tools owned by his parents, the damage would not be covered. However, coverage does apply if the property is rented. Thus, if you rent a portable television set and accidentally drop it, the damage is covered.
- *Property Owned by or Rented to a Tenant.* Coverage does not apply to property owned by or rented to a tenant of an insured or to a resident in the named insured's household.
- *Business Liability.* Property damage arising out of a business engaged in by an insured is excluded. Thus, if you operate a lawn-maintenance business and accidentally cut down a shrub while mowing a customer's lawn, the damage is not covered.
- *Act or Omission in Connection with the Premises.* Property damage caused by an act or omission in connection with a premises owned, rented, or controlled by the insured, other than an insured location, is not covered. For example, without an endorsement, farmland owned by the insured is not covered under the homeowners policy. Thus, if the insured should accidentally damage the tractor of the tenant who is farming the land, coverage does not apply.
- *Motor Vehicles, Aircraft, Watercraft, or Hovercraft.* Property damage that results from the ownership, maintenance, or use of a motor vehi-

cle, aircraft, watercraft, or hovercraft is not covered. For example, if you run over a neighbor's 10-speed bicycle with your auto, the loss is not covered.

Loss Assessment

The homeowners policy provides coverage of $1000 for certain loss assessments. Higher limits are available by endorsement. For example, assume that you belong to a homeowners association that rents a hall for a monthly meeting. Someone is injured at one of the meetings and is awarded a judgment of $110,000. If the association's liability policy has policy limits of only $100,000, the $10,000 balance will be split among the association members and each member would be assessed a portion of the $10,000 balance. The homeowners policy would pay your loss-assessment charge up to $1000.

ENDORSEMENTS TO A HOMEOWNERS POLICY

Some property owners have special needs or desire broader coverage than that provided by a standard homeowners policy. Numerous endorsements can be added to a homeowners policy to meet individual needs, including the following:

- Inflation guard endorsement
- Earthquake endorsement
- Personal property replacement cost loss settlement endorsement
- Scheduled personal property endorsement (with agreed value loss settlement)
- Personal injury endorsement
- Watercraft endorsement
- Home business insurance coverage endorsement

Inflation Guard Endorsement

Some homeowners are underinsured because inflation has increased the replacement cost of their home. If a loss occurs and you do not carry insurance at least equal to 80 percent of the replacement cost of the dwelling, you will be penalized because the full replacement cost will not be paid.

To deal with inflation, you should add an **inflation guard endorsement** to your homeowners policy if it is not included by your insurer. The inflation guard endorsement is designed for use with the ISO homeowner forms and provides for an annual pro rata increase in the limits of liability under Coverages A, B, C, and D. The percentage increase is selected by the insured, such as 4 percent or 6 percent. For example, if the policyowner selects a 6 percent inflation guard endorsement, the various limits are increased by 6 percent annually. This specified annual percentage increase is prorated throughout the policy year. Thus, a house originally insured for $200,000 would be covered for $206,000 at the end of six months.

Earthquake Endorsement

An **earthquake endorsement** can be added that covers earthquakes, landslides, volcanic eruption, and earth movement. A single earthquake is defined as all earthquake shocks that occur within a 72-hour period. A deductible must be satisfied. The base deductible is 5 percent of the limit that applies *either* to the dwelling (Coverage A) or to personal property (Coverage C), whichever is greater. There is a minimum deductible of $250. The deductible can be increased with a reduction in premiums. There is no other deductible that applies to an earthquake loss. The deductible does not apply to Coverage D (loss of use) and to additional coverages. In some states where earthquakes occur frequently, or the risk of an earthquake is high, higher deductibles of 10 to 25 percent are typically used.

Although earthquakes can cause catastrophic losses, a high percentage of property owners in earthquake zones do not have earthquake insurance. Insurers in California selling homeowners insurance must offer earthquake insurance on new policies, but the majority of homeowners do not carry earthquake insurance. The major reasons for their reluctance to purchase earthquake coverage are high cost, high deductibles, a mistaken belief that earthquakes will not occur, and the belief that the federal government will provide disaster relief.

After the earthquake in Northridge, California, in 1994, property insurers were reluctant to offer earthquake insurance because of the fear of bankruptcy. California insurers paid out more in earthquake claims than they collected in premiums for the previous 25 years.

As a result of the crisis in the homeowners insurance market, California enacted legislation in 1995 that allows insurers to offer a limited earthquake policy with a maximum deductible of 15 percent of the dwelling coverage.[2] A privately funded, state-run earthquake pool was also created to deal with the problem.

Personal Property Replacement Cost Loss Settlement Endorsement

An unendorsed homeowners policy pays losses to personal property on the basis of actual cash value. However, a **personal property replacement cost loss settlement endorsement** can be added to the policy. *Claims are paid on the basis of replacement cost with no deduction for depreciation.* The endorsement applies to personal property, awnings, carpets, domestic appliances, and outdoor equipment.

The replacement cost endorsement for personal property has several important limitations. The amount paid is limited to the *smallest* of the following amounts:

- Replacement cost at the time of loss
- Full repair cost
- Coverage C amount, if applicable
- Any special dollar limits in the policy (such as theft limits on jewelry, furs, and silverware)
- For loss to any item, the limit of liability that applies to the item.

If the cost to repair or replace exceeds $500, the property must actually be repaired or replaced to receive replacement cost. Otherwise, only the actual cash value is paid.

The replacement cost endorsement excludes certain types of property, such as antiques, fine arts, and similar property; collector's items and souvenirs; property that is not in good or workable condition; and obsolete property stored or not used.

As a general rule, you should consider adding the replacement cost endorsement for personal property to your homeowners policy. You usually cannot find used property that replaces exactly the property lost. Also, because of depreciation, the amount paid for a loss based on actual cash value policy is substantially less than that payable based on replacement cost. Most insureds typically are unaware of the big difference between replacement cost and actual cash value.

Scheduled Personal Property Endorsement (with Agreed Value Loss Settlement)

The homeowners policy has limits on the amounts paid for certain personal property losses. Also, insureds may desire broader coverage than the homeowners policy provides. If you own valuable jewelry, furs, silverware, cameras, musical instruments, fine arts, antiques, or a stamp or coin collection, you can list the property in a schedule and insure it for a specific amount agreed to by the insurer.

Under the scheduled **personal property endorsement (with agreed valued loss settlement)**, the insurer agrees to pay the stated amount for a scheduled item if a total loss occurs. The endorsement insures property against risks of direct physical loss, which means the property is insured on an "all risk," or "open perils" basis. *All direct physical losses to scheduled property are covered except those losses specifically excluded.* For example, if a diamond ring insured for $25,000 is stolen; the amount paid is $25,000. Likewise, if a grand piano insured for $75,000 is severely damaged in a tornado; the amount paid is $75,000.

Personal Injury Endorsement

The homeowners policy only covers legal liability arising out of bodily injury or property damage to someone else. Personal injury coverage, which should not be confused with bodily injury, can be added to the homeowners policy as an endorsement.

Personal injury means legal liability arising out of the following:

- False arrest, detention, or imprisonment
- Malicious prosecution
- Wrongful eviction, wrongful entry, or invasion of the right of private occupancy of a room, dwelling, or premises
- Oral or written publication of material that slanders a person or organization, or an organization's products or services
- Oral or written publication of material that violates a person's right to privacy

For example, if you have a person arrested who is later found innocent, or if you make false statements that damage a person's reputation, you may be liable for damages. These losses are not covered under a homeowners policy but would be covered by the personal injury endorsement.

Watercraft Endorsement

The **watercraft endorsement** covers watercraft that are otherwise excluded under the homeowners policy. The endorsement provides liability and medical payments coverage on any inboard or inboard-outdrive powered watercraft; sailing vessels 26 feet or more in length; and watercraft powered by one or more outboard motors exceeding 25 total horsepower.

Home Business Insurance Coverage Endorsement

A growing number of home owners operate a business out of their homes. A standard homeowners policy provides only limited coverage on business property, and legal liability arising out of a business operation is excluded. A **home business insurance coverage endorsement** can be added that covers both business property and legal liability arising out of a home-based business. This type of endorsement increases the coverage on business property on the residence premises from $2500 to the Coverage C limit on personal property. Coverage on business property away from the premises is increased from $500 to $5000. The endorsement also provides coverage for accounts receivable, valuable papers and records, and the loss of business income and extra expenses when loss from an insured peril causes the business to be suspended.

The home business insurance endorsement covers business liability loss exposures that are normally found in a commercial package policy for a business firm. Liability coverage includes (1) bodily injury and property damage liability, (2) personal and advertising injury, and (3) products and completed operations exposures associated with the home business. These coverages are discussed in Chapter 14.

In addition to the preceding endorsements, dozens of additional endorsements are available to meet the specific needs of homeowners. One new endorsement provides coverage for *identity theft*. Some insurers now include this coverage in their homeowner policies. Others sell the coverage either as a separate policy or as an endorsement to a homeowners or renters policy (see Insight 9.2).

COST OF HOMEOWNERS INSURANCE

As an informed consumer, you should understand how the cost of a homeowners policy is determined. Also, certain underwriting factors determine if an applicant for a homeowners policy is acceptable for insurance. Major rating and underwriting factors include the following:

- Construction
- Location
- Fire-protection class
- Construction costs
- Age of home
- Type of policy
- Deductible amount
- Insurance score
- CLUE report

Construction

Construction of the home is an extremely important rating factor. The more fire-resistant the home is, the lower the rate. Thus, wooden homes cost more to insure than brick homes. However, earthquake insurance costs are substantially less for wooden homes.

Location

Location of the home is another important rating factor. For rating purposes, the loss experience of each rating territory is determined. Insureds who reside in territories with high losses from fires, storms, natural disasters, or crime must pay higher rates than insureds who reside in low-loss territories.

Fire-Protection Class

The fire-protection class affects the rates charged. The Insurance Services Office (ISO) rates the quality of public fire departments from one to ten. A lower number results in a lower rate. Accessibility of the home to the fire department and water supply and fire hydrants is also important. Homes in rural areas generally have higher rates than homes in large cities.

Construction Costs

Construction costs have a significant effect on rates. The costs of labor and materials vary widely in the

INSIGHT 9.2

Identity Theft Insurance Can Protect Your Good Name

Identity theft occurs when a thief uses your name, driver's license, Social Security number, ATM account number, credit card number, or other identification for fraudulent purposes. The number of identity theft victims is much higher than originally believed. According to a Federal Trade Commission survey released in September 2003, 27.3 million Americans have been victims of identity theft in the last five years, including 9.9 million in the last year alone. According to the survey, last year's identity theft losses to business firms and financial institutions totaled almost $48 billion, and consumer victims reported $5 billion in out-of-pocket expenses.[a]

Consumers whose identities are stolen can spend months or even years and thousands of dollars trying to restore good name and credit record. Victims may lose job opportunities, be refused loans for education, housing, cars, or even be arrested for crimes they didn't commit. Victims often experience humiliation, anger, and frustration as they try to reclaim their identities and clean up their credit records. One student who experienced identity theft said the following: [b]

"My wallet was stolen in December 1998. There's been no end to the problems I've faced since then. The thieves used my identity to write checks, use a debit card, open a bank account with a line of credit, open credit accounts with several stores, obtain cell phones and run up huge bills, print fraudulent checks on a personal computer bearing my name, and more. I've spent the last two years trying to repair my credit report (a very frustrating process) and have suffered the ill effects of having a marred credit history. I've recently been denied a student loan because of inaccurate information on my credit report."

Identity theft insurance reimburses crime victims for the cost of restoring their identity and cleaning up their credit record. Insureds are reimbursed for lost wages, phone calls, notary and certified mailing costs, attorney fees with the prior consent of the insurer, and other specified expenses. Some insurers now include the coverage in their homeowners policies. Others make it available as a separate policy or as an endorsement to a homeowners policy. Coverage varies depending upon the insurer. One company provides expense reimbursement limits from $500 up to $25,000 per covered person to restore a victim's credit history. The following expenses are covered:

- Lost wages up to a certain limit because of time off to deal with identity theft

- Loan reapplication fees to reapply for loans turned down because of erroneous credit information that reflects the identity theft

- Phone charges for calling financial institutions, business firms, and law enforcement agencies to discuss the identity theft

- Certified mail and notary costs for completing and delivering fraud affidavits

- Attorney fees incurred with the insurer's prior consent because of the cost of defending suits brought incorrectly by business firms and collection agencies, removing criminal or civil judgments wrongly entered against the insured, and challenging information on a credit report.

[a] *FTC Releases Survey of Identity Theft in U.S. 27.3 Million Victims in Past 5 Years, Billions in Losses for Businesses and Consumers,* press release, September 3, 2003.

[b] Consumer complaint to the FTC, February 22, 2001.

United States. The higher the cost of repairing or rebuilding your home, the higher your premium is likely to be.

Type of Policy

The type of policy is extremely important in determining the total premium. The Homeowners 3 policy (special form) is more expensive than the Homeowners 2 policy (broad form) because the coverage is broader. The Homeowners 5 policy (com-

prehensive form) is the most expensive contract because the dwelling, other structures, and personal property are covered on an "all risk" or "open perils" basis. All direct physical damage losses are covered except those losses specifically excluded.

Deductible Amount

The deductible amount has an important effect on cost. The higher the deductible, the lower the premium. A flat $250 deductible applies to all covered

EXHIBIT **9.2**
Distribution of FICO Scores

Distribution of Borrower Credit Scores by Risk Tier		
Risk Tier	Credit Score – Banking	% of Borrowers
A (prime)–Good	660+	70%
A – Fair	620–659	18%
B	580–619	9%
C	550–579	2.7%
D	520–549	0.3%
Source: HSH Associates, National Home Equity Assoc.		

• 70% of borrowers have good credit
• They also tend to file fewer insurance claims

29%

20%

16%

11%   11%

7%

5%

1%

<= 499   500–549   550–599   600–649   650–699   700–749   750–799   800+

Higher Risk   Lower Risk

SOURCE: Excerpted from Robert P. Hartwig and Claire Wilkinson, *The Use of Credit Information in Personal Lines Insurance Underwriting*, Insurance Issues Series (New York: Insurance Information Institute, June 2003), Vol. 1, No. 2, Exhibit 2.

losses. The deductible can be increased with a reduction in premiums. The deductible does not apply to a fire department service charge, coverage for credit or ATM cards, scheduled property that is specifically insured, and the personal liability coverages under Section II.

Insurance Score

Many insurers also use the applicant's *credit record* for purposes of underwriting and rating. The applicant's credit record is used to determine an insurance score. An ***insurance score*** *is a credit-based score that is highly predictive of future claim costs.* Insurance scores predict the average claim behavior for a group of insureds with essentially the same credit history. Insureds as a group with poor credit and low insurance scores generally file more homeowner claims than insureds with good credit and higher insurance scores.

Several credit organizations calculate insurance scores for insurers. One of the most important is the

Fair, Isaac and Company (FICO). Exhibit 9.2 shows a distribution of FICO scores by Fair Isaac. The majority of consumers have good credit records.

Insurers claim there is a strong and statistically significant relationship between insurance scores and underwriting experience. The lower the insurance score, the more likely insureds as a group are likely to file homeowners claims. Actuarial studies generally support this conclusion. For example, one study by Tillinghast Towers-Perrin, a major actuarial consulting firm, examined the relationship between insurance scores and loss ratios (cost of claims filed relative to the premiums collected). Tillinghast reviewed nine samples of data from eight insurers. The study showed that in eight out of nine samples, the probability that a statistically significant correlation exists between insurance scores and loss ratios exceeded 99 percent. *That is, insureds with low insurance scores, as a group, accounted for a high proportion of the dollars paid out in claims.* Exhibit 9.3 shows the insurance scores and relative performance for three insurers from the Tillinghast

EXHIBIT **9.3**

Tillinghast Towers-Perrin Study: Relationship between Insurance Scores and Loss Ratio Relativities for Three Homeowners Insurers

Homeowners Company A

SOURCE: Tillinghast Towers-Perrin

Homeowners Company B

SOURCE: Tillinghast Towers-Perrin

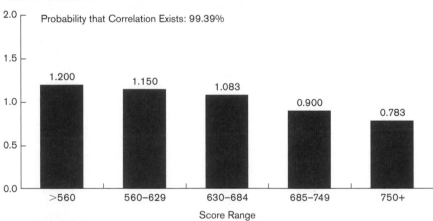

Homeowners Company C

SOURCE: Tillinghast Towers-Perrin

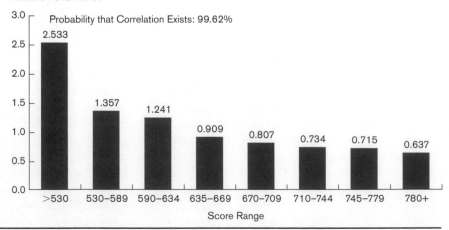

SOURCE: Excerpted from Robert P. Hartwig and Claire Wilkinson, *The Use of Credit Information in Personal Lines Insurance Underwriting,* Insurance Issues Series (New York: Insurance Information Institute, June 2003), Vol. 1, No. 2, Exhibits 8, 9, 10.

EXHIBIT 9.4
Tips for Buying a Homeowners Policy

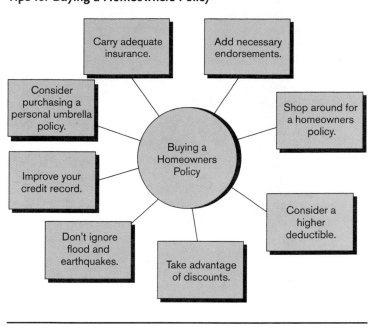

study. As insurance scores decline, claimants as a group tend to file more claims.

The use of credit records and insurance scores for purposes of rating and underwriting is highly controversial. The majority of states have enacted legislation that place restrictions on the uses of credit records by insurers. Chapter 28 discusses this important issue in greater detail.

CLUE Report

For purposes of underwriting and rating, insurers also use reports that reveal the prior claim history of a home. CheckPoint is a commercial firm that prepares Comprehensive Loss Underwriting Exchange (CLUE) reports for insurers that show the claims history on homes that insurers are asked to insure. CLUE is a database that contains up to five years of information on property claims, which includes the date of loss, type of loss, and amounts paid.

The use of CLUE reports is controversial. Critics claim that insurers are terrified of rising losses from mold claims and water damage and do not wish to insure homes that have experienced such

losses. Also, some homebuyers have found it difficult to obtain homeowners insurance because the CLUE report indicated a history of previous claims on the home they would like to purchase. Likewise, some homeowners selling their homes may not get the best price if the home has been rejected by several insurers because of previous claims.

However, in rebuttal, insurers claim they can rate more accurately based on personal characteristics and claim history by using CLUE reports in their underwriting. Also, insurers can detect fraudulent claims more easily and the filing of numerous claims by some homeowners.

Suggestions for Buying a Homeowners Policy

As a careful insurance consumer, you should remember certain suggestions when purchasing a homeowners policy (see Exhibit 9.4).

Carry Adequate Insurance   The first suggestion is to carry adequate amounts of property insurance on both your home and personal property. This consideration is particularly important if a room is added or home improvements are made because the value of the home may be substantially increased. The home must be insured for at least 80 percent of its replacement cost to avoid a penalty if a partial loss occurs. *However, you should seriously consider insuring your home for 100 percent of replacement cost.* Few homeowners can afford an additional out-of-pocket payment equal to 20 percent of replacement cost if a total loss occurs.

Add Necessary Endorsements Certain endorsements may be necessary depending on your needs, local property conditions, or high values for certain types of personal property. To deal with inflation, you should add an *inflation guard endorsement* to your homeowners policy if your insurer does not include it. An *earthquake endorsement* is desirable if you live in an earthquake zone. The *personal property replacement cost endorsement* is also desirable because you are indemnified on the basis of replacement cost with no deduction for depreciation. In addition, if you own valuable property, such as jewelry, furs, fine art, or a valuable coin or stamp collection, you should add the *scheduled personal property endorsement* to your policy. Each item is listed and specifically insured for a certain amount.

Shop Around for a Homeowners Policy Another important suggestion is to shop around for a homeowners policy. Because considerable price variation occurs among insurers, you can often reduce your homeowners premium by shopping around. Consequently, it pays to get a premium quote from several insurers before you buy a homeowners policy. Several Internet sites provide premium quotes (see Internet Resources). Some states also publish shoppers' guides to assist consumers who purchase homeowners policies. These guides indicate the wide variation in premiums charged by insurers. For example, the Arizona Department of Insurance surveyed 64 insurers in selected cities in Arizona to determine the cost of homeowners insurance. Exhibit 9.5 provides premium data for a $200,000 dwelling located in Phoenix, Arizona and Mesa, Arizona. *The cost difference between the lowest- and highest-cost policy for a $200,000 frame dwelling is 430 percent in Phoenix, Arizona and*

453 percent in Mesa, Arizona. Clearly, it pays to shop around.

Consider a Higher Deductible Another suggestion for reducing premiums is to purchase a policy with a higher deductible. The standard homeowners deductible is $250. *A higher deductible can substantially reduce your premiums.* You can usually get a discount of 10 percent with a $500 deductible and a 20 to 30 percent discount with a $1000 deductible. For example, Patrick has a $1000 deductible in his homeowners policy instead of the standard $250, which saves him $180 annually. In other words, Patrick saves $180 each year but loses only $750 in coverage. That additional $750 is very expensive coverage.

Take Advantage of Discounts When you shop for a homeowners policy, you should inquire whether you are eligible for any discounts or credits, which can further reduce your premiums. Insurers offer a wide variety of discounts based on numerous factors, including age of the home, fire and smoke alarms, sprinkler system, dead-bolt locks, and fire extinguishers.

The appendix to this chapter provides additional suggestions for reducing the cost of a homeowners policy.

Don't Ignore Flood and Earthquakes The homeowners policy covers hurricanes, tornadoes, windstorms, and fire losses. However, floods and earthquakes are specifically excluded. Although federal flood insurance is available, and an earthquake endorsement can be added to the homeowners policy, most property owners are not insured against these two perils. If you reside in a flood or earthquake zone, you should seriously consider covering such perils in your personal risk management program.

Improve Your Credit Record Another important suggestion is to improve your credit record. As noted earlier, many insurers use an applicant's credit record and insurance score for purposes of underwriting and rating. Applicants with good or superior credit records may be able to purchase a homeowners policy more cheaply than applicants with poor credit records. A good credit record can also result in lower interest rates on mortgage loans, auto loans, and credit cards.

EXHIBIT 9.5
2003 Homeowners Premium Comparison Survey

Name of Insurer	Phoenix, AZ		Mesa, AZ	
	Masonry	Frame	Masonry	Frame
Electric IC	$437.00 (1)	$437.00 (1)	$ 419.00 (3)	$ 419.00 (3)
Teachers IC	477.00 (2)	491.00 (2)	407.00 (2)	419.00 (2)
Horace Mann IC	498.00 (3)	512.00 (3)	423.00 (4)	436.00 (4)
Pharmacists Mutual IC	501.00 (4)	561.00 (5)	501.00 (7)	561.00 (9)
Armed Forces Ins Exchange	519.00 (5)	549.00 (4)	316.00 (1)	332.00 (1)
Austin Mutual IC	525.00 (6)	642.00 (9)	431.00 (5)	525.00 (6)
Amex AC	590.00 (7)	590.00 (6)	480.00 (6)	480.00 (5)
American National P&C Co	596.00 (8)	596.00 (7)	624.00 (16)	624.00 (14)
Western Home IC	620.00 (9)	620.00 (8)	568.00 (10)	568.00 (10)
Nationwide Mutual Fire IC	655.00 (10)	655.00(10)	556.00 (9)	556.00 (8)
Balboa IC	697.00 (11)	731.00 (14)	697.00 (29)	731.00 (31)
Union IC of Providence	703.00 (12)	703.00 (11)	585.00 (12)	585.00 (11)
Unigard Indemnity Co	716.00 (13)	716.00 (12)	697.00 (28)	697.00 (26)
Prudential P&C IC	723.00 (14)	781.00 (17)	617.00 (15)	665.00 (21)
Church Mutual IC	725.00 (15)	814.00 (21)	725.00 (33)	814.00 (44)
Centre IC	727.00 (16)	727.00 (13)	554.00 (8)	554.00 (7)
American Commerce IC	759.00 (17)	849.00 (24)	624.00 (17)	697.00 (25)
Amica Mutual IC	773.00 (18)	773.00 (15)	676.00 (26)	676.00 (23)
First American P&C IC	779.00 (19)	779.00 (16)	588.00 (13)	588.00 (12)
Liberty Mutual Fire IC	789.00 (20)	789.00 (18)	634.00 (21)	634.00 (17)
Kansas City Fire and Marine IC	791.00 (21)	807.00 (19)	608.00 (14)	618.00 (13)
Omaha P&C IC	810.00 (22)	810.00 (20)	642.00 (22)	642.00 (18)
Hartford Cas IC	816.00 (23)	846.00 (23)	704.00 (31)	729.00 (29)
Economy Premier AC	820.00 (24)	876.00 (28)	665.00 (25)	708.00 (27)
Country Mutual IC	839.00 (25)	839.00 (22)	628.00 (19)	628.00 (16)
United Services Auto Assoc	840.00 (26)	937.00 (36)	579.00 (11)	644.00 (19)
Allstate Indemnity Co	840.00 (27)	867.00 (26)	702.00 (30)	723.00 (28)
American National General IC	859.00 (28)	859.00 (25)	898.00 (51)	898.00 (47)
Metropolitan P&C IC	866.00 (29)	925.00 (35)	631.00 (20)	672.00 (22)
Allstate IC	867.00 (30)	897.00 (33)	751.00 (39)	776.00 (36)
Owners IC	871.00 (31)	957.00 (38)	883.00 (46)	967.00 (53)
Pacific Indemnity IC	872.00 (32)	872.00 (27)	1,075.00 (57)	1,075.00 (57)
Homesite Indemnity Co	874.00 (33)	913.00 (34)	712.00 (32)	743.00 (34)
Century-National IC	878.00 (34)	878.00 (29)	741.00 (36)	741.00 (33)
EMCASCO IC	878.00 (35)	878.00 (30)	733.00 (35)	733.00 (32)
Western Agricultural IC	880.00 (36)	880.00 (31)	652.00 (23)	652.00 (20)
Farmers IC of AZ	890.00 (37)	890.00 (32)	625.00 (18)	625.00 (15)
Standard Fire IC	904.00 (38)	992.00 (42)	664.00 (24)	730.00 (30)
Brotherhood Mutual IC	916.00 (39)	998.00 (44)	743.00 (37)	807.00 (41)
Newport IC	923.00 (40)	971.00 (39)	923.00 (52)	971.00 (54)

Exhibit 9.5 (continued)
2003 Homeowners Premium Comparison Survey

Name of Insurer	Phoenix, AZ		Mesa, AZ	
	Masonry	Frame	Masonry	Frame
Shelby Cas IC	$ 924.00 (41)	$ 975.00 (40)	$746.00 (38)	787.00 (38)
American International IC	947.00 (42)	947.00 (37)	808.00 (44)	808.00 (42)
Depositors IC	962.00 (43)	981.00 (41)	779.00 (42)	795.00 (39)
State Farm Fire and Cas Co	993.00 (44)	993.00 (43)	769.00 (41)	769.00 (35)
American Family Mutual IC	1,008.00 (45)	1,008.00 (45)	682.00 (27)	682.00 (24)
Hartford IC of the Midwest	1,009.00 (46)	1,067.00 (48)	762.00 (40)	804.00 (40)
Sentry Ins A Mutual Co	1,012.00 (47)	1,012.00 (46)	786.00 (43)	786.00 (37)
Hartford Underwriters IC	1,043.00 (48)	1,083.00 (52)	895.00 (48)	929.00 (49)
Twin City Fire IC	1,043.00 (49)	1,083.00 (53)	895.00 (49)	929.00 (50)
USAA Cas IC	1,053.00 (50)	1,175.00 (56)	727.00 (34)	809.00 (43)
Great American Spirit IC	1,062.00 (51)	1,062.00 (47)	927.00 (53)	927.00 (48)
Federal IC	1,075.00 (52)	1,075.00 (49)	1,075.00 (58)	1,075.00 (58)
Great Northern IC	1,075.00 (53)	1,075.00 (50)	1,075.00 (59)	1,075.00 (59)
Vigilant IC	1,075.00 (54)	1,075.00 (51)	1,075.00 (60)	1,075.00 (60)
Auto-Owners IC	1,102.00 (55)	1,206.00 (57)	1,117.00 (61)	1,219.00 (61)
CSE Safeguard IC	1,126.00 (56)	1,218.00 (58)	889.00 (47)	959.00 (52)
Employers Mutual Cas Co	1,141.00 (57)	1,141.00 (54)	954.00 (54)	954.00 (51)
American Fire and Cas Co	1,146.00 (58)	1,146.00 (55)	829.00 (45)	829.00 (45)
West American IC	1,237.00 (59)	1,237.00 (59)	895.00 (50)	895.00 (46)
Farmers Ins Exchange	1,374.00 (60)	1,374.00 (60)	977.00 (55)	977.00 (55)
Hartford Fire IC	1,401.00 (61)	1,455.00 (61)	1,197.00 (62)	1,244.00 (62)
Ohio Cas IC	1,480.00 (62)	1,480.00 (62)	1,069.00 (56)	1,069.00 (56)
American Bankers IC of FL	2,041.00 (63)	2,041.00 (63)	1,705.00 (63)	1,705.00 (63)
Scottsdale IC	2,315.00 (64)	2,315.00 (64)	2,315.00 (64)	2,315.00 (64)

Coverages: Dwelling Coverage C: $200,000; Other Structures Coverage: $20,000; Contents Coverage: $150,000; Additional Living Expense Coverage: $20,000; Personal Liability Coverage: $100,000; Medical Payments Coverage: $1,000; $250 Flat Deductible

Characteristics: A two-story, single family dwelling containing single-cylinder dead-bolt locks, one fire extinguisher, and two smoke detectors. Above average condition, masonry or frame (composition roof), built in October 2001.

Source: Excerpted from Arizona Department of Insurance, *2003 Homeowners Premium Comparison Survey*, January 2003 Edition.

Consider Purchasing a Personal Umbrella Policy A basic homeowners policy provides only $100,000 of personal liability insurance, which is insufficient in the event of a catastrophic liability loss. A **personal umbrella policy** provides an additional $1 million to $10 million of liability insurance after the underlying coverage is exhausted. It also covers liability arising out of personal injury, including coverage for libel, slander, and defamation of character. The homeowners policy does not cover personal injury without an endorsement. Also, in addition to coverage on your home and personal activities, the personal umbrella policy provides excess liability insurance on your cars, boats, and recreational vehicles. The personal umbrella policy is explained in greater detail in Chapter 12.

CASE APPLICATION

Lucia and her husband, Geraldo, recently purchased a new home for $250,000. The home is insured under an HO-3 policy for $250,000 with no endorsements attached. The home is located in an area where property values have increased steadily over the years. Lucia collects antiques for a hobby. Geraldo has a stamp collection that contains several rare stamps. The couple also owns a 30-foot sailboat that they use on weekends.

a. Assume you are a risk management consultant who has been asked to evaluate the couple's HO-3 policy. Identify three endorsements that Lucia and Geraldo may wish to purchase to modify their HO-3 policy.
b. Explain how the above HO-3 policy would be modified by each endorsement identified in your answer to (a) above.
c. For each of the following losses, indicate whether Section II of the homeowners policy would provide full coverage for the loss. If full coverage would not be provided, explain why.

(1) Lucia entertains members of a local garden club in her home and serves the guests a buffet luncheon. Two guests become seriously ill and sue Lucia, alleging she had served them contaminated food. The court awards each guest damages of $60,000.
(2) Geraldo is an architect. The roof of a new addition to a client's home collapses. The client alleges that the roof collapsed because of Geraldo's faulty design. The cost of rebuilding is $40,000. The client seeks to recover that amount from Geraldo.
(3) During a visit to a friend's home, Lucia accidentally breaks a figurine that she picked up to admire. The figurine has a value of $475. The friend is seeking payment from Lucia.

SUMMARY

- Section II of the homeowners policy protects the named insured, resident relatives, and other persons for legal liability arising out of their personal acts.

- Insured locations include the residence premises described in the declarations, other residences acquired during the policy period, a residence where the insured is temporarily residing, vacant land other than farmland, cemetery or burial plots, land on which a residence is being built, and occasional rental of a premises for other than business purposes.

- Personal liability insurance (Coverage E) protects the insured against a claim or suit for damages because of bodily injury or property damage caused by the insured's negligence. The company will defend the insured and pay out those sums that the insured is legally obligated to pay up to the policy limits.

- Medical payments to others (Coverage F) pays the reasonable medical expenses of another person who may be accidentally injured on the premises, or by the activities of an insured, resident employee, or animal owned by or in the care of an insured. It is not necessary to prove negligence and establish legal liability before the medical expenses are paid. The coverage does not apply to injuries of the named insured and regular residents of the household, other than residence employees.

- Section II also provides four additional coverages: (1) claim expenses, (2) first-aid expenses, (3) damage to property of others, and (4) coverage for a loss-assessment charge.

- Numerous endorsements can be added to a homeowners policy to meet individual needs, including the following:

    Inflation guard endorsement

    Earthquake endorsement

    Personal property replacement cost loss settlement endorsement

    Scheduled personal property endorsement (with agreed value loss settlement)

    Personal injury endorsement

    Watercraft endorsement

    Home business insurance coverage endorsement

- The cost of a homeowners policy depends on numerous factors. These include construction, location, fire-protection class, construction costs, age of the home, type of policy, deductible amount, insurer, and insurance score.

■ Certain suggestions should be followed when shopping for a homeowners policy:

>   Carry adequate insurance.
>
>   Add necessary endorsements.
>
>   Shop around for a homeowners policy.
>
>   Consider a higher deductible.
>
>   Take advantage of discounts.
>
>   Don't ignore floods and earthquakes.
>
>   Improve your credit record.
>
>   Consider purchasing a personal umbrella policy.

KEY CONCEPTS AND TERMS

Claim expenses
Contractual liability
Damage to property
  of others
Earthquake endorsement
First-aid expenses
Home business insurance
  coverage endorsement
Inflation guard
  endorsement
Insurance score
Medical payments
  to others
Occurrence

Personal injury
  endorsement
Personal liability
Personal property
  replacement cost loss
  settlement endorsement
Personal umbrella
  policy
Scheduled personal
  property endorsement
  (with agreed value loss
  settlement)
Watercraft endorsement

REVIEW QUESTIONS

1. What is the meaning of an *occurrence* under Section II of the homeowners policy?

2. Briefly explain the personal liability coverage (Coverage E) in Section II of the homeowners policy.

3. a. Briefly explain the coverage for medical payments to others (Coverage F) in Section II of the home owners policy.
   b. Identify the people who are covered for medical payments to others (Coverage F) in the homeowners policy.

4. Personal liability (Coverage E) and medical payments to others (Coverage F) provide protection to insureds at various insured locations. Identify the insured locations under Section II in the homeowners policy.

5. List the major exclusions that apply to personal liability (Coverage E) and medical payments to others (Coverage F) in the homeowners policy.

6. Section II of the homeowners policy provides several additional coverages. One additional coverage is called *damage to the property of others*. Briefly describe this coverage.

7. Briefly describe the following endorsements that can be added to a homeowners policy:
   a. Earthquake endorsement
   b. Inflation guard endorsement
   c. Personal property replacement cost loss settlement endorsement.
   d. Scheduled personal property endorsement (with agreed value loss settlement)

8. Homeowners insurance premiums are based on a number of factors. Identify the major factors that determine the cost of a homeowners policy.

9. Many insurers now use insurance scores in the underwriting and rating of a homeowners policy.
   a. Explain the meaning of an insurance score.
   b. Why do insurers use insurance scores in underwriting and rating?

10. Briefly explain the suggestions that consumers should follow when shopping for a homeowners policy.

APPLICATION QUESTIONS

1. Indicate whether the following losses are covered under Section II of the homeowners policy. Assume there are no special endorsements. Give reasons for your answers.
   a. The insured's dog bites a neighbor's child and also chews up the neighbor's coat.
   b. The insured accidentally injures another player while playing softball.
   c. A guest slips on a waxed kitchen floor and breaks an arm.
   d. A neighbor's child falls off a swing in the insured's yard and breaks an arm.
   e. The insured accidentally falls on an icy sidewalk and breaks a leg.
   f. While driving to the supermarket, the insured injures another motorist with the automobile.
   g. A ward of the court, age 10, in the care of the insured, deliberately breaks a neighbor's window.

h. The insured paints houses for a living. A can of paint accidentally falls onto a customer's roof and discolors it.

i. The insured falls asleep while smoking a cigarette in a rented hotel room, and the room is badly damaged by the fire.

j. The insured borrows a camera, and it is stolen from a motel room while the insured is on vacation.

2. Joseph is the named insured under a Homeowners 3 policy (special form) with a liability limit of $100,000 per occurrence and a $1000 limit for medical payments to others. For each of the following situations, explain whether the loss is covered under Section II of Joseph's homeowners policy.

a. Joseph is a self-employed accountant who works in his home. One of Joseph's clients sues him for negligence in the preparation of a tax return and is awarded a $3000 judgment against him.

b. A maid who works for Joseph's wife falls from a ladder in the home and is injured. The maid incurs medical expenses of $1000. The maid sues Joseph for $10,000 alleging that his wife is negligent. The employer does not have workers compensation insurance.

c. Joseph's 25-year-old son, who recently married and now lives in his own apartment, negligently kills another hunter in a hunting accident. The son is sued for $1 million in a wrongful-death accident.

3. Martha rents an apartment and is the named insured under a Homeowners 4 policy (contents broad form) with a liability limit of $100,000 per occurrence and $1000 medical payments. For each of the following situations, indicate to what extent, if any, the loss is covered under Section II of Martha's homeowners policy. Assume there are no special endorsements, and each situation is an independent event.

a. Martha is at a party at a friend's house. She accidentally burns a hole in the living room couch with her cigarette. It will cost $500 to repair the damaged couch.

b. Martha rents a snowmobile at a ski resort and accidentally collides with a skier. Martha is sued for $200,000 by the injured skier.

4. Explain whether each of the following losses would be covered under Section II in the homeowners policy. If the exposure is not covered, explain how coverage can be obtained.

a. The insured owns a restaurant in a large city. The insured is sued by several customers who allege they became seriously ill from a contaminated banana cream pie served at the restaurant.

b. While operating a 30-foot sailboat, the insured injures a swimmer.

c. The insured is sued by his ex-wife, who alleges her reputation has been ruined because the insured lied about her relationship with another man.

5. Jerry and Lois Gower own and operate the Gower Painting Co. The couple is insured under a Homeowners 3 policy with no special endorsements. The policy has a $100,000 per occurrence limit for personal liability and a $1000 limit for medical payments to others. For each of the following situations, indicate to what extent, if any, the loss is covered under Section II of their homeowners policy?

a. Jerry left a ladder standing against a house that he was painting. When Jerry went to lunch, a small child, age 7, climbed the ladder and was seriously injured when the ladder collapsed. Jerry is sued by the child's parents for $200,000. Jerry hired an attorney to defend him and was charged a fee of $10,000.

b. Lois accidentally fell off the roof of a second story house that she was painting and injured her leg. She incurred medical expenses of $3000.

c. The couple's daughter, Jennifer, age 22, attends college at a large Midwestern university. While playing softball, Jennifer made a hard slide into second base and accidentally injured the opposing player. The injured player claims Jennifer intended to injure her and sues Jennifer for $50,000.

d. Lois has a basset hound, Huey, for a pet. Huey is a friendly, docile dog and loves people. One morning, Lois carelessly left the backyard gate open, and Huey escaped from the fenced yard. A neighbor tried to catch the dog, and Huey bit him on the hand and leg. The neighbor incurred medical bills of $800. Lois is later sued by the neighbor for $50,000 when the dog bite became infected and did not heal.

e. Jerry is playing golf with a friend who is riding in a golf cart that he is operating. The cart overturned when Jerry carelessly ran into a wooded area on the outside of the fairway and hit a tree. Jerry's friend is seriously injured and sues Jerry for $150,000.

INTERNET RESOURCES

- The **Insurance Information Institute** provides timely information on homeowners insurance and other personal property insurance coverages. Articles on homeowners insurance and other property and liability coverages can be accessed directly online. Visit the site at

  http://www.iii.org

- **Insure.com** provides news, premium quotes, and other consumer information on homeowners insurance. The site also provides news releases about events that affect the insurance industry. Visit the site at

  http://www.insure.com

- **Insurance.com** provides premium quotes on a variety of insurance products, including homeowners and renters insurance, auto insurance, life insurance, and health insurance. You can even get quotes on pet insurance. Visit the site at

  http://www.insurance.com

- **INSWEB** provides premium quotes on homeowners, auto, and other insurance products. You can comparison shop from your computer. In addition, the site provides information and articles from industry, consumer, and regulatory groups. Visit the site at

  http://www.insweb.com

- **Quicken.com** provides timely information on homeowners, condominium, renters, and auto insurance. The site also provides premium quotes for homeowners, auto, and life insurance, as well as other personal insurance lines. Visit the site at

  http://www.quicken.com/insurance

SELECTED REFERENCES

"Automated Underwriting Tools: Credit & CLUE" *Hot Topics & Insurance Issues,* Insurance Information Institute, January 2004.

"Catastrophes: Insurance Issues," *Hot Topics & Insurance Issues,* Insurance Information Institute, February 2004.

Fair, Isaac and Company, Inc. *Predictiveness of Credit History for Insurance Loss Relativities,* A Fair, Isaac Paper, October 1999.

Fire, Casualty & Surety Bulletins, Personal Lines volume, Dwelling section. Erlanger, KY: National Underwriter Company. The bulletins are updated monthly.

Hamilton, Karen L., and Cheryl L. Ferguson. *Personal Risk Management and Property-Liability Insurance,* First Edition. Malvern, PA.: American Institute for Chartered Property Casualty Underwriters/Insurance Institute of America, 2002.

Hartwig, Robert P., and Claire Wilkinson. *The Use of Credit Information in Personal Lines Insurance Underwriting.* New York: Insurance Information Institute, Insurance Issues Series, Vol. 1, No. 2, June 2003.

"Homeowners Insurance, Rising Cost of Homeowners Insurance," *Facts and Statistics,* Insurance Information Institute.

Wiening, Eric A., George E. Rejda, Constance M. Luthardt, and Cheryl L. Ferguson. *Personal Insurance,* First Edition. Malvern, PA.: American Institute for Chartered Property Casualty Underwriters/ Insurance Institute of America, 2002.

NOTES

1. The discussion of Section II liability coverages in this chapter is based largely on the *Fire, Casualty & Surety Bulletins,* Personal Lines volume, Dwelling section (Erlanger, KY: National Underwriter Company); and the copyrighted HO-3 policy and subsequent coverage modifications drafted by the Insurance Services Office (ISO). The HO-3 policy and various policy provisions are used with the permission of ISO.

Students may take a self-administered test on this chapter at

www.aw-bc.com/rejda

APPENDIX

TWELVE WAYS TO SAVE MONEY ON A HOMEOWNERS POLICY*

The price you pay for your homeowners insurance can vary by hundreds of dollars depending on the size of your house and the insurance company from which you buy your policy. Here are 12 steps you can take to save money.

1. **Shop around.** Prices vary from company to company, so it pays to shop around. Get quotes from several companies. You can call the companies directly or access information on the Internet. The state insurance department may also provide comparisons of prices charged by major insurers.

   You buy insurance to protect you financially and provide peace of mind. It is important to pick a company that is financially stable. Check the financial health of insurance companies such as A. M. Best (http://www.ambest.com) and Standard and Poor's (http://www.standard andpoors.com/ratings).

   Get quotes from different types of insurance companies. Some sell through exclusive agents. These agencies have the same name as the insurance company. Some sell through independent agents who offer policies from several insurance companies. Others do not use agents. They sell directly to consumers over the phone or via the Internet.

   But don't shop price alone. You want a company that answers your questions and handles claims fairly and efficiently. Ask friends and relatives for their recommendations. Contact your state insurance department to find out whether it makes available consumer complaint ratios by company.

2. **Raise your deductible.** The higher your deductible, the more money you save on your premium. Consider a deductible of at least $500. If you can afford to raise it to $1000, you may save as much as 25 percent.

   If you live in a disaster-prone area, your insurance policy may have a separate deductible for damage from major disasters. If you live near the East Coast, you may have a separate windstorm deductible; if you live in a state vulnerable to hail storms, you may have a separate deductible for hail; and if you live in an earthquake-prone area, your earthquake endorsement has a deductible.

3. **Buy your home and auto policies from the same insurer.** Most companies that sell homeowners

*This appendix is adapted from "How Can I Save Money?" Insurance Information Institute, http://www.iii.org/individuals/homei/hbs/save/

insurance also sell auto and umbrella liability insurance. (An umbrella liability policy will give you extra liability coverage.) Some insurance companies will reduce your premium by 5 percent to 15 percent if you buy two or more insurance policies from them. But make certain this combined price is lower than buying individual coverages from different companies.

4. **Make your home more disaster-resistant.** Find out from your insurance agent or company representative what you can do to make your home more resistant to windstorms and other natural disasters. You may be able to save on premiums by adding storm shutters and shatter-proof glass, reinforcing your roof, or buying stronger roofing materials. Older homes can be retrofitted to make them better able to withstand earthquakes. In addition, consider modernizing your heating, plumbing, and electrical systems to reduce the risk of fire and water damage.

5. **Don't confuse what you paid for your house with rebuilding costs.** The land under your house isn't at risk from theft, windstorm, fire, and the other perils covered in your homeowners policy. So don't include its value in deciding how much homeowners insurance to buy. If you do, you'll pay a higher premium than you should.

6. **Ask about discounts for home security devices.** You can usually get discounts of at least 5 percent for a smoke detector, burglar alarm, or dead-bolt locks. Some companies may cut your premiums by as much as 15 percent or 20 percent if you install a sophisticated sprinkler system and a fire and burglar alarm that rings at the police, fire, or other monitoring stations. These systems aren't cheap, and not every system qualifies for a discount. Before you buy one, find out what kind your insurer recommends, how much the device would cost, and how much you'd save on premiums.

7. **Seek out other discounts.** Many companies offer discounts, but they don't all offer the same discount or the same amount of discount in all states. Ask your agent or company representative about discounts available to you. For example, if you're at least 55 years old and retired,

you may qualify for a discount of up to 10 percent at some companies. If you've completely modernized your plumbing or electrical system recently, some companies may also provide a price break.

8. **See if you can get group coverage.** Does your employer administer a group insurance program? Check to see if a homeowners policy is available and is a better deal than you can find elsewhere. In addition, professional, alumni, and business groups may offer an insurance package at a reduced price.

9. **Stay with the same insurer.** If you've been insured with the same company for several years, you may receive a discount for being a long-term policyholder. Some insurers will reduce premiums by 5 percent if you stay with them for three to five years and by 10 percent if you're a policyholder for six years or more. To ensure you're getting a good deal, periodically compare this price with the prices of policies from other insurers.

10. **Review policy limits and the value of your possessions annually.** You want your policy to cover any major purchases or additions to your home. But you don't want to spend money for coverage you don't need. If your five-year-old fur coat is no longer worth the $5000 you paid for it, you'll want to reduce or cancel your floater (extra insurance for items whose full value is not covered by standard homeowners policies) and pocket the premium savings.

11. **Look for private insurance if you are in a government plan.** If you live in a high-risk area—one that is especially vulnerable to coastal storms, fires, or crime—and you've been buying your homeowners insurance through a government plan, find out from insurance agents, company representatives, or your state department of insurance which insurance companies might be interested in your business. You may find there are steps you can take that will allow you to buy insurance at a lower price in the private market.

12. **When you're buying a home, consider the cost of homeowners insurance.** The price you pay

for homeowners insurance depends in part on the cost of rebuilding your home and the likelihood that it will be damaged by natural disasters or burn down. You may pay less if you buy a house close to a fire hydrant or in a community that has a professional rather than a volunteer fire department. It may also be cheaper if your home's electrical, heating, and plumbing systems are less than 10 years old. If you live in the East, consider a brick home because it's more wind-resistant. If you live in an earthquake-prone area, look for a wooden frame house because it is more likely to withstand this type of disaster. Choosing wisely could cut your premiums by 5 percent to 15 percent.

Remember that flood insurance and earthquake damage are not covered by a standard homeowners policy. If you buy a house in a flood-prone area, you'll have to pay for a flood insurance policy that costs an average of $400 a year. The Federal Emergency Management Agency provides useful information on flood insurance on its Web site (http://www.fema.gov). A separate earthquake policy is available from most insurance companies. The cost of the coverage will depend on the likelihood of earthquakes in your area and the construction features of your home.

If you have questions about insurance for any of your possessions, be sure to ask your agent or company representative. For example, if you run a business out of your home, be sure you have adequate coverage. Most homeowners policies cover business equipment in the home, but only up to $2500 and they offer no business liability insurance.

CHAPTER 10

AUTOMOBILE INSURANCE

"A careful driver is one who honks his horn when he goes through a red light."

Henry Morgan

LEARNING OBJECTIVES

After studying this chapter, you should be able to

◆ Identify the parties that are insured for liability coverage under the Personal Auto Policy (PAP).

◆ Describe the liability coverage in the PAP.

◆ Explain the medical payments coverage in the PAP.

◆ Describe the uninsured motorists coverage in the PAP.

◆ Explain the coverage for damage to your auto in the PAP.

◆ Explain the duties imposed on the insured after an accident or loss.

Michael, age 32, is an accountant who lives in Chicago, IL. He drives to work on a busy expressway. One morning, it was snowing heavily, visibility was poor, and the expressway was coated with ice. Like many motorists, he carelessly ignored the hazardous road conditions. While driving at a high rate of speed, he lost control of his car and smashed into another car. The other driver was seriously injured, and her car was damaged beyond repair. Although Michael was not injured, his car was badly damaged. He received a citation from the police for reckless driving. Michael reported the accident to his auto insurer, who subsequently paid the injured driver for her bodily injuries and property damage to her car. Michael's insurer also paid for the damage to his car less a small deductible.

Michael's policy protected him against the financial consequences of his negligent act. Auto insurance provides similar protection to millions of motorists. It is one of the most important coverages to emphasize in a personal risk management program. Legal liability arising out of an auto accident can reach catastrophic levels. Medical expenses, pain and suffering, the unexpected death of a family member, and physical damage to an expensive car are additional costs that must also be recognized.

This chapter discusses the major provisions of the Personal Auto Policy (PAP) drafted by the Insurance Services Office (ISO). The PAP policy is widely used throughout the United States. Some insurers, such as State Farm and Allstate, have designed their own forms that differ somewhat from the PAP form, but the differences are relatively minor.

OVERVIEW OF PERSONAL AUTO POLICY

In this section we discuss the major provisions in the 1998 Personal Auto Policy (PAP) drafted by the Insurance Services Office (ISO), which is widely used throughout the United States.[1] However, at the time of this writing, ISO has designed a new 2005 Personal Auto Policy that will eventually replace the older 1998 policy. The 2005 PAP will be introduced in most jurisdictions beginning in 2005. The 2005 PAP will be discussed later in the chapter.

Eligible Vehicles

Only certain types of vehicles are eligible for coverage under the PAP. An eligible vehicle is a four-wheel motor vehicle owned by the insured or leased by the insured for at least six continuous months. Thus, a private passenger auto, station wagon, or sport utility vehicle owned by the insured is eligible for coverage.

A pickup or van is eligible for coverage if the vehicle has a gross vehicle weight of 10,000 pounds or less and is not used for the delivery and transportation of goods and materials. The limitation on use does not apply if (1) such use is incidental to the named insured's business of installing, maintaining, or repairing furnishings or equipment (such as a plumber who transports work tools and supplies in a van) or (2) the vehicle is used in ranching or farming.

Your Covered Auto

An extremely important provision is the definition of **your covered auto.** Four classes of vehicles are considered to be covered autos:

- Any vehicle shown in the declarations
- A newly acquired auto

- A trailer owned by the named insured
- A temporary substitute vehicle

Any Vehicle Shown in the Declarations   Any vehicle shown on the declarations page is a covered auto. Covered autos include a private passenger auto, station wagon, sport utility vehicle, pickup, or van owned by the named insured. A private passenger auto, pickup, or van leased for at least six months is a covered auto as well.

Newly Acquired Auto   A newly acquired private passenger auto, pickup, or van is a covered auto if it is acquired by the named insured during the policy period. As stated earlier, a pickup or van must (1) have a gross vehicle weight of 10,000 pounds or less, and (2) must not be used to transport business materials unless the materials are incidental to the named insured's business, and that business is installing, maintaining, or repairing furnishing or equipment, or is farming or ranching.

With respect to *liability coverage, medical payments coverage, uninsured motorists coverage,* and any other coverage (except coverage for damage to your auto), a newly acquired auto has the same coverage as the broadest coverage provided for any vehicle shown in the declarations. Coverage begins on the date that you become the owner. However, if the newly acquired auto is *an additional vehicle,* you must notify the insurer within 14 days after you become the owner for the coverage to be effective from the purchase date. If the newly acquired auto is a *replacement auto* that replaces a vehicle shown in the declarations, coverage is automatically provided on the replacement vehicle without having to ask the company first to insure it. As a result, liability coverage, medical payments coverage, and the uninsured motorists coverage apply automatically to the replacement vehicle without first having to notify the insurer.

With respect to coverage for damage to your auto, however, a different set of rules applies. The PAP contains notification provisions that apply separately to collision losses and to other-than-collision losses. Collision coverage for a newly acquired auto becomes effective on the date that you become the owner. *However, you must ask the insurer to insure the vehicle within 14 days after you become the* *owner if the declarations page indicates that at least one auto is insured for collision coverage.* In such a case, the newly acquired auto has the broadest coverage provided for any auto shown in the declarations. A similar provision applies to coverage for other-than-collision losses.

The time requirement for notifying the insurer is reduced if there is no collision coverage on any vehicle. *If the declarations page does not indicate coverage for at least one auto, a newly acquired auto is automatically insured for collision coverage for only four days after you become the owner.* You must notify the insurer within the four-day period. If a loss occurs before you notify the insurer, a $500 collision deductible must be met. A similar provision applies to coverage for other-than-collision losses.

Trailer Owned by the Named Insured   A trailer owned by the named insured is also a covered auto. A trailer is a vehicle designed to be pulled by a private passenger auto, pickup, or van and also includes a farm wagon or farm implement while being towed by such vehicles. For example, you may be pulling a boat trailer that overturns and injures another motorist. The liability coverage in the PAP would cover the loss.

Temporary Substitute Vehicle   A temporary substitute vehicle is also a covered auto. A **temporary substitute vehicle** is a nonowned auto or trailer that you are temporarily using because of mechanical breakdown, repair, servicing, loss, or destruction of a covered vehicle. For example, if you drive a loaner car furnished by a repair shop or the car of a friend while your car is in the garage for repairs, your PAP covers the nonowned vehicle.

Summary of PAP Coverages

The PAP consists of a declarations page, a definitions page, and the following six parts:

Part A: Liability Coverage
Part B: Medical Payments Coverage
Part C: Uninsured Motorists Coverage
Part D: Coverage for Damage to Your Auto
Part E: Duties after an Accident or Loss
Part F: General Provisions

PART A: LIABILITY COVERAGE

Liability coverage (Part A) is the most important part of the PAP. It protects a covered person against a suit or claim arising out of the negligent ownership or operation of a covered vehicle.

Insuring Agreement

In the insuring agreement, the insurer agrees to pay any damages for bodily injury or property damage for which an insured is legally responsible because of an auto accident. The PAP is typically written with split limits. **Split limits** *mean that the amounts of insurance for bodily injury liability and property damage liability are stated separately.* For example, split limits of $250,000/$500,000/$100,000 mean that you have bodily injury liability coverage of $250,000 for each person and a maximum of $500,000 of bodily injury coverage for each accident. You also have $100,000 of property damage liability coverage. (Practitioners frequently refer to such limits as 250/500/100.)

Liability coverage can also be written with a single limit by adding an appropriate endorsement to the policy. A **single limit** *applies to both bodily injury and property damage liability: the total amount of insurance applies to the entire accident without a separate limit for each person.* For example, a single limit of $500,000 would apply to both bodily injury and property damage liability.

The amount paid as damages includes any prejudgment interest awarded against the insured. Many states now allow plaintiffs (injured persons) to receive interest on the judgment from the time the suit is entered to the time the judgment is determined. Any prejudgment interest is considered part of the damages awarded and is subject to the policy limit of liability.

The insurer also agrees to defend you and pay all legal defense costs. The defense costs are paid in addition to the policy limits. *However, the insurer's duty to settle or defend the claim ends when the limit of liability has been exhausted by payment of judgments or settlements.* This provision means that the insurer cannot deposit the policy limits into an escrow account and walk away without defending the insured. The obligation to defend ends when the policy limits are exhausted by payment of a judgment against the insured or settlement with a claimant. The duty to defend also ends if the claim is settled within the policy limits.

In addition, the insurer has no obligation to defend any claim not covered by the policy. For example, if you intentionally cause bodily injury or property damage and are sued, the insurer has no obligation to defend you because intentional acts are specifically excluded.

Insured Persons

The following four groups are insured under the liability section of the PAP:

- The named insured and any resident family member
- Any person using the named insured's covered auto with permission
- Any person or party, but only for liability arising out of an insured person's use of a covered auto on behalf of that person or organization
- Any person or organization legally responsible for the named insured's or family members' use of any auto or trailer (other than a covered auto or one owned by that person or organization)

First, the named insured and resident family members are insured for liability coverage. The named insured also includes a spouse if a resident of the same household. In recognition of the widespread divorce and separation found today, the PAP limits coverage for 90 days to a spouse who no longer resides in the named insured's household and is not listed as a named insured in the policy. If a spouse ceases to be a resident of the same household and is not listed as a named insured, the spouse is covered for 90 days following the change in residency, or until the spouse obtains a separate PAP or the policy period ends, whichever occurs first. If both spouses are named in the declarations as named insureds in the same PAP, the policy covers both spouses even though one spouse no longer resides in the same residence.

For example, Jennifer and James are married and live in the same residence. Jennifer is the named insured under her PAP policy. Assume that James is not listed as a named insured in her policy. He is still considered a named insured because he is Jennifer's husband. If the couple separates and James moves into another apartment, he is covered for 90 days under Jennifer's policy, or until he purchases his own policy, if earlier. However, if both were named insureds under the same PAP, James would be covered as a named insured until the policy expires, or until he purchases his own policy, if earlier.

A family member is a person related to the named insured by blood, marriage, or adoption who resides in the same household, including a ward or foster child. *Thus, the husband, wife, and children are covered while using any auto, owned or non-owned.* If the children are attending college and are temporarily away from home, they are still insured under their parents' policy.

Second, any other person using the named insured's covered auto is also insured provided that person can establish a reasonable belief that permission to use the covered auto exists. For example, John may have permitted his girlfriend, Susan, to drive his car several times over the past six months. If Susan takes John's car without his express permission, she is covered under his policy as long as she can show a reasonable belief that John would have given her permission to use the car.

Third, any person or organization legally responsible for the acts of a covered person while using a covered auto is also insured. For example, if Mark drives his car on an errand for his employer and injures someone, the employer is covered for any suit or claim.

Finally, coverage applies to any person or organization legally responsible for the named insured's or family members' use of any auto or trailer (other than a covered auto or one owned by the person or organization). For example, Mark may borrow the car of a fellow worker to mail a package for his employer. If Mark injures someone while driving that car, the employer is also covered for any suit or claim. However, the PAP does not extend coverage to the employer when the named insured is using an auto owned by the employer. So if Mark is driving to the post office in a company car, the employer is not insured under Mark's PAP.

Supplementary Payments

In addition to the policy limits and a legal defense, certain **supplementary payments** can be paid.

- Up to $250 for the cost of a bail bond
- Premiums on appeal bonds and bonds to release attachments
- Interest accruing after a judgment
- Up to $200 daily for the loss of earnings
- Other reasonable expenses

Premiums on a bail bond can be paid up to $250 because of an auto accident that results in property damage or bodily injury. However, payment is not made for a traffic violation such as a speeding ticket except if an accident occurs. For example, assume Richard is drunk and injures another motorist in an auto accident. If he is arrested, and bail is set at $2500, the insurer will pay the bail bond premium up to a maximum of $250.

Premiums on an appeal bond and a bond to release an attachment of property in any suit defended by the insurer are also paid as supplementary payments. If interest accrues after a judgment is awarded, the interest is also paid as a supplementary payment. Any prejudgment interest, however, is part of the liability limits.

The insurer will also pay up to $200 daily for the loss of earnings (but not other income) due to attendance at a hearing or trial at the company's request.

Finally, other reasonable expenses incurred at the insurer's request are paid. For example, you may be a defendant in a trial and be requested to testify. If you have meal or transportation expenses, they would be paid as a supplemental payment.

Exclusions

A lengthy list of exclusions applies to the liability coverage under the PAP. They are summarized as follows:

1. *Intentional injury or damage.* Intentional bodily injury or property damage is specifically excluded. For example, a driver changes lanes suddenly without signaling and cuts sharply in front of Richard's car. Richard is enraged and deliberately rams the vehicle. The intentional property damage to the other driver's car is not covered by Richard's PAP. Unfortunately, "road rage" is widespread nationally and is responsible for numerous motor vehicle deaths (see Insight 10.1).
2. *Property owned or transported.* Liability coverage is not provided to any person for damage

INSIGHT 10.1

How to Increase the Odds of Being Killed or Injured While Driving

You read the sport pages. Rowdy and violent fans, often intoxicated, frequently curse the players, throw debris on the field, start fights, assault umpires, and engage in other types of aggressive behavior. Is this violent behavior limited only to sporting events? Hardly. Road rage is another symptom of the underlying violence and anger that many Americans exhibit. *Road rage, or aggressive driving, includes a variety of driving offenses, including tailgating, obscene gestures, cursing and screaming, horn blowing, high speed duels, erratic lane changes, and even gun play. Some accidents result in fist fights and assaults.* Increased traffic congestion, drunk drivers, and tired drivers only aggravate the problem.

If you want to increase the odds of being killed or injured while driving, lose your temper, drive aggressively, and engage in road rage tantrums. According to the National Highway Traffic Safety Administration, *the deaths of nearly 28,000 of the 41,907 people who were killed in highway crashes*

in 1996 were associated with road rage.[a] Moreover, according to the AAA Foundation for Traffic Safety, *there were over 10,000 aggressive driving incidents from 1990 through mid-1996 where an angry motorist intentionally injured or killed another motorist in response to a grievance.*[b] In 1998, Arizona enacted a law making aggressive driving a crime by defining aggressive driving as speeding plus committing two other infractions, such as erratic lane changes, failure to yield, tailgating, and being an immediate hazard to another driver. New York addresses the road rage problem in prelicensing and defensive driving courses. The preceding statistics are sobering. If you want to stay alive while driving, keep your cool!

[a] "Auto Safety and Crashworthiness," *Hot Topics & Insurance Issues*, Insurance Information Institute, September 2003.
[b] Ibid.

---

to property owned or being transported by that person. For example, the suitcase and camera belonging to a friend may be damaged in an auto accident while you and your friend are on vacation together. The damage would not be covered.

3. *Property rented, used, or in the insured's care.* Damage to property rented to, used by, or in the care of the insured is not covered. For example, if you rent some skis that are damaged in an auto accident, the property damage is not covered. The exclusion, however, does not apply to property damage to a residence or private garage. For example, if you rent a house and carelessly back into a partly opened garage door, the property damage to the door would be covered.

4. *Bodily injury to an employee.* Bodily injury to an employee of the insured who is injured during the course of employment is also excluded. The intent here is to cover the employee's injury under a workers compensation law. However, a domestic employee injured during the course of employment would be covered if workers compensation benefits are not required or available.

5. *Use as a public or livery conveyance.* There is no liability coverage on a vehicle while it is being used as a public or livery conveyance. The intent here is to exclude coverage if the insured makes the vehicle available for hire to the general public. However, the exclusion does not apply to share-the-expense carpools.

6. *Vehicles used in the automobile business.* If a person is employed or engaged in the automobile business, liability arising out of the operation of vehicles in the automobile business is excluded. The automobile business refers to the selling, repairing, servicing, storing, or parking of vehicles designed for use mainly on public highways. It also includes road testing and delivery. For example, assume you take your car to a garage for repairs. If a mechanic has an accident and injures someone while road testing your car, your PAP liability coverage does not protect the mechanic. (However, if you are sued because you are the car owner, you are covered.) The intent of this exclusion is to exclude loss exposures that should be covered under the auto repair firm's liability policy, such as a garage policy.

The preceding exclusion does not apply to the operation, ownership, or use of a covered auto by the named insured, any resident family member, or any partner, agent, or employee of the named insured or family member. For example, if an auto mechanic has an accident while driving his or her car to pick up a part, the mechanic's PAP would cover the loss.

7. *Other business vehicles.* Liability coverage does not apply to any vehicle maintained or used in any other business (other than farming or ranching). This exclusion is similar to the preceding automobile business exclusion except it applies to all other business use with certain exceptions. The intent here is to exclude liability coverage for commercial vehicles and trucks that are used in a business. For example, if you drive a city bus or operate a large cement truck, your PAP liability coverage does not apply.

    The exclusion does not apply to an owned or nonowned private passenger auto, pickup, or van. Thus, you are covered if you drive your car on company business.

8. *Using a vehicle without reasonable belief of permission.* If a person uses a vehicle without a reasonable belief that he or she has permission to do so, the liability coverage does not apply. The exclusion does not apply to a family member who is using a covered auto owned by the named insured.

9. *Nuclear energy exclusion.* Liability of insureds who are covered under special nuclear energy contracts is also excluded.

10. *Vehicle with fewer than four wheels.* Liability coverage does not apply to any vehicle that has fewer than four wheels or is designed for use mainly off public roads. Thus, motorcycles, mopeds, motorscooters, minibikes, and trail bikes are excluded. However, the exclusion does not apply if the vehicle is being used in a medical emergency or to any *nonowned* golf cart.

11. *Vehicle furnished or made available for the named insured's regular use.* Liability coverage excludes a vehicle other than a covered auto that is owned by, furnished, or made available for the named insured's regular use. You can occasionally drive another person's car and still have coverage under your policy. *However, if the nonowned auto is driven regularly or is furnished or made available for your regular use, your PAP liability coverage does not apply.* For example, if your employer furnishes you with a car, or if a car is available for your regular use in a company carpool, the liability coverage does not apply. The key point is not how frequently you drive someone else's car, but whether it is furnished or made available for your regular use.

    For an additional premium, the **extended non-owned coverage endorsement** can be added to the PAP that covers the insured while operating a nonowned auto on a regular basis.

12. *Vehicle owned by, furnished, or made available for the regular use of any family member.* This exclusion is similar to the preceding exclusion. However, it does not apply to the named insured and spouse. For example, if Mary borrows a car owned and insured by her son who lives with her, the liability coverage under Mary's PAP would cover her while driving the son's car.

13. *Racing vehicle.* Liability coverage does not apply to any vehicle while it is located inside a racing facility for the purpose of competing in or preparing for a prearranged racing or speed contest.

Limit of Liability

As noted earlier, the PAP is typically written with split limits. That is, the amounts of insurance for bodily injury liability and property damage liability are stated separately. The maximum amount paid for bodily injury to each person is the amount shown in the declarations. Subject to that limit for each person, the maximum amount paid for bodily injury to all persons resulting from any one auto accident is the amount shown in the declarations. The maximum amount paid for property damage resulting from any one auto accident is also shown in the declarations.

Out-of-State Coverage

An important provision applies if the accident occurs in a state other than where the covered auto is principally garaged. If the accident occurs in a state that has a financial responsibility law with higher liability limits than the limits shown in the declarations, the PAP automatically provides the higher specified limits.

EXHIBIT **10.1**
Primary and Excess Insurance

Ken is the named insured and borrows Karen's car with her permission. Both policies will cover any loss. Ken has $50,000 of liability insurance and Karen has $100,000. Ken negligently injures another motorist and must pay damages of $125,000. *The rule is that insurance on the borrowed car is primary, and other insurance is excess.*
Each company pays as follows:

Karen's insurer (primary)	$100,000
Ken's insurer (excess)	25,000
Total	$125,000

Karen's insurer pays $100,000 while Ken's insurer pays the remaining $25,000.

If the state has a compulsory insurance or similar law that requires a nonresident to have insurance whenever he or she uses a vehicle in that state, the PAP provides the required minimum amounts and types of coverage. This provision assures compliance with an out-of-state no-fault law and the payment of required benefits. No-fault auto insurance laws are discussed in Chapter 11.

Other Insurance

In some cases, more than one liability policy covers a loss. If other applicable liability insurance applies to an *owned vehicle*, the insurer pays only its pro rata share of the loss. The insurer's share is the proportion that its limit of liability bears to the total applicable limits of liability under all policies. However, if the insurance applies to a *nonowned vehicle*, the insurer's insurance is excess over any other collectible insurance (see Exhibit 10.1).

PART B: MEDICAL PAYMENTS COVERAGE

Medical payments coverage is frequently included in the PAP. Benefits are paid without regard to fault.

Insuring Agreement

Under this provision, the company will pay all reasonable medical and funeral expenses incurred by an insured for services rendered within three years from the date of the accident. Covered expenses include medical, surgical, X-ray, dental, and funeral expenses. The benefit limits typically range from $1000 to $10,000 per person and apply to each insured who is injured in the accident.

Medical payments coverage is not based on fault. Thus, if you are injured in an auto accident and are at fault, medical payments can still be paid to you and to other injured passengers in the car.

Insured Persons

Two groups are insured for medical payments coverage:

- Named insured and family members
- Other persons while occupying a covered auto

The named insured and family members are covered if they are injured while occupying any motor vehicle or are injured as pedestrians when struck by a motor vehicle designed for use mainly on public roads. For example, if the parents and children are injured in an auto accident while on vacation, their medical expenses are covered up to the policy limits. If the named insured or any family member is struck by a motor vehicle or trailer while walking, his or her medical expenses are also paid. However, if you are injured by a farm tractor, snowmobile, or bulldozer, your injury is not covered, because these vehicles are not designed for use mainly on public roads.

Other persons are also covered for their medical expenses while occupying a covered auto. For example, if you own your car and are the named insured, all passengers in your car are covered for their medical expenses under your policy. However, if you are operating a *nonowned vehicle*, other passengers in the car (other than family members) are not covered for their medical expenses under your policy. The intent here is to have other passengers in the nonowned vehicle seek protection under their own insurance or under the medical expense coverage that applies to the nonowned vehicle.

Exclusions

Medical payments coverage has numerous exclusions. They are summarized as follows:

1. *Motorized vehicle with fewer than four wheels.* Bodily injury while occupying a motorized vehicle with fewer than four wheels is excluded.
2. *Public or livery conveyance.* If a covered auto is used as a public or livery conveyance, the medical payments coverage does not apply. The exclusion does not apply to a share-the-expense carpool.
3. *Using the vehicle as a residence.* Coverage does not apply if the injury occurs while the vehicle is being used as a residence or premises. For example, if you own and occupy a camper trailer as a residence in a campground while on vacation, medical expense coverage does not apply if you burn yourself while cooking on a stove in the trailer.
4. *Injury occurring during course of employment.* Coverage does not apply if the injury occurs during the course of employment, and workers compensation benefits are required or available.
5. *Vehicle furnished or made available for the named insured's regular use.* Coverage does not apply to any injury sustained while occupying or when struck by a vehicle (other than a covered auto) that is owned by the named insured or is furnished or made available for the named insured's regular use. The intent here is to avoid providing "free" medical payments coverage on an owned or regularly used car not described in the policy.
6. *Vehicle furnished or made available for the regular use of any family member.* A similar exclusion applies to any vehicle (other than a covered auto) that is owned by any family member or is furnished or made available for the regular use of any family member. The exclusion does not apply to the named insured and spouse. For example, if a son living at home owns a car that is not insured for medical payments coverage, and the parents are injured while occupying the son's car, the parent's medical expenses would be covered under their policy.
7. *Using a vehicle without a reasonable belief of permission.* Coverage does not apply if the injury occurs while occupying a vehicle without a reasonable belief of being entitled to do so. The exclusion does not apply to a family member who is using a covered auto owned by the named insured.
8. *Vehicle used in the business of an insured.* Coverage does not apply to any injury sustained while occupying a vehicle when it is being used in the business of an insured. The intent here is to exclude medical payments coverage for non-owned trucks and commercial vehicles used in the business of an insured person. The exclusion does not apply to a private passenger auto (owned or nonowned), to an owned pickup or van, or to a trailer used with any of the preceding vehicles.
9. *Nuclear weapon, radiation, or war.* Bodily injury from a nuclear weapon, nuclear radiation, or war is not covered.
10. *Racing vehicle.* Coverage does not apply to a bodily injury sustained while occupying a vehicle located inside a racing facility for the purpose of competing in or preparing for a prearranged racing or speed contest.

Other Insurance

If other automobile medical payments insurance applies to an *owned vehicle,* the insurer pays its pro rata share of the loss based on the proportion that its limits bear to the total applicable limits.

However, medical payments coverage is excess with respect to a *nonowned vehicle.* For example, assume that Kim is driving her car and picks up Patti for lunch. Kim loses control of the car and hits a tree, and Patti is injured. Patti's medical bills are $6000. Kim has $2000 of medical expenses coverage, and Patti has $5000. Kim's insurer pays the first $2000 as primary insurer, and Patti's insurer pays the remaining $4000 as excess insurance.

PART C: UNINSURED MOTORISTS COVERAGE

Some motorists are irresponsible and drive without liability insurance. According to an Insurance Research Council (IRC) study released in 2001, an

ExHIBIT 10.2
Percentage of Uninsured Motorists 1995–1997 Average

State	Percent Uninsured	State	Percent Uninsured
Colorado	32%	Rhode Island	11%
New Mexico	30%	Delaware	11%
South Carolina	28%	Arkansas	11%
Alabama	25%	Wisconsin	11%
Mississippi	25%	Hawaii	10%
California	22%	Kentucky	10%
District of Columbia	21%	Iowa	10%
Florida	20%	Pennsylvania	9%
Texas	18%	Vermont	9%
Tennessee	18%	Montana	9%
Oklahoma	17%	Connecticut	9%
Alaska	16%	Kansas	9%
Maryland	16%	Utah	9%
Arizona	16%	New Hampshire	9%
Nevada	15%	Louisiana	8%
New Jersey	15%	West Virginia	8%
Washington	15%	Idaho	8%
Missouri	13%	New York	7%
Georgia	13%	North Dakota	7%
Michigan	13%	Nebraska	7%
Illinois	13%	Wyoming	7%
Ohio	13%	Massachusetts	7%
Oregon	12%	South Dakota	6%
Virginia	12%	North Carolina	6%
Indiana	12%	Maine	4%
Minnesota	12%	Nationwide	14%

Source: Insurance Research Council, *IRC Study Estimates 14% of Drivers Are Uninsured,* News Release, February 1, 2001.

estimated 14 percent of the drivers in the United States were uninsured during the years 1995 to 1997. The percentage of uninsured drivers, however, varies widely by state. The IRC study showed that the estimated percentage of uninsured drivers ranged a high of 32 percent in Colorado to a low of 4 percent in Maine (see Exhibit 10.2).

The **uninsured motorists coverage** pays for the bodily injury (and property damage in some states) caused by an uninsured motorist, by a hit-and-run driver, or by a negligent driver whose insurance company is insolvent.

Insuring Agreement

The insurer agrees to pay compensatory damages that an insured is legally entitled to receive from the owner or operator of an uninsured motor vehicle because of bodily injury caused by an accident. Damages include medical bills, lost wages, and compensation for a permanent disfigurement resulting from the accident. Several important points must be emphasized with respect to this coverage.

1. *The coverage applies only if the uninsured motorist is legally liable.* If the uninsured motorist is not liable, the insurer will not pay for the bodily injury.
2. *The insurer's maximum limit of liability for any single accident is the amount shown in the declarations.* You cannot receive duplicate payments for the same elements of loss under the uninsured motorists coverage and Part A (liability coverage) or Part B (medical payments coverage)

of the policy, or any underinsured motorists coverage provided by the policy. Also, you cannot receive a duplicate payment for any element of loss for which payment has been made by or on behalf of persons or organizations legally responsible for the accident. Finally, the insurer will not pay you for any part of a loss if you are entitled to be paid for that part of the loss under a workers compensation or disability benefits law.

3. *The claim is subject to arbitration if the insured and insurer disagree over the amount of damages or whether the insured is entitled to receive any damages.* However, both the insured and insurer must agree to arbitration. Under this provision, each party selects an arbitrator. The two arbitrators select a third arbitrator. A decision by two of the three arbitrators is binding on all parties. However, the decision is binding only if the damages awarded do not exceed the state's minimum financial responsibility law limits.

4. *Some states also include coverage for property damage from an uninsured motorist in their uninsured motorists law.* In these states, if an uninsured driver runs a red light and smashes into your car, the property damage to the car would be covered under the uninsured motorists coverage, subject to any applicable deductible.

There is considerable variation among the states that include property damage coverage in their uninsured motorists law. In some states, property damage coverage is an optional coverage that is purchased separately from the regular uninsured motorists coverage. In other states, both bodily injury and property damage coverages are included together in the uninsured motorists coverage; however, the insured may have the option of waiving the coverage if it is not desired. In some states, both bodily injury and property damage coverage are mandatory under the state's uninsured motorists law. Finally, the property damage is subject to a deductible.

Insured Persons

Three groups are insured under the uninsured motorists coverage:

■ The named insured and his or her family members

■ Any other person while occupying a covered auto
■ Any person legally entitled to recover damages

First, the named insured and his or her family members are covered if they are injured by an uninsured motorist. Second, any other person who is injured while occupying a covered auto is also insured; the coverage applies only if the individual is occupying a covered auto. Finally, any person legally entitled to recover damages is insured. An individual may not be physically involved in the accident but may be entitled to recover damages from the person or organization legally responsible for the bodily injury of the insured person. For example, if the named insured is killed by an uninsured motorist, the surviving spouse could still collect damages under the uninsured motorists coverage.

Uninsured Vehicles

An extremely important provision defines an uninsured motor vehicle. Four groups of vehicles are considered to be uninsured vehicles:

1. An uninsured vehicle is a motor vehicle or trailer for which no bodily injury liability insurance policy or bond applies at the time of the accident.

2. A bodily injury liability policy or bond may be in force on a vehicle. However, the amount of insurance on that vehicle may be less than the amount required by the state's financial responsibility law in the state where the named insured's covered auto is principally garaged. This vehicle is also considered to be an uninsured motor vehicle.

3. A hit-and-run vehicle is also considered to be an uninsured vehicle. Thus, if the named insured or any family member is struck by a hit-and-run driver while occupying a covered auto or a non-owned auto, or while walking, the uninsured motorists coverage will pay for the injury.

4. Another uninsured vehicle is one to which a bodily injury liability policy applies at the time of the accident, but the insurer or bonding company denies coverage or becomes insolvent. For example, if you have a valid claim against a negligent driver, but his or her insurer becomes insolvent before the claim is paid, your uninsured motorists coverage would pay the claim.

Exclusions

The uninsured motorists coverage has several general exclusions, summarized as follows:

1. *No uninsured motorists coverage on vehicle.* Coverage does not apply to an insured while occupying or when struck by a motor vehicle owned by that insured, which is not insured for coverage under this policy.
2. *Primary coverage under another policy.* Family members are not covered while they are occupying a vehicle owned by the named insured, which is insured for uninsured motorists' coverage on a primary basis under another policy. The intent here is to have such family members seek protection under the policy insuring the vehicle that they are occupying.
3. *Settling a claim without the insurer's consent.* If an insured or legal representative settles a bodily injury claim without the insurer's consent, coverage does not apply. The purpose of this exclusion is to protect the insurer's subrogation rights.
4. *Using the vehicle as a public or livery conveyance.* If an insured occupies a covered auto when it is being used as a public or livery conveyance, coverage does not apply. The exclusion does not apply to a share-the-expense carpool.
5. *No reasonable belief of permission.* Coverage does not apply to any insured who is using a vehicle without a reasonable belief that he or she is entitled to do so. This exclusion does not apply to a family member who is using a covered auto owned by the named insured.
6. *No benefit to workers compensation insurer.* The uninsured motorists coverage cannot directly or indirectly benefit a workers compensation insurer or self-insurer. A workers compensation insurer may have a legal right of action against a third party who has injured an employee. If an uninsured driver injures an employee who receives workers compensation benefits, the workers compensation insurer could sue the uninsured driver or attempt to make a claim under the injured employee's uninsured motorists coverage. This exclusion prevents the uninsured motorists coverage from providing benefits to the workers compensation insurer.

7. *No punitive damages.* The PAP excludes payment for punitive or exemplary damages under the uninsured motorists coverage.

Other Insurance

The PAP contains a number of provisions that apply when more than one uninsured motorist coverage provision applies to the loss. These provisions are summarized as follows:

- The maximum amount paid is limited to the highest limit of any of the policies that provide uninsured motorists coverage.
- If an insurer provides uninsured motorist coverage on a *vehicle not owned by the named insured, the insurance provided is excess over any collectible insurance providing insurance on a primary basis.* For example, Jeffrey has an uninsured motorist coverage limit of $25,000, and Ashley has an uninsured motorist coverage limit of $50,000. If Jeffrey is injured by an uninsured driver while occupying Ashley's car and has bodily injuries of $60,000, Ashley's policy is primary and pays $50,000. Jeffrey's insurer pays the remaining $10,000 as excess insurance.
- When the named insured's policy and the other policy provide uninsured motorists coverage on a *primary basis,* each policy pays its pro rata share of the loss. Each insurer's share is the proportion that its limit of liability bears to the total of all applicable limits of liability for coverage provided on a primary basis.
- When the named insured's policy and the other policy provide uninsured motorists coverage on an *excess basis,* each policy also pays its pro rata share of the loss. Each insurer's share is the proportion that its limit of liability bears to the total of all applicable limits of liability for coverage provided on an excess basis.

Underinsured Motorists Coverage

Underinsured motorists coverage can be added to the PAP to provide more complete protection. Underinsured motorists coverage applies when a negligent third-party driver carries liability insurance, but the limits carried are less than the insured's actual damages for bodily injury.

An underinsured vehicle is defined as a vehicle to which a liability policy or bond applies at the time of the accident, but the liability limits carried are less than the limits provided by the insured's underinsured motorists coverage. The maximum amount paid for the bodily injury under the coverage varies among the states. *In general, the maximum amount paid is the underinsured motorist's coverage limit less the amount paid by the negligent driver's insurer.* For example, assume that Kristen adds the underinsured motorists coverage to her policy in the amount of $100,000. She is injured by a negligent driver who has liability limits of $25,000/$50,000, which satisfy the state's minimum required limits. If her bodily injury damages are $100,000, she would receive only $25,000 from the negligent driver's insurer, because that amount is the applicable limit of liability. However, she would receive another $75,000 from her insurer under the underinsured motorists coverage.

However, assume that Kristen's bodily injury damages are $125,000. The maximum amount she would collect under the underinsured motorists coverage is still only $75,000, which is the difference between the $100,000 limit under her underinsured motorists coverage and the $25,000 collected from the negligent driver's insurer (see preceding rule). To collect the full amount of her injury, Kristen should have carried limits of at least $125,000.

The underinsured motorist coverage endorsement is not uniform among the states. In some states, the underinsured motorists coverage can be added as an endorsement to the PAP to complement the coverage provided by the uninsured motorists coverage. In other states, a single endorsement provides both uninsured and underinsured coverage and replaces the uninsured motorist coverage that is part of the standard PAP. In addition, some states make the underinsured motorists coverage mandatory, while other states make it optional. Finally, the available or required limits for the underinsured motorists coverage also vary by state.

PART D: COVERAGE FOR DAMAGE TO YOUR AUTO

Part D (**coverage for damage to your auto**) provides coverage for the damage or theft of an automobile.

Insuring Agreement

The insurer agrees to pay for any direct and accidental loss to a covered auto or nonowned auto, including its equipment, less any deductible. If two autos insured under the same policy are damaged in the same accident, only one deductible must be met. If the deductible amounts are different, the higher deductible will apply. *Two optional coverages are available: (1) collision coverage and (2) other-than-collision coverage (also called comprehensive).* A collision loss is covered only if the declarations page indicates that collision coverage is provided for that auto. Likewise, coverage for an other-than-collision loss is in force only if the declarations page indicates that other-than-collision coverage is provided for that auto.

Collision Loss Collision *is defined as the upset of your covered auto or nonowned auto or its impact with another vehicle or object.* The following are examples of a collision loss:

- You lose control of your car on an icy street, and it overturns.
- Your car hits another car, a telephone pole, a tree, or a building.
- Your car is parked, and you find the rear fender dented when you return.
- You open the car door in a parking lot, and the door is damaged when it hits the vehicle parked next to you.

Collision losses are paid regardless of fault. If you cause the accident, your insurer will pay for the damage to your car, less any deductible. If the other driver damages your car, you can either collect from the negligent driver (or from his or her insurer), or look to your insurer to pay the claim. If you collect from your own insurer, you must give up subrogation rights to your insurer, who will then attempt to collect from the negligent party who caused the accident. If the entire amount of the loss is recovered, your insurer will refund the deductible.

Other-Than-Collision Loss The PAP can be written to cover an **other-than-collision loss.** The PAP distinguishes between a collision and an other-than-collision loss. This distinction is important because some car owners do not wish to pay for collision coverage on their cars. Also, the deductibles under the two coverages may be different. Other-than-collision coverage is frequently written with a lower deductible.

Loss from any of the following perils is considered to be an other-than-collision loss:

- Missiles or falling objects
- Fire
- Theft or larceny
- Explosion or earthquake
- Windstorm
- Hail, water, or flood
- Malicious mischief or vandalism
- Riot or civil commotion
- Contact with a bird or animal
- Glass breakage

These losses are self-explanatory, but a few comments are in order. Theft of the vehicle is covered, including the theft of equipment, such as hub caps, tires, or a stereo set. Theft of an air bag from a covered vehicle parked on the street is also covered.

In addition, colliding with a bird or animal is not a collision loss. Thus, if you hit a bird or deer with your car, the physical damage to the car is considered to be an other-than-collision loss.

Finally, if glass breakage is caused by a collision, you can elect to have it covered as a collision loss. This distinction is important because both coverages (collision loss and other-than-collision loss) are written with deductibles. Without this qualification, you would have to pay two deductibles if the car has both body damage and glass breakage in the same accident. By treating glass breakage as part of the collision loss, only the collision deductible must be satisfied.

Nonowned Auto   The Part D coverages also apply to a nonowned auto. A **nonowned auto** *is a private passenger auto, pickup, van, or trailer not owned by or furnished or made available for the regular use of the named insured or family member, while it is in the custody of or is being operated by the named insured or family member.* For example, if Tyler borrows Mike's car, Tyler's collision coverage and other-than-collision coverage on his car apply to the borrowed car. However, Tyler's insurance is excess over any physical damage insurance on the borrowed car.

The Part D coverages apply only if the nonowned auto is not furnished or made available for

the regular use of the named insured or family member. You can occasionally drive a borrowed automobile, and your physical damage insurance will cover the borrowed vehicle. *However, if the vehicle is driven on a regular basis or is furnished or made available for your regular use, the Part D coverages do not apply.* The key point here is not how frequently you drive a nonowned auto, but whether the vehicle is furnished or made available for your regular use.

The Part D coverages also apply to a temporary substitute vehicle, which is also considered to be a nonowned auto. A temporary substitute vehicle is a nonowned auto or trailer that is used as a temporary replacement for a covered auto that is out of normal use because of its breakdown, repair, servicing, loss, or destruction. *Thus, the Part D coverages that apply to a covered auto also apply to a temporary substitute vehicle for that auto.* Hence, if your car is in the shop for repairs, and you are furnished a loaner car, your physical damage insurance also applies to the loaner car.

If you have an accident while operating a nonowned auto, the PAP provides the broadest coverage applicable to any covered auto shown in the declarations. For example, assume that you own two cars. One vehicle is insured for both a collision loss and an other-than-collision loss, and the other is insured only for an other-than-collision loss. If you drive a nonowned auto, the borrowed vehicle is covered for both collision and other-than-collision losses.

Collision Damage Waiver (CDW) on Rental Cars
Our discussion of collision insurance on nonowned cars would not be complete without a brief discussion of the collision damage waiver (CDW) on rental cars. This coverage is sometimes called a loss damage waiver (LDW). When you rent a car and check the CDW box, you are relieved of financial responsibility if the rental car is damaged or stolen. However, the rental agreement contains numerous restrictions. The CDW may be void even when checked if you cause an accident by speeding, driving while intoxicated, or driving on unpaved roads. The CDW is expensive and can easily increase the daily rental cost by $10 to $20 or some higher amount.

Should you purchase the CDW if you rent a car? Many consumer experts say the CDW is not needed if (1) you carry collision and comprehensive insurance on your own car because the coverages also apply to the rental car, and (2) certain credit cards cover the physical damage or theft of a rental car on an excess basis if the card is used to rent the car.

The preceding view that the CDW may be unnecessary is not uniform among all financial advisors. In particular, the Independent Insurance Agents & Brokers of America, an association of independent property/casualty insurance agents and brokers, says consumers in general should purchase the CDW, as least for short-term rentals. Because of numerous restrictive provisions in the rental agreement, incomplete protection under the PAP, and credit card limitations, the organization believes consumers generally should buy the CDW even if it is costly (see Insight 10.2)

Deductible The collision coverage is typically written with a straight deductible of $250, or some higher amount. Coverage for other-than-collision losses is also normally written with a deductible. Deductibles are designed to reduce small claims, hold down premiums, and encourage the insured to be careful in protecting the car from damage or theft.

Transportation Expenses

Part D also pays for temporary transportation expenses. The insurer will pay, without application of a deductible, up to $20 daily to a maximum of $600 for temporary transportation expenses incurred by the insured because of loss to a covered auto. Payments can be made for a train, bus, taxi, rental car, or other transportation expense. *Payments are made for other-than-collision losses only if the declarations indicate that other-than-collision coverage is provided on that auto. Likewise, payments are made for collision losses only if the declarations indicate that collision coverage is provided for that auto.*

The coverage also includes payment of any expenses for which the insured is legally responsible because of loss to a nonowned auto, such as the loss of daily rent on a rental car.

Finally, if the loss is caused by the total theft of a covered auto or nonowned auto, expenses incurred during the first 48 hours after the theft occurred are not covered. If the loss is caused by a peril other than theft, expenses incurred during the first 24 hours after the auto has been withdrawn from use are not covered.

Coverage for *towing and labor costs* can be added by an endorsement. This coverage pays for towing and labor costs if a covered auto or nonowned auto breaks down, provided the labor is performed at the place of breakdown. The maximum amount paid is $25, $50, or $75 for each breakdown depending on the amount of insurance purchased. For example, if you call a repair truck because your car fails to start, the labor costs and any towing costs will be paid up to the policy limits. Labor costs, however, are covered only for work done at the place of the breakdown. The cost of repairs at a service station or garage is not covered.

Exclusions

Numerous exclusions apply to the Part D coverages, summarized as follows:

1. *Use as a public or livery conveyance.* Loss to a covered auto or any nonowned auto is excluded if the vehicle is being used as a public or livery conveyance. Again, the exclusion does not apply to a share-the-expense carpool.

2. *Damage from wear and tear, freezing, and mechanical or electrical breakdown.* There is no coverage for any damage due to wear and tear, freezing, mechanical or electrical breakdown, or road damages to tires. The intent here is to exclude the normal maintenance cost of operating an automobile and to cover tire defects under the tire manufacturer's warranty. However, the exclusion does not apply to the total theft of a covered auto or any nonowned auto. For example, if a stolen car is recovered but the electrical system is damaged by a thief who hotwired the car, the loss is covered.

3. *Radioactive contamination or war.* Damage from radioactive contamination or war is excluded.

4. *Electronic equipment designed for the reproduction of sound.* The PAP excludes electronic equipment and accessories designed for the reproduction of sound, such as radios, stereos, tape decks, or compact disc players. However, this exclusion does not apply to equipment and accessories permanently installed in a covered auto or

INSIGHT 10.2

The Top 10 Reasons to Purchase the Rental Car Collision Damage Waiver (CDW)

It has been debated for years whether or not a person renting a vehicle should purchase the collision (or loss) damage waiver from the rental company. *Our recommendation is that consumers, in general, **should** purchase the CDW/LDW, at least for short-term rentals. Our reasons are given below.*

- **Loss Valuation.** The personal auto policy (PAP) covers the lesser of the actual cash value of the vehicle or the amount necessary to repair or replace the damaged property. However, the rental agreement may contractually obligate you to reimburse the rental company for the full value of the vehicle. Also, the PAP also does not pay for any *betterment* (increased value of new parts replacing old ones) of the vehicle, nor any *diminution* of value (if the market value of the vehicle after repairs is less than that before the accident).

- **Loss Settlement.** As implied above, there may be disagreement over the value of the vehicle or the amount charged for labor and materials to repair it. The insurance company has the right to ". . . *inspect and appraise the damaged property before its repair or disposal.*" However, the rental company, unlike you, is not contractually obligated to the insurer—it may choose to make the repairs immediately, potentially resulting in a lack of PAP coverage because of failure to comply with this contractual condition. In any case, purchase of the CDW usually allows the renter to walk away without the headaches involved in adjusting an auto claim.

- **Loss Payment.** The rental agreement may require immediate reimbursement for damages, and it is customary practice for the rental company to charge your credit card. This can create a significant debt, *max* out the card's credit limit (perhaps shortening a vacation or business trip), or result in litigation.

- **Loss Damage Waivers (LDW).** Rental agreements often make the renter responsible for *any* loss in value beyond normal wear and tear, regardless of the cause and regardless of fault. In order for your PAP to respond, you must insure at least one vehicle for both collision and other-than-collision (often called *comprehensive*) coverage. If not, your policy will not respond to the rental car damage and loss of use claims.

- **Indirect Losses.** You most likely will be responsible for the rental company's loss of rental income on the damaged unit. Your policy has limited coverage for these charges.

- **Administrative Expenses.** The rental contract may make the insured liable for various *administrative* or loss-related expenses such as towing (e.g., one insured was charged for a 230-mile tow), appraisal, claims adjustment, and storage. some of these expenses may not be covered by the PAP.

- **Other Insurance.** The PAP says that it is excess over: (1) any coverage provided by the owner of the auto, (2) any other applicable physical damage insurance, and (3) any other source of recovery applicable to the loss, such as travel policies or credit card coverages. The potential controversy over who pays what is obvious and can result in litigation. In addition, keep in mind that many states have statutes, proprietary policy forms, and/or case law precedents that may govern rental car exposures.

- **Excluded Vehicles & Territories.** The PAP normally does not provide physical damage coverage for motorcycles, mopeds, motor homes, or other vehicles that are not private passenger autos, pickups, vans, or trailers. In addition, use of covered vehicles is limited to the U.S., its territories and possessions, Puerto Rico, and Canada (the rental agreement may also exclude operation outside a specific geographical area).

- **Excluded Uses & Drivers.** The PAP may have limitations on use of vehicles that are not otherwise excluded by the rental agreement CDW or LDW. Also, the PAP may include an exclusionary endorsement for certain drivers or may apply only to designated individuals—the CDW will probably also only apply to certain individuals, but operators for which no PAP coverage is available may be afforded protection under the rental agreement by adding them as designated drivers.

- **Additional and/or Future Costs.** The PAP will include a deductible in the range of $100–$500 or higher. In addition, payment for damage to a rental car may result in a significant premium increase (if not nonrenewal) via surcharges or loss of credits.

Although most CDW/LDW fees are considered outrageous, if not unconscionable, **we advise you to purchase the CDW/LDW for short-term rentals.** If anything, this will give you peace of mind while on vacation or business, and it could save you from a lot of inconvenience and lost time and money.

Source: "Virtual University," © Independent Insurance Agents & Brokers of America, Inc. The current version of this article can be found at IIABA's Virtual University, http://www.iiaba.net/VU/Lib/Ins/PL/Auto/WilsonTop10CDW.htm

nonowned auto. For example, the theft of a permanently installed radio would be covered.

5. *Other electronic equipment.* The PAP excludes electronic equipment that receives or transmits audio, visual, or data signals. Such equipment includes citizens band radios, telephones, two-way mobile radios, scanning monitor receivers, television monitor receivers, video cassette recorders, audio cassette recorders, and personal computers. This exclusion does not apply to electronic equipment necessary for the operation of the auto or to a permanently installed telephone. Note that the telephone must be permanently installed. Consequently, a portable cell phone that many people use while driving in their cars would not be covered.

   Safety experts believe that drivers can be easily distracted while using a cell phone, which increases the chance of an auto accident. The extent to which the use of cell phones contributes to auto accidents is controversial. However, empirical research studies suggest that using a cell phone while driving can be extremely dangerous (see Insight 10.3).

6. *Tapes, records, and discs.* Loss to stereo tapes, records, discs, or other media designed for use with the electronic equipment described previously is also excluded. An endorsement can be added to the PAP to cover excluded tapes and electronic equipment.

7. *Government destruction or confiscation.* The PAP excludes the total loss to a covered auto or nonowned auto due to destruction or confiscation by a governmental or civil authority. For example, if a federal drug agency confiscates a drug dealer's car, the loss would not be covered.

8. *Trailer, camper body, or motor home.* The PAP excludes loss to a trailer, camper body, or motor home not shown in the declarations. This exclusion also applies to facilities and equipment, such as cooking, dining, plumbing or refrigeration equipment, and awnings or cabanas. For example, damage to a stove or refrigerator is not covered.

   The exclusion does not apply to a nonowned trailer. Likewise, it does not apply to a trailer or camper body acquired during the policy period provided that you notify the insurer within 14 days after you become the owner.

9. *Loss to a nonowned auto used without reasonable belief of permission.* Loss to a nonowned auto is not covered when it is used by the named insured or his or her family member without a reasonable belief of permission.

10. *Radar detection equipment.* Equipment for the detection or location of radar or laser is excluded. This exclusion is justified on the basis that radar detection equipment circumvents state and federal speed laws.

11. *Custom furnishings or equipment.* Loss to customized furnishings or equipment in or upon a pickup or van is not covered. Such furnishings or equipment include special carpeting, furniture or bars, height-extending roofs, and custom murals or paintings. However, an endorsement can be added that covers the excluded furnishings or equipment.

12. *Nonowned auto used in the automobile business.* Loss to a nonowned auto maintained or used by someone engaged in the business of selling, repairing, servicing, storing, or parking vehicles designed for use on public highways is specifically excluded. For example, if a mechanic damages a customer's car while road testing it, the loss is not covered under the mechanic's PAP. Instead, this business loss exposure should be covered under a commercial garage policy.

13. *Racing vehicle.* Loss to a covered auto or nonowned auto is not covered while it is located inside a racing facility for the purpose of competing in or preparing for a prearranged racing or speed contest.

14. *Rental car.* Loss to or loss of use of a vehicle rented by the named insured or family member is not covered if a state law or rental agreement precludes the car rental agency from recovering from the named insured or family member.

Limit of Liability

The amount paid for a physical damage loss to a covered vehicle is the lower of (1) actual cash value of the damaged or stolen property, or (2) amount necessary to replace the property with other property of like kind and quality. If the cost of repairs exceeds the vehicle's actual cash value, the vehicle may be declared a total loss, and the amount paid is the

INSIGHT 10.3

Using a Cell Phone While Driving Can Be Dangerous to Your Health

The majority of drivers with cell phones use them while driving at least part of the time. Do cell phones distract drivers and cause auto accidents? According to a 2000 survey by the Insurance Research Council, 91 percent of Americans believe that talking on a cell phone while driving distracts drivers and increases the chance of an accident.[a] Research studies suggest that using a cell phone while driving can be dangerous. Consider the following:[b]

- According to the *New England Journal of Medicine,* talking on a cell phone while driving quadruples the chances of being involved in a motor vehicle accident, which is a risk similar to driving while drunk.

- According to the Harvard Center for Risk Analysis, six percent of the auto accidents in the United States each year may be attributed to cell phone use, which results in 2600 deaths and 330,000 injuries.

- Research commissioned by Direct Line, a British insurer, found that talking on a mobile phone while driving is more dangerous than driving while drunk. Drivers' reaction times, on average, were 30 percent slower when talking on a hand-held mobile phone compared to being drunk and almost 50 percent slower than under normal driving conditions.

- Even if an accident does not occur, using a cell phone while driving can be dangerous. Progressive Insurance found that 46 percent of 837 drivers surveyed who used cell phones while driving admitted swerving into another lane, 23 percent tailgated another vehicle, another 18 percent almost hit another car, and 10 percent ran a red light. (To digress, the author frequently sees drivers trying to make a tight left-hand turn on a busy intersection with only one hand on the steering wheel and the other hand on their cell phone, which can easily result in an accident.)

- In 2003, the National Transportation Safety Board recommended that all states should prohibit drivers with learners' permits or graduated licenses from using cell phones while driving. The board's recommendation

came after an accident in which a 20-year-old driver with little driving experience flipped over her new sport utility vehicle (SUV) on to a minivan, killing her and four others. An investigation revealed that she was speaking on a cell phone when a gust of wind hit the SUV, causing it to overturn. The cell phone and inexperience contributed to her lack of control.

- Proponents of cell phones, however, claim that other distractions are more important, such as eating, drinking, reading newspapers, talking with passengers, and changing the radio. A 2001 study funded by the American Automobile Association and conducted by the University of North Carolina suggested that drivers are more distracted by changing radio stations or inserting a CD than by using their cell phone; the study concluded that cell phones account for only one percent of the accidents.[c] Proponents also claim that cell phones provide numerous benefits to drivers, including faster notification of emergency personnel in a traffic accident, quicker roadside assistance when a car breaks down, and increased personal security.

In 2001, New York passed a law that requires motorists to use a hands-free system, such as use of a headset, for making cell phone calls while driving. In addition to New York, ten states have passed legislation that restricts the use of cell phones while driving (Arizona, California, Florida, Illinois, Massachusetts, Mississippi, New Jersey, Oklahoma, Oregon, and Rhode Island). Other states require law enforcement officers to provide information about cell phones when an auto accident occurs (California, Florida, Iowa, Maryland, Massachusetts, Michigan, Minnesota, Montana, Nebraska, New Jersey, Oklahoma, Oregon, Pennsylvania, Tennessee, Texas, and Utah).[d]

[a] "Cell Phones and Driving," *Hot Topics & Insurance Issues,* Insurance Information Institute, February 2003.
[b] Ibid.
[c] Ibid.
[d] Ibid.

actual cash value less the deductible. If a total loss occurs, there is an adjustment for depreciation and physical condition in determining the actual cash value. In practice, insurers declare a vehicle to be a total loss if the estimated cost of repairs plus the salvage value exceeds the actual cash value of the car.

For a partial loss, such as a smashed fender, only the amount necessary to repair or replace the damaged property with property of like kind and quality will be paid. The car can be repaired with parts manufactured by the original equipment manufacturer (*OEM*) or with generic auto parts (also called *after market parts*). Some policyholders believe that generic auto parts are of lower quality than OEM parts, which has resulted in a number of lawsuits against auto insurers. The majority of states now require insurers to notify policyholders when generic auto parts are used to repair the vehicle. Insurance company practices differ in this regard. In some cases, policyholders can pay the difference between OEM parts and generic parts and have the vehicle repaired with OEM parts. Some auto insurers offer policyholders a choice between OEM parts and generic parts by an endorsement to the policy. Some insurers always use OEM parts, while others use OEM parts for repairing new or late model cars. You should call your agent and inquire about the claim settlement practices of your company so you know what to expect if your car is damaged.

The PAP also has limits on the amount paid for certain losses. Loss to a nonowned trailer is limited to $500. However, under the new 2005 PAP (discussed later), the maximum payment for loss to a nonowned trailer is increased to $1500. Loss to equipment designed for the reproduction of sound, which is installed in locations not used by the auto manufacturer for such equipment, is limited to $1000.

Betterment If the value of the vehicle is increased after repairs are completed (such as repainting the entire car when only one fender and door are damaged), the insurer will not pay for the **betterment** or increase in value.

Diminution in Value A car damaged in an auto accident may have a reduced market or resale value. In recent years, many insureds have requested payment for the loss in market value. The Insurance Services Office has prepared a clarifying endorsement that insurers can add to the policy. The endorsement states that any loss in market or resale value (also called **diminution in value**) from a direct and accidental physical damage loss to a covered auto is not covered.

Finally, many consumers purchase new cars on a lease arrangement. The value of a new car declines substantially during the first year because of depreciation. Also, the collision deductible on a leased car may be $500 or even higher. If a leased car is totaled in an accident shortly after purchase, the amount paid by the insurer may be substantially less than the payoff amount of the lease. As a result, you could owe a bank or other financial institution hundreds or even thousands of dollars. This risk can be handled by **gap insurance**, *which pays the difference between the amount your insurer pays for a totaled car and the amount owed on the lease or loan* (see Insight 10.4).

Payment of Loss

The insurer has the option of paying for a physical damage loss in money (including any sales tax) or repairing or replacing the damaged or stolen property. If the car or its equipment is stolen, the insurer will pay the expense of returning the stolen car to the named insured and will also pay for any damage resulting from the theft. The insurer also has the right to keep all or part of the recovered stolen property at an agreed or appraised value.

Other Sources of Recovery

If other insurance covers a physical damage loss, the insurer pays only its pro rata share. The insurer's share is the proportion that its limit of liability bears to the total of all applicable limits.

With respect to a nonowned auto (including a temporary substitute), the Part D coverages are excess over any other collectible source of recovery. *Thus, any physical damage insurance on the borrowed car is primary, and your physical damage insurance is excess.* If you borrow a car and damage it, the owner's physical damage insurance (if any) applies first, and your collision insurance is excess, subject to any deductible. For example, assume that you borrow a friend's car and damage it in an accident. The owner's collision deductible is $500, and your collision deductible is $250. If repairs to the borrowed car are $2000, the owner's PAP pays $1500 ($2000 − $500), and your PAP pays $250 ($500 − $250). The remaining $250 of loss would have to be paid either by the owner or by you. In short, if the owner's collision deductible is larger than your deductible, your insurer pays the difference between the two deductibles.

Appraisal Provision

The PAP contains an **appraisal provision** for handling disputes over the amount of a physical damage

INSIGHT 10.4

Save Yourself Some Grief—Make Certain You Have Gap Insurance on a Leased Car

Gap insurance can prevent financial grief if a leased car is a total loss. Insurers total out a car when the cost of repairs and salvage value exceed its actual cash value. Your car may be totaled because of a collision, theft, tornado, fire, or some other peril. If a car is totaled, the amount paid by the insurer may be substantially less than the amount owed on the lease or loan. Gap insurance pays the difference between the amount paid by your insurer and the amount owed on the lease or loan. The difference can be substantial as shown by the following:

Lease or loan payoff at the time of loss	$20,000
Actual cash value of car	15,000
Your deductible	500
Payment from insurer	14,500
Gap	5,500
Gap insurance pays	5,500

You should check to see if gap insurance is included in the lease you sign. You normally do not actually buy a gap policy if you lease a car. The new car dealer typically buys a master policy from an insurer and includes the cost in the monthly lease payment. However, you should make certain by checking with the car dealer before you lease a car.

If you have a car loan instead of a lease, you may want to buy gap insurance to avoid a substantial gap payment if your car is totaled before the loan is paid off. Your agent should be able to assist you, or gap insurance may be available on the Internet. However, according to the Insurance Information Institute, gap insurance may not be available in some states.

loss. This provision is particularly important in the case of damage to a low-mileage car or to a car in above-average condition. The insured may claim that the car is worth more than the amount stated in the various publications of car prices that auto dealers use. To resolve the dispute, either party can demand an appraisal of the loss. Each party selects a competent and impartial appraiser. The two appraisers then select an umpire. Each appraiser states separately the actual cash value of the car and the amount of the loss. If the appraisers fail to agree, they submit their differences to the umpire. A decision by any two parties is binding on all. Each party pays his or her appraiser, and the umpire's expenses are shared equally. Finally, by agreeing to an appraisal, the insurer does not waive any rights under the policy.

PART E: DUTIES AFTER AN ACCIDENT OR LOSS

You should know what to do if you have an accident or loss. Some obligations are based on common sense, while others are required by law and by the provisions of the PAP. You should first determine if anyone is hurt. If someone is injured, an ambulance should be called immediately. If there are bodily injuries, or the property damage exceeds a certain amount (such as $200), you must notify the police in most jurisdictions. You should give the other driver your name, address, and the name of your agent and insurer and request the same information from him or her. You should also get the name and address of any witnesses.

You should not admit fault. The question of who caused the accident will be determined by the insurers involved or by a court of law.

Your insurance agent should be promptly notified of the accident, even if there are no injuries or property damage. Failure to report the accident promptly to your insurer could jeopardize your coverage if you are later sued by the other driver.

After the accident occurs, a number of duties are imposed on you. You must cooperate with the insurer in the investigation and settlement of a claim. You must send to the insurer copies of any legal papers or notices received in connection with the accident. If you are claiming benefits under the uninsured motorists, underinsured motorists, or medical payments coverages, you may be required to take a physical examination at the insurer's expense. You must also authorize your insurer to obtain medical reports and other pertinent records. Finally, you must submit a proof of loss at the insurer's request.

Some additional duties are imposed on you if you are seeking benefits under the uninsured motorists coverage. The police must be notified if a hit-and-run driver is involved. Also, if you bring a lawsuit against the uninsured driver, you must send copies of the legal papers to your insurer.

If your car is damaged, and you are seeking indemnification under Coverage D, other duties are imposed on you. You must take reasonable steps to protect the vehicle from further damage; your insurer will pay for any expense involved. You must also permit the insurer to inspect and appraise the car before it is repaired.

PART F: GENERAL PROVISIONS

This section contains a number of general provisions. Only two of them are discussed here.

Policy Period and Territory

The PAP provides coverage only in the United States, its territories or possessions, Puerto Rico, and Canada. The policy also provides coverage while a covered auto is being transported between the ports of the United States, Puerto Rico, or Canada. For example, if you rent a car while vacationing in England, Germany, or Mexico, you are not covered. Additional auto insurance must be purchased to be covered while driving in foreign countries. If you intend to drive in Mexico, you should first obtain liability insurance from a Mexican insurer. A motorist from the United States who has not purchased insurance from a Mexican insurer could be detained in jail after an accident, have his or her automobile impounded, and be subject to other penalties as well.

Termination

An important provision applies to termination of the insurance by either the insured or insurer. There are four parts to this provision:

- Cancellation
- Nonrenewal
- Automatic termination
- Other termination provisions

All states place restrictions on the insurer's right to cancel or nonrenew an auto insurance policy. Many states, however, have laws that differ from the termination provisions contained in the PAP. In such cases, an endorsement is added to the PAP to make the auto policy conform to state law.

Cancellation   The named insured normally can cancel at any time by returning the policy to the insurer or by giving advance written notice of the effective date of **cancellation.**

The insurer also has the right of cancellation. If the policy has been in force for *fewer than 60 days*, the insurer can cancel by sending a cancellation notice to the named insured. At least 10 days' notice must be given if the cancellation is for nonpayment of premiums and at least 20 days' notice is required in all other cases. Thus, the insurer has 60 days to investigate a new insured to determine whether he or she is acceptable.

After the policy has been in force for 60 days, or it is a renewal or continuation policy, the insurer can cancel for only three reasons: (1) the premium has not been paid, (2) the driver's license of any insured has been suspended or revoked during the policy period, or (3) the policy was obtained through material misrepresentation.

Nonrenewal   The insurer may also discontinue coverage by not renewing the policy when it comes up for renewal. If the insurer decides not to renew, the named insured must be given at least 20 days' notice before the end of the policy period.

Automatic Termination   If the insurer decides to renew the policy, an automatic termination provision becomes effective. This means that if the named insured does not accept the insurer's offer to renew, the policy automatically terminates at the end of the current policy period. Thus, once the insurer bills the named insured for another period, the insured must pay the premium, or the policy automatically terminates on its expiration date. However, some insurers may provide a short grace period to pay the renewal premium.

Finally, if other insurance is obtained on a covered auto, the PAP insurance on that auto automatically terminates on the day the other insurance becomes effective.

Other Termination Provisions Many states place additional restrictions on the insurer's right to cancel or not renew. If state law requires a longer period of advance notice to the named insured or modifies any termination provision, the PAP is modified to comply with those requirements. Also, if the policy is canceled, the named insured is entitled to any premium refund; however, making or offering to make a premium refund is not a condition for cancellation. Finally, the effective date of cancellation stated in the cancellation notice is the end of the policy period.

2005 PERSONAL AUTO POLICY

As stated earlier, the Insurance Services Office (ISO) has revised the 1998 PAP, and a new 2005 PAP will be introduced in most jurisdictions beginning in 2005. ISO also has revised several endorsements that can be added to the PAP.

The 2005 PAP is similar to the 1998 PAP with certain key changes. The major changes are summarized as follows:[2]

- *Minimum liability limits shown.* The 2005 PAP will show the state's actual minimum liability insurance limits that motorists must carry under a compulsory insurance law or financial responsibility law. A number of courts have held that the 1998 form is ambiguous because it refers to minimum liability requirements without actually listing the specific limits. The 2005 PAP will show the state's required minimum limits.
- *Clarification of other insurance provisions.* The other insurance provisions that appear in the liability, medical payments, and uninsured motorists sections of the PAP are clarified to mean that any coverage provided on a nonowned auto, *including any vehicle used as a temporary substitute for a covered auto,* is excess over any other collectible insurance.
- *Extension of medical payments coverage to a nonowned pickup or van.* Medical payments coverage under the new 2005 PAP is extended to cover medical expenses sustained while occupying a nonowned pickup or van being used in the business of an insured. The older 1998 PAP provided medical payments coverage only on an owned pickup or van used in the business of an insured. The 2005 PAP provides medical pay-

ments coverage on both owned and nonowned pickups or vans being used in the business of an insured. Agents requested an expansion of coverage so that medical payments coverage would track more closely with the liability and physical damage coverages.

- *Increase in the physical damage limit for a nonowned trailer.* The maximum amount paid for a physical damage loss to a nonowned trailer is increased from $500 to $1500, which reflects the higher market value of such trailers.
- *Uninsured motorists exclusion narrowed.* The 1998 PAP does not provide uninsured motorist coverage for a bodily injury sustained by an insured if such insured or legal representative settles the claim without the insurer's consent. The intent here is to protect the insurer's subrogation rights against the uninsured driver. The 2005 PAP narrows the exclusion and states that the exclusion applies if the insured or legal representative settles the bodily injury claim without the insurer's consent, but only if such settlement prejudices the insurer's right to recover the loss payment. Several court decisions have indicated that these side agreements may not have a significant impact on an insurer.
- *Expansion of coverage of electronic equipment.* The 2005 PAP expands coverage of electronic equipment. New cars often include electronic equipment such as navigational systems, video entertainment systems, and Internet access systems. Because the electronic equipment is permanently attached to the vehicle, insureds expect that the PAP will cover such equipment. The 2005 PAP first lists and then excludes certain types of electronic equipment. The excluded equipment includes:
  - Radios and stereos
  - Tape decks
  - Compact disk systems
  - Navigation systems
  - Internet access systems
  - Personal computer
  - Video entertainment systems
  - Telephones
  - Televisions
  - Two-way mobile radios
  - Scanners, or
  - Citizens band radios.

However, the above exclusion does not apply to electronic equipment that is permanently installed in a covered auto or a nonowned auto. Thus, there is coverage if such electronic equipment is permanently installed in the vehicle.

- *Relaxation of duties after an accident or loss provision.* In Part E (duties after an accident or loss), the 1998 PAP has a lead-in provision that states that insurer has no duty to provide coverage unless there is full compliance with certain specified duties. These duties include promptly notifying the insurer of the accident and cooperating with the insurer in the investigation and settlement of the claim. The 2005 PAP relaxes the lead-in provision and states that the insurer has no duty to provide coverage only if the failure to comply with the listed duties is prejudicial to the insurer. Many courts have held that the lead-in provision in the 1998 PAP is too harsh because the insured's failure to comply with every duty may not affect or harm the insurer's position. The 2005 PAP recognizes this

principle and specifies that the insurer is relieved of its duty to cover the loss only if the failure to comply is prejudicial to the insurer.

INSURING MOTORCYCLES AND OTHER VEHICLES

The PAP excludes coverage for motorcycles, mopeds, and similar vehicles. However, a **miscellaneous-type vehicle endorsement** can be added to the PAP to insure motorcycles, mopeds, motorscooters, golf carts, motor homes, dune buggies, and similar vehicles. One exception is a snowmobile, which requires a separate endorsement to the PAP. The miscellaneous-type vehicle endorsement can be used to provide the same coverages found in the PAP.

You should be aware of several points if the miscellaneous-type vehicle endorsement is added to the PAP. First, the liability coverage does not apply to a nonowned vehicle. Although other persons are covered while operating your motorcycle with your

---

CASE APPLICATION

Kim, age 20, is a college student who recently purchased her first car from a friend who had financial problems. The vehicle is a high-mileage 1994 Toyota Tercel with a current market value of $1000. Assume you are a financial planner and Kim asks your advice concerning the various coverages in the PAP.

a. Briefly describe the major coverages that are available in the PAP.
b. Which of the available coverages in (a) should Kim purchase? Justify your answer.
c. Which of the available coverages in (a) should Kim not purchase? Justify your answer.
d. Assume that Kim purchases the PAP coverages that you have recommended. To what extent, if any, would Kim's insurance cover the following situations?
  (1) Danielle, Kim's roommate, borrows Kim's car with her permission and injures another motorist. Danielle is at fault.

  (2) Kim is driving under the influence of alcohol and is involved in an accident where another motorist is seriously injured.
  (3) During the football season, Kim charges a fee to transport fans from a local bar to the football stadium. Several passengers are injured when Kim suddenly changes lanes without signaling and hits another car.
  (4) Kim drives her boyfriend's car on a regular basis. While driving the boyfriend's car, she is involved in an accident in which another motorist is injured. Kim is at fault.
  (5) Kim rents a car in England where she is participating in a summer study program. The car is stolen from a dormitory parking lot.

e. Kim also owns a motorcycle. To what extent, if any, does Kim's PAP cover the motorcycle?

permission, the liability coverage does not apply if you operate a nonowned motorcycle (other than as a temporary substitute vehicle).

Second, a passenger hazard exclusion can be elected, which excludes liability for bodily injury to any passenger on the motorcycle. When the exclusion is used, the insured pays a lower premium. For example, if a passenger on your motorcycle is thrown off and is injured, the liability coverage on the motorcycle does not apply.

Finally, the amount paid for any physical damage losses to the motorcycle is limited to the lowest of (1) the stated amount shown in the endorsement, (2) the actual cash value, or (3) the amount necessary to repair or replace the property (less any deductible).

SUMMARY

- The Personal Auto Policy (PAP) consists of a declarations page, a definitions page, and six major parts:

    Part A: Liability Coverage

    Part B: Medical Payments Coverage

    Part C: Uninsured Motorists Coverage

    Part D: Coverage for Damage to Your Auto

    Part E: Duties After an Accident or Loss

    Part F: General Provisions

- Liability coverage protects the insured from bodily injury and property damage liability arising out of the negligent operation of an automobile or trailer.

- A covered auto includes any vehicle shown in the declarations; newly acquired vehicles; a trailer owned by the insured; and a temporary substitute auto.

- Insured persons include the named insured and spouse, resident family members, other persons using a covered auto if a reasonable belief that permission to use the vehicle exists, and any person or organization legally responsible for the acts of a covered person.

- Medical payments coverage pays all reasonable medical, dental, and funeral expenses incurred by an insured person for services rendered within three years from the date of the accident.

- Uninsured motorists coverage pays for the bodily injury of a covered person caused by an uninsured motorist, a hit-and-run driver, or a negligent driver whose insurer is insolvent.

- Underinsured motorists coverage can be added as an endorsement to the PAP. The coverage applies when a negligent driver carries liability insurance, but the liability limits carried are less than the limit provided by the underinsured motorists coverage.

- Coverage for damage to your auto pays for a direct physical loss to a covered auto or nonowned auto less any deductible. A collision loss or other-than-collision loss is covered only if the declarations page indicates that such coverages are in effect.

- Certain duties are imposed on the insured after an accident occurs. A person seeking coverage must cooperate with the insurer in the investigation and settlement of a claim and send to the insurer copies of any legal papers or notices received in connection with the accident.

- After the policy has been in force for 60 days, or it is a renewal or continuation policy, the insurer can cancel the policy only if the premium has not been paid, the driver's license of an insured has been suspended or revoked during the policy period, or the policy was obtained through material misrepresentation. The insurer can also discontinue coverage by not renewing the policy. If the insurer decides not to renew the policy when it comes up for renewal, the named insured must be given at least 20 days' notice of its intention not to renew.

- Motorcycles and mopeds can be insured by adding the miscellaneous-type vehicle endorsement to the personal auto policy.

KEY CONCEPTS AND TERMS

Appraisal provision
Betterment
Cancellation
Collision
Coverage for damage to your auto
Diminution in value
Extended nonowned coverage endorsement
Gap insurance
Liability coverage
Medical payments overage
Miscellaneous-type vehicle endorsement
Nonowned auto
Nonrenewal
Other-than-collision loss
Personal Auto Policy (PAP)
Single limit
Split limits
Supplementary payments
Temporary substitute vehicle
Underinsured motorists coverage
Uninsured motorists coverage
Your covered auto

REVIEW QUESTIONS

1. The personal auto policy (PAP) contains several coverages that meet the insurance needs of typical insureds. For each of the following coverages, briefly describe the type of coverage provided, and give an example of a loss that would be covered.
   a. Part A: Liability Coverage
   b. Part B: Medical Payments Coverage
   c. Part C: Uninsured Motorists Coverage
   d. Part D: Coverage for Damage to Your Auto

2. The PAP provides coverage for *your covered auto*. Identify the four classes of vehicles that are considered to be covered autos.

3. The PAP provides liability coverage to four groups. Identify the four groups of persons or parties who can be insured under the PAP.

4. In addition to the policy limits and a legal defense, the PAP provides for certain supplementary payments. Briefly describe the supplementary payments that can be paid under the liability section of the PAP.

5. a. List the major exclusions that apply to liability coverage (Part A) in the PAP.
   b. List the major exclusions that apply to medical payments coverage (Part B) in the PAP.

6. Describe the major features of the uninsured motorists coverage (Part C) in the PAP.

7. Coverage for damage to your auto (Part D) in the PAP provides for two optional coverages: (1) collision coverage, and (2) other-than-collision coverage.
   a. What is a collision loss? Explain your answer.
   b. What is other-than-a-collision loss? Explain your answer.
   c. List the major exclusions that apply to coverage for damage to your auto (Part D).

8. Coverage for damage to your auto (Part D) in the PAP also covers the insured while driving a non-owned auto.
   a. Explain the meaning of a nonowned auto.
   b. If the insured drives a nonowned auto on a regular basis, does the insured's PAP provide coverage? Explain your answer.

9. Explain the duties imposed on the insured after an accident or loss occurs.

10. Does the PAP cover you if you are driving a vehicle in a foreign country? Explain your answer.

APPLICATION QUESTIONS

1. Fred has a PAP with the following coverages:
   Liability coverages: $100,000/$300,000/$50,000
   Medical payments coverage: $5000 each person
   Uninsured motorists coverage: $25,000 each person
   Collision loss: $250 deductible
   Other-than-collision loss: $100 deductible
   With respect to each of the following situations, indicate whether the loss is covered and the amount payable, if any, under the policy. Assume that each situation is a separate event.

   a. Fred's son, age 16, is driving a family car, runs a red light, and kills a pedestrian. The family of the deceased pedestrian sue for $500,000.
   b. Fred borrows a friend's car to go to the supermarket. He fails to stop at a red light and negligently smashes into another motorist. The other driver's car, valued at $10,000, is totally destroyed. In addition, damages to the friend's car are $3000.
   c. Fred's daughter, Heather, attends college in another state and drives a family auto. Fred tells her that no other person is to drive the family car. Heather lets her boyfriend drive the car, and he negligently injures another motorist. The boyfriend is sued for $50,000.
   d. Fred's wife is driving a family car in a snowstorm. She loses control of the car on an icy street and smashes into the foundation of a house. The property damage to the house is $20,000. The damage to the family car is $5000. Fred's wife has medical expenses of $3000.
   e. Fred is walking across a street and is struck by a motorist who fails to stop. He has bodily injuries in the amount of $15,000.
   f. Fred's car is being repaired for faulty brakes. While road testing the car, a mechanic injures another motorist and is sued for $50,000.
   g. Fred's car hits a cow crossing a highway. The cost of repairing the car is $2500.
   h. A thief breaks a car window and steals a camera and golf clubs locked in the car. It will cost $400 to replace the damaged window. The stolen property is valued at $500.
   i. Fred's wife goes shopping at a supermarket. When she returns, she finds that the left rear fender has been damaged by another driver who did not leave a name. The cost of repairing the car is $1000.

j. Fred works for a construction company. While driving a large cement truck, he negligently injures another motorist. The injured motorist sues Fred for $20,000.

k. Fred's son drives a family car on a date. He gets drunk, and his girlfriend drives him home. The girlfriend negligently injures another motorist who has bodily injuries in the amount of $200,000.

l. Stereo tapes valued at $500 are stolen from Fred's car. The car was locked when the theft occurred.

m. While driving a rented golf cart, Fred accidentally injures another golfer with the cart.

2. Karen is the named insured under a PAP that provides coverage for bodily injury and property damage liability, medical payments, and the uninsured motorists coverage. For each of the following situations, briefly explain whether the claim is covered by Karen's PAP.

a. Karen ran into a telephone pole and submitted a medical expense claim for Jason, a passenger in Karen's car at the time of the accident.

b. Karen loaned her car to Scott. While operating Karen's car, Scott damaged Gray's car in an accident caused by Scott's negligence. Karen is sued by Gray for damages.

c. Karen's husband ran over a bicycle while driving the car of a friend. The owner of the bicycle demands that Karen's husband pay for the damage.

d. In a fit of anger, Karen deliberately ran over the wagon of a neighbor's child that had been left in Karen's driveway after repeated requests that the wagon be left elsewhere. The child's parents seek reimbursement.

3. Janet has a PAP with the following coverages:

Liability coverages: $100,000/$300,000/$50,000

Medical payment coverage: $5000 each person

Uninsured motorists coverage: $25,000 each person

Collision loss: $250 deductible

Other-than-collision loss: $100 deductible

Towing and labor cost coverage: $25 each disablement

To what extent, if any, is each of the following losses covered under Janet's PAP? Treat each event separately.

a. Janet rents a car while on vacation. She is involved in an accident with another motorist when she fails to yield the right of way. The injured motorist is awarded a judgment of $100,000. The rental agency carries only liability limits of $30,000 on the rental car. The rental agency carries no collision insurance on its cars and is seeking $15,000 from Janet for repairs to the rental car.

b. Janet borrows her friend's car with permission. She is in an accident with another motorist in which she is at fault. The cost of repairing the friend's car is $2000. The friend's auto policy has a $500 deductible for collision losses and $100 for other-than-collision losses.

c. Janet is employed as a salesperson and is furnished a company car. She is involved in an accident with another motorist while driving the company car during business hours. The injured motorist claims Janet is at fault and sues her for $100,000. Damage to the company car amounts to $5000.

d. Janet's car will not start because of a defective battery. A wrecker tows the car to a service station where the battery is replaced. Towing charges are $60. The cost of replacing the battery is $100.

4. Michael was driving a neighbor's pickup truck to get a load of firewood. A child darted out between two parked cars and ran into the street in front of the truck. In an unsuccessful attempt to avoid hitting the child, Michael lost control of the vehicle and hit a telephone pole. The child was critically injured, the pickup truck was badly damaged, and the telephone pole collapsed. Michael has liability coverage and collision coverage under his PAP. The neighbor also has a PAP with liability coverage and collision coverage on the pickup.

a. If Michael is found guilty of negligence, which insurer will pay first for the bodily injuries to the child and the property damage to the telephone pole? Explain.

b. Which insurer will pay for the physical damage to the neighbor's pickup? Explain.

5. Pablo traded in his 1998 Ford for a new Ford. One week later, he hit an oily spot in the road on his way to work and skidded into a parked car. The 1998 Ford was insured under the PAP with full coverage, including a $250 deductible for a collision loss. At the time of the accident, Pablo had not notified his insurer of the trade-in. The physical damage to the parked car was $8000. Damage to Pablo's car was $5000. Will Pablo's PAP cover either or both of these losses? Explain.

6. James, age 18, lives at home and occasionally drives the car of his friend, Mary. Mary carries $300,000 of liability insurance on her car under a PAP. James is

also insured under his mother's PAP, which provides $500,000 of liability coverage. Assume that James has an accident while using Mary's car and is found to be legally liable in the amount of $400,000. How much, if any, will each policy pay? Explain your answer.

7. Patrick has a PAP with liability limits of $50,000/$100,000/$25,000. Patrick failed to stop at a red light and hit a van. The van sustained damages of $15,000. Three passengers in the van were injured and incurred the following bodily injuries:

Passenger A, $15,000

Passenger B, $60,000

Passenger C, $10,000

Patrick was also injured and incurred medical bills of $10,000. His car sustained damages of $10,000. Because of his injury, Patrick was unable to work and lost $5000 in wages. How much will Patrick's insurer pay under the liability coverage (Part A) section of his PAP? Explain your answer.

INTERNET RESOURCES

■ **All Quotes Insurance.Com** uses the power of technology to find solutions to your insurance needs. The database contains hundreds of qualified insurance providers that provide competitive quotes. You can get quotes on auto, homeowners, life, health, disability income and other insurance products. Visit the site at

www.allquotesinsurance.com

■ The **Insurance Research Council (IRC),** a division of the American Institute for CPCU, provides the insurance industry and the public with timely research studies that are relevant to public policy issues dealing with risk and insurance. Visit the site at

http://www.ircweb.org

■ The **RAND Institute for Civil Justice** is an organization within the RAND Corporation that conducts independent, objective research and analysis concerning the civil justice system. Many research studies deal with auto insurance and the insurance industry. Visit the site at

http://www.rand.org/centers/icj/

■ **Geico Direct** sells auto insurance directly over the phone (800-861-8380). The company claims that a 15-minute call can save you 15 percent or more on auto insurance rates. Geico Direct also has a Web site that provides similar premium quotes online. Visit the site at

http://www.geico.com

■ The **Insurance Information Institute** provides timely information on auto insurance and other personal property insurance coverages. Numerous consumer brochures and articles on auto insurance and other property and liability coverages can be accessed directly online. Visit the site at

http://www.iii.org

■ **Insure.com** provides premium quotes for auto insurance, homeowners insurance, and other insurance products. The site also provides timely information and news releases about auto insurance and events that affect the insurance industry. Visit the site at

http://www.insure.com

■ **INSWEB** provides premium quotes for auto, homeowners, and other insurance products. You can comparison shop from your computer. In addition, the site has a learning center and provides information and articles from industry, consumer, and regulating groups. Visit the site at

http://www.insweb.com

■ The **Progressive Casualty Insurance Company** has a user-friendly site that gives auto insurance quotes for most states. Progressive claims its rates are highly competitive. Progressive also provides comparison rates from other insurers. Visit the site at

http://www.progressiveinsurance.com

■ The **National Association of Insurance Commissioners (NAIC)** has a link to all state insurance departments, which provide a considerable amount of consumer information on auto insurance. On the home page, click on "State Insurance Web Sites." For starters, check out New York, Wisconsin, and California. Visit the site at

http://www.naic.org

SELECTED REFERENCES

"Automated Underwriting Tools: Credit & CLUE," *Hot Topics & Insurance Issues,* Insurance Information Institute, January 2004.

Fair, Isaac and Company, Inc. *Predictiveness of Credit History for Insurance Loss Relativities,* A Fair, Isaac Paper, October 1999.

Fire, Casualty & Surety Bulletins, Personal Lines volume, Personal Auto section. Erlanger, KY: National Underwriter Company. The bulletins are updated monthly.

Hamilton, Karen L., and Cheryl L. Ferguson. *Personal Risk Management and Property-Liability Insurance,* First Edition. Malvern, PA.: American Institute for Chartered Property Casualty Underwriters/Insurance Institute of America, 2002.

Hartwig, Robert P., and Claire Wilkinson. *The Use of Credit Information in Personal Lines Insurance Underwriting,* Insurance Information Institute, Insurance Issues Series, Vol. 1, No. 2, June 2003.

Wiening, Eric A., George E. Rejda, Constance M. Luthardt, and Cheryl L. Ferguson. *Personal Insurance,* First Edition. Malvern, PA.: American Institute for Chartered Property Casualty Underwriters/Insurance Institute of America, 2002.

NOTES

1. The material in this chapter is based on *Fire, Casualty & Surety Bulletins*, Personal Lines volume, Personal Auto section (Erlanger, KY: National Underwriter Company); and the 1998 edition of the Personal Auto Policy (copyrighted) by the Insurance Services Office. The Personal Auto Policy is used with the permission of the Insurance Services Office.

2. This section is based on Rob Olson, International Risk Management Institute (IRMI), *Personal Lines Pilot #7: ISO Files 2005 Personal Auto Multistate Forms,* February 19, 2004, and Rob Olson, International Risk Management Institute (IRMI), *Personal Lines Pilot #8: ISO's 2005 Personal Auto Program, Part II,* March 18, 2004. The *Personal Lines Pilot* is an e-mail newsletter for personal lines insurance professionals at http://www.IRMI.com. The 2005 Personal Auto Policy is used with the permission of the Insurance Services Office (ISO).

Students may take a self-administered test on this chapter at
www.aw-bc.com/rejda

CHAPTER 11

AUTOMOBILE INSURANCE AND SOCIETY

"The current system of paying for auto injuries suffers from two fundamental problems: premiums are too high and victims with serious injuries rarely receive full compensation."

Joint Economic Committee, 105th Congress

LEARNING OBJECTIVES

After studying this chapter, you should be able to

◆ Describe each of the following approaches for compensating auto accident victims:
  Financial responsibility laws
  Compulsory insurance laws
  Unsatisfied judgment fund
  Uninsured motorists coverage
  Low-cost auto insurance
  "No pay, No play laws"

◆ Explain the meaning of no-fault auto insurance and the rationale for no-fault insurance laws.

◆ Describe each of the following methods for providing auto insurance to high-risk drivers:
  Automobile insurance plan
  Joint underwriting association (JUA)
  Reinsurance facility

◆ Identify the major factors that determine the cost of auto insurance to consumers.

◆ Explain the suggestions that consumers should follow in shopping for auto insurance.

James, age 26, graduated from a small liberal arts college and accepted a job with a public relations firm in Minneapolis, Minnesota. Shortly after he moved to Minneapolis, a drunk driver ran a red light and smashed into his car. James was seriously injured, and his car was damaged beyond repair. James incurred medical bills in excess of $50,000 and was unable to work for three months. When he tried to collect damages from the negligent driver, he discovered that the driver was uninsured and unemployed and had a lengthy history of alcohol abuse. In short, James had to eat the loss.

James had an unfortunate and costly introduction to the auto insurance reparations system. Each year, millions of motorists are injured or killed in auto accidents in the United States. Society then has the problem of compensating these victims for their bodily injuries and property damage caused by negligent drivers. Society also has the burden of providing auto insurance to irresponsible drivers, including drunk drivers, high-risk drivers, and drivers who habitually break traffic laws. Society must also deal with the problem of compensating innocent accident victims who are injured by uninsured drivers. Finally, some consumer groups believe that auto insurance rates are too high, which has led to cries for legislative reform.

This chapter discusses the preceding problems in depth. Four areas are emphasized: (1) the various approaches for compensating auto accident victims, (2) no-fault auto insurance as an alternative to the tort liability system, (3) methods for providing auto insurance to high-risk drivers, and (4) suggestions for buying auto insurance.

APPROACHES FOR COMPENSATING AUTO ACCIDENT VICTIMS

In many cases, innocent persons who are injured in auto accidents are unable to recover financial damages from the negligent motorists. Although accident victims may have bodily injuries or suffer property damage, they may recover nothing or receive less than full indemnification. To deal with this problem, the states use a number of approaches to provide some protection to accident victims from irresponsible and reckless drivers. They include the following:[1]

- Financial responsibility laws
- Compulsory insurance laws
- Unsatisfied judgment funds
- Uninsured motorists coverage
- Low-cost auto insurance
- "No pay, no play" laws
- No-fault auto insurance

Financial Responsibility Laws

All states have enacted some type of financial responsibility law or compulsory insurance law that requires motorists to furnish proof of financial responsibility up to certain minimum dollar limits. A **financial responsibility law** *does not require proof of financial responsibility until after the driver has his or her first accident or until after conviction for certain offenses, such as driving under the influence of alcohol.* Proof

EXHIBIT **11.1**
Financial Responsibility and Compulsory Auto Insurance Limits by State

State	Liability Limits[1]	State	Liability Limits[1]	State	Liability Limits[1]
Alabama	20/40/10	Kentucky	25/50/10	North Dakota	25/50/25
Alaska	50/100/25	Louisiana	10/20/10	Ohio	12.5/25/7.5
Arizona	15/30/10	Maine	50/100/25	Oklahoma	10/20/10
Arkansas	25/50/25	Maryland	20/40/15	Oregon	25/50/10
California[2]	15/30/5	Massachusetts	20/40/5	Pennsylvania	15/30/5
Colorado	25/50/15	Michigan	20/40/10	Rhode Island	25/50/25
Connecticut	20/40/10	Minnesota	30/60/10	South Carolina	15/30/10
Delaware	15/30/5	Mississippi	10/20/5	South Dakota	25/50/25
D.C.	25/50/10	Missouri	25/50/10	Tennessee[7]	25/50/10
Florida[3]	10/20/10	Montana	25/50/10	Texas	20/40/15
Georgia	25/50/25	Nebraska	25/50/25	Utah	25/50/15
Hawaii	20/40/10	Nevada	15/30/10	Vermont	25/50/10
Idaho	25/50/15	New Hampshire[4]	25/50/25	Virginia	25/50/20
Illinois	20/40/15	New Jersey[5]	15/30/5	Washington	25/50/10
Indiana	25/50/10	New Mexico	25/50/10	West Virginia	20/40/10
Iowa	20/40/15	New York[6]	25/50/10	Wisconsin[4]	25/50/10
Kansas	25/50/10	North Carolina	30/60/25	Wyoming	25/50/20

[1] The first two figures refer to bodily injury liability and the third figure to property damage liability. For example, 20/40/10 means coverage up to $40,000 for all persons injured in an accident, subject to a limit of $20,000 for one individual, and $10,000 coverage for property damage.

[2] Low-cost policy limits for Los Angeles and San Francisco low-income drivers in the California Automobile Assigned Risk Plan are 10/20/3. This is a pilot program effective from July 1, 2000, until January 1, 2007.

[3] Only property damage liability is compulsory.

[4] Liability insurance not compulsory; limits are for financial responsibility.

[5] Drivers may choose a Standard or Basic Policy. Basic Policy limits are 10/10/5.

[6] 50/100 if injury results in death.

[7] Although legally defined as financial responsibility, Tennessee's law is similar to a compulsory law because drivers can be fined if stopped by police or after crashes if they cannot show proof of financial responsibility.

NOTE: Data are from Alliance of American Insurers; American Insurance Association; National Association of Independent Insurers; Insurance Information Institute.

SOURCE: *The I.I.I. Fact Book 2004* (New York, NY: Insurance Information Institute, 2004), p. 47.

of financial responsibility is typically required under the following circumstances:

- After an accident involving bodily injury or property damage over a certain amount
- Upon failure to pay a final judgment resulting from an auto accident
- Following a conviction for certain offenses, such as drunk driving or reckless driving

Under these conditions, if a motorist cannot demonstrate that he or she meets the state's financial respon-

sibility law requirements, the state can revoke or suspend the motorist's driving privileges.

Evidence of financial responsibility can be provided by producing evidence of an auto liability insurance policy with at least certain minimum limits, such as $25,000/$50,000/$25,000.[2] Other ways in which the financial responsibility law can be satisfied are by posting a bond, by depositing securities or money in the amount required by law, or by showing that the person is a qualified self-insurer. Exhibit 11.1 shows the minimum liability insurance requirements in the various states.

Although financial responsibility laws provide some protection against irresponsible motorists, they have two major defects:

- *There is no guarantee that all accident victims will be paid.* The accident victim may not be paid if he or she is injured by an uninsured driver, hit-and-run driver, or driver of a stolen car. An irresponsible motorist often drives without a license, so the law fails to achieve the objective of getting the irresponsible driver off the road.
- *Accident victims may not be fully indemnified for their injuries.* Most financial responsibility laws require only minimum liability insurance limits, which are relatively low. If the bodily injury exceeds the minimum limit, the accident victim may not be fully compensated.

Compulsory Insurance Laws

Liability insurance is compulsory in 47 states and the District of Columbia. A **compulsory insurance law** *requires motorists to carry at least a minimum amount of liability insurance before the vehicle can be licensed or registered.*

Some people believe that compulsory insurance laws provide greater protection against uninsured drivers because motorists must provide evidence of financial responsibility before an accident occurs. However, a study by the National Association of Independent Insurers (NAII) casts doubt on the effectiveness of these laws. The study concludes that compulsory liability insurance laws do not reduce the number of uninsured drivers, auto losses, or insurance premiums. More specifically, the study notes the following defects:[3]

- *Substantial numbers of motorists continue to operate vehicles without insurance.* In 1995, about 15 percent of the entire driver population in the nation had no liability insurance. However, of the 43 states that required drivers to buy such insurance, 13 states had estimated uninsured motorist populations higher than the countrywide norm. In five of these jurisdictions, more than 20 percent of the drivers were uninsured.
- *Despite compulsory insurance laws, claim frequency and loss costs associated with financially* *irresponsible drivers continue to increase in those states requiring such insurance.*
- *The injury loss experience connected to drivers without liability insurance is on average worse in compulsory states than in noncompulsory states.* Drivers with insurance in the compulsory states are 21 percent more likely to file an injury claim in an accident caused by someone without coverage.

Unsatisfied Judgment Funds

Five states—Maryland, Michigan, New Jersey, New York, and North Dakota—have established unsatisfied judgment funds for compensating innocent accident victims. An **unsatisfied judgment fund** *is a state fund for compensating auto accident victims who have exhausted all other means of recovery.* These funds have certain common characteristics:[4]

- The accident victim must obtain a judgment against the negligent motorist and must show that the judgment cannot be collected.
- The maximum amount paid by the fund generally is limited to the state's compulsory insurance law. The amount paid may also be reduced by collateral sources of recovery, such as workers compensation benefits.
- The negligent driver is not relieved of legal responsibility when the fund makes a payment to the accident victim. Negligent drivers must repay the fund or lose their driver's license until the fund is reimbursed for the payments.

The method of financing benefits varies from state to state. Funds can be obtained by charging a fee to each motorist, by assessing insurers based on the amount of auto liability insurance written in the state, by assessing the uninsured motorists in the state, and by surcharging drivers with convictions for moving vehicle violations.

Uninsured Motorists Coverage

Uninsured motorists coverage is another approach for compensating injured auto accident victims. The injured person's insurer agrees to pay the accident victim who has a bodily injury (or property damage in some states) caused by an uninsured motorist, by a hit-and-run driver, or by a negligent driver whose insurer is insolvent.

Uninsured motorists coverage has the following advantages.

- *Motorists have some protection against an uninsured driver.* Many states require the coverage to be mandatorily included in all auto liability insurance policies sold within the state. In other states, coverage is included in the policy unless the insured voluntarily declines the protection by signing a written waiver.
- *Claim settlement is faster and more efficient than a tort liability lawsuit.* Although the accident victim must establish negligence by the uninsured driver, it is not necessary to sue the negligent driver and win a judgment.

Uninsured motorist's coverage, however, has several defects as a technique for compensating injured auto accident victims. They include the following:

- *Unless higher limits are purchased, the maximum amount paid is limited to the state's financial responsibility or compulsory insurance law requirement.* The minimum limits are relatively low. Thus, the accident victim may not be fully compensated for his or her loss.
- *The injured person must establish that the uninsured motorist is legally liable for the accident.* This task may be difficult in some cases and expensive if an attorney must be hired.
- *Property damage is not covered in many states.* Unless you have collision coverage, you would collect nothing for any property damage to your car caused by an uninsured motorist in those states.

Low-Cost Auto Insurance

As stated earlier, compulsory insurance laws generally have not been effective in reducing the number of uninsured drivers. A few states have enacted new laws to deal with the problem.[5] Many drivers are uninsured because of the high cost of auto insurance. **Low-cost auto insurance** provides minimum amounts of liability insurance at reduced rates to motorists who cannot afford regular insurance or have few financial assets to protect.

California has a pilot program for drivers in California's assigned risk program. The program was enacted into law in July 2000 and will expire January 1, 2007. The law requires all auto insurers in the state to take their fair share of applicants. Bodily injury liability coverage is available up to $10,000 per person, up to $20,000 per accident, and $3000 for property damage liability. Collision and comprehensive insurance are not offered.

California's program was not initially effective because the policies were still expensive for low-income drivers; such drivers had few financial assets to protect; and medical care coverage was not provided. Legislation enacted in 2003 reduced premiums and provided for an optional uninsured motorists coverage and medical payments coverage. Despite these changes, however, the program has had limited success in reducing the number of uninsured drivers. By the end of 2003, only about 5600 low-cost policies were in force.

New Jersey has a basic policy that offers $15,000 in personal injury protection, up to $250,000 for catastrophic medical bills, and $5000 in property damage liability. Policyholders have the option to purchase $10,000 of bodily injury liability insurance. The uninsured and underinsured coverage and collision and comprehensive insurance are not available. In addition, in 2003, New Jersey began offering a low-cost auto policy with an annual premium of $365 that provides the same benefits as the basic policy; the low-cost policy is limited to the poorest drivers in the state who are eligible for Medicaid.

Colorado earlier had a low-cost plan for families with annual incomes up to $31,000, which provided a maximum benefit of $25,000 for medical expenses or personal injury protection under its no-fault law. However, Colorado repealed its no-fault law in July 2003 and replaced it with a tort liability law. Colorado's law now requires minimum liability limits of at least $25,000/$50,000/$15,000. At the time of this writing, Colorado does not have a low-cost liability policy for low-income consumers.

"No Pay, No Play" Laws

Another approach is enactment of **"no pay, no play" laws,** which prohibit uninsured motorists from suing negligent drivers for noneconomic damages, such as compensation for pain and suffering. More than 20 states are considering the proposal as a method for reducing the number of uninsured drivers. A few states have enacted such laws. In Michigan, uninsured drivers who are 50 percent or more at fault cannot collect noneconomic damages in an auto accident. California prohibits suits by both uninsured drivers and drunk drivers. Louisiana requires uninsured drivers to pay the first $10,000 of out-of-pocket medical expenses and the first $10,000 in property damage before uninsured drivers can sue the other party. New Jersey prohibits uninsured drivers, drunk drivers, and motorists who commit intentional acts from filing lawsuits for economic and noneconomic damages. In addition, Iowa's law prohibits motorists from collecting noneconomic damages for injuries resulting from the accident if the motorist used the vehicle to commit a felony.

No-Fault Auto Insurance

No-fault auto insurance is another method for compensating injured accident victims. Because of dissatisfaction and defects in the traditional tort liability system, about half of the states, the District of Columbia, and Puerto Rico currently have no-fault laws in effect. Although no-fault laws vary among the states, certain characteristics are common.

Definition of No-Fault Insurance No-fault auto insurance *means that after an auto accident involving a bodily injury, each party collects from his or her own insurer regardless of fault*. It is not necessary to determine who is at fault and prove negligence before a loss payment is made. Regardless of who caused the accident, each party collects from his or her own insurer.

In addition, a true no-fault law places some restriction on the right to sue the negligent driver who caused the accident. If a bodily injury claim is below a certain **monetary threshold** (such as $2000), an injured motorist would not be permitted to sue but instead would collect from his or her own insurer. However, if the bodily injury claim exceeds the threshold amount, the injured person has the right to sue the negligent driver for damages. If the negligent driver is insured, the negligent driver's insurance company will usually cover the loss.

In some states, a verbal rather than monetary threshold is used. A **verbal threshold** *means that a suit for damages is allowed only in serious cases, such as those involving death, dismemberment, disfigurement, or permanent loss of a bodily member or function*. Thus, if the injured person has a less severe injury than those listed, the injured person would not be permitted to sue but instead would collect from his or her insurer.

Basic Characteristics of No-Fault Plans No-fault plans vary widely among the states with respect to the type of law, benefits provided, and restrictions on the right to sue.[6] Proposals for new types of no-fault plans are continually emerging.

1. *Types of no-fault plans*. Several types of no-fault plans and proposals exist. They include the following:

- Pure no-fault plan
- Modified no-fault plan
- Add-on plan
- Choice no-fault plan

Under a **pure no-fault plan**, *accident victims could not sue at all, regardless of the amount of the claim, and no payments would be made for pain and suffering*. In effect, the tort liability system would be abolished, because accident victims could not sue for damages. Instead, injured persons would receive unlimited medical benefits and lost wages from their insurers. No state has enacted a pure no-fault plan at this time, but Michigan's law comes closest to this concept.

Under a **modified no-fault plan**, *an injured person has the right to sue a negligent driver only if the bodily injury claim exceeds the dollar or verbal threshold*. Otherwise, the accident victim collects from his or her own insurer. Thus, modified no-fault plans only partially restrict the right to sue.

An **add-on plan** *pays benefits to an accident victim without regard to fault, and the injured person still has the right to sue the negligent driver who caused the accident*. This plan also includes the right to sue for pain and suffering. Because the injured person retains the right to sue, add-on plans are not true no-fault laws.

Three states (Kentucky, New Jersey, and Pennsylvania) have **choice no-fault plans.** Under such laws, motorists can elect to be covered under the state's no-fault law and pay lower premiums or can retain the right to sue under the tort liability system and pay higher premiums.

Slightly more than half of the jurisdictions with no-fault laws have enacted modified plans where restrictions are placed on the right to sue. The remainder have add-on plans or choice no-fault laws. As noted earlier, no state has enacted a pure no-fault plan, and three states have choice no-fault laws.

2. *No-fault benefits.* No-fault benefits are provided by adding an endorsement to the auto insurance policy. The endorsement is typically called "basic reparations benefits coverage" or "personal injury protection coverage (PIP)" which describes the no-fault benefits. Benefits are restricted to the injured person's *economic loss,* such as medical expenses, a percentage of lost wages, and certain other expenses. The injured person can sue for *noneconomic loss* (such as pain and suffering and inconvenience) only if the dollar threshold is exceeded or the verbal threshold is met.

The following benefits are typically provided:

- Medical expenses
- Loss of earnings
- Essential services expenses
- Funeral expenses
- Survivors' loss benefits

Medical expenses are paid usually up to some maximum limit. Michigan has no limit on medical benefits. Rehabilitation expenses incurred by an injured accident victim are also paid.

Payments are made for the loss of earnings. The no-fault benefits are typically limited to a stated percentage of the disabled person's weekly or monthly earnings, with a maximum limit in terms of dollar amount and duration.

Benefits are also paid for **essential services expenses** *ordinarily performed by the injured person.* Examples include housework, cooking, lawn mowing, and house repairs.

Funeral expenses are paid up to some dollar limit. In some states, funeral expenses are included as part of the medical expense limit. In other states, funeral expenses are a separate benefit.

Survivors' loss benefits *are payable to eligible survivors, such as a surviving spouse and dependent children.* The survivors typically receive periodic income payments or a lump sum to compensate them for the death of a covered person.

A number of states also require that **optional no-fault benefits** above the prescribed minimums be made available. Likewise, many states require insurers to offer **optional deductibles** that may be used to restrict or eliminate certain no-fault coverages.

3. *Right to sue.* In those states with add-on plans, there are no restrictions on the right to sue. The accident victim can receive first-party no-fault benefits from his or her insurer and still sue the negligent driver for damages.

All states permit a lawsuit in the event of a serious injury. A serious injury typically is an injury that results in death, dismemberment, disfigurement, bone fracture, permanent loss of a bodily function or organ, or permanent disability. Under these circumstances, the injured person can sue for damages, including payment for pain and suffering.

In those states with modified no-fault laws, the right to sue is restricted. In general, the accident victim can sue the negligent driver for general damages, including pain and suffering, only if a dollar or verbal threshold is met.

Finally, the three states with choice no-fault laws allow motorists to elect coverage under the state's no-fault law with lower premiums and restrictions on lawsuits or, alternatively, to retain the right to sue under the tort liability system with higher premiums.

4. *Exclusion of property damage.* With the exception of Michigan, no-fault laws cover only bodily injury and not property damage. Thus, if a negligent driver smashed into your car, you would still be permitted to sue for the property damage to your car. It is argued that the defects inherent in the tort liability system with respect to bodily injuries are not normally present to the same degree in property damage claims; thus, a lawsuit for property damage does not normally result in long court delays, expensive legal fees, and defects similar to those now found in bodily injury lawsuits. Also, the size of a property

damage claim settlement is relatively small when compared to bodily injury liability settlements.

Arguments for No-Fault Laws Proponents of no-fault laws argue that an alternative system is needed because of defects in the present tort liability system. These defects include the following:

- *Difficulty in determining fault.* Critics argue that auto accidents occur suddenly and unexpectedly, and determination of fault is often difficult. Under a no-fault law, it is not necessary to determine fault. Each party collects from his or her insurer if the bodily injury claim is below a certain dollar threshold or does not meet the description of a verbal threshold.

- *Inequity in claim payments.* Under the present system, small claims are often overpaid, whereas serious claims may be underpaid. As a result, auto accident victims with serious injuries often recover less than the full amount of their economic losses. *Claimants with minor injuries receive compensation that averages two to three times their economic loss while claimants who are severely injured receive much less—just over half on average.*[7]

- *High transactions costs and attorney fees.* Critics also argue that the present tort system incurs high transactions costs and attorney fees. A Joint Economic Committee Study showed that for each premium dollar paid for bodily injury liability, attorneys (representing both plaintiffs and defendants) receive more than 28 cents of the premium dollar. Overhead expenses, state taxes and fees, and commissions and selling expenses eat up another 28 cents. Fraudulent and excessive claims account for about 13 cents out of each premium dollar. *Only 31 cents of each premium dollar is paid to injured claimants for medical bills, lost wages, and pain and suffering related to actual economic loss* (see Exhibit 11.2).

- *Fraudulent and excessive claims.* The Joint Economic Committee Study showed that the present system is flawed because of fraudulent and excessive claims. Two types of abuse are present. First, explicit fraud occurs, including staged auto accidents, fake claims, and collusion

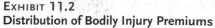

EXHIBIT 11.2
Distribution of Bodily Injury Premiums

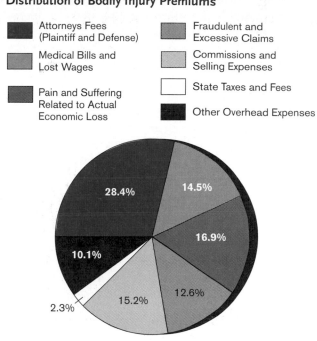

- Attorneys Fees (Plaintiff and Defense)
- Medical Bills and Lost Wages
- Pain and Suffering Related to Actual Economic Loss
- Fraudulent and Excessive Claims
- Commissions and Selling Expenses
- State Taxes and Fees
- Other Overhead Expenses

28.4% 14.5% 16.9% 10.1% 12.6% 2.3% 15.2%

SOURCE: "Auto Choice: Impact on Cities and the Poor," *Joint Economic Committee Study*, 105th Congress, Washington, DC (March 1998).

among doctors, attorneys, and chiropractors. Second, the present system encourages injured victims to inflate their claims above their actual losses to increase their damage awards. Because payments for noneconomic losses (pain and suffering) are difficult to calculate, one rule of thumb currently followed is to calculate such losses as two to three times the claimant's economic losses (medical bills and lost wages). *Because pain and suffering awards are based on a multiple of medical expenses and wage loss, claimants have a powerful incentive to inflate their claims.* According to one estimate, fraudulent and excessive auto insurance claims cost each American household $200 annually in additional premiums.[8]

- *Delay in payments.* Under the present system, many claims are not paid promptly because of the time consumed by investigation, negotiation, and waiting for a court date. Moreover, hiring an attorney does not necessarily speed up payment. An Insurance Research Council (IRC) study of closed claims in 1997 showed that claimants without attorneys received payments significantly more quickly than claimants with attorneys. *Thirty-one percent of bodily injury claimants without an attorney received a final payment from their insurers within 30 days of the injury report, compared with only 1 percent of claimants represented by attorneys.*[9]

In addition, hiring an attorney does not necessarily mean that injured claimants will be better off financially than claimants without attorneys. *According to the IRC study, claimants repre-sented by attorneys received lower net payments than claimants without attorneys after deducting legal fees and economic losses (such as medical expenses and lost wages).* On average, claimants with attorneys received net payments of $708, whereas claimants without attorneys received net payments of $1449 (see Exhibit 11.3). Although claimants with attorneys received substantially higher gross payments, they incurred average legal fees of 32 percent of the award. This group also incurred higher economic losses (primarily medical expenses) to be paid out of their claim settlement.[10]

Exhibit 11.3
Net Payment to Bodily Injury Claimants by Attorney Representation

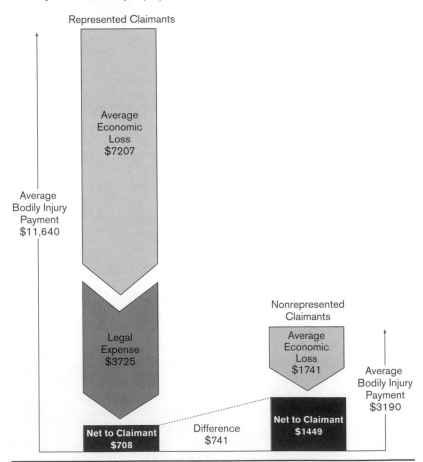

SOURCE: *Injuries in Auto Accidents, an Analysis of Auto Insurance Claims, Executive Summary* (Malvern, PA: Insurance Research Council, 1999), fig. 1.6, p. 9.

Arguments Against No-Fault Laws   Supporters of the present system argue that no-fault laws are also defective. Major arguments against no-fault laws include the following:

- *Defects of the negligence system are exaggerated.* Generations of judges, lawyers, and juries have successfully applied negligence concepts to auto accidents. A large proportion of fatal crashes and serious accidents involve alcohol where fault can usually be determined without difficulty. Also, the fact that most claims are settled out of court suggests that the present system is working fairly well.

- *Claims of efficiency and premium savings are exaggerated.* Predictions of greater efficiency and premium savings from no-fault laws are exaggerated and unreliable. In many states with no-fault laws, premiums have increased more rapidly than in tort liability states.

- *Court delays are not universal.* Court delays are a problem only in certain large metropolitan areas, and this delay can be reduced by providing for more adequate courts and improved procedures. The courts are burdened because of an increase in the number of divorce cases, drug and other criminal cases, and other types of civil suits.

- *Safe drivers may be penalized.* A no-fault plan can penalize safe drivers and provide a bonus for irresponsible motorists who cause accidents. The rating system may inequitably allocate the accident costs to the drivers who are not at fault, and their premiums may go up as a result.

- *There is no payment for pain and suffering.* Plaintiff attorneys argue that the true cost to the accident victim cannot be measured only by the actual dollar amount of medical expenses and loss of wages. Pain and suffering should also be considered in determining the amount of damages.

- *The tort liability system needs only to be reformed.* This reform could be accomplished by increasing the number of judges and courtrooms, limiting the fees of attorneys, and using arbitration rather than the courts to settle small cases. Rather than replacing the tort liability system with a new system of no-fault, the tort liability system needs only to be reformed, not abandoned.

Evaluation of No-Fault Laws   A few states have repealed their no-fault laws because low dollar thresholds resulted in additional lawsuits. Other states have changed their plans over time. A study of no-fault plans by the Institute for Civil Justice provides valuable information concerning the effectiveness of no-fault plans. The major conclusions are as follows:[11]

- *No-fault plans reduce transaction costs (attorney fees and claim processing costs).* All no-fault plans reduce transaction costs. However, a no-fault plan that absolutely banned compensation for noneconomic loss would eliminate about three-fourths of the transaction costs. Alternative plans that allow some access to the liability system would reduce transaction costs by 20 to 40 percent, depending on the plan design.

- *No-fault plans match the compensation received for an injury more closely with the economic loss sustained.* No-fault plans increase the fraction of economic loss that is compensated and reduce the amount paid for noneconomic loss. Economic loss includes medical bills, lost wages, and other losses measured in monetary terms. Injured people with smaller claims tend to recover amounts that approximate their medical costs and lost wages. However, seriously injured people recover a larger share of their losses because they can collect both no-fault benefits and liability compensation.

- *No-fault plans eliminate compensation for noneconomic loss, such as pain and suffering, for injured people below the threshold.* Noneconomic losses include pain and suffering, disfigurement, and other losses not measured in monetary terms.

- *No-fault plans generally pay benefits more quickly.* On average, no-fault plans pay benefits to injured people about two months faster than under the traditional system.

- *No-fault plans can yield substantial savings over the traditional system, or such plans can increase costs depending on the plan design.* Under different no-fault alternatives, total injury coverage costs may decrease. Such costs, however, may be higher under no-fault plans, depending on the threshold and level of no-fault benefits. This is especially true in states that have relatively low dollar thresholds. Whether a particular no-fault plan will reduce total injury costs will depend on the provisions in the plan and plan design.

- *On the negative side, fraudulent no-fault auto insurance claims have increased substantially over time in a number of states.* In particular, fraudulent no fault claims are a major problem in New York. According to the Insurance Research Council, one in four PIP claims in New York includes an element of fraud.[12] In addition, the amount of an average PIP claim in New York is substantially higher than in other no-fault states. The increase in fraudulent claims is due largely to staged accidents, excessive use of medical diagnostic tests, phony pain clinics, and corrupt physicians, lawyers, and chiropractors.

To reduce the fraud problem, New York recently enacted new regulations that shorten the time period for reporting an auto accident and the submission of medical bills. As a result of the reduction in notification time, insurers can examine the plan of treatment sooner, which provides fewer opportunities for unnecessary diagnostic tests and fraudulent claims.

AUTO INSURANCE FOR HIGH-RISK DRIVERS

Some drivers have difficulty obtaining auto insurance through normal market channels. This is especially true of younger drivers, who account for a disproportionate number of auto accidents, drivers who have poor driving records, and drivers with one or more convictions for drunk driving. These drivers can obtain auto insurance in the **shared market** (also called the **residual market**). The shared market refers to plans in which auto insurers participate to make insurance available to drivers who are unable to obtain coverage in the standard markets.

High-risk drivers who have difficulty in obtaining auto insurance in the standard markets can purchase the insurance from a number of sources. They include the following:

- Automobile insurance plan
- Joint underwriting association (JUA)
- Reinsurance facility

- Maryland Automobile Insurance Fund
- Specialty automobile insurers

Automobile Insurance Plan

Most states have an **automobile insurance plan** (also called an **assigned risk plan**) that makes auto insurance available to motorists who are unable to obtain insurance in the voluntary market. Under such a plan, all auto insurers in the state are assigned their proportionate share of high-risk drivers based on the total volume of auto insurance written in the state. For example, if insurer A writes 5 percent of the auto insurance premiums in the state, insurer A must accept 5 percent of the high-risk applicants in the automobile insurance plan (see Exhibit 11.4). The premiums charged, however, are substantially higher than those charged in the voluntary markets. It is not uncommon for high-risk drivers to pay two or three times the standard premium.

Exhibit 11.4
Example of an Automobile Insurance Plan (Generalized)

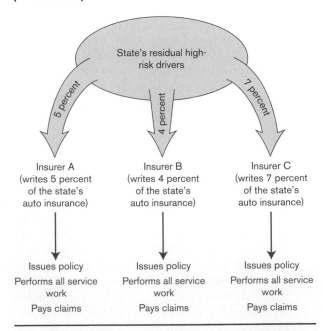

SOURCE: Adapted from Karen L. Hamilton and Cheryl L. Ferguson, *Personal Risk Management and Property-Liability Insurance,* First Edition, (Malvern, PA.: American Institute for Chartered Property Casualty Underwriters/Insurance Institute of America, 2002), Exhibit 9-5, p. 9.37.

The major advantage of automobile insurance plans is that a high-risk driver generally has at least one source for obtaining liability insurance. Thus, the social objective of protecting innocent accident victims is at least partially met. Nevertheless, such plans have several disadvantages, which include the following:

- *Despite higher premiums paid by high-risk drivers, auto insurance plans have incurred substantial underwriting losses.* Thus, good drivers in the voluntary markets are subsidizing the substandard drivers.
- *High premiums may cause many high-risk drivers to go uninsured.* This effect is the exact opposite of what the plans are intended to accomplish.
- *Many drivers who are "clean risks" with no driving convictions are arbitrarily placed in the plans.* This can happen when poor territorial loss experience or inadequate rate increases granted by regulatory officials cause insurers to restrict the writing of auto insurance in a given territory or state in the voluntary market.

Joint Underwriting Association

A few states have established joint underwriting associations to make auto insurance available to high-risk drivers. A **joint underwriting association (JUA)** is an organization of auto insurers operating in the state in which high-risk business is placed in a common pool, and each company pays its pro rata share of pool losses and expenses. The JUA influences the design of the high-risk auto policy and sets the rates that are charged. All underwriting losses are proportionately shared by the companies on the basis of premiums written in the state.

A limited number of insurance companies are designated as servicing insurers to administer the high-risk JUA business. Each agent or broker is assigned a company that provides claim services and other services to the policyowners. Although only a limited number of large insurers are servicing insurers, all insurers share in the underwriting losses, as noted earlier.

Reinsurance Facility

A few states have established a **reinsurance facility** (or **pool**) for placing high-risk drivers. Under this arrangement, the insurance company must accept all applicants for insurance, both good and bad drivers. If the applicant is considered a high-risk driver, the insurer has the option of placing the driver in the reinsurance pool. Although the high-risk driver is in the reinsurance pool, the original insurer services the policy. Underwriting losses in the reinsurance facility are shared by all auto insurers in the state.

Maryland Automobile Insurance Fund

The **Maryland Automobile Insurance Fund** is a state fund that makes auto insurance available to Maryland motorists who are unable to obtain insurance in the voluntary markets. The state fund came into existence because of high rates charged by private insurers, large numbers of motorists who had been placed in the assigned risk plan, and difficulties experienced by high-risk drivers in obtaining insurance. The fund provides insurance only to drivers who have been canceled or refused insurance by private insurers.

Specialty Auto Insurers

Specialty auto insurers are insurers that specialize in insuring motorists with poor driving records. These insurers typically insure drivers who have been canceled or refused insurance, teenage drivers, and drivers convicted of drunk driving. The premiums are substantially higher than premiums paid in the standard market. The actual premium paid is based on the individual's driving record, typically over the past three years. The higher the number of chargeable accidents or moving vehicle traffic violations, the higher the premium charged. The liability insurance limits are at least equal to the financial responsibility law requirement in the state, and many insurers offer higher limits on an optional basis. In addition, because the drivers have a high probability of being involved in an accident, medical payments coverage often has relatively low limits, and collision insurance may require a high deductible.

COST OF AUTO INSURANCE

Auto insurance is expensive. Auto insurers have substantially increased their rates in recent years because of rising medical costs, higher motor vehicle repair costs, soaring jury awards in motor vehicle

Exhibit 11.5
Average Consumer Expenditures on Auto Insurance

* Insurance Information Institute estimates.

Note: Data are from National Association of Insurance Commissioners and Insurance Information Institute.

Source: Insurance Information Institute.

liability cases, and insurance fraud and abuse (see Exhibit 11.5). You should be aware of the factors that determine auto insurance premiums and what you can do to reduce the premiums. This section discusses the major factors that determine the cost of auto insurance.

The major rating factors for determining private passenger auto premiums are as follows:

- Territory
- Age, gender, and marital status
- Use of the auto
- Driver education
- Good student discount
- Number and types of cars
- Individual driving record
- Insurance score

Territory

A base rate for liability insurance is first established, determined largely by the territory where the auto is principally used and garaged. Each state is divided into rating territories—for example, a large city, a

part of a city, a suburb, or a rural area. Claims data are compiled for each territory in determining the basic rate. Thus, a city driver normally pays a higher rate than a rural driver because of the higher number of auto accidents in congested cities. In addition, because of increased litigation, higher claim costs, large numbers of vehicles, and traffic congestion, average annual auto insurance premiums are substantially higher in certain states, such as New Jersey and New York (see Exhibit 11.6).

Age, Gender, and Marital Status

Age, gender, and marital status are important in determining the total premium. Most states permit these factors to be used in determining premiums.

Age is an extremely important rating factor because young drivers account for a disproportionate number of auto accidents. In 2002, drivers under age 25 accounted for about 14 percent of all licensed drivers; however, this group accounted for about 23 percent of the drivers in all accidents and about 21 percent of all fatal accidents (see Exhibit 11.7).

Exhibit 11.6
Average Expenditures for Auto Insurance by State, 2001

State	Liability	Collision	Comprehensive	Average Expenditure	Rank[1]
Alabama	$321.98	$288.34	$123.47	$ 605.32	39
Alaska	489.55	338.07	142.06	826.10	10
Arizona	457.96	273.20	183.10	822.35	11
Arkansas	335.18	259.27	154.74	620.90	33
California[2]	404.48	282.42	108.46	688.89	23
Colorado	466.02	269.69	199.38	807.51	12
Connecticut	569.32	297.08	127.10	912.19	5
Delaware	564.23	254.26	111.34	850.56	8
District of Columbia[3]	543.86	381.97	230.40	1,011.76	3
Florida	482.16	245.30	108.33	788.02	13
Georgia	355.86	334.52	157.84	703.07	22
Hawaii	490.84	229.42	90.86	705.10	21
Idaho	293.31	202.45	133.92	523.38	48
Illinois	357.64	277.16	112.77	682.59	25
Indiana	338.67	246.21	113.30	614.86	35
Iowa	267.31	192.18	136.95	512.66	49
Kansas	266.62	233.71	199.91	555.90	44
Kentucky	406.59	246.08	114.10	645.21	27
Louisiana	482.39	309.34	175.48	838.96	9
Maine	299.44	216.46	105.39	545.42	46
Maryland	457.05	271.26	124.73	783.77	14
Massachusetts[4]	588.45	292.69	132.32	936.01	4
Michigan	293.92	415.63	162.43	735.12	18
Minnesota	421.70	211.52	175.41	735.20	17
Mississippi	337.45	283.48	163.44	637.62	30
Missouri	339.33	264.57	133.24	633.52	31
Montana	307.18	210.45	202.91	572.06	42
Nebraska	284.71	199.75	183.54	553.83	45
Nevada	540.99	291.08	133.88	851.15	7
New Hampshire	368.93	256.18	104.60	685.62	24
New Jersey[3,5]	599.80	388.83	193.91	1,027.71	1
New Mexico	392.95	254.38	167.58	662.27	26
New York	681.48	301.25	178.54	1,014.96	2
North Carolina	315.75	242.48	109.71	564.76	43
North Dakota	234.47	195.59	203.72	497.79	51
Ohio	356.73	232.49	93.45	613.75	36
Oklahoma	345.83	255.95	160.99	621.58	32
Oregon	396.38	218.81	109.93	642.52	28
Pennsylvania	434.41	255.22	118.26	726.41	19
Rhode Island	568.85	328.48	129.71	880.06	6

EXHIBIT 11.6 (continued)
Average Expenditures for Auto Insurance by State, 2001

State	Liability	Collision	Comprehensive	Average Expenditure	Rank[1]
South Carolina	$360.32	$234.33	$150.22	$616.87	34
South Dakota	263.99	190.52	193.65	510.42	50
Tennessee	321.39	273.18	112.24	610.65	37
Texas[6]	418.86	272.79	128.59	735.46	16
Utah	365.91	250.76	122.52	640.12	29
Vermont	311.41	254.12	117.21	602.52	40
Virginia	357.51	221.63	109.35	610.14	38
Washington	462.21	241.69	132.34	749.74	15
West Virginia	418.40	262.81	159.87	706.90	20
Wisconsin	304.10	200.52	125.49	573.46	41
Wyoming	261.61	221.50	199.49	527.63	47
Countrywide	**$412.96**	**$270.98**	**$133.49**	**$717.70**	

[1] Ranked by average expenditure.
[2] Preliminary.
[3] The District of Columbia and New Jersey are entirely urban and their results cannot be directly compared to states with rural areas.
[4] Data incorporates Safe Driver Plan credits and surcharges.
[5] Historically, New Jersey has paid 2 to 4 times the national average in dividends, and at times as high as 6 times the national average, which reduces the average expenditure paid by New Jersey policyholders.
[6] Due to the absence of county mutual data, Texas results are not comparable to results from other states.

NOTE: Average Expenditure = Total premiums written/Liability Car-Years. A car-year is equal to 365 days of insured coverage for a single vehicle.

NOTE: Data are reprinted with permission from State Average Expenditures and Premiums for Personal Automobile Insurance in 2001, published by the National Association of Insurance Commissioners. Further reprint or redistribution strictly prohibited without written permission of NAIC.

SOURCE: Adapted from *The I.I.I. Fact Book 2004* (New York, NY: Insurance Information Institute, 2004), pp. 40–42.

EXHIBIT 11.7
Accidents by Age of Drivers, 2002

Age Group	Number of Drivers	Percent of Total	Drivers in Fatal Accidents	Percent of Total	Drivers in All Accidents	Percent of Total
Under 20	9,508,000	4.9%	6,100	11.6%	2,420,000	11.5%
20–24	16,768,000	8.7	5,900	11.2	2,090,000	9.4
25–34	33,734,000	17.5	10.300	19.5	7,020,006	22.9
35–44	41,040,000	21.2	10,300	19.5	6,670,000	21.7
45–54	38,711,000	20.0	8,300	15.7	5,130,000	16.7
55–64	25,609,000	13.2	5,300	10.1	2,760,000	9.0
65–74	15,812,000	8.1	2,000	5.3	1,490,000	4.9
Over 70	12,118,000	6.3	3,700	7.0	1,120,000	3.6
Total	**193,300,000**	**100.0%**	**52,700**	**100.0%**	**30,700,000**	**100.0%**

NOTE: Percent of total columns may not add due to rounding.

NOTE: Data are from National Safety Council.

SOURCE: Adapted from *The I.I.I. Fact Book 2004* (New York, NY: Insurance Information Institute, 2004), p. 102.

Drivers over age 65 are also involved in a high percentage of fatal accidents (see Exhibit 11.8).

Gender is also important. Insurers generally charge female drivers lower rates than males, but the rate gap is narrowing, especially at the younger ages. In recent years, female drivers have experienced higher accident rates than male drivers. However, male drivers are involved in a higher proportion of accidents where someone is killed.[13]

Marital status is also important for some age groups, because young married male drivers tend to have relatively fewer accidents than unmarried male drivers in the same age category.

Certain credits and rate discounts may be allowed with respect to the rating factor of age. A premium credit may be given if a youthful driver of a family car is attending a school or college more than 100 miles away from home and does not have a car at school. Also, female drivers ages 30 through 64 may be eligible for a rate discount if they are the only drivers in their households. Older drivers are also eligible for rate discounts from many insurers.

Use of the Auto

Use of the auto is another important rating factor. Insurers classify vehicles on the basis of how the car is driven, such as the following:

- Pleasure use—not used in business or customarily driven to work, unless the one-way mileage to work is under 3 miles.
- Drive to work—not used in business, but is driven 3 to 15 miles to work each day.
- Drive to work—not used in business, but is driven 15 or more miles each way.
- Business use—customarily used in business or professional pursuits.
- Farm use—principally garaged on a farm or ranch, and not used in any other business or driven to school or work.

A car classified for farm use has the lowest rating factor, followed next by pleasure use of the car. Driving the car to work or using it for business purposes requires a higher rating factor.

Exhibit 11.8
Motor Vehicle Deaths per 100,000 Persons by Age, 2002

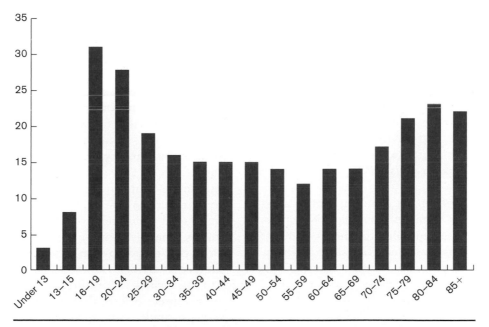

Note: Data are from Insurance Institute for Highway Safety.
Source: Adapted from *The I.I.I. Fact Book 2004* (New York: NY: Insurance Information Institute, 2004), p. 102.

Driver Education

If a youthful operator successfully completes an approved driver education course, he or she can receive a driver training credit, such as 10 or 15 percent. The rate credit is based on the premise that driver education courses for teenage drivers can reduce accidents.

Good Student Discount

A **good student discount** can also reduce premiums. The cost reduction is based on the premise that good students are better drivers. The psychological makeup and intellectual capacity of the superior student also contribute to the safer operation of an auto. Also, a superior student will probably spend more time studying and less time driving.

To qualify for the discount, the individual must be a full-time student in high school or college, be at least age 16, and meet one of the following:

- Rank in the upper 20 percent of the class
- Have a B average, or the equivalent
- Have at least a 3.0 average
- Be on the dean's list or honor roll

A school official must sign a form indicating that the student has met one of the scholastic requirements.

Number and Types of Cars

A **multicar discount** is available if the insured owns two or more cars. This discount is based on the assumption that two cars owned by the same person will not be driven as frequently as only one car owned by that person or family.

The year, make, and model also affect the cost of physical damage insurance on the car. As the car gets older, premiums for physical damage insurance decline.

Also, the cost of repairs is an important rating factor for physical damage insurance. New cars are rated based on susceptibility to damage and cost of repairs. Cars that are damage-resistant and relatively easy to repair generally have lower rates.

Individual Driving Record

Many insurers have **safe driver plans** where the premiums paid are based in large part on the individual driving record of the insured and vehicle operators who live with the insured. The insured who has a clean driving record qualifies for a lower rate than drivers who have poor records. A clean driving record means that the driver has not been involved in any accident where he or she is at fault and has not been convicted of a serious traffic violation in the last three years. A driver without a clean record must pay higher premiums.

Points are assessed for accidents and traffic violations, and rate surcharges are applied accordingly. Points are charged for a conviction of drunk driving, failure to stop and report an accident, homicide or assault involving an automobile, driving on a suspended or revoked driver's license, and other offenses. The actual premium paid is based on the total number of accumulated points.

Most insurers impose a surcharge for a chargeable accident that exceeds a given amount, such as $500. The surcharge generally lasts three years. For example, the base premium may be surcharged 10 percent for the first accident and 25 percent for the second.

Insurance Score

Another important rating factor is an insurance score based on the applicant's credit record. *An insurance score is a credit-based score that proponents claim is highly predictive of future claim costs.* An insurance score is a statistical analysis of an individual's credit record that indicates the likelihood of filing an insurance claim within a specified future time period. The insurance score is based on an individual's credit history and is then combined with other rating factors for purposes of underwriting and rating. Insurers claim there is a high correlation between insurance scores and the likelihood of an auto accident. Drivers as a group with poor credit tend to file relatively more claims than drivers with good credit; conversely, drivers as a group with good credit tend to file relatively fewer claims. Actuarial studies generally support this conclusion. For example, a credit study by the Casualty Actuarial Society shows that drivers with the worst credit (category A) had the highest loss ratio (see Exhibit 11.9). Thus, auto insurers believe that use of credit enables insurers to underwrite applicants at rates that reflect their specific risk.

Credit organizations, such as Fair Isaac and ChoicePoint, calculate insurance scores for auto

EXHIBIT 11.9
Casualty Actuarial Society Credit Study

Personal Automobile Loss Ratio by Credit Category

Category	Earned Premium	Incurred Loss	Loss Ratio
A	$74,279	$75,333	101.4%
B	158,922	124,723	78.5%
C	69,043	47,681	69.1%
D	91,746	52,688	57.4%
Total	**$393,990**	**$300,425**	**76.3%**

Category A – Unacceptable Credit Rating
Category B – No established credit history (or does not meet the definition of A, C or D)
Category C – Good Credit Rating
Category D – Excellent Credit Rating

NOTE: Data are from Casualty Actuarial Society.

SOURCE: Excerpted from Robert P. Hartwig and Claire Wilkinson, *The Use of Credit Information in Personal Lines Insurance Underwriting,* Insurance Issues Series (New York: Insurance Information Institute, June 2003), Vol. 1, No. 2, Exhibit 13.

insurers based on the applicant's credit history. A mathematical formula assigns weights to various credit factors and then summarizes the results in a three digit number. The formulas used to calculate insurance scores are proprietary, but typically include late payments, outstanding debt, past due amounts, public records, payment patterns, and similar credit factors.

The use of insurance scores for purposes of underwriting and rating in auto insurance is highly controversial. Critics claim that the correlation between credit history and driving records does not necessarily indicate a cause and effect relationship; credit scores do not accurately reflect your driving behavior; and erroneous credit reports can have a devastating impact on your premiums. The majority of states have enacted legislation that place restrictions on the use of credit records by insurers. Chapter 28 discusses this important issue in greater detail.

SHOPPING FOR AUTO INSURANCE

As a careful insurance consumer, you should remember certain suggestions when you buy an auto insurance policy (see Exhibit 11.10).

Carry Adequate Liability Insurance

The most important rule in purchasing auto insurance is to carry adequate liability insurance. If you carry minimum limits to satisfy the state's financial or compulsory insurance law, such as $25,000/$50,000/$25,000, you are seriously underinsured. Even if you carry higher limits of $100,000/$300,000/$50,000, you are still underinsured in the event of a bad accident. A negligent driver who is underinsured could have a deficiency judgment filed against him or her, under which both present and future income and assets could be attached to satisfy the judgment. You can avoid this problem by carrying adequate liability limits.

You should also consider purchasing a personal umbrella policy, which will provide another $1 million to $10 million of liability insurance on your car on an excess basis after the underlying insurance limit is exhausted. The personal umbrella policy is discussed in Chapter 12.

Carry Higher Deductibles

Another important suggestion is to carry higher deductibles for collision and other-than-collision losses (also called comprehensive). Some insureds carry deductibles as low as $100, which is too low in

EXHIBIT 11.10
Tips for Buying Auto Insurance

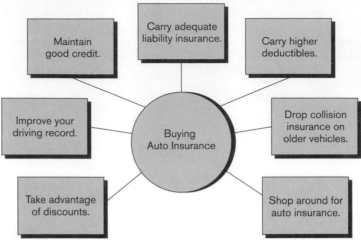

view of the rapid inflation in car prices over time. Many insureds have $250 deductibles. Increasing the deductible from $250 to $500, however, will reduce your collision and comprehensive cost by 15 to 30 percent. If you can afford an expensive car with a market value of $20,000 or more, you might even consider a $1000 collision deductible.

Drop Collision Insurance on Older Vehicles

You should consider dropping collision insurance on your car if it is an older model with a low market value. The cost of repairs after an accident will often exceed the value of an older car, but the insurer will pay no more than its current market value (less the deductible). One rough rule of thumb is that when a standard auto (such as a Chevrolet, Ford, or Dodge) is more than six years old, you should drop the physical damage insurance on the car.

Shop Around for Auto Insurance

Another important suggestion is to shop carefully for auto insurance. There is intense price competition among insurers. Contact several insurers and compare premiums. Many state insurance departments publish shoppers' guides to help insurance consumers make better purchase decisions. State insur-

ance departments also have Web sites that provide information on auto insurance rates in different cities within the state. For example, Exhibit 11.11 compares the rates of 15 insurers that write 74 percent of the coverage in Nebraska for six different classes of drivers in southeast and southwest Omaha. As you can see, rates among insurers vary widely for the same coverages. The savings by shopping around and comparing rates can be substantial.

Take Advantage of Discounts

When shopping for auto insurance, you should determine whether you are eligible for one or more discounts. All insurers do not offer the same discounts, and certain discounts are not available in all states. Common discounts include the following:

- *Multicar discount*—10 to 15 percent
- *No accidents in three years*—5 to 10 percent
- *Drivers over age 50*—5 to 15 percent
- *Defensive driving course*—5 to 10 percent
- *Antitheft device*—5 to 50 percent discount for comprehensive (other-than-collision)
- *Automatic seat belt and air bag*—20 to 60 percent for medical payments
- *Antilock brakes*—5 to 10 percent
- *Good student discount*—5 to 25 percent

EXHIBIT 11.11
Auto Insurance Premiums for Omaha, Nebraska (Six-Month Premiums)

Type of Car and Coverage Limits

2003 Ford Taurus SE 4-Door Sedan

Liability Limits of:		
	$100,000/$300,000	Bodily Injury
	$100,000	Property Damage
	$5,000	Medical Payments
	$100,000/$300,000	Underinsured Motorist
	$100,000/$300,000	Uninsured Motorist
	$250	Collision Deductible
	$100	Comprehensive Deductible

Hypothetical Drivers

Example 1: 17-year-old male, principal driver, pleasure use, driving fewer than 12,000 miles annually. No violations or accidents in the last three years.

Example 2: 17-year-old female, principal driver, pleasure use, driving fewer than 12,000 miles annually. No violations or accidents in the last three years.

Example 3: 21-year-old male, principal driver, pleasure use, driving fewer than 12,000 miles annually. No violations or accidents in the last three years.

Example 4: 21-year-old female, principal driver, pleasure use, driving fewer than 12,000 miles annually. No violations or accidents in the last three years.

Example 5: 44-year-old married male or female, principal driver, pleasure use, driving fewer than 12,000 miles annually. No violations or accidents in the last three years.

Example 6: 65-year-old married male or female, principal driver, pleasure use, driving fewer than 12,000 miles annually. No violations or accidents in the last three years.

Premiums: Southeast Omaha

Company	Example 1 17-yr-old Single Male	Example 2 17-yr-old Single Female	Example 3 21-yr-old Single Male	Example 4 21-yr-old Single Female	Example 5 44-yr-old Married Male or Female	Example 6 65-yr-old Married Male or Female
Allied Property & Casualty Ins. Co.	$2,150	$1,414	$1,510	$1,108	$ 551	$ 496
Allstate Property & Casualty Ins. Co.	2,812	1,980	1,514	1,187	863	741
AMCO Insurance Company	2,278	1,498	1,600	1,173	583	526
American Family Mutual Ins. Co.	2,011	1,423	1,246	878	583	528
American Standard Ins. Co. of Wisconsin	3,110	2,390	2,355	1,600	1,066	969
Farm Bureau Mutual Ins. Co.[1]	1,376	1,092	766	738	494	448
Farmers Insurance Exchange[2]	N/A	N/A	2,420	1,766	683	593
Farmers Mutual Ins. Co. of Nebraska	1,727	1,088	926	743	471	393
Mid-Century Ins. Co.[1]	3,649	3,002	2,686	2,447	1,499	1,360
Motor Club Ins. Association	1,969	1,277	1,248	831	542	490
Progressive Northern Ins. Co.	3,611	2,645	754	553	353	380
Shelter Mutual Ins. Co.	1,718	1,083	972	703	491	443
State Farm Fire and Cas Co.	2,663	1,935	1,191	910	628	552
State Farm Mutual Auto Ins. Co.	2,126	1,543	1,191	910	628	552
United Services Automobile	1,604	950	848	643	459	439

EXHIBIT 11.11 (continued)
Auto Insurance Premiums for Omaha, Nebraska (Six-Month Premiums)

| | Premiums: Southwest Omaha | | | | | |
| | Example 1 | Example 2 | Example 3 | Example 4 | Example 5 | Example 6 |
Company	17-yr-old Single Male	17-yr-old Single Female	21-yr-old Single Male	21-yr-old Single Female	44-yr-old Married Male or Female	65-yr-old Married Male or Female
Allied Property & Casualty Ins.. Co.	$2,050	$1,349	$1,436	$1,053	$ 524	$473
Allstate Property & Casualty Ins. Co.	3,325	2,354	1,784	1,401	1,018	876
AMCO Insurance Company	2,183	1,436	1,530	1,121	558	504
American Family Mutual Ins.. Co.	2,011	1,423	1,246	878	583	528
American Standard Ins. Co. of Wisconsin	3,110	2,390	2,355	1,600	1,066	969
Farm Bureau Mutual Insurance Co.[1]	1,265	1,005	705	679	455	413
Farmers Insurance Exchange[2]	N/A	N/A	1,557	1,154	447	390
Farmers Mutual Ins. Co. of Nebraska	1,727	1,088	926	743	471	393
Mid-Century Ins. Co.	2,410	1,972	1,746	1,602	977	890
Motor Club Ins. Association	1,969	1,277	1,248	831	542	490
Progressive Northern Ins. Co.	3,265	2,389	684	501	322	346
Shelter Mutual Ins. Co.	1,541	972	872	631	441	398
State Farm Fire and Cas. Co.	2,132	1,550	954	729	505	444
State Farm Mutual Auto Ins. Co.	1,701	1,236	954	729	505	444
United Services Automobile	1,510	895	799	607	434	415

[1]The collision deductible was changed from $250 to $200 because the company does not offer a $250 deductible.
[2]Rates do not include a membership fee.
Rates in effect as of August 1, 2003 for a six month premium term.
SOURCE: Nebraska Department of Insurance, *2003 Auto Rate Guide.*

- *Auto and homeowners policy with same insurer—* 5 to 15 percent
- *College student away from home without a car—* 10 to 40 percent

Improve Your Driving Record

If you are a high-risk driver and are paying exorbitant premiums, having a clean driving record over the past three years will substantially reduce your premiums. In the meantime, you should consider other alternatives. Although physical damage insurance on a new or late-model car can easily double the premiums for a high-risk driver, an older car can be driven without collision insurance. You might also consider riding a motorcycle or bicycle or using

mass transit. Nevertheless, there is no substitute for a good driving record.

To maintain a good driving record, you should not drive after you have been drinking alcohol. Impaired drivers account for a relatively high proportion of auto accidents in which someone is seriously injured or killed. A conviction for driving under the influence (DUI) can have a devastating effect on the premiums you are charged. Premiums can easily double or triple after a DUI conviction.

Finally, based on a national survey by the Transportation Department, certain occupations are more likely to be involved in auto accident than other groups. Students, medical doctors, and attorneys have the worst driving records, while pilots, firefighters, and farmers generally are involved in fewer

INSIGHT 11.1

More Drivers Are on the Roads; Who Are You Most Likely to Run Into? A Student? A Politician? A Librarian?

America is a nation of drivers. The Transportation Department's latest national survey showed that, for the first time, the typical American family has more vehicles in the garage than licensed drivers in the house. Many Americans have firm beliefs about which professions and occupations speed, or drive aggressively, or are the most accident-prone. Quality Planning Corporation released statistics derived from a study of more than one million drivers across the country. The analysis reveals who has the most accidents and who gets the most speeding tickets. There are some surprises in the numbers.

Perhaps predictably, it is students who top the charts as the most likely to get into an accident, and who have the highest number of speeding violations. Students consistently score much higher across both categories than all other occupations, but noticeably so in the case of accidents, where their lack of experience and low aversion to risk result in scores that are well ahead of medical doctors, attorneys, architects, and real estate agents, who round out the Top Five occupations most likely to be involved in an accident. At the bottom end of the accident-prone table are homemakers, politicians, pilots, fireman, and farmers. **Students are 3.5 times more likely to be involved in an accident than farmers.**

Politicians and Members of Clergy Lead Charmed Lives
When it comes to speeding tickets, the Top Five roster changes significantly. Scores for doctors, attorneys, and real estate agents drop appreciably. In their place, top-scoring students are joined by manual laborers, architects, enlisted military, and politicians are those who break the law most frequently. Law enforcement officers and firemen rank near the bottom on both accidents and speeding tickets. Politicians, who rank fourth for speeding violations, somehow manage to avoid collisions, ranking 38 for accidents.

Commenting on the statistics, Dr. Daniel Finnegan, president and founder of QPC, noted, "The numbers blow big

holes in the conventional wisdom about which professions are accident-prone or dangerous drivers. Interestingly, it appears that it is educated professionals who are most likely to be involved in accidents. Fortunately for those unlucky enough to be involved in an accident, individuals from two professions which are most helpful after such an incident—doctors and lawyers—are most likely to be on the scene."

The Data
Forty different occupations were compared, and the Top Five and Bottom Five in each occupation are presented here:

Accidents

Top 5 Occupations	Bottom 5 Occupations
1. Student	36. Homemaker
2. Medical doctor	37. Politician
3. Attorney/lawyer	38. Pilot
4. Architect	39. Fireman
5. Real Estate agent	40. Farmer

Speeding Violations

Top 5 Occupations	Bottom 5 Occupations
1. Student	36. Teacher/professor
2. Enlisted military	37. Clerical/secretary
3. Manual laborer	38. Law enforcement
4. Politician	39. Librarian
5. Architect	40. Homemaker

SOURCE: Adapted from Quality Planning Corporation, *More Drivers Are on the Roads; Who Are You Most Likely to Run Into? A Student? A Politician? A Librarian?*, Press Release, October 30, 2003.

accidents (see Insight 11.1). Students also top the charts for speeding violations.

Maintain Good Credit

Another important suggestion is to maintain good credit. As we noted earlier, many auto insurers use an applicant's credit record for purposes to

underwriting or rating. Applicants with good or superior credit records may be able to purchase auto insurance more cheaply than applicants with poor credit records. A good credit record can also result in lower interest rates on credit cards and mortgage loans and higher credit limits. If your credit history is poor, clean it up if you wish to pay lower premiums.

CASE APPLICATION

Paige, age 26, has purchased a new Ford sedan. She has a clean driving record. Collision coverage on the car in a small midwestern city where she lives would cost approximately $630 every six months with a $100 deductible, $566 with a $250 deductible, $492 with a $500 deductible, and $368 with a $1000 deductible. The state has a compulsory insurance law that requires minimum liability limits of $25,000/$50,000/$25,000. Paige would like to purchase collision insurance with a $100 deductible because the out-of-pocket cost to repair her car in an accident where she is at fault would be relatively small. She also would like to purchase only minimum liability limits, because she has few financial assets to protect. Paige is also concerned that she might be seriously injured by a driver who has no insurance.

Assume that Paige asks your advice concerning her auto insurance coverages. Based on the above facts, answer the following questions.

a. Paige wants to know why auto insurance costs so much. Explain to her the factors that determine auto insurance rates.
b. Do you recommend that Paige purchase collision insurance with a $100 deductible? Explain your answer.
c. Do you agree with Paige that only minimum liability limits should be purchased because she has few financial assets to protect? Explain your answer.
d. Assume that Paige adds the uninsured motorist coverage to her policy. Would she be completely protected against the financial consequences of a bodily injury caused by an uninsured driver? Explain your answer.
e. Paige would like to reduce her auto premiums because her monthly car payments are high. Explain to Paige the various methods for reducing or holding down auto insurance premiums.

SUMMARY

- Financial responsibility laws require motorists to show proof of financial responsibility after an accident involving bodily injury or property damage over a certain amount, for conviction of certain offenses, and for failure to pay a final judgment resulting from an auto accident. Most motorists meet the financial responsibility law requirements by carrying auto liability insurance limits of a certain amount.

- Compulsory insurance laws require motorists to carry auto liability insurance at least equal to a certain amount before the vehicle can be licensed or registered.

- Five states have unsatisfied judgment funds to compensate accident victims who have exhausted all other means of recovery. The accident victim must obtain a judgment against the negligent driver who caused the accident and show that the judgment cannot be collected.

- Uninsured motorists coverage is another approach for compensating auto accident victims. Uninsured motorists coverage compensates the accident victim who has bodily injuries caused by an uninsured motorist, by a hit-and-run driver, or by a negligent driver whose company is insolvent.

- No-fault auto insurance means that after an auto accident involving a bodily injury, each party collects from his or her own insurer, regardless of fault. There are several types of no-fault plans: pure no-fault plan; modified no-fault plan; add-on plan; and choice no-fault plan.

- The arguments for no-fault auto insurance laws are summarized as follows:
    Difficulty in determining fault
    Inequity in claim payments
    High transaction costs and attorney fees
    Fraudulent and excessive claims
    Delay in payments

- The arguments against no-fault auto insurance laws are summarized as follows:
    Defects of the negligence system are exaggerated.
    Claims of efficiency and premium savings are exaggerated.
    Court delays are not universal.
    Safe drivers may be penalized.
    There is no payment for pain and suffering.
    The tort liability system needs only to be reformed.

- Several approaches are used to provide auto insurance to high-risk drivers:
    Automobile insurance plan
    Joint underwriting association (JUA)

Reinsurance facility

Maryland Automobile Insurance Fund

Specialty automobile insurers

■ The premium charged for auto insurance is a function of numerous variables, including:

Territory

Age, gender, and marital status

Use of the auto

Driver education

Good student discount

Number and types of cars

Individual driving record

Insurance score

■ Consumer experts suggest several rules to follow when shopping for auto insurance:

Carry adequate liability insurance.

Carry higher deductibles.

Drop collision insurance on older vehicles.

Shop around for auto insurance.

Take advantage of discounts.

Improve your driving record.

Maintain good credit.

KEY CONCEPTS AND TERMS

Add-on plan	Multicar discount
Assigned risk plan	No-fault auto insurance
Automobile insurance plan	"No pay, no play" laws
Choice no-fault plan	Optional deductibles
Compulsory insurance law	Optional no-fault benefits
Essential services expenses	Pure no-fault plan
Financial responsibility law	Reinsurance facility (or pool)
Good student discount	Safe driver plans
Insurance score	Shared market (residual market)
Joint underwriting association (JUA)	Specialty auto insurers
Low-cost auto insurance	Survivors' loss benefits
Maryland Automobile Insurance Fund	Uninsured motorists coverage
Modified no-fault plan	Unsatisfied judgment fund
Monetary threshold	Verbal threshold

REVIEW QUESTIONS

1. a. What is a financial responsibility law?
   b. What is a compulsory insurance law?

2. a. Describe the characteristics of unsatisfied judgment funds.
   b. How are unsatisfied judgment funds financed?

3. a. Describe the characteristics of a low-cost auto insurance plan.
   b. What is a "no pay, no play" law?

4. a. Explain the meaning of no-fault auto insurance.
   b. What is the difference between a monetary threshold and a verbal threshold?
   c. Describe the major types of no-fault laws.
   d. List the arguments for and against no-fault auto insurance.

5. Describe the characteristics of automobile insurance plans.

6. What is a joint underwriting association (JUA)?

7. Describe the characteristics of a reinsurance facility.

8. Describe the characteristics of specialty auto insurers.

9. a. Identify the factors that determine the premiums charged for auto insurance.
   b. Explain the significance of an applicant's credit score in auto insurance underwriting and rating.

10. Explain the suggestions that consumers should follow when shopping for an auto insurance policy.

APPLICATION QUESTIONS

1. All states have financial responsibility or compulsory insurance laws that require motorists to carry at least minimum amounts of auto liability insurance.
   a. What are the various ways in which proof of financial responsibility can be satisfied in a state with a financial responsibility law?
   b. Does a financial responsibility law or compulsory insurance law guarantee that injured auto accident victims will be adequately compensated for your injuries? Explain your answer.
   c. How effective are compulsory insurance laws in reducing the problem of uninsured drivers?

2. Uninsured motorists coverage is another approach to the problem of uninsured drivers.
   a. Explain the advantages of the uninsured motorists coverage in meeting the problem of uninsured drivers.
   b. Explain the defects of the uninsured motorists coverage as a technique for compensating people who are injured by uninsured drivers.

3. About half the states have passed some type of no-fault auto insurance law to compensate injured auto accident victims.
   a. Describe the no-fault benefits that are typically paid in a state with a no-fault law.
   b. Why have no-fault auto insurance laws been enacted into law?
   c. Explain the arguments against no-fault auto insurance laws.
   d. How well have no-fault auto insurance laws worked? Explain your answer.

4. Society has the problem of providing auto insurance to high-risk drivers, including irresponsible drivers, drunk drivers, and drivers who habitually break traffic laws. An automobile insurance plan (assigned risk plan) is one approach to the problem of providing auto insurance to high-risk drivers.
   a. What is an automobile insurance plan?
   b. Describe the eligibility requirements for obtaining insurance from an automobile insurance plan.
   c. Explain the process for assigning high-risk drivers to individual insurers.
   d. Explain the disadvantages of automobile insurance plans.

INTERNET RESOURCES

- **All Quotes Insurance.Com** uses the power of technology to find solutions to your insurance needs. The database contains hundreds of qualified insurance providers that provide competitive quotes. You can get quotes on auto, homeowners, life, health, disability income and other insurance products. Visit the site at

  www.allquotesinsurance.com

- **The Insurance Research Council (IRC),** a division of the American Institute for CPCU, provides the insurance industry and the public with timely research studies that are relevant to public policy issues dealing with risk and insurance. Visit the site at

  http://www.ircweb.org

- **The RAND Institute for Civil Justice** is an organization within the RAND Corporation that conducts independent, objective research and analysis concerning the civil justice system. Many research studies deal with auto insurance and the insurance industry. Visit the site at

  http://www.rand.org/centers/icj/

- **Geico Direct** sells auto insurance directly over the phone (800-624-8341). The company claims that a 15-minute call can save you 15 percent or more on auto insurance rates. Geico Direct's Web site provides similar premium quotes online. Visit the site at

  http://www.geico.com

- The **Insurance Information Institute** provides timely information on auto insurance and other personal property and liability insurance coverages. Numerous consumer brochures and articles on auto insurance and other property and liability coverages can be accessed directly online. Visit the site at

  http://www.iii.org

- **Insure.com** provides premium quotes for auto insurance, homeowners insurance, and other insurance products. The site also provides timely information and news releases about auto insurance and events that affect the insurance industry. Visit the site at

  http://www.insure.com

- **INSWEB** provides premium quotes for auto, homeowners, and other insurance products. You can comparison shop from your computer. In addition, the site has a learning center and provides information and articles from consumer, industry, and regulatory groups. Visit the site at

  http://www.insweb.com

- The **Progressive Casualty Insurance Company** has a user-friendly site that gives auto insurance quotes in most states. Progressive claims its rates are highly competitive. Progressive also provides comparison rates from other insurers. Visit the site at

  http://www.progressiveinsurance.com

SELECTED REFERENCES

Abrahamse, Allan, and Stephen Carrol. "The Effects of a Choice Auto Insurance Plan on Insurance Costs and Compensation." *CPCU Journal,* vol. 51, no. 1 (Spring 1998), pp. 19–39.

"Automated Underwriting Tools: Credit and CLUE," *Hot Topics & Insurance Issues,* Insurance Information Institute, March 2004.

Carrol, Stephen J., and James S. Kakalik. "No-Fault Approaches to Compensating Auto Accident Victims." *The Journal of Risk and Insurance,* vol. 60, no. 2 (June 1993), pp. 265–287.

———. *No-Fault Automobile Insurance: A Policy Perspective.* Santa Monica, CA: RAND, Institute for Civil Justice, 1991.

Carrol, Stephen J., James S. Kakalik, Nicholas M. Pace, and John L. Adams. *No-Fault Approaches to Compensating People Injured in Automobile Accidents.* Santa Monica, CA: RAND, Institute for Civil Justice, 1991.

"Compulsory Auto Insurance," *Hot Topics & Insurance Issues,* Insurance Information Institute, February 2004.

Fair, Isaac and Company, Inc. *Predictiveness of Credit History for Insurance Loss Relativities,* A Fair, Isaac Paper, October 1999.

Fire, Casualty & Surety Bulletins, Personal Lines volume, Personal Auto section. Erlanger, KY: National Underwriter Company. The bulletins are updated monthly.

Hamilton, Karen L., and Cheryl L. Ferguson. *Personal Risk Management and Property-Liability Insurance,* First Edition. Malvern, PA.: American Institute for Chartered Property Casualty Underwriters/Insurance Institute of America, 2002.

Hartwig, Robert P., and Claire Wilkinson. *The Use of Credit Information in Personal Lines Underwriting Insurance,* Insurance Information Institute, Insurance Issues Series, Vol. 1, No. 2, June 2003.

Hartwig, Robert P. *Update on New York's No-Fault Fraud & Abuse Problem,* Insurance Information Institute, Insurance Fraud Briefing, New York Alliance against Insurance Fraud, Albany, NY, March 25, 2003.

Lascher, Jr., Edward I., and Michael R. Powers, ed. *The Economics and Politics of No-Fault Insurance.* Boston, MA: Kluwer Academic Publishers, 2001.

Maroney, Patrick, Kevin Eastman, and Ann Butler. "An Analysis of the Auto Choice Reform Act of 1997." *Risk Management and Insurance Review,* vol.2, no.2 (Winter 1999), pp. 60–71.

"No-Fault Auto Insurance." *Hot Topics & Insurance Issues.* New York: Insurance Information Institute, November 2003.

Schmidt, Joan T., and Jia-Hsing Yeh. "An Economic Analysis of Auto Compensation Systems: Choice Experiences from New Jersey and Pennsylvania." *The Journal of Risk & Insurance,* vol. 70, no. 4 (December 2003), pp. 601–628.

U.S. Congress, Joint Economic Committee. "Auto Choice: Impact on Cities and the Poor," *Joint Economic Committee Study,* 105th Congress, Washington, DC, March 1998.

Wiening, Eric A., George E. Rejda, Constance M. Luthardt, and Cheryl L. Ferguson. *Personal Insurance,* First Edition. Malvern, PA.: American Institute for Chartered Property Casualty Underwriters/Insurance Institute of America, 2002.

NOTES

1. A complete discussion of these laws can be found in *Fire, Casualty & Surety Bulletins*, Personal Lines volume, Personal Auto section (Erlanger, KY: National Underwriter Company). Discussion of financial responsibility laws is based on this source.

2. The first two figures refer to bodily injury liability limits, and the third figure refers to property damage liability. The liability limits apply to each accident.

3. NAII data as cited in Tony Attrino, "Compulsory Auto Laws Blasted," *National Underwriter,* Property & Casualty/Risk & Benefits Management ed., September 7, 1998, pp. 2, 65.

4. Eric A. Wiening, George E. Rejda, Constance M. Luthardt, and Cheryl L. Ferguson, *Personal Insurance,* First Edition (Malvern, PA.: American Institute for Chartered Property Casualty Underwriters/Insurance Institute of America, 2002), pp. 2.8–2.10.

5. This section is based on "Compulsory Auto Insurance," *Hot Topics & Insurance Issues,* Insurance Information Institute, February 2004.

6. This section is based on "No-Fault Automobile Insurance," in *Fire, Casualty & Surety Bulletins*, Personal Lines volume, Personal Auto section (Erlanger, KY: National Underwriter Company). The bulletins are updated monthly.

7. "No-Fault Auto Insurance." *Hot Topics & Insurance Issues.* New York: Insurance Information Institute, November 2003.

8. "Auto Choice: Relief for Businesses and Consumers," *Joint Economic Committee Study,* 105th Congress, Washington, DC, July 1998.

9. *Injuries in Auto Accidents, an Analysis of Auto Insurance Claims, Executive Summary* (Malvern, PA: Insurance Research Council, 1999), p. 9.

10. Ibid., p. 8.

11. Stephen J. Carrol, et al., *No-Fault Approaches to Compensating People Injured in Automobile Accidents* (Santa Monica, CA: RAND, Institute for Civil Justice, 1991), pp. xvi, 43.

12. "No-Fault Auto Insurance." *Hot Topics & Insurance Issues.* New York: Insurance Information Institute, November 2003.

13. *The I.I.I. Fact Book 2004* (New York: Insurance Information Institute, 2004), p. 103.

Students may take a self-administered test on this chapter at
www.aw-bc.com/rejda

CHAPTER 12

OTHER PROPERTY AND LIABILITY INSURANCE COVERAGES

"Variety is the very spice of life."

William Cowper,
Olney Hymns (1779)

LEARNING OBJECTIVES

After studying this chapter, you should be able to

◆ Describe the following ISO dwelling forms:
   Dwelling Property 1 (basic form)
   Dwelling Property 2 (broad form)
   Dwelling Property 3 (special form)

◆ Explain how a mobile home can be insured.

◆ Identify the types of property that can be insured under a personal articles floater.

◆ Explain how recreational boats can be insured.

◆ Explain the basic provisions of the national flood insurance program.

◆ Describe the basic characteristics of title insurance.

◆ Explain the major characteristics of a personal umbrella policy.

Raymond, age 45, is an avid fisherman who competes regularly in fishing contests. He recently purchased a new motorboat with a 350 horsepower engine for $25,000. However, before he took possession, he contacted his insurance agent. The agent explained that the homeowners policy would provide only limited coverage for the boat and that the boat should be specifically insured under a separate policy. The homeowners policy would pay only a maximum of $1500 for a covered physical damage loss, and personal liability coverage under the homeowners policy would not apply. Raymond wisely took his agent's advice and insured the boat under a separate boat owners policy.

Raymond had a specialized need for insurance that required a certain coverage. Likewise, some property owners have special needs that require special insurance coverages. This chapter discusses several property and liability insurance coverages designed to meet specific needs. Topics discussed include the Insurance Services Office (ISO) dwelling program, mobile home insurance, inland marine floaters, insurance on boats, title insurance, and federal flood insurance. The chapter concludes with a discussion of the personal umbrella policy.

ISO DWELLING PROGRAM

Although the majority of homeowners are insured under a homeowners policy, certain dwellings are ineligible for coverage under a homeowners policy. For example, if the home is not occupied by the owner but is rented to a tenant, the property owner is ineligible for a homeowners policy. Also, some property owners do not need a homeowners policy, or they may want a less costly policy. Most of these homes can be insured under a dwelling policy drafted by the Insurance Services Office (ISO).

The ISO dwelling forms are narrower in coverage than the current homeowners forms. One major difference is that the dwelling forms do not include coverage for theft or for personal liability insurance without appropriate endorsements. In contrast, the homeowners forms automatically include theft coverage and personal liability insurance as part of a standard policy.

The ISO dwelling program has been changed several times since its inception in 1977. The following section discusses the latest Dwelling 2002 program, which became effective in August 2003.

The current ISO dwelling program has three major forms:[1]

- Dwelling Property 1—Basic Form
- Dwelling Property 2—Broad Form
- Dwelling Property 3—Special Form

Dwelling Property 1 (Basic Form)

The basic form provides coverages similar to the homeowners policies discussed in Chapter 8. Coverage A insures the dwelling shown in the declarations; materials and supplies located on or next to the described location used to construct or repair the dwelling; and if not otherwise covered in the policy, building equipment and outdoor equipment used to service the described location.

Coverage B covers other structures set apart from the dwelling by clear space, such as a detached garage or storage shed. The coverage does not apply to any land damage, including land on which the other structures are located.

Coverage C covers the personal property of the named insured and resident family members while the property is on the described location. Up to 10 percent of the Coverage C limit can be applied to cover personal property anywhere in the world.

Coverage D covers the fair rental value if a loss makes part of the dwelling rented to others unfit for normal use. A maximum of 20 percent of the insurance on the dwelling can be applied to cover the loss of rents, subject to a maximum monthly limit of 1/12 of that amount.

The basic form covers only a limited number of perils that apply to both the dwelling and personal property:

- *Fire or lightning*
- *Internal explosion*
- *Windstorm or hail*
- *Explosion*
- *Riot or civil commotion*
- *Aircraft*
- *Vehicles*
- *Smoke*
- *Volcanic eruption*
- *Vandalism or malicious mischief*

All covered property losses are paid on an actual cash value basis. However, for losses to the dwelling and other structures, some states require that a modified loss settlement endorsement appear in the policy. Under this endorsement, if the building is repaired or replaced at the same site within 180 days of the loss, the insurer pays the lesser of (1) the limit of liability, or (2) the amount actually spent to repair or replace using common construction materials and methods. If the insured elects not to repair or replace the building, the insurer pays the lowest of the limit of liability, the market value, or the amount it would cost to repair or replace.

Dwelling Property 2 (Broad Form)

The broad form provides broader coverage than the basic form. Covered losses to the dwelling and other structures are indemnified on the basis of *replacement* cost rather than actual cash value. The replacement *cost* provisions are similar to those found in the homeowner contracts. The broad form also adds a new benefit for additional living expense (Coverage E). If a covered loss makes the property unfit for normal use, the additional increase in living expenses is paid.

The broad form includes all of the perils listed in the basic form plus the following additional perils:

- *Damage by burglars*
- *Falling objects*
- *Weight of ice, snow, or sleet*
- *Accidental discharge or overflow of water or steam*
- *Explosion of a steam or hot water heating system, an air conditioning or automatic fire protective sprinkler system, or an appliance for heating water*
- *Freezing of a plumbing, heating, air conditioning or automatic fire protective sprinkler system, or household appliance*
- *Sudden and accidental damage from an artificially generated electrical current*
- *Volcanic eruption*

Dwelling Property 3 (Special Form)

The special form provides the broadest coverage in the ISO dwelling program. The dwelling and other structures are insured against risk of direct loss to covered property. This means that coverage is provided on an "all risk" or "open perils" basis. *All direct physical losses to the dwelling and other structures are covered except those losses specifically excluded.* However, personal property is covered for the same named perils found in the broad form discussed earlier.

Endorsements to the Dwelling Program

Several endorsements can be added to a dwelling form, depending on the needs and desires of the property owner. They include *theft coverage,* which can be written on a limited or broad basis by an endorsement. Personal liability insurance is also available by adding a *personal liability supplement* to the policy, which provides personal liability insurance similar to the liability coverages found in the homeowners policy.

MOBILE HOME INSURANCE

Mobile homes generally cost less than conventional housing. Because of cost, some families have purchased mobile homes as an alternative to conventional housing. Mobile homes are also purchased as a vacation home or second home.

Under the ISO program, **mobile home insurance** is written by adding an endorsement to either a Homeowners 2 or Homeowners 3 policy, which tailors the homeowners policy to meet the special characteristics of mobile homes. A number of specialty insurers also write a mobile home insurance based on their own forms tailored to the mobile home exposures. The following discussion of mobile home insurance is based on the ISO program.[2]

Eligibility

A mobile home typically must be at least 10 feet wide and 40 feet long, must be capable of being towed on its own chassis, and must be designed for year-round living. These requirements are imposed to eliminate coverage for camper trailers pulled by automobiles and insured under an auto insurance policy.

Coverages

Coverages on a mobile home are similar to those found in a homeowners policy. Coverage A insures mobile homes on a *replacement cost basis*. It also insures floor coverings, household appliances, dressers, cabinets, and other built-in furniture when installed on a permanent basis.

Some mobile homes have depreciated to the point where replacement cost coverage is inappropriate. In such cases, an optional actual cash value endorsement can be added. Under this endorsement, the insurer has the option of (1) paying the cost of repairs, (2) replacing the damaged property with similar property, but not necessarily from the same manufacturer, or (3) paying the amount in money. If paid in money, the insurer pays the lowest of the difference in actual cash value before and after the loss, the cost of repairs, or the cost to replace the property with similar property.

Coverage B insures other structures and is 10 percent of Coverage A, with a minimum limit of $2000. Coverage C insures unscheduled personal property and is 40 percent of Coverage A. Coverage D provides for loss-of-use coverage and is 30 percent of the Coverage A limit.

An additional coverage pays up to $500 for the cost incurred in transporting the mobile home to a safe place to avoid damage when it is endangered by a covered peril, such as a forest fire. No deductible applies to this coverage. The $500 limit can be increased to a higher limit by an endorsement.

Finally, Coverages E and F provide for comprehensive personal liability insurance and medical payments to others. This coverage is similar to the coverage provided in the homeowner contracts.

INLAND MARINE FLOATERS

Many people own certain types of valuable personal property—such as jewelry, furs, and cameras—that are frequently moved from one location to another. This property can be insured by an appropriate inland marine floater. An **inland marine floater** *is a policy that provides broad and comprehensive protection on property frequently moved from one location to another.*

Basic Characteristics of Inland Marine Floaters

Although inland marine floaters are not uniform, they have certain common characteristics:[3]

- *Coverage can be tailored to the specific type of personal property to be insured.* For example, under the personal articles floater, several types of property can be insured, such as jewelry, coins, or stamps. The insured can select the appropriate coverage needed.
- *Desired amounts of insurance can be selected.* The homeowners policy has several limits on personal property. For example, there is a $200 limit on money and coins, a $1500 limit on stamp collections, and a $2500 limit for the theft of silverware or goldware. Higher limits are available through a floater policy.
- *Broader and more comprehensive coverage can be obtained.* For example, the personal articles floater insures against risks of direct physical loss to covered property. Consequently, all direct physical losses are covered except those losses specifically excluded.
- *Most floaters cover insured property anywhere in the world.* This protection is especially valuable for global travelers.
- *Inland marine floaters are often written without a deductible.*

Personal Articles Floater

The **personal articles floater (PAF)** is an inland marine floater that provides comprehensive protection on valuable personal property.[4] The coverage also can be added as an endorsement to a homeowners policy. When written as a separate contract, the PAF insures certain optional classes of personal property on an "all-risks" or "open perils" basis. *All direct physical losses are covered except certain losses specifically excluded.*

The classes of personal property that can be covered include the following:

- *Jewelry*. Because of moral hazard, insurance on jewelry is underwritten carefully. Each item is described with a specific amount of insurance.
- *Furs*. Each item is listed separately with a specific amount of insurance.
- *Cameras*. Most photographic equipment can be covered under the PAF. Each item must be individually described and valued.
- *Musical instruments*. Musical instruments, cases, amplifying equipment, and similar articles can also be covered. Instruments played for pay are not covered unless a coverage option is activated in the policy.
- *Silverware*. The PAF can also be written to cover silverware and goldware.
- *Golfer's equipment*. Golf clubs and equipment are covered anywhere in the world. Golfer's clothes in a locker are also covered when the insured is playing golf.
- *Fine arts*. Fine arts include paintings, etchings, lithographs, antique furniture, rare books, rare glass, bric-a-brac, and manuscripts. Coverage of scheduled fine arts is on a valued basis. The amount of insurance listed in the schedule for that item is the amount paid for a total loss.
- *Stamp and coin collections*. Stamp and coin collections can be insured on a *blanket basis;* the stamps or coins are not described, and the insurance applies to the entire collection. The amount paid is the market value of the stamps and coins at the time of loss, with a $1000 maximum limit on any unscheduled coin collection and a $250 maximum limit on any single stamp or coin.

However, if the stamps or coins are valuable, they can be individually *scheduled*. The agreed value amount is then the amount paid if a loss occurs.

Scheduled Personal Property Endorsement

Coverage provided by a PAF can be added to a homeowners policy by use of a **scheduled personal property endorsement.** The endorsement provides essentially the same coverages provided by the freestanding personal articles floater.

WATERCRAFT INSURANCE

Millions of Americans own or operate boats for pleasure and recreation. The homeowners policy, however, provides only limited coverage of boats. Coverage on a boat, its equipment, and boat trailer is limited to $1500. Direct loss from windstorm or hail is covered only if the boat is inside a fully enclosed building. Theft of the boat or its equipment away from the premises is excluded. Also, boats are covered only against a limited number of named (broad form) perils, and more comprehensive protection may be desired. Finally, legal liability arising out of the operation or ownership of larger boats is not covered under the homeowners policy. For these reasons, boat owners often purchase separate insurance contracts that provide broader protection.[5]

Insurance on recreational boats generally can be classified into two categories:

- Boat owners package policy
- Yacht insurance

Boat Owners Package Policy

Many insurers have designed a **boat owners package policy** that combines physical damage insurance on the boat, medical expense insurance, liability insurance, and other coverages into one policy. Although the package policies are not uniform, they have certain common characteristics.

Physical Damage Coverage A boat owners policy provides physical damage insurance on the boat on an "all-risks" or "open perils" basis. *All direct physical losses are covered except certain losses specifically excluded.* Thus, if the boat collides with another boat, is stranded on a reef, or is damaged by heavy winds, the loss is covered. Certain exclusions apply, including wear and tear, gradual deterioration, mechanical breakdown, use of the boat for commercial purposes, and use of the boat (except sailboats in some policies) in any race or speed contest.

Liability Coverage   The insured is covered for property damage and bodily injury liability arising out of the negligent ownership or operation of the boat. For example, if an operator carelessly damages another boat, swamps another boat, or accidentally injures some swimmers, the loss is covered. Certain exclusions apply, including intentional injury, use of the boat for commercial purposes, and use of the boat (sailboats sometimes excepted) in any race or speed test.

Medical Expense Coverage   This coverage is similar to that found in auto insurance contracts. The coverage pays the reasonable and necessary medical expenses of a covered person who is injured while in the boat or while boarding or leaving the boat. Most policies impose a limit of one to three years during which time the medical expenses must be incurred. In addition, many boat owners policies cover the medical expenses of water-skiers who are injured while being towed. If not covered, coverage can be obtained by an endorsement to the policy.

Uninsured Boaters Coverage   Some boat owners policies have an optional uninsured boaters coverage for bodily injury caused by an uninsured boater, which is similar to the uninsured motorists coverage in auto insurance.

Yacht Insurance

Yacht insurance is designed for larger boats, such as cabin cruisers, inboard motorboats, and sailboats over 26 feet in length. Yacht policies are not standard, but certain coverages typically appear in all policies. The following section summarizes the major provisions of a yacht policy of one insurer.

Property Damage   This coverage insures the yacht and its equipment for property damage on an "all-risks" or "open perils" basis. The policy covers accidental direct physical loss or damage to the yacht except certain losses specifically excluded. Thus, if the yacht is damaged or sinks because of heavy seas, high winds, or collision with another vessel, the loss is covered. Exclusions include wear and tear; weath-

ering; damage from insects, mold, animals, and marine life; marring, scratching, denting, and blistering; and freezing or extremes of temperature. A deductible applies to property damage losses.

Liability Coverage   Liability coverage insures the legal liability of an insured arising out of the ownership, operation, or maintenance of the yacht. For example, collision with another boat or damage to a dock or marina would be covered. The coverage also includes the cost of raising, removing, or destroying a sunken or wrecked yacht.

Medical Payments Coverage   This coverage pays for necessary and reasonable medical expenses because of accidental bodily injury. Covered expenses include medical, hospital, ambulance, professional nursing, and funeral costs.

Uninsured Boater   This coverage pays the bodily injury damages up to the policy limit that the insured is legally entitled to recover from an uninsured owner or operator of another yacht.

Other Coverages   The policy may also include additional coverages. These coverages include coverage for legal liability incurred by the insured to maritime workers who are injured in the course of employment and who are covered under the U.S. Longshoremen's and Harbor Workers' Compensation Act; physical damage insurance on a vessel trailer listed in the declarations; and coverage for personal property while aboard the yacht. Personal property includes clothing, personal effects, fishing gear, and sports equipment, but not money, jewelry, traveler's checks, or other valuables.

GOVERNMENT PROPERTY INSURANCE PROGRAMS

Government insurance programs are often necessary because certain perils are difficult to insure privately, and coverage may not be available at affordable premiums from private insurers. Two government insurance programs merit a brief discussion:

- National flood insurance program
- FAIR plans

National Flood Insurance Program

Buildings in flood zones are difficult to insure privately because the ideal requirements of an insurable risk discussed in Chapter 2 are not easily met. The exposure units in flood zones are not independent of each other, and the potential for a catastrophic loss is present. Thus, premiums for flood insurance in flood-prone areas would be too high for most insureds to pay. Also, adverse selection is a problem because only property owners in flood zones are likely to seek protection. For these reasons, financial assistance from the federal government is needed.

Because of increasing flood losses and the escalating costs of disaster relief to the taxpayers, Congress created the **National Flood Insurance Program (NFIP)** in 1968.[6] The purposes of the legislation are to reduce flood damage in communities by flood-plain management ordinances and to provide flood insurance to property owners.

Flood insurance can be purchased from agents or brokers who represent private insurers. Agents or brokers who are not affiliated with private insurers can write federal flood insurance directly with the NFIP.

Most flood insurance policies are written with private insurers. Under the *write-your-own program* enacted in 1983, private insurers sell federal flood insurance under their own names, collect the premiums, and receive an expense allowance for policies written and claims paid. The federal government is responsible for all underwriting losses. The NFIP is self-supporting for the average historical loss year, which means that unless a widespread disaster occurs, claims and operating expenses are paid by flood insurance premiums, not by the taxpayers.

Federal law requires individuals to purchase flood insurance if they have federal guaranteed financing to build, buy, refinance, or repair structures located in special flood zones in the participating community. This financing requirement includes federal FHA and VA loans as well as most conventional mortgage loans.

Eligibility Requirements   Most buildings and their contents can be covered by flood insurance if the community agrees to adopt and enforce sound flood control and land use measures.

When a community joins the program, it is provided with a flood hazard boundary map that shows the general area of flood losses, and residents are allowed to purchase limited amounts of insurance at subsidized rates under the emergency portion of the program.

A flood insurance rate map is then prepared that divides the community into specific zones to determine the probability of flooding in each zone. When this map is prepared, and the community agrees to adopt more stringent flood control and land use measures, the community enters the regular phase of the program. Higher amounts of flood insurance can then be purchased.

Definition of Flood   In the Standard Flood Insurance Policy, flood is defined, in part, as:

> *A general and temporary condition of partial or complete inundation of two or more acres of normally dry land area or of two or more properties (at least one of which is your property) from overflow of inland or tidal waters, from unusual and rapid accumulation or runoff of surface waters from any source, or from mudflow.*

For example, flood damage caused by an overflow of rivers, streams, or other bodies of water, by abnormally high waves, or by severe storms is covered. Note that the accumulation or runoff of surface water can come from any source, such as melting snow, ice, or heavy rain. If the flooding causes damage from mudslides or mudflow, the loss is also covered.

Amounts of Insurance   Under the *emergency program*, maximum coverage on single-family dwellings is limited to $35,000 on the building and $10,000 on the contents. For other residential and nonresidential buildings, maximum coverage is limited to $100,000 on the building and $100,000 on the contents (see Exhibit 12.1).

Under the *regular program*, maximum coverage on single-family dwellings is limited to $250,000 on the building and $100,000 on the contents. Commercial structures can be insured up to a limit of $500,000 on the building and $500,000 on the contents.

Single family dwellings and residential condominium buildings can be indemnified on a replacement cost basis if certain conditions are met. The insured must carry insurance equal to 80 percent of

Exhibit 12.1
Amount of Federal Flood Insurance under the Emergency and Regular Programs

Building Coverage	Emergency Program	Regular Program
Single-family dwelling*	$ 35,000*	$250,000
Other residential*	35,000*	250,000
Other residential	100,000*	250,000
Non-residential	100,000*	500,000
Contents Coverage		
Residential	$ 10,000	$100,000
Nonresidential including Small Business	100,000	$500,000

*Under the Emergency Program, higher limits of building coverage are available in Alaska, Hawaii, the U.S. Virgin Islands, and Guam.

SOURCE: Federal Emergency Management Agency (FEMA).

the replacement cost of the dwelling at the time of loss, or the maximum amount of insurance available at the inception of the policy, whichever is less. If the amount of insurance carried is less than 80 percent of the full replacement cost at the time of loss, the amount paid is subject to a coinsurance penalty. Losses to contents are always adjusted on an actual cash value basis (replacement cost less depreciation).

Waiting Period With certain exceptions, there is a 30-day waiting period for new applications and for endorsements to increase the amount of insurance on existing policies. Without a waiting period, property owners in flood zones could delay purchasing insurance until an imminent flood threatens their property.

Deductible A $500 deductible applies separately to both the building and contents. Higher deductibles are available with a saving in premiums.

Premiums The cost of the protection is relatively low. The preferred risk policy is available for slightly more than $100 annually. The average flood insurance policy costs about $400 annually and is less expensive than interest on federal disaster loans.[7]

There are numerous misconceptions and myths about the federal flood insurance program. Insight 12.1 discusses some common misunderstandings about the program.

FAIR Plans

During the 1960s, major riots occurred in many cities in the United States, resulting in millions of dollars in property damage. Subsequently, many property owners in riot-prone areas were unable to obtain property insurance at affordable premiums. This problem resulted in the creation of **FAIR plans** (Fair Access to Insurance Requirements), which were enacted into law as a result of the Urban Property and Reinsurance Act of 1968. *The basic purpose of a FAIR plan is to make property insurance available to urban property owners who are unable to obtain coverage in the normal markets.* FAIR plans typically provide coverage for fire and extended-coverage insurance, vandalism, malicious mischief, and, in some states, crime insurance and sprinkler leakage. FAIR plans have been established in 31 states and the District of Columbia.

In addition, seven states have beach and windstorm plans that are in operation along the Atlantic and Gulf Coast seaboard, where property is highly vulnerable to damage from severe windstorms and hurricanes.[8]

INSIGHT 12.1

Myths and Facts About the National Flood Insurance Program

To clear up misconceptions, the National Flood Insurance Program (NFIP) has compiled the following list of common myths about the program.

1. **Myth: You can't buy flood insurance if you are located in a high-flood-risk area.**
   Fact: You can buy federal flood insurance no matter where you live if your community belongs to the NFIP, except in Coastal Barrier Resource System (CBRS) areas. The program was created in 1968 to provide affordable flood insurance to people who live in areas with the greatest risk of flooding, called Special Flood Hazard Areas (SFHAs). In fact, under the National Flood Insurance Act, lenders must require borrowers whose property is located within an SFHA to purchase flood insurance as a condition of receiving a federally backed mortgage loan. There is an exemption for conventional loans on properties within CBRS areas.

2. **Myth: You can't buy flood insurance immediately before or during a flood.**
   Fact: You can purchase flood coverage at any time. There is a 30-day waiting period after you've applied and paid the premium before the policy becomes effective, with the following exceptions: (1) If the initial purchase of flood insurance is in connection with the making, increasing, extending, or renewing of a loan, there is no waiting period. The coverage becomes effective at the time of the loan, provided that application and payment of premium are made at or prior to loan closing. (2) If the initial purchase of flood insurance is made during the 13-month period following the effective date of a revised flood map for a community, there is a one-day waiting period.
   The policy does not cover a "loss in progress," defined by the NFIP as a loss occurring as of 12:01 A.M. on the first day of the policy term. In addition, you cannot increase the amount of insurance coverage you have during a loss in progress.

3. **Myth: Homeowners insurance policies cover flooding.**
   Fact: Unfortunately, many homeowners do not find out until it is too late that their homeowners policies do not cover flooding.

4. **Myth: Flood insurance is only available for homeowners.**
   Fact: Flood insurance is available to protect homes, condominiums, apartments, and nonresidential buildings, including commercial structures. A maximum of $250,000 of building coverage is available for single-family residential buildings, and $250,000 per unit for residential condominiums. The limit for contents coverage on all residential buildings is $100,000, which is also available to renters.
   Commercial structures can be insured to a limit of $500,000 for the building and $500,000 for the contents.

5. **Myth: You can't buy flood insurance if your property has been flooded.**
   Fact: You are still eligible to purchase flood insurance, provided that your community is participating in the NFIP.

6. **Myth: Only residents of high-risk flood zones need to insure their property.**
   Fact: Even if you live in an area that is not flood-prone, it's advisable to have flood insurance. Between 25 percent and 30 percent of the NFIP's claims come from outside high-flood-risk areas. The NFIP's Preferred Risk Policy, available for just over $100 per year, is designed for residential properties located in low- to moderate-flood-risk zones.

7. **Myth: Federal flood insurance can only be purchased through the NFIP directly.**
   Fact: NFIP flood insurance is sold through private insurance companies and agents and is backed by the federal government.

8. **Myth: The NFIP does not offer any type of basement coverage.**
   Fact: Yes, it does. The NFIP defines a basement as any area of a building with a floor that is below ground level on all sides. While flood insurance does not cover basement improvements, such as finished walls, floors, or ceilings, or personal belongings that may be kept in a basement, such as furniture and other contents, it does cover structural elements, essential equipment, and other basic items normally located in a basement.

Myths and Facts About the National Flood Insurance Program

The following items are covered under building coverage, as long as they are connected to a power source and installed in their functioning location:

- Sump pumps
- Well water tanks and pumps, cisterns and the water in them
- Oil tanks and the oil in them, natural gas tanks and the gas in them
- Pumps and/or tanks used in conjunction with solar energy
- Furnaces, hot water heaters, air conditioners, and heat pumps
- Electrical junction and circuit breaker boxes, and required utility connections
- Foundation elements
- Stairways, staircases, elevators, and dumbwaiters
- Unpainted drywalls and sheet rock walls and ceilings, including fiberglass insulation
- Cleanup

The following items are covered under contents coverage:

- Clothes washers
- Clothes dryers
- Food freezers and the food in them

9. **Myth: Federal disaster assistance will pay for flood damage.**
Fact: Before a community is eligible for disaster assistance, it must be declared a federal disaster area. Federal disaster declarations are issued in less than 50 percent of flooding incidents. The premium for an NFIP policy, averaging about $400 a year, is less expensive than interest on federal disaster loans.

Furthermore, if you are uninsured and receive federal disaster assistance after a flood, you must purchase flood insurance to remain eligible for future disaster relief.

10. **Myth: The NFIP encourages coastal development.**
Fact: One of the NFIP's primary objectives is to guide development away from high-flood-risk areas. NFIP regulations minimize the impact of structures that are built in SFHAs by requiring them not to cause obstructions to the natural flow of floodwaters. Also, as a condition of community participation in the NFIP, those structures built within SFHAs must adhere to strict floodplain management regulations.

In addition, the Coastal Barrier Resources Act (CBRA) of 1982 relies on the NFIP to discourage building in fragile coastal areas by prohibiting the sale of flood insurance in designated CBRA areas. While the NFIP does not prohibit property owners from buildng along coastal areas, any federal financial assistance, including federally-backed flood insurance, is prohibited. However, the law does not prohibit privately financed development or insurance.

11. **Myth: The NFIP does not cover flooding resulting from hurricanes or the overflow of rivers or tidal waters.**
Fact: The NFIP defines covered flooding as a general and temporary condition during which the surface of normally dry land is partially or completely inundated. Two properties in the area or two or more acres must be affected. Flooding can be caused by:

- The overflow of inland or tidal waters
- The unusual and rapid accumulation or runoff of surface waters from any source, such as heavy rainfall
- Mudslides or mudflows, caused by flooding, that could be described as a river of liquid mud
- The collapse or destabilization of land along the shore of a lake or other body of water, resulting from erosion or the effect of waves, or water currents exceeding normal, cyclical levels

12. **Myth: Wind-driven rain is considered flooding.**
Fact: No, it isn't. Rain entering through wind-damaged windows, doors, or a hole in a wall or roof, resulting in standing water or puddles, is considered windstorm damage rather than flood damage. Federal flood insurance covers only damage caused by the general condition of flooding (defined above), typically caused by storm surge, wave wash, tidal waves, or the overflow of any body of water over normally dry land areas. Buildings that sustain this type of damage usually have a watermark, showing how high the water rose before it subsided. Although the Standard Flood Insurance Policy (SFIP) specifically excludes wind and hail damage, homeowners policies provide such coverage.

SOURCE: Adapted from "Myths and Facts About the NFIP," Federal Emergency Management Agency, March 2, 2004.

Each state with a FAIR plan has a pool or syndicate that provides basic property insurance to persons who cannot obtain insurance in the regular markets. The pools or syndicates are operated by private insurers. Each insurer in the pool or syndicate is assessed its proportionate share of losses and expenses based on the proportion of property insurance premiums written in the state.

FAIR plan premiums are higher than premiums paid in the standard market. However, basic insurance is made available where coverage otherwise would not exist. All FAIR plans cover fire, vandalism, riot, and windstorm. About a dozen states provide some type of homeowners policy, which includes personal liability coverage. The FAIR plan in California covers brush fires.

Before a building is insured under a FAIR plan, it must meet certain underwriting standards. If these standards are met, a policy is issued. If the building is substandard, the property owner must make certain improvements that reduce the risk of fire, theft, or water damage, such as upgrading the electrical wiring, heating, or plumbing systems, repairing the roof, or improving security. If the property owner does not correct the conditions that make the home prone to losses, the FAIR plan administrator may deny coverage.

TITLE INSURANCE

Our discussion of property insurance coverages would not be complete without a brief description of title insurance. **Title insurance** *protects the owner of property or the lender of money for the purchase of property against any unknown defects in the title to the property under consideration.* Defects to a clear title can result from an invalid will, incorrect description of the property, defective probate of a will, undisclosed liens, easements, and numerous other legal defects that occurred sometime in the past. In particular, the problem of a forged title has increased in recent years. Without a clear title, the owner could lose the property to someone with a superior claim or incur other losses because of an unknown lien, unmarketability of the title, and attorney expenses. Title insurance is designed to provide protection against these losses.

Any liens, encumbrances, or easements against real estate are normally recorded in a courthouse in the area where the property is located. This information is recorded in a legal document known as an *abstract,* which is a history of ownership and title to the property. When real estate is purchased, the purchaser may hire an attorney to search the abstract to determine whether there are any defects to a clear title to the property. However, the purchaser is not fully protected by this method, because there may be an unknown lien, encumbrance, or other title defect not recorded in the abstract. The owner could still incur a loss despite a diligent and careful title search. Thus, the owner needs a stronger guarantee that he or she will be indemnified if a loss occurs. Title insurance can provide that guarantee.

Title insurance policies have certain characteristics that distinguish them from other contracts:

- *The policy provides protection against title defects that have occurred in the past, prior to the effective date of the policy.*
- *The policy is written by the insurer based on the assumption that no losses will occur.* Any known title defects or facts that have a bearing on the title are listed in the policy and excluded from coverage.
- *The premium is paid only once when the policy is issued.* No additional premiums are required.
- *The policy term runs indefinitely into the future.* As long as the title defect occurred before the issue date of the policy, any insured loss is covered, no matter when it is discovered in the future.
- *If a loss occurs, the insured is indemnified in dollar amounts up to the policy limits.* The policy does not guarantee possession by the owner, removal of any title defects, or a legal remedy against known defects.

The policy limit is usually the purchase price of the property. If the property appreciates in value over the years, the homeowner could be underinsured at the time of loss. This consideration is especially important in those areas where inflation in housing prices is occurring.

PERSONAL UMBRELLA POLICY

Personal liability claims occasionally reach catastrophic levels and can exceed the liability limits of a homeowners or auto insurance policy. For example, catastrophic losses can result from a chain-reaction

EXHIBIT 12.2
**Typical Underlying Coverage Amounts Required to Qualify
for a Personal Umbrella Policy**

Auto liability insurance	$250,000 / $500,000 / $50,000 or $500,000 single limit
Personal liability insurance (separate contract or homeowners policy)	$100,000 or $300,000
Large watercraft	$500,000

accident on an icy highway where cars collide and several people are killed or injured; a boating accident in which a boat is swamped by another boat and several people are injured or drown; or a defamation-of-character lawsuit by someone who claims that his or her reputation is ruined.

The **personal umbrella policy** *provides protection against a catastrophic lawsuit or judgment.* Most insurers write this coverage in amounts ranging from $1 million to $10 million. Coverage is broad and covers catastrophic liability loss exposures arising out of the home, cars, boats, recreational vehicles, sports, and other personal activities.

Basic Characteristics

Although personal umbrella policies differ among insurers, they share several common characteristics, including the following:[9]

- Excess liability insurance
- Broad coverage
- Self-insured retention or deductible
- Reasonable cost

Excess Liability Insurance   *The personal umbrella policy provides excess liability insurance over underlying insurance contracts that apply.* The umbrella policy pays only after the underlying insurance limits are exhausted. The insured is required to carry certain minimum amounts of liability insurance on the underlying contracts. Although the required amounts vary among insurers, the amounts shown in Exhibit 12.2 are typical.

If the required amounts of underlying insurance are not maintained, the umbrella insurer pays only the amount that it would have paid had the underlying insurance been kept in force.

Broad Coverage   *The umbrella policy provides broad coverage of personal liability loss exposures.* The policy covers bodily injury and property damage liability, as well as personal injury. **Personal injury** typically includes false arrest, detention, or imprisonment; malicious prosecution; wrongful eviction or wrongful entry; libel, slander, and defamation of character; and oral or written publication of material that violates a person's right to privacy.

In addition, the umbrella policy covers certain losses not covered by any underlying contract after a self-insured retention or deductible is met. In addition to the policy limits, most umbrella policies pay legal defense costs as well.

Self-insured Retention   The umbrella policy typically contains a self-insured retention or deductible. The **self-insured retention,** *or deductible, applies only to losses covered by the umbrella policy but not by any underlying contract.* The self-insured retention is typically $250 but can be higher. Examples of claims not covered by the underlying contracts but insured under an umbrella policy include libel, slander, defamation of character, and a variety of additional claims (see Insight 12.2).

To illustrate, assume that Andrea has a $1 million personal umbrella policy and an auto insurance policy with limits of $250,000 per person and $500,000 per accident for bodily injury liability. If she negligently injures another motorist and must pay damages of $650,000, the auto policy pays the first $250,000. The umbrella policy pays the remaining $400,000, because the underlying limit of $250,000 per person under the auto policy has been exhausted. The self-insured retention does not apply here.

Now assume that Andrea is sued by her ex-husband for defamation of character and must pay

INSIGHT 12.2

Examples of Claims Covered by Personal Umbrella Policy

The following are examples of claims covered by personal umbrella insurance:

- The mast on a boat broke and seriously injured a guest on the boat. The amount of the judgment that exceeded the limit of the insured's watercraft policy was paid by the insured's personal umbrella insurer.

- The insured caused an accident involving a school bus and injured several children. The resulting judgments resulted in damages that far exceeded the insured's personal auto policy (PAP) liability limit. The insured's personal umbrella policy covered the amount in excess of the PAP limit up to the umbrella liability limit.

- The insured slandered two police officers. Although the insured's homeowners policy did not cover this loss, the insured's personal umbrella policy provided protection.

- The insured rented a car in France and was involved in a serious accident. Personal umbrella coverage responded

to the loss, although the PAP coverage did not apply because the accident occurred overseas.

- The insured's son rented a motorcyle and was involved in a serious accident. The underlying automobile and home-owners contracts did not cover the resulting third-party claim, but the personal umbrella policy covered the loss.

Although in the first two examples, the claims were covered under the boat and auto policies, the umbrella policy covered amounts over and above the limits on these policies (subject to its limit). In the last three examples, the personal umbrella policy provided broader coverage than that of the home-owners or auto policies and thus provided the only liability coverage available to the insured.

SOURCE: Eric A. Weining, George E. Rejda, Consance M. Luthardt, and Cheryl L. Ferguson, *Personal Insurance*, First Edition, (Malvern, PA.: American Institute for Chartered Property Casualty Underwriters/Insurance Institute of America, 2002), pp 9.14–9.15

damages of $50,000. If there is no underlying coverage and the self-insured retention is $250, her umbrella policy would pay $49,750. The self-insured retention must be paid by Andrea in this case.

Reasonable Cost   An umbrella policy is also reasonable in cost. The actual cost depends on several variables, including the number of cars, boats, and motorcycles to be covered. For most families, the annual premium for a $1 million umbrella policy is less than $250.

ISO Personal Umbrella Policy

In 1998, the Insurance Services Office (ISO) introduced a standard personal umbrella policy. Member companies can use the ISO policy or develop their own umbrella policy. The following discussion summarizes the basic characteristics of the ISO policy.

Persons Insured   The ISO umbrella policy covers the following people:

- *Named insured and spouse if a resident of the same household*

- *Resident relatives, including a ward or foster child*
- *Household residents younger than age 21 in the care of the named insured or an insured age 21 or older*
- *Any person using an auto, recreational motor vehicle, or watercraft that is owned by the named insured and covered under the umbrella policy*
- *Any other person or organization legally responsible for the named insured or family member while using an auto or recreational motor vehicle covered under the policy. For example, if James does volunteer work and negligently injures another motorist while delivering food baskets for a local church, the church is also covered.*

Coverages   The umbrella policy pays for damages in excess of the retained limit for bodily injury, property damage, or personal injury for which the insured is legally liable because of a covered loss. The **retained limit** *is (1) the total limits of the underlying insurance or any other insurance available to an insured, or (2) the deductible stated in the declarations if the loss is covered by the umbrella* *policy but not by any underlying insurance or other insurance.*

In addition to the liability limit, the policy pays legal defense costs; expenses incurred by the insurer while defending the suit; premiums on any required bonds; reasonable expenses incurred by an insured at the insurer's request, including the loss of earnings up to $250 daily; and interest on any unpaid judgment.

Exclusions The ISO policy contains numerous exclusions. Major exclusions include the following:

- *Expected or intentional injury.* Expected or intentional injury is excluded. However, the exclusion does not apply to intentional bodily injury resulting from reasonable force to protect people or property, such as firing a gun at an intruder who is breaking into the home.
- *Certain personal injury losses.* The policy excludes coverage for certain personal injury losses, such as libel and slander that the insured knows to be false or which occurred prior to the policy's inception. It also excludes criminal acts and acts committed against an employee, such as discrimination in hiring, firing, or promotion.
- *Rental of the premises.* With certain exceptions, the ISO policy excludes liability arising out of rental of the residence premises to someone else. This exclusion does not apply to the occasional rental of the residence premises, such as a professor who goes on a sabbatical leave and rents out his or her home for six months. The exclusion also does not apply if part of the residence premises is rented as an office, school, studio, or private garage.
- *Business liability.* The policy excludes liability arising out of business activities by the insured. This exclusion does not apply to an insured who performs civic or public activities without compensation other than reimbursement for expenses, such as a Girl or Boy Scout leader. Likewise, it does not apply to minors younger than age 18 (21 if a full-time student) who are self-employed, such as in delivering newspapers, mowing lawns, baby-sitting, or removing snow.
- *Professional services.* The policy excludes liability arising out of the rendering of or failure to render professional services.
- *Aircraft, watercraft, and recreational vehicles.* The policy excludes liability arising out of the ownership or use of aircraft, except model or hobby aircraft. Also excluded are activities involving watercraft or recreational motor vehicles unless coverage is provided by underlying insurance.
- *No reasonable belief.* The ISO personal umbrella policy excludes coverage for a person using an auto, recreational motor vehicle, or watercraft without a reasonable belief that he or she is entitled to do so. This exclusion does not apply to a family member who uses a vehicle owned by the named insured, such as a teenager who drives a family car without first getting permission.
- *Vehicles used in racing.* The policy excludes the use of autos, recreational motor vehicles, or watercraft in a prearranged race or speed contest. The exclusion does not apply to sailboats or to watercraft involved in predicted log cruises.
- *Communicable disease, sexual molestation, or use of a controlled substance.* The policy excludes liability arising out of the transmission of a communicable disease; sexual molestation; corporal punishment; physical or mental abuse; or the use or sale of a controlled substance, such as methamphetamine, cocaine, marijuana, and narcotic drugs (except prescription drugs).
- *Directors and officers.* The ISO policy excludes acts or omissions of an insured as an officer or member of a board of directors. This exclusion does not apply to nonprofit organizations in which the insured receives no compensation other than reimbursement for expenses.
- *Care, custody, and control.* The policy excludes coverage for damage to property rented to, used by, or in the care, custody, and control of the insured to the extent that the insured is required by contract to provide insurance for such property. The exclusion does not apply to property damage caused by fire, smoke, or explosion.

In addition, the ISO personal umbrella policy excludes liability arising out of bodily injury to the named insured or any family member; damage to property owned by an insured; bodily injury to any person eligible to receive workers compensation benefits; and liability arising out of the escape of fuel from a fuel system, absorption or inhalation of lead, or lead contamination.

CHAPTER 12 / OTHER PROPERTY AND LIABILITY INSURANCE COVERAGES

CASE APPLICATION

Ben recently retired and purchased an older house near a river. Although the house needs major repairs, it will be his major residence. The river overflows occasionally, which has caused substantial damage to several homes in the area. Ben lives alone, but he keeps two Rottweiler dogs on the premises as watchdogs. He also has a small 15-horsepower boat, which is used for fishing.

An insurance agent has informed Ben that the house cannot be insured under a Homeowners 3 (HO-3) policy because the underwriter would not approve the application. The agent stated he would try to get the underwriter to approve a Dwelling Property 3 policy (DP-3). If that policy cannot be obtained, the agent indicated that he would try to get a Dwelling Property 1 policy (DP-1). As a last resort, the agent stated that coverage might be available through the state's FAIR plan.

a. Assume you are a personal insurance advisor. Identify the major loss exposures that Ben faces.
b. Explain the major differences among the HO-3, DP-3, and DP-1 policies discussed by the agent.
c. To what extent will each of the coverage alternatives discussed by the agent cover the loss exposures identified in (a)?
d. Assume that Ben obtains a DP-3 policy. Do you recommend that he also purchase the personal liability supplement? Explain.
e. Assume that Ben obtains a DP-1 policy. Do you recommend that he also purchase flood insurance through the National Flood Insurance Program? Explain.

SUMMARY

- The ISO dwelling program is designed for dwellings that are ineligible for coverage under a homeowners policy and for persons who do not want or need a homeowners policy.

- The *Dwelling Property 1 policy* is a basic form that provides coverage for a limited number of named perils. The *Dwelling Property 2 policy* is a broad form that includes all perils covered under the basic form and some additional perils. The *Dwelling Property 3 policy* is a special form that covers the dwelling and other structures against risks of direct loss to property. All direct physical losses are covered except for those losses specifically excluded; personal property is covered on a named-perils basis.

- A mobile home can be insured by an endorsement to a Homeowners 2 or Homeowners 3 policy. Thus, the coverages on a mobile home are similar to those found in homeowner contracts.

- An *inland marine floater* provides broad and comprehensive protection on personal property that is frequently moved from one location to another. Although inland marine floaters are not uniform, they share certain common characteristics. Insurance can be tailored to the specific types of personal property to be insured; desired amounts of insurance and type of coverage can

be selected; broader and more comprehensive coverage can be obtained; most floaters cover insured property anywhere in the world; and floaters are often written without a deductible.

- The *personal articles floater (PAF)* insures certain optional classes of personal property on an "all-risks" or "open perils" basis. All direct physical losses are covered except certain losses specifically excluded. The classes are jewelry, furs, cameras, musical instruments, silverware, golfer's equipment, fine arts, postage stamps, and coin collections. Individual items are listed and insured for specific amounts.

- The *scheduled personal property endorsement* is an endorsement that can be added to the homeowners policy that provides essentially the same coverages provided by the personal articles floater.

- Insurance on recreational boats generally can be divided into two categories. A *boat owners package policy* combines physical damage insurance, medical expense insurance, liability insurance, and other coverages into one contract. *Yacht insurance* is designed for larger boats such as cabin cruisers and inboard motorboats. Yacht insurance provides physical damage insurance on the boat and equipment, liability insurance, medical payments insurance, and other coverages.

- The flood peril is difficult to insure privately because of the problems of a catastrophic loss, prohibitively high premiums, and adverse selection. Federal flood insurance is available to cover buildings and personal property in flood zones.

- Under the *write-your-own program,* private insurers write flood insurance, collect premiums, and pay claims. They are then reimbursed for any losses by the federal government.

- *FAIR plans* provide basic property insurance to individuals who are unable to obtain coverage in the normal markets. If the property meets certain underwriting standards, it can be insured at standard or surcharged rates. In some cases, the owner may be required to make certain improvements in the property before the policy is issued.

- *Title insurance* protects the owner of property or secured lender against any unknown defects in the title to the property.

- The *personal umbrella policy* is designed to provide protection against a catastrophic lawsuit or judgment. The major features of the personal umbrella policy are as follows:

    The policy provides excess liability insurance over basic underlying insurance contracts.

    Coverage is broad and includes protection against certain losses not covered by the underlying contracts.

    A self-insured retention must be met for certain losses covered by the umbrella policy but not by any underlying contract.

    The umbrella policy is reasonable in cost.

KEY CONCEPTS AND TERMS

Boat owners package policy
Dwelling Property 1 (basic form)
Dwelling Property 2 (broad form)
Dwelling Property 3 (special form)
FAIR plans
Flood
Inland marine floater

Mobile home insurance
National Flood Insurance Program (NFIP)
Personal articles floater (PAF)
Personal injury
Personal umbrella policy
Retained limit
Self-insured retention
Title insurance
Yacht insurance

REVIEW QUESTIONS

1. The ISO dwelling program has three major forms. Describe the characteristics of each of the following:
   a. Dwelling Property 1 (basic form)
   b. Dwelling Property 2 (broad form)
   c. Dwelling Property 3 (special form)

2. A dwelling policy can be modified by adding certain endorsements. Describe the coverage provided by the personal liability supplement that can be added to a dwelling policy.

3. Describe the basic characteristics of inland marine floaters.

4. The personal articles floater (PAF) provides comprehensive protection for valuable personal property. Give three examples of property that might require coverage under a PAF instead of a standard homeowners policy.

5. Identify the coverages found in a typical boat owners package policy.

6. Why are buildings in flood zones difficult to insure by private insurers?

7. The National Flood Insurance Program (NFIP) has numerous provisions. Briefly explain each of the following:
   a. Write-your-own program
   b. Meaning of a flood
   c. Waiting period

8. What is the purpose of a FAIR plan?

9. Describe the basic characteristics of title insurance.

10. Briefly explain the basic characteristics of a personal umbrella policy.

APPLICATION QUESTIONS

1. Pedro owns a sixplex apartment building and lives in one unit. The building is insured under the Dwelling Property 1 (basic form) policy for $160,000. The replacement cost of the building is $200,000. Explain to what extent, if any, Pedro will recover for the following losses:
   a. A fire occurs in one of the apartments because of defective wiring. The actual cash value of the damage is $10,000, and the replacement cost is $12,000.

b. The tenants move out because the apartment is unfit for normal living. It will take three months to restore the apartment to its former condition. The apartment is rented for $600 monthly.

c. A tenant's personal property is damaged in the fire. The actual cash value of the damaged property is $5000, and its replacement cost is $7000.

2. Mathew owns a mobile home that is insured by an endorsement to a Homeowners 3 policy. Explain to what extent, if at all, this policy would pay for each of the following losses:

a. A severe windstorm damages the roof of the mobile home.

b. A built-in range and oven are also damaged in the storm.

c. A window air conditioner is badly damaged in the storm.

d. Mathew must move to a furnished apartment for three months while the mobile home is being repaired.

3. Morgan has an outboard motorboat insured under a boat owners package policy. Indicate whether each of the following losses would be covered under Morgan's policy. If the loss is not covered, or not completely covered, explain why.

a. Morgan's boat was badly damaged when it struck a log floating in the water.

b. An occupant in Morgan's boat was injured and incurred medical expenses when the boat struck a concrete abutment.

c. The motor was stolen when the boat was docked at a marina.

d. A small child in Morgan's boat was not wearing a life jacket. The child fell overboard and drowned. The child's parents have sued Morgan.

4. Dan has a personal umbrella policy with a $1 million limit. The self-insured retention is $250. Dan has a homeowners policy with no special endorsement and an auto insurance policy. The policies have the following liability limits:

Homeowners policy: $300,000
Personal auto policy: $250,000/$500,000/$50,000

The liability limits meet the umbrella insurer's requirements with respect to the minimum amounts of liability insurance on the underlying contracts. Indicate whether each of the following losses would be covered under Dan's personal umbrella policy. If

the loss is not covered, or not covered fully, explain why.

a. Dan coaches a Little League baseball team. A team member sitting behind third base was struck in the face by a line drive and lost the sight in one eye. Dan is sued by the parents, who allege that his coaching is inadequate. The team member is awarded damages of $1 million.

b. Dan is a member of the board of directors for the local Young Men's Christian Association (YMCA). Dan is sued by a YMCA member who was seriously injured when a trampoline collapsed. The injured member is awarded damages of $500,000.

c. Dan accuses a male teenager, age 14, of stealing his racing bike valued at $2000. The police arrest the youth and book him. The police later arrest the actual thief and recover the bicycle. Dan is sued by the youth's parents for false arrest. The teenager is awarded damages of $100,000.

d. Dan fails to stop at a red light, and his car strikes another motorist. The injured motorist is awarded damages of $200,000.

5. Lori has a personal umbrella policy with a $1 million limit. The self-insured retention is $250. Lori has a homeowners policy with no special endorsement and an auto insurance policy. The policies have the following liability limits:

Homeowners policy: $300,000
Personal auto policy: $250,000/$500,000/ $50,000

The liability limits meet the umbrella insurer's requirements with respect to the minimum amounts of liability insurance on the underlying contracts. Indicate the amount, if any, that would be paid by Lori's umbrella policy for each of the following losses.

a. Lori's dog bites a small child. The parents sue Lori and are awarded damages of $25,000.

b. Lori failed to stop at a red light, and her car hit a school bus. Two children are severely injured. A court awards each child damages in the amount of $350,000.

c. Lori is a volunteer for a local nonprofit charity. While being interviewed on television with other guests, Lori called one of the guests a "bag lady." The guest sues Lori for defamation of character and is awarded damages of $25,000.

d. Lori is a member of the board of directors for a local bank. She receives an annual fee of $50,000 for her service as a board member. She is also a member of the board's audit committee. The shareholders sue Lori and other board members for not discovering several fraudulent accounting transactions that caused millions of dollars of losses to the shareholders. A court awards the shareholders damages of $5 million.

INTERNET RESOURCES

- The **Federal Emergency Management Agency (FEMA)** provides valuable consumer information about the National Flood Insurance Program. Check out this site at

  http://www.fema.gov

- The **Insurance Information Institute (III)** provides valuable consumer information on a number of property and liability insurance contracts for individuals and families. A timely feature is "Hot Topics & Insurance Issues." The III sponsors a site at

  http://www.iii.org

- Another site with lots of useful information about home, auto, and other property and liability insurance coverages is sponsored by the **Independent Insurance Agents & Brokers of America.** You can find this site at

  http://www.independentagent.com

- **Insure.com** provides consumers with information on a variety of insurance products, including homeowners and auto insurance. Check out this interesting site at

  http://www.insure.com

- **INSWEB** provides premium quotes for auto, homeowners, and other insurance products. The site has a learning center and provides information and articles from consumer, industry, and regulatory groups. Visit the site at

  http://www.insweb.com

- The **National Association of Insurance Commissioners (NAIC)** has a link to all state insurance departments, which provide a considerable amount of consumer information for auto, homeowners, and other personal insurance coverages. Click on "State Insurance Web Sites." For starters, check out New York, Wisconsin, and California. Visit the site at

  http://www.naic.org

SELECTED REFERENCES

Chesebrough, John R., and George E. Rejda. "Personal Umbrella Liability Insurance—A Critical Analysis." *CPCU Journal,* vol. 48, no. 2 (June 1995), pp. 98–104.

Fire, Casualty & Surety Bulletins. Fire and Marine volume and Casualty and Surety volume. Erlanger, KY: National Underwriter Company. See also the Personal Lines volume and Guide to Policies I volume. The bulletins are published monthly.

"Personal Umbrella Liability Policy." *The CPCU Handbook of Insurance Policies,* 4th ed. Malvern, PA: American Institute for CPCU, 2001, pp. 102–108.

Hamilton, Karen L., and Cheryl L. Ferguson. *Personal Risk Management and Property-Liability Insurance,* First Edition. Malvern, PA.: American Institute for Chartered Property Casualty Underwriters/Insurance Institute of America, 2002.

Wiening, Eric A., George E. Rejda, Constance M. Luthardt, and Cheryl L. Ferguson. *Personal Insurance,* First Edition. Malvern, PA.: American Institute for Chartered Property Casualty Underwriters/Insurance Institute of America, 2002.

NOTES

1. The ISO dwelling program is described in detail in *Fire, Casualty & Surety Bulletins*, Personal Lines volume, Dwelling section. The dwelling property forms by the Insurance Services Office were also used by the author in preparing this section.
2. For a detailed explanation of mobile homes, see "Mobile Home Insurance," *Fire, Casualty & Surety Bulletins*, Personal Lines volume, Dwelling section.
3. Eric A. Wiening, George E. Rejda, Constance M. Luthardt, and Cheryl L. Ferguson, *Personal Insurance,* First Edition (Malvern, PA.: American Institute for Chartered Property Casualty Underwriters/Insurance Institute of America, 2002), p. 9.4.
4. Discussion of the personal articles floater is based on *Fire, Casualty & Surety Bulletins*, Personal Lines volume, Misc. Personal section.
5. Insurance on pleasure boats is based on *Fire, Casualty & Surety Bulletins*, Companies and Coverages volume, Aircraft-Marine section; and the yacht policy discussed in the *CPCU Handbook of Insurance Policies,* 4th ed. (Malvern, PA: American Institute for CPCU, 2001), pp. 95–101.

6. Current details of the federal flood insurance program can be found in the *Fire, Casualty & Surety Bulletins,* Fire and Marine volume, Catastrophe section. See also, Federal Emergency Management Agency, *Flood Insurance* at http://www.fema.gov/nfip/

7. Federal Emergency Management Agency.

8. FAIR plans exist in Arkansas (rural), California, Connecticut, Delaware, District of Columbia, Florida (joint underwriting association), Georgia, Hawaii, Illinois, Indiana, Iowa, Kansas, Kentucky, Louisiana, Maryland, Massachusetts, Michigan, Minnesota, Mississippi (rural), Missouri, New Jersey, New Mexico, New York, North Carolina, Ohio, Oregon, Pennsylvania, Rhode Island, Virginia, Washington, West Virginia, and Wisconsin. Beach and windstorm plans exist in Alabama, Florida, Louisiana, Mississippi, North Carolina, South Carolina, and Texas.

9. Discussion of the personal umbrella policy is based on John R. Chesebrough and George E. Rejda, "Personal Umbrella Liability Insurance—A Critical Analysis," *CPCU Journal,* vol. 48, no. 2 (June 1995), pp. 98–104; "Personal Umbrella Liability Insurance," in *Fire, Casualty & Surety Bulletins,* Companies and Coverage volume, Personal Packages section (Erlanger, KY: National Underwriter Company); and "Personal Umbrella Liability Policy," *The CPCU Handbook of Insurance Policies,* 4th ed. (Malvern, PA: American Institute for CPCU, 2001), pp. 102–108.

Students may take a self-administered test on this chapter at
www.aw-bc.com/rejda

PART FOUR

COMMERCIAL PROPERTY AND LIABILITY RISKS

CHAPTER 13

COMMERCIAL PROPERTY INSURANCE

"Protecting the company assets in the event of a loss is a key function of the risk manager's job. Commercial property insurance is the primary technique for financing the risks associated with damage or destruction of these assets."

Rebecca A. McQuade
Director of Risk Management, PACCAR Inc.

LEARNING OBJECTIVES

After studying this chapter, you should be able to

◆ Explain the basic provisions in the building and personal property coverage form, including
Covered property
Additional coverages
Optional coverages

◆ Identify the causes of loss that are covered under the following forms:
Causes-of-loss basic form
Causes-of-loss broad form
Causes-of-loss special form

◆ Explain the basic provisions in the business income (and extra expense) coverage form, including
Meaning of a business income loss
Coverage of extra expenses

◆ Explain the basic coverages in an ocean marine policy, including
Hull insurance
Cargo insurance
Protection and indemnity (P&I) insurance
Freight insurance

◆ Identify the types of property that can be covered by an inland marine insurance policy.

◆ Describe the major provisions in a businessowners policy (BOP), including
  Coverages provided
  Additional coverages
  Optional coverages

*N*athan, age 38, is the general manager of Contemporary Furniture and Fashion, a local retail firm that specializes in the sale of contemporary furniture, modern art, and household accessories. Recently, an electrical circuit in the building shorted out, which caused a severe fire and extensive property damage. The store was expected to be closed for at least three months. When Nathan called his insurance agent to report the fire, the agent stated that the property damage to the building and inventory was fully covered except for a modest deductible. Nathan was also relieved to hear that the insurance on the business would cover a large part of the business income lost during the three-month shutdown period.*

Like Contemporary Furniture and Fashion, business firms own valuable commercial real estate; business personal property, such as office furniture, computers, machinery, and supplies; and inventories of finished products. This property can be damaged or destroyed if a loss occurs. In addition, firms may experience a substantial loss of business income or incur sizable extra expenses in the event of a loss.

This chapter discusses commercial property insurance, with special emphasis on the commercial property insurance program developed by the Insurance Services Office (ISO). More specifically, it focuses on the commercial package policy, the building and personal property coverage form, business income insurance, and other property coverages. The chapter also discusses ocean marine and inland marine insurance, which covers transportation and other commercial risks. It concludes with an analysis of the businessowners policy, which is designed for owners of small- to medium-sized business firms.

ISO COMMERCIAL PROPERTY PROGRAM

The Insurance Services Office (ISO) has designed a commercial property program that makes available package policies tailored to meet the specific needs of business firms, such as a **commercial package policy (CPP)**. *A package policy is one that combines two or more coverages into a single policy.* If both property and liability insurance coverages are combined into a single policy, it is also known as a *multiple-line policy*. In contrast, a policy that provides only one type of coverage is known as a *monoline policy*.

When compared with individual policies, a package policy has several advantages. There are fewer gaps in coverage; insureds pay relatively lower premiums because individual policies are not purchased; savings in insurer expenses can be passed on to the policyholder; and the insured has the convenience of a single policy.

This section discusses the format of the commercial package policy, which is widely used by business firms. The CPP can be used to insure motels, hotels, apartment houses, office buildings, retail stores, churches and schools, processing firms such as dry cleaners, manufacturing firms, and a wide variety of other commercial firms. The CPP can be specifically designed to cover most property and liability loss exposures in a single policy, with the major exceptions of workers compensation and surety bonds.

Under the ISO program, each commercial package policy contains (1) a common policy declarations page, (2) a common policy conditions page, and (3) two or more coverage parts.[1] Exhibit 13.1 shows in greater detail the various parts of a commercial package policy.

Common Policy Declarations

Each commercial package policy contains a *common policy declarations page* that shows the name and address of the insured, policy period, description of the insured property, a list of coverage parts that apply, and the premium amount.

Common Policy Conditions

Each commercial package policy also contains a *common policy conditions page* that applies to all commercial lines of insurance. The common conditions are summarized as follows:

- *Cancellation.* Either party can cancel by giving the other party advance notice. The insurer can cancel by giving notice of cancellation for non-payment of premiums at least 10 days in advance and 30 days in advance for any other reason. If the insurer cancels, a pro rata refund of the premium is made. If the insured cancels, the refund may be less than pro rata.
- *Changes.* Any changes in the policy can be made only by an endorsement issued by the insurer.
- *Examination of books and records.* The insurer has the right to audit the insured's books and records any time during the policy period and up to three years after the policy period ends.

- *Inspections and surveys.* The insurer has the right to make inspections and surveys that relate to insurability of the property and premiums to be charged.
- *Premiums.* More than one party may be named as an insured in the declarations page. The *first named insured* in the declarations is the party responsible for the payment of premiums.
- *Transfer of rights and duties.* The insured's rights and duties under the policy cannot be transferred without the insurer's written consent. One exception is that the rights and duties can be transferred to a legal representative if an individual named insured should die.

Coverage Parts

Each commercial package policy contains two or more of the following *coverage parts:*

- Commercial property coverage form(s)
- Commercial general liability coverage form
- Crime coverage form
- Equipment breakdown protection coverage form
- Inland marine coverage form(s)
- Auto coverage form
- Farm coverage form(s)

Each coverage part, in turn, contains (1) its own declarations page that applies to that coverage, (2) the specific conditions that apply to that coverage part, (3) coverage forms that describe the various coverages provided, and (4) where applicable, a causes-of-loss form that describes the various perils that are covered.

BUILDING AND PERSONAL PROPERTY COVERAGE FORM

The **building and personal property coverage form** is widely used to cover a direct physical damage loss to commercial buildings and business personal property. Discussion is based on the current (2002) edition of the form.

Covered Property

The insured selects the property to be covered. Covered property can include the following:

EXHIBIT 13.1
Components of the ISO Commercial Package Policy (CPP)

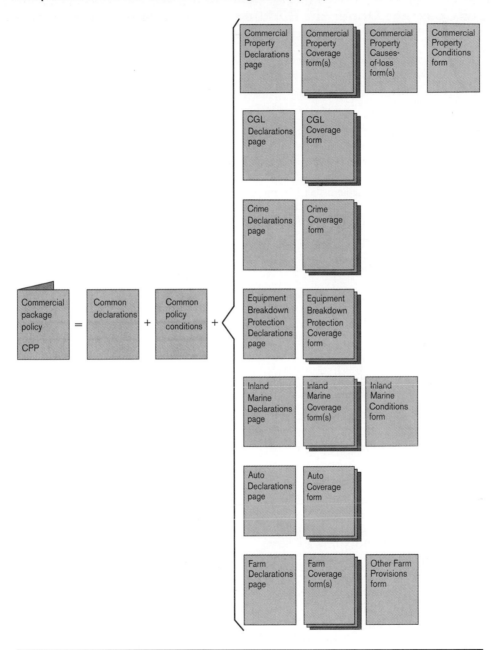

SOURCE: Arthur L. Flitner and Jerome Trupin, *Commercial Insurance*, First Edition (Malvern, PA: American Institute for CPCU/Insurance Institute of America, 2002), p. 1.11.

INSIGHT 13.1

Examples of Coverage Under the Building and Personal Property Coverage Form

The building and personal property coverage form can be used to cover a building, business personal property, and personal property of others. Most business firms do not require coverage in all three categories. Depending on its needs, a firm can elect only those coverages desired.

Examples

1. Worldwide Realty, Inc., is the owner of a building rented to others. It has purchased coverage for the building only.
2. Sue Brown, doing business as Sue's Leather Restoring, operates in Worldwide Realty's building. Sue has no need for building insurance because she is only a tenant. She has purchased coverage for her own business personal property and for the personal property of others in her care, custody, or control.

3. Smith and Jones, LLP, a law firm operating in Worldwide Realty's building, has purchased coverage only for its own business personal property because it does not have an insurable interest in the building and does not have any personal property of others in its possession.
4. City Laundry, Inc., a commercial laundry, owns and occupies the building adjacent to Worldwide Realty's building. City Laundry has purchased coverage for the building, its business personal property, and the personal property of others in its care, custody, or control.

SOURCE: Adapted from Jerome Trupin and Arthur L. Flitner, *Commercial Property Risk Management and Insurance*, 6th ed., vol. 1 (Malvern, PA: American Institute for CPCU, 2001), pp. 3.6–3.7.

- Building
- Named insured's business personal property
- Personal property of others in the care, custody, or control of the insured

For coverage to apply, the declarations page must show a limit of insurance for that category. Depending on its needs, a business firm can elect one or all three coverages (see Insight 13.1).

Building   The form covers the building described in the declarations and includes any completed additions and fixtures and permanently installed machinery and equipment. Certain outdoor fixtures are also covered, such as light poles, flagpoles, and mailboxes. Finally, equipment used to maintain or service the building (such as fire-extinguishing equipment, appliances for cooking and dishwashing, floor buffers, and vacuum cleaners) is also covered.

Business Personal Property   Business personal property of the named insured inside or on the building or within 100 feet of the premises is also covered. It includes furniture and fixtures; computer systems, machinery and equipment; stock or inventory; and all other personal property owned by the insured and used in the insured's business.

In addition, the insured's interest in the personal property of others is covered to the extent of labor, materials, and other charges. For example, a machine shop may repair a piece of machinery owned by a customer. If parts and labor are $1000 and the machinery is damaged from an insured peril before it is delivered to the customer, the insured's interest of $1000 is covered.

The insured's use interest in improvements and betterments as a tenant is also covered as business personal property. Improvements and betterments include fixtures, alterations, installations, or additions that are made part of the building at the insured's expense and cannot be removed legally. An example of an improvement is the installation of a new air conditioning unit by an insured who leases a building to open a new bar and restaurant.

Finally, business personal property includes leased personal property, which the insured has a contractual obligation to insure. An example would be leased computer equipment, for which the insured is required to provide insurance.

Personal Property of Others   Personal property of others in the care, custody, or control of the insured is also covered. For example, if a tornado destroys a machine shop and equipment belonging to customers is damaged, the loss would be covered.

Additional Coverages   Several additional coverages are provided, summarized as follows:

- *Debris removal*. The cost of debris removal is paid up to certain limits specified in the policy. Debris removal coverage does not apply to the cost of extracting pollutants from land or water.
- *Preservation of property*. If property is moved to another location for safekeeping because of a covered loss, any direct physical loss or damage to the property while being moved or while stored at the other location is covered. Coverage applies only if the loss or damage occurs within 30 days after the property is first moved.
- *Fire department service charge*. A maximum of $1000 can be paid for a fire department service charge. No deductible applies to this coverage.
- *Pollutant cleanup and removal*. The insurer also pays the cost to clean up and remove pollutants from land or water at the described premises if the release or discharge of the pollutants results from a covered cause of loss. The maximum paid is limited to $10,000 during each separate 12-month policy period.
- *Increased cost of construction*. Another additional coverage is the increased cost of construction because of an ordinance or law. The additional coverage applies only to buildings insured on a replacement-cost basis. The maximum amount of additional insurance that applies to each described building insured under this form is $10,000, or 5 percent of the limit of insurance that applies to that building, whichever is less.
- *Electronic data*. The current (2002) edition of the form adds a separate additional coverage for electronic data. The policy pays the cost to replace or restore electronic data destroyed or corrupted by a covered cause of loss, including CDs, floppy disks, hard drives, and similar equipment. Covered causes of loss include damage caused by a computer virus except if caused by an employee or leased employee. The maximum paid is $2500 during any policy year.

Extensions of Coverage   If a coinsurance requirement of 80 percent or higher is shown in the declarations, or a value-reporting period symbol is shown on the declarations page, the insurance can be extended to cover other property. The extensions of coverage are summarized as follows:

- *Newly acquired or constructed property*. Insurance on the building is extended to cover new buildings while being built on the described premises and to newly acquired buildings at other locations. The insurance applies for a maximum period of 30 days and is limited to a maximum of $250,000 for each building. In addition, the insurance on business personal property ($100,000 maximum) can be applied to business personal property at newly acquired locations. This insurance also applies for a maximum period of 30 days.
- *Personal effects and property of others*. Insurance on business personal property can be extended to cover the personal effects of the named insured, officers, partners, or employees. However, the extension does not apply to theft. The extension also applies to personal property of others in the named insured's care, custody, or control. The maximum paid is limited to $2500.
- *Valuable papers and records (other than electronic data)*. Insurance on business personal property can also be extended to cover the costs of researching, replacing, or restoring lost information on lost or damaged valuable papers and records. The maximum paid is limited to $2500 at each described premises.
- *Property off the premises*. Covered property that is temporarily at a location not owned, leased, or operated by the insured is covered up to $10,000. The extension of coverage does not apply to property in or on a vehicle or to property in the care, custody, or control of salespersons. However, if the property is in the care, custody, or control of salespersons at a trade show, fair, or exhibition, the extension of coverage will apply.
- *Outdoor property*. Outdoor fences, radio and television antennas, detached signs, and trees, plants, and shrubs are covered up to a maximum of $1000, but not more than $250 for any single tree, shrub, or plant. The insurance applies only

to losses caused by fire, lightning, explosion, riot or civil commotion, or aircraft.

■ *Nonowned detached trailers.* Coverage can also be extended to nonowned detached trailers under certain circumstances. The trailer must be used in the business and in the insured's care, custody, and control; the insured must also have a contractual obligation to pay for any loss or damage to the trailer. However, coverage ceases if the trailer is attached to any motor vehicle whether in motion or not. For example, a construction company may rent a U-Haul trailer that is used as a temporary office while at a worksite; coverage applies as long as the trailer is not attached to any motorized vehicle. The maximum paid under this extension is $5000.

Other Provisions

Numerous additional provisions are included in the building and personal property coverage form, but it is beyond the scope of this text to discuss each of them. Several important provisions, however, are summarized here.

Deductible   A standard deductible of $250 applies to each occurrence. Higher deductible amounts are available. Only one deductible must be satisfied if several buildings or different types of business personal property are damaged in the same occurrence.

Coinsurance   If a coinsurance percentage is stated in the declarations, the coinsurance requirement must be met to avoid a coinsurance penalty. To reduce misunderstanding and confusion, the form contains several excellent examples of how coinsurance works.

Optional Coverages   Three optional coverages are preprinted in the form, which eliminates the need for separate endorsements.

■ *Agreed value.* This option suspends the coinsurance clause and substitutes a new agreement that covers any loss in the same proportion that the limit of insurance bears to the agreed value shown in the declarations. For example, if the agreed value for an item is $100,000, and the limit of insurance is $100,000, then any loss is

covered in full less any deductible up to the limit of insurance.

■ *Inflation guard.* This option automatically increases the amount of insurance by an annual percentage shown in the declarations.

■ *Replacement cost.* Under the replacement cost option, there is no deduction for depreciation if a loss occurs. However, this option does not apply to the property of others; contents of a residence; manuscripts; works of art, antiques, and similar property; and stock (unless designated in the declarations). Replacement cost insurance generally is recommended when buildings and their contents are insured. Otherwise, the loss is paid on an actual cash value basis.

CAUSES-OF-LOSS FORMS

A *causes-of-loss form* must be added to the policy to have a complete contract. Insureds can select one of the following forms:

■ Causes-of-loss basic form
■ Causes-of-loss broad form
■ Causes-of-loss special form

Causes-of-Loss Basic Form

The **causes-of-loss basic form** provides coverage for 11 basic causes of loss to covered property:

■ Fire
■ Lightning
■ Explosion
■ Windstorm or hail
■ Smoke
■ Aircraft or vehicles
■ Riot or civil commotion
■ Vandalism
■ Sprinkler leakage
■ Sinkhole collapse
■ Volcanic action

These perils are self-explanatory, but two comments are in order. *Sprinkler leakage* provides coverage for the accidental leakage or discharge of any substance from an automatic sprinkler system for fire protection. For example, if the sprinkler system in a department store accidentally leaks water that damages the stock, the loss is covered.

Sinkhole collapse means the sudden sinking or collapse in underground empty spaces created by the action of water on limestone or dolomite rock formations. Although damage caused by the sinkhole collapse is covered, the cost of filling the sinkhole is specifically excluded.

Causes-of-Loss Broad Form

The **causes-of-loss broad form** includes all causes of loss covered by the basic form plus several additional causes:

- Falling objects
- Weight of snow, ice, or sleet
- Water damage

The broad form also covers collapse of a building as an additional coverage. Collapse is covered only if caused by the following:

- Certain specified causes of loss
- Hidden decay
- Hidden insect or vermin damage
- Weight of people or personal property
- Weight of rain that collects on a roof
- Use of defective materials or methods in construction or remodeling if collapse occurs during the course of construction or remodeling

Causes-of-Loss Special Form

The **causes-of-loss special form** insures against "risks of direct physical loss" (formerly called "all-risks").

INSIGHT 13.2

Advantages of the Special Causes-of-Loss Form

The special form insurance provides coverage for risks of direct physical loss to covered property. *The burden of proof as to coverage falls on the insurer—not the insured.* As long as the insured can demonstrate that a direct physical loss has occurred to covered property, the cause of loss is presumed to be covered unless the *insurer* can prove that an exclusion applies.

In contrast, the basic and broad forms place the burden of proof on the insured. Unless the *insured* can prove that one of the named perils caused the loss, the insurer has no obligation to pay. Which party has the burden of proof can make a major difference when the cause of loss is not entirely clear.

Insured and students of insurance sometimes ask for examples of "all-risks" type losses that would not be covered under a broad form. Some examples include the following:

- *Theft.* Because many types of theft are not excluded, those that are not excluded are covered.
- *Friendly fire.* The named peril "fire" is generally held to mean only *hostile fire*. No such limitation applies to the special form and most other "all-risks" forms because they do not exclude damage by friendly fire. Although court decisions are eroding the doctrine of friendly fire, an insured that has suffered a loss caused by a friendly fire might have to institute a lawsuit to prevail under a named perils policy.
- *Vehicle damage.* The aircraft or vehicles peril of the basic and broad forms contains a contact requirement. However, vehicles can harm property without making contact with the damaged property. The special form covers damage by vehicles whether or not direct physical contact occurs. It also covers damage caused by vehicles regardless of whether the insured owns or operates the damage-causing vehicle. The basic and broad forms exclude coverage when the vehicle is owned by the insured or operated in the course of the insured's business.
- *Water damage caused by ice dam.* When melting snow or ice backs up under roof shingles (usually because gutters are clogged with ice, a phenomenon referred to as "ice damming"), the resulting water damage is covered by the special form but not by the basic form or the broad form.

These examples help to illustrate the breadth of "all-risks" coverage. **The key point is this: A cause of loss that is not specifically excluded is covered.**

Another advantage is the relatively small additional premium charged for special form coverage instead of broad form coverage. The vast majority of risk managers and experienced insurance producers therefore prefer the special form.

SOURCE: Adapted from Jerome Trupin and Arthur L. Flitner, *Commercial Property Risk Management and Insurance*, 6th ed., vol. 1 (Malvern, PA: American Institute for CPCU, 2001), pp. 5.30–5.31.

That is, all direct physical damage losses to insured property are covered unless specifically excluded or limited in the form itself. The burden of proof falls on the insurer to show that the loss is not covered because of a specific exclusion or limitation that applies. In addition, collapse is included as an additional coverage.

The special form provides for three additional extensions of coverage. First, personal property in transit is covered for certain causes of loss while the property is in or on a motor vehicle owned, leased, or operated by the insured. The maximum paid is $5000.

Second, if the damage results from a covered water damage loss or from other liquids, the cost of tearing out and replacing part of the building or structure to repair the leaking water system or appliance is covered.

Finally, the special form covers glass damage as an additional extension of coverage. The insurer will pay for the cost of boarding up openings if repair or replacement of the damaged glass is delayed. The insurer will also pay the expense of removing or replacing obstructions when glass that is part of the building is being repaired or replaced. The cost of removing or replacing window displays, however, is not covered.

Because of its advantages, most risk managers prefer the special form (see Insight 13.2).

REPORTING FORMS

A firm may have sharp fluctuations in its inventories throughout the year. A **reporting form** requires the insured to report periodically the value of the insured inventory. As long as the report is accurate, the amount of insurance on the inventory is automatically adjusted based on the amount of insured values.

Under the ISO commercial property program, the *value reporting form* is used to insure fluctuations in inventory. An advance premium is paid at the inception of the policy based on the limit of insurance. The final premium is determined at the end of the policy period based on the values reported. The insured has the option of reporting daily, weekly, monthly, quarterly, or at the end of the policy year. As long as the insured reports the correct values, the full amount of the loss is covered up to the policy limits. For example, assume that the insured correctly reports an inventory of $1 million at the last reporting date, and the inventory is increased to $5 million before the next reporting date. If a total loss occurs, the entire inventory of $5 million would be covered up to the policy limit (less the deductible).

The value reporting form contains a *full reporting clause* (honesty clause) that requires the insured to report the values honestly. If the insured is dishonest or careless and underreports, he or she will be penalized if a loss occurs. *If the insured underreports the property values at a location, and a loss occurs at that location, recovery is limited to the proportion that the last value reported bears to the correct value that should have been reported.* For example, if the actual inventory on hand is $500,000, and the insured reports only $400,000, only four-fifths of any loss will be paid (less the deductible).

BUSINESS INCOME INSURANCE

Business firms often experience a consequential, or indirect, loss as a result of a direct physical damage loss to covered property, such as the loss of profits, rents, or extra expenses during the period of restoration. **Business income insurance** (formerly called *business interruption insurance*) is designed to cover the loss of business income, expenses that continue during the shutdown period, and extra expenses because of a direct physical loss to insured property.

Two basic ISO forms are used to insure business income losses:[2]

- Business income (and extra expense) coverage form
- Extra expense coverage form

Business Income (and Extra Expense) Coverage Form

The **business income (and extra expense) coverage form** is used to cover the loss of business income whether the income is derived from retail or service operations, manufacturing, or rents. When a firm has a business income loss, profits are lost, and certain expenses may still continue, such as rent, interest, insurance premiums, and some salaries. The present form covers both the loss of business income and extra expenses that result from a physical damage loss to covered property.

Loss of Business Income The business income and extra expense coverage form covers the loss of business income due to the suspension of operations during the period of restoration. The suspension of operations must result from the direct physical loss or damage to property caused by an insured peril at the described premises. The insured perils are listed in the causes-of-loss form attached to the policy. *Business income is defined as the net profit or loss (before income taxes) that would have been earned plus continuing normal operating expenses, including payroll.* In effect, the amount paid represents the profit (or loss) that would have occurred if the suspension of operations had not occurred, plus expenses that continue during the period of suspension. For example, assume that a retail shoe store has a fire and must suspend operations for six months. All regular employees are laid off during the shutdown period. Assume also that the firm's estimated sales and expenses for the 12 months of the policy period are as shown in Exhibit 13.2.

Assuming that income is earned equally over the period, the store's normal net income for 12 months is estimated to be $100,000. Thus, if the store is shut down for only six months, it will lose net income of $50,000. During the shutdown period, assume the firm also has continuing expenses of $20,000, such as the payment of rent, interest, utilities, and other expenses. Thus, the total loss payment would be $70,000. This can be summarized as follows.

Net income lost during the period of suspension	$50,000
Continuing expenses during the period of suspension	+ 20,000
Amount paid	$70,000

The loss payment of $70,000 represents the loss of net income plus an amount for continuing expenses.

Extra Expenses The business income form also covers extra expenses. **Extra expenses** are the necessary expenses incurred by the firm during the period of restoration that would not have been incurred if the loss had not taken place. Examples of covered expenses are the cost of relocating temporarily to

EXHIBIT 13.2
Estimated Sales and Expenses for the 12 Months of the Policy Period

Sales	$800,000
Less cost of goods sold	−400,000
Gross income	$400,000
Less expenses	−300,000
Net income before taxes	$100,000

another location, increased rent at another location, and the rental of substitute equipment.

Additional Coverages The business income form provides several additional coverages, summarized as follows:

- *Action of civil authority.* Loss of business income and extra expenses caused by action of a civil authority that prohibits access to the described premises because of a covered cause of loss are also paid. The coverage for business income begins 72 hours after the time of that action and continues for up to three consecutive weeks after the coverage begins.
- *Alterations and new buildings.* The loss of business income as a result of a direct physical damage loss to a new building on the premises (whether completed or under construction) is covered. The loss of business income because of alterations or additions to existing buildings is covered as well.
- *Extended business income.* A business that reopens may experience reduced earnings after the repairs are completed, and additional time may be needed to rebuild a customer base. For example, a restaurant that reopens after a fire may need time to attract former customers back. The extended business income provision covers the reduction in earnings for a limited period after the business reopens. The extended period begins on the date the property is repaired and operations are resumed and ends after 30 consecutive days or when business income returns to normal, whichever occurs first.
- *Interruption of computer operations.* Coverage also applies to the suspension of operations

caused by an interruption of computer operations from a covered cause of loss. For example, business operations may be temporarily suspended because a "hacker" breaks into the company's computer system, causing it to crash. The maximum paid is $2500 during any policy year.

Coinsurance The business income coverage form can be purchased with coinsurance of 50, 60, 70, 80, 90, 100, or 125 percent. *The basis for coinsurance is the sum of net income that would have been earned plus continuing normal operating expenses, including payroll, for the 12 months following the inception of the policy or the last anniversary date, whichever is later.* This sum is then multiplied by the coinsurance percentage to determine the required amount of insurance. For example, assume that net income and operating expenses for the 12 months of the current policy term are $400,000, and that the coinsurance percentage is 50 percent; the required amount of insurance would be $200,000.

The actual coinsurance percentage selected depends on the length of time it takes to resume operations, and on the period of time during which most of the business is done. If the firm expects to be shut down for more than one year, the 125 percent option should be selected. If the firm expects to be shut down for no more than six months and business is uniform throughout the year, a coinsurance percentage of 50 percent should be selected. However, when seasonal peak periods are considered, this percentage may be inadequate, because 50 percent of the firm's business may not occur within a consecutive six-month period. Thus, when business income is seasonal or has peak periods, a coinsurance percentage higher than 50 percent is advisable to provide greater protection during a prolonged shutdown period that continues during the peak period.

Ordinary payroll is covered under the business income coverage form unless it is excluded by an endorsement to the policy. The endorsement can exclude ordinary payroll, or it can be covered for a limited period, such as 90 days. Limiting or excluding ordinary payroll reduces the premium.

Optional Coverages The business income form also has coverages that can be activated by an appropriate entry on the declarations page. The optional coverages are summarized as follows:

- *Maximum period of indemnity.* This optional coverage eliminates coinsurance and pays for the loss of business income for a maximum period of 120 days. The amount paid cannot exceed the policy limit. This option can be used by smaller firms that will not be shut down for more than 120 days if a loss occurs.
- *Monthly limit of indemnity.* This optional coverage eliminates coinsurance and limits the maximum monthly amount that will be paid for each consecutive 30-day period to a fraction of the policy limit. The fractions are one-third, one-fourth, and one-sixth. For example, if the fraction selected is one-third, and the policy limit is $120,000, the maximum paid for each consecutive 30-day period is $40,000.
- *Business income agreed value.* This option suspends the coinsurance clause and places no limit on the monthly amount paid, provided that the agreed amount of business income insurance is carried. The agreed amount is the coinsurance percentage (50 percent or higher) multiplied by an estimate of net income and operating expenses for the 12 months of the policy period.
- *Extended period of indemnity.* This option extends the recovery period following completion of repairs from 30 days to a longer period stated in the declarations. The extended period of indemnity can be 60, 90, 120, 150, 180, 270, or 360 days. This option is advantageous for those firms that need a longer recovery period to recapture old business and resume normal operations.

Extra Expense Coverage Form

Certain firms such as banks, newspapers, and dairies must continue to operate after a loss occurs; otherwise, customers will be lost to competitors. The **extra expense coverage form** is a separate form that can be used to cover the extra expenses incurred by the firm in continuing operations during a period of restoration. The extra expense form does not cover the loss of business income because of the interruption of operations. However, the additional expenses to continue operating are covered, subject to certain limits stated in the declarations on the amount of insurance that can be used. A common limitation is 40 percent, 80 percent, and 100 percent. A maximum of 40 percent can be paid when the recovery period is 30 days or less, 80 percent when the recovery period is longer than 30 days but does not exceed 60 days, and 100 percent when the recovery period is longer than 60 days.

Business Income from Dependent Properties

Some firms depend on a single supplier for raw materials and supplies or on a single customer to purchase most or all of the firm's products. The insured's business may incur a loss because of property damage incurred by the sole supplier or customer. An appropriate endorsement can be added to a business income policy that covers loss of income at the insured's location that results from direct damage to property at other locations.

There are four types of dependent properties situations for which this coverage may be needed.[3]

- *Contributing location.* A contributing location is a location that furnishes materials or services to the insured. For example, the insured may depend on one supplier for raw materials. If the supplier's factory is damaged, the insured's business may be forced to shut down.
- *Recipient location.* A recipient location is a location that purchases the insured's products or services. For example, a specialized cheese manufacturer may sell most of its cheese production to a resort hotel. If the hotel is closed because of fire, the cheese factory may have to shut down.
- *Manufacturing location.* A manufacturing location is a location that manufactures products for delivery to the insured's customers. If the manufacturer's plant is damaged, the products cannot be delivered, and the insured would incur a loss.
- *Leader location.* A leader location is a location that attracts customers to the insured's place of business. For example, a major department store in a shopping center may have a fire. As a result, smaller stores in the shopping center may experience a decline in sales.

Miscellaneous Business Income Coverages

Several specialized business income coverages are available to cover the loss of certain types of business income or extra expenses. The *leasehold interest coverage form* covers the loss that may result from the cancellation of a valuable lease when the building is damaged by a covered cause of loss. *Tuition fees insurance* covers the loss of tuition if a school or college has a covered loss and is out of operation for a semester. *Weather insurance* covers losses due to weather conditions, such as the loss of business because of excessive rain or snow.

OTHER COMMERCIAL COVERAGES

The building and personal property coverage form discussed earlier is designed to meet the commercial property and liability insurance needs of most business firms. However, many firms have certain needs that require the use of specialized coverages, which include the following:

- Builders risk insurance
- Condominium insurance
- Equipment breakdown insurance
- Difference in conditions (DIC) insurance

Builders Risk Insurance

A building under construction is exposed to numerous perils, especially the peril of fire. Under the simplified commercial property program by ISO, the **builders risk coverage form** can be used to insure buildings under construction. This form can be used to cover the insurable interest of a general contractor, subcontractor, or building owner.

Under the builders risk coverage form, insurance is purchased equal to the *full value* of the completed building. Because the building is substantially overinsured during the initial stages of construction, the rate charged is adjusted to reflect the average value exposed.

If desired, a *builders risk reporting form* can be attached as an endorsement, which requires the builder to report monthly the value of the building under construction. The initial premium reflects the value of the building at the inception of the policy period and not the completed value of the building. As construction progresses, the amount of insurance on the building is increased based on the reported values. The premiums are adjusted during the policy period based on the values reported by the builder.

Condominium Association Coverage Form

Owners of individual residential condominium units have a common interest in the building, which includes the exterior walls, the roof, and the plumbing, heating, and air conditioning systems. However, property insurance on the building and other condominium property is purchased in the name of the condominium owners association (named insured).

The **condominium association coverage form** covers the following types of property:

- Building
- Named insured's business personal property
- Personal property of others

The form covers the condominium building and equipment used to maintain or service the building, such as fire extinguishing equipment and outdoor furniture. If required by the condominium association agreement, the form also covers fixtures, improvements and alterations that are part of the building, and appliances within individual units (such as a dishwasher, stove, or dishwashers). However, insurance on the building does not cover the unit-owner's personal property (such as furniture, clothes, and household contents). The unit owner's personal property is normally insured under the Homeowners 6 policy (unit-owner's form).

The form also covers the named insured's business personal property. The named insured is the condominium owners association. One example of business personal property is equipment in a condominium health club, such as treadmills, weights, stationary bikes, and similar equipment. Another example is furniture in a community clubhouse.

Finally, the form covers personal property of others in the named insured's care, custody, and control. For example, if the association leases several riding lawn mowers, snowblowers, and other equipment to maintain the grounds, the equipment is covered.

Condominium Commercial Unit-Owners Coverage Form

Business or professional firms may own individual units in a commercial condominium. For example, a physician, dentist, or business firm may own individual office space in a commercial office building that is legally organized as a condominium.

The **condominium commercial unit-owners coverage form** covers the following categories of property:

- Business personal property of the unit owner
- Personal property of others

Business personal property includes the following:

- Furniture
- Fixtures and improvements that are part of the building and owned by the unit owner
- Machinery and equipment
- Stock
- All other personal property owned by the unit owner and used in the business
- Labor, materials, or services furnished by the unit owner on personal property of others
- Leased personal property that the unit owner has a contractual obligation to insure

The condominium form also covers the personal property of others in the care, custody, and control of the unit owner. The personal property must be in or on the building described in the declarations or within 100 feet of the described premises if in the open or in a vehicle.

Equipment Breakdown Insurance

Equipment breakdown insurance (formerly known as *boiler and machinery insurance*) covers losses due to the accidental breakdown of covered equipment. Such equipment includes steam boilers; air conditioning and refrigeration equipment; electrical generating equipment; pumps, compressors, turbines, and engines; machinery used in manufacturing; and electrically powered computer equipment.

The causes-of-loss forms discussed earlier exclude steam boiler explosions, electrical breakdown, and mechanical breakdown. The **equipment breakdown protection coverage form** can be used to provide such coverage. Coverage can be written separately as a monoline policy, or it can be part of a commercial package policy. The following discussion is based on the current edition of the ISO form, which became effective in July 2001.

Covered Cause of Loss   The covered cause of loss is a breakdown to covered equipment. A *breakdown* is a direct physical loss that causes damage to covered equipment. *Covered equipment* refers to the boiler,

INSIGHT 13.3

Examples of Equipment Breakdown Losses

Steam boiler explosions can cause extensive damage not only to the boiler itself but to the building that houses it. In one case, a heating boiler in a telephone company switching office exploded and tore through the roof, leaving the building looking as if it had been struck by a military missile.

Boilers can sustain serious damage as a result of a malfunction even when they don't explode. Severe overheating of a boiler in a factory, caused by low-water conditions in the boiler, resulted in damage to the furnace tubes and a portion of the rear tube sheet. The physical damage loss was $27,000, and the business income loss was $30,000.

Although boiler explosions provided the original impetus for equipment breakdown coverage, other types of equipment can suffer serious damage in many other ways.

- A short circuit in the aluminum bus (an electrical conductor) in an apartment building caused extensive damage to the building's electrical cables and wiring. Residents were temporarily relocated. The physical damage loss was $120,000, and the extra expense loss was $72,000.

- The rotating cylinder door assembly of a 400-pound commercial washing machine opened during the extract cycle, damaging the basket and inner and outer shells. The cost to repair the physical damage amounted to $61,000.
- A portion of an air conditioning compressor became detached and fell into the evaporator, puncturing several tubes. The cooling water from the tubes contaminated the refrigerant and caused severe damage to the driving motor windings. The loss amounted to $45,000.
- Voltage fluctuation caused two terminal boards in an office building's phone computer to short-circuit. The resulting loss amounted to $52,000.

SOURCE: Arthur L. Flitner and Jerome Trupin, *Commercial Insurance,* First Edition (Malvern, PA: American Institute for Chartered Property Casualty Underwriters/Insurance Institute of America, 2002), p 6.4. Originally adapted with permission from *Whistle Stop,* a publication of The Hartford Steam Boiler Inspection and Insurance Company, Hartford, CT. Reprinted here with permission of The Hartford Steam Boiler Inspection and Insurance Company.

machinery, or electrical or mechanical equipment insured under the policy, including communication equipment and computer equipment. Covered equipment also includes equipment owned by a public or private utility used solely to support utility services to the premises. Insight 13.3 gives examples of covered equipment breakdown losses.

Coverages Provided   The current ISO form contains numerous coverages that can be included or omitted depending on the needs of the business firm. A specific coverage is in force if the declarations page indicates either a limit of insurance, or if the word "INCLUDED" is shown for the coverage. If neither is indicated, there is no coverage for that benefit.

- *Property damage.* The form pays for direct damage to covered property located at the premises described in the declarations. Covered property is property owned by the insured or property in the insured's care, custody, or control for which the insured is legally liable.
- *Expediting expenses.* Expediting expenses are the reasonable extra costs the insured must pay to make temporary repairs or to expedite the permanent repair or replacement of the damaged

property. For example, the extra transportation charges to speed up delivery of a replacement part would be covered.

- *Business income and extra expense—extra expense only.* This coverage pays for the loss of business income and extra expenses. Business income refers to the loss of business income and extra expenses incurred during the period of restoration. However, if shown in the declarations, only extra expenses can be covered. For example, a firm may have its own power plant and an emergency standby connection with an outside public utility firm in case power is interrupted because of a covered loss. The extra costs of the outside power would be covered.
- *Spoilage damage.* This coverage pays for spoilage damage to raw materials, property in process, or finished products. For example, the loss of refrigeration in a meatpacking plant that results in the spoilage of meat would be covered.
- *Utility interruption.* This coverage extends the protection provided by the business income and extra expense coverages. For example, if a power generator owned by a local public utility has a mechanical failure, and the insured firm loses power and must shut down its business

operations, the resulting loss of business income would be covered. However, the insured must select a waiting period—such as 12 hours—before coverage applies.

- *Newly acquired premises.* Coverage automatically applies to newly acquired premises leased or purchased. The insured is required to notify the insurer of the newly acquired premises as soon as practicable.

- *Ordinance or law coverage.* This coverage pays for the increase in loss that results from an ordinance or law regulating the demolition, construction, repair, or use of the building. The form describes in detail what losses will be paid or not paid because of some ordinance or law.

- *Errors and omissions.* If the insured has made an unintentional error or mistake in describing the property or premises to be insured, the loss or damage will still be covered.

- *Brands and labels.* If there is a loss to covered property, the insurer may take any part of the property at an agreed or appraised value. This coverage allows the insured to stamp the word *salvage* on the merchandise or to remove the brand or label from the damaged merchandise at the insurer's expense. The insurer pays the reasonable cost provided the total cost of the activity and the value of the damaged property do not exceed the limit of insurance for such coverage.

- *Contingent business income and extra expense— extra expense only coverage.* This coverage extends the firm's business income coverage to insure the loss of income that results from a breakdown at a nonowned premises critical to the firm's operation. For example, if a business firm is located in a shopping mall and a breakdown of an electrical generator in another store causes a total blackout in the mall, the firm may have to shut down. The loss of business would be covered.

Difference in Conditions Insurance

Difference in conditions (DIC) insurance is an "all-risks" policy that covers other perils not insured by basic property insurance contracts.[4] DIC insurance is written as a separate contract to supplement the coverage provided by the underlying contracts. As such, it excludes perils covered by the underlying contracts (such as fire and extended coverage perils, vandalism and malicious mischief, and sprinkler leakage). However, most other insurable perils are covered. The policy can also be written to include coverage for flood, earthquake, and building collapse. A substantial deductible must be satisfied for losses not covered by the underlying contracts.

DIC insurance has two major advantages. First, it can be used to fill gaps in coverage. Many large multinational corporations use a DIC policy to insure their overseas property. Many foreign countries require property insurance to be purchased locally; if the local coverage is inadequate, a DIC policy can fill the gap in coverage.

Second, DIC insurance can be used to insure unusual and catastrophic exposures that are not covered by the underlying contracts. Some unusual losses that have been paid include the following:[5]

- An accident caused molasses to spill into a machine. The cost to clean the machine was $38,000.
- Dust collected on a roof, solidified, and the weight caused the roof to collapse.
- A city water main broke, which flooded the basement of an industrial plant, causing hundreds of thousands of dollars of damage.

Finally, DIC is less expensive than the purchase of separate contracts for flood and earthquake. It costs less because it is excess over the underlying coverages, and it does not require either coinsurance or insurance to full value.

TRANSPORTATION INSURANCE

Billions of dollars of goods are shipped by business firms each year. These goods are exposed to damage or loss from numerous transportation perils. The goods can be protected by ocean marine and inland marine contracts. **Ocean marine insurance** *provides protection for goods transported over water.* All types of ocean-going vessels and their cargo can be insured by ocean marine contracts; the legal liability of ship owners and cargo owners can also be insured.

Inland marine insurance *provides protection for goods shipped on land.* It includes insurance on imports and exports, domestic shipments, and means of transportation such as bridges and tunnels. In addition, inland marine insurance can be used to insure fine art, jewelry, furs, and other property.[6]

Ocean Marine Insurance

Ocean marine insurance is one of the oldest forms of transportation insurance. Ocean marine contracts are incredibly complex, reflecting basic marine law, trade, customs, and court interpretations of the various policy provisions.

Ocean marine insurance can be divided into four major classes to reflect the various insurable interests:

- **Hull insurance** *covers physical damage to the ship or vessel.* It is similar to collision insurance that covers physical damage to an automobile caused by a collision. Hull insurance is always written with a deductible. In addition, it contains a **collision liability clause** (also called a **running down clause**) that covers the owner's legal liability if the ship collides with another vessel or damages its cargo. However, the running down clause does not cover legal liability arising out of injury or death to other persons, damage to piers and docks, and personal injury and death of crew members.
- **Cargo insurance** *covers the shipper of the goods if the goods are damaged or lost.* The policy can be written to cover a single shipment. If regular shipments are made, an open-cargo policy can be used that insures the goods automatically when a shipment is made. The shipper is required to report periodically the shipments that are made. The open-cargo policy has no expiration date and remains in force until it is canceled.
- **Protection and indemnity (P&I) insurance** *is usually written as a separate contract that provides comprehensive liability insurance for property damage or bodily injury to third parties.* P&I insurance protects the ship owner for damage caused by the ship to piers, docks, and harbor installations, damage to the ship's cargo, illness or injury to the passengers or crew, and fines and penalties.

- **Freight insurance** *indemnifies the ship owner for the loss of earnings if the goods are damaged or lost and are not delivered.*

Basic Concepts in Ocean Marine Insurance

Ocean marine insurance is based on certain fundamental concepts. The following section discusses these concepts and related contractual provisions.

Implied Warranties   Ocean marine contracts contain three implied warranties:

- Seaworthy vessel
- No deviation from planned course
- Legal purpose

The ship owner implicitly warrants that the vessel is seaworthy, which means that the ship is properly constructed, maintained, and equipped for the voyage to be undertaken.

The warranty of no deviation means that the ship cannot deviate from its original course. However, an intentional deviation is permitted in the event of an unavoidable accident, to avoid bad weather, to save the life of an individual on board, or to rescue persons from some other vessel.

The warranty of legal purpose means that the voyage should not be for some illegal venture, such as smuggling drugs into a country.

The implied warranties are based on court decisions and are just as binding as any written warranty stated in the contract. The three implied warranties are strictly applied in hull insurance. However, in cargo insurance, the insured usually has no knowledge of the ship in which the goods are shipped. Insurers may insert a clause stating that the insurance is not voided by a deviation of which the insured has no knowledge or by any unintentional error in describing the vessel or voyage.

Covered Perils   An ocean marine policy provides broad coverage for certain specified perils, including **perils of the sea,** such as damage or loss from bad weather, high waves, collision, sinking, and stranding. Other covered perils include loss from fire, enemies, pirates, thieves, jettison (throwing goods overboard to save the ship), barratry (fraud by the master or crew at the expense of the ship or cargo owners), and similar perils.

Ocean marine insurance can also be written on an "all-risks" basis. All unexpected and fortuitous losses are covered except those losses specifically excluded. Common exclusions are losses due to delay, war, inherent vice (tendency of certain types of property to decompose), and strikes, riots, or civil commotion.

Particular Average   In marine insurance, the word *average* refers to a partial loss. A **particular average** *is a loss that falls entirely on a particular interest,* as contrasted with a general average, a loss that falls on all parties to the voyage. Under the *free-of-particular-average clause* (FPA), partial losses are not covered unless the loss is caused by certain perils, such as stranding, sinking, burning, or collision of the vessel.

The FPA clause can be written with a percentage, such as 3 percent. If the loss exceeds the stated percentage, the entire loss is payable. For example, if cargo is insured for $100,000, a partial loss under $3000 falls entirely on the insured; if the loss is $3000 or more, the insurer pays the loss in full.

General Average   A **general average** *is a loss incurred for the common good and consequently is shared by all parties to the venture.* For example, if a ship damaged by heavy waves is in danger of sinking, part of the cargo may be jettisoned to save the ship. The loss falls on all parties to the voyage: the ship owner, cargo owners, and freight interests. In this context, *freight* refers to the revenue that a cargo ship earns. Each party must pay its share of the loss based on the proportion that its interest bears to the total value in the venture. For example, assume that the captain must jettison $1 million of steel to save the ship. Also assume that the various interests are as follows:

Value of steel	$ 2 million
Value of other cargo	3 million
Value of ship and freight	+15 million
Total	$20 million

The owner of the steel would absorb 2/20 of the loss, or $100,000. The owners of the other cargo would pay 3/20 of the loss, or $150,000. Finally, the ship and freight interests would pay 15/20 of the loss, or $750,000.

Certain conditions must be satisfied to have a general average loss:[7]

- *Imminent peril.* There must be an imminent peril to all interests in the venture—ship, cargo, and freight.
- *Voluntary.* The sacrifice must be voluntary, and the special expense incurred must be reasonable.
- *Preservation of at least part of the value.* The effort must be successful. At least part of the value must be saved.
- *Free from fault.* Any party that claims a general average contribution from other interests in the voyage must be free from fault with respect to the risk that threatens the venture.

Coinsurance   Although an ocean marine policy does not contain a specific coinsurance clause, losses are settled as if there were a 100 percent coinsurance clause. An ocean marine policy is a valued contract, by which the face amount is paid if a total loss occurs. If the insurance carried does not equal the full value of the goods at the time of loss, the insured must share in the loss. Thus, if $50,000 of cargo insurance is carried on goods worth $100,000, only one-half of any partial loss will be paid. The policy face is paid in the event of a total loss.

Inland Marine Insurance

Inland marine insurance grew out of ocean marine insurance. Ocean marine insurance first covered property from the point of embarkation to the place where the goods landed. As commerce and trade developed, goods had to be shipped over land as well. Inland marine insurance developed in the 1920s to cover property being transported over land, means of transportation such as bridges and tunnels, and property of a mobile nature.

Nationwide Marine Definition

As inland marine insurance developed, conflicts arose between fire insurers and marine insurers. To resolve the confusion and conflict, the companies drafted a **nationwide marine definition** in 1933 to define the property that marine insurers could write. The definition was approved by the National Association of Insurance Commissioners (NAIC) and was later revised and broadened in 1953. In 1976, the NAIC drafted a new definition of marine insurance that has been adopted by most states. At present, marine insurers can write insurance on the following types of property:

- Imports
- Exports
- Domestic shipments
- Means of transportation and communication
- Personal property floater risks
- Commercial property floater risks

Major Classes of Inland Marine Insurance

Commercial property that can be insured by inland marine contracts can be conveniently classified into the following categories:[8]

- Domestic goods in transit
- Property held by bailees
- Mobile equipment and property
- Property of certain dealers
- Means of transportation and communication

Domestic Goods in Transit   Domestic goods may be shipped by a common carrier, such as a trucking company, railroad, or airline, or by the company's own trucks. The goods can be damaged because of fire, lightning, flood, earthquake, or other perils. They can also be damaged from the collision, derailment, or overturn of the transportation vehicle. These losses can be insured by an inland marine policy.

Although a common carrier is legally liable for safe delivery of the goods, liability does not extend to all losses. For example, a common carrier is not responsible for losses due to acts of God (such as lightning), acts of public authority, acts of public enemies (war), improper packaging by the shipper, and inherent vice.

In addition, shipping charges are reduced if the shipper agrees to limit the carrier's liability for the goods at less than their full value (called a *released bill of lading*). Consequently, the shipper can save money by agreeing to a released bill of lading and then purchase insurance to cover the shipment.

Property Held by Bailees   Inland marine insurance can be used to insure property held by a bailee. A **bailee** *is someone who has temporary possession of*

property that belongs to another. Examples of bailees are dry cleaners, laundries, and television repair shops. Under common law, bailees are legally liable for damage to customers' property only if they or their employees are negligent. However, to ensure customer goodwill, many bailees purchase bailee's customers insurance that covers the damage or loss to customers' property while in the bailee's possession regardless of fault, normally from certain named perils.

Mobile Equipment and Property   Inland marine property floaters can be used to cover property that is frequently moved from one location to another, such as a tractor, crane, or bulldozer. Also, plumbing, heating, or air conditioning equipment can be covered while being transported to a job site or while being installed.

In addition, a property floater policy can be used to insure certain other types of property, such as fine arts, livestock, theatrical property, computers, and signs.

Property of Certain Dealers   Inland marine insurance is also used to insure the property of certain dealers. Specialized inland marine policies or inland marine "block" policies are used to insure the property of jewelers, furriers, and dealers in diamonds, fine art, cameras, and musical instruments, and other dealers. Most policies provide coverage on an "all-risks" basis.

Means of Transportation and Communication   Means of transportation and communication *refer to property at a fixed location that is used in transportation or communication.* Inland marine insurance can be used to cover bridges, tunnels, piers, docks, wharves, pipelines, power transmission lines, radio and television towers, outdoor cranes, and similar equipment for loading, unloading, or transporting. For example, a bridge may be damaged by a flood, an ice jam, or a ship that collides with it; a television tower or power line may be blown over in a windstorm; or a fire may start in a tunnel when a gasoline truck overturns and explodes. These losses can be insured under inland marine contracts.

The commercial property loss exposures just described can be insured by a wide variety of inland marine contracts. For purposes of regulation, inland marine contracts are classified into two categories: (1) *filed forms* and (2) *nonfiled forms*. With filed forms, the policy forms and rates are filed with the state insurance department. Filed forms are typically used in situations where there are a large number of potential insureds and the loss exposures are reasonably homogeneous.

In contrast, nonfiled forms refer to policy forms and rates that are not filed with the state insurance department. Nonfiled forms are used in situations where the insured has specialized or unique needs, the number of potential insureds is relatively small, and the loss exposures are diverse.[9]

Filed Inland Marine Forms

Under the ISO simplified commercial inland marine program, the various policy forms and rates are filed with the state insurance department.

Numerous forms can be used in the ISO commercial inland marine insurance program. The major forms are summarized here:

- The **accounts receivable coverage form** indemnifies the firm if it is unable to collect outstanding customer balances because of damage or destruction of the records. A firm may incur a sizable loss if its accounts receivable records are lost because of a fire, theft, or other peril, and the amount owned by customers cannot be collected.
- The **camera and musical instrument dealers coverage form** is used to cover stock in trade consisting principally of cameras or musical instruments and related equipment and accessories. The property of others in the insured's care, custody, or control is also covered.
- The **commercial articles coverage form** covers photographic equipment and musical instruments that are used commercially by photographers, professional musicians, motion picture producers, production companies, and other persons.
- The **equipment dealers form** covers the stock in trade of dealers in agricultural implements and construction equipment. The form can also be extended to cover furniture, fixtures, office supplies, and machinery used in the business.
- The **film coverage form** covers exposed motion picture film as well as magnetic or video tapes.
- The **floor plan coverage form** refers to a financing plan in which the dealer borrows money to buy merchandise to display and sell, but the title is held by the lending institution or manufacturer. The form can be used to cover the interest of the dealer, lending institution, or both interests.
- The **jewelers block coverage form** covers jewelry, watches, and precious stones of retail and wholesale jewelers, jewelry manufacturers, and diamond wholesalers.
- The **mail coverage form** covers securities in transit by first-class mail, registered or certified mail, or express mail. It is designed for stock brokerage firms, banks, and other financial institutions that ship securities by mail.
- The **physicians and surgeons equipment coverage form** covers the medical, surgical, or dental equipment of physicians and dentists, including furniture, fixtures, and improvements.
- The **signs coverage form** covers neon, mechanical, and electrical signs. Each covered sign must be scheduled.
- The **theatrical property coverage form** covers costumes, stage scenery, and similar property used in theatrical productions. For example, a New York play may be presented in another city, which requires the shipment of stage props and scenery to that city. The theatrical property can be covered under this form.
- The **valuable papers and records coverage form** covers loss to valuable papers and records, such as student transcripts at a university, plans and blueprints of an architectural firm, and prescription records in a drugstore. The form covers the cost of reconstructing the damaged or destroyed records. It can also be used to insure the loss of irreplaceable records, such as a rare manuscript.

Nonfiled Inland Marine Forms

Nonfiled forms are also available to meet the specialized or unique needs of commercial firms. Only a few of them are discussed here.

Shipment of Goods We noted earlier that inland marine insurance can be used to cover the domestic shipment of goods. An **annual transit policy** can be used by manufacturers, wholesalers, and retailers to cover the shipment of goods on public trucks, railroads, and coastal vessels. Both outgoing and incoming shipments can be insured. Although these forms are not standardized, they have similar characteristics. They can be written either on an "all-risks" or a named-perils basis.

Although a transit policy provides broad coverage, it contains certain exclusions. The policy can be written to cover the theft of an entire shipment, but pilferage of the goods generally is not covered. Other common exclusions are losses from strikes, riots or civil commotion, leakage and breakage (unless caused by an insured peril), marring, scratching, dampness, molding, and rotting.

A **trip transit policy** is used by firms and individuals to cover a single shipment. For example, an electrical transformer worth several thousand dollars that is shipped from an Eastern factory to the West Coast or the household goods of executives who are transferred can be insured under a variation of the trip transit policy.

Bailee Forms   As stated earlier, a bailee is someone who has temporary possession of property that belongs to others. A *bailee's liability policy* can be used to cover the firm's liability for the property of customers, such as clothes in a laundry. A bailee's liability policy, however, covers the loss only if the firm is legally liable. In contrast, a *bailee's customers policy* can be used to cover the loss or damage to the property of others regardless of legal liability. A bailee's customers policy generally is designed for firms that hold the property of others that have high value, such as fur coats. A covered loss is paid regardless of legal liability, and the goodwill of customers is maintained.

Business Floaters   A **business floater** is an inland marine policy that covers property that frequently moves (floats) from one location to another. Numerous business floaters are available. For example, a *contractors equipment floater* can be used to insure the property of contractors, such as bulldozers, tractors, cranes, earthmovers, and scaffolding equipment. A *garment contractors floater* covers garments and parts of garments that are sent by a garment manufacturer for processing to outside firms, such as buttonhole makers, pleaters, or embroiderers.

Means of Transportation and Communication
Inland marine contracts can be used to cover bridges, tunnels, towers, pipelines, power lines, and similar property. For example, a toll bridge lost revenues because a ship ran into a bridge pylon, forcing the bridge to close. A business income policy can be written to cover the loss of income.

This type of property can be insured either on a risk-of-direct-physical-loss basis or on a named-perils basis, depending on the specific needs of the insured.

BUSINESSOWNERS POLICY (BOP)

The **businessowners policy (BOP)** is a package policy specifically designed for small- to medium-sized retail stores, office buildings, apartment buildings, and similar firms. The Insurance Services Office (ISO) has revised the BOP several times since its inception in 1976. The latest changes occurred in 2002, when ISO introduced a new BOP policy. The current edition became effective in July 2002.[10]

The BOP is a package policy that provides both property and liability insurance coverages. The following section discusses the property insurance coverages; the liability insurance coverages are discussed in the following chapter.

Eligible Firms

The BOP can be written to cover buildings and business personal property of the owners of apartments and residential condominium associations; office and office condominium associations; retail establishments; and eligible mercantile, service, or processing firms such as appliance firms, beauty parlors, and photocopy services. BOP coverage is also available for certain contractors, "limited-cooking" restaurants, and convenience stores.

Certain business firms are ineligible for a BOP because the loss exposures are outside those contemplated for the average small- to medium-sized firm. They include auto repair or service stations; dealers in automobiles, motorcycles, or mobilehomes; parking lots; bars; places of amusement such as a bowling alley; and banks and financial institutions.

BOP Coverages

The current version of the BOP is a *special form*, which insures property on an "all risks" or "open perils" basis; all losses are covered except those losses specifically excluded. However, if desired, named-perils coverage is available by an endorsement to the policy; only those perils named in the policy are covered.

The present BOP is a self-contained policy that incorporates the property coverages, liability coverages, and policy conditions into one contract. The following discussion summarizes the basic characteristics of the BOP.

1. *Buildings.* The BOP covers the buildings that are described in the declarations, including completed additions, fixtures and outdoor fixtures, and permanently installed machinery and equipment. The building coverage also includes personal property in apartments or rooms furnished by the named insured as a landlord, and personal property owned by the named insured to maintain or service the premises, such as fire-extinguishing equipment and refrigerating and dishwashing appliances. The limit of insurance on the building is automatically increased each year by a stated percentage shown in the declarations to keep pace with inflation.

2. *Business personal property.* Business personal property is also covered. It includes property owned by the named insured used in the business; property of others in the insured's care, custody, and control; tenant's improvements and betterments; and leased personal property for which the named insured has a contractual responsibility to insure. Business personal property also includes exterior building glass if the named insured is a tenant, and no limit of insurance is shown in the declarations. The glass must be owned by the named insured or in the insured's care, custody, and control. A peak season provision provides for a temporary increase of 25 percent of the amount of insurance when inventory values are at their peak.

In addition, business personal property at newly acquired locations is covered for a maximum of $100,000 for 30 days. This provision provides automatic protection until the BOP can be endorsed to cover the new location. Business personal property in transit or temporarily away from the insured location is covered up to a maximum of $5000.

3. *Covered causes of loss.* The latest edition of the BOP insures property against "risks of direct physical loss," which means that all direct physical losses are covered unless specifically excluded or limited in the form itself.

The BOP can also be issued on a named perils basis by an endorsement. Covered causes of loss include fire, lightning, explosion, windstorm or hail, smoke, aircraft or vehicles, riot or civil commotion, vandalism, sprinkler leakage, sinkhole collapse, volcanic action, and certain transportation perils. The named perils endorsement also includes an optional coverage for burglary and robbery.

4. *Additional coverages.* The BOP provides several additional coverages that might be needed by the typical businessowner:

- Debris removal
- Preservation of covered property after a loss occurs
- Fire department service charge
- Collapse
- Water damage, other liquids, powder or molten material damage
- Business income, extended business income, and extra expense
- Pollutant clean-up and removal
- Loss of business income because of action by a civil authority
- Money orders and counterfeit paper currency ($1000 maximum)
- Forgery and alteration losses ($2500 maximum)
- Increased cost of construction because of an ordinance or law ($10,000 maximum for each described building insured on a replacement cost basis)
- Business income from dependent properties ($5000 maximum)
- Glass expenses incurred to put up temporary plates or board up openings if repair or replacement of damaged glass is delayed
- Fire extinguisher systems recharge expense ($5000 maximum in any one occurrence)

5. *Optional coverages.* The BOP provides several optional coverages to meet the specialized needs of businessowners by payment of an additional premium:

- Outdoor signs
- Money and securities
- Employee dishonesty
- Equipment breakdown

6. *Deductible.* A standard deductible of $500 per occurrence applies to all property coverages. Optional deductibles of $250, $1000, and $2500 are also available if desired. The deductible does not apply, however, to the fire department service charge, business income losses, extra expenses, action by a civil authority, and recharge expense for a fire extinguisher system.

7. *Business liability insurance.* The businessowners policy also has business liability coverage similar to the commercial general liability policy (CGL). The businessowner is insured for bodily injury and property damage liability, and advertising and personal injury liability. Medical expense insurance is also provided. Commercial general liability insurance is discussed in Chapter 14.

CASE APPLICATION

Kimberly owns and operates a tennis shop in a resort area. The business is seasonal. A large part of the annual revenues are due to sales in June, July, and August. Kimberly keeps the shop open during the remaining months of the year, but the inventory carried during those months is reduced. During the summer months, the amount of inventory on hand is substantially increased. Kimberly has the business insured under the special form businessowners policy (BOP) with no special endorsements attached.

a. Assume you are a risk management consultant. Identify the major loss exposures that Kimberly faces.

b. Assume that a covered loss occurs in July, which damages part of the inventory. Does the BOP provide any protection for the increase in inventory during the summer months? Explain your answer.

c. Kimberly plans to hire an additional employee during the summer months when sales are increasing. She is concerned about possible employee theft and dishonesty. Explain to Kimberly how this loss exposure can be handled under the BOP.

d. A fire damaged the building. As a result, Kimberly incurred a business income loss because the business was closed for three months.

e. Vandals broke the exterior glass window to the business, which caused substantial damage to the building.

SUMMARY

- Under the ISO commercial property insurance program, a commercial package policy contains a common declarations page, a common policy conditions page, and two or more coverage parts. Each coverage part, in turn, has its own declarations page, policy conditions, coverage forms, and a causes of loss form.

- A *commercial package policy* combines two or more coverage parts into a single policy. When compared with individual policies, a package policy has fewer gaps in coverage; premiums are relatively lower because individual policies are not purchased; savings in insurer expenses can be passed on to the policyholder; and the insured has the convenience of a single policy.

- The coverage parts available under the ISO commercial property program include the following:

  Commercial property coverage form(s)

  Commercial general liability coverage form

  Crime coverage form

  Equipment breakdown protection coverage form

  Inland marine coverage form(s)

  Auto coverage form

  Farm coverage form(s)

- The *building and personal property coverage form* can be used to insure the commercial building, business personal property, and personal property of others in the care and custody of the insured.

- Under the ISO commercial property insurance program, a causes-of-loss form must be added to a commercial policy to form a complete contract. There are three causes-of-loss forms:

    Causes-of-loss basic form

    Causes-of-loss broad form

    Causes-of-loss special form

- The *business income (and extra expense) coverage form* covers the loss of business income due to the suspension of business operations because of a covered loss. Business income is the net profit or loss before income taxes that would have been earned if the loss had not occurred, plus normal operating expenses, including payroll. Extra expenses incurred as a result of a loss are also covered.

- The *extra expense coverage form* covers only the extra expenses incurred by the firm in continuing operations during the period of restoration. Loss of profits is not covered.

- Certain miscellaneous commercial coverages are important to business firms that have unique or specialized needs, including builders risk insurance, condominium insurance, equipment breakdown protection insurance, and difference in conditions insurance.

- Ocean marine insurance can be classified into four categories that reflect the various insurable interests:

    Hull insurance

    Cargo insurance

    Protection and indemnity (P&I) insurance

    Freight insurance

- A particular average loss in marine insurance is a loss that falls entirely on a particular interest, as contrasted with a general average loss that falls on all parties to the voyage.

- Inland marine contracts are used to insure the following classes of commercial property:

    Domestic goods in transit

    Property held by bailees

    Mobile equipment and property

    Property of certain dealers

    Means of transportation and communication

- For purposes of regulation, inland marine contracts are classified into filed forms and nonfiled forms. Filed forms are policy forms and rates that are filed with the state insurance department. Nonfiled forms are not filed with the state insurance department.

- Filed inland marine forms include the following:

    Accounts receivable coverage form

    Camera and musical instrument dealers coverage form

    Commercial articles coverage form

    Equipment dealers form

    Film coverage form

    Floor plan coverage form

    Jewelers block coverage form

    Mail coverage form

    Physicians and surgeons equipment coverage form

    Signs coverage form

    Theatrical property coverage form

    Valuable papers and records coverage form

- Nonfiled inland marine forms include the following:

    Annual transit policy

    Trip transit policy

    Bailee forms

    Business floaters

    Means of transportation and communication

- The *businessowners policy* is a package policy for small- to medium-sized business firms. It covers the building, business personal property, loss of business income, extra expenses, and business liability exposures. Optional coverages are available for outdoor signs, money and securities, employee dishonesty, and equipment breakdown.

KEY CONCEPTS AND TERMS

Annual transit policy
Bailee
Builders risk coverage form
Building and personal property coverage form

Business floater
Business income (and extra expense) coverage form
Business income insurance

Businessowners policy (BOP)

Cargo insurance

Causes-of-loss forms (basic, broad, special)

Collision liability clause (running down clause)

Commercial package policy (CPP)

Condominium association coverage form

Condominium commercial unit-owners coverage form

Difference in conditions (DIC) insurance

Equipment breakdown protection coverage form

Extra expense coverage form

Freight insurance

General average

Hull insurance

Implied warranties

Inland marine insurance

Means of transportation and communication

Nationwide marine definition

Ocean marine insurance

Package policy

Particular average

Perils of the sea

Protection and indemnity (P&I) insurance

Reporting form

Trip transit policy

REVIEW QUESTIONS

1. a. What is a package policy?
    b. Explain the advantages of a commercial package policy to a business firm as compared to the purchase of separate policies?

2. Identify the causes of loss that are covered under the following forms:
    a. Causes-of-loss basic form
    b. Causes-of-loss broad form
    c. Causes-of-loss special form

3. Explain the following provisions in the *building and personal property coverage form:*
    a. Covered property
    b. Additional coverages
    c. Optional coverages

4. The *business income (and extra expense) coverage form* contains a number of policy provisions. Explain the following provisions:
    a. Business income loss
    b. Coverage of extra expenses

5. Briefly describe the following commercial property insurance coverages:
    a. Builders risk insurance
    b. Condominium insurance
    c. Equipment breakdown insurance
    d. Difference in conditions (DIC) insurance

6. Explain the following ocean marine insurance coverages:
    a. Hull insurance
    b. Cargo insurance
    c. Protection and indemnity (P&I) insurance
    d. Freight insurance

7. a. What is the difference between a particular average loss and a general average loss in ocean marine insurance?
    b. What conditions must be fulfilled to have a general average loss?

8. Identify the major types of commercial property that can be insured under an inland marine insurance policy.

9. Briefly describe the following inland marine coverages:
    a. Accounts receivable coverage form
    b. Valuable papers and records coverage form
    c. Bailee's customer policy

10. The *businessowners policy* (BOP) contains a number of coverages. Explain the following:
    a. Coverage of buildings
    b. Coverage of business personal property
    c. Covered causes of loss
    d. Additional coverages provided by the BOP

APPLICATION QUESTIONS

1. Michael owns a television repair shop that is insured under a commercial package policy. The policy includes the *building and personal property coverage form* and the *causes-of-loss broad form*. The declarations page indicates that coverage applies to both the building and the named insured's business property. Explain whether or not the following losses would be covered under his policy.
    a. A fire occurs on the premises, and the building is badly damaged.
    b. A burglar steals some money and securities from an unlocked safe.
    c. A business computer and fax machine are damaged by vandals who break into the shop after business hours.
    d. A tornado touched down near the store. Several television sets of customers in the shop for repair were damaged in the storm.

2. Never-Die Battery manufactures batteries for industrial and consumer use. The company purchased a

commercial package policy (CPP) to cover its property exposures. In addition to common policy conditions and declarations, the policy contains a *building and personal property coverage form and an equipment breakdown protection coverage form.* The policy also contains the *causes-of-loss broad form.* With respect to each of the following losses, indicate whether or not the loss is covered.

a. An explosion occurred that damaged the building where finished batteries are stored.

b. Because of the explosion, the company incurred expenses for special delivery of replacement parts for machines used to manufacture the batteries.

c. The explosion injured several employees who received emergency treatment at a local hospital.

d. An automatic sprinkler system accidentally discharged in the finished goods building. Some recently manufactured batteries were ruined because of water damage and corrosion.

3. Ben owns a retail shoe store that is insured for $90,000 under the *business income (and extra expense) coverage form* with a 50 percent coinsurance provision. Because of a fire, Ben was forced to close the store for one month before it could be reopened. If the fire had not occurred, Ben's estimated net profits and operating expenses for the 12-month period after the policy's inception date would have been $180,000. However, for the one-month period that the store was closed, Ben had a business income loss of $12,000 (loss of net income plus continuing operating expenses). How much will Ben recover for the business income loss? Explain your answer.

4. a. Janet is the risk manager of Daily News, a daily publication in a highly competitive market. She wants to be certain that the newspaper will continue to be published if the company's printing facilities are damaged or destroyed by a covered cause of loss. What type of insurance can Janet purchase to cover the added cost of continuing to print the paper after a physical damage loss has occurred?

b. James opened a book store in a mall. His store was located between a theater and a department store. James counts on the theater and department store to generate walk-in business for his store. James knows that if either of the other businesses closes,

his store would incur a substantial financial loss. What type of insurance can James purchase to cover this type of loss exposure?

5. The *Mary Queen*, an ocean-going oil tanker, negligently collided with a large freighter. The *Mary Queen* is insured by an ocean marine hull insurance policy with a running down clause. For each of the following losses, explain whether the ocean marine coverage would apply to the loss.

a. Damage to the *Mary Queen*

b. Damage to the freighter

c. Death or injury to the crew members on the freighter

6. An Ocean Transfer cargo ship was forced to jettison some cargo in a severe ocean storm. The various interests in the voyage at the time the property was jettisoned are the following:

Value of the ship	$4.0 million
Value of iron ore	$2.0 million
Value of lumber and wood chips	$2.0 million

Assume the captain must jettison iron ore valued at $800,000. What is the amount that Ocean Transfer must pay under the principle of a general average loss? Explain your answer.

7. The inventory at Jennifer's business fluctuates over time. Jennifer's property insurance policy requires the periodic reporting of inventory values. Jennifer believes she can save money by underreporting the value of the inventory. Last period, she reported only $200,000 when the actual value was $400,000. Shortly after filing the last report, the value of the inventory increased to $500,000. The inventory was totally destroyed when a fire occurred. Ignoring any deductible, what is the amount that Jennifer's insurer will pay? Explain your answer.

8. Richard owns and operates a small furniture store. In addition to Richard, the firm employs two sales representatives. Richard's agent advises him that the store can be insured under a *businessowners policy* (BOP). Identify the various loss exposures to Richard's furniture store that can be covered by the businessowners policy.

INTERNET RESOURCES

■ **A. M. Best Company** is a rating organization that rates insurers and publishes books and periodicals relating to the insurance industry, including property and liability insurance. Visit the site at

http://www.ambest.com

■ The **American Insurance Association** is a trade and service organization for property and liability insurers that provides a forum for discussing problems as well as safety, promotional, and legislative issues. Visit the site at

http://www.aiadc.org

■ The **Independent Insurance Agents & Brokers of America** sponsors a site that provides a considerable amount of information on commercial property and liability insurance. The site is designed for agents, risk managers, and consumers. Visit the site at

http://www.independentagent.com

■ The **Insurance Institute for Highway Safety/Highway Loss Data Institute** is a nonprofit organization that compiles, processes, and provides the public with insurance data on human and economic losses resulting from highway accidents. Visit the site at

http://www.hwysafety.org

■ The **Insurance Information Institute** is a primary source of information, analysis, and referral on subjects dealing with property and liability insurance. Visit the site at

http://www.iii.org

■ The **Inland Marine Underwriters Association** provides a forum for discussing common problems encountered by inland marine insurers. Visit the site at

http://www.imua.org

■ The **Insurance Services Office (ISO)** provides statistical information, actuarial analysis, policy language, and technical information to participants in property and liability insurance markets. ISO has drafted a considerable number of commercial property forms, as discussed in this chapter. Visit the site at

http://www.iso.com

■ The **Insurance Research Council** is a division of the American Institute for CPCU. It provides the public and the insurance industry with timely research information relating to property and liability insurance. Visit the site at

http://www.ircweb.org

■ The **Property Casualty Insurers Association of America— PCI** is the nation's premier trade association of property and casualty insurers. Established in 2004 by a merger of the Alliance of American Insurers (Alliance) and the National Association of Independent Insurers (NAII), PCI advocates the public policy position of its members on important issues and provides members with targeted industry information. Visit the site at

http://www.pciaa.net/sitehome.nsf/main

■ The **Risk and Insurance Management Society (RIMS)** is the premier organization of corporate risk managers that makes known to insurers the insurance needs of business and industry, supports loss prevention, and provides a forum for discussing common objectives and problems. RIMS also publishes *Risk Management Magazine*. Visit the site at

http://www.rims.org

SELECTED REFERENCES

Fire, Casualty & Surety Bulletins, Fire and Marine volume. Erlanger, KY: National Underwriter Company. The various commercial coverages are discussed in the Commercial Property section, Business Income section, Inland Marine section, and Boiler & Machinery section.

Flitner, Arthur L., and Arthur E. Brunck. *Ocean Marine Insurance,* 2nd ed., vols. 1 and 2. Malvern, PA: Insurance Institute of America, 1992.

Flitner, Arthur L., and Jerome Trupin. *Commercial Insurance,* First Edition. Malvern, PA: American Institute for Chartered Property Casualty Underwriters/ Insurance Institute of America, 2002.

The CPCU Handbook of Insurance Policies, 4th ed. Malvern, PA: American Institute for CPCU, 2001.

Trupin, Jerome, and Arthur L. Flitner. *Commercial Property Insurance and Risk Management,* 6th ed. Malvern, PA: American Institute for Chartered Property Casualty Underwriters/Insurance Institute of America, 2001.

NOTES

1. This chapter is based on *Fire, Casualty & Surety Bulletins*, Fire and Marine volume, Commercial Property section (Erlanger, KY: National Underwriter Company); Arthur L. Flitner and Jerome Trupin, *Commercial Insurance*, First Edition (Malvern, PA: American Institute for Chartered Property Casualty Underwriters/Insurance Institute of America, 2002); Jerome Trupin and Arthur L. Flitner, *Commercial Property Insurance and Risk Management*, 6th ed., (Malvern, PA: American Institute for Chartered Property Casualty Underwriters/Insurance Institute of America, 2001); and *The CPCU Handbook of Insurance Policies*, 4th ed. (Malvern, PA: American Institute for CPCU, 2001). The author also drew on the various copyrighted commercial property and liability forms of the Insurance Services Office (ISO). The forms are used with the permission of ISO.

2. This section is based on *Fire, Casualty & Surety Bulletins*, Fire and Marine volume, Business Income section (Erlanger: KY: National Underwriter Company); and Trupin and Flitner, chs. 8–9.

3. Trupin and Flitner, p. 9.36.

4. DIC insurance is discussed in detail in Trupin and Flitner, pp. 7.24–7.30.

5. William H. Rodda et al., *Commercial Property Risk Management and Insurance*, 2nd ed., vol. 1 (Malvern: PA: American Institute for Property and Liability Underwriters, 1983), pp. 221–222.

6. Transportation insurance is discussed in detail in *Fire, Casualty & Surety Bulletins*, Fire and Marine volume, Inland Marine section; Trupin and Flitner, ch. 10; and Philip Gordis, *Property and Casualty Insurance*, 33rd ed. (Indianapolis, IN: Rough Notes Co., 1995), chs. 16 and 20. The author drew on these sources in preparing this section.

7. Gordis, pp. 336–337.

8. Bernard L. Webb et al., *Commercial Insurance*, 3rd ed. (Malvern, PA: Insurance Institute of America, 1996), pp. 157–160.

9. Ibid., pp. 162–163.

10. The businessowners policy is discussed in *Fire, Casualty & Surety Bulletins*, Fire and Marine volume, Commercial Property section; and Trupin and Flitner, ch. 14.

Students may take a self-administered test on this chapter at
www.aw-bc.com/rejda

CHAPTER 14

COMMERCIAL LIABILITY INSURANCE

"The litigious nature of American society is a risk that can impact a company's bottom line. Liability insurance is a key tool for managing this risk."

William B. Hedrick,
Senior Vice President, Marsh USA, Inc.

LEARNING OBJECTIVES

After studying this chapter, you should be able to

◆ Identify the major liability loss exposures of business firms.

◆ Describe the basic coverages provided by the commercial general liability (CGL) policy.

◆ Explain the coverage provided by a workers compensation and employers liability policy.

◆ Describe the important provisions of a commercial umbrella policy.

◆ Identify the liability coverages provided by a businessowners policy (BOP).

◆ Describe the basic characteristics of a malpractice liability policy for physicians.

*C*harles, age 55, is the manager of the meat department in a large supermarket in Seattle, Washington. During a recent weekend, the meat department inadvertently sold several packages of contaminated chicken. Five customers who purchased the chickens became ill from bacteria poisoning. Charles fears that the customers will sue the supermarket for damages. He was relieved when the company's risk manager stated that the firm's general liability insurance policy would cover any claims.

Like supermarkets, many business firms operate in an intensely competitive environment where liability lawsuits are routine. The suits range from small nuisance claims to multimillion-dollar demands. Firms are sued because of defective products, injuries to customers, property damage, pollution of the environment, sexual harassment, discrimination against employees, and numerous other reasons. Commercial liability insurance can provide firms with the protection needed to deal with these loss exposures.

This chapter discusses the major liability loss exposures of business firms and the commercial coverages available for insuring these exposures. Topics covered include the commercial general liability (CGL) policy, the employment practices liability policy, workers compensation and employers liability policy, and other commercial liability coverages.

GENERAL LIABILITY LOSS EXPOSURES

General liability refers to the legal liability arising out of business operations other than auto or aviation accidents and employee injuries. The major general liability loss exposures of business firms include the following:

- Premises and operations
- Products liability
- Completed operations
- Contractual liability
- Contingent liability

Premises and Operations

Legal liability can arise out of the *ownership and maintenance of the premises* where the firm does business. Firms are legally required to maintain the premises in a safe condition and are responsible for the actions of their employees. Customers in a store legally are considered to be *invitees*, and the highest degree of care is owed to them. The customers must be warned and protected against any dangerous condition on the premises. For example, a firm can be held liable if a customer trips on a torn carpet and breaks a leg, or if a ceiling collapses and injures a customer.

Legal liability can also arise out of the firm's operations, either on or off the premises. For example, employees unloading lumber in a lumberyard may accidentally damage a customer's truck, or a construction worker on a high-rise building may carelessly drop a tool that injures a pedestrian.

Products Liability

Products liability *refers to the legal liability of manufacturers, wholesalers, and retailers to persons who are injured or incur property damage from defective* *products.* Firms can be successfully sued on the basis of negligence, breach of warranty, and strict liability. These topics were discussed earlier in Chapter 7, and additional treatment is not needed here.

Completed Operations

Completed operations *refers to liability arising out of faulty work performed away from the premises after the work or operation is completed.* Contractors, plumbers, electricians, repair shops, and similar firms can be held liable for bodily injuries and property damage to others after their work is completed. When the work is in progress, it is part of the operations exposure. However, after the work is completed, it is a completed operations exposure. For example, a hot water tank may explode if it is improperly installed, or ductwork in a supermarket may collapse and injure a customer because of improper installation.

A general liability policy provides coverage for both products liability and completed operations. Both products liability and completed operations loss exposures are now included in a definition called **products-completed operations hazard.** *The policy covers liability losses that occur away from the premises and arise out of the insured's product or work after the insured has relinquished possession of the product or the work has been completed.* For example, assume that an electrical outlet is improperly installed, and a fire breaks out one month later. The installer's liability is insured under the products-completed operations coverage.

Contractual Liability

Contractual liability *means that the business firm agrees by a written or oral contract to assume the legal liability of another party.* For example, a manufacturing firm rents a building, and the lease specifies that the building owner is to be held harmless for any liability arising out of use of the building. Thus, by a written lease, the manufacturing firm assumes some potential legal liability that ordinarily would be the owner's responsibility.

Contingent Liability

Contingent liability *refers to liability arising out of work done by independent contractors.* As a general rule, business firms are not legally liable for work done by independent contractors. However, a firm can be held liable if (1) the activity is illegal, (2) the situation or type of work does not permit delegation of authority, or (3) the work done by the independent contractor is inherently dangerous.[1] For example, a general contractor may hire a subcontractor to perform a blasting operation. If someone is injured by the blast, the general contractor can be held liable even though the subcontractor is primarily responsible.

Other General Liability Loss Exposures

Business firms are often exposed to other important general liability loss exposures, as summarized here.

- *Environmental pollution.* Chemical, manufacturing, and other firms may pollute the environment with smoke, fumes, acids, toxic chemicals, waste materials, and other pollutants. In addition, leaking underground storage tanks are a major liability exposure for many firms.
- *Fire legal liability.* Another important loss exposure is **fire legal liability.** A firm may rent or use property such as a building that belongs to another party. If a fire occurs because of the negligence of the firm or its employees, the firm can be held legally liable for the loss.
- *Liquor liability.* Under a **liquor liability law** (also called a **dramshop law**), bars, restaurants, taverns, and other establishments that sell liquor can be held legally liable for injuries caused by intoxicated customers. However, general liability policies typically exclude liquor liability coverage for firms in the business of manufacturing, selling, distributing, or serving of alcoholic beverages.
- *Directors and officers liability.* Officers and directors of business firms are often sued by employees, stockholders, competing firms, government agencies, and other parties. Numerous lawsuits have been initiated by angry stockholders who claimed that they incurred a financial loss because of mismanagement by officers and directors. A **directors and officers liability policy** can be used to cover the legal liability of directors and officers.
- *Personal and advertising injury.* Business firms can be sued for personal and advertising injury.

Personal and advertising injury *refers to false arrest, detention or imprisonment, malicious prosecution, unlawful entry or eviction, libel, slander, defamation of character, violation of privacy, using ideas that belong to another in your ads, and infringement of a copyright or trade slogan in your ads.* For example, a department store may be successfully sued by an innocent customer who is erroneously arrested for shoplifting. Likewise, a firm may be sued because of copyright infringement in its advertising.

- *Property in the insured's care, custody, or control.* Liability can also arise out of damage to property in the insured's care, custody, or control. General liability policies usually exclude coverage for this exposure. This exclusion can be a problem for firms that work on the property of others, such as an auto repair garage or a television repair shop. In some cases, a bailees customers policy can be used to cover liability for damage to personal property in the care, custody, or control of the insured.
- *Sexual harassment.* Employers are frequently sued by employees on the grounds of sexual harassment. Such suits are expensive to defend. To reduce the possibility of a sexual harassment suit, many employers have adopted strict rules that prohibit certain actions, such as lewd or suggestive language.
- *Employment practices.* Employers are also sued by employees because of discrimination, failure to hire or promote, wrongful termination, and other employment-related practices.

COMMERCIAL GENERAL LIABILITY POLICY

The **commercial general liability (CGL) policy** is widely used by business firms to cover their general liability loss exposures. The CGL policy has two coverage forms: an occurrence form and a claims-made form. The following section discusses both forms of the CGL policy drafted by the Insurance Services Office (ISO). Discussion is based on the current edition of the CGL, which became effective in most states in October 2001.[2]

Overview of the CGL Occurrence Policy

The CGL occurrence policy can be written alone or as part of a commercial package policy. The occurrence form contains five major sections:

- Section I—Coverages
  Coverage A: Bodily injury and property damage liability
  Coverage B: Personal and advertising injury liability
  Coverage C: Medical payments
  Supplementary payments: Coverages A and B
- Section II—Who Is an Insured?
- Section III—Limits of Insurance
- Section IV—Commercial General Liability Conditions
- Section V—Definitions

Section I—Coverages

Section I provides coverage for bodily injury and property damage liability, personal and advertising injury liability, medical payments, and certain supplementary payments.

Coverage A: Bodily Injury and Property Damage Liability The insurer agrees to pay on behalf of the insured all sums up to the policy limits that the insured is legally obligated to pay because **of bodily injury or property damage** to which the insurance applies. The bodily injury or property damage must be caused by an occurrence. An **occurrence** *is defined as an accident, including continuous or repeated exposure to substantially the same general harmful conditions.* For example, an explosion occurs in a store, and several customers are injured, or a meat company processes a batch of contaminated hamburger, and over a period of time several persons become violently ill. These incidents would be considered occurrences and would be covered by the CGL.

In addition, the current CGL policy contains a provision for a known loss. Under this provision, coverage does not apply when a loss is known or is apparent before the policy's inception date, such as a loss in progress. Bodily injury or property damage is covered only if (1) it is caused by an occurrence during the policy period, and (2) no insured or employee authorized to receive notice of an occurrence or claim knew prior to the policy inception date that the bodily injury or property damage had occurred in whole or in part. For example, if an insured knew that prior to the policy period, actions by the firm were causing bodily injury or property damage, any bodily injury or property damage claims arising out of the known occurrence would not be covered.

Defense Costs   The insurer also pays legal defense costs. The insurer has the right to investigate a claim or suit and settle it at its discretion. The insurer's duty to defend ends when the applicable limits of insurance are paid out. Legal defense costs are generally paid in addition to the policy limits.

Exclusions   A lengthy list of exclusions applies to both bodily injury and property damage liability. Major exclusions include the following:

- *Expected or intended injury*. Bodily injury or property damage that is expected or intended by the insured is not covered. However, the exclusion does not apply to bodily injury that results from the use of reasonable force to protect persons or property.
- *Contractual liability*. The policy excludes liability assumed by a contract or agreement. However, the exclusion does not apply to liability that the insured would have in the absence of the contract or agreement or to liability assumed by an *insured contract*. An insured contract refers to a lease of the premises, a sidetrack agreement, an easement or license agreement, an obligation to indemnify a municipality, an elevator maintenance agreement, or a tort liability assumption (liability imposed by law in the absence of any contract or agreement) for bodily injury and property damage.
- *Liquor liability*. The exclusion applies only to firms in the business of manufacturing, distributing, selling, serving, or furnishing alcohol. For example, if a bartender continues to serve a drunken customer who injures another person, the bar owner is not covered for any claim or suit. However, the liquor exclusion does not apply to firms that are not in the liquor business. For example, an insured that serves drinks at a company-sponsored party would be covered. Coverage can be obtained by firms in the liquor manufacturing and distribution business by adding the liquor liability coverage form to the policy.
- *Workers compensation*. Any legal obligation of the insured to pay benefits under a workers compensation law or similar law is excluded.
- *Employers liability*. The policy excludes liability for bodily injury to an employee arising out of and in the course of employment. It also excludes a claim by a spouse or close relative who is seeking damages as a result of a job-related injury to an employee of the insured. For example, a suit by a spouse who seeks damages for the loss of consortium (loss of companionship, affection, and comfort) following a work-related injury is not covered.
- *Pollution exclusion*. Bodily injury or property damage arising out of the discharge or seepage of pollutants is also excluded. This exclusion also applies to cleanup costs that are incurred because of a government order. Coverage can be obtained by a pollution endorsement or by adding a separate pollution liability coverage form to the policy.
- *Aircraft, auto, and watercraft exclusion*. Liability arising out of the ownership or operation of aircraft, autos, and watercraft is specifically excluded. The intent here is to exclude legal liability covered by other policies. The exclusion does not apply to watercraft while ashore on premises owned or rented by the insured and to nonowned watercraft less than 26 feet in length and not used to carry people or property for a fee. In addition, the exclusion does not apply to bodily injury to customers resulting from parking automobiles on the premises or next to the premises, which is important for firms that park the cars of customers. However, physical damage to the car being parked is not covered because of the care, custody, or control exclusion (discussed later).
- *Mobile equipment*. Mobile equipment is not covered when the equipment is (a) being transported by an insured's auto or (b) used in or in preparation for any racing, speed, or demolition contest, or in any stunting activity. For example, a bulldozer is excluded while being transported to a job site on a trailer.

- *War.* Bodily injury or property damage due to war is specifically excluded. War is defined to include civil war, insurrection, rebellion, or revolution. The exclusion applies only to liability assumed by a contract or agreement.
- *Damage to property.* The CGL policy excludes property owned, rented, or occupied by the insured, premises that the insured sells or abandons, property loaned to the named insured, and personal property in the insured's care, custody, or control. Other excluded losses are property damage to that particular part of real property on which the insured, contractors, or subcontractors are working and part of any property that must be restored, repaired, or replaced because the insured's work is performed incorrectly.
- *Property damage to the insured's product.* The policy excludes **property damage to the insured's product** if the damage results from a defect in the product. For example, a defective hot water tank may explode. The damage to the tank itself is not covered. However, property damage from the explosion would be covered under the manufacturer's liability policy.
- *Property damage to the insured's work.* The policy also excludes **property damage to the insured's work** that is included in the "products-completed operations hazard." The insured's work refers to the work or operations of the insured as well as material, parts, and equipment used in the work. For example, an employee of a heating contractor may improperly install a gas furnace that later explodes after it was installed. Although the property damage to the customer's building is covered, the value of the employee's work is specifically excluded. The exclusion does not apply if the work is performed by a subcontractor on behalf of the insured.
- *Property damage to impaired property.* The policy also excludes **property damage to impaired property** that is not physically damaged. If property is impaired because of a defect in the insured's product or work, or failure to perform, the loss is not covered. Impaired property is tangible property that cannot be used or is less useful because (1) it incorporates the insured's product or work, or (2) the insured fails to per-

form the terms of a contract or agreement, and (3) the property can be restored to use by correction of the insured's product or work or fulfillment of the contract. For example, assume that the insured manufactures airplane parts, and a faulty part causes several jets to be grounded. The planes are considered impaired property. The loss of use of the jets is not covered by the insured's CGL policy.

- *Recall of products.* Damages and expenses arising out of the recall of defective products are also excluded. In recent years, firms have incurred substantial losses in recalling defective products such as automobiles, drugs, or food products. The CGL specifically excludes such losses.
- *Personal and advertising injury.* Coverage A does not apply to bodily injury arising out of personal and advertising injury. For example, Coverage A would not apply to a customer who is falsely arrested for shoplifting and later submits a claim that he or she was physically injured in the same incident. (However, there would be coverage for the incident under Coverage B— Personal and Advertising Injury Liability.)

In addition to the preceding exclusions, CGL policies typically include an endorsement that excludes suits by aggrieved employees against their employers because of sexual harassment, wrongful discharge, failure to promote, and similar employment practices. Specific coverage for these loss exposures must be purchased (discussed later).

Coverage B: Personal and Advertising Injury Liability
Under this coverage, the insurer agrees to pay those sums that the insured is legally obligated to pay as damages because of personal and advertising injury. This term is defined in the policy and includes the following:

- False arrest, detention, or imprisonment
- Malicious prosecution
- Wrongful eviction or entry
- Oral or written publication that slanders or libels
- Oral or written publication that violates a person's right to privacy
- Use of another's advertising idea in your advertisement

- Infringing upon another's copyright, slogan, or trade dress (total image and appearance of a product, including graphics, size, and shape)

For example, if a customer is falsely arrested for stealing, coverage applies if the firm is sued. Likewise, if a marketing manager uses an ad based on advertising ideas owned by an outside ad agency, coverage applies if the firm is sued.

Coverage C: Medical Payments   Medical payments cover the medical expenses of persons who are injured in an accident on the premises or on ways next to the premises, or as a result of the insured's operations. The medical expenses must be incurred within one year of the accident and are paid without regard to legal liability. For example, if a customer falls on a slippery floor in a supermarket, the medical expenses are covered up to the policy limits.

Supplementary Payments: Coverages A and B   Certain supplementary payments are included under Coverages A and B in addition to the policy limits:

- All expenses incurred by the insurer
- Up to $250 for the cost of a bail bond because of an accident or traffic violation arising out of the use of a vehicle to which the insurance applies
- Cost of bonds to release attachments
- Actual loss of earnings by the insured up to $250 a day because of time off from work
- All costs taxed against the insured in the suit such as court costs
- Prejudgment interest
- All interest that accrues after entry of the judgment

Section II—Who Is an Insured?

The CGL policy can be used to insure a variety of individuals and organizations. If designated in the declarations, insureds include the following:

- Owner and spouse if a sole proprietorship
- Partners, members, and their spouses if a partnership or joint venture
- Members and managers if a limited liability company
- Officers, directors, and stockholders if a corporation

- A trust and trustees, but only with respect to their duties as trustees

The following are also insured under the policy:

- Volunteer workers, but only while performing duties related to the named insured's business
- Employees acting within the scope of their employment
- Any person or organization acting as a real estate manager
- A legal representative if the named insured should die
- Drivers of mobile equipment owned by the named insured
- Any newly acquired or formed organization, other than a partnership, joint venture, or limited liability company

Section III—Limits of Insurance

The limits of insurance state the maximum amount that the insurer will pay regardless of the number of insureds, claims made or suits brought, or persons or organization making such claims or bringing suits. Several limits apply (see Exhibit 14.1).

1. *General aggregate limit.* The **general aggregate limit** is the maximum amount that the insurer will pay for the sum of the following: damages under Coverage A, except bodily injury and property damage included in the "products-completed operations hazard"; damages under Coverage B; and medical expenses under Coverage C.
2. *Products-completed operations aggregate limit.* The **products-completed operations aggregate limit** is the maximum amount that the insurer will pay under Coverage A because of bodily injury and property damage included in the "products-completed operations hazard."
3. *Personal and advertising injury limit.* This limit is the maximum amount that the insurer will pay under Coverage B for personal injury and advertising injury.
4. *Each-occurrence limit.* The **each-occurrence limit** is the maximum amount that the insurer will pay for the sum of all damages under Coverage A and the medical expenses under Coverage C arising out of any one occurrence.

EXHIBIT 14.1
Illustration of the CGL Limits of Insurance

SOURCE: Arthur L. Flitner and Jerome Trupin, *Commercial Insurance*, First Edition (Malvern, PA: American Institute for Chartered Property Casualty Underwriters/Insurance Institute of America, 2002), Exhibit 9.1, p. 9.6.

5. *Damage to rented premises.* This limit is the maximum amount that the insurer will pay under Coverage A for property damage to rented premises from a single fire.

6. *Medical expense limit.* This limit is the maximum amount that the insurer will pay under medical expenses because of a bodily injury sustained by any one person.

Section IV—Commercial General Liability Conditions

This section states the various conditions that apply to the general liability coverage form. The conditions include provisions dealing with bankruptcy; duties in the event of an occurrence, claim, or suit; legal action against the insurer; other insurance; premium audit; and numerous additional conditions.

Section V—Definitions

This section in the CGL policy defines more precisely the various terms used in the policy. Numerous definitions are stated in some detail. However, space limitations preclude a discussion of these definitions here.

Overview of the CGL Claims-Made Policy

The Insurance Services Office (ISO) also offers a claims-made policy, which is similar to the occurrence policy with the major exceptions of payment of claims on a claims-made basis, inclusion of an extended reporting period (Section V), and moving of the definitions to Section VI.

Meaning of "Claims-Made"   An **occurrence policy** is one that covers claims arising out of occurrences that take place during the policy period, regardless of when the claim is made. In contrast, the **claims-made policy** *covers only claims that are first reported during the policy period, provided the event occurred after the retroactive date (if any) stated in the policy.* The retroactive date is an extremely important concept that is discussed later.

To illustrate the difference between the two concepts, assume a building contractor purchased an occurrence policy three years ago, and the policy has been kept in force up to the present time. The contractor replaces the occurrence policy with a claims-made policy. If the contractor were sued because of a defect in a building constructed three years earlier, the occurrence policy would cover the claim. However, assuming no retroactive coverage, the claims-made policy would not cover the loss because it occurred prior to the inception date of the policy.

Rationale for Claims-Made Policies   Insurers have resorted to claims-made policies because of the problem of **long-tail claims.** The long-tail refers to a relatively small number of claims that are reported years after the policy was first written. Under an occurrence policy, the insurer that provided coverage when the incident occurred was responsible for the claim. As a result, insurers had to pay claims on policies that expired years earlier. This made it difficult for actuaries to estimate accurately the correct premiums to charge and the correct loss reserve to establish for incurred but not yet reported (IBNR) claims. Under a claims-made policy, premiums, losses, and loss reserves can be estimated with greater accuracy.

Retroactive Date   A claims-made policy can be written to cover events that occur prior to the inception of the policy. Coverage will depend on the retroactive date, if any, inserted in the policy. To be covered, the occurrence must take place after the retroactive date, and the claim must be reported during the current policy term. If the occurrence takes place before the retroactive date, the claims-made policy will not respond.

For example, assume that the retroactive date is the date of the original claims-made policy. The issue date of the original claims-made policy is January 1, 2002. The most recent claims-made policy is issued on January 1, 2004. The insured would be covered for all occurrences that take place after January 1, 2002, and are reported during the current policy period.

Extended Reporting Periods   The claims-made policy also contains a provision that extends the period for reporting claims. *The purpose is to provide coverage under an expired claims-made policy for claims first reported after the policy expires.* The extended reporting period does not extend the period of protection. To be covered, the injury must occur after the retroactive date but before the end of the policy period. Injuries that occur before the retroactive date or after the policy expires are not covered.

The **basic extended reporting period** is automatically provided without an extra charge whenever one of the following occurs:

- The policy is canceled or not renewed.
- The insurer renews or replaces the policy with a retroactive date that is later than the retroactive date in the original policy.
- The claims-made policy is replaced with an occurrence policy.

The basic extended reporting period provides for two separate reporting periods or "tails." The first tail is a five-year period after the policy expires; the second tail is a 60-day period after the expiration date.

The five-year tail applies to claims arising out of an occurrence reported to the company during the policy period or no later than 60 days after the end of the policy period. (However, the occurrence must take place during the policy period or after the retroactive date.) For example, assume that a customer in a supermarket slips and falls on a wet floor during the policy period. The insured reports the occurrence promptly to the company, but no actual claim is made against the insured during the policy period. Any resulting claim arising out of that reported occurrence is covered by the expired policy if the claim is made before the end of the five-year period.

The second tail of 60 days applies to all other claims; these claims result from occurrences that take place during the policy period (or after the retroactive date), but are not reported to the insurer during the policy period. Coverage applies if the occurrence is reported to the insurer within 60 days after the policy expires. For example, referring back to our earlier example, the insured may have been unaware that the customer fell, so the incident was not reported to the company. However, if a claim is made against the insured after the policy expires, coverage applies if the occurrence is reported to the insurer within 60 days after the expiration date.

If the insured wants a longer reporting period after the policy expires, the supplemental extended reporting period can be added by an endorsement and payment of an additional premium. The insured must request the endorsement in writing within 60 days after the policy expires.

EMPLOYMENT-RELATED PRACTICES LIABILITY INSURANCE

Employers are frequently sued by employees and potential employees because of wrongful termination, discrimination, sexual harassment, failure to promote, failure to hire, and other employment-related practices. In recent years, the number of such suits has increased substantially, and the median

EXHIBIT **14.2**
Median Compensatory Award for Employment-Practice Liability Cases

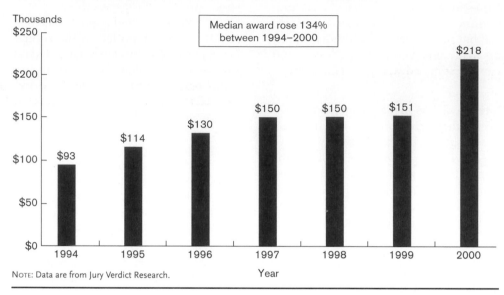

NOTE: Data are from Jury Verdict Research.

SOURCE: From Robert P. Hartwig, *Liability Trends, Issues and Jury Verdicts: Impact on Insurance Liability and Excess Casualty Markets*, Insurance Information Institute, Risk & Insurance Management Society Annual Meeting, Chicago, IL., April 8, 2003.

awards for damages have also increased (see Exhibit 14.2). General liability insurance policies generally exclude or offer limited protection against liability arising out of the employment practices of employers. Many insurers now offer a separate policy or have specific endorsements to deal with these exposures.

ISO makes available **an employment-related practices liability coverage form,** which deals with employment practices loss exposures. The following discussion is based on the ISO form.

Insuring Agreement

The ISO form is a claims-made policy. The insurer agrees to pay damages arising out of an injury if a claim is first made during the policy period or during a 30-day grace period after the policy period ends. An *injury*, as defined in the policy, includes any of the following:

- Refusal to employ, termination of employment, demotion or failure to promote, reassignment, negative evaluation, and defamation or humiliation
- Coercing a person to commit an unlawful act or omission within the scope of employment
- Work-related sexual harassment

- Other work-related verbal, physical, mental, or emotional abuse, such as discrimination based on race, age, and gender

Co-payment

The ISO form includes a co-payment provision that requires the insured to pay part of the damages and legal defense costs up to some maximum limit. For example, assume that the co-payment percentage is 20 percent, and the maximum co-payment charge is $25,000. If actual damages and legal defense costs amount to $100,000, the insured would pay $20,000. If the actual claim is $200,000, the insured would pay a maximum of $25,000.

Legal Defense

The ISO form also provides for a legal defense, although legal defense costs are included as part of the policy limit. Payment of legal defense costs reduces the amount of insurance available to pay damages.

Note that a claim cannot be settled without the insured's consent. This provision is designed to protect the employer's image and reputation. However, if the insurer works out a settlement with a claimant but the employer refuses to settle, any final settlement above the initial settlement is the employer's responsibility.

Exclusions

The ISO form contains a number of exclusions. Liability arising out of the following is excluded:

- Criminal, fraudulent, or malicious acts
- Contractual liability
- Workers compensation and similar laws
- Failure to comply with the Americans with Disabilities Act
- Violation of laws applicable to employers, such as the Age Discrimination in Employment Act, and the Family and Medical Leave Act of 1993
- Strikes and lockouts
- Liability of an insured who commits a sexual harassment offense. (For example, an employer but not the supervisor would be covered if an immediate supervisor sexually harasses an employee.)
- Termination of employment, job relocation, or assignment due to business decisions
- Intentional discrimination or coercion
- Retaliatory actions (such as actions taken against an employee who files a complaint with a governmental authority)

Because of the growing number of sexual harassment suits filed in recent years, interest in employment practices liability insurance is increasing. Most insurers will check an employer's program on sexual harassment very carefully before writing such insurance.

WORKERS COMPENSATION INSURANCE

Millions of workers are injured or become sick each year because of job-related accidents and disease. All states have workers compensation laws that provide benefits to workers who have a job-related injury or occupational disease. Employers can meet their legal obligations to injured workers by purchasing a workers compensation policy, by self-insurance, or by purchasing the coverage from a competitive or monopolistic state fund in some states.

Workers compensation insurance provides medical care, cash benefits, survivor benefits, and reha-

bilitation services to workers who are injured or die from job-related accidents or disease. The benefits paid are based on the principle of **liability without fault.** *The employer is held absolutely liable for job-related accidents and disease regardless of fault.* Workers receive benefits according to state law and are not required to sue their employers to receive benefits. The benefits are extremely important to workers who are injured or die as a result of job-related accidents or disease. Insight 14.1 provides in greater detail some basic facts about workers compensation laws.

This section discusses the current version of the **workers compensation and employers liability insurance policy** drafted by the National Council on Compensation Insurance.[3] The historical development of workers compensation as a form of social insurance is treated in Chapter 24.

The workers compensation and employers liability policy provides the following coverages:

- Part One: Workers Compensation Insurance
- Part Two: Employers Liability Insurance
- Part Three: Other-States Insurance

Part One: Workers Compensation Insurance

Part One refers to **workers compensation insurance.** Under this section, the insurer agrees to pay all workers compensation benefits and other benefits that the employer must legally provide to covered employees who have a job-related injury or an occupational disease. There are no policy limits for Part One. The insurer instead pays all benefits required by the workers compensation law of any state listed in the declarations.

Under certain conditions, the employer is responsible for payments made by the insurer that exceed regular workers compensation benefits. These situations generally involve fines or penalties associated with intentional misconduct by the employer. The employer must reimburse the insurer for any payments that exceed regular workers compensation benefits because of the following:

- Serious and willful misconduct by the employer
- Knowingly employing workers in violation of law
- Failure to comply with a health or safety regulation

INSIGHT 14.1

Basic Facts about Workers Compensation

Workers compensation benefits are payable to workers injured on the job and survivors of workers injured on the job. Workers compensation is the "exclusive remedy" for providing compensation for such injuries or fatalities. To qualify for workers compensation benefits, the injury or fatality must arise out of and in the course of employment. Background and facts about workers compensation:

- It is the nation's oldest social insurance compensation.

- It is a state-based program that protects injured workers and their survivors against the financial consequences of work-related accidents, disease, and deaths.

- The percentage of the workforce eligible to receive workers compensation benefits is estimated at 97%.

- Workers compensation does not exclude any type of treatment or service. The only coverage criteria are that the injury, illness, or death is work-related, and that the treatment or service provided is reasonable and necessary.

- Generally, employers are mandated by law to provide workers compensation coverage for their employees.

- Workers compensation is financed by employers, either through self-insurance or, more commonly, by securing insurance with an insurer licensed to write workers compensation insurance.

Although each state's workers compensation program and laws differ, common features include:

- All state workers compensation laws require payment of all reasonable and necessary medical treatment, at no cost to the worker, with no co-payments or deductibles, for as long as necessary to rehabilitate the injured worker, even for life.

- All workers compensation laws also provide tax-free benefits for lost wages, typically at two-thirds of a worker's wage.

- The duration, and sometimes the level of wage loss benefits depends on whether there is any permanent injury and, if so, the extent of permanency.

- All workers compensation laws also provide benefits for the survivors and dependents of workers whose deaths were work-related; these benefits continue for the life of the surviving spouse or until remarriage.

- Dependency benefits are usually provided until at least age 18 but sometimes longer, as in the case of a dependent who's attending college or another educational institution.

Source: Excerpted from American Insurance Association, "Protecting Workers Compensation from Terrorism," *AIA Advocate*, February 10, 2003.

■ Discharge, coercion, or discrimination against any employee in violation of the workers compensation law

Part Two: Employers Liability Insurance

Part Two refers to **employers liability insurance,** which covers employers against lawsuits by employees who are injured in the course of employment, but whose injuries (or disease) are not compensable under the state's workers compensation law. This part is similar to other liability insurance policies where negligence must be established before the insurer is legally obligated to pay.

Employers liability insurance is needed for several reasons. First, a few states do not require workers compensation insurance for smaller employers with fewer than a certain number of employees, such as three or fewer. In such cases, an employer is covered under the employers liability section if an employee with a work-related injury or disease sues for damages.

Second, an injury or disease that occurs on the job or at the work place may not be considered to be work related, and, therefore, would not be covered under the state's workers compensation law. However, the injured employee may still believe that the employer should be held accountable, and the employer would be covered if sued.

Third, some state workers compensation laws permit lawsuits by spouses and dependents for the *loss of consortium*. The employer would be covered under Part Two in such a case.

Finally, in a growing number of cases, employers are confronted with lawsuits because of *third-party over cases*. An injured employee may sue a negligent third party, and the third party, in turn, sues the employer for contributory negligence. The lawsuit would be covered under Part Two (unless the employer assumed the liability of the third party). For example, assume that a machine is defective, and its operator is injured. In addition to the payment of workers compensation benefits, the state may allow the injured employee to sue the negligent third party. If the injured employee sues the manufacturer of the defective machine, the manufacturer, in turn, could sue the employer for failure to provide proper operating instructions or failure to enforce safety rules. The employer would be covered in such cases.

The employers liability section of the ISO policy also contains several exclusions. Major exclusions include:

- Liability assumed under contract
- Punitive damages
- Bodily injury to an employee employed in violation of the law
- Obligations imposed on the employer because of a workers compensation, occupational disease, unemployment compensation, or disability benefits law
- Intentional injury caused by the employer
- Bodily injury outside the United States or Canada
- Damages arising out of coercion, demotion, evaluation, reassignment, harassment, discrimination, or termination of any employee
- Bodily injury to any person subject to the Longshore and Harbor Workers Compensation Act
- Bodily injury to any person subject to the Federal Employers Liability Act
- Bodily injury to a master or crew member of any vessel
- Fines or penalties because of violation or federal or state law
- Damages payable under the Migrant and Seasonal Agricultural Worker Protection Act

Part Three: Other-States Insurance

Part Three of the workers compensation and employers liability policy provides **other-states insurance.** Workers compensation coverage (Part One) applies only to those states listed on the information page (declarations page) of the policy. However, the

employer may face a workers compensation claim under the law of another state. This possibility could arise if an employee is injured while on a business trip in a state that was not considered when the workers compensation policy was first written, or if the law of a particular state is broadened so that employees are now covered under that state's workers compensation law. Also, the employer's operations may be expanded in a particular state, which brings the employees under the state's workers compensation law.

Other-states insurance applies only if one or more states are shown on the information page of the policy. The information page is the equivalent of a declarations page. *In such cases, if the employer begins work in any of the states listed, the policy applies as if that state were listed in the policy for workers compensation purposes.* Thus, the employer has coverage for any workers compensation benefits that it may have to make under that state's workers compensation law.

The terrorist attack on the World Trade Center in New York City on September 11, 2001, raised several questions with respect to which state workers compensation law should apply to workers who are traveling or who reside in other states. The terrorist attack also raised other questions concerning the compensability of terrorism injuries under state workers compensation laws (see Insight 14.2).

Voluntary Compensation Coverage

Some employers wish to provide workers compensation benefits to employees even though they are not required by law to do so. A **voluntary compensation endorsement** can be added to the policy by which the insurer agrees to pay workers compensation benefits to employees not covered under the law.

In summary, workers compensation insurance is an important commercial coverage that provides considerable economic security to workers who are disabled by a job-related accident or disease. Weekly cash benefits are paid during the period of disability; medical care is unlimited; rehabilitation services and survivor benefits are also available.

In addition, because of experience rating and loss prevention programs, workers compensation programs promote occupational safety and health.

INSIGHT 14.2

Compensability of Terrorism Injuries Under State Workers Compensation Laws

Compensability of Injuries

Terrorist strikes that injure people at work raise several compensability issues under state workers compensation laws. *The basic test for determining whether an injury is work-related is whether the injury arose "out of and in the course of" employment.* States have developed different interpretations of that basic test.

Classes of Risk Tests

The interpretations can be broadly classified as follows:

- *"Positional risk" test:* The most lenient requires only that the employment required the employee to be in the location where the injury occurred.
- *"Increased risk" test:* Requires that the employment conditions increased the risk of injury beyond the risk faced by those not in the employment.
- *"Actual risk" test:* Requires that the risk causing the injury be a risk peculiar to the employment and not one to which the general public would be equally exposed.

Although it appears that New York applies the positional risk test, the injuries and deaths resulting from the World Trade Center attacks arguably could satisfy all three tests or, at least, all but the most restrictive actual risk test. The World Trade Center towers had been targeted by terrorists once before and were regarded by many as prime targets for terrorists. Therefore, employment in the World Trade Center may have increased the risk of suffering a terrorist attack. However, many more suffered injury than just those who worked in the targeted buildings.

Choice of Jurisdiction

Terrorist attacks also raise questions about the appropriate jurisdiction for pursuing workers compensation claims.

Many employees may have worked for employers headquartered in other states, may have been present while traveling from other states, may have been hired in other states, or may have resided in other states. *Under the laws of many states, those factors may present an injured worker or the survivors of an injured worker with a choice of jurisdictions.* The decision may hinge on factors such as which state applies more liberal compensability tests or provides more liberal benefits.

Nature of Injuries

Finally, terrorist attacks may present unique questions concerning the nature of injuries. Many in New York may have been injured fleeing the destruction and breathing dust and smoke. Injured employees may suffer psychological or emotional injuries such as post-traumatic stress disorder. Psychological or emotional injuries may strike many employees who experienced no physical injuries but witnessed the injury of others or only narrowly escaped injury.

States apply different standards to the treatment of different types of injury, particularly mental or emotional injuries. For example, some states provide no compensation for so-called mental injuries, injuries for which there are no physical symptoms. Some states provide compensation for mental injuries that flow from an actual physical injury, while others provide no compensation at all for mental injuries.

However, the effectiveness of individual states in reducing the number of job-related injuries and disease varies widely. A recent study by the Work Loss Data Institute shows wide variation in the effectiveness of workers compensation programs among the states. The study awarded grades to individual states and jurisdictions based on several variables, including overall injury rates, duration of disability, and key injuries such as a carpel tunnel syndrome and lower back strain. As shown in Exhibit 14.3, nine states received grades of A or A– (Arizona, Arkansas, Georgia, Indiana, Iowa, Minnesota, Nevada, Oregon, and Utah). Eight jurisdictions received a grade of F (California, Louisiana, New Jersey, New York, Puerto Rico, Rhode Island, Texas, and West Virginia).

COMMERCIAL AUTO INSURANCE

Legal liability arising out of the ownership and use of cars, trucks, and trailers is another important loss exposure for many firms. This section examines sev-

EXHIBIT 14.3
State Safety and Loss Report Card

State	Grade	State	Grade
Alabama	C	Missouri	C
Alaska	B–	Montana	C–
Arizona	A	Nebraska	B
Arkansas	A–	Nevada	A
California	F	New Jersey	F
Connecticut	B	New Mexico	B+
Delaware	D	New York	F
Florida	B	North Carolina	B+
Georgia	A	Oklahoma	D+
Guam	D–	Oregon	A–
Hawaii	D	Puerto Rico	F
Illinois	D	Rhode Island	F
Indiana	A	South Carolina	C
Iowa	A	Tennessee	B–
Kansas	B	Texas	F
Kentucky	D	Utah	A
Louisiana	F	Vermont	C–
Maine	C	Virgin Islands	C
Maryland	D	Virginia	C+
Massachusetts	D–	Washington	C
Michigan	D+	West Virginia	F
Minnesota	A	Wisconsin	B+

Source: "State Report Cards for Workers Compensation," 2003 edition, © Work Loss Data Institute, Encinitas, CA.

eral commercial auto coverages that can be used to meet this exposure.[4]

Business Auto Coverage Form

The ISO **business auto coverage form** is widely used by business firms to insure their commercial auto exposures. Firms have considerable flexibility with respect to the autos that can be covered. There are nine numerical classifications, each of which is referred to as a symbol:

1. Any auto
2. Owned autos only
3. Owned private passenger autos only
4. Owned autos other than private passenger autos only
5. Owned autos subject to no-fault plans
6. Owned autos subject to a compulsory uninsured motorists law
7. Specifically described autos
8. Hired autos only
9. Nonowned autos only

If one or more of the symbols 1 through 6 are selected, there is automatic coverage on any new owned autos that the firm acquires during the policy period. If symbol 7 is used, new cars are covered only if two conditions are met: (1) the insurer must already cover all autos that the insured owns for the coverage provided, or the new auto must replace one that the insured previously owned that had such coverage, and (2) the firm informs the insurer within 30 days after acquisition that it wants the auto insured for that coverage.

Liability Insurance Coverage   The insured is covered for a bodily injury or property damage claim to which the insurance applies, which is caused by an accident that results from the ownership, maintenance, or use of a covered auto. For example, if an employee drives a company car during the course of employment and injures another motorist, the employer has coverage for any resulting lawsuit.

In addition, the insurer pays all covered pollution cost or expense to which the insurance applies.

To be covered, the pollution cost or expense must be caused by an accident that results from the ownership, maintenance, or use of a covered auto. However, the pollution cost or expense is covered only if there is either bodily injury or property damage to which the insurance applies, which is caused by the same accident. For example, a company employee driving a company car may negligently smash into an oil truck on a crowded expressway, which causes the truck to overturn spilling oil over the environment. The pollution cost that the insured must legally pay is covered.

Finally, the insurer agrees to defend the insured and pay all legal defense costs. Defense costs are in addition to the policy limit. The duty to defend or settle ends when the limit of insurance is exhausted by the payment of judgments or settlements.

Physical Damage Coverage   The insured has a choice of physical damage coverages that can be used to insure covered autos against damage or loss. Several physical damage coverages are available, summarized as follows:

- *Comprehensive coverage.* The insurer will pay for loss to a covered auto or its equipment from any cause except the covered auto's collision with another object or its overturn.
- *Specified causes-of-loss coverage.* Only losses from certain specified perils are covered: fire, lightning, or explosion; theft; windstorm, hail, or earthquake; flood; mischief or vandalism; or the sinking, burning, collision, or derailment of any conveyance transporting the covered auto.
- *Collision coverage.* Loss caused by the covered auto's collision with another object or its overturn is covered under this provision.

Coverage for towing and labor costs can be added if desired. The company will pay up to the limit shown in the declarations for towing and labor costs incurred each time a covered auto of the private passenger type is disabled. However, the labor must be performed at the place of disablement.

In addition, if a damaged covered auto has comprehensive coverage, the coverage applies to glass breakage, to loss caused by hitting a bird or animal, and to loss caused by falling objects or missiles. If glass breakage results from a collision, the insured can elect to have it covered as a collision loss. Without this option, the insured would have to meet two deductibles if both glass breakage and body damage result from the same collision. By treating glass breakage as part of the collision loss, only the collision deductible must be satisfied.

The insurer will also pay up to $20 per day (after 48 hours) up to a maximum of $600 for transportation expenses incurred by the insured because of the total theft of a covered auto of the private passenger type. The coverage applies only to covered autos that are insured for either comprehensive or specified causes-of-loss coverage.

Nonownership Liability Coverage

Salespersons, repair and maintenance employees, employees who make deliveries, inspection personnel, and other employees frequently drive their automobiles on company business. A business firm can be held legally liable for property damage or bodily injury caused by employees while they are using their own cars on company business. If the employee carries liability insurance on his or her car, the firm is protected as an additional insured. The liability limits may be inadequate, however, or the policy may have lapsed. The firm may also be exposed to liability claims arising from the operation of other nonowned autos—for example, a restaurant or hotel that parks cars for the guests. These nonownership exposures can also be insured by selecting the appropriate covered auto designation symbol or combination of symbols.

Garage Coverage Form

The **garage coverage form** is a specialized form for auto dealers. Auto dealers include both franchised auto dealers (such as a Chevrolet or Toyota dealer) and nonfranchised dealers (such as a used car dealer). The major coverages include liability coverage, garagekeepers coverage, and physical damage coverage.

Liability Coverage   The insurer agrees to pay all sums that an insured must legally pay as damages because of bodily injury or property damage to which this insurance applies caused by an accident in the course of garage operations. *Garage operations* are defined to include garage business locations, autos covered under the form, and all operations necessary or incidental to a garage business. As such, the liability section includes coverage for premises and operations liability, auto liability, incidental contractual liability, and products and completed operations.

The insured has a choice of autos that can be covered, and numerical symbols are used to denote the covered autos, an approach similar to the business auto policy.

The liability section of the garage policy contains numerous exclusions. Only two of them are discussed here. *First, damage to the property of others in the insured's care, custody, or control is excluded.* Thus, damage to a customer's car on an automobile servicing hoist, or damage to a customer's car while it is being road tested by a mechanic, would not be covered. These common exposures can be covered by adding garagekeepers coverage to the policy.

Second, there is no coverage for property damage to any of the insured's products if the product is defective at the time it is sold. For example, assume that a dealer sells a tire that has a hidden defect. The defective tire later blows out, and the car is damaged in a collision. This exclusion eliminates coverage for the defective tire, but the property damage caused by the defective tire would be covered. The intent of this exclusion is to cover property damage or bodily injury caused by a defective product but not any damage to the product itself.

Garagekeepers Coverage As noted earlier, the garage coverage form excludes coverage for property of others in the care, custody, or control of the insured. Adding garagekeepers coverage to the policy can eliminate this exclusion. The insurer agrees to pay all sums the insured must legally pay as damages for loss to a customer's car left in the insured's care while the insured is attending, servicing, repairing, parking, or storing the vehicle in its garage operations.

Three coverages are available: (1) comprehensive coverage, (2) specified causes of loss coverage, and (3) collision coverage. These coverages are based on the legal liability of the insured. For example, if a customer's car were stolen because the dealer carelessly left the garage door unlocked, the loss would be covered. It is possible, however, to broaden the coverage on customers' autos without regard to legal liability by payment of an additional premium. This coverage is called a direct coverage option, which indemnifies customers for their losses even though the garage has no legal liability to do so. The insured checks a box on the declarations page to activate the option.

Physical Damage Coverage Physical damage insurance on covered autos can also be included in the garage policy. The following three coverages are available:

- *Comprehensive coverage.* The company will pay for a loss from any cause except for the covered auto's collision with another object or its overturn.
- *Specified causes of loss coverage.* Covered perils are fire, lightning or explosion, theft, windstorm, hail, earthquake, flood, mischief or vandalism, and the sinking, burning, collision, or derailment of any conveyance transporting the covered auto.
- *Collision coverage.* Loss caused by the covered auto's collision with another object or its overturn is covered under this provision.

AVIATION INSURANCE

Major commercial airlines own fleets of expensive jets, and the liability exposure is enormous. Occasionally, a commercial jet will crash accidentally because of mechanical or human error, killing hundreds of passengers and causing extensive property damage to surrounding buildings. Legal liability losses arising out of the crash of a fully loaded jet airliner can be catastrophic. In addition, some firms own aircraft used on company business. Company planes sometimes crash, resulting in death or bodily injury to the passengers, as well as death or injury to people on the ground and substantial property damage to surrounding buildings where the crash occurs. Finally, thousands of Americans own or operate small planes, which may crash because of pilot error or inexperience.

Most states apply the common-law rules of negligence to aviation accidents. However, some states have absolute or strict liability laws that hold the owners or operators of aircraft absolutely liable for aviation accidents. As a result of international treaties and agreements among countries, absolute liability is also imposed on commercial airlines for aviation accidents that occur during international flights.

Aviation Insurers

Aviation insurance is highly specialized and is underwritten by a relatively small number of insurer organizations. Most of the domestic aviation market is accounted for by two multicompany aviation pools: United States Aircraft Insurance Group (USAIG) and Associated Aviation Underwriters (AAU). Both pools underwrite and manage aviation insurance on behalf of the individual insurers that belong to the pool. The two pools account for most of the aviation insurance that is written for commercial airlines, aircraft manufacturers, and large domestic airports.

Aviation Insurance for Private Business and Pleasure Aircraft

AAU offers a policy designed for the owners and operators of private business and pleasure aircraft. The policy provides physical damage coverage for damage to the aircraft and liability coverage for property damage and bodily injury arising out of the ownership or use of the insured aircraft.[5]

Physical Damage Coverage   A plane on the ground can be damaged by fire, collapse, theft, vandalism, or other perils. While taxiing, the plane can collide with vehicles, buildings, or other aircraft. The most severe exposure is present when the plane is in flight. A plane can collide with another plane; it can be struck by lightning or damaged by turbulent winds; or it can experience mechanical difficulties from a fire or explosion. Planes can also be damaged or destroyed by acts of terrorism.

Physical damage insurance provides coverage for direct damage to the aircraft. The insured has a choice of physical damage coverages. There are three insuring agreements for physical damage to the aircraft:

- *"All-risks" basis.* All physical damage losses to the aircraft, including disappearance, are covered except those losses excluded.
- *"All-risks" basis, not in flight.* The aircraft is covered on an "all-risks" basis only when it is on the ground and not in flight. Fire or explosion following a crash is not covered.
- *"All-risks" basis, not in motion.* The aircraft is covered on an "all-risks" basis only when it is standing still. Fire or explosion after a crash is not covered.

Although aircraft can be covered on an "all-risks" basis, certain exclusions apply. Excluded losses include damage to tires (unless caused by fire, theft, or vandalism), wear and tear, deterioration, mechanical or electrical breakdown, and failure of installed equipment. However, these exclusions do not apply if a covered loss occurs.

Liability Coverage   Liability coverage pays for bodily injury or property damage arising out of the insured's ownership, maintenance, or use of the insured aircraft. Coverage also applies to bodily injury arising out of the premises where the aircraft is stored or parked.

Liability coverage contains several important exclusions. Excluded losses are liability assumed in a contract, workers compensation, and damage to property in the insured's care, custody, and control (except personal effects of passengers up to $250 and damage to an aircraft hangar or its contents up to $5000). Also excluded are damage or injury from noise, such as sonic boom, interference with the quiet enjoyment of property, and pollution losses.

BAILEE'S CUSTOMER POLICY

A bailee is someone who has temporary possession of property that belongs to another party. Bailees—such as laundries or dry cleaners, for example—are legally liable for damage to the customers' goods only if they or their employees are guilty of negligence. However, the customers expect to be paid for the loss or damage to their goods regardless of who is at fault. If the customers are not reimbursed, the bailee may lose future business. In the case of a destructive fire or tornado, the business may be financially ruined if customers are not reimbursed for their damaged property.

A **bailee's customer policy** is a generic name for a policy that covers loss or damage to the property of customers regardless of the bailee's legal liability. Although the policies are not standard, they can be written to meet the needs of a particular bailee, including laundries and dry cleaners, tailors, television repair shops, and upholsterers.

A bailee's customer policy can be written either as an "all-risk" ("open perils") policy or as a named-perils policy. Under an "all-risk" policy, all losses are covered except those losses specifically excluded. A named-perils policy typically includes coverage for fire and lightning, wind and hail, explosion, smoke, strike, riot and civil discussion, vandalism, burglary and hold-up, transportation risks, and confusion of goods (inability to identify the goods even though they are not physically damaged). For example, if a suit or dress is damaged in a fire or tornado, or if the garment is damaged when a delivery truck overturns, the loss would be covered.

A named-perils policy typically excludes theft from an unattended vehicle unless the vehicle is locked and there is visible evidence of a forced entry, loss resulting from misdelivery or an unaccountable shortage where evidence of theft is absent, dishonest acts of the named insured or employees, and processing damage (unless caused by fire or explosion). For example, if a dress is damaged by cleaning fluid or it shrinks in the cleaning process, the loss is not covered.

COMMERCIAL UMBRELLA POLICY

Because firms are often sued for large amounts, they may seek protection against catastrophic loss exposures not adequately insured under standard liability policies. A **commercial umbrella policy** can provide protection against catastrophic liability judgments that might otherwise bankrupt a firm.

The Insurance Services Office (ISO) has designed an umbrella policy for commercial firms. The following discussion summarizes the major provisions in the ISO **commercial liability umbrella coverage form.**[6]

Coverages

The ISO commercial umbrella policy pays the ultimate net loss in excess of the retained limit for bodily injury, property damage, and personal and advertising injury to which the insurance applies. The **ultimate net loss** *is the total sum the insured is legally obligated to pay.* The **retained limit** *refers to (1) the available limits of underlying insurance listed in the declarations, or (2) the self-insurance retention, whichever applies.*

If the loss is covered by both an underlying insurance contract and the umbrella policy, the umbrella policy pays only after the underlying limits are exhausted. For example, assume that an umbrella policy has a limit of $5 million. Assume also that the underlying limit under a commercial general liability (CGL) policy is $1 million for each occurrence, and a judgment against the insured amounts to $3 million. The underlying insurance would pay $1 million, and the umbrella policy would pay the remaining $2 million.

If the loss is not covered by any underlying insurance but is covered by the umbrella policy, the insured must satisfy a **self-insured retention (SIR)**. The SIR can range from $500 for small firms to $1 million or more for large corporations. For example, assume that a firm's SIR amount is $25,000. A customer in the firm's store who is falsely accused and arrested for shoplifting wins a judgment against the insured in the amount of $100,000. If the loss is not covered by any underlying contract, the insured would pay $25,000. The umbrella policy would pay the remaining $75,000.

Legal defense costs are also paid when the underlying insurance does not provide coverage, or the underlying limits are exhausted.

Required Underlying Coverages

Insureds are required to carry certain minimum amounts of liability insurance before the umbrella insurer will pay any claims. The following underlying coverages and limits are typically required:

Commercial general liability insurance

$1,000,000 (each occurrence)
$2,000,000 (general aggregate)
$2,000,000 (products and completed-
             operations aggregate)

Business auto liability insurance

$1,000,000 (combined single limit)

Employers liability insurance

$500,000 (bodily injury per accident)
$500,000 (bodily injury by disease per
          employee)
$500,000 (disease aggregate)

The commercial umbrella policy applies when the loss exceeds the underlying limits.

Exclusions

The ISO commercial umbrella form contains a lengthy list of exclusions. Under bodily injury and property damage liability, losses arising out of the following are excluded:

- Expected or intended injury
- Contractual liability (with certain exceptions)
- Liquor liability
- Any obligation of the insured under a workers compensation or similar law
- Any obligation of the insured under the Employees Retirement Income Security Act (ERISA)
- Any auto that is not a covered auto
- Bodily injury to an employee in the course of employment
- Liability arising out of employment-related practices
- Pollution
- Liability arising out of aircraft or watercraft unless provided by underlying insurance
- Racing activities
- War
- Care, custody, or control exclusion
- Damage to your product
- Damage to your work
- Damage to impaired property or property not physically impaired
- Recall of products, work, or impaired property
- Bodily injury arising out of personal and advertising injury
- Liability arising out of professional services

A lengthy set of exclusions also applies to personal and advertising injury liability. Under personal and advertising injury, claims arising out of the following are not covered:

- Acts caused by or at the direction of the insured with the knowledge that the act would violate the rights of another
- Oral or written publication of material that the insured knows to be false
- Oral or written publication of material whose first publication occurred before the policy period
- Criminal acts of the insured
- Breach of contract except an implied contract to use someone else's idea in your ad

- Failure of the product to perform as stated in the ad
- Wrong description of the price or products
- An insured whose business is advertising, broadcasting, publishing, or telecasting
- Pollutants
- Employment-related practices, such as failure to hire, harassment, and humiliation
- Professional services

LIABILITY INSURANCE, BUSINESSOWNERS POLICY

The businessowners policy (BOP) discussed in Chapter 13 also contains a **business liability coverage form** that provides general liability insurance to business firms. The liability coverage is written on an occurrence basis, and with certain exceptions, it is similar to the commercial general liability coverage form discussed earlier.[7]

Basic Coverages

The BOP liability form contains two basic coverages: (1) business liability and (2) medical expenses. Business liability includes coverage for bodily injury, property damage, and personal and advertising injury. Coverage for medical expenses is also provided. Thus, if a customer in a retail shoe store falls and breaks an arm, the customer's medical expenses would be paid without regard to legal liability up to the medical expense limit.

Amount of Insurance

The minimum amount of insurance provided for liability insurance and medical expenses is $300,000 for each occurrence, which can be increased to $500,000, $1 million, or $2 million. This limit is the maximum that the insurer will pay for both liability and medical expense losses.

The BOP has a medical expense limit of $5000 per person. In addition, there is a separate limit of $50,000 for property damage caused by fire or explosion to premises rented to or temporarily occupied by the named insured with the permission of the owner. Higher limits are available by an endorsement.

In addition, the BOP has two aggregate limits on the total amount of covered claims that can be paid during the policy period. *The first aggregate limit applies to bodily injury or property damage losses that are included in the products-completed operations hazard and is equal to twice the liability and medical expenses limit. The second aggregate limit applies to all other covered losses (including medical expenses and personal and advertising injury losses) and is also equal to twice the liability and medical expenses limit.* The aggregate limit, however, does not apply to property damage to premises rented or temporarily occupied by the named insured if the damage arises out of a fire or explosion. Damage to rented premises from a fire or explosion is subject to a separate limit described in the declarations.

Legal Defense

The insurer pays the legal costs of defending the insured. The duty to defend applies only to claims covered under the policy. The legal costs are in addition to the amount that the insurer is legally obligated to pay because of the insured's negligence.

The definition of an insured also includes employees while they are acting within the scope of their activities. This feature protects a negligent employee who might be named in the lawsuit along with the employer.

Exclusions

In general, the business liability coverage exclusions are similar to the CGL policy. The liability coverage excludes claims arising out of expected or intentional injury; contractual liability; liquor liability; workers compensation and similar laws; pollution, aircraft, auto, or watercraft; professional services; damage to the named insured's products or work, damage to impaired property, and recall of products.

Although liability coverage excludes professional services, a pharmacist's professional liability endorsement is available to a retail druggist or drugstore. In addition, the exclusion of autos does not apply to the parking of an auto on or next to the premises owned or rented by the named insured. This exception is especially important if the firm has employees who park the cars of customers; however,

there is no coverage for damage to a customer's car driven by an employee because of the care, custody, or control exclusion. Finally, the liquor liability exclusion applies only if the named insured is in the business of manufacturing, distributing, selling, serving, or furnishing alcohol beverages. There is coverage if alcohol is served at functions incidental to the insured's business. Thus, if the company has a Christmas party and an intoxicated employee injures someone, the firm is covered if a lawsuit ensues.

PROFESSIONAL LIABILITY INSURANCE

Chapter 7 examined the problem of lawsuits against physicians, surgeons, attorneys, accountants, professors, and other professionals. This section briefly discusses some professional liability insurance coverages that provide protection against a malpractice lawsuit or lawsuit involving a substantial error or omission.

Physicians Liability Insurance

Physicians, surgeons, and dentists require substantial amounts of **physicians liability insurance** that covers acts of malpractice or omission resulting in harm or injury to patients. The *physicians, surgeons, and dentists professional liability coverage form* drafted by the ISO covers acts of malpractice by physicians and surgeons. This policy has the following characteristics:[8]

- *The insuring agreement provides broad coverage.* The insurer agrees to pay all sums that the insured is legally obligated to pay as damages because of injury caused by a medical incident. A *medical incident* is any act or omission in the furnishing of professional medical or dental services by the insured, an employee of the insured, or any person acting under the personal direction or supervision of the insured. For example, if Dr. Jones operates on a patient and the patient is paralyzed after the operation, Dr. Jones would be covered for a malpractice lawsuit.
- *Liability is not restricted to accidental acts of the physician or surgeon.* In many cases, the physician or surgeon deliberately intends to do a

INSIGHT 14.3

Florida Doctor Operates on Wrong Side of Head

A woman remained in serious condition at Florida Hospital Orlando after surgery for a brain hemorrhage in which her doctor accidentally began working on the wrong side of her skull.

Hospital officials remained tightlipped about their internal investigation into the mistake and said it's too early to explain why the error occurred. A neurosurgeon was operating on the unidentified woman when he drilled into the wrong area of her skull.

Hospital officials say he quickly realized the mistake and completed the operation in the correct location. At the family's request, officials are not releasing many specifics of the incident.

"(The patient) came in with a life-threatening condition, and she's had a successful surgery," said Dr. Monica Reed, Florida Hospital chief medical officer. "She is improving and progressing" as expected for someone who suffered a brain hemorrhage.

Reed said given the volume of surgeries done at Florida Hospital's facilities every year—numbering about 50,000—

wrong-site surgeries are rare. Nationwide, the Joint Commission on the Accreditation of Healthcare Organizations counted 58 wrong-site procedures in 2001—up from 50 nationally in 2000.

Reed said similar problems have happened before at the hospital. She could not discuss specific instances but said Florida Hospital reports its mistakes to the appropriate agencies for investigation.

"Any time you look at a process that involves human beings, you're going to have something like this," Reed said.

In Lake County, Leesburg Regional Medical Center has implemented an aggressive system to prevent such mishaps, including stickers with the words "no cut" on them and widely labeling "no" on a patient's skin with a marker.

SOURCE: Adapted from "Florida Doctor Operates on Wrong Side of Head," *Lincoln Journal Star*, February 27, 2002, p. 2A.

certain act; however, the professional diagnosis or the performance of the act may be faulty, and the patient is injured (see Insight 14.3). For example, Dr. Jones may intend to operate on a patient by using a certain surgical procedure. If the patient is harmed or injured by the operation, Dr. Jones would still be covered for his willful, intentional act to operate in a certain way.

- *The policy covers the physician for liability arising out of the negligent acts of an employee*; however, a nurse typically is not included as an insured under the physician's policy but must secure his or her own professional liability policy. For example, if the office nurse gives a wrong shot to a patient, and the patient is harmed, the physician has liability coverage for the incident. However, the nurse is not covered under the physician's policy for the incident.

- *There is a maximum limit per medical incident and an aggregate limit for each coverage.* For example, a patient and the patient's family may file separate claims against a physician for damages arising out of the same medical incident.

Under current forms, the per-medical-incident limit is the maximum that would be paid for both claims. The aggregate limit is the maximum amount that would be paid as damages during any policy year.

- *Professional liability insurance is not a substitute for other necessary forms of liability insurance.* General liability insurance is also needed to cover liability arising out of a hazardous condition on the premises or acts of the insured that are not professional in nature. For example, a patient may trip on a torn carpet in the doctor's office and break an arm. The professional liability policy would not cover this event.

- *Current forms permit the insurer to settle the claim without the physician's or surgeon's consent.* Payment of a claim could be viewed as an admission of guilt. Older forms required the insurer to obtain the physician's consent before a claim could be settled. However, current forms permit the insurer to settle without the physician's consent because an occasional claim against a physician in certain high-risk categories is not viewed as being overly detrimental to his or her character.

- *An extended reporting period endorsement can be added.* A physician with a claims-made policy may retire, change insurers, or drop the malpractice insurance. To protect the physician, an extended reporting period endorsement can be added, which covers future claims arising out of incidents that occurred during the period in which the claims-made policy was in force.

In summary, a professional liability policy for physicians and surgeons provides considerable protection. The insurance is expensive, however. Malpractice insurance covering certain high-risk specialties can cost $75,000 or more each year in certain parts of the country. Physicians have responded to the medical malpractice problem by practicing defensive medicine, by abandoning high-risk specialties such as obstetrics and neurosurgery, and by pushing for legislation to limit malpractice awards.

Errors and Omissions Insurance

Errors and omissions insurance provides protection against loss incurred by a client because of negligent acts, errors, or omissions by the insured. Professionals who need errors and omissions insurance include insurance agents and brokers, travel agents, real estate agents, stockbrokers, attorneys, consultants, engineers, architects, and other individuals who give advice to clients. The errors and omissions coverage is designed to meet the needs of each profession.

This type of coverage can be illustrated by the *insurance agents and brokers errors and omissions policy*. The policy has a number of provisions. First, the insurer agrees to pay all sums that the insured is legally obligated to pay because of any negligent act, error, or omission by the insured (or by any other person for whose acts the insured is legally liable) in the conduct of business as general agents, insurance agents, or insurance brokers. For example, assume that Mark is an independent agent who fails to renew a property insurance policy for a client. The policy lapses, and a subsequent loss is not covered. If the client sues for damages, Mark would be covered for the omission. The policy is normally sold with a sizable deductible so that the agent has an incentive to minimize mistakes and errors.

Errors and omissions policies are generally issued on a claims-made basis covering claims made against the agent or broker only because of errors during the current policy period (and after the retroactive date).

Finally, the policy contains relatively few exclusions. However, claims that result from dishonest, fraudulent, criminal, or malicious acts by the insured, libel and slander, bodily injury, and destruction of tangible property are specifically excluded.

DIRECTORS AND OFFICERS LIABILITY INSURANCE

Officers and directors of corporations are increasingly being sued by shareholders, employees, competing firms, government agencies, and other parties because of alleged mismanagement. A **directors and officers liability (D&O) policy** provides financial protection for the directors and officers and the corporation if the directors and officers are sued for mismanagement of the company's affairs. Most corporations have bylaws that require the company to bear the financial responsibility of indemnifying directors and officers for alleged mismanagement. A D&O policy reimburses the company for its costs in defending and settling lawsuits against directors and officers.

D&O policies are not uniform, but they have certain common features. The following discussion summarizes the major characteristics of D&O policies.

Insuring Agreement Most policies contain the following insuring agreements:

- *Personal liability of directors and officers.* The first agreement covers the personal liability of directors and officers. The policy agrees to pay damages on behalf of insured persons because of a wrongful act. Insured persons include directors and officers and employees.

  The definition of a wrongful act varies among insurers. One policy defines a wrongful act broadly as any employment practices wrongful act; errors and omissions by a director or officer; any matter against an insured person solely because the person is a director or officer; errors and omissions by insured persons in their

INSIGHT 14.4

Directors & Officers Liability Insurance Premiums Skyrocket as Shareholders Claims Increase, According to Tillinghast Study

On the heels of similar increases from the previous year, purchasers of Directors & Officers (D&O) liability insurance paid nearly 30 percent more for their D&O coverage, according to Tillinghast-Towers *Perrin's 2002 Directors & Officers Liability Survey*. This sustained increase in premiums reflects continued concern over high-profile bankruptcies, corporate scandals, and D&O lawsuits—particularly securities and shareholder litigation. The survey, which included 2275 participants, is the 25th in a series of studies on D&O liability claims and insurance purchasing patterns and the only study of its type produced for the marketplace. Tillinghast's primary objective in conducting the study is to help organizations assess probable exposures to claims against their directors and officers, as well as to assist companies with developing appropriate financial protection programs.

Claim frequency and claim severity appeared to stabilized for most types of claims, although shareholder claims severity was up significantly. Among closed claims, U.S. participants paid an average of $5.72 million, up only slightly from $5.65 last year. However, the average indemnity paid for shareholder claims increased significantly to $23.35 million, compared with $17.18 million last year and $9.62 million two years ago.

Premiums: The Upward Trend Continues

The hard market trends seen in 2001 have spilled over into 2002, as D&O insurance purchasers faced a big jump in premium rates, with increases in the double and triple digits. Additionally, insurers implemented tougher underwriting guidelines for D&O insurance in 2002.

"In light of recent events, a dramatic surge in premiums is not really that surprising. Declining stocks on Wall Street and the unprecedented, large corporate scandals that have plagued businesses over the past year were clearly the main drivers of the rate increases," say Mark Larsen, survey leader and Tillinghast consultant. "Until we see some improvement in the stock market and shareholders believe that good corporate governance has taken hold, we can expect to see this trend continue into 2003, and possibly beyond."

Other key findings from the survey revealed:

- **Shareholders drive disclosure scrutiny:** Inadequate or inaccurate disclosure, including financial reporting and claims related to stock offerings, was most frequently at issue in U.S. shareholder claims, up from 38.8 percent last year to 46.4 percent this year.
- **First decrease in limits in almost a decade:** Even though some respondents purchased higher limits, the survey found a decrease in average D&O policy limits for the

first time in eight years. This change indicates that most organizations faced tough risk management decisions when evaluating D&O coverage as a result of dramatic premium increases during the past few years.

- **Discrimination ranked #1 issue:** Discrimination in employment was the most frequently cited D&O issue among U.S. participants, accounting for 43 percent of employee claims, which is down slightly from last year (46.1 percent), and 27.1 percent of overall claims.

Insurance Coverage: Taking a Closer Look

Among both U.S. and Canadian participants in the survey, the purchase of D&O insurance was common, with 97 percent and 90 percent of businesses respectively, having secured coverage. The average amount of coverage carried by U.S. participants was $18.9 million in total limits, which was down slightly from last year ($20.1 million). Survey participants that opted not to carry coverage reported seeing a lack of need for coverage and the high cost, as the primary reasons for not purchasing.

"Current market conditions indicate that purchasers should take a longer-term view of D&O coverage," says Jim Swanke, leader of Tillinghast's Self-Insured Organizations practice. "Purchasers should be mindful of the financial strength and reputation of all D&O insurers in their programs and diligently evaluate the amount of coverage limits they purchase."

Claims: A Leveling Off

The 2002 survey suggests a leveling off of claim frequency and stabilization in claim severity as indicated by the average payments and legal costs in 2002. The U.S. indemnity payment for closed claims averaged $5.72 million, up from $5.65 million last year, and the average legal costs in the U.S. were down from $0.54 million in 2001 to $0.52 million in 2002.

Private firms with fewer than 500 shareholders were less than half as likely to experience a D&O claim as their publicly traded counterparts. Companies with a history of M&A or divestiture activity were more than twice as likely to experience a claim against their directors and officers.

"In response to rising D&O claims, Tillinghast expects the insurance industry will maintain tougher standards for underwriting, even for firms that are actually considered good risks. Insurers have and will continue to be increasingly selective as to which risks qualify for full coverage," says Eric Speer, Tillinghast Region Manager for the Americas.

SOURCE: Adapted from Tillinghast-Towers Perrin, *Directors & Officers Liability Insurance Premiums Skyrocket as Shareholders Claims Increase, According to Tillinghast Study*, Press Release, New York, NY, April 24, 2003.

capacity as a director or officer of an outside entity; and any employment practices wrongful act, or other errors and omissions by the corporation.

- *Corporate reimbursement coverage.* The second insuring agreement pays on behalf of the corporation. This coverage reimburses the corporation for loss resulting from the company's obligation to reimburse directors and officers to the extent required or permitted by law for suits alleging wrongful acts by such directors and officers.

D&O policies are written on a claims-made basis. The policies typically have a discovery or extended reporting period in the event the insurer cancels the policy or refuses to renew. The reporting period varies by insurers—such as 90 days to 12 months—and applies only to claims for wrongful acts committed prior to termination of the policy but reported during the reporting period.

Exclusions   D&O policies contain numerous exclusions. Common exclusions are as follows:

- Bodily injury and property damage (covered under the CGL policy)
- Libel and slander (covered under the CGL policy)
- Personal profit, such as profit from insider trading
- Certain violations of the Securities Exchange Act of 1934 or similar provisions of state law
- Return of salaries or bonuses illegally received without stockholder approval
- Deliberate dishonesty by an insured
- Failure to procure or maintain insurance
- Violation of ERISA law
- Illegal discrimination

Boards of directors have been under heavy attack recently because of lax corporate governance, inadequate oversight of management, corporate fraud and greed, and deceptive and illegal accounting practices. According to a recent study by Tillinghast-Towers Perrin, a major actuarial consulting firm, most D&O claims are due to (1) discrimination in employment, and (2) suits by shareholders because of inadequate or inaccurate disclosure, including financial reporting and claims related to stock offerings. As a result, D&O premiums have increased substantially, and underwriting has tightened (see Insight 14.4).

CASE APPLICATION

a. Lastovica Construction is insured under a commercial general liability (CGL) policy. The firm agreed to build a new plant for the Smith Corporation. A heavy machine used by Lastovica Construction accidentally fell from the roof of the partially completed plant. Bill, an employee of the construction firm, was severely injured when the falling machine crushed his foot. Heather, a pedestrian, was also injured by the machine while walking on a public sidewalk in front of the building.

   (1) Heather sued both Lastovica Construction and the Smith Corporation for her injury. Indicate the extent, if any, of the CGL insurer's obligation to provide a legal defense for Lastovica Construction.

   (2) What legal defense could the Smith Corporation use to counter Heather 's claim based on the nature of its relationship with Lastovica Construction? Explain your answer.

   (3) Does Lastovica Construction have any responsibility for Bill's medical expenses and lost wages? Explain.

b. James owns a restaurant that is insured under a claims-made CGL policy. The policy term is January 1, 2003, through December 31, 2003. On December 15, 2003, a customer became violently ill from eating a piece of banana cream pie that had become contaminated. On February 1, 2004, the customer made a claim against James for the illness. James had no prior notice that the customer had become ill. Explain with reasons whether James's policy will cover the loss.

SUMMARY

- General liability refers to the legal liability of business firms arising out of business operations other than liability for auto or aviation accidents or employee injuries. Important general liability loss exposures are as follows:

    Premises and operations
    Products liability
    Completed operations
    Contractual liability
    Contingent liability

- Legal liability can arise out of the *ownership and maintenance of the premises* where the firm does business. *Products liability* means that the firm can be held liable for property damage or bodily injury arising out of a defective product. *Completed operations liability* refers to liability arising out of faulty work performed away from the premises after the work is completed. *Contractual liability* means that the business firm agrees to assume the legal liability of another party by a written or oral contract. *Contingent liability* means that the firm can be held liable for work by independent contractors.

- Other important general liability loss exposures include environmental pollution; property in the insured's care, custody, or control; fire legal liability; liability arising out of a liquor or dramshop law; directors and officers liability; personal and advertising injury; and liability arising out of sexual harassment and employment practices.

- The *commercial general liability (CGL) policy* can be used to cover most general liability loss exposures of business firms. The CGL provides coverage for the following:

    Bodily injury and property damage liability
    Personal and advertising injury liability
    Medical payments
    Supplementary payments

- An *occurrence policy* covers liability claims arising out of occurrences that take place during the policy period, regardless of when the claim is made.

- A *claims-made policy* covers only claims that are first reported during the policy period or extended reporting period, provided that the event occurred after the retroactive date, if any, stated in the policy.

- Insurers have resorted to claims-made policies because of the problem of the *long tail*. The long tail refers to the relatively small number of claims that are reported years after the policy is first written. As a result of these claims, it is difficult to estimate premiums, losses, and loss reserves accurately. A claims-made policy enables an insurer to estimate premiums and losses more accurately.

- *Employment-related practices liability insurance* covers employers against suits arising out of wrongful termination, discrimination against employees, sexual harassment, and other employment-related practices.

- All states have workers compensation laws that require covered employers to provide workers compensation benefits to employees who become disabled because of work-related accidents or occupational disease. The workers compensation insurer pays all benefits that the employer must legally provide to employees who are occupationally disabled.

- The *business auto coverage form* can be used by business firms to insure their liability exposures from automobiles. The employer can select those autos to be covered under the policy.

- The *garage coverage form* is designed to meet the insurance needs of auto dealers. The major coverages include liability insurance, garagekeepers insurance, and physical damage insurance. *Garagekeepers insurance* covers the garage owner's liability for damage to customers' autos while the autos are in the dealer's care for service, repairs, or storage.

- Aviation insurance covering private business and pleasure aircraft provides physical damage coverage on the aircraft and liability coverage for injury to passengers and people on the ground.

- A *bailee's customer policy* can be used to cover the loss or damage to the property of customers regardless of the bailee's legal liability.

- A *commercial umbrella policy* provides protection to firms against a catastrophic judgment. An umbrella policy is excess insurance over the underlying coverages.

- A businessowners policy provides business liability coverage and medical expense coverage to small- to medium-sized business firms. The insured's employees are also covered for their negligent acts while acting within the scope of their employment.

- Physicians liability insurance is designed to cover professional liability arising out of a medical error or omission. The policy has several important features:

    Coverage is broad.

    Liability is not restricted to accidental acts.

    The insured is protected against the negligent acts of employees.

    There is a maximum limit for each medical incident and an aggregate limit for each coverage.

    Professional liability insurance is not a substitute for other necessary forms of liability insurance.

    Current forms permit the company to settle a claim without the physician's or surgeon's consent.

    An extended reporting period endorsement can be added.

- A **directors and officers (D&O) liability policy** provides financial protection for the directors and officers and the corporation if the directors and officers are sued for mismanagement of the company's affairs.

KEY CONCEPTS AND TERMS

Advertising injury
Aviation insurance
Bailee's customer policy
Basic extended reporting period
Bodily injury or property damage
Business auto coverage form
Business liability coverage form
Claims-made policy
Commercial general liability (CGL) policy
Commercial umbrella policy
Completed operations
Contingent liability
Contractual liability
Directors and officers (D&O) liability policy
Each occurrence or per occurrence limit
Employers liability insurance
Employment-related practices liability coverage
Errors and omissions insurance
Fire legal liability
Garage coverage form
General aggregate limit
Liquor liability law (dramshop law)
Long-tail claims
Medical payments
Occurrence
Occurrence policy
Other-states insurance
Personal injury
Physicians liability insurance
Products-completed operations aggregate limit
Products-completed operations hazard
Products liability
Property damage to impaired property
Property damage to the insured's product
Property damage to the insured's work
Retained limit
Self-insured retention (SIR)
Ultimate net loss
Voluntary compensation endorsement
Workers compensation and employers liability insurance

REVIEW QUESTIONS

1. Identify the major general liability loss exposures of business firms.

2. Define each of the following:
    a. Products liability
    b. Completed operations
    c. Contractual liability
    d. Contingent liability

3. Briefly describe the meaning of "products and completed operations hazard."

4. The commercial general liability policy (CGL) contains several coverages. Briefly explain each of the following coverages:
    a. Bodily injury and property damage liability
    b. Personal and advertising injury liability
    c. Medical payments

5. Explain the difference between an occurrence policy and a claims-made policy.

6. A workers compensation policy contains several coverages. Briefly explain each of the following coverages:
    a. Part one: workers compensation insurance
    b. Part two: employers liability insurance
    c. Part three: other states insurance

7. a. Identify the major coverages in the business auto coverage form.
    b. Describe the major characteristics of the garage coverage form.

8. Briefly describe the following coverages that appear in an aircraft policy:
    a. Physical damage coverage
    b. Liability coverage

9. a. What is a bailee?
   b. Why is liability insurance needed by a bailee?
   c. Briefly describe the basic characteristics of a bailees customer policy.

10. Explain the following characteristics in a commercial umbrella policy:
    a. Coverages provided
    b. Required underlying coverages
    c. Self-insured retention (SIR)

11. Briefly describe the major characteristics of a physicians liability insurance policy.

12. Explain the two insuring agreements that typically appear in a directors & officers (D&O) liability policy.

APPLICATION QUESTIONS

1. Ben owns an appliance and furniture store and is insured under a commercial general liability policy written on an occurrence basis. Explain whether Ben's CGL policy would provide coverage for each of the following situations:
   a. Ben forcibly detained a customer whom he erroneously accused of shoplifting. One month later, after the policy had expired, the customer sued Ben for defamation of character.
   b. Ben's employees were delivering a large desk to a customer's house. The customer's front door and the desk were scratched and damaged when the desk hit the door. The customer immediately filed a claim for the damage to the door and the desk.
   c. An advertising firm sues Ben for using copyrighted material without permission when the material first appears in a special holiday ad. Ben maintains that the ad material is original and belongs to him.
   d. Unknown to Ben, an automatic dishwasher had a defective part. One week after the dishwasher was installed in a customer's house, it malfunctioned and caused considerable water damage to the kitchen carpet. The homeowner holds Ben responsible for the damage.
   e. An employee accidentally knocked over a heavy lamp that injured a customer's foot. The customer later presents a bill for medical expenses to Ben for payment.

2. Jill operates a sporting goods store in a rented location at a shopping mall. She is insured under a CGL policy with the following limits:

General aggregate limit	$1,000,000
Products-completed operations aggregate limit	1,000,000
Personal and advertising injury limit	250,000
Each-occurrence limit	300,000
Damage to rented premises	100,000
Medical expense limit (any one person)	5,000

   A propane tank that Jill kept in the store exploded. Indicate the dollar amount, if any, that Jill's insurer will pay for each of the following losses:
   a. Three customers were injured by flying debris with medical expenses of $6000, $7500, and $5000, respectively.
   b. A fire resulted from the explosion. Damages to the rented building are $50,000.
   c. A customer injured by the explosion sues Jill for $200,000 for the bodily injury.

3. Allison owns and operates a small retail food store in a suburban shopping center. The store is insured for liability coverage under a businessowners policy. Explain whether the following situations are covered under Allison's businessowners policy. Treat each situation separately.
   a. A clerk accidentally injures a customer with a shopping cart. Both Allison and the clerk are sued.
   b. A customer slips on a wet floor and breaks a leg.
   c. Allison has a customer arrested for shoplifting. The customer is innocent and sues for damages.
   d. A woman returns a spoiled package of gourmet cheese and demands her money back.
   e. Allison has a Christmas party for her employees after the store closes. One employee gets drunk and injures another motorist while driving home. The injured motorist sues both Allison and the employee.

4. A surgeon is insured under a physicians, surgeons, and dentists professional liability policy. Explain whether the following situations are covered by the professional liability policy. Treat each situation separately.
   a. An office nurse gives a patient a wrong drug. Both the physician and the nurse are sued.
   b. The surgeon sets the broken arm of a patient. The patient sues because the arm becomes deformed and crooked.

c. A patient waiting to see the doctor is injured when the legs of an office chair collapse.

5. Delivery Service purchased a commercial umbrella policy with a $10 million liability limit and a $100,000 self-insured retention. The umbrella insurer required Delivery Service to carry a $1 million per-occurrence limit on its general liability policy and a $1 million per-occurrence limit on its business auto policy. A Delivery Service driver was intoxicated while driving a company van and killed another motorist. The court ruled that Delivery Service must pay damages in the amount of $5 million. How much, if any, of this amount will the umbrella insurer pay? Explain your answer.

6. Electrical Services is an electrical contractor that employs 10 electricians. Electrical Services faces numerous loss exposures. One general liability loss exposure arises out of faulty work that an electrician performs in a customer's home, which can cause property damage to the home. Identify the general liability loss exposure to which this example refers.

7. Fast Pizza hires college students who drive their own cars to deliver pizzas to customers. Fast Pizza is concerned that the company may be liable for damages caused by company employees while they are driving their cars on company business. Identify a liability coverage form that Fast Pizza could purchase to deal with this exposure.

INTERNET RESOURCES

- The **Defense Research Institute** is a service organization created to improve the administration of justice and the skills of defense attorneys. Visit the site at

  http://www.dri.org

- The **RAND Institute for Civil Justice** is a research unit within the RAND Organization that conducts independent, objective research on the civil justice system. Visit the site at

  http://www.rand.org

- The **Insurance Information Institute** is a primary source of information, analysis, and referral on subjects dealing with property and liability insurance. Visit the site at

  http://www.iii.org

- The **Insurance Services Office (ISO)** provides statistical information, actuarial analyses, policy language, and technical information to participants in property and liability insurance markets. ISO drafted the commercial general liability policy discussed in this chapter. Visit the site at

  http://www.iso.com

- The **National Council on Compensation Insurance** develops and administers rating plans and systems for workers compensation insurance. Visit the site at

  http://www.ncci.com

- The **National Safety Council** provides national support and leadership in the field of safety; publishes safety materials of all kinds; and conducts a public information and publicity program to support safety. Visit the site at

  http://www.nsc.org

- The **Risk and Insurance Management Society (RIMS)** is the premier professional organization for corporate risk managers and buyers of insurance. RIMS makes known to insurers the insurance needs of business and industry, supports loss prevention programs, and provides a forum for discussing common risk management objectives and problems. RIMS also publishes *Risk Management Magazine*. Visit the site at

  http://www.rims.org

SELECTED REFERENCES

Fire, Casualty & Surety Bulletins. Erlanger, KY: National Underwriter Company, Casualty & Surety volume. The bulletins are published monthly. Detailed information on all forms of commercial liability insurance can be found in this volume.

Wells, Alexander T., and Bruce D. Chadbourne. *Introduction to Aviation Insurance and Risk Management,* 2nd ed. (Malabar, FL: Krieger Publishing Company, 2000).

NOTES

1. Emmett J. Vaughan, and Therese M. Vaughan, *Fundamentals of Risk and Insurance,* 9th ed. (New York: Wiley, 2003), p. 584.

2. This section is based on *Fire, Casualty & Surety Bulletins*, Casualty and Surety volume, Public Liability section (Erlanger, KY: National Underwriter Company); and Arthur L. Flitner and Jerome Trupin, *Commercial Insurance*, First Edition. (Malvern, PA: American Institute for Chartered Property Casualty Underwriters/Insurance Institute of America, 2002). The author also drew on the various commercial general liability forms of the Insurance Services Office (copyrighted) that appeared in *The CPCU Handbook of Insurance Policies*, 4th ed. (Malvern, PA: American Institute for CPCU, 2001). The author drew heavily on these sources in the preparation of this chapter.

3. The workers compensation and employers liability policy is discussed in detail in *Fire, Casualty & Surety Bulletins*, Casualty and Surety volume, Workers Compensation section (Erlanger, KY: National Underwriter Company).

4. This section is based on the *Fire, Casualty & Surety Bulletins*, Casualty and Surety volume, Auto section (Erlanger, KY: National Underwriter Company), and the ISO business auto coverage form and garage coverage form.

5. Aviation insurance is discussed in *Fire, Casualty & Surety Bulletins*, Companies & Coverages volume, Aircraft-Marine section (Erlanger, KY: National Underwriter). See also Alexander T. Wells and Bruce D. Chadbourne, *Introduction to Aviation Insurance and Risk Management*, 2nd ed. (Malabar, FL: Krieger Publishing Company, 2000).

6. A detailed discussion of the commercial umbrella policy can be found in *Fire, Casualty & Surety Bulletins*, Casualty and Surety volume, Public Liability section (Erlanger, KY: National Underwriter). See also Flitner and Trupin, *Commercial Insurance*, pp. 13.5–13.12.

7. A detailed discussion of the businessowners policy can be found in *Fire, Casualty & Surety Bulletins*, Fire and Marine volume, Commercial Property section (Erlanger, KY: National Underwriter Company).

8. Professional liability insurance for physicians is discussed in *Fire, Casualty & Surety Bulletins*, Casualty and Surety volume, Public Liability section (Erlanger, KY: National Underwriter Company).

Students may take a self-administered test on this chapter at www.aw-bc.com/rejda

CHAPTER 15

CRIME INSURANCE AND SURETY BONDS

"Right now, some of your employees are stealing and you don't even realize it."

John Case
Employee Theft—The Profit Killer

LEARNING OBJECTIVES

After studying this chapter, you should be able to

◆ Define theft, robbery, and safe burglary.

◆ Identify the insuring agreements in the commercial crime coverage form and give an example of where each can be used.

◆ Explain the difference between the discovery form and the loss sustained form.

◆ Identify the basic insuring agreements in a financial institution bond for a commercial bank.

◆ Show how surety bonds differ from insurance.

◆ Identify the major types of surety bonds and give an example of where each can be used.

*M*egan, age 25, works as a cashier in a 24-hour convenience store in Tucson, Arizona. Around midnight, a male customer pulled a gun on Megan and demanded all of the cash in the cash register. As a matter of company policy, all employees are instructed never to resist a holdup but to surrender the cash. Megan gave the thief an undisclosed amount of cash. The store manager later told Megan that the company has a crime insurance policy that covers holdups and other crimes.

The above example shows that most firms need protection against crime loss exposures. Business firms lose billions of dollars annually because of robbery, burglary, larceny, and employee theft. Other crimes are widespread, including fraud, embezzlement, and illegal activities. Computer crimes are also increasing.

This chapter discusses the Insurance Services Office (ISO) commercial crime insurance program that protects business firms against robbery, burglary, employee theft, and other crime losses. It concludes with a discussion of surety bonds that provide indemnification to an injured party if the bonded party fails to perform an agreed upon act.

ISO COMMERCIAL CRIME INSURANCE PROGRAM

In 1986, the Insurance Services Office (ISO) introduced a simplified-language program to replace the older commercial crime forms. Since then, the program has been modified several times. The latest changes became effective in 2002. The following discussion is based on this program.

Crime coverage can either be added to a package policy or purchased separately as a stand-alone (monoline) policy. There are five basic crime coverage forms and policies: (1) commercial crime coverage form, (2) commercial crime policy, (3) government crime coverage form, (4) government crime policy, and (5) employee theft and forgery policy. Each coverage form or policy is written in two versions—a discovery version and a loss-sustained version (see Exhibit 15.1). The *discovery version* covers a loss that is discovered during the policy period or within 60 days after the policy expires even though the loss may have occurred before the policy's inception date. The *loss-sustained version* covers a loss that occurs during the policy period (or a loss that would have been covered under a prior policy if the insurance had been kept in force), and the loss is dis-

covered during the policy period or within one year after the policy expires. These two versions are discussed in greater detail later in the chapter.

The commercial crime coverage form and the commercial crime policy are designed for most private firms and nonprofit organizations other than financial institutions, such as banks and savings and loan institutions.

The government crime coverage form and government crime policy are designed for governmental

Exhibit 15.1
ISO Commercial Crime Coverage Forms and Policies

- Commercial Crime Coverage Form (discovery version and loss-sustained version)
- Commercial Crime Policy (discovery version and loss-sustained version)
- Government Crime Coverage Form (discovery version and loss-sustained version)
- Government Crime Policy (discovery version and loss-sustained version)
- Employee Theft and Forgery Policy (discovery version and loss-sustained version)

entities, such as states, cities, counties, state universities, and public utilities.

The employee theft and forgery policy is designed for business firms that need coverage only for employee theft and forgery losses. With certain exceptions, the crime coverage forms and policies follow a similar format with respect to insuring agreements, exclusions, and policy conditions.

It is beyond the scope of the text to discuss each of the five crime coverage forms and policies in detail. Instead, the fundamentals of commercial crime insurance can be illustrated by a discussion of the ISO commercial crime coverage form.[1]

COMMERCIAL CRIME COVERAGE FORM

The **commercial crime coverage form** can be added to a package policy to cover the crime exposures of business firms. Alternatively, a separate commercial crime policy can be purchased that provides essentially the same coverages.

Basic Definitions

Most property crimes against business firms are due to robbery, burglary, or theft. The commercial crime coverage form has a definitions page that defines key terms. **Robbery** is the unlawful taking of property from the care and custody of a person by someone who (1) has caused or threatens to cause that person bodily harm, or (2) has committed an obviously unlawful act witnessed by that person.

Safe burglary is the unlawful taking of property from within a locked safe or vault by someone who unlawfully enters the safe or vault as evidenced by marks of forcible entry upon the exterior. For coverage to apply, there must be marks of forcible entry upon the exterior of the safe. The definition of safe burglary also includes the unlawful taking of a safe or vault from the premises. Coverage applies if the entire safe is taken from inside the premises, which some burglars may do.

Theft is a broader term and is defined as the unlawful taking of money, securities, or other property to the deprivation of the insured. It includes robbery and burglary as well as shoplifting and employee theft.

Insuring Agreements

The commercial crime coverage form contains several insuring agreements. Firms can select one or more of the following coverages:

- Employee Theft
- Forgery or Alteration
- Inside the Premises—Theft of Money and Securities
- Inside the Premises—Robbery or Safe Burglary of Other Property
- Outside the Premises
- Computer Fraud
- Funds Transfer Fraud
- Money Orders and Counterfeit Currency

Employee Theft   This coverage pays for the loss of money, securities, and other property that results directly from theft committed by an employee. The theft is covered even if the employee cannot be identified, or the employee is acting alone or in collusion with other persons. For example, if an employee steals money from a cash register, the loss is covered. Other types of employee theft are common, especially for small business firms (see Insight 15.1).

Coverage of employee theft also includes the theft of other property. **Other property** *is any tangible property other than money or securities that has intrinsic value. However, other property does not include any property excluded under the policy.* For example, if an employee in an appliance store steals a television set, the loss is covered.

The insuring agreement applies on a *blanket basis* to all persons who meet the definition of an employee—that is, covered employees are not specifically named in the policy. If desired, employers can use a *schedule approach,* which identifies covered employees in the policy by name or by position. Most employers prefer to cover employees on a blanket basis.

Forgery or Alteration   This coverage pays for a loss that results directly from forgery or from the alteration of checks, drafts, promissory notes, or similar instruments made or drawn by the insured or insured's agent. For example, if a burglar steals some company checks and forges the insured's name, the resulting loss is covered. Likewise, if a check signed

Taking Home More Than a Paycheck: Employee Theft Costs U.S. Employers $20 Billion–$40 Billion a Year

Jim Lashley has always paid close attention to the behind-the-scenes paperwork needed to keep his landscape company on task. The 36-year-old Orlando, Fla., business owner handles the money, invoices and checks for Landscape Supply Co. Only his accountant is privy to the quarterly records.

For 10 years, Lashley's hands-on management was the ultimate insurance against employee theft or fraud. Or so he thought.

About two years ago, Lashley's secretary at the time began secretly diverting installation orders to her boyfriend. She also went to Lashley's sod provider and opened a line of credit for supplies. Because she had no intention of paying back the sod provider, Lashley said, she was able to secure dozens of sod-installation jobs at a fraction of the going rate.

In the end, her actions cost Lashley roughly 20 jobs and at least $10,000. The sod provider also had to swallow a $5,000 supply bill.

"She'd been with me for two years before all of this started," Lashley said. "I trusted her."

At one time or another, nearly every small business experiences some type of employee theft or fraud. Whether it's a theft of money, incoming business, inventory or intellectual property, small businesses are especially vulnerable to being swindled.

Often, a small company lacks the resources to supervise every employee. For instance, a small business may rely on one person to complete accounting and bookkeeping transactions in addition to opening mail, making deposits, writing checks and overseeing petty cash. This type of unrestricted access lends itself to the possibility of theft.

According to the U.S. Chamber of Commerce, employee theft costs U.S. employers $20 billion to $40 billion annually. Nearly 90 percent of all businesses report that they have experienced employee theft of some kind. Unfortunately, 75 percent of employee-related crimes go unnoticed.

To avoid becoming a victim, small-business owners should learn to recognize and avoid potential problems.

Start by dividing responsibilities among two or more employees. If one person writes checks or disburses cash, for example, then another person should be in charge of handling the accounts-payable records, said Judith Dacey, president of Small Business Resources Inc. in Orlando.

Dacey, a certified public accountant, also recommends business owners do extensive background checks before hiring a new employee. Call former employers and ask whether they would rehire the worker.

"Small-business owners tend to skip this step," Dacey said. "But it's one of the most important. Make sure and ask each reference, 'Can I trust this person?'"

Owners also should keep an eye on the vacation schedule, their accounting records and any changes in an employee's personal life.

An employee who takes very brief vacations or no vacation at all should draw your attention. Employee-perpetrated crimes are most often discovered while the employee is away on vacation and other employees are filling in.

Examine accounting records frequently and double-check vendor payments. Keep an eye out for missing or altered documentation or weak and disorganized records. Require employees to file original invoices and contracts—not copies. It's also not a bad idea to have some documents, such as bank statements, mailed directly to your home.

Changes in your employees' personal lives can also cause a trusted employee to go bad. Watch for employees who are under some new stress, such as large medical bills, excessive use of alcohol or large investment losses.

SOURCE: From Sarah Hale, *Sentinel* Staff Writer. "Taking Home More Than a Paycheck: Employee Theft Costs U.S. Employers $20 Billion–$40 Billion a Year," *Orlando Sentinel*, Monday, March 11, 2002.

by the insured is altered from $100 to $1000, that loss too is covered.

Note that this coverage applies only *to forgery or alteration of the insured's checks or instruments* and not to losses that result from the acceptance of forged checks or the instruments of others.[2]

Inside the Premises—Theft of Money and Securities This coverage pays for the loss of money and securities inside the premises or banking premises that result directly from theft, disappearance, or destruction. Coverage also applies to (1) damage to the premises or its exterior resulting from the actual or attempted theft of money or securities if the insured owns the premises or is liable for damage to it, and (2) damage to a locked safe, vault, cash register, or cash box because of actual or attempted theft or unlawful entry.

Coverage is broad because of the words "theft, disappearance, or destruction." For example, losses that occur when a cashier inside a liquor store is held up, money is destroyed in a fire or tornado, or a cash register or safe is damaged in a burglary are all covered. In addition, damage to the premises or its exterior is covered if the insured owns the building or is liable for any damage to it.

Inside the Premises—Robbery or Safe Burglary of Other Property This provision complements the previous insuring agreement of money and securities. This coverage pays for the loss or damage to *other property* inside the premises by the actual or attempted robbery of a custodian, or by safe burglary inside the premises. The term "custodian" is defined in the policy and includes the named insured, partners, and employees but not a janitor or watchperson. For example, if the owner of a pawn shop is robbed of several guns, the loss is covered. Likewise, if a cashier in a liquor store sees a customer take a bottle or liquor and then sprint out of the store without paying, that loss too is covered.

Safe burglary of other property inside the premises is also covered. As stated earlier, **safe burglary** *is the unlawful taking of (1) property from within a locked safe or vault by a person unlawfully entering the safe as evidenced by marks of forcible entry upon its exterior, or (2) a safe or vault from inside the premises*. For example, if a burglar breaks into a locked safe and steals a diamond ring owned by the insured, the loss is covered.

Note that the burglary coverage in this insuring agreement applies only to safe burglary of other property inside the premises. For coverage to apply, property classified as other property must be in a locked safe or vault. Thus, if a burglar breaks into a clothing store and steals several suits and dresses off the rack, the burglary loss of other property would not be covered.

If broader coverage of burglary losses is desired, the policy can be endorsed with an optional insuring agreement to cover such losses. One optional agreement is **inside the premises—robbery or burglary of other property.** This agreement covers actual or attempted burglary as well as robbery of a watchperson.

Outside the Premises The **outside the premises** insuring agreement covers the theft, disappearance, or destruction of money and securities outside the premises while in the custody of a messenger or an armored-car company. A messenger is someone who has care and custody of the property outside the premises. For example, if an employee is robbed while taking the daily cash receipts to the bank, the loss is covered. Likewise, the loss of money or securities in the custody of an armored-car company is also covered. The amount payable is limited to the amount of loss that cannot be recovered from the armored-car company.

In addition, actual or attempted robbery of other property outside the premises in the care of a messenger or armored-car company is covered. For example, if an employee is robbed while taking the insured's diamond ring and other jewelry to a bank, the loss is covered. A $5000 limit applies.

Computer Fraud This provision covers the loss of money, securities, and other property if a computer is used to transfer property fraudulently from inside the premises or banking premises to a person or place outside the premises. For example, if a computer hacker breaks into a business computer and a check is issued to a fictitious person and cashed, the loss is covered.

Funds Transfer Fraud The current edition of the crime coverage form adds a new insuring agreement for the fraudulent transfer of funds. The insuring agreement covers the loss of funds that result directly from fraudulent instructions that direct a financial institution to transfer or pay funds from the insured's account. For example, assume that a bank transfers funds from the insured's account to a bank in Switzerland. If the instruction to transfer the funds (such as electronic, cable, or telephone) is fraudulently made without the insured's knowledge or consent, the loss of money or securities is covered.

Computer crime losses and incidents have increased dramatically in recent years. Because of the limitations of traditional property and general liability policies, many business firms desire more comprehensive coverage of their computer loss exposures. The computer fraud and fund transfer fraud coverages just discussed do not cover all major

Specialized Cyber-Risk Coverages for Computer Loss Exposures

According to the CERT Centers at Carnegie Mellon University's Software Engineering Institute, the number of computer incidents rose 377 percent between 2000 and 2002. An incident may involve one site or possibly thousands of sites. Another study by the Computer Security Institute found that 250 respondents reported computer losses over $200 million. Respondents included U.S. corporations, government agencies, financial institutions, medical institutions, and universities.

Cyber insurance coverages are now available to deal with the growing number of network security risks that have the potential to shutdown a network, destroy vital data, or steal customer information. Specialized cyber-risk coverages are stand-alone policies tailored to meet specific business needs. Depending on the insurer, the following coverages are available:

- *Loss and corruption of data.* This coverage pays for the destruction or damage of data from computer viruses, malicious code, and Trojan horses.
- *Business income losses.* This coverage pays for the loss of business income resulting from an attack on the company's computer network, which limits the company's ability to conduct business, such as a denial-of-service computer attack. Coverage also includes extra expenses, forensic expenses, and dependent business interruption losses.
- *Liability losses.* This coverage pays legal defense costs, judgments and settlements, and sometimes, punitive damages, as a result of the following:
  — Breach of privacy due to the theft of data, such as credit cards or financial data.

— Transmission of a computer virus resulting from a computer attack that causes loss to third parties.
— Failure of computer security measures that cause network systems to be unavailable to third parties.
— Rendering of Internet professional services.
— Allegations of copyright or trademark infringement, libel, slander, defamation, or other media on the company's Web site.
- *Cyber extortion.* This coverage covers the "settlement" of an extortion threat against a company's network, including the cost of hiring a security firm to track down and negotiate with blackmailers.
- *Public relations costs.* This coverage pays the public relations costs associated with a cyber attack and restoring public confidence.
- *Criminal rewards.* This coverage pays the cost of posting a criminal reward fund for information leading to the arrest and conviction of the cyber-criminal who attacked the company's computer system.
- *Cyber-terrorism coverages.* This coverage covers terrorist acts as defined by the Terrorism Risk Insurance Act of 2002. In some cases, coverage can be further extended to terrorist acts beyond those contemplated in the Act.
- *Identity theft losses.* This coverage provides access to an identity theft call center in the event of stolen customer or employee personal information.

Source: Adapted from "Cyber Insurance," *Hot Topics & Insurance Issues,* Insurance Information Institute, 2003.

computer loss exposures. Several insurers have designed specialized **cyber-risk insurance** contracts tailored to meet specific computer loss exposures of business firms (see Insight 15.2).

Money Orders and Counterfeit Paper Currency

This coverage pays for losses resulting directly from the good-faith acceptance of money orders that are not paid upon presentation or from counterfeit currency acquired in the course of business. For example, if a sales clerk accepts a $50 counterfeit bill in exchange for merchandise, the loss is covered.

Exclusions

The commercial crime coverage form contains numerous exclusions. It is beyond the scope of the text to discuss each exclusion. However, certain exclusions merit a brief discussion and are summarized here.

- *Dishonest acts or theft committed by the named insured, partners, or members.* Loss due to dishonest acts or theft by the insured or the insured's partners or members is specifically excluded.

- *Dishonest acts or theft by employees, managers, directors, trustees, or representatives.* With the exception of the employee theft insuring agreement, dishonest acts or theft committed by employees, managers, directors, trustees, or representatives are excluded.
- *Indirect loss.* An indirect loss that results from a covered loss is excluded. For example, if the business is temporarily closed because of a burglary, the loss of business income under this form is not covered.
- *Employee canceled under prior insurance.* This exclusion applies only to the employee theft insuring agreement. There is no coverage for any loss caused by an employee for whom coverage has been canceled under a previous policy and not reinstated since the last cancellation.
- *Inventory shortages.* This exclusion applies only to the employee theft insuring agreement. There is no coverage for any loss if proof of loss depends on an inventory computation or on a profit and loss computation. The intent here is to exclude inventory losses that may be due to errors in record keeping rather than employee dishonesty.
- *Trading losses.* This exclusion applies only to the employee theft insuring agreement. Trading losses whether in the named insured's name or in a fictitious account are specifically excluded. Thus, unauthorized trading in stocks, bonds, futures, and derivatives is not covered. However, unauthorized trading losses can be catastrophic. An endorsement is available to cover trading losses that meet the criteria for employee theft.

Policy Conditions

The policy conditions section in the commercial crime coverage form contains numerous conditions. Four important policy conditions are discussed here.

Cancellation as to Any Employee   This provision states that the insurance coverage as to any employee is immediately canceled once the insured has knowledge that the employee has committed a theft or dishonest act. The insured must notify the insurer of any theft or dishonest act even though the loss does not exceed the deductible. The insurance coverage ceases immediately on that employee.

The firm could encounter some serious coverage problems if a minor loss is not reported. If the dishonest employee is later involved in another loss, and the insurer becomes aware of the earlier loss, the insured would have no coverage.

Discovery Form   As stated earlier, the crime coverage forms and policies are written in two versions—a discovery version and a loss-sustained version.

The **discovery form** *covers losses that are discovered during the policy period or within 60 days after the policy's expiration date, regardless of when the loss occurred.* Thus, losses that occur prior to a policy's inception date are covered if they are discovered within the policy period or within 60 days after termination or cancellation of the policy. In the case of employee benefit plans, the discovery period extends to one year after the policy's expiration date.

Employee theft can go undetected for years. The discovery form can be especially valuable for a business firm that has been in business for several years but is uninsured for employee theft losses. If the new insurance were written on a discovery basis, it would cover any losses that occurred years earlier but were only discovered during the current policy period (or within 60 days after expiration of the policy).

However, an underwriter may have reason to believe that large undiscovered losses might exist prior to the policy's inception date. To deal with adverse selection, a **retroactive date endorsement** could be added to the policy, which covers losses that occur only after the retroactive date and are discovered during the current policy period. If the retroactive date is the same as the policy's inception date, losses that occurred prior to the policy's inception date would not be covered.[3]

Loss-Sustained Form   The **loss-sustained form** *covers losses that occur during the policy period and are discovered during the policy period or within one year after the policy expires.* For example, if an employee steals $10,000 in cash during the policy period, the loss is covered if it is discovered during the current policy period or within one year after the policy's expiration date.

Loss Sustained During Prior Insurance   When commercial crime insurance is written on a loss-sustained basis, the policy contains an important condition called **loss sustained during prior insurance.** *Under this provision, the current policy provides coverage for a loss that occurred during the term of the prior policy but was discovered only after the discovery period under the prior policy had expired.* This provision enables an employer to change insurers without penalty. This provision applies only if there is no break in the continuity of coverage under both policies. Another requirement is that the loss is one that would have been covered by the current policy if it had been in force when the loss occurred.

The maximum recovery under this provision is limited to the policy limit under the previous policy, or the limit of insurance under the current policy, whichever is less. For example, assume that the policy limit under the previous policy is $10,000, and the policy limit under the current policy is $25,000. The current policy will pay only a maximum of $10,000 for any covered loss that occurred while the previous policy was in force.

FINANCIAL INSTITUTION BONDS

Commercial banks, savings and loan institutions, credit unions, stock brokerage firms, and other financial institutions are faced with crime loss exposures that can result in enormous financial losses. These exposures include bank holdups, employee dishonesty, forgery and alteration of checks, acceptance of counterfeit money, theft of securities, armored-car exposures, and numerous additional crime exposures. Because of the size and complexity of their crime exposures, financial institutions use some type of financial institution bond to deal with these exposures. In its application to financial institutions, the word "bond" is synonymous with "insurance policy" and should not be confused with surety bonds discussed later.

The Surety Association of America makes available a number of financial institution bonds that banks and other financial institutions can use. One widely used form is **Standard Form No. 24, Financial Institution Bond,** which is designed for commercial banks, savings banks, and savings and loan institutions. The following discussion is based on this form.

The financial institution bond contains a number of insuring agreements. Agreements A, B, C, and F are part of the basic bond coverage. Agreements D, F, and coverage for data processing organizations are optional.[4]

- Insuring Agreement A—Fidelity
- Insuring Agreement B—On Premises
- Insuring Agreement C—In Transit
- Insuring Agreement D—Forgery or Alteration
- Insuring Agreement E—Securities
- Insuring Agreement F—Counterfeit Currency
- Coverage for Data Processing Organizations

Fidelity Coverage

Most losses under a financial institution bond are fidelity losses due to employee dishonesty. **Fidelity coverage** covers losses resulting directly from the dishonest or fraudulent acts of employees acting alone or in collusion with others. *To be covered as a fidelity loss, the employee must commit a dishonest or fraudulent act with the manifest intent to cause the insured to sustain loss, and to obtain financial benefit for the employee or some other party.* For example, if a bank teller steals cash from a bank register or vault, the loss is covered.

On Premises Coverage

This provision covers the loss of property on the premises from robbery, burglary, misplacement, mysterious unexplained disappearance, theft, and a number of additional perils. For example, if a bank robber threatens a bank teller with bodily harm and escapes with $25,000, the loss is covered. Loss or damage to furnishings, fixtures, and office equipment as a result of burglary, robbery, vandalism, or malicious mischief is also covered.

In-Transit Coverage

This provision covers in-transit losses, which include losses from robbery, larceny, theft, misplacement, mysterious unexplained disappearance, and other specified perils. The property must be in the custody of a natural person acting as a messenger or in the custody of a transportation company. For example, if a bank loses money in an armored car robbery, the loss is covered.

Forgery or Alteration Coverage

This optional provision covers loss from forgery or alteration of most negotiable instruments and certain financial instruments specified in the bond. For example, if a bank officer's name is forged on a check payable to a fictitious person, the loss is covered.

Securities Coverage

This optional provision covers losses to the insured because securities accepted in good faith have been forged, altered, lost, or stolen. For example, if a bank in good faith accepts some stolen stock certificates as collateral for a loan and tries to sell the certificates when the borrower defaults, any resulting loss is covered.

Counterfeit Money

This provision covers loss to the insured from counterfeit money. For example, if a bank teller accepts a fake $100 bill, the loss to the bank is covered.

Coverage for Data Processing Organizations

This coverage is optional and must be deleted by a rider if there are no data processing organizations to be covered. This provision covers data processing organizations while acting on behalf of the insured in the data processing of checks and other accounting records of the insured.

SURETY BONDS

A **surety bond** *is a bond that usually provides monetary compensation if the bonded party fails to perform certain promised acts.* For example, a contractor may be financially overextended and unable to complete a building project. A public official may embezzle public funds, or the executor of an estate may illegally convert part of the estate assets to his or her own use. Surety bonds can be used to meet these loss exposures.

Parties to a Surety Bond

There are always three parties to a surety bond:

- Principal
- Obligee
- Surety (obligor)

The **principal** *is the party who agrees to perform certain acts or fulfill certain obligations.* For example, a construction company may agree to build an office building for a commercial bank. The construction company may be required to obtain a performance bond before the contract is awarded. The construction company would be known as the principal.

The **obligee** *is the party who receives the proceeds of the bond if the principal fails to perform.* In the previous example, the bank would be reimbursed for any loss that resulted from failure of the construction company to complete the building on time or according to contract specifications.

The surety is the final party to the bond. The **surety** (**obligor**) *is the party who agrees to answer for the debt, default, or obligation of another.* For example, the construction company may have purchased a performance bond from a commercial insurer. If the construction company (principal) fails to perform, the bank (obligee) would be reimbursed for any loss by the commercial insurer (surety).

Comparison of Surety Bonds and Insurance

Surety bonds are similar to insurance contracts in that both provide protection against specified losses. However, there are some important differences between them, as listed in Exhibit 15.2.

Types of Surety Bonds

Different types of surety bonds can be used to meet specific needs and situations. Although surety bonds are not uniform and have different characteristics, they can generally be grouped into the following categories:[5]

- Contract bonds
  - Bid bond
  - Performance bond
  - Payment bond
  - Maintenance bond
- License and permit bonds
- Public official bonds
- Judicial bonds
  - Fiduciary bond
  - Court bond
- Federal surety bonds
- Miscellaneous surety bonds

Exhibit 15.3 compares the various types of contract bonds.

EXHIBIT **15.2**
Comparison of Insurance and Surety Bonds

Insurance

---

1. There are two parties to an insurance contract.

2. The insurer expects to pay losses. The premium reflects expected loss costs.

3. The insurer normally does not have the right to recover a loss payment from the insured.

4. Insurance is designed to cover unintentional losses that ideally are outside of the insured's control.

Surety Bonds

---

1. There are three parties to a surety bond.

2. The surety theoretically expects no losses to occur. The premium is viewed as a service fee, by which the surety's credit is substituted for that of the principal.

3. The surety has the legal right to recover a loss payment from the defaulting principal.

4. The surety guarantees the principal's character, honesty, integrity, and ability to perform. These qualities are within the principal's control.

Contract Bonds A **contract bond** *guarantees that the principal will fulfill all contractual obligations.* There are several types of contract bonds. Under a *bid bond*, the owner (obligee) is guaranteed that the party awarded a bid on a project will sign a contract and furnish a performance bond.

Under a **performance bond,** the owner is guaranteed that work will be completed according to the contract specifications. For example, if a building is not completed, the surety is responsible for completion of the project and the extra expense in hiring another contractor. Performance bonds are especially important in the construction industry where a large number of construction firms fail each year.

A *payment bond* guarantees that the bills for labor and materials used in building the project will be paid by the contractor when the bills are due.

A *maintenance bond* guarantees that poor workmanship by the principal will be corrected, or defective materials will be replaced. This maintenance guarantee is often included in a performance bond for one year without additional charge.

Exhibit 15.3 compares the various types of contract bonds.

License and Permit Bonds These types of bonds are commonly required of persons who must obtain a license or permit from a city or town before they can engage in certain activities. A **license and permit bond** *guarantees that the person bonded will comply with all laws and regulations that govern his or her activities.* For example, a liquor store owner may post a bond guaranteeing that liquor will be sold according to the law. A plumber or electrician may post a bond guaranteeing that the work performed will comply with the local building code.

Public Official Bonds This type of bond is usually required by law for public officials who are elected or appointed to public office. A **public official bond** *guarantees that public officials will faithfully perform their duties for the protection of the public.* For example, a state treasurer must comply with state law governing the deposit of public funds.

Judicial Bonds Judicial bonds *guarantee that the party bonded will fulfill certain obligations specified by law.* There are several types of judicial bonds. A **fiduciary bond** guarantees that the person who is responsible for the property of another will faithfully perform all required duties, give an accounting of all property, and make up any deficiency for which the courts hold the fiduciary liable. For example, administrators of estates, receivers or liquidators, or guardians of minor children may be required to post a bond guaranteeing their performance.

A **court bond** is designed to protect one person (obligee) against loss in the event that the person bonded does not prove that he or she is legally entitled to the remedy sought against the obligee. For example, an **attachment bond** guarantees that if the court rules against the plaintiff who has attached the property of the defendant in a lawsuit, the defendant will be reimbursed for damages as a result of having the property attached.

Finally, a **bail bond** is another type of court bond. If the bonded person fails to appear in court at the appointed time, the entire bond is forfeited.

Federal Surety Bonds These bonds are required by federal agencies that regulate the actions of business firms such as manufacturers, wholesalers, and large

Exhibit 15.3
Comparison of Contract Bonds

	Obligee	Principal	Guarantee
Bid Bond	The owner of the party calling for the bid	The bidder	The bidder will enter into the contract and provide a performance bond if the bid is accepted.
Performance Bond	The property owner or the party having the work done	The contractor	The contract will be performed by the contractor according to plans and specifications.
Payment Bond	Same as performance bond	The contractor	The project will be free of liens—that is, certain bills for labor and materials will be paid.
Maintenance Bond	Same as performance bond	The contractor	The work will be free from defects in materials and workmanship for a specified period.

Source: Donald S. Malecki et al., *Commercial Liability Insurance and Risk Management*, 3rd ed., vol. 2 (Malvern, PA: American Institute for CPCU, 1996), p. 209.

import firms. A **federal surety bond** *guarantees that the bonded party will comply with federal standards.* The bond also guarantees the payment of taxes or duties that accrue if the bonded party fails to pay.

Miscellaneous Surety Bonds This category consists of bonds that cannot be classified in any other group. For example, an *auctioneer's bond* guarantees the accounting of sales proceeds by an auctioneer; a *lost-instrument bond* guarantees the obligee against loss if the original instrument (such as a lost stock certificate) shows up later in the possession of another party; and an *insurance agent bond* indemnifies an insurer for any penalties that result from the unlawful acts of agents.

CASE APPLICATION

The ISO commercial crime coverage form can be used to insure specific crime exposures of most business firms. Assume that you are a risk management consultant. For each of the following losses, identify an appropriate insuring agreement that would have covered the loss.

a. Jennifer owns a restaurant and is taking the daily cash receipts to the bank. While walking to her car, she is confronted by a person with a gun and is told to hand over the cash. Fearing for her life, she surrenders the money.

b. Travis owns a large supermarket. When the store was closed, a burglar broke into a locked safe and stole several thousand dollars.

c. Rebecca is a cashier at a 24-hour convenience store. In the early morning, a drug addict confronts her with a knife and threatens her with bodily harm if she does not give him all the cash in the cash drawer.

d. Alan is executive director of Day Watch, a nonprofit organization that provides day care to the homeless. Three employees have access to the cash that the shelter receives from charitable donations. One employee disappeared for several weeks. Alan discovered that the employee had stolen a substantial amount of cash.

e. Josh sells merchandise over the Internet. Josh is concerned that a thief might break into his business computer and transfer company funds to a fictitious person.

SUMMARY

- *Theft* is the unlawful taking of money, securities, or other property to the deprivation of the insured. Robbery and burglary are forms of theft.

- *Robbery* is the unlawful taking of property from the care and custody of a person by one who has (1) caused or threatened to cause that person bodily harm or (2) committed an obviously unlawful act witnessed by that person.

- *Safe burglary* is the unlawful taking of property from within a locked safe or vault by someone who unlawfully enters the safe or vault as evidenced by marks of forcible entry upon the exterior. The definition of safe burglary also includes the unlawful taking of a safe or vault from the premises.

- There are five basic ISO crime coverage forms and policies:

    Commercial Crime Coverage Form
    Commercial Crime Policy
    Government Crime Coverage Form
    Government Crime Policy
    Employee Theft and Forgery Policy

    Each crime coverage form or policy is written in two versions—a discovery version and a loss-sustained version.

- The *discovery form* covers losses that are discovered during the policy period or within 60 days after the policy's expiration date, regardless of when the loss occurred.

- The *loss-sustained form* covers losses that occur during the policy period and are discovered during the policy period or within one year after the policy expires.

- The commercial crime coverage form contains several insuring agreements. Firms can select one or more of the following coverages:

    Employee Theft
    Forgery or Alteration
    Inside the Premises—Theft of Money and
        Securities
    Inside the Premises—Robbery or Safe Burglary
    of Other Property
    Outside the Premises
    Computer Fraud
    Funds transfer fraud
    Money Orders and Counterfeit Currency

- *Loss sustained during prior insurance* is a provision by which the current policy provides coverage for a loss that occurred during the term of the prior policy but was discovered only after the discovery period under the prior policy had expired. The purpose is to enable an insured to change insurers without penalty. The provision applies only if there is no break in the continuity of coverage under both policies, and the loss is one that would have been covered by the current policy if it had been in force when the loss occurred.

- The financial institution bond is designed for banks and similar institutions. The following coverages are available:

    Insuring Agreement A—Fidelity
    Insuring Agreement B—On Premises
    Insuring Agreement C—In Transit
    Insuring Agreement D—Forgery or Alteration
    Insuring Agreement E—Securities
    Insuring Agreement F—Counterfeit Currency
    Coverage for Data Processing Organizations

- There are three parties to a surety bond. The *principal* is the party who agrees to perform certain obligations. The *obligee* is the party who receives the proceeds of the bond if the principal fails to perform. The *surety* (obligor) is the party who agrees to answer for the debt, default, or obligation of another.

- Surety bonds are similar to insurance contracts in that losses are expected. However, there are several major differences between surety bonds and insurance.

    There are two parties to an insurance contract; there are three parties to a surety bond.

    The insurer expects to pay losses; the surety theoretically expects no losses to occur.

    The insurer normally does not have the right to recover a loss payment from an insured; the surety has the right to recover from a defaulting principal.

    Insurance covers unintentional losses outside of the insured's control; the surety guarantees the principal's character and ability to perform, which are within the principal's control.

- Surety bonds guarantee the performance of the principal. They include various contract bonds, license and permit bonds, public official bonds, judicial bonds, federal surety bonds, and miscellaneous surety bonds.

KEY CONCEPTS AND TERMS

Attachment bond
Bail bond
Cancellation as to any employee
Commercial crime coverage form
Contract bond
Court bond
Discovery form
Federal surety bond
Fidelity coverage
Fiduciary bond
Financial institution bond
Inside the premises—theft of money and securities
Inside the premises—robbery or burglary of other property
Judicial bonds
License and permit bonds
Loss-sustained form
Loss sustained during prior insurance
Obligee
Other property
Outside the premises
Performance bond
Principal
Public official bond
Retroactive date endorsement
Robbery
Safe burglary
Surety bonds
Surety (obligor)
Theft

REVIEW QUESTIONS

1. Define robbery, safe burglary, and theft.

2. Briefly describe the following insuring agreements in the commercial crime coverage form:
   a. Employee theft
   b. Forgery or alteration
   c. Inside the premises—theft of money and securities
   d. Inside the premises—robbery or safe burglary of other property
   e. Outside the premises

3. a. Explain the difference between a discovery form and a loss-sustained form.
   b. What is the purpose of the retroactive date endorsement that might be attached to a policy written on a discovery basis?

4. Identify the major exclusions in the commercial crime coverage form.

5. An important policy provision is called *cancellation as to any employee*. Explain the meaning of this provision.

6. When commercial crime insurance is written on a loss-sustained basis, the policy contains a provision called *loss sustained during prior insurance*. Explain the meaning of this provision.

7. Briefly describe the following insuring agreements that appear in a financial institutions bond.
   a. Fidelity coverage
   b. On premises coverage
   c. In transit coverage
   d. Forgery or alteration

8. Identify the three parties to a surety bond.

9. How do surety bonds differ from insurance contracts?

10. Identify three types of surety bonds and give an example where each can be used.

APPLICATION QUESTIONS

1. Patrick is the owner of a liquor store that is insured under an ISO commercial crime coverage form with the following insuring agreements:
   - Employee Theft
   - Inside the Premises—Theft of Money and Securities
   - Inside the Premises—Robbery or Safe Burglary of Other Property
   - Outside the Premises

   For each of the following losses, indicate whether any of the above insuring agreements would cover the loss. Explain your answer.
   a. Patrick withdrew money from a bank on a Friday afternoon to cash the payroll checks of customers over the weekend. He drove back to the liquor store and parked his car in the store's parking lot. As he was walking toward the liquor store, he was robbed of the cash at gunpoint.
   b. A television surveillance tape revealed that a newly hired employee was stealing money from the cash register.
   c. Patrick suspected that one employee was taking liquor from the stock of inventory without paying. A physical inventory revealed a shortage of five cases of Canadian whiskey.
   d. A burglar forced open a locked safe and money inside the safe was taken. Also, the interior of the store was badly damaged in the burglary.
   e. Because of the burglary, the business was closed for two days. Patrick's sales receipts for the week were substantially reduced.
   f. A robber threatened a cashier with a knife and demanded the cash receipts. The cashier resisted paying and was severely cut and injured. The thief escaped with a substantial amount of cash.

g. A customer paid for merchandise by giving the cashier a $50 money order drawn on a commercial bank. When the money order was presented to the bank for payment, the bank refused to pay because the money order had been stolen.

2. Kathy owns a large retail electrical store that sells light fixtures, lamps, and electrical equipment. The firm is not insured for employee theft. A risk management consultant recommended adding an ISO commercial crime coverage form to the firm's package policy, including coverage for employee theft. The crime form was issued on a *discovery basis* on July 1, 2004, without a retroactive date endorsement. The coverage amount for employee theft is $25,000. A routine audit in December 2004 by an accounting firm revealed that one of the bookkeepers had embezzled $20,000 over a three-month period in 2002.
   a. What dollar amount, if any, will the insurer pay for the loss?
   b. Would your answer to part (a) be the same or different if the crime coverage form were issued on a loss-sustained basis? Explain.

3. Richard owns several retail stores. The employees are insured for employee theft under a commercial crime coverage form with an insurance limit of $10,000. Richard discovered that Vera, a long-time accountant, had embezzled $5000 from the firm to pay the gambling debts of her son, who had been threatened with bodily harm. Vera agreed to repay the firm, and the embezzlement was not reported to the insurer. Several months later, Vera stole $3000 from the company's cash receipts and then disappeared. What is the liability of the insurer, if any for the preceding losses? Explain your answer.

4. Vasquez Construction has been awarded a contract by a local school board to build a new public school and must provide a performance bond.
   a. With respect to the performance bond, identify the principal, surety, and obligee.
   b. If Vasquez Construction fails to complete the building according to the terms of the contract, what would be the surety's obligation?
   c. Does the surety have any recourse against Vasquez Construction in this example? Explain your answer.

INTERNET RESOURCES

■ The **Coalition Against Insurance Fraud** is an alliance of consumer, law enforcement, and insurance industry groups that attempts to reduce all types of insurance fraud by public advocacy and education. Visit the site at
http://www.insurancefraud.org

■ The **Insurance Committee for Arson Control** is an industry group that works to increase public awareness of arson and what can be done to reduce the arson problem. The organization also helps insurers recognize arson-prone risks and resist payment of fraudulent arson claims. Visit the site at
http://www.arsoncontrol.org

■ The **National Association of Surety Bond Producers** is a trade association of surety bond producers. Visit the site at
http://www.nasbp.org

■ The **National Insurance Crime Bureau** is a nonprofit organization dedicated to combating crime and vehicle theft. Visit the site at
http://www.nicb.org

■ The **Surety Association of America** is a statistical, rating, development, and advisory organization for surety companies. Visit the site at
http://www.surety.org

■ The **Surety Information Office** is a source of information about contract surety bonds. Visit the site at
http://www.sio.org

SELECTED REFERENCES

Fire, Casualty & Surety Bulletins. Casualty and Surety volume, Crime section and Surety section. Erlanger, KY: National Underwriter Company. The bulletins are updated monthly. Detailed information on commercial crime insurance and surety bonds can be found in this volume.

Flinter, Arthur L., and Jerome Trupin. *Commercial Insurance,* First Edition. Malvern, PA: American Institute for Chartered Property Casualty Underwriters/Insurance Institute of America, 2002, Ch. 5.

Trupin, Jerome, and Arthur L. Flitner. *Commercial Property Insurance and Risk Management,* 6th ed., vol. 2. Malvern, PA: American Institute for Chartered Property Casualty Underwriters/Insurance Institute of America, 2001, chs. 11, 12, 15.

NOTES

1. The commercial crime coverages discussed in this chapter are based on Arthur L. Flitner and Jerome Trupin, *Commercial Insurance,* First Edition (Malvern, PA: American Institute for Chartered Property Casualty Underwriters/Insurance Institute of America, 2002), Ch. 5; Jerome Trupin and Arthur L. Flitner, *Commercial Property Insurance and Risk Management,* 6th ed., vol. 2 (Malvern, PA: American Institute for Chartered Property Casualty Underwriters/Insurance Institute of America, 2001), chs. 11, 12; and *Fire, Casualty & Surety Bulletins,* Casualty and Surety volume, Crime section and Surety section (Erlanger, KY: National Underwriter Company). The author also drew on the copyrighted commercial crime coverage forms and contractual provisions of the Insurance Services Office (ISO). The material is used with the permission of the Insurance Services Office.

2. Trupin and Flitner, p. 11.15.

3. Trupin and Flitner, pp. 11.39, 11.40.

4. The discussion of financial institution bonds is based on *Fire, Casualty & Surety Bulletins,* Casualty and Surety volume, Financial Institutions section (Erlanger, KY: National Underwriter Company). The author also drew on the Standard Form No. 24 (revised to January, 1986), Financial Institution Bond, the Surety Association of America, for purposes of discussing relevant contractual provisions.

5. Discussion of surety bonds is based on *Fire, Casualty & Surety Bulletins,* Casualty and Surety volume, Surety section (Erlanger, KY: National Underwriter Company).

Students may take a self-administered test on this chapter at
www.aw-bc.com/rejda

PART FIVE
LIFE AND HEALTH RISKS

CHAPTER 16

FUNDAMENTALS OF LIFE INSURANCE

"My idea of walking into the jaws of death is marrying some woman who's lost three husbands."

Kin Hubbard

LEARNING OBJECTIVES

After studying this chapter, you should be able to

◆ Explain the meaning of premature death.

◆ Describe the financial impact of premature death on different types of families.

◆ Explain the needs approach for estimating the amount of life insurance to own.

◆ Explain the yearly renewable term method for providing life insurance protection.

◆ Show how the level-premium method can provide lifetime insurance protection.

*T*odd and Susan are married and have two preschool children. Todd earns $35,000 annually as an accountant. Susan earns $20,000 annually as a part-time school nurse. Both incomes are needed to maintain their present standard of living. The couple has little savings. Late one evening, an uninsured drunk driver ran a red light and smashed into Todd's car killing him instantly. Todd had only $50,000 of life insurance on his life. Can the family survive on the $50,000 left to them? Probably not. Although Social Security survivor benefits are payable, the monthly cash payments are not large enough to replace his earnings. In addition, other financial factors must be considered, such as payment of funeral expenses, the remaining mortgage balance, car loans, credit card debts, and funding the children's college education. Clearly, $50,000 will not go far. Todd's untimely and unexpected death will create financial insecurity for the surviving family members.

This chapter discusses the risk of premature death and how life insurance can alleviate the financial consequences of premature death. Topics discussed include the meaning of premature death, the financial impact of premature death on the different types of families, and an analysis of the various methods for estimating the amount of life insurance to own. The chapter concludes with a discussion of the basic methods for providing life insurance to an individual, which include the yearly renewable term method and the level-premium method.

PREMATURE DEATH

Meaning of Premature Death

Premature death *can be defined as the death of a family head with outstanding unfulfilled financial obligations,* such as dependents to support, children to educate, and a mortgage to pay off. Premature death can cause serious financial problems for the surviving family members because their share of the deceased breadwinner's earnings is lost forever. If replacement income from other sources is inadequate, or if the accumulated financial assets available to the family are also inadequate, the surviving family members will be exposed to great financial insecurity.

Costs of Premature Death

As stated in Chapter 1, certain costs are associated with premature death. These costs are worth repeating. First, the family's share of the deceased bread-

winner's earnings is lost forever. Second, additional expenses are incurred because of funeral expenses, uninsured medical bills, estate settlement costs, and federal estate taxes for large estates. Third, because of insufficient income, some families will experience a reduction in their standard of living (see Insight 16.1). Finally, certain noneconomic costs are incurred, such as emotional grief, loss of a parental role model, and counseling and guidance for the children.

Chances of Dying Prematurely

The problem of premature death has declined over time due to significant breakthroughs in medical science, improvements in health because of economic growth and higher real incomes, and improvements in public health and sanitation. As a result, life expectancy has increased over the past century (See Exhibit 16.1). Life expectancy is the average total number of years that a person can expect to live.

INSIGHT 16.1

Get Life Insurance—Before It's Too Late

Dear Ann Landers: I am a 43-year-old widow with two children, 10 and 11 years of age. My husband passed away due to a sudden seizure. He was only 37. Although "Tom" made a good living, we were just getting by and never managed to save anything. The only life insurance Tom had was through his work and that wasn't much. When he died, I received benefits for one year. After paying the funeral expenses and outstanding debts, there was nothing left.

Tom and I had discussed life insurance and decided it was something we could not afford at the time, so we waited. Now, it is too late. And it isn't only life insurance: If only we had paid out an extra $15 a month for insurance on our mortgage, it would have paid off the house. A few extra dollars on our auto loan would have paid off our car.

My children and I get by on Social Security benefits, which is a lot less than what Tom was earning. I wish I could

be a stay-at-home mom, but that's not possible. I have to work. Because of the Social Security benefits, I am allowed to make only a specified amount of money per year. *Our total income is less than half of what it was. It is difficult to explain to two young children why we have to cut back on so many things.* I am doing everything I can to hold on to our home so that when the children are ready for college, I can sell it and pay their tuition.

My message to your readers is, HAVE LIFE INSURANCE. All the "if onlys" in the world won't help if you don't. My Tom was 37 years old. It can happen anytime, anywhere to anyone.

—Finding My Way in Tampa, Fla.

SOURCE: Adapted from Ann Landers, "Get Life Insurance—Before It's Too Late," *Lincoln Journal Star*, October 1, 1999.

Thus, a female baby born today with a life expectancy of 80 years has a 50 percent chance that she will die before age 80 and a 50 percent chance that she will still be alive beyond age 80.

A recent report shows that life expectancy in 2001 climbed to an all-time high of 77.2 years and

increased for both males and females and for blacks and whites as well (see Insight 16.2). Although life expectancy has increased, large numbers of Americans still die each year from three major causes of death—heart disease, cancer, and strokes.

EXHIBIT **16.1**
Improvements in Life Expectancy over the Past Century

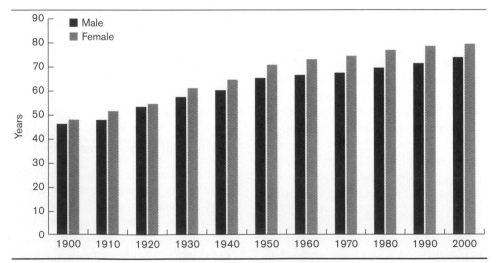

SOURCE: TIAA-CREFF Institute, "Trends in Longevity and Retirement Planning," *Quarterly* (Summer 2003), p. 2.

INSIGHT 16.2

New Study Finds Life Expectancy in the U.S. Hits New High

American's life expectancy hit an all-time high in 2001, while age-adjusted deaths hit an all-time low, according to a new report released by HHS Secretary Tommy G. Thompson.

The report from HHS' Centers for Disease Control and Prevention (CDC) documents that the national age-adjusted death rate decreased slightly from 869 deaths per 100,000 population in 2000 to 855 deaths per 100,000 in 2001. There were declines in mortality among most racial, ethnic, and gender groups.

Meanwhile, life expectancy hit a new high of 77.2 years in 2001, up from 77 in 2000, and increased for both men and women as well as whites and blacks. For men, life expectancy increased from 74.3 years in 2000 to 74.4 years in 2001; for women, life expectancy increased from 79.7 years to 79.8 years. Record high life expectancies were observed for white men and for both black men and women.

"This report highlights some encouraging progress, including a continued reduction in death rates from the Nation's three leading killers—heart disease, cancer, and stroke," Secretary Thompson said. "At the same time, it reminds us that we need to do more to reduce the health disparities that disproportionately affect certain racial and ethnic groups."

It includes a new sub-category for homicide—deaths from terrorism—that was added as a result of the September 11 attacks. Although the overall U.S. homicide rate increased nearly 17 percent between 2000 and 2001, the increase is attributable entirely to the murders resulting from the September 11 attacks on America. In fact, nonterrorism homicide rates actually declined slightly between 2000 and 2001.

Among leading causes of death, there were declines in mortality from heart disease (nearly 4 percent), cancer (2 percent), stroke (nearly 5 percent), and accidents/unintentional injuries (nearly 2 percent). The biggest decline in mortality among leading causes of death was for influenza/pneumonia (more than 7 percent).

The age-adjusted death rate from HIV/AIDS declined nearly 4 percent between 2000 and 2001, a bigger decline than the year before and continuing a trend that has occurred since 1995. Over this 6-year period, mortality from HIV has declined nearly 70 percent after increasing over 191 percent between 1987 and 1994.

However, HIV remains the sixth leading cause of death for people ages 25–44, and a leading cause of death among African-Americans in this age group.

"People with HIV are living longer, no question about it, and that is something we're very pleased about," said CDC Director Julie Gerberding. "However, much remains unclear. What is the long-term efficacy of anti-AIDS drugs, for example? Also, since new HIV infections continue to occur, we must remain focused on HIV prevention and keep positive trends in perspective."

SOURCE: Adapted from National Center for Health Statistics, "HHS Study Finds Life Expectancy in the U.S. Rose to 77.2 Years in 2001, Annual Mortality Report Also Includes New Category for Terrorism Homicide" *HHS News*, March 14, 2003.

Although heart disease is a leading cause of death, cardiovascular death rates have plummeted in recent years. This decline is due largely to a reduction in cigarette smoking, better control of blood pressure, decreases in cholesterol levels, and improved medical treatments for heart attacks and strokes.

Economic Justification of Life Insurance

The purchase of life insurance is economically justified if the insured earns an income, and others are dependent on that earning capacity for at least part of their financial support. If the breadwinner dies prematurely, life insurance can be used to restore the family's share of the deceased breadwinner's earnings.

It should also be noted that a life insurance policy is a valued policy that pays a stated sum to a named beneficiary and is not a contract of indemnity. *The insured event is the uncertainty of the time of death.* We must all die, but the time of death is uncertain.

As stated earlier, a family head may die with outstanding financial obligations and dependents to support, which may result in financial insecurity for the surviving dependents. However, the financial impact of premature death of the breadwinner is not uniform but depends on the type of family in which the breadwinner dies.

FINANCIAL IMPACT OF PREMATURE DEATH ON DIFFERENT TYPES OF FAMILIES

The composition of the family has changed significantly over time. As a result, premature death has a more severe financial impact on certain types of families than on others. The major types of families in the United States can be classified as follows:

- Single people
- Single-parent families
- Two-income earners
- Traditional families
- Blended families
- Sandwiched families

Single People

The number of single people has increased in recent years. Younger adults are postponing marriage, often beyond age 30, and many young and middle-aged adults are single again because of divorce.

Premature death of a single person who has no dependents to support or outstanding financial obligations is not likely to create a financial problem for others. Other than needing a modest amount of life insurance for burial purposes and uninsured medical bills, this group does not need large amounts of life insurance.

Single-Parent Families

The number of single-parent families with children under age 18 has increased in recent years because of the large number of children born outside of marriage, divorce, legal separation, and death. Premature death of the family head in a single-parent family can cause great financial insecurity for the surviving children. *The need for large amounts of life insurance on the family head is great.* However, many single-parent families, especially families with female heads, have incomes below the poverty line, and their ability to purchase large amounts of life insurance is limited.

Two-Income Earners

Families in which both spouses work outside the home have largely replaced the traditional family in which only one spouse is in the paid labor force.

Both incomes are necessary to maintain the family's standard of living. In two-income families with dependent children, the premature death of one income earner can cause considerable financial insecurity because both incomes are normally needed to maintain the family's standard of living. *Both income earners need substantial amounts of life insurance on their lives.* The life insurance can replace the lost earnings if one family head dies prematurely.

However, in two-income families without children, premature death of one income earner is not likely to cause economic insecurity for the surviving spouse. The surviving spouse is already in the workforce and is earning an income. In addition, career couples without children do not have to pay child-care costs or college education costs. The need for large amounts of life insurance by income earners within this group is considerably less.

Traditional Families

Traditional families are families in which only one parent is in the labor force, and the other parent stays at home to take care of dependent children. Premature death can cause great financial insecurity in families with dependent children in which only one parent is in the paid labor force. *The working parent in the labor force needs substantial amounts of life insurance.* If the working spouse dies with an insufficient amount of life insurance, the family may have to adjust its standard of living downward.

In addition, the nonemployed spouse who is caring for the dependent children also needs life insurance. The cost of hiring child care services can be a heavy financial burden to the surviving working spouse if the nonemployed spouse should die.

Blended Families

A blended family is one in which a divorced person, widow, or widower with children remarries, and the new spouse also has children. Premature death of a working spouse in a blended family can cause great financial insecurity. *The need for life insurance on both family heads within this group is great.* Both spouses may be in the labor force at the time of remarriage. The death of one spouse may result in a reduction in the family's standard of living since the family's share of that income is lost.

Sandwiched Families

A sandwiched family is one in which a son or daughter with children provides financial support or other services to one or both parents. Thus, the son or daughter is "sandwiched" between the younger and older generations. Premature death of a working spouse in a sandwiched family can result in the loss of financial support to both the surviving children and aged parent(s). *A working spouse in a sandwiched family needs a substantial amount of life insurance.*

AMOUNT OF LIFE INSURANCE TO OWN

Once you determine that you need life insurance, the next step is to calculate the correct amount of life insurance to own. In 2000, the average amount of life insurance coverage per insured household was only $196,200, which represents only 35 months of disposable personal income per insured household.[1] The correct amount of life insurance to own, however, is an individual matter, because family needs and financial goals vary widely. Some life insurers and financial planners have proposed certain arbitrary rules for determining the amount of life insurance to own, such as six to ten times annual earnings. These rules are meaningless, however, because they do not take into account that family size, income, financial goals, and needs vary from family to family.

Three approaches can be used to estimate the amount of life insurance to own:

- Human life value approach
- Needs approach
- Capital retention approach

Human Life Value Approach

As noted earlier, the family's share of the deceased breadwinner's earnings is lost forever if the family head dies prematurely. This loss is called the human life value. **Human life value** *can be defined as the present value of the family's share of the deceased breadwinner's future earnings*. It can be calculated by the following steps:

1. Estimate the individual's average annual earnings over his or her productive lifetime.

2. Deduct federal and state income taxes, Social Security taxes, life and health insurance premiums, and the costs of self-maintenance. The remaining amount is used to support the family.
3. Determine the number of years from the person's present age to the contemplated age of retirement.
4. Using a reasonable discount rate, determine the present value of the family's share of earnings for the period determined in step 3.

For example, assume that Josh, age 25, is married and has two children. He earns $25,000 annually and plans to retire at age 65. (For the sake of simplicity, assume that his earnings remain constant.) Of this amount, $10,000 is used for federal and state taxes, life and health insurance, and Josh 's personal needs. The remaining $15,000 is used to support his family. This stream of future income is then discounted back to the present to determine Josh's human life value. Using a reasonable discount rate of 6 percent, the present value of $1 payable annually for 40 years is $15.05. Therefore, Josh has a human life value of $225,750 ($15,000 × $15.05 = $225,750). This amount represents the present value of the family's share of Josh's earnings that would be lost if he should die prematurely. As you can see, the human life has an enormous economic value when earning capacity is considered. The major advantage of the human life value concept is that it crudely measures the economic value of a human life.

However, the human life value approach has several limitations as a tool for determining the amount of life insurance to own. First, other sources of income are ignored, such as Social Security survivor benefits. Second, in its simplest form, work earnings and expenses are assumed to be constant, and employee benefits are ignored. Third, the amount of money allocated to the family can quickly change because of divorce, birth of a child, or death of a family member. Also, the long run discount rate is critical; the human life value can be substantially increased by assuming a lower rate. Finally, the effects of inflation on earnings and expenses are ignored.

Needs Approach

The second method for estimating the amount of life insurance to own is the **needs approach.** The various family needs that must be met if the family head should die are analyzed, and the amount of money needed to meet these needs is determined. The total amount of existing life insurance and financial assets is then subtracted from the total amount needed. The difference, if any, is the amount of new life insurance that should be purchased. The most important family needs are the following:

- Estate clearance fund
- Income during the readjustment period
- Income during the dependency period
- Life income to the surviving spouse
- Special needs
  - Mortgage redemption fund
  - Educational fund
  - Emergency fund
- Retirement needs

Estate Clearance Fund An **estate clearance fund** or cleanup fund is needed immediately when the family head dies. Immediate cash is needed for burial expenses; uninsured medical bills; installment debts; estate administration expenses; and estate, inheritance, and income taxes.

Income During the Readjustment Period The **readjustment period** is a one- or two-year period following the breadwinner's death. During this period, the family should receive approximately the same amount of income received while the family head was alive. The purpose of the readjustment period is to give the family time to adjust its living standard to a different level.

Income During the Dependency Period The **dependency period** follows the readjustment period; it is the period until the youngest child reaches age 18. The family should receive income during this period so that the surviving spouse can remain at home, if necessary, to care for the children. The income needed during the dependency period is substantially reduced if the surviving spouse is already in the labor force and plans to continue working.

Life Income to the Surviving Spouse Another important need is to provide life income to the surviving spouse, especially if he or she is older and has been out of the labor force for many years. Two

income periods must be considered: (1) income during the blackout period, and (2) income to supplement Social Security benefits after the blackout period. The **blackout period** *refers to the period from the time that Social Security survivor benefits terminate to the time the benefits are resumed.* Social Security benefits to a surviving spouse terminate when the youngest child reaches age 16 and start again when the spouse attains age 60.

If a surviving spouse has a career and is already in the labor force, the need for life income is greatly reduced or even eliminated. However, this conclusion is not true for an older spouse under age 60 who has been out of the labor force for years, and for whom Social Security survivor benefits have temporarily terminated. The need for income during the blackout period is especially important for this group.

Special Needs Families should also consider certain special needs, including a mortgage redemption fund, an educational fund, and an emergency fund.

- *Mortgage redemption fund*. It is often desirable to provide the family with a mortgage-free home. The amount of monthly income needed by surviving family members is greatly reduced when monthly mortgage payments or rent payments are not required.
- *Educational fund*. The family head may wish to provide an educational fund for the children. If the children plan to attend a private college or university, the cost will be considerably higher than at a public institution.
- *Emergency fund*. A family should also have an emergency fund. An unexpected event may occur that requires large amounts of cash, such as major dental work, home repairs, or a new car.

Retirement Needs Because the family head may survive to retirement, a family should consider the need for adequate retirement income. Most retired workers are eligible for Social Security retirement benefits and may also be eligible for retirement benefits from an employer. If retirement income from these sources is inadequate, you can obtain additional income from cash-value life insurance, individual investments, a retirement annuity, or an individual retirement account (IRA). We will discuss retirement products in Chapter 20.

Exhibit 16.2
How Much Life Insurance Do You Need?

What You Will Need	Jennifer Smith		Your Needs	
Cash needs				
Funeral costs	$ 10,000		$	
Uninsured medical bills	3,000			
Installment debts	12,000			
Probate costs	3,000			
Federal estate taxes	0			
State inheritance taxes	0			
Total estate clearance fund		$ 28,000		$
Income needs				
Readjustment period	14,400			
Dependency period	108,000			
Life income to surviving spouse	0			
Retirement income	0			
Total income needs		$ 122,400		$
Special needs				
Mortgage redemption fund	110,000			
Emergency fund	25,000			
College education fund	100,000			
Total special needs		$ 235,000		$
Total needs		$ 385,400		$

What You Have Today	Jennifer Smith		Your Assets	
Checking account and savings	$ 10,000		$	
Mutual funds and securities	25,000			
IRAs and Keogh plan	4,200			
Section 401(k) plan and employer savings plan	4,500			
Private pension death benefit	10,000			
Current life insurance	50,000			
Other financial assets	0			
Total assets		$ 103,700		$
Additional life insurance needed				
Total needs		$ 385,400		$
Less total assets		103,700		
Additional life insurance needed		**$ 281,700**		$

Illustration of the Needs Approach

Exhibit 16.2 provides a worksheet that you can use to determine the amount of life insurance you need. The first part of the worksheet shows the amount needed to meet your various cash needs, income needs, and special needs. The second part analyzes your present financial assets for meeting these needs. The final part determines the amount of additional life insurance needed, which is calculated by subtracting total assets from total needs. For example,

Jennifer and Scott Smith are married and have a son, age 1. Jennifer, age 33, earns $40,000 annually as a marketing analyst for a large oil company. Scott, age 35, earns $30,000 as an elementary school teacher. Jennifer would like her family to be financially secure if she dies prematurely.

Cash Needs   Jennifer estimates that her family will need at least $10,000 for funeral expenses. Although she is currently insured under a group health insurance plan, certain medical services are excluded, and she must pay an annual deductible and coinsurance charges. Thus, she estimates that the family will need $3000 for uninsured medical expenses. She is also making monthly payments on a car loan and credit card debts. Installment debts currently total $12,000. In addition, she estimates that the cost of probating her will and attorney fees will be $3000, and that no federal estate taxes will be payable.

Income Needs   Jennifer also wants to provide monthly income to her family during the readjustment and dependency periods until her son reaches age 18. Jennifer and Scott's net take-home pay is approximately $4000 each month. Jennifer believes that her family can maintain its present standard of living if it receives 75 percent of that amount, or $3000 monthly. Thus, she wants the family to receive $3000 monthly for 17 years during the readjustment and dependency periods.

The family's need for $3000 per month is reduced if other sources of income are available. Scott's net take-home pay is about $1800 monthly. In addition, Scott and his son are eligible for Social Security survivor benefits. Scott's benefits are payable until his son reaches age 16, whereas his son's benefits are payable until age 18. In this example, we assume that only the son will receive Social Security survivor benefits. Because Scott's earnings substantially exceed the maximum annual limit allowed under the Social Security earnings test, he will lose all of his Social Security survivor benefits. However, his son will continue to receive benefits until age 18. The Social Security Administration has prepared a simplified form that will give you an estimate of the Social Security survivor benefits payable if you should die. (Call 800-772-1213 for a form to determine your estimated benefits.) Jennifer's son will receive an estimated $600 each

month from Social Security until age 18. Thus, the family would receive a total of $2400 monthly from Scott's take-home pay and the son's Social Security benefit. Because their income goal is $3000 monthly, there is a monthly shortfall of $600. Jennifer's family needs an additional $14,400 to provide monthly income of $600 during the two-year readjustment period, and another $108,000 to provide monthly income for an additional 15 years during the dependency period. Thus, the family needs a total of $122,400 to meet the monthly goal of $3000 during the readjustment and dependency periods.

If Jennifer considers the time value of money, it will take less than $122,400 of life insurance to accomplished the desired income goal. Likewise, if she takes inflation into account, she must increase the amount of life insurance just to maintain the real purchasing power of the benefits. *However, she can ignore both present value and future inflation if she assumes that one offsets the other. Thus, in our example, we assume that the life insurance proceeds are invested at an interest rate equal to the rate of inflation.* Such an assumption builds into the program an automatic hedge against inflation that preserves the real purchasing power of the death benefit. In most cases, the death proceeds can be invested at a return exceeding the rate of inflation. The calculations are also simplified, and the use of present value tables and assumptions concerning future inflation rates are unnecessary.

In addition, Scott is currently in the labor force and plans to continue working if Jennifer should die. Thus, there is no need to provide additional income during the blackout period.

A final need to consider is retirement income. Scott will receive Social Security retirement benefits and a lifetime pension from the school district's retirement plan. He also has an individual retirement account (IRA) that will provide additional retirement income. Jennifer believes that Scott's total retirement income will be sufficient to meet his needs, so he does not need additional retirement income.

In summary, after considering Scott's take-home pay and Social Security survivor benefits, Jennifer determines that she will need an additional $122,400 to meet the income goal of $3000 monthly during the readjustment and dependency periods. Additional income during the blackout period is not needed.

Special Needs Jennifer would like the mortgage paid off if she should die; the current mortgage balance is $110,000. She also wants to establish an emergency fund of $25,000 for the family and an educational fund of $100,000 for her son. Thus, her special needs total $235,000.

Determining the Amount of New Life Insurance Needed After determining total family needs, the next step is to add up all financial assets that can be used to satisfy these needs. Jennifer has a checking account and personal savings in the amount of $10,000. She owns several mutual funds and individual stocks with a current market value of $25,000. She has an individual retirement account with a current balance of $4200, and $4500 in a Section 401(k) plan sponsored by her employer; a lump-sum pension benefit of $10,000 is also payable when she dies. She is insured for $40,000 under her employer's group life insurance plan, and she has an individual life insurance policy in the amount of $10,000. Total financial assets available upon her death are $103,700.

Total family needs are $385,400, but her current financial assets are only $103,700. Thus, Jennifer needs an additional $281,700 of life insurance to protect her family.

The major advantage of the needs approach is that it is a reasonably accurate method for determining the amount of life insurance to own when specific family needs are recognized. The needs approach also considers other sources of income and financial assets. The major disadvantage, however, is that future projections over the insured's lifetime require numerous assumptions and the use of a computer. Dynamic programming models with changing assumptions are complex and usually are not needed by the typical insured.

Capital Retention Approach

The **capital retention approach** (also called *capital needs analysis*) is another method for estimating the amount of life insurance to own. Unlike the needs approach, which assumes liquidation of the life insurance proceeds, the capital retention approach preserves the capital needed to provide income to

the family. The income-producing assets are then available for distribution later to the heirs.

The amount of life insurance needed based on the capital retention approach can be determined by the following steps:

- Prepare a personal balance sheet.
- Determine the amount of income-producing capital.
- Determine the amount of additional capital needed (if any).

Prepare a Personal Balance Sheet The first step is to prepare a personal balance sheet that lists all assets and liabilities. The balance sheet should include all death benefits from life insurance and from other sources. For example, Enrique, age 35, has a wife and two children, ages 3 and 5. Enrique earns $60,000 annually. If he should die, he wants his family to receive $30,000 annually. He also wants to establish an emergency fund and educational fund, and pay off the mortgage, auto loan, and charge accounts. Enrique's personal balance sheet, including death benefits from life insurance and his pension plan, is as follows:

Assets	
House	$125,000
Automobiles	15,000
Personal and household property	45,000
Securities and investments	28,000
Checking account	2,000
Individual and group life insurance	200,000
Private pension death benefit	20,000
Total	$435,000

Liabilities	
Mortgage	$100,000
Auto loan	10,000
Charge accounts and other bills	5,000
Total	$115,000

Determine the Amount of Income-Producing Capital The next step is to determine the amount of income-producing assets that can provide income to the family. This step is performed by subtracting the liabilities, cash needs, and non-income-producing capital from total assets. Enrique has $55,000 of capital that can produce income for the family. This situation is illustrated as follows:

Total assets		$435,000
Less:		
Mortgage payoff	$100,000	
Auto loan and credit card debts	15,000	
Final expenses	10,000	
Emergency fund	10,000	
Educational fund	60,000	
Non-income-producing capital (automobiles, personal and household property, value of home)	185,000	
Total deductions		−380,000
Capital now available for income		$ 55,000

In the preceding illustration, the home is not an income-producing asset. Unless the home is sold or rented, it ordinarily does not produce cash income for the family. Thus, the home is considered to be part of *non-income-producing capital* that is subtracted from total assets to arrive at the amount of liquid assets that can produce income for the family.

Determine the Amount of Additional Capital Needed

The final step is to determine the amount of additional capital (if any) that is needed. This step involves a comparison of the income objective with other sources of income, such as Social Security survivor benefits. In Enrique's case, his family would have an income shortage of $14,700 annually based on his present financial situation. Assuming the liquid assets and life insurance proceeds can be invested to earn 6 percent annually, Enrique needs an additional $245,000 of life insurance to meet his financial goals. This calculation is summarized as follows:

Income objective for family	$ 30,000
Less:	
Capital now available for income ($55,000 × 6%)	−3,300
Social Security survivor benefits	−12,000
Income shortage	$ 14,700
Total new capital required ($14,700/0.06)	$245,000

The capital retention approach has the advantages of simplicity, ease of understanding, and preservation of capital. In addition, investment income earned on the emergency and educational funds can be used as a partial hedge against inflation, or it can be accumulated to offset rising educational costs. The major disadvantage, however, is that a larger amount of life insurance is required to produce a given amount of income.

Interactive Calculators on the Internet

Many life insurers and premium quoting services have interactive calculators on their Web sites that calculate the amount of life insurance needed. You make assumptions about inflation, rates of return on the death proceeds, amount of income needed by the family, and other assumptions. However, the quality of the interactive calculators varies widely. Some calculators are extremely limited, and questions concerning the amount of accumulated assets and other sources of income are often ignored. Other calculators are more detailed and enable you to estimate more accurately the amount of life insurance needed, especially for special needs, such as estimated college expenses in a private or public university.

In addition, depending on the type of calculator used, the amount of life insurance needed varies widely. *One study of 11 calculators produced recommendations ranging from $73,329 to $3.8 million for a male family head, age 35, and from $0 to $2.3 million for his spouse the same age.*[2] However, despite their limitations, the interactive calculators are worth checking out as a first starting point for estimating the amount of life insurance needed.

Opportunity Cost of Buying Life Insurance

The previous discussion shows that most family heads generally need substantial amounts of life insurance on their lives. However, this conclusion must be qualified by considering the opportunity cost of purchasing life insurance. Opportunity cost refers to what the insured person gives up when life insurance premiums are paid. Since income is limited, the purchase of life insurance reduces the amount of discretionary income available for other high priority needs. Many families today are heavily in debt and have little savings. Monthly mortgage payments, car loans, credit cards debts, utility costs, food, clothing, and taxes absorb most or all of the family's disposable income. The children also may have special medical or dental needs that are expensive to provide. Parents with children in college have an additional financial burden because of the payment of college tuition and other costs. Moreover, saving for retirement reduces the amount available for new life insurance purchases. Thus, after payment of other high priority expenses, family heads often have only a limited amount of discretionary income available to purchase life insurance. *As a result, the optimal amounts of life insurance that should be purchased may not be possible.* However, as will be pointed out later, inexpensive term insurance can play an important role in providing financial security to those families with limited amounts of income to spend on life insurance.

Summary

As stated earlier, most families need substantial amounts of life insurance to prevent or reduce financial insecurity from premature death. Unfortunately, research studies show that many families are seriously underinsured. *One study showed that 26 percent of American households own no life insurance (see Insight 16.3).* Another study by LIMRA International reported that *45 percent of the widows and 37 percent of the widowers said that the life insurance on their spouse was inadequate.*[3]

A more recent study based on an economic life cycle model also underscores the problem of underinsurance. Using 1995 Survey of Consumer Finances (SCF) data, Gokhale and Kotlikoff compared the actual amount of life insurance owned by the households surveyed with the amount recommended by their life cycle model. Four groups of survivors were studied—wives, husbands, primary earners, and secondary earners. *The authors concluded that over 30 percent of the wives and almost a third of the secondary earners, most of whom are wives, would experience a severe (40% or greater) reduction in their standard of living if their spouse died without any insurance protection. Another one-fifth of the wives and one-fifth of the secondary earners would*

experience a significant (20% to 40%) decline in their standard of living if their spouse died.[4]

The reasons for underinsurance vary. Some family heads believe that life insurance costs too much. However, the cost of life insurance, especially term insurance, has declined dramatically in recent years, which many consumers fail to recognize. Other alleged reasons for underinsurance include a lack of understanding by households concerning the correct amount of life insurance to own; the assumption that interactive calculators accurately reflect the thinking of policyowners may be incorrect (for example, paying off the mortgage and all debts when the family head dies); and the preferences of households to spend the money needed to be fully insured on other things (such as taking a vacation instead of buying more life insurance).[5] This latter point, of course, reflects the opportunity cost of buying life insurance discussed earlier. It is clear that greater consumer education on the amount of life insurance to own is necessary.

METHODS FOR PROVIDING LIFE INSURANCE PROTECTION

Two basic methods can be used to provide life insurance to individuals: the yearly renewable term method and the level-premium method.[6]

Yearly Renewable Term Method

Yearly renewable term insurance *provides life insurance protection for only one year.* The insured is permitted to renew the policy for successive one-year periods with no evidence of insurability. That is, evidence of good health or a physical examination is not required when the policy is renewed.

The pure premium for yearly renewable term insurance is determined by the death rate at each attained age. For the sake of simplicity, interest and operating expenses of the insurer are ignored in this discussion. The insurance protection is for one year only, and individuals within the group must pay their pro rata share of death claims. Based on the Commissioners 1980 Standard Ordinary Table of Mortality, the death rate for males at age 30 is 1.73 for each 1000 lives. If 100,000 males, age 30, are insured for $1000 for one year, the insurance

INSIGHT 16.3

Life Insurance Study Reveals Crisis of Underinsurance

A study conducted by Roper Starch Worldwide and commissioned by the Life and Health Insurance Foundation for Education (LIFE) reveals that more than 25 million American households have no life insurance coverage. *Today, only 74 percent of all households own some form of life insurance, down from 83 percent in 1976.* Much of the drop is due to the continued decline in ownership of individual life insurance. For the first time, the proportion of households with group coverage now surpasses the percentage with individual coverage.

In addition, many households that have coverage appear to be underinsured. For instance, married people with a single income say that most households need five times the primary wage earner's income in life insurance, but they personally have only three times their income. Yet, even five times one's income may not be enough. While individual needs vary, most insurance professionals recommend life insurance coverage equal to seven to ten times a person's income.

"There's a real crisis of underinsurance in this country," said David F. Woods, president of *LIFE*. "This study underscores the fact that millions of people are exposing their families to potential financial hardship. If a parent or spouse were to die unexpectedly, how would these families continue to pay their mortgages and daily expenses, or put their children through college?"

According to the study, people who feel that their households are inadequately insured cite several reasons for not owning more life insurance.

The top reason is cost. "What a lot of consumers don't realize is that the cost of life insurance has actually gone down," said Woods. "With the variety of insurance products on the market today, price shouldn't be an obstacle when obtaining adequate coverage."

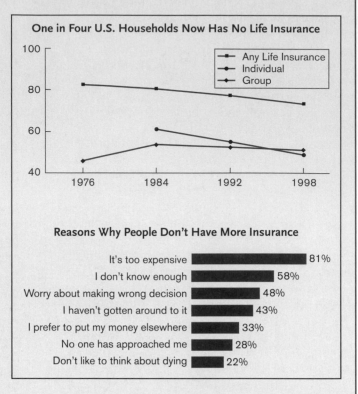

One in Four U.S. Households Now Has No Life Insurance

- Any Life Insurance
- Individual
- Group

Reasons Why People Don't Have More Insurance

It's too expensive	81%
I don't know enough	58%
Worry about making wrong decision	48%
I haven't gotten around to it	43%
I prefer to put my money elsewhere	33%
No one has approached me	28%
Don't like to think about dying	22%

The second most commonly cited reason for not having more insurance is a lack of knowledge. Almost 60 percent of people say that not knowing enough about insurance is a reason they haven't secured additional coverage for their households. Nearly half the public haven't purchased more insurance because they are worried about making a wrong decision, and 43 percent say they simply haven't gotten around to it.

SOURCE: Adapted from Society of Financial Service Professionals, "New LIFE Study Reveals Crisis of Underinsurance," *Society Page* (April 1999), pp. 22–23.

---

company must pay 173 death claims, or $173,000. If interest and expenses are ignored, each insured must pay a premium of $1.73 ($173,000/100,000 = $1.73). You will notice that the $1.73 in premiums is the same as the death rate at age 30. At age 31, the male death rate is 1.78 per 1000 lives. If the 99,827 survivors want the protection for another year, the insurer must pay 178 death claims, or $178,000. Each of the 99,827 insureds must pay

their pro rata share of the death claims, or $1.78 ($178,000/99,827 = $1.78). Finally, if the 99,649 survivors wish to insure their lives for another year, the insurer must pay $183,000 in death claims. Each insured's share of the total death claims would be $1.83 ($183,000/99,649 = 1.83).

You can see that the yearly renewable term insurance premium increases as the individual gets older. *The premium increase is gradual during the early years, but it rises sharply during the later years.* The following illustration shows the pure premiums for $1000 of yearly renewable term insurance for males at various attained ages. (Interest and expenses are again ignored.)

Age 30	$1.73
Age 40	$3.02
Age 50	$6.71
Age 60	$16.08
Age 70	$39.51
Age 80	$98.84

Because premiums increase with age, yearly renewable term insurance premiums eventually become prohibitive in cost, so some insureds may drop their insurance. The healthier members may drop their life insurance as the premiums increase, but the unhealthy persons will continue to renew their policies despite the premium increase. This situation leads to adverse selection against the insurer. The insurer may then have a disproportionate number of impaired lives in the group, which drives the death rate up even more.

You can see that under the yearly renewable method, the premiums are substantial at the older ages. Therefore, if the insured wants lifetime protection, the yearly renewable term method is impractical because the premiums are prohibitive in cost at the older ages. Some other method must be used to provide lifetime protection. This method is called the level-premium method.

Level-Premium Method

Under the **level-premium method,** premiums do not increase from year to year but remain level throughout the premium paying period, and the insured has lifetime protection to age 100. Under this method, premiums paid during the early years of the policy are higher than is necessary to pay current death claims, while those paid in the later years are inadequate for paying death claims. The redundant or excess premiums paid during the early years are invested at compound interest, and the accumulated funds are then used to supplement the inadequate premiums paid during the later years of the policy. Because the method of investing and accumulating the fund is regulated by state law, it is referred to as

a **legal reserve.** The legal reserve technically is a composite liability account of the insurer and should not be allocated to individual contracts. However, for our purposes, we can view the legal reserve as the aggregate of the individual accounts established for the individual policyowners.[7]

As stated earlier, under the level-premium method, premiums do not increase with age. *A level premium is possible because the excess premiums are invested at compound interest and are used to supplement the deficiency in premiums during the later years.* In contrast, under the yearly renewable term method, the premiums are very low during the early years but gradually increase to a point where they become prohibitive in cost. For this reason, lifetime protection cannot be provided to most insureds under the yearly renewable term method.

Fundamental Purpose of the Legal Reserve   The excess premiums paid during the early years are reflected in a legal reserve. The concept of a legal reserve can be illustrated in greater detail by Exhibit 16.3, which represents the legal reserve under an ordinary life policy. The legal reserve steadily increases over time and is equal to the face amount of the policy at age 100. If the insured is still alive at age 100, the face amount of the policy is paid to the policyowner at that time. *The difference between the face amount of the policy and the legal reserve is called the* **net amount at risk.** The net amount at risk represents the pure insurance portion of the policy. It declines over time as the legal reserve increases.

EXHIBIT 16.3

Relationship Between the Net Amount at Risk and Legal Reserve

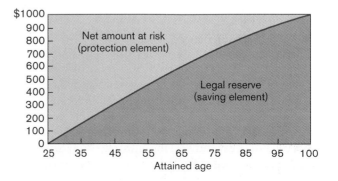

INSIGHT 16.4

New 2001 CSO Mortality Table

The National Association of Insurance Commissioners (NAIC) requested the Society of Actuaries (SOA) and the American Academy of Actuaries to construct a new mortality table for use in the current statutory valuation system. The SOA collected annual mortality data for 1990–1995 from 21 insurers that participated in the study. Supplemental data from other sources were also used, especially at the younger and older ages where mortality experience was scarce. The mortality experience was then projected to 2001 based on recent trends in mortality improvement. The actuaries also added an overall load of 15 percent as a mortality margin.

There are separate tables for smokers, nonsmokers, and a composite table that does not distinguish between smokers and nonsmokers for both males and females, for a total of six tables.

The 2001 CSO table reduces the statutory reserve requirements by approximately 20 percent. As a result, the

new table will have a significant impact on basic reserves and tax reserves on new policies sold and on nonforfeiture or cash surrender requirements as well. The new table will also affect the guideline premiums paid by policyowners and maximum charges by insurers for the cost of insurance. Another possible impact is more competitive term insurance rates.

As of August 14, 2003, three states had adopted the new table; another 21 states plan to adopt the table; and 11 states are considering adoption. The 2001 CSO table will be used as the minimum standard for all policies issued on or after January 1, 2009.

SOURCE: Adaptation of American Academy of Actuaries, *Report of the American Academy of Actuaries' Commissioners' Standard Ordinary Task Force, Presented to the National Association of Insurance Commissioners' Life and Health Actuarial Task Force*, Philadelphia, PA, June 2002.

Thus, from a conceptual standpoint, the death claim can be viewed as consisting of two elements: a legal reserve (saving element) and the net amount at risk (protection element).[8] As the legal reserve increases, the net amount at risk declines. *It follows that the fundamental purpose of the legal reserve is to provide lifetime protection.* As the death rate increases with age, the legal reserve also increases, and the net amount at risk declines, which produces a cost of insurance within practical limits.[9] Therefore, by the level-premium method, the insurer can provide the insured with lifetime protection.

Because the legal reserve is so important in providing lifetime protection, it is a liability item on an insurer's balance sheet. Insurers must calculate their minimum legal reserve liabilities for individual policies according to certain standards. In the past, the states required insurers to use the 1980 Commissioners Standard Ordinary (CSO) mortality table to value their legal reserves. However, because of the increase in life expectancy, the older 1980 CSO mortality table became outdated. As a result, actuaries have developed a new 2001 CSO mortality table, which will be used in the future to value legal reserves (see Insight 16.4).

Cash Values Cash values should not be confused with the legal reserve. Under the level-premium method, a legal reserve results. Because of the legal reserve, cash values become available. The policyowner may no longer want the insurance, and the policy can be surrendered for its cash surrender value. However, cash values and the legal reserve are not the same thing and are computed separately. Because of the loading for expenses and high first-year acquisition expenses, cash values are initially below the legal reserve. The policyowner, however, has the right to borrow the cash value or exercise one of the cash surrender options. Chapter 18 discusses the cash surrender options in greater detail.

You should also remember that cash values are the by-product of the level-premium method, not the purpose of it. The fundamental purpose of the level-premium method is to provide lifetime protection and not to build up a savings account in the form of cash values. This is not to say that an individual cannot save by purchasing cash-value life insurance. Indeed, in the aggregate, large amounts are annually saved by policyowners in the form of accumulated cash values. However, the savings feature is incidental to the fundamental goal of lifetime protection.

CASE APPLICATION 1

Scott, age 28, and Brenda, age 25, are married and have a daughter, age 3. Scott has the following cash and income needs:

Cash Needs

Estate clearance	$20,000
Mortgage redemption	90,000
Emergency fund	20,000
Education fund	50,000

Income Needs

Readjustment period	$2000 monthly
Dependency period	2000 monthly
Blackout period	1000 monthly

Brenda is employed outside the home. Her monthly net take-home pay is $1500 after taxes and other deductions. She plans to continue working if Scott should die.

Based on the assumption that the life insurance proceeds can be invested at a rate of interest equal to the rate of inflation, answer the following questions:

a. How much additional life insurance, if any, is needed to meet Scott's cash needs if his present life insurance and financial assets total $100,000?

b. Ignoring the availability of Social Security survivor benefits, how much additional life insurance, if any, is needed to provide the desired amount of income during the readjustment and dependency periods?

c. In the above example, how much additional life insurance, if any, is needed if Social Security survivor benefits of $500 monthly are paid to the child until age 18?

d. How much additional life insurance, if any, is needed to provide the desired amount of income during the blackout period if Brenda does not work outside the home?

CASE APPLICATION 2

Althea, age 35, is a registered nurse who earns $40,000 annually. She is married and has two children, ages 2 and 5. If she should die, she wants her family to receive $20,000 annually. She also wants to set up a final expense fund of $10,000, establish an educational fund of $100,000, and pay off the mortgage, automobile loan, and outstanding credit card balances. Her husband, Nicholas, is capable of supporting himself if she should die. Althea's personal balance sheet, including life insurance and a pension death benefit, is as follows:

Assets

Condominium	$150,000
Personal property	40,000
Two automobiles	18,000
Mutual funds	55,000
Checking account	2,000
Individual and group life insurance	180,000
Pension death benefit	15,000
Total	$460,000

Liabilities

Mortgage	$125,000
Auto loan	8,000
Credit card balance	2,000
Total	$135,000

Estimated Social Security survivor benefits are $12,080 annually. Assume that the life insurance proceeds and liquid funds can earn 6 percent annually. Using the capital retention method, calculate the amount of additional life insurance that Althea should purchase to attain her financial goals.

SUMMARY

- Premature death means that a family head dies with outstanding unfulfilled financial obligations, such as dependents to support, children to educate, or a mortgage to pay off. Great financial insecurity may result if a family head dies prematurely.

- At least four costs are associated with premature death:

    There is the loss of the human life value. The family's share of the deceased breadwinner's future income is lost forever.

    Additional expenses may be incurred, such as burial costs, expenses of the last illness, and probate and estate settlement costs.

    Because of insufficient income, some families may experience a reduction in their standard of living.

    Noneconomic costs are incurred, such as the emotional grief of the surviving dependents and the loss of a role model and guidance for the children.

- The purpose of life insurance can be economically justified if a person has an earning capacity, and someone is dependent on those earnings for at least part of his or her financial support.

- The financial impact of premature death on the family varies by family type. Premature death can cause considerable economic insecurity if a family head dies in a single-parent family, in a family with two-income earners with children, or in a traditional, blended, or sandwiched family. In contrast, if a single person without dependents or an income earner in a two-income family without children dies, financial problems for the survivors are unlikely.

- The human life value is defined as the present value of the family's share of the deceased breadwinner's future earnings. This approach crudely measures the economic value of a human life.

- The needs approach can be used to determine the amount of life insurance to own. After considering other sources of income and financial assets, the various family needs are converted into specific amounts of life insurance. The most important family needs are as follows:

    Estate clearance fund

    Income during the readjustment period

    Income during the dependency period

    Life income to the surviving spouse

    Special needs: mortgage redemption fund, education fund, emergency fund

    Retirement needs

- The capital retention approach for estimating the amount of life insurance to own is based on the assumption that income-producing capital will be preserved and not liquidated.

- Under the yearly renewable term method for paying premiums, life insurance protection is provided for one year only. The policy can be renewed for successive one-year periods with no evidence of insurability. The method is not suitable for lifetime protection because premiums increase with age until they reach prohibitively high levels.

- Under the level-premium method, premiums do not increase from year to year but remain level throughout the premium-paying period. The insured has lifetime protection to age 100. Under this method, premiums paid during the early years are higher than are necessary to pay current death claims. The excess premiums paid during the early years are invested and used to supplement the inadequate premiums paid during the later years.

- The legal reserve is a liability item for an insurer that reflects the excess premiums paid during the early years of the policy. It steadily increases until it reaches the face amount of the policy by age 100. The fundamental purpose of the legal reserve is to provide lifetime protection.

- Because a legal reserve is necessary for lifetime protection, cash values become available. However, cash values are the by-product of the level-premium method, not the purpose of it. Because the insured has paid more than is actuarially necessary during the early years of the policy, he or she should receive something back if the policy is surrendered.

KEY CONCEPTS AND TERMS

Blackout period
Capital retention approach
Cash values
Dependency period
Estate clearance fund
Human life value
Legal reserve
Level-premium method for paying premiums

Needs approach
Net amount at risk
Premature death
Readjustment period
Yearly renewable term insurance method for paying premiums

REVIEW QUESTIONS

1. a. Explain the economic justification for the purchase of life insurance.
   b. Explain the meaning of premature death.
   c. Identify the costs associated with premature death.

2. Explain the financial impact of premature death on the different types of families in the United States.

3. a. Define the human life value.
   b. Describe the steps in determining the human life value of a family need.

4. The needs approach is widely used for determining the amount of life insurance to purchase. Describe the following needs for a typical family head:
   a. Cash needs
   b. Income needs
   c. Special needs

5. Explain the capital retention approach for determining the amount of life insurance to own.

6. Explain why the yearly renewable term method for paying premiums is not appropriate for lifetime protection.

7. Explain how the level-premium method can provide lifetime protection to an insured.

8. What is the meaning of *net amount at risk?*

9. a. Why does a level-premium policy develop a legal reserve?
   b. Explain the fundamental purpose of a legal reserve.

10. Are cash values and the legal reserve the same thing? Explain your answer.

APPLICATION QUESTIONS

1. Richard, age 45, is married with two children in high school. He estimates that his average annual earnings over the next 20 years will be $60,000. He estimates that one-third of his average annual earnings will be used to pay taxes, insurance premiums, and the costs of self-maintenance. The remainder will be used to support his family. Richard wants to calculate his human life value and believes a 6 percent discount rate is appropriate. The present value of $1 payable for 20 years at a discount rate of 6 percent is $11.47. Calculate Richard's human life value.

2. a. The human life value is one method for estimating the amount of life insurance to own. Keeping all other factors unchanged, explain the effect, if any, of each of the following:
      (1) The discount rate used to calculate the human life value is increased.
      (2) The amount of average annual income going to the family is increased.
      (3) The period over which income is paid to the family is reduced.
   b. Explain the limitations of the human life value approach as a method for determining the amount of life insurance to own.

3. Kelly, age 32, is married and has a one-year old son. She earns $45,000 annually as a marketing analyst. Her employer provides group life insurance in the amount of twice the employee's salary. Kelly also participates in her employer's 401(k) plan. She has the following financial needs and objectives for her family if she should die:
   - Funeral costs and uninsured medical bills $10,000
   - Income support for her son   2,000
                                    monthly for 17 years
   - Pay off mortgage on home   150,000
   - Pay off car loan and credit card debts   15,000
   - College education fund for son   150,000

   Kelly has the following financial assets:
   - Checking account   2,000
   - IRA account   8,000
   - 401(k) plan   25,000
   - Individual life insurance   25,000
   - Group life insurance   90,000

   a. Ignoring the availability of Social Security survivor benefits, how much additional life insurance, if any, should Kelly purchase to meet her financial goals based on the needs approach? (Assume that the rate of return earned on the policy proceeds is equal to the rate of inflation.)
   b. How much additional life insurance, if any, is needed if estimated Social Security survivor benefits in the amount of $800 monthly are payable until her son attains age 18?

4. Shannon, age 35, is a single parent with a son, age 3. She earns $40,000 annually as the director of public relations at a local community college. After attending a public lecture on death and dying, she decides to purchase additional life insurance so that her son will be financially secure if she should die. Shannon's sister has agreed to be the legal guardian

for her son if Shannon should die. Shannon does not know how much life insurance to purchase. She has the following financial goals:

Pay funeral expenses	$10,000
Pay off credit card debts and car loan	15,000
Establish an educational fund for her son	100,000
Income support for the son paid to Shannon's sister as legal guardian monthly for 15 years	2,000

Shannon has little savings. However, she owns a $25,000 individual life insurance policy purchased by her parents and is also insured for $40,000 under the college's group life insurance plan. She also participates in the college's retirement plan and has an account balance of $30,000. Estimated Social Security survivor benefits are $700 monthly until Shannon's son attains age 18. Based on the needs approach, how much additional life insurance, if any, should Shannon purchase to attain her financial goals? (Assume that the rate of return earned on the policy proceeds is equal to the rate of inflation.)

5. Janet, age 28, is married and has a son, age 3. She wants to determine how much life insurance she should own based on the capital retention approach. She would like to provide $30,000 each year before taxes to her family if she should die. She owns a house jointly with her husband that has a current market value of $250,000 with a mortgage of $100,000. She also owes $16,000 on a car loan and credit cards. She would like to have the mortgage, car loan, and credit card debts paid off if she should die. She has no investments, and her checking account balance is only $1,000. She owns an individual life insurance policy in the amount of $100,000 that her parents purchased for her when she was a baby. Estimated Social Security survivor benefits are $10,000 annually. Janet assumes the life insurance proceeds can be invested at 5 percent interest. Based on the capital retention approach, how much additional life insurance, if any, should Janet purchase to meet her financial goals?

INTERNET RESOURCES

■ **A. M. Best Co.** is a major rating organization that rates the financial strength of insurance companies. The company also publishes periodicals, reports, and books

relating to the insurance industry, including *Best's Review*. This publication provides considerable information about life insurance products and the insurance industry. Visit the site at

http://www.ambest.com

■ The **American Council of Life Insurers** represents the life insurance industry on issues dealing with legislation and regulation at the federal and state level. The site provides consumer information on the purposes and types of life insurance. Visit the site at

http://www.acli.com

■ The **Life Office Management Association (LOMA)** provides extensive information dealing with the management and operations of life insurers and financial services companies. Visit the site at

http://www.loma.org

■ **LIMRA International, Inc.** is the principal source of life insurance sales and marketing statistics. The organization provides news and information about the financial services field, conducts research, and publishes a wide range of publications. Visit the site at

http://www.limra.com

■ The **National Association of Insurance and Financial Advisors** represents sales professionals in life and health insurance and the financial services industry. The organization promotes ethical standards, supports legislation in the interest of policyowners and agents, and provides agent education seminars. Visit the site at

http://www.naifa.org/index.html

■ The **National Underwriter Company** publishes books and periodicals about life insurance products. The company publishes the *National Underwriter*, Life & Health/Financial Services edition, a weekly trade publication, which provides timely news about the life insurance industry. Visit the site at

www.nationalunderwriter.com

■ The **Society of Financial Service Professionals** represents individuals who have earned the professional Chartered Life Underwriter (CLU) and Chartered Financial Consultant (ChFC) designations. The site provides timely information on life insurance products. Visit the site at

www.financialpro.org

■ **The American College** offers professional certification and graduate degree programs in the financial services industry. It offers numerous programs and courses leading to the award of professional designations (CLU, ChFC, and others). Visit the site at

http://www.amercoll.edu

SELECTED REFERENCES

Black, Kenneth, Jr., and Harold D. Skipper, Jr. *Life Insurance,* 13th ed. Upper Saddle River, NJ: Prentice-Hall, 2000.

Elger, John F., "Calculating Life Insurance Need: Don't Let the Tools Fool You," *Journal of Financial Service Professionals,* Vol. 57, No. 3 (May 2003), pp. 38–40.

Gokhale Jagadeesh and Laurence J. Kotlikoff, "The Adequacy of Life Insurance," *Research Dialogue,* Issue No. 72, New York: TIAA-CREF Institute, July 2002.

Graves, Edward E., ed. *McGill's Life Insurance,* 5th ed. Bryn Mawr, PA: The American College, 2004.

LIMRA International. *1998 Survivor Study, Fulfilling the Promise: The Role of the Life Insurance Company and Agent.* Windsor, CT: LIMRA International, 1998.

LIMRA International. *1998 Survivor Study—The Financial Impact of Death.* Windsor, CT: LIMRA International, 1999.

Mitchell, James O., "The Adequacy of Life Insurance Coverage in U.S. Households," *Journal of Financial Service Professionals,* Vol. 57, No. 3 (May 2003), pp. 54–63.

TIAA-CREF Institute, "The Adequacy of Life Insurance," *Quarterly* (Autumn 2002), pp. 18–22.

Todd, Jerry D. "Integrative Life Insurance Needs Analysis," *Journal of Financial Service Professionals,* Vol. 58, No. 2 (March 2004), pp. 57–66.

Wiening, Eric A., George E. Rejda, Constance M. Luthardt, and Cheryl L. Ferguson. *Personal Insurance,* First Edition. Malvern, PA: American Institute for Chartered Property Casualty Underwriters/Insurance Institute of America, 2002.

NOTES

1. *Life Insurers Fact Book 2001* (Washington, DC: American Council of Life Insurers, 2001), p. 104.

2. John F. Elger, Calculating Life Insurance Need: Don't Let the Tools Fool You," *Journal of Financial Service Professionals,* Vol. 57, No. 3 (May 2003), Table 3, p. 40.

3. *1998 Survivor Study—The Financial Impact of Death* (Windsor, CT: LIMRA International, 1999), p. 5.

4. TIAA-CREF Institute, "The Adequacy of Life Insurance," *Quarterly* (Autumn 2002), p. 22.

5. James O. Mitchell, "The Adequacy of Life Insurance Coverage in U.S. Households," *Journal of Financial Service Professionals,* Vol. 57, No. 3 (May 2003), p. 61.

6. Edward E. Graves, ed., *McGill's Life Insurance,* 4th ed. (Bryn Mawr, PA: The American College 2002, ch. 2)

7. Ibid. The legal reserve technically is a liability item that must be offset by sufficient assets. Otherwise, regulatory authorities may declare the insurer to be insolvent.

8. This separation is only a theoretical concept. In practice, the death claim paid by the insurer does not consist of two separate benefits that equal the face value of the policy. An ordinary life insurance policy is an undivided contract, and the death benefit is the face amount of insurance.

9. The *cost of insurance* is a technical term that is obtained by multiplying the net amount at risk by the death rate at the insured's attained age. Under the level-premium method, the cost of insurance can be kept within reasonable bounds at all ages.

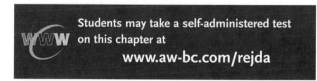

CHAPTER 17

TYPES OF LIFE INSURANCE

"The number of different types of life insurance contracts on the market is large . . . The effect of this proliferation is confusion and frustration for the buyer."

Joseph M. Belth
Life Insurance: A Consumer's Handbook

LEARNING OBJECTIVES

After studying this chapter, you should be able to

◆ Describe the basic characteristics of term insurance.

◆ Explain the major characteristics of ordinary life insurance.

◆ Describe the basic characteristics of variable life insurance.

◆ Explain the basic characteristics of universal life insurance.

◆ Show how variable universal life insurance differs from universal life insurance.

◆ Describe the basic characteristics of current assumption whole life insurance.

*A*shley, age 28, is a single parent with two preschool children. She earns $25,000 annually as a secretary for a local trucking company. Her husband died unexpectedly from a heart attack one year ago. A small life insurance policy on his life paid the funeral expenses. Although the family receives Social Security survivor benefits, money is tight. Ashley is trying to reassess her life insurance needs to protect her family. A life insurance agent recently met with her and presented several proposals. However, Ashley does not understand clearly the various proposals and the best type of life insurance for her to buy.

The material in this chapter will help Ashley understand the major forms of life insurance sold today. The chapter discusses three principal areas. Traditional life insurance is discussed first, which includes term, whole life, and endowment insurance. Next, the chapter discusses variations of whole life insurance, which include variable life insurance, universal life insurance, and variable universal life insurance. The chapter concludes with a discussion of other types of life insurance that have unique features or meet special needs.

TYPES OF LIFE INSURANCE

From a generic viewpoint, life insurance policies can be classified as either **term insurance** or **cash-value life insurance.** Term insurance provides temporary protection, while cash-value life insurance has a savings component and builds cash values. Numerous variations and combinations of these two types of life insurance are available today.

Term Insurance

Term insurance has several basic characteristics.[1] First, the period of protection is temporary, such as 1, 5, 10, or 20 years. Unless the policy is renewed, the protection expires at the end of the period.

Most term insurance policies are **renewable,** which means that the policy can be renewed for additional periods without evidence of insurability. The premium is increased at each renewal and is based on the insured's attained age. The purpose of the renewal provision is to protect the insurability of the insured. However, the renewal provision results in adverse selection against the insurer. Because premiums increase with age, insureds in good health tend to drop their insurance, while those in poor

health will continue to renew, regardless of the premium increase. To minimize adverse selection, many insurers have an age limitation beyond which renewal is not allowed, such as age 70 or 80. Some insurers, however, permit term policies to be renewed to age 95 or 99.

Most term insurance policies are also **convertible,** which means the term policy can be exchanged for a cash-value policy without evidence of insurability. There are two methods for converting a term policy. Under the *attained-age method,* the premium charged is based on the insured's attained age at the time of conversion. Under the *original-age method,* the premium charged is based on the insured's original age when the term insurance was first purchased. Most insurers offering the original-age method require the conversion to take place within a certain time period, such as five years, from the issue date of the term policy. The policyowner must also pay the difference between the premiums paid on the term policy and those that would have been paid on the new policy, with interest on the difference at a specified rate.[2] The purpose of the financial adjustment is to place the insurer in the same financial position it would have achieved if the policy had been issued at the original age. Because of the financial adjustment required, few term insurance policies are converted based on the original-age method.

Finally, term insurance policies have no cash-value or savings element. Although some long-term policies develop a small reserve, it is used up by the contract expiration date.

Types of Term Insurance   A wide variety of term insurance products are sold today. They include the following:

- Yearly renewable term
- 5-, 10-, 15-, or 20-year term
- Term to age 65
- Decreasing term
- Reentry term

Yearly renewable term insurance is issued for a one-year period, and the policyowner can renew for successive one-year periods to some stated age without evidence of insurability. Premiums increase with age at each renewal date. Most yearly renewable term policies also allow the policyowner to convert to a cash-value policy with no evidence of insurability.

Term insurance can also be issued for *5, 10, 15, or 20 years, or for longer periods*. The premiums paid during the term period are level, but they increase when the policy is renewed.

A *term to age 65 policy* provides protection to age 65, at which time the policy expires. The policy can be converted to a permanent plan of insurance, but the decision to convert must be exercised before age 65. For example, the insurer may require conversion to a permanent policy before age 60. Because premiums are level, the policy develops a small reserve that is used up by the end of the period.

Decreasing term insurance is a form of term insurance where the face amount gradually declines each year. Although the face amount declines over time, the premium is level throughout the period. In some policies, the premiums are structured so that the policy is fully paid for a few years before the coverage expires. For example, a 20-year decreasing term policy may require premium payments for 17 years. This method avoids paying a relatively large premium for only a small amount of insurance near the end of the term period. Finally, decreasing term insurance can be written as a separate policy, or it can be added as a rider to an existing contract.

Reentry term (also called *revertible term*) is another important term insurance product. Under a reentry term policy, renewal premiums are based on select (lower) mortality rates if the insured can periodically demonstrate acceptable evidence of insurability. Select mortality rates are based on the mortality experience of recently insured lives. However, to remain on the low-rate schedule, the insured must periodically show that he or she is in good health and is still insurable. The rates are substantially increased if the insured cannot provide satisfactory evidence of insurability.

Uses of Term Insurance   Term insurance is appropriate in three situations. *First, if the amount of income that can be spent on life insurance is limited, term insurance can be effectively used.* Because of mortality improvements and keen price competition, term insurance rates have declined sharply in recent years. Substantial amounts of life insurance can be purchased for a relatively modest annual premium outlay (see Exhibit 17.1).

Second term insurance is appropriate if the need for protection is temporary. For example, decreasing term insurance can be effectively used to pay off the mortgage if the family head dies prematurely.

Finally, term insurance can be used to guarantee future insurability. A person may desire large amounts of permanent insurance, but may be financially unable to purchase the needed protection today. Inexpensive term insurance can be purchased, which can be converted later into a permanent insurance policy without evidence of insurability.

Limitations of Term Insurance   Term insurance has two major limitations. *First, term insurance premiums increase with age at an increasing rate and eventually reach prohibitive levels.* Thus, term insurance is not suitable for individuals who need large amounts of life insurance beyond age 65 or 70. For example, based on the rates of one insurer, the premium for a $500,000 annually renewable term policy for a male nonsmoker, age 25, is $353. The premium increases to $2914 at age 65 and $9805 at age 75.

Second, term insurance is inappropriate if you wish to save money for a specific need. Term insurance policies do not accumulate cash values. Thus, if you wish to save money for a child's college educa-

EXHIBIT 17.1
Illustrative Examples of Term Life Insurance Premiums, $250,000

	Female Premiums						Male Premiums				
Age	10 Year	15 Year	20 Year	25 Year	30 Year	Age	10 Year	15 Year	20 Year	25 Year	30 Year
35	$ 103	$ 125	$ 145	$ 183	$ 205	35	$ 123	$ 138	$ 165	$ 223	$ 253
40	$ 123	$ 158	$ 185	$ 238	$ 260	40	$ 148	$ 183	$ 225	$ 288	$ 335
45	$ 190	$ 215	$ 253	$ 330	$ 385	45	$ 225	$ 300	$ 360	$ 450	$ 513
50	$ 253	$ 290	$ 363	$ 490	$ 495	50	$ 338	$ 455	$ 525	$ 743	$ 828
55	$ 365	$ 413	$ 550	$ 835	$ 1,015	55	$ 500	$ 670	$ 768	$ 1,640	$ 2,330
60	$ 503	$ 615	$ 845	$ 2,135	$ 2,400	60	$ 783	$ 990	$1,335	$ 3,630	$ 3,630
65	$ 775	$ 975	$1,593	$ 3,900	$ 3,900	65	$1,330	$1,650	$2,693	$ 5,250	$ 5,250
70	$1,338	$1,600	$2,970	$ 7,220	$ 7,220	70	$2,473	$3,175	$4,860	$ 8,790	$ 8,790
75	$2,275	$4,870	$5,820	$10,370	$12,420	75	$4,400	$7,443	$9,600	$13,260	$15,030

NOTE: The premiums are guaranteed annual premiums for a nonsmoker. Final premiums and coverage availability will vary depending on age, sex, state availability, hazardous activities, and personal and family health history.

SOURCE: Quotesmith.com, Inc.

tion or accumulate a fund for retirement, term insurance is inappropriate unless it is supplemented with an investment plan.

Decreasing term insurance also has several disadvantages and should not be used to meet all of your insurance needs. If you become uninsurable, you must convert the remaining insurance to a permanent plan to freeze the insurance at its present level. If the policy is not converted, the insurance protection continues to decline even though you are uninsurable. Moreover, decreasing term insurance does not provide for changing needs, such as a birth or adoption of a child. Nor does it provide an effective hedge against inflation. Because of inflation, the amount of life insurance in most families should be periodically increased just to maintain the real purchasing power of the original policy.

Whole Life Insurance

In contrast to term insurance, which provides short-term protection, **whole life insurance** *is a cash-value policy that provides lifetime protection*. From a historical or traditional perspective, the following two types of whole life insurance merit some discussion:

- Ordinary life insurance
- Limited-payment life insurance

Ordinary Life Insurance Ordinary life insurance (also called straight life and continuous premium whole life) provides lifetime protection to age 100, and the death claim is a certainty. If the insured is still alive at age 100, the face amount of insurance is paid to the policyowner at that time.[3]

In addition, premiums do not increase from year to year but remain level throughout the premium paying period. Under an ordinary life policy, the policyowner is overcharged for the insurance protection during the early years and undercharged during the later years when premiums are inadequate to pay death claims. As stated in Chapter 16, the excess premiums are reflected in a liability item for insurers known as a legal reserve. The legal reserve makes it possible to provide lifetime protection.

Ordinary life insurance also has an investment or saving element called a **cash surrender value.** The cash values are due to the overpayment of insurance premiums during the early years. As a result, the policyowner builds a cash equity in the policy. The policy may be surrendered for its cash value, or the cash value may be borrowed under a loan provision. The

INSIGHT 17.1

Another Look at Cash Value Life Insurance as an Investment

Substantial amounts of cash value life insurance are sold currently as an investment or tax shelter. Agents often cite the investment attributes of cash value insurance, which include forced saving, safety of principal, favorable income tax treatment, liquidity, protection against claims of creditors, and a reasonable rate of return. Despite these alleged advantages, however, cash value life insurance has two major defects as an appealing investment: (1) *the effective rate of return on the cash value is not disclosed to policyowners,* (2) *the loading for expenses when compared to competing investments is relatively high.*

One of the most important investment considerations is the rate of return earned on the investment. The annual total return (capital gains and dividends) on mutual funds and individual stocks can be easily determined and is readily available to investors. However, this is not true for cash value life insurance. The problem is that part of the premium must be used to pay for the cost of the insurance protection, sales expenses, and administrative costs, while the remainder can be allocated to the cash value. Various techniques, such as the Linton Yield and the yearly-rate-of return method by Professor Joseph Belth, are available for estimating the rate of return on the cash value after deducting the cost of insurance (see Chapter 19). However, these techniques are complex, and most policyowners are not aware of them and how they can be used. *Moreover, the life insurance industry has consistently opposed any legislation that would require the disclosure of the*

true effective annual rate of return on a cash value policy. Some policies, such as a universal life policy, quote a specific interest rate that is credited to the policy, such as a current interest rate of 5 percent. However, such rates are gross rates and do not reflect the true net rate of return after deductions for the cost of insurance and other policy expenses.

Is the rate of return on a cash value policy reasonable? The Consumer Federation of America has analyzed more than 5000 cash value policies for consumers and has issued several reports. One study of 57 cash value policies shows negative rates of return during the early years. *The average rate of return on these policies was −90% in year one, −61.7% in year two, −22.3% in year three and −1.2% in year four.*[a]

The annual rates of return are negative during the early years because there is little or no cash value in a policy because of relatively high first-year acquisition expenses and other continuing policy expenses.

Cash value policies generally must be held for at least 15 years for the rate of return to become attractive. The same study shows the following average annual rates of return for the 57 policies over longer periods:

Years Policy Held	Average Annual Rate of Return
5	−14.5%
10	2.3%
15	5.1%
20	6.1%

---

cash values are relatively small during the early years, but increase over time. For example, in many ordinary life policies, a $100,000 policy issued at age 20 would have at least $50,000 of cash value at age 65.

Finally, ordinary life insurance contains cash surrender or nonforfeiture options, dividend options (if participating), and settlement options that can be used to meet a wide variety of financial needs and objectives. These options are discussed in Chapter 18.

Uses of Ordinary Life Insurance   Ordinary life insurance is appropriate in two general situations: (1) when lifetime protection is needed, and (2) when additional savings are desired.

An ordinary life policy is appropriate when lifetime protection is needed. This means that the need for life insurance will continue beyond age 65 or 70.

Some financial planners and consumer experts point out that the average person does not need large amounts of life insurance beyond age 65, because the need for life insurance declines with age. This view is an oversimplification of a complex issue and can be misleading. Some persons may need substantial amounts of life insurance beyond age 65. For example, an estate clearance fund is still needed at the older ages; there may be a sizable federal estate tax problem if the estate is large, so substantial amounts of life insurance may be needed for estate liquidity; a divorce settlement may require the purchase and maintenance of a life insurance policy on a divorced spouse, regardless of age; and the policyowner may wish to leave a sizable bequest to a surviving spouse, children, or charity, regardless of when death occurs. Because an ordinary life policy can provide lifetime

Another Look at Cash Value Life Insurance as an Investment

The annual rate of return can be considered "reasonable" only if you are willing to hold the policy for at least 15 or 20 years. You will lose most or all of your money if you surrender the policy or let it lapse during the early years. The Consumer Federation of America estimates that about 25% of the policyowners who buy cash value life insurance let the policies lapse in the first three years, and nearly 50% give up their policies in the first 10 years.[b] As a result, buyers of cash value life insurance lose billions of dollars annually by terminating their policies prematurely.[c]

The second problem is that the expense loading is relatively high when compared to mutual funds and other investments. For example, variable universal life insurance is widely sold today as an investment and tax shelter. The prospectus for one policy sold by a leading insurer shows that the loading for sales expenses for the first five years is 6.75% of the target premium. The target premium is the premium that keeps the policy in force for a specified number of years. In addition, state premium taxes and federal taxes are 3.25% of the premium. Thus, sales expenses and taxes are 10 percent of the target premiums paid for the first five policy years.

The same prospectus also shows various deductions from the cash value for policy expenses and investment management fees. These deductions include a monthly contract fee of $30; a monthly fee of 7 cents per $1000 of the policy face amount plus the face amount of any term insurance rider; a mortality and expense risk fee for certain mortality and expense guarantees; an investment management fee on the separate account in which the funds are invested; and other fees. These deductions can absorb as much as 2% of the cash value. The policy also has a deferred surrender charge that applies for the first 10 years. Finally, there is a monthly deduction for the cost of insurance. *As you can see, selling expenses, monthly fees, contract fees, surrender charges, and other expenses have a severe impact on the rate of return on cash value life insurance policies.*

The Consumer Federation of America recommends that a new cash value life insurance policy should be purchased as an investment only if (1) you are willing to hold the policy for at least 20 years, and (2) you have made maximum annual contributions to your employer's Section 401(k) plan or individual retirement account (IRA), which provide favorable income tax treatment at a much lower cost.

[a] James H. Hunt, *Analysis of Cash Value Life Insurance Policies,* Consumer Federation of America, July 1997.
[b] Ibid.
[c] Ibid.

protection, these objectives can be realized even though the insured dies at an advanced age.

Ordinary life insurance can also be used to save money. Some insureds wish to meet their protection and savings needs by an ordinary life policy. As stated earlier, ordinary life insurance builds cash values that can be obtained by surrendering the policy or by borrowing the cash value.

Substantial amounts of cash value life insurance are sold today primarily as an investment and as a method to save money. Insight 17.1 discusses the investment merits of cash value life insurance in greater detail.

Limitation of Ordinary Life Insurance *The major limitation of ordinary life insurance is that some people are still underinsured after the policy is purchased.* Because of the savings feature, some persons may voluntarily purchase or else be persuaded by

a life insurance agent to purchase an ordinary life policy when term insurance would be a better choice. For example, assume that Mark, age 30, is married with two dependents to support. He estimates that he can spend only $500 annually on life insurance. This premium would purchase about $56,000 of ordinary life insurance. The same premium would purchase about $500,000 of yearly renewable term insurance from many insurers. It is difficult to justify the purchase of an ordinary life insurance policy if it leaves the insured inadequately covered.

Limited-Payment Life Insurance A limited-payment policy is another type of traditional whole life insurance. The insurance is permanent, and the insured has lifetime protection. The premiums are level, but they are paid only for a certain period. For example, Shannon, age 25, may purchase a 20-year limited payment policy in the amount of $25,000. After 20 years, the policy is completely paid up, and no additional premiums are required even though the coverage remains in force. A paid-up policy should not be confused with one that *matures*. A policy matures when the face amount is paid as a death claim or as an endowment. A policy is *paid up* when no additional premium payments are required.

The most common limited-payment policies are for 10, 20, 25, or 30 years. A policy paid up at age 65 or 70 is another form of limited-payment insurance. An extreme form of limited-payment life insurance is **single-premium whole life insurance,** which provides lifetime protection with a single premium. Because the premiums under a limited-payment policy are higher than those paid under an ordinary life policy, the cash values are also higher.

A limited-payment policy should be used with caution. It is extremely difficult for a person with a modest income to insure his or her life adequately with a limited-payment policy. Because of the relatively high premiums, the amount of permanent life insurance that can be purchased is substantially lower than if an ordinary life policy were purchased. If permanent life insurance is desired, most people will find that their need for permanent protection can be better met by an ordinary life policy.

Endowment Insurance

Endowment insurance is another traditional form of life insurance. An endowment policy pays the face amount of insurance if the insured dies within a specified period; if the insured survives to the end of the endowment period, the face amount is paid to the policyowner at that time. For example, if Stephanie, age 35, purchased a 20-year endowment policy and died any time within the 20-year period, the face amount would be paid to her beneficiary. If she survives to the end of the period, the face amount is paid to her.

At the present time, endowment insurance is relatively unimportant in terms of total life insurance in force. Endowment insurance accounts for less than 1 percent of the life insurance in force. Because of the Deficit Reduction Act of 1984 (DEFRA), most new endowment policies cannot meet the tax definition of life insurance. If this definition is not met, the investment income credited to the cash sur-

render value is subject to current taxation. Thus, adverse tax consequences have discouraged the purchase of new endowment policies, and most life insurers have discontinued the sale of new endowment policies. Even so, many older endowment policies are still in force, and some contracts are still used in tax-qualified retirement plans. Although endowment policies are no longer readily available in the United States, they remain popular in many foreign countries.

VARIATIONS OF WHOLE LIFE INSURANCE

Life insurers have experienced keen competition from mutual funds, commercial banks, and other financial institutions. To remain competitive and to overcome the criticisms of traditional cash-value policies, insurers have developed a wide variety of whole life products that combine insurance protection with an investment component. Important variations of whole life insurance include the following:

- Variable life insurance
- Universal life insurance
- Variable universal life insurance
- Current assumption whole life insurance
- Indeterminate-premium whole life insurance

Variable Life Insurance

Variable life insurance *can be defined as a fixed-premium policy in which the death benefit and cash values vary according to the investment experience of a separate account maintained by the insurer.* The death benefit and cash surrender values will increase or decrease with the investment experience of the separate account. Although there are different policy designs, variable life policies have certain common features. They are summarized as follows:

- *A variable life policy is a permanent whole life contract with a fixed premium.* The premium is level and is guaranteed not to increase.
- *The entire reserve is held in a separate account and is invested in common stocks or other investments.* The policyowner has the option of investing the cash value in a variety of investments, such as a common stock fund, bond

fund, balanced fund, money market fund, or international fund. If the investment experience is favorable, the face amount of insurance is increased. If the investment experience is poor, the amount of life insurance could be reduced, but it can never fall below the original face amount.

- *Cash surrender values are not guaranteed, and there are no minimum guaranteed cash values.* The actual cash values depend on the investment experience. Thus, although the insurer bears of the risk of excessive mortality and expenses, the policyowner bears the risk of poor investment results.

Universal Life Insurance

Universal life insurance is another important variation of whole life insurance. **Universal life insurance** (also called flexible premium life insurance) *can be defined as a flexible premium policy that provides protection under a contract that unbundles the protection and saving components.* Except for the first premium, the policyowner determines the amount and frequency of payments. The premiums, less explicit expense charges, are credited to a cash value account (also called an accumulation fund) from which monthly mortality charges are deducted and to which monthly interest is credited. In addition, universal life policies typically have a monthly deduction for administrative expenses.

Universal life insurance has certain characteristics, which include the following:[4]

- Unbundling of component parts
- Two forms of universal life insurance
- Considerable flexibility
- Cash withdrawals permitted
- Favorable income-tax treatment

Unbundling of Component Parts A distinct characteristic is the separation or unbundling of three components—protection component, saving component, and expense component. The policyowner receives an annual disclosure statement that shows the premiums paid, death benefit, and value of the cash value account. The statement also shows the mortality charge, expense charges, and interest credited to the cash value account.

- *Premiums.* As noted earlier, except for the first premium, the policyowner determines the frequency and amount of premium payments. Most policies have a *target premium,* which is a suggested level premium that will keep the policy in force for a specified number of years. However, the policyowner is not obligated to pay the target premium. Most policies also have a *no-lapse guarantee,* which guarantees that the policy will remain in force for a certain number of years, such as 15 or 20 years, if at least the minimum premium is paid. The minimum premium is specified in the policy and, depending on the insurer, may be less than or equal to the target premium.
- *Mortality charge.* A monthly mortality charge is deducted from the cash value account for the cost of the insurance protection. The cost of insurance is determined by multiplying the applicable monthly mortality rate by the net amount at risk (difference between the current death benefit and cash value). The policy contains a table that shows the maximum rate per $1000 of insurance that the company can charge. Most insurers charge less than the maximum rate. However, the insurer has the right to increase the current mortality charge up to the maximum guaranteed rate stated in the policy.
- *Expense charges.* Insurers typically deduct 5 to 10 percent of each premium for expenses. There is also a monthly fee for administrative expenses, such as $5 or $6. In addition, there is a relatively high surrender charge that applies if the policy is terminated during the early years. The surrender charge declines annually and disappears after a period of time, such as 10, 15, or 20 years. As a result, the policyowner can lose a substantial amount of money if the policy is surrendered during the early years. Finally, there is a charge for each partial cash withdrawal, such as $25.

Some insurers sell *low load policies* that are sold directly to the public by calling a toll-free telephone number or by applying over the Internet. Most of the first-year premium is credited to the accumulation account and earns interest at the quoted rate. To recover expenses, the policy typically has a *back-end surrender charge.* The surrender charge is usually applied

EXHIBIT 17.2
Universal Life Insurance Death Benefits

Source: Kenneth Black, Jr., and Harold D. Skipper, Jr., Life Insurance, 13th ed., © 2000.
Reprinted by Permission of Pearson Education, Inc., Upper Saddle River, NJ.

over a shorter period, such as five years instead of a longer period.

■ *Interest rate.* Interest earnings credited to the cash value account depend on the interest rate. There are two rates of interest. The guaranteed cash value is credited with a contractually *guaranteed minimum interest rate,* such as 3 or 4 percent. The cash values, however, may be credited with a higher *current rate,* such as 4½ or 5 percent. The current rate is not guaranteed but changes periodically depending on market conditions and company experience.

If the policyowner borrows the cash value, the amount borrowed is usually credited with a lower rate of interest. The cash value representing the amount borrowed is credited with either the minimum interest rate or a rate 1 to 2 percent below the policy loan rate.

Two Forms of Universal Life Insurance   There are two forms of universal life insurance (see Exhibit 17.2). *Option A pays a level death benefit during the early years.* As the cash value increases over time, the net amount at risk declines. However, the death benefit increases during the later years of the policy. If the death benefit did not increase, the policy would not meet the *corridor test* required by the Internal Revenue Code. As a result, the policy would not receive favorable income-tax treatment. The corridor test is a complex test that disqualifies a policy for favorable income-tax treatment if the cash values are excessive relative to the net amount at risk.

Option B provides for an increasing death benefit. The death benefit is equal to a constant net amount at risk plus the accumulated cash value. If the cash value increases over time, the death benefit will increase. Please note that an increasing death benefit each year is not guaranteed. The illustration of Option B in Exhibit 17.2 is based on the assumption that the policyowner pays at least the target premiums and that the interest rate assumptions are realized. In reality, the premiums paid by the policyowner may vary, and interest rates will change periodically. Thus, actual cash values will fluctuate and could even decline to zero, especially if premiums are discontinued and interest rates decline. As a result of fluctuations in the cash value account, the death benefit will fluctuate and may not necessarily increase each year.

Considerable Flexibility Compared to traditional whole life products, universal life insurance provides considerable flexibility, which includes the following:

- The policyowner determines the frequency and amount of premium payments. Premiums can be discontinued if there is sufficient cash value to pay mortality costs and expenses.
- The death benefit can be increased or decreased. Evidence of insurability is required to increase the amount of insurance.
- The policy can be changed from a level death benefit to a death benefit equal to a specified face amount plus the policy cash value (with evidence of insurability).
- The policyowner can add cash to the policy at any time, subject to maximum guideline limits that govern the relationship of the cash value to the death benefit (tax law limitations).
- Policy loans are permitted at competitive interest rates.
- If the policy permits, additional insureds can be added.

Cash Withdrawals Permitted Part or all of the cash value can be withdrawn. Interest is not charged, but the death benefit is reduced by the amount of the withdrawal. Most insurers charge a surrender fee for each cash withdrawal, such as $25. As noted earlier, policy loans are also permitted.

Favorable Income-Tax Treatment Universal life insurance enjoys the same favorable federal income-tax treatment as traditional cash-value policies. The death benefit paid to a named beneficiary is normally received income-tax free. Interest credited to the cash value account is not taxable to the policyowner in the year credited.

Universal Life Insurance Illustration To illustrate how universal life insurance works, assume that Jason, age 25, buys a universal life policy with a level death benefit of $100,000. The annual planned premium is $445, which can be changed. For the sake of simplicity, assume that the mortality charge, expense charge, and crediting of interest are made annually. (However, in practice, there is a monthly deduction for mortality and expense charges and monthly crediting of interest.)

Each premium is subject to a 5 percent premium expense charge. The policy has a monthly administrative charge of $6. The policy provides for a maximum mortality charge, but the current mortality charge is only about two-thirds of the maximum rate. The policy has a guaranteed interest rate of 4.5 percent and a current interest rate of 5.5 percent that is not guaranteed.

When Jason pays the first premium of $445, there is a premium expense charge of approximately $22 (5 percent of $445). There is also an administrative charge of $72 ($6 monthly). The first year mortality charge is $113 ($1.13 per $1000 of the specified $100,000 death benefit). The remaining $238 is credited with $13 of interest (5.5 percent on $238). Thus, the cash value account at the end of the first year is $251. This calculation is summarized as follows:

Annual premium	$445
Less:	
Premium expense charges	−22
Administrative charges	−72
Mortality cost	−113
	$238
Interest at 5.5 percent	13
Cash value account end of year	$251

However, if Jason surrenders the policy at the end of the first year, the surrender value is zero because of the surrender charge. A declining surrender charge applies if the policy is terminated within 16 years after the issue date. Exhibit 17.3 shows in greater detail the cash-value accumulation based on the guaranteed and current interest rates.

Limitations of Universal Life Universal life insurance has several limitations. Consumer experts point out the following limitations:[5]

- *Misleading rates of return.* The advertised rates of return on universal life insurance are

EXHIBIT 17.3
$100,000 Universal Life Policy, Level Death Benefit, Male Age 25, Nonsmoker,
5.5 Percent Assumed Interest

Age	Year	Premium Outlay	Guaranteed Assumptions			Illustrated Assumptions		
			Death Benefit	Cash Value	Cash Surrender Value	Death Benefit	Cash Value	Cash Surrender Value
26	1	$445.00	$100,000	$222	$0	$100,000	$251	$0
27	2	445.00	100,000	454	0	100,000	516	0
28	3	445.00	100,000	698	140	100,000	796	238
29	4	445.00	100,000	953	395	100,000	1,092	534
30	5	445.00	100,000	1,219	661	100,000	1,392	834
31	6	445.00	100,000	1,498	991	100,000	1,709	1,202
32	7	445.00	100,000	1,788	1,331	100,000	2,041	1,584
33	8	445.00	100,000	2,079	1,673	100,000	2,393	1,987
34	9	445.00	100,000	2,383	2,028	100,000	2,764	2,409
35	10	445.00	100,000	2,689	2,385	100,000	3,143	2,839
36	11	445.00	100,000	2,994	2,740	100,000	3,542	3,288
37	12	445.00	100,000	3,300	3,097	100,000	3,964	3,761
38	13	445.00	100,000	3,609	3,457	100,000	4,396	4,244
39	14	445.00	100,000	3,919	3,818	100,000	4,853	4,752
40	15	445.00	100,000	4,232	4,181	100,000	5,323	5,272
41	16	445.00	100,000	4,557	4,557	100,000	5,832	5,832
42	17	445.00	100,000	4,872	4,872	100,000	6,369	6,369
43	18	445.00	100,000	5,190	5,190	100,000	6,924	6,924
44	19	445.00	100,000	5,495	5,495	100,000	7,509	7,509
45	20	445.00	100,000	5,790	5,790	100,000	8,114	8,114
46	21	445.00	100,000	6,069	6,069	100,000	8,739	8,739
47	22	445.00	100,000	6,325	6,325	100,000	9,376	9,376
48	23	445.00	100,000	6,568	6,568	100,000	10,025	10,025
49	24	445.00	100,000	6,785	6,785	100,000	10,687	10,687
50	25	445.00	100,000	6,976	6,976	100,000	11,363	11,363
51	26	445.00	100,000	7,133	7,133	100,000	12,052	12,052
52	27	445.00	100,000	7,242	7,242	100,000	12,729	12,729
53	28	445.00	100,000	7,280	7,280	100,000	13,390	13,390
54	29	445.00	100,000	7,241	7,241	100,000	14,033	14,033
55	30	445.00	100,000	7,106	7,106	100,000	14,668	14,668
56	31	445.00	100,000	6,866	6,866	100,000	15,282	15,282
57	32	445.00	100,000	6,498	6,498	100,000	15,873	15,873
58	33	445.00	100,000	5,981	5,981	100,000	16,445	16,445
59	34	445.00	100,000	5,282	5,282	100,000	16,989	16,989

Exhibit 17.3 (continued)
**$100,000 Universal Life Policy, Level Death Benefit, Male Age 25, Nonsmoker,
5.5 Percent Assumed Interest**

			Guaranteed Assumptions			Illustrated Assumptions		
Age	Year	Premium Outlay	Death Benefit	Cash Value	Cash Surrender Value	Death Benefit	Cash Value	Cash Surrender Value
60	35	445.00	100,000	4,370	4,370	100,000	17,483	17,483
61	36	445.00	100,000	3,562	3,562	100,000	18,111	18,111
62	37	445.00	100,000	2,567	2,567	100,000	18,723	18,723
63	38	445.00	100,000	1,362	1,362	100,000	19,298	19,298
64	39	445.00	0*	0	0	100,000	19,839	19,839
65	40	445.00				100,000	20,322	20,322
66	41	445.00				100,000	20,819	20,819
67	42	445.00				100,000	21,233	21,233
68	43	445.00				100,000	21,570	21,570
69	44	445.00				100,000	21,824	21,824
70	45	445.00				100,000	21,951	21,951
71	46	445.00				100,000	21,915	21,915
72	47	445.00				100,000	21,721	21,721
73	48	445.00				100,000	21,327	21,327
74	49	445.00				100,000	20,695	20,695
75	50	445.00				100,000	19,772	19,772
76	51	445.00				100,000	18,478	18,478
77	52	445.00				100,000	16,780	16,780
78	53	445.00				100,000	14,574	14,574
79	54	445.00				100,000	11,770	11,770
80	55	445.00				100,000	8,215	8,215
81	56	445.00				100,000	3,685	3,685
82	57	445.00				0*	0	0

NOTE: This illustration assumes that the nonguaranteed elements currently illustrated will continue unchanged for all years shown. This is not likely to occur, and actual results may be more or less favorable. Illustrated values are based on nonguaranteed elements that are subject to change. Guaranteed values are based on a guaranteed interest rate of 4.5 percent. Illustrated values are based on a current interest rate of 5.5 percent. Premiums are assumed to be paid at the beginning of the year. Benefiits values, and ages are shown at the end of the year.

*Coverage will terminate under current assumptions. Additional premiums would be required to continue coverage.

misleading. For example, insurers may advertise current rates of interest of 4½ or 5 percent on universal life policies. *However, the advertised rates are gross rates and not net rates.* The advertised gross rate overstates the true rate of return on the saving component because it does not reflect deductions for sales commissions, expenses, and the cost of the insurance protection. As a result of these deductions, the effective yearly return is substantially lower than the advertised rate and is often negative for several years after the policy is purchased.

- *Decline in interest rates.* Many earlier sales presentations showed sizable future cash values based on relatively high interest rates. However, interest rates have declined sharply in recent years. *As a result, the earlier cash-value and premium-payment projections based on higher interest rates are misleading and invalid.* Actual cash values will be substantially less than the projected values based on higher interest rates when the policy was first sold.

- *Right to increase the mortality charge.* As stated earlier, insurers can increase the current mortality charge for the cost of insurance up to some maximum limit. Other expenses may be hidden in the mortality charge. If the insurer's expenses increase, the mortality charge could be increased to recoup these expenses. The increase may not be noticed or questioned because the insured may believe the increase is justified because he or she is getting older.

- *Lack of firm commitment to pay premiums.* Another limitation is that some policyowners do not have a firm commitment to pay premiums. As a result, the policy may lapse because of nonpayment of premiums. As stated earlier, premiums can be reduced or skipped in a universal life policy. However, at some point, money must be added to the account, or the policy will lapse. Many insurers have experienced an increase in lapsed universal life policies, which is partly due to the lack of a firm commitment by policyowners to make fixed and regular premium payments.

Variable Universal Life Insurance

Variable universal life insurance is an important variation of whole life insurance. It is a popular type of cash value insurance that has been widely sold in recent years. Most variable universal life policies are sold as investments or tax shelters.

Variable universal life insurance is similar to a universal life policy with two major exceptions:

- The policyowner determines how the premiums are invested, which provide considerable investment flexibility.

- The policy does not guarantee a minimum interest rate or minimum cash value. One exception, however, is that the variable annuity may have a fixed income account, which may guarantee a minimum interest rate on the account value.

Selection of Investments by Policyowner   *A variable universal life policy allows the policyowner to invest the premiums in a wide variety of investments.* The premiums are invested in one or more *separate accounts,* which are similar to mutual funds in their daily operations. Insurers typically have ten or more separate accounts available. These accounts typically include a common stock fund, bond fund, balanced fund, international fund, real estate fund, money market fund, and other accounts. Some insurers also use the mutual funds of investment companies as subaccounts, such as mutual funds sold by Fidelity Investments and the Vanguard Group. Depending on the policyowner's investment goals and tolerance for risk, the premiums can be invested accordingly. The premiums purchase accumulation units, which reflect the value of the underlying investments.

The policyowner can switch out of the different funds without incurring an income-tax liability, such as switching out of a bond fund into a money market fund if interest rates rise.

No Minimum Interest Rate or Cash Value Guarantees   Unlike a universal life policy, *a variable universal life policy has no guaranteed minimum interest rate and no guaranteed minimum cash value.* When you buy a universal life policy, the cash value account earns a stated rate of interest determined by the insurer from time to time; there is also a minimum interest rate guarantee. However, when you buy a variable universal life policy, you select one or more separate accounts, and the policy cash values reflect the value of these accounts. There is no minimum interest rate or cash value guarantee. However, as stated earlier, a fixed income account may guarantee a minimum interest rate on the account value, such as 3 percent.

Relatively High Expense Charges   Variable universal life insurance policies have relatively high expense charges, which reduce the investment returns and erode the favorable tax treatment under the policy. Variable universal life insurance is typically sold as a tax shelter. Investment earnings are not currently taxable as income to the policyowner. If the policy stays in force until death, no federal income taxes are ever payable even if the separate account has sizable capital gains. However, according to the Consumer Federation of America,

VARIATIONS OF WHOLE LIFE INSURANCE

the various expense charges can more than offset the favorable income-tax treatment that variable universal life insurance now enjoys. A study of variable universal life policies by the Consumer Federation of America (CFA) showed the following charges:[6]

- *Front-end load.* Many policies have front-end loads for sales commissions and expenses, typically ranging from 5 percent to 11 percent.
- *Back-end surrender charge.* Policies purchased from agents typically have back-end surrender charges. The surrender charge usually exceeds the first year premium and declines to zero over a ten- to twenty-year period. Many policies have surrender charges that are level for the first five years, and then start to decline.
- *State premium taxes and federal taxes.* State premium taxes that vary by state and federal taxes average about 3 percent of premiums.
- *Investment management fees.* Deductions from the separate accounts are made daily for investment management fees. For the policies studied, investment management fees ranged from .20 percent to 1.62 percent.
- *Mortality and expense charges.* Mortality and expense (M&E) charges are also deducted for certain insurer guarantees. The variable universal life insurer guarantees the death benefit even though the stock market and other markets are declining; the insurer also guarantees future expense charges regardless of inflation. For example, one insurer guarantees until age 70, or five years if later, that the death benefit will be paid even though the net cash surrender value is negative, provided a certain level of premiums is paid. The CFA study showed that M&E charges ranged from .60 percent to .90 percent of the cash value.
- *Administrative costs.* Administrative costs are deducted monthly from the separate accounts, typically $5 to $10.

In addition to the above charges, there is a monthly deduction for the cost of insurance. The applicable mortality rate is multiplied by the net amount at risk (face amount minus the cash value) to determine the insurance charge.

Substantial Investment Risk   Variable universal life insurance is a risky type of life insurance to own.

There is a substantial investment risk. Consumers Union refers to variable universal life insurance as a form of "insurance roulette." The investment risk falls entirely on the policyowner. Investment returns vary widely, depending on how the funds are invested. If the investment experience is poor, cash values can decline to zero. This is particularly important for policyowners who are making only minimum premium payments or have discontinued premium payments. If the premiums are invested largely in common stocks and the separate account declines sharply because of a severe stock market decline, the policyowner may have to pay additional premiums to keep the policy in force.

Variable universal life insurance policyowners lost billions of dollars during the unprecedented three-year stock market decline of 2000–2002, one of the most severe market declines in the history of the United States. Many policyowners invested large amounts of money in variable universal life policies during the strong bull market prior to 2000, only to see their cash value accounts decline sharply during the subsequent three-year bear market that followed. However, during the market decline, insurers continued to make monthly deductions from the separate accounts for the cost of insurance and expense charges. As a result, accumulation units purchased at higher stock market prices had to be liquidated at lower prices to pay for the cost of insurance and other expenses, in effect "buying high and selling low." Investing in the stock market may be a fine way to save money, especially for retirement, but not when your life insurance protection is at stake.

The Consumer Federation of America (CFA) believes variable universal life insurance policies are complex and difficult to understand and recommends that consumers seeking tax-advantaged investments should first consider investing in a Section 401(k) plan or Roth IRA (see Insight 17.2). These retirement products are discussed later in the text.

Current Assumption Whole Life Insurance

Current assumption whole life insurance (also called interest-sensitive whole life) is a nonparticipating whole life policy in which the cash values are based on the insurer's current mortality, investment, and expense experience. A nonparticipating policy is a policy that does not pay dividends.

INSIGHT 17.2

Variable Universal Life Insurance: Is It Worth It?

A report prepared by the Consumer Federation of America's life insurance expert—actuary James H. Hunt, former Vermont insurance commissioner—addresses the question, is variable universal life insurance (VUL) worth it? The report's answer is that a VUL policy is extremely difficult to understand and comparison shop but can provide good value if intelligently purchased, held, and managed.

"Variable universal life insurance policies are so complex that they are difficult for most consumers to purchase intelligently," said Hunt. "Those seeking tax-sheltered investments should look first to 401-Ks or even to Roth IRAs," he added.

Variable universal life insurance combines features of term insurance and a mutual fund. It represents the most popular type of cash value life insurance sold in recent years. In 2000, for example, variable life captured 57 percent of the market for new cash value policies, as measured by premiums paid. And, well over 90 percent of these variable life premiums represented VUL policies worth $9 billion. While the decline in stock prices lowered VUL sales more recently, when these prices rebound so should VUL sales.

"Many consumers who, several years ago, replaced whole life policies by transferring policy values to VUL policies have lost billions of dollars," said Hunt. "On the other hand, those who are now replacing VUL policies with universal life policies could also lose billions of dollars if stock prices increase in the future," he added.

To help consumers evaluate new or existing VUL policies and other cash value insurance policies, the nonprofit Consumer Federation offers a Rate of Return Service provided by Hunt. In the past 15 years, Hunt has analyzed more than 5000 policies. The cost of this analysis per policy ranges from $55 to $75. Consumers can learn more about the service by calling 1-202-387-0087 or by consulting www.evaluate lifeinsurance.org or www.consumerfed.org.

High Charges May More than Offset Tax Benefits

As well as insurance protection, the main attraction of a VUL policy is providing a tax shelter—under current law, VUL investment earnings do not represent taxable income, and if the policy is held to death, no income taxes are ever assessed. The main cost of a VUL policy, however, which can more than offset the tax benefits, is an array of charges:

- Federal and state premium taxes that vary among states but average around 3 percent of premiums;
- M&E (mortality and expense) charges assessed against cash values that range, among policies studied, from 60 to 90 basis points (with 100 basis points equaling 1 percentage point);
- Investment management assets charges that vary, among policies studied, from 20 to 162 basis points; and
- Surrender charges that typically exceed the first year's premium and last from 10 to 15 years.

Common Features Although current assumption whole life products vary among insurers, they share some common features, summarized as follows:[7]

- *An accumulation account is used to reflect the cash value under the policy.* The accumulation account is credited with the premiums paid less expenses and mortality charges plus interest based on current rates.
- *If the policy is surrendered, a surrender charge is deducted from the accumulation account.* A surrender charge that declines over time, such as 10 to 20 years, is deducted from the accumulation account to determine the net cash surrender value.
- *A guaranteed interest rate and current interest rate are used to determine cash values.* The minimum cash values are based on the guaranteed

interest rate, such as 4 or 4.5 percent. However, the accumulation account is credited with a higher interest rate based on current market conditions and company experience.

- *A fixed death benefit and maximum premium level at the time of issue are stated in the policy.* (However, under the low-premium version discussed next, both are subject to change.)

In addition to having the preceding characteristics, current assumption whole life products generally can be classified into two categories: (1) low-premium products and (2) high-premium products.

Low-Premium Products Under the low-premium version, the initial premium is substantially lower than the premium paid for a regular, nonparticipating whole life policy. The low premium is initially

INSIGHT 17.2 (continued)

Variable Universal Life Insurance: Is It Worth It?

For consumers who bought VUL policies in recent years, the report recommends the following:z

- Hold the policies at least through the surrender charge period;
- "Dollar cost average" through market weakness;
- Be informed about the level of asset charges on "name accounts" and consider changing to an index fund; and
- Never surrender a VUL policy with a loss without looking into a transfer of the loss in the policy—the excess of premiums over the surrender value—to a variable annuity.

When and How VUL Policies Should be Purchased

The report recommends that consumers considering a VUL policy purchase should first compare an attractive VUL policy to a combination of term insurance and a low-cost mutual fund. In general, purchasing a VUL policy can make sense if one plans on taking substantial "tax-free" withdrawals or loans as retirement income and intends to maintain the policy until death. (And in general, VUL policies are more attractive than a combination of term insurance and a variable annuity, because the latter is expensive and its earnings will be taxable to someone, someday.)

Those wishing to purchase a VUL policy should look first to an insurer that deals directly with the public and charges no or low commissions. Low-load insurers include Ameritas (800-552-3553), USAA Life (800-531-8000), and TIAA-CREF (800-223-1200). The report notes that Ameritas is particularly attractive because it makes available the low-cost Vanguard separate accounts while allowing buyers to change their minds about investment purchases at minimum cost. TIAA-CREF policies also have very low asset charges.

When shopping for a VUL policy, the report specifically recommends that consumers:

- Decide on the amount of the premium you would like to pay and how frequently;
- Decide on the amount of insurance you would like to have and whether you want Option A or Option B. In seeking to maximize the tax-advantaged investment aspects of a policy, ask or the lowest Option B insurance amount that is not a Modified Endowment contract (MEC), and ask that Option A be illustrated beginning in policy year eight.
- Eliminate any riders, which usually offer poor value, such as a rider or your spouse. A term life rider on the insured person can be effective in lowering commission costs, but some term riders cost nearly double what careful shopping can achieve.
- Request an illustration at some hypothetical gross earnings rate, such as 8 percent. Specify that you would like the illustration to assume that 100 percent of your investment allocations be in the lowest cost, index account even if later you intend a different selection.
- Compare the columns of cash surrender values among competing illustrations. In general, the higher the surrender values the better the policy.
- Read the full CFA report, which provides many examples of what different insurers charge for VUL policies as well as much analysis and advice (see www.consumerfed.org).

SOURCE: Adapted from Consumer Federation of America, *New CFA Report Answers Question—Is Variable Universal Life Insurance Worth It?*, Press Release, February 24, 2003.

---

guaranteed only for a certain period, such as five years. However, after the initial guaranteed period expires, a *redetermination provision* allows the insurer to recalculate the premium based on the same or different actuarial assumptions with respect to mortality, interest, and expenses (hence, the name "current assumption whole life"). If the new premium is higher than the initial premium, the policyowner generally has the option of paying the higher premium and maintaining the same death benefit. Alternatively, the policyowner can continue to pay the lower premium, but the death benefit is reduced.

High-Premium Products   Although premiums are higher under the second category, these policies typically contain a *vanishing premium provision* in

which the premiums vanish after a certain time period, such as ten years. The premium vanishes when the accumulation account exceeds the net single premium needed to pay up the contract based on current interest and mortality costs.[8] *However, the policy remains paid up only if current interest and mortality experience remain unchanged or are more favorable than initially assumed.* If the accumulation account falls below the minimum cash surrender value, additional premiums are required.

Indeterminate-Premium Whole Life Insurance

An **indeterminate-premium whole life policy** *is a generic name for a nonparticipating policy that permits the insurer to adjust premiums based on* *anticipated future experience.* The maximum premium that can be charged is stated in the policy. The actual premium paid when the policy is issued is considerably lower and may be guaranteed for some initial period, such as three to five years. The intent is to have the actual premium paid reflect current market conditions. After the initial guaranteed period expires, the insurer can increase premiums up to the maximum limit if future anticipated experience with respect to mortality, investments, and expenses is expected to worsen. However, the premiums may not change if future experience is expected to be similar to past experience. Conversely, if future experience is expected to improve, then the insurer can further reduce the premiums if it desires to do so.

Exhibit 17.4 summarizes the basic characteristics of the major forms of life insurance. This chart helps to clarify the major types of life insurance and how they differ.

OTHER TYPES OF LIFE INSURANCE

A wide variety of additional life insurance products are sold today. Some policies are designed to meet special needs or have unique features. Others combine term insurance and cash-value life insurance to meet these needs.

Modified Life Insurance

A **modified life policy** is a whole life policy in which premiums are lower for the first three to five years and higher thereafter. The initial premium is slightly higher than for term insurance, but considerably lower than for an ordinary life policy issued at the same age.

There are several variations of the modified life policy. Under one version, the premium increases only once at the end of three or five years, and a dividend is paid that can be used to offset most or all of the premium increase. Under another version, the premiums gradually increase each year for five years and remain level thereafter. Finally, term insurance can be used for the first three to five years, which automatically converts into an ordinary life policy at a slightly higher premium than for a regular ordinary life policy issued at the same age.

The major advantage of a modified life policy is that insureds can purchase permanent insurance immediately even though they cannot afford the higher premiums for a regular whole life policy. Modified life insurance is particularly attractive to persons who expect that their incomes will increase in the future and that higher premiums will not be financially burdensome.

Preferred Risks

Many life insurers sell policies at lower rates to individuals known as **preferred risks.** These people are individuals whose mortality experience is expected to be lower than average. The policy is carefully underwritten and is sold only to individuals whose health history, weight, occupation, and habits indicate more favorable mortality than the average. The insurer may also require the purchase of a minimum amount of insurance, such as $100,000. If an individual qualifies for a preferred rate, substantial savings are possible.

A discount for nonsmokers is a current example of a preferred risk policy. Most insurers offer substantially lower rates to nonsmokers in recognition of the more favorable mortality that can be expected of this group.

Second-to-Die Life Insurance

Second-to-die life insurance (also called survivorship life) is a form of life insurance that insures two or more lives and pays the death benefit upon the death of the second or last insured. The insurance usually is whole life, but it can be term. Because the death proceeds are paid only upon the death of the second or last insured, the premiums are substantially lower than if two individual policies were issued.

Second-to-die life insurance is widely used at the present time in estate planning. As a result of an unlimited marital deduction, the deceased's entire estate can be left to a surviving spouse free of any federal estate tax. However, when the surviving spouse dies, a sizable federal estate tax may be payable. A second-to-die policy would provide estate liquidity and the cash to pay estate taxes.

EXHIBIT 17.4
Comparison of Major Life Insurance Contracts

	Term Insurance	Ordinary Life Insurance	Variable Life Insurance	Universal Life Insurance	Variable Universal Life Insurance	Current Assumption Whole Life Insurance
Death benefit paid	Level or decreasing death benefit	Level death benefit	Guaranteed minimum death benefit plus increased amount from favorable investment returns	Either level or an increasing death benefit	Either level or an increasing death benefit	Level death benefit
Cash value	No cash value	Guaranteed cash values	Cash value depends on investment performance (not guaranteed).	Guaranteed minimum cash value plus excess interest credited to the account	Cash value depends on investment performance (not guaranteed).	Guaranteed minimum cash value plus excess interest credited
Premiums paid	Premiums increase at each renewal	Level premiums	Fixed level premiums	Flexible premiums	Flexible premiums	Premiums paid may vary based on insurer experience; guaranteed maximum premium
Policy loans	No	Yes	Yes	Yes	Yes	Yes
Partial withdrawal of cash value	No	No	No	Yes	Yes	Yes
Surrender charge	No	No	Yes	Yes	Yes	Yes

Juvenile Insurance

Juvenile insurance refers to life insurance purchased by a parent or adult on the lives of children younger than a certain age, such as age 14 or 15. Insurers generally require the child to be at least one month old before he or she can be insured. Some insurers, however, will insure a child as young as one day old.

The major disadvantage in insuring children is that the family head may be inadequately insured. Scarce premium dollars that could be used to increase the life insurance on the family head are instead diverted to the children.

Arguments for life insurance on children are not convincing. One argument is that insurance on children is less expensive because it is purchased at a younger age. This argument is deceptive. Although insurance premiums on children are lower, they are paid over a much longer time period. Premiums at the older ages are higher, but they are paid for shorter periods of time. Moreover, when present values are taken into account, the child's policy can be more expensive. One study indicated that the present value of the premiums for a $20,000 life-paid-up-at-age-65 policy issued by one insurer on a child at age 15 is $5584 at a 4 percent discount rate. However, the present value of the premiums for the same type of policy issued by the same insurer at age 35 is only $3905.[9] In short, a juvenile insurance policy may be no bargain when it comes to cost.

Another argument is that life insurance should be purchased to guarantee the future insurability of the children. This argument has slightly greater validity, but only if the husband and wife are adequately insured. Unfortunately, a guaranteed insurability option cannot be purchased separately but must be added to the permanent life insurance policy. Even if future insurability cannot be guaranteed, the odds are that the children will still be able to purchase insurance in the future. More than 90 percent of all new policies sold are issued at standard rates.

Savings Bank Life Insurance

Savings bank life insurance (SBLI) is a type of life insurance that was sold originally by mutual savings banks in three states—Massachusetts, New York,

and Connecticut. More recently, however, SBLI is also sold directly to consumers over the phone or through Internet Web sites in those states and in additional states as well.

A number of SBLI products are available, including term and whole life insurance, insurance for children and seniors, and tax-deferred annuities.

Maximum limits on the amount of savings bank life insurance on an individual's life have been substantially raised. Applicants can now purchase a substantial amount of life insurance in those states where SBLI is sold. In Massachusetts, the amount of term insurance on a single life ranges from $100,000 to $5 million. In addition, SBLI products in Massachusetts are sold directly to consumers in a number of surrounding states, including Maine, New Hampshire, New Jersey, Pennsylvania, and Rhode Island.

In Connecticut, substantial amounts of SBLI life insurance can also be purchased. Applicants can purchase individual term insurance up to a maximum of $5 million. Whole life insurance can be purchased in amounts up to $5 million as well.

In 1998, New York passed legislation that allowed savings bank life insurance to be sold by one mutual life insurance company. The company is now called the SBLI USA Mutual Life Insurance Company. SBLI USA now sells to consumers in New York and in other jurisdictions as well, including New Jersey, Pennsylvania, South Dakota, and Puerto Rico. The legislation increased substantially the amount of life insurance on an individual life. Individual term insurance policies are available in amounts ranging from $100,000 to $1 million or more. Group life insurance plans are available in amounts ranging from $25,000 to $100,000. Whole life insurance is also available in amounts ranging from $2000 to $1 million.

The objective of SBLI is to provide low-cost insurance to consumers by holding down operating costs and the payment of high sales commissions. The cost of life insurance to consumers is an important topic that will be discussed in Chapter 19.

Industrial Life Insurance

Industrial life insurance (sometimes called *debit insurance*) is a class of life insurance that is issued in small amounts, and the premiums are payable weekly or monthly. In the past, the premiums were collected at the insured's home by an agent of the company. More than nine out of ten such policies were cash-value policies.

In recent years, industrial life insurance has also been called **home service life insurance,** reflecting the fact that individual policies are serviced by agents who call at the policyowner's home to collect the premiums. In most cases, however, home collections are no longer made. The policyowner remits the premiums to the agent or to the company. The amount of life insurance per policy generally ranges from $5000 to $25,000. Home service life insurance is relatively unimportant and accounts for less than 1 percent of all life insurance in force.

Group Life Insurance

Group life insurance is a type of insurance that provides life insurance on a group of people in a single master contract. Physical examinations are not required, and certificates of insurance are issued as evidence of insurance.

Group life insurance is important in terms of total life insurance in force. Most group life contracts provide term insurance coverage. In 2002, group life insurance accounted for 42 percent of all life insurance in force in the United States.[10] It is an important employee benefit provided by employers and will be discussed in greater detail in Chapter 22.

CASE APPLICATION

Sharon, age 28, is a single parent who earns $28,000 annually as a secretary at a local university. She is the sole support of her son, age 3. Sharon is concerned about the financial well-being of her son if she should die. Although she finds it difficult to save, she would like to start a savings program to send her son to college. She is currently renting an apartment but would like to own a home someday. A friend has told her that life insurance might be useful in her present situation. Sharon knows nothing about life insurance, and the amount of income available for life insurance is limited. Assume you are a financial planner who is asked to make recommendations concerning the type of life insurance that Sharon should buy. The following types of life insurance policies are available:

- Five-year renewable and convertible term
- Life-paid-up-at-age 65
- Ordinary life insurance
- Universal life insurance

a. Which of these policies would best meet the need for protection of Sharon's son if she should die prematurely? Explain your answer.

b. Which of these policies best meets the need to accumulate a college fund for Sharon's son? Explain your answer.

c. Which of these policies best meets the need to accumulate money for a down payment on a home? Explain your answer.

d. What major obstacle does Sharon face if she tries to meet all of her financial needs by purchasing cash-value life insurance?

e. Sharon decides to purchase the five-year term policy in the amount of $300,000. The policy has no cash value. Identify a basic characteristic of a typical term insurance policy that would help Sharon accumulate a fund for retirement.

SUMMARY

- *Term insurance* provides temporary protection and is typically renewable and convertible without evidence of insurability. Term insurance is appropriate when income is limited, or when there are temporary needs. Because term insurance usually has no cash values, it cannot be used for retirement or savings purposes.

- There are several traditional forms of whole life insurance. *Ordinary life insurance* is a form of whole life

insurance that provides lifetime protection to age 100. The premiums are level and are payable for life. The policy develops an investment or saving element called a cash surrender value, which results from the overpayment of premiums during the early years. An ordinary life policy is appropriate when lifetime protection is desired or additional savings are desired.

- A *limited-payment policy* is another traditional form of whole life insurance. The insured also has lifetime protection, but the premiums are paid only for a limited period, such as 10, 20, or 30 years, or until age 65.

- *Endowment insurance* pays the face amount of insurance if the insured dies within a specified period. If the insured survives to the end of the endowment period, the face amount of insurance is paid to the policyowner at that time.

- *Variable life insurance* is a fixed-premium policy in which the death benefit and cash surrender value vary according to the investment experience of a separate account maintained by the insurer. The entire reserve is held in a separate account and is invested in common stocks or other investments. The cash surrender values are not guaranteed.

- *Universal life insurance* is another variation of whole life insurance. Conceptually, universal life can be viewed as a flexible-premium policy that provides lifetime protection under a contract that separates the protection and saving components. Universal life insurance has the following features:

    Unbundling of protection, savings, and expense components

    Two forms of universal life insurance

    Considerable flexibility

    Cash withdrawals permitted

    Favorable income-tax treatment

- *Variable universal life insurance* is similar to universal life insurance with two major exceptions. First, the cash values can be invested in a wide variety of investments. Second, there is no minimum guaranteed interest rate, and the investment risk falls entirely on the policyowner.

- *Current assumption whole life insurance* is a nonparticipating whole life policy in which the cash values are based on the insurer's current mortality, investment, and expense experience. An accumulation account is credited with a current interest rate that changes over time.

- An *indeterminate-premium whole life policy* is a nonparticipating policy that permits the insurer to adjust premiums based on anticipated future experience. The initial premiums are guaranteed for a certain time period and can then be increased up to some maximum limit.

- A *modified life policy* is a whole life policy in which premiums are lower for the first three to five years and are higher thereafter.

- Many insurers sell policies with lower rates to preferred risks. The policies are carefully underwritten and sold only to individuals whose health history, weight, occupation, and habits indicate more favorable mortality than average. Minimum amounts of insurance must be purchased.

- *Second-to-die life insurance* (*survivorship life*) insures two or more lives and pays the death benefit upon the death of the second or last insured.

- *Juvenile insurance* refers to life insurance purchased by a parent or other adult on the lives of children younger than a certain age, such as age 15 or 16.

- *Savings bank life insurance* is sold in Massachusetts, New York, and Connecticut, and other states as well. It is also sold directly to consumers over the phone or Internet.

- *Industrial life insurance* is a type of insurance in which the policies are sold in small amounts, and the premiums earlier were paid to an agent at the policyowner's home.

- *Group life insurance* provides life insurance on people in a group under a single master contract.

KEY CONCEPTS AND TERMS

Cash surrender value	Preferred risks
Cash-value life insurance	Reentry term
Convertible	Renewable
Current assumption whole life insurance	Savings bank life insurance
Endowment insurance	Second-to-die life insurance
Group life insurance	Single-premium whole life insurance
Indeterminate-premium whole life policy	Term insurance
Industrial (home service) life insurance	Universal life insurance
Juvenile insurance	Variable life insurance
Limited-payment policy	Variable universal life insurance
Modified life policy	Whole life insurance
Ordinary life insurance	

REVIEW QUESTIONS

1. a. Briefly explain the basic characteristics of term insurance policies.

   b. Identify the major types of term insurance policies sold today.

2. a. Explain the situations that justify the purchase of term insurance.

   b. What are the major limitations of term insurance?

3. a. Briefly explain the basic characteristics of ordinary life policies.

   b. Why does an ordinary life insurance policy develop a legal reserve?

4. a. Explain the situations that justify the purchase of ordinary life insurance.

   b. What is the major limitation of ordinary life insurance?

5. Describe the basic characteristics of variable life insurance.

6. a. Explain the basic characteristics of universal life policies.

   b. Explain the limitations of universal life insurance.

7. a. What is a variable universal life insurance policy?

   b. How does variable universal life insurance differ from a typical universal life insurance policy?

   c. Identify the various expense charges that policyowners must pay under a variable universal life insurance policy.

8. Describe the basic features of current assumption whole life insurance.

9. What is a preferred risk policy?

10. Should life insurance be purchased on the lives of children? Explain your answer.

APPLICATION QUESTIONS

1. Megan, age 28, is married and has a son, age one. She recently purchased a cash-value life insurance policy that has the following characteristics:
   — The frequency and amount of premium payments are flexible.
   — The insurance and saving components are separate.
   — The interest rate credited to the policy is tied to current market conditions, but the policy guarantees a minimum interest rate.
   — The policy has a back-end surrender charge that declines to zero over some time period.

   Based on the above characteristics, what type of life insurance did Megan purchase? Explain your answer.

2. Todd, age 35, would like to save money for a comfortable retirement. He is considering purchasing a cash-value life insurance policy that has the following characteristics:

   — The premiums are invested in separate accounts selected by the policyowner.
   — Interest income and capital gains are not currently taxable to the policyowner.
   — The frequency and amount of premium payments can be changed as financial circumstances change.
   — A mortality and expense (M&E) charge is periodically deducted from the cash value account.

   Based on the above characteristics, what type of life insurance is Todd considering purchasing? Explain your answer.

3. For each of the following situations, describe a life insurance policy that can be used to meet the situation. Treat each situation separately.
   a. An increasing face amount of insurance if the investment results are favorable
   b. Insuring the human life value of an individual, age 35, at the lowest possible annual premium
   c. A policy that permits the policyowner to determine how the premiums are to be invested
   d. A policy that allows cash withdrawals for a down payment on a home or payment of college tuition for the children
   e. A policy that is sold to insureds whose mortality experience is expected to be lower than average
   f. A policy in which premiums are lower for the first three to five years and higher thereafter, which may appeal to insureds whose incomes are expected to increase
   g. A policy designed to pay estate taxes upon the death of the last surviving spouse

4. Susan, age 35, is a single parent with two preschool children. She would like to purchase a traditional life insurance policy with a face amount of $100,000. She is considering the following policies:
   (1) Five-year renewable and convertible term insurance that is renewable until age 65
   (2) Ordinary life insurance
   (3) Twenty-payment whole life insurance
   (4) Life paid-up-at-age-65
   a. Which of these contracts requires the highest and lowest current annual premium outlay?
   b. If Susan intends to keep the insurance until age 65, under which of these contracts will the annual premium increase?
   c. Which of these contracts will allow Susan to continue her life insurance protection beyond age 65? Explain your answer.

d. If Susan has only a limited amount of income to spend on life insurance, which life insurance policy should she purchase?

5. Richard, age 35, is married and has two children, ages 2 and 5. He is considering the purchase of additional life insurance. He has the following financial goals and objectives:
 • Paying off the mortgage on his home, which has 25 years to run.
 • Accumulation of a sizeable retirement fund.
 • Payment of monthly income to the family if he should die.
 • Withdrawal of funds from the policy when the children reach college age.

For each of the following life insurance policies, indicate which of the above financial goals, if any, could be met if the policy is purchased. Treat each policy separately.
a. Decreasing term insurance
b. Ordinary life insurance
c. Universal life insurance
d. Variable universal life insurance

INTERNET RESOURCES

■ The **American Council of Life Insurers** represents the life insurance industry on issues dealing with legislation and regulation at the federal and state levels. The site provides consumer information on the purposes and types of life insurance. Visit the site at

http://www.acli.com

■ The **Consumer Federation of America (CFA)** is a nonprofit organization that represents numerous consumer groups. This site is one of the best sources for obtaining meaningful consumer information about life insurance policies and other insurance products. CFA makes available a low-cost life insurance evaluation service by which individual life insurance policies can be evaluated for a small fee. Visit the site at

http://www.consumerfed.org

■ **INSWEB** provides timely information and premium quotes for life insurance as well as homeowners, auto, and other insurance products. Visit the site at

http://www.insweb.com

■ **Insure.com** provides up-to-date information, premium quotes, and other consumer information on life insur-

ance. The site also provides news releases about events that affect the insurance industry. Visit the site at

http://www.insure.com

■ The **National Underwriter Company** publishes books and other documents on life insurance products. The company publishes the *National Underwriter,* Life & Health/Financial Services edition, a weekly trade publication that provides timely news about the life insurance industry and new life insurance products. Visit the site at

http://www.nationalunderwriter.com

■ The **National Association of Insurance Commissioners (NAIC)** has a link to all state insurance departments, which provide a considerable amount of consumer information on the types of life insurance discussed in this chapter. Click on State Insurance Web Sites. For starters, check out New York, Wisconsin, and California. Visit the site at

http://www.naic.org

SELECTED REFERENCES

Belth, Joseph M. *Life Insurance: A Consumer's Handbook,* 2nd ed. Bloomington, IN: Indiana University Press, 1985.

Black, Kenneth, Jr., and Harold D. Skipper, Jr. *Life Insurance,* 13th ed. Upper Saddle River, NJ: Prentice-Hall, 2000.

Graves, Edward E., ed. *McGill's Life Insurance,* 5th ed. Bryn Mawr, PA: The American College, 2004.

Hunt, James H. *Variable Universal Life Insurance: Is It Worth It?* Consumer Federation of America, February 2003.

Life Insurers Fact Book, 2003. Washington, DC: American Council of Life Insurers, 2004.

Weining, Eric A., George E. Rejda, Constance M. Luthardt, and Cheryl L. Ferguson. *Personal Insurance,* First Edition. Malvern, PA.: American Institute for Chartered Property Casualty Underwriters/Insurance Institute of America, 2002.

NOTES

1. These characteristics are discussed in greater detail in Edward E. Graves, ed., *McGill's Life Insurance,* 5th ed. (Bryn Mawr, PA: The American College,

2004); and Kenneth Black, Jr., and Harold D. Skipper, Jr., *Life Insurance,* 13th ed. (Upper Saddle River, NJ: Prentice-Hall, 2000), ch. 4.

2. Black and Skipper, p. 79.

3. Because of increases in longevity, some insurers are now extending the period of protection to some later age, such as 103.

4. This section is based on Graves, ch. 5; Black and Skipper, pp. 114–127; and Joseph M. Belth, ed., "The War Over Universal Life—Part 1," *Insurance Forum,* vol. 8, no. 11 (November 1981).

5. Limitations of universal life are discussed in detail in Belth, ed., "The War Over Universal Life—Part 1," *Insurance Forum,* vol. 8, no. 11 (November 1981); "The War Over Universal Life—Part 2," *Insurance Forum,* vol. 8, no. 12 (December 1981); and "Universal Life Insurance," *Consumer Reports* (August 1986).

6. *New CFA Report Answers Question—Is Variable Universal Life Insurance Worth it?,* Consumer Federation of America, February 24, 2003.

7. This section is based on Black and Skipper, pp. 97–101.

8. Ibid., p. 100.

9. Glenn L. Wood, et al., *Personal Risk Management and Insurance,* 4th ed., vol. 2 (Malvern, PA: American Institute for Property and Liability Underwriters, 1989), p. 29.

10. *Life Insurers Fact Book, 2003* (Washington, DC: American Council of Life Insurers, 2003), p. 98.

Students may take a self-administered test on this chapter at

www.aw-bc.com/rejda

CHAPTER 18

LIFE INSURANCE CONTRACTUAL PROVISIONS

"Nearly every family buys life insurance; yet few policyholders ever read a life insurance contract with any effort to understand its provisions."

Mehr and Gustavson,
Life Insurance: Theory and Practice

After studying this chapter, you should be able to

◆ Describe the following contractual provisions that appear in life insurance policies:
  Incontestable clause
  Suicide clause
  Grace period provision

◆ Identify the dividend options that typically appear in participating life insurance policies.

◆ Explain the cash-surrender options (nonforfeiture options) that appear in cash-value policies.

◆ Describe the various settlement options for the payment of life insurance death benefits.

◆ Describe the following riders that can be added to a life insurance policy:
   Waiver of premium
   Guaranteed purchase option
   Accidental death benefit rider
   Cost-of-living rider
   Accelerated death benefits rider

*R*aymond, age 30, and Jennifer, age 28, are married and have a daughter, age one. Raymond recently purchased a $500,000 term insurance policy that requires an annual premium payment of $400. One week after the second annual premium was due, Raymond died unexpectedly in a hit-and-run auto accident. He did not pay the premium on the policy before he died. Jennifer is concerned that the insurer will not pay the death claim because the premium had not been paid. Raymond's life insurance agent, however, assured her that the death benefits would be paid. Raymond died during the grace period for paying premiums, and the policy was still in force.

In the preceding case, Jennifer's financial security was affected by a life insurance contractual provision dealing with the grace period. Life insurance policies contain dozens of contractual provisions that affect the insured and beneficiary and payment of the death proceeds. Some contractual provisions are mandatory and must be included in every life insurance policy. Other provisions are optional.

This chapter discusses some common life insurance contractual provisions. It is divided into three major parts. The first part discusses life insurance contractual provisions that can have important financial consequences for consumers. The second part analyzes the basic options that frequently appear in life insurance policies, including dividend options, nonforfeiture options, and settlement options. The final part discusses additional benefits and riders that can be added to a life insurance policy.

LIFE INSURANCE CONTRACTUAL PROVISIONS

Life insurance policies contain numerous contractual provisions. This section discusses the major contractual provisions that life insurance consumers should understand.

Ownership Clause

The owner of a life insurance policy can be the insured, the beneficiary, a trust, or another party. In most cases, the applicant, insured, and owner are the same person. Under the **ownership clause,** *the policyowner possesses all contractual rights in the policy* *while the insured is living.* These rights include naming and changing the beneficiary, surrendering the policy for its cash value, borrowing the cash value, receiving dividends, and electing settlement options. These rights generally can be exercised without the beneficiary's consent.

The policy also provides for a change of ownership. The policyowner can designate a new owner by filing an appropriate form with the company. The insurer may require the policy to be endorsed to show the new owner.

Entire-Contract Clause

The **entire-contract clause** *states that the life insurance policy and attached application constitute the entire contract between the parties.* All statements in the application are considered to be representations rather than warranties. No statement can be used by the insurer to void the policy unless it is a material misrepresentation and is part of the application. In addition, the insurer cannot change the policy terms unless the policyowner consents to the change.

There are two basic purposes of the entire-contract clause. First, it prevents the insurer from amending the policy without the knowledge or consent of the owner by changing its charter or bylaws. Second, it also protects the beneficiary. A statement made in connection with the application cannot be used by the insurer to deny a claim unless the statement is a material misrepresentation and is part of the application.

Incontestable Clause

The **incontestable clause** *states that the insurer cannot contest the policy after it has been in force two years during the insured's lifetime.* After the policy has been in force for two years during the insured's lifetime, the insurer cannot later contest a death claim on the basis of a material misrepresentation, concealment, or fraud when the policy was first issued. The insurer has two years in which to discover any irregularities in the contract. With few exceptions, if the insured dies, the death claim must be paid after the contestable period expires. For example, if Tony, age 25, applies for a life insurance policy, conceals the fact that he has high blood pressure, and dies within the two-year

period, the insurer could contest the claim on the basis of a material concealment. But if he dies *after* expiration of the period, the insurer must pay the claim.

The purpose of the incontestable clause is to protect the beneficiary if the insurer tries to deny payment of the claim years after the policy was first issued. Because the insured is dead, he or she cannot refute the insurer's allegations. As a result, the beneficiary could be financially harmed if the claim is denied on the grounds of a material misrepresentation or concealment.

The incontestable clause is normally effective against fraud. If the insured makes a fraudulent misstatement to obtain the insurance, the company has two years to detect the fraud. Otherwise, the death claim must be paid. However, there are certain situations where the fraud is so outrageous that payment of the death claim would be against the public interest. In these cases, the insurer can contest the claim after the contestable period runs out. They include the following:[1]

- The beneficiary takes out a policy with the intent of murdering the insured.
- The applicant for insurance has someone else take a medical examination.
- An insurable interest does not exist at the inception of the policy.

Suicide Clause

Most life insurance policies contain a suicide clause. The **suicide clause** *states that if the insured commits suicide within two years after the policy is issued, the face amount of insurance will not be paid; there is only a refund of the premiums paid.* In some life insurance policies, suicide is excluded for only one year. If the insured commits suicide after the period expires, the policy proceeds are paid just like any other claim.

In legal terms, death is normally considered an unintentional act because of the strong instinct of self-preservation. Thus, there is a presumption against suicide. Consequently, the burden of proving suicide always rests on the insurer. To deny payment of the claim, the insurer must prove conclusively that the insured has committed suicide (see Insight 18.1).

INSIGHT 18.1

Is This Death a Suicide?

Facts

A 20-year-old Marine served in a fighter squadron as a radar technician. He was familiar with .45-caliber semi-automatic pistols and had given instructions on their use. The Marine was a happy-go-lucky, cheerful person who sometimes tried to "shake up" his friends by placing a .45 to his head and pulling the trigger. One day when the Marine was apparently in good spirits, he suddenly put a pistol to his head, said "Here's to it" to a friend, and pulled the trigger. The gun fired, killing the Marine. The insurance company that insured him claimed the death was a suicide.

Decision

The death is not a suicide.

Reasoning

The company must prove that the death was intentional. The burden of proof was not met here (*Angelus v. Government Personnel Life Ins. Co.,* 321 P.2d 545 [Wash. 1958]).

Source: *Business Law Text and Cases: The Legal Environment,* 3e by Frascona, Joseph L., ©1987. Reprinted by permission of Pearson Education, Inc., Upper Saddle River, NJ.

The purpose of the suicide clause is to reduce adverse selection against the insurer. By having a suicide clause, the insurer has some protection against the individual who wishes to purchase life insurance with the intention of committing suicide.

Grace Period

A life insurance policy also contains a **grace period** *during which the policyowner has a period of 31 days to pay an overdue premium.* Universal life and other flexible-premium policies have longer grace periods, such as 61 days. The insurance remains in force during the grace period. If the insured dies within the grace period, the overdue premium is deducted from the policy proceeds.

The purpose of the grace period is to prevent the policy from lapsing by giving the policyowner additional time to pay an overdue premium. The policyowner may be temporarily short of funds or may have forgotten to pay the premium. In such cases, the grace period provides considerable financial flexibility.

Reinstatement Clause

A policy may lapse if the premium has not been paid by the end of the grace period, or if an automatic premium loan provision is not in effect. The **reinstatement provision** *permits the owner to reinstate a lapsed policy.* The following requirements must be fulfilled to reinstate a lapsed policy:

- Evidence of insurability is required.
- All overdue premiums plus interest must be paid from their respective due dates.
- Any policy loan must be repaid or reinstated, with interest from the due date of the overdue premium.
- The policy must not have been surrendered for its cash value.
- The policy must be reinstated within a certain period, typically three or five years from the date of lapse.

It may be advantageous for a policyowner to reinstate a lapsed policy rather than purchase a new one. First, the premium is lower because the reinstated policy was issued at an earlier age. Second, the acquisition expenses incurred in issuing the policy must be paid again under a new policy. Third, cash values and dividends are usually higher under the reinstated policy; the new policy may not develop any cash values until the end of the third year. Fourth, the incontestable period and suicide period under the old policy may have expired. Reinstatement of a lapsed policy does not reopen the suicide period, and a new incontestable period generally applies only to statements contained in the application for reinstatement. Statements contained in the original application cannot be contested after the original contestable period expires. Finally, the reinstated policy may contain more favorable policy provisions, such as a 6 percent interest rate on policy loans.

A major disadvantage of reinstating a lapsed policy is that a substantial cash outlay is required if the policy lapsed several years earlier. Also, most life insurers have reduced premiums over time and have developed new products. As a result, it may cost less to purchase a new policy even though the insured is older when the new purchase is made. As a practical matter, most lapsed policies are not reinstated because of the required cash outlay.

Misstatement of Age or Sex Clause

Under the **misstatement of age or sex clause,** *if the insured's age or sex is misstated, the amount payable is the amount that the premiums paid would have purchased at the correct age and sex.* For example, assume that Troy, age 35, applies for a $20,000 ordinary life policy, but his age is incorrectly stated as age 34. If the premium is $20 per $1000 at age 35 and $19 per $1000 at age 34, the insurer will pay only 19/20 of the death proceeds. Thus, only $19,000 would be paid (19/20 × $20,000 = $19,000).

Beneficiary Designation

The beneficiary is the party named in the policy to receive the policy proceeds. The principal types of beneficiary designations are as follows:

- Primary and contingent beneficiary
- Revocable and irrevocable beneficiary
- Specific and class beneficiary

Primary and Contingent Beneficiary A **primary beneficiary** *is the beneficiary who is first entitled to receive the policy proceeds on the insured's death.* A **contingent beneficiary** *is entitled to the proceeds if the primary beneficiary dies before the insured.* If the primary beneficiary dies before receiving the guaranteed number of payments under an installment settlement option, the remaining payments are paid to the contingent beneficiary.

In many families, the husband will name his wife primary beneficiary (and vice versa), and the children will be named as contingent beneficiaries. The legal problem in naming *minor children* as beneficiaries is that they lack the legal capacity to receive the policy proceeds directly. Most insurers will not pay the death proceeds directly to minor children.[2] Instead, they will require a guardian to receive the proceeds on the minor's behalf. If a court of law appoints a *guardian,* payment of the proceeds may be delayed and legal expenses will be incurred. One solution is to have a *guardian* named in the will who can legally receive the proceeds on the children's behalf. Another approach is to pay the proceeds to a *trustee* (such as a commercial bank with a trust department), which has the discretion and authority to use the funds for the children's welfare.

The insured's estate can be named as primary or contingent beneficiary. However, many financial planners do not recommend designation of the estate as beneficiary. The death proceeds may be subject to attorney fees and other probate expenses, federal estate taxes, state inheritance taxes, and claims of creditors. Payment of the proceeds may also be delayed until the estate is settled.

Revocable and Irrevocable Beneficiary Most beneficiary designations are revocable. A **revocable beneficiary** *means that the policyowner reserves the right to change the beneficiary designation without the beneficiary's consent.* The revocable beneficiary has only the expectation of benefits, and the policyowner can change the beneficiary whenever desired. All policy rights under the contract can be exercised without the consent of the revocable beneficiary.

In contrast, an **irrevocable beneficiary** *is one that cannot be changed without the beneficiary's consent.* If the policyowner wishes to change the beneficiary designation, the irrevocable beneficiary must consent to the change. However, most policies today provide that the interest of a beneficiary, even an irrevocable beneficiary, terminates if the beneficiary dies before the insured. Thus, if the irrevocable beneficiary dies before the insured, all rights to the policy proceeds revert to the policyowner, who can then name a new beneficiary.

Specific and Class Beneficiary A **specific beneficiary** means the beneficiary is specifically named and identified. In contrast, under a **class beneficiary,** a specific person is not named but is a member of a group designated as beneficiary, such as "children of the insured." A class designation is appropriate whenever the insured wishes to divide the policy proceeds equally among members of a particular group.

Most insurers restrict the use of a class designation because of the problem of identifying members

LIFE INSURANCE CONTRACTUAL PROVISIONS

of the class. Although all insurers permit the designation of children as a class, they will not permit this designation to be used when the class members cannot be identified, or the relationship to the insured is remote. For example, the class designation "my children" means that all children of the insured share in the policy proceeds, whether legitimate, illegitimate, or adopted. But if "children of the insured" is used as the designation, the insured's children by any marriage would be included, but the spouse's children by a former marriage would be excluded. Thus, a class designation must be used with great care.

Change-of-Plan Provision

Life insurance policies may contain a **change-of-plan provision** that allows policyowners to exchange their present policies for different contracts. The purpose of this provision is to provide flexibility to the policyowner. The original policy may no longer be appropriate if family needs and financial objectives change.

If the change is to a *higher-premium policy*, such as changing from an ordinary life to a limited-payment policy, the policyowner must pay the difference in the policy reserve under the new policy and the policy reserve under the original policy. Evidence of insurability is not required, because the pure insurance protection (net amount at risk) is reduced.

In addition, based on company practice, the policyowner may be allowed to change to a *lower-premium policy*, such as changing from a limited-payment policy to an ordinary life policy. In such a case, the insurer refunds the difference in cash values under the two policies to the policyowner. Evidence of insurability is required in this type of change, because the pure insurance protection is increased (higher net amount at risk).

Exclusions and Restrictions

A life insurance policy contains remarkably few exclusions and restrictions. *Suicide* is excluded only for the first two years. During a period of war, some insurers may insert a **war clause** in their policies, which excludes payment if the insured dies as a direct result of war. The purpose of the war clause is to reduce adverse selection against the insurer when

large numbers of new insureds may be exposed to death during wartime.

In addition, **aviation exclusions** may be present in some policies. Most newly issued policies do not contain any exclusions with respect to aviation deaths, and aviation death claims are paid like any other claim. However, some insurers exclude aviation deaths other than as a fare-paying passenger on a regularly scheduled airline. Military aviation may also be excluded or be covered only by payment of an extra premium. In addition, a private pilot who does not meet certain flight standards may have an aviation exclusion rider inserted in the policy, or be charged a higher premium.

During the initial underwriting of the policy, the insurer may discover *certain undesirable activities or hobbies* of the insured. These activities may be excluded or covered only by payment of an extra premium. Some excluded activities are auto racing, skydiving, scuba diving, flying a hang glider, and travel or residence in a dangerous country.

Payment of Premiums

Life insurance premiums can be paid annually, semiannually, quarterly, or monthly. If the premium is paid other than annually, the policyowner must pay a carrying charge, which can be relatively expensive when the true rate of interest is calculated. For example, the semiannual premium may be 52 percent of the annual premium and so could be viewed as a carrying charge of only 4 percent. However, the actual charge is 16.7 percent. Assume that your annual premium is $1000. You pay the semiannual premium of $520 and defer payment of $480. Six months later, the $480 and $40 carrying charge are due. This means that you are paying $40 for the use of $480 for six months, which is the equivalent of an annual percentage rate of 16.7 percent.[3]

Assignment Clause

A life insurance policy is freely assignable to another party. There are two types of assignments. *Under an* **absolute assignment,** *all ownership rights in the policy are transferred to a new owner.* For example, the policyowner may wish to donate a life insurance policy to a church, charity, or educational institution. This goal can be accomplished by an absolute assignment. The new owner can then exercise the ownership rights in the policy.

Under a **collateral assignment,** *the policyowner assigns a life insurance policy as collateral for a loan.* The assignment form used is typically the American Bankers Association's assignment form. *Under this form, only certain rights are transferred to the creditor to protect its interest, and the policyowner retains the remaining rights.* The party to whom the policy is assigned can receive the policy proceeds only to the extent of the loan; the balance of the proceeds is paid to the beneficiary.

The purpose of the assignment clause is to protect the insurer from paying the policy proceeds twice if an unrecorded assignment is presented to the insurer after the death claim is paid to the beneficiary. If the insurer is not notified of the assignment, the proceeds are paid to the named beneficiary when the policy matures as a death claim or endowment. Under general rules of law, the insurer is relieved of any further obligation under the policy, even though a valid assignment is in existence at the insured's death. However, if the insurer is notified of the assignment, a new contract exists between the insurer and assignee (one who receives the assignment, such as a bank), and the insurer then recognizes the assignee's rights as being superior to the beneficiary's rights.

Policy Loan Provision

Cash-value life insurance contains a **policy loan provision** that allows the policyowner to borrow the cash value. The interest rate is stated in the policy. Older policies typically have a 5 or 6 percent loan rate. Newer policies typically have an 8 percent loan rate. However, all states permit insurers to charge a variable policy loan interest rate based on the National Association of Insurance Commissioner's model bill. If a variable rate is used, limits exist on the maximum rate that can be charged. The maximum interest rate is the greater of Moody's Composite Yield on seasoned corporate bonds two months prior to the determination date or the interest rate credited to the cash value plus 1 percent.[4] The policy loan rate can be revised as often as every three months.

On newly issued participating contracts, many insurers will reduce the dividend based on the amount of cash value borrowed. This step has the effect of indirectly increasing the effective interest rate on the policy loan. Under interest-sensitive policies, such as universal life and variable universal life, the current interest rate credited to the cash values that are borrowed is typically reduced, which again increases the effective interest rate on the loan.

Interest on a policy loan must either be paid annually or added to the outstanding loan if not paid. If the loan is not repaid by the time the policy matures as a death claim or endowment, the face amount of the policy is reduced by the amount of indebtedness. With the exception of a policy loan to pay a premium, the insurer can defer granting the loan for up to six months, but this is rarely done.

Persons who borrow their cash values often believe that they are paying interest on their own money. *This view is clearly incorrect. The cash value legally belongs to the insurer.* Although you have the contractual right to surrender or borrow the cash value, the cash legally belongs to the insurer. Interest must be paid on the loan because the insurer assumes a certain interest rate when premiums, legal reserves, dividends, and surrender values are calculated. The insurer's assets must be invested in interest-bearing securities and other investments so that the contractual obligations can be met. *A policyowner must pay interest on the loan to offset the loss of interest to the insurer.* If the loan had not been granted, the insurer could have earned interest on the funds.

Notice, too, that policy loan provisions make it necessary for the insurer to keep some assets in lower-yielding, liquid investments to meet the demand for policy loans. Because these funds could have been invested in higher-yielding investments, policy-owners who borrow should pay interest because higher yields must be forsaken to maintain liquidity.

Advantages of Policy Loans   The major advantage of a policy loan is the relatively low rate of interest that is paid. This is especially true for older contracts. The low policy loan rates of 5, 6, or 8 percent are substantially lower than credit card rates. There is also no credit check on the policyowner's ability to repay the loan; there is no fixed repayment schedule; and the policyowner has complete financial flexibility in determining the amount and frequency of loan repayments.

Disadvantages of Policy Loans The major disadvantage is that the policyowner is not legally required to repay the loan, and the policy could lapse if the total indebtedness exceeds the available cash value. Rather than repay the loan, the policyowner may let the policy lapse or may surrender the policy for any remaining cash value. Finally, if the loan has not been repaid by the time the policy matures, the face amount of insurance is reduced by the amount of the debt.

Automatic Premium Loan

The automatic premium loan provision can be added to most cash-value policies. *Under the* **automatic premium loan provision,** *an overdue premium is automatically borrowed from the cash value after the grace period expires, provided the policy has a loan value sufficient to pay the premium.* The policy continues in force just as before, but a premium loan is now outstanding. Interest is charged on the premium loan at the stated contractual rate. Premium payments can be resumed at any time without evidence of insurability.

The basic purpose of an automatic premium loan is to prevent the policy from lapsing because of nonpayment of premiums. The policyowner may be temporarily short of funds or may forget to pay the premium. Thus, the automatic premium loan provides considerable financial flexibility to the policyowner.

The automatic premium loan provision, however, has two major disadvantages. First, it may be overused. The policyowner may get into the habit of using the automatic premium loan provision too frequently. If the cash values are relatively modest and are habitually borrowed over an extended period, they could eventually be exhausted, and the contract would terminate. Second, the policy proceeds will be reduced if the premium loans are not repaid by the time of death.

DIVIDEND OPTIONS

Life insurance policies frequently contain dividend options. If the policy pays dividends, it is known as a **participating policy.** Both stock and mutual insurers issue participating policies, which gives the policyowner the right to share in the divisible surplus of the insurer. The dividend represents largely a refund of part of the gross premium if the insurer has favorable experience with respect to mortality, interest, and expenses. In contrast, a policy that does not pay dividends is known as a **nonparticipating policy.**

Policy dividends are derived from three principal sources: (1) the difference between expected and actual mortality experience; (2) excess interest earnings on the assets required to maintain legal reserves; and (3) the difference between expected and actual operating expenses. Because the dividends paid are determined by the insurer's actual operating experience, they cannot be guaranteed.

There are several ways in which dividends can be taken:

- Cash
- Reduction of premiums
- Dividend accumulations
- Paid-up additions
- Term insurance (fifth dividend option)

Cash

A dividend is usually payable after the policy has been in force for a stated period, typically one or two years. The policyowner receives a check equal to the dividend, usually on the anniversary date of the policy.

Reduction of Premiums

The dividend can be used to reduce the next premium coming due. The dividend notice will indicate the amount of the dividend, and the policyowner must then remit the difference between the premium and actual dividend paid. This option is appropriate whenever premium payments become financially burdensome. It can also be used if the policyowner has a substantial reduction in income and expenses must be reduced.

Dividend Accumulations

The dividend can be retained by the insurer and accumulated at interest. The policy guarantees a minimum interest rate such as 3 percent, but a higher rate may be paid based on current market conditions. The accumulated dividends generally can be withdrawn at any time. If not withdrawn, they are added to the amount paid when the policy matures as a death claim, or the contract is surrendered for its cash value. The dividend itself is not taxable for income-tax purposes. However, the interest income on the accumulated dividends is taxable income and must be reported annually for federal and state income-tax purposes. Thus, the accumulation option may be undesirable for policyowners who wish to minimize income taxes.

Paid-up Additions

Under the **paid-up additions option,** *the dividend is used to purchase a small amount of paid-up whole life insurance.* For example, assume that Paige, age 20, owns an ordinary life policy. If a dividend of $50 were paid, about $200 of paid-up whole life insurance could be purchased.

The paid-up additions option has some favorable features. *First, the paid-up additions are purchased at net rates, not gross rates;* there is no loading for expenses. *Second, evidence of insurability is not required.* Thus, if the insured is substandard in health or is uninsurable, this option may be appealing, because additional amounts of life insurance can be purchased without demonstrating insurability.

One disadvantage, however, is that *paid-up additions are a form of single premium whole life insurance.* Consumer experts point out that rarely is a single premium policy appropriate for most insureds. For example, if a $100,000 ordinary life insurance policy is desired, the insured normally does not pay a single premium of $40,000 to obtain the protection. Consequently, why should a $40 dividend be used to buy a $100 paid-up addition? Because most people are underinsured, a better approach would be to use the dividends to purchase another policy if the applicant is insurable. A reasonable approach would be to accumulate the dividends either under the interest option or paid-up additions option for several years. The accumulated cash could then be used to purchase a new policy.[6]

Term Insurance (Fifth Dividend Option)

Some insurers offer a fifth dividend option by which the dividend is used to purchase term insurance. Two forms of this option are typically used. *The dividend can be used to purchase one-year term insurance equal to the cash value of the basic policy, and the remainder of the dividend is then used to buy paid-up additions or is accumulated at interest.* This option may be appropriate if the policyowner regularly borrows the cash value. The face amount of the policy would not be reduced by the amount of any outstanding loans at the time of death.

A second form of this option is to use the dividend to purchase yearly renewable term insurance. The actual amount of term insurance purchased depends on the amount of the dividend, the insured's attained age, and the insurer's term insurance rates. However, it is not uncommon for a $40 dividend to purchase $10,000 or more yearly renewable term insurance under this option. Unfortunately, this desirable option is offered by only a small proportion of companies.

Other Uses of Dividends

The dividends can also be used to convert a policy into a *paid-up contract.* If the paid-up option is used, the policy becomes paid-up whenever the reserve value under the basic contract plus the reserve value of the paid-up additions or deposits equal the net single premium for a paid-up policy at the insured's attained age. For example, an ordinary life policy issued at age 25 could be paid up by age 48 by using this option.

The dividend can also be used to *mature a policy as an endowment.* When the reserve value under the basic policy plus the reserve value of the paid-up additions or deposits equal the face amount of insurance, the policy matures as an endowment. For example, a $50,000 ordinary life policy issued at age 25 would mature as an endowment at age 58 by using this option.[7]

Finally, keep in mind that the use of dividend options will vary among policyowners. There is no best dividend option. The best option to use is the one that best meets your financial goals and objectives (see Insight 18.2).

NONFORFEITURE OPTIONS

If a cash-value policy is purchased, the policyowner pays more than is actuarially necessary for the life insurance protection. Thus, the policyowner should get something back if the policy is surrendered. The payment to a withdrawing policyowner is known as a nonforfeiture value or cash surrender value.

INSIGHT 18.2

Which Dividend Option Is Best for Consumers?

Consumers may be confused concerning the best dividend option to select in a participating life insurance policy. In reality, there is no best dividend option. *The best dividend option is one that best meets your financial goals and objectives.* If money is tight and premiums are financially burdensome, dividends can be paid in cash or used to reduce premiums. If you are substandard in health or uninsurable, the paid-up additions option in a cash value policy is attractive if you need additional insurance. The paid-up additions are purchased at net rates with no loading.

If you have a cash value policy and wish to accumulate funds for retirement, the paid-up additions option is appropriate. The paid-up additions can also pay up a policy prior to retirement. Another advantage, according to the Consumer Federation of America, is that the interest rate credited to paid-up additions may be higher than the interest rate credited to accumulated dividends retained by the insurer under the interest option.[a]

If income-tax considerations are important, you should not use the dividend accumulations option. Although the dividends are not taxable, the interest earnings on the dividends are taxed as ordinary income. In this case, the paid-up additions option is more appropriate because the dividend becomes the legal reserve under the paid-up addition. Interest earnings credited to the legal reserve are not taxed as current income to the policyowner. Moreover, as stated earlier, the interest rate credited to paid-up additions may be higher than the interest rate credited to the accumulated dividends under the dividend accumulations option.

Finally, if you need more life insurance, you can use the fifth dividend option if it is available. In short, no single dividend option is best for all policyowners. Each policyowner should choose an option best suited to his or her financial situation.

[a]James H. Hunt, *Evaluating Cash Value Life Insurance Policies,* Consumer Federation of America, September 21, 2001.

All states have standard **nonforfeiture laws** that require insurers to provide at least a minimum nonforfeiture value to policyowners who surrender their policies. There are three **nonforfeiture options** or cash surrender options:

- Cash value
- Reduced paid-up insurance
- Extended term insurance

Cash Value

The policy can be surrendered for its cash value, at which time all benefits under the policy cease. A policy normally does not build any cash value until the end of the second or third year, although some policies have a small cash value at the end of the first year. The cash values are small during the early years because the relatively high first-year acquisition expenses incurred by the insurer in selling the policy have not yet been recovered. However, over a long period, the cash values accumulate to substantial amounts.

The insurer can delay payment of the cash value for six months if the policy is surrendered. This provision is required by law and is a carryover from the Great Depression of the 1930s, when cash demands on life insurers were excessive. Insurers generally do not delay payment of the cash value because of fear that confidence in the company will be undermined.

The cash surrender option can be used if the insured no longer needs life insurance. Although it is usually not advisable to surrender a policy for cash because other options may be more appropriate, there are circumstances where the cash surrender option can be used. For example, if an insured is retired and no longer has any dependents to support, the need for substantial amounts of life insurance may be reduced. In such a case, the cash surrender option could be used if cash is needed.

Reduced Paid-up Insurance

Under the **reduced paid-up insurance** *option, the cash surrender value is applied as a net single premium to purchase a reduced paid-up policy.* The amount of insurance purchased depends on the insured's attained age, the cash surrender value, and the mortality and interest assumptions stated in the original contract. The reduced paid-up policy is the same as the original policy, but the face amount of insurance is reduced. If the original policy is participating, the reduced paid-up policy also pays dividends.

The reduced paid-up insurance option is appropriate if life insurance is still needed but the policyowner does not wish to pay premiums. For example, assume that Mark has a $100,000 ordinary life policy that he purchased at age 21. He is now age 65 and wants to retire, but he does not want to pay premiums after retirement. The cash surrender value can be used to purchase a reduced paid-up policy of about $83,000.

Extended Term Insurance

Under the **extended term insurance** *option, the net cash surrender value is used as a net single premium to extend the full face amount of the policy (less any indebtedness) into the future as term insurance for a certain number of years and days.* In effect, the cash value is used to purchase a paid-up term insurance policy equal to the original face amount (less any indebtedness) for a limited period. The length of the term insurance protection is determined by the insured's attained age when the option is exercised, the net cash surrender value, and the premium rates for extended term insurance. For example, in our earlier illustration, if Mark stopped paying premiums at age 65, the cash value would be sufficient to keep the $100,000 policy in force for another 15 years and 272 days. If he is still alive after that time, the policy is no longer in force.

If the policy lapses for nonpayment of premiums, and the policyowner has not elected another option, the extended term option automatically goes into effect in most policies. This means that many policies are still in force even though the policyowners mistakenly believe the policy is not in force because of nonpayment of premiums. However, if the automatic premium loan provision has been added to the policy, it has priority over the extended term option.

A whole life or endowment policy contains a table of nonforfeiture values that indicates the benefits under the three options at various ages.

EXHIBIT 18.1
Nonforfeiture Options (Dollar Amount for Each $1000 of Ordinary Life Insurance Issued at Age 21)

End of Policy Year	Cash or Loan Value	Paid-up Insurance	Extended Term Insurance	
			Years	Days
1	$ 0.00	$ 0	0	0
2	0.00	0	0	0
3	4.79	15	1	315
4	16.21	48	6	161
5	27.91	81	11	15
6	39.91	113	14	275
7	52.20	145	17	158
8	64.78	176	19	157
9	77.66	206	20	342
10	90.84	236	22	29
11	104.33	265	22	351
12	118.13	294	23	231
13	132.25	322	24	54
14	146.69	350	24	191
15	161.43	377	24	290
16	176.47	403	24	356
17	191.79	429	25	28
18	207.38	454	25	42
19	223.22	478	25	36
20	239.29	502	25	13
Age 60	563.42	806	17	26
Age 65	608.49	833	15	272

Exhibit 18.1 illustrates the nonforfeiture values for an ordinary life policy issued at age 21.

SETTLEMENT OPTIONS

Settlement options refer to the various ways that the policy proceeds can be paid. The policyowner may elect the settlement option prior to the insured's death, or the beneficiary may be granted the right. In addition, most policies permit the cash surrender value to be paid under the settlement options if the policy is surrendered. The most common settlement options are as follows:

- Cash
- Interest option
- Fixed-period option
- Fixed-amount option
- Life income options

Cash

When insureds die, cash may be needed immediately for funeral expenses and other expenses. The policy proceeds can be paid in a lump sum to a designated beneficiary or beneficiaries. Interest is paid on the policy proceeds from the date of death to the date of payment. The payment of interest is especially important in those cases where the life insurance proceeds are large, and the proceeds are paid several weeks or months after the insured's death. As a practical matter, most policy proceeds are paid in a lump sum within weeks following the insured's death.

Interest Option

Under the **interest option,** *the policy proceeds are retained by the insurer, and interest is periodically paid to the beneficiary.* The interest can be paid monthly, quarterly, semiannually, or annually. Most insurers guarantee a minimum interest rate on the policy proceeds retained under the interest option. If the policy is participating, a higher rate of interest is

paid based on excess interest earnings. For example, an insurer may pay 5 percent on the proceeds even though the contractual rate is only 3 percent.

The beneficiary can be given withdrawal rights, by which part or all of the proceeds can be withdrawn. The beneficiary may also be given the right to change to another settlement option.

The interest option provides considerable flexibility, and it can be used in a wide variety of circumstances. In particular, it can be effectively used if the funds will not be needed until some later date. For example, educational funds could be retained at interest until the children are ready for college. Meanwhile, the interest income can supplement the family's income.

Fixed-Period Option

Under the **fixed-period (installment-time) option,** *the policy proceeds are paid to a beneficiary over some fixed period of time.* Payments can be made monthly, quarterly, semiannually, or annually. Both principal and interest are systematically liquidated under this option. If the primary beneficiary dies before receiving all payments, the remaining payments will be paid to a contingent beneficiary or to the primary beneficiary's estate.

Exhibit 18.2 illustrates the fixed-period option of one insurer for each $1000 of proceeds at a guaranteed interest rate of 3 percent. The length of the

EXHIBIT 18.2
Fixed-Period Option (Minimum Monthly Income Payments per $1000 Proceeds, 3 Percent Interest)

Period (Years)	Monthly Payment	Period (Years)	Monthly Payment	Period (Years)	Monthly Payment
1	$84.50	11	$8.86	21	$5.32
2	42.87	12	8.24	22	5.15
3	29.00	13	7.71	23	4.99
4	22.07	14	7.26	24	4.84
5	17.91	15	6.87	25	4.71
6	15.14	16	6.53	26	4.59
7	13.17	17	6.23	27	4.48
8	11.69	18	5.96	28	4.37
9	10.54	19	5.73	29	4.27
10	9.62	20	5.51	30	4.18

period determines the amount of each payment. If the fixed period is five years, a $100,000 policy would provide a monthly income of $1791. However, the monthly benefit would be only $962 if a ten-year period is elected.

The fixed-period option can be used in those situations where income is needed for a definite time period, such as during the readjustment, dependency, and blackout periods. The fixed-period option, however, should be used with caution. It is extremely inflexible. Partial withdrawals by the beneficiary normally are not allowed because of the administrative expense of recomputing the amount of the payment during the fixed period. However, many insurers will permit the beneficiary to withdraw the commuted value of the remaining payments in a lump sum.

Fixed-Amount Option

Under the **fixed-amount (installment-amount) option**, *a fixed amount is periodically paid to the beneficiary*. The payments are made until both the principal and interest are exhausted. If excess interest is paid, the period is lengthened, but the amount of each payment is unchanged.

For example, assume that the death benefit is $100,000, the credited interest rate is 3 percent annually, and the desired monthly benefit is $2900. The actual monthly payout schedule would be calculated by the insurer. In this case, the beneficiary would receive $2900 monthly for 36 months. At that time, the principal and interest would be exhausted.

The fixed-amount option provides considerable flexibility. The beneficiary can be given limited or unlimited withdrawal right and the right to switch the unpaid proceeds to another option. The beneficiary may also be allowed to increase or decrease the fixed amount. It is also possible to arrange a settlement agreement, by which the periodic payments can be increased at certain times, such as when grown children start college. Unless there is some compelling reason for using the fixed-period option, the fixed-amount option is recommended because of its greater flexibility.

Life Income Options

Death benefits can also be paid to the beneficiary under a life income option. The cash surrender value can also be disbursed under a **life income option**. The major life income options are as follows.

Life Income   *Under this option, installment payments are paid only while the beneficiary is alive and cease on the beneficiary's death.* Although this option provides the highest amount of installment income, there may be a substantial forfeiture of the proceeds if the beneficiary dies shortly after the payments start. Because there is no refund feature or guarantee of payments, other life income options are usually more desirable.

Life Income with Period Certain   Under this option, a life income is paid to the beneficiary with a certain number of guaranteed payments. *If the primary beneficiary dies before receiving the guaranteed number of payments, the remaining payments are paid to a contingent beneficiary.* For example, assume that Karen is receiving $1000 monthly under a life income option with 10 years certain. If she dies after receiving only one year of payments, the remaining nine years of payments will be paid to a contingent beneficiary or to her estate.

Life Income with Refund   Under this option, a lifetime income is paid to the beneficiary. *If the beneficiary dies before receiving payments equal to the amount of insurance, the difference is refunded in installments or in a lump sum to another beneficiary.* For example, assume Paige has $100,000 of life insurance paid to her under the refund option. If she dies after receiving payments of only $10,000, the remaining $90,000 is paid to another beneficiary or to her estate.

Joint-and-Survivor Income   *Under this option, income payments are paid to two persons during their lifetimes, such as a husband and wife.* For example, Richard and Margo may be receiving $1200 monthly under a joint-and-survivor income annuity. If Richard dies, Margo continues to receive $1200 monthly during her lifetime. There are also variations of this option, such as a joint-and-two-thirds annuity or a joint-and-one-half annuity. Thus, the monthly income of $1200 would be reduced to $800 or $600 on the death of the first person.

Various life income options for single lives are illustrated in Exhibit 18.3, which shows the amount

EXHIBIT 18.3
Life Income Options (Minimum Monthly Income Payments per $1000 Proceeds)

Adjusted Age		Period Certain			
Male	Female	None	10 Years	20 Years	Refund
50	55	$ 4.62	$4.56	$4.34	$4.36
51	56	4.72	4.65	4.40	4.44
52	57	4.83	4.75	4.46	4.52
53	58	4.94	4.85	4.53	4.61
54	59	5.07	4.96	4.59	4.69
55	60	5.20	5.07	4.66	4.79
56	61	5.33	5.19	4.72	4.88
57	62	5.48	5.31	4.78	4.99
58	63	5.64	5.43	4.84	5.09
59	64	5.80	5.57	4.90	5.20
60	65	5.98	5.70	4.96	5.32
61	66	6.16	5.85	5.02	5.44
62	67	6.36	5.99	5.07	5.57
63	68	6.57	6.14	5.13	5.71
64	69	6.79	6.30	5.17	5.85
65	70	7.03	6.45	5.22	6.00
66	71	7.28	6.62	5.26	6.15
67	72	7.54	6.78	5.30	6.31
68	73	7.83	6.95	5.33	6.48
69	74	8.13	7.11	5.36	6.66
70	75	8.45	7.28	5.39	6.85
71	76	8.79	7.45	5.41	7.05
72	77	9.16	7.62	5.43	7.26
73	78	9.55	7.79	5.45	7.48
74	79	9.96	7.95	5.46	7.71
75	80	10.41	8.11	5.48	7.95

of minimum monthly income paid by one insurer for each $1000 of insurance proceeds.

Females usually receive lower periodic payments under the life income options than males because of a longer life expectancy. For example, if the proceeds are $100,000, a female beneficiary, age 65, would receive $570 monthly under the life income option with 10 years certain, while a male beneficiary of the same age would receive $645.

Exhibit 18.4 illustrates the minimum monthly payments under the joint-and-survivor income option of one insurer for each $1000 of insurance proceeds. If the insurance proceeds are $200,000 and the male and female beneficiary are both age 65, a monthly payment of $996 would be paid until the last annuitant dies.

Advantages of Settlement Options

The major advantages of settlement options are summarized as follows:

- *Periodic income is paid to the family.* Settlement options can restore part or all of the family's share of the deceased breadwinner's earnings. The financial security of the family can then be maintained.

EXHIBIT 18.4
Joint-and-Survivor Life Income Option (Minimum Monthly Income Payments per $1000 Proceeds)

Male Adjusted Age	Female Adjusted Age						
	55	60	65	70	75	80	85 and Over
55	$4.16	$4.34	$4.51	$4.65	$4.76	$4.84	$4.88
60	4.26	4.51	4.75	4.98	5.16	5.29	5.37
65	4.35	4.65	4.98	5.31	5.61	5.84	5.98
70	4.41	4.76	5.17	5.62	6.07	6.44	6.68
75	4.46	4.84	5.32	5.88	6.48	7.03	7.42
80	4.48	4.89	5.41	6.05	6.79	7.52	8.07
85 and over	4.50	4.92	5.46	6.15	6.99	7.85	8.53

- *Principal and interest are guaranteed.* The insurance company guarantees both principal and interest. There are no investment worries and administrative problems, because the funds are invested by the insurer.
- *Settlement options can be used in life insurance planning.* Life insurance can be programmed to meet the policyowner's needs and objectives.
- *An insurance windfall can create problems for the beneficiary.* The funds may be spent unwisely; bad investments may be made; and others may try to get the funds. Many insurers now offer money market accounts for investment of the death proceeds so that beneficiaries are not forced to make immediate decisions concerning disposition of the funds.

Disadvantages of Settlement Options

The major disadvantages of settlement options are summarized as follows:

- *Higher yields often can be obtained elsewhere.* Interest rates offered by other financial institutions may be considerably higher.
- *The settlement agreement may be inflexible and restrictive.* The policyowner may have a settlement agreement that is too restrictive. The beneficiary may not have withdrawal rights or the right to change options. For example, the funds may be paid over a 20-year period under the fixed-period option with no

right of withdrawal. An emergency may arise, but the beneficiary could not withdraw the funds.

- *Life income options have limited usefulness at the younger ages.* Life income options should rarely be used before age 65 or 70, which restricts their usefulness at the younger ages. If a life income option is elected at a young age, the income payments are substantially reduced. Also, using a life income option is the equivalent of purchasing a single-premium life annuity, which may be purchased at a lower cost from another insurer.

Use of a Trust

The policy proceeds can also be paid to a trustee, such as the trust department of a commercial bank. Under certain circumstances, it may be desirable to have the policy proceeds paid to a trustee rather than disbursed under the settlement options. This would be the case if the amount of insurance is substantial; if considerable flexibility and discretion in the amount and timing of payments are needed; if there are minor children or mentally handicapped adults who cannot manage their own financial affairs; or if the amounts paid must be periodically changed as the beneficiary's needs and desires change. These advantages are partly offset by the payment of a trustee's fee, and the investment results cannot be guaranteed.

ADDITIONAL LIFE INSURANCE BENEFITS

Other benefits can often be added to a life insurance policy by the payment of an additional premium. These benefits provide valuable protection to the policyowner.

Waiver-of-Premium Provision

A **waiver-of-premium provision** can be added to a life insurance policy. In some policies, the waiver-of-premium provision is automatically included. Under this provision, if the insured becomes totally disabled from bodily injury or disease before some stated age, all premiums coming due during the period of disability are waived. During the period of disability, death benefits, cash values, and dividends continue as if the premiums had been paid.

Before any premiums are waived, the insured must meet the following requirements:

- Become disabled before some stated age, such as before age 60 or 65
- Be continuously disabled for six months (Some insurers have a waiting period of four months.)
- Satisfy the definition of total disability
- Furnish proof of disability satisfactory to the insurer

On older policies, there is a retroactive refund of premiums paid by the policyowner during the first six months of disability if all premiums are being waived. Newer waiver-of-premium provisions, however, may not provide a retroactive refund.

The insured must also satisfy the definition of disability stated in the policy. Some common definitions of disability are as follows:

- The insured cannot engage in *any gainful occupation* for which he or she is reasonably fitted by education, training, and experience.
- During the first two years, total disability means that the insured cannot perform all duties of *his or her occupation*. After the initial period, total disability means that the insured cannot engage in any occupation reasonably fitted by education, training, and experience.
- Total disability is the entire and irrecoverable loss of sight of both eyes, or the use of both hands or both feet, or one hand and one foot.

The first definition of total disability appears in many older life insurance policies. *Under this definition, the insured is considered totally disabled if he or she cannot work in any gainful occupation reasonably fitted by education, training, and experience.* For example, assume that Dr. Brown is a chemistry professor who has throat cancer and cannot teach. If he can find some other job for which he is reasonably fitted by training and education, such as a research scientist for a chemical firm, he would not be considered disabled. However, if he cannot work in any occupation reasonably fitted by his education, training, and experience, then he would be considered totally disabled.

The second definition of total disability is more liberal and is found in many newer life insurance policies. *For the first two years of disability, total disability means the insured cannot perform all the duties of his or her own occupation.* After the initial period expires, the definition becomes stricter. *The insured is considered totally disabled only if he or she cannot engage in any occupation reasonably fitted by education, training, and experience.* For example, assume that Dr. Pudwill is a dentist whose hand is severely injured in a hunting accident. For the first two years, he would be considered totally disabled, because he is unable to perform all duties of his occupation. Premiums during this initial period would be waived. However, after the initial period expires, if he could work in any occupation for which he is reasonably fitted by his education and training, he would not be considered totally disabled. Thus, if he could get a job as a research scientist or as a professor in a dental school, he would not be considered disabled. He would then have to resume premium payments.

Total disability can also be defined in terms of the loss of use of bodily members. For example, if Jason loses his eyesight in an explosion, or if both legs are paralyzed from some crippling disease, he would be considered totally disabled.

Before any premiums are waived, the insured must furnish satisfactory proof of disability to the insurer. The insurer may also require continuing proof of disability once each year. If satisfactory proof of disability is not furnished, no further premiums will be waived.

If you have adequate amounts of disability-income insurance, the waiver-of-premium rider is not needed. If you become disabled, the life insurance premiums could be treated like any other monthly expense that must be paid, such as housing, utilities, and food. However, most breadwinners are substantially underinsured against the risk of long-term disability. Thus, many financial planners recommend adding this provision to a life insurance policy, especially if the face amount of life insurance is large. During a period of long-term disability, premium payments can be financially burdensome. Because most persons are underinsured for disability-income benefits, waiver of premiums during a period in which income is reduced is highly desirable.

Guaranteed Purchase Option

The **guaranteed purchase option** *permits the policy-owner to purchase additional amounts of life insurance at specified times in the future without evidence of insurability*. The guaranteed purchase option is also called the *guaranteed insurability option*. The purpose of the option is to guarantee the insured's future insurability. The insured may need additional life insurance in the future and may be unable to afford the additional insurance today. The guaranteed purchase option guarantees the purchase of specified amounts of life insurance in the future at standard rates, even though the insured may become substandard in health or uninsurable.

Amount of Insurance The typical option allows the policyowner to purchase additional amounts of life insurance every three years up to some maximum age without evidence of insurability, such as age 45. In most cases, the additional insurance increases the face amount of the original policy. However, some insurers issue a new policy for each option exercised. For example, the guaranteed purchase option of one insurer allows additional purchases of life insurance when the insured attains ages 25, 28, 31, 34, 37, 40, or 43. The amount of life insurance that can be purchased at each option date is limited to the face amount of the basic policy subject to some minimum and maximum amount. For example, assume that Heather, age 22, purchases a $25,000 ordinary life policy with a guaranteed purchase option and becomes uninsurable after the policy is issued. Assuming that she elects to exer-

cise each option, she would have the following amounts of insurance:

Age 22	$25,000 (basic policy)
	+
Age 25	$25,000
Age 28	25,000
Age 31	25,000
Age 34	25,000
Age 37	25,000
Age 40	25,000
Age 43	25,000
Total insurance at age 43	$200,000

Although uninsurable, Heather has increased her insurance coverage from $25,000 to $200,000.

Advance Purchase Privilege Most insurers have some type of advance purchase privilege, by which an option can be immediately exercised on the occurrence of some event. If the insured marries, has a birth in the family, or legally adopts a child, an option can be immediately exercised prior to the next option due date. Some insurers will provide automatic term insurance for 90 days if the insured marries or a child is born. The insurance expires after 90 days unless the guaranteed insurability option is exercised.

If an option is exercised under the advance purchase privilege, the number of total options is not increased. If an option is exercised early, each new purchase eliminates the next regular option date. Finally, the policyowner typically has only 30 to 60 days to exercise an option. If the option expires without being used, it cannot be exercised at some later date. In some insurers, failure to exercise an option may terminate all subsequent options. This provision protects the insurer from adverse selection.

Other Considerations Two additional points should be noted concerning the guaranteed purchase option. The first is whether the waiver-of-premium rider can be added to the new insurance without furnishing evidence of insurability. Insurer practices vary in this regard. The most liberal provision permits the waiver-of-premium rider to be added to the new insurance if the original policy contains such a provision. If premiums are being waived under the original policy, they are also waived for the new insurance. Thus, in our earlier example, if premiums are being waived under Heather's original policy of $25,000, the premiums for the new life insurance purchased will also be waived. A less liberal approach permits the disabled insured to purchase additional life insurance with each option, but not to waive the new premiums under the waiver-of premium rider.

Second, the additional insurance is normally not subject to a new incontestable clause or to a new suicide provision.

Accidental Death Benefit Rider

The **accidental death benefit rider** (also known as **double indemnity**) *doubles the face amount of life insurance if death occurs as a result of an accident.* In some policies, the face amount is tripled. The cost of the rider is relatively low. For example, at one insurer, the rider costs $69 annually when added to a $100,000 policy issued to a male age 35. Thus, if the insured dies as a result of an accident, $200,000 will be paid.

Requirements for Collecting Benefits   Before a double indemnity benefit is paid, several requirements must be satisfied:

- Death must be caused directly and independently of any other cause by accidental bodily injury.
- Death must occur within 90 days of the accident.
- Death must occur before some specified age, such as age 60, 65, or 70.

The first requirement is that accidental injury must be the direct cause of death. If death occurs from some other cause, such as disease, the double indemnity benefit is not paid. For example, assume that Sam is painting his two-story house. If the scaffold collapses and Sam is killed, a double indemnity benefit would be paid because the direct cause of death is an accidental bodily injury. However, if Sam died from a heart attack and fell from the scaffold, the double payment would not be made. In this case, heart disease is the direct cause of death, not accidental bodily injury.

The second requirement is that death must occur within 90 days of the accident. The purpose of

this requirement is to establish the fact that accidental bodily injury is the proximate cause of death. However, because modern medical technology can prolong life for extended periods, many insurers are using longer time periods, such as 120 or 180 days.

Finally, the accidental death must occur before some specified age. To limit their liability, insurers typically impose some age limitation. Although some policies provide lifetime accidental death benefits, coverage usually terminates on the policy anniversary date just after the insured reaches a certain age, such as age 70.

Financial planners generally do not recommend purchase of the double indemnity rider. Although the cost is relatively low, there are three major objections to the rider. *First, the economic value of a human life is not doubled or tripled if death results from an accident.* Therefore, it is economically unsound to insure an accidental death more heavily than death from disease. *Second, most persons will die as a result of a disease and not from an accident.* Because most persons are underinsured, the premiums for the double indemnity rider could be better used to purchase an additional amount of life insurance, which would cover both accidental death and death from disease. *Finally, the insured may be deceived and believe that he or she has more insurance than is actually the case.* For example, a person with a $50,000 policy and a double indemnity rider may erroneously believe that he or she has $100,000 of life insurance.

Cost-of-Living Rider

The **cost-of-living rider** *allows the policyowner to purchase one-year term insurance equal to the percentage change in the consumer price index with no evidence of insurability.* The amount of term insurance changes each year and reflects the cumulative change in the consumer price index (CPI) from the issue date of the policy. However, insurers may limit the amount of insurance that can be purchased each year, such as a maximum of 10 percent of the policy face value. The policyowner pays the entire premium for the term insurance.

For example, assume that Luis, age 28, buys a $100,000 ordinary life insurance policy and that the CPI increases 5 percent during the first year. He would be allowed to purchase $5000 of one-year term insurance, and the total amount of insurance in force would be $105,000. The term insurance can be converted to a cash-value policy with no evidence of insurability.

Accelerated Death Benefits Rider

Many insurers now make available a living benefits rider that can be added to a life insurance policy. The **accelerated death benefits rider** *allows insureds who are terminally ill or who suffer from certain catastrophic diseases to collect part or all of their life insurance benefits before they die, primarily to pay for the medical care they require.* Benefits may also be payable if the insured is receiving long-term care in a nursing home or hospital.

Although accelerated death benefits riders are not uniform, they generally can be classified as follows:

- Terminal illness rider
- Catastrophic illness rider
- Long-term care rider

The *terminal illness rider* allows terminally ill insureds with a limited life expectancy (24 months or less) to receive part or all of the policy proceeds. Insurers generally allow the rider to be added without an extra premium, but any lump sums advanced are discounted for interest to reflect the time value of money. The face amount of insurance, cash values if any, and premiums are reduced after the payment is made. For example, based on the rider of one insurer, Dr. Harry Crockett, age 59, who is terminally ill with cancer, requests 50 percent of his $100,000 term insurance policy. After the benefit is discounted for interest, he receives $46,296. After the payment is made, premiums are reduced 50 percent, and the face amount is reduced to $50,000.

The *catastrophic illness rider* allows insureds who have certain catastrophic diseases to collect part or all of the policy face amount. Covered diseases typically include AIDS, life-threatening cancer, coronary artery disease, kidney failure, and similar types of catastrophic diseases.

The *long-term care rider* allows insureds who require long-term care to collect part of their life

CASE APPLICATION

Sonja, age 25, recently purchased a $100,000 ordinary life insurance policy on her life. The waiver-of-premium rider and guaranteed purchase option are attached to the policy. For each of the following situations, indicate the extent of the insurer's obligation, if any, to Sonja or to Sonja's beneficiary. Identify the appropriate policy provision or rider that applies in each case. Treat each event separately.

a. Sonja fails to pay the second annual premium due on January 1. She dies 15 days later.
b. Sonja commits suicide three years after the policy was purchased.
c. At Sonja's death, the life insurer discovers that Sonja deliberately lied about her age. Instead of being 25 years old, as she indicated, she was actually 26 years old at the time the policy was purchased.
d. Two years after the policy was purchased, Sonja is told that she has leukemia. She is uninsurable but would like to obtain additional life insurance.

e. Sonja is seriously injured in an auto accident. After six months, she is still unable to return to work. She has no income from her job, and the insurance premium payments are financially burdensome.
f. Sonja has a mentally disabled son. She wants to make certain that her son will have a continuous income after her death.
g. Sonja lets her policy lapse. After four years, she wants to get the policy reinstated. Her health is fine. Point out to Sonja how she can reinstate her life insurance.
h. Sonja wants to retire and does not wish to pay the premiums on her policy. Indicate the various options that are available to her.
i. Ten years after the policy was purchased, Sonja is fired from her job. She is unemployed and is in desperate need of cash.
j. When Sonja applied for life insurance, she concealed the fact that she had high blood pressure. She dies five years later.

insurance prior to death. The rider may cover care in a skilled nursing facility, intermediate care facility, or custodial care facility. Some riders also cover certain types of home care. To illustrate, based on the rider of one insurer, a monthly benefit can be paid equal to 2 percent of the face amount of insurance up to a maximum of 50 percent of the face amount. Thus, if the face amount is $200,000, a monthly benefit of $4000 could be paid up to 25 months.

As an alternative, terminally ill insureds may be able to sell their policies to private firms. A number of firms will buy the life insurance policies of terminally ill insureds at a discount (called a **viatical settlement**), especially policies owned by AIDS patients. The cash enables AIDS victims to pay their medical bills and other expenses. However, critics argue that the states do not adequately regulate such purchases, and that there is potential for abuse.

SUMMARY

- The *ownership clause* states that the policyowner possesses all contractual rights in the policy while the insured is living.

- The *entire-contract clause* states that the life insurance policy and attached application constitute the entire contract between the parties.

- The *incontestable clause* states that a life insurer cannot contest the policy after it has been in force two years during the insured's lifetime.

- The *suicide clause* states that if the insured commits suicide within two years after the policy is issued, the face amount is not paid. There is only a refund of the premiums paid.

- The *grace period* allows the policyowner a period of 31 days to pay an overdue premium. Universal life and other flexible premium policies usually have longer grace periods, such as 61 days. The insurance remains in force during the grace period.

- There are several types of beneficiary designations. A *primary beneficiary* is the party who is first entitled to receive the policy proceeds upon the insured's death. A *contingent beneficiary* is entitled to the proceeds if the primary beneficiary dies before the insured or dies before receiving the guaranteed number of payments under an installment settlement option. A *revocable*

beneficiary designation means that the policyowner can change the beneficiary without the beneficiary's consent. An *irrevocable beneficiary* designation is one that cannot be changed without the beneficiary's consent.

- A *dividend* represents a refund of part of the gross premium if the experience of the company is favorable. Dividends paid to policyowners are not taxable and can be taken in several ways:

    Cash

    Reduction of premiums

    Dividend accumulations

    Paid-up additions

    Term insurance (in some companies)

- There are three *nonforfeiture* or cash surrender options:

    Cash value

    Reduced paid-up insurance

    Extended term insurance

- The cash value can be borrowed under the policy loan provision. An automatic premium loan provision can also be added to the policy, by which an overdue premium is automatically borrowed from the cash value.

- *Settlement options* are the various ways that the policy proceeds can be paid. The most common settlement options are as follows:

    Cash

    Interest option

    Fixed-period option

    Fixed-amount option

    Life income options

- A *waiver-of-premium provision* can be added to a life insurance policy, by which all premiums coming due during a period of total disability are waived. Before any premiums are waived, the insured must meet the following requirements:

    Become disabled before some stated age, such as age 60 or 65

    Be continuously disabled for six months

    Satisfy the definition of total disability

    Furnish proof of disability satisfactory to the insurer

- The *guaranteed purchase option* permits the policyowner to purchase additional amounts of life insurance at specified times without evidence of insurability. The purpose of the option is to guarantee the insured's future insurability.

- The *accidental death benefit rider (double indemnity rider)* doubles the face amount of life insurance if death occurs as a result of an accident. Consumer experts generally do not recommend purchase of the double indemnity rider.

- The *cost-of-living rider* allows the policyowner to purchase one-year term insurance equal to the percentage change in the consumer price index with no evidence of insurability.

- The *accelerated death benefits rider* pays part of the life insurance death benefit to a terminally ill insured before death occurs to help pay for medical and other expenses.

KEY CONCEPTS AND TERMS

Absolute assignment
Accelerated death benefits rider
Accidental death benefit rider (double indemnity)
Automatic premium loan provision
Aviation exclusions
Change-of-plan provision
Class beneficiary
Collateral assignment
Contingent beneficiary
Cost-of-living rider
Dividend accumulations option
Entire-contract clause
Extended term insurance
Fixed-amount (installment-amount) option
Fixed-period (installment-time) option
Grace period
Guaranteed purchase option

Incontestable clause
Interest option
Irrevocable beneficiary
Life income option
Misstatement of age or sex clause
Nonforfeiture laws
Nonforfeiture options
Nonparticipating policy
Ownership clause
Paid-up additions option
Participating policy
Policy loan provision
Primary beneficiary
Reduced paid-up insurance
Reinstatement provision
Revocable beneficiary
Settlement options
Specific beneficiary
Suicide clause
Viatical settlement
Waiver-of-premium rider
War clause

REVIEW QUESTIONS

1. Briefly explain the following life insurance contractual provisions.
   a. Suicide clause
   b. Grace period
   c. Reinstatement clause

2. a. Describe the incontestable clause in a life insurance policy.
   b. What is the purpose of the incontestable clause?

3. a. Explain the requirements for reinstating a lapsed life insurance policy.
   b. What are the advantages and disadvantages of reinstating a lapsed life insurance policy?

4. Explain the following beneficiary designations.
   a. Primary and contingent beneficiary
   b. Revocable and irrevocable beneficiary
   c. Specific and class beneficiary

5. A life insurance policy is freely assignable to another party. Explain the following types of assignments:
   a. Absolute assignment
   b. Collateral assignment

6. a. Describe the policy loan provision that appears in a typical cash-value life insurance policy.
   b. Why is interest charged on a policy loan?
   c. List the advantages and disadvantages of a policy loan.

7. A life insurance policy that pays dividends is known as a *participating policy*.
   a. Identify the sources from which dividends can be paid.
   b. List the various dividend options in a typical life insurance policy.
   c. Can an insurer guarantee the payment of a dividend? Explain your answer.

8. All states have nonforfeiture laws that require the payment of a cash surrender value when a policy is surrendered. Briefly explain the following nonforfeiture options that are found in a typical life insurance policy.
   a. Cash value option
   b. Reduced paid-up insurance
   c. Extended term insurance

9. In addition to cash, life insurance death benefits can be paid under other settlement options. Briefly explain the following settlement options.
   a. Interest option
   b. Fixed-period option
   c. Fixed amount option
   d. Life income options

10. Explain the definition of total disability that is found in a typical waiver-of-premium provision.

APPLICATION QUESTIONS

1. Richard, age 35, owns an ordinary life insurance policy in the amount of $250,000. The policy is a participating policy that pays dividends. Richard has a number of financial goals and objectives. For each of the following situations, identify a dividend option that could be used to meet Richard's goals. Treat each situation separately.
   a. Richard finds the premium payments are financially burdensome. He wants to reduce his annual premium outlay.
   b. Richard has leukemia and is uninsurable. He needs additional life insurance protection.
   c. Richard wants to accumulate additional cash for a comfortable retirement.
   d. Richard would like to have a paid-up policy at the time of retirement.
   e. Richard has substantial earned income that places him in a high marginal income-tax bracket. He wants the insurer to retain the dividends, but he does not want to pay an income tax on the investment earnings.

2. Kathy, age 29, is married and has a son, age 3. She owns a $100,000 ordinary life insurance policy with a waiver-of-premium provision, guaranteed purchase option, and accelerated death benefits rider. Kathy has several financial goals and objectives for her family. For each of the following situations, identify an appropriate contractual provision or policy benefit that will enable Kathy to meet her financial goals. Treat each situation separately.
   a. If Kathy dies, she wants the policy proceeds to be paid in the form of monthly income to the family until her son attains age 18.
   b. Kathy is totally disabled in an auto accident when she failed to stop at a red light. After six months, she has not recovered and remains totally disabled. As a result, she cannot return to her former job or work in any occupation based on her previous training and experience. She finds that the premium payments for life insurance are financially burdensome.
   c. When she retires, Kathy would like to have the cash value in the policy paid to her in the form of lifetime income. She wants the payments to continue for at least 10 years.
   d. Kathy is terminally ill from a serious heart condition. Kathy's physician believes she will die within one year. Kathy has no savings and health insurance, and her medical bills are soaring. She needs $50,000 to pay all medical bills and other financial obligations.
   e. Three years after the policy was issued, Kathy was diagnosed with breast cancer. As a result, she is now uninsurable. She would like to purchase additional life insurance to protect her family.

3. Jim, age 32, purchased a $300,000 five-year renewable and convertible term insurance policy. In answering the health questions, Jim told the agent that he had not visited a doctor within the last five years. However, he had visited the doctor two months earlier. The doctor told Jim that he had a serious heart disease. Jim did not reveal this information to the agent when he applied for life insurance. Jim died three years after the policy was purchased. At that time, the life insurer discovered the heart ailment. Explain the extent of the insurer's obligation, if any, with respect to payment of the death claim.

4. Additional riders and benefits often can be added to a life insurance policy to provide greater protection to the insured. Describe each of the following riders and options:
   a. Waiver-of-premium rider
   b. Guaranteed purchase option
   c. Double indemnity rider
   d. Cost-of-living rider
   e. Accelerated death benefits rider

INTERNET RESOURCES

- **Consumer Federation of America (CFA)** is a nonprofit organization that represents numerous consumer groups. This site is one of the best resources for obtaining meaningful consumer information about life insurance and other insurance products. CFA makes available a low-cost life insurance evaluation service by which individual life insurance policies can be evaluated for a small fee. Visit the site at

   http://www.consumerfed.org

- The **American Council of Life Insurers** represents the life insurance industry on issues dealing with legislation and regulation at the federal and state levels. The site provides consumer information on the purposes and types of life insurance. Visit the site at

   http://www.acli.com

■ **INSWEB** provides timely information and premium quotes for life insurance as well as for homeowners, auto, and other insurance products. Visit the site at

http://www.insweb.com

■ **Insure.com** provides up-to-date information, premium quotes, and other consumer information on life insurance. The site also provides news releases about events that affect the insurance industry. Visit the site at

http://www.insure.com

■ **The National Underwriter Company** publishes books and other documents on life insurance products. The company publishes the *National Underwriter,* Life & Health/Financial Services edition, a weekly trade publication that provides news about the life insurance industry. Visit the site at

http://www.nationalunderwriter.com

■ The **National Association of Insurance Commissioners (NAIC)** has a link to all state insurance departments, which provide a considerable amount of consumer information on life insurance. Click on State Insurance Web sites. For starters, check out New York, Wisconsin, and California. Visit the site at

http://www.naic.org

■ The **Viatical Association of America** is a trade association that represents viatical settlement brokers and funding companies. A viatical settlement enables terminally ill individuals to obtain cash from their life insurance policies. Visit the site at

http://www.viatical.org

SELECTED REFERENCES

Anderson, Buist M. *Anderson on Life Insurance.* Boston, MA: Little, Brown, 1991. See also the *September 1996 Supplement to Anderson on Life Insurance.*

Belth, Joseph M. *Life Insurance: A Consumer's Handbook,* 2nd ed. Bloomington, IN: Indiana University Press, 1985.

Black, Kenneth, Jr., and Harold D. Skipper, Jr. *Life Insurance,* 13th ed. Upper Saddle River, NJ: Prentice-Hall, 2000.

Crawford, Muriel L. *Life and Health Insurance Law,* 8th ed. Boston, MA: Irwin/McGraw-Hill, 1998.

Graves, Edward E., ed. *McGill's Life Insurance,* 5th ed. Bryn Mawr, PA: The American College, 2004.

Graves, Edward E., and Burke A. Christensen, eds. *McGill's Legal Aspects of Life Insurance,* 3rd ed. Bryn Mawr, PA: The American College, 2002.

Wiening, Eric A., George E. Rejda, Constance M. Luthardt, and Cheryl L. Ferguson. *Personal Insurance,* First Edition. Malvern, PA.: American Institute for Chartered Property Casualty Underwriters/ Insurance Institute of America, 2002.

NOTES

1. Edward E. Graves, ed., *McGill's Life Insurance,* 4th ed. (Bryn Mawr, PA: The American College, 2002), p. 747.

2. There are exceptions. In some states, minors can receive a limited amount of proceeds.

3. See Joseph M. Belth, ed., "Special Issue on Fractional Premiums," *Insurance Forum,* vol. 25, no. 12 (December 1998).

4. Black, Kenneth, Jr., and Harold D. Skipper, Jr., *Life Insurance,* 13th ed. (Upper Saddle River, NJ: Prentice-Hall, 2000), p. 237.

5. Robert I. Mehr and Sandra G. Gustavson, *Life Insurance, Theory and Practice,* 4th ed. (Plano, TX: Business Publications, Inc., 1987), p. 206.

Students may take a self-administered test on this chapter at
www.aw-bc.com/rejda

CHAPTER 19

BUYING LIFE INSURANCE

"When you buy life insurance, it's relatively easy to compare first-year premium costs. But that figure tells you nothing about what the policy will cost over the long run."

Consumers Union

LEARNING OBJECTIVES

After studying this chapter, you should be able to

◆ Explain the defects in the traditional net cost method for determining the cost of life insurance.

◆ Explain the interest-adjusted surrender cost index and net payment cost index for determining the cost of life insurance.

◆ Explain the yearly rate-of-return method for determining the annual rate of return on the saving component in a life insurance policy.

◆ Describe the suggestions to follow when purchasing life insurance.

Mathew, age 32, is divorced and has a daughter, age 2. He earns $40,000 annually as an accountant for a national consumer products company. Mathew wants to update his life insurance program. Recently, a life insurance agent presented several proposals. However, Mathew does not know how to evaluate the various plans. Moreover, like most insurance consumers, he is unaware of the importance of performing a cost comparison of the different policies.

This chapter is designed to answer the questions that Mathew may have concerning the purchase of life insurance. Most consumers buy life insurance without much thought. They are often unaware of the huge cost variations among insurers and frequently purchase life insurance from the first agent who persuades them to buy. As a result, they may pay more than is necessary for their insurance protection. The purchase of a high-cost rather than a low-cost policy can cost thousands of dollars over a lifetime.

This chapter discusses the fundamentals of buying life insurance. Specific topics covered include the various methods for determining the cost of life insurance, the rate of return earned on the saving component of a cash-value policy, taxation of life insurance, and suggested guidelines for buying life insurance.

DETERMINING THE COST OF LIFE INSURANCE

The cost of life insurance is a complex subject. In general, cost can be viewed as the difference between what you pay for a life insurance policy and what you get back. If you pay premiums and get nothing back, the cost of the insurance equals the premiums paid. However, if you pay premiums and later get something back, such as cash values and dividends, your cost will be reduced. Thus, in determining the cost of life insurance, four major factors must be considered: (1) annual premiums, (2) cash values, (3) dividends, and (4) time value of money. Two widely used cost methods that consider some or all of the preceding factors are the *traditional net cost method* and the *interest-adjusted cost method*. Although the following discussion is based on cash-value life insurance, the same cost methods can be used to determine the cost of term insurance.

Traditional Net Cost Method

From a historical perspective, life insurers previously used the **traditional net cost method** to illustrate the net cost of life insurance. Under this method, the annual premiums for some time period are added together. Total expected dividends to be received during the same period and the cash value at the end of the period are then subtracted from the total premiums to determine the net cost of life insurance. For example, assume that the annual premium for a $10,000 ordinary life insurance policy issued to a female, age 20, is $132.10. Estimated dividends over a 20-year period are $599, and the cash surrender value at the end of the twentieth year is $2294 (see Exhibit 19.1). The average cost per year is minus $12.55 (−$1.26 per $1000).

The traditional net cost method has several defects and is misleading. The most glaring defects are as follows:

EXHIBIT 19.1
Traditional Net Cost Method

Total premiums for 20 years	$2642
Subtract dividends for 20 years	−599
Net premiums for 20 years	$2043
Subtract the cash value at the end of 20 years	−2294
Insurance cost for 20 years	−$251
Net cost per year (−$251 ÷ 20)	−$12.55
Net cost per $1000 per year (−$12.55 ÷ 10)	−$1.26

- *The time value of money is ignored.* Interest that the policyowner could have earned on the premiums by investing them elsewhere is ignored.
- *The insurance is often shown to be free (to have a negative cost).* This is contrary to common sense, because no life insurer can provide free life insurance and remain in business.
- *The steepness of the dividend scale is ignored.* Some insurers pay small dividends at first and then pay ballooning dividends in later years. The timing and amount of each dividend are ignored.
- *The dividend scale is assumed to remain unchanged.* For most insurers, dividends will change over time.
- *The net cost is based on the assumption that the policy will be surrendered.* The assumption that the policyowner will keep the insurance exactly 20 years (or some other period) and then surrender the policy is questionable.

Interest-Adjusted Cost Method

The **interest-adjusted cost method** developed by the National Association of Insurance Commissioners is a more accurate measure of life insurance costs. *Under this method, the time value of money is taken into consideration by applying an interest factor to each element of cost.*

There are two principal types of interest-adjusted cost indexes, the *surrender cost index* and the *net payment cost index*. The surrender cost index is useful if you believe that you may surrender the policy at the end of 10 or 20 years, or some other time period.

The net payment cost index is useful if you intend to keep your policy in force, and cash values are of secondary importance to you.

Surrender Cost Index The **surrender cost index** *measures the cost of life insurance if you surrender the policy at the end of some time period, such as 10 or 20 years* (see Exhibit 19.2).

The annual premiums are accumulated at 5 percent interest, which recognizes the fact that the policyowner could have invested the premiums elsewhere. Although not shown, the annual dividends are also accumulated at 5 percent interest, which considers interest earnings on the dividends as well as the amount and timing of each dividend. Assume that the accumulated value of the dividends at the end of 20 years is $824. Using the same policy as before, the net premiums for 20 years adjusted for interest are $3762.

The next step is to subtract the cash value at the end of 20 years from the net premiums, which results in a total insurance cost of $1468. The policyowner pays this amount for the insurance protection for 20 years, after considering the time value of money.

The final step is to convert the total interest-adjusted cost for 20 years into an annual cost. This is

EXHIBIT 19.2
Surrender Cost Index

Total premiums for 20 years, each accumulated at 5%	$4586
Subtract dividends for 20 years, each accumulated at 5%	−824
Net premiums for 20 years	$3762
Subtract the cash value at the end of 20 years	−2294
Insurance cost for 20 years	$1468
Amount to which $1 deposited annually at the beginning of each year will accumulate to in 20 years at 5%	$34.719
Interest-adjusted cost per year ($1468 ÷ $34.719)	$42.28
Cost per $1000 per year ($42.28 ÷ 10)	$4.23

done by dividing the total interest-adjusted cost by an *annuity due* factor of 34.719. This factor means that a $1 deposit at the *beginning* of each year at 5 percent interest will accumulate to $34.719 at the end of 20 years. By dividing the total interest-adjusted cost of $1468 by $34.719, you end up with an annual interest-adjusted cost of $42.28, or $4.23 for each $1000 of insurance. As you can see, the interest-adjusted cost is positive, which means that it costs something to own life insurance when forgone interest is considered. In this case, the average annual cost is $42.28 if the policy is surrendered after 20 years.

Net Payment Cost Index   The **net payment cost index** *measures the relative cost of a policy if death occurs at the end of some specified time period, such as 10 or 20 years. It is based on the assumption that you will not surrender the policy.* Therefore, it is the appropriate cost index to use if you intend to keep your life insurance in force.

The net payment cost index is calculated in a manner similar to the surrender cost index except that the cash value is not subtracted (see Exhibit 19.3).

If the policy is kept in force for 20 years, the policy has an annual cost of $108.36 ($10.84 per $1000) after interest is considered.

Substantial Cost Variation Among Insurers

There are enormous cost variations in cash-value life insurance based on the interest-adjusted cost indexes.

EXHIBIT 19.3
Net Payment Cost Index

Total premiums for 20 years, each accumulated at 5%	$4586
Subtract dividends for 20 years, each accumulated at 5%	−824
Insurance cost for 20 years	$3762
Amount to which $1 deposited annually at the beginning of each year will accumulate to in 20 years at 5%	$34.719
Interest-adjusted cost per year ($3762 ÷ $34.719)	$108.36
Cost per $1000 per year ($108.36 ÷ 10)	$10.84

Exhibit 19.4 shows the 10-year interest-adjusted costs for selected insurers for a $100,000 participating whole life policy issued to a male, age 35.

In the interpretation of these indexes, the lower the index number, the less costly is the policy. As shown in Exhibit 19.4, the surrender cost index ranged from a low of $1.24 per $1000 for USAA Life to a high of $2.97 per $1000 for Massachusetts Mutual Life. The net payment cost index ranged from a low of $8.24 per $1000 for Manufacturers Life to a high of $10.47 for General American. *This wide variation in cost highlights the point stated earlier—you can save thousands of dollars over a long period by paying careful attention to the cost index when you shop for life insurance.*

Unfortunately, most consumers do not consider interest-adjusted cost data when they buy life insurance. Instead, they use premiums as a basis for comparing costs. However, using premiums alone pro- vides an incomplete comparison. Interest-adjusted cost data will give you more accurate information about the expected cost of a policy.

Obtaining Cost Information

If you are solicited to buy life insurance, you can ask the agent to give you interest-adjusted cost data on the policy. Cost data can also be obtained by calling certain price quoting services at their toll-free numbers. In addition, cost data are readily available on the Internet (see Internet Resources). Finally, most policy illustrations include interest-adjusted cost data.

If you use interest-adjusted cost data, keep in mind the following points:

- *Shop for a policy and not an insurer.* Some insurers have excellent low-cost policies at certain ages and amounts, but they are not as competitive when other ages and amounts are considered.
- *Compare only similar plans of insurance.* You should compare policies of the same type with the same benefits. Otherwise, the comparison can be misleading.
- *Ignore small variations in the cost index numbers.* Small cost differences can be offset by other policy features or by services that you can expect to get from an agent or insurer.

EXHIBIT 19.4
Comparison of Life Insurance Costs for Selected Companies

	Surrender Cost Index			Net Payment Index	
1	USAA Life	1.24	1	Manufacturers	8.24
2	Government Personnel Mut. Life	1.59	2	United Heritage Life	8.32
3	Country Life	1.74	3	John Hancock Mutual Life	8.71
4	Phoenix Home Life Mutual	1.92	4	Phoenix Home Life Mutual	9.08
5	Mutual Life of New York	2.10	5	Columbus Life	9.16
6	Columbian Mutual Life	2.35	6	State Farm	9.29
7	National Life Vermont	2.39	7	American Family Life	9.43
8	AmerUs Life	2.40	8	Country Life	9.55
9	John Hancock Mutual Life	2.47	8	Security Mutual of New York	9.55
10	Western-Southern Life	2.49	9	United Farm Family Life	9.57
11	Ohio National Life	2.51	10	Phoenix Home Life Mut. (Home Life)	9.65
12	Mutual Trust Life	2.54	11	Farm Family Life	9.66
12	Security Mutual of New York	2.54	12	Mutual Life of New York	9.82
13	Farm Family Life	2.56	13	Ohio National Life	9.83
13	Manufacturers Life	2.56	14	Berkshire Life	10.17
14	United Farm Family Life	2.60	15	New York Life	10.19
15	Penn Mutual Life	2.64	16	USAA Life	10.24
16	American Family Life	2.84	17	Farmers & Traders Life	10.28
17	State Farm	2.87	18	Knights of Columbus	10.40
18	Massachusetts Mutual Life	2.97	19	General American	10.47

NOTE: The indexes shown are the annual costs over a 10-year period for a $100,000 participating whole life policy issued to a male, age 35.

SOURCE: Adapted from Kim Kelleher, "Looking at Whole Life," *Best's Review*, Life/Health edition (July 1998), p. 53. Copyrighted by A. M. Best Company. Used with permission.

- *Cost indexes apply only to a new policy.* The cost data should not be used to determine whether to replace an existing policy with a new one. Other factors should be considered as well (see Insight 19.1).
- *The type of policy you buy should not be based solely on a cost index.* You should buy the type of policy that best meets your needs, such as term, whole life, or some combination. Once you have decided on the type of policy, then compare costs.

NAIC Policy Illustration Model Regulation

Our discussion of life insurance costs would not be complete without a brief discussion of the Life Insurance Policy Illustration Model Regulation drafted by the National Association of Insurance Commissioners (NAIC).

The majority of states have adopted the model regulation. The model act requires insurers to present certain information to applicants for life insurance. The policy illustration contains a *narrative summary* that describes the basic characteristics of the policy, including how the policy functions, underwriting class, death benefit option, payment of premiums, and any riders. The narrative summary also describes the elements of the policy that are not guaranteed, federal tax guidelines for the policy, key definitions, and interest-adjusted cost data.

In addition, the policy illustration has a *numeric summary* that shows the premium outlay, value of the accumulation account, cash surrender values, and death benefit. Three policy values must be provided

INSIGHT 19.1

Should You Replace a Life Insurance Policy?

If you already own a life insurance policy, a health insurance policy, or an annuity contract, you should be careful if you are considering replacing it. Although the relative financial strength of the original company and the replacing company is an important factor in your decision, you should consider other factors as well:

- If you consider replacing life or health insurance, *your state of health and other items affecting your eligibility should be reviewed.* You may not qualify for new insurance, or you may qualify only at high rates.
- *You should determine the cost of getting out of the original policy.* Many policies contain substantial surrender charges.
- *You should determine the cost of getting into the replacement policy.* Many policies involve substantial front-end expenses.
- *You should determine whether the cost of continuing the original policy is reasonable.* If the cost is reasonable, there may be little if any advantage in replacing it. [A procedure for making such a determination is described in Appendix E of the text.]
- *You should consider the tax implications of a replacement.* In some situations, the termination of a life insurance policy or may trigger an income tax liability. You may be able to defer the tax, but you should consult your tax adviser.
- *You should consider the incontestability clause.* For example, if a life insurance policy is more than two years

old, the company usually is barred from alleging that the policy is void because of false statements you made in the application. Thus, the original policy may not be contestable, while the replacement policy may be contestable for two years.

- *You should also be aware of the suicide clause.* Suicide usually is excluded during the first two years of a life insurance policy. Thus, the original policy may currently cover suicide, while the replacement policy may not cover suicide for two years.
- *If someone recommends replacement, you should try to determine the amount of compensation the person making the recommendation will receive if you follow the advice.* Some who recommend replacement are motivated by a genuine desire to help you reduce your expenses or avoid the problems that may arise if your original company gets into financial trouble. However, in the current environment of public concern about the financial strength of insurance companies, some persons may descend on the policyowners of a troubled company like sharks who detect blood in the water. The fact that a person receives a commission does not necessarily mean he or she is giving bad advice, but you should be on guard.

SOURCE: Adapted from Joseph M. Belth, ed., "The Replacement Problem," The Insurance Forum, vol. 30, no. 9 (September 2003), p. 250.

based on (1) current interest rate credited to the policy, (2) guaranteed minimum interest rate under the policy, and (3) midpoint interest rate. The illustration also shows the number of years the insurance protection will remain in force under the three sets of interest assumptions. The applicant and agent must sign the illustration and indicate they have discussed and they understand that the nonguaranteed elements in the policy are subject to change and can be higher or lower than the values shown in the illustration.

Certain deceptive sales practices are prohibited in the illustration of policy values: insurers are prohibited from using anticipated gains from improvements in mortality in the sales illustration; the term "vanishing premium" cannot be used; and the values shown in the illustration must be justified by a self-support test.

Finally, the insurer must provide an annual report on the policy and notify the policyowners when a change occurs in the dividend scale or individual pricing elements that would negatively affect the policy values. The model regulation should reduce misunderstanding of policy values by policyowners and reduce deceptive sales practices by agents.

RATE OF RETURN ON SAVING COMPONENT

Another important consideration is the rate of return earned on the saving component of a traditional whole life insurance policy. Consumers normally do not know the annual rate of return they earn on the saving component in their policies. A consumer who buys a traditional cash-value policy with a low return can lose a considerable amount of money over the life of the policy. Thus, the annual rate of return you earn on the saving component is critical if you intend to invest money in a life insurance policy over a long period of time.

Linton Yield

The **Linton yield** is one method that can be used to determine the rate of return on the saving portion of a cash-value policy. It was developed by M. Albert Linton, a well-known life insurance actuary. *In essence, the Linton yield is the average annual rate of return on a cash-value policy if it is held for a specified number of years.* It is based on the assumption that a cash-value policy can be viewed as a combination of insurance protection and a savings fund. To determine the average annual rate of return for a given period, it is first necessary to determine that part of the annual premium that is deposited in the savings fund. This amount can be determined by subtracting the cost of the insurance protection for that year from the annual premium (less any dividend). The balance of the premium is the amount that can be deposited into the savings fund. Thus, the average annual rate of return is the compound interest rate that is required to make the savings deposits equal the guaranteed cash value in the policy at the end of a specified period.

Calculation of the Linton yield is complex and requires specific information. Unfortunately, current rates of return based on the Linton yield are not readily available to consumers. However, a 1997 Consumer Federation of America study of 109 cash-value policies based on the Linton yield showed that the annual rates of return vary widely. *The study showed that the average annual rates of return for the 109 policies ranged from a minus 87.9 percent for the first year to 8.2 percent for the twentieth year* (see Exhibit 19.5). The study concluded that consumers lose billions of dollars annually by terminating their policies early. The Consumer Federation of America recommends that consumers should not purchase a cash-value policy unless they plan to hold it for at least 20 years.

Annual rates of return based on the Linton yield are usually negative during the early years of the policy. These negative returns reflect the heavy first-year acquisition and administrative expenses when

EXHIBIT 19.5
Average Annual Rates of Return for 109 Cash-Value Policies by Year of Policy

Year	Rate of Return (%)
1	−87.9
2	−54.9
3	−18.9
4	0.0
5	5.6
6	7.3
7	7.7
8	7.7
9	7.6
10	9.8
11	8.0
12	8.0
13	8.0
14	7.9
15	8.1
16	7.8
17	7.8
18	7.8
19	7.8
20	8.2

SOURCE: Consumer Federation of America, *Rates of Return on Cash-Value Policies Vary Widely*, press release, July 16, 1997.

the policy is first sold. An agent receives a commission, and there may be a medical examiner's fee, an inspection report, and other expenses involved in issuing the policy. As a result of these expenses, most cash-value policies have little or no cash value at the end of the first year, and the cash values remain relatively low during the early years. Thus, if you surrender the policy or allow it to lapse during the early years, you will lose a substantial amount of money.

Because current information on Linton yields is not readily available, this method has limited usefulness as a consumer tool.[1] We must therefore consider other methods. The yearly rate-of-return method discussed next is a simple, but valuable methodology that can enable you to calculate the annual rate of return on the saving component in your policy.

Yearly Rate-of-Return Method

Professor Joseph M. Belth has developed the **yearly rate-of-return method** for calculating the saving component of a cash-value policy.[2] The yearly rate of return is based on the following formula:

$$i = \frac{(CV + D) + (YPT)(DB - CV)(.001)}{(P + CVP)} - 1$$

where

i = yearly rate of return on the saving component, expressed as a decimal
CV = cash value at end of policy year
D = annual dividend
YPT = assumed yearly price per $1000 of protection (see benchmark prices in Exhibit 19.6)
DB = death benefit
P = annual premium
CVP = cash value at end of preceding policy year

The first expression in the numerator of the formula is the amount available in the policy at the end of the policy year. The second expression in the numerator is the assumed price of the protection component, which is determined by multiplying the amount of protection by an assumed price per $1000 of protection. Assumed prices per $1000 of protection for various ages are benchmarks derived from certain U.S. population death rates (see Exhibit 19.6). Finally, the expression in the denominator of the formula is the amount available in the policy at the beginning of the policy year.

For example, assume that Mark purchased a $100,000 participating ordinary life policy at age 35. He is now age 42 at the beginning of the eighth policy year. He would like to know the yearly rate of return on the saving component for the eighth year of the policy. The annual premium is $1500. The cash value in the policy is $7800 at the end of the seventh policy year and $9200 at the end of the eighth policy year. The eighth-year dividend is $400. Because Mark is age 42 at the beginning of the eighth policy year, the benchmark price is $4.00 per $1000 (see again Exhibit 19.6).

Based on the preceding information, the yearly rate of return for the eighth policy year is calculated as follows:

$$i = \frac{(9200 + 400) + (4)(100,000 - 9200)(.001)}{(1500 + 7800)} - 1$$

$$= \frac{(9600) + (4)((90,800)(.001)}{(9300)} - 1$$

$$= \frac{9600 + 363}{9300} - 1$$

$$= \frac{9963}{9300} - 1 = 1.071 - 1 = .071 = 7.1\%$$

The yearly rate of return for the eighth policy year is 7.1 percent, assuming that the yearly price per $1000 of protection is $4.

The major advantage of Belth's method is simplicity—you do not need a computer. The information needed can be obtained by referring to your policy and premium notice, or by contacting your agent or insurer. The same methodology can be used to evaluate an existing life insurance policy. (See Appendix E at the end of the text.)

EXHIBIT 19.6
Benchmark Prices

Age	Benchmark Price
Under 30	$ 1.50
30–34	2.00
35–39	3.00
40–44	4.00
45–49	6.50
50–54	10.00
55–59	15.00
60–64	25.00
65–69	35.00
70–74	50.00
75–79	80.00
80–84	125.00

NOTE: The benchmark prices were derived from certain U. S. population death rates. The benchmark figure for each five-year age bracket is close to the death rate per $1000 at the highest age in that bracket.

SOURCE: Adapted from Joseph M. Belth, *Life Insurance: A Consumer's Handbook,* 2nd ed. (Bloomington, IN: Indiana University Press, 1985), table 9, p. 84. Reprinted by permission of the author.

TAXATION OF LIFE INSURANCE

Treatment of life insurance buying would be incomplete without a discussion of the taxation of life insurance. This section discusses briefly the taxation of life insurance.

Federal Income Tax

Life insurance proceeds paid in a lump sum to a designated beneficiary are generally received income-tax free by the beneficiary. If the proceeds are periodically liquidated under the settlement options, the payments consist of both principal and interest. The principal is received income-tax free, but the interest is taxable as ordinary income.

Premiums paid for individual life insurance policies generally are not deductible for income-tax purposes. Dividends on life insurance policies are received income-tax free. However, interest on dividends retained under the interest option is taxable to the policyowner. If the dividends are used to buy paid-up additions, the cash value of the paid-up additions accumulates income-tax free unless the contract is terminated with a policy gain (discussed later). Thus, compared with the interest option, the paid-up additions option provides a small tax advantage.

In addition, the annual increase in cash value under a permanent life insurance policy is presently income-tax free. However, if the policy is surrendered for its cash value, any gain is taxable as ordinary income. If the cash value exceeds the premiums paid less any dividends, the excess is taxed as ordinary income.

Federal Estate Tax

If the insured has any ownership interest in the policy at the time of death, the entire proceeds are included in the gross estate of the insured for federal estate-tax purposes. Examples include the right to change the beneficiary, the right to borrow the cash value or surrender the policy, and the right to elect a settlement option. The proceeds are also included in the insured's gross estate if they are payable to the estate. They can be removed from the gross estate if the policyowner makes an *absolute assignment* of the policy to someone else and has no incidents of ownership in the policy at the time of death. However, if the assignment is made within three years of death, the proceeds will be included in the deceased's gross estate for federal estate-tax purposes.

A federal estate tax is payable if the decedent's taxable estate exceeds certain limits. After the taxable estate is determined, a tentative tax is calculated. The tentative tax is reduced or eliminated by a tax credit called a *unified credit*. For individuals who die in 2004, the amount of the credit is $555,800, which eliminates the federal estate tax completely on taxable estates of $1,500,000 or less. However, as a result of the Economic Growth and Tax Relief Reconciliation Act of 2001, the amount of property exempt from taxation will gradually increase in the future until the federal estate tax disappears in 2010. For 2004, the maximum exempt amount is $1,500,000. The exempt amount will gradually increase to $3,500,000 in 2009. The estate tax will then be repealed in 2010. The exempt amount will increase gradually according to the following schedule:

Year	Exempt Amount	Unified Credit
2004	$1,500,000	$ 555,800
2005	1,500,000	555,800
2006	2,000,000	780,800
2007	2,000,000	780,800
2008	2,000,000	780,800
2009	3,500,000	1,455,800
2010	*Estate tax repealed*	

In addition, federal estate tax rates on taxable estates will decrease in the future and then will be eliminated. The highest federal estate tax rates will decline according to the following schedule:

Year	Highest Estate Tax Rate (%)	On Amounts Over
2004	48	$2,000,000
2005	47	2,000,000
2006	46	2,000,000
2007	45	1,500,000
2008	45	1,500,000
2009	45	1,500,000
2010	0	*Estate tax repealed*

Although the federal estate tax is scheduled to expire in 2010, estate planners are not certain that the tax will actually disappear. Because of complex congressional budget rules, all tax cut provisions, including repeal of the federal estate tax, will no longer apply after December 31, 2010. Unless Congress acts to change the legislation, the federal estate tax and other tax changes will revert back to 2000 levels.

To determine whether a federal estate tax is payable, the gross estate must first be calculated. The *gross estate* includes the value of the property you own when you die, one-half of the value of the property owned jointly with your spouse, life insurance death proceeds in which the insured has any incidents of ownership, and certain other items. The gross estate can be reduced by certain deductions in determining the *taxable estate*. Allowable deductions include funeral and administrative expenses, claims against the estate, estate settlement and probate costs, charitable contributions, and certain other deductions.

In addition, the gross estate can be reduced by the *marital deduction,* which is a deduction of the value of the property included in the gross estate but passed on to the surviving spouse. This property is taxed later, when the surviving spouse dies. For example, assume that Richard dies in 2004 and has a gross estate of $2.7 million. He leaves $1 million of property outright to his spouse. Thus, the marital deduction is $1 million. Assume that debts, funeral expenses, and administrative costs total $200,000. The taxable estate is $1.5 million, and the tentative federal tax is $555,800. However, as a result of the unified credit of $555,800, the federal estate tax is zero (see Exhibit 19.7).

SHOPPING FOR LIFE INSURANCE

Developing a sound life insurance program involves seven steps, as illustrated in Exhibit 19.8 and discussed next.

Determine Whether You Need Life Insurance

The first step is to determine whether you need life insurance. If you are married or single with one or more dependents to support, you may need a substantial amount of life insurance. You may also need

EXHIBIT 19.7
Calculating Federal Estate Taxes*

Gross estate		$2,700,000
Less:		
Debts	$150,000	
Administrative costs	40,000	
Funeral expenses	10,000	
		−200,000
Adjusted gross estate		$2,500,000
Less:		
Marital deduction		−1,000,000
Taxable estate		$1,500,000
Tentative tax		$ 555,800
Less:		
Applicable credit		−555,800
Federal estate tax		$ 0

*Individual dies in 2004.

EXHIBIT 19.8
Shopping for Life Insurance

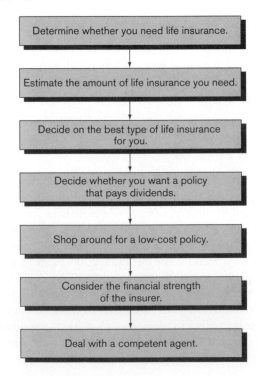

life insurance if you have a temporary need, such as paying off the mortgage on your home. In addition, if you have accumulated substantial assets, large amounts of life insurance may be needed to provide estate liquidity and to pay federal estate taxes that are due within nine months of your death.

However, if you are single and no one is presently dependent on you for financial support, you do not need life insurance, other than a modest amount for burial purposes. The arguments for buying life insurance when you are young and insurable are not compelling. Even if your situation should change and you need life insurance in the future, *more than nine out of ten applicants for life insurance are accepted at standard rates.* Thus, it is a waste of money to buy life insurance when it is not needed.

Estimate the Amount of Life Insurance You Need

The needs approach and capital retention approach are practical methods for determining the amount of life insurance needed. Persons with dependents often need surprisingly large amounts of life insurance. In determining the amount needed, you must consider your family's present and future financial needs, potential survivor benefits from Social Security, and other financial assets currently owned.

If you carry a sufficient amount of life insurance, it is unnecessary to purchase additional life insurance as supplemental coverage. These coverages include accidental death insurance from life insurers, accidental death and dismemberment insurance offered by commercial banks, credit life insurance on consumer loans, and life insurance sold by mail. In addition, flight insurance sold at airports is a bad buy for most consumers because commercial jets rarely crash.

Decide on the Best Type of Life Insurance for You

The next step is to select the best type of life insurance policy for you. *The best policy is the one that best meets your financial needs.* If the amount of money you can spend on life insurance is limited, or if you have a temporary need, consider only term insurance. If you need lifetime protection, consider ordinary life insurance or universal life insurance. If you believe that you cannot save money without being forced to do so, also consider ordinary life

insurance or universal life insurance as a savings vehicle. However, remember that the annual rates of return on cash-value policies can vary enormously.

Also, avoid purchasing a policy that you cannot afford. A large percentage of new life insurance policies lapse for nonpayment of premiums during the first two years. The lapse rate for policies in force for less than two years was about 14 percent in 2000.[3] *If you drop the policy after a few months or years, you will lose a substantial sum of money. Be sure you can afford the premium.*

Decide Whether You Want a Policy That Pays Dividends

In recent decades, participating life insurance policies that pay dividends generally have been better buys than nonparticipating policies because of high interest rates that permitted insurers to raise their dividends. However, interest rates have declined in recent years, and many insurers have reduced their dividends because excess interest earnings have declined. Thus, if you believe that interest rates will be higher in the future, you should consider a participating policy because excess interest has a powerful impact on dividends. However, if you believe that interest rates will remain at lower levels in the future, then consider a nonparticipating policy. Policies that do not pay dividends generally require a lower premium outlay.

Shop Around for a Low-Cost Policy

One of the most important suggestions is to shop carefully for a low-cost policy. There is enormous variation in the cost of life insurance. You should not purchase a life insurance policy from the first agent who approaches you. *Instead, you should compare the interest-adjusted cost of similar policies from several insurers before you buy.* Otherwise, you may be overpaying for the insurance protection. If you make a mistake and purchase a high-cost policy, this mistake can cost you thousands of dollars over your lifetime.

When you shop for a low-cost policy, you should also consider **low-load life insurance.** Some life insurers sell insurance directly to the public by using telephone representatives or fee-only financial

INSIGHT 19.2

Warning: Internet Shopping May Not Produce the Best Prices

The Consumer Federation of America [CFA] released a comparative study of 25 web-based Internet sites offering comparative term life insurance information. The results show tremendous differences in the quality and reliability of these sites in finding the most economical term life insurance policies. "We chose term life insurance to test the reliability of the Internet as a shopping tool because of the straightforward and comparative nature of the product," said J. Robert Hunter, CFA's Director of Insurance and report co-author. "Clearly, shopping around can pay off, but the best deal is very much dependent on where you land on the web," said Hunter.

Of the 25 sites analyzed, nine (36 percent) are so inadequate and potentially misleading that they are not recommended by CFA. These sites are **Insure Rate, Intelli-quote, Insure One, Compusurance, SpeedInsure, 4freequotes, Answerfinancial, Ebix,** and **SelectOne.** In addition, some sites are merely referral services to put a consumer in touch with an agent.

The analysis of 25 Internet sites showed a range of offerings from simply providing information to consumers about term life insurance policies, to selling insurance directly from the site on commission, to simply generating leads for agents. "For many consumers shopping on the Internet is still a new experience, and it is difficult to immediately discern which of these sites truly offer fair prices," said Hunter. "Our study clearly indicates that shopping around can save hundreds of dollars on term life insurance, but the wrong site can cause you to inadvertently pay too much thinking that you are getting a good deal."

Other findings include:

- *Five best sites for term insurance shopping.* **Term4Sale** was the highest recommended site because of its very complete list of insurers, including no-load insurers, and ease of use. **Compulife** is also favored because of its extensive listing of all life insurers in the U.S., and because it quotes premiums for low-load insurers. **InsWeb, Accuquote,** and **Quotesmith** are also recommended.

- *Seventy-two percent of sites fail to show lowest prices.* For the hypothetical male consumer used for the research, the actual low-cost insurer was CNA Life. However, only seven (28 percent) of the sites actually displayed CNA Life as the low-cost insurer. The sites that properly identified the actual low-cost insurer are **Accuquote, Insweb, NetQuote, Quicken, Quotesmith, Youdecide.com,** and **Term4sale.**

- *Lowest priced term insurance is often absent.* Because many sites make a profit by commissions on insurance sales, they do not include no-load insurance companies. No-load companies are usually low-cost providers, so their quotes can be useful. Term4Sale.com is one site that provides quotes for no-load companies.

- *Methodology.* Each website was searched for a $500,000 ten-year term policy for a hypothetical 40-year-old male in excellent health. Research was terminated for any site that was too difficult to navigate, or asked for too much personal information.

SOURCE: Adapted from Consumer Federation of America, *Warning: Internet Shopping May Not Produce the Best Prices, New CFA Study Rates 36 Percent of Term Insurance Websites as "NOT RECOMMENDED,"* press release, August 1, 2001.

---

planners. The major advantage is that marketing expenses account for only 10 to 25 percent of the first year's premium rather than 90 to 125 percent on policies sold by agents. Two major low-load insurers that sell policies by phone are Ameritas Direct (800-689-6830) and USAA Life (800-531-8000).

In summary, shopping for a low-cost policy can save you thousands of dollars. However, the quality of available cost information varies widely, as does the quality of Internet sites. In particular, a Consumer Federation of America study of online sites for term insurance concluded that some sites are difficult to use and are not recommended; not all sites show the lowest premium quotes; some sites do not include quotes from low-load insurers; and certain sites are more useful to consumers than others (see Insight 19.2).

Consider the Financial Strength of the Insurer

In addition to cost, you should consider the financial strength of the insurer issuing the policy. Some life insurers have become insolvent and have gone out of

EXHIBIT 19.9
Rating Categories of Major Rating Agencies

Rank Number	Ratings				
	Best	Fitch	Moody's	S&P	Weiss
1	A++	AAA	Aaa	AAA	A+
2	A+	AA+	Aa1	AA+	A
3	A	AA	Aa2	AA	A−
4	A−	AA−	Aa3	AA−	B+
5	B++	A+	A1	A+	B
6	B+	A	A2	A	B−
7	B	A−	A3	A−	C+
8	B−	BBB+	Baa1	BBB+	C
9	C++	BBB	Baa2	BBB	C−
10	C+	BBB−	Baa3	BBB−	D+
11	C	BB+	Ba1	BB+	D
12	C−	BB	Ba2	BB	D−
13	D	BB−	Ba3	BB−	E+
14	E	B+	B1	B+	E
15	F	B	B2	B	E−
16		B−	B3	B−	F
17		CCC+	Caa1	CCC	
18		CCC	Caa2	CC	
19		CCC−	Caa3	R	
20		CC/C	Ca		
21		DDD	C		
22		DD/D			

NOTE: The ratings in a given rank are not necessarily equivalent to one another.

SOURCE: Joseph M. Belth, ed., "The Financial Strength of Life-Health Insurance Companies," *The Insurance Forum*, vol. 30, no. 9 (September 2003), p. 247.

business. Although all states have state guaranty funds that pay the claims of insolvent life insurers, there are limits on the amount guaranteed. Although death claims are paid promptly, you may have to wait years before you can borrow or withdraw your cash value. Thus, it is important to buy life insurance only from financially sound insurers.

A number of rating organizations periodically grade and rate life insurers on their financial strength (see Exhibit 19.9). The companies are rated based on the amount of their capital and surplus, legal reserves, quality of investments, past profitability, competency of management, and numerous other factors. However, the various ratings are not always a reliable guide for consumers and can be confusing. There are wide variations in the grades given by the different rating agencies. Joseph M. Belth, a nationally known consumer expert in life insurance, recommends that an insurer should receive a high rating from at least two of the following four rating agencies before a policy is purchased. The following are considered high ratings for someone who is conservative:[4]

Best: A++, A+, A
Fitch: AAA, AA+, AA, AA−
Moody's: Aaa, Aa1, Aa2, Aa3, A1
S&P: AAA, AA+, AA, AA−, A+
Weiss: A+, A, A−, B+, B, B−

Deal with a Competent Agent

You should also deal with a competent agent when you buy life insurance. Selling life insurance is a tough job, and only a relatively small proportion of new life insurance agents are successful.

Most new agents receive only a minimum amount of training before they are licensed to sell life insurance. New agents also are often placed under intense pressure to sell life insurance. Even mature agents are expected to sell a certain amount of insurance. As a result, some agents have engaged in deceptive sales practices by misrepresenting the insurance to clients or by recommending policies that maximize commissions rather than meeting the client's needs. Because of deceptive sales practices by

agents, several major life insurers have been subject to heavy fines by state insurance departments and class action litigation by angry policyowners.

To reduce the possibility of receiving bad advice or being sold the wrong policy, you should consider the professional qualifications of the agent. An agent who is a **Chartered Life Underwriter (CLU)**, **Chartered Financial Consultant (ChFC)**, or **Certified Financial Planner (CFP)** should be technically competent to give proper advice. More importantly, agents who hold the preceding professional designations are expected to abide by a code of ethics that places their clients' interests ahead of their own. Agents who are currently studying for these professional designations should also be considered.

CASE APPLICATION

A participating ordinary life policy in the amount of $10,000 is sold to an individual, age 35. The following cost data are given:

Annual premium	$230
Total dividends for 20 years	$1613
Cash value at end of 20 years	$3620
Accumulated value of the annual premiums at 5 percent for 20 years	$7985
Accumulated value of the dividends at 5 percent for 20 years	$2352
Amount to which $1 deposited annually at the beginning of each year will accumulate in 20 years at 5 percent	$34.719

a. Based on this information, compute the annual net cost for each $1000 of life insurance at the end of 20 years using the *traditional net cost method*.

b. Compute the annual *surrender cost index* for each $1000 of life insurance at the end of 20 years.

c. Compute the annual *net payment cost index* for each $1000 of life insurance at the end of 20 years.

SUMMARY

- There are enormous cost variations among similar life insurance policies. Purchase of a high-cost policy can cost thousands of extra dollars over the insured's lifetime for the same amount of insurance protection.

- The traditional net cost method for illustrating the cost of life insurance has several defects:

    The time value of money is ignored.

    The insurance is often shown to be free.

    The steepness of the dividend scale is ignored.

    The dividend scale is assumed to remain unchanged.

    The net cost is based on the assumption that the policy will be surrendered.

- The interest-adjusted method is a more accurate measure of life insurance costs. The time value of money is taken into consideration by applying an interest factor to each element of cost. If you are interested in surrendering the policy at the end of a certain period, the surrender cost index is the appropriate cost index to use. If you intend to keep your policy in force, the net payment cost index should be used.

- Annual rates-of-return data on the saving component in traditional cash-value life insurance policies are not readily available to consumers. However, the yearly rate-of-return method can be helpful to consumers in this regard.

- Life insurance death proceeds paid in a lump sum to a designated beneficiary are generally received income-tax free by the beneficiary. Premiums for individual life insurance are not income-tax deductible. If a policy is surrendered for its cash value, any gain is taxable as ordinary income. If the cash value exceeds the premiums paid less any dividends, the excess is taxed as ordinary income.

- If the insured has any ownership interest in the policy at the time of death, the entire proceeds are included in his or her gross estate for federal estate-tax purposes. A federal estate tax is payable if the decedent's taxable estate exceeds certain limits. The exempt amount will gradually rise in the future. The federal estate tax is scheduled to expire in 2010.

- Life insurance experts typically recommend several rules to follow when shopping for life insurance:

   Determine whether you need life insurance.

   Estimate the amount of life insurance you need.

   Decide on the best type of insurance for you.

   Decide whether you want a policy that pays dividends.

   Shop around for a low-cost policy.

   Consider the financial strength of the insurer.

   Deal with a competent agent.

KEY CONCEPTS AND TERMS

Certified Financial Planner (CFP)
Chartered Financial Consultant (ChFC)
Chartered Life Underwriter (CLU)
Interest-adjusted cost method

Linton yield
Low-load life insurance
Net payment cost index
Surrender cost index
Traditional net cost method
Yearly rate-of-return method

REVIEW QUESTIONS

1. Explain the defects in the traditional net cost method for determining the cost of life insurance.

2. a. Why is the interest-adjusted cost method a more accurate measure of the cost of life insurance?
   b. Briefly describe the *surrender cost index* as a method for determining the cost of life insurance.
   c. Briefly describe the *net payment cost index* as a method for determining the cost of life insurance.
   d. Where can you obtain interest-adjusted cost information?

3. Why is the rate of return on the saving component in most cash-value policies negative during the early years of the policy?

4. Briefly explain the *Linton Yield* as a method for determining the rate of return on the saving component of a cash-value policy.

5. Briefly explain the yearly rate-of-return method that policyowners can use to determine the rate of return on the saving component of a cash-value policy.

6. Explain the federal income-tax treatment of a cash-value policy with respect to each of the following:
   a. Payment of premiums
   b. Annual dividends
   c. Annual increase in the cash value
   d. Payment of death proceeds to a stated beneficiary

7. Explain the federal estate-tax treatment of life insurance death proceeds.

8. Describe the suggestions that consumers should follow when life insurance is purchased.

9. The states require life insurers to disclose certain policy information to applicants for life insurance. Describe the types of information that appear on a typical disclosure statement.

10. What is a *low-load* life insurance policy? Explain.

APPLICATION QUESTIONS

1. Nicole, age 25, is considering the purchase of a $20,000 participating ordinary life insurance policy. The annual premium is $248.60. Projected dividends over the first 20 years are $814. The cash value at the end of 20 years is $4314. If the premiums are invested at 5 percent interest, they will accumulate to $8631 at the end of 20 years. If the dividends are invested at 5 percent interest, they will accumulate to $1163 at the end of 20 years. A $1 deposit at the beginning of each

year at 5 percent interest will accumulate to $34.719 at the end of 20 years.
   a. Based on the *traditional net cost method,* calculate the net cost per $1000 per year.
   b. Based on the *surrender cost index,* calculate the net cost per $1000 per year.
   c. Based on the *net payment cost index,* calculate the net cost per $1000 per year.

2. Todd, age 40, is considering the purchase of a $100,000 participating ordinary life insurance policy. The annual premium is $2280. Projected dividends over the first 20 years are $15,624. The cash value at the end of 20 years is $35,260. If the premiums are invested at 5 percent interest, they will grow to $79,159 at the end of 20 years. If the dividends are invested at 5 percent interest, they will accumulate to $24,400 at the end of 20 years. A $1 deposit at the beginning of each year at 5 percent interest will accumulate to $34.719 at the end of 20 years.
   a. Based on the *traditional net cost method,* calculate the net cost per $1000 per year.
   b. Based on the *surrender cost index,* calculate the net cost per $1000 per year.
   c. Based on the *net payment cost index,* calculate the net cost per $1000 per year.

3. John, age 52, is overweight, smokes, and had a mild heart attack five years ago. Ignoring the advice of his physician, he refuses to exercise, lose weight, and quit smoking. John owns a $25,000 participating ordinary life policy that he purchased 20 years ago. A life insurance agent approached John and proposed that he replace the older policy with a new life insurance policy. The agent claims the new policy is superior to the older policy that was purchased years ago. Despite John's health problems, the agent claims that John can get life insurance from his company. What factors should John consider before replacing the older policy with a new policy?

4. Allison is trying to complete her income tax return. A number of questions have come up about life insurance. Explain the tax treatment of each of the following.
   a. Allison was the beneficiary named in her grandfather's life insurance policy. Her grandfather died this year and Allison received a lump-sum payment of $50,000. She wonders if she has to report the $50,000 as taxable income.
   b. Allison purchased a $100,000 cash value life insurance policy on her own life six years ago. This year, the cash value increased by $380. Allison wonders if the cash value increase must be reported as taxable income. The policy remains in force.
   c. Allison's annual life insurance premium is $350. Allison itemizes her income tax deductions. She wonders if her life insurance premium is a tax deductible expense.
   d. Allison's ordinary life insurance policy is a participating policy. This year she received $120 in policyowner dividends. She wonders if she is required to report the $120 as taxable income.

INTERNET RESOURCES

- **Ameritas Direct** sells life insurance and annuities directly to consumers without traditional agents. Visit the site at
  http://www.ameritasdirect.com

- **Consumer Federation of America** makes available a low-cost life insurance evaluation service by which individual life insurance policies can be evaluated for a small fee. Visit the site at
  http://www.consumerfed.org

- **Insure.com** provides premium quotes on life insurance and news releases about events that affect the insurance industry. Visit the site at
  http://www.insure.com

- **Insurance.com** is an online independent insurance agency that provides premium quotes on life insurance, health insurance, and other insurance products. Visit the site at
  http://www.insurance.com

- **Insweb** provides timely information and premium quotes for life insurance and other insurance products. Visit the site at
  http://www.insweb.com

- **QuickQuote** provides premium quotes on life insurance, health insurance, and numerous other insurance products. Visit the site at
  http://www.quickquote.com

■ **Select Quote** monitors over 1400 insurers that sell term life insurance. It claims that it makes only the strongest and competitively price policies available to consumers. It also represents a wide range of insurers that specialize in insuring people with different risks, such as a pilot, scuba diver, or diabetic. Visit the site at

http://www.selectquote.com

■ **Term4Sale** is considered to be one of the best consumer sites for obtaining term insurance quotes. Visit the site at

http://www.term4sale.com

SELECTED REFERENCES

Belth, Joseph M. *Life Insurance: A Consumer's Handbook,* 2nd ed. Bloomington, IN: Indiana University Press, 1985.

Black, Kenneth, Jr., and Harold D. Skipper, Jr. *Life Insurance,* 13th ed. Upper Saddle River, NJ: Prentice-Hall, 2000.

Consumer Federation of America. *Warning: Internet Shopping May Not Produce the Best Prices, New CFA Study Rates 36 Percent of Term Insurance Websites as "NOT RECOMMENDED,"* press release, August 1, 2001.

Consumer Federation of America. *Rates of Return on Cash Value Life Insurance Policies Vary Widely, CFA Report Shows Why Consumers Lose Billions of Dollars Annually,* press release, July 16, 1997.

Graves, Edward E., ed. *McGill's Life Insurance,* 5th ed. Bryn Mawr, PA: The American College, 2004.

Hunt, James H. *Analysis of Cash Value Life Insurance Policies.* Washington, DC: Consumer Federation of America, July 1997.

Hunt, James H. *Evaluating Cash Value Life Insurance Policies.* Washington, DC: Consumer Federation of America, September 28, 2001.

Hunt, James H. *Variable Universal Life Insurance: Is It Worth It?* Consumer Federation of America, February 2003.

Hunter, J. Robert, and James H. Hunt. *Term Life Insurance on the Internet: An Evaluation of On-Line Quotes.* Washington, DC: Consumer Federation of America, 2001.

NOTES

1. However, the Consumer Federation of America will analyze a life insurance policy based on the Linton yield for a small fee.

2. This section is based on Joseph M. Belth, *Life Insurance: A Consumer's Handbook,* 2nd ed. (Bloomington, IN: Indiana University Press, 1985), pp. 89–91, 208–209.

3. *Life Insurers Fact Book, 2001* (Washington, DC: American Council of Life Insurers, 2001), table 7.6, p. 103.

4. Joseph M. Belth, ed., "The Financial Strength of Life-Health Insurance Companies," *The Insurance Forum,* vol. 30, no. 9 (September 2003), p. 247.

CHAPTER 20

ANNUITIES AND INDIVIDUAL RETIREMENT ACCOUNTS

"Buy an annuity cheap, and make your life interesting to yourself and everybody else that watches the speculation."

Charles Dickens

LEARNING OBJECTIVES

After studying this chapter, you should be able to

◆ Show how an annuity differs from life insurance.

◆ Describe the basic characteristics of a fixed annuity and a variable annuity.

◆ Explain the major characteristics of an equity-indexed annuity.

◆ Describe the basic characteristics of a traditional tax-deductible individual retirement account (IRA).

◆ Explain the basic characteristics of a Roth IRA.

◆ Explain the income tax treatment of a traditional IRA and a Roth IRA.

Raymond, age 27, graduated from a large southern university and accepted a job as a computer specialist with a computer software firm with an annual salary of $45,000. He has several financial goals, which include saving money for a comfortable retirement. Unfortunately, Raymond is ineligible to participate in the company's Section 401(k) retirement plan for one year. A financial planner recommended that Raymond invest in an individual retirement account (Roth IRA). He could start saving immediately for retirement; the investment income would accumulate income-tax free; and the retirement fund would grow to a sizable amount. The planner pointed out that if Raymond saved $3000 each year for 40 years, and the IRA account earned an average annual return of 6 percent, he would have more than $492,000 in his account at age 67. If the contributions were invested in a Roth IRA, he could receive the retirement benefits free of current income taxes, but his contributions would not be deductible.

Like Raymond, millions of workers dream of achieving financial independence and a comfortable retirement. Planning for a comfortable retirement should receive high priority in a personal risk management program. Retirement planning is especially important today because the proportion of older people in the population is increasing; the period of retirement for many workers is growing longer because of increased life expectancy; and studies show that many workers are not saving enough for a comfortable retirement.

This chapter discusses the timely topic of retirement planning and shows how annuities and IRAs can ensure a comfortable retirement. Two major areas are emphasized. The first part discusses the annuity concept and the different types of annuities sold today. The second part discusses the characteristics of IRAs, including the traditional tax-deductible IRA and the Roth IRA.

INDIVIDUAL ANNUITIES

The vast majority of workers who retire today receive Social Security retirement benefits. Some workers also receive benefits from their employers' retirement plans. Individual annuities can also be purchased to provide additional retirement income. An annuity is a tax-deferred product. Although the premiums are paid with after-tax dollars, the investment income accumulates income-tax free and is not taxed until benefits are paid to the annuitant. The investment returns of tax-deferred compounding over long periods can be impressive (see Exhibit 20.1).

Annuity Principle

An **annuity** *can be defined as a periodic payment that continues for a fixed period or for the duration of a designated life or lives.* The person who receives the periodic payments or whose life governs the duration of payment is known as the **annuitant.**

An annuity is the opposite of life insurance. Life insurance creates an immediate estate and provides protection against dying too soon before financial assets can be accumulated. In contrast, an annuity provides protection against living too long and exhausting one's savings while the individual is still

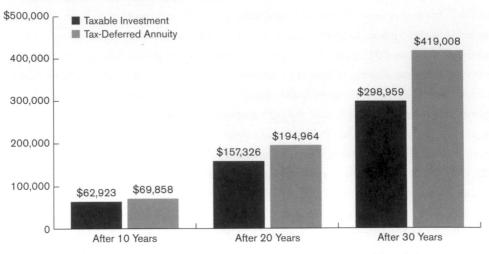

EXHIBIT 20.1
Tax Advantage of a Tax-Deferred Annuity

NOTE: The hypothetical example assumes a $5000 annual investment, a 6% annual rate of return and a 31% combined federal and state tax bracket. Annual investments are made at the beginning of the year with after-tax dollars. Investment returns occur at the end of the year and are taxed at that time.

SOURCE: Calculated from the Investment Growth Calculator, Fidelity Investments.

alive. Thus, *the fundamental purpose of an annuity is to provide a lifetime income that cannot be outlived.* It protects against the loss of income because of excessive longevity and the exhaustion of savings.

Annuities are possible because the risk of excessive longevity is pooled by the group. Individuals acting alone cannot be certain that their savings will be sufficient during retirement. Some will die early before exhausting their savings, whereas others will still be alive after exhausting their principal. Although the insurance company cannot predict how long any particular member of the group will live, it can determine the approximate number of annuitants who will be alive at the end of each successive year. Thus, the company can calculate the amount that each person must contribute to the pool. Interest can be earned on the funds before they are paid out to the annuitants. Also, some annuitants will die early, and their unliquidated principal can be used to provide additional payments to annuitants who survive beyond their life expectancy. Thus, annuity payments consist of three sources: (1) premium payments, (2) interest earnings, and (3) the unliquidated principal of annuitants who die early. By pooling the risk of excessive longevity, insurers

can pay a lifetime income to annuitants that cannot be outlived.

Annuitants tend to be healthy individuals who generally live longer than most persons. Because of the higher life expectancy of annuitants, actuaries use special annuity tables to calculate annuity premiums.

TYPES OF ANNUITIES

Insurers sell a wide variety of individual annuities. For sake of convenience and understanding, the major annuities sold today can be classified as follows:

- Fixed annuity
- Variable annuity
- Equity-indexed annuity

Fixed Annuity

A **fixed annuity** pays periodic income payments that are guaranteed and fixed in amount. During the **accumulation period** prior to retirement, premiums are credited with interest. There are typically two interest rates: a guaranteed minimum interest rate and a current interest rate. The *guaranteed rate* is the minimum interest rate that will be credited to the fixed annuity, such as 3 percent. The *current rate* is higher and is based on current market conditions, such as 4 percent. The current rate is guaranteed only for a limited period, typically one to five years.

As an inducement to purchase the annuity, many insurers sell *bonus annuities,* which initially increase the amount of interest credited to the annuity. The bonus interest generally ranges from 3 percent to 4 percent of the amount deposited. For example, an investor who deposits $100,000 into an annuity with a 3 percent bonus would receive an additional $3000 of interest the first year. However, there is no such thing as a free lunch. The bonus is paid for by reduced renewal interest rates credited to the annuity in the future or by higher expense fees.

Because interest rates have declined dramatically in recent years, many insurers have found it difficult to pay a guaranteed minimum interest rate of 3 percent on fixed annuities. In early 2003, the National Association of Insurance Commissioners (NAIC) proposed legislation that would replace the current 3 percent guaranteed minimum rate with a rate that would float with the yield on a five-year treasury note. The guaranteed rate could not exceed 3 percent or fall below 1 percent. A number of states have already adopted the proposed legislation.

The **liquidation period** (also called the **payout period**) follows the accumulation period and refers to the period in which the funds are being paid out. During the liquidation period, the accumulated cash can be *annuitized* or paid to the annuitant in the form of a guaranteed lifetime income. However, the periodic payments are fixed in amount and generally do not change. As a result, fixed annuities provide little or no protection against inflation.

Payment of Benefits   A fixed annuity can be purchased so that the income payments start immediately. This type of fixed annuity is called an immediate annuity. An **immediate annuity** *is one where the first payment is due one payment interval from the date of purchase.* For example, if the income is paid monthly, the first payment starts one month from the purchase date, or one year from the purchase date if the income is paid annually. Immediate annuities are typically purchased in a lump sum by

people near retirement. Because of the wide variation in monthly payments, financial planners recommend generally that consumers shop around before purchasing an immediate annuity.

A fixed annuity can also be purchased that defers the income payments until some later date. A **deferred annuity** *provides income payments at some future date.* This type of annuity is essentially a plan for accumulating a sum of money prior to retirement on a tax-deferred basis. If the annuitant dies during the accumulation period prior to retirement, a death benefit is typically paid equal to the sum of the gross premiums paid or the cash value if higher. At the maturity date of the contract, the annuitant can receive the funds in a lump sum or have them paid out under one of the settlement options (discussed later).

A fixed annuity that defers the income payments until a future date can be purchased with a lump sum, or the contract may permit flexible premium payments. A deferred annuity purchased with a lump sum is called a **single-premium deferred annuity.** In contrast, a **flexible-premium annuity** allows the annuity owner to vary the premium payments; there is no requirement that the owner must deposit a specified amount each year. Thus, the annuity owner has considerable flexibility in the payment of premiums.

Annuity Settlement Options   The annuity owner has a choice of **annuity settlement options.** Cash can be withdrawn in a lump sum or in installments, or the funds can be annuitized or paid out as life income. As a practical matter, relatively few annuities are annuitized.

The following settlement options are typically available:

- *Cash option.* The funds can be withdrawn in a lump sum or in installments. The taxable portion of the distribution (discussed later) is subject to federal and state income taxes. The cash option also leads to adverse selection against the insurer because those in poor health will take cash rather than annuitize the funds.

- *Life annuity (no refund).* A **life annuity (no refund)** option provides a life income to the annuitant only while the annuitant remains alive. *No additional payments are made after the annuitant dies.* This type of settlement option

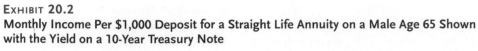

EXHIBIT 20.2
Monthly Income Per $1,000 Deposit for a Straight Life Annuity on a Male Age 65 Shown with the Yield on a 10-Year Treasury Note

SOURCE: Immediateannuity.com

pays the highest amount of periodic income payments because it has no refund features. It is suitable for someone who needs maximum lifetime income and has no dependents or has provided for them through other means. However, because of the risk of forfeiting the unpaid principal if death occurs early, relatively few annuity owners elect this option.

Because interest rates have declined sharply in recent years, the amount of monthly income payable under a life annuity with no refund (also called a straight life annuity) has also declined. Exhibit 20.2 compares the amount of monthly income under a straight life annuity with yields on a 10-year Treasury note.

- *Life annuity with guaranteed payments.* A **life annuity with guaranteed payments** (also called a **life annuity with period certain**) pays a life income to the annuitant with a certain number of guaranteed payments, such as 5, 10, 15, or 20 years. If the annuitant dies before receiving the guaranteed number of payments, the remaining payments are paid to a designated beneficiary. This option can be used by someone who needs lifetime income but who also wishes to provide income to the beneficiary in the event of an early death. Because of the guaranteed

payments, the periodic income payments are less than the income paid by a life annuity with no refund.

- *Installment refund option.* An **installment refund option** pays a life income to the annuitant. If the annuitant dies before receiving total income payments equal to the purchase price of the annuity, the payments continue to the beneficiary until they equal the purchase price. A **cash refund option** is another version of this option. If the annuitant dies before receiving total payments equal to the purchase price of the annuity, the balance is paid in a lump sum to the beneficiary.

- *Joint-and-survivor annuity.* A **joint-and-survivor annuity option** pays benefits based on the lives of two or more annuitants, such as a husband and wife or a brother and sister. The annuity income is paid until the last annuitant dies. Some contracts pay the full amount of the original income payments until the last survivor dies. Other plans pay only two-thirds or one-half of the original income after the first annuitant dies.

Exhibit 20.3 provides examples of monthly income payments for a $100,000 immediate annuity issued to a male age 65.

Variable Annuity

A second type of annuity is a variable annuity. A **variable annuity** pays a lifetime income, but the income payments vary depending on common stock prices. *The fundamental purpose of a variable annuity is to provide an inflation hedge by maintaining the real purchasing power of the periodic payments during retirement.* It is based on the assumption of a positive correlation between the cost of living and common stock prices over the long run.

Basic Characteristics of a Variable Annuity Premiums are invested in a portfolio of common stocks or other investments that presumably will increase in value during a period of inflation. The premiums are used to purchase **accumulation units** during the period prior to retirement, and the value of each accumulation unit varies depending on common stock prices. For example, assume that the accumulation unit is initially valued at $1, and the annuitant makes a monthly premium payment of $100. During the first month, 100 accumulation units are purchased.[1] If common stock prices increase during the second month, and the accumulation unit rises to $1.10, about 91 accumulation units can be purchased. If the stock market declines during the third

month, and the accumulation unit declines to $0.90, 111 accumulation units can be purchased. Thus, accumulation units are purchased over a long period of time in both rising and falling markets.

At retirement, the accumulation units are converted into **annuity units.** The number of annuity units remains constant during the liquidation period, but the value of each unit will change each month or year depending on the level of common stock prices. For example, at retirement, assume that the annuitant has 10,000 accumulation units. Assume that the accumulation units are converted into 100 annuity units.[2] As stated earlier, the number of annuity units remains constant, but the value of each unit will change over time. Assume that the annuity unit is initially valued at $10 when the annuitant retires. A monthly income of $1000 will be paid. During the second month, if the annuity unit increases in value to $10.10, the monthly income also increases to $1010. During the third month, if the annuity units decline in value to $9.90 because of a stock market decline, the monthly income is reduced to $990. Thus, the monthly income depends on the level of common stock prices.

Guaranteed Death Benefit Variable annuities typically provide a guaranteed death benefit that protects the principal against loss due to market declines. *The typical death benefit states that if the annuitant dies before retirement, the amount paid to the beneficiary will be the higher of two amounts: the amount invested in the contract or the value of the account at the time of death.* Thus, if the annuitant dies during a market decline, the beneficiary receives an amount at least equal to the total amount invested in the contract.

Some variable annuities go one step further and pay enhanced death benefits. Enhanced benefits either (1) guarantee the principal (contributions made) plus interest or (2) periodically adjust the value of the account to lock in investment gains. For example, the annuity may contain a *rising-floor death benefit* by which the death benefit is periodically reset. Thus, a 5 percent rising-floor benefit may be periodically reset so that the beneficiary will receive the principal plus 5 percent interest.

A second example is the *stepped-up benefit* by which the contract periodically locks in investment gains, such as every five years. For example, assume

EXHIBIT 20.3
Examples of Monthly Income Annuity Payments from an Immediate Annuity, $100,000 Purchase Price, Male, Age 65

Annuity Settlement Option	Estimated Monthly Income
Life income with no refund	$698
Life income with 5 years guaranteed payments	692
Life income with 10 years guaranteed payments	675
Life income with 15 years guaranteed payments	649
Life income with 20 years guaranteed payments	619
Joint and survivor option[a]	605
Joint and survivor option with 20 years guaranteed	592

[a] Both annuitants are age 65.

SOURCE: WebAnnuities.com. Data shown are estimates as of May 2004.

that $10,000 is invested in year 1, and the account is now worth $15,000 in year 5. The new death benefit is $15,000, even though the annuity owner has invested only $10,000.

Finally, an *enhanced earning benefit* is a newer type of death benefit that pays an additional amount for income taxes when the annuitant dies. The amount paid covers the income tax that heirs must pay on accumulated earnings in the annuity. For example, assume that $100,000 invested in a variable annuity grows to $200,000, and the annuitant dies. The designated beneficiary must pay an income tax on the $100,000 gain. The enhanced death benefit would pay an additional amount, such as 40 percent or $40,000, to help pay the income tax on the gain.

During the sharp stock market decline of 2000–2002, investors in variable annuities lost billions of dollars. However, because of the death benefit, amounts invested in a variable annuity are paid to a designated beneficiary if the annuitant dies before retirement. As a result, the variable annuity death benefit has become more important to investors in recent years (see Insight 20.1).

Fees and Expenses   Variable annuity owners pay a number of fees and expenses. Some fees consist of investment management and administrative fees; other fees are insurance charges that pay for the guarantees and other services provided. In addition, most variable annuities have surrender charges.

Specifically, variable annuities typically contain the following fees and expenses:

- *Investment management charge.* This charge is a payment to the investment manager and asset-management company for the brokerage services and investment advice provided in the management of the investment portfolio.
- *Administrative charge.* This charge covers the paperwork, record keeping, and periodic reports to the annuity owner.
- *Mortality and expense risk charge.* This fee, called the "M&E" fee, pays for (1) the mortality risk associated with the guaranteed death benefit and excessive longevity; (2) a guarantee that annual expenses will not exceed a certain percentage of assets after the contract is issued; and (3) an allowance for profit.

- *Surrender charge.* Most annuities have a surrender charge if the annuity is surrendered during the early years of the contract. This charge helps to pay agents and brokers who sell variable annuities. It is usually a percentage of the account value and declines over time. The surrender charge is typically 7 percent of the account value for the first year, declining one percentage point for each year until it reaches zero for the eighth and later years. Most variable annuities permit partial withdrawals each year of as much as 10 percent of the account value without imposition of a surrender charge.

In addition to these charges, some annuities have a front-end load of 4 or 5 percent; the annuity may have an annual contract fee, such as $25 or $50; and there may be a charge if funds are transferred from one subaccount to another. *In the aggregate, total fees and expenses in most variable annuities are high and can easily exceed 2 percent of assets. As a result, long-run total returns may be significantly reduced in high-cost annuities.*

Some annuities, however, have relatively low annual expenses, and a small number do not have a surrender charge. Exhibit 20.4 shows the names and telephone numbers for a selected group of low-cost variable annuities.

Investment Performance of Variable Annuities   Variable annuities give the annuity owner several investment choices, similar to mutual funds. The premiums are invested in investment portfolios called "subaccounts," such as a growth stock fund, corporate bond fund, international stock fund, or money market fund. The funds can be transferred from one account to another without triggering unfavorable income-tax consequences.

The investment performance of variable annuities varies widely depending on the insurer, type of investment, and total expense rate. Exhibit 20.5 shows average annual total returns and average expense rates for various subaccounts for the five-year period ending December 31, 2003. The five-year annualized return ranged from .17 percent for growth and income accounts to 8.84 percent for international bond accounts.

INSIGHT 20.1

Annuity Death Benefit Starts Paying Its Way

When the stock market was roaring, many investors scoffed at variable annuities, the insurance industry's version of mutual funds.

Because variable annuities added insurance protection to mutual funds, they carried higher fees than pure mutual funds did and, in most cases, the insurance features were not being used.

But after the markets began to slide three years ago, one of those features, known as the death benefit, has become a prized possession. A form of life insurance, it provides a silver lining for anyone who put money into a variable annuity.

An investor who in the spring of 2000 put $100,000 into a mutual fund based on the Standard & Poor's 500-stock index would now have only about $60,000 left in the account. But because of the death benefit, the same investment in a variable annuity is still worth $100,000 — at least on paper.

To collect on the $100,000, an investor has to die; the proceeds go to his estate. That may not be very appealing, but there is no cushion for the mutual fund investor. If he dies, his estate would get just the $60,000.

"Almost everybody was very critical of variable annuities as being a ripoff," said Andrew Kligerman, an analyst at Bear, Stearns. "But now they can see real value."

Gary Holloway, who runs a custom copying business in Norman, Okla., put $100,000 into a variable annuity two years ago, after taking heavy losses on a handful of high-technology stocks and aggressive mutual funds. For him, the death benefit was a big selling point. "I'm sure I'll predecease my wife," said Mr. Holloway, who is 52 and had a health scare a few years ago. "The market is funny right now. Who knows what could happen? But she's still guaranteed the death benefit, the $100,000."

The variable-annuity death benefit seemed superfluous to many critics during the bull market because investors who put money into the stock market for long periods—say, 20 or 30 years—never ended up with less money than they started with. Since the variable annuity was designed as a long-term, retirement investment vehicle, the obvious question was, why pay the roughly quarter of a percent that insurers charged for the death benefit?

The answer is that bad things often happen over the short run. Markets collapse and otherwise healthy people may die unexpectedly.

"In the roaring bull market, some people felt the death benefit was really an unnecessary expense," said John Walters, executive vice president for variable annuities and mutual funds at the Hartford Financial Services Group. But, Mr. Walters said, people are taking a different view during the bear market.

In the last few years, insurers have paid hundreds of millions of dollars in death benefits on variable annuities. In 2000, the year the market peaked, for example, Hartford paid $5.4 million. But last year, the payouts jumped to $258 million, up from $101 million the previous year.

For many investors, analysts and insurers say, the death benefit has always provided some psychological value. Variable annuities had traditionally been bought by conservative investors who were more inclined to put their money into certificates of deposit and money market funds than into the stock market. Even during the market boom, these investors, they say, willingly paid an extra fee for the death benefit rather than plunge into the market without a safety net.

"It gave some comfort," said Colin Devine, an analyst at Salomon Smith Barney. "People wanted some security for their retirement nest egg. Say you died. Your wife is still here. You want to know that she'll get the principal."

In the palmy days of the market, the insurance companies calculated that the probability of paying death benefits was slight. Consequently, Mr. Kligerman said, most companies set aside very little in reserves, money that regulators require insurers to designate for expected losses, to pay death benefits.

"The market was so strong that it appeared there wasn't much loss potential," Mr. Kligerman said. Death benefits are paid only when there is a loss.

Now that the odds have shifted, the insurers are confirming the value—or, in their case, the expense—of the death benefit by increasing their reserves almost every quarter since the downturn began. By the end of 2002, Mr. Kligerman said, the death benefit reserves for seven big insurance companies came to nearly $1 billion. According to the Financial Research Corporation of Boston, about 100 insurance companies sell variable annuities, suggesting that actual reserves for death benefits are considerably higher.

Variable annuities present something of a puzzle to thoughtful investors. They are sold as retirement vehicles with deferred taxation on earnings like nondeductible IRAs, and they appeal most to people in their 50s and 60s. But analysts say that for most of these investors, a comparable mutual fund would probably earn more by retirement time. That is because the additional fees for the variable annuity's insurance features—the death benefit and a seldom-used provision for periodic payments for life—are a significant drag on performance.

Still, owning variable annuities has been a blessing for the survivors of investors in the last few years. Despite higher fees, the investors' nest eggs have been preserves.

SOURCE: Excerpted from Joseph B. Treaster, "Annuity Death Benefiit Start Paying Its Way," © 2003 The New York Times Co. Reprinted by permission.

EXHIBIT 20.4
Five Low-Cost Variable Annuities

Name	Total Annual Expenses	Sales Load	Surrender Charge	Minimum Investment	Telephone Number
Vanguard Variable Annuity Plan	0.60%[a]	None	None	5000	800-522-5555
Lifetime Variable Select (TIAA-CREF)	0.66%[b]	None	None	$2500	800-223-1200
USAA Variable Annuity	1.05%[c]	None	None	1000	800-531-4440
Fidelity Retirement Reserves	1.11%[d]	None	None	2500	800-544-2442
Schwab Signature Annuity	1.13%[e]	None	None	5000	800-838-0650

[a] Vanguard Equity Index Portfolio. An annual fee of $25 applies to contracts less than $25,000.
[b] Stock Index Account.
[c] Premiums are invested in the Vanguard Midcap Index Fund. An annual contract fee of $30 is also charged.
[d] Index 500 Portfolio.
[e] Schwab S&P 500 Fund.

Equity-Indexed Annuity

An equity-indexed annuity is a newer type of annuity that offers the guarantees of a fixed annuity and limited participation in stock market gains. An **equity-indexed annuity** *is a fixed, deferred annuity that allows the annuity owner to participate in the* *growth of the stock market and also provides downside protection against the loss of principal and prior interest earnings if the annuity is held to term.* Term periods typically range from one to ten years. The annuity value is linked to the performance of a stock market index, typically Standard and Poor's 500

EXHIBIT 20.5
Annuity Fund Performances and Fees
Averages and returns for periods ended Dec. 31, 2003.

TYPE OF FUND	AVERAGE FUND EXPENSE	AVERAGE TOTAL EXPENSE	4TH QTR. TOTAL RETURN	ONE-YEAR TOTAL RETURN	THREE-YEAR ANNUALIZED RETURN	FIVE-YEAR ANNUALIZED RETURN
Aggressive Growth	1.03%	2.35	+11.61%	+34.77%	− 7.38%	+ 0.69%
Balanced	0.84	2.16	+ 7.23	+ 17.72	− 0.23	+ 1.8
Corporate Bond	0.72	2.04	+ 0.85	+ 5.74	+ 6.12	+ 4.63
Growth	1.00	2.34	+11.56	+30.49	− 5.54	+ 0.59
Government Bond General	0.76	2.08	− 0.28	+ 0.96	+ 4.85	+ 4.2
Growth & Income	0.81	2.14	+11.84	+26.27	− 3.05	+ 0.17
High-Yield Bond	0.87	2.21	+ 4.94	+21.73	+ 5.8	+ 1.63
International Bond	1.14	2.45	+ 4.59	+17.82	+10.41	+ 8.8
International Stock	1.02	2.36	+13.34	+30.74	− 4.98	+ 2.03
Money Market	0.56	1.88	− 0.18	− 0.46	+ 0.58	+ 1.92
Specialty Fund	1.82	3.08	+14.97	+45.65	+20.56	+ 1.18
U.S. Diversified Equity Avg.	0.96	2.29	+11.63	+30.21	− 5.28	+ 0.50

SOURCE: Excerpted from Laura Saunders Egodigwe, "Annuities Await Repercussions," *The Wall Street Journal*, January 8, 2004, p. R25.

Composite Stock Index. If the stock market rises, the annuity is credited with part of the gain in the index, which does not include the reinvestment of dividends. If the stock market declines, the annuity earns at least a minimum return, which typically is 3 percent on 90 percent of the principal invested.

The key elements of an equity-indexed annuity are as follows: (1) the participation rate, (2) the cap on the maximum percentage of gain credited to the contract, (3) the indexing method used, and (4) the guaranteed minimum value.

Participation Rate   The *participation rate* is the percent of increase in the stock index that is credited to the contract. The insurer periodically determines the participation rate, which is subject to change. Participation rates generally range from 25 percent to 90 percent of the gain in the stock index. A few insurers have participation rates of 100 percent. Investors usually receive only part of the increase in the stock index (excluding the reinvestment of dividends). For example, if the participation rate is 80 percent and the stock index rises 10 percent during the measuring period, the annuity value increases by 8 percent.

Cap on the Maximum Percentage of Gain   The *cap* is the maximum percentage of gain that is credited to the contract. For example, assume the annuity has a participation rate of 80 percent and a 10 percent cap. If the index rises 10 percent, the annuity has an 8 percent return. However, if the stock market soars and the index rises 20 percent, the maximum gain is capped at 10 percent (instead of 16 percent). Thus, investors should seek annuities with no caps, which will allow larger gains to be realized during periods when stock prices increase rapidly.

Indexing Method   The *indexing method* refers to the method for crediting excess interest to the annuity. Insurers use several indexing methods for crediting interest, only one of which is discussed here. Under the *annual reset method* (also known as the *ratchet method*), interest earnings are calculated based on the annual change in the stock index; the index value starting point is also reset annually. Thus, if the stock index decreases during any contract year, the decrease does not have to be recov-

ered before any additional growth in the index will be credited to the contract.

Guaranteed Minimum Value   Equity-indexed annuities with terms longer than one year have a guaranteed minimum value that provides downside protection against the loss of principal if the annuity is held to term. This minimum value typically is 90 percent of the single premium (less partial withdrawals) accumulated at 3 percent interest. *The result is a guaranteed minimum value at the end of the term.* For example, an annuity with a seven-year term would have a guaranteed minimum value of 110.69 percent of the single premium at the end of the term (assuming no withdrawals). However, because the minimum guarantee applies to only 90 percent of the single premium, an investor who surrenders the contract during the first three or four policy years may experience a loss of principal. If it is held to term, the principal is guaranteed against loss.

TAXATION OF INDIVIDUAL ANNUITIES

An individual annuity purchased from a commercial insurer is a nonqualified annuity. A *nonqualified annuity* is an annuity that does not meet the Internal Revenue Code requirements. As such, it does not qualify for most income-tax benefits that qualified employer retirement plans receive.

Premiums for individual annuities are not income-tax deductible and are paid with after-tax dollars. However, the investment income is tax deferred and accumulates free of current income taxes until the funds are actually distributed.

The taxable portion of any distribution is taxable as ordinary income. In addition, the taxable portion of a premature distribution before age 59½ is subject to a 10 percent penalty tax, with certain exceptions.[3]

The periodic annuity payments from an individual annuity are taxed according to the General Rule. Under this rule, the *net cost* of the annuity payments is recovered income-tax free over the payment period. The amount of each payment that exceeds the net cost is taxable as ordinary income.

An exclusion ratio must be calculated to determine the nontaxable and taxable portions of the annuity payments. The **exclusion ratio** is determined by dividing the investment in the contract by the expected return:

$$\frac{\text{Investment in the contract}}{\text{Expected return}} = \text{Exclusion ratio}$$

The *investment in the contract (basis)* is the total cost of the annuity, which generally is the total amount of the premiums or other consideration paid for the annuity less any nontaxable distributions previously received.[4] The *expected return* is the total amount that the annuitant can expect to receive under the contract. It is determined by multiplying the annual payments the annuitant will receive by the life expectancy of the annuitant, which is obtained from actuarial tables provided by the IRS.

As an example, assume that Ben, age 65, purchased an immediate annuity for $108,000 that pays a lifetime monthly income of $1000. The annuity has no refund features. Investment in the contract is $108,000. Based on the IRS actuarial table, Ben has a life expectancy of 20 years. Expected return is $240,000 (20 × 12 × $1000). The exclusion ratio is 0.45 ($108,000 ÷ $240,000). Each year, until the net cost is recovered, Ben receives $5400 tax free (45% × $12,000), and $6600, which is taxable. After the net cost is recovered, the total payment would be taxable.

In summary, annuities can be attractive to investors who have made maximum contributions to other tax-advantaged plans and who wish to save additional amounts on a tax-deferred basis. Also, because of the surrender charge, the investor should expect to remain invested for 10 or more years.

However, annuities are not for everyone, especially a variable annuity. You should not purchase a variable annuity if you will need the funds before age 59½; the period of investing is less than 15 years; and you have not made maximum annual contributions to other tax-advantaged plans, such as a Section 401(k) plan and an IRA. Other considerations are important as well (see Insight 20.2).

INDIVIDUAL RETIREMENT ACCOUNTS

An **individual retirement account (IRA)** allows workers with taxable compensation to make annual contributions to a retirement plan up to certain limits and receive favorable income-tax treatment.

The Economic Growth and Tax Relief Reconciliation Act of 2001 has substantially increased the tax advantages of IRAs. Maximum annual contribution limits are increased, and special catch-up rules allow older workers to make additional contributions. There are two basic types of IRA plans:

- Traditional IRA
- Roth IRA

Traditional IRA

A **traditional IRA** is an IRA that allows workers to take a tax deduction for part or all of their IRA contributions. The investment income accumulates income-tax free on a tax-deferred basis, and the distributions are taxed as ordinary income.

Eligibility Requirements   There are two eligibility requirements for establishing a traditional tax-deductible IRA. *First, the participant must have earned income during the year.* Earned income includes wages and salaries, bonuses, commissions, self-employment income, and taxable alimony and separate maintenance payments. However, earned income does not include investment income, pension or annuity income, Social Security, and rental income. For example, if a person receives only Social Security and investment income, he or she could not make an IRA contribution for that year.

Second, the participant must be under age 70½. No IRA contributions are allowed for the tax year in which the participant attains age 70½ or any later year.

Annual Contribution Limits   Prior to 2002, the maximum annual IRA contribution was limited to $2000 or 100 percent of earned income, whichever was less. Recent changes in the tax code substantially increased the maximum annual contribution to an IRA. Special catch-up rules also allow workers age 50 and over to make additional contributions.

For 2004, the maximum annual IRA contribution is increased to $3000 or 100 percent of earned compensation, whichever is less. Older workers age 50 and over can contribute a maximum of $3500 to

INSIGHT 20.2

Ten Questions to Answer Before You Buy a Variable Annuity

Variable annuities are a valuable retirement tool if used properly. However, variable annuities are not for everyone. Before you buy an annuity, you should answer the following questions:

- **What are the annual fees and expenses?** Most variable annuities have relatively high annual fees and expenses. According to *Morningstar*, the average total variable annuity expense charge for the industry was 2.26% in early 2003.[a] Other investments, especially no-load mutual funds, typically have lower annual expense charges. Before you buy, you should shop for an annuity with relatively low annual expenses.

- **Are you willing to be locked into the annuity for at least 15 years?** Most annuities have back-end surrender charges that extend over long periods, typically seven to ten years. You will lose a substantial amount of money if you surrender the annuity during the early years. Also, the favorable income tax advantages of a variable annuity require a long holding period of at least 15 years for the tax benefits to offset the high fees and expenses.

- **Have you made maximum annual contributions to your employer's 401(k) plan or other qualified retirement plan and to an individual retirement account?** Most employers make a partial matching contribution to qualified retirement plans, and you are passing up "free money" if you don't contribute the maximum allowed. Also, an IRA may have lower annual expense charges than a variable annuity.

- **Have you considered your tolerance for risk?** The value of your annuity depends on the investment experience of the underlying subaccounts. If the premiums are invested in a stock account, the value of your annuity can decline substantially in a severe market decline. Depending on your tolerance for risk, your "comfort" level may be adversely affected.

- **Are you willing to tolerate fluctuations in monthly income?** Variable annuity retirement benefits also fluctuate with the investment experience of the underlying subaccounts. If the funds are invested in a stock market account, a substantial market decline can be financially painful. Common stocks are also sensitive to interest rates. If interest rates rise because of inflationary expectations or a change in Federal Reserve monetary policy, your variable annuity benefits may decline.

- **Will you need the funds before age 59 1/2?** You should not buy a variable annuity if the funds will be needed before age 59 1/2. Cash withdrawals before age 59 1/2 generally are subject to a 10% federal tax penalty on the taxable portion of the distribution. You should have available cash to cover three to six months of living expenses, which reduces the need to withdraw funds from your annuity.

- **Is your combined federal and state income tax bracket at least 28 percent?** If you are in a lower tax bracket, high variable annuity fees and expenses can dilute the tax advantages of a deferred annuity.

- **Are you aware that capital gains are taxed as ordinary income when annuity distributions are made?** The taxable portion of a variable annuity distribution is taxed as ordinary income, which can be as high as 37.6% for 2004 and 2005. In contrast, long-term capital gains in a taxable account are taxed currently at a maximum capital gains rate of 15 percent.

- **Are you aware that if you should die, your heirs will be taxed on the variable annuity earnings just as you would?** In contrast, mutual funds in a taxable account pass to the heirs free of income taxes because of a "stepped-up" cost basis. As a result, heirs don't pay income taxes on the accumulated gains.

- **Should you invest your IRA contributions in a variable annuity?** As a general rule, the answer is no. IRAs already receive favorable income-tax treatment. Investing IRA contributions in a variable annuity results in an unnecessary duplication of fees and expenses.

[a]As of March 31, 2003, the Morningstar Principia data base tracked 19,368 variable annuity accounts.

their plans. This provision will help older workers who have saved little or nothing for their retirement. If the participant has a nonworking or low-earning spouse, the maximum annual IRA contribution is increased to $6000 (**spousal IRA**). However, the maximum annual contribution to each account is limited to $3000.

The maximum annual amounts that can be contributed to an IRA will increase in the future according to the following schedule:

Year	Maximum Annual Contribution for Workers Under Age 50	Maximum Annual Contribution for Workers Age 50 and Older
2004	3000	$3500
2005	4000	4500
2006	4000	5000
2007	4000	5000
2008	5000	6000

After 2008, the annual IRA contribution limit will be indexed for inflation in increments of $500. IRA catch-up limits are not indexed for inflation.

Income Tax Deduction of Traditional IRA Contributions Traditional IRA contributions may be (1) fully income-tax deductible, (2) partly deductible, or (3) not deductible at all. A full deduction is allowed in two general situations. *First a worker who is not covered by an employer-sponsored retirement plan can make a fully deductible IRA contribution up to the annual statutory maximum.* For 2004, the maximum tax-deductible IRA contribution is the lower of $3000 ($3500 if age 50 or older), or 100 percent of compensation.

Second, even if the worker is covered by the employer's retirement plan, a full deduction is allowed if the worker's modified adjusted gross income is below certain thresholds. Modified adjusted gross income generally is the adjusted gross income figure shown on your tax return without taking into account the IRA deduction and certain other items.[5] For 2004, a full deduction is allowed if the taxpayer's modified adjusted gross income is $45,000 or less ($65,000 or less for married couples filing jointly). As discussed later, the income limits for a full tax deduction will rise gradually in the future.

The full IRA tax deduction is gradually phased out as a person's modified adjusted gross income increases. For 2004, the phase-out range is $45,000 to $55,000 for single taxpayers and $65,000 to $75,000 for married taxpayers filing jointly. For example, in 2004, a single taxpayer with a modified adjusted gross income of $50,000 could contribute $3000 to an IRA but could deduct only $1500.

The phase-out limits will gradually increase in the future according to the following schedules:

Year	Single Taxpayer
2004	$45,000–$55,000
2005 or later	$50,000–$60,000

Year	Married Taxpayer Filing Jointly
2004	$65,000–$75,000
2005	$70,000–$80,000
2006	$75,000–$85,000
2007 and later	$80,000–$100,000

Taxpayers with incomes that exceed the phase-out limits can contribute to a traditional IRA but cannot deduct their contributions. This type of IRA is called a **nondeductible IRA.** In such cases, a Roth IRA (discussed later) should be considered.

Special Phase-out Rule for Spouses A special phase-out rule applies to married couples in situations where one spouse is not an active participant in an employer-sponsored retirement plan, but the other spouse is an active participant. *As a result, most homemakers can make a fully deductible contribution to a traditional IRA even though the other spouse is covered under a retirement plan at work.* For 2004, the maximum annual IRA deduction for a spouse who is not an active participant is $3000, ($3500 if age 50 or older) even if the other spouse is covered under a retirement plan at work. Eligibility for a full deduction is limited to married couples with modified adjusted gross incomes of $150,000 or less. The tax deduction is phased out for married couples with modified adjusted gross incomes between $150,000 and $160,000.

For example, Josh, age 35, is covered under a Section 401(k) retirement plan at work. His wife, Ashley, age 32, is a full-time homemaker. For 2004, their modified adjusted gross income is $125,000. For 2004, Ashley can make a tax-deductible IRA contribution of $3000 because she is not considered an active participant, and the couple's combined modified adjusted gross income is less than $150,000. However, Josh cannot make a tax-deductible contribution because his income exceeds the income threshold for active participants.

Saver's Credit The law also provides a temporary income tax credit to encourage low- and middle-income workers to contribute to an IRA or other qualified retirement plan. The tax credit is equal to the applicable percentage times the amount of qualified retirement savings contributed to the plan. The maximum credit rate is 50 percent, and the maximum annual contribution that can be counted is $2000. Thus, the maximum tax credit a worker can receive for a tax year is $1000 (50% x $2000). The maximum credit of $1000 annually is available for single taxpayers with an adjusted gross income of $15,000 or less ($30,000 or less for married couples filing jointly). The tax credit declines as income increases and is limited to single workers with an

EXHIBIT 20.6
Topping It Off with a Saver's Credit

Saver's Credit[a]
For tax years 2002 through 2006, the tax credit for making contributions to an IRA or workplace savings plan is as follows:

Joint Filers Adjusted Gross Income (AGI)	Head of Household Filers AGI	Other Filers AGI	Credit	Maximum Credit
$0–$30,000	$0–$22,500	$0–$15,000	50%	$1,000
$30,001–$32,500	$22,501–$24,375	$15,001–$16,250	20%	$400
$32,501–$50,000	$24,376–$37,500	$16,251–$25,000	10%	$200
Over $50,000	Over $37,500	Over $25,000	0%	$0

[a]To be eligible for a tax credit, you must be age 18 or older, cannot be a full-time student, and cannot be claimed as a dependent on someone else's tax return.
SOURCE: Fidelity Investments, © 2001 FMR Corp. All Rights Reserved. Reprinted by permission.

adjusted gross income of $25,000 or less and to married couples with $50,000 or less (see Exhibit 20.6). Unless extended by Congress, the saver's credit will expire at the end of 2006.

Withdrawal of Funds With certain exceptions, distributions from a traditional IRA before age 59½ are considered to be premature distributions. A 10 percent tax penalty must be paid on the amount of the distribution included in gross income. However, the penalty tax does not apply to distributions that result from any of the following:

- Death of the individual
- Disability of the individual
- Substantially equal payments paid over the life expectancy of the individual or the individual and his or her beneficiary
- Portions of any distributions treated as a return of nondeductible contributions
- Distributions used to pay for unreimbursed medical expenses in excess of 7½ percent of adjusted gross income
- Distributions used to pay medical insurance premiums for the worker, spouse, and dependents if the worker has received unemployment compensation benefits for 12 consecutive weeks
- Distributions to pay for qualified education expenses
- Qualified acquisition costs for a first-time home buyer (maximum of $10,000)

Distributions from a traditional IRA must start no later than April 1 of the year following the calendar year in which the individual attains age 70½. The funds can be withdrawn in a lump sum or in installments. A minimum annual distribution requirement must be met. The minimum annual distribution payment is based on the life expectancy of the individual or the joint life expectancy of the individual and his or her beneficiary. The Internal Revenue Service (IRS) has developed life expectancy tables for purposes of determining the minimum annual distribution. If the distributions are less than the amount required by law, a 50 percent excise tax is imposed on the excess accumulation. The purpose of this requirement is to force participants in traditional IRAs to have the funds paid out over a reasonable period so that the federal government can collect taxes on the tax-deferred amounts.

Taxation of Distributions Distributions from a traditional IRA are taxed as ordinary income, except for any nondeductible IRA contributions, which are received income-tax free. Part of the distribution is not taxable if nondeductible contributions are made. The other part is taxable and must be included in the taxpayer's income. A complex formula and an IRS worksheet must be used to compute the nontaxable and taxable portions of each distribution.

In addition, as noted earlier, a 10 percent tax penalty applies to premature distributions taken before age 59½.

Establishing a Traditional IRA   Traditional IRAs can be established with a variety of financial organizations. You can set up an IRA with a bank, mutual fund, stock brokerage firm, or life insurer. Contributions to a traditional IRA can be made anytime during the year or up to the due date for filing a tax return, not including extensions.

There are two types of traditional IRAs: (1) an individual retirement account, and (2) an individual retirement annuity.

- *Individual Retirement Account.* An individual retirement account is a trust or custodial account set up for the exclusive benefit of the account holder or beneficiaries. The trustee or custodian must be a bank, a federally insured credit union, a savings and loan institution, or an entity approved by the IRS to act as trustee or custodian. Contributions must be in cash, except for rollover contributions (discussed later) that can be in the form of property other than cash. No part of the contributions can be used to purchase a life insurance policy. Likewise, IRA assets cannot be pledged as collateral for a loan.
- *Individual Retirement Annuity.* A traditional IRA can also be established by purchasing an individual retirement annuity from a life insurer. The annuity must meet certain requirements. The annuity owner's interest in the contract must be nonforfeitable. The contract must be nontransferable by the owner. In addition, the annuity must permit flexible premiums so that if earnings change, the IRA contributions can be changed as well. Contributions cannot exceed the annual maximum limit, and the distributions must begin by April 1 of the year following the year in which the annuity owner reaches age 70½.

IRA Investments   IRA contributions can be invested in a variety of investments, including certificates of deposit, mutual funds, and individual stocks and bonds in a self-directed brokerage account. Contributions can also be invested in U.S. gold and silver coins, certain precious metals. However, the contributions cannot be invested in insurance contracts or collectibles, such as baseball cards or antiques.

IRA Rollover Account   A *rollover* is a tax-free distribution of cash or other property from one retirement plan, which is then deposited into another retirement plan. The amount you roll over is tax free but generally becomes taxable when the new plan pays out that amount to you or to your beneficiary. For example, if you quit your job and receive a lump-sum distribution from your employer's qualified retirement plan, the funds can be rolled over or deposited into a special **IRA rollover account.** If you receive the funds directly, the employer must deduct 20 percent for federal income taxes. The tax can be deferred, however, if the employer transfers the funds directly into the IRA rollover account.

The assets in the IRA rollover account can be paid out as income when the worker retires. Exhibit 20.7 shows how long the payments will last given selected rates of return and withdrawal rates.

Roth IRA

A **Roth IRA** is another type of IRA that provides substantial tax advantages. The annual contribution limits discussed earlier for a traditional IRA also apply to a Roth IRA. However, for 2004, the maximum annual contribution that an individual can make to all IRA accounts (both traditional and Roth) is $3000 for workers under age 50 ($3500 if age 50 or older), not counting rollover contributions. However, as stated earlier, the maximum annual contribution limits will rise in the future.

Unlike a traditional IRA, the annual contributions to a Roth IRA are not tax deductible. However, the investment income accumulates income-tax free, and qualified distributions are not taxable if certain requirements are met. A qualified distribution is any distribution from a Roth IRA that (1) is made after a five-year holding period beginning with the first tax year for which a Roth contribution is made, and (2) is made for any of the following reasons:

- The individual is age 59½ or older.
- The individual is disabled.
- The distribution is paid to a beneficiary or to the estate after the individual's death.
- The distribution is used to pay qualified first-time home buyer expenses (maximum of $10,000).

EXHIBIT 20.7
How Long the Money Will Last (in Years)

Withdrawal	Rate of Return											
	1%	2%	3%	4%	5%	6%	7%	8%	9%	10%	11%	12%
12%	7	8	8	8	8	9	9	10	10	11	12	13
11	8	8	9	9	9	10	10	11	12	13	14	15
10	9	9	10	10	10	11	12	13	14	15	17	19
9	10	10	11	11	12	13	14	15	16	18	21	26
8	11	11	12	13	14	15	16	18	20	24	30	*
7	12	13	14	15	16	18	20	22	27	36	*	*
6	14	15	16	18	19	22	25	31	44	*	*	
5	17	18	20	22	24	29	36	*	*	*		
4	20	22	25	28	33	42	*	*	*			
3	25	28	33	39	*	*	*	*				
2	35	40	50	*	*	*	*					
1	*	*	*	*	*	*						

NOTE: For example, if you have saved $700,000 for retirement and initially withdraw 4 percent of the money ($28,000), your money will last 42 years, assuming a 6 percent annual return. The table assumes that your initial withdrawal is increased each year to keep up with an inflation rate of 3 percent, the historical average.

SOURCE: Reprinted by permission from the Kiplinger's Personal Finance Website (www.kiplinger.com).© October 1, 1998, The Kiplinger Washington Editor's, Inc.

Unlike a traditional IRA, contributions to a Roth IRA can be made after age 70½, and the minimum distribution rules after attainment of age 70½ do not apply to Roth IRAs.

Income Limits   Roth IRAs have generous income limits. The maximum annual IRA contribution can be made by single taxpayers with modified adjusted gross incomes of $95,000 or less, and by married couples filing jointly with modified adjusted gross incomes of $150,000 or less. Maximum annual IRA contributions are phased out for single taxpayers with modified adjusted gross incomes between $95,000 and $110,000, and for married couples filing jointly with modified adjusted gross incomes between $150,000 and $160,000.

Conversion to a Roth IRA   A traditional IRA can be converted into a Roth IRA. The right to convert is limited to taxpayers with annual adjusted gross incomes of $100,000 or less. Although the amount converted is taxed as ordinary income, qualified distributions from the Roth IRA are received income-tax free. Many investment firms, including Fidelity Investments and Charles Schwab, provide interactive calculators on their Web sites that investors can use to determine if conversion to a Roth IRA is financially desirable.

In summary, a traditional or Roth IRA can provide substantial tax advantages, and regular contributions can substantially increase a person's retirement income. However, you may be confused concerning whether to establish a traditional IRA or a Roth IRA. Insight 20.3 discusses the factors to consider in determining which type of IRA is right for you.

INSIGHT 20.3

Traditional vs. Roth: Which Is Right for You?

You know you want to invest in an IRA, but you are confused about which type of IRA is best for you—a Traditional or a Roth? What's the difference? The main difference between the Traditional and Roth IRA is the way they are taxed.

With a Traditional IRA you can deduct your annual contribution from your taxes. For example, if you earn $50,000 a year and put $3000 in a traditional IRA, you will only have to pay tax on $47,000 in income to the IRS. If your 2003 gross income is between $40,000 and $50,000 ($60,000 to $70,000 for joint filers), the amount you can contribute on a tax-deductible basis gradually decreases. Above $50,000 ($70,000 for joint filers) all contributions must be in after-tax dollars. For the 2004 tax year, you may deduct your entire contribution if your adjusted gross income (AGI) is $45,000 or less (or $65,000 or less if you're married, filing jointly).

Taxpayers who are 50 years and older are permitted to contribute an additional $500 in years 2002–2005, and $1000 in 2006–2010. At 59 1/2, you may begin withdrawing funds but will be forced to pay taxes.

With a Roth IRA, since contributions are made with after-tax money, you can withdraw them at any time without further tax or penalty. After age 59 1/2, all earnings can be withdrawn tax-free, so long as the account has been open at least five years. If the account has not been open five years, withdrawn earnings will be subject to ordinary taxes but not penalties. (If the Roth IRA had been converted from a traditional IRA, earnings are subject to income tax at withdrawal, and the amount relating to the taxable part of your conversion will be subject to the penalty unless an exception applies.)

In other words, the Roth offers tax-*exempt* rather than simply tax-*deferred* earnings. While both allow you to accumulate wealth without paying taxes along the way on your profits, the traditional IRA ultimately sticks you with a tax bill for those profits (plus your initial contributions if those were deducted when made). The Roth doesn't. As long as you follow the rules, *you never pay taxes on your gains.* So paying the piper now before contributing to the Roth may work out to be better for you than paying him later on from your investment profits.

IRAs At-a-Glance

A Roth IRA May Be Appropriate if:
- You're single and your AGI is less than $95,000 (for a full contribution), or your AGI is between $95,000 and $110,000 (for a partial contribution).
- You're married and filing jointly and your AGI is less than $150,000 (for a full contribution), or your AGI is between $150,000 and $160,000 (for a partial contribution).

Note: If your earnings are too high to make you eligible for a Roth IRA, you can open a Traditional IRA, although your contributions won't be tax deductible.
- You can convert assets from a Traditional IRA to a Roth IRA if your household's adjusted gross income is under $100,000.

- Your AGI is over $110,000 (or $150,000 if married filing jointly).
- You're over 50, and want to contribute $500 over the regular contribution limit for the years between 2003 and 2005; this amount increases to $1000 per year starting in 2006.
- You wish to continue making contributions after 70.
- Your beneficiaries, other than your spouse, will be subject to mandatory distributions, but they will pay no income tax on your Roth IRA funds as long as the account has been open at least five years.
- You're are in an employer-sponsored retirement plan.

Roth IRAs Are Best if:
- You believe you may be in a higher tax bracket when you withdraw the money.
- You might want to withdraw your original contributions before retirement.
- You might need to draw from retirement savings for education costs or a first home.
- You may want to use your retirement savings for estate building.

A Traditional IRA May Be Appropriate if:
- You are under age 70 1/2 and have earned income.
- Your 2003 gross income is between $40,000 and $50,000 ($60,000 to $70,000 for joint filers), the amount you can contribute on a tax-deductible basis gradually decreases. Above $50,00 ($70,000 for joint filers) all contributions must be in after-tax dollars. For the 2004 tax year, you may deduct your entire contribution if your adjusted gross income (AGI) is $45,000 or less (or $65,000 or less if you're married, filing jointly).

Note: Anyone can make *after-tax* contributions of up to $3000 per year ($3500 if age 50+) from earned income. If your AGI is above the limits, you may still contribute, but you may not deduct your contributions.
- You prefer to defer taxes until retirement, when withdrawals will be taxed as income.
- Generally, if you're filing singly or jointly and you're not an active participant in an employer-sponsored retirement plan, your contributions are fully tax-deductible regardless of your AGI.
- Your earnings are too high to make you eligible for a Roth IRA. You can open a Traditional IRA, although your contributions won't be tax-deductible.

Traditional IRAs Are Best if:
- You can deduct your contributions.
- You believe you may be in the same or a lower tax bracket in retirement.
- You may need to draw from retirement savings for education costs or a first home.
- You want to consolidate your retirement assets using a Rollover IRA.

Source: Teachers Insurance and Annuity—College Retirement Equities Fund, New York, NY, 2004.

CASE APPLICATION 1

Investors can invest in a wide variety of annuities and can also use different annuity settlement options to meet specific retirement needs. For each of the following retirement objectives, identify either (1) a specific annuity or (2) an annuity settlement option that can be used to meet the objective. Treat each situation separately.

a. James, age 35, is a sales representative and plans to retire at age 65. His monthly income varies from month to month. He would like to invest in an annuity that allows him to change the frequency and amount of premium payments.

b. Nancy, age 65, plans to retire in six months. She has $200,000 in a savings account. She would like to receive lifetime monthly income that is guaranteed.

c. John, age 28, makes maximum annual contributions to his employer's retirement plan and also to a Roth IRA. He wants to invest additional funds that receive favorable income tax treatment and also wants to select the types of investments in which the premiums are invested.

d. Jennifer, age 63, plans to retire in 90 days. She has $100,000 invested in an annuity and would like to receive lifetime monthly income to supplement her Social Security benefits. However, she is concerned that she might die before she receives the amount invested.

e. Fred, age 70, recently retired and has $50,000 to invest for additional income. He wants the retirement benefits to be protected against the risk of inflation after he retires.

f. Mary, age 75, is a widow with no dependents who needs additional retirement income. She has $25,000 to invest in an annuity. She wants to receive the maximum amount of monthly annuity income possible.

g. Kathy, age 32, would like to invest in the stock market, but she is conservative and risk averse. She would like to participate in any stock market gains, but she also wants her principal guaranteed against loss.

CASE APPLICATION 2

Scott and Allison are married and file a joint tax return. Scott is a graduate student who works part-time and earned $10,000 in 2004. He is not eligible to participate in his employer's retirement plan because he is a part-time worker. Allison is a high school teacher who earned $42,000 in 2004 and is an active participant in the school district's retirement plan. Assume you are a financial planner and the couple asks for your advice. Based on the preceding facts, answer each of the following questions.

a. Is Scott eligible to establish and deduct contributions to a traditional IRA? Explain your answer.

b. Is Allison eligible to establish and deduct contributions to a traditional IRA? Explain your answer.

c. Assume that Scott graduates and the couple's modified adjusted gross income is $120,000. Both Scott and Allison participate in their employers' retirement plans. Can either Scott or Allison, or both, establish a Roth IRA? Explain your answer.

d. Allison has a baby and withdraws from the labor force to raise the child. She is no longer an active participant in the school district's retirement plan. Scott receives a promotion and continues to participate in his employer's retirement plan. His annual salary is $110,000. Can Allison make a tax-deductible contribution to a traditional IRA? Explain your answer.

e. Explain to Scott and Allison the advantages of a Roth IRA over a traditional IRA.

SUMMARY

■ An annuity provides periodic payments to an annuitant, which continue for either a fixed period or for the duration of a designated life or lives. The fundamental purpose of a life annuity is to provide lifetime income that cannot be outlived.

■ A *fixed annuity* pays periodic income payments to an annuitant that are guaranteed and fixed in amount. A fixed annuity can be purchased so that the income payments start immediately or can be deferred to some later date. Deferred annuities typically provide for flexible premiums.

■ Annuity settlement options typically include the following:

    Cash

    Life income (no refund)

    Life income with guaranteed payments

    Installment refund option

    Joint-and-survivor annuity option

■ A *variable annuity* pays a lifetime income, but the income payments will vary depending on the investment experience of the subaccount in which the premiums are invested. The purpose of this type of annuity is to provide an inflation hedge by maintaining the real purchasing power of the periodic payments.

■ During the *accumulation period*, variable annuity premiums purchase accumulation units, which are then converted into *annuity units* at retirement. The number of annuity units remains constant during retirement, but the value of the annuity units changes periodically so that the income payments will change over time.

■ Variable annuities typically pay a guaranteed death benefit if the annuitant dies before retirement. The typical death benefit is the higher of two amounts: the amount invested in the contract or the value of the account at the time of death.

■ Variable annuities have numerous fees and charges. These charges include an investment management fee, a charge for administrative expenses, a management and expense risk charge for the guaranteed death benefit and other guarantees, and a surrender charge that declines over time. In the aggregate, total fees and expenses can be substantial.

■ An *equity-indexed annuity* is a fixed, deferred annuity that allows the annuity owner to participate in the growth of the stock market and also provides downside protection against the loss of principal and prior interest earnings if the annuity is held to term.

■ The key elements of an equity-indexed annuity are (1) the participation rate, (2) the cap on the maximum percentage of gain credited to the contract, (3) the indexing method used, and (4) the guaranteed minimum value.

■ An *exclusion ratio* is used to determine the nontaxable and taxable portions of the periodic annuity payments. The exclusion ratio is determined by dividing the investment in the contract by the expected return.

■ The major types of IRAs are (1) a traditional IRA, and (2) a Roth IRA.

■ A *traditional IRA* allows workers to deduct part or all of their IRA contributions. The investment income accumulates income-tax free on a tax-deferred basis, and the distributions are taxed as ordinary income.

■ To be eligible for a traditional IRA, the participant must have taxable compensation and be younger than age 70½.

■ For 2004, the maximum annual IRA contribution is limited to $3000 ($3500 if age 50 or older) or 100 percent of earned income, whichever is less. If the participant has a nonworking or low-earning spouse, the maximum annual IRA contribution is increased to $6000 ($7000 if age 50 or older).

■ IRA contributions to a traditional IRA are income-tax deductible if the participant (1) is not an active participant in an employer-sponsored retirement plan or (2) has taxable compensation below certain income thresholds.

■ Distributions from a traditional IRA are taxed as ordinary income, except for any nondeductible IRA contributions, which are received income-tax free.

■ With certain exceptions, distributions from a traditional IRA before age 59½ are considered to be a premature distribution. A 10 percent tax penalty must be paid on the amount of the distribution included in gross income.

■ Distributions from a traditional IRA must start no later than April 1 of the year following the calendar year in which the individual attains age 70½.

- IRA contributions to a *Roth IRA* are not income-tax deductible. However, the income accumulates free of taxation, and qualified distributions are received income-tax free if certain requirements are met.

- A qualified distribution from a Roth IRA is any distribution that (1) is made after a five-year holding period beginning with the first tax year for which a Roth contribution is made, and (2) is paid when the individual attains age 59½, becomes disabled, dies, or is used to pay qualified first-time home buyer expenses. Unlike a traditional IRA, contributions to a Roth IRA can be made after age 70½, and the minimum distribution rules after attainment of age 70½ do not apply.

KEY CONCEPTS AND TERMS

Accumulation period	Installment refund option
Accumulation unit	IRA rollover account
Annuitant	Joint-and-survivor annuity
Annuity	option
Annuity settlement options	Life annuity (no refund)
Annuity unit	Life annuity with
Cash refund option	guaranteed payments
Deferred annuity	Liquidation period
Equity-indexed annuity	Nondeductible IRA
Exclusion ratio	Roth IRA
Fixed annuity	Single-premium deferred
Flexible-premium annuity	annuity
Immediate annuity	Spousal IRA
Individual retirement	Traditional IRA
account (IRA)	Variable annuity

REVIEW QUESTIONS

1. How does an annuity differ from life insurance?

2. Describe the major characteristics of a fixed annuity.

3. Identify the annuity settlement options that are typically found in a fixed annuity.

4. Describe the basic characteristics of a variable annuity.

5. Explain the major characteristics of an equity-indexed annuity.

6. Explain the eligibility requirements for a traditional IRA.

7. What are the annual contribution limits to an IRA?

8. Explain the basic characteristics of a traditional IRA.

9. Describe the major characteristics of a Roth IRA.

10. What is an IRA rollover?

APPLICATION QUESTIONS

1. Although both fixed and variable annuities can provide lifetime income to annuitants, they differ in important ways. Compare and contrast (1) a fixed annuity with (2) a variable annuity with respect to each of the following:
   a. Determining how the premiums are invested
   b. Stability of income payments after retirement
   c. Death benefits if the annuitant dies before retirement

2. An equity-indexed annuity and a variable annuity are both similar and different in many respects.
   a. Explain the major similarities between an equity-indexed annuity and a variable annuity.
   b. Identify the major differences between an equity-indexed annuity and a variable annuity.

3. Mario, age 65, purchased an immediate annuity for $120,000 that pays a lifetime monthly income of $1000. The annuity has no refund feature. Based on the IRS actuarial table, Mario has a life expectancy of 20 years. If Mario receives 12 monthly payments of $1000 the first year, how much taxable income must he report on his tax return?

4. Travis, age 25, graduated from college and obtained a position as a tax accountant. He is ineligible to participate in his employer's retirement plan for one year.
   a. Assume that Travis has a starting salary of $45,000 for 2004 and does not participate in the employer's retirement plan. Is Travis eligible to establish a traditional tax-deductible IRA? Explain your answer.
   b. Assume the same facts in (a). Is Travis eligible to establish a Roth IRA? Explain your answer.

5. A traditional IRA and a Roth IRA have both similarities and differences. Compare and contrast (1) a traditional IRA with (2) a Roth IRA with respect to each of the following:
   a. Income-tax treatment of IRA contributions and distributions
   b. Income limits for eligibility

c. Determining how the IRA contributions are invested

d. Eligibility, if any, of a nonworking spouse in the home to make an IRA contribution

INTERNET RESOURCES

■ **Annuity.com** provides annuity quotes online and timely information about fixed, equity indexed, variable, and other tax-deferred annuities. Visit the site at

http://www.annuity.com

■ **Annuityshopper.com** provides online annuity rates for immediate annuities from major insurers. The site claims consumers can save thousands of dollars by shopping for immediate annuities through its service. Visit the site at

http://www.annuityshopper.com

■ **Charles Schwab** provides informative articles and information on retirement planning, annuities, and individual retirement accounts (IRAs). Visit the site at

http://www.schwab.com

■ **Fidelity Investments** offers timely information on retirement planning, annuities, and IRAs, including interactive calculators for making IRA decisions. Visit the site at

http://www.fidelity.com

■ **Insure.com** provides timely information on annuities, IRAs, and other insurance products. The site provides a list of companies that have weak financial ratings. Visit the site at

http://www.insure.com

■ The **Roth IRA Web site** is devoted to Roth IRAs and provides a considerable amount of consumer information on this type of IRA. The site provides links to articles, books, tapes, calculators, IRS documents, and a message board on Roth IRAs. Visit the site at

http://www.rothira.com

■ **WebAnnuities.com** claims it is the nation's leading annuity broker. The company has helped more than 10,000 consumers purchase the safest and most reliable life income annuities for their retirement. Visit the site at

www.webannuities.com

■ **TIAA-CREF** is an excellent source of accurate information on retirement planning, annuities, and IRAs. Visit the site at

http://www.tiaa-cref.org

■ The **Vanguard Group** provides timely information on variable annuities, IRAs, and retirement planning. Visit the site at

http://www.vanguard.com

SELECTED REFERENCES

Actuarialfoundation.org. *Getting Ready to Retire: What You Need to Know About Annuities,* 2002.

Black, Kenneth Jr., and Harold D. Skipper, Jr. *Life & Health Insurance,* 13th ed. Upper Saddle River, NJ: Prentice-Hall, 2000, ch. 8.

Graves, Edward E., ed. *McGill's Life Insurance,* 5th ed. Bryn Mawr, PA: The American College, 2004.

Kaster, Nicholas, and Glenn Sulzer. *Saving for the Future, Roth and Traditional IRAs.* Chicago, IL: CCH, Inc., 2002.

Littell, David A., and Kenn Beam Tacchino. *Planning for Retirement Needs,* 6th ed. Bryn Mawr, PA: The American College, 2003

Pope, Elizabeth, et al. *2004 U.S. Master Pension Guide.* Chicago, IL: CCH Inc., 2004.

NOTES

1. A deduction for administrative expenses and sales expenses is ignored. Some individual variable annuity contracts have a front-end load.

2. The actual number of annuity units will depend on the market value of the account, attained age of the annuitant, number of guaranteed payments, conversion rates, assumed investment return, and other factors.

3. The 10 percent penalty tax does not apply to individuals who attain age 59½ or become totally disabled; when the distribution is received by a beneficiary or estate after the individual dies; when the distribution is part of substantially equal payments paid over the life expectancy of the individual or individual and beneficiary; or when the distribution is from an annuity contract under a qualified personal injury settlement. Certain other exceptions also apply.

4. The procedure for determining the total cost of an annuity is complex. Total cost must be reduced by (1) any refunded premiums, rebates, dividends, or unrepaid loans that you received by the later of the annuity starting date or the date on which you received your first payment; (2) any additional premiums paid for double indemnity or disability payments; and (3) any other tax-free amounts you received under the contract or plan before the later of the dates specified in item 1. In addition, an adjustment must be made for any refund features in the annuity. The IRS provides worksheets for making these calculations.

5. Modified adjusted gross income is essentially the adjusted gross income figure shown on your tax return without taking into account any IRA deductions, student loan interest deduction, foreign earned income exclusion, foreign housing exclusion or deduction, exclusion of qualified bond interest, and exclusion of employer-paid adoption expenses.

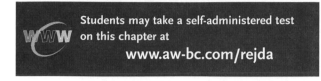

Students may take a self-administered test on this chapter at

www.aw-bc.com/rejda

CHAPTER 21

INDIVIDUAL HEALTH INSURANCE COVERAGES

"They had me on the operating table all day. They looked into my stomach, my gallbladder, they examined everything inside of me. Know what they decided? I need glasses."

Joe E. Lewis

LEARNING OBJECTIVES

After studying this chapter, you should be able to

◆ Explain the major health care problems in the United States.

◆ Explain the basic characteristics of individual major medical insurance.

◆ Describe the key characteristics of long-term care insurance.

◆ Describe the major characteristics of disability-income contracts.

◆ Describe the guidelines to follow when purchasing individual health insurance.

Tim, age 40, is a self-employed carpet layer who was diagnosed as having a brain tumor that required immediate surgery. The surgeon's fee, hospital expenses, and other medical bills totaled $150,000. Like many small business firms, Tim had no health insurance. In addition, he was unable to work for more than one year and did not have a disability-income policy to restore his lost earnings. In short, because of the lack of health insurance, Tim was exposed to serious financial insecurity as result of the unexpected surgery. He eventually had to declare bankruptcy.

As Tim's experience demonstrates, health insurance should be given high priority in any personal risk management program. If you become seriously ill or are injured, you face two major financial problems: payment of your medical bills and the loss of earned income. A serious illness can produce catastrophic medical bills. Without proper protection, you may have to pay thousands of dollars out of your own pocket. In addition, an extended disability can result in the loss of thousands of dollars of earned income.

This chapter is the first of two chapters dealing with private health insurance. The discussion in Chapter 21 is limited to individual health and disability-income insurance coverages. Chapter 22 discusses the various group health insurance plans provided by employers. Although group health insurance accounts for more than 90 percent of the total medical expense premiums paid, a considerable amount of individual insurance is still sold. Individual plans are especially important for individuals and families who are not covered by group insurance.

This chapter discusses the health care problems in the United States. It also discusses individual health insurance coverages to deal with these problems. These coverages include major medical insurance, basic hospital-surgical plans, long-term care insurance, and disability-income insurance. The chapter concludes with a discussion of guidelines to follow when individual health insurance is purchased.

HEALTH CARE PROBLEMS IN THE UNITED STATES

The United States provides the highest quality health care in the world, and the health of Americans has improved remarkably. Despite major breakthroughs in medicine, the health care delivery system is a source of considerable frustration. The present system has four major problems:

- Rising health care expenditures
- Large number of uninsured persons in the population
- Uneven quality of medical care
- Considerable waste and inefficiency

Rising Health Care Expenditures

Total health care expenditures have increased substantially over time. *According to the Centers for Medicare & Medicaid Services, health care spending in the United States totaled an estimated $1.5 trillion in 2002; this figure is expected to increase sharply to $3.1 trillion by 2012 (see Exhibit 21.1). As a percentage of gross domestic product (GDP),*

EXHIBIT **21.1**
Projected National Health Expenditures and Percentage of Gross Domestic Product (GDP)

NHE in Billions

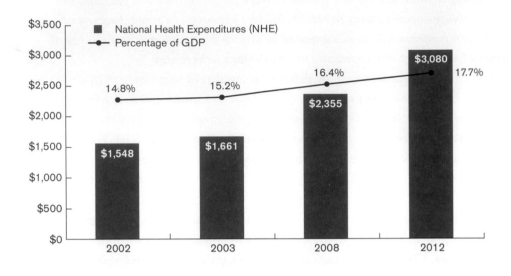

NOTE: Data are from Centers for Medicare and Medicaid Services, 2003.

SOURCE: Blue Cross and Blue Shield Association, *Medical Cost Reference Guide, Revised June 2003.*

total health care spending is projected to increase to almost 18 percent of GDP by 2012, up from 14.8 percent of GDP in 2002. Thus, roughly one in seven dollars of the nation's income is now spent on health care.

Several factors account for the increase in health care spending. According to the Blue Cross and Blue Shield Association, health care expenditures in the United States are rising currently because of the following key factors.[1]

- *Rising hospital costs.* More than half of the increase in private insurance spending in 2001 was due to rising hospital costs, especially the cost of outpatient care as outpatient visits continue to grow. Inpatient services, however, are the largest single component of health care costs. Rising hospital inpatient costs are due largely to the increased use of expensive technology; higher labor costs because of the current

shortage of nurses; consolidation of hospitals; and increased costs per hospital admission.

- *Prescription drug costs.* Prescription drugs continue to be a major driver of health care costs. The cost of prescription drugs increased 11 percent from 2000 to 2001. Rising pharmaceutical costs are due to the increased use of prescription drugs, price inflation, and switching to higher cost drugs.

- *New technology.* New technology is a major driver of health care costs. During the 1990s, the federal government estimates that 10 percent to 40 percent of the growth in personal health care spending was attributable to changes in technology. One example of new technology is a new drug-eluting stent, which opens clogged coronary arteries.

- *Physician cost trends.* The number of specialists has increased over time. Specialist charges average more than twice the charges by primary care physicians, and specialist charges are growing at a much faster rate. Patient visits to specialists have also increased, especially visits by older patients. In addition, rising physician fees are partly due to growing payroll expenses for nonphysician personnel. Also, medical malpractice premiums have increased sharply for certain specialists.

- *Cost shifting by Medicare and Medicaid.* The Medicare and Medicaid programs do not pay the full cost of providing health care to Medicare and Medicaid patients. As a result, costs are shifted from Medicare and Medicaid to private paying patients who must pay more for the care they receive.
- *State mandated benefits.* The states have mandated that insurers must provide certain benefits in health insurance contracts. Examples include coverage for mental health, alcoholism and drug addition, chiropractic services, and care for newly born infants. As a result of mandated benefits, individuals and employers must pay for benefits that they might not otherwise purchase.
- *Higher administrative costs.* From 1998 to 2002, health plan administrative costs increased an average of 4.6 percent each year. The fastest growing components of administrative costs were customer service, information technology, and medical management.
- *Other factors.* Other factors that also drive up health care costs include the cost of hospital inpatient care for uninsured patients and health care fraud and abuse.

Large Number of Uninsured Persons in the Population

Another serious problem is the large number of persons who are uninsured for medical care. According to the 2003 Current Population Survey, the percentage of the population without health insurance increased in 2002, the second consecutive year of increase. *An estimated 15.2 percent of the population, or 43.6 million people, were without health insurance coverage during the entire year in 2002, up from 14.6 percent in 2001, or an increase of 2.4 million people.*[2] Groups with large numbers of uninsured persons include the following:

- *Low income persons living in poverty (32.4%)*
- *Hispanics (32.4%)*
- *Foreign-born population (33.3%)*
- *Blacks and Asians who reported a single race (20.2% and 18.4%, respectively)*
- *Young adults, ages 18 to 24 (29.6%)*

In addition, many states have a high proportion of uninsured persons. These states include Texas (24.1%), New Mexico (22.0%), California (18.7%), Louisiana (18.6%), and Oklahoma (18.2%).[3]

The sobering statistics show that large numbers of people in the United States are exposed to severe economic insecurity from poor health. Proposals for reducing the proportion of uninsured persons are endless and include universal health insurance; tax credits for workers to purchase health insurance; tax subsidies for small employers; state health insurance plans; expansion of Medicaid and Medicare; and numerous other proposals. It is beyond the scope of the text, however, to discuss these proposals in detail.

Uneven Quality of Medical Care

Another problem is that the quality of medical care is uneven and varies widely depending on the physician, geographic location, and type of disease being treated. A new report by the National Committee for Quality Assurance (NCQA) shows that there are severe "quality gaps" in the nation's health care system that prevent millions of patients from receiving the best medical care possible.[4] The term "quality gap" means that millions of patients do not receive the care that medical science has shown to be effective in treating certain diseases, such as high blood pressure, diabetes, and smoking-related heart disease; stated differently, many doctors are not following the recommended guidelines in treating common ailments (see Insight 21.1). As a result of the quality gap, the financial impact on the nation is severe. The NCQA concludes that quality gaps cause 57,000 avoidable deaths, nearly 41 million sick days, and more than $11 billion in lost productivity.[5]

Another quality-of-care study shows that medical injuries to inpatients during their hospital stays kill thousands of patients annually. According to a study by Zahn and Miller, hospital-related injuries

INSIGHT 21.1

Study Shows U.S. Doctors Are Not Following Guidelines

Doctors fail to take nearly half the recommended steps for treating common illnesses such as high blood pressure and diabetes, suggesting that health care in the United States isn't nearly as good as many people thought, researchers say.

Treatment guidelines, many written by medical specialty organizations, outline recommended approaches to many common ailments, ranging from painkillers and exercise for arthritis to surgery for breast cancer.

However, the guidelines are often ignored, indicating that even people who have good insurance and doctor's they like don't always get the best care, said Elizabeth McGlynn, a researcher with the Rand Corp. think-tank, who led a study published in today's New England Journal of Medicine.

"I think most people assume the big problem is, 'Can you get in to see a doctor if you are ill?'" she said. But that turned out to be just the first step: "Once you're in the door, there is no guarantee you will get the full mix of services you need to protect your health."

Her study documents a broad range of lapses in treating and preventing run-of-the-mill illnesses. For instance, patients studied did not receive one-third of the recommended immunizations, one-third of the standard medicines for heart diseases, or half of the recommended care for diabetes.

The report, based on a review of medical records for 6712 people in 12 cites, looked only at how often their doctors followed the rules, not whether they suffered any ill effects from the lapses.

"This study showed that there is a substantial discrepancy between what we say doctors ought to be doing and what they are doing," said Dr. Earl Steinberg, an adjunct professor at John Hopkins University and head of a company that develops computer programs for doctors.

The presidents of the American Academy of Family Physicians and of the American College of Physicians said their organizations have been discussing the problem for some time.

"I don't think that it surprises anybody in the health profession to know that there is no real uniformity of health care," said Dr. James Martin, AAFP president.

One problem is that there are so many guidelines and so many steps. The study looked at 30 medical conditions, plus preventive care. All of those guidelines added up to 439 actions, recommendations or other steps.

"The days of everyone being able to keep it all in your own head are long gone," Martin said.

He also noted that a recent article in the journal *Public Health* estimated that if the average doctor did everything recommended for annual health exams, the check up would last 90 minutes instead of 15 to 20.

He and the ACP's president, Dr. Munsey S. Wheby, said affordable electronic systems that help doctors keep track of the latest guidelines could play a big part in solving the problem. Such systems run into six figures, Martin said.

The study found that alcoholics got the least amount of standard care. Their doctors took only 11 percent of the recommended steps, such as proposing treatment programs for them.

Also at the bottom of the scale were broken hips, irregular heartbeats, and heartburn and ulcers, which were grouped together. Each had 10 or fewer items in their guidelines, but doctors followed them only about one-quarter to one third of the time.

On the other hand, even though doctors treating pregnant women had 39 steps, they followed them about 73 percent of the time. McGlynn credited a detailed form distributed widely by the American College of Obstetrics and Gynecologists.

Source: Janet McConnaughey, "Study Shows U.S. Doctors Are Not Following Guidelines," *Lincoln Journal Star*, June 26, p.4A. Reprinted with permission of The Associated Press.

Percentage of treatment guidelines that doctors followed, by ailment

100% of guidelines met
90%
Senile cataract — 80%
Breast cancer
Prenatal care
Low back pain — 70%
Coronary artery disease
Depression — 60%
Osteoarthritis
Colorectal cancer
Asthma
High cholesterol — 50% of guidelines met
Diabetes
Headache
Urinary tract infection — 40%
STD or vaginitis
30%
Atrial fibrillation
Hip fracture — 20%
Treatment for alcoholism
10% of guidelines met

kill about 32,000 patients each year and add more than $9 billion to the nation's health bill.[6] The study focused on 18 types of medical injuries, such as accidental laceration, trauma or injury to newborns, foreign objects left in the body, post-surgical hemorrhage, and transfusion reactions.

Waste and Inefficiency

A final problem is waste and inefficiency in the present system. The administrative costs of delivering health insurance benefits are excessively high; there is excessive paperwork by both health care providers and insurers; claim forms are not uniform nationally; a considerable amount of medical care provided by physicians is considered inappropriate; defensive medicine by physicians often results in unnecessary tests and procedures; there is duplication of expensive technology in hospitals in many cities; and fraud and abuse by health care providers are widespread.

INDIVIDUAL HEALTH INSURANCE COVERAGES

As stated earlier, most people with health insurance are covered under group health insurance plans. Group health insurance premiums account for more than 90 percent of all health insurance premiums. Chapter 22 discusses group health insurance coverages in some detail. Although group health insurance is a major source of protection, individual coverages are also important. Millions of Americans are insured under individual medical expense plans. Some people are not employed and require individual coverage; workers retire and need supplemental health insurance; and college students frequently attain a limiting age under their parents' group health insurance plans and must obtain their own coverage. In addition, long-term care insurance and disability-income insurance are important individual coverages that merit discussion. In this section, we discuss the following individual coverages:

- Hospital-surgical insurance
- Major medical insurance
- Long-term care insurance
- Disability-income insurance

HOSPITAL-SURGICAL INSURANCE

Many older individual medical expense plans still in force are **hospital-surgical insurance** plans. These plans are also called basic plans because they cover routine medical expenses and are not designed to cover catastrophic losses. Lifetime aggregate limits are relatively low, such as $100,000. Maximum benefits for each illness are also relatively low, such as a maximum of $20,000 for each covered event. The types of medical expenses covered vary widely among insurers. Most policies cover the following:

- *Hospital Expenses.* A typical policy covers *inpatient hospital expenses.* Some older plans pay actual room and board charges up to some maximum daily limit, such as $400 per day for a maximum of 365 days. Most insurers, however, have moved away from this approach. Newer plans cover the cost of a semiprivate room, subject to any deductible or coinsurance requirements. For example, the plan may pay 80 percent of the cost of a semiprivate room after a hospital deductible of $150 is met, with a maximum daily limit of $400.

  Individual plans also cover a variety of *miscellaneous hospital expenses,* such as X-rays, inpatient drugs, and laboratory tests. For example, the plan may pay 80 percent of the miscellaneous charges up to a maximum of $10,000. Another approach is to pay a maximum benefit for miscellaneous charges that is some multiple of the maximum daily room-and-board benefit, such as 10 times the daily benefit.

- *Surgical Expenses.* Hospital-surgical plans also cover surgical expenses. Some older plans still in force use a schedule approach by which common surgical procedures are listed in a schedule with a maximum dollar amount paid for each procedure. The current approach, however, is to reimburse surgeons on the basis of their **reasonable and customary charges.** Many insurers consider a fee to be reasonable and customary if it does not exceed the 80th or 90th percentile for a similar procedure performed by other surgeons in the same area. The insured must pay that portion of the fee that exceeds the upper limit.

- *Outpatient Services.* Individual plans commonly cover certain *outpatient services,* such as emergency treatment within 72 hours of an injury; diagnostic x-rays, and lab expenses. The plans also have maximum limits on the amounts paid for outpatient services.
- *Physicians' Visits.* Many plans provide coverage for physicians' visits, which pay for *nonsurgical treatment* provided by a physician to a patient while in the hospital. For example, a family physician may visit a patient who is hospitalized because of the flu. There are maximum limits on the amount paid for each visit, such as a maximum of $75 for each visit but not to exceed 21 visits for a single confinement.

At the present time, basic individual hospital-surgical plans have a limited presence in today's market and are relatively unimportant. Most basic plans still in existence are guaranteed renewable that do not permit an insurer to cancel. However, because of the rapid increase in health care costs over time and low maximum benefits, relatively few individual basic plans are sold currently. Most new individual medical expense plans sold currently are major medical insurance plans, which we discuss in the following section.

MAJOR MEDICAL INSURANCE

Insureds often desire broader coverage than that provided by the basic coverages just discussed. **Major medical insurance** is designed to pay a high proportion of the covered expenses of a catastrophic illness or injury. A typical individual major medical policy has the following characteristics:

- Broad coverage
- High maximum limits
- Benefit period
- Deductible
- Coinsurance
- Exclusions

Broad Coverage

Major medical insurance provides broad coverage of all reasonable and necessary medical expenses and other related expenses from a covered illness or injury. The policy covers eligible expenses incurred while in the hospital, in the doctor's office, or at home. Eligible medical expenses include hospital room and board charges, miscellaneous hospital services and supplies, treatment by licensed physicians and surgeons, prescription drugs, durable medical equipment, and numerous other expenses.

High Maximum Limits

Major medical policies are also written with high lifetime limits of $500,000, $1 million, $2 million, or some higher amount. Some plans have no maximum limits. High limits are necessary to meet the crushing financial burden of a major catastrophic illness or injury.

Benefit Period

The maximum amount paid under a major medical policy depends partly on the length of the benefit period. A **benefit period,** *such as three years, refers to the length of time that major medical benefits will be paid after the deductible is satisfied.* When the benefit period ends, the insured must then satisfy a new deductible to establish a new benefit period. For example, assume that Jennifer has a $1 million major medical expense policy with a $500 deductible and a three-year benefit period. Assume that she is severely injured in an auto accident and satisfies the deductible on the first day of her injury. A three-year benefit period for that illness is then established. At the end of three years, Jennifer must again satisfy a new deductible if the maximum amount of $1 million has not been paid.

The purpose of the benefit period is to provide a definite time period within which eligible medical expenses for a specific disease or injury must be incurred in order to be reimbursed under the policy.

Deductible

A major medical policy usually contains a deductible that must be satisfied before benefits are paid. The purpose of the deductible is to eliminate payment of small claims and the relatively high administrative expenses of processing small claims. By eliminating small claims, the insurer can provide high policy limits and still keep the premiums reasonable.

The following types of deductible provisions are commonly found in individual major medical policies:

- Calendar-year deductible
- Family deductible
- Common-accident provision

Most major medical policies have a calendar-year deductible. A **calendar-year deductible** *is an aggregate deductible that has to be satisfied only once during the calendar year.* All covered medical expenses incurred by the insured during the calendar year can be applied toward the deductible. Once the deductible is met, no additional deductible has to be satisfied during the calendar year. To avoid paying for two deductibles in a short period, most plans have a carryover provision. This provision means that unreimbursed medical expenses incurred during the last three months of the calendar year that are applied to this year's deductible can also be carried over and applied to next year's deductible.

The **family deductible** *specifies that medical expenses for all family members are accumulated for purposes of satisfying the deductible.* The accumulation period typically is one month, but a longer period could be used. For example, a $100 monthly deductible may be used. If medical expenses for the entire family exceed $100 during the month, the major medical policy starts to pay.

Individual major medical policies also contain a **common-accident provision.** *Only one deductible has to be satisfied if two or more family members are injured in a common accident, such as an automobile accident.*

Coinsurance

Major medical policies contain a **coinsurance provision** *that requires the insured to pay a certain percentage of eligible medical expenses in excess of the deductible.* Coinsurance is also called a *percentage participation clause* in health insurance. A typical plan requires the insured to pay 20 percent or 25 percent of covered expenses in excess of the deductible. For example, assume that Megan has covered medical expenses in the amount of $10,500. She has a $1 million major medical policy with a $500 deductible and an 80-20 coinsurance provi-

sion. The insurer will pay $8000 of the total bill, and Megan will pay $2000 (plus the deductible). This is summarized as follows:

Covered expenses	$10,500
Less the deductible	−500
Remaining expenses	$10,000
80% paid by insurer	8000
20% paid by Megan	$ 2000

The purposes of the coinsurance clause are to reduce premiums and to prevent overutilization of policy benefits. Also, the insured is less likely to demand unnecessary medical services if he or she pays part of the cost.

Major medical policies also contain a **stop-loss limit** by which 100 percent of the eligible medical expenses are paid after the insured incurs a certain amount of out-of-pocket expenses, such as $2000. *The purpose of the stop-loss limit is to reduce the financial burden of a catastrophic loss.* For example, if Megan's covered medical expenses in excess of the deductible are $100,000 and the stop-limit is $2000, her major medical policy would pay $98,000. She would pay only $2000 (plus the deductible). Without the stop-limit, Megan would have to pay $20,000 (plus the deductible).

Exclusions

All major medical policies contain exclusions. Some common exclusions are as follows:

- Expenses caused by war or military conflict
- Elective cosmetic surgery
- Dental care, except as a result of an accident
- Eye and hearing examinations, eyeglasses, and hearing aids
- Pregnancy and childbirth, except complications of pregnancy (Maternity can be covered with a rider.)
- Expenses covered by workers compensation and similar laws
- Services furnished by governmental agencies unless the patient has an obligation to pay
- Experimental surgery

To control cost, major medical plans typically contain **internal limits** for certain types of expenses. There may be annual or lifetime limits on the amount paid for certain diseases, such as alcoholism and drug addiction. For example, one plan limits inpatient coverage for alcoholism and drug addiction to no more than 45 days of treatment during any successive 12-month period.

Major Medical Insurance and Managed Care

Many individual major medical plans have incorporated elements of managed care into the plan design. Managed care is a generic term for medical expense plans that provide benefits to insureds in a cost-effective manner. For example, the plan may require precertification and approval for nonemergency admission into a hospital; certain types of surgery must be done on an outpatient basis, and an insured may be required to use a preferred provider or pay higher out-of-pocket costs for the benefits received. **Preferred providers** are physicians, hospitals, and other health-care providers who are part of a plan network and agree to provide medical services to plan members at discounted fees. Insureds who go outside the network for care must pay higher-out-of-pocket costs for the care received.

LONG-TERM CARE INSURANCE

Long-term care insurance is another coverage that is rapidly growing in popularity. **Long-term care insurance** pays a daily or monthly benefit for medical or custodial care received in a nursing facility, in a hospital, or at home.

Chance of Entering a Nursing Home

Many older Americans will spend some time in a nursing home. The need for care in a nursing home increases after age 65. *One study by the Milbank Memorial Fund found that the proportion of the elderly attaining age 65 who are likely to use nursing homes ranges from 39 percent to 49 percent, depending on the database. Estimates of the elderly living in a nursing home for at least two years after age 65 range from 16 percent to 25 percent.*[7]

The cost of long-term care in a nursing home is staggering. Most long-term facilities charge $50,000 to $80,000 or even more for each year of care. Except for the first 100 days, Medicare does not cover long-term care in a nursing facility, and custodial care is excluded altogether. In addition, most elderly are not initially eligible for long-term care under the Medicaid program, which is a welfare program that imposes strict eligibility requirements and a stringent means test. As a result, many older Americans have purchased long-term care policies to meet the crushing financial burden of an extended stay in a nursing facility.

Basic Characteristics

Numerous insurers sell long-term care policies. The policies sold currently usually have certain generic characteristics.[8]

Types of Policies   Long-term care policies generally can be classified into three major categories: (1) facility-only policies, (2) home health care only policies, and (3) comprehensive policies that combine care in a nursing facility and home health care into a single policy.

- A *facility-only policy* typically covers care in a nursing home, assisted-living facility, Alzheimer's facility, or hospice as long as the insured satisfies the benefit trigger (discussed later).
- A *home health care policy* covers care received outside of an institution and typically covers home health care, adult day care, and respite care. Respite care is a benefit that provides occasional full-time care to an insured who is receiving home health care services, which allows a caregiver to take a needed break.
- A *comprehensive policy* typically covers care in a nursing home, assisted living facility, and hospice and also makes available optional benefits for home health care and adult day care. All three types of policies generally provide for a care coordinator who evaluates the various options for providing care and recommends the most appropriate services for an insured.

Aggregate Benefits   Purchasers of long term care insurance have a choice of benefits, such as daily benefits of $150, $200, $250, or even higher, which are paid over a maximum period of two, three, or four years, or over the insured's lifetime. Some plans have a choice of lifetime maximum benefits, such as $150 daily and a $350,000 lifetime limit.

Elimination Period   An **elimination period** is a waiting period during which time benefits are not paid. Elimination periods can range from zero to 365 days. Common elimination periods are 30, 60, 100, or 180 days. A longer elimination period can substantially reduce premiums.

Eligibility for Benefits   Tax-qualified policies have two *benefit triggers* that determine whether the insured is chronically ill and eligible for benefits. *The insured must meet only one of the two triggers to receive benefits.* The first trigger requires the insured to be unable to perform a certain number of **activities of daily living,** commonly called ADLs. Six common **ADLs** are eating, bathing, dressing, transferring from a bed to a chair, using the toilet, and maintaining continence. Benefits are paid if the insured cannot perform a certain number of ADLs listed in the policy without assistance from another person, such as two out of the six ADLs.

The second trigger is that the insured needs substantial supervision to be protected against threats to health and safety because of a *severe cognitive impairment.* For example, benefits can be triggered if the insured has a short- or long-term memory impairment; or becomes disoriented with respect to persons, place, time, or abstract reasoning; or has errors in judgment with respect to safety awareness.

Finally, non tax-qualified policies often have more liberal eligibility requirements and make benefits available if a *medical necessity trigger* is met. This means that benefits can be paid if a physician certifies that long-term care is needed even if the insured does not meet any of the benefit triggers described earlier.

Inflation Protection   Protection against inflation is usually made available as an optional benefit. For example, based on an inflation rate of 5 percent annually, a daily charge of $110 will increase to $292 in 20 years.[9] Protection against inflation is especially important if the policy is purchased at a younger age.

Two methods are used to provide protection against inflation. One method allows the insured to purchase additional amounts of insurance in the future without evidence of insurability. For example, one insurer allows the insured to exercise four options, one every five years, to increase his or her coverage 20 percent each time an option is exercised.

A second method provides for an automatic benefit increase by which the daily benefit is increased by a fixed percentage, such as 5 percent for the next 10 or 20 years. The dollar amount of the annual increase will depend on whether the inflation adjustment is based on simple or compound interest. A daily benefit of $100 will increase to $200 in 20 years based on 5 percent simple interest; however, if the benefit is compounded, it will increase to $265. Adding an automatic benefit increase to the policy is expensive and could double the amount of the annual premium in some cases.

Guaranteed Renewable Policy   The policies sold currently are guaranteed renewable. Once issued, the policy cannot be canceled. However, rates can be increased for the underwriting class in which the insured is placed.

Expensive Coverage   Long-term care insurance is expensive, especially at the older ages. For example, one insurer charges $1,548 for a policy sold in Nebraska to a person age 65 with a $100 daily benefit, three-year benefit period, 90-day elimination period, and compound interest inflation protection. The same policy sold at age 80 would cost $4,645 annually. Most long-term care is paid for out-of-pocket by patients and their families (see Exhibit 21.2).

Taxation of Long-Term Care Insurance   Long-term care insurance that meets certain requirements receives favorable income tax treatment. The coverage can be an individual or group plan. Employer-paid premiums are deductible by the employer under a group plan and are not taxable to the employee.

Annual premiums paid by an individual for either individual or group coverage are deductible as medical expenses if the premiums paid plus other unreimbursed medical expenses exceed 7½ percent of the individual's adjusted gross income. However, certain annual limits apply. For 2004, the maximum annual deduction ranged from $260 for people age 40 or below to $3250 for people over age 70. These limits are indexed for inflation.

Most long-term care policies are written on a *reimbursement basis,* which reimburse the insured for actual expenses incurred up to the policy limits,

EXHIBIT 21.2
Sources of Payment for Long Term Care, 2000

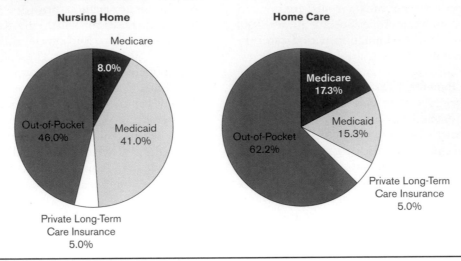

SOURCE: *Centers for Medicare & Medicaid Services,* Office of the Actuary, National Health Statistics Group.

and the benefits paid are income-tax free. However, a few policies are written on a *per diem basis,* which pay the stated daily benefit regardless of actual expenses incurred if benefits are triggered. In this case, the tax-free benefits are limited to $230 daily (2004 limit). However, higher daily benefits are tax-free to the extent that long-term care expenses exceed that amount. The insured must have proof of actual costs paid.

DISABILITY-INCOME INSURANCE

Disability-income insurance is another important form of individual health insurance. A serious disability can result in a substantial loss of work earnings. Unless you have replacement income from disability-income insurance, or income from other sources, you may be financially insecure. Many workers seldom think about the financial consequences of a long-term disability. However, the probability of becoming disabled before age 65 is much higher than is commonly believed, especially at the younger ages. For example, *the probability that a person age 25 will be totally disabled for at least 90 days prior to age 65 is 54 percent* (see Exhibit 21.3).

The financial loss to the family from long-term total and permanent disability can be substantially greater than the financial loss that results from premature death at the same age. In the case of premature death, the family loses its share of the deceased family head's future earnings, and funeral expenses

EXHIBIT 21.3
Probability of Becoming Disabled for at Least 90 Days Before Age 65

Age	Probability
25	54%
30	52
35	50
40	48
45	44
50	39
55	32
60	9

NOTE: Based on 1985 Commissioners Disability Table.

SOURCE: Adapted with permission from Edward E. Graves, ed., *McGill's Life Insurance,* 3rd ed. (Bryn Mawr, PA: The American College, 2000), table 7-2, p. 168. Copyright © 2000 by The American College. All Rights Reserved.

are also incurred. However, in the case of total and permanent disability, earned income is lost; medical bills are being incurred; savings are reduced or depleted; employee benefits may be lost; and additional expenses are incurred, such as getting someone to care for the disabled person. It is clear that disability-income insurance should be a high priority in a personal risk management program.

Disability-income insurance provides income payments when the insured is unable to work because of sickness or injury. An individual policy pays monthly income benefits to an insured who becomes totally disabled from a sickness or accident. The amount of disability insurance you can buy is related to your earnings. To prevent overinsurance and to reduce moral hazard and malingering, most insurers limit the amount of disability income sold to no more than 60 to 80 percent of your gross earnings.

Meaning of Total Disability

The most important policy provision in a disability income policy is the meaning of "total disability." Most policies require the worker to be totally disabled to receive benefits.

Definitions of Total Disability   There are several definitions of total disability. The most important include the following:

- Inability to perform all duties of the insured's own occupation
- Inability to perform the duties of any occupation for which the insured is reasonably fitted by education, training, and experience
- Inability to perform the duties of any gainful occupation
- Loss-of-income test

The most liberal definition defines total disability in terms of your own occupation. **Total disability** *is the complete inability of the insured to perform each and every duty of his or her own occupation.* An example would be a surgeon whose hand is blown off in a hunting accident. The surgeon could no longer perform surgery and would be totally disabled under this definition.

The second definition is more restrictive. In this case, *total disability is the complete inability to perform the duties of any occupation for which the*

insured is reasonably fitted by education, training, and experience. Thus, if the surgeon who lost a hand in a hunting accident could get a job as a professor in a medical school or as a research scientist, he or she would not be considered disabled because these occupations are consistent with the surgeon's training and experience.

The third definition is the most restrictive and is commonly used for hazardous occupations where a disability is likely to occur. *Total disability is defined as the inability to perform the duties of any gainful occupation.* The courts generally have interpreted this definition to mean that the person is totally disabled if he or she cannot work in any gainful occupation reasonably fitted by education, training, and experience.

Finally, some insurers use a loss-of-income test to determine if the insured is disabled. *You are considered disabled if your income is reduced as a result of a sickness or accident.* A disability-income policy containing this definition typically pays a percentage of the maximum monthly benefit equal to the percentage of earned income that is lost. For example, assume that Karen earns $5000 monthly and has a disability-income contract with a maximum monthly benefit of $3000. If Karen's work earnings are reduced to $2500 monthly because of the disability (50 percent), the policy pays $1500 monthly (50 percent of $3000).

Most insurers now combine the first two definitions. *For the initial period of disability—typically two years—total disability is defined in terms of the insured's own occupation. After the initial period of disability expires, the second definition is applied.* For example, Dr. Myron Pudwill is a dentist who can no longer practice because of arthritis in his hands. For the first two years, he would be considered totally disabled. However, after two years, if he could work as a dental supply representative or as a professor in a dental school, he would no longer be considered disabled because he is reasonably fitted for these occupations by his education and training.

Finally, the policy may also contain a definition of *presumptive disability.* A total disability is presumed to exist if the insured suffers the total and irrecoverable loss of sight in both eyes, or the total loss or use of both hands, both feet, or one hand and one foot.

Partial Disability Some disability-income policies also pay partial disability benefits. **Partial disability** *is defined as the inability of the insured to perform one or more important duties of his or her occupation.* Partial disability benefits are paid at a reduced rate for a shorter period. For example, a person may be totally disabled from an automobile accident. If the person recovers and goes back to work on a part-time basis to see if recovery is complete, partial disability benefits may be paid.

Residual Disability Newer policies frequently include a residual disability benefit, or this provision can be added as an additional benefit. **Residual disability** *means that a pro rata disability benefit is paid to an insured whose earned income is reduced because of an accident or sickness.* The typical residual disability provision has a time and duties test that considers both income and occupation. One common residual disability provision is as follows:[10]

1. You are not able to do one or more of your important daily business duties, or you are not able to do your usual daily business duties for as much time as it would normally take for you to do them.
2. Your loss of monthly income is at least 25 percent of your prior monthly income.
3. You are under the care and attendance of a physician.

However, some insurers use an alternative definition of residual disability that considers only the loss of earned income. In this definition, **residual disability** *means that you are engaged in your regular or another occupation, and your income is reduced because of an accident or sickness by at least 20 percent of your prior income.*

Finally, most insurers consider a loss of earned income in excess of 75 or 80 percent to be a loss of 100 percent, in which case the full monthly benefit for total disability is paid.

One major advantage of the residual disability definition is the payment of a partial benefit if the insured returns to work but earnings are reduced. For example, Nicholas is a salesperson who earns $4000 monthly. He is seriously injured in an auto accident. When he returns to work, his earnings are only $3000 monthly, or a reduction of 25 percent. If his disability-income policy pays a monthly benefit of $2000 for total disability, a residual benefit of $500 is paid, and his total monthly income is $3500.

Benefit Period

The benefit period is the length of time that disability benefits are payable after the elimination period is met. The insured has a choice of benefit periods, such as 2, 5, 10 years, or up to age 65 or 70 (provided the insured is still performing his or her occupation).

Most disabilities are relatively short. In fact, the majority of disabilities have durations of less than two years.[11] However, this fact does not mean that a two-year benefit period is adequate. The longer the disability lasts, the less likely the disabled person will recover. For example, a person who became disabled at age 22 and remains disabled for two years has a 41 percent chance of remaining disabled for at least five more years.[12] Thus, because of uncertainty concerning the duration of disability, you should elect a longer benefit period—ideally, one that pays benefits to age 65.

Elimination Period

Individual policies normally contain an elimination period (waiting period), during which time benefits are not paid. Insurers offer a range of elimination periods, such as 30, 60, 90, 180, or 365 days. Most insurers have stopped offering elimination periods that are shorter than 14 days, and elimination periods of 30 or more days are now the rule.

High-quality disability-income policies are expensive and can cost as much as 2 to 3 percent of your annual earnings. Increasing the elimination period from 30 to 90 days can substantially reduce the premiums. For example, in one plan, a male accountant who purchases a monthly benefit of $4250 to age 65 will pay $4036 annually for a policy with a 30-day elimination period. However, if he elects a 90-day elimination period, the annual premium would be about $1888, or 53 percent less. The majority of employers have sick leave or short-term disability plans that would provide some income during the longer elimination period. One disadvantage, however, is that a group disability-income plan is usually not convertible into an individual policy if the worker becomes unemployed. Thus, group insurance is not a satisfactory substitute for a high-quality disability-income policy.

Finally, to make disability-income insurance more affordable, *some insurers sell policies with initially lower rates that gradually increase with age.* This approach is similar to term life insurance rates that increase as the insured gets older.

Waiver of Premium

Most policies automatically include a **waiver-of-premium** provision. If the insured is totally disabled for 90 days, future premiums will be waived as long as the insured remains disabled. In addition, there may be a refund of the premiums paid during the initial 90-day period. If the insured recovers from the disability, premium payments must be resumed.

Rehabilitation Provision

Disability-income policies typically include a rehabilitation provision. The insurer and insured may agree on a vocational rehabilitation program. To encourage rehabilitation, part or all of the disability-income benefits are paid during the training period. At the end of training, if the insured is still totally disabled, the benefits continue as before. But if the individual is fully rehabilitated and is capable of returning to work, the benefits will terminate. The costs of rehabilitation are usually paid by the company.

Accidental Death, Dismemberment, and Loss-of-Sight Benefits

Some disability-income policies pay accidental death, dismemberment, and loss-of-sight benefits in the event of an accident. The maximum amount paid, known as the principal sum, is based on a schedule. For example, the principal sum is paid for loss of both hands or both feet or sight of both eyes.

Optional Disability-Income Benefits

Several optional benefits can be added to a disability-income policy. They include the following:

- *Cost-of-living rider.* Under this option, the disability benefits are periodically adjusted for increases in the cost of living, usually measured by the Consumer Price Index. Two limitations generally apply to the cost-of-living adjustment. First, the annual increase in benefits may be limited to a certain maximum percentage (such as 5 percent per year). Second, there may be a maximum limit on the overall increase in benefits (such as a 100 percent maximum increase in benefits). The rider is expensive and can increase the basic premium by 25 to 40 percent.
- *Option to purchase additional insurance.* Your income may increase, and you may need additional disability-income benefits. Under this option, the insured has the right to purchase additional disability-income benefits at specified times in the future with no evidence of insurability. The premium is generally based on the insured's age at the time the additional benefits are purchased.
- *Social Security rider.* Social Security disability benefits are difficult to obtain because of a strict definition of disability and stringent eligibility requirements. The Social Security rider pays you an additional amount if you are turned down for Social Security disability benefits.
- *Return of premium.* This rider pays back some of the premiums paid into the policy. For example, after 10 years, you would receive 80 percent of the premiums paid, less any claims. The option is controversial and is not recommended. Disability-income insurance is designed to provide income protection and should not be viewed as being similar to cash-value life insurance. The option is also expensive and can increase the already high cost of a policy by 30 to 100 percent.

Tighter Disability-Income Market

Although disability-income insurance is important, it is becoming more difficult to obtain. Disability-income insurers have experienced an explosion of claims and high underwriting losses in recent years. As a result, the market for disability-income insurance has tightened and is more restrictive. The underwriting losses are due to several factors, including an excessive number of claims by physicians with noncancellable policies that could not be repriced; a substantial increase in claims for alcohol and drug abuse and emotional disorders; liberal policy provisions; inadequate rates; payment of lifetime benefits; and liberal claims treatment of physicians and attorneys.

Some insurers have withdrawn from the disability-income market, while others have redesigned their policies. Disability insurers have also reduced the maximum benefit period available under the own-occupation definition of disability to two years; the amount of insurance has been cut back from a maximum of 80 percent of income to 60 or 65 percent; new policies sold to physicians do not pay lifetime benefits, and monthly payments are capped; elimination periods have been increased; and underwriting standards have tightened.

INDIVIDUAL MEDICAL EXPENSE CONTRACTUAL PROVISIONS

All states have laws that require certain contractual provisions to appear in individual medical expense insurance contracts, while other provisions are optional. It is beyond the scope of this text to analyze in detail all contractual provisions. Instead, attention is focused on those provisions that are commonly found in newly issued contracts and are relevant to insurance consumers.

Renewal Provisions

A renewal provision refers to the length of time that an individual policy can remain in force. Renewal provisions include the following:[13]

- Optionally renewable
- Nonrenewable for stated reasons only
- Guaranteed renewable
- Noncancellable

Optionally Renewable   This provision gives the insured the least protection with respect to continuation of coverage. Under an **optionally renewable policy,** *the insurer has the right to terminate a policy on any anniversary date, or in some cases, on a premium date.* The policy is renewable only with the consent of the insurer. Instead of nonrenewal, the

insurer may specify the conditions that must be met before the policy is renewed. These conditions could include a policy amendment that excludes certain types of losses or injuries to certain parts of the body, or coverage for certain occurrences may be limited.

Nonrenewable for Stated Reasons Only   This provision provides greater protection. The insurer may refuse to renew the coverage, but only for certain reasons stated in the policy, such as:

- The policyowner attains a certain age.
- The policyowner is no longer employed.
- The insurer decides to nonrenew all policies with the same form number as the policyowner's policy.

Guaranteed Renewable   Most individual medical expense policies are guaranteed renewable. This type of renewal provision provides considerable protection to the insured. A **guaranteed renewable policy** *is one in which the insurer guarantees to renew the policy to some stated age. However, the insurer has the right to increase premium rates for the underwriting class in which the insured is placed.* The policy cannot be canceled, and renewal of the policy is at the insured's sole discretion.

Noncancellable   A noncancellable policy provides the greatest protection to the insured. A **noncancellable policy** *is one that cannot be canceled. The insurer guarantees renewal of the policy to some stated age, and the premiums are guaranteed and cannot be increased during that period.* A noncancellable medical expense policy allows the insured to keep the insurance in force by the timely payment of premiums until at least age 50, or if the policy is issued after age 44, for at least five years from the issue date. Provided the insured pays the premiums on time, the insurer cannot cancel, refuse to renew, or increase premium rates stated in the policy, or unilaterally make any changes in the policy provisions.

The Health Insurance Portability and Accountability Act of 1996 now requires most new individual medical expense policies to be issued on a guaranteed renewable basis. Insurers are allowed to nonrenew such policies only under certain conditions, including nonpayment of premiums, fraud or misrepresentation, or discontinuation of the type of coverage provided by the policy.[14]

Preexisting-Conditions Clause

To control adverse selection, individual medical expense policies usually contain some type of **preexisting-conditions clause**. A preexisting condition is a physical or mental condition for which the insured received treatment or that existed during some specified time period—such as five years—prior to the effective date of the policy. Preexisting conditions are not covered until the policy has been in force for a specified period, such as two years, unless the condition is disclosed in the application and not excluded by a rider.

The preexisting-conditions exclusion usually applies to health conditions not disclosed in the application. If the condition is disclosed in the application, it usually would be covered unless the insurer excludes the condition by attaching an exclusionary rider.

Many states have placed restrictions on the types of preexisting-conditions clauses that insurers can use. For example, a state may limit exclusions for a preexisting condition to 12 months, with a six-month look-back period (how far back the insurer can go to see whether the condition existed before the policy inception date).

In addition, the Health Insurance Portability and Accountability Act of 1996 (HIPPA) guarantees the availability of individual health insurance coverage with no preexisting-conditions limitations to certain individuals who have lost their group health insurance coverage. HIPPA is discussed in Chapter 22.

Notice of 10-Day Right to Examine Policy

If you are not satisfied with the policy, you have 10 days to send it back after receiving it. The entire premium will be refunded, and the policy will be void.

Claims

A number of important provisions in an individual medical expense policy deal with claims. Under the *notice of claim provision,* you are required to give written notice to the insurer within 20 days after a covered loss occurs or as soon as is reasonably pos-

sible. Under the *claim forms provision,* the insurer is required to send you a claim form within 15 days after notice is received. Finally, under the *proof-of-loss provision,* you must send written proof of loss to the insurer within 90 days after a covered loss occurs. If it is not reasonably possible to provide proof of loss within 90 days, your claim will not be affected if the proof is sent as soon as possible. However, in any event, you must provide proof of loss within one year unless you are legally incapable of doing so.

Grace Period

A grace period is a required provision. The **grace period** *is a 31-day period after the premium due date to pay an overdue premium.* If the premium is paid after the due date but within the grace period, coverage is still in force.

Reinstatement

If the premium is not paid within the grace period, the health insurance policy lapses. The **reinstatement provision** *permits the insured to reinstate a lapsed policy.* If the insured pays the premium to the insurance company or agent, and an application is not required, the policy is reinstated. However, if an application for reinstatement is required, the policy is reinstated only when the insurer approves the application. If the insurer has not previously notified the insured that the application for reinstatement has been denied, the policy is then automatically reinstated on the forty-fifth day following the date of the conditional receipt. The reinstated policy is subject to a 10-day waiting period for sickness, but accidents are covered immediately.

Time Limit on Certain Defenses

The time limit on certain defenses is a required provision and has the same effect as the incontestable clause in life insurance. The **time limit on certain defenses** *states that after the policy has been in force for two years, the insurer cannot void the policy or deny a claim on the basis of misstatements in the application, except for fraudulent misstatements.* After two years, the insurer could deny a claim if it could prove that the insured made a fraudulent misstatement when the policy was first issued.

SHOPPING FOR HEALTH INSURANCE

High-quality individual health insurance plans are expensive. You should not waste money buying health insurance coverages that do not provide meaningful protection. Certain guidelines should be followed when you are purchasing health insurance (see Exhibit 21.4). They include the following:

- Insure for the catastrophic loss.
- Consider group health insurance first.
- Purchase a policy that has a preferred provider network.
- Don't ignore disability-income insurance.
- Avoid limited policies.
- Watch out for restrictive policy provisions and exclusions.
- Use deductibles and elimination periods to reduce premiums.

Insure for the Catastrophic Loss

The most important rule is to purchase health insurance that provides protection against a catastrophic loss that can destroy you financially. The cost of a serious illness or injury can prove ruinous. Open-heart surgery can cost more than $100,000; a kidney or heart transplant can cost more than $400,000; and the cost of a crippling auto accident requiring several major operations, plastic surgery, and rehabilitation can exceed $200,000. Unless you have adequate health insurance or financial assets to meet these expenditures, you will be financially insecure. The inability to pay for catastrophic medical bills is a major cause of personal bankruptcy. *Thus, you should purchase a high-quality individual major medical policy or be covered under a group major medical plan.* To limit your out-of-pocket expenses, make certain that the major medical policy has a stop-loss limit that requires the insurer to pay 100 percent of all covered expenses in excess of the stop-loss limit.

Consider Group Health Insurance First

In dealing with the risk of poor health, you should first consider whether group health insurance is available. You may be eligible to participate in a group health insurance plan sponsored by your employer or be a member of another group that offers group insurance.

Group health insurance is preferable to individual coverage for several reasons. First, employers frequently make available a number of group health insurance plans to their employees, ranging from tra-

Exhibit 21.4
Guidelines for Health Insurance Shoppers

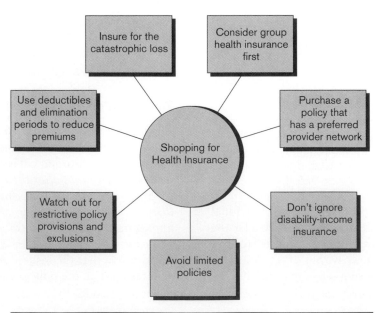

INSIGHT 21.2

Don't Delay Applying for Disability-Income Insurance

Applicants for disability-income insurance frequently have certain health impairments, such as lower back problems or arthritic knees, which may make them substandard or uninsurable for disability-income insurance but not for life insurance. As a result, the percentage of applicants for disability-income insurance who are classified as substandard or uninsurable is substantially higher than for life insurance. Typically, in life insurance, 3 to 5 percent of all applicants are classified as substandard and rated up because of health conditions. *In disability-income insurance, however, 15 to 25 percent of all applicants have health impairments that result in* *extra premiums, an exclusionary rider, or a combination of both.* Moreover, in life insurance, only 1 to 3 percent of the applicants are considered uninsurable. *In contrast, in disability-income insurance, 5 to 10 percent of the applicants are considered uninsurable.*[a] These sobering statistics point out the advantage of applying for disability-income insurance when you are young and healthy, when fewer health impairments are present.

[a] Charles E. Soule, *Disability-Income Insurance, The Unique Risk*, 5th ed. Bryn Mawr, PA: The American College, 2002, p. 23.

ditional group indemnity plans to managed care plans, such as those involving health maintenance organizations (HMOs) and preferred provider organizations (PPOs). The various group indemnity plans have different deductible amounts, coinsurance requirements, and stop-loss limits. HMOs typically have no deductible or coinsurance requirements, or the amounts paid out-of-pocket are relatively low. Depending on your financial circumstances and need for protection, you can select the plan that best meets your needs and ability to pay.

Second, group health insurance is typically broader in coverage than individual protection and has fewer exclusions and restrictions. Also, there is usually no individual underwriting in group health insurance.

Third, employers usually pay a large part of the monthly premiums, which makes the plan financially attractive to the employees and their families. Some employers pay the entire cost.

Finally, group health insurance plans provide substantial tax advantages to employees. The employer's contributions do not result in taxable income to the employee, and the employee's contributions can often be made with *before-tax dollars.* These tax advantages should not be ignored.

Purchase a Policy That Has a Preferred Provider Network

Another important suggestion is to shop for a policy that has a preferred provider network. Insurers frequently establish networks of health care providers who agree to provide medical services to the insureds at discounted fees. Preferred providers include physicians, dentists, hospitals, pharmaceutical firms, and other health care providers who are part of the network. If you see a preferred provider, your out-of-pocket cost will be substantially less than if you see a provider outside the network.

Don't Ignore Disability-Income Insurance

You should not ignore the importance of disability-income insurance in your health insurance program. A substantial amount of earned income is lost each year because of sickness and injury, but not replaced by disability-income and sick-leave benefits.

You should consider purchasing an individual guaranteed renewable or noncancellable disability-income policy that will pay at least two-thirds of your earnings up to age 65 with an elimination period of 30 to 90 days. Even if you are covered under a group short-term or long-term disability-income plan, you should still consider an individual policy.

Finally, you should not delay in applying for disability-income insurance. As workers become older, they often develop health impairments that make them substandard or uninsurable for disability-income insurance but not necessarily for life insurance. As a result of strict underwriting, applicants for disability-income insurance are more likely to be considered substandard or uninsurable than in life insurance (see Insight 21.2).

INSIGHT 21.3

How to Get Health Insurance if You Are Uninsurable

The majority of states have special high-risk pools that provide health insurance to people who are medically uninsurable. Applicants must show they have been refused health insurance elsewhere before they are accepted. Two eligibility requirements are commonly imposed. First, the applicant must be a resident of the state. Second, the applicant must provide proof of one or more of the following: (1) be rejected by at least one insurer, (2) be presently insured under a plan with a higher premium than the pool premium, (3) be presently insured with a restrictive rider or rated policy, or (4) be offered a policy with a restrictive waiver or rider.

Major medical benefits are typically provided. A calendar-year deductible and 80 to 20 percent coinsurance are common. The plans typically have an annual stop-loss limit that caps annual out-of-pocket expenses.

The insurance is expensive, with maximum rates generally ranging from 125 to 400 percent of individual standard rates. Despite the high premiums, the pools have incurred substantial underwriting losses. Health insurers doing business in a particular state are assessed their pro rata share of excess losses. In many states, the insurers can deduct all or part of the assessments from the state premium taxes paid. General revenue appropriations and taxes on tobacco and cigarettes are also used to fund excess losses in some states.

The major advantage of these pools is that they provide health insurance coverage to the medically uninsurable. The pools, however, are not a viable solution to the national problems of health insurance affordability and accessibility. They have incurred substantial underwriting deficits; the assessment method of funding such deficits is defective since the true cost is hidden and is shifted indirectly to taxpayers through premium tax offsets or to policyowners through higher premiums; only a small fraction of the medically uninsurable have obtained insurance through the pools; and high premiums make the insurance unaffordable to many applicants.

SOURCE: George E. Rejda and Michael McNamara, *Personal Financial Planning*, p. 365. Boston: Addison-Wesley, a division of Pearson Education, 1998.

Avoid Limited Policies

A **limited policy** covers only certain diseases or accidents, pays limited benefits, or places serious restrictions on the right to receive the benefits. A **hospital indemnity policy** is one example of a limited policy. It pays a fixed daily or monthly benefit if you are confined to a hospital. For example, the plan may pay $3000 monthly ($100 daily) if you are hospitalized; no health questions are asked, and the first month's premium is only $1. It sounds like a good deal, but in health insurance, there is no such thing as a "free lunch." The policy is limited. Most people will never collect benefits for an extended period. The average hospital stay for patients insured by private insurance is less than five days. Even if you are confined for only five days, the benefit paid would be only $500. During that time, you may have incurred several thousands of dollars of medical expenses, but only a small amount would be paid by the hospital indemnity benefit. In addition, the policy covers you only while you remain in the hospital. If you recover at home, no payment is made.

A **cancer policy** is another example of a limited policy. If you are insured under a high-quality individual or group major medical policy, you do not need a cancer policy. Consumer experts argue that it is illogical to insure yourself more heavily against only one disease because you do not know how you will become disabled.

Accident-only policies should also be avoided because they are limited in coverage and benefits. A list of these policies is endless, but includes accident insurance offered by sponsors of credit cards, travel accident policies to cover you while on vacation, and airline accident policies sold over the counter or from vending machines in airports.

Watch Out for Restrictive Policy Provisions and Exclusions

If you are shopping for an individual policy, you should be aware of any restrictions on coverage that might apply. Two common restrictions are a preexisting-conditions clause and an **exclusionary rider.** An individual policy with a preexisting-conditions clause longer than one year should not be purchased. If possible, you should also avoid buying an individual policy in which an exclusionary rider appears. If you have been treated for certain diseases, such as cancer or heart disease, the insurer may add a rider to the policy that excludes the condition.

As a last resort, if you are uninsurable and cannot obtain either individual or group coverage, you may be eligible for coverage from a state high-risk pool for the uninsurable (see Insight 21.3). The majority of states operate such high-risk pools. Information on enrolling is available from your state insurance department.

Use Deductibles and Elimination Periods to Reduce Premiums

High-quality individual health insurance coverages are expensive. A comprehensive major medical policy that covers the entire family can cost $6000 to $8000 annually. You can reduce your premiums by purchasing a policy with a substantial deductible. If you can afford it, an annual deductible of $500 or $1000 will substantially reduce your premiums. Likewise, premiums for a disability-income policy can be substantially reduced by buying a policy with an elimination period of 90 days or longer.

Finally, you should contact more than one insurer before purchasing a policy. Although price is important, it should not be the only consideration. A low-premium policy may contain restrictive provisions, pay limited benefits, or reflect a restrictive claims policy.

CASE APPLICATION

Lorri, age 28, is a registered nurse who earns $4000 monthly working in a hospital. She is seriously injured in an automobile accident in which she is at fault and is expected to be off work for at least one year. She has a guaranteed renewable disability-income policy that pays $2800 monthly up to age 65 for accidents and sickness after a 90-day elimination period. A residual disability benefit is included in the policy. Lorri's policy contains the following provisions:

- *Total disability means:* (a) your inability during the first 24 months to perform substantially all of the important duties of your occupation; and you are not working at any gainful occupation; (b) after the first 24 months that benefits are payable, it means your inability to engage in any gainful occupation.
- *Gainful occupation means:* Any occupation or employment for wage or profit that is reasonably consistent with your education, training, and experience.

a. If Lorri is off work for one year because of the accident, indicate the extent, if any, of the insurer's obligation to pay disability benefits.

b. Assume that Lorri is disabled for one year, recovers, and returns to work part-time. If she earns $2000 monthly after returning to work, indicate the extent, if any, of the insurer's obligation to pay her disability benefits.

c. Assume that after two years, Lorri is unable to return to work as a full-time hospital nurse. A drug manufacturer offers her a job as a lab technician, which she accepts. Indicate the extent, if any, of the insurer's obligation to continue paying her disability benefits.

d. Following the accident, could Lorri's insurer cancel her policy or increase her premiums? Explain your answers.

SUMMARY

- The health care delivery system in the United States has four major problems:

  Rising health care expenditures

  Large number of uninsured in the population

  Uneven quality of medical care

  Waste and inefficiency

- Individual health insurance policies can generally be classified into the following categories:

  Hospital-surgical insurance

  Major medical insurance

  Long-term care insurance

  Disability-income insurance

- Individual hospital-surgical policies typically cover hospital expenses, surgical expenses, outpatient diagnostic

X-rays and lab expenses, and physician's in-hospital expenses.

- Major medical insurance is designed to cover the expenses of a catastrophic illness or injury. A typical major medical plan has certain characteristics:

  Broad coverage

  High maximum limits

  Benefit period

  Deductible

  Coinsurance

  Exclusions

- Long-term care insurance pays a daily or monthly benefit for medical or custodial care in a nursing facility or at home.

- Disability-income policies provide for the periodic payment of income to an individual who is totally disabled. The benefits are paid after an elimination period is satisfied. The insured generally has a choice of benefit periods. In addition, after 90 days, all premiums are waived if the insured is totally disabled.

- The definition of disability is stated in a disability-income policy. For the first two years, total disability is typically defined as the inability to perform all duties of the insured's own occupation. After that time, total disability is defined as the inability to perform the duties of any occupation for which the insured is reasonably fitted by education, training, and experience.

- Health insurance policies contain certain contractual provisions. Some provisions are required by state law, while others are optional.

- A renewal provision refers to the length of time that an individual medical expense policy can remain in force. Renewal provisions include the following:

  Optionally renewable

  Nonrenewable for stated reasons only

  Guaranteed renewable

  Noncancellable

- Consumer experts recommend certain rules to follow when health insurance is purchased:

  Insure for the catastrophic loss.

  Consider group insurance first.

  Purchase a policy that has a preferred provider network.

  Don't ignore disability-income insurance.

  Avoid limited policies.

Watch out for restrictive policy provisions and exclusions.

Use deductibles and elimination periods to reduce premiums.

KEY CONCEPTS AND TERMS

Accident-only policy
Activities of daily living (ADLs)
Benefit period
Benefit triggers
Calendar-year deductible
Cancer policy
Coinsurance provision
Common-accident provision
Disability-income insurance
Elimination (waiting) period
Exclusionary rider
Family deductible
Grace period
Guaranteed renewable policy
Hospital indemnity policy
Hospital-surgical insurance plan
Internal limits
Limited policy
Long-term care insurance
Major medical insurance
Noncancellable policy
Nonrenewable for stated reasons only
Optionally renewable policy
Partial disability
Preexisting-conditions clause
Preferred provider
Reasonable and customary charges
Reinstatement provision
Residual disability
Schedule approach
Stop-loss limit
Time limit on certain defenses
Total disability
Waiver of premium

REVIEW QUESTIONS

1. What are the four major problems in health care in the United States?

2. Identify the benefits that are typically included in a basic hospital-surgical expense policy.

3. a. Describe the basic characteristics of major medical insurance.

   b. Why are deductibles and coinsurance used in a major medical policy?

4. Briefly explain the basic characteristics of long-term care insurance.

5. a. Explain the various definitions of disability that are found in disability-income insurance.

b. Briefly explain the following disability-income insurance provisions:
   (1) Residual disability
   (2) Benefit period
   (3) Elimination period
   (4) Waiver of premium

6. Identify the optional benefits that can be added to a disability-income policy.

7. Explain the following renewal provisions that appear in individual medical expense policies:
   a. Optionally renewable
   b. Nonrenewable for stated reasons only
   c. Guaranteed renewable
   d. Noncancellable

8. Explain the meaning of a preexisting condition.

9. Explain the time limit on certain defenses contractual provision.

10. Briefly describe the guidelines that consumers should follow when individual health insurance is purchased.

APPLICATION QUESTIONS

1. Brittany, age 28, purchased an individual major medical insurance policy with a lifetime limit of $1 million, a calendar-year deductible of $250, and an 80-20 percent coinsurance provision. Brittany had emergency surgery for an inflamed appendix. Covered medical expenses are $30,750. Brittany also lost $1000 in wages because she could not work for one week.
   a. What is the amount paid by the insurer? Explain.
   b. What is the amount paid by Brittany? Explain.
   c. Would your answer to (b) above change if Brittany's policy contained an annual stop-loss limit of $3000? Explain.

2. Fred and Janet and their two daughters, Kelly and Karen, are insured under an individual major medical policy that covers the entire family. The policy has a calendar-year deductible of $500 that applies to each covered person, an 80-20 percent coinsurance provision, and a common accident provision.
   a. Janet had gallbladder surgery and incurred covered medical expenses of $15,500. How much will Janet receive from her insurer?
   b. Fred, Kelly, and Karen were injured in the same bobsledding accident. Covered medical expenses are $2500 for George, $900 for Kelly, and $600 for Karen. How much of the loss will be paid by the insurer? Show your calculations.

3. Mark, age 25, is insured under an individual major medical policy with a lifetime limit of $2 million. The plan has a calendar-year deductible of $500, 80-20 percent coinsurance, and an annual stop-loss limit of $2000. Mark recently had outpatient arthroscopic surgery on his knee, which he injured in a skiing accident. The surgery was performed in an outpatient surgical center. Mark incurred the following medical expenses.

Outpatient X-rays and diagnostic tests	$700
Covered charges in the surgical center	9,800
Surgeon's fee	3,000
Outpatient prescription drugs	300
Physical therapy expenses	700

In addition, Mark could not work for two weeks and lost $2000 in earnings.
   a. Based on the above information, how much of the loss will be paid by the insurance company?
   b. If Mark's policy did not contain a stop-loss limit, how much will the insurance company pay? Show your calculations.

4. Jeff currently earns $3000 per month. He has an individual disability-income policy that will pay $2000 monthly if he is totally disabled. Disability is defined in terms of the worker's own occupation. The policy has a 30-day elimination period and also provides residual disability benefits.
   a. If Jeff is severely injured in an auto accident and cannot work for four months, how much will he collect under his policy?
   b. Assume Jeff returns to work but can only work part-time until he recovers completely. If he earns $200 monthly, what is the amount, if any, that Jeff can collect under his policy? Explain your answer.

INTERNET RESOURCES

■ **America's Health Insurance Plans (AHIP)** is a national trade association that represents nearly 1300 member companies that provide health insurance coverage to more than 200 million Americans. The site provides considerable information on health-care issues in the United States. Visit the site at

http://www.aahp.org/

- **eHealthInsurance.com** offers online applications for major medical insurance from several leading insurers. It allows you to shop privately for health insurance without sales pressure. Visit the site at

  http://www.ehealthinsurance.com

- **INSWEB** provides timely information and premium quotes for individual health insurance, small group health insurance, and Medicare supplement policies. Applicants fill out health forms, and the site provides quotes from multiple insurers. Visit the site at

  http://www.insweb.com

- **Insure.com** provides up-to-date information, premium quotes, and other consumer information on health insurance and other insurance products. The site also provides news releases about events that affect the insurance industry. Visit the site at

  http://www.insure.com

- The **National Association of Health Underwriters** is a professional association of health insurance professionals who sell and service medical expense, major medical, and disability-income insurance. Visit the site at

  http://www.nahu.org

- **QuickQuote** provides premium quotes on life insurance, health insurance, and numerous other insurance products. Visit the site at

  http://www.quickquote.com

- **Quotesmith.com** provides life and health insurance quotes for individuals, families, students, and small groups. Quotes on auto and homeowners insurance are also available. Visit the site at

  http://www.quotesmith.com

- The **National Association of Insurance Commissioners (NAIC)** has a link to all state insurance departments, which provide a considerable amount of consumer information on the health insurance coverages discussed in this chapter. Click on State Insurance Web sites. For starters, check out New York, Wisconsin, and California. Visit the site at

  http://www.naic.org

SELECTED REFERENCES

Beam, Burton T., Jr., and Thomas P. O'Hare. *Meeting the Financial Need of Long-Term Care.* Bryn Mawr, PA: The American College, 2003.

Black, Kenneth, Jr., and Harold D. Skipper, Jr. *Life Insurance,* 13th ed. Upper Saddle River, NJ: Prentice-Hall, 2000, chs. 7, 9, 10.

Health Insurance Association of America. *Guide to Disability-Income Insurance.* Washington, DC: Health Insurance Association of America, 1999.

Health Insurance Association of America. *Guide to Health Insurance.* Washington, DC: Health Insurance Association of America, 2001.

Health Insurance Association of America. *Health Insurance Nuts and Bolts: An Introduction to Health Insurance Operations.* Washington, DC: Health Insurance Association of America, 2001.

Health Insurance Association of America. *The Health Insurance Primer: An Introduction to How Health Insurance Works.* Washington, DC: Health Insurance Association of America, 2000.

Health Insurance Association of America. *Source Book of Health Insurance Data, 2002.* Washington, DC: Health Insurance Association of America, 2002.

O'Hare, Thomas P. *Individual Medical Expense Insurance,* 3rd ed. Bryn Mawr, PA: The American College, 2004.

Rejda, George E. "Problem of Poor Health," in *Social Insurance and Economic Security,* 6th ed. Upper Saddle River, NJ: Prentice-Hall, 1999, ch. 8.

Soule, Charles E. *Disability Income Insurance: The Unique Risk,* 5th ed. Bryn Mawr, PA: The American College, 2002.

U.S. Bureau of the Census. *Health Insurance Coverage 2002, Current Population Reports,* P60–223, Washington, DC, September 2003.

NOTES

1. BCBSHealthIssues.com, *Medical Cost Reference Guide, Revised June 2003.*
2. U.S. Census Bureau, *Numbers of Americans With and Without Health Insurance Rise, Census Bureau Reports,* U.S. Department of Commerce News, September 30, 2003.

3. U.S. Bureau of the Census, *Health Insurance Coverage 2002, Current Population Reports,* P60-223, Washington, DC (September 2003).

4. Rhonda L. Rundle, "Quality Gap in Health Care Kills 57,000 Each Year in U.S.," *The Wall Street Journal,* September 18, 2003, p. D3.

5. Ibid.

6. Chunliu Zhan and Marlene R. Miller, "Excess Length of Stay, Charges, and Mortality Attributable to Medical Injuries during Hospitalization," *JAMA,* Journal of the American Medical Association, Vol. 290, No. 14 (October 8, 2003).

7. Robyn I. Stone, *Long-Term Care for the Elderly with Disabilities: Current Policy, Emerging Trends, and Implications for the Twenty-First Century* (New York: Milbank Memorial Fund, 2000), p. 10.

8. Burton T., Beam Jr. and Thomas P. O'Hare, *Meeting the Financial Need of Long-Term* (Bryn Mawr, PA: The American College, 2003), ch. 6.

9. *A Shopper's Guide to Long-Term Care Insurance* (Kansas City, MO: National Association of Insurance Commissioners, 2003).

10. Kenneth Black, Jr., and Harold D. Skipper, Jr., *Life Insurance,* 13th ed. (Upper Saddle River, NJ: Prentice-Hall, 2000), pp. 157–158.

11. Edward E. Graves, ed., *McGill's Life Insurance,* 3rd ed. (Bryn Mawr, PA: The American College, 2000), p. 181.

12. Ibid., table 7-4, p. 170.

13. *The Health Insurance Primer: An Introduction to How Health Insurance Works* (Washington, DC: Health Insurance Association of America, 2000), pp. 83–84.

14. Ibid., p. 84.

Students may take a self-administered test on this chapter at
www.aw-bc.com/rejda

CHAPTER 22

EMPLOYEE BENEFITS: GROUP LIFE AND HEALTH INSURANCE

"Employee benefits are an extremely important part of almost everyone's financial security."

Jerry S. Rosenbloom
The Handbook of Employee Benefits

After studying this chapter, you should be able to

◆ Explain the underwriting principles followed in group insurance.

◆ Describe the basic characteristics of group term life insurance.

◆ Explain the major characteristics of the following group medical expense plans:
   Basic medical expense insurance
   Major medical insurance
   Dental insurance

◆ Show how short-term disability income plans differ from long-term disability plans.

◆ Describe the basic characteristics of the following managed care plans:
   Health maintenance organizations (HMOs)
   Preferred provider organizations (PPOs)
   Point of service plans (POS)

◆ Describe the major characteristics of cafeteria plans.

*E*mployee benefits are very important in a personal risk management program. Employee benefits are employer-sponsored plans that pay benefits if a worker dies, becomes sick or disabled, or retires. The various benefits provide considerable financial security to employees and their families. They are also important in calculating total employee compensation. Although the starting salaries in many companies may be relatively low, generous employee benefits can substantially increase employees' total compensation packages. For example, Megan, age 25, is an English major who graduated from college and accepted an entry-level job with a national book publisher at an annual salary of $30,000. However, when employer contributions for life insurance, health and dental insurance, retirement, vacation, and other benefits are factored in, Megan's total annual compensation increases substantially to $36,000—an increase of 20 percent.

This chapter is the first of two chapters dealing with employee benefit plans. Chapter 22 is limited to employer-sponsored group life and health insurance plans. Retirement plans are discussed in Chapter 23. Topics discussed in this chapter include group life insurance, group medical expense plans, group dental insurance, group disability-income plans, and the Health Insurance Portability and Accountability Act. The chapter concludes with a discussion of cafeteria plans.

GROUP INSURANCE

Group insurance differs from individual insurance in several respects. *A distinctive characteristic is the coverage of many persons under one contract.* A master contract is formed between the insurer and the group policyowner for the benefit of the individual members. In most plans, the group policyowner is the employer. Employees receive a certificate of insurance that shows they are insured.

A second characteristic is that group insurance usually costs less than comparable insurance purchased individually. Employers usually pay part or all of the cost, which reduces or eliminates premium payments by the employees. In addition, administrative and marketing expenses are reduced as a result of mass distribution methods.

Another characteristic is that individual evidence of insurability is usually not required. Group selection of risks is used, not individual selection. The insurer is concerned with the insurability of the group as a whole rather than with the insurability of any single member within the group.

Finally, experience rating is used in group insurance plans. If the group is sufficiently large, the actual loss experience of the group is a major factor in determining the premiums charged.

Basic Underwriting Principles

Because individual evidence of insurability is usually not required, group insurers must observe certain underwriting principles so that the loss experience of the group is favorable. These principles are as follows:[1]

- Insurance incidental to the group
- Flow of persons through the group
- Automatic determination of benefits
- Minimum participation requirements
- Third-party sharing of cost
- Simple and efficient administration

Insurance Incidental to the Group   Insurance must be incidental to the group; that is, the group should not be formed for the sole purpose of obtaining insurance. This requirement is necessary to reduce adverse selection against the insurer. If the group is formed for the specific purpose of obtaining insurance, a disproportionate number of unhealthy persons would join the group to obtain low-cost insurance, and the loss experience would be unfavorable.

Flow of Persons Through the Group   Ideally, there should be a flow of younger persons into the group and a flow of older persons out of the group. Without a flow of younger persons into the group, the average age of the group will increase, and premium rates will likewise increase. Higher premiums may cause some younger and healthier members to drop out of the plan, while the older and unhealthy members will still remain, which would lead to still higher losses and increased rates. However, turnover of employees should not be so significant that administrative costs are high.

Automatic Determination of Benefits   Benefits should be automatically determined by some formula that precludes individual selection of insurance amounts. The amount of insurance can be based on earnings, position, length of service, or some combination of these factors. *The purpose of this requirement is to reduce adverse selection against the insurer.* If individual members were permitted to select the amount of insurance, unhealthy persons would likely select larger amounts, while healthier persons would likely select smaller amounts. The result would be a disproportionate amount of insurance on the impaired lives. However, many group insurance plans allow employees to select their own benefit levels up to certain maximum limits. If additional amounts of insurance are desired above the maximum allowed, evidence of insurability is usually required.

Minimum Participation Requirements   A minimum percentage of the eligible employees must participate in the plan. If the plan is a **noncontributory plan,** the premiums are paid entirely by the employer, and 100 percent of the eligible employees must be covered. If the plan is a **contributory plan,** the employee

pays part or all of the cost and a large proportion of the eligible employees must elect to participate in the plan. In a contributory plan, it may be difficult to get 100 percent participation, so a lower percentage such as 50 to 75 percent is typically required.

There are two reasons for the minimum participation requirement. First, if a large proportion of eligible employees participate, adverse selection is reduced, because the possibility of insuring a large proportion of unhealthy lives is reduced. Second, if a high proportion of eligible members participate, the expense rate per insured member or per unit of insurance can be reduced.

Third-Party Sharing of Cost   Ideally, individual members should not pay the entire cost of their protection. In most groups, the employer pays part of the cost. A third-party sharing of cost avoids the problem of a substantial increase in premiums for older members. In a plan in which the members pay the entire cost, younger persons help pay for the insurance provided to older persons. Once they become aware of this fact, some younger persons may drop out of the plan and obtain their insurance more cheaply elsewhere. Older unhealthy members will still remain, causing premiums to increase even more. However, if the employer absorbs any increase in premiums because of adverse mortality experience, premiums paid by the employees can be kept fairly stable. In addition, a third-party sharing of cost makes the plan more attractive to individual members and encourages greater participation in the plan.

Simple and Efficient Administration   The group plan should be simple and efficiently administered. Premiums are collected from the employees by payroll deduction, which reduces the insurer's administrative expenses and keeps participation in the plan high.

Eligibility Requirements in Group Insurance

Insurers typically require that certain eligibility requirements must be satisfied before the insurance is in force. The eligibility requirements generally are designed to reduce adverse selection against the insurer.

Eligible Groups   Types of groups eligible for group insurance are determined by insurance company policy and state law. Eligible groups include individual employer groups, multiple-employer groups, labor unions, creditor-debtor groups, and miscellaneous groups, such as fraternities, sororities, and alumni groups.

Group insurers usually require the group to be a certain size before the group is insured. Traditionally, this size was ten lives, but some insurers now insure groups with as few as two or three members. There are two reasons for a minimum-size requirement. First, the insurer has some protection against insuring a group that consists largely of substandard individuals, so that the financial impact of one impaired life on the loss experience of the group is reduced. Second, certain fixed expenses must be met regardless of the size of the group. The larger the group, the broader the base over which these expenses can be spread, and the lower the expense rate per unit of insurance.

Eligibility Requirements   Before employees can participate in a group insurance plan, they must meet certain eligibility requirements, including the following:

- Be full-time employees
- Satisfy a probationary period
- Apply for insurance during the eligibility period
- Be actively at work when insurance becomes effective

Employers generally require the workers to be employed full-time before they can participate in the plan. A *full-time worker* is one who works the required number of hours established by the employer as a normal work week, which is at least 30 hours. However, some group plans today permit part-time workers to be covered. In some group insurance plans, new employees may have to satisfy a **probationary period**, which is a period of one to six months, before he or she can participate in the plan. The purpose of the probationary period is to eliminate transient workers who will be with the firm for only a short period. It is administratively expensive to maintain records and insure workers who will not be working permanently for the firm.

After the probationary period (if any) expires, the employee is eligible to participate in the plan.

However, if the plan is contributory, the employee must request coverage either before or during the eligibility period. The **eligibility period** is a period of time—typically 31 days—during which the employee can sign up for the insurance without furnishing evidence of insurability.

Finally, the employee must be *actively at work* on the day the insurance becomes effective. The employee who is actively at work is presumably meeting certain minimum health standards, which also gives the insurer some protection against adverse selection.

GROUP LIFE INSURANCE PLANS

Group life insurance is a popular and relatively inexpensive employee benefit. At the end of 2002, $6.9 trillion of group life insurance was in force, which accounted for 42 percent of the total life insurance in force in the United States.[2]

The major types of group life insurance plans are the following:

- Group term life insurance
- Group accidental death and dismemberment insurance (AD&D)
- Group universal life insurance

Group Term Life Insurance

Group term life insurance is the most important form of group life insurance. More than 90 percent of the group life insurance in force is group term life insurance. The insurance provided is *yearly renewable term insurance,* which provides low-cost protection to the employees during their working careers.

The amount of term insurance on an employee's life is typically one to five times the annual salary or earnings. The term insurance remains in force as long as the employee is part of the group. If the employee quits or is laid off, he or she has the right to convert the group term insurance to an individual cash-value policy within 31 days without evidence of insurability. However, the group term insurance normally cannot be converted into an individual term insurance policy.[3] As a practical matter, relatively few employees convert their group insurance because of the problem of cost and because group insurance will probably be provided by another employer. Those employees who do convert are usually substandard in health or uninsurable, which results in strong adverse selection against the insurer.

Most group plans allow a modest amount of life insurance to be written on the employee's spouse and dependent children. Because of state law and tax considerations, the amount of dependent life insurance is relatively low. The insurance on the spouse's life can be converted to an individual cash-value policy. Some states require that the conversion option should also apply to the insurance on the children.

Most employers provide a reduced amount of term insurance on retired employees. The amount of insurance may be a flat amount, such as $10,000, or it may be a percentage of the amount of insurance at the date of retirement, such as 50 percent.

Group term insurance has the major advantage of providing low-cost protection to employees that can be used to supplement individual life insurance policies. However, it has two major disadvantages. First, the insurance is temporary and terminates when the individual is no longer part of the group. Second, it is expensive for an older worker to convert to an individual policy after retirement.

Finally, group term life insurance is used by commercial banks and other lending institutions to insure the lives of debtors. Credit life insurance provides for the cancellation of any outstanding debt if the borrower dies. The lending institution is both the policyowner and beneficiary. The unpaid balance of the loan is paid to the creditor at the debtor's death. Many financial planners do not recommend the purchase of credit life insurance because of excessive rates. Although the rates are regulated by the states, many debtors are overcharged for their protection (see Insight 22.1).

Group Accidental Death and Dismemberment (AD&D) Insurance

Many group life insurance plans also provide **group accidental death and dismemberment (AD&D) insurance** that pays additional benefits if the employee dies in an accident or incurs certain types of bodily injury. The AD&D benefit is some multiple of the group life insurance benefit, such as one or two times the insurance on the employee's life. The full

AD&D benefit, called the *principal sum,* is paid if the employee dies in an accident. In addition, a percentage of the principal sum is paid for certain types of dismemberments, such as one-half the principal sum for the loss of a hand, foot, or eye because of accidental bodily injury.

Many plans also make available **voluntary accidental death and dismemberment insurance** in which employees can voluntarily purchase additional amounts of AD&D insurance. The employees normally pay the entire cost of the voluntary coverage.

Group Universal Life Insurance

In addition to group term life insurance, some employers make available **group universal life insurance** for their employees. These plans are similar to individual universal life insurance policies, but have some important differences. The major characteristics of group universal life plans are summarized as follows:[4]

- *Plan design.* Two approaches are used in the plan design. Under the first approach, there is only one plan. The employee who wants only term insurance pays only the mortality and expense charges. The employee who wants to accumulate cash values must pay higher premiums. Under the second approach, two plans are used—term insurance and universal life insurance. The employee who wants only term insurance pays into the term insurance plan. The employee who wants universal life insurance must pay higher premiums so that cash values are accumulated. The employee may be required to pay initial premiums equal to two or three times the cost of the pure insurance protection.
- *Amount of insurance.* Universal life insurance is issued on a guaranteed basis up to certain limits with no evidence of insurability. Employees generally select the amount of guaranteed coverage equal to some multiple of their salaries, such as one to five times their annual salary. Higher amounts of insurance require evidence of insurability, usually based on a simplified medical questionnaire.
- *Mortality and expense charges.* Most group universal life plans have guaranteed mortality charges for three years; after that time, the group is experience-rated. Expense charges must

INSIGHT 22.1

Credit Insurance Overcharges Cost Consumers Billions of Dollars Annually

In 2000, consumers paid about $6 billion for credit insurance, but they would have paid only $3.5 billion if states had implemented the credit insurance rate standards of their insurance commissioners' own deliberative body, the National Association of Insurance Commissioners. *Consumers thereby paid $2.5 billion in overcharges in 2000—or 75 percent more than they should have had to pay. For one of the coverages—credit unemployment insurance—the overcharge was 1000 percent.*

Poor Value for Consumers

"In many states, credit life and credit disability insurance offers such poor value that consumers should not purchase it unless they are over age 50 or in poor health or both," said James Hunt, CFA's Life Actuary and coauthor of the report. "In most states, officials should lower maximum rates allowed, better enforce those rate caps, limit the sale of excessive amounts of credit life insurance and correct unfair refunds when debts are refinanced," said Hunt.

Consumer credit insurance is insurance sold in connection with a loan. The main coverages are credit life, credit disability, credit involuntary unemployment, credit leave of absence and credit property. Credit life insurance pays off the loan if the borrower dies, while credit disability, credit involuntary unemployment and credit leave of absence make the monthly loan payments in the event the borrower becomes disabled, involuntarily unemployed, or takes an approved family leave from work, respectively. Credit property pays to repair or replace property purchased (or pledged as collateral) with the loan.

Low Loss Ratio

The single most important measure of the reasonableness of credit insurance benefits in comparison to the cost is the *loss ratio*. The loss ratio is the ratio of benefits (also known as claims) paid by credit insurers to the premiums paid by consumers for the product. *The National Association of Insurance Commissioners (NAIC) model statutes and regulations for credit insurance specify a 60 percent minimum loss ratio. Yet, by 2000,* *the loss ratios for the major credit coverages were far below 60 percent.*

- *In 2000, the loss ratio for all coverages combined was only 34.2 percent, down from 42.5 percent in 1995.*
- *The 2000 premium and loss ratios by coverage were*

Credit Life	$2.1 billion	40.7%
Credit Disability	$2.3 billion	46.1%
Credit Unemployment	$1.1 billion	5.8%
Credit Property	$0.5 billion	14.7%

- *Total premiums for the four major coverages have been around $6 billion a year for the past several years. If a 60 percent loss ratio standard had been enforced, consumers would have paid only $3.5 billion in 2000. Overcharges came to $2.5 billion, meaning that consumers paid 75 percent more premiums than they should have.*
- *The countrywide credit life loss ratio peaked at about 45 percent in 1993 and declined to less than 41 percent in 2000. The countrywide credit disability loss peaked in 1991 at about 59 percent and dropped to about 46 percent in 2000.*
- *From 1995 to 2000, while the amount of credit unemployment sold jumped from $600 million to $1.1 billion, the loss ratios dropped from a low of 18.2 percent to only 5.8 percent.*

Credit insurance is regulated by the states—typically by state insurance commissioners. In almost every state, the law empowers the insurance commissioner to disapprove credit life and credit disability insurance premiums if the benefits provided are not reasonable in relation to the premiums. Most states establish minimum loss ratios as the basis for this standard. *Yet, the report found that almost half the states were failing to enforce existing loss ratio standards.* And other states without loss ratio standards were failing to protect credit insurance consumers from excessive charges.

Source: Adapted from *Credit Insurance Overcharges Hit $2.5 Billion Annually*, Consumer Federation of America, press release, November 15, 2001.

---

also be paid. These charges are generally lower than the expenses assessed against individual policies. Finally, there is a minimum interest rate guarantee on the cash values. Higher current rates are paid that change over time.

- *Premium flexibility.* Premiums can be reduced, increased, or even eliminated if the cash value is sufficient to pay current mortality and expense charges.
- *Loans and withdrawals.* Employees can make policy loans and withdrawals. The loan or withdrawal amount must be at least equal to a certain minimum amount, such as $250 or $500. The policy loan rate usually is based on some

index, such as Moody's composite bond yield. Interest credited to the cash values on the amounts borrowed is also reduced, such as 2 percent less than Moody's composite bond yield.

- *Options at retirement.* The retired employee has the option of continuing the universal life coverage, and the insurer bills the retired employee directly. The employee also has the option of terminating the coverage and withdrawing the cash value; electing a settlement option for liquidation of the cash value in the form of annuity income; or decreasing the amount of pure insurance so that the cash value is sufficient to keep the policy in force with no additional premiums required.
- *Dependent coverage.* A term insurance rider can be added to cover dependents, such as $10,000 to $50,000 on the spouse and $5000 to $10,000 on each child.

GROUP MEDICAL EXPENSE INSURANCE

Group medical expense insurance is an employee benefit that pays the cost of hospital care, physicians' and surgeons' fees, and related medical expenses. These plans are extremely important in providing financial security to employees and their families. Group plans currently account for more than 90 percent of the total premiums paid for medical expense insurance.

Group medical expense insurance is available from a number of sources. Major sources include the following:

- Commercial insurers
- Blue Cross and Blue Shield plans
- Managed Care organizations
- Self-insured plans by employers

Commercial Insurers

Commercial life and health insurers sell both individual and group medical expense plans. Some property and casualty insurers also sell medical expense coverages. Most individuals and families insured by commercial insurers are covered under group plans. The business is highly concentrated. Most of the business is written by a small number of insurers.

Commercial insurers also sponsor managed care plans that provide benefits to members in a cost-effective manner, including health maintenance organizations (HMOs) and preferred provider organizations (PPOs). Managed care plans are discussed in greater detail later in the chapter.

Blue Cross and Blue Shield Plans

Blue Cross and Blue Shield plans are medical expense plans that cover hospital expenses, physician's and surgeon's fees, ancillary charges, and other medical expenses. Major medical insurance is also available. The various plans sell individual, family, and group coverages. Most insureds are covered by group plans.

Blue Cross plans cover hospital expenses and other related expenses. The plans typically provide service benefits rather than cash benefits to the insured. Blue Cross plans usually pay the full cost of a semiprivate room, and payment is made directly to the hospital rather than to the insured.

Blue Shield plans cover physicians' and surgeons' fees and related medical expenses. Most plans today write both Blue Cross and Blue Shield coverages. The joint plans offer both basic medical expense benefits and major medical insurance. Finally, like commercial insurers, Blue Cross and Blue Shield plans also sponsor managed care plans, including HMOs and PPOs.

In the majority of states, Blue Cross and Blue Shield plans are nonprofit organizations that receive favorable tax treatment and are regulated under special legislation. However, to raise capital and become more competitive, several Blue Cross and Blue Shield plans have converted to a for-profit status with stockholders and a board of directors. In addition, many nonprofit plans own profit-seeking affiliates. Blue Cross and Blue Shield plans are discussed in greater detail in Chapter 25.

Managed Care Organizations

Managed care organizations are another source of group medical expense benefits. Managed care organizations generally are for-profit organizations that make available managed care plans to employers. Managed care is a generic term for medical expense benefits that are provided to covered employees in a cost effective manner. There is great emphasis on controlling costs, and the care provided by physicians is carefully monitored.

Managed care organizations typically sponsor **health maintenance organizations (HMOs)** and other types of managed care plans. Health maintenance organizations (HMOs) are managed care plans that provide broad, comprehensive health care services to the members for a fixed prepaid fee. As stated earlier, there is great emphasis on controlling costs. HMOs and other managed care plans are discussed later in this chapter.

Self-insured Plans by Employers

Many employers self-insure part or all of the health insurance benefits provided to their employees. **Self-insurance** (also called **self-funding**) *means that the employer pays part or all of the cost of providing health insurance to the employees.*

Self-insured plans are usually established with stop-loss insurance and an administrative services only contract. *Stop-loss insurance means that a commercial insurer will pay claims that exceed a certain dollar amount up to some maximum limit.* This arrangement protects employees when claims exceed a center level.

An *administrative services only (ASO) contract is a contract between an employer and a commercial insurer (or other third party) in which the insurer provides only administrative services.* These services can include plan design, claims processing, actuarial support, and record keeping.

Employers self-insure their medical expense plans for several reasons, including the following:

- *Under the Employee Retirement Income Security Act of 1974 (ERISA), self-insured plans generally are not subject to state regulation. Thus, a national employer does not have to comply with separate state laws.*
- *Costs may be reduced or increase less rapidly because of savings in state premium taxes, commissions, and the insurer's profit.*
- *The employer retains part or all of the funds needed to pay claims and earns interest until the claims are paid.*

- *Self-insured plans are exempt from state laws that require insured plans to offer certain state-mandated benefits.*

TYPES OF GROUP MEDICAL EXPENSE PLANS

Group medical expense plans have changed rapidly over time. Older plans were often called **traditional group indemnity plans** or fee-for-service plans. These plans permitted insureds considerable freedom in selecting their own physicians and other health care providers; the plans paid cash indemnity benefits for covered services up to certain maximum limits; and cost containment was not heavily stressed. It should be noted, however, that newer group indemnity plans have several cost-containment provisions, such as preadmission certification by which a covered person must be approved for admission into a hospital and second surgical opinions. In addition, traditional indemnity plans also use preferred provider networks to control costs. Preferred provider networks are discussed later in the chapter.

Two types of traditional group indemnity plans that merit some discussion are (1) basic medical expense insurance and (2) major medical insurance.

Basic Medical Expense Insurance

Basic medical expense insurance *is a generic name for group plans that provide only basic benefits.* The benefits are sufficient to pay routine medical expenses but generally are not designed to cover a catastrophic loss. Group basic medical expense plans typically provide the following benefits:

- Hospital expense insurance
- Surgical expense insurance
- Physicians' visits
- Miscellaneous benefits

Hospital expense insurance covers medical expenses incurred while in a hospital. Some older indemnity plans pay actual room and board charges up to some stated maximum, such as $500 per day. Newer plans typically pay **service benefits** in which the full cost of a semiprivate room is paid if the employee is hospitalized, subject to any deductible or coinsurance requirement. In addition to daily room and board benefits, most plans provide full or partial payment (generally up to some maximum dollar amount) for miscellaneous hospital charges, such as drugs, X-rays, and operating room charges.

Surgical expense insurance is usually included in a basic plan to help pay surgeons' and physicians' fees for surgical operations. Several methods are used to compensate surgeons. Older plans may use a *schedule approach* in which the various surgical operations are listed in a schedule, and a maximum dollar amount is specified for each procedure. A variation of the schedule approach is a *relative-value schedule* in which units or points are assigned to each operation based on the degree of difficulty. A conversion factor is then used to convert the relative value of the operation into a specific dollar amount paid to the physician.

Newer plans typically reimburse physicians on the basis of their **reasonable and customary charges.** A physician is paid his or her usual fee as long as it is considered reasonable and customary. Many insurers consider a fee to be reasonable and customary if it does not exceed the 85th or 90th percentile amount for a similar medical procedure performed by other physicians in the same area. However, insurers differ in how usual and customary fees are calculated. As a result, patients often must pay substantial amounts out-of-pocket because of "balance billing" by physicians for the remainder of the fee not paid by insurance.

Group basic medical expense plans also provide benefits for *physicians' visits* other than for surgery. Most plans cover physicians' visits only while the employee is hospitalized, but some plans cover office or home visits as well. The amount paid can be a fixed amount, or it can be based on the physician's reasonable and customary charges.

Finally, basic plans provide a wide variety of miscellaneous benefits. Depending on the plan, basic benefits may cover home health care visits by medical specialists, extended-care facility benefits, radiation therapy, diagnostic X-rays, CAT scans and magnetic resonance imaging (MRI), and supplemental accident benefits.

Basic medical expense plans have declined in relative importance over time. Employers that still provide basic benefits to their employees usually

supplement them with major medical benefits. We discuss group major medical insurance in the following section.

Major Medical Insurance

Most employers with group health insurance plans typically provide major medical insurance to their employees. **Major medical insurance** is designed to pay a high proportion of the covered expenses of a catastrophic illness or injury. **Major medical insurance** can be written as a supplement to a basic medical expense plan, or it can be combined with a basic plan to form a comprehensive major medical policy.

Supplemental Major Medical Insurance Supplemental major medical insurance *is designed to supplement the benefits provided by a basic plan.* Some medical expenses are not covered under a basic plan, or the benefits paid may be exhausted under the basic plan. Medical expenses not covered under a basic plan may be eligible for reimbursement under the supplemental major medical plan.

Supplemental major medical insurance plans have characteristics similar to the individual major medical policies described in Chapter 21, but the benefits have much higher limits and are more comprehensive.

Most supplemental major medical plans have high lifetime limits, such as $1 million to $5 million. A few plans have no limits at all. These high limits reflect the rapid increase in medical costs over time.

A **coinsurance provision** of 80 percent is typically found in supplemental major medical plans. However, the coinsurance provision is modified by a **stop-loss limit,** which places a dollar limit on the maximum amount that an individual must pay. Under a stop-loss provision, once the individual's annual out-of-pocket expenses exceed a certain amount, such as $2000, all remaining eligible medical expenses are paid in full.

A **corridor deductible** may be used to integrate a basic medical expense plan with a supplemental major medical plan. Before the supplemental major medical plan pays any benefits, a corridor deductible must be met. A *corridor deductible applies only to eligible medical expenses not covered by the basic medical expense plan.* As noted earlier, some medical expenses are not covered under a basic plan, or the expenses may be covered but the benefits paid by the basic plan are exhausted. These expenses may be eligible for reimbursement under the supplemental major medical plan, subject to a corridor deductible. This type of deductible can be illustrated by the following example:

Total medical expenses	$50,000
Paid by basic medical expense plan	40,000
Remaining medical expenses	$10,000
Corridor deductible paid by	
the insured	500
Balance of medical expenses	
to be paid	$9500
80 percent paid by supplemental	
major medical plan	7600
20 percent paid by the insured	$1900

Comprehensive Major Medical Insurance Many employers have comprehensive major medical plans for their employees. **Comprehensive major medical insurance** *is a combination of basic benefits and major medical insurance in one policy.* This type of plan is widely used by employers who want both basic benefits and major medical protection in a single policy. This type of plan is characterized by a deductible, such as $200 or $300 per year, by high maximum limits of $1 million to $5 million, and by coinsurance. In addition, the deductible and coinsurance provisions may not be applied to certain medical expenses. For example, in one plan, the deductible does not apply to hospital expenses. The first $3000 of covered hospital expenses are paid in full, and a coinsurance rate of 80 percent is applied to the remaining hospital expenses.

A **calendar-year deductible** is widely used in comprehensive major medical plans. The deductible has to be met only once during the calendar year. All covered medical expenses incurred by the insured during the year can be used to satisfy the deductible.

The deductible applies separately to the employee and each family member. However, to minimize the financial impact on the family, the major medical plan may contain a **family deductible provision.** Under this provision, additional deductibles for family members are waived if two or three separate deductibles have been satisfied by individual family members during the year.

Traditional group indemnity plans just discussed have declined in relative importance in recent years. In 2002, traditional indemnity plans enrolled only 6 percent of all covered employees, down from 22 percent in 1996. In contrast, managed care plans have grown rapidly over time. The following section discusses managed care plans.

MANAGED CARE PLANS

Employers and insurers have designed a variety of managed care plans to hold down the escalation in health care costs. **Managed care** *is a generic name for medical expense plans that provide covered services to the members in a cost-effective manner.* Under managed care plans, the employees' choice of physicians and hospitals may be limited to certain health care providers; cost control and cost reduction are heavily emphasized; utilization review is done at all levels; the quality of the care provided by physicians is carefully monitored and evaluated; health care providers share in the financial results through various risk-sharing techniques; and preventive care and healthy lifestyles are emphasized.

Managed care plans have grown rapidly over time. The proportion of workers covered by the major types of managed care plans increased from 58 percent in 1993 to about 93 percent at the beginning of 2001.[5]

There are several types of managed care plans. They include the following:

- Health maintenance organizations (HMOs)
- Preferred provider organizations (PPOs)
- Point-of-service (POS) plans
- Exclusive provider organizations (EPOs)

Health Maintenance Organizations (HMOs)

A *health maintenance organization (HMO) is an organized system of health care that provides comprehensive services to its members for a fixed, prepaid fee.* Many employers sponsor HMOs that provide comprehensive medical services to covered employees.

Basic Characteristics HMOs have several basic characteristics that distinguish them from traditional group indemnity plans.

- *Organized health care plan.* An HMO has the responsibility for organizing and delivering comprehensive health care services to its members. The HMO owns or leases medical facilities, enters into agreements with hospitals and physicians to provide medical services, hires ancillary personnel, and has general managerial control over the various services provided.
- *Broad, comprehensive health services.* An HMO provides broad, comprehensive health care services to the members. Most services generally are covered in full, with relatively few maximum limits on individual services. However, many HMOs limit the amount paid for the treatment of alcoholism and drug addiction. Covered services include hospital care, surgeons' and physicians' fees, maternity care, laboratory and X-ray services, outpatient, special-duty nursing, and numerous other services. Office visits to HMO physicians are covered either in full or at a nominal charge for each visit.
- *Restrictions on the choice of physician.* Traditional HMOs typically limit the choice of physicians and other health care providers to providers who are part of the HMO network. However, as discussed later, some HMOs allow employees to select health care providers outside of the plan network by payment of higher out-of-pocket costs. In addition, because HMOs operate in limited geographical areas, there may be limited coverage for medical care received outside of the area. HMOs typically cover only emergency medical treatment received outside of the geographical area of the HMO.
- *Payment of a fixed, prepaid fee.* HMO members pay a fixed, prepaid fee (usually monthly) for the medical services provided. High deductibles and coinsurance requirements are usually not emphasized. However, to control costs, many HMOs impose a coinsurance requirement for certain diseases, such as alcoholism and drug addiction. Some HMOs now impose an inpatient hospital deductible. In addition, there may be a nominal fee for certain services, such as $15 for an office visit.
- *Heavy emphasis on controlling costs.* HMOs place a heavy emphasis on controlling the cost of covered services. HMOs typically pay network physicians or medical groups a capitation fee. A

capitation fee *is a method of payment by which a physician or hospital receives a fixed annual payment for each plan member regardless of the frequency or type of service provided.* As such, HMO providers have no financial incentive to provide unnecessary medical care because their financial compensation does not increase.

Some HMOs pay physicians a salary, which also holds down costs because the provider has no financial incentive to provide unnecessary services. HMOs also contract with specialists and other providers to provide certain medical services at negotiated fees. In addition, a **gatekeeper physician** generally controls access to an expensive specialist. A gatekeeper physician is a primary care physician who determines whether medical care from a specialist is necessary. However, some HMOs now allow patients to bypass the primary care physician and see a specialist directly. Finally, HMOs emphasize preventive care and healthy lifestyles, which also tend to hold down costs.

Types of HMOs   There are several types of HMOs:

- *Staff model.* Under a staff model, physicians are employees of the HMO and are paid a salary and possibly an incentive bonus to hold down costs.
- *Group model.* Under a group model, physicians are employees of another group that has a contract with the HMO to provide medical services to its members. The HMO pays the group of physicians a monthly or annual capitation fee for each member. As stated earlier, a capitation fee is a fixed amount for each member regardless of the number of services provided. In return, the group agrees to provide all covered services to the members during the year. The group model typically has a closed panel of physicians that requires members to select physicians affiliated with the HMO.
- *Network model.* Under a network model, the HMO contracts with two or more independent group practices to provide medical services to covered members. The HMO pays a fixed monthly fee for each member to the medical group. The medical group then decides how the fees will be distributed among the individual physicians.

■ *Individual practice association plan (IPA).* A final type of HMO is an **individual practice association plan (IPA).** An IPA is an open panel of physicians who work out of their own offices and treat patients on a fee-for-service basis. However, the individual physicians agree to treat HMO members at reduced fees. Physicians may be paid a capitation fee for each member or may be paid a reduced fee. For example, they may be paid only 90 percent of their usual fee for an office visit. In addition, to encourage cost containment, most IPAs have risk-sharing agreements with the participating physicians. Payments may be reduced if the plan experience is poor. A bonus is paid if the plan experience is better than expected.

Preferred Provider Organizations

A **preferred provider organization (PPO)** is a plan that contracts with health care providers to provide medical services to the members at reduced fees. The employer, insurer, or other group negotiates contracts with physicians, hospitals, and other providers of care to provide certain medical services to the plan members at discounted fees. To encourage patients to use PPO providers, deductibles and co-payment charges are reduced. In addition, the patient may be charged a lower fee for certain routine treatments, or offered increased benefits such as preventive health care services.

PPOs should not be confused with HMOs. There are three important differences.[6] *First, PPO providers typically do not provide medical care on a prepaid basis, but are paid on a fee-for-service basis as their services are used.* However, as stated earlier, the fees charged are below the provider's regular fee.

Second, unlike an HMO, patients are not required to use a preferred provider but have freedom of choice every time they need care. However, the patients have a financial incentive to use a preferred provider because the deductible and co-payment charges are reduced. In addition, if the health care provider's actual charge exceeds the negotiated fee, the provider absorbs the excess amount. Savings can be substantial. For example, if a surgeon who participates in a PPO charges a normal fee of $4000 for a knee operation but the negotiated fee is only $3000,

the patient does not have to pay the additional $1000. The surgeon absorbs this amount.

Finally, most PPOs do not use a gatekeeper physician, and employees do not have to get permission from a primary care physician to see a specialist.

PPOs offer the major advantage of controlling health care costs because provider fees are negotiated at a discount. PPOs also help physicians to build up their practice. Patients benefit because they pay less for their medical care. Enrollments in PPOs have increased rapidly over time and accounted for 54 percent of all employee enrollments in 2003.

Point-of-Service Plans

A **point-of-service (POS)** plan is another important type of managed care plan. A point-of-service (POS) plan is typically structured as an HMO, but members are allowed to go outside the network for medical care. *If patients see providers who are in the network, they pay little or nothing out of pocket, which is similar to an HMO. However, if the patients receive care from providers outside the network, the care is covered, but the patients must pay substantially higher deductibles and co-payments.* For example, a patient who sees a physician outside the network may be required to pay a $500 annual deductible and a coinsurance charge of 30 percent. If the patient sees a participating physician within the network, there is no additional charge.

The POS plan has the major advantage of preserving freedom of choice for plan members; it also eliminates the fear that plan members will not be able to see a physician or specialist of their choice. The major disadvantage is the substantially higher cost that a member must pay to see a provider outside the network.

Exclusive Provider Organizations

An **exclusive provider organization (EPO)** is a plan that does not cover medical care received outside a network of preferred providers. If patients receive medical care outside the network, they must pay the entire cost themselves. Preferred providers who are in the network are reimbursed on a fee-for-service basis based on a schedule of negotiated fees.

Exhibit 22.1
Total Health Benefit Cost per Active Employee, 1994–2003

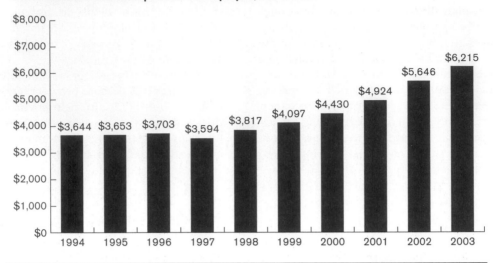

Source: *Surprise Slow-Down in US Health Benefit Cost Increase,* Mercer Human Resource Consulting, National Survey of Employer-Sponsored Health Plans. Used with permission.

Advantages of Managed Care Plans

Managed care plans have a number of advantages. Managed care plans generally have lower hospital and surgical utilization rates than traditional group indemnity plans; plan members pay substantially lower out-of-pocket costs if they use network providers; and employees do not have to file claim forms.

Proponents of managed care also maintain that managed care plans have reduced the rate of increase in health care costs over time because of the heavy emphasis on cost control. While this may have been true earlier, it is not true today. At the time of this writing, health care costs continue to increase. *According to a survey of employer health plans by Mercer Human Resource Consulting, total health benefit costs per active employee increased from $5646 in 2002 to $6215 in 2003, or an increase of 10.1 percent (see Exhibit 22.1).* The average increase expected in 2004 is 13 percent.

According to Mercer Human Resource Consulting, employer health care costs are rising for several reasons:[7] (1) the average age of the labor force is increasing, which results in higher medical costs as workers age; (2) health care providers have

more leverage in negotiating higher reimbursement rates than they did a few years ago; (3) mergers and acquisitions and general consolidation in the managed care industry have reduced competition; (4) new medical technology, such as genomics and new electronic diagnostic techniques, drive up health care costs, and (5) plan designs of the past decade have insulated employees from the true cost of medical care because financial involvement generally is limited only to the payment of deductibles or copayment charges. For example, many employees believe that a copayment charge of $10, $15, or $25 is the true cost of a prescription drug when the actual cost may be ten times higher. Cost insulation creates an environment in which employees have no incentive to hold down costs or reduce overutilization of plan benefits.

Disadvantages of Managed Care Plans

According to many critics, the major disadvantage of managed care plans is that the quality of care is being reduced because of the heavy emphasis on cost control. Critics argue that access to specialists may

EXHIBIT 22.2
Estimated Deaths Attributable to Failure to Deliver Recommended Care:
Selected Measures/Conditions (U.S. Population)

Measure	Avoidable Deaths Each Year
Beta-Blocker Treatment	1,700
Breast Cancer Screening	2,500
Cervical Cancer Screening	700
Cholesterol Management-Control	6,500
Controlling High Blood Pressure	28,300
Diabetes Care–HbA1c Control	13,600
Prenatal Care	1,500
Smoking Cessation	2,700
Total	**57,500**

SOURCE: Table 1, National Committee for Quality Assurance, *The State of Health Care Quality, 2003,* Washington, DC, 2003.

be delayed because some gatekeeper physicians do not promptly refer sick patients to specialists because of the additional cost to the plan; some patients who should be hospitalized are not admitted into a hospital; and certain diagnostic tests are not performed. In addition, critics agree that for-profit HMOs often skimp on preventive care to maximize profits.

Many physicians criticize managed care plans because of the restrictions placed on their freedom to treat patients. HMO physicians must often obtain approval from plan administrators or insurers before certain diagnostic tests or procedures can be given; they may have to argue for additional days of hospital coverage for patients who are too sick to be released; referral to a specialist may be denied or delayed; and prescription drugs may be limited only to certain drugs on an approved list. In addition, physicians argue that some HMOs impose a "gag rule" on the right of the doctor to discuss with patients alternative methods of treatment not approved by the HMO. Thus, many plan physicians believe the traditional doctor–patient relationship is being seriously compromised by outside third parties. As a result, a rising number of doctors are cutting their links to HMOs.

In addition, managed care plans commonly provide financial incentives to health care providers to hold down costs, such as an incentive bonus based on the profitability of the plan. Critics argue that network physicians often have a financial conflict of interest between providing the highest-quality medical care to their patients and holding down costs to increase plan profits and the amount of their bonus.

Finally, many workers are unaware of the various restrictions and limitations in managed care plans, and state regulation of HMOs varies widely.

Although many physicians and patients are dissatisfied with managed care plans, studies show that the quality of health care plans is improving. The National Committee for Quality Assurance (NCQA), a major accreditation organization, conducts an annual survey of managed care plans and rates the plans based on the quality of services provided. The 2003 survey showed that the quality of health care plans has improved significantly for millions of Americans over time.[8] Despite improvements, however, serious problems remain. The NCQA concluded that there are severe "quality gaps" in the nation's health care system that prevent millions of patients from receiving the best medical care possible. The term "quality gap" means that

Exhibit 22.3
National Employee Enrollment in Health Care Plans, 1993–2003
(% of All Covered Employees)

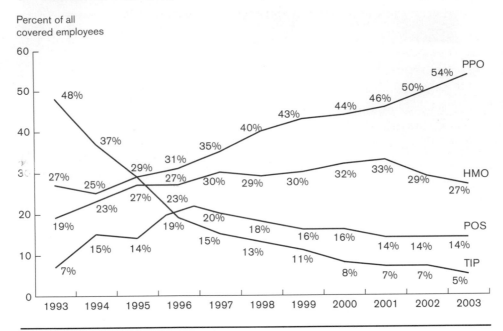

Source: *Surprise Slow-Down in US Health Benefit Cost Increase*, Mercer Human Resource Consulting, National Survey of Employer-Sponsored Health Plans. Used with permission.

health care providers often fail to provide the recommended health care services that medical science has shown to be effective in treating certain diseases. As a result, quality gaps cause more than 57,000 avoidable deaths each year, nearly 41 million sick days, and more than $11 billion in lost productivity (see Exhibit 22.2).[9]

Current Developments in Managed Care Plans

Managed care plans are constantly changing. Some current developments that merit discussion include (1) declining HMO enrollments, (2) changes in plan design, and (3) new cost management strategies.

Declining HMO Enrollments HMO enrollments grew steadily in the 1980s and early 1990s. *More recently, however, HMO enrollments declined from 33 percent of all covered employees in 2001 to*

27 percent in 2003. Enrollments in traditional indemnity plans (TIP) have also declined (see Exhibit 22.3). In contrast, enrollments in PPOs continue to increase. Employers have become dissatisfied with HMOs in recent years because of substantially higher HMO premiums and plan costs.[10]

The decline in HMO enrollments is also due to employee dissatisfaction. Many employees are dissatisfied because of higher premiums, higher deductibles and copayment charges, and disruptions brought about by network changes in physicians and health care plans. Some physicians drop out of HMOs or their contracts are not renewed, while mergers in the managed care industry often cause changes in health care plans. The result is employee dissatisfaction and withdrawal from the HMO.

Changes in Plan Design To control costs, employers have increased their cost-sharing provisions

INSIGHT 22.2

Defined-Contribution Health Plan that Puts Employee in Charge of Spending Catches On

Under a defined-contribution health plan, each employee gets a set medical budget—say $2000 a year—which can be spent on virtually any health service. Once that initial money is used up, the employee pays for medical costs up to a certain amount out of his or her own pocket, like a deductible. Beyond that level, the employer begins paying again (see box).

The plan's structure is supposed to motivate employees to ask about medical fees and even shop around to minimize their spending. "Nobody spends other people's money the way they spend their own money," says Maureen Cotter, a health-care consultant at Watson Wyatt Worldwide in Washington, D.C. who has been working with many employers considering a defined-contribution program.

But in shifting the responsibility for health-care spending from companies to individuals, these new plans have also raised fears that employees will suffer. There are safeguards, such as spending caps, that protect employees who face catastrophic health expenses. But whether workers will short-change their own health to save a buck—skipping an expensive MRI, for example, or not filling a prescription—remains to be seen.

Medtronic Inc., a medical-device maker based in Minneapolis, offered 10,000 of its employees a defined-contribution plan marketed by a small company in the same city called **Definity Health** Corp. About 1300 workers signed up for it at the beginning of 2001. Now, after a year on the plan, Debra Schmidt, a 43-year-old Medtronic administrative assistant, says she is making out better than she was on her HMO plan.

Ms. Schmidt, who has asthma and a thyroid problem, sees an endocrinologist every three months and an asthma specialist once or twice a year. With her HMO, she says, "I had to call, I had to go to the general practitioner first, then pay a copay there, then get a referral. I was taking more out of my pocket," she says. Then, the endocrinologist she liked dropped out of the HMO network.

Now, under the Definity plan, Ms. Schmidt chooses whichever doctor she wants and never has to seek a referral or get permission to see a specialist. She pays $77 a month for Definity's plan, compared with $162 a month in premiums for her HMO.

At the beginning of the year, Medtronic put $2000 into Ms. Schmidt's Definity medical account. When she visited a doctor or filled a prescription, the entire bill was subtracted from the $2000. Because her family used a lot of medical services and pharmaceuticals in 2001, her $2000 budget was used up by August. Ms. Schmidt knew she would be a chronic

In the Driver's Seat
An example of how a defined-contribution health plan works:

- Employee John gets a medical account of $2000 from his employer to be used on virtually any health service.
- Every medical or pharmaceutical bill is deducted from the $2000.
- After the $2000 is used up, John is responsible for his own health-care costs, up to $1000.
- After John has used up his $1000, his company begins paying again at 100% if he stays in the network.
- If John doesn't use up his initial $2000, he can roll it into the following year.

user of medical services, so her $77 monthly premium reflects her choice of a $1000 deductible, which kicks in after the initial $2000 that Medtronic put in is used up.

So, beginning in August, Ms. Schmidt had to pay for services and pharmaceuticals herself, up to $1000. "That took us through Thanksgiving," she says. For the rest of 2001, Medtronic picked up 100% of her medical bills if she stayed in the network, and 80% if she went outside.

Davie Ness, vice president of compensation and benefits at Medtronic, says employees on the plan use a 24-hour nurse phone line four times more often than people in other plans. Apparently, they are calling first to inquire about a medical condition rather than rushing off to see a doctor.

Definity says it, too, has witnessed consumers making money-saving choices. On average, it says, each of its 6600 members is filling six prescriptions a year, compared with an industry average of eight or nine. Does this indicate they might be endangering their health? No, Definity says, arguing that much of the lower use reflects members using more over-the-counter remedies for colds and allergies.

Medtronic says it's still too early to know whether Definity will be a money saver. But at another employer, Ridgeview Medical Center, a Minneapolis hospital system where most of the 700 employees signed up with Definity in 2001, the system saved $480,000 in the first eight months. The results came from fewer employee visits to emergency rooms, as well as fewer expensive tests such as CT scans.

Source: Adapted from Barbara Martinez, "Health Plan That Puts Employees in Charge of Spending Catches On," *The Wall Street Journal*, January 8, 2002, pp. B1, B4. © 2002. Reprinted with permission via Copyright Clearance Center.

by requiring employees to pay higher deductibles, higher coinsurance and copayment charges, and higher maximum annual out-of-pocket expenses. Employers are also redesigning their health care plans to make them more cost effective. Two important changes in plan design include (1) three-tier copayment charges for prescription drugs, and (2) consumer directed health plans.

- *Three-tier copayment charges for prescription drugs.* To control the substantial increase in the cost of prescription drugs, many employers now use a three-tier pricing system. Copayment charges are lower if employees use less expensive generic drugs. If employees use a brand-name drug that is on an approved list (called a formulary), copayment charges are higher. If the brand name drug is not included in the formulary, the copayment charge is even higher.
- *Consumer-directed health care plans.* Some large employers are now making consumer-directed health care plans available to employees as an option. We noted earlier that employees are often insulated from the true cost of medical care. A consumer-directed health plan is designed to make employees more sensitive to the cost of medical care and to give them a financial incentive to avoid unnecessary care and seek out low-cost providers. Under such plans, employees have an employer-funded account to pay for routine medical expenses; in addition, employees are covered for a serious illness or injury under a high-deductible or major medical plan. A *defined contribution plan* is one example of a consumer-directed health care plan (see Insight 22.2).

New Cost Management Strategies

In addition to changes in plan design, employers are using new cost management strategies to hold down costs. These strategies include (1) collective purchasing arrangements, (2) tiered networks, and (3) disease management programs.[11]

- *Collective purchasing arrangements.* Some larger employers are using collective purchasing arrangements to hold down costs. This means that larger employers band together and collectively negotiate for lower rates.

- *Tiered networks.* In addition to prescription drugs, many PPOs are now using tiered networks for other health care providers. A tiered network is a plan in which employees receive a higher reimbursement rate or pay a lower copayment charge if they participate in a narrower network than that found in a typical PPO. The objective is to encourage patients to use less costly hospitals and doctors instead of more expensive providers. Proponents argue that if patients have to pay more for their care out-of-pocket, they will opt for less expensive services. Insight 22.3 discusses a tiered network plan in which patients pay higher out-of-pocket costs for hospital stays in hospitals that are not part of the network.
- *Disease management programs.* Many large employers have health care web sites that provide employees with information on self-care, health risk assessment, health care decision tools, and management of certain diseases. The top three disease management programs offered provide information about diabetes, heart disease, and asthma.[12]

HEALTH SAVINGS ACCOUNTS

Congress recently enacted the Medicare Prescription Drug, Improvement, and Modernization Act of 2003, which provides a prescription drug benefit for beneficiaries and updates the program. The new law also allows all eligible persons under age 65 to establish health savings accounts and receive favorable income tax treatment. A **health savings account (HSA)** *is tax-exempt trust or custodial account established exclusively for the purpose of paying qualified medical expenses of the account beneficiary who is covered under a high-deductible health insurance plan.* To have a qualified HSA, you must purchase a high-deductible health insurance policy and cannot be covered by another low-deductible plan. The annual deductible for an individual must be at least $1000, and annual out-of-pocket expenses cannot exceed $5000. For family coverage, the annual deductible must be at least $2000, and annual out-of-pocket expenses cannot exceed $10,000. The family deductible applies to the entire family and not to each family member.

Insurers Begin Charging More for Some Hospitals and Doctors

Some insurance companies are trying yet another tactic to drive down health care costs, using tiered medical coverage to steer patients from high-priced hospitals and doctors to less expensive ones.

The new plans establish price categories for hospitals and doctors in the same way that many plans now are "tiering" prescription drugs, requiring patients to pay more themselves for the costlier alternatives.

The rationale is the same: If some of the money comes from their own pockets, patients will opt for cheaper services.

Consumer advocates and hospital executives fear the plans will force people to make medical decisions based on cost rather than quality. The insurers say the wide differences in prices for similar services aren't always justified. Hospital prices, in particular, can vary by thousands of dollars in the same city.

CompCareBlue, a unit of BlueCross & BlueShield United of Wisconsin, began offering a tiered product last month. Michael Bernstein, CompCareBlue's president, called it "probably the most elegant way for consumers to understand the price differences."

He said all the hospitals included in the plan provide quality care, and that some major academic medical centers are included in the policy's low-cost option.

"We think every hospital in the network measures up on quality," said Bernstein. "We based the program solely on cost to us, because we didn't feel equipped to make quality distinctions."

Plans typically have two tiers—one less expensive and one more—with a third category for out-of-network services.

One plan option, offered by CompCareBlue would require patients to pay nearly $3000 for an out-of-network hospital stay. Treatment at the hospital in the least-expensive tier would cost the patient $300. Other plans have less dramatic differences, mandating patients to pay a $250 per-stay premium for more expensive hospitals.

Tiered hospitalization plans cost 5 percent to 15 percent less than traditional policies, which will require the same co-payment or patient fee no matter what the hospital's charge is.

Bernstein said his company's plan was designed for employers that want to continue to offer coverage to workers without the premium rate hikes that are accompanying the rise in health care costs.

Hospital costs are becoming a bigger factor in those costs. Spending on hospital inpatient services increased 7.1 percent last year—nearly three times the 2000 increase, according to a survey by the Center for Studying Health System Change, a Washington, D.C.-based research institute. Outpatient services costs rose 16.3 percent, outpacing prescription drug spending, which grew 13 percent.

Hewitt Associates estimates health care costs will grow 15.4 percent in 2003 after rising 13.7 percent this year and 10.2 percent in 2001.

Other companies that began offering tiered plans this year are PacifiCare of California, Blue Shield of California and Waltham-Mass.-based Tufts Health Plan.

Jamie Court, executive director of the Foundation for Taxpayer and Consumer Rights, said the new plans hurt poorer patients.

"These products create a barrier to access for those with great medical need but little money," he said.

Insurers hope hospitals that charge more will feel the competitive need to lower prices. Hospital officials say it's not that simple.

"These programs don't lower costs, they simply shift them to the consumer," said Carmela Coyle, senior vice president for policy at the American Hospital Association.

She said an institution's location, specialties or staff all are important factors that a patient should be able to consider without regard to cost.

Hospitals in the Tufts Health Plan are divided into two categories: community hospitals and academic medical centers, with the latter costing consumers about $250 more per stay.

HSA contributions can made by individuals, their employers, and family members Contributions to the HSA account are tax deductible up to certain limits; investment earnings accumulate income-tax free; and distributions from the account are tax free if used to pay for qualified medical expenses. If the employer contributes to the plan, the contributions are excludable from the employee's gross income.

For 2004, total contributions for individual coverage are limited to the annual deductible, or $2600 ($5150 for family coverage), whichever is lower. For 2004, individuals between ages 55 and 65 can make an additional catch up contribution of $500, which will gradually rise to $1000 in 2009. As stated earlier, distributions from the account that are used to pay nonreimbursable qualified medical expenses are not taxable. Distributions prior to age 65 for nonqualified withdrawals generally are subject to an income tax and a 10 percent tax penalty. Finally, once an individual attains age 65 or goes on Medicare, he or she can no longer contribute to an HSA.

Patients' Bill of Rights

Because of dissatisfaction with managed care plans, federal legislation has been introduced that would protect the rights of patients in managed care plans. Legislation is considered necessary because of the denial of care and widespread dissatisfaction with managed care plans voiced by both patients and physicians.

Several proposals have been introduced. One proposal includes the following:

- Allows patients harmed by the denial of care the right to sue the managed care plan.
- Requires health plans to pay for emergency-room care even if the hospital is outside the network.
- Allows women to see obstetricians and gynecologists without prior approval and to designate them as primary-care physicians.
- Requires health plans to pay routine health care costs associated with clinical trials.
- Defines "medical necessity" and prohibits plans from interfering with a doctor's care if the services provided are medically necessary.
- Requires health plans to pay for an overnight hospital stay for a patient who has a mastectomy if the doctor and patient want it.
- Allows patients who are pregnant or undergoing a plan of treatment the right to keep their doctors for 90 days even if the doctor leaves the network.
- Allows patients to appeal denials first through an internal process and then to outside experts.

Finally, it should be noted that most states already have laws that require health insurance plans to include most of the provisions contained in the various federal proposals (except for the right of consumers to sue health insurance plans directly).

GROUP MEDICAL EXPENSE CONTRACTUAL PROVISIONS

Group medical expense insurance plans contain numerous contractual provisions that can have a significant financial impact on the insured. Three important provisions deal with (1) preexisting conditions, (2) coordination of benefits, and (3) continuation of group health insurance.

Preexisting Conditions

Group medical expense plans often contain a **preexisting-conditions** provision that excludes coverage for a medical condition for a limited period after the worker enters the plan. The purposes of this provision are to reduce adverse selection against the insurer and to control employer costs.

In 1996, Congress enacted the **Health Insurance Portability and Accountability Act (HIPAA),** which places restrictions on the right of insurers and employers to deny or limit coverage for preexisting conditions.

The following discussion summarizes the major provisions of the law dealing with preexisting conditions:

- Employer-sponsored group health insurance plans cannot exclude or limit coverage for a preexisting condition for more than 12 months (18 months for late enrollees). A *preexisting condition is defined as a medical condition diagnosed or treated during the previous six months.* A preexisting condition exclusion cannot be applied to pregnancy, newly born children, or adopted children.
- After the initial 12-month period expires, no new preexisting condition period can be imposed on workers who maintain continuous coverage with no more than a 63-day gap in coverage, even if the workers should change jobs or health care plans.

- *Insurers and employers must give credit for previous coverage of less than 12 months with respect to any preexisting condition exclusion found in the new health plan.* For example, a worker with a preexisting condition who was previously insured for eight months under a group plan when he or she changes jobs or health plans would face a maximum additional exclusion of four months for a preexisting condition, rather than the normal 12 months.
- Discrimination based on health status is prohibited. Employers that offer health insurance to employees and dependents cannot exclude, drop from coverage, or charge higher premiums based on health status. Health status is broadly defined to include the individual's medical condition; physical and mental illness; medical history; claims experience; evidence of insurability, including conditions arising out of acts of domestic violence; genetic information; and disability.
- The law also guarantees the availability of group health insurance to small employers. Commercial insurers, HMOs, and other groups issuing health insurance coverages are prohibited from denying coverage to firms that employ between 2 and 50 employees.

Because of limits on preexisting conditions and credit for previous and continuous coverage, employees will no longer be afraid to change jobs for fear of losing their group health insurance protection. As a result, they can change jobs and still be assured of health insurance coverage. Thus, the law makes the health insurance protection "portable."

However, portability does not mean that employees can take their present group health insurance benefits with them when they change jobs. **Portability** *means that when employees change jobs, the new employer or health plan must give them credit for previous and continuous health insurance coverage.* When the employees leave their present job, the insurer or employer must provide information showing how long they were covered while working at that job. The worker then presents this documentation to the new employer or health plan. If a worker has been covered for 12 months or more by a previous employer or health plan and does not

have a gap in coverage of more than 63 days, the worker is eligible for coverage under the new employer's plan even though he or she has a preexisting condition.

Coordination of Benefits

Group medical insurance plans typically contain a **coordination-of-benefits provision,** which specifies the order of payment when an insured is covered under two or more group health insurance plans. Total recovery under all plans is limited to 100 percent of covered expenses. The purpose is to prevent overinsurance and duplication of benefits if an insured is covered by more than one plan.

The coordination-of-benefit provisions in most group plans are based on rules developed by the National Association of Insurance Commissioners (NAIC). These rules are complex and are beyond the scope of this text to discuss in detail. The following summarizes the major provisions based on the NAIC rules.

- *Coverage as an employee is usually primary to coverage as a dependent.* For example, Karen and Chris Swift both work, and each is insured as a dependent under the other's group medical insurance plan. If Karen incurs covered medical expenses, her plan pays first. She then submits any unreimbursed expenses (such as the deductible and coinsurance payments) to Chris's insurer for payment. No more than 100 percent of the eligible medical expenses are paid under both plans.
- With respect to dependent children, if the parents are married or are not separated, *the plan of the parent whose birthday occurs first during the year is primary; the plan of the parent with the later birthday is secondary.* For example, if Karen's birthday is in January and Chris's birthday is in July, Karen's plan would pay first if their son is hospitalized. Chris's plan would be secondary.
- If the parents of dependent children are not married, or are separated (regardless of whether they have ever been married), or are divorced, and there is no court decree specifying who is responsible for the child's health care expenses, the following rules apply:

— The plan of the parent who is awarded custody pays first.

— The plan of the step-parent who is the spouse of the parent awarded custody pays second.

— The plan of the parent without custody pays third.

— The plan of the step-parent who is the spouse of the parent without custody pays last.

Continuation of Group Health Insurance

Employees often quit their jobs, are laid off, or are fired. If a qualifying event occurs that results in a loss of coverage, employees and covered dependents can elect to remain in the employer's health insurance plan for a limited period under the Consolidated Omnibus Budget Reconciliation Act of 1985 (also known as COBRA). The **COBRA law** applies to firms with 20 or more employees. *A qualifying event includes termination of employment for any reason (except gross misconduct), divorce or legal separation, death of the employee, and attainment of a maximum age by dependent children.* If the worker loses his or her job or no longer works the required number of hours, the terminated worker and his or her covered dependents can elect to remain in the employer's plan for as long as 18 months. However, the worker must pay 102 percent of the group insurance rate. If the worker dies or is divorced or legally separated or has a child who is no longer eligible for coverage, covered dependents have the right to remain in the group plan for up to three years.

After the period of protection under COBRA expires, some workers with preexisting conditions may be unable to obtain individual health insurance. The Health Insurance Portability and Accountability Act guarantees individual health insurance to eligible persons with no evidence of insurability if certain conditions are met. Eligible persons with health problems are guaranteed individual health insurance if they can meet the following requirements: (1) have employment-based health insurance for at least 18 months, (2) are ineligible for COBRA or have exhausted their COBRA coverage, and (3) are ineligible for coverage under any other employment-based health plan. The insurance provided is a guaranteed renewable policy.

GROUP DENTAL INSURANCE

Group dental insurance helps pay the cost of normal dental care and also covers damage to teeth from an accident. Dental insurance has the principal advantage of helping employees meet the costs of regular dental care. It also encourages insureds to see their dentists on a regular basis, thereby preventing or detecting dental problems before they become serious.

Types of Plans

There are two basic types of group dental insurance plans.[13] Under a **scheduled dental insurance plan,** the various dental services are listed in a schedule, and a flat dollar amount is paid for each service. If the dentist charges more than the specified amount, the patient must pay the difference.

Under a **nonscheduled dental insurance plan** (also called **comprehensive dental insurance**), most dental services are covered, including oral examinations, X-rays, cleaning, fillings, extractions, inlays, bridgework and dentures, oral surgery, root canals, and orthodontia. Dentists are reimbursed on the basis of their reasonable and customary charges subject to any limitations on benefits stated in the plan.

Cost Controls

To control costs and reduce adverse selection against the insurer when the plan is initially installed, several cost controls are used. They include the following:

- Deductibles and coinsurance
- Maximum limit on benefits
- Waiting periods
- Exclusions
- Predetermination-of-benefits provision

Most dental insurance plans use *deductibles* and **coinsurance** to control costs. The coinsurance percentage may vary depending on the type of service. To encourage regular visits to a dentist, many plans do not impose any coinsurance requirements for one or two routine dental examinations each year. However, fillings and oral surgery may be paid only at a rate of 80 percent, while the cost of orthodontia or dentures is may be paid at a lower rate of 50 percent.

Maximum limits on benefits are also used to control costs. There may be a maximum annual limit on the amount paid, such as $2000 during the calendar year. Another approach is to impose a lifetime maximum on certain types of dental services, such as a lifetime maximum of $5000 for dentures.

Waiting periods for certain types of services are used to control costs as well. For example, some plans do not cover dentures until the employee is insured for at least one year, and there may be only one replacement of dentures for each five-year period.

Certain *exclusions* are used to reduce costs. Common exclusions include cosmetic dental work, such as capping a tooth; replacement of lost or stolen dental devices, such as dentures or a space retainer; and benefits provided under a workers compensation or similar law.

A *predetermination-of-benefits provision* is also used to control costs. Under this provision, if the cost of dental treatment exceeds a certain amount, such as $300, the dentist submits a plan of treatment to the insurer. The insurer then specifies the services covered and how much the plan will pay. The employee is informed of the amount the plan will pay and then makes a decision on whether to proceed with the proposed plan of treatment.

Finally, it should be pointed out that, just as in medical expense insurance, there are dental HMOs, PPOs, and self-funded plans by employers that provide dental insurance to employees.

GROUP DISABILITY-INCOME INSURANCE

Group disability-income insurance pays weekly or monthly cash payments to employees who are disabled from accidents or illness. There are two basic types of plans: (1) short-term plans and (2) long-term plans.

Short-Term Plans

Many employers have short-term plans that pay disability benefits for relatively short periods ranging from 13 weeks to two years. The majority of short-term plans sold today pay benefits for a maximum period of 26 weeks. In addition, most plans have a short elimination period of one to seven days for sickness, while accidents are typically covered from the first day of disability. The elimination period reduces nuisance claims, holds down costs, and discourages malingering and excessive absenteeism.

Most short-term plans cover only **nonoccupational disability,** which means that an accident or illness must occur off the job. *Disability is usually defined in terms of the worker's own occupation. You are considered totally disabled if you are unable to perform all of the duties of your own occupation.* Partial disability is seldom covered under a group short-term plan; you must be totally disabled to qualify.

The amount of disability-income benefits is related to the worker's normal earnings and is typically equal to some percentage of weekly earnings, such as 50 to 70 percent. Thus, if Amy's weekly earnings are $600 and the plan replaces 70 percent of earnings, she would collect a maximum weekly benefit of $420 if she becomes disabled.

In addition, short-term plans have relatively few exclusions. As noted earlier, a disability that occurs on the job is usually not covered, because occupational disability is covered under a workers compensation law. Also, except for very small groups, preexisting conditions are covered immediately. Most plans also cover alcoholism, drug addiction, and nervous and mental disorders.

Long-Term Plans

Many employers also have long-term plans that pay benefits for longer periods, typically ranging from two years to age 65. However, if the disability occurs beyond age 65, benefits are paid for a limited period. For example, under the plan of one disability insurer, if the worker is younger than 60 at the time of disability, the maximum benefit period is to age 65. However, if a worker age 66 becomes disabled, the maximum benefit period is only 21 months.

A dual definition of disability is typically used to determine whether a worker is totally disabled. *For the first two years, you are considered disabled if you are unable to perform all of the duties of your own occupation. After two years, you are still considered disabled if you are unable to work in any occupation for which you are reasonably fitted by education, training, and experience.* In addition, in contrast to short-term plans, long-term plans typically cover both occupational and nonoccupational disability.

The disability-income benefits are usually paid monthly, and the maximum monthly benefits are substantially higher than the benefits paid by short-term plans. The maximum monthly benefit is generally limited to 50 to 70 percent of the employee's normal earnings. Most plans commonly pay maximum monthly benefits of $2000, $3000, $4000, or even higher amounts. A waiting period of three to six months is typically required before the benefits are payable.

To reduce malingering and moral hazard, other disability-income benefits paid by the employer are taken into consideration. If the disabled worker is also receiving Social Security or workers compensation benefits, the long-term disability benefit is reduced accordingly. However, many plans limit the reduction only to the amount of the initial Social Security disability benefit. Thus, if Social Security disability benefits are increased because of increases in the cost of living, the long-term disability-income benefit is not reduced further.

Some long-term plans have additional supplemental benefits. Under the *cost-of-living adjustment,* benefits paid to disabled employees are adjusted annually for increases in the cost of living. However, there may be a maximum limit on the percentage increase in benefits.

Under the *pension accrual benefit,* the plan makes a pension contribution so that the disabled employee's pension benefit remains intact. For example, if both Carlos and his employer contribute 6 percent of his salary into a pension plan, and Carlos becomes disabled, the plan would pay an amount equal to 12 percent of his monthly salary into the company's pension plan for as long as he remains disabled. Thus, Carlos would still receive his pension at the normal retirement age.

Finally, if the disabled worker dies, the plan may pay monthly *survivor income benefits* to an eligible surviving spouse or children for a limited period—such as two years—following the disabled worker's death.

CAFETERIA PLANS

The final part of this chapter deals with cafeteria plans. **Cafeteria plans** *allow employees to select those employee benefits that best meet their specific needs.* Instead of a single benefits package that applies to all employees, cafeteria plans allow employees to select among the various group life, medical expense, disability, dental, and other plans that are offered. Cafeteria plans also allow employers to introduce new benefits to meet the specific needs of certain employees.

Although cafeteria plans vary among employers, they share certain common characteristics. First, in many plans, the employer gives each employee a certain number of dollars or credits that can be spent on the different benefits or taken as cash. If taken as cash, the employer's credits are taxed as income to the employee.

Second, many cafeteria plans are also *premium-conversion plans,* which is a generic name for a plan that allows employees to make their premium contributions for plan benefits with before-tax dollars. Premium-conversion plans are commonly used for group health and dental insurance. Employees elect to reduce their salaries, and the salary reduction is used to pay for plan benefits. In effect, employee premium contributions are paid with before-tax dollars. As a result, taxes are reduced, and disposable income is increased.

Third, cafeteria plans typically allow employees to establish flexible spending accounts. A **flexible spending account** *is an arrangement that permits employees to pay for certain unreimbursed medical expenses with before-tax dollars.* The employee agrees to a salary reduction, which is used to pay for certain expenses permitted by the Internal Revenue

Code with before-tax dollars. These expenses include unreimbursed medical and dental expenses, plan deductibles, coinsurance charges, eye glasses, hearing aids, cosmetic surgery, and other expenses not covered under a typical group plan. More recently, the Internal Revenue Service issued a ruling that allows reimbursement for the purchase of over-the-counter pain drugs. One disadvantage, however, is that amounts in the flexible spending account not used by the employee by the end of the year are forfeited to the employer. However, at the time of this writing, federal legislation has been introduced that would allow workers to carry over any unused funds up to $500 to the next plan year; workers would also have the option of withdrawing the funds and paying taxes on the money or depositing the money in a 401(k) plan or similar retirement plan.

Many employers now provide debit cards that employees can use to pay for unreimbursed expenses out of their account balances. The debit card allows employees to be reimbursed immediately for their uncovered out-of-pocket expenses.

Finally, if the cafeteria plan meets certain requirements specified in the Internal Revenue Code, the employer's credits are not currently taxable to the employee.

Cafeteria plans have certain advantages, including the following:

- Employees can select those benefits that best meet their specific needs.
- Employees generally pay their share of the cost of benefits with before-tax dollars, which reduces taxes and increases take-home pay.
- Employers can more easily control rising employee benefit costs. For example, an employer may limit the number of benefit dollars or credits given to each employee or offer the employees a medical expense plan with a higher deductible.

Cafeteria plans also have certain disadvantages, including the following:

- The employer may incur higher initial development and administrative costs in establishing a cafeteria plan rather than a traditional employee benefits plan.
- Administrative complexity is increased. The employee benefits manager must have knowledge of the details of a large number of plans and must be able to answer the specific questions of employees concerning these plans.

CASE APPLICATION

Karen Swift is president of an accounting firm that has ten employees. The only employee benefit provided by the firm is a paid two-week vacation for employees with one or more years of service. The firm's profits have substantially increased, and Karen would like to provide some additional benefits to the employees. Karen needs advice concerning the types of benefits to provide. Assume you are an employee benefits consultant. Based on the following considerations, answer the following questions:

a. Karen would like to provide life insurance for the employees equal to two times their salaries. She wants to minimize the cost of this benefit. What type of life insurance do you recommend?

b. Several employees have expressed an interest in having some life insurance in force on their lives after retirement. Explain to Karen how employees can keep their life insurance after retirement.

c. Karen would also like to provide health insurance benefits to the employees. Identify the major types of group health insurance plans that she might consider.

d. Assume that Karen is considering both a preferred provider plan (PPO) and a health maintenance organization plan (HMO). Explain the major differences between these two plans to Karen.

e. Are there any other group insurance benefits that Karen should consider? Explain your answer.

f. Karen would like to give the employees a choice of benefits. Explain to Karen how this goal can be accomplished.

SUMMARY

- Group insurance provides benefits to a number of persons under a single master contract. Low-cost protection is provided, because the employer pays part or all of the premiums. Evidence of insurability is usually not required. Larger groups are subject to experience rating, by which the group's loss experience determines the premiums charged.

- Certain underwriting principles are followed in group insurance to obtain favorable loss experience:

    Insurance should be incidental to the group.

    There should be a flow of persons through the group.

    The benefits should be determined by some formula that precludes individual selection of insurance amounts.

    A minimum percentage of eligible employees should participate in the plan.

    There should be a third-party sharing of costs.

    There should be simple and efficient administration.

- Most groups today are eligible for group insurance benefits. However, employees must meet certain eligibility requirements:

    Be full-time employees.

    Satisfy a probationary period in some plans.

    Apply for insurance during the eligibility period.

    Be actively at work when the insurance becomes effective.

- There are several types of group life insurance plans:

    Group term life insurance

    Group accidental death and dismemberment (AD&D) insurance

    Group universal life insurance

- Group medical expense plans are available from a number of sources, including:

    Commercial insurers

    Blue Cross and Blue Shield

    Health maintenance organizations (HMOs)

    Self-insured plans by employers

- Group basic medical expense insurance provides only basic benefits, which typically include:

    Hospital expense insurance

    Surgical expense insurance

    Physicians' visits insurance

    Coverage for miscellaneous benefits

- Group major medical insurance is designed to cover catastrophic losses. There are two basic types of group major medical plans:

    Supplemental major medical insurance

    Comprehensive major medical insurance

- Managed care is a generic name for a medical expense plan that provides necessary medical care in a cost-effective manner.

- A health maintenance organization (HMO) is a managed care plan that provides broad, comprehensive services to its members for a fixed, prepaid fee. A typical HMO has the following characteristics:

    Organized plan to deliver health services to the members

    Broad, comprehensive health services

    Restrictions on the choice of physician

    Payment of a fixed, prepaid fee

    Heavy emphasis on controlling costs

- A preferred provider organization (PPO) is a plan that contracts with health care providers to provide certain medical services to its members at discounted fees. Members pay lower deductibles and coinsurance charges if preferred providers are used.

- A point-of-service (POS) plan is a managed care plan that allows members to receive medical care outside the network of preferred providers. However, the patient must pay substantially higher deductible and co-payment charges.

- An exclusive provider organization (EPO) is a managed care plan that does not cover medical care received outside the network of preferred providers.

- Group medical expense plans contain certain contractual provisions that may have a financial impact on the insured. Major provisions include the following:

    Preexisting-conditions provision

    Coordination-of-benefits provision

    Continuation of group health insurance under the COBRA law

- There are two basic types of group dental insurance plans:

Scheduled plans

Nonscheduled plans (comprehensive plans)

- Many employers provide disability-income benefits to covered employees. There are two basic types of plans:

    Short-term disability-income plans

    Long-term disability-income plans

- Cafeteria plans allow employees to select those benefits that best meet their specific needs. Flexible spending accounts in a cafeteria plan allow employees to pay for the benefits with before-tax dollars.

KEY CONCEPTS AND TERMS

Basic medical expense insurance
Blue Cross and Blue Shield plans
Cafeteria plans
Calendar-year deductible
Capitation fee
COBRA law
Coinsurance provision
Comprehensive major medical insurance
Contributory plan
Coordination-of-benefits provision
Corridor deductible
Eligibility period
Exclusive provider organization (EPO)
Experience rating
Family deductible provision
Flexible spending account
Gatekeeper physician
Group accidental death and dismemberment (AD&D) insurance
Group dental insurance
Group disability-income insurance
Group medical expense insurance
Group term life insurance
Group universal life insurance
Health Insurance Portability and Accountability Act (HIPAA)
Health maintenance organization (HMO)
Health savings account (HSA)
Hospital expense insurance
Individual practice association (IPA) plan
Major medical insurance
Managed care
Master contract
Noncontributory plan
Nonoccupational disability
Nonscheduled dental insurance plan (comprehensive dental insurance)
Point-of-service (POS) plan
Portability
Preexisting condition
Preferred provider organization (PPO)
Probationary period
Reasonable and customary charges
Scheduled dental insurance plan
Self-insurance (self-funding)
Service benefits
Stop-loss limit
Supplemental major medical insurance
Surgical expense insurance
Traditional group indemnity plan
Voluntary accidental death and dismemberment insurance

REVIEW QUESTIONS

1. Describe the basic underwriting principles that are followed in group insurance.

2. Explain the typical eligibility requirements that employees must meet in group insurance plans.

3. Briefly describe the following types of group life insurance plans:
   a. Group term life insurance
   b. Group accidental death and dismemberment insurance (AD&D)
   c. Group universal life insurance

4. a. Describe the major characteristics of Blue Cross and Blue Shield plans.
   b. Why do many employers self-insure (self-fund) their group medical expense plans?

5. a. Identify the benefits provided by basic medical expense plans.
   b. Briefly describe the major characteristics of the following group major medical insurance plans.
      1. Supplemental major medical insurance
      2. Comprehensive major medical insurance

6. a. What is a managed care plan?
   b. Briefly explain the basic characteristics of the following types of managed care plans:
      (1) Health maintenance organizations (HMOs)
      (2) Preferred provider organizations (PPOs)
      (3) Point-of-service (POS) plans
      (4) Exclusive provider organizations (EPOs)

7. The Health Insurance Portability and Accountability Act (HIPAA) places restrictions on the employer's right to deny or limit coverage for preexisting conditions.
   a. How is a preexisting condition defined under HIPAA?
   b. Describe the major provisions under HIPAA that deal with preexisting conditions.

8. Briefly explain each of the following group medical expense provisions:
   a. Coordination of benefits
   b. Continuation of group health insurance under the COBRA law.

9. Briefly explain the basic characteristics of the following group dental insurance plans:
   a. Scheduled dental insurance plan
   b. Comprehensive dental insurance

10. Briefly describe the major characteristics of the following group disability-income plans:
    a. Short-term disability-income plans
    b. Long-term disability-income plans

11. Describe the basic characteristics of cafeteria plans in an employee benefits program.

APPLICATION QUESTIONS

1. Group term life insurance and group universal life insurance have different characteristics and objectives. Compare (1) group term insurance with (2) group universal life insurance with respect to each of the following:
   a. Period of protection provided
   b. Right to continue the coverage after termination of employment
   c. Availability of employer contributions
   d. Right to obtain a policy loan

2. Margo, age 35, was severely injured in an auto accident. She is covered under her employer's preferred provider organization (PPO) plan. The plan provides major medical insurance with a $2 million lifetime limit, a calendar-year deductible of $300, a coinsurance requirement of 80-20 percent, and an annual stop-loss limit of $2,000. As a result of the accident, Margo incurred the following medical expenses:

Cost of ambulance to the hospital	$ 500
Hospital bill for a three-day stay	$15,300
Surgery for a broken leg	$ 5,000
Prescription drugs outside the hospital	$ 300
Physical therapy for the broken leg	$ 1,200

In addition, Margo could not work for one month and lost $3000 in earnings.
   a. Based on the above, how much will Margo collect for her injury if she receives medical care from health care providers who are part of the PPO network?

   b. Assume that Margo's broken leg does not heal properly, and she needs another operation. Margo would like a different surgeon with an outstanding professional reputation to perform the operation. The surgeon is not a member of the PPO network. Will Margo's plan pay for the surgery? Explain your answer.

3. Jane, age 28, and John, age 30, are married and have a son, age one. Jane is covered under her employer's group medical expense plan as an employee. Jane is also covered under John's plan as a dependent. The son is covered under both plans as a dependent. Jane's birthday is January 10, while John's birthday is November 15. Both plans have the same coordination-of-benefits provision.
   a. If Jane is hospitalized, which plan is primary? Which plan is excess?
   b. If the son is hospitalized, which plan is primary? Which plan is excess?
   c. Assume that the couple gets a divorce, and Jane is awarded custody of her son. A court decree states that John must provide health insurance on his son. If the son is hospitalized after the divorce, which plan is primary? Which plan is excess?

4. Jason, age 25, graduated from college and accepted a job as an accountant with a large employer. The company is subject to the Health Insurance Portability and Accountability Act (HIPAA) of 1996. The employer's group health insurance plan contains a provision that excludes preexisting conditions for 12 months. Jason had major surgery three months before he was hired in which a malignant tumor was removed from his lung. The surgeon explained that the risk of new tumors developing, although slight, was possible. Based on the preceding information, answer the following questions.
   a. Six months after he was hired, Jason had surgery to have another malignant tumor removed from his lung. Does the group health insurance plan have to pay for the surgery? Explain your answer.
   b. Would your answer to (a) above change if the second surgical operation occurred 18 months after Jason was hired? Explain your answer.
   c. After working for the company for two years, Jason lost his job when his company merged with another firm. After six weeks, Jason found another job as an accountant. Jason enrolled in the new employer's group health insurance plan, which also

excludes preexisting conditions for 12 months. The new employer is also subject to HIPAA. Assume that Jason must have his lungs x-rayed to detect any new tumors. Can the new group health insurance plan exclude coverage of the medical condition? Explain your answer.

5. Many employers have both group short-term and long-term disability-income plans. Compare (1) short-term plans with (2) long-term plans with respect to each of the following:
   a. Definition of disability under the plan
   b. Elimination period
   c. Length of the benefit period
   d. Offsets if other disability-income benefits are received

6. When group dental insurance plans are initially installed, the insurer is exposed to a high degree of adverse selection. Describe the various cost controls that can be incorporated into the dental plan to control for adverse selection.

INTERNET RESOURCES

■ **America's Health Insurance Plans (AHIP)** is a national trade association that prepresents nearly 1300 member companies that provide health insurance coverage to more than 200 million Americans. The site provides considerable information on health-care issues in the United States. Visit the site at

http://www.aahp.org

■ **Blue Cross and Blue Shield** plans are nonprofit corporations that provide medical, hospital, and surgical benefits to plan members in specific geographical areas. The various plans account for a substantial portion of the group health insurance market. Visit the site at

http://www.bcbs.com

■ The **Employee Benefit Research Institute (EBRI)** is a nonprofit organization devoted exclusively to the dissemination of data, policy research, and educational material on economic security and employee benefits. Visit the site at

http://www.ebri.org

■ **Healthgrades.com** used a star system to rate hundreds of hospitals based on specific procedures. The stars range from a high of five to a low of one. Hospitals that have fewer complications for a specific procedure receive a higher grade. Information on physicians and nursing homes is also available. Visit the site at

http://www.healthgrades.com

■ The **International Foundation of Employee Benefit Plans** is a nonprofit educational organization that provides programs, publications, and research studies to individuals in the employee benefits field. The organization cosponsors the Certified Employee Benefit Specialist (CEBS) program. Visit the site at

http://www.ifebp.org

■ **Medicare.gov** provides timely information on the Medicare program. The site also includes information on nursing homes and Medigap policies. Visit the site at

http://www.medicare.gov

■ The **Centers for Disease Control and Prevention (CDC)** is the leading federal agency for protecting the health and safety of people in the United States and abroad. CDC provides credible statistics to enhance health decisions and to promote good health. CDC serves as the national focus for application of disease prevention and control, environmental health, and educational activities to improve health. Visit the site at

http://www.cdc.gov/nchs

■ The **National Committee for Quality Assurance (NCQA)** provides information to employers and consumers on the quality of their health care plans. NCQA issues a report card on the quality of care provided and has an accreditation program for health care plans. Visit the site at

http://www.ncqa.org

SELECTED REFERENCES

Beam, Burton T., Jr. *Group Benefits: Basic Concepts and Alternatives,* 10th ed. Bryn Mawr, PA: The American College, 2004.

Black, Kenneth, Jr., and Harold D. Skipper, Jr. *Life & Health Insurance,* 13th ed. Upper Saddle River, NJ: Prentice-Hall, 2000, chs. 19–20.

Health Insurance Association of America. *Health Insurance Nuts and Bolts: An Introduction to Health Insurance Operations.* Washington, DC: Health Insurance Association of America, 2001.

Health Insurance Association of America. *The Health Insurance Primer: An Introduction to How Health Insurance Works.* Washington, DC: Health Insurance Association of America, 2000.

Panszczyk, Linda, et al. *2004 U.S. Master Employee Benefits Guide.* Chicago, IL: CCH Incorporated, 2004.

Rosenbloom, Jerry S., ed., *The Handbook of Employee Benefits,* 5th ed. New York: McGraw-Hill, 2001.

Source Book of Health Insurance Data, 2002. Washington, DC: Health Insurance Association of America.

NOTES

1. Burton T. Beam, Jr. *Group Benefits: Basic Concepts and Alternatives,* 9th ed. (Bryn Mawr, PA: The American College, 2002), ch. 4.
2. *Life Insurer's Fact Book, 2003* (Washington, DC: American Council of Life Insurers, 2003), p. 98.
3. In a few states, the terminating employee is allowed to purchase term insurance for a limited period (such as one year), after which he or she must convert to some form of cash-value life insurance.
4. Beam, ch. 11.
5. *Source Book of Health Insurance Data, 2002.* (Washington, DC: Health Insurance Association of America, 2002), p. 53.
6. Beam, Ch. 11.
7. Blaine Bos, *2002 Mercer National Survey of Employer-Sponsored Health Plans,* Mercer Human Resource Consulting, 2002.
8. National Committee for Quality Assurance, *The State of Health Care Quality: 2003* Washington, DC, 2003.
9. Ibid.
10. Blaine Bos, *2002 Mercer National Survey of Employer-Sponsored Health Plans,* Mercer Human Resource Consulting, 2002.
11. Ibid.
12. Ibid.
13. Beam, Ch. 13.

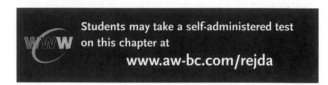

Students may take a self-administered test on this chapter at

www.aw-bc.com/rejda

CHAPTER 23

EMPLOYEE BENEFITS: RETIREMENT PLANS

"Retirement at age 65 is ridiculous. When I was 65, I still had pimples."

George Burns

"When some fellers decide to retire, nobody knows the difference."

Kin Hubbard

LEARNING OBJECTIVES

After studying this chapter, you should be able to

◆ Explain the basic features of private retirement plans, including:
   Minimum age and service requirements
   Retirement ages
   Vesting rules

◆ Distinguish between defined-contribution and defined-benefit retirement plans.

◆ Describe the basic characteristics of Section 401(k) plans.

◆ Explain the major features of profit-sharing plans.

◆ Describe the basic characteristics of Keogh plans for the self-employed.

◆ Identify the major features of SIMPLE retirement plans for small employers.

Josh, age 26, is a bank teller for a large national bank. He earns $40,000 annually and recently became eligible to participate in the bank's retirement plan. The bank has a Section 401(k) retirement plan for eligible employees. Josh has a number of questions about the plan, including the amount he can contribute, the amount contributed by the bank, investment options, and the retirement age. He also wants to know whether he will receive anything if he should quit his job prior to retirement.

Like Josh, many employees are bewildered by the complexities of private retirement plans. This chapter deals with the questions that Josh and others may have concerning the basic features of private retirement plans. Although they may seem complicated, private retirement plans are extremely important in maintaining the worker's economic security during retirement. When added to Social Security retirement benefits, private retirement benefits enable retirees to attain a higher standard of living during retirement.

This chapter discusses the fundamentals of private retirement plans. It is divided into two major parts. The first part discusses the fundamentals of private retirement plans, including minimum age and service requirements, retirement ages, and vesting rules. The second part describes the major types of private retirement plans, including defined-contribution and defined-benefit plans, Section 401(k) plans, profit-sharing plans, and retirement plans for the self-employed.

FUNDAMENTALS OF PRIVATE RETIREMENT PLANS

Millions of workers participate in private retirement plans. These plans have an enormous social and economic impact on the nation. Retirement benefits increase the economic security of both individuals and families during retirement. Retirement contributions are also an important source of capital funds to the financial markets. These funds are invested in new plants, machinery, equipment, housing developments, shopping centers, and other worthwhile economic investments.

Federal legislation and the Internal Revenue Code have had a great influence on the design and growth of private retirement plans. The **Employee Retirement Income Security Act of 1974 (ERISA)** established minimum pension standards to protect the rights of covered workers. More recently, the

Economic Growth and Tax Relief Reconciliation Act of 2001 increased the tax advantages of private retirement plans for both employees and employers. The Internal Revenue Service (IRS) also exerts a significant influence on private retirement plans. The IRS continuously issues new rules and regulations that affect the design and growth of private retirement plans. The following discussion is based on current IRS requirements at the time of this writing.[1]

Favorable Income Tax Treatment

Private retirement plans that meet certain IRS requirements are called **qualified plans** and receive favorable income tax treatment. The employer's contributions are tax deductible up to certain limits as an ordinary business expense; the employer's contributions are not considered taxable income to the employees; the investment earnings on plan assets accumulate on a tax-deferred basis; and the pension benefits attributable to the employer's contributions are not taxed until the employee retires or receives the funds. The tax advantages of qualified plans to employees are substantial, especially if the employee starts early (see Exhibit 23.1).

Minimum Coverage Requirements

A qualified plan must benefit workers in general and not only **highly compensated employees.**[2] Certain **minimum coverage requirements** must be satisfied to receive favorable tax treatment. The coverage rules are complex and beyond the scope of the text to discuss in detail. However, to reduce discrimination in favor of highly compensated employees, a qualified retirement plan must meet one of the following tests:

- *Ratio percentage test.* The plan must benefit a percentage of non-highly compensated employees that is at least 70 percent of the highly compensated employees covered by the plan. Thus, if a plan covers 100 percent of the highly compensated employees, it must also cover at least 70 percent of the non-highly compensated employees. Likewise, if the plan covers only 50 percent of the highly compensated employees, it must also cover at least 35 percent (50% × 70%) of the non-highly compensated employees.

   For example, Ajax Manufacturing has 1000 eligible employees, and 100 employees are highly compensated. Assume that 100 percent of the highly compensated employees (100) are covered by the plan. The ratio percentage test is satisfied if at least 70 percent of the non-highly compensated employees, or 630 employees (70% × 900), are also covered by the plan.
- *Average benefits test.* Under this test, two requirements must be met: (1) the plan must benefit a reasonable classification of employees and must not discriminate in favor of highly compensated employees, and (2) the average benefit for the non-highly compensated employees must be at least 70 percent of the average benefit provided to all highly compensated employees.

The minimum coverage tests typically come into play when an employer establishes a retirement plan for employees in one location (e.g. the Philadelphia office) but not in another location (e.g. the Boston office). The coverage tests are also important if an employer establishes a retirement plan for some workers based on job classification but not location.

Minimum Age and Service Requirements

Most pension plans have a **minimum age and service requirement** that must be met before employees can participate in the plan. *Under present law, all eligible employees who have attained age 21 and have completed one year of service must be allowed to participate in the plan.* One exception is that the plan can require two years of service if there is 100 percent immediate vesting (discussed later) upon entry into the plan.

For purposes of determining eligibility, a year of service is a 12-month period during which the employee works at least 1000 hours. An hour of service is any hour for which the employee works or is entitled to be paid.

Retirement Ages

A typical pension plan has three retirement ages:

- Normal retirement age
- Early retirement age
- Deferred retirement age

Normal Retirement Age The **normal retirement age** is the age that a worker can retire and receive a full, unreduced pension benefit. Age 65 is the normal retirement age in most plans. However, as a result of an amendment to the Age Discrimination in Employment Act, most employees cannot be forced to retire at some stated mandatory retirement age. To remain qualified, a private pension plan cannot impose a mandatory retirement age.

Early Retirement Age An **early retirement age** is the earliest age that workers can retire and receive a retirement benefit. The majority of employees currently retire before age 65. For example, a typical plan may permit a worker with 10 years of service to retire at age 55.

In a defined benefit plan (discussed later), the retirement benefit is actuarially reduced for early retirement. The actuarial reduction is necessary for three reasons: (1) the worker's full benefit will not

EXHIBIT **23.1**
Tax Advantage of a Tax-Deferred Retirement Plan

Total
Account Value:
$324,180
Years Until
Retirement:
40

Total
Account Value:
$141,760
Years Until
Retirement:
30

Total
Account Value:
$18,128
Years Until
Retirement:
10

Total
Account Value:
$57,266
Years Until
Retirement:
20

Total
investment:
$12,000

Total
investment:
$24,000

Total
investment:
$36,000

Total
investment:
$48,000

NOTE: This hypothetical example is based on a $100 monthly contribution to a tax-deferred retirement plan and an 8 percent rate of return compounded monthly. Your own plan account may earn more or less than this example and income taxes will be due when you withdraw funds from your account.

SOURCE: Fidelity.com, *The Benefits of Starting Early, 2003.*

have accrued by the early retirement date; (2) the retirement benefit is paid over a longer period of time; and (3) early retirement benefits are paid to some workers who would have died before reaching the normal retirement age.

Deferred Retirement Age

The **deferred retirement age** is any age beyond the normal retirement age. A relatively small number of older employees continue working beyond the normal retirement age. However, under current law with certain exceptions, workers can defer retiring with no maximum age limit as long as they can do their jobs. Employees who continue working beyond the normal retirement age continue to accrue benefits under the plan.

Benefit Formulas

Qualified retirement plans are designed to pay retirement benefits, which, together with Social Security

retirement benefits, will generally restore about 50 to 60 percent of the worker's gross earnings prior to retirement. A benefit formula is used to determine contributions or benefits.

Defined-Contribution Formulas

In a **defined-contribution formula,** *the contribution rate is fixed, but the retirement benefit is variable.* For example, both the employer and employee may contribute 6 percent of pay into the plan. Although the contribution rate is known, the retirement benefit will vary depending on the worker's current age, earnings, investment returns, and retirement age.

A fixed percentage of salary is typically used to determine the retirement contributions. For example, both the employee and employer may contribute 6 percent of salary into the plan. Each employee has an individual account, and the actual retirement benefit will depend on the value of the employee's account at retirement.

Defined-Benefit Formulas   In a **defined-benefit plan,** *the retirement benefit is known, but the contributions will vary depending on the amount needed to fund the desired benefit.* For example, assume a worker, age 50, is entitled to a retirement benefit at the normal retirement age equal to 50 percent of average pay for the highest three consecutive years of earnings. An actuary then determines the amount that must be contributed to produce the desired benefit.

In a defined-benefit plan, the benefit amount can be based on **career-average earnings,** which is an average of the worker's earnings while participating in the plan, or it can be based on a **final pay average,** which generally is an average of the worker's earnings over a three- to five-year period prior to retirement.

When a new defined-benefit pension plan is installed, some older workers may be close to retirement. To pay more adequate retirement benefits, defined-benefit plans may give credit for service with the firm prior to the installation of the plan. The **past-service credits** provide additional pension benefits. The actual amount paid, however, will depend on the benefit formula used to determine benefits.

In a defined-benefit plan, numerous formulas can be used to determine the retirement benefit. They include the following:

- *Unit-benefit formula.* The unit-benefit formula is widely used at the present time. Under this formula, both earnings and years of service are considered. For example, the plan may pay a retirement benefit equal to 1 percent of the worker's final average pay multiplied by the number of years of service. Thus, a worker with a final average monthly salary of $4000 and 30 years of service would receive a monthly retirement benefit of $1200.
- *Flat percentage of annual earnings.* Under this formula, the retirement benefit is a fixed percentage of the worker's earnings, such as 25 to 50 percent. The benefit may be based on career-average earnings or on an average of final pay.
- *Flat dollar amount for each year of service.* Under this formula, a flat dollar amount is paid for each year of credited service. For example, the plan may pay $40 monthly at the normal retirement age for each year of credited service. If the employee has 30 years of credited service, the

monthly pension is $1200. This formula is not widely used except in union-negotiated retirement plans.

- *Flat dollar amount for all employees.* This formula is sometimes used in collective bargaining plans by which a flat dollar amount is paid to all employees regardless of their earnings or years of service. Thus, the plan may pay $600 monthly to each worker who retires.

Years of service are extremely important in determining the total pension benefit. Frequent job changes and withdrawal from the labor force for extended periods can significantly reduce the size of the pension benefit. This is especially true for women who may have prolonged breaks in employment due to family considerations.

Vesting Provisions

Vesting *refers to the employee's right to the employer's contributions or benefits attributable to the contributions if employment terminates prior to retirement.* The employee is always entitled to the value of his or her contributions if employment terminates prior to retirement. However, the right to the employer's contributions, or benefits attributable to the contributions, depends on the extent to which vesting has been attained.

Qualified defined-benefit plans and other retirement plans (except defined-contribution plans as discussed below) must meet one of the following **minimum vesting standards:**

- *Cliff vesting.* Under this rule, the worker must be 100 percent vested after five years of service.
- *Graded vesting.* Under this rule, the rate of vesting must meet the following minimum standard:

Years of Service	Percentage Vested
3	20
4	40
5	60
6	80
7	100

However, for *qualified defined-contribution plans* with voluntary employee contributions and matching employer contributions, recent legislation shortens the time period for acquiring a fully vested status. Faster vesting is designed to encourage greater participation by lower- and middle-income employees. Beginning in 2002, defined-contribution plans with voluntary employee contributions and matching employer contributions must meet one of the following minimum vesting schedules.

- *Employer contributions must be 100 percent vested after three years (rather than five years).*
- *Employer contributions must be 20 percent vested after two years of service. The percentage of vesting increases 20 percent for each year of service until full vesting is attained after six years (rather than seven years).*

It should be noted that the preceding rules for faster vesting apply only to matching employer contributions as defined in the Internal Revenue Code. Employee voluntary (elective) contributions are always 100 percent vested. *As such, the definition of employer matching contributions refers only to defined-contribution plans.*[3] For all other retirement plans (such as a defined-benefit plan), the older five-year cliff vesting and seven-year graded vesting schedules discussed earlier remain in effect.

From the employer's viewpoint, the basic purpose of vesting is to reduce labor turnover. Employees have an incentive to remain with the firm until a vested status has been attained. In a defined-benefit plan, if employees terminate their employment before full vesting is attained, the forfeitures generally are used to reduce the employer's future pension contributions. However, in a defined-contribution plan, forfeitures can either be reallocated to the accounts of the remaining participants or used to reduce future employer contributions.

Limits on Contributions and Benefits

For 2004, under a *defined-contribution plan,* the maximum annual addition that can be made to an employee's account is limited to 100 percent of compensation, or $41,000, whichever is lower. This figure is indexed for inflation in increments of $1000. Annual additions include all employer and employee contributions and any forfeitures allocated to the employee's account.

For 2004, *under a defined-benefit plan,* the maximum annual benefit is limited to 100 percent of the worker's average compensation for the three highest consecutive years of compensation, or $165,000, whichever is lower. This latter figure is indexed for inflation in increments of $5000.

There is also a maximum limit on the annual compensation that can be counted when determining benefits and contributions under all plans. For 2004, the maximum annual compensation that can be counted in the contribution or benefit formula is $205,000 (indexed for inflation in increments of $5000).

Participants in defined-benefit plans are protected against the loss of pension benefits up to certain limits if the pension plan should terminate. The **Pension Benefit Guaranty Corporation (PBGC)** is a federal corporation that guarantees the payment of vested or nonforfeitable benefits up to certain limits if a private pension plan is terminated. For plans terminated in 2004, the maximum guaranteed pension at age 65 is $44,386 per year.

Early Distribution Penalty

A 10 percent tax penalty applies to funds withdrawn early from a qualified plan before age 59½. The 10 percent penalty tax applies to the amount included in gross income. However, the early distribution penalty does not apply to distributions that are:

- Made after age 59½
- Made after the death or total and permanent disability of the employee
- Made after attaining age 55 and separation from service
- Made as part of a series of substantially equal payments paid over the worker's life expectancy or joint life expectancy of the worker and beneficiary after separation from service
- Distributions for certain medical expenses
- Payments to an alternate payee as a result of a qualified domestic relations order
- Payments made in connection with certain employee stock ownership plans (ESOPs)

In addition, several additional exceptions to the early distribution penalty apply to individual retirement accounts (IRAs), simplified employee pensions (SEPs), and SIMPLE retirement plans (discussed later). The early distribution penalty does not apply to

- Distributions to pay for qualified elementary and secondary education expenses
- Distributions to pay for a first-time home purchase ($10,000 limit)
- Distributions to pay health insurance premiums by an individual who is receiving unemployment insurance benefits

Minimum Distribution Requirements

Pension contributions cannot remain in the plan indefinitely. Plan distributions must start no later than April 1 of the calendar year following the year in which the individual attains age 70½. However, participants older than 70½ who are still working can delay receiving minimum distributions from a qualified retirement plan. The required beginning date of a participant who is still employed after age 70½ is April 1 of the calendar year that follows the calendar year in which he or she retires. *The preceding rule does not apply to individual retirement accounts (IRAs) and certain other qualified plans.*

Finally, the minimum distribution rules do not apply to Roth IRAs.

Funding of Pension Benefits

Qualified private pension plans use advance funding to finance the pension benefits. **Advance funding** *means the employer systematically and periodically sets aside funds prior to the employee's retirement.* This type of funding increases the security of benefits for the active employees because funds are periodically set aside prior to retirement, and the contributions and investment income receive favorable income-tax treatment.

A qualified plan must also meet certain minimum funding standards. In a defined-benefit plan, the employer must make an annual contribution at least equal to the normal cost of the plan, plus an amount sufficient to amortize any unfunded liabilities over a period of years, which can range from 5 to 40 years depending on the liability and when it occurred.[4] **Normal cost** is the amount necessary to

fund the pension costs attributable to the current year's operation of the plan. Liabilities under the plan may arise because of an unfunded initial past-service liability, changes in actuarial assumptions, and plan experience. If the employer fails to meet the minimum funding standard, a tax penalty is imposed.

In addition, changes in the interest rate used to value pension liabilities has a significant impact on defined benefit plans. In recent years, interest rates have declined dramatically. As interest rates decline, the present value of future pension benefits increases, and pension plan liabilities increase. In addition, because of the severe stock market decline in 2000–2002, defined benefit pension plans that invested heavily in common stocks lost billions of dollars. As a result, the majority of defined benefit corporate pension plans are not fully funded. a fully funded plan is a plan in which plan assets are at least equal to 100 percent of the benefits of the benefits accrued to date. *A study of 472 defined benefit plans with 1000 or more participants by Watson Wyatt Worldwide, a major consulting firm, concluded that nearly two-thirds of the plans were underfunded in 2002 (see Insight 23.1).*

To deal with the funding problem, Congress enacted legislation in 2004 that provides temporary funding relief for two years for defined benefit plans. In determining the value of defined benefit pension liabilities, employers earlier were required to use an interest rate derived from the 30-year U.S. Treasury bond rate. However, the Treasury no longer issues 30-year bonds, and the rate of interest on such bonds has declined dramatically, which resulted in substantially higher employer contributions. The new legislation allows employers to use a higher interest rate based on a blend of long-term corporate bonds to calculate their pension liabilities instead of a lower rate based on 30-year treasury bonds. As a result, the higher interest assumption reduces required employer contributions. The legislation also allows two years of funding relief from higher pension contributions to some troubled pension plans, including those in the airline and steel industries.

The minimum funding standard also applies to defined-contribution pension plans. However, because there is no past-service liability, the minimum

INSIGHT 23.1

Nearly Two-Thirds of Corporate Pension Plans Underfunded, Watson Wyatt Research Finds

The percentage of employers with fully funded pension plans declined from 84 percent in 1998 to 37 percent in 2002, according to a new Watson Wyatt study. The decline in 2002 would have been even greater if Congress had not passed the *Job Creation and Worker Assistance Act of 2002,* which increased the maximum interest rate companies can use to determine the present value of benefits earned to date under the plan (the higher the interest rate, the lower the present value of future benefits).

"With almost two-thirds of pension plans falling short, we expect to see many companies struggling in the midst of a very bad economy to make massive cash contributions to improve their funding levels," says Kevin Wagner, a retirement practice director for Watson Wyatt. *A fully funded pension plan is one where the market value of plan assets is sufficient to cover at least 100 percent of benefits accrued by employees to date.*

The downward trend is expected to continue in 2002. "If interest rates remain low and the overall performance of the stock market remains weak, the percentage of companies with underfunded pension plans is likely to increase even further," Wagner says.

The study shows that companies are making changes to their funding practices to improve their position over the long-term, including making plan contributions that exceed the minimum funding levels required by the Employee Retirement Income Security Act (ERISA). In 1992, 57 percent of companies were funding their plans at the ERISA minimum, compared to 30 percent in 2002.

While the decline in fully funded plans was significant, Wagner says companies should not overreact. "Companies need to avoid knee-jerk responses to this drop. Despite a couple of bad years, pension plans have been financially efficient over the past decade and they are critical components of companies' HR programs," he says. "The best course of action is to focus on developing appropriate funding policies that balance the capital need of the underfunded pension plans against the overall capital needs of the organization, keeping long-term goals in mind."

Wagner also believes the Treasury Department needs to act quickly to replace the 30-year Treasury bond rate with a composite high-quality long-term corporate bond rate that can be used to determine funding requirements. "Waiting until late this year to find a permanent replacement rate could have a dramatic and damaging impact on pension plans and plan participants," said Wagner.

SOURCE: Excerpted from Watson Wyatt Worldwide, *Nearly Two-Thirds of Corporate Pension Plans Underfunded, Watson Wyatt Research Finds,* Press Release, March 26, 2003. For more information visit watsonwyatt.com.

funding standard is met provided the employer makes the required contribution each year based on the plan's contribution formula.

Integration with Social Security

Many qualified private pension plans are integrated with Social Security. Because employers pay half of the total Old-Age, Survivors, and Disability Insurance (OASDI) payroll tax, they argue that OASDI retirement benefits should be considered in the calculation of private pension benefits. As a result, pension costs can be reduced. Also, integration provides a method for increasing pension benefits for highly compensated employees without increasing the cost of providing benefits to lower-paid employees.

The Internal Revenue Service has prescribed complex integration rules (called *permitted dis-*

parity rules) that must be followed when a qualified retirement plan is integrated with OASDI. Only one of them—an *excess plan*—is discussed here. In a defined-contribution plan, the pension contribution rate can be higher for employees with earnings above a specified integration level than for employees with earnings below that level. The maximum integration level is the OASDI wage base. Thus, if the integration level is set at the OASDI wage base ($87,900 for 2004), highly compensated employees can receive an additional 5.7 percent of compensation in excess of the wage base, provided that the employer makes contributions at least equal to 5.7 percent of total compensation for all employees.

For example, the Smith Corporation has a defined-contribution pension plan that has a contribution rate of 6 percent of compensation, plus

5.7 percent of compensation in excess of the taxable OASDI wage base ($87,900 in 2004). The rule described above is met. Thus, if Kristin earns $100,000, the contribution made on her behalf will be $6690. This amount is 6 percent of $100,000 ($6000) plus 5.7 percent of $12,100 ($100,000 minus $87,900), or $690.

If the employer cannot afford to contribute at least 5.7 percent of total compensation for all employees, the maximum disparity must be reduced. For example, if the contribution rate for all employees is 4 percent of total compensation, then an additional contribution of 4 percent of compensation in excess of the integration level can be made.

Finally, as noted earlier, the maximum integration level is the OASDI wage base. The integration level can be set lower, but this approach generally reduces the maximum disparity allowed.

Top-Heavy Plans

Special rules apply to top-heavy plans. A **top-heavy plan** is a retirement plan in which more than 60 percent of the plan assets are in accounts attributed to key employees. A plan is considered top-heavy if the present value of the cumulative accrued benefits for the key employees exceeds 60 percent of the present value of the cumulative accrued benefits under the plan for all covered employees. (Accrued benefits are measured in terms of benefits for defined-benefit plans and account balances for defined-contribution plans.)

A top-heavy plan must meet certain additional requirements to retain its qualified status. These requirements include the following:

- A special rapid vesting schedule must be used for nonkey employees (100 percent vesting after three years, or 20 percent after two years and 20 percent for each year thereafter).
- Certain minimum benefits or contributions must be provided for nonkey employees.

The Economic Growth and Tax Relief Reconciliation Act of 2001 has modified significantly the top-heavy rules. The legislation changes the definitions of a top-heavy plan and a key employee to reduce the number of plans considered top-heavy. The law also provides for an adjustment in the minimum benefit or contribution rules so that the cost to employers can be reduced.

TYPES OF QUALIFIED RETIREMENT PLANS

A wide variety of qualified retirement plans are available today to meet the specific needs of employers. The most important include the following:

- Defined-contribution plans
- Defined-benefit plans
- Section 401(k) plans
- Section 403(b) plans
- Profit-sharing plans
- Retirement plans for the self-employed
- Simplified employee pension (SEP) plans
- SIMPLE retirement plans

The following sections discuss the basic characteristics of these plans.

DEFINED-CONTRIBUTION PLANS

As noted earlier, a **defined-contribution plan** is a retirement plan in which the contribution rate is fixed, but the actual retirement benefit varies, depending on the worker's age of entry into the plan, contribution rate, investment returns, and the age of normal retirement.

One example of a defined-contribution plan is a money purchase plan. A **money purchase plan** is an arrangement in which each participant has an individual account, and the employer's contribution is a fixed percentage of the participant's compensation. For example, the money purchase formula may specify an annual contribution by the employer of 10 percent of base pay to the employee's account. If the plan is contributory, both the employee and employer usually contribute at the same rate, such as 5 percent of base pay.

Defined-contribution plans are widely used by business firms today. Most new plans today are defined-contribution plans. One financial advantage to the firm is that past-service credits are typically not granted for service prior to the plan's inception date, which reduces the employer's cost. Defined-contribution plans are also widely used by nonprofit organizations and state and local governments, where pension costs must be budgeted as a percentage of payroll.

In this type of pension plan, each employee has an individual account, and the retirement contributions and investment income are credited to the account. The employee receives periodic statements that show the account value and investment returns. Amounts forfeited by employees who terminate their employment before they attain full vesting are used to reduce future employer contributions or are reallocated to the accounts of the remaining employees.

However, from the employee's perspective, a defined-contribution plan has several disadvantages. Retirement benefits can only be estimated; the benefit formula may produce an inadequate benefit if the worker enters the plan at an advanced age; and any investment losses must be borne by the employee. Also, some employees do not understand the factors to consider in choosing a particular investment, such as a stock fund, bond fund, money market fund, and other investment options.

In addition, because of fear and the desire to protect principal, some employees invest a large proportion of their retirement contributions in a **stable value fund.** This type of fund is a fixed-income fund that credits the contributions with a specified rate of interest but offers limited opportunities for the growth of principal. As a result, the retirement benefits may be inadequate.

DEFINED-BENEFIT PLANS

Traditional Defined-Benefit Plans

From a historical perspective, employers typically established defined-benefit plans that paid guaranteed benefits to retired workers. As we noted earlier, a defined-benefit plan is a retirement plan in which the retirement benefit is known in advance, but the contributions vary depending on the amount needed to fund the desired benefit. Such plans typically pay benefits based on a *unit-benefit formula* that considers both earnings and years of participation in the plan. For example, the plan may provide a retirement benefit payable at the normal retirement age equal to 1.5 percent of final pay for each year of credited service. Assume Jennifer retires at age 65 and has 25 years of credited service and final pay of $50,000 based on an average of her three highest consecutive years of earnings. She would receive an annual lifetime pension of $18,750.

Defined-benefit retirement plans have the major advantages of guaranteeing the worker's retirement benefit; the retirement benefits reflect more accurately the effects of inflation because the benefits are usually based on a final-pay formula; the plans are usually noncontributory, which means that only the employer contributes to the plan; and the investment risk falls directly on the employer, not the employee. In addition, defined-benefit plans favor workers who enter the plan at older ages because the employer must contribute a relatively larger amount for older workers than for younger workers.

Defined-benefit plans have declined in relative importance over the years. Because of actuarial considerations, they are more complicated and expensive to administer and fund than defined-contribution plans. Also, these plans initially have large unfunded past-service liabilities because of past-service credits that are expensive to fund. In contrast, defined-contribution plans do not provide past-service credits for service prior to the plan's inception.

Cash-Balance Plans

Many employers have converted their traditional defined-benefit plans to a cash-balance plan. A **cash-balance plan** *is a defined-benefit plan in which the benefits are defined in terms of a hypothetical account balance; actual retirement benefits will depend on the value of the participant's account at retirement.*

In a typical cash-balance plan, the employer establishes "hypothetical accounts" for plan participants. The accounts are hypothetical because the contributions and interest credits are bookkeeping credits. Actual contributions are not allocated to the participants' accounts, and the accounts do not reflect actual investment gains or losses. The investment credits are also hypothetical and are based on an interest rate stated in the plan or on some external index.

Each year, the participants' accounts are credited with (1) a *pay credit,* such as 4 percent of compensation, and (2) an *interest credit,* such as 5 percent of the account balance. The interest credit can be based on a fixed rate or on a variable rate pegged to some index, such as a one-year Treasury bill rate. Investment gains and losses on the plan's assets do not directly affect the benefits promised to the participants. Thus, the employer bears the investment risks and realizes any investment gains. For example, assume that the employer makes a contribution of 4 percent of pay each year to the participants' accounts. If James earns $50,000 annually, his "account" is credited with $2000. Each year, his account balance will be credited with a stated interest rate, such as 5 percent. At retirement, James can elect to receive a life annuity that will pay him a life income. Instead of an annuity, the cash-balance plan may allow him to elect a lump-sum payment equal to the account balance, which can then be rolled over into an IRA.

Many employers have converted traditional defined-benefit plans into cash-balance plans in an effort to hold down pension costs. Also, younger workers benefit because they can understand the plan better; benefits accrue at a faster pace than under a traditional defined-benefit plan; and the benefits are portable for workers who leave before retirement age.

However, critics argue that the switch to a cash-balance plan can reduce expected pension benefits for older workers by 20 percent to 50 percent. Here's why. The benefits earned under the traditional defined-benefit formula may exceed the benefit amount earned under the new cash-balance formula. *In this situation, older participants may not earn any additional benefits until their benefits under the new cash-balance plan formula exceed the benefits earned under the old formula. It may take several years before additional benefits accrue under the new plan.* Actuaries call this effect a "wear away," because you wear away the old benefit before earning a new benefit. As a result, many older workers believe cash balance plans are discriminatory because the cash balance formula produces a benefit that is substantially lower than the traditional defined benefit formula. This can be illustrated by Exhibit 23.2, which shows that a worker, age 55, at the time of conversion receives a substantially lower benefit under a

Exhibit 23.2
How Conversion to a Cash Balance Plan Potentially Lowers Annuity Benefits

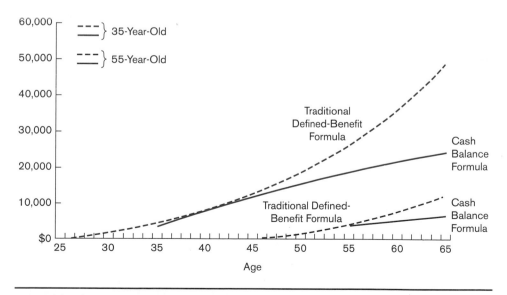

NOTE: Model results are based on the assumption of $40,000 salary and 10-year tenure at conversion for both the 35-year-old and the 55-year-old worker at conversion.

SOURCE: United States General Accounting Office, *Private Pensions, Implication of Conversion to Cash Balance Plans,* GAO/HEHS-00-185 (September 2000), Figure 4, p. 26

cash balance formula as compared to a younger worker, age 35.

Many older workers believe that cash balance pension plans are discriminatory and have sued their employers. Insight 23.2 discusses the court decision in one suit against a major corporation in which the judge ruled that the switch to a cash balance plan illegally harmed older workers.

SECTION 401(K) PLANS

Section 401(k) plans are becoming increasingly popular among employees as a tax-deferred saving plan. A **Section 401(k) plan** *is a qualified cash or deferred arrangement (CODA) that allows eligible employees the option of putting money into the plan or receiving the funds as cash.* Plan contributions are not currently taxable as income to plan participants.

A Section 401(k) plan can be a qualified profit-sharing plan, savings or thrift plan, or stock bonus plan. A plan can be established that includes both employer and employee contributions, or the employee contributions alone.

In a typical plan, both the employer and employees contribute, and the employer matches part or all of the employee's contributions. For example, for each dollar contributed by the employee, the employer may contribute 25 or 50 cents, or some higher amount.

Most plans allow the employees to determine how the funds are invested. Employees typically have a choice of investments, such as a common stock fund, bond fund, fixed-income fund, and other funds.

Many plans also allow the contributions to be invested in company stock. However, it is risky to invest a large proportion of 401(k) funds in the company's stock. For example, thousands of Enron employees who invested a large part of their 401(k) contributions in Enron Corporation stock lost substantial amounts of money when the company declared bankruptcy in late 2001. The workers lost not only their jobs but also a major part of their retirement savings.

Annual Limit on Elective Deferrals

Eligible employees can voluntarily elect to have their salaries reduced if they participate in a Section 401(k) plan. The salary reduction is technically called an "elective deferral." The amount of salary deferred is then invested in the employer's Section 401(k) plan. The amounts deferred accumulate free of current income taxes until the funds are withdrawn. However, Social Security taxes must be paid on the contributions to the plan. The funds are taxed as ordinary income when withdrawals are made.

For 2004, the maximum limit on elective deferrals in a Section 401(k) plan is $13,000 for workers under age 50. Workers who are age 50 or older before the end of the plan year can make an additional catch-up contribution or $3,000. The maximum dollar limit on elective deferrals will increase in the future according to the following schedule:

Year	Participants Under Age 50	Participants Age 50 and Older
2004	$13,000	$16,000
2005	14,000	18,000
2006	15,000	20,000

Beginning in 2007, the maximum dollar limits will be indexed for inflation in increments of $500.

Actual Deferral Percentage Test

To prevent discrimination in favor of highly compensated employees in a Section 401(k) plan, an **actual deferral percentage (ADP) test** must be satisfied. That is, the actual percentage of salary deferred for highly compensated employees is subject to certain limitations. In general, the eligible employees are divided into two groups: (1) highly compensated employees, and (2) other eligible employees. The percentage of salary deferred for each employee is totaled and then averaged to get an ADP for each group. The ADPs of both groups are then compared. The rules for calculating the ADPs are complex and beyond the scope of this text to discuss in detail. However, Exhibit 23.3 shows the permissible ADPs for highly compensated employees based on these rules. For example, if the non-highly compensated group has an ADP of 6 percent, the ADP for the highly compensated group is limited to 8 percent for favorable tax treatment.

INSIGHT 23.2

Judge Says I.B.M. Pension Shift Illegally Harmed Older Workers

A federal court ruled that I.B.M. violated age discrimination laws in the way it changed its traditional pension plan in the 1990s. The decision could cast doubt over similar changes hundreds of companies have made in plans covering millions of workers, and I.B.M. said it would appeal.

Judge G. Patrick Murphy of Federal District Court in the Southern District of Illinois ruled that I.B.M. had discriminated against its older workers in several ways when it converted its pension plan because the changes would leave them with smaller benefits at retirement than younger workers would have when they eventually retired.

I.B.M. changed its plan twice. In 1995, it switched to a hybrid called a pension equity plan, and in 1999 it converted to what is called a cash-balance plan. That type of plan combines some features of traditional pensions, which provide a defined benefit at retirement, with other features of 401(k) retirement plans. Both of I.B.M.'s changes took away some benefits from older workers and gave them less time than their younger colleagues to build up new ones.

Even though I.B.M. made various concessions after the 1999 changes caused an uproar, Judge Murphy found that those concessions still offered insufficient protection to older workers.

The lawsuit has been certified a class action, covering about 130,000 I.B.M. workers and retirees in the United States. *Court documents show that I.B.M. projected it would save billions of dollars in pension costs over the years after the changes took effect.* Some of that was to be used to create pensions for executives.

"All cash-balance plans would be viewed as age discriminatory" if the ruling is upheld on appeal, said David M. Spee, senior consulting actuary with Watson Wyatt, a consulting firm that has helped IBM and other companies make changes to their pension plans. Cash-balance plans, which are more common than pension equity plans, cover more than two million employees at hundreds of companies.

The corporate world had hoped that disputes over cash-balance pensions would be resolved this year by regulations being written by the Internal Revenue Service. The I.R.S. approach has been that cash-balance pension plans are not inherently discriminatory and can be designed to treat older workers fairly.

"The court's decision is in sharp tension with the Treasury's regulatory position," said J. Mark Iwry, a senior fellow at the Brookings Institution and a former benefits tax counsel at the Treasury Department.

It was unclear what effect the new ruling might have on the creation of those regulations. There are also bills pending in Congress that would resolve the legal issues raised by pension conversions.

An I.B.M. spokeswoman said the company planned an immediate appeal. She said it was not clear whether an appeal could be granted before Judge Murphy addressed the question of compensation.

"We stand by our plan and believe it does not discriminate on the basis of age," said the spokeswoman, Kendra Collins. "Under the court's interpretation of the law, every cash-balance plan is illegal."

In his ruling, Judge Murphy considered whether I.B.M.'s pension changes treated employees equitably by looking at the amount of benefits older and younger workers would have earned by the time they retired. Both the cash-balance model and the pension equity plan failed this test.

In their traditional design, pension plans reward institutional loyalty by allowing workers to build up to the biggest part of their benefit in the years just before they retire. Cash-balance pensions were designed in the 1980s in a different way, letting employees build up their benefits at a steadier rate year by year. In cash-balance plans, the yearly gain is based on interest rates. In pension equity plans, the amount earned each year is linked to each employee's pay.

In either case, younger employees have many years to build up their benefits, Judge Murphy wrote. But employees who are close to retirement age when the pension plan is converted have few years and therefore cannot earn as much. He offered several examples in his ruling.

In addition, Judge Murphy found that certain calculations I.B.M. had done while converting its pension plan had either worsened the effect on older workers or given advantages to younger employees that older ones did not receive. One was the calculation of the benefit amount each worker had earned under the traditional pension plan at the time it was converted.

Judge Murphy also faulted the way I.B.M. dealt with a situation known to pension professionals as wearaway, a period when a new pension plan has been adopted but some employees, in effect, earn no new benefits.

SOURCE: Adapted from Mary Williams Walsh, "Judge Says I.B.M. Pension Shift Illegally Harmed Older Workers," *The New York Times on the Web*, August 1, 2003. © 2003 by The New York Times Co. Reprinted with permission.

Exhibit 23.3
Permissible Actual Deferral Percentages (ADPs) for Highly Compensated Employees

ADP for Non-HCE	ADP for HCE
1%	2%
2	4
3	5
4	6
5	7
6	8
7	9
8	10
9	11.25
10	12.50
11	13.75
12	15

Source: Nicholas Kaster et al., *2003 U.S Master Pension Guide* (Chicago, IL: CCH Incorporated, 2003), p. 834.

Limitations on Distributions

As noted earlier, a 10 percent penalty tax applies to an early distribution of funds before age 59½ with certain exceptions. Exceptions include death or disability of the employee, payments that are part of a life or joint life annuity payout, separation from service after age 55, payments for medical expenses deductible under the Internal Revenue Code, and payments to a qualified payee under a qualified domestic relations order.

The plan may permit the withdrawal of funds for a hardship withdrawal. The IRS recognizes four reasons for a hardship withdrawal:

- Certain unreimbursable medical expenses
- Purchase of a primary residence
- Payments for post-secondary education expenses
- Payments to prevent eviction or foreclosure on your home

The 10 percent penalty tax still applies to a hardship withdrawal. However, 401(k) plans typically have a *loan provision* that allows funds to be borrowed without a tax penalty.

Despite the substantial tax penalties for a premature distribution, many employees often use their 401(k) funds and other retirement funds for purposes other than retirement, such as spending the funds outright, paying off debts, or buying a home. Employees who take money out of their retirement plans early will receive a substantially lower amount of income during retirement. As a result, they may be exposed to serious financial insecurity during retirement.

In summary, a 401(k) plan can play an important role in your retirement plans. However, employees often make serious mistakes in their 401(k) plans. These mistakes should be avoided (see Insight 23.3).

SECTION 403(B) PLANS

Section 403(b) plans are retirement plans designed for employees of public educational systems and tax-exempt organizations, such as hospitals, nonprofit groups, and churches. These plans are also known as **tax-sheltered annuities (TSA)**. Under the plan, eligible employees voluntarily elect to reduce their salaries by a fixed amount. The salary reduction is called an "elective deferral," which is then invested in the 403(b) plan. Employers may make a matching contribution, such as 50 cents for each dollar contributed by the employee by salary reduction. For example, if Kathy earns $3000 monthly and elects to defer $200 monthly, only $2800 is subject to income taxes. The $200 salary reduction plus any employer contributions are then invested in the 403(b) plan.

A 403(b) plan can be funded by purchasing an annuity from an insurance company or by investing in mutual funds. If an annuity is used, the employer must purchase the annuity, and the employee's rights under the contract must be nonforfeitable. *Non-forfeitable* means that the amounts contributed by the employer cannot be taken away from the employee. Employee salary reductions are always nonforfeitable. In addition, the annuity must nontransferable. *Nontransferable* means the annuity contract cannot be sold, assigned, or pledged as collateral for a loan.

Current law places a maximum annual dollar limit on elective deferrals under a 403(b) plan. For 2004, the maximum limit on elective deferrals for workers under age 50 is $13,000. Employees age 50 and older can make an additional catch-up contribution of $3000. The maximum dollar limit on elective

INSIGHT 23.3

Ten Common 401(k) Mistakes

Here are 10 ways we often mismanage our 401(k) plans. Each has the potential to cost us thousands of dollars in the amount we accrue for retirement.

- **Failure to participate at all.** According to the Profit Sharing/401k Council of America (PSCA), in 1999 82.5 percent of all eligible employees participated in their 401(k) plans. For various reasons, then, 17.5 percent of all eligible employees failed to contribute one nickel to their plans. It would be nice to think those folks saved for retirement elsewhere. Unfortunately, there are no data to confirm they did. And those who didn't almost certainly face a bleak retirement future.

- **Failure to contribute enough to receive the maximum employer match.** An employer's matching contribution represents free money. It provides an immediate and totally risk-free, tax-deferred return on your savings. By not contributing enough to receive the maximum possible match from your employer, you leave money on the table. Not only do you miss out on that money, but you miss out on the compounded growth that money could have earned—a loss that could easily amount to thousands of dollars.

- **Borrowing from your 401(k).** Many plans offer a loan feature. There are some emergency situations in which borrowing from a 401(k) may be appropriate. However, such loans will only serve to reduce the balance that would have been available in the plan at retirement had the loan not been taken. While the loaned money is out of your 401(k) account, it is not growing, which will ultimately reduce your retirement assets.

- **Trying to time the market.** Many plans today offer a 24-hour ability to change investments when desired. Some participants use this feature to switch from one investment to another as they anticipate changes in the marketplace. This is called market timing. Even the pros can't time the market with any consistent degree of success. Long-term investors should be consistent and stick with an appropriate investment allocation.

- **Being too conservative.** Younger participants tend to have more invested in equities than do older participants. Still, many participants are too conservative for the long haul. History indicates that a larger return is available in stocks, and the risk of loss in the equities market declines over time. Consequently, those with 10 or more years until retirement should be willing to have a high proportion of their investments in equities to ensure the maximum accumulation possible in their 401(k) accounts.

- **Being too aggressive.** As we get closer to retirement, we have to become more aware of short-term risk in the equities market. Otherwise, we may have to cash in our plans when stocks are at a low. In the short term, stocks can and do plunge dramatically. Therefore, to avoid having to sell during one of those drops, we should protect our stash by steadily decreasing our exposure to stocks beginning five to 10 years before we retire. Then, money we know we will take from our plan for living expenses in the next five years should remain out of the stock market.

- **Holding too much company stock.** We may think our employer is the next Microsoft, but banking most of our retirement money on that belief keeps too many eggs in one basket. The business could suffer a severe setback. Try to have no more than 15 percent to 25 percent of your plan assets in company stock.

- **Failure to allocate or rebalance.** Investing is a personal issue, and each of us must establish an *asset allocation* of stocks, bonds, and cash that's appropriate for our age, ability to sleep at night, and retirement plans. Once established, we must recognize that over time our investment performance will cause that allocation to change. That means we must rebalance our holdings to re-establish the desired allocation. If we don't do that (once a year is good), then an imbalance could adversely affect our total accumulation during one of the inevitable gyrations in the marketplace.

- **Keeping a default election.** Many plans today have a default election. That means you must opt out of the plan. If you don't, you're automatically enrolled, and your contribution will be made to a default option, usually an ultraconservative choice such as a money market fund. Some folks allow that automatic election to stand, and thus condemn themselves to low returns.

- **Keeping the money during a job change.** A study by Hewitt Associates revealed that 68 percent of plan participants who changed jobs in 1999 took cash withdrawals from their tax-deferred retirement accounts rather than leaving their money in the plan or rolling their balances into their new employer's plans or into IRAs. Those tax-deferred savings are thus *lost forever*, and can only mean fewer retirement dollars and higher taxes and penalties.

SOURCE: Adapted from David Braze, *Ten Common 401(k) Mistakes, The Motley Fool*, www.fool.com, September 24, 2001.

deferrals will increase in the future according to the following schedule:

Year	Participants under Age 50	Participants Age 50 and Older
2004	$13,000	$16,000
2005	14,000	18,000
2006	15,000	20,000

Beginning in 2007, the above limits will be adjusted for increases in the cost-of-living.

PROFIT-SHARING PLANS

Many employers have profit-sharing plans to provide retirement income to eligible employees. A **profit-sharing plan** *is a defined-contribution plan in which the employer's contributions are typically based on the firm's profits.* However, there is no requirement that the employer must actually earn a profit to contribute to the plan.

Employers establish profit-sharing plans for several reasons. Eligible employees are encouraged to work more efficiently; the employer's cost is not affected by the age or number of employees; and there is greater flexibility in employer contributions. If there are no profits, there are no contributions.

The profit-sharing contributions can be discretionary—based on an amount determined annually by the board of directors—or they can be based on a formula, such as a certain percentage of profits above a certain level. There are annual limits, however, on the amount that can be contributed into an employee's account. *For 2004, the maximum employer tax-deductible contribution is limited to 25 percent of the employee's compensation or $41,000, whichever is less.*

The profit-sharing funds are typically distributed to the employees at retirement, death, disability, or termination of employment (only the vested portion), or after a fixed number of years (at least two years). Amounts forfeited by employees who leave the company before they attain full vesting are reallocated to the accounts of the remaining participants.

A 10 percent tax penalty applies to a distribution to a participant younger than age 59½. To avoid the tax penalty, many plans have loan provisions that permit employees to borrow from their accounts.

RETIREMENT PLANS FOR THE SELF-EMPLOYED

Sole proprietors and partners can establish qualified retirement plans and enjoy most of the favorable tax advantages now available to participants in qualified corporate pension plans. Retirement plans for the owners of unincorporated business firms are commonly called **Keogh plans.** The contributions to the plan are income-tax deductible up to certain limits, and the investment income accumulates on a tax-deferred basis. The amounts deposited and the investment earnings are not taxed until the funds are distributed.

With certain exceptions, the same rules that apply to qualified corporate pension plans now apply to retirement plans for the self-employed.

Limits on Contributions and Benefits

For 2004, if the Keogh plan is a defined-contribution plan, the maximum annual contribution by a self-employed individual is limited to 25 percent of compensation or $41,000, whichever is lower. However, for purposes of determining the amount that can be contributed, self-employment net earnings must be reduced by (1) one-half of the Social Security self-employment tax and (2) the actual contributions into the plan. This latter adjustment presents a problem because the amount of the Keogh deduction and the amount of net earnings are dependent on each other. Fortunately, the IRS has prepared a worksheet to help you make the correct calculation. *However, for our purposes here, the maximum annual contribution into a defined-contribution Keogh plan is limited to 20 percent of net earnings after subtracting one-half of the Social Security self-employment tax.* If the 20 percent figure is used, the resulting amount is exactly equal to 25 percent of compensation after the two adjustments are made.

For example, after deducting one-half of the Social Security payroll tax, Shannon has net self-employment earnings of $50,000. She can make a maximum tax-deductible contribution of $10,000 into the plan, which reduces her taxable earnings to

$40,000. This amount is exactly equal to 25 percent of her net income after the contribution is made ($10,000/$40,000 = 25%).

For 2004, if the Keogh plan is *a defined-benefit plan*, a self-employed individual can fund for a maximum annual benefit equal to 100 percent of average compensation for the three highest consecutive years of compensation, or $165,000, whichever is lower. This latter figure is indexed for inflation.

For example, assume that Nancy, age 50, establishes a defined-benefit plan that will provide a retirement benefit equal to 50 percent of her net income at age 65. If average net income for the three highest consecutive years is $50,000, she can fund for a maximum annual benefit of $25,000. An actuary then determines the amount that she can contribute annually into the plan to reach that goal. In this case, based on 7 percent interest and certain actuarial assumptions, Nancy could contribute $10,847 annually into the plan.

Other Requirements

Certain other requirements must also be met, including the following:

- All employees at least age 21 and with one year of service must be included in the plan. A two-year waiting period can be required if the plan provides for full and immediate vesting upon entry.
- Certain annual reports must be filed with the IRS.
- A 10 percent tax penalty applies to the withdrawal of funds prior to age 59½ (except for certain distributions as noted earlier).
- Plan distributions must start no later than April 1 of the year following the calendar year in which the self-employed person attains age 70½.
- If the plan is top-heavy, the special top-heavy rules discussed earlier must also be met.

SIMPLIFIED EMPLOYEE PENSION (SEP)

A **simplified employee pension (SEP)** is a retirement plan in which the employer contributes to an IRA established for each eligible employee; however, the annual contribution limits are substantially higher. SEP plans are popular with smaller employers because the amount of required paperwork is minimal.

In one type of plan, called a **SEP-IRA,** the employer contributes to an IRA owned by each employee. The SEP-IRA must cover all qualifying employees who are at least age 21, have worked for the employer in at least three of the immediately preceding five years, and have received at least $450 (indexed limit for 2004) from the employer in compensation during the tax year.

For 2004, the maximum annual tax-deductible employer contribution to a SEP-IRA is limited to 25 percent of the employee's compensation, or $41,000, whichever is less. There is full and immediate vesting of all employer contributions under the plan.

SIMPLE RETIREMENT PLANS

Smaller employers are eligible to establish a Savings Incentive Match Plan for Employees, or SIMPLE for short. The **SIMPLE retirement plan** is limited to employers that employ 100 or fewer eligible employees and do not maintain another qualified plan. Under a SIMPLE plan, smaller employers are exempt from most nondiscrimination and administrative rules that apply to qualified plans. A SIMPLE plan can be structured either as an IRA or as a 401(k) plan. Only the IRA arrangement is discussed here (SIMPLE-IRA).

Eligible Employees

All employees who have earned at least $5000 from the employer during any two previous years and who are reasonably expected to earn at least $5000 during the current year must be allowed to participate in a SIMPLE plan. Self-employed individuals can also participate.

Employee Contributions

For 2004, eligible employees can elect to contribute a maximum of $9000 into a SIMPLE plan. Participants age 50 and older in 2004 can elect an additional catch-up contribution of $1500, for a total of $10,500. The amount elected by the employee can be expressed as a percentage of compensation or as a specific dollar amount.

The maximum annual contribution limits will rise in the future according to the following schedule:

Year	Participants Under Age 50	Participants Age 50 and Older
2004	$ 9,000	$10,500
2005	10,000[a]	12,000
2006	10,000	12,500[b]

[a] Beginning in 2006, indexed for inflation in increments of $500.
[b] Beginning in 2007, indexed for inflation in increments of $500.

Employer Contributions

Employers can choose between two options and can switch options each year if certain notification requirements are met:

- *Matching option.* The employer matches the employee's contributions on a dollar-for-dollar basis up to 3 percent of the employee's compensation for the year.
- *Nonelective contribution option.* The employer must make a nonelective contribution of 2 percent of compensation for all eligible employees.

If employers elect the matching option, they can reduce the matching contribution to 1 percent of compensation provided the employees are notified within a reasonable time before the 60-day election period during which employees can decide whether to participate in the plan. The employer is allowed to contribute at the lower rate for any two years during a five-year period ending with that year. The option to contribute at a lower matching rate is especially helpful to firms that are strapped for cash during lean years.

All contributions go into an IRA account and are fully and immediately vested. Withdrawals of funds by SIMPLE participants under age 59½ are subject to a 10 percent tax penalty. However, withdrawals during the first two years of participation are subject to a stiff 25 percent tax penalty.

FUNDING AGENCY AND FUNDING INSTRUMENTS

An employer must also select a funding agency when a pension plan is established. A **funding agency** *is a financial institution that provides for the accumulation or administration of the funds that will be used to pay pension benefits.* If the funding agency is a commercial bank or individual trustee, the plan is

called a *trust-fund plan.* If the funding agency is a life insurer, the plan is called an *insured plan.* If both funding agencies are used, the plan is called a *combination plan.*

The employer must select a funding instrument to fund the pension plan. A **funding instrument** *is a trust agreement or insurance contract that states the terms under which the funding agency will accumulate, administer, and disburse the pension funds.* Funding instruments include the following:[5]

- Trust-fund plan
- Deposit-administration plan
- Immediate-participation guarantee (IPG) plan
- Group deferred annuity
- Guaranteed investment contract (GIC)

Trust-Fund Plan

The majority of pension assets are in trust-fund plans. Under a **trust-fund plan,** all contributions are deposited with a trustee, who invests the funds according to the trust agreement between the employer and trustee. The trustee can be a commercial bank or an individual trustee. Annuities are not usually purchased when the employees retire, and the pension benefits are paid directly out of the fund. The trustee does not guarantee the adequacy of the fund, nor are there any guarantees of principal and interest rates. A consulting actuary periodically determines the adequacy of the fund.

Deposit-Administration Plan

A **deposit-administration plan** is an insured plan. All pension contributions are deposited in an unallocated fund. When the worker retires, an immediate annuity is purchased out of the plan's assets.

A **separate account** is a variation of the deposit-administration plan. Under a separate account, the pension funds are segregated, so that the account assets are not commingled with the insurer's general assets. The pension funds can be invested in an equity account or fixed-income account.

Immediate-Participation Guarantee Plan

An **immediate-participation guarantee (IPG) plan** is another insured plan. All pension contributions are deposited in an unallocated fund. The fund immediately reflects any unfavorable plan experience with respect to mortality, investments, and expenses. Annuities generally are not purchased when the workers retire; the pension benefits are paid directly out of the plan's assets. The insurer does not guarantee the adequacy of the fund. However, the insurer periodically evaluates the fund to determine whether it is sufficient to continue paying the promised benefits to the retired workers. If the fund declines to a level that is inadequate for paying full benefits to the retired workers, annuities would then be purchased for them.

Group Deferred Annuity

A group deferred annuity is an insured plan that has declined in importance in recent years. Under a **group deferred annuity,** a single-premium deferred annuity is purchased each year equal to the retirement benefit earned for that year. For example, under a defined-benefit pension plan, the worker may earn for the current year a monthly retirement benefit of $25 starting at age 65. A benefit equal to that amount would be purchased for that year. The benefit amount paid at retirement is the sum of the benefits payable under all deferred-annuity contracts that have been purchased on the worker's behalf.

Group deferred annuities are not widely used today because newer and more flexible pension products have been developed. Most plans have changed to other methods of funding, but older deferred annuities purchased before the change still remain in force.

Guaranteed Investment Contract

A **guaranteed investment contract** (GIC) is an arrangement in which the insurer guarantees an interest rate for a number of years on a lump-sum deposit. Guaranteed investment contracts have been popular with employers because of the interest rate guarantee by the insurer. In addition, the principal is guaranteed against loss. Finally, most guaranteed investment contracts make annuity options or other payment options available, but the employer is not required to use these options.

CASE APPLICATION

Richard, age 40, is the owner of Auto Repair, Inc. Because of a competitive labor market, he wants to establish a retirement plan for his employees. He is considering several retirement plans, including (1) a *defined-contribution plan,* (2) a *Section 401(k) plan,* and (3) a *SEP-IRA.* Assume you are a financial planner and Richard asks for your advice. Answer the following questions.

a. Explain to Richard the advantages and disadvantages of each of the three retirement plans.
b. Michael, age 28, is a mechanic for Auto Repair who earned $50,000 in 2004. Assume that the firm establishes a defined-contribution plan with a contribution rate of 6 percent of compensation by both the employee and employer. For 2004, what is the maximum tax-deductible contribution the firm can make to Michael's account?
c. Susan, the company's office manager, is 28 years old, and earns $35,000. She has worked for the company for three years. Can Richard exclude her from participating in the defined-contribution plan to hold down pension costs? Explain your answer.
d. Assume Auto Repair selects a Section 401(k) plan. The plan allows participants to defer 6 percent of their salary up to annual maximum limit ($13,000 for 2004 for participants under age 50). The employer makes a matching contribution of 50 cents for each dollar contributed. James, age 25, is a mechanic who has decided to defer only 3 percent of his salary because of substantial personal debts. What advice would you give to James?
e. Richard's wife, Maria, age 35, is self-employed as a freelance writer. After deducting half of the Social Security self-employment payroll tax, she has a net income of $50,000 for the current tax year. What is the maximum tax-deductible contribution Maria can make to a defined-contribution Keogh plan?

SUMMARY

- Qualified retirement plans receive favorable income-tax treatment. Employer contributions are tax-deductible and not considered taxable income to employees; investment earnings accumulate income-tax free; and pension benefits attributable to the employer's contributions are not taxed until the employee retires or receives the funds.
- Under the tax law, qualified pension plans must meet certain minimum coverage requirements, which are designed to reduce discrimination in favor of highly compensated employees.
- To meet the minimum coverage requirement, a retirement plan must satisfy one of the following tests:

    Ratio percentage test

    Average benefit test

- All employees who are at least age 21 and have one year of service must be allowed to participate in a qualified retirement plan.
- A retirement plan has a normal retirement age, an early retirement age, and a deferred retirement age. Most employees cannot be forced to retire at some mandatory retirement age. Benefits generally continue to accrue for employees who work beyond the normal retirement age.
- The benefits in a defined-benefit plan are typically based on the following benefit formulas:

    Unit-benefit formula

    Flat percentage of annual earnings

    Flat dollar amount for each year of service

    Flat dollar amount for all employees

- A qualified private pension plan must meet one of the following minimum vesting standards:

    Cliff vesting

    Graded vesting

- For 2004, under a *defined-contribution plan*, the maximum annual addition to an employee's account is limited to 100 percent of compensation, or $41,000, whichever is lower.
- For 2004, under a *defined-benefit plan*, the maximum annual benefit is limited to 100 percent of the worker's average compensation for the three highest consecutive years of compensation, or $165,000, whichever is lower.

- A *defined-contribution plan* is a retirement plan in which the contribution rate is fixed, but the actual retirement benefit varies, depending on the worker's age of entry into the plan, contribution rate, investment returns, and the age of normal retirement.
- A *defined-benefit plan* is a retirement plan in which the retirement benefit is known, but the contributions vary depending on the amount needed to fund the desired benefit. Defined-benefit plans typically pay benefits based on a unit-benefit formula that considers both earnings and years of participation in the plan.
- A *cash-balance plan* is a defined-benefit plan in which the benefits are defined in terms of a hypothetical account balance. The participant's account is credited with a pay credit and an interest credit. Actual retirement benefits will depend on the value of the participant's account at retirement.
- A *Section 401(k) plan* is a qualified cash or deferred arrangement (CODA) that allows eligible employees the option of putting money into the plan or receiving the funds as cash. The employee typically agrees to a salary reduction, which reduces the employee's taxable income. For 2004, the maximum salary reduction is limited to $13,000 for participants under age 50 and to $16,000 for participants age 50 and older. These limits will increase in the future. The contributions deposited in the plan accumulate income-tax free until the funds are withdrawn.
- A *Section 403(b) plan* is a retirement plan for employees of public schools and tax-exemption organizations. This plan is also called a *tax-sheltered annuity*. Eligible employees can voluntarily elect to reduce their salaries by a fixed amount, which is then invested in the plan. For 2004, the maximum elective deferral for workers under age 50 is $13,000 ($16,000 for workers age 50 and older).
- A *profit-sharing plan* is a defined-contribution plan in which the employer's contributions are typically based on the firm's profits.
- A self-employed individual can establish a *Keogh plan* and receive favorable federal income-tax treatment. The contributions to the plan are income-tax deductible, and the investment income accumulates on a tax-deferred basis.
- A *simplified employee pension (SEP)* is a retirement plan in which the employer contributes to an individual

retirement account (IRA) established for each eligible employee. For 2004, the maximum annual tax-deductible employer contribution to a SEP-IRA is limited to 25 percent of the employee's compensation, or $41,000, whichever is less. There is full and immediate vesting of all employer contributions under the plan.

- Under a *SIMPLE plan,* for 2004, eligible employees can elect to contribute up to $9000. Employees age 50 and older can contribute a maximum of $10,500. The maximum annual contribution limit will increase in the future. The employer has the option of either matching the employee's contributions on a dollar-for-dollar basis up to 3 percent of compensation, or making a nonelective contribution of 2 percent of compensation for all eligible employees.

- The major types of funding instruments to fund a pension plan are as follows:

  Trust-fund plan

  Deposit-administration plan

  Immediate-participation guarantee (IPG) plan

  Group deferred annuity

  Guaranteed investment contract (GIC)

KEY CONCEPTS AND TERMS

Actual deferral percentage (ADP) test
Advance funding
Average benefit test
Career-average earnings
Cash-balance plan
Deferred retirement age
Defined-benefit plan
Defined-contribution formula
Defined-contribution plan
Deposit-administration plan
Early retirement age
Economic Growth and Tax Relief Reconciliation Act of 2001
Employee Retirement Income Security Act of 1974 (ERISA)
Final average pay
Funding agency
Funding instrument
Group deferred annuity
Guaranteed investment contract (GIC)
Highly compensated employees
Immediate-participation guarantee (IPG) plan
Keogh plans
Minimum age and service requirement
Minimum coverage requirements
Minimum vesting standards
Money purchase plan
Normal cost
Normal retirement age
Past-service credits
Pension Benefit Guaranty Corporation (PBGC)
Profit-sharing plan
Qualified plan
Ratio percentage test
Section 401(k) plan
Section 403(b) plan
Separate account
SEP-IRA
SIMPLE retirement plan
Simplified employee pension (SEP)
Stable value fund
Taxpayer Relief Act of 1997
Top-heavy plan
Trust-fund plans
Vesting

REVIEW QUESTIONS

1. a. What are the federal income-tax advantages to employers in a qualified retirement plan?

   b. What are the federal income-tax advantages to employees in a qualified retirement plan?

2. A qualified retirement plan must meet certain minimum coverage requirements to receive favorable income-tax treatment. Explain the *ratio percentage test,* which satisfies the minimum coverage requirement.

3. Explain the following retirement ages in a typical qualified retirement plan:

   a. Early retirement age

   b. Normal retirement age

   c. Deferred retirement age

4. Briefly explain the basic characteristics of a defined-contribution retirement plan.

5. a. Briefly explain the basic characteristics of a traditional defined-benefit retirement plan.

   b. What is a cash-balance retirement plan?

6. a. Describe the basic characteristics of a Section 401(k) plan.

   b. Describe the basic characteristics of a Section 403(b) plan (also called a tax-sheltered annuity).

7. Explain the major characteristics of a profit-sharing plan.

8. Describe the basic features of a Keogh plan for the self-employed.

9. Briefly explain the major characteristics of a simplified employee pension (SEP).

10. Briefly explain the basic characteristics of a SIMPLE retirement plan.

APPLICATION QUESTIONS

1. Qualified retirement plans must meet certain requirements to receive favorable federal income-tax treatment. Briefly explain each of the following:
   a. Minimum age and service requirements
   b. Vesting provisions
   c. Limitations on contributions and benefits
   d. Early distribution tax penalty

2. Fine Furniture has 1000 employees who are eligible to participate in the firm's defined-contribution retirement plan. Of this number, 100 employees are considered highly compensated, and 900 employees are non-highly compensated employees. The retirement plan covers all highly compensated employees. What is the minimum number of non-highly employees who must be covered under the plan in order to satisfy the *ratio percentage test*?

3. A national labor union representing pipeline construction workers has a defined-benefit pension plan for its members. Ron, age 65, is a heavy equipment operator who wants to retire. He has been a member of the union for 30 years. The pension plan has a unit-benefit formula, which provides a retirement benefit equal to 1.5 percent of the worker's final average compensation for each year of credited service. Final average compensation is based on the worker's highest three years of earnings. Ron's final average compensation is $70,000. How much will Ron receive each month when he retires?

4. Scott, age 35, is the owner of a local retail firm that sells carpets and other floor coverings. The company employs five people. One employee is a college student who works only part-time. The student earned $4000 last year, and his earnings are expected to be the same this year. Assume that Scott installs a SIMPLE retirement plan. For 2004, the plan permits eligible employees under age 50 to contribute a maximum of $9000 into the plan. Employees age 50 and older can make an additional catch-up contribution of $1500. The company also makes a matching contribution into the plan. Based on this information, answer the following questions.
   a. Does Scott have to include the part-time student in the SIMPLE plan? Explain your answer.
   b. One employee who earns $40,000 elects to contribute $9000 into the plan. What is the amount of the company's contribution?
   c. If the company experiences financial problems in a business recession, can Scott reduce the company's contributions to the plan? Explain your answer.

5. Brandon, age 26, is a self-employed carpenter. One month ago, Brandon hired his brother, age 20, to help in the business because of a local housing boom. Brandon wants to accumulate a retirement fund and decides to adopt a Keogh plan to fund his retirement. Brandon's gross earnings are $120,000. After deducting allowable business deductions and one-half of the Social Security self-employment payroll tax, Brandon's net earnings are $80,000.
   a. What is the maximum tax-deductible contribution Brandon can make to the Keogh plan?
   b. Does Brandon have to include his brother in his Keogh plan? Explain your answer.

6. An employer must select a *funding agency* and a *funding instrument* when a pension plan is established.
   a. What is a funding agency?
   b. Briefly describe each of the following funding instruments:
      (1) Trust-fund plan
      (2) Deposit-administration plan
      (3) Immediate participation guarantee (IPG) plan
   c. What is a guaranteed investment contract (GIC)?

INTERNET RESOURCES

- The **American Benefits Council** is an organization that represents plan sponsors and technical professionals in the employee benefits field. The site provides an analysis of proposed legislation affecting private pension plans and other employee benefits. Visit the site at
  http://www.appwp.org

- The **Employee Benefit Research Institute (EBRI)** is a nonprofit organization that makes available research studies and notes on qualified retirement plans. Visit the site at
  http://www.ebri.org

- **Fidelity Investments** provides a substantial amount of timely information on retirement planning and qualified retirement plans, including 401(k) plans. Visit its 401(k) site at
  http://www.401k.com

- The **Pension Benefit Guaranty Corporation** is a federal corporation that protects the retirement benefits of workers in defined-benefit pension plans. The site provides timely information on defined-benefit pension plans. Visit the site at

  http://www.pbgc.gov

- The **Employee Benefits Security Administration (EBSA)** is an agency of the U.S. Department of Labor that provides information and statistics on qualified retirement plans. Visit the site at

  http://www.dol.gov/ebsa

- **Charles Schwab** provides informative articles and information on retirement planning, annuities, and individual retirement accounts (IRAs). Visit the site at

  http://www.schwab.com

- The **Vanguard Group** provides timely information on retirement planning, variable annuities, and IRAs. Visit the site at

  http://www.vanguard.com

- **TIAA-CREF** has an excellent site that provides a considerable amount of information on retirement planning and retirement options. Visit the site at

  http://www.tiaa-cref.org

SELECTED REFERENCES

Allen, Jr., Everett T. et al. *Pension Planning: Pension, Profit-Sharing, and Other Deferred Compensation Plans,* 9th ed. New York, NY: McGraw-Hill/Irwin, 2003.

Commerce Clearing House. *Law, Explanation and Analysis, Economic Growth, and Tax Relief Reconciliation Act of 2001.* Chicago, IL: CCH Inc., 2001.

Littell, David A., and Kenn Beam Tacchino. *Planning for Retirement Needs,* 6th ed. Bryn Mawr, PA: The American College, 2003.

Pope, Elizabeth, et al. *2004 U.S. Master Pension Guide,* Chicago, IL: CCH Inc., 2004.

Rosenbloom, Jerry S., ed. *The Handbook of Employee Benefits,* 5th ed. New York: McGraw-Hill, 2001.

NOTES

1. This chapter is based on Commerce Clearing House, *Law, Explanation and Analysis, Economic Growth, and Tax Relief Reconciliation Act of 2001* (Chicago, IL: CCH Inc., 2001); Elizabeth Pope, et al., *2004 U.S. Master Pension Guide* (Chicago, IL: CCH Inc., 2004); and David A. Littell and Kenn Beam Tacchino, *Planning for Retirement Needs,* 6th ed. (Bryn Mawr, PA: The American College, 2003). IRS documents for taxpayers are also used.

2. For 2004, highly compensated employees are employees who (1) owned 5 percent of the company at any time during the year or preceding year or (2) had compensation from the employer in excess of $90,000 (indexed for inflation) during the preceding year, and if the employer so elects, were in the top-paid group of employees for the preceding year (that is, the highest 20 percent of employees based on compensation).

3. Commerce Cleaning House, *Law, Explanation and Analysis, Economic Growth, and Tax Relief Reconciliation Act of 2001* (Chicago, IL: CCH Inc., 2001), pp. 206–207.

4. Vincent Amoroso, "Costing and Funding Retirement Benefits," in Jerry S. Rosenbloom, ed., *The Handbook of Employee Benefits,* 5th ed. (New York: McGraw-Hill, 2001), p. 1139.

5. Amoroso, pp. 1111–1118.

Students may take a self-administered test on this chapter at **www.aw-bc.com/rejda**

CHAPTER 24

SOCIAL INSURANCE

"Economic security is one of the unfulfilled needs of humans. Social security programs have been designed to aid people in their quest for economic security."

Robert J. Myers
Social Security, 4th ed.

LEARNING OBJECTIVES

After studying this chapter, you should be able to

◆ Explain the reasons why social insurance programs are established.

◆ Describe the basic characteristics of social insurance programs.

◆ Identify the major benefits provided by the Old-Age, Survivors, and Disability Insurance (OASDI) program.

◆ Identify the major benefits under the Medicare program.

◆ Describe the basic objectives and important provisions of state unemployment insurance programs.

◆ Explain the basic objectives and major provisions of workers compensation programs.

S ocial insurance programs are compulsory government insurance programs with certain characteristics that distinguish them from private insurance and other government insurance programs. The various programs provide a safety net against the financial insecurity that can result from premature death, unemployment, poor health, job-related disabilities, and old age. Social insurance programs are especially valuable to individuals and families with limited incomes. For example, Carlos, age 30, died instantly in an auto accident in early 2004. He left behind a widow and son, age one. At the time of his death, Carlos had annual covered earnings under Social Security in the amount of $20,000. As a result, his widow and son are currently receiving monthly Social Security survivor benefits of approximately $1280, which enable them to maintain at least a minimum standard of living.[1]

This chapter discusses the major social insurance programs in the United States. The programs discussed include the Social Security program (OASDI), Medicare, state unemployment insurance programs, and workers compensation programs.

SOCIAL INSURANCE

Reasons for Social Insurance

Although the United States has a highly developed system of private insurance, social insurance programs are necessary for several reasons.

- *Social insurance programs are enacted to solve complex social problems.* A social problem affects most or all of society and is so serious that direct government intervention is necessary. For example, the Social Security program came into existence because of the Great Depression of the 1930s, when massive unemployment required a direct government attack on economic insecurity.
- *Social insurance programs are necessary because certain risks are difficult to insure privately.* For example, unemployment is difficult to insure privately because it does not completely meet the requirements of an insurable risk. However, the risk of unemployment can be insured by state unemployment insurance programs.
- *Social insurance programs provide a base of economic security to the population.* Social insurance programs provide a layer of financial protection to most persons against the long-term financial consequences of premature death, old age, occupational and nonoccupational disability, and unemployment.

Basic Characteristics of Social Insurance

Social insurance programs in the United States have certain characteristics that distinguish them from other government insurance programs:[2]

- Compulsory programs
- Floor of income
- Emphasis on social adequacy rather than individual equity
- Benefits loosely related to earnings
- Benefits prescribed by law
- No means test
- Full funding unnecessary
- Financially self-supporting

Compulsory Programs With few exceptions, social insurance programs are compulsory. A compulsory program has two major advantages. First, the goal of providing a floor of income to the population can be achieved more easily. Second, adverse selection is reduced, because both healthy and unhealthy lives are covered.

Floor of Income Social insurance programs are generally designed to provide only a floor of income with respect to the risks that are covered. Most persons are expected to supplement social insurance benefits with their own personal program of savings, investments, and private insurance.

The concept of a floor of income is difficult to define. One extreme view is that the floor of income should be so low as to be virtually nonexistent. Another extreme view is that the social insurance benefit by itself should be high enough to provide a comfortable standard of living, so that private insurance benefits would be unnecessary. A more realistic view is that social insurance benefits, when combined with other income and financial assets, should be sufficient for most persons to maintain a reasonable standard of living. Any group whose basic needs are still unmet would be provided for by supplemental public assistance (welfare) benefits.

Social Adequacy Rather Than Individual Equity Social insurance programs pay benefits based largely on social adequacy rather than on individual equity. **Social adequacy** *means that the benefits paid should provide a certain standard of living to all contributors. This means that the benefits paid are heavily weighted in favor of certain groups, such as low-income persons, large families, and the presently retired aged.* In technical terms, the actuarial value of the benefits received by these groups exceeds the actuarial value of their contributions. In contrast, the individual equity principle is followed in private insurance. **Individual equity** *means that contributors receive benefits directly related to their contributions; the actuarial value of the benefits is closely related to the actuarial value of the contributions.*

The basic purpose of the social adequacy principle is to provide a floor of income to all covered persons. If low-income persons received social insurance benefits actuarially equal to the value of their tax contributions (individual equity principle), the benefits paid would be so low that the basic objective of providing a floor of income to everyone would not be achieved.

Benefits Loosely Related to Earnings Social insurance benefits are loosely related to the worker's earnings. The higher the worker's covered earnings, the greater will be the benefits. The relationship between higher earnings and higher benefits is loose and disproportionate, but it does exist. Thus, some consideration is given to individual equity.

Benefits Prescribed by Law Social insurance programs are prescribed by law. The benefits or benefit formulas, as well as the eligibility requirements, are established by law. In addition, the administration or supervision of the program is performed by government.

No Means Test Social insurance benefits are paid as a matter of right without any demonstration of need. A formal means test is not required. A **means test** is used in public assistance—welfare applicants must show that their income and financial assets are below certain levels as a condition of benefit eligibility. By contrast, applicants for social insurance benefits have a statutory right to the benefits if they fulfill certain eligibility requirements.

Full Funding Unnecessary It is unnecessary for social insurance programs to be fully funded. For example, **a fully funded program** under Social Security means that the accumulated assets plus the present value of future contributions payable over the next 75 years will be sufficient to discharge all liabilities for benefits payable over the next 75 years. According to the *Wall Street Journal,* the Social Security program has unfunded liabilities for retirees of $11.9 trillion.[3] However, the combined OASDI trust fund balance at the end of calendar 2002 totaled only about $1.4 trillion. To be fully funded, a substantially higher trust fund balance would be required.

A fully funded Social Security program is unnecessary for several reasons. First, because the program will operate indefinitely and not terminate in the predictable future, full funding is unnecessary. Second, because the Social Security program is compulsory, new workers will always enter the program and pay taxes to support it. Third, the federal government can use its taxing and borrowing powers to raise additional revenues if the program has financial problems. Finally, from an economic viewpoint, full funding would require substantially higher Social Security taxes, which would be deflationary and cause substantial unemployment. In contrast, private pension plans must emphasize full funding, because private pension plans can terminate.

Financially Self-supporting Social insurance programs in the United States are designed to be financially self-supporting. This means the programs should be almost completely financed from the earmarked contributions of covered employees, employers, and the self-employed, and interest on the trust-fund investments.

OLD-AGE, SURVIVORS, AND DISABILITY INSURANCE (OASDI)

The Old-Age, Survivors, and Disability Insurance (OASDI) program, commonly known as **Social Security,** is the most important social insurance program in the United States. Social Security was enacted into law as a result of the Social Security Act of 1935. More than nine out of ten workers are working in occupations covered by Social Security, and about one in six persons receives a monthly cash benefit.[4]

Covered Occupations

The following groups are covered under the Social Security program:

- *Employees in private firms.* Virtually all private-sector employees are covered under the program at the present time.
- *Federal civilian employees.* Federal civilian employees hired after 1983 are covered on a compulsory basis. However, federal civilian employees hired before 1984 are covered only for Hospital Insurance under Medicare but not for OASDI.
- *State and local government employees.* State and local government employees can be covered by a voluntary agreement between the state and the federal government. The majority of state and local government employees are now covered. However, state and local government employees hired after March 1986 are covered for Hospital Insurance (HI) under the Medicare program and must pay the Hospital Insurance tax.

  After July 1, 1991, all state and local government employees who are not participating in a public retirement system are covered on a com-

pulsory basis. However, students employed in public schools, colleges, and universities can be excluded.

- *Employees of nonprofit organizations.* All employees of nonprofit charitable, educational, and religious organizations are covered if they are paid at least $100 during the year.
- *Self-employment.* Self-employed persons are covered if their net annual earnings are $400 or more.
- *Domestic employment in private homes.* Domestic employees are covered only if they earn $1400 or more in 2004.
- *Other groups.* Ministers are covered on a self-employment basis unless they elect out because of conscience or religious principles. U.S. military personnel are covered on a compulsory basis. Finally, railroad workers subject to the Railroad Retirement Act are not required to pay OASDI taxes directly. However, because of certain coordinating provisions, railroad employees are, in reality, covered compulsorily for OASDI and HI under Medicare.

Determination of Insured Status

Before you or your family can receive benefits, you must have credit for a certain amount of work in covered employment. Credits can be earned anytime during the year. For 2004, you receive one **credit** (also called a **quarter of coverage**) for each $900 of covered earnings. A maximum of four credits can be earned each year. The amount of covered earnings required to earn one credit will automatically increase each year as average wages in the national economy rise.

To become eligible for the various benefits, you must attain an insured status. There are three types of insured status:

- Fully insured
- Currently insured
- Disability insured

Retirement benefits require a fully insured status. Survivor benefits require either a fully insured or currently insured status, although certain survivor benefits require a fully insured status. Disability benefits require a disability-insured status.

Fully Insured To be eligible for retirement benefits, you must be fully insured. You are **fully insured** for retirement benefits if you have 40 credits. However, for people born before 1929, fewer credits are required as shown by the following:

Year of Birth	Credits Needed
1929 or later	40
1928	39
1927	38
1926	37
1925	36
1924	35

Currently Insured You are **currently insured** if you have earned at least 6 credits during the last 13 calendar quarters ending with the quarter of death, disability, or entitlement to retirement benefits.

Disability Insured The number of credits required to be **disability insured** depends on your age when you become disabled. If you are *age 31 or older,* you must have earned a certain number of credits as shown by the following:

Disabled at Age	Credits Needed
31 through 42	20
43	21
44	22
45	23
46	24
47	25
48	26
49	27
50	28
51	29
52	30
53	31
54	32
55	33
56	34
57	35
58	36
59	37
60	38
61	39
62 or older	40

In addition, at least 20 of the credits must be earned during the past 10 years immediately before you became disabled.

Workers younger than age 31 can acquire a disability-insured status with fewer credits. For *ages 24 through 30,* you must have worked half the time between age 21 and the time you become disabled. For example, a worker disabled at age 27 needs credit for three years of work out of the past six years.

If you become *disabled before age 24,* you must have earned six credits during the three-year period ending when your disability begins. Finally, blind persons are required only to have a fully insured status. They are not required to meet the recent-work test requirement that applies to other disability applicants.

TYPES OF BENEFITS

The total program consists of Social Security (OASDI) and Medicare. The OASDI program pays monthly retirement, survivor, and disability benefits to eligible beneficiaries. The Medicare program covers the medical expenses of almost all persons aged 65 and older and certain disabled beneficiaries younger than age 65. We discuss only OASDI cash benefits at this point; Medicare is covered later in the chapter.

Retirement Benefits

Social Security retirement benefits are an important source of income to most retired workers. Without these benefits, poverty and economic insecurity among the aged would be substantially increased.

Full Retirement Age For persons born in 1937 or earlier, the **full retirement age** for unreduced benefits is age 65. However, the full retirement age will gradually increase in the future to age 67 to improve the financial solvency of the OASDI program and to allow for the increase in life expectancy (see Exhibit 24.1).

Early Retirement Age Workers and their spouses can retire as early as age 62 with actuarially reduced benefits (see again Exhibit 24.1).

EXHIBIT 24.1
Social Security Full Retirement Age and Reduction in Benefits by Age

No matter what your full retirement age (also called "normal retirement age") is, you may start receiving benefits as early as age 62.

Year of Birth[a]	Full Retirement Age	Age 62 Reduction Months[b]	Monthly % Reduction*	Total % Reduction at Age 62
1937 or earlier	65	36	.555	20.00
1938	65 and 2 months	38	.548	20.83
1939	65 and 4 months	40	.541	21.67
1940	65 and 6 months	42	.535	22.50
1941	65 and 8 months	44	.530	23.33
1942	65 and 10 months	46	.525	24.17
1943–1954	66	48	.520	25.00
1955	66 and 2 months	50	.516	25.84
1956	66 and 4 months	52	.512	26.66
1957	66 and 6 months	54	.509	27.50
1958	66 and 8 months	56	.505	28.33
1959	66 and 10 months	58	.502	29.17
1960 and later	67	60	.500	30.00

[a] If you were born on January 1st, you should refer to the previous year.

[b] If you were born on the 1st of the month, we figure the benefit as if your birthday were in the previous month.

SOURCE: Social Security Online, www.socialsecurity.gov.

The actuarial reduction in benefits for early retirement at age 62 will gradually increase to 30 percent in the future when the higher full retirement age provisions become fully effective.

Monthly Retirement Benefits   Monthly retirement benefits can be paid to retired workers and their dependents. Eligible persons include the following:

- *Retired worker.* Monthly retirement benefits can be paid at the full retirement age to a fully insured worker. Reduced benefits can be paid as early as age 62.
- *Spouse of a retired worker.* The spouse of a retired worker can also receive monthly benefits if she or he is at least age 62 and has been married to the retired worker for at least one year. A

divorced spouse is also eligible for benefits based on the retired worker's earnings if she or he is at least age 62, and the marriage lasted at least 10 years.

- *Unmarried children younger than age 18.* Monthly benefits can also be paid to unmarried children of a retired worker who are younger than age 18 (or 19 if full-time elementary or high school students).
- *Unmarried disabled children.* Unmarried disabled children age 18 or older are also eligible for benefits based on the retired worker's earnings if they were severely disabled before age 22 and continue to remain disabled.
- *Spouse with dependent children younger than age 16.* A spouse at any age can receive a monthly benefit if the spouse is caring for an eligible child younger than age 16 (or is caring for a child of any age who was disabled before age 22) who is receiving a benefit based on the retired worker's earnings. The mother's or father's benefit terminates when the youngest child attains age 16 (unless the mother or father is caring for a child disabled before age 22).

Retirement Benefit Amount The monthly retirement benefit is based on the worker's **primary insurance amount (PIA)**, which is the monthly amount paid to a retired worker at the full retirement age or to a disabled worker. The PIA, in turn, is based on the worker's **average indexed monthly earnings (AIME)**, which is a method that updates the worker's earnings based on increases in the average wage in the national economy. The indexing of covered wages results in a relatively constant replacement rate so that workers retiring today and in the future will have about the same proportion of their work earnings replaced by OASDI benefits.

Earnings are indexed by taking into account changes in average wages in the national economy since the worker actually earned the money. The indexing year is the second year before the worker reaches age 62, becomes disabled, or dies, whichever occurs first. For example, assume that Vicki is a registered nurse who retired at age 62 in 2004. The critical year for setting the index factor is the second year before she attained age 62 (2002). To illustrate the method for one year, assume that Vicki's earnings in 1964 were $4800. If her actual earnings in

1964 are multiplied by the index factor for that year (7.26612), her indexed earnings for 1964 are $34,877. This procedure is carried out for each year during the measurement period, except that actual dollar amounts are counted for and after the indexing year. The index factors change each year as average wages in the national economy change.

For persons born after 1928, the highest 35 years of indexed earnings are used to calculate the worker's AIME for retirement benefits. (For those born earlier, fewer years are counted.) The AIME is then used to determine the worker's primary insurance amount. A weighted benefit formula is used, which weights the benefits heavily in favor of low-income groups. This weighting reflects the social adequacy principle discussed earlier.

Exhibit 24.2 provides examples of monthly OASDI retirement benefits for selected beneficiary designations.

Delayed Retirement Credit To encourage working beyond the full retirement age, a delayed retirement credit is available. The primary insurance amount is increased by a certain percentage if you delay receiving retirement benefits beyond the full retirement age. The percentage increase varies depending on the year of birth. For example, if you were born in 1939 or 1940, the primary insurance amount is increased by 7 percent (prorated monthly) for each year of delay beyond the full retirement age. The credit will gradually increase in the future to a maximum of 8 percent for workers born in 1943 or later.

Automatic Cost-of-Living Adjustment The cash benefits are automatically adjusted each year for changes in the cost of living, which maintains the real purchasing power of the monthly benefits during periods of inflation. Whenever the consumer price index for all urban wage earners and clerical workers on a quarterly basis increases from the third quarter of the previous year to the third quarter of the present year, the benefits are automatically increased by the same percentage for the December benefits (payable in January). The cost-of-living increase for benefits payable in January 2004 was 2.1 percent.

Earnings Test The OASDI program has an **earnings test (retirement test)** that can result in a reduc-

Exhibit 24.2
Examples of Monthly OASDI Retirement Benefits at the Full Retirement Age

The following table shows approximate monthly benefits at full retirement age for you and your spouse. It is assumed that you have worked steadily since age 22 and received average pay raises throughout your working career. It is also assumed that your earnings, and the general level of wages and salaries in the country, will stay the same until you retire. This way, *the table shows the value of your benefits in today's dollars.*

Your spouse may, instead, qualify for a higher retirement benefit based on her or his own work record.

Your Age in 2004	Who Receives Benefits	Your Present Annual Earnings				
		$20,000	$35,000	$50,000	$65,000	$87,900 and Higher
65	You	$830	$1,193	$1,521	$1,659	$1,825
	Spouse	415	596	760	829	912
64	You	852	1,225	1,564	1,711	1,888
	Spouse	426	612	782	855	944
63	You	860	1,237	1,580	1,733	1,919
	Spouse	430	618	790	866	959
62	You	851	1,224	1,564	1,721	1,913
	Spouse	425	612	782	860	956
61	You	854	1,228	1,567	1,734	1,942
	Spouse	427	614	783	867	971
55	You	861	1,240	1,575	1,753	2,008
	Spouse	430	620	787	876	1,004
50	You	866	1,250	1,582	1,762	2,003
	Spouse	433	625	791	881	1,016
45	You	872	1,260	1,588	1,770	2,050
	Spouse	436	630	794	885	1,025
40	You	879	1,273	1,596	1,781	2,067
	Spouse	439	636	798	890	1,033
35	You	885	1,282	1,603	1,790	2,078
	Spouse	442	641	801	895	1,039
30	You	888	1,288	1,606	1,794	2,080
	Spouse	444	644	803	897	1,040

Source: *2004 Guide to Social Security and Medicare* (Louisville, KY: William M. Mercer, November, 2003), p. 12.

tion or loss of monthly benefits for workers with earned incomes above certain annual limits. The earnings test has been changed several times. The most recent change occurred in 2000, which eliminated the earnings test for beneficiaries who attain the full retirement age. As a result, hundreds of thousands of older workers can continue to work without losing any benefits. The earnings test applies to the following:

- *Beneficiary under the full retirement age.* If a beneficiary is under the full retirement age, $1 in benefits will be deducted for each $2 of earnings in excess of the annual limit. For 2004, the annual limit is $11,640. The annual limit is increased annually based on increases in average wages in the national economy.

- *Calendar year in which the beneficiary attains the full retirement age.* The earnings test is liberalized for this age group. In the calendar year in which the beneficiary attains the full retirement age, $1 in benefits will be deducted for each $3 of earnings above the annual limit. For 2004, the annual limit is $31,080. *However, only earnings before the month in which the beneficiary attains the full retirement age are counted.* For example, assume that Jason attains the full retirement age in July 2004. During the first six months of 2004, Jason earned $34,080. Because his earnings are $3000 over the annual limit, he will lose $1000 in benefits.

The annual limit for this age group will increase in the future based on increases in average wages in the national economy.

■ *Earnings test eliminated after attainment of the full retirement age.* A recent change in the law eliminated the earnings test in and after the month the beneficiary attains the full retirement age. *Beneficiaries who have attained the full retirement age or beyond can earn any amount and receive full OASDI benefits.* As an alternative, beneficiaries who continue working beyond the full retirement age can elect to receive a delayed retirement credit instead of monthly cash benefits.

The earnings test does not apply to investment income, dividends, interest, rents, or annuity payments. The purpose of this exception is to encourage private savings and investments to supplement OASDI benefits.

Survivor Benefits

Survivor benefits can be paid to the dependents of a deceased worker who is either fully or currently insured. For certain survivor benefits, a fully insured status is required.

■ *Unmarried children younger than age 18.* Survivor benefits can be paid to unmarried children younger than age 18 (younger than 19 if full-time elementary or high school students).

■ *Unmarried disabled children.* Unmarried children age 18 or older who become severely disabled before age 22 are eligible for survivor benefits based on the deceased parent's earnings.

■ *Surviving spouse with children younger than age 16.* A widow, widower, or surviving divorced spouse is entitled to a monthly benefit if she or he is caring for an eligible child who is younger than age 16 (or who is disabled before age 22) and is receiving a benefit based on the deceased

worker's earnings. The benefits terminate for the surviving spouse when the youngest child reaches age 16, or the disabled child dies, marries, or is no longer disabled.

■ *Surviving spouse age 60 or older.* A surviving spouse age 60 or older is also eligible for survivor benefits. The deceased worker must be fully insured. A surviving divorced spouse age 60 or older is also eligible for survivor benefits if the marriage lasted at least 10 years.

■ *Disabled widow or widower, ages 50 through 59.* A disabled widow, widower, or surviving divorced spouse who is age 50 or older can receive survivor benefits under certain conditions. The person must be disabled at the time of the worker's death or become disabled no later than seven years after the mother's or father's benefits end. The deceased must be fully insured.

■ *Dependent parents.* Dependent parents age 62 and older can also receive survivor benefits based on the deceased's earnings. The deceased worker must be fully insured.

■ *Lump-sum death benefit.* A lump-sum death benefit of $255 can be paid when a worker dies. The benefit, however, can be paid only if there is an eligible surviving widow, widower, or entitled child.

The value of Social Security survivor benefits is substantial. For an average wage earner with a family, the value of the survivor benefits is currently equivalent to $354,000 of private life insurance.[5] The benefits, however, are paid monthly and not in a lump sum.

Disability Benefits

Disability-income benefits can be paid to disabled workers who meet certain eligibility requirements, including the following:

■ Be disability insured
■ Meet a five-month waiting period
■ Satisfy the definition of disability

A disabled worker must be disability insured and must also meet a five-month waiting period. Benefits begin after a waiting period of five full calendar months. Therefore, the first payment is for the sixth full month of disability.

The definition of disability stated in the law must also be met. A strict definition of disability is used in the program: *The worker must have a physical or mental condition that prevents him or her from doing any substantial gainful work and is expected to last (or has lasted) at least 12 months or is expected to result in death.* The impairment must be so severe that the worker is prevented from doing any substantial gainful work in the national economy. In determining whether a person can do substantial gainful work, his or her age, education, training, and work experience can be taken into consideration. If the disabled person cannot work at his or her own occupation but can engage in other substantial gainful work, the disability claim will not be allowed.[6]

The major groups eligible to receive OASDI disability-income benefits are as follows:

- *Disabled worker.* A disabled worker under the full retirement age receives a benefit equal to 100 percent of the primary insurance amount. The worker must meet the definition of disability, be disability insured, and satisfy a full five-month waiting period.
- *Spouse of a disabled worker.* Benefits can be paid to the spouse of a disabled worker at any age if she or he is caring for a child younger than age 16 or a child who became disabled before age 22 and is receiving benefits based on the disabled worker's earnings. If no eligible children are present, the spouse must be at least age 62 to receive benefits.
- *Unmarried children younger than age 18.* Disability benefits can be paid to unmarried children younger than age 18 (or younger than 19 if a full-time elementary or high school student).
- *Unmarried disabled children.* Unmarried children age 18 or older who became severely disabled before age 22 are also eligible for benefits, based on the disabled worker's earnings.

In summary, the OASDI program provides valuable retirement, survivor, and disability benefits to workers and their families. The benefits are especially valuable during periods of national emergency. In particular, the terrorist attacks in the United States on September 11, 2001 caused the deaths of thousands of workers. The OASDI program responded quickly by paying survivor benefits to the victims' families. Insight 24.1 provides an update of the benefits paid because of the terrorist attacks.

Taxation of OASDI Benefits

Some beneficiaries who receive monthly cash benefits must pay an income tax on part of the benefits. The amount of benefits subject to taxation depends on your combined income. *Combined income* (also called *provisional income*) is the sum of your adjusted gross income, plus tax-free interest, plus one-half of your Social Security benefits. If your combined income exceeds certain dollar thresholds, some benefits are taxable.

If you file a federal tax return as an individual and your combined income is between $25,000 and $34,000, up to 50 percent of the benefits are subject to taxation. If your combined income exceeds $34,000, up to 85 percent of your benefits are subject to taxation.

If you are married and file a joint tax return and have a combined income between $32,000 and $44,000, up to 50 percent of the benefits are subject to taxation. If your combined income exceeds $44,000, up to 85 percent of the benefits are subject to taxation.

For married taxpayers who file separate tax returns and have lived together anytime during the year, the dollar threshold is zero. If not living together, you are considered to be a single person.

The Social Security Administration will send you a form each year that shows the amount of Social Security benefits received. The Internal Revenue Service has prepared a detailed worksheet to determine the amount of benefits, if any, to include in your taxable income.

Financing Social Security Benefits

Social Security benefits are financed by a payroll tax paid by employees, employers, and the self-employed; interest income on the trust fund investments; and by revenues derived from the taxation of part of the monthly cash benefits.

In 2004, a worker paid a payroll tax of 6.2 percent on covered earnings up to a maximum of $87,900. The maximum taxable earnings base will automatically increase in the future if wages in the national economy increase. In addition, a worker

INSIGHT 24.1

Social Security and September 11th: Two Years Later—2003

- **Social Security is America's family protection plan.** It is more than a retirement program; it provides valuable survivors and disability protection for workers and their families.
- **As a result of September 11th, Social Security received 5629 individual benefit claims from 2281 families.** Most of the assistance went to family members of those killed in the terrorist attacks. However, Social Security also helped workers get disability and retirement benefits.
  - *Survivors Benefits:* When a worker dies, certain surviving family members may be eligible for Social Security survivors benefits. **Social Security is currently paying monthly benefits to 2375 surviving children and 853 surviving spouses. In addition to monthly benefits, one-time payments were made to 1800 members of victims' families.**
  - *Disability Benefits:* When a worker is unable to work due to a disability that lasts or may be expected to last at least one year or to result in death, the disabled worker and certain family members may be eligible for Social Security disability benefits. **Social Security is currently paying monthly benefits to 498 individuals disabled by the terrorist attacks of September 11th and 81 of their dependent spouses or children**

- **Nearly $67 million in benefits have been paid to people affected by the September 11, 2001 tragedies.**
  - The first payments to surviving family members (benefits for the month of September) were paid on October 3, 2001.
  - As of August 2003, Social Security is paying more than $3 million per month.
- **Social Security responded to the September 11th terrorist attacks by activating special emergency procedures to give the fastest possible service to the families of the victims of the tragedies at the World Trade Center, the Pentagon and in Pennsylvania.**
  - These procedures allowed for acceptance of documents as proof of death that, under other circumstances, would not have been accepted. Airplane manifests, lists of employees furnished by employers and other statements that placed the worker at the scene of the attacks were accepted.
  - Social Security employees helped families at special assistance centers that were established in New York, Arlington, VA and Shanksville, PA.

SOURCE: "Social Security and September 11th: Two Years Later—2003," *Press Office Fact Sheet*, September 2003.

---

pays a Medicare tax of 1.45 percent on all of earned income, including earnings that exceed the OASDI wage base. The employee's contribution is matched by an identical contribution from the employer.

The self-employed pay a tax rate that is twice the employee rate. However the self-employed are allowed certain deductions, which reduce the effective tax rate.

Long-Range OASDI Actuarial Deficit   It has always been the intent of Congress that the OASDI program should be actuarially sound. Although the present program is currently running an annual surplus, the program will experience a serious long-range actuarial deficit in the years ahead. Based on and the intermediate cost estimate in the 2004 Board of Trustees Report, the OASDI trust funds will experience serious financial problems in the future. The annual cost of OASDI benefits repre-

sents 4.3 percent of the gross domestic product (GDP) today and is projected to increase to 6.6 percent of GDP in 2078. *The projected 75-year actuarial deficit in the combined Old-Age and Survivors Insurance (OASI) and Disability Insurance (DI) trust funds is 1.89 percent of taxable payroll, down slightly from 1.92 percent in last year's report. The program continues to fail a long-range test of financial balance by a wide margin. Projected OASDI tax income will begin to fall short of outlays in 2018 and will be sufficient to finance only 73 percent of the scheduled annual benefits by 2042, when the combined OASDI trust fund is projected to be exhausted.*[7]

Reducing the Long-Range Deficit   Reducing the long-range deficit will require some hard choices. Based on the 2004 Board of Trustees Report, the Social Security program can be actuarially balanced over the next 75 years in various ways, *which include an immediate increase in scheduled program revenues of 15 percent or an immediate reduction in benefits of 13 percent, or some combination of the two. Greater adjustment in scheduled benefits and revenues will be required if the changes are delayed or gradually phased in.*[8]

Four basic approaches for reducing or eliminating the deficit include (1) increasing payroll taxes, (2) decreasing benefits, (3) using general revenues to fund benefits, and (4) prefunding future benefits by personal savings accounts or by direct investment of the trust funds in private investments. The proposals can be implemented individually or in combination with each other. Examples of changes that will increase revenues or reduce costs include the following:

- Extend Social Security coverage on a compulsory basis to new state and local government employees.
- Increase the number of years used in calculating retirement benefits from 35 to 38.
- Speed up scheduled increases in the full retirement age, or increase it beyond age 67.
- Reduce benefits for future retirees across the board.
- Increase the Social Security taxable earnings base to cover a larger percentage of earnings.
- Subject all Social Security benefits to the federal income tax.
- Invest part of the trust fund assets in private investments, such as common stock.

In addition, the general revenues of the federal government could be used to fund the program. It was proposed earlier to use part of the projected future surplus in the unified budget to reduce the long-range deficit. However, the projected surplus has vanished because of a business downswing in 2001–2002; recent federal income-tax cuts; and increased federal spending to finance the war in Iraq, homeland security, and the war on terrorism. As a result, the unified budget is expected to run deficits for several years in the future. Thus, increased reliance on general revenue financing to reduce the long-range deficit is unlikely.

The preceding proposals are controversial. Their impact on the long-range deficit will vary depending on the proposal selected. The American Academy of Actuaries has designed an interactive

Social Security program that allows you to make hypothetical changes in the OASDI program and gives an estimate of the impact on the long-range deficit (see Insight 24.2).

Voluntary Personal Retirement Accounts Under this proposal, each worker could use part of the Social Security payroll tax to establish a personal retirement account. The tax contributions would be invested in a common stock fund or some other approved investment. At retirement, the worker would receive benefits from the individual account and traditional Social Security. If the worker died before retirement, the deceased worker's spouse or beneficiary would inherit the assets.

The President's Commission to Strengthen Social Security has proposed three reform models for Congress and the public to consider:[9]

- *Model 1. Workers can voluntarily invest 2 percent of taxable wages in a personal account. In exchange, there would be a comparable reduction in traditional Social Security benefits. No other changes would be made to traditional Social Security. This approach would reduce the long-range deficit but not eliminate it.*
- *Model 2. Workers can voluntarily invest 4 percent of taxable wages up to $1000 annually in a personal account. In exchange, there would be a comparable reduction in traditional Social Security benefits. However, for future retirees, Social Security benefits would be indexed for annual price changes instead of wage growth. The Commission claims that future retirees will receive combined benefits that are at least as high as benefits paid to today's retirees without raising taxes or requiring additional worker contributions. The Commission also claims that long-range solvency will be restored.*
- *Model 3. Workers could contribute 2.5 percent of taxable wages up to $1000 annually to a personal account (with a comparable reduction in traditional benefits) but only if they contribute an additional 1 percent of taxable wages. The Commission believes that benefits will reach or exceed current scheduled benefits and wage replacement ratios under this model. The Commission also claims that the plan achieves long-range solvency by adding to revenues and by slowing the growth in benefits.*

INSIGHT 24.2

How Would You Fix Social Security?

There are no easy solutions for saving Social Security. The long-range actuarial deficit can be eliminated only by increasing revenues, reducing benefits, or both. The American Academy of Actuaries has an interactive program on its Web site (www.actuary.org/socialsecurity) that allows you to make hypothetical changes in the Social Security program. The program then shows the estimated change in the long-range actuarial deficit based on the Board of Trustees Reports. Also shown are arguments for and against the proposed change. One major advantage is that you can propose changes in Social Security that are consistent with your political, economic, and ideological beliefs. The following are examples of the proposed changes and the estimated reduction in the long-range deficit.

	Reduction in Long-Range Deficit
Benefit Reductions	
• Gradually increase the retirement age for full benefits to age 70 by 2030 and index thereafter.	68%
• Accelerate the increase in retirement age to 67 and index thereafter.	26
• Reduce the annual cost-of-living adjustment (COLA) by 1/2 percentage point.	37
• Reduce benefits by 5 percent for future retirees.	26
• Reduce benefits for those whose total retirement income exceeds $45,000 annually.	85
Revenue Increases	
• Increase the payroll tax on employees and employers by 1/2 percentage point each.	53
• Increase wages subject to Social Security taxes to $95,000.	26
• Eliminate the cap on taxable wages.	77
• Tax Social Security benefits like pension benefits.	16
• Cover new state and local government employees.	11
Investing in the Private Sector	
• Invest 40 percent of the Social Security trust fund in private investments, such as stocks.	48
• Create personal retirement accounts (Deposit 1 percentage point of the payroll tax into a private account)	Cost not estimated

SOURCE: Adapted from American Academy of Actuaries, *The Social Security Game*, www.actuary.org/socialsecurity.

Personal retirement accounts are controversial. Proponents of personal accounts claim that the real rate of return on OASDI payroll taxes under the present system is relatively low. Most single workers will earn a real rate of return under 2 percent (see Exhibit 24.3). In addition, the age an average earner must attain to receive back in benefits all of the taxes paid for the retirement portion of Social Security will also increase in the future (see Exhibit 24.4). Proponents believe that personal accounts will allow younger workers to earn substantially higher real rates of return, especially if the tax contributions are invested in common stocks.

Proponents of personal accounts also argue that low-income workers can accumulate sizable financial assets over time and that the workers would legally own the assets. If a worker dies before retirement, the assets would be paid to the decedent's spouse or beneficiary.

Critics of personal accounts, however, argue that the risk to workers will increase. Workers would have to bear any investment losses, and the present OASDI program with its safety net and income guarantees would be dramatically altered. In addition, critics argue that substantial amounts of general revenues will be needed to finance the transaction

EXHIBIT 24.3
Real Rates of Return for All Retirees[a]

Birth Year	Single Male (Medium Wages)	Single Female (Medium Wages)	Single Earner Couple (Medium Wages)	Two-Earner Couple (Medium/ Low Wages)
1970	1.13%	1.59%	3.42%	2.24%
1980	0.91	1.36	3.31	2.08
1990	0.88	1.29	3.14	1.97
2000	0.86	1.25	3.02	1.88

NOTE: May 27, 2001, calculation by the Social Security Office of the Actuary.

[a]Assumes no change in the law, retirement at age 65.

SOURCE: President's Commission to Strengthen Social Security, *The Interim Report of the President's Commission to Strengthen Social Security*, Washington, DC, August 10, 2001.

EXHIBIT 24.4
What Age Must You Reach to Get Back What You've Paid In?

Year of Birth	Age an Average Earner Gets Back Taxes Paid into the Retirement Portion of Social Security	Total Life Expectancy for Individual Reaching Age 65	
		MALE	FEMALE
1875	65.2	77.7	79.7
1895	66.1	78.2	82.4
1915	67.8	79.7	83.9
1936	81.8	81.3	84.6
1945	85.2	81.9	85.0
1955	89.7	82.5	85.6
1965	91.9	83.0	86.1

NOTE: Data are from Congressional Research Service, "Social Security: The Relationship of Taxes and Benefits for Past, Present, and Future Retirees," June 22, 2001. Under the intermediate assumptions of the 2001 Trustees Report and taking into account benefit increases and continued accrual of interest after retirement but not the taxation of benefits. The retirees are assumed to begin work at age 22 and retire in January of the year in which they turn 65. Assumes contributions earn interest equal to the long-term government bond rate.

SOURCE: President's Commission to Strengthen Social Security, *The Interim Report of the President's Commission to Strengthen Social Security*, Washington, DC, August 10, 2001.

costs of the new program, which will increase the size of the federal debt. Critics also argue that the reduction in future OASDI benefits will be substantial, and that workers will receive less at retirement if the expected investment gains are not realized. Finally, critics argue that the proposal would result in a horrendous administrative problem for a large number of workers.

MEDICARE

Medicare is an important part of the Social Security program that covers the medical expenses of almost all persons age 65 and older. Medicare also covers disabled persons younger than age 65 who have been entitled to disability benefits for at least 24 months (they need not be continuous). In addition, the program covers persons younger than age 65 who need long-term kidney dialysis treatment or a kidney transplant.

The Medicare program has been changed several times since its enactment in 1965. The latest and most sweeping changes occurred in late 2003 when Congress passed **The Medicare Prescription Drug, Improvement, and Modernization Act of 2003.** The new law adds a prescription drug benefit to Medicare, provides substantial subsidies to employers and insurers to encourage participation in the program, allows private plans to compete with Medicare, and modernizes the program. The key provision in the law that adds a prescription drug benefit to the program, however, does not become effective until 2006.

The new legislation is complex and controversial. Some provisions will not become effective until future years. The major coverages and key provisions in the current Medicare program include the following:

- Hospital Insurance (Part A)
- Medical Insurance (Part B)
- Medicare Advantage (formerly Medicare + Choice)
- New prescription drug benefit

Hospital Insurance (Part A)

Hospital Insurance (Part A) provides coverage for hospital stays and other benefits as well. Part A benefits include the following:

- *Inpatient hospital care.* Inpatient care in a hospital is covered for up to 90 days for each benefit period. A *benefit period* starts when the patient first enters the hospital and ends when the patient has been out of the hospital or skilled nursing facility for 60 consecutive days. For the first 60 days, Medicare pays all covered costs except for an initial inpatient hospital deductible ($876 in 2004). The deductible is paid only once during the benefit period no matter how many times the patient is hospitalized. For the 61st through 90th day, Medicare pays all covered costs except for a daily coinsurance charge ($219 in 2004). If the patient is still hospitalized after 90 days, a *lifetime reserve* of 60 additional days is available. Lifetime reserve days are subject to a daily coinsurance charge

($438 in 2004). The inpatient hospital deductible and coinsurance charges are adjusted annually to reflect changes in hospital costs.

- *Skilled nursing facility care.* Inpatient care in a skilled nursing facility is covered up to maximum of 100 days in a benefit period. The first 20 days of covered services are paid in full. For the next 80 days, the patient must pay a daily coinsurance charge ($109.50 in 2004). To be eligible for coverage, the patient must be hospitalized first for at least three days and must require skilled nursing care. Intermediate care and custodial care are not covered.

- *Home health care services.* Health care services in the patient's home are covered if the patient requires skilled care and meets certain conditions. Covered services include skilled nursing care, physical therapy, occupational therapy, speech-language therapy, home health aide services, medical social services, durable medical equipment, medical supplies, and other services. No cost-sharing provisions apply to covered services, but the patient must pay 20 percent of the Medicare-approved amount for durable medical equipment.

- *Hospice care.* Hospice care is available for beneficiaries with a terminal illness. Benefits include drugs for pain relief and symptom control, medical and support services from a Medicare-approved hospice, and other services not otherwise covered by Medicare. Hospice care is usually given in the patient's home. However, short-term hospital and inpatient respite care are covered when necessary. Respite care is care given to a hospice patient so that the usual caregiver can rest for a short period.

- *Blood transfusions.* Part A also pays for the cost of inpatient blood transfusions in a hospital or skilled nursing facility during a covered stay. The first three pints of blood are not covered. However, the patient cannot be charged for the first three pints if the blood is replaced by the patient or someone else.

Hospitals are reimbursed for inpatient services under a prospective payment system. Hospital care is classified into **diagnosis-related groups (DRGs),** and a flat amount is paid for each type of care depending on the diagnosis group in which the case is placed. Thus, a flat, uniform amount is paid to each hospital for the same type of care or treatment. However, the amount paid varies among different geographical locations and by urban and rural facilities.

The purpose of the DRG system is to create a financial incentive to encourage hospitals to operate more efficiently. Hospitals can keep the payment amounts that exceed their costs, but they must absorb any costs in excess of the DRG flat amounts.

Medical Insurance (Part B)

Medical Insurance (Part B) is a voluntary program that covers physicians' fees and related medical services. Beneficiaries who are covered under Part A on the basis of their covered earnings are automatically covered under Part B unless they voluntarily decline the coverage.

Part B pays for several types of services that are medically necessary. Covered services include the following:

- *Physicians' services.* Physicians' services are covered in the doctor's office, hospital, or elsewhere. Medical supplies furnished by a doctor in the office, services of the office nurse, and drugs administered by a doctor are also covered.
- *Outpatient hospital services.* Outpatient hospital services for diagnosis and treatment are covered, such as care in an emergency room or outpatient clinic in a hospital. Laboratory tests, X-rays, and diagnostic hospital services as an outpatient are also covered.
- *Home health care services.* Part B also provides home health care services. These services are similar to those provided by Part A.
- *Other medical and health care services.* Other covered services include diagnostic tests, X-rays and radiation treatment, limited ambulance services, prosthetic devices, and durable medical equipment used at home.

Part B has numerous exclusions, including most dental care, dentures, routine foot care, and hearing aids. Eyeglasses are covered only if the patient needs corrective lenses after a cataract operation.

Amount Paid by Part B   In 2004, Part B of Medicare paid 80 percent of the approved charges for most

covered services after a $100 calendar-year deductible is met. For some services, Part B pays all allowable costs in full, such as flu shots and pneumonia shots if the health-care provider accepts an assignment. For other *outpatient services,* the patient pays an amount that varies according to the service provided but cannot exceed $876 per service in 2004.

Under the new Medicare law, the Part B deductible will increase in the future. *Beginning in 2005, the Part B deductible will increase from $100 to $110 and will be indexed thereafter to the growth in Part B spending.*

For services provided by physicians, Part B also pays 80 percent of the Medicare-approved amount after the annual deductible is met. The approved fee is usually less than the physician's actual fee. The approved amount is based on a complex relative-value fee schedule that determines payment based on the time, skill, and intensity of the services provided; the cost of practicing medicine; and medical malpractice costs. Geographical variations in the cost of practicing medicine are also considered.

Medical payments to physicians are made on an assigned or nonassigned basis. By accepting an assignment, a physician agrees to accept the Medicare-approved amount as payment in full. The patient is not liable for any additional out-of-pocket costs other than the calendar-year deductible and coinsurance payments. However, physicians who do not accept an assignment of a Medicare claim cannot charge more than 15 percent above the allowable charge. Many physicians refuse to accept new Medicare patients because the Medicare-approved payments are often less than the physician's actual cost of treatment.

Part B Monthly Premium   Beneficiaries with Part B coverage must pay a monthly premium for the benefits provided ($66.60 in 2004), which is supplemented by the federal government out of its general revenues. Under previous law, all Part B beneficiaries paid 25 percent of the cost of program, and the federal government paid the rest. *However, the new Medicare law introduces a means test based on income into the program; beginning in 2007, the Part B premium will increase for Medicare beneficiaries with annual incomes in excess of $80,000 for individuals and $160,000 for couples.* Actual Part B premium amounts will not become available until the end of 2006.

Under the new law, all beneficiaries with annual incomes under $80,000 ($160,000 for couples) will continue to receive the 75 percent premium subsidy. The subsidy declines to 65 percent for beneficiaries with annual incomes between $80,000 and $100,000; 50 percent for beneficiaries with annual incomes between $100,000 and $150,000; 35 percent for beneficiaries with annual incomes between $150,000 and $200,000; and 20 percent for beneficiaries with annual incomes over $200,000. The income thresholds for couples will be twice the individual threshold limit. Threshold limits will increase annually based on the consumer price index. The new premiums will be phased-in over a five-year period beginning in 2007.

The means testing of Part B premiums based on income represents a significant departure from a basic social insurance principle, which is the payment of cash benefits to eligible applicants without a formal means test. Public assistance and other welfare programs require applicants to meet a means test before the benefits are paid, and the benefit amount is related to the applicant's income. The new Medicare law introduces a welfare element into the Part B program because Part B premiums for some beneficiaries will increase because of their incomes. As a result, the social insurance character of Part B will be diluted when the new means test becomes operational.

Financing of Medicare

Hospital Insurance (Part A) is financed largely by a payroll tax paid by covered employees, employers, and the self-employed, plus a relatively small amount of general revenues. As stated earlier, the payroll tax for covered employees and employers is 1.45 percent on all covered earnings, even those that exceed the maximum Social Security earnings base. Medical Insurance (Part B) is financed by monthly premiums and the general revenues of the federal government.

Medicare Financial Crisis Hospital Insurance (Part A) of Medicare will experience a serious financial crisis in the future. *The 2004 Board of Trustees Report shows that the projected 75-year actuarial deficit in the Hospital Insurance (HI) Trust Fund is now 3.12 percent of taxable payroll, up significantly from 2.40 percent in last year's report. The increased*

deficit is due mainly to higher actual and projected hospital expenditures, lower actual and projected taxable payroll, and new Medicare legislation. The fund also fails a long-range test of close actuarial balance by a wide margin. The projected date of exhaustion of the HI Trust Fund has been moved up to 2019 as compared to 2026 in last year's report. In addition, HI tax income falls short of outlays beginning this year (2004), as compared to 2013 in last year's report. HI could be brought into actuarial balance over the next 75 years by an immediate increase of 108 percent in program income or an immediate 48 percent reduction in program outlays, or some combination of the two. Greater adjustments will be required if the changes are delayed or phased in gradually.[10]

The unsatisfactory financial condition is due to several factors, including an increase in the number of Medicare beneficiaries, inflation in hospital costs exceeding the overall rate of inflation, fraud and abuse by health-care providers, increased home-health care costs, and an inefficient and inflationary fee-for-service method of reimbursement.

To hold down Medicare costs, Congress earlier reduced payments to hospitals and physicians, placed spending limits on specified services, placed limits on fee increases paid to physicians, implemented the diagnosis-related group method in which flat amounts are paid to hospitals for each specific case, and introduced other cost-reduction measures as well. Despite these efforts, however, Medicare costs continue to increase. The new Medicare law contains provisions that will allow private plans to compete with the Medicare program (discussed later). One major objective is to stimulate competition so that, hopefully, the escalation in Medicare costs can be slowed.

Medicare Advantage Program (formerly Medicare + Choice)

As an alternative to the original Medicare program, Congress enacted the Medicare + Choice program (part C) in 1997, which allows beneficiaries to enroll in private health maintenance organizations (HMOs) that contract with Medicare. The private plans provide regular Medicare benefits and often additional benefits as well, such as prescription drugs outside the hospital. Under the new law, the Medicare + Choice program has been renamed the

Medicare Advantage program. Beginning in 2006, Medicare Advantage plans will be expanded to include regional preferred provide organizations (PPOs) that will enable beneficiaries in both urban and rural areas to have multiple choices of Medicare health coverage.

At the beginning of 2004, Medicare beneficiaries had the following choices:

- *Original Medicare Plan.* Beneficiaries can elect the original Medicare plan, which is the traditional plan run by the federal government that provides Part A and Part B benefits. Beneficiaries can elect any provider that accepts Medicare patients. Medicare pays its share of the bill, and the beneficiary pays the balance. Some services are not covered.
- *Medicare Managed Care Plans.* Beneficiaries can also elect a Medicare managed care plan, such as a health maintenance organization (HMO). The plan may provide extra benefits, such as prescription drugs outside the hospital.

  Managed care plans are operated by private insurers. In most plans, patients can see only doctors, specialists, or hospitals that are part of the plan network. If patients receive care outside of the service area of the plan, they may have to pay more for the service provided, or it may not be covered.

  The plan may also require members to choose a primary care physician and get a referral to see a specialist. Physicians can join or leave managed care plans at any time. At the end of each year, Medicare managed care plans can leave the Medicare program or change their benefits. However, new plans may become available.
- *Medicare Preferred Provider Organization Plans (PPOs).* Beneficiaries also have the option of receiving care from a Medicare PPO. In addition to Medicare services, the PPO may provide additional benefits, such as coverage for prescription drugs. In most PPO plans, patients receive treatment from physicians, specialists, and hospitals that belong to the plan network. However, patients are free to use health care providers that are outside the network, but they must pay higher out-of-pocket costs. Plan members do not need a referral from a primary care physician to see a specialist.

- *Medicare Specialty Plans.* These plans provide more focused care for Medicare beneficiaries with certain diseases, such as congestive heart failure, diabetes, or end-stage renal disease. A specialty plan provides Medicare health care services as well as more focused care to manage a specific disease or condition. The objective is to provide efficient, cost effective, and high quality care to Medicare beneficiaries with certain diseases.
- *Private Fee-for-Service Plans.* In some areas of the country, private insurers offer private fee-for-service plans. Patients can go to any Medicare-approved physician or hospital that accepts Medicare beneficiaries and accepts the terms of the plan's payment schedule. Patients may receive additional benefits not covered by the original Medicare plan, such as extra days in a hospital or prescription drugs. However, the private company rather than Medicare determines the amounts paid for covered services and how much the patient has to pay for the services provided. In addition, patients may have to pay premiums when they join a private fee-for-service plan and other costs as well, such as copayments and coinsurance. These costs are different from those paid under the original Medicare plan. Finally, at the end of each year, companies offering private fee-for-service plans can decide to join, leave, or continue to offer the plan.

New Prescription Drug Benefit

Beginning in 2006, Medicare beneficiaries will have access to a voluntary prescription drug benefit for the first time in the history of the program. This benefit will provide significant savings for seniors and younger disabled beneficiaries. A drug discount card will be used during the interim period.

Key Provisions The prescription drug program is complex and controversial. The key provisions are summarized as follows:

- *Interim drug discount card.* Medicare-approved discount cards are now available that beneficiaries can use before the prescription drug program becomes effective in 2006. The discount card will provide an estimated discount of 10 percent to 20 percent off the retail price of

EXHIBIT 24.5
Out-of-Pocket Drug Spending in 2006 for Medicare Beneficiaries Under New Medicare Legislation

Note: Benefit levels are indexed to growth in per capita expenditures for covered Part D drugs. As a result, the Part D deductible is projected to increase from $250 in 2006 to $445 in 2013; the catastrophic threshold is projected to increase from $5100 in 2006 to $9066 in 2013.

SOURCE: The Henry J. Kaiser Family Foundation, November 2003. This material is reprinted with permission of the Henry J. Kaiser Family Foundation. The Kaiser Family Foundation, based in Menlo Park, CA is a nonprofit, independent national health care philantropy and is not associated with Kaiser Permanente or Kaiser Industries.

prescription drugs. Low-income beneficiaries with no coverage for prescription drugs from other sources will receive an annual subsidy of $600 to help them pay for their drugs during the interim period

- *Prescription drug benefit.* Beginning in 2006, beneficiaries can enroll in a private stand-alone drug plan or a private health plan. The estimated monthly premium is $35. After a $250 annual deductible is met, Medicare will pay 75 percent of the drug costs between the deductible and $2250.
- *Coverage gap.* Beneficiaries will pay 100 percent for the cost of drugs between $2250 and $5100, which is equivalent to $3600 in out-of-pocket spending.
- *Catastrophic coverage.* Medicare will pay 95 percent of drug costs in excess of $5100, or require a modest copayment. Exhibit 24.5 shows the interaction of these provisions under the new Medicare law.
- *Low-income subsidies.* Monthly premiums, the annual deductible, and the coverage gap are waived for low-income beneficiaries with incomes under 135 percent of the federal

poverty line. Low-income beneficiaries, however, would pay $2 for each generic prescription and $5 for all other prescriptions. To qualify, beneficiaries cannot have more than $6000 in fluid assets ($9000 for couples).

Other low income beneficiaries with limited assets and incomes between 135 percent and 150 percent of the poverty line will receive premium and deductible assistance and have limited cost sharing.

- *Coverage options.* The new law has several options for obtaining prescription drug coverage. Beneficiaries in the original Medicare plan will be able to enroll voluntarily in a *Prescription Drug Plan (PDP),* which is a private stand-alone drug plan that contracts with Medicare to provide drug coverage to beneficiaries in a certain area. Beneficiaries will also have the option of enrolling in a private *Medical Advantage Plan,* which can be a local health maintenance organization (HMO) or a regional preferred provider organization (PPO). Medical Advantage plans will provide drug benefits in addition to other benefits. Finally, beneficiaries who are now covered for prescription drugs under the group plans of former employers can elect to remain in the employer's plan, and Medicare will provide a tax-free subsidy to help employers pay for the drug coverage provided.

■ *Retiree coverage.* The Congressional Budget Office has estimated that millions of beneficiaries now covered for prescription drugs under employer plans could lose their coverage if the employers discontinued providing drug benefits after the new law becomes effective. Employers that continue to provide drug coverage for retirees when the Medicare drug benefit begins in 2006 will receive tax-free subsidies. The subsidies are estimated to be worth as much as $70 billion and are designed to encourage employers to continue to provide drug coverage for retirees.

Other Provisions The new law contains additional provisions that deal with prescription drugs. Other provisions are designed to encourage private plans to compete with Medicare. Some important provisions that merit a brief discussion include the following:

■ *Importing drugs from foreign countries.* Importing drugs from foreign countries is not allowed. However, drugs could be imported from Canada if the Department of Health and Human Services (HHS) certifies that the drugs are safe, something that HHS has refused to do at the time of this writing.

■ *Prohibiting federal government to negotiate drug prices.* The federal government is prohibited from using its purchasing power to negotiate lower drug prices with pharmaceutical firms.

■ *Role of private firms.* Private firms will administer the program on a regional basis. The new law provides substantial subsidies to private insurers to encourage them to participate in the program, which includes PPOs and private-fee-for-service plans.

■ *Competition from private plans.* Beginning in 2010, the original Medicare plan will face competition from private plans in a demonstration project in six metropolitan areas. The demonstration project will last six years. The areas selected must have at least two private plans that enroll at least 25 percent of the Medicare beneficiaries. For beneficiaries who remain in

the original Medicare plan, premium increases are limited to a maximum of 5 percent annually and are waived for low-income beneficiaries. The federal government will provide a backup drug plan in any region that does not have at least one private health plan and one stand alone drug plan.

Health Savings Accounts As stated in Chapter 22, the new Medicare law allows all eligible persons under age 65 to establish health savings accounts and receive favorable income tax treatment. A **health savings account (HSA)** *is a tax-exempt trust or custodial account established exclusively for the purpose of paying qualified medical expenses of the account beneficiary who is covered under a high-deductible health insurance plan.* To receive favorable tax treatment, you must purchase a high-deductible health insurance policy and cannot be covered by another low-deductible plan. The annual deductible for an individual must be at least $1000, and annual out-of-pocket expenses cannot exceed $5000. For family coverage, the annual deductible must be at least $2000, and annual out-of-pocket expenses cannot exceed $10,000.

HSA contributions can be made by individuals, employers, and family members. Contributions to the HSA account are income-tax deductible up to certain limits; investment earnings accumulate income-tax free; and distributions from the account are tax-free if used to pay for qualified medical expenses. Any employer contributions are not taxed as income to the employee.

For 2004, total contributions for individual coverage are limited to the annual deductible, or $2600 ($5150 for family coverage), whichever is lower. For 2004, individuals between ages 55 and 65 can make additional catch-up contributions.

Medigap Insurance

Because of numerous exclusions, deductibles, cost-sharing provisions, and limitations on approved charges, Medicare does not pay all medical expenses. As a result, most Medicare beneficiaries either have post-retirement health benefits from their former employers or have purchased a Medigap policy or Medicare supplement policy that pays part or all of the covered charges not paid by Medicare.

Medigap policies are sold by private insurers and are strictly regulated by federal law. There are various standard policies, each of which offers a different combination of benefits. The basic policy has a core package of benefits. The remaining policies have a different combination of benefits, but they all include the core package. Each policy has a letter designation ranging from A through J. Insurers are not allowed to change the various combinations of benefits or the letter designations.

Insurers must provide an open enrollment period of six months from the date the applicant first enrolls in Medicare Part B and is age 65 or older. Applicants cannot be turned down or charged higher premiums because of poor health if they buy a policy during that period. Once the Medigap open enrollment period ends, beneficiaries may not be able to buy a policy of their choice but may have to accept whatever an insurer is willing to provide.

The new Medicare law also has provisions that affect Medigap insurance. At the time of this writing, there are ten standard Medigap policies. In 2006, Medigap plans will include two new plans to help beneficiaries with their out-of-pocket costs. No new Medigap policies with drug coverage may be sold.

UNEMPLOYMENT INSURANCE

Unemployment insurance programs are federal-state programs that pay weekly cash benefits to workers who are involuntarily unemployed. Each state has its own unemployment insurance program. The various state programs arose out of the unemployment insurance provisions of the Social Security Act of 1935.

Unemployment insurance has several basic objectives:

- Provide cash income during involuntary unemployment
- Help unemployed workers find jobs
- Encourage employers to stabilize employment
- Help stabilize the economy

Weekly cash benefits are paid to unemployed workers during periods of **short-term involuntary unemployment,** thus helping them maintain their economic security. A second objective is to help unemployed workers find jobs; applicants for bene-

fits must register for work at local employment offices, and officials provide assistance in finding suitable jobs. A third objective is to encourage employers to stabilize their employment through experience rating (discussed later). Finally, unemployment benefits help stabilize the economy during recessionary periods.

Coverage

Most private firms, state and local governments, and nonprofit organizations are covered for unemployment benefits. A *private firm* is subject to the federal unemployment tax if it employs one or more employees in each of at least 20 weeks during the calendar year (or preceding calendar year), or it pays wages of $1500 or more during a calendar quarter of either year. Most jobs in *state and local government* are also covered for unemployment insurance benefits. However, state and local governments are not required to pay the federal unemployment tax but instead may elect to reimburse the system for the benefits paid to government employees. In addition, *nonprofit charitable, educational, or religious organizations* are covered if they employ four or more workers for at least one day in each of 20 different weeks during the current or prior year. The nonprofit organization has the right either to pay the unemployment tax or to reimburse the states for the benefits paid.

Agricultural firms are covered if they have a quarterly payroll of at least $20,000 or employ ten or more workers in at least 20 weeks during the current or prior year. *Domestic employment* in a private household is covered if the employer pays domestic wages of $1000 or more in a calendar quarter during the current or prior year.

Eligibility Requirements

An unemployed worker must meet the following eligibility requirements to receive benefits:

- Have qualifying wages and employment during the base year
- Be able and available for work
- Actively seek work
- Be free from disqualification
- Serve a one-week waiting period

The applicant must earn qualifying wages of a specified amount during his or her base year. In most states, the base year is the first four of the last five calendar quarters preceding the unemployed worker's claim for benefits. Most states also require employment in at least two calendar quarters during the base year. The purpose of this requirement is to limit benefits to workers with a current attachment to the labor force.

The applicant must be physically and mentally capable of working and must be available for work. The claimant must register for work at a public employment office and actively seek work.

The applicant must not be disqualified from receiving benefits. Disqualifying acts include voluntarily quitting his or her job without good cause, direct participation in a labor dispute, being discharged for misconduct, or refusing suitable work.

Finally, a one-week waiting period must be satisfied in most states. The waiting period eliminates short-term claims, holds down costs, and provides time to obtain the claimant's wage record and process the claim.

Benefits

A weekly cash benefit is paid for each week of total unemployment. The benefit paid varies with the worker's past wages, within certain minimum and maximum dollar amounts. Most states use a formula that pays weekly benefits based on a fraction of the worker's high quarter wages. For example, a fraction of $\frac{1}{26}$ results in the payment of benefits equal to 50 percent of the worker's full-time wage in the highest quarter (subject to minimum and maximum amounts). For instance, assume that Jennifer earns $400 weekly or $5200 during her highest quarter. Applying the fraction of $\frac{1}{26}$ to this amount produces a weekly unemployment benefit of $200, or 50 percent of her full-time weekly wage. Several states also pay a dependent's allowance for certain dependents.

During the second quarter of calendar 2003, the average weekly benefit amount ranged from $107 in Puerto Rico to $358 in Massachusetts. The average weekly benefit for the United States was $263 during the same period.[11] In virtually all jurisdictions, the maximum duration of regular benefits is limited to 26 weeks.

During periods of high unemployment, some workers exhaust their regular unemployment benefits. A permanent federal-state program of extended benefits pays additional benefits to unemployed workers who exhaust their regular benefits during periods of high unemployment in individual states. Under the **extended-benefits program,** claimants can receive up to 13 additional weeks of benefits or one-half the total amount of regular benefits, whichever is less. There is an overall limit of 39 weeks for both regular and extended benefits. The costs of the extended benefits are shared equally by the federal government and the states.

Financing

State unemployment insurance programs are financed largely by payroll taxes paid by employers on the covered wages of employees. A few states also require the employees to contribute. All tax contributions are deposited in the Federal Unemployment Trust Fund. Each state has a separate account, which is credited with the unemployment-tax contributions and the state's share of investment income. Unemployment benefits are paid out of each state's account.

For 2004, covered employers paid a federal payroll tax of 6.2 percent on the first $7000 of annual wages paid to each covered employee. Employers can credit toward the federal tax any contributions paid under an approved unemployment insurance program and any tax savings under an approved experience-rating plan. The total employer credit is limited to a maximum of 5.4 percent. The remaining 0.8 percent is paid to the federal government and used for state and federal administrative expenses, for financing the federal government's share of the extended-benefits program, and for maintaining a loan fund from which states can temporarily borrow when their accounts are depleted.

Because of a desire to strengthen their unemployment reserves and maintain fund solvency, the majority of states have a taxable wage base that exceeds $7000.

Experience rating is also used, by which firms with favorable employment records pay reduced tax rates. The major argument in support of experience rating is that firms have a financial incentive to stabilize their employment. However, some cyclical and seasonal firms have little control over their employment, and experience rating provides little financial incentive for them to stabilize employment. Also, labor unions are opposed to experience rating,

Exhibit 24.6
Insured Unemployment as a Percent of Total Employment: Regular State Programs

NOTE: Recessions from peak to trough are shown by shaded bands.

SOURCE: U.S. Department of Labor, Employment Training Administration, *Unemployment Insurance Chartbook,* October 2003, Chart A.12.

because some business firms may resist benefit increases and contest some valid claims.

Problems and Issues

State unemployment insurance programs have numerous problems and issues. Some important problems are summarized as follows:

- *Decline in the proportion of total unemployed who receive benefits.* Only a relatively small proportion of the total unemployed receive state unemployment insurance benefits at any time. Exhibit 24.6 shows the proportion of the total unemployed who file for regular state unemployment benefits, commonly called the recipiency rate. The recipiency rate increased slightly in recent years to 43 percent in 2002. However, it is still below the higher levels of the 1950s and 1960s when more than 50 percent of the total unemployed received unemployment benefits.

According to the Advisory Council on Unemployment Compensation, the decline in recipiency rates is due to: (1) tighter eligibility requirements and more restrictive policy changes at both the state and federal level, (2) a decline in the percentage of unionized workers for whom unemployment insurance claims historically have been high, (3) a decline in the proportion of workers employed in the manufacturing sector in which claim rates also have been high, and (4) the increasing percentage of the unemployed who live in states in which the receipt of unemployment benefits is below the national average.[12]

- *Inadequate unemployment trust fund balances.* Many states have relatively low trust fund balances for paying benefits. During previous recessions, many states found their trust fund balances inadequate for paying benefits because of higher unemployment and a longer duration of payments. States can borrow from their fed-

Exhibit 24.7
Average High Cost Multiples, by State Calendar Year 2002

US Avg = 0.62

NM VI VT MS DE ME NH AZ WY MT HI LA OR IN UT PR GA IA FL OK DC AK NV NJ SD SC NE WI KS MD RI WA VA ID CO CT TN WV MI KY AL CA OH MA PA ND AR MO NC MN IL TX NY

Source U.S. Department of Labor, Employment Training Administration, *Unemployment Insurance Chartbook,* October 2003, Chart B.3.

eral unemployment account if their trust fund balances decline to a level where benefit obligations cannot be met.

One widely used measure to estimate the adequacy of a state's unemployment trust account is known as an average high-cost multiple. The *average high-cost multiple* is a measure of solvency and indicates how many years a state can pay unemployment benefits if it paid benefits equivalent to the average amount paid out during the three highest-cost 12-month periods during the previous 20 years, without collecting any additional revenue. The Interstate Commission of Employment Security Administrators has recommended an average high-cost multiple of 1.5. This means that a state would have enough money in its trust fund account to pay benefits for 1.5 years at a rate equivalent to the average amount paid out during the previous three worst 12-month periods without the benefit of any revenue inflow. *However, in calendar 2002, only 10 of 53 jurisdictions had an average high-cost multiple of 1.5 or higher. The*

average for the United States was only .62, which meant that the states, on average, could pay benefits for only six months (see Exhibit 24.7). New Mexico had the highest average high-cost multiple, while both New York and Texas had outstanding loans and negative trust fund balances.

- *Imperfect experience-rating formulas.* Unemployment insurance tax rates are experience rated, which encourages employers to reduce layoffs, gives employers an incentive to police fraudulent claims, and allocates the cost of unemployment to those firms that are responsible for the unemployment.

  In reality, these objectives have not been completely met because of "imperfect" experience-rating formulas. That is, the employers responsible for the unemployment are not charged for all benefits paid to former employees. Employers are often not charged the full cost of benefit payments because of numerous reasons, such as partial forgiveness of charges for employers with negative balances in their reserve accounts, payments made on behalf of firms going out of business, special industry tax rates, caps on changes in annual employer tax rates, and low state taxable wage bases.

In addition, employers that pay maximum tax rates because of layoffs are incurring benefit costs that must be funded by other employers. Under the present system, low-cost firms with positive balances in their reserve accounts subsidize high-cost firms with negative balances in their account. This subsidy is unfair to low-cost firms, and it reduces the financial incentive for high-cost firms that pay maximum tax rates to reduce their unemployment.

WORKERS COMPENSATION

Many workers are injured or become sick each year because of job-related accidents or disease. In addition to pain and suffering, disabled workers must deal with the loss of earned income, payment of medical bills, partial or permanent loss of bodily functions or limbs, and job separation.

Workers compensation is a social insurance program that provides medical care, cash benefits, and rehabilitation services to workers who are disabled from job-related accidents or disease. The benefits are extremely important in reducing the economic insecurity that may result from a job-related disability.

Development of Workers Compensation

Under the *common law of industrial accidents*, dating back to 1837, workers injured on the job had to sue their employers and prove negligence before they could collect damages. However, an employer could use three common law defenses to block lawsuits from injured workers:

- Contributory negligence doctrine
- Fellow-servant doctrine
- Assumption-of-risk doctrine

Under the **contributory negligence doctrine,** an injured worker could not collect damages if he or she contributed in any way to the injury. Under the **fellow-servant doctrine,** the injured worker could not collect if the injury resulted from the negligence

of a fellow worker. And under the **assumption-of-risk doctrine,** the injured worker could not collect if he or she had advance knowledge of the dangers inherent in a particular occupation and still chose to work in that occupation. As a result of the harsh common law, relatively few disabled workers collected adequate amounts for their injuries.

The enactment of *employer liability laws* between 1885 and 1910 was the next step in the development of workers compensation. These laws reduced the effectiveness of the common law defenses, improved the legal position of injured workers, and required employers to provide safe working conditions for their employees. However, injured workers were still required to sue their employers and prove negligence before they could collect for their injuries.

Finally, the states passed *workers compensation laws* as a solution to the growing problem of work-related accidents. In 1908, the federal government passed a workers compensation law covering certain federal employees, and by 1920, most states had passed similar laws. All states today have workers compensation laws.

Workers compensation is based on the fundamental principle of **liability without fault.** *The employer is held absolutely liable for job-related injuries or disease suffered by the workers, regardless of who is at fault.* Disabled workers are paid for their injuries according to a schedule of benefits established by law. The workers are not required to sue their employers to collect benefits. The laws provide for the prompt payment of benefits to disabled workers regardless of fault and with a minimum of legal formality. The costs of workers compensation benefits are therefore considered to be a normal cost of production, which is included in the price of the product.

Objectives of Workers Compensation

State workers compensation laws have several basic objectives:

- Broad coverage of employees for job-related accidents and disease
- Substantial protection against the loss of income
- Sufficient medical care and rehabilitation services
- Encouragement of safety
- Reduction in litigation

A fundamental objective is to provide broad coverage of employees for job-related accidents and disease. That is, workers compensation laws should cover the vast majority occupations or job-related accidents and disease.

A second objective is to provide substantial protection against the loss of income. The cash benefits are designed to restore a substantial proportion of the disabled worker's lost earnings, so that the disabled worker's previous standard of living can be maintained.

A third objective is to provide sufficient medical care and rehabilitation services to injured workers. Workers compensation laws require employers to pay hospital, surgical, and other medical costs incurred by injured workers. Also, the laws provide for rehabilitation services to disabled employees so they can be restored to productive employment.

Another objective is to encourage firms to reduce job-related accidents and to develop effective safety programs. Experience rating is used to encourage firms to reduce job-related accidents and disease, because firms with superior accident records pay relatively lower workers compensation premiums.

Finally, workers compensation laws are designed to reduce litigation. The benefits are paid promptly to disabled workers without requiring them to sue their employers. The objective is to reduce or eliminate the payment of legal fees to attorneys, and time-consuming and expensive trials and appeals.

Complying with the Law

All states except Texas have compulsory laws that require covered employers to provide specified benefits to workers who become disabled from a job-related accident or disease. Employers can comply with state law by purchasing a workers compensation policy, by self-insuring, or by obtaining insurance from a monopoly or competitive state fund.

Most firms purchase a workers compensation policy from a private insurer. The policy pays the benefits that the employer must legally provide to workers who have a job-related accident or disease.

Self-insurance is allowed in most states. Many large firms self-insure their workers compensation losses to save money. In addition, group self-insurance is often available to smaller firms that pool their risks and liabilities.

Finally, workers compensation insurance can be purchased from a state fund in certain states. In some jurisdictions, covered employers generally must purchase workers compensation insurance from a **monopoly state fund** or self-insure the risk. Other states have a **competitive state fund** that competes with private insurers.[13]

Covered Occupations

Although most occupations are covered by workers compensation laws, certain occupations are excluded or have incomplete coverage. Because of the nature of the work, most states exclude or provide incomplete coverage for farm workers, domestic servants, and casual employees. Some states have numerical exemptions, by which small firms with fewer than a specified number of employees (typically three to five) are not required to provide workers compensation benefits. However, employers can voluntarily cover employees in an exempted class.

Eligibility Requirements

Two principal eligibility requirements must be met to receive workers compensation benefits. First, the disabled person must work in a covered occupation. Second, the worker must have a job-related accident or disease. *This means the injury or disease must arise out of and in the course of employment.* The courts have gradually broadened the meaning of this term over time. The following situations are usually covered under a typical workers compensation law:

- An employee who travels is injured while engaging in activities that benefit the employer.
- The employee is injured while performing specified duties at a specified location.
- The employee is on the premises and is injured going to the work area.
- The employee has a heart attack while lifting some heavy materials while at work.

Workers Compensation Benefits

Workers compensation laws provide four principal benefits:

- Unlimited medical care
- Disability income
- Death benefits
- Rehabilitation services

Unlimited Medical Care Medical care generally is covered in full in virtually all states with no time or monetary limitations. However, the majority of states have medical fee schedules that limit the amounts paid for certain medical procedures.

Medical care is expensive. To hold down medical costs, many states allow employers to use managed care arrangements to treat injured employees. The use of health maintenance organizations (HMOs) and preferred provider organizations (PPOs) has also increased over time.

Disability Income Disability-income benefits can be paid after the disabled worker satisfies a waiting period that usually ranges from three to seven days. If the injured worker is still disabled after a certain number of days or weeks, most states pay disability benefits retroactively to the date of injury.

The weekly cash benefit is based on a percentage of the injured worker's average weekly wage, typically two-thirds, and the degree of disability. There are four classifications of disability: (1) temporary total, (2) permanent total, (3) temporary partial, and (4) permanent partial. Temporary total disability claims are the most common and account for the majority of all cash claims. For example, a worker in Nebraska may break a leg and be totally disabled for three months. After a one-week waiting period, the disabled worker would receive two-thirds of his or her weekly wage up to a maximum of $562 weekly.

Death Benefits Death benefits can be paid to eligible survivors if the worker dies as a result of a job-related accident or disease. Two types of benefits are paid. First, a burial allowance is paid. Second, weekly income benefits can be paid to eligible surviving dependents. The weekly benefit is based on a proportion of the deceased worker's wages (typically two-thirds) and is usually paid to a surviving spouse for life or until she or he remarries. Upon remarriage, the widow or widower typically gets one or two years of payments in a lump sum. A weekly benefit can also be paid to each dependent child until a specified age, such as age 18 or later.

Rehabilitation Services All states provide rehabilitation services to restore disabled workers to productive employment. In addition to weekly disability benefits, workers who are being rehabilitated are compensated for board and room, travel, books, and equipment. Training allowances may also be paid in some states.

Second-Injury Funds

Some states have provisions for a second-injury fund. The purpose is to encourage employers to hire handicapped workers. If a second-injury fund did not exist, employers would be reluctant to hire handicapped workers because of the higher benefits that might have to be paid if a second injury occurs.

For example, assume that a worker with a pre-existing injury or handicap is injured in a job-related accident. When combined with the first injury, the second injury produces a disability more severe than that caused by the second injury alone. Thus, the workers compensation benefits that must be paid are higher than if only the second injury had occurred. The employer pays only for the second injury, and the second-injury fund pays the additional benefits that are required.

Problems and Issues

Workers compensation programs faces numerous problems and issues at the present time. Three timely problems that merit some discussion are as follows:

- *Continued threat of terrorism* Workers compensation insurers must still deal with the risk of terrorism. Because of the terrorist attacks on September 11, 2001, insurers paid out about $2 billion in workers compensation claims, or 5 percent of the total September 11 losses. It is estimated that claim costs for future acts of terrorism could cost insurers anywhere from $300,000 to $1 million per employee, depending on the state.[14] Employers that have a heavy concentration of employees in a single building in major metropolitan areas, such as New York, are especially vulnerable and are now considered high risk. This classification applied earlier only to dangerous occupations, such as roofing. Because of the possibility of catastrophe losses, all but the largest insurers are now limiting coverage, which is forcing some employers to self-insure more of the exposure or to deal with several insurers to obtain the desired coverage.[15]

■ *Substantial underwriting losses.* Workers compensation insurers have incurred substantial underwriting losses in recent years. According to the Insurance Information Institute, the financial results for 2002 show that the combined ratio for workers compensation insurance is 110. This means that workers compensation insurers paid out almost $1.10 in claims and expenses for each dollar of premium collected.[16] One reason for the heavy losses is that the high cost of medical care, which accounts for more than 50 percent of an average workers compensation claim, continues to rise at double digit rates (12.0% in 2002). Payments for lost wages have also increased.

■ *Increased litigation.* Although a fundamental objective of workers compensation is to reduce lawsuits, attorneys are involved in a substantial percentage of claims, especially high-cost claims. A study of claims in 13 states by the National Council on Compensation Insurance revealed that 80 to 90 percent of the high-cost claims involved attorneys. High-cost claims included permanent total disability cases, permanent partial disability cases, and negotiated awards.[17]

The increased litigation is due to (1) suits by injured workers who are dissatisfied with their workers compensation awards and then sue for higher amounts; (2) denial of claims by some employers, which results in lawsuits by the injured workers; and (3) court decisions that have eroded the **exclusive remedy doctrine.** This doctrine states that workers compensation benefits should be the sole and exclusive remedy for injured workers; workers have a statutory right to receive benefits without proving negligence, but in turn, they give up the right to sue the employer. This doctrine has been eroded by court decisions in recent years. As a result, injured employees often can receive both workers compensation benefits and a tort damage award based on negligence.

CASE APPLICATION

Sam, age 35, and Kathy, age 33, are married and have a son, age 1. Sam is employed as an accountant and earns $60,000 annually. Kathy is an associate professor of finance at a large university and earns $110,000 annually. Both are currently and fully insured under the OASDI program. Assume you are a financial planner who is asked to give them advice concerning OASDI and other social insurance programs. Answer each of the following questions based on the following situations. Treat each situation separately.

a. Sam is killed instantly in an automobile accident. To what extent, if any, would the surviving family members be eligible to receive OASDI survivor benefits?

b. Kathy has laryngitis that damaged her vocal cords. As a result, she can no longer teach. She is offered a research position in the business research bureau of the university where she is employed. To what extent, if any, would Kathy be eligible to receive OASDI disability benefits?

c. A deranged student fired a handgun at Kathy because she gave him a grade of D+. As a result, Kathy was seriously injured and is expected to be off work for at least one year while she is recovering. To what extent, if any, would existing social insurance programs in the United States provide income during the period of temporary disability?

d. Sam would like to retire at age 62 and still work part-time as an accountant. He has been informed that the OASDI earnings test would be relevant in his case. Explain how the earnings test might affect his decision to work part-time after retirement.

e. Sam resigned from his job to find a higher-paying position. Explain whether Sam could receive unemployment insurance benefits during the period of temporary unemployment before he finds a new job.

SUMMARY

- Social insurance programs are compulsory insurance programs with certain characteristics that distinguish them from other government insurance programs. Social insurance programs in the United States have the following characteristics:

    Compulsory programs

    Floor of income

    Emphasis on social adequacy rather than individual equity

    Benefits loosely related to earnings

    Benefits prescribed by law

    No means test

    Full funding unnecessary

    Financially self-supporting

- The Old-Age, Survivors, and Disability Insurance (OASDI) program, commonly called Social Security, is the most important social insurance program in the United States. The program pays monthly cash benefits to eligible beneficiaries who retire or become disabled. The program also pays survivor benefits to eligible surviving family members.

- The current Medicare program consists of (1) Hospital Insurance (Part A), (2) Supplementary Medical Insurance (Part B), and (3) Medicare Advantage Program, and (4) new prescription drug benefit.

- Unemployment insurance programs are federal-state programs that pay weekly cash benefits to workers who are involuntarily unemployed. Unemployment insurance programs have several objectives:

    Provide cash income to unemployed workers during periods of involuntary unemployment

    Help unemployed workers find jobs

    Encourage employers to stabilize employment

    Help stabilize the economy

- Unemployed workers must meet certain eligibility requirements to receive weekly cash benefits:

    Have qualifying wages and employment during the base year

    Be able and available for work

    Actively seek work

    Be free from disqualification

    Serve a one-week waiting period in most states

- Workers compensation is a social insurance program that provides medical care, cash benefits, and rehabilitation services to workers who become disabled from job-related accidents or disease. Workers compensation laws have the following objectives:

    Broad coverage of employees for job-related injuries and disease

    Substantial protection against the loss of income

    Sufficient medical care and rehabilitation services

    Encouragement of safety

    Reduction in litigation

- Workers compensation laws typically pay the following benefits:

    Unlimited medical care

    Weekly disability-income benefits

    Death benefits to survivors

    Rehabilitation services

KEY CONCEPTS AND TERMS

Assumption-of-risk doctrine

Average indexed monthly earnings (AIME)

Competitive state fund

Contributory negligence doctrine

Credit (quarter of coverage)

Currently insured

Diagnosis-related groups (DRGs)

Disability insured

Earnings test (retirement test)

Exclusive remedy doctrine

Experience rating

Extended-benefits program

Fellow-servant doctrine

Full retirement age

Fully funded program

Fully insured

Health savings account (HSA)

Hospital Insurance (Part A)

Individual equity

Liability without fault

Means test

Medical Insurance (Part B)

Medicare

Medicare Advantage plans

Medigap policy

Monopoly state fund

Primary insurance amount (PIA)

Second-injury fund

Short-term involuntary unemployment

Social adequacy

Social Security (OASDI)

Unemployment insurance

Workers compensation

REVIEW QUESTIONS

1. Explain the reasons for social insurance programs in the United States.

2. Describe the basic characteristics of social insurance programs.

3. The OASDI program has several types of insured status. Briefly explain the meaning of the following:
   a. Fully insured
   b. Currently insured
   c. Disability insured

4. The OASDI program provides several major benefits. Briefly describe each of the following:
   a. Retirement benefits
   b. Survivor benefits
   c. Disability benefits

5. Explain the definition of disability used in the OASDI program.

6. a. The Medicare program provides several basic benefits. Identify the major benefits that are available under each of the following:
   (1) Hospital Insurance (Part A)
   (2) Medical Insurance (Part B)
   b. Briefly describe the major choices available to Medicare beneficiaries under the Medicare Advantage program.

7. Explain the basic objectives of state unemployment insurance programs.

8. Explain the eligibility requirements for receiving unemployment insurance benefits.

9. Describe the basic objectives of workers compensation laws.

10. Identify the major benefits provided under a typical workers compensation law.

APPLICATION QUESTIONS

1. The OASDI program provides retirement benefits to covered employees and their dependents.
   a. Briefly describe the eligibility requirements for OASDI retirement benefits.
   b. Explain whether each of the following persons would be eligible for OASDI retirement benefits based on the retired worker's earnings record. Treat each item separately.
      (1) A retired worker's unmarried son, age 25, who became totally disabled at age 15 because of an auto accident.
      (2) A spouse, age 63, of a retired worker who is no longer caring for an unmarried child under age 18.
      (3) A retired worker's spouse, age 45, who is caring for the 12-year-old daughter of the retired worker
      (4) A divorced spouse, age 55, who was married to a retired worker for six years.

2. The OASDI program pays survivor benefits to eligible family members based on the deceased worker's earnings record.
   a. Describe the eligibility requirements for OASDI survivor benefits.
   b. Explain whether each of the following persons would be eligible for OASDI survivor benefits based on the deceased worker's earnings record. Treat each item separately.
      (1) A surviving spouse, age 35, who is caring for an unmarried child under age 16.
      (2) A son, age 19, who is attending college full-time.
      (3) A surviving spouse, age 55, who has no children under age 16 in her care.
      (4) A surviving spouse, age 60, who has been out of the labor force for several years.
      (5) A dependent parent, age 80, who was receiving financial help from the deceased worker.

3. The OASDI program pays disability benefits to a disabled worker and eligible family members.
   a. Describe the eligibility requirements for OASDI disability.
   b. Explain whether each of the following persons would be eligible for disability-income benefits. In each case, assume that the disabled worker is disability-insured. Treat each item separately.
      (1) A worker, age 22, who is injured in an auto accident and is expected to return to work within three months.
      (2) The disabled worker's spouse, age 25, who is caring for a dependent child under age 16; the disabled worker is currently receiving benefits.
      (3) The disabled worker's daughter, age 16, who is attending high school full-time.

(4) A university professor, age 50, who can no longer teach because of chronic laryngitis but can work as a research scientist for a drug company.

(5) A worker, age 40, with a crushed foot who expects to be off work for at least one year.

4. The original Medicare program consists of Hospital Insurance (Part A) and Medical Insurance (Part B). For each of the following losses, indicate whether the loss is covered under Part A or Part B of Medicare. (Ignore any deductible or coinsurance requirements. Treat each event separately.)

a. Mary, age 66, is hospitalized for five days because of a heart attack.

b. John, age 62, has prostate cancer and visits his family doctor for treatment.

c. Marion, age 80, is a patient in a skilled nursing facility. She has been confined to the nursing home for more than two years.

d. Don, age 72, has a hearing impairment and obtains a hearing aid from a local firm.

e. Sarah, age 68, has a speech impairment and is confined to her home because of a stroke. A licensed speech therapist visits her in the home and provides services to restore her speech.

f. Fred, age 78, has an arthritic hip that makes it painful to walk and needs surgery to have the hip replaced.

g. Michael, age 65, is covered under the original Medicare program. His spouse, age 62, has cancer and requires chemotherapy.

5. A critic of state unemployment insurance programs stated that "unemployment insurance programs are designed to maintain economic security for unemployed workers, but several critical problems must be resolved."

a. What type of unemployment is covered under a typical state unemployment insurance program?

b. Describe some situations that may disqualify a worker for unemployment benefits.

c. Why has the proportion of unemployed workers who receive unemployment benefits declined over time?

6. Workers compensation laws provide considerable financial protection to workers who have a job-related accident or disease.

a. Explain the fundamental legal principle on which workers compensation laws are based.

b. List the various ways that covered employers can comply with the state's workers compensation law.

c. Explain the eligibility requirements for collecting workers compensation benefits.

d. Explain why lawsuits by injured employees against their employers have increased in many states.

INTERNET RESOURCES

■ The **Employment and Training Administration (ETA)** is a federal agency in the U.S. Department of Labor that provides detailed information and data on state unemployment compensation programs. Visit the site at

http://www.doleta.gov

■ The **Centers for Medicare & Medicaid Services (CMS)**, which is part of the U.S. Department of Health and Human Services, administers the Medicare program. CMS provides timely information and data on the Medicare program to consumers, health care professionals, and the media, including actuarial cost estimates for the program. Visit the site at

http://www.cms.hhs.gov

■ **Medicare.gov** is the official government site for people on Medicare. The site provides information on the basics of Medicare, nursing homes, participating physicians, Medicare publications, and prescription drug assistance programs. Visit the site at

http://www.medicare.gov

■ The **National Academy of Social Insurance** is a professional organization that attempts to improve public understanding of social insurance programs. It publishes timely and important research studies on Social Security and Medicare. Visit the site at

http://www.nasi.org

■ The **National Council on Compensation Insurance Holdings, Inc.** develops and administers rating plans and systems for workers compensation insurance. Visit the site at

http://www.ncci.com

■ The **Office of the Chief Actuary** in the Social Security Administration provides actuarial cost estimates of the OASDI program and determines the annual cost-of-living adjustments in benefits. The site provides a number of timely publications. Visit the site at

http://www.ssa.gov/OACT/index.html

- The **Social Security Administration (SSA)** is an independent federal agency that administers the Social Security program. Its Web site provides current information on OASDI retirement, survivor, and disability benefits and recent changes in the program. Visit the site at

http://www.socialsecurity.gov

- The **Social Security Advisory Board** is an independent, bipartisan board that advises the president and members of Congress on matters relating to Social Security. Its Web site provides timely and relevant reports dealing with Social Security. Visit the site at

http://www.ssab.gov

- The **Workers Compensation Research Institute** is an independent, not-for-profit research organization providing high-quality, objective information about public policy issues involving workers compensation systems. Visit the site at

http://www.wcrinet.org/about.html

SELECTED REFERENCES

2004 Guide to Social Security and Medicare. Louisville, KY: William M. Mercer, November 2003.

Alliance of American Insurers. *Survey of Workers' Compensation Laws, 2003 – 2004 Edition.* Downers Grove, IL: Alliance of American Insurers, 2003.

Emsellem, Maurice, et al. *Failing the Unemployed, A State by State Examination of Unemployment Insurance Systems.* Washington, DC: Center on Budget and Policy Priorities, March 2002.

Insurance Information Institute. "Workers Compensation," *Hot Topics & Insurance Issues* at http://iii.org/media/hottopics/insurance/workerscomp/

Klingel, Stephen J. "Critical Issues Facing Workers Compensation," *Workers Compensation Issue Report 2003.* National Council on Compensation Insurance: Boca Raton, Florida, 2003.

National Academy of Social Insurance. *The Report of Private Health Plans in Medicare: Lessons from the Past, Looking to the Future,* Final Report of Study Panel on Medicare and Markets. Washington, DC: National Academy of Social Insurance, November 2003.

Myers, Robert J. *Social Security,* 4th ed. Philadelphia, PA: Pension Research Council and University of Pennsylvania Press, 1993.

National Bipartisan Commission on the Future of Medicare. *Building a Better Medicare for Today and Tomorrow.* Washington, DC, Final Version, March 16, 1999.

President's Commission to Strengthen Social Security. *Strengthening Social Security and Creating Personal Wealth for All Americans, Report of the President's Commission,* Washington, DC, December 21, 2001.

President's Commission to Strengthen Social Security. *The Interim Report of the President's Commission to Strengthen Social Security,* Washington, DC, August 2001.

Rejda, George E. *Social Insurance and Economic Security,* 6th ed. Upper Saddle River, NJ: Prentice-Hall, 1999.

———. "State Unemployment Compensation Programs," in Jerry S. Rosenbloom, ed., *The Handbook of Employee Benefits,* 5th ed. New York: McGraw-Hill, 2001, ch. 24.

Social Security and Medicare Board of Trustees. *Status of the Social Security and Medicare Programs: A Summary of the 2004 Annual Reports,* Washington, DC, March 2004.

U.S. Congress, House, Committee on Ways and Means. *2003 Green Book, Background Material and Data on Programs within the Jurisdiction of the Committee on Ways and Means.* Washington, DC, U.S. Government Printing Office, 2003.

NOTES

1. *2004 Guide to Social Security and Medicare* (Louisville, KY: William M. Mercer, November 2003), p. 37.
2. George E. Rejda, *Social Insurance and Economic Security,* 6th ed. (Upper Saddle River, NJ: Prentice-Hall, 1999), pp. 18–25.
3. "Bush's Medicare Gamble," *The Wall Street Journal,* June 23, 2003, p. A14.
4. This section is based largely on Rejda, chs. 5 and 6.
5. Social Security Administration, SSA Publication no. 05–10055, April 2000.

6. A more liberal rule applies to blind workers. A blind worker age 55 or older must be unable to perform work that requires skills or abilities comparable to those required by the work that he or she did regularly before age 55 (or before he or she became blind, if later than age 55).

7. Data cited are from Social Security and Medicare Board of Trustees, *Status of Social Security and Medicare Programs, A Summary of the 2004 Annual Reports* (March 2004).

8. Ibid.

9. The President's Commission to Strengthen Social Security, *Strengthening Social Security and Creating Personal Wealth for All Americans, Report of the President's Commission*, Washington, DC, December 21, 2001.

10. Social Security and Medicare Board of Trustees, *Status of Social Security and Medicare Programs, A Summary of the 2004 Annual Reports* (March 2004).

11. Data obtained from U.S. Department of Labor, Employment and Training Division at http://www.ows.doleta.gov/unemploy/finance.asp

12. *Advisory Council on Unemployment Compensation, Report and Recommendations* (Washington, DC: Advisory Council on Unemployment Compensation, 1994), pp. 31–32.

13. As of January 2001, exclusive or monopoly funds existed in North Dakota, Ohio, Washington, West Virginia, Wyoming, Puerto Rico, and the Virgin Islands. In January 2001, competitive state funds existed in Arizona, California, Colorado, Hawaii, Idaho, Kentucky, Louisiana, Maine, Maryland, Michigan, Minnesota, Missouri, Montana, New Mexico, New York, Oklahoma, Oregon, Pennsylvania, Rhode Island, Texas, and Utah.

14. Insurance Information Institute, "Workers Compensation," *Hot Topics & Insurance Issues, May 2004.*

15. Ibid.

16. Ibid.

17. "Attorneys Involved in Most High-Cost Workers Compensation Claims," *1996 Issues Report, Vital Workers Compensation Information* (Boca Raton, FL: National Council on Compensation Insurance, 1996).

Students may take a self-administered test on this chapter at **www.aw-bc.com/rejda**

PART SIX
THE INSURANCE INDUSTRY

CHAPTER 25

TYPES OF INSURERS AND MARKETING SYSTEMS

"Insurers are increasingly using multiple distribution channels to sell their products."

Insurance Information Institute

After studying this chapter, you should be able to

- Describe the major types of private insurers, including the following:

Stock insurers	Lloyd's Associations
Mutual insurers	Blue Cross and Blue Shield plans
Reciprocal exchanges	Health maintenance organizations

- Explain why some life insurers have demutualized or formed holding companies in recent years.

- Explain the difference between an agency building system and a nonbuilding agency system as marketing systems in life insurance.

- Describe the direct response system for selling life insurance.

- Describe the different marketing systems in property and liability insurance, including the following:

Independent agency system	Direct response system
Exclusive agency system	Mixed systems
Direct writer	

Jennifer, age 24, is a senior at a large Eastern university. The university recently sponsored a job fair for students seeking employment after graduation. Jennifer signed up for an interview with a large global insurer. She was surprised to hear that in addition to insurance, insurers sell mutual funds and other investments; annuities; individual retirement accounts; 401(k) plans and other qualified retirement plans; and a wide variety of other financial products as well. She was also surprised to hear that insurers own banks, issue credit cards, and make real estate loans and home equity loans to individuals.

Thousands of life and health and property and liability insurers are doing business in the United States today. As part of the financial services industry, private insurers have a profound impact on the American economy. Private insurers sell financial and insurance products that enable individuals and families to attain a high degree of economic security. The insurance industry also provides millions of jobs for workers and is an important source of capital to business firms. In addition, indemnification for losses is one of the most important economic functions of insurers; insureds are restored completely or partially to their previous financial position, thereby maintaining their economic security.

The chapter discusses the role of private insurance companies in the financial services industry. Topics discussed include an overview of the financial services industry, the major types of private insurers, the major marketing methods for selling insurance, and the role of agents and brokers in the sales process.

OVERVIEW OF PRIVATE INSURANCE IN THE FINANCIAL SERVICES INDUSTRY

The financial services industry consists of thousands of financial institutions that provide financial products and services to the public. Financial institutions include commercial banks, savings and thrift institutions, credit unions, life and health insurers, property and casualty insurers, mutual funds, securities brokers and dealers, private and state pension funds, various government-related financial institutions, finance companies, and other financial firms.

There are various ways of measuring the relative importance of private insurance in the financial services industry. One common method is to determine the percentage of industry assets held by each financial sector. Exhibit 25.1 shows the amount of assets held by various financial institutions at the end of 2002. The banking sector held 27 percent of the total assets; mutual funds and securities brokers and dealers accounted for 19 percent of the assets; and the insurance industry held 11 percent of the total assets, down from 13 percent in 1997. However, this figure is somewhat misleading and understates the relative financial importance of the insurance

EXHIBIT **25.1**
Assets of Financial Services Sectors, by Industry, Year-End 2002

($ billions)	
Sector	*Assets*
Banking	
Commercial banking (1)	$7,342.5
Savings institutions (2)	1,357.4
Credit unions	560.8
Bank personal trusts and estates	807.9
Total	**$10,068.6**
Insurance	
Life insurance companies	$3,331.2
All other insurers	915.5
Total	**$4,246.7**
Securities	
Mutual and closed-end funds	$6,013.3
Securities broker/dealers (3)	1,335.4
Total	**$7,348.7**
Pensions	
Private pension funds (4)	$3,657.7
State and local government pension funds	1,966.5
Total	**$5,624.2**
Government-related	
Government lending enterprises	$2,543.3
Federally-related mortgage pools	3,158.2
Total	**$5,701.5**
Other	
Finance companies	$1,185.1
Real estate investment trusts	92.8
Mortgage companies	32.1
Asset-backed securities issuers	2,398.6
Funding corporations	1,153.5
Total	**$4,8621.1**
Total All Sectors	**$37,851.8**

(1) Commercial banking includes U.S.-chartered commercial banks, foreign banking offices in the United States, bank holding companies, and banks in U.S.-affiliated areas.

(2) Savings institutions include savings and loan associations, mutual savings banks and federal banks.

(3) Securities broker/dealers include investment banks.

(4) Private pension funds include defined-benefit and contribution plans [including 401(k)s] and the Federal Employees Retirement Thrift Savings Plan.

NOTE: Data are from the Board of Governors of the Federal Reserve System.

SOURCE: Insurance Information Institute, *The Financial Services Fact Book 2004.* See http://www.financialservicesfacts.org.

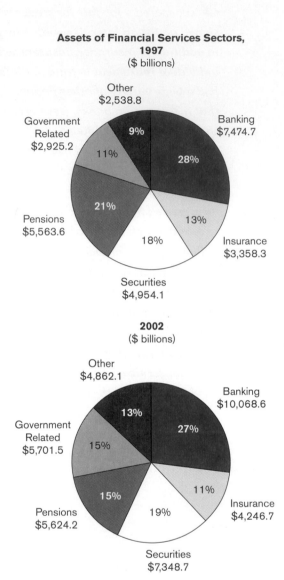

Assets of Financial Services Sectors, 1997
($ billions)

Other $2,538.8
Banking $7,474.7
Government Related $2,925.2
Pensions $5,563.6
Securities $4,954.1
Insurance $3,358.3

9% · 28% · 13% · 18% · 21% · 11%

2002
($ billions)

Other $4,862.1
Banking $10,068.6
Government Related $5,701.5
Pensions $5,624.2
Securities $7,348.7
Insurance $4,246.7

13% · 27% · 11% · 19% · 15% · 15%

industry because private insurers also control a large amount of private pension assets (shown separately).

The financial services industry is changing rapidly. Two trends clearly stand out—consolidation and convergence of financial products and services. *Consolidation* means that the number of firms in the financial markets has declined over time because of mergers and acquisitions. Because of competitive reasons, the number of firms competing in major financial markets has declined. The number of commercial banks declined from about 25,000 before World War II to about 8100 in 2001; the number of securities dealers and brokerage firms declined from 9515 in 1987 to about 7000 in 2001.[1] Likewise, the number of life insurers doing business in the United States declined from 1944 in 1992 to 1171 at year-end 2002, or a decline of about 40 percent.[2] The number of property and casualty insurers (3163 in 2001) is expected to decline by 30 percent over the next decade.[3]

A second clear trend is the convergence of financial products and services. *Convergence* means that financial institutions can now sell a wide variety of financial products outside their core business area, which was difficult to do earlier because of federal restrictions. Prior to enactment of the Financial Modernization Act in 1999 (also known as the Gramm-Leach-Bliley Act), banks, investment firms, and insurers generally did not have the freedom to compete freely in all financial markets. Banks generally provided only banking services and related products; securities dealers typically sold only stocks, bonds, and other investments; and insurers generally sold only insurance products. The Financial Modernization Act now allows financial institutions, including private insurers, to compete in other financial markets outside their core business area.

TYPES OF PRIVATE INSURERS

A large number of private insurers are currently doing business in the United States. As noted earlier, 1171 life and health insurers were operating in the United States near the end of 2002. These insurers sell a wide variety of life and health insurance products, annuities, private pension plans and related financial products. Exhibit 25.2 shows the top 20 U.S. life and health insurance groups and companies ranked by revenues and assets in 2002.

In addition, as stated earlier, there were 3163 property and casualty insurers operating in the United States in 2001. These insurers sell property and casualty insurance and related lines, including inland marine coverages and surety and fidelity bonds. Exhibit 25.3 shows the top 20 U.S. property and casualty companies ranked by revenues and assets in 2002.

There are various ways of classifying the different types of insurers. In terms of legal organization and ownership, the major types of private insurers can be classified as follows.

- Stock insurers
- Mutual insurers
- Reciprocal exchanges
- Lloyd's Associations
- Blue Cross and Blue Shield Plans
- Health maintenance organizations (HMOs)

Stock Insurers

A **stock insurer** *is a corporation owned by stockholders who participate in the profits and losses of the insurer.* The stockholders elect a board of directors, who in turn appoint executive officers to manage the corporation. The board of directors has the ultimate responsibility for the corporation's financial success.

The types of insurance that a stock insurer can write are determined by its charter. In property and liability insurance, the majority of stock insurers are multiple-line insurers that write most types of insurance, with the exception of life and health insurance. Some states also permit the writing of life and health insurance.

A stock insurer cannot issue an assessable policy. As assessable policy permits the insurer to assess the policyowners additional premiums if losses are excessive. Instead, the stockholders must bear all losses. But they also share in the profits: if the business is profitable, dividends can be declared and paid to the stockholders. The value of the stock may also increase if the business is profitable.

EXHIBIT 25.2
Top 20 U.S. Life and Health Insurance Groups and Companies, by Revenues, 2002

($ millions)			
Rank	Group	Revenues	Assets
1	MetLife	$34,055	$277,385
2	Prudential Financial	26,797	292,746
3	New York Life Insurance	24,721	117,228
4	Mass. Mutual Life Ins.	20,247	94,267
5	TIAA-CREF	19,791	261,588
6	Northwestern Mutual	15,916	102,935
7	AFLAC	10,257	45,058
8	UnumProvident	9,560	45,260
9	John Hancock Financial Services	8,911	97,864
10	Principal Financial	8,868	89,861
11	Guardian Life of America	8,136	29,856
12	Conseco	6,148	6,905
13	Thrivent Financial for Lutherans	5,618	44,823
14	Lincoln National	4,636	93,133
15	Mutual of Omaha Ins.	4,353	15,203
16	Pacific LifeCorp	3,816	57,305
17	Jefferson-Pilot	3,480	30,609
18	Torchmark	2,738	12,361
19	Phoenix Companies	2,453	25,246
20	Unitrin	2,298	7,706

SOURCE: Insurance Information Institute, *The Financial Services Fact Book 2004*. See http://www.financialservicesfacts.org.

Mutual Insurers

A **mutual insurer** *is a corporation owned by the policyowners*. The policyowners elect the board of directors, who appoint the executives who manage the corporation. Because relatively few policyowners bother to vote, the board of directors has effective management control of the company.

A mutual insurer may pay a dividend or give a rate reduction in advance. In life insurance, a dividend is largely a refund of a redundant premium that can be paid if the mortality, investment, and operating experience is favorable. However, because the mortality and investment experience cannot be guaranteed, the dividends legally cannot be guaranteed by insurers.

There are several types of mutual insurers, including the following:

- Assessment mutual
- Advance premium mutual
- Factory mutual
- Fraternal insurer

Assessment Mutual An **assessment mutual** *is an insurer that has the right to assess policyowners an additional amount if the experience is unfavorable*. Relatively few assessment mutuals are in existence today, partly because of the practical problem of collecting the assessments. Those insurers still doing business are smaller insurers that operate in limited

EXHIBIT 25.3
Top 20 U.S. Property and Casualty Companies, by Revenues, 2002

Rank	Group	Revenues	Assets
	($ millions)		
1	American Intl. Group	$67,723	$561,000
2	State Farm Insurance Cos.	49,654	117,811
3	Berkshire Hathaway	42,353	169,544
4	Allstate	29,579	117,426
5	Loews	16,898	75,509
6	Nationwide	15,949	129,565
7	Hartford Fin. Services	15,907	182,043
8	Liberty Mutual Insurance Group	14,544	55,827
9	Progressive	9,294	13,564
10	USAA	9,222	38,203
11	Chubb	9,140	34,114
12	St. Paul Cos.	8,918	39,920
13	Safeco	7,065	34,656
14	American Family Ins. Group	5,145	10,840
15	Fidelity National Financial	5,083	5,246
16	First American Corp.	4,704	3,398
17	American Financial Group	3,750	19,500
18	Auto-Owners Insurance	3,514	8,175
19	Erie Insurance Group	3,440	10,271
20	Allmerica Financial	3,419	26,518

SOURCE: Insurance Information Institute, *The Financial Services Fact Book 2004.* See http://www.financialservicesfacts.org.

geographical areas and write only a limited number of lines of insurance.

Advance Premium Mutual An **advance premium mutual** *is owned by the policyowners, but it does not issue assessable policies.* Once the insurer's surplus (difference between assets and liabilities) exceeds a certain amount, the states will not permit a mutual insurer to issue an assessable policy. The advance premium mutual is generally larger and financially stronger than the assessment mutual described earlier. The premiums charged are expected to be sufficient to pay all claims and expenses. Any additional costs because of poor experience are paid out of the company's surplus.

In life insurance, most mutual insurers pay dividends annually to the policyowners. In property and liability insurance, dividends to policyowners are not paid on a regular basis. Property and liability insurers instead may charge lower initial premiums that are closer to the actual amount needed for claims and expenses.

Factory Mutual A **factory mutual** *is a specialized insurer that insures only superior properties.* There is great emphasis on loss prevention. Before a factory can be insured, it must meet stringent underwriting standards. The factory typically must be of superior construction, have an approved sprinkler system, and meet other requirements.

A factory mutual provides periodic inspection and engineering services to its insureds. Because the costs of these loss-control services are high, only the larger risks are eligible for the insurance.

Fraternal Insurer   A **fraternal insurer** *is a mutual insurer that provides life and health insurance to members of a social or religious organization.* To qualify as a fraternal insurer under a state's insurance code, the insurer must have some type of social or religious organization in existence, such as a lodge or a religious, charitable, or benevolent society. Examples of fraternals are the Knights of Columbus, Catholic Workmen, and Aid Association for Lutherans.

Fraternal insurers sell only life and health insurance to their members. The assessment principle was originally used to pay death claims. Today, most fraternals operate on the basis of the level premium and legal reserve system that is used by commercial life insurers. Fraternal insurers also sell term life insurance. Because fraternals are nonprofit or charitable organizations, they receive favorable tax treatment.

Changing Corporate Structure of Mutual Insurers
The corporate structure of mutual insurers—especially life insurers—is changing rapidly. Three trends are clearly evident:

- Increase in company mergers
- Demutualization of mutual insurers
- Formation of mutual holding companies.

1. *Increase in company mergers.* We noted earlier that the number of active life insurers has declined sharply in recent years. Most of the decline is due to company mergers and acquisitions. A merger means that one insurer is absorbed by another insurer or that two or more existing insurers are merged into an entirely new company. Mergers occur because insurers wish to reduce their operating costs and general overhead costs. They also occur because some insurers wish to acquire a line of new insurance or enter a new area of business.
2. *Demutualization.* **Demutualization** *means that a mutual insurer is converted into a stock insurer.* Some mutual insurers have become stock insurers for the following reasons:[4]

- The ability to raise new capital is increased.
- Stock insurers have greater flexibility to expand by acquiring new companies or by diversification.
- Stock options can be offered to attract and retain key employees.
- Conversion to a stock insurer may provide tax advantages.

There are three principal methods by which a mutual insurer can convert to a stock insurer—pure conversion, merger, or bulk reinsurance (see Exhibit 25.4).[5] In a *pure conversion,* a mutual insurer amends its articles of incorporation and is reorganized as a stock insurer. In a *merger,* a mutual insurer and stock insurer are joined together as a single company, and the stock insurer is the surviving company. In *bulk reinsurance,* a mutual insurer cedes all of its assets and liabilities to a stock company, and the mutual insurer is then dissolved (see Exhibit 25.1).

3. *Mutual holding company.* Demutualization is cumbersome, expensive, and slow, and it requires the approval of regulatory authorities. As an alternative, many states have enacted legislation that allows a mutual insurer to form a holding company. A **holding company** *is a company that directly or indirectly controls an authorized insurer.* A mutual insurer is reorganized as a holding company that owns or acquires control of stock insurance companies that could issue common stock (see Exhibit 25.5). The mutual holding company would own at least 51 percent of the subsidiary stock insurer if the latter issues common stock.

Mutual holding companies are highly controversial. Proponents argue that they offer numerous advantages:

- Insurers have an easier and less expensive way to raise new capital to expand or remain competitive.
- Insurers can enter new areas of insurance more easily, such as a life insurer acquiring a property and liability insurer.
- Stock options can be given to attract and retain key employees.

Critics of mutual holding companies, however, argue that policyowners may be financially hurt by the change; the mutual holding structure

Exhibit 25.4
Alternative Modes of Demutualization

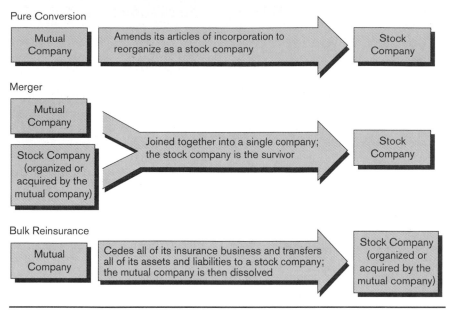

could result in a reduction of dividends and other financial benefits to policyowners. Critics also argue that a conflict of interest may arise between top management and the policyowners. For example, top management may be given company stock or stock options for earning higher operating profits, which could result in

Exhibit 25.5
Mutual Holding Company Illustration

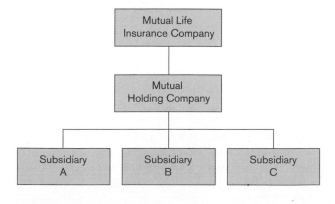

lower dividends or higher premiums for policy-owners (see Insight 25.1).

Reciprocal Exchanges

A reciprocal exchange is another type of private insurer. A **reciprocal exchange** *can be defined as an unincorporated mutual.* A reciprocal insurer has several distinct characteristics. *First, in its purest form, insurance is exchanged among the members; each member of the reciprocal insures the other members and, in turn, is insured by them.* Thus, there is an exchange of insurance promises—hence the name reciprocal exchange.

Second, a reciprocal is managed by an attorney-in-fact. The attorney-in-fact is usually a corporation that is authorized by the subscribers to seek new members, pay losses, collect premiums, handle reinsurance arrangements, invest the funds, and perform other administrative duties. However, the attorney-in-fact is not personally liable for the payment of claims and is not the insurer. The reciprocal exchange is the insurer.

INSIGHT 25.1

Holding Company Schemes: The Feeling Isn't Mutual

Insurers wishing to preserve their mutual structure sometimes form a mutual holding company (MHC). An MHC is a corporation that allows insurance companies to sell stock for up to a 49 percent stake of the company *without* passing proceeds onto policyholders. MHCs are prohibited in some states, mainly because they give many stock options to senior management, coupled with a lack of accountability to shareholders. So, in effect, MHCs will give you obscure "membership interests" that don't really give you any options, because assets are transferred to the holding company and away from you. Policyholders get no voting rights in the new company. Although companies seeking to convert to MHCs often tell policyholders that the company will still be mutual after the conversion, in reality, policyholders lose a major advantage of the mutual structure: the lack of conflicts of interest between policyholders and stockholders.

Some smaller insurance companies have used subscription rights to demutualize. This is legal only in Pennsylvania and Illinois. Subscription rights allow policyholders to purchase stock at the initial public offering (IPO) price without paying a commission. Generally, access to IPOs is limited to large institutional investors, so proponents of subscription rights say policyholders have a rare opportunity to participate in the process.

SOURCE: Insure.com, Inc., a subsidiary of Quotesmith.com, Inc. used with permission.

Third, from a historical perspective, reciprocals can be classified as pure or modified. Historically, the reciprocals that operated earlier were of the pure type. A separate account was kept for each member. The account was credited with the member's premiums and share of investment earnings and debited for the member's share of losses and expenses. The balance in the account could be paid to a terminating member. Thus, in its purest form, insurance was provided "at cost" to the member.

Most reciprocals today are of the modified type. In the modified form, a reciprocal is similar to an advance premium mutual. Individual accounts are not set up for each member to reflect the profit or losses of the reciprocal. In effect, the financial operations of the reciprocal are similar to a mutual insurer, with the exception of management by an attorney-in-fact.

Most reciprocals are relatively small and account for only a small percentage of the total property and liability insurance premiums written. In addition, most reciprocals specialize in a limited number of lines of insurance. However, a few reciprocals are multiple-line insurers and can be large.

Lloyd's Associations

Insurance can also be purchased from a Lloyd's Association. There are two basic types of **Lloyd's Associations:**

- Lloyd's of London
- American Lloyds

Lloyd's of London **Lloyd's of London** is a major worldwide ocean marine insurer that writes a wide variety of risks and is extremely important as a professional reinsurer. Lloyd's is also famous for writing insurance on diverse exposure units such as a pianist's fingers, a Kentucky Derby winner's legs, and a hole-in-one at a professional golf tournament.

Lloyd's of London has several important characteristics. *First, Lloyd's technically is not an insurance company, but is an association that provides physical facilities and services to the members for selling insurance.* Lloyd's by itself does not write insurance; the insurance is written by the syndicates that belong to Lloyd's. In this respect, Lloyd's is similar to the New York Stock Exchange, which does not buy or sell securities, but provides a marketplace and other services to the members.

Second, the insurance is actually written by the various syndicates that belong to Lloyd's. The syndicates are managed by an underwriting agent who is responsible for appointing a professional underwriter for each major type of business. The syndicates tend to specialize in marine, aviation, automobile, and other property and liability insurance lines. The unusual exposure units that have made

EXHIBIT 25.6
Lloyd's of London: Split of 2001 Premiums by Business Type

Lloyd's famous account for only a small part of the total business. Likewise, life insurance accounts only for a small fraction of the total business and is limited to short-term contracts (see Exhibit 25.6).

Third, the individual members (called Names) who belong to the various syndicates have unlimited liability with respect to insurance written as individuals. Names pledge their personal fortunes to pay their agreed-upon share of the insurance written as individuals and have unlimited liability.

Lloyd's has experienced severe underwriting losses in previous years because of natural disasters, asbestos liability claims, mismanagement, and the September 11, 2001 terrorist attack on the World Trade Center in New York. Because of unlimited liability, many individual Names could not pay their share of claims and were financially ruined. Lloyds returned to profitability in 2002.

Lloyd's has also considered a proposal that would eliminate the unlimited personal liability of new members. Although the present system provides tax advantages to individual Names, it often results in angry protests and lawsuits when catastrophic losses result in the bankruptcy of some Names.

Another characteristic is that corporations with limited liability can join Lloyd's of London. Because of the underwriting losses mentioned earlier and the need to raise new capital, corporations are now permitted to join Lloyd's of London. Unlike the individual Names, however, corporations have limited liability. The infusion of new capital from corporations has substantially increased the ability of Lloyd's to write new business.

Individual members must also meet stringent financial requirements. Each member must make a substantial underwriting deposit. All premiums are deposited into a premium trust fund, and withdrawals are allowed only for claims and expenses. A central guarantee fund pays the loss if an individual member is financially insolvent.

Finally, Lloyd's is licensed only in a small number of jurisdictions in the United States. In the other states, Lloyd's must operate as a nonadmitted insurer. This means that a surplus lines broker or agent can place business with Lloyd's, but only if the insurance cannot be obtained from an admitted insurer in the state. Despite the lack of licensing, Lloyd's does a considerable amount of business in the United States. In particular, Lloyd's of London reinsures a large number of American insurers and is an important professional reinsurer.

American Lloyds Private underwriters in the United States have formed associations similar to Lloyd's of London. The American Lloyds associations, however, differ from Lloyd's of London in several respects. First, the number of individual underwriters is smaller. Second, the liability of an individual underwriter is limited. Each underwriter is responsible only for his or her share of the loss and not that of any insolvent member. Third, the personal net worth and financial strength of an underwriter are considerably lower than that of a Lloyd's of London member. Fourth, an American Lloyds association does not operate through a syndicate, but is managed by an attorney-in-fact. Finally, the financial reputation of an American Lloyds association is not as good as that of Lloyd's of London. Several associations have failed, and some states, such as New York, forbid the formation of new associations.

Blue Cross and Blue Shield Plans

Blue Cross and Blue Shield plans are another type of insurer organization. In most states, Blue Cross plans typically are organized as nonprofit, community-oriented prepayment plans that provide coverage primarily for hospital services. Blue Shield plans generally are nonprofit, prepayment plans that provide payment for physicians' and surgeons' fees and other medical services. In recent years, the majority of Blue Cross and Blue Shield plans have merged into single entities. In late 2000, 50 plans jointly wrote Blue Cross and Blue Shield benefits. However, a few separate Blue Cross plans and Blue Shield plans were still in operation.

Although most members are insured through group plans, individual and family coverages are also available. Blue Cross and Blue Shield plans also sponsor health maintenance organizations (HMOs) and preferred provider organizations (PPOs).

In the majority of states, Blue Cross and Blue Shield plans are nonprofit organizations that receive favorable tax treatment and are regulated under special legislation. However, to raise capital and become more competitive, a few Blue Cross and Blue Shield plans have converted to a for-profit status with stockholders and a board of directors. In addition, many nonprofit Blue Cross and Blue Shield plans own profit-seeking affiliates.

Health Maintenance Organizations

HMOs are organized plans of health care that provide comprehensive health care services to their members. HMOs provide broad health care services to a specified group for a fixed prepaid fee; cost control is emphasized; choice of health care providers may be restricted; and less costly forms of treatment are often provided. The characteristics of HMOs have already been discussed in Chapter 22, so additional treatment is not needed here.

AGENTS AND BROKERS

A successful sales force is the key to success in the financial services sector. Most policies today are sold by agents and brokers.

Agents

An **agent** *is someone who legally represents the insurer and has the authority to act on the insurer's behalf.* An agent can bind the principal by expressed powers, by implied powers, and by apparent authority. If you buy insurance, you will probably purchase the insurance from an agent. However, there is an important difference between a life insurance agent and a property and liability insurance agent. A life insurance agent usually does not have the authority to bind the company. He or she is merely a soliciting agent who induces persons to apply for life insurance. The applicant for life insurance must be approved by the company before the insurance becomes effective.

In contrast, a property and liability insurance agent typically has the power to bind the company immediately with respect to certain types of coverage. *This relationship is normally created by a binder, which is temporary evidence of insurance until the policy is actually issued.* Binders can be oral or written. For example, if you telephone an agent and request insurance on your motorcycle, the insurance can become effective immediately.

Brokers

In contrast to an agent who represents the insurer, a **broker** *is someone who legally represents the insured.* A broker legally does not have the authority to bind the insurer. Instead, he or she can solicit or accept applications for insurance and then attempt to place the coverage with an appropriate insurer. But the insurance is not in force until the insurer accepts the business.

A broker is paid a commission from the insurers where the business is placed. Many brokers are also licensed as agents, so that they have the authority to bind their companies as agents.

Brokers are extremely important in property and liability insurance at the present time. Large brokerage firms have knowledge of highly specialized insurance markets, provide risk management and loss control services, and control the accounts of large corporate insurance buyers.

Brokers are also important in the surplus lines markets. *Surplus lines refer to any type of insurance for which there is no available market within the state, and the coverage must be placed with a nonadmitted insurer.* A **nonadmitted insurer** *is an insurer not licensed to do business in the state.* A **surplus lines broker** *is a special type of broker who is licensed to place business with a nonadmitted insurer.* An individual may be unable to obtain the coverage from an admitted insurer because the loss exposure is too great, or the required amount of insurance is too large. A surplus lines broker has the authority to place the business with a surplus lines insurer if the coverage cannot be obtained in the state from an admitted company.

Finally, brokers are important in the area of employee benefits, especially for larger employers. Large employers often obtain their group life and medical expense coverages through brokers.

TYPES OF MARKETING SYSTEMS

Marketing systems refer to the various methods for selling insurance. Insurers employ actuaries, claims adjusters, underwriters, and other home office personnel, but unless insurance policies are profitably sold, the insurer's financial survival is unlikely. Thus, an efficient marketing system is essential to an insurance company's survival.

Life Insurance Marketing Systems

Marketing systems for the sale of life insurance have changed dramatically over time. Traditional methods for selling life insurance have been substantially modified, and new marketing models have emerged. At the time of this writing, the major life insurance marketing systems can be classified as follows.[6]

- Agency building system
- Nonbuilding agency system
- Direct response system

Agency Building System An **agency building system** is a system by which an insurer builds its own agency force by recruiting, financing, training, and supervising new agents. The new agents generally represent only the insurer.

Several types of agency building systems exist. Two basic types are the general agency system and managerial system.

- *General agency system.* Under the **general agency system,** the general agent is an independent contractor who represents only one insurer. The general agent is in charge of a territory and is responsible for recruiting, training, and motivating new agents. The general agent receives a commission based on the amount of business produced.

   Most insurers provide some financial assistance to the general agent. For example, the insurer may pay part or all of the expenses of hiring and training new agents, and it therefore has considerable control over the selection of agents and their training. The insurer may also provide an allowance for agency office expenses and other expenses.
- *Managerial system.* The **managerial system** is another type of agency building system. Under this system, branch offices are established in various areas. The branch manager is an employee of the company who has the responsibility for hiring and training new agents. In some companies, sales by the manager are not allowed or

are discouraged; in other companies, sales are allowed but are usually not expected.

The manager is paid a salary and commission based on the volume and quality of the insurance sold and the number of productive agents hired. Under this system, the company pays the expenses of the branch office, including the financing of new agents.

Nonbuilding Agency System A **nonbuilding agency system** is a marketing system by which an insurer sells its products through established agents who are already engaged in selling life insurance. Under this system, an insurer enters into contracts with successful agents who agree to sell the insurer's products.

Examples of these nonbuilding agency systems abound. Only one of them—the personal-producing general agent—is discussed here.

Today, a considerable amount of new life insurance is sold by personal-producing general agents. A **personal-producing general agent** is a successful agent who is hired primarily to sell insurance under a contract that provides both direct and overriding commissions. A personal-producing general agent is an above-average salesperson or "super-producer" with a proven sales record. He or she is hired to sell insurance and not to recruit and train new agents. The personal-producing general agent usually receives higher commissions than the typical agent. In return, he or she is expected to sell a certain amount of insurance for a particular insurer. In addition, a personal-producing general agent may have contracts with more than one insurer. Finally, such agents typically pay their own expenses.

Direct Response System The **direct response system** is a marketing system by which life and health insurance is sold directly to customers without the services of an agent. Potential customers are solicited by television radio, mail, newspapers, and other media. Some insurers use *telemarketing* to sell their products. Many insurers also have Web sites through which life and health insurance can be sold directly to the customer.

Direct response insurers engage heavily in market research and testing. New computer technology enables them to gather relevant information about consumers and to maintain extensive records.

The direct response system has several advantages. It enables insurers to gain access to large markets; acquisition costs can be held down; and uncomplicated products can be sold effectively. One disadvantage, however, is that complex products are often difficult to sell because an agent's services may be required.

Finally, in addition to the preceding methods, substantial amounts of new individual life insurance, annuities, long-term care insurance, and other financial products are now being sold to employees in group insurance plans. Premiums are deducted from the employee's wages. Workers who are no longer employed can keep the insurance in force by paying premiums directly to the insurance company.

Property and Liability Insurance Marketing Systems

The major methods for marketing property and liability insurance include the following:

- Independent agency system
- Exclusive agency system
- Direct writer
- Direct response system
- Multiple distribution systems

Independent Agency System The **independent agency system,** which is sometimes called the American agency system, has several basic characteristics. First, *the independent agency is a business firm that usually represents several unrelated insurers*. Agents are authorized to write business on behalf of these insurers and in turn are paid a commission based on the amount of business produced.

Second, the agency owns the *expirations or renewal rights to the business*. If a policy comes up for renewal, the agency can place the business with another insurer if it chooses to do so. Likewise, if the contract with an insurer is terminated, the agency can place the business with other insurers.

Third, the independent agent is *compensated by commissions that vary by line of insurance*. The commission rate on renewal business typically is the same as that paid on new business. If a lower renewal rate is paid, the insurer would lose business, because the agent would place the insurance with another insurer at the time of renewal. A second commission called a *contingent or profit-sharing commission* (or bonus) may also be paid to the agent based on favorable loss experience.

In addition to selling, independent agents perform other functions. They are frequently authorized to adjust small claims. Larger agencies may also provide loss control services to their insureds, such as accident prevention and loss control engineers. Also, for some lines, the agency may bill the policyowners and collect the premiums. However, most insurers use *direct billing,* by which the policyowner is billed directly by the insurer. This is particularly true of personal lines of insurance, such as auto and homeowners.

Exclusive Agency System   *Under the* **exclusive agency system,** *the agent represents only one insurer or group of insurers under common ownership.* The agent is generally prohibited by contract from representing other insurers.

Agents under the exclusive agency system do not usually own the expirations or renewal rights to the policies. There is some variation, however, in this regard. Some insurers do not give their agents any ownership rights in the expirations. Other insurers may grant limited ownership of expirations while the agency contract is in force, but this interest terminates when the agency contract is terminated.[7] In contrast, under the independent agency system, the agency has complete ownership of the expirations.

Another difference is the payment of commissions. Exclusive agency insurers generally pay a lower commission rate on renewal business than on new business. This approach results in a strong financial incentive for the agent to write new business and is one factor that helps explain the rapid growth of exclusive agency insurers. In contrast, as noted earlier, insurers using the independent agency system typically pay the same commission rate on new and renewal business.

Also, exclusive agency insurers provide strong support services to new agents. A new agent usually starts as an employee during a training period to learn the business. After the training period, the agent becomes an independent contractor who is then paid on a commission basis.

The functions performed by exclusive agents vary among insurers. Some insurers limit exclusive agents to selling insurance, while others permit them to adjust small first-party claims as well. Virtually all exclusive agency insurers use the direct billing method and are responsible for issuance of the policy.

Direct Writer   A direct writer is often erroneously confused with an exclusive agency insurer. A **direct writer** *is an insurer in which the salesperson is an employee, not an independent contractor.* The insurer pays all the selling expenses, including the employee's salary and Social Security taxes. Similar to exclusive agents, an employee of a direct writer represents only one insurer.

Employees of direct writers are usually compensated on a "salary plus" arrangement. Some companies pay a basic salary plus a commission directly related to the amount of insurance sold. Others pay a salary and a bonus that represent both selling and service activities of the employee.

Direct Response System   Property and liability insurers also use the direct response system to sell insurance. As noted earlier, a direct response insurer sells directly to the public by television, telephone, mail, newspapers, and other media. Many property and liability insurers also operate Web sites that provide information and premium quotes.

The direct response system is used primarily to sell personal lines of insurance, such as auto and homeowners insurance. However, it is not as effective in the marketing of commercial property and liability coverages because of their complexity and rating considerations.

Multiple Distribution Systems   The distinctions between the traditional marketing systems are breaking down as insurers search for new ways to sell insurance. To increase their profits, many property and liability insurers use more than one distribution system to sell insurance. These systems are referred to as **multiple distribution systems.** For example, some insurers that have traditionally used the independent agency system now sell insurance directly to consumers over the Internet or by television and mail advertising. Other insurers that have used only exclusive agents (also called captive

INSIGHT 25.2

Payroll Plan Lets Workers Save Money and Checks

When Kenneth Kraut's auto insurance comes due four times a year, he writes a check and mails it.

He may soon be free of the bother, thanks to his employer.

Kraut, a flavor chemist in Somerset, New Jersey, now can have the insurance payments deducted a bit at a time from his biweekly paychecks. In addition to removing a worry, he saves 5 percent off the top of his premium.

"It's a great convenience. It's kind of like a forced savings," Kraut said. "It's small amounts per paycheck. This way you're not hit all at once with a big bill."

Kraut's company, Flavor Dynamics Inc., is among a growing number of small businesses around the country now able to offer discounts on optional employee benefits through automatic payroll deductions. The offerings aren't new, but in the past they've generally been available only to large companies able to negotiate volume discounts.

The program was introduced by Ceridian Corp., a Minnesota-based payroll services company that joined with RewardsPlus of America Corp. in Baltimore to develop the plan for small business clients.

Flavor Dynamics, a family-owned business with 20 employees, that makes flavorings for the food industry, jumped at the chance to sign up, said Marilyn De Rovira, a company vice president.

The program gives employees convenience and price breaks on services they might be buying elsewhere, De Rovira said. Companies like Flavor Dynamics are able to offer benefits that attract employees, she said.

The program from Ceridian's Small Business Solutions unit includes auto, homeowners, pet, life and long-term care insurance, home security, mortgages, and home equity loans at prices 5 percent to 15 percent below what individuals would pay on their own. There are no startup fees or administrative expenses.

"The program enables us to assist small business owners in retaining their most valuable asset—their employees—by providing them with optional benefits at a low cost," said Robert Digby, senior vice president of marketing for Bloomington, Minnesota-based Ceridian.

For Flavor Dynamics, the program helps De Rovira and her husband, Dolf, who own the business, compete for employees.

"There's such stiff competition with employees and trying to make them happy," Mrs. De Rovira said. "I thought this would be something that would be very interesting for them."

Source: Adapted from Karren Mills, "Payroll Plan Lets Workers Save Money and Checks," *Lincoln Journal Star*, May 16, 1999, p. 3D. Reprinted with permission from the Associated Press.

agents) in the past to sell insurance are now using independent agents as well. Other insurers are marketing property and liability insurance through banks and to consumer groups through employers and through professional and business associations. The lines between the traditional distribution systems will continue to blur in the future as insurers develop new systems to sell insurance.

MASS MERCHANDISING

Some property and liability insurers use mass merchandising to market their insurance. **Mass merchandising** *is a plan for insuring individuals in a group under a single program of insurance at reduced premiums*. Property and liability insurance is sold on a group basis to employers, labor unions, trade associations, and other groups.

Mass-merchandising plans have several distinct characteristics. First, property and liability insurance is sold to individual members of a group; auto and homeowners insurance are popular lines that have been used in such plans. Second, individual underwriting is used; individuals applying for coverage must meet the insurer's underwriting standards. Third, rate reductions of 5 to 15 percent are typically given because of a lower commission scale for agents and savings in administrative expenses. In addition, premiums are paid by payroll deduction. Finally, employers usually do not contribute to the plans; any employer contributions result in taxable income to the employees.

Insight 25.2 provides a practical illustration of a mass-merchandising plan that allows employees to pay for various types of insurance through convenient payroll deduction.

CASE APPLICATION

Acme Insurance is a medium-sized stock property and liability insurer that specializes in the writing of commercial lines of insurance. The board of directors has appointed a committee to determine the feasibility of forming a new subsidiary insurer that would sell only personal lines of insurance, primarily homeowners and auto insurance. The new insurance company would have to meet certain management objectives. One member of the board of directors believes the new insurer should be legally organized as a mutual insurer. Assume you are an insurance consultant who is asked to serve on the committee. To what extent, if any, would each of the following objectives of the board of directors be met by formation of a mutual property and liability insurer? Treat each objective separately.

a. Acme Insurance must legally own the new insurer.
b. The new insurer should be able to sell common stock periodically in order to raise capital and expand into new markets.
c. The policies sold should pay dividends to the policyowners.
d. The new insurer should be licensed to do business in all states.

SUMMARY

- There are several basic types of insurers:

   Stock insurers

   Mutual insurers

   Reciprocal exchanges

   Lloyd's Associations

   Blue Cross and Blue Shield Plans

   Health maintenance organizations (HMOs)

- An *agent* is someone who legally represents the insurer and has the authority to act on the insurer's behalf. In contrast, a *broker* is someone who legally represents the insured.

- *Surplus lines* refer to any type of insurance for which there is no available market within the state, and the coverage must be placed with a nonadmitted insurer. A *nonadmitted insurer* is a company not licensed to do business in the state. A *surplus lines broker* is a special type of broker who is licensed to place business with a nonadmitted insurer.

- In life insurance, several basic marketing methods are used:

   Agency building system

   Nonbuilding agency system

   Direct response system

- In property and liability insurance, a number of marketing systems are used:

   Independent agency system

   Exclusive agency system

   Direct writer

   Direct response system

   Multiple distribution systems

- Mass merchandising is a plan by which property and liability insurance is sold on a group basis. Individual members of a group are insured under a single program of insurance at reduced premiums. There is, however, individual underwriting.

KEY CONCEPTS AND TERMS

Advance premium mutual
Agency building system
Agent
Assessment mutual
Broker
Contingent or profit-sharing commission
Demutualization
Direct response system
Direct writer
Exclusive agency system
Expirations or renewal rights to business
Factory mutual
Fraternal insurer
General agency system
Holding company
Independent agency system
Lloyd's Associations
Lloyd's of London
Managerial system
Mass merchandising
Multiple distribution systems
Mutual insurer
Nonadmitted insurer
Nonbuilding agency system
Personal-producing general agent
Reciprocal exchange
Stock insurer
Surplus lines broker

REVIEW QUESTIONS

1. Describe the basic characteristics of stock insurers.

2. a. Describe the basic features of mutual insurers.

   b. Identify the major types of mutual insurers.

3. The corporate structure of mutual insurers is changing. Briefly describe three major trends that have an impact on the corporate structure of mutual insurers.

4. Explain the basic characteristics of Lloyd's of London.

5. Describe the basic characteristics of a reciprocal exchange.

6. Explain the legal distinction between an agent and a broker.

7. Briefly describe the basic characteristics of the following marketing systems in life and health insurance:

   a. Agency building system

   b. Nonbuilding agency system

   c. Direct response system

8. Briefly describe the basic characteristics of the following marketing systems in property and liability insurance:

   a. Independent agency system

   b. Exclusive agency system

   c. Direct writer

   d. Direct response system

   e. Multiple distribution systems

9. Who owns the policy expirations or the renewal rights to the business under the independent agency system?

10. What is a mass-merchandising plan in property and liability insurance?

APPLICATION QUESTIONS

1. A group of investors are discussing the formation of a new property and casualty insurer. The proposed company would market a new homeowners policy that combines traditional homeowner coverages with unemployment benefits if the policyowner becomes involuntarily unemployed. Each investor would con-tribute at least $100,000 and would receive a proportionate interest in the company. In addition, the company would raise additional capital by selling ownership rights to other investors. Management wants to avoid the expense of hiring and training agents to sell the new policy and wants to sell the insurance directly to the public by selective advertising in personal finance magazines.

   a. Identify the type of insurance company that best fits the above description.

   b. Identify the marketing system that management is considering adopting.

2. Compare a stock insurer with a mutual insurer with respect to each of the following:

   a. Identification of the parties who legally own the company

   b. Right to assess policyowners additional premiums

   c. Right of policyowners to elect the board of directors

3. A luncheon speaker stated that "the number of life insurers has declined sharply during the past decade because of the increase in company mergers and acquisitions, demutualiztion of insurers, and formation of mutual holding companies."

   a. Why have the number of mergers and acquisitions among insurers increased over time?

   b. What is the meaning of *demutualization?*

   c. Briefly explain the advantages of demutualization to a mutual life insurer.

   d. What is a mutual holding company?

   e. What are the advantages of a mutual holding company to an insurer?

4. A newspaper reporter wrote that "Lloyds of London is an association that provides physical facilities and services to the members for selling insurance. The insurance is underwritten by various syndicates who belong to Lloyd's." Describe Lloyd's of London with respect to each of the following:

   a. Liability of individual members and corporations

   b. Types of insurance written

   c. Financial safeguards to protect insureds

5. Property and liability insurance can be marketed under different marketing systems. Compare the independent agency system with the exclusive agency system with respect to each of the following:

   a. Number of insurers represented

   b. Ownership of policy expirations

   c. Differences in the payment of commissions

INTERNET RESOURCES

■ **The American College** is an accredited, nonprofit educational institution that provides graduate and undergraduate education, primarily on a distance learning basis, to people in the financial services field. The organization awards the professional Chartered Life Underwriter (CLU) designation, the Chartered Financial Consultant (ChFC) designation, and other professional designations. Visit the site at
http://www.amercoll.edu

■ The **American Council of Life Insurers (ACLI)** represents the life insurance industry on issues dealing with legislation and regulation. ACLI also publishes statistics on the life insurance industry in an annual fact book. Visit the site at
http://www.acli.com

■ The **American Institute for CPCU** is an independent, nonprofit organization that offers educational programs and professional certification to people in all segments of the property and liability insurance business. The organization awards the professional CPCU designation and other designations. Visit the site at
http://www.aicpcu.org

■ The **American Insurance Association (AIA)** is an important property and casualty trade association that represents more than 400 insurers. The site lists available publications, position papers on important issues in property and casualty insurance, press releases, insurance-related links, and names of state insurance commissioners. Visit the site at
http://www.aiadc.org

■ The **Insurance Information Institute (III)** has an excellent site for obtaining information on the property and liability insurance industry. It provides timely consumer information on auto, homeowners, and business insurance, and other types of property and liability insurance. Visit the site at
http://www.iii.org

■ The **Insurance Information Institute (III)** also publishes a new fact book on the financial services industry. The publication has detailed information on the role of insurers in the financial services industry. Visit the site at
http://www.financialservicesfacts.org/financial

■ The **Insurance Journal** is a definitive online source of timely information on the property/casualty industry. A free online newsletter is available that provides breaking news on important developments in property and casualty insurance. Visit the site at
http://www.insurancejournal.com

■ **Insure.com** provides a considerable amount of timely information on the insurance industry. The stories reported are directed toward insurance consumers. Consumers can get premium quotes on life, health, auto, and homeowners insurance. Visit the site at
http://www.insure.com

■ **InsWeb** offers insurance quotes from the nation's strongest insurers. You can obtain quotes for auto and homeowners insurance, term life insurance, individual health insurance, and other products as well. Visit the site at
http://www.insweb.com

■ **LIMRA International, Inc.,** is the principal source of industry sales and marketing statistics in life insurance. Its site provides news and information about LIMRA and the financial services field, conducts research, and produces a wide range of publications. Visit the site at
http://www.limra.com

■ **Lloyd's of London** provides a considerable amount of information about its history and chronology, global insurance operations, financial results, and key events on its website. The site also provides information to the news media. Visit the site at
http://www.lloydsoflondon.co.uk

■ The **National Association of Mutual Insurance Companies** is a trade association that represents mutual property and casualty insurance companies. Visit the site at
http://www.namic.org

■ **Towers Perrin** is one of the world's largest actuarial and management consulting firms. The Tillinghast business of Towers Perrin provides a substantial amount of information on the insurance industry and advises other organizations on risk financing and self-insurance. Visit the site at
http://www.towersperrin.com

SELECTED REFERENCES

Black, Kenneth, Jr., and Harold D. Skipper, Jr. *Life Insurance,* 13th ed. Upper Saddle River, NJ: Prentice-Hall, 2000, chs. 23–24.

Carson, James M., Mark D. Forester, and Michael J. McNamara. "Changes in Ownership Structure: Theory and Evidence from Life Insurer Demutualizations," *Journal of Insurance Issues,* Vol. 21, No. 1 (1998), pp. 1–22.

Life Insurers Fact Book, 2003. Washington, DC: American Council of Life Insurers, 2003.

The Financial Services Fact Book 2003. New York: Insurance Information Institute, 2003.

The Fact Book 2004, Insurance Information Institute, New York: Insurance Information Institute, 2004.

Graves, Edward E., ed. *McGill's Life Insurance,* 5th ed. Bryn Mawr, PA: The American College, 2004.

Viswanathan, Krupa S., and J. David Cummins. "Ownership Structure Changes in the Insurance Industry: An Analysis of Demutualization," *The Journal of Risk and Insurance,* Vol. 70, No. 3 (September 2003), pp. 401–437.

Webb, Bernard L., et al. *Insurance Operations and Regulation,* 1st ed. Malvern, PA: American Institute for Chartered Property Casualty Underwriters/ Insurance Institute of America, 2002.

NOTES

1. *The Financial Services Fact Book 2003* (New York: Insurance Information Institute, 2003).
2. *Life Insurers Fact Book 2003* (Washington, DC: American Council of Life Insurers, 2003).
3. *The Financial Services Fact Book 2003.*
4. Edward E. Graves, ed., *McGill's Life Insurance,* 4th ed. (Bryn Mawr, PA: The American College, 2002), pp. 602–604.
5. Ibid., pp. 604–607.
6. Kenneth Black, Jr., and Harold D. Skipper, Jr., *Life and Health Insurance,* 13th ed. (Upper Saddle River, NJ: Prentice-Hall, 2000), pp. 603–613.
7. Bernard L. Webb, et al., *Insurance Operations and Regulation,* 1st ed., (Malvern, PA: American Institute for Chartered Property and Casualty Underwriters/Insurance Institute of America, 2002), p. 3.11.

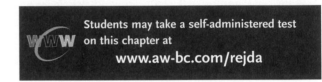

Students may take a self-administered test on this chapter at
www.aw-bc.com/rejda

CHAPTER 26

INSURANCE COMPANY OPERATIONS

"People who work for insurance companies do a lot more than sell insurance."

Insurance Information Institute

After studying this chapter, you should be able to

- Explain the rate-making function of insurers.

- Explain the steps in the underwriting process.

- Describe the steps in the process of settling a claim.

- Explain the reasons for reinsurance and the various types of reinsurance treaties.

- Explain the importance of insurance company investments and identify the various types of investments of insurers.

B rittany, age 25, is a senior at a large Western university. The university has a job placement office where recruiters from major corporations interview students for possible employment. Brittany has signed up for interviews with several insurance companies to learn about job opportunities in that industry. One recruiter explained that insurers hire new employees with a variety of educational backgrounds, and that a wide variety of jobs are available in the industry today. Brittany is surprised to learn of the wide diversity of employment opportunities in the insurance industry. Jobs currently exist in rate making, underwriting, sales, claims, finance, information technology, accounting, legal, and numerous other areas.

This chapter deals with these occupational areas in the insurance industry. To make insurance available to the public, insurers must engage in a wide variety of specialized functions or operations. This chapter discusses the major functional operations of insurers.

INSURANCE COMPANY OPERATIONS

The most important insurance company operations consist of the following:

- Rate making
- Underwriting
- Production
- Claim settlement
- Reinsurance
- Investments

Insurers also engage in other operations, such as accounting, legal services, loss control, and data processing.

The sections that follow discuss each of these functional areas in some detail.

RATE MAKING

Rate making *refers to the pricing of insurance.* Insurance pricing differs considerably from the pricing of other products. When other products are sold, the company generally knows in advance what its costs of production are, so that a price can be established to cover all costs and yield a profit. However, the insurance company does not know in advance

what its actual costs are going to be. The premium charged for the insurance may be inadequate for paying all claims and expenses during the policy period. It is only after the period of protection has expired that an insurer can determine its actual losses and expenses. Of course, the insurer hopes that the premium paid in advance will be sufficient to pay all claims and expenses and yield a profit.

The person who determines rates and premiums is known as an **actuary.** An actuary is a highly skilled mathematician who is involved in all phases of insurance company operations, including planning, pricing, and research. In life insurance, the actuary studies important statistical data on births, deaths, marriages, disease, employment, retirement, and accidents. Based on this information, the actuary determines the rates for life and health insurance policies. The objectives are to calculate premiums that will make the business profitable, enable the company to compete effectively with other insurers, and allow the company to pay claims and expenses as they occur. A life insurance actuary must also determine the legal reserves a company needs for future obligations.[1]

Professional certification as an actuary is attained by passing a series of examinations administered by the Society of Actuaries, which qualifies the actuary as a Fellow of the Society of Actuaries.

In property and liability insurance, actuaries also determine the rates for different lines of insurance.

Rates are based on the company's past loss experience and industry statistics. Statistics on hurricanes, tornadoes, fires, diseases, crime rates, traffic accidents, and the cost of living are also carefully analyzed. Many companies use their own loss data in establishing the rates. Other companies obtain loss data from rating organizations, such as the Insurance Services Office (ISO). These organizations calculate historical or prospective loss costs that individual companies can use in calculating their rates.

Actuaries in property and liability insurance also determine the adequacy of loss reserves,[2] allocate expenses, and compile statistics for company management and for state regulatory officials. Also, actuaries help resolve management problems in underwriting, sales, claims, and product development.

To become a certified actuary in property and liability insurance, the individual must pass a series of examinations administered by the Casualty Actuarial Society. Successful completion of the examinations enables the actuary to become a Fellow of the Casualty Actuarial Society.

UNDERWRITING

Underwriting *refers to the process of selecting and classifying applicants for insurance.* The underwriter is the person who decides to accept or reject an application. The fundamental objective of underwriting is to produce a profitable book of business. The underwriter constantly strives to select certain types of applicants and to reject others so as to obtain a profitable portfolio of insurable risks.

Statement of Underwriting Policy

Underwriting starts with a clear statement of underwriting policy. An insurer must establish an underwriting policy that is consistent with company objectives. The objective may be a large volume of business with low unit profits or a smaller volume with a larger unit of profit. Classes of business that are acceptable, borderline, or prohibited must be clearly stated. The amounts of insurance that can be written on acceptable and borderline business must also be determined.

The insurer's underwriting policy is determined by top-level management in charge of underwriting.

The **line underwriters**—persons who make daily decisions concerning the acceptance or rejection of business—are expected to follow official company policy. The underwriting policy is stated in detail in an *underwriting guide* that specifies the lines of insurance to be written; territories to be developed; forms and rating plans to be used; acceptable, borderline, and prohibited business; amounts of insurance to be written; business that requires approval by a senior underwriter; and other underwriting details.

Basic Underwriting Principles

As noted earlier, the goal of underwriting is to produce a profitable volume of business. To achieve this goal, certain underwriting principles are followed. Three important principles are as follows:

- Selection of insureds according to the company's underwriting standards
- Proper balance within each rate classification
- Equity among policyowners

The first principle is that the underwriter must select prospective insureds according to the company's underwriting standards. This means that the underwriters should select only those insureds whose actual loss experience will not exceed the loss experience assumed in the rating structure. For example, a factory mutual may wish to insure only high-grade factories, and expects that its actual loss experience will be well below average. Underwriting standards are established with respect to eligible factories, and a rate is established based on a relatively low loss ratio.[3] Assume that the expected loss ratio is established at 30 percent, and the rate is set accordingly. The underwriters ideally should insure only those factories that can meet the stringent underwriting requirements, so that the actual loss ratio for the group will not exceed 30 percent.

The purpose of the underwriting standards is to reduce adverse selection against the insurer. There is an old saying in underwriting, "select or be selected against." Adverse selection is the tendency of people with a higher-than-average chance of loss to seek insurance at standard (average) rates, which if not controlled by underwriting, will result in higher-than-expected loss levels.

The second underwriting principle is to have a proper balance within each rate classification. This means that a below-average insured in an underwriting class should be offset by an above-average insured, so that on balance, the class or manual rate for the group as a whole will be adequate for paying all claims and expenses. For example, much of the underwriting today is **class underwriting**, especially for personal lines of insurance. Exposure units with similar loss-producing characteristics are grouped together and placed in the same underwriting class. Each exposure unit within the class is charged the same rate. However, all exposure units are not completely identical. Some will be above average for the class as a whole, while others will be below average. The underwriter must select a proper balance of insureds so that the class rate (average rate) will be adequate for paying all claims and expenses.

A final underwriting principle is equity among the policyowners. This means that equitable rates should be charged, and that each group of policyowners should pay its own way in terms of losses and expenses. Stated differently, one group of policyowners should not unduly subsidize another group. For example, a group of 20-year-old persons and a group of 80-year-old persons should not pay the same premium rate for individual life insurance. If identical rates were charged to both groups, younger persons would be subsidizing older persons. This would be inequitable. Once the younger persons became aware that they were being overcharged, they would seek other insurers whose classification systems are more equitable. The first insurer would then end up with a disproportionate number of older, unhealthy persons, and the underwriting results would be unprofitable. Thus, because of competition, there must be rate equity among the policyowners.

Steps in Underwriting

After the insurer's underwriting policy is established, it must be communicated to the sales force. Initial underwriting starts with the agent in the field.

Agent as First Underwriter   This step is often called field underwriting. The agent is told what types of applicants are acceptable, borderline, or prohibited. For example, in auto insurance, an agent may be told not to solicit applicants who have been convicted for drunk driving, who are single drivers under age 21, or who are young drivers who own high-powered sports cars. In property insurance, certain exposures, such as bowling alleys and restaurants, may have to be submitted to a company underwriter for approval.

In property and liability insurance, the agent often has authority to bind the company immediately, subject to subsequent disapproval of the application and cancellation by a company underwriter. Thus, it is important that the agent follow company policy when soliciting applicants for insurance. To encourage a submission of only profitable business, a *contingent or profit-sharing commission* is often paid based on the agent's favorable loss experience.

In life insurance, the agent must also solicit applicants in accordance with the company's underwriting policy. The agent may be told not to solicit applicants who are drug addicts, active alcoholics, or persons who work in hazardous occupations.

Sources of Underwriting Information   The underwriter requires certain types of information in deciding whether to accept or reject an applicant for insurance. The type of information varies by type of insurance. In property insurance, both the physical features of the property and personal characteristics of the applicant must be considered. Physical features include the type of construction, occupancy of the building, quality of fire protection, water supply, and exposure from surrounding buildings.

With respect to personal characteristics of the applicant, information that reveals the presence of *moral hazard* is particularly important. The underwriter wants to screen out applicants who may intentionally cause a loss or inflate a claim. Thus, the applicant's present financial condition, past loss record, living habits, and moral character are especially important in the underwriting process.

Underwriting information can be obtained from a wide variety of sources. Important sources of information include the following:

- Application
- Agent's report
- Inspection report
- Physical inspection
- Physical examination and attending physician's report
- Medical Information Bureau (MIB)

The *application* is a basic source of underwriting information. It varies depending on the type of insurance. For example, in life insurance, the application will show the individual's age, gender, weight, occupation, personal and family health history, and any hazardous hobbies, such as sky diving.

An *agent's report* is another source of information. Most companies require the agent to give an evaluation of the prospective insured. For example, in life insurance, the agent may be asked to state how long he or she has known the applicant, to estimate the applicant's annual income and net worth, to judge whether the applicant plans to lapse or surrender existing life insurance, and to determine whether the application is the result of the agent's solicitation.

An *inspection report* may be required, especially if the underwriter suspects moral hazard. An outside firm investigates the applicant for insurance and makes a detailed report to the company. The report may include the applicant's present financial condition, drinking habits, marital status, amount of outstanding debts, delinquent bills, policy record, felony convictions, and additional information, such as whether the applicant has ever declared bankruptcy.

A *physical inspection* may also be required before an application for property and liability insurance is approved. The agent or company representative may physically inspect the property to be insured and then submit a report to the underwriter. For example, in workers compensation insurance, an inspection may reveal unsafe working conditions, such as dangerous machinery; violation of safety rules, such as not wearing goggles when a grinding machine is used; and an excessively dusty or toxic plant.

In life insurance, a physical examination will reveal whether the applicant is overweight, has high blood pressure, or has any abnormalities in the heart, respiratory system, urinary system, or other parts of the body. An *attending physician's report* may also be required, which is a report from a physician who has treated the applicant in the past.

A final source of underwriting information in life insurance is a **Medical Information Bureau (MIB) report.** Companies that belong to the bureau report any health impairments, which are then recorded and made available to member companies. For ex-

ample, if an applicant for life insurance has high blood pressure, this information would be recorded in the MIB files, which are coded and do not reveal the decision made by the submitting company.

Making an Underwriting Decision   After the underwriter evaluates the information, an underwriting decision must be made. There are three basic underwriting decisions with respect to an initial application for insurance:

- Accept the application
- Accept the application subject to certain restrictions or modifications
- Reject the application

First, the underwriter can accept the application and recommend that the policy be issued. A second option is to accept the application subject to certain restrictions or modifications. Several examples illustrate this second type of decision. Before a crime insurance policy is issued, the applicant may be required to place iron bars on windows or install an approved central station burglar alarm system; the applicant may be refused a homeowners policy and offered a more limited dwelling policy; a large deductible may be inserted in a property insurance policy; or a higher rate for life insurance may be charged if the applicant is substandard in health. If the applicant agrees to the modifications or restrictions, the policy is then issued.

The third decision is to reject the application. However, excessive and unjustified rejection of applications reduces the insurer's profitability and alienates the agents who solicited the business. If an application is rejected, the rejection should be based on a clear failure to meet the insurer's underwriting standards.

Many insurers now use computerized underwriting for certain personal lines of insurance that can be standardized, such as auto and homeowners insurance. As a result, underwriting decisions can be expedited.

Other Underwriting Considerations

Other factors are considered in underwriting. They include the following:

- *Rate adequacy and underwriting.* When rates are considered adequate for a class, insurers are more willing to underwrite new business. However, if rates are inadequate, prudent underwriting requires a more conservative approach to the acceptance of new business. If moral hazard is excessive, the business generally cannot be insured at any rate.

In addition, in commercial property and liability insurance, the underwriters have a considerable impact on the price of the product. A great deal of negotiation over price takes place between the line underwriter and the agent concerning the proper pricing of a commercial risk.

Finally, the critical relationship between adequate rates and underwriting profits or losses results in periodic underwriting cycles in certain lines of insurance, such as commercial general liability and commercial multiperil insurance. If rates are adequate, underwriting profits are higher, and underwriting is more liberal. Conversely, when rates are inadequate, underwriting losses occur, and underwriting becomes more restrictive.

- *Reinsurance and underwriting.* Availability of reinsurance may result in more liberal underwriting. However, if reinsurance cannot be obtained on favorable terms, the underwriting may be more restrictive.
- *Renewal underwriting.* In life insurance, policies are not cancelable. In property and liability insurance, most policies can be canceled or not renewed. If the loss experience is unfavorable, the insurer may either cancel or not renew the policy. Most states have placed restrictions on the insurer's right to cancel.

PRODUCTION

The term **production** refers to the sales and marketing activities of insurers. Agents who sell insurance are frequently referred to as **producers.** This word is used because an insurance company can be legally chartered, personnel can be hired, and policy forms printed, but nothing is produced until a policy is sold. The key to the insurer's financial success is an effective sales force.

Agency Department

Life insurers have an agency or sales department. This department is responsible for recruiting and training new agents and for the supervision of general agents, branch office managers, and local agents.

Property and liability insurers have marketing departments. To assist agents in the field, special agents may also be appointed. A *special agent* is a highly specialized technician who provides local agents in the field with technical help and assistance with their marketing problems. For example, a special agent may explain a new policy form or a special rating plan to agents in the field.

In addition to development of an effective sales force, an insurance company engages in a wide variety of marketing activities. These activities include the development of a marketing philosophy and the company's perception of its role in the marketplace; identification of short-run and long-run production goals; marketing research; development of new products to meet the changing needs of consumers and business firms; development of new marketing strategies; and advertising of the insurer's products.

Professionalism in Selling

The marketing of insurance has been characterized by a distinct trend toward professionalism in recent years. This means that the modern agent should be a competent professional who has a high degree of technical knowledge in a particular area of insurance and who also places the needs of his or her clients first. The professional agent identifies potential insureds, analyzes their insurance needs, and recommends the best solution to the problem. After the sale, the agent has the responsibility of providing follow-up service to clients to keep their insurance programs up to date. Finally, a professional agent abides by a code of ethics.

Several organizations have developed professional designation programs for agents and other personnel in the insurance industry. In life and health insurance, The American College has established the **Chartered Life Underwriter (CLU)** program. An individual must pass eight professional examinations to receive the CLU designation.

The American College also awards the **Chartered Financial Consultant (ChFC)** designation for professionals who are working in the financial services industry. To earn the ChFC designation, students must pass eight professional examinations.

A similar professional program exists in property and liability insurance. The American Institute for CPCU has established the **Chartered Property Casualty Underwriter (CPCU)** program. The CPCU program also requires an individual to pass eight examinations.

Other professionals are also important in the insurance industry. Many financial planners are also licensed as insurance agents. The **Certified Financial Planner (CFP)** designation is granted by the Certified Financial Planner Board of Standards, Inc. Many agents in property and liability insurance have been awarded the **Certified Insurance Counselor (CIC)** designation sponsored by the Society of Certified Insurance Counselors.

CLAIM SETTLEMENT

Every insurance company has a claims division or department for adjusting claims. This section examines the basic objectives in adjusting claims, the different types of claim adjustors, and the various steps in the claim-settlement process.

Basic Objectives in Claim Settlement

From the insurer's viewpoint, there are several basic objectives in settling claims.[4]

- Verification of a covered loss
- Fair and prompt payment of claims
- Personal assistance to the insured

The first objective in settling claims is to verify that a covered loss has occurred. This step involves determining whether a specific person or property is covered under the policy, and the extent of the coverage. This objective is discussed in greater detail later in the chapter.

The second objective is the fair and prompt payment of claims. If a valid claim is denied, the fundamental social and contractual purpose of protecting the insured is defeated. Also, the insurer's reputation may be harmed, and the sales of new policies may be adversely affected. Fair payment means that the insurer should avoid excessive claim settlements and

should resist the payment of fraudulent claims, because they will ultimately result in higher premiums. If the insurer follows a liberal claims policy, all policyowners will suffer because a rate increase will become necessary.

The states have passed laws that prohibit unfair claim practices. These laws are patterned after the National Association of Insurance Commissioners' Model Act. Some unfair claim practices prohibited by these laws include the following:[5]

- Refusing to pay claims without conducting a reasonable investigation.
- Not attempting in good faith to provide prompt, fair, and equitable settlements of claims in which liability has become reasonably clear.
- Compelling insureds or beneficiaries to institute lawsuits to recover amounts due under its policies by offering substantially less than the amounts ultimately recovered in suits brought by them.

A third objective is to provide personal assistance to the insured after a covered loss occurs. Aside from any contractual obligations, the insurer should also provide personal assistance after a loss occurs. For example, the claims adjustor could assist the agent in helping a family find temporary housing after a fire occurs.

Types of Claims Adjustors

The person who adjusts a claim is known as a **claims adjustor.** The major types of adjustors include the following:

- Agent
- Company adjustor
- Independent adjustor
- Adjustment bureau
- Public adjustor

An **agent** often has authority to settle small first-party claims up to some maximum limit.[6] The insured submits the claim directly to the agent, who has the authority to pay up to some specified amount. This approach to claim settlement has several advantages: it is speedy, it reduces adjustment expenses, and it preserves the policyowner's good will.

A **company adjustor** can settle a claim. The adjustor is usually a salaried employee who represents only one company. After notice of the loss is received, the company adjustor will investigate the claim, determine the amount of loss, and arrange for payment.

An **independent adjustor** can also be used to settle claims. An independent adjustor is a person who offers his or her services to insurance companies and is compensated by a fee. The company may use an independent adjustor in certain geographical areas where the volume of claims is too low to justify a branch office with a staff of full-time adjustors. An independent adjustor may also be used in highly specialized areas where a company adjustor with the necessary technical skills and knowledge is not available.

An **adjustment bureau** can be used to settle claims. An adjustment bureau is an organization for adjusting claims that is supported by insurers that use its services. Claims personnel employed by an adjustment bureau are highly trained individuals who adjust claims on a full-time basis. An adjustment bureau is frequently used when a catastrophic loss, such as a hurricane, occurs in a given geographical area, and a large number of claims are submitted at the same time.

A **public adjustor** can be involved in settling a claim. *A public adjustor, however, represents the insured rather than the insurance company and is paid a fee based on the amount of the claim settlement.* A public adjustor may be employed by the insured if a complex loss situation occurs and technical assistance is needed, and also in those cases where the insured and insurer cannot resolve a dispute over a claim.

Steps in Settlement of a Claim

There are several important steps in settling a claim:

- Notice of loss must be given.
- The claim is investigated.
- A proof of loss may be required.
- A decision is made concerning payment.

Notice of Loss   The first step is to notify the insurer of a loss. A provision concerning notice of loss is usually stated in the policy. A typical provision requires the insured to give notice immediately or as soon as possible after the loss has occurred. For example, the homeowners policy requires the insured to give immediate notice; a medical expense policy may require the insured to give notice within 30 days after

the occurrence of a loss, or as soon afterward as is reasonably possible; and the personal auto policy requires that the insurer must be notified promptly of how, when, and where the accident or loss happened. The notice must also include the names and addresses of any injured persons and of witnesses.

Investigation of the Claim   After notice is received, the next step is to investigate the claim. An adjustor must determine that a covered loss has occurred and must also determine the amount of the loss. A series of questions must be answered before the claim is approved. The most important questions include the following:[7]

- Did the loss occur while the policy was in force?
- Does the policy cover the peril that caused the loss?
- Does the policy cover the property destroyed or damaged in the loss?
- Is the claimant entitled to recover?
- Did the loss occur at an insured location?
- Is the type of loss covered?
- Is the claim fraudulent?

The last question dealing with fraudulent claims is especially important. Insurance fraud is widespread, especially in auto and health insurance. Dishonest people frequently submit claims for bodily injuries that have never occurred.

Filing a Proof of Loss   An adjustor may require a proof of loss before the claim is paid. A proof of loss is a sworn statement by the insured that substantiates the loss. For example, under the homeowners policy, the insured may be required to file a proof of loss that indicates the time and cause of the loss, interest of the insured and others in the damaged property, other insurance that may cover the loss, and any change in title or occupancy of the property during the term of the policy.

Decision Concerning Payment   After the claim is investigated, the adjustor must make a decision concerning payment. There are three possible decisions. *The claim can be paid.* In most cases, the claim is paid promptly according to the terms of the policy. *The claim can be denied.* The adjustor may believe that the policy does not cover the loss or that the claim is fraudulent. Finally, the claim may be valid, but there may be a dispute between the insured and

How Many Complaints Have Been Filed Against Your Insurance Company?

Consumers often experience considerable frustration in their efforts to obtain accurate and timely information on complaints against specific insurers. Some state insurance departments provide detailed information on complaints and rank the insurers operating in the state based on a complaint index. However, not all states provide complaint data to the public.

The National Association of Insurance Commissioners (NAIC) has a Web site that provides a wealth of information to consumers with respect to complaints against specific insurers. *Go to the NAIC Consumer Information Source at http://www.naic.org/cis/. Type in the company name, state, and business type. After locating the company, click on Closed Complaints.* Note that this Web site may change if the NAIC makes changes to its current site.

The information provided is based on closed consumer complaint reports. Four types of complaint data are available:

- *Complaint counts by state.* This source shows the total number of complaints in each state for a specific insurer. For example, in 2003, one major property and casualty insurer in Illinois had 461 complaints from insureds and other parties.
- *Complaint counts by code.* This source shows the total number of complaints by type of coverage, reason the complaint was filed, and disposition of the complaint.

- *Complaint ratio report.* This source is valuable because it compares a specific insurer with all insurers nationally using a single index number. This source compares the ratio of the insurer's market share of complaints to the insurer's market share of premiums for a specific policy type. For the above insurer, the national median complaint ratio in 2003 for homeowners insurance was 1.00. The insurer in question received a score of 0.33, which was well below the national median. The index score is also shown visually in a graph.
- *Complaint trend report.* This source shows whether complaints against the insurer are increasing or decreasing. The information presented shows the total number of complaints in the database for consecutive years with the percentage change in complaint counts between years. For example, the total number of complaints for the above insurer increased from 2286 in 2002, to 3308 in 2003, or an increase of 45 percent.

Information on complaints is especially valuable if you are shopping around for auto, homeowners, or health insurance and want to avoid insurers that have bad reputations for paying claims or for providing other services to policyowners.

insurer over the amount to be paid. *In the case of a dispute, a policy provision may specify how the dispute is to be resolved.* For example, if a dispute arises under the homeowners policy, both the insured and insurer select a competent appraiser. The two appraisers select an umpire. If the appraisers cannot agree on an umpire, a court will appoint one. An agreement by any two of the three is then binding on all parties.

When there is disagreement over the claim settlement, consumers may file a complaint with the state insurance department. All states, however, do not provide complaint information on specific insurers. The National Association of Insurance Commissioners (NAIC) now has a Web site that permits consumers to check the complaint record of individual insurers (see Insight 26.1).

REINSURANCE

Reinsurance is another important insurance operation. This section discusses the meaning of reinsur-

ance, the reasons for reinsurance, and the different types of reinsurance contracts.

Definitions

Reinsurance *is the shifting of part or all of the insurance originally written by one insurer to another insurer.* The insurer that initially writes the business is called the **ceding company.** The insurer that accepts part or all of the insurance from the ceding company is called the **reinsurer.** The amount of insurance retained by the ceding company for its own account is called the **retention limit** or **net retention.** The amount of the insurance ceded to the reinsurer is known as a **cession.** Finally, the reinsurer in turn may reinsure part or all of the risk with another insurer. This is known as a **retrocession.** In this case, the second reinsurer is called a **retrocessionaire.**

Reasons for Reinsurance

Reinsurance is used for several reasons. The most important reasons include the following.

- Increase underwriting capacity
- Stabilize profits
- Reduce the unearned premium reserve
- Provide protection against a catastrophic loss

Reinsurance also enables an insurer to retire from a territory or class of business and to obtain underwriting advice from the reinsurer.

Increase Underwriting Capacity Reinsurance can be used to increase the insurance company's underwriting capacity to write new business. The company may be asked to assume liability for losses in excess of its retention limit. Without reinsurance, the agent would have to place large amounts of insurance with several companies or not accept the risk. This is awkward and may create ill will on behalf of the policyowner. Reinsurance permits the primary company to issue a single policy in excess of its retention limit for the full amount of insurance.

Stabilize Profits Reinsurance can be used to stabilize profits. An insurer may wish to avoid large fluctuations in annual financial results. Loss experience can fluctuate widely because of social and economic conditions, natural disasters, and chance. Reinsurance can be used to level out the effects of poor loss experience. For example, reinsurance may be used to cover a large exposure. If a large, unexpected loss occurs, the reinsurer would pay the portion of the loss in excess of some specified limit. Another arrangement would be to have the reinsurer reimburse the ceding insurer for losses that exceed a specified loss ratio during a given year. For example, an insurer may wish to stabilize its loss ratio at 70 percent. The reinsurer then agrees to reimburse the ceding insurer for part or all the losses in excess of 70 percent up to some maximum limit.

Reduce the Unearned Premium Reserve Reinsurance can be used to reduce the unearned premium reserve. For some insurers, especially newer and smaller ones, the ability to write large amounts of new insurance may be restricted by the unearned premium reserve requirement. The **unearned premium reserve** *is a liability item on the insurer's balance sheet that represents the unearned portion of gross premiums on all outstanding policies at the time of valuation.* In effect, the unearned premium

reserve reflects the fact that premiums are paid in advance, but the period of protection has not yet expired. As time goes on, part of the premium is considered earned, while the remainder is unearned. It is only after the period of protection has expired that the premium is fully earned.

As noted earlier, an insurer's ability to grow may be restricted by the unearned premium reserve requirement. This is because the entire gross premium must be placed in the unearned premium reserve when the policy is first written. The insurer also incurs relatively heavy first-year acquisition expenses in the form of commissions, state premium taxes, underwriting expenses, expenses in issuing the policy, and other expenses. In determining the size of the unearned premium reserve, there is no allowance for these first-year acquisition expenses, and the insurer must pay them out of its surplus. (Policyholders' surplus is the difference between assets and liabilities.[8])

For example, a one-year property insurance policy with an annual premium of $1200 may be written on January 1. The entire $1200 must be placed in the unearned premium reserve. At the end of each month, one-twelfth of the premium, or $100, is earned and the remainder is unearned. On December 31, the entire premium is fully earned. However, assume that first-year acquisition expenses are 30 percent of the gross premium, or $360. This amount will come out of the insurer's surplus up front. Thus, the more business it writes, the greater is the short-term drain on its surplus. A rapidly growing insurer's ability to write new business could eventually be impaired.

Reinsurance reduces the level of the unearned premium reserve required by law and temporarily increases the insurer's surplus position. As a result, the ratio of policyholders' surplus to net written premiums is improved, which permits the insurer to continue to grow.

Provide Protection Against a Catastrophic Loss Reinsurance also provides financial protection against a catastrophic loss. Insurers often experience catastrophic losses because of natural disasters, industrial explosions, commercial airline disasters, and similar events. Reinsurance can provide considerable protection to the ceding company that experiences a catastrophic loss. The reinsurer pays part or all of the losses that exceed the ceding company's retention up to some specified maximum limit.

Exhibit 26.1
September 11, 2001 Insurance Industry Loss Estimates[a]
($ billions)

Total:
$40.2 Billion

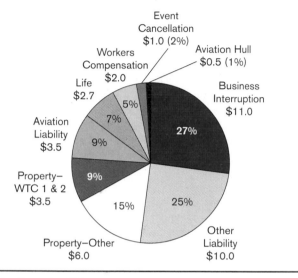

[a] As of September, 2002.

NOTE: Data are from Morgan Stanley and Insurance Information Institute.

SOURCE: *The I.I.I. Insurance Fact Book 2004* (New York: Insurance Information Institute, 2004), p. 83.

The tragic terrorist attacks on September 11, 2001, clearly show the importance of reinsurance to the insurance industry. The attacks caused the loss of thousands of lives and billions of dollars of property damage. Total losses exceeded $80 billion. Insured losses totaled $40.2 billion, which was the largest single catastrophe for the insurance industry in the history of the United States. Most insurance lines were dramatically affected. Exhibit 26.1 shows an updated impact of these losses on major lines of insurance.

Reinsurers paid out at least half of the insured losses, or more than $20 billion, and incurred severe underwriting losses in 2001. As a result, reinsurers increased premiums sharply, and the reinsurance market tightened. Although payments from reinsurers reduced the adverse financial impact of the terrorist attacks on primary insurers, the industry

believed that additional financial help was necessary. Congress responded by enacting the Terrorism Risk Insurance Act of 2002. The Act established a federal reinsurance program that provides a federal backup for property and casualty insurers in the event of future terrorist attacks. Exhibit 26.2 summarizes the key provisions of the federal reinsurance program.

Other Reasons for Reinsurance An insurer can use reinsurance to retire from the business or from a given line of insurance or territory. Reinsurance permits the insurer's liabilities for existing insurance to be transferred to another carrier; thus, the policyowner's coverage remains undisturbed.

Finally, reinsurance can enable an insurer to obtain the underwriting advice and assistance of the reinsurer. An insurer may wish to write a new line of insurance, but it may have little experience with

EXHIBIT **26.2**
Summary of Key Features of the Terrorism Risk Insurance Act of 2002

The new law provides a federal backup for future terrorist attacks for property and casualty insurers. Unless extended by Congress, the federal reinsurance program expires at the end of 2005.

- Insurers are required to offer terrorism coverage in all commercial property and casualty policies through 2004. The Secretary of the Treasury has the discretion to extend the availability-of-coverage requirement to the end of 2005.

- Insurers must clearly disclose to the policyowners the premiums charged for covered terrorist loss and the federal share of compensation for insured losses. With the exception of workers compensation insurance, policyowners can decline the coverage.

- The law provides a federal backstop for terrorism losses. After the insurer meets an annual deductible, the federal government pays 90 percent of the losses that exceed the deductible amount, and the insurer pays the remaining 10 percent. The deductible is based on a percentage of direct earned premiums. For 2003, the deductible is 7 percent of direct earned premiums; the deductible increases to 10 percent in 2004 and 15 percent in 2005.

- The law places a $100 billion annual cap on payments by the federal government for terrorist losses. If the federal government pays for insured losses during the year, the Secretary of the Treasury is required to recoup the federal payments, which is the difference between total industry costs and certain fixed dollars amounts ($10 billion in 2002 and 2003, $12.5 billion for 2004, and $15 billion 2005). Recoupment of federal assistance is not required if the aggregate payments by all insurers for losses covered under the Act exceed $10 billion in 2003, $12.5 billion in 2004, and $15 billion in 2005. Recoupment is accomplished by surcharging the policyowners. However, the surcharge cannot exceed 3 percent of the annual premium for the policy.

SOURCE: Robert P. Hartwig, *The Long Shadow of September 11: Terrorism and Its Impacts on Insurance and Reinsurance Markets* (New York: Insurance Information Institute, March 2002).

respect to underwriting the line. The reinsurer can often provide valuable assistance with respect to rating, retention limits, policy coverages, and other underwriting details.

Types of Reinsurance

There are two principal forms of reinsurance: (1) facultative and (2) treaty.

Facultative Reinsurance   Facultative reinsurance *is an optional, case-by-case method that is used when the ceding company receives an application for insurance that exceeds its retention limit.* Before the policy is issued, the primary insurer shops around for reinsurance and contacts several reinsurers. The primary insurer is under no obligation to cede insurance, and the reinsurer is under no obligation to accept the insurance. But if a willing reinsurer can be found, the primary insurer and reinsurer can then enter into a valid contract.

Facultative reinsurance is frequently used when a large amount of insurance is desired. Before the application is accepted, the primary insurer determines whether reinsurance can be obtained. If available, the policy can then be written.

Facultative reinsurance has the advantage of flexibility, because a reinsurance contract can be arranged to fit any kind of case. It can increase the insurer's capacity to write large amounts of insurance. The reinsurance tends to stabilize the insurer's operations by shifting large losses to the reinsurer.

The major disadvantage of facultative reinsurance is that it is uncertain. The ceding insurer does not know in advance if a reinsurer will accept any part of the insurance. There is also a further disadvantage of delay, because the policy will not be issued until reinsurance is obtained. In times of bad loss experience, the reinsurance market tends to tighten, and the avoidability and affordability of reinsurance may be a problem. Therefore, facultative reinsurance has the further disadvantage of being unreliable.

Treaty Reinsurance   Treaty reinsurance *means the primary insurer has agreed to cede insurance to the reinsurer, and the reinsurer has agreed to accept the business.* All business that falls within the scope of the agreement is automatically reinsured according to the terms of the treaty.

Treaty reinsurance has several advantages to the primary insurer. It is automatic, and no uncertainty or delay is involved. It is also economical, because it is not necessary to shop around for reinsurance before the policy is written.

Treaty reinsurance could be unprofitable to the reinsurer. The reinsurer generally has no knowledge about the individual applicant and must rely on the underwriting judgment of the primary insurer. The primary insurer may write bad business and then reinsure it. Also, the premium received by the reinsurer may be inadequate. Thus, if the primary insurer has a poor selection of risks or charges inadequate rates, the reinsurer could incur a loss. However, if the primary insurer consistently cedes unprofitable business to its reinsurers, the ceding insurer will find it difficult to operate because reinsurers will not want to do business with it.

There are several types of reinsurance treaties and arrangements, including the following:

- Quota-share treaty
- Surplus-share treaty
- Excess-of-loss treaty
- Reinsurance pool

Quote-Share Treaty   Under a **quota-share treaty,** the ceding insurer and reinsurer agree to share premiums and losses based on some proportion. *The ceding insurer's retention limit is stated as a percentage rather than as a dollar amount.* For example, Apex Fire Insurance and Geneva Re may enter into a quota-share treaty by which premiums and losses are shared 50 percent and 50 percent. Thus, if a $100,000 loss occurs, Apex Fire pays $100,000 to the insured but is reimbursed by Geneva Re for $50,000.

Premiums are also shared based on the same agreed-on percentages. However, the reinsurer pays a **ceding commission** to the primary insurer to help compensate for the expenses incurred in writing the business. Thus, in the previous example, Geneva Re would receive 50 percent of the premium less a ceding commission that is paid to Apex Fire.

The major advantage of quota-share reinsurance is that the unearned premium reserve is reduced. For smaller insurers and other insurers that wish to reduce the drain on surplus, a quota-share treaty can be especially effective. The principal disadvantage is that a large share of potentially profitable business is ceded to the reinsurer.

Surplus-Share Treaty   Under a **surplus-share treaty,** the reinsurer agrees to accept insurance in excess of the ceding insurer's retention limit, up to some maximum amount. *The retention limit is referred to as a line and is stated as a dollar amount.* If the amount of insurance on a given policy exceeds the retention limit, the excess insurance is ceded to the reinsurer up to some maximum limit. The primary insurer and reinsurer then share premiums and losses based on the fraction of total insurance retained by each party. Each party pays its respective share of any loss regardless of its size.

For example, assume that Apex Fire Insurance has a retention limit of $200,000 (called a line) for a single policy, and that four lines, or $800,000, are ceded to Geneva Re. Apex Fire now has a total underwriting capacity of $1 million on any single exposure. Assume that a $500,000 property insurance policy is issued. Apex Fire takes the first $200,000 of insurance, or two-fifths, and Geneva Re takes the remaining $300,000, or three-fifths. These fractions then determine the amount of loss paid by each party. If a $5000 loss occurs, Apex Fire pays $2000 (two-fifths), and Geneva Re pays the remaining $3000 (three-fifths). This situation can be summarized as follows:

Apex Fire	$ 200,000	(1 line)
Geneva Re	800,000	(4 lines)
Total underwriting capacity	$1,000,000	
$500,000 policy issued		
Apex Fire	$200,000	(2/5)
Geneva Re	$300,000	(3/5)
$5000 loss occurs		
Apex Fire	$2000	(2/5)
Geneva Re	$3000	(3/5)

Under a surplus-share treaty, premiums are also shared based on the fraction of total insurance retained by each party. However, the reinsurer pays a ceding commission to the primary insurer to help compensate for the acquisition expenses.

The principal advantage of a surplus-share treaty is that the primary insurer's underwriting capacity is increased. The major disadvantage is the increase in administrative expenses. The surplus-share treaty is more complex and requires greater record keeping.

Excess-of-Loss Treaty An **excess-of-loss treaty** is designed largely for catastrophic protection. Losses in excess of the retention limit are paid by the reinsurer up to some maximum limit. The excess-of-loss treaty can be written to cover (1) a single exposure, (2) a single occurrence, such as a catastrophic loss from a tornado, or (3) excess losses when the primary insurer's cumulative losses exceed a certain amount during some stated time period, such as a year. For example, assume that Apex Fire Insurance wants protection for all windstorm losses in excess of $1 million. Assume that an excess-of-loss treaty is written with Franklin Re to cover single occurrences during a specified time period. Franklin Re agrees to pay all losses exceeding $1 million but only to a maximum of $10 million. If a $5 million hurricane loss occurs, Franklin Re would pay $4 million.

Reinsurance Pool Reinsurance can also be provided by a reinsurance pool. A **reinsurance pool** *is an organization of insurers that underwrites insurance on a joint basis.* Reinsurance pools have been formed because a single insurer alone may not have the financial capacity to write large amounts of insurance, but the insurers as a group can combine their financial resources to obtain the necessary capacity. For example, the combined hull and liability loss exposures on a large commercial jet can exceed $500 million if the jet should crash. Such high limits are usually beyond the financial capability of a single insurer. However, a reinsurance pool for aviation insurance can provide the necessary capacity. Reinsurance pools also exist for nuclear energy exposures, oil refineries, marine insurance, insurance in foreign countries, and numerous other types of exposures.

The method for sharing losses and premiums varies depending on the type of reinsurance pool. Pools work in two ways.[9] First, each pool member agrees to pay a certain percentage of every loss. For example, if one insurer has a policyowner that incurs a $500,000 loss, and there are 50 members in

the pool, each insurer would pay 2 percent, or $10,000 of the loss, depending on the agreement.

A second arrangement is similar to the excess-of-loss reinsurance treaty. Each pool member is responsible for its own losses below a certain amount. Losses exceeding that amount are shared by all members in the pool.

ALTERNATIVES TO TRADITIONAL REINSURANCE

Some insurers and reinsurers are now using the capital markets as an alternative to traditional reinsurance. The financial capacity of the property and casualty industry to pay catastrophic losses from hurricanes, earthquakes, and other natural disasters is limited. Rather than rely solely on the limited financial capacity of the insurance industry to pay catastrophic claims, some insurers and reinsurers are using the capital markets to gain access to the capital of institutional investors. Having access to the capital markets substantially increases the funds available to pay catastrophe losses.

Securitization of Risk

There is an increasing use of the securitization of risk to obtain funds to pay for a catastrophe loss. **Securitization of risk** means *that an insurable risk is transferred to the capital markets through the creation of a financial instrument, such as a catastrophe bond, futures contract, options contract, or other financial instrument.* These instruments are also called risk-linked securities that transfer insurance-related risks to the capital markets. Insurers were among the first financial institutions to experiment with the securitization of risk.

Catastrophe Bonds

Catastrophe bonds are an excellent example of the securitization of risk. **Catastrophe bonds** *are corporate bonds that permit the issuer of the bond to skip or defer scheduled payments if a catastrophic loss occurs.* The bonds are complex financial instruments issued by insurers and reinsurers and are designed to provide funds for catastrophe natural disaster losses.

The bonds pay relatively high interest rates and help institutional investors to diversify their portfolios because natural disasters occur randomly and are not correlated with the stock market or other economic factors.

Catastrophe bonds are made available to institutional investors in the capital markets through an entity called a *special purpose reinsurance vehicle (SPRV)*, which is specifically established for that purpose. The insurer purchases reinsurance from the SPRV and pays reinsurance premiums to the SPRV. The SPRV issues the catastrophe bonds, holds the premiums collected from insurers and the proceeds from the bond sales in a trust, and invests the funds in U.S. Treasuries or other high quality assets. The bonds pay relatively high interest rates. *However, if a catastrophe loss occurs, the investors could forfeit the interest and even the principal, depending on how the bonds are structured.* The catastrophe bonds sold currently are indexed products where the loss of principal is based on formulas that consider the severity of a catastrophic loss and its location, such as earthquake losses in California, rather than on the actual losses experienced by the insurer.[10]

Catastrophe bonds are typically purchased by institutional investors seeking higher-yielding, fixed-income securities. The bonds generally are not available for direct purchase by individual retail investors. Insurers to date have transferred only a small portion of their catastrophe loss exposures to the capital markets. According to the Swiss Reinsurance Company, outstanding catastrophe bonds represented only about 2.5 to 3.0 percent of the worldwide catastrophe reinsurance coverage in 2002.[11]

According to the U.S. Government Accounting Office (GAO), there are several reasons that help explain the limited use of catastrophe bonds: (1) some insurers believe that the costs of issuing a catastrophe bond, which include high rates of return paid to investors and administrative costs, are significantly higher than the cost of traditional reinsurance; (2) certain statutory accounting standards that give credit on an insurer's balance sheet for traditional reinsurance purchases are currently not permitted for catastrophe bonds; and (3) some institutional investors perceive catastrophe bonds to be relatively illiquid.[12]

EXHIBIT 26.3
Growth of Life Insurers' Assets

SOURCE: *Life Insurers Fact Book 2003* (Washington, DC: American Council of Life Insurers, 2003), Figure 2.1, p. 13.

INVESTMENTS

The investment function is extremely important in the overall operations of insurance companies. Because premiums are paid in advance, they can be invested until needed to pay claims and expenses.

Life Insurance Investments

Assets held by life insurers have increased substantially over time. In 2002, U.S. life insurers held about $3.4 trillion in assets (see Exhibit 26.3). The funds available for investment are derived primarily from premium income, investment earnings, and maturing investments that must be reinvested.

A life insurer divides its assets into two accounts. The assets in the *general account* support the contractual obligations for guaranteed fixed dollar benefits, such as life insurance death benefits. The assets in the *separate account* support the liabilities for investment-risk products, such as variable annuities, variable life insurance, and private pension benefits.

State laws place restrictions on the types of assets in the general account. Because of the long-term nature of life insurance products, most investments are in bonds, mortgages, and real estate; only a small percentage of the assets are invested in stocks. In contrast, state laws generally have fewer restrictions on the investment of assets in the separate account. As such, almost three-fourths of the assets in the separate account are invested in stocks (see Exhibit 26.4).

Life insurance investments have an important economic and social impact on the nation for several reasons. First, life insurance contracts are long-term, and the liabilities of life insurers extend over long periods of time, such as 50 or 60 years. Thus, safety of principal is a primary consideration. Consequently, as stated earlier, the majority of investments in the general account are in bonds.

Second, investment income is extremely important in reducing the cost of insurance to policyowners because the premiums can be invested and earn interest. The interest earned on investments is reflected in the payment of dividends to policyowners, which reduces the cost of life insurance.

Finally, life insurance premiums also are an important source of capital funds to the economy. These funds are invested in shopping centers,

EXHIBIT 26.4
Asset Distribution of Life Insurers 2002

SOURCE: *Life Insurers Fact Book 2003* (Washington, DC: American Council of Life Insurers, 2003), Figure 2.2, p. 20.

housing developments, office buildings, hospitals, new plants, and other economic and social ventures.

Property and Liability Insurance Investments

In 2002, property and liability insurance company investments totaled about $848 billion.[13] Most assets are invested in securities that can be quickly sold to pay claims if a major catastrophe occurs—primarily high-quality stocks and bonds rather than real estate (see Exhibit 26.5).

In addition, in 2002, net premiums written for all lines totaled about $377.2 billion.[14] Premiums

EXHIBIT 26.5
Investments of Property and Casualty Insurers, 2002

Instruments by Type

Real Estate and Mortgages 1.40%
Preferred stock 1.71%
Other 4.59%
Cash and short-term investments 8.54%
Common stock 16.41%
Bonds 67.35%

Bond Portfolio[1]
(Represents 67.35% of total investments)

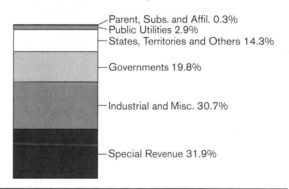

Parent, Subs. and Affil. 0.3%
Public Utilities 2.9%
States, Territories and Others 14.3%
Governments 19.8%
Industrial and Misc. 30.7%
Special Revenue 31.9%

[1]As of December 31. 2002.

NOTE: Data are from A. M. Best Company, Inc.

SOURCE: *The I.I.I. Insurance Fact Book 2004* (New York: Insurance Information Institute, 2004), p. 22

are typically paid in advance, so they can be invested until needed for claims and expenses.

Two important points must be stressed when the investments of property and liability insurers are analyzed. *First, in contrast to life insurance, property and liability insurance contracts generally are short-term in nature.* The policy period in most contracts is one year or less, and property claims are usually settled quickly. Also, in contrast to life insurance claims, which are generally fixed in amount, property and liability claim payments can vary widely depending on catastrophic losses, inflation, medical costs, construction costs, auto repair costs, economic conditions, and changing value judgments by society. For these reasons, the investment objective of liquidity is extremely important to property and liability insurers.

Second, investment income is extremely important in offsetting unfavorable underwriting experience. The investment of capital and surplus funds, along with the funds set aside for loss reserves and the unearned premium reserve, generate investment earnings that usually permit an insurer to continue its insurance operations despite an underwriting deficit.

OTHER INSURANCE COMPANY FUNCTIONS

Insurers also perform other functions. They include accounting, legal, loss control services, and electronic data processing.

Accounting

The **accounting department** is responsible for the financial accounting operations of an insurer. Accountants prepare financial statements, develop budgets, analyze the company's financial operations, and keep track of the millions of dollars that flow into and out of a typical company each year. Periodic reports are prepared dealing with premium income, operating expenses, claims, investment income, and dividends to policyowners. Accountants also prepare statutory annual statements that must be filed with state insurance departments. If the company is publicly traded, accountants must also prepare accounting statements based on Generally Accepted Accounting Principles (GAAP) for investors.

Legal Function

Another important function of insurance companies is the *legal function*. In life insurance, attorneys are widely used in advanced underwriting and estate planning. Attorneys also draft the legal language and policy provisions in insurance policies and review all new policies before they are marketed to the public. Other activities include providing legal assistance to actuarial personnel who testify at rate hearings; reviewing advertising and other published materials; providing general legal advice concerning taxation, marketing, investments, and insurance laws; and lobbying for legislation favorable to the insurance industry.

Attorneys must also keep abreast of the frequent changes in state and federal laws that affect the company and its policyowners. These include laws on consumerism, cost disclosure, affirmative action programs, truth in advertising, and similar legislation. Finally, attorneys must keep up with current court cases and legal precedents.

Loss-Control Services

Loss control is an important part of risk management, and a typical property and liability insurer provides numerous loss-control services. These services include advice on alarm systems, automatic sprinkler systems, fire prevention, occupational safety and health, prevention of boiler explosions, and other loss-prevention activities. In addition, loss-control specialists can provide valuable advice on the construction of a new building or plant to make it safer and more resistive to damage, which can result in a substantial rate reduction. Loss control specialists can also assist underwriters.

Electronic Data Processing

Another important functional area is **electronic data processing (EDP)**. Computers have revolutionized the insurance industry by speeding up the processing and storage of information and by eliminating many routine tasks. Computers are widely used in accounting, policy processing, premium notices,

---

CASE APPLICATION

Reinsurance can be used by an insurer to solve several problems. Assume you are an insurance consultant who is asked to give recommendations concerning the type of reinsurance plan or arrangement to use. For each of the following situations, indicate the type of reinsurance plan or arrangement that the ceding insurer should use, and explain the reasons for your answer.

a. Company A is an established insurer and is primarily interested in having protection against a catastrophic loss arising out of a single occurrence.

b. Company B is rapidly growing new company and desires a plan of reinsurance that will reduce the drain on its surplus from writing a large volume of new business.

c. Company C has received an application to write a $50 million life insurance policy on the life of the chief executive officer of a major corporation. Before the policy is issued, the life insurer wants to make certain that adequate reinsurance is available.

d. Company D would like to increase its underwriting capacity to underwrite new business.

information retrieval, telecommunications, simulation studies, market analysis, training and education, sales, and policyowner services. Information can quickly be obtained on premium volume, claims, loss ratios, investments, and underwriting results.

SUMMARY

- Rate making refers to the pricing of insurance. Insurance rates are determined by actuaries.

- Underwriting refers to the process of selecting and classifying applicants for insurance. There are several important underwriting principles:

  Selection of insureds according to the company's underwriting standards

  Proper balance within each rate classification

  Equity among policyowners

- In determining whether to accept or reject an applicant for insurance, underwriters have several sources of information. Important sources include the application, agent's report, inspection report, physical inspection, physical examination, attending physician's report, and the Medical Information Bureau.

- Production refers to the sales and marketing activities of insurers. Agents who sell insurance are called producers.

- From the insurer's viewpoint, there are several basic objectives in settling claims:

  Verification of a covered loss

  Fair and prompt payment of claims

  Personal assistance to the insured

- The person who adjusts a claim is known as a claims adjustor. The major types of adjustors are as follows:

  Agent

  Company adjustor

  Independent adjustor

  Adjustment bureau

  Public adjustor

- Several steps are involved in settling a claim:

  Notice of loss must be given to the company.

  The claim is investigated by the company.

  A proof of loss may be required.

  A decision is made concerning payment.

- Reinsurance is the shifting of part or all of the insurance originally written by one insurer to another insurer. Reinsurance is used for several reasons:

  To increase the company's underwriting capacity

  To stabilize profits

  To reduce the unearned premium reserve

  To provide protection against a catastrophic loss

- Facultative reinsurance means the primary company shops around for reinsurance. The primary company is under no obligation to reinsure, and the reinsurer is under no obligation to accept the insurance. But if the primary company and reinsurer enter into a valid contract, it is known as a facultative treaty. In contrast, under treaty reinsurance, if the business falls within the scope of the agreement, the primary company must cede insurance to the reinsurer, and the reinsurer must accept the ceded coverage.

- The most important types of automatic reinsurance treaties are as follows:

  Quota-share treaty

  Surplus-share treaty

  Excess-of-loss treaty

  Reinsurance pool

- Other important insurance company operations include investments, accounting, legal services, loss-control services, and electronic data processing.

KEY CONCEPTS AND TERMS

Actuary
Adjustment bureau
Catastrophe bonds
Ceding commission
Ceding company
Certified Financial Planner (CFP)
Certified Insurance Counselor (CIC)
Cession
Chartered Financial Consultant (ChFC)
Chartered Life Underwriter (CLU)
Chartered Property Casualty Underwriter (CPCU)
Claims adjustor
Class underwriting
Company adjustor
Electronic data processing (EDP)
Excess-of-loss treaty
Facultative reinsurance
Independent adjustor
Line underwriter
Loss control
Medical Information Bureau (MIB) report
Producers
Production
Public adjustor
Quota-share treaty
Rate making

Reinsurance
Reinsurance pool
Reinsurer
Retention limit (net retention)
Retrocession
Retrocessionaire

Securitization of risk
Surplus-share treaty
Treaty reinsurance
Underwriting
Unearned premium reserve

REVIEW QUESTIONS

1. How does rate making, or the pricing of insurance, differ from the pricing of other products?

2. a. Define the meaning of underwriting.
   b. Briefly explain the basic principles of underwriting.

3. Identify the major sources of information available to underwriters.

4. Explain the basic objectives in the settlement of claims.

5. Describe the steps involved in the settlement of a claim.

6. Briefly describe the following types of claims adjustors:
   a. Agent
   b. Company adjustor
   c. Independent adjustor
   d. Adjustment bureau
   e. Public adjustor

7. a. What is the meaning of reinsurance?
   b. Briefly explain the reasons for reinsurance.
   c. Explain the meaning of "securitization of risk."

8. Distinguish between facultative reinsurance and treaty reinsurance.

9. Briefly explain the following types of reinsurance treaties:
   a. Quota-share treaty
   b. Surplus-share treaty
   c. Excess-of-loss treaty
   d. Reinsurance pool

10. Briefly describe the following insurance company operations:
    a. Production
    b. Accounting
    c. Legal services
    d. Loss control
    e. Electronic data processing

APPLICATION QUESTIONS

1. Delta Insurance is a property insurer that enters into a surplus-share reinsurance treaty with Eversafe Re. Delta has a retention limit of $200,000 on any single building, and nine lines of insurance are ceded to Eversafe. A building valued at $1,600,000 is insured with Delta. Shortly after the policy was issued, a severe windstorm caused a $800,000 loss to the building.
   a. How much of the loss will Delta pay?
   b. How much of the loss will Eversafe pay?
   c. What is the maximum amount of insurance that Delta can write on a single building? Explain your answer.

2. Liability Insurance Company writes a substantial amount of commercial liability insurance. A large construction company requests $100 million of liability insurance to cover its business operations. Liability Insurance has a reinsurance contract with Bermuda Re that enables the coverage to be written immediately. Under the terms of the contract, Liability Insurance pays 25 percent of the losses and retains 25 percent of the premium. Bermuda Re pays 75 percent of the losses and retains 75 percent of the premium, less a ceding commission that is paid to Liability Insurance. Based on the preceding, answer the following questions.
   a. What type of reinsurance contract best describes the reinsurance arrangement that Liability Insurance has with Bermuda Re?
   b. If a $50 million covered loss occurs, how much will Bermuda Re have to pay? Explain your answer.
   c. Why does Bermuda Re pay a ceding commission to Liability Insurance?

3. Property Insurance Company is a new property insurer. The company is growing rapidly because of a new homeowners policy that combines traditional homeowner coverages with insurance that pays off the mortgage if the insured dies or becomes totally disabled. Premiums written have increased substantially; new agents have been hired; and the company is considering expanding into additional states. However, its growth has been hampered by statutory accounting rules that require an insurer to write off its first-year acquisition expenses immediately but do not allow the full recognition of premium income

until the policy period has expired. In this case, explain how reinsurance will enable Property Insurance to continue to grow in an orderly fashion.

4. Richard lives in a sparsely populated county in northern Vermont. He owns and operates an adjustment bureau that adjusts property insurance claims in the area. Property insurers that market insurance in northern Vermont cannot afford to hire full-time claims adjustors for the area because it is not cost effective. A small property insurer contracts with Richard's company to adjust claims for homeowners who incur losses in the county where Richard lives. Richard's company is paid a fee for each claim that he adjusts and settles. What type of claims adjustor best describes Richard's company?

5. Felix is a property claims adjustor for a large property insurer. Janet is a policyowner who recently notified the company that the roof of her home incurred substantial hail damage because of a recent storm that caused severe property damage to homes in the area. Janet owns her home and is insured under a standard homeowners policy with no special endorsements. What questions should Felix ask before the claim is approved?

INTERNET RESOURCES

- The **American Institute for CPCU** is an independent, nonprofit organization that offers educational programs and professional certification to people in all segments of the property and liability insurance business. The organization awards the professional CPCU designation and other designations. Visit the site at

  http://www.aicpcu.org

- The **American Council of Life Insurers (ACLI)** represents the life insurance industry on issues dealing with legislation and regulation. ACLI also publishes statistics on the life insurance industry in an annual fact book. Visit the site at

  http://www.acli.com

- **The American College** is an accredited, nonprofit educational institution that provides graduate and undergraduate education, primarily on a distance learning basis, to people in the financial services industry. The organization awards the professional Chartered Life

Underwriter (CLU) designation, the Chartered Financial Consultant (ChFC) designation, and other professional designations. Visit the site at

http://www.amercoll.edu

- The **American Insurance Association (AIA)** is an important property and casualty trade association that represent more than 400 companies writing more than $118 billion annually in premiums. The site lists available publications, position papers on important issues in property and casualty insurance, press releases, insurance-related links, and names of state insurance commissioners. Visit the site at

  http://www.aiadc.org

- The **Insurance Information Institute (III)** has an excellent site for obtaining information on the property and liability insurance industry. It provides timely consumer information on auto, homeowners, and business insurance, and other types of property and liability insurance. Visit the site at

  http://www.iii.org

- The **Life Office Management Association (LOMA)** provides extensive information dealing with the management and operations of life insurers and financial services companies. Visit the site at

  http://www.loma.org

- **LIMRA International, Inc.** is the principal source of industry sales and marketing statistics in life insurance. Its site provides news and information about LIMRA and the financial services field, conducts research, and publishes a wide range of publications. Visit the site at

  http://www.limra.com

- The **National Association of Insurance Commissioners (NAIC)** provides considerable information on complaints against specific insurers. Go to NAIC Consumer Information Source, type in the company name, state, and business type. After locating the company, click on Closed Complaints. Visit the site at

  http://www.naic.org/cis/

- The **National Association of Mutual Insurance Companies** is a trade association that represents mutual insurance companies in property and casualty insurance. Visit the site at

  http://www.namic.org

■ **Towers Perrin** is one of the world's largest actuarial and management consulting firms. The Tillinghast business of Towers Perrin provides a substantial amount of information on the insurance industry and advises other organizations on risk financing and self-insurance. Visit the site at

http://www.towersperrin.com

SELECTED REFERENCES

Black, Kenneth, Jr., and Harold D. Skipper, Jr. *Life Insurance,* 13th ed. Upper Saddle River, NJ: Prentice-Hall, 2000, chs. 25–26.

Graves, Edward E., ed. *McGill's Life Insurance,* 5th ed. Bryn Mawr, PA: The American College, 2004.

Insurance Information Institute. "Reinsurance," *Hot Topics & Insurance Issues,* January 2004.

United States General Accounting Office. *Catastrophe Insurance Risk, The Role of Risk-Linked Securities and Factors Affecting Their Use,* GAO-02-941, September 2002.

United States General Accounting Office. *Catastrophe Insurance Risk, Status of Efforts to Securitize Natural Catastrophe and Terrorism Risk,* GAO-03-1033, September 2003.

Webb, Bernard L., et al. *Insurance Operations and Regulation,* 1st ed. Malvern, PA: American Institute for Chartered Property Casualty Underwriters/Insurance Institute of America, 2002.

NOTES

1. A legal reserve is a liability item on a company's balance sheet that measures the insurer's obligations to its policyowners. State laws require a company to maintain policy reserves at a level that is sufficient to pay all policy obligations as they fall due.

2. In property and liability insurance, a loss reserve is an estimated liability item that represents an amount for claims reported but not yet paid, claims in the process of settlement, and claims that have already occurred but have not been reported. See Chapter 27 for a further discussion of loss reserves.

3. A loss ratio is the ratio of incurred losses and loss adjustment expenses to earned premiums. For example, if incurred losses and loss adjustment expenses are $70 and earned premiums are $100, the loss ratio is 0.70, or 70 percent.

4. For additional information on claim settlement, see Bernard L. Webb, et al. *Insurance Operations and Regulation,* 1st ed. (American Institute for Chartered Property Casualty Underwriters/Insurance Institute of America, 2002), Chs. 13–15.

5. Webb, et al., pp. 13.47–13.48.

6. A first-party claim is a claim submitted by the insured to the insurer, such as fire damage to property owned by the insured.

7. Robert I. Mehr, Emerson Cammack, and Terry Rose, *Principles of Insurance,* 8th ed. (Homewood, IL: Richard D. Irwin, 1985), pp. 616–617.

8. Technically, for a stock insurer, policyholders' surplus is the sum of capital stock (value of the contributions of original stockholders), plus surplus (the amount paid in by the organizers in excess of the par value of the stock), plus any retained earnings. In the case of a mutual insurer, there is no capital account. Policyholders' surplus is the excess of assets over liabilities.

9. *Sharing the Risk,* 3rd ed. (New York: Insurance Information Institute, 1989), pp. 119–120.

10. Insurance Information Institute, "Reinsurance," *Hot Topics & Insurance Issues,* January 2004.

11. U.S. General Accounting Office, *Catastrophe Insurance Risks, Status of Efforts to Securitize Natural Catastrophe and Terrorism Risk,* GAO-03-1033, September 2003.

12. Ibid.

13. *The I.I.I. Insurance Fact Book 2004* (New York: Insurance Information Institute, 2004), p. 21.

14. Ibid, p. 7.

Students may take a self-administered test on this chapter at
www.aw-bc.com/rejda

CHAPTER 27

INSURANCE PRICING

*"Actuaries hold an insurance company's
profits in their hands."*

Insurance Careers

After studying this chapter, you should be able to

◆ Explain the major objectives of rate making.

◆ Describe the basic methods for determining rates in property and liability insurance,
including the following:
Judgment rating
Class rating
Merit rating

◆ Explain how an underwriting profit or loss for a property and liability insurer is determined.

◆ Explain the basic concepts used in life insurance, including the following:
Net single premium
Net level premium
Gross premium

◆ Identify the various reserves that insurers must maintain by law.

*W*arren, age 42, is the executive director of the actuarial science program at a large Southern university. He has been asked to speak to a group of freshmen about career opportunities in actuarial science. Warren explained that insurance pricing, or rate making, is one of the most important functions of an insurance company. He explained that actuaries hold the profits of an insurance company in their hands. Actuaries must analyze vast amounts of statistics and loss data to determine the correct rates to charge. The actual rates must be high enough to pay all claims and expenses and earn a profit for the insurer. However, if the rates are too high, the insurer may find itself at a competitive disadvantage.

This chapter discusses the important rate-making function of insurers. Major topics covered include the objectives of rate making, the basic rating methods used in property and liability insurance and life insurance, and the various reserves that insurers must maintain by law.

OBJECTIVES OF RATE MAKING

Rate making, or insurance pricing, has several basic objectives. Because insurance rates—primarily property and liability rates—are regulated by the states, certain statutory or regulatory requirements must be satisfied. Also, due to the overall goal of profitability, certain business objectives must be stressed in rate making. Thus, rate-making goals can be classified into two basic categories—regulatory objectives and business objectives.

Regulatory Objectives

The goal of insurance regulation is to protect the public. The states have rating laws that require insurance rates to meet certain standards. In general, rates charged by insurers must be adequate, not excessive, and not unfairly discriminatory.

Adequate Rates The first regulatory requirement is that rates must be adequate. *This means the rates charged by insurers should be high enough to pay all losses and expenses.* If rates are inadequate, an insurer may become insolvent and fail. As a result, policyowners, beneficiaries, and third-party claimants may be financially harmed if their claims are not paid. However, rate adequacy is complicated by

the fact that the insurer does not know its actual costs when the policy is sold. The premium is paid in advance, but it may not be sufficient to pay all claims and expenses during the policy period. It is only after the period of protection has expired that an insurer can determine its actual costs.

Not Excessive The second regulatory requirement is that the rates must not be excessive. *This means that the rates should not be so high that policyowners are paying more than the actual value of their protection.* Exorbitant prices are not in the public interest.

Not Unfairly Discriminatory The third regulatory requirement is that the rates must not be unfairly discriminatory. *This means that exposures that are similar with respect to losses and expenses should not be charged substantially different rates.*[1] For example, if two healthy males, age 30, buy the same type and amount of life insurance from the same insurer, they should not be charged two different rates. However, if the loss exposures are substantially different, it is not unfair rate discrimination to charge different rates. Thus, if two males, age 30 and age 65, apply for the same type and amount of life insurance, it is not unfair to charge the older male a higher rate because of the higher probability of death.

Business Objectives

Insurers are also guided by certain business objectives in designing a rating system. The rating system should also meet the following objectives:[2]

- Simplicity
- Stability
- Responsiveness
- Encouragement of loss control

Simplicity The rating system should be easy to understand so that producers can quote premiums with a minimum amount of time and expense. This is especially important in the personal lines market, where the relatively small premiums do not justify a large amount of time and expense in the preparation of premium quotations. In addition, commercial insurance purchasers should understand how their premiums are determined so that they can take active steps to reduce their insurance costs.

Stability Rates should be stable over short periods so that consumer satisfaction can be maintained. If rates change rapidly, insurance consumers may become irritated and dissatisfied. They may then look to government to control the rates or to enact a government insurance program.

Responsiveness The rates should also be responsive over time to changing loss exposures and changing economic conditions. To meet the objective of rate adequacy, the rates should increase when loss exposures increase. For example, as a city grows, auto insurance rates should increase to reflect the greater traffic and increased frequency of automobile accidents. Likewise, the rates should reflect changing economic conditions. Thus, if inflation causes liability awards to increase, liability insurance rates should be increased to reflect this trend.

Encouragement of Loss Control The rating system should also encourage loss-control activities that reduce both loss frequency and severity. This point is important because loss control tends to keep insurance affordable. Profits are also stabilized. As you will see later, certain rating systems provide a strong financial incentive to the insured to engage in loss control.

BASIC DEFINITIONS IN RATE MAKING

Before proceeding, you should be familiar with some basic terms that are widely used in rate making. A **rate** is the price per unit of insurance. An **exposure unit** is the unit of measurement used in insurance pricing. It varies by line of insurance. For example, in fire insurance, the exposure unit is $100 of coverage; in products liability insurance, it is $1000 of sales; and in auto collision insurance, it is one car-year, which is one car insured for a year.

The **pure premium** refers to that portion of the rate needed to pay losses and loss-adjustment expenses. **Loading** refers to the amount that must be added to the pure premium for other expenses, profit, and a margin for contingencies. The **gross rate** consists of the pure premium and a loading element. Finally, the **gross premium** paid by the insured consists of the gross rate multiplied by the number of exposure units. Thus, if the gross rate is 10 cents per $100 of property insurance, the gross premium for a $500,000 building would be $500.

RATE MAKING IN PROPERTY AND LIABILITY INSURANCE

There are three basic rate-making methods in property and liability insurance—judgment, class, and merit rating. Merit rating in turn can be broken down into schedule rating, experience rating, and retrospective rating. Thus, the basic rating methods can be conveniently classified as follows:[3]

- Judgment rating
- Class rating
- Merit rating
    Schedule rating
    Experience rating
    Retrospective rating

Judgment Rating

Judgment rating *means that each exposure is individually evaluated, and the rate is determined largely by the underwriter's judgment.* This method is used when the loss exposures are so diverse that a class rate cannot be calculated, or when credible loss statistics are not available.

Judgment rating is widely used in ocean marine insurance and in some lines of inland marine insurance. Because the various ocean-going vessels, ports of destination, cargoes carried, and dangerous waters are so diverse, ocean marine rates are determined largely by judgment.

Class Rating

The second type of rating method is class rating. Most rates used today are class rates. **Class rating** *means that exposures with similar characteristics are placed in the same underwriting class, and each is charged the same rate.* The rate charged reflects the *average loss experience* for the class as a whole. Class rating is based on the assumption that future losses to insureds will be determined largely by the same set of factors. For example, major classification factors in life insurance include age, gender, health, and whether the applicant smokes or is a nonsmoker. Accordingly, healthy persons who are the same age and gender and who do not smoke are placed in the same underwriting class and charged the same rate for life insurance. Smokers are placed in a different underwriting class and charged higher rates.

The major advantage of class rating is that it is simple to apply. Also, premium quotations can be quickly obtained. As such, it is ideal for the personal lines market.

Class rating is also called *manual rating,* because the various rates are published in a rating manual. Class rating is widely used in homeowners insurance, private passenger auto insurance, workers compensation, and life and health insurance.

There are two basic methods for determining class rates: the **pure premium method** and **loss ratio methods.**

Pure premium method As stated earlier, the pure premium is that portion of the gross rate needed to pay losses and loss-adjustment expenses. The *pure premium can be determined by dividing the dollar amount of incurred losses and loss-adjustment expenses by the number of exposure units.* Incurred losses include all losses paid during the accounting period, plus amounts held as reserves for the future payment of losses that have already occurred during the same period. Thus, incurred losses include all losses that occur during

the accounting period whether or not they have been paid by the end of the period. Loss-adjustment expenses are the expenses incurred by the company in adjusting losses during the same accounting period.

To illustrate how a pure premium can be derived, assume that in auto collision insurance, 500,000 automobiles in a given underwriting class generate incurred losses and loss-adjustment expenses of $30 million over a one-year period. The pure premium is $60. This can be illustrated by the following:

Pure premium =

$$\frac{\text{Incurred losses and loss-adjustment expenses}}{\text{Number of exposure units}}$$

$$= \frac{\$30,000,000}{500,000}$$

$$= \$60$$

The final step is to add a loading for expenses, underwriting profit, and a margin for contingencies. The expense loading is usually expressed as a percentage of the gross rate and is called the expense ratio. The final gross rate can be determined by dividing the pure premium by 1 minus the expense ratio. For example, if expenses are 40 percent of the gross rate, the final gross rate is $100. This can be illustrated by the following:[4]

$$\text{Gross rate} = \frac{\text{Pure premium}}{1 - \text{Expense ratio}}$$

$$= \frac{\$60}{1 - 0.40}$$

$$= \$100$$

Loss ratio method *Under the loss ratio method, the actual loss ratio is compared with the expected loss ratio, and the rate is adjusted accordingly.* The actual loss ratio is the ratio of incurred losses and loss-adjustment expenses to earned premiums.[5] The expected loss ratio is the percentage of the premiums that is expected to be used to pay losses. For example, assume that a line of insurance has incurred losses and loss-adjustment expenses in the amount of $800,000, and earned premiums are $1 million. The actual loss ratio is 0.80, or 80 percent. If the expected loss ratio is 0.70, or 70 percent, the rate must be increased 14.3 percent. This can be illustrated by the following:

$$\text{Rate change} = \frac{A - E}{E}$$

where A = Actual loss ratio
E = Expected loss ratio

$$= \frac{0.80 - 0.70}{0.70}$$

$$= 0.143, \text{ or } 14.3\%$$

Merit Rating

The third principal type of rating method in property and liability insurance is merit rating. **Merit rating** *is a rating plan by which class rates (manual rates) are adjusted upward or downward based on individual loss experience.* Merit rating is based on the assumption that the loss experience of a particular insured will differ substantially from the loss experience of other insureds. Thus, class rates are modified upward or downward depending on individual loss experience.

There are several different types of merit rating plans:

- Schedule rating
- Experience rating
- Retrospective rating

Schedule Rating Under a **schedule rating** *plan, each exposure is individually rated. A basis rate is determined for each exposure, which is then modified by debits or credits for undesirable or desirable physical features.* Schedule rating is based on the assumption that certain physical characteristics of the insured's operations will influence the insured's future loss experience. Thus, the physical characteristics of the exposure to be insured are extremely important in schedule rating.

Schedule rating is used in commercial property insurance for large, complex buildings, such as an industrial plant. Each building is individually rated based on the following factors:

- Construction
- Occupancy
- Protection

- Exposure
- Maintenance

Construction refers to the physical characteristics of the building. A building may be constructed with frame, brick, fire-resistive, or fire-proof materials. A frame building is charged a higher rate than a brick or fire-resistive building. Also, tall buildings and buildings with large open areas may receive debits because of the greater difficulty of extinguishing or containing a fire.

Occupancy refers to use of the building. The probability of a fire is greatly influenced by its use. For example, open flames and sparks from torches and welding equipment can quickly cause a fire. Also, if highly combustible materials or chemicals are stored in the building, the fire will be more difficult to contain.

Protection refers to the quality of the city's water supply and fire department. It also includes protective devices installed in the insured building. Rate credits are given for a fire alarm system, security guard, automatic sprinkler system, fire extinguishers, and similar protective devices.

Exposure refers to the possibility that the insured building will be damaged or destroyed from a fire that starts in an adjacent building and spreads to the insured building. The greater the exposure from surrounding buildings, the greater are the charges applied.

Finally, *maintenance* refers to the housekeeping and overall maintenance of the building. Debits are applied for poor housekeeping and maintenance. Thus, debits may be given if oily rags or other debris are scattered about.

Experience Rating Experience rating is another form of merit rating. Under **experience rating**, *the class or manual rate is adjusted upward or downward based on past loss experience.* The most distinctive characteristic of experience rating is that *the insured's past loss experience is used to determine the premium for the next policy period.* The loss experience over the past three years is typically used to determine the premium for the next policy year. If the insured's loss experience is better than the average for the class as a whole, the class rate is reduced. If the loss experience is worse than the class average, the rate is increased. In determining the magnitude of the rate change, the actual loss experience is modified by a *credibility factor*[6] based on the volume of experience.

For example, assume that a retail firm has a general liability insurance policy that is experience rated. Annual premiums are $30,000, and the expected loss ratio is 30 percent. If the actual loss ratio over the past three years is 20 percent, and the credibility factor (C) is 0.29, the firm will receive a premium reduction of 9.7 percent. This can be illustrated by the following:

$$\text{Premium change} = \frac{A - E}{E} \times C$$
$$= \frac{0.20 - 0.30}{0.30} \times 0.29$$
$$= -9.7\%$$

Thus, the premium for the next policy period is $27,090. As you can see, experience rating provides a financial incentive to reduce losses, because premiums can be reduced by favorable loss experience.

Experience rating is generally limited only to larger firms that generate a sufficiently high volume of premiums and more credible experience. Smaller firms are normally ineligible for experience rating. This rating system is frequently used in general liability insurance, workers compensation, commercial auto liability insurance, and group health insurance.

Retrospective Rating The final form of merit rating is retrospective rating. Under a **retrospective rating** plan, *the insured's loss experience during the current policy period determines the actual premium paid for that period*. Under this rating plan, a provisional premium is paid at the beginning of the policy period. At the end of the period, a final premium is calculated based on actual losses that occur during the policy period. There is a minimum premium and maximum premium that must be paid. In practice, the actual premium paid generally will fall somewhere between the minimum and maximum premium, depending on the insured's loss experience during the current policy period.

Retrospective rating is widely used by large firms in workers compensation insurance, general liability insurance, auto liability and physical damage insurance, and burglary and glass insurance.

RATE MAKING IN LIFE INSURANCE

Our discussion of rate making so far has applied largely to property and liability insurance. This section briefly examines the fundamentals of life insurance rate making.[7]

Net Single Premium

Life insurance policies can be purchased with a single premium, or with annual, semiannual, quarterly, or monthly premiums. Although most policies are not purchased with a single premium, the net single premium forms the foundation for the calculation of all life insurance premiums.

The **net single premium** (**NSP**) *can be defined as the present value of the future death benefit*. It is that amount, which together with compound interest, will be sufficient to pay all death claims. In calculating the NSP, only mortality and investment income are considered. Insurance company expenses or the loading element are considered later, when the gross premium is calculated.

The NSP is based on three basic assumptions: (1) premiums are paid at the beginning of the policy year, (2) death claims are paid at the end of the policy year, and (3) the death rate is uniform throughout the year.

Certain assumptions must also be made concerning the probability of death at each attained age. Although life insurers generally develop their own mortality data, we will use the Commissioners 1980 Standard Ordinary Mortality Table in our illustrations (see Exhibit 27.1).

Also, since we are assuming that premiums are paid in advance, and that death claims are paid at the end of the policy year, the amount needed to pay death benefits is discounted for compound interest. It is assumed that the amounts needed for death claims can be discounted annually at 5 percent compound interest.

Term Insurance The NSP for term insurance can be calculated easily. The period of protection is only for a specified period or to a stated age. The face amount is paid if the insured dies within the specified period, but nothing is paid if the insured dies after the period of protection expires.

The NSP for *yearly renewable term insurance* is considered first. Assume that a $1000 yearly renewable term insurance policy is issued to a male age 45. *The cost of each year's insurance is determined by multiplying the probability of death by the amount of insurance multiplied by the present value of $1 for the time period the funds are held.* By referring to the 1980 CSO mortality chart in Exhibit 27.1, we see that out of 10 million males alive at age zero, 9,210,289 are still alive at the beginning of age 45. Of this number, 41,907 persons will die during the year. Therefore, the probability that a person age 45 will die during the year is 41,907/9,210,289. This fraction is then multiplied by $1000 to determine the amount of money the insurer must have on hand from each policyowner at the end of the year to pay death claims. However, because premiums are paid in advance, and death claims are paid at the end of the year, the amount needed can be discounted for one year. From Exhibit 27.2, we see that the present value of $1 at 5 percent interest is 0.9524. Thus, if the probability of death at age 45 is multiplied by $1000, and the sum is discounted for one year's interest, the resulting net single premium is $4.33. This calculation is summarized as follows:

Age 45, NSP

$$\frac{41,907}{9,210,289} \times \$1000 \times 0.9524 = \$4.33$$

If $4.33 is collected in advance from each of the 9,210,289 persons who are alive at age 45, this amount together with compound interest will be sufficient to pay all death claims.

If the policy is renewed for another year, the NSP at age 46 would be calculated as follows:

Age 46, NSP

$$\frac{45,108}{9,168,382} \times \$1000 \times 0.9524 = \$4.69$$

The NSP for a yearly renewable term insurance policy issued at age 46 is $4.69. Premiums for subsequent years are calculated in the same manner.

Now consider the NSP for a *five-year term insurance policy* in the amount of $1000 issued to a person age 45. In this case, the company must pay the death claim if the insured dies any time within the five-year period. However, death claims are paid at the end of the year in which they occur and not at the end of the five-year period. Consequently, the cost of each year's mortality must be computed separately and then added together to determine the net single premium.

The cost of insurance for the first year is determined exactly as before, when we calculated the net single premium for yearly renewable term insurance. Thus, we have the following equation:

Age 45, first-year insurance cost

$$\frac{41,907}{9,210,289} \times \$1000 \times 0.9524 = \$4.33$$

The next step is to determine the cost of insurance for the second year. Referring back to Exhibit 27.1, we see that at age 46, 45,108 people will die during the year. Thus, for the 9,210,289 persons who are alive at age 45, the probability of dying during age 46 is 45,108/9,210,289. Note that the denominator does not change but remains the same for each probability fraction. Because the amount needed to pay second-year death claims will not be needed for two years, it can be discounted for two years at 5 percent interest. Thus, for the second year, we have the following calculation:

Age 46, second-year insurance cost

$$\frac{45,108}{9,210,289} \times \$1000 \times 0.9070 = \$4.44$$

For each of the remaining three years, we follow the same procedure (see Exhibit 27.3). If the insurer collects $22.74 in a single premium from each of the 9,210,289 persons who are alive at age 45, that sum together with compound interest will be sufficient to pay all death claims during the five-year period.

Ordinary Life Insurance   In calculating the NSP for an ordinary life policy, the same method described earlier for the five-year term policy is used except that the calculations are carried out to the end of the mortality table (age 99). Thus, in our illustration, the NSP for a $1000 ordinary life insurance policy issued at age 45 would be $270.84.

EXHIBIT **27.1**
Commissioners 1980 Standard Ordinary Mortality Table, Male Lives

Age at Beginning of Year	Number Living at Beginning of Designated Year	Number Dying During Designated Year	Age at Beginning of Year	Number Living at Beginning of Designated Year	Number Dying During Designated Year
0	10,000,000	41,800	25	9,663,007	17,104
1	9,958,200	10,655	26	9,645,903	16,687
2	9,947,545	9,848	27	9,629,216	16,466
3	9,937,697	9,739	28	9,612,750	16,342
4	9,927,958	9,432	29	9,596,408	16,410
5	9,918,526	8,927	30	9,579,998	16,573
6	9,909,599	8,522	31	9,563,425	17,023
7	9,901,077	7,921	32	9,546,402	17,470
8	9,893,156	7,519	33	9,528,932	18,200
9	9,885,637	7,315	34	9,510,732	19,021
10	9,878,322	7,211	35	9,491,711	20,028
11	9,871,111	7,601	36	9,471,683	21,217
12	9,863,510	8,384	37	9,450,466	22,681
13	9,855,126	9,757	38	9,427,785	24,324
14	9,845,369	11,322	39	9,403,461	26,236
15	9,834,047	13,079	40	9,377,225	28,319
16	9,820,968	14,830	41	9,348,906	30,758
17	9,806,138	16,376	42	9,318,148	33,173
18	9,789,762	17,426	43	9,284,975	35,933
19	9,772,336	18,177	44	9,249,042	38,753
20	9,754,159	18,533	45	9,210,289	41,907
21	9,735,626	18,595	46	9,168,382	45,108
22	9,717,031	18,365	47	9,123,274	48,536
23	9,698,666	18,040	48	9,074,738	52,089
24	9,680,626	17,619	49	9,022,649	56,031

SOURCE: Kenneth Black, Jr., and Harold D. Skipper, Jr., *Life Insurance*, 13th ed., 2000, pp. 698–699. Reprinted by permission of Prentice-Hall, Inc., Upper Saddle River, NJ.

Net Annual Level Premium

Most life insurance policies are not purchased with a single premium because of the large amount of money required. Consumers generally find it more convenient to pay for their insurance in installment payments. If premiums are paid annually, the net single premium must be converted into a net annual level premium, which must be the mathematical equivalent of the net single premium. The net annual level premium cannot be determined by simply dividing the net single premium by the number of years over which the premiums are to be paid. Such a

division would produce an insufficient premium, for two reasons. First, the net single premium is based on the assumption that the entire premium is paid in advance at the beginning of the period. If premiums are paid in installments, and some insureds die early, the insurer would suffer the loss of future premiums.

Second, installment payments result in the loss of interest income because of the smaller amounts that are invested. Thus, the mathematical adjustment for the loss of premiums and interest is accomplished by dividing the net single premium by the present value of an appropriate life annuity due of $1. To be more precise, the **net annual level pre-**

Exhibit 27.1 (continued)
Commissioners 1980 Standard Ordinary Mortality Table, Male Lives

Age at Beginning of Year	Number Living at Beginning of Designated Year	Number Dying During Designated Year	Age at Beginning of Year	Number Living at Beginning of Designated Year	Number Dying During Designated Year
50	8,966,618	60,166	75	4,898,907	314,461
51	8,906,452	65,017	76	4,584,446	323,341
52	8,841,435	70,378	77	4,261,105	328,616
53	8,771,057	76,396	78	3,932,489	329,936
54	8,694,661	83,121	79	3,602,553	328,012
55	8,611,540	90,163	80	3,274,541	323,656
56	8,521,377	97,655	81	2,950,885	317,161
57	8,423,722	105,212	82	2,633,724	308,804
58	8,318,510	113,049	83	2,324,920	298,194
59	8,205,461	121,195	84	2,026,726	284,248
60	8,084,266	129,995	85	1,742,478	266,512
61	7,954,271	139,518	86	1,475,966	245,143
62	7,814,753	149,965	87	1,230,823	220,994
63	7,664,788	161,420	88	1,009,829	195,170
64	7,503,368	173,628	89	814,659	168,871
65	7,329,740	186,322	90	645,788	143,216
66	7,143,418	198,944	91	502,572	119,110
67	6,944,474	211,390	92	383,472	97,191
68	6,773,084	223,471	93	286,281	77,900
69	6,509,613	235,453	94	208,381	61,660
70	6,274,160	247,892	95	146,721	48,412
71	6,026,268	260,937	96	98,309	37,805
72	5,765,331	274,718	97	60,504	29,054
73	5,490,613	289,026	98	31,450	20,693
74	5,201,587	302,680	99	10,757	10,757

mium (**NALP**) *is determined by dividing the net single premium by the present value of a life annuity due (PVLAD) of $1 for the premium-paying period.* Thus, we obtain the following:

$$NALP = \frac{NSP}{PVLAD \text{ of } \$1 \text{ for the premium-paying period}}$$

The concept of a life annuity due requires a brief explanation. The annual premium payments can be viewed as being similar to a life annuity, except that the payments flow from the insured to the insurer.

Both life annuity payments and premium payments are similar in that both are paid during the lifetime of a specified individual, or for a stated period of time. Both cease on death (unless the annuity has a refund feature), and both are discounted for compound interest. The major exception is that the first premium is due immediately (because premiums are paid in advance), while the first annuity payment is due one payment interval from the date of purchase.[8] Thus, the annual payments are the equivalent of a regular life annuity plus one payment that is made immediately. However, to distinguish the premium payments from the annuity payments, we refer to

EXHIBIT 27.2
Present Value of $1 at 5 Percent Compound Interest

Number of Years	5%	Number of Years	5%
1	0.9524	21	0.3589
2	0.9070	22	0.3418
3	0.8638	23	0.3256
4	0.8227	24	0.3101
5	0.7835	25	0.2953
6	0.7462	26	0.2812
7	0.7107	27	0.2678
8	0.6768	28	0.2551
9	0.6446	29	0.2429
10	0.6139	30	0.2314
11	0.5847	35	0.1813
12	0.5568	40	0.1420
13	0.5303	45	0.1113
14	0.5051	50	0.0872
15	0.4810	53	0.0753
16	0.4581	54	0.0717
17	0.4363	55	0.0683
18	0.4155		
19	0.3957		
20	0.3769		

SOURCE: Adapted with permission from Insurance Institute of America, Inc. *Insurance Company Finance*, Exhibit 2-7, p. 64, © 1986.

the series of premium payments as a *life annuity due*. If the annual level premiums are to be paid for life—such as in an ordinary life policy—the premium is called a *whole life annuity due*. If the annual premiums are to be paid for only a temporary period—such as in the case of term insurance or limited payments policies—the premium is called a *temporary life annuity due*.[9]

Term Insurance Consider the net annual level premium for a five-year term insurance policy in the amount of $1000 issued at age 45. Recall that the net single premium for a five-year term insurance policy at age 45 is $22.74. This sum must be divided by the present value of a five-year *temporary life annuity due of $1*. For the first year, a $1 payment is due immediately. For the second year, the probability that a person age 45 will still be *alive* at age 46 to make the second payment of $1 must be determined. Referring back to Exhibit 27.1, 9,210,289 persons are alive at age 45. Of this number, 9,168,382 are still alive at age 46. Thus, the probability of survival is 9,168,382/9,210,289. This fraction is multiplied by $1, and the resulting sum is then discounted for one year's interest. Thus, the present value of the second payment is $0.948. Similar calculations are performed for the remaining three years. The calculations are summarized as follows:

EXHIBIT 27.3
Figuring the NSP for a Five-Year Term Insurance Policy

Age	Probability of Death		Amount of Insurance		Present Value of $1 at 5%		Cost of Insurance
45	$\frac{41,907}{9,210,289}$	×	$1000	×	0.9524	=	$ 4.33 (year 1)
46	$\frac{45,108}{9,210,289}$	×	$1000	×	0.9070	=	4.44 (year 2)
47	$\frac{48,536}{9,210,289}$	×	$1000	×	0.8638	=	4.55 (year 3)
48	$\frac{52,089}{9,210,289}$	×	$1000	×	0.8227	=	4.65 (year 4)
49	$\frac{56,031}{9,210,289}$	×	$1000	×	0.7835	=	4.77 (year 5)
						NSP =	$22.74

Age 45 $1 due immediately   = $1.000

Age 46 $\dfrac{9,168,382}{9,210,289} \times \$1 \times 0.9524 = 0.948$

Age 47 $\dfrac{9,123,274}{9,210,289} \times \$1 \times 0.9070 = 0.898$

Age 48 $\dfrac{9,074,738}{9,210,289} \times \$1 \times 0.8638 = 0.851$

Age 49 $\dfrac{9,022,649}{9,210,289} \times \$1 \times 0.8227 = \underline{0.806}$

PVLAD of $1 = $4.503

The present value of a five-year temporary life annuity due of $1 at age 45 is $4.50. If the net single premium of $22.74 is divided by $4.50, the net annual level premium is $5.05.

$$\text{NALP} = \frac{\text{NSP}}{\text{PVLAD of \$1}} = \frac{\$22.74}{\$4.50} = \$5.05$$

Ordinary Life Insurance The net annual level premium for a $1000 ordinary life insurance policy issued at age 45 is calculated in a similar manner. The same procedure is used except that the calculations are extended to the end of the mortality table. Thus, the present value of a *whole life annuity due of $1* for ages 45 through 99 must be calculated. If the calculations are performed, the present value of a whole life annuity due of $1 at age 45 is $15.312. The net single premium ($270.84) is then divided by the present value of a whole life annuity due of $1 at age 45 ($15.312), and the net annual level premium is $17.69.

Gross Premium The gross premium is determined by adding a loading allowance to the net annual level premium. The loading must cover all operating expenses, provide a margin for contingencies, and, in the case of stock life insurers, provide for a contribution to profits. If the policy is a participating policy, the loading must also reflect a margin for dividends.

Three major types of expenses are reflected in the loading allowance: (1) production expenses, (2) distribution expenses, and (3) maintenance expenses.[10] Production expenses are the expenses incurred before the agent delivers the policy, such as policy printing costs, underwriting expenses, and the cost of the medical examination. Distribution expenses are largely selling expenses, such as the first-year commission, advertising, and agency allowances. Maintenance expenses are the expenses incurred after the policy is issued, such as renewal commissions, costs of collecting renewal premiums, and state premium taxes.

RESERVES IN PROPERTY AND LIABILITY INSURANCE

The remainder of this chapter focuses largely on the various financial reserves of insurance companies. Insurers are required by law to maintain certain reserves on their balance sheets. Because premiums are paid in advance, but the period of protection extends into the future, insurers must establish certain reserves to assure that the premiums collected in advance will be available to pay future losses.

Property and liability insurers are required to maintain two principal types of financial reserves:

- Unearned premium reserve
- Loss reserves

Unearned Premium Reserve

The **unearned premium reserve** *is a liability item that represents the unearned portion of gross premiums on all outstanding policies at the time of valuation.* An insurer is required by law to place the entire gross premium in the unearned premium reserve when the policy is first written, and renewal premiums must be placed in the same reserve.

Reasons for the Unearned Premium Reserve *The fundamental purpose of the unearned premium reserve is to pay for losses that occur during the policy period.* Premiums are paid in advance, but the period of protection extends into the future. To assure policyowners that future losses will be paid, the unearned premium reserve is required.

The unearned premium reserve is also needed so that premium refunds can be paid to the policyowners in the event of cancellation. If the insurer cancels the policy, a full pro rata premium refund based on the unexpired portion of the policy term must be paid to the policyowner. Thus, the unearned premium reserve must be adequate so the premium refunds can be made in the event of cancellation.

Finally, if the business is reinsured, the unearned premium reserve serves as the basis for determining the amount that must be paid to the reinsurer for carrying the reinsured policies to the end of their terms. In practice, however, the amount paid to the reinsurer may be considerably less than the unearned premium reserve, because the reinsurer does not incur heavy first-year acquisition expenses in acquiring the reinsured policies.

Methods of Calculation   Several methods can be used to calculate the unearned premium reserve. Only one of them is described here. Under the **annual pro rata method,** it is assumed that the policies are written uniformly throughout the year. For purposes of determining the unearned premium reserve, it is assumed that all policies are issued on July 1, which is the average issue date. Therefore, on December 31, the unearned premium reserve for all one-year policies is one-half of the premium income attributable to these policies. For two-year policies, the unearned premium reserve is three-fourths of the premium income, and for three-year policies, it is five-sixths of the premium income.

Equity in Unearned Premium Reserve   The law requires an insurer to place the entire gross premium in the unearned premium reserve. As will be shown later, this results in a redundant or excessive reserve, because most of the expenses incurred in writing the business are incurred when the policy is first written. Relatively lower expenses are incurred after the policy is issued. However, because of its emphasis on insurer solvency, the law prohibits an insurer from taking credit in advance for these prepaid expenses. Although the premium is being earned gradually over the policy period, the initial acquisition and underwriting expenses cannot be amortized over the same period. Instead, they are treated as cash expenses and charged off immediately. Therefore, because the unearned premium reserve must be established on the basis of a gross premium rather than a net premium, it is substantially overstated. *This overstatement or redundancy in the unearned premium reserve is called the* **equity in the unearned premium reserve.** Authorities estimate that the unearned premium reserve may be overstated by 20 to 40 percent, with 35 percent being a typical or average estimate of the equity in this reserve.

Effect on Underwriting Profit or Loss   The equity in the unearned premium reserve is important in determining the true underwriting profit or loss of a property-casualty insurer. For example, assume that a new property insurer begins operating on January 1. It plans to sell only one-year property insurance policies. In establishing the rates, the insurer has an expected loss ratio of 60 percent, an expected expense ratio of 35 percent, and expects to earn an underwriting profit of 5 percent. The *loss ratio is the ratio of incurred losses and loss-adjustment expenses to earned premiums.* The *expense ratio is the ratio of expenses incurred to written premiums.* Also assume that the business is written uniformly throughout the year, and the annual pro rata method is used to determine the unearned premium reserve.

During the year, $10 million of property insurance premiums are written. On December 31, earned premiums are $5 million, and the unearned premium reserve is $5 million. Incurred losses and loss adjustment expenses incurred total $3 million, and expenses incurred are $3.5 million. On December 31, what is the insurer's underwriting profit or loss? The law requires the company to use a *statutory underwriting formula* to determine its underwriting results. Investment gains or losses are not considered in the formula. The statutory formula is as follows:

Statutory underwriting profit or loss =

$$\begin{array}{c} \text{Earned} \\ \text{premiums} \end{array} - \begin{array}{c} \text{Losses incurred and} \\ \text{loss-adjustment} \\ \text{expenses incurred} \end{array} - \begin{array}{c} \text{Expenses} \\ \text{incurred} \end{array}$$

In our illustration, the company has a statutory underwriting loss of $1.5 million. This can be illustrated as follows:

($000 omitted)		
Premiums written		$10,000
Deduct unearned premiums		−5,000
Earned premiums		$ 5,000
Losses incurred (60% of earned premiums)	$3,000	
Expenses incurred (35% of premiums written)	$3,500	
Total losses and expenses		−6,500
Statutory underwriting loss		($ 1,500)

Although the insurer's actual loss and expense experience conforms exactly to the experience anticipated in the rating structure, it has a statutory underwriting loss rather than a 5 percent underwriting profit. This result is due to the statutory method for determining a profit or loss. As noted earlier, the first-year acquisition expenses cannot be amortized over the policy term but must be immediately charged off as a cash expense. This requirement produces a statutory underwriting loss in our example.

The statutory underwriting loss of $1.5 million is a charge against the insurer's surplus. Thus, a rapidly growing insurer will experience a surplus drain because of a continuous increase in the unearned premium reserve. The opposite is true for an insurer whose premium volume is declining. The insurer will have a gain in its surplus account as the business runs off the books. The equity in the unearned premium reserve will flow into the insurer's surplus with the passage of time as the policy terms run off. Thus, to correct for the distortion that may result from the statutory formula, an **adjusted underwriting profit or loss** (called a *trade profit or loss*) is often used by financial analysts to determine the true underwriting results.

One method for determining the insurer's adjusted underwriting profit or loss is to consider the equity in the unearned premium reserve. The increased equity in the unearned premium reserve can be added to the statutory profit or loss to determine the adjusted underwriting profit or loss. Returning to our earlier illustration, assume that the insurer experienced an increase of $5 million in the unearned premium reserve. If an estimated equity of 35 percent in the unearned premium reserve is also assumed, the insurer has an adjusted underwriting profit rather than a loss. This can be illustrated as follows:

($000 omitted)	
Statutory underwriting loss	$−1500
Equity in the unearned premium reserve	1750
Adjusted underwriting profit	$ 250

After adjusting the statutory formula for the equity in the unearned premium reserve, the insurer has an adjusted underwriting profit of $250,000, which is exactly 5 percent of earned premiums.

Recent Underwriting Results   Based on the statutory formula method for determining underwriting profits, the property and liability industry is not highly profitable. Even when based on generally accepted accounting principles (GAAP), the annual rate of return is generally lower than for other industries. Insight 27.1 shows that, from 1993–2002, the Fortune 500 companies have earned a higher annual rate of return each year than the returns earned by property and casualty and life and health insurers.

In addition, because of the terrorist attacks on September 11, 2001, the property and casualty insurance industry incurred heavy underwriting losses for 2001. Since that time, underwriting losses have declined on a relative basis. At the time of this writing, early estimates indicate the industry is approaching profitability. This can be illustrated by the combined ratio. The **combined ratio** *is the sum of the loss ratio and expense ratio.* If the combined ratio is below 100, the property and casualty industry has an underwriting gain; if it exceeds 100, the industry has an underwriting loss. According to preliminary estimates by the Insurance Information Institute, the combined ratio is expected to fall to 100 in 2004, down from an estimated 101.7 in 2003 and well below the 115.7 result for 2001, which reflects the terrorist attacks for that year (see Exhibit 27.4). For 2004, an estimated combined ratio of 100 means that property and casualty insurers will pay out roughly $1 in losses and expenses for each $1 in premiums taken in as a result of their underwriting operations.[11]

Loss Reserves

The loss reserve is another important liability reserve for property-liability insurers. A loss reserve is the estimated cost of settling claims that have already occurred but have not been paid as of the valuation date. More specifically, the **loss reserve** *is an estimated amount for (1) claims reported and adjusted but not yet paid, (2) claims reported and filed but not yet adjusted, and (3) claims incurred but not yet reported to the company.* The loss reserve is especially important to casualty insurers because bodily injury and property damage liability lawsuits may take a long time to settle—often several years. In contrast, property insurance claims, auto collision and comprehensive losses, and other first-party

EXHIBIT **27.4**
Terrorism Losses to Hike Combined Ratio to Record Levels (Combined Ratio)

SOURCE: Robert P. Hartwig, Insurance Information Institute, Industry Financials and Outlook, *Special Report: Earlybird Forecast* 2004 (New York: Insurance Information Institute, 2004).

insurance claims are settled more quickly; hence loss reserves are relatively small for property insurers.

Loss reserves generally can be classified as case reserves, reserves based on the loss ratio method, and incurred-but-not-reported reserves.

Case Reserves   Case reserves are loss reserves that are established for each individual claim when it is reported. Major types of case reserves include the following:[12]

- Judgment method
- Average value method
- Tabular method

Under the judgement method, a claim reserve is established for each individual claim. The amount of the loss reserve can be based on the judgement of someone in the claims department, or it can be estimated by a computer program. Many insurers now use computer programs that apply certain rules to calculate the size of the loss reserve. The details of an individual claim are entered into the computer, and the computer program estimates the size of the required loss reserve.

Under the *average value method,* an average value is assigned to each claim. This method is used when the number of claims is large, the average claim amount is relatively small, and the claims are quickly settled. For example, loss reserves for auto physical damage claims are often based on this method.

Under the *tabular value method,* loss reserves are determined for certain claims for which the amounts paid depend on the length of life, duration of disability, remarriage of the beneficiary, and similar factors. This method is often used to establish loss reserves involving total permanent disability, partial permanent disability, survivor benefits, and similar claims. The loss reserve is called a *tabular reserve* because the duration of the benefit period is based on data derived from mortality, morbidity, and remarriage tables.

Loss Ratio Method   Case reserves just discussed establish loss reserves for individual claims. In contrast, the *loss ratio method* establishes aggregate loss reserves for a specific line of insurance, such as workers compensation. Under the loss ratio method,

INSIGHT 27.1

Profitability of Insurance Industry and Other Selected Industries

Annual Rate of Return: Net Income After Taxes As a Percent of Equity, 1993–2002

Year	Property/casualty insurance		Life/health insurance[4]	Selected other industries[1]			Fortune 500 combined Industrials & service[6]
	Statutory accounting[2]	GAAP accounting[3]		Diversified financial[5]	Commercial banks	Electric & gas utilities	
1993	10.6%	11.0%	NA	17.1%	14.9%	11.1%	11.9%
1991	5.6	5.6	NA	18.4	15.6	11.3	13.7
1995	9.0	8.7	11.0%	18.2	15.6	11.9	14.0
1996	9.5	9.3	10.0	18.5	16.5	11.5	14.1
1997	11.9	11.6	12.0	14.9	16.9	10.4	13.9
1998	9.0	8.5	11.0	19.8	16.0	10.2	13.4
1999	6.7	6.0	13.0	21.0	18.0	11.9	15.2
2000	6.4	5.9	10.0	21.3	16.7	11.8	14.6
2001	−1.6	−1.2	7.0	19.3	14.0	10.5	10.4
2002	3.2	2.2	1.0	19.5	17.3	7.9	10.2

[1] Return on equity on a GAAP accounting basis, Fortune. [2] Net income after taxes, divided by year-end policyholder's surplus. Calculated by the Insurance Information Institute from A. M. Best Company, Inc. data. Statutory accounting is used by insurers when preparing the Annual Statements they submit to regulators. Data include state funds beginning in 2000, representing a break in the series. [3] Return on average net worth, Insurance Services Office, Inc (ISO). [4] Return on equity on a GAAP accounting basis, Fortune. Combined stock and mutual companies as calculated by the Insurance Information Institute. [5] Companies whose major source of revenue comes from providing diversified financial services. These companies are not specifically chartered as insurance c companies, banks or savings institutions, or brokerage or securities companies, but they may earn revenue from these sources. [6] Fortune 500 Combined Industrial and Services Businesses median return on equity.

NA=Data not available.

NOTE: Data are from A.M. Best Company, Inc.; Insurance Services Office, Inc. (ISO); and Fortune.

SOURCE: Excerpted from *The I.I.I. Insurance Fact Book 2004* (Insurance Information Institute, 2004), p. 20.

a formula based on the expected loss ratio is used to estimate the loss reserve. The expected loss ratio is multiplied by premiums earned during some time period. Loss and loss-adjustment expenses paid to date are then subtracted from the ultimate loss figure to determine the current loss reserve. The loss ratio method is required by law for certain lines of insurance, such as workers compensation, where the expected loss ratio ranges from 65 percent to 75 percent of earned premiums.

Incurred-But-Not-Reported (IBNR) Reserve. Many losses occur near the end of the accounting period but are not reported until the next period. The **incurred-but-not-reported (IBNR) reserve** *is a re-serve that must be established for claims that have already occurred but have not yet been reported.* For example, on December 31, a certain number of auto accidents have already occurred but have not been reported to the insurer. Loss reserves must be established for these losses that will be reported during the next accounting period.

LIFE INSURANCE POLICY RESERVES

Policy reserves are the major liability item of life insurers. This section briefly examines the nature, purposes, and types of life insurance policy reserves.[13]

Nature of the Reserve

Under a level-premium plan of life insurance, the premiums paid during the early years of the contract are higher than are necessary to pay death claims, while those paid during the later years are insufficient to pay death claims. The excess premiums collected during the early years of the contract must be accounted for and held for future payment to the policyowners' beneficiary. The excess premiums paid during the early years result in the creation of a policy reserve. *Policy reserves are a liability item on the company's balance sheet that must be offset by assets equal to that amount.* Policy reserves are considered a liability item because they represent an obligation of the insurer to pay future policy benefits to policyowners. The policy reserves held by the insurer plus future premiums and future interest earnings will enable the insurer to pay all future policy benefits if the actual experience conforms to the actuarial assumptions used in calculating the reserve. Policy reserves are often called *legal reserves,* because state insurance laws specify the minimum basis for calculating them.

Purposes of the Reserve

The policy reserve has two fundamental purposes. *First, it is a formal recognition of the insurer's obligation to pay future benefits.* The policy reserve plus future premiums and interest earnings must be sufficient to pay all future policy benefits.

Second, the reserve is a legal test of the insurer's solvency. The insurer must hold assets equal to its legal reserves and other liabilities. This requirement is the legal test of the insurer's ability to meet its present and future obligations to its policyowners. Policy reserves should not, therefore, be viewed as a fund. Rather, they are a liability item that must be offset by assets.

Definition of the Reserve

The **policy reserve** *can be defined as the difference between the present value of future benefits and the present value of future net premiums.* The net single premium is equal to the present value of future benefits. At the inception of the policy, the net single premium is also equal to the present value of future net premiums. The net single premium can be con-

verted into a series of annual installment payments without changing this relationship. However, once the first installment premium payment is made, this statement is no longer true. The present value of future benefits and the present value of future net premiums are no longer equal to each other. The present value of future benefits will increase over time, because the date of death is drawing closer, while the present value of future net premiums will decline, because fewer premiums will be paid. Thus, the difference between the two is the policy reserve.

This situation is illustrated in Exhibit 27.5, which shows the prospective reserve (defined later) for an ordinary life policy issued at age 45. At the inception of the policy, the net single premium is equal to the present value of future benefits and the present value of future net premiums.

The present value of future benefits increases over time, while the present value of future net premiums declines, and the reserve is the difference between them. At age 100, the reserve is equal to the policy face amount. If the insured is still alive at that time, the face amount of insurance is paid to the policyowner.

Types of Reserves

The reserve can be viewed either retrospectively or prospectively. If we refer to the past experience, the reserve is known as a retrospective reserve. The **retrospective reserve** *represents the net premiums collected by the insurer for a particular block of policies, plus interest earnings at an assumed rate, less the amounts paid out as death claims.*[14] Thus, the retrospective reserve is the excess of the net premiums accumulated at interest over the death claims paid out.

The reserve can also be viewed prospectively when we look to the future. The **prospective reserve** *is the difference between the present value of future benefits and the present value of future net premiums.* The retrospective and prospective methods are the mathematical equivalent of each other. Both methods will produce the same level of reserves at the end of any given year if the same set of actuarial assumptions is used.

Reserves can also be classified based on the time of valuation. At the time the reserves are valued, they can be classified as terminal, initial, and mean.

EXHIBIT 27.5
Prospective Reserve—Ordinary Life Insurance

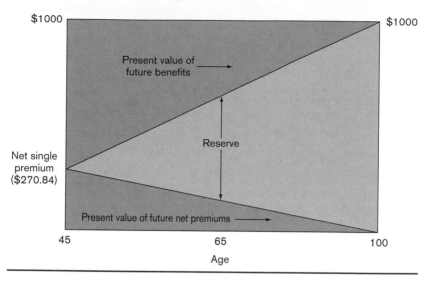

A **terminal reserve** *is the reserve at the end of any given policy year*. It is used by companies to determine cash surrender values as well as the net amount at risk for purposes of determining dividends. The **initial reserve** *is the reserve at the beginning of any policy year*. It is equal to the preceding terminal reserve plus the net level annual premium for the current year. The initial reserve is also used by insurers to determine dividends. Finally, the **mean reserve** *is the average of the terminal and initial reserves*. It is used to indicate the insurer's reserve liabilities on its annual statement.

CASE APPLICATION

Assume that you are asked to explain how premiums in a life insurance policy are calculated. Based on the following information, answer the questions below.

a. Compute the net single premium for a five-year term insurance policy in the amount of $1000 issued at age 40.

b. Compute the net annual level premium for the same policy as in part (a).

c. Is the net annual level premium the actual premium paid by the policyowner? Explain your answer.

Age at Beginning of Year	Number Living at Beginning of Designated Year	Number Dying During Designated Year	Present Value of $1 at 5%	
			Year	Factor
40	9,377,225	28,319	1	0.9524
41	9,348,906	30,758	2	0.9070
42	9,318,148	33,173	3	0.8638
43	9,284,975	35,933	4	0.8227
44	9,249,042	38,753	5	0.7835

SUMMARY

- State rating laws require insurance rates to meet certain standards. The rates charged by insurers must be adequate, not excessive, and not unfairly discriminatory.

- The rating system should also meet certain business objectives. The rates should be simple, stable, and responsive, and should encourage loss prevention.

- Three major rating methods are used in property and liability insurance: judgment, class, and merit rating.

- Judgment rating means that each exposure is individually evaluated, and the rate is determined largely by the underwriter's judgment.

- Class rating means that exposures with similar characteristics are placed in the same underwriting class, and each is charged the same rate. The rate charged reflects the average loss experience for the class as a whole. Most personal lines of insurance are class rated.

- Merit rating is a rating plan by which class rates are adjusted upward or downward based on individual loss experience. It is based on the assumption that the loss experience of a particular insured will differ substantially from the loss experience of other insureds.

- There are three principal types of merit rating plans:

    Schedule rating

    Experience rating

    Retrospective rating

- Under *schedule rating,* each exposure is individually rated, and debits and credits are applied based on the physical characteristics of the exposure to be insured. *Experience rating* means that the insured's past loss experience is used to determine the premium for the next policy period. *Retrospective rating* means the insured's loss experience during the current policy period determines the actual premium paid for that period.

- In life insurance rate making, the *net single premium* is the present value of the future death benefit. The *net annual level premium* must be the mathematical equivalent of the net single premium. The net annual level premium is determined by dividing the net single premium by the present value of a life annuity due of $1 for the premium-paying period. A loading for expenses must be added to the net annual level premium to determine the gross premium.

- The unearned premium reserve in property and casualty insurance is a liability reserve that represents the unearned portion of gross premiums on all outstanding policies at the time of valuation. The fundamental purpose of the unearned premium reserve is to pay for losses that occur during the policy period.

- A loss reserve is the estimated cost of settling claims that have already occurred but have not been paid as of the valuation date.

- In life insurance, a policy reserve is defined as the difference between the present value of future benefits and the present value of future net premiums. Policy reserves or legal reserves are a formal recognition of the insurer's obligation to pay future benefits. Also, the reserve is a legal test of an insurer's solvency, because the insurer must hold assets equal to its legal reserves and other liabilities.

KEY CONCEPTS AND TERMS

Adjusted underwriting
  profit or loss
Annual pro rata
  method
Case reserves
Class rating (manual
  rating)
Combined ratio
Earned premiums
Equity in the
  unearned premium
  reserve
Expense ratio
Experience rating
Exposure unit
Gross premium
Gross rate
Incurred-but-not-
  reported (IBNR)
  reserve
Initial reserve
Judgment rating
Loading
Loss ratio
Loss ratio method of
  rating

Loss reserve
Mean reserve
Merit rating
Net annual level
  premium (NALP)
Net single premium
  (NSP)
Policy reserve
Prospective reserve
Pure premium
Pure premium method
  of rating
Rate
Retrospective rating
Retrospective
  reserve
Schedule rating
Temporary life annuity
  due
Terminal reserve
Unearned premium
  reserve

REVIEW QUESTIONS

1. a. Explain the regulatory objectives of rate making.
   b. Explain the business objectives of rate making.

2. What is judgment rating?

3. a. Explain the meaning of class rating.
   b. Briefly describe the following methods for determining class rates:
      1. Pure premium method
      2. Loss ratio method

4. a. Explain the meaning of merit rating.
   b. Identify the three basic types of merit rating plans.

5. a. Explain the meaning of the *net single premium* in life insurance.
   b. Explain the three assumptions on which calculation of the net single premium is based.

6. How is the net annual level premium computed?

7. In life insurance, a loading for expenses must be added to the net annual level premium to determine the gross premium. Identify the major types of expenses that are included in the loading allowance.

8. a. Explain the meaning of the *unearned premium reserve*.
   b. What are the purposes of the unearned premium reserve?

9. a. What is a loss reserve?
   b. Identify the different types of loss reserves in property and liability insurance.

10. Why does a legal reserve develop under the level-premium method for paying life insurance premiums?

APPLICATION QUESTIONS

1. A property insurer writes a considerable amount of property insurance on commercial warehouses. The expected loss ratio for the next policy period is 60 percent. The actual loss ratio, however, is 68 percent. Based on the *loss ratio method*, what change, if any, is needed in the level of rates? Show your calculations.

2. A large casualty insurer writes a substantial amount of private passenger auto insurance. An actuary analyzed claims data for a specific class of drivers for a recent one-year policy period. The claims data showed that the insurer paid out $30 million for incurred losses and loss adjustment expenses for each 100,000 cars insured for one year. Based on the *pure premium method*, calculate the pure premium. Show your calculations.

3. For the last calendar year, a property insurer reported the following financial information for a specific line of insurance:

Premiums written	$25,000,000
Expenses incurred	5,000,000
Incurred losses and loss adjustment expenses	14,000,000
Earned premiums	20,000,000

   a. Calculate the loss ratio.
   b. Calculate the expense ratio.
   c. Calculate the combined ratio.
   d. Does the insurer have a statutory underwriting profit or loss? Explain your answer.

4. Merit rating is used in property and liability insurance where the final premiums paid depend at least partly on the loss experience of the individual insured. Describe the basic characteristics of each of the following types of merit-rating plans.
   a. Schedule rating
   b. Experience rating
   c. Retrospective rating

5. a. Why are property and casualty insurers required to maintain certain loss reserves?
   b. Briefly explain the following methods for determining loss reserves:
      (1) Judgment method
      (2) Average value method
      (3) Tabular method
   c. Explain the loss ratio method for determining loss reserves for a specific line of insurance.
   d. What is an incurred-but-not-reported (IBNR) loss reserve?

6. Based on the 1980 CSO mortality table, the probability of death for a male age 45 is 41,907/9,210,289, or .00455. Assume that premiums are paid at the beginning of the year, death claims are paid at the end of the year, and the discount rate is 5 percent. Calculate the *net single premium* for a one-year term insurance policy in the amount of $1,000 issued to a

male age 45. (Note: The present value of $1 payable in one year at 5 percent interest is 0.9524).

INTERNET RESOURCES

- The **American Academy of Actuaries** is a public policy and communications organization that represents actuaries in all practice specialties. The site provides timely studies on important insurance problems and issues. Visit the site at

  http://www.actuary.org

- The **American Society of Pension Actuaries** is an organization formed to educate pension actuaries, consultants, and other professionals in the employee benefits field. Visit the site at

  http://www.aspa.org

- The **Casualty Actuarial Society** is a professional organization that promotes education in actuarial science and provides statistics on property and casualty insurance. Visit the site at

  http://www.casact.org

- The **Conference of Consulting Actuaries** is an organization that consists of consulting actuaries in all disciplines. Visit the site at

  http://www.ccactuaries.org

- The **Insurance Information Institute** is a primary source for information, statistics, and analysis on topics in property and casualty insurance. Visit the site at

  http://www.iii.org

- **Insurance Journal**, the *Property Casualty Magazine* is a free online journal that provides breaking regional and national news on the property/casualty industry. Breaking news and current developments are sent daily to your e-mail address. Visit the site at

  http://www.insurancejournal.com

- The **Insurance Services Office (ISO)** provides statistical information, actuarial analyses and consulting, policy language, and related information to participants in the property and casualty insurance markets. Visit the site at

  http://www.iso.com

- The **Society of Actuaries** is a professional organization that educates and qualifies individuals to become actuaries, provides continuing education programs, and enforces a professional code of conduct. Membership is obtained by successful completion of a rigorous set of examinations leading to the designation of Associate or Fellow in the Society. Visit the site at

  http://www.soa.org

- **Towers Perrin** is one of the world's largest actuarial and management consulting firms. The Tillinghast business of Towers Perrin provides a substantial amount of information on the insurance industry and advises other organizations on risk financing and self-insurance. Visit the site at

  http://www.towersperrin.com

SELECTED REFERENCES

Black, Kenneth, Jr., and Harold D. Skipper, Jr. *Life Insurance,* 13th ed. (Upper Saddle River, NJ: Prentice-Hall, 2000), chs. 27–30.

Graves, Edward E., ed. *McGill's Life Insurance,* 5th ed. Bryn Mawr, PA: The American College, 2004.

The I.I.I. Insurance Fact Book. 2004. New York, NY: Insurance Information Institute, 2004.

Webb, Bernard L., et al. *Insurance Operations and Regulations,* First Edition. Malvern, PA: American Institute for Chartered Property Casualty Underwriters/ Insurance Institute of America, 2002.

NOTES

1. Robert J. Gibbons, George E. Rejda, and Michael W. Elliott, *Insurance Perspectives* (Malvern, PA: American Institute for Chartered Property Casualty Underwriters, 1992), p. 119.
2. Bernard L. Webb, Connor M. Harrison, and James J. Markam, *Insurance Operations,* 2nd ed., vol. 2 (Malvern, PA: American Institute for Chartered Property Casualty Underwriters, 1997), pp. 89–90.
3. The basic rate-making methods are discussed in some detail in Webb et al., chs. 10 and 11. See also Bernard L. Webb, J. J. Launie, Willis Park Rokes, and Norman A. Baglini, *Insurance Company Operations,* 3rd ed., vol. 2 (Malvern, PA: American Institute for Property and Liability Underwriters, 1984), chs. 9 and 10.
4. An equivalent method for determining the final rate is to divide the pure premium by the permissible loss

ratio. The *permissible loss ratio* is the same as the expected loss ratio. If the expense ratio is 0.40, the permissible loss ratio is 1 – 0.40, or 0.60. Thus, if the pure premium of $60 is divided by the permissible loss ratio of 0.60, the resulting gross rate is also $100.

$$\text{Gross rate} = \frac{\text{Pure premium}}{\text{Permissable loss ratio}} = \frac{\$60}{0.60} = \$100$$

5. Earned premiums are the premiums actually earned by a company during the accounting period, rather than the premiums written during the same period.

6. The credibility factor (C) refers to the statistical reliability of the data. It ranges from a value of 0 to 1 and increases as the number of claims increases. If the actuary believes that the data are highly reliable and can accurately predict future losses, a credibility factor of 1 can be used. However, if the data are not completely reliable as a predictor of future losses, a credibility factor of less than 1 is used.

7. This section is based on Kenneth Black, Jr., and Harold D. Skipper, Jr., *Life Insurance*, 13th ed. (Upper Saddle River, NJ: Prentice-Hall, 2000), pp. 714–727, 732–736; and Edward E. Graves, ed., *McGill's Life Insurance*, 4th ed. (Bryn Mawr, PA: The American College, 2002), chs. 11 and 13. The author drew heavily on these sources in preparing this section.

8. For example, if an immediate life annuity is purchased with annual payments, the first payment would be due one year from the purchase date.

9. Dan M. McGill, *Life Insurance*, rev. ed. (Homewood, IL: Richard D. Irwin, 1967), p. 208.

10. Ibid., pp. 247–248.

11. Data for 2004 are preliminary. See Robert P. Hartwig, Industry Financials and Outlook, *Special Report: Earlybird Forecast 2004*, Insurance Information Institute, 2004.

12. For a detailed explanation of loss reserves, see Bernard L. Webb, et al., *Insurance Operations and Regulation*, First Edition (Malvern, PA: American Institute for Chartered Property Casualty Underwriters/ Insurance Institute of America, 2002), ch. 12.

13. Life insurance reserves are discussed in greater detail in Black and Skipper, ch. 29, and Graves, ch. 12.

14. Graves, p. 344.

Students may take a self-administered test on this chapter at **www.aw-bc.com/rejda**

CHAPTER 28

GOVERNMENT REGULATION OF INSURANCE

"There are serious shortcomings in state laws and regulatory activities with respect to protecting the interests of insurance consumers."

U.S. General Accounting Office

LEARNING OBJECTIVES

After studying this chapter, you should be able to

◆ Explain the major reasons why insurers are regulated.

◆ Identify key legal cases legislative acts that have had an important impact on insurance regulation.

◆ Identify the major areas that are regulated.

◆ Explain the objectives of rate regulation and the different types of rating laws.

◆ Explain the major arguments for and against state regulation of insurance.

Jason, age 25, filled out an application for auto insurance and paid the agent $250 for the first premium. The application included collision coverage on the car. Shortly thereafter, Jason was involved in an auto accident in which he was at fault, and his car was badly damaged. The insurer denied payment on the grounds that no auto policy was ever issued. A complaint to the state insurance department revealed that the agent did not remit the application and premium to the insurer. Further investigation revealed that the agent did not remit the premiums of other policyholders as well. As a result, the state insurance department revoked the agent's license and fined the insurer for inadequate supervision of agents. The insurance department also recommended that the insurer pay for the damage to Jason's car.

One important function of state insurance departments is to protect consumers. In the preceding case, the state insurance department helped Jason resolve his claim dispute with the insurance company because of a dishonest agent. To protect consumers, the states regulate the market activities of insurers. Certain federal laws also apply to insurers.

This chapter discusses the fundamentals of insurance regulation. Topics covered include the reasons why insurers are regulated, the various methods for regulating insurers, and the specific areas that are regulated. The chapter concludes with a discussion of current issues in insurance regulation.

REASONS FOR INSURANCE REGULATION

Insurers are regulated by the states for several reasons, including the following:

- Maintain insurer solvency
- Compensate for inadequate consumer knowledge
- Ensure reasonable rates
- Make insurance available

Maintain Insurer Solvency

Insurance regulation is necessary to maintain the solvency of insurers. Solvency is important for several reasons. First, premiums are paid in advance, but the period of protection extends into the future. If an insurer goes bankrupt and a future claim is not paid, the insurance protection paid for in advance is worthless. Therefore, to ensure that claims will be paid, the financial strength of insurers must be carefully monitored.

A second reason for stressing solvency is that individuals can be exposed to great financial insecurity if insurers fail and claims are not paid. For example, if the insured's home is totally destroyed by a tornado and the loss is not paid, he or she may be financially ruined. Thus, because of possible financial hardship to insureds, beneficiaries, and third-party claimants, regulation must stress insurer solvency.

Finally, when insurers become insolvent, certain social and economic costs are incurred. Examples include the loss of jobs by insurance company employees, a reduction in premium taxes paid to the states, and a "freeze" on the withdrawal of cash values by life insurance policyowners. These costs can be minimized if insolvencies are prevented.

Insurer solvency is an important issue that is discussed in greater detail later in the chapter.

Compensate for Inadequate Consumer Knowledge

Regulation is also necessary because of inadequate consumer knowledge. Insurance contracts are technical, legal documents that contain complex clauses and provisions. Without regulation, an unscrupulous insurer could draft a contract so restrictive and legalistic that it would be worthless.

Also, most consumers do not have sufficient information for comparing and determining the monetary value of different insurance contracts. It is difficult to compare dissimilar policies with different premiums because the necessary price and policy information is not readily available. For example, individual health insurance policies vary widely by cost, coverages, and benefits. The average consumer would find it difficult to evaluate a particular policy based on the premium alone.

Without good information, consumers cannot select the best insurance product. This failure can reduce the impact that consumers have on insurance markets as well as the competitive incentive of insurers to improve product quality and lower price. Thus, regulation is needed to produce the same market effect that results from knowledgeable consumers who are purchasing products in highly competitive markets.

Finally, some agents are unethical, and state licensing requirements are minimal. Thus, regulation is needed to protect consumers against unscrupulous agents.

Ensure Reasonable Rates

Regulation is also necessary to ensure reasonable rates. Rates should not be so high that consumers are being charged excessive prices. Nor should they be so low that the solvency of insurers is threatened. In most insurance markets, competition among insurers results in rates that are not excessive. Unfortunately, this result is not always the case. In some insurance markets with relatively few insurers, such as credit and title insurance, rate regulation is needed to protect consumers against excessive rates. Regulation also protects consumers against some insurers who may attempt to increase rates to exorbitant levels after a natural disaster occurs so as to recoup their underwriting losses.

Make Insurance Available

Another regulatory goal is to make insurance available to all persons who need it. Insurers are often unwilling to insure all applicants for a given type of insurance because of underwriting losses, inadequate rates, adverse selection, and a host of additional factors. However, the public interest may require regulators to take actions that expand private insurance markets so as to make insurance more readily available. If private insurers are unable or unwilling to supply the needed coverages, then government insurance programs may be necessary.

HISTORICAL DEVELOPMENT OF INSURANCE REGULATION

In this section, the development of insurance regulation by the states is briefly reviewed. You should pay careful attention to certain landmark legal decisions and legislative acts that have had a profound impact on insurance regulation.

Early Regulatory Efforts

Insurance regulation first began when state legislatures granted charters to new insurers, which authorized their formation and operation. The new insurers were initially subject to few regulatory controls. The charters required only that the companies issue periodic reports and provide public information concerning their financial conditions.

The creation of state insurance commissions was the next step in insurance regulation. In 1851, New Hampshire became the first state to create a separate insurance commission to regulate insurers. Other states followed suit. In 1859, New York created a separate administrative agency headed by a single superintendent who was given broad licensing and investigative powers. Thus, initial insurance regulation developed under the jurisdiction and supervision of the states.

Paul v. Virginia

The case of *Paul v. Virginia* in 1868 was a landmark legal decision that established the right of the states to regulate insurance.[1] Samuel Paul was an agent in Virginia who represented several New York insurers. Paul was fined for selling fire insurance in Virginia without a license. He appealed the case on the grounds that Virginia's law was unconstitutional. He argued that because insurance was interstate commerce, only the federal government had the right to regulate insurance under the commerce clause of the U.S. Constitution. The Supreme Court disagreed. The Court ruled that issuance of an insurance policy was not interstate commerce. Therefore, the insurance industry was not subject to the commerce clause of the Constitution. *Thus, the legal significance of Paul v. Virginia was that insurance was not interstate commerce, and that the states rather than the federal government had the right to regulate the insurance industry.*

South-Eastern Underwriters Association Case

The precedent set in *Paul v. Virginia,* which held that insurance is not interstate commerce, was overturned by the Supreme Court in 1944. The **South-Eastern Underwriters Association (SEUA)** was a cooperative rating bureau that was found guilty of price fixing and other violations of the Sherman Antitrust Act. *In the landmark case of U.S. v. South-Eastern Underwriters Association, the Supreme Court ruled that insurance was interstate commerce when conducted across state lines and was subject to federal regulation.*[2] The Court's decision that insurance was interstate commerce and subject to federal antitrust laws caused considerable turmoil for the industry and state regulators. The decision raised serious doubts concerning the legality of private rating bureaus, and the power of the states to regulate and tax the insurance industry.

McCarran-Ferguson Act

To resolve the confusion and doubt that existed after the SEUA decision, Congress passed the **McCarran-Ferguson Act** (Public Law 15) in 1945. *The McCarran-Ferguson Act states that continued regulation and taxation of the insurance industry by the states are in the public interest. It also states that federal antitrust laws apply to insurance only to the extent that the insurance industry is not regulated by state law.* Therefore, as long as state regulation is in effect, federal antitrust laws will not apply to insurance. However, the exemption from antitrust laws is not absolute. The Sherman Act forbids any acts or agreements to boycott, coerce, or intimidate. In these areas, insurers are still subject to federal law.

At present, the states still have the primary responsibility for regulating insurance. However, Congress can repeal the McCarran-Ferguson Act, which would then give the federal government primary authority over the insurance industry. There have been strong pressures from some politicians and consumer groups to repeal the McCarran-Ferguson Act, but Congress to date has not done so. This important issue is discussed later in the chapter.

METHODS FOR REGULATING INSURERS

Three principal methods are used to regulate insurers: legislation, courts, and state insurance departments.

Legislation

All states have insurance laws that regulate the operations of insurers. These laws regulate (1) formation of insurance companies, (2) licensing of agents and brokers, (3) financial requirements for maintaining solvency, (4) insurance rates, (5) sales and claim practices, (6) taxation, and (7) rehabilitation or liquidation of insurers. Also, laws have been passed to protect the rights of consumers, such as laws restricting the right of insurers to terminate insurance contracts and laws making insurance more widely available.

Insurers are also subject to regulation by certain federal agencies and laws. Only a few are mentioned here. The Federal Trade Commission has authority to regulate mail-order insurers in those states where they are not licensed to do business. The Securities and Exchange Commission has issued regulations concerning the sale of variable annuities and variable life insurance and has jurisdiction over the sale of insurance company securities to the public. The Employee Retirement Income Security Act of 1974 (ERISA) applies to the private pension plans of insurers.

Courts

State and federal courts periodically hand down decisions concerning the constitutionality of state insurance laws, the interpretation of policy clauses and provisions, and the legality of administrative actions by state insurance departments. As such, the various court decisions can affect the market conduct and operations of insurers in an important way.

State Insurance Departments

All states, the District of Columbia, and U.S. territories have a separate insurance department or bureau. An insurance commissioner, who is elected or appointed by the governor, has the responsibility to administer state insurance laws. Through administrative rulings, the state insurance commissioner wields considerable power over insurers doing business in the state. The insurance commissioner has the power to hold hearings, issue cease-and-desist orders, and revoke or suspend an insurer's license to do business.

The state insurance commissioners belong to an important organization known as the **National Association of Insurance Commissioners (NAIC)**. The NAIC, founded in 1871, meets periodically to discuss industry problems that might require legislation or regulation. The NAIC has drafted model laws in various areas and has recommended adoption of these proposals by state legislatures. Although the NAIC has no legal authority to force the states to adopt the recommendations, most states have accepted all or part of them.

WHAT AREAS ARE REGULATED?

Insurers are subject to numerous laws and regulations. The principal areas regulated include the following:

- Formation and licensing of insurers
- Solvency regulation
- Rate regulation
- Policy forms
- Sales practices and consumer protection

Formation and Licensing of Insurers

All states have requirements for the formation and licensing of insurers. A new insurer is typically formed by incorporation. The insurer receives a charter or certificate of incorporation from the state, which authorizes its formation and legal existence.

After being formed, insurers must be licensed to do business. The licensing requirements for insurers are more stringent than those imposed on other new firms. If the insurer is a capital stock insurer, it must meet certain minimum capital and surplus requirements, which vary by state and by line of insurance. A new mutual insurer must meet a minimum surplus requirement (rather than capital and surplus, as there are no stockholders), and other requirements.

A license can be issued to a domestic, foreign, or alien insurer. A **domestic insurer** is an insurer domiciled in the state; it must be licensed in the state as well as in other states where it does business. A **foreign insurer** is an out-of-state insurer that is chartered by another state; it must be licensed to do business in the state. An **alien insurer** is an insurer chartered by a foreign country. It must also meet certain licensing requirements to operate in the state.

Solvency Regulation

In addition to minimum capital and surplus requirements, insurers are subject to other financial regulations designed to maintain solvency.

Admitted Assets   An insurer must have sufficient assets to offset its liabilities. Only admitted assets can be shown on the insurer's balance sheet. **Admitted assets** *are assets that an insurer can show on its statutory balance sheet in determining its financial condition.* All other assets are nonadmitted.

Most assets are classified as admitted assets. These assets include cash, bonds, common and preferred stocks, mortgages, real estate, and other legal investments. Nonadmitted assets include premiums overdue by 90 or more days, office furniture and supplies, and certain investments or amounts that exceed statutory limits for certain types of securities. Nonadmitted assets are excluded because their liquidity is uncertain. As a result, policyholders' statutory surplus is decreased by an increase in non- admitted assets.

Reserves   Reserves *are liability items on an insurer's balance sheet and reflect obligations that* *must be met in the future.* The states have regulations for the calculation of reserves. The various methods for calculating reserves were discussed in Chapter 27.

Surplus The surplus position is also carefully monitored. **Policyowners' surplus** *is the difference between an insurer's assets and its liabilities.* The surplus of a capital stock insurer consists of two items: (1) a capital stock account that represents the value of the shares issued to the stockholders, and (2) paid-in surplus that represents amounts paid in by stockholders in excess of the par value of the stock. Both items together represent policyowners' surplus. Because a mutual insurer has no stockholders, policyowners' surplus is simply the difference between assets and liabilities.

In property and liability insurance, policyowners' surplus is important for several reasons. First, the amount of new business an insurer can write is limited by the amount of policyowners' surplus. One conservative rule is that a property insurer can safely write $2 of new net premiums for each $1 of policyowners' surplus. Second, policyowners' surplus is necessary to offset any substantial underwriting or investment losses. Finally, policyowners' surplus is required to offset any deficiency in loss reserves that may occur over time.

In life insurance, policyowners' surplus is less important because of the substantial safety margins in the calculation of premiums and dividends, conservative interest assumptions used in calculating legal reserves, conservative valuation of investments, greater stability in operations over time, and less likelihood of a catastrophic loss.

Risk-Based Capital To reduce the risk of insolvency, life and health insurers must meet certain risk-based capital standards based on a model law developed by the NAIC. The NAIC has drafted a similar model law for property and liability insurers. Only the standards for life insurers are discussed here.

Risk-based capital (RBC) *means that insurers must have a certain amount of capital, depending on the riskiness of their investments and insurance operations. Insurers are monitored by regulators based on how much capital they have relative to their risk-based capital requirements.* For example, insurers that invest in less-than-investment-grade corporate bonds ("junk bonds") must set aside more capital than if Treasury bonds were purchased.

The risk-based capital requirements in life insurance are based on a formula that considers four types of risk:

- *Asset risk.* Asset risk is the risk of default of assets for affiliated investments; the parent company must hold an equivalent amount of risk-based capital that provides protection against the financial downturn of affiliates. The asset risk also represents the risk of default for bonds and other debt assets and a loss in market value for equity (common stock) assets.
- *Insurance risk.* Insurance risk is the equivalent of underwriting risk and reflects the amount of surplus needed to pay excess claims because of random fluctuations and inaccurate pricing for future claim levels (risk of fluctuations in experience).
- *Interest rate risk.* Interest rate risk reflects possible losses due to changing interest rates. The impact of interest rate changes is greatest on those products where the contractual guarantees favor the policyowners and where policyowners are likely to respond to changes in interest rates by withdrawing funds from the insurer. Examples include a decline in the market value of assets supporting contractual obligations because of a rise in interest rates, and liquidity problems caused by policyowners withdrawing funds because of changing interest rates.
- *Business risk.* Business risk represents the wide range of general business risks that life insurers face, such as guaranty fund assessments and insolvency because of bad management.

The NAIC requires a comparison of a company's total adjusted capital with the amount of required risk-based capital. *Total adjusted capital* is essentially the company's net worth (assets minus liabilities) with certain adjustments.

The model act requires certain regulatory and company actions that must be taken if an insurer's total adjusted capital falls below its RBC levels.

Action Level	RBC Ratio	Required Action
No action	200% or higher	Nothing
Company action level	150%–200%	Insurer must file a report with the regulator outlining the corrective actions to be taken.
Regulatory action level	100%–150%	Regulator must examine insurer; insurer must file an action plan.
Authorized control level	70%–100%	Regulator is authorized to seize insurer.
Mandatory control level	Less than 70%	Regulator is required to seize insurer.

The effect of the RBC requirements is to raise the minimum amount of capital for many insurers and decrease the chance that a failing insurer will exhaust its capital before it can be seized by regulators. Thus, the overall result is to limit an insurer's financial risk and reduce the cost of insolvency. As a practical matter, the vast majority of insurers have total adjusted capital that exceeds their risk-based capital requirements.

Investments Insurance company investments are regulated with respect to types of investments, quality, and percentage of total assets or surplus that can be invested in different investments. The basic purpose of these regulations is to prevent insurers from making unsound investments that could threaten the company's solvency and harm the policyowners.

Life insurers typically invest in common and preferred stocks, bonds, mortgages, real estate, and policy loans. The laws generally place maximum limits on each type of investment based on a percentage of assets or surplus.

Property and casualty insurers invest in common and preferred stock, tax-free municipal and special revenue bonds, government and corporate bonds, cash, and other short-term investments. The percentage of assets invested in real estate is relatively small (slightly over 1 percent in 2000). Most assets are invested in highly liquid securities—for example, high-quality stocks and bonds rather than real estate—that can be sold quickly to pay claims if a catastrophe loss occurs.

Dividend Policy In life insurance, the annual gain from operations can be distributed in the form of dividends to policyowners, or it can be added to the insurer's surplus for present and future needs. Many states limit the amount of surplus a participating life insurer can accumulate. The purpose of this limitation is to prevent life insurers from accumulating a substantial surplus at the expense of dividends to policyowners.

Reports and Examinations Annual reports and examinations are used to maintain insurer solvency. Each insurer must file an annual report with the state insurance department in states where it does business. The annual report provides detailed financial information to regulatory officials with respect to assets, liabilities, reserves, investments, claim payments, risk-based capital, and other information.

Insurance companies are also periodically examined by the states. Depending on the state, domestic insurers generally are examined one or more times every three to five years by the state insurance department. However, state regulations have the authority to conduct an examination at any time when considered necessary. Licensed out-of-state insurers are also periodically examined.

Liquidation of Insurers If an insurer is financially impaired, the state insurance department assumes control of the company. With proper management, the insurer may be successfully rehabilitated. If the insurer cannot be rehabilitated, it is liquidated according to the state's insurance code.

Most states have adopted the Insurers Supervision, Rehabilitation, and Liquidation Model Act drafted by the NAIC in 1977 or similar types of legislation. The Act is designed to achieve uniformity among the states in the liquidation of assets and payment of claims of a defunct insurer and provides for a comprehensive system for rehabilitation and liquidation.

If an insurer becomes insolvent, some claims may still be unpaid. All states have **guaranty funds** that provide for the payment of unpaid claims of insolvent property and casualty insurers. In life insurance, all states have enacted guaranty laws and guarantee associations to pay the claims of policyowners of insolvent life and health insurers.

The **assessment method** is the major method used to raise the necessary funds to pay unpaid claims. Insurers are generally assessed after an insolvency occurs. New York is an exception because it maintains a permanent preassessment solvency fund, which assesses property and casualty insurers prior to any insolvency. A few states have preassessment funds for workers compensation. Insurers can recoup part or all of the assessments paid by special state premium tax credits, refunds from the state guaranty funds, and higher insurance premiums. The result is that taxpayers and the general public indirectly pay the claims of insolvent insurers.

The guaranty funds limit the amount that policyowners can collect if an insurer goes broke. For example, in life insurance, the guaranty fund may place a limit of $100,000 on cash values and $300,000 on the combined benefits from all policies. Some state funds also do not protect out-of-state residents when an insurer domiciled in the state goes broke.

Rate Regulation

Rate regulation is another important area of insurance regulation. Property and liability insurance rates must meet certain statutory standards. As noted in Chapter 27, rates must be adequate, reasonable (not excessive), and not unfairly discriminatory. However, there are wide variations among states with respect to implementation of these objectives.

Rate regulation is far from uniform. Some states have more than one rating law, depending on the type of insurance. The principal types of rating laws are the following:

- Prior-approval laws
- File-and-use laws
- Open-competition laws
- Flex-rating laws

Prior-Approval Laws Many states have some type of prior-approval law for regulating rates. Under a **prior-approval law,** rates must be filed and approved by the state insurance department before they can be

used. In most states, if the rates are not disapproved within a certain period, such as 30 or 60 days, they are deemed to be approved.

Insurance companies have criticized prior-approval laws on several grounds. There is often considerable delay in obtaining a needed rate increase, because state insurance departments are often understaffed. The rate increase that is granted may be inadequate, and needed rate increases can be denied for political purposes. In addition, the statistical data required by the state insurance department to support a rate increase may not be readily available.

File-and-Use Laws This type of law is more liberal than the laws discussed earlier. Under a **file-and-use law,** insurers are required only to file the rates with the state insurance department, and the rates can be used immediately. Regulatory authorities have the authority to disapprove the rates later if they violate state law. This type of rating law overcomes the problem of delay that exists under a prior-approval law.

A variation of file and use is a **use-and-file law**. Under this law, insurers can put into effect rate changes, but the rates must be filed with the regulatory authorities within a certain period after first being used, such as 15 to 60 days.

Open-Competition Laws Open-competition laws (also called no-filing laws) are the most liberal of all rating laws. Under an open-competition law, insurers are not required to file their rates with the state insurance department. However, insurers may be required to furnish rate schedules and supporting data to state officials. The fundamental assumption underlying an open-competition law is that market forces will determine the price and availability of insurance rather than the discretionary acts of regulatory officials.

Flex-Rating Laws Some states have enacted an innovative rating law known as flex rating. Under a **flex-rating law,** prior approval of rates is required only if the rate increase or decrease exceeds a specific predetermined range. Rate changes of up to 10 to 25 percent are typically permitted without prior approval. The purpose of a flex-rating law is to allow insurers to make rate changes more rapidly in response to changing market conditions.

Commercial Lines Deregulation   Many states have passed legislation that exempts insurers from filing rates and policy forms for large commercial accounts with the state insurance department for approval. In most states, the legislation applies to commercial auto, general liability, and commercial multiperil lines. Proponents of deregulation of commercial lines believe that insurers can design new products more quickly to meet the insurance needs of corporations; insurers can save money because rates and policy forms do not have to be filed for a commercial account with offices in several states; and risk managers can get specific coverages more quickly.

Life Insurance Rate Regulation   Life insurance rates are not directly regulated by the states.[3] Rate adequacy in life insurance is indirectly achieved by regulations that require legal reserves to be at least a minimum size. Minimum legal reserve requirements affect the rates that must be charged to pay death claims and expenses.

Policy Forms

The regulation of new policy forms is another important area of insurance regulation. Because insurance contracts are technical and complex, the state insurance commissioner has the authority to approve or disapprove new policy forms before the contracts are sold to the public. The purpose is to protect the public from misleading, deceptive, and unfair provisions.

Sales Practices and Consumer Protection

The sales practices of insurers are regulated by laws concerning the licensing of agents and brokers, and by laws prohibiting twisting, rebating, and unfair trade practices.

Licensing of Agents and Brokers   All states require agents and brokers to be licensed. Depending on the type of insurance sold, applicants must pass one or more written examinations. The purpose is to ensure that agents have knowledge of the state insurance laws and the contracts they intend to sell. If the agent is incompetent or dishonest, the state insurance commissioner has the authority to suspend or revoke the agent's license.

All states have legislation requiring the continuing education of agents. The continuing education requirements are designed to upgrade an agent's knowledge and skills.

Twisting   All states forbid twisting. **Twisting** *is the inducement of a policyowner to drop an existing policy in another company due to misrepresentation or incomplete information.* Twisting laws apply largely to life insurance policies; the objective here is to prevent policyowners from being financially harmed by replacing one life insurance policy with another.

All states have replacement regulations so that policyowners can make an informed decision concerning the replacement of an existing life insurance policy. These laws are based on the premise that replacement of an existing life insurance policy generally is not in the policyowner's best interest. For example, a new front-end load for commissions and expenses must be paid; a new incontestable clause and suicide clause must be satisfied; and higher premiums based on the policyowner's higher attained age may have to be paid. *In some cases, however, switching policies can be financially justified.* However, deceptive sales practices by some agents of certain insurers have resulted in the replacement of life insurance policies that were financially harmful to the policyowners. At the time of this writing, some insurers are still settling class action lawsuits by policyowners who were deceived by unethical agents.

Rebating   State insurance codes also forbid rebating. **Rebating** *is giving to an individual a premium reduction or some other financial advantage not stated in the policy as an inducement to purchase the policy.* One obvious example is a partial refund of the agent's commission to the policyowner. The basic purpose of antirebate laws is to ensure fair and equitable treatment of all policyowners by preventing one insured from obtaining an unfair price advantage over another.

Consumer groups, however, believe that antirebating laws are harmful to consumers. Critics argue that (1) rebating will increase price competition and lower insurance rates; (2) present antirebating laws protect the incomes of agents rather than consumers; and (3) insurance purchasers are denied the right to negotiate price with insurance agents.

Unfair Trade Practices Insurance laws prohibit a wide variety of *unfair trade practices,* including misrepresentation, twisting, rebating, deceptive or false advertising, inequitable claim settlement, and unfair discrimination. The state insurance commissioner has the legal authority to stop insurers from engaging in unfair trade practices and deceptive advertising. Insurers can be fined, an injunction can be obtained, or, in serious cases, the insurer's license can be suspended or revoked.

Complaint Division State insurance departments typically have a complaint division or department for handling consumer complaints. The department will investigate the complaint and try to obtain a response from the alleged offending insurer or agency. Most consumer complaints involve claims. An insurer may refuse to pay a claim, or it may dispute the amount payable. Although state insurance departments respond to individual complaints, the departments generally lack direct authority to order insurers to pay disputed claims where factual questions are an issue. *However, you should phone or write your state insurance department if you feel you are being treated unfairly by your insurer or agent.* This consideration is especially true for auto insurance disputes where certain insurers have significantly higher complaint ratios than others (see Insight 28.1).

Readable Policies Greater protection of the consumer is also evidenced by the trend toward more *readable policies.* To make insurance contracts more understandable, the states have approved policies in which the language is less technical and is therefore simpler and easier to understand. The development of more readable policies will undoubtedly benefit most consumers.

Publications and Brochures. State insurance departments typically provide a wide variety of publications and brochures for consumers. The publications provide considerable information on life, health, auto, homeowners, and long-term care insurance, and other insurance products as well. Many states also publish rate information on auto and homeowners insurance on the Internet so that consumers can make meaningful cost comparisons.

Taxation of Insurers

Insurers pay numerous local, state, and federal taxes. Two important taxes are the federal income tax and the state premium tax. Insurers pay federal income taxes based on complex formulas and rules established by federal legislation and the Internal Revenue Service. The states also levy a premium tax on gross premiums received from policyowners, such as 2 percent of the premium paid.

The primary purpose of the premium tax is to raise revenues for the states, not to provide funds for insurance regulation. However, many state insurance departments are underfunded and receive only a small fraction of the premium taxes collected. Critics of state regulation argue that if state regulation is to become more effective, more money must be spent on insurance regulation.

Most states also have **retaliatory tax laws** that affect premium taxes and other taxes. For example, assume that the premium tax is 2 percent in Nebraska and 3 percent in Iowa. If insurers domiciled in Nebraska are required to pay a 3 percent premium tax on business written in Iowa, then domestic insurers in Iowa doing business in Nebraska must also pay a 3 percent tax on business written in Nebraska even though Nebraska's rate is 2 percent. The purpose of a retaliatory tax law is to protect domestic insurers in the state from excessive taxation by other states where they do business.

STATE VERSUS FEDERAL REGULATION

Critics of state regulation argue that the McCarran-Ferguson Act should be repealed and replaced by federal regulation. Certain advantages are claimed for federal regulation.

Advantages of Federal Regulation

The following arguments are offered in support of federal regulation of insurance:

- *Uniformity of laws.* Federal regulation can provide greater uniformity of laws. Under state regulation, insurers doing business in more than one state must observe different state laws. Under federal regulation, the laws would be uniform.

INSIGHT 28.1

2003 Annual Ranking of Automobile Insurance Complaints in New York State (based on 2002 data)

The New York State Insurance Department makes available annual rankings of auto insurers doing business in New York. The rankings shown here are based on the complaint ratios of 51 insurance companies or groups of companies. The ratios are based on calendar year 2002 data.

The *complaint ratio* represents the number of private passenger auto insurance complaints upheld against an insurer and closed by the department in 2002, divided by the insurer's 2001–2003 average private passenger auto insurance premium volume in New York State. Insurers with the fewest upheld complaints per million dollars of premiums appear at the top of the list. *The insurer with the lowest ratio is ranked first in the report; the insurer with the highest ratio is ranked last. The lower the ratio, the better is the insurer's performance. Insurers with the lowest and highest ratios for 2002 are shown below.* Data for 2001 and 2000 are shown for comparison purposes.

Lowest Complaint Ratios—Top 25

Company or Group	Complaint Ratio	Current Ranking*	2001 Ranking	2000 Ranking
Atlantic	0.00	1	4	20
Electric	0.00	2	25	45
Amica	0.01	3	6	6
USAA	0.06	4	9	7
Erie	0.08	5	1	1
New York Central Mutual***	0.09	6	12	9
Preferred Mutual	0.11	7	21	10
Merchants Mutual	0.11	8	20	40
Chubb	0.14	9	8	5
Response	0.14	10	26	17
State-Wide	0.14	11	14	16
GMAC	0.15	12	32	27
Allmerica	0.15	13	17	13
CNA	0.17	14	33	22
National Grange	0.17	15	7	8
White Mountains	0.18	16	16	28
Allianz	0.18	17	43	42
American Modern	0.18	18	**	**
Travelers****	0.18	19	13	18
State Farm	0.19	20	11	14
Prudential	0.20	21	30	33
Progressive	0.20	22	34	32
Nationwide	0.20	23	24	44
Royal and SunAlliance	0.20	24	19	31
Utica	0.23	25	29	35

* Based on calendar year 2002 data.
** Not ranked in that year due to low premium volume
*** In this report, the Central Services Group will be referred to as New York Central Mutual Fire. New York Central Mutual Fire writes over 99% of the group's private passenger auto business.
**** In 2002, Citigroup spun off its Travelers property/casualty business.

INSIGHT 28.1 (continued)

2003 Annual Ranking of Automobile Insurance Complaints in New York State (based on 2002 data)

Prior Year Complaint Rankings of Bottom Ten New York State Private Passenger Auto Insurance Companies

Company or Group	Complaint Ratio	Current Ranking*	2001 Ranking	2000 Ranking
Credit Suisse Group	0.70	42	45	41
Eveready	0.75	43	3	38
Sentry	1.30	44	37	15
St. Paul	1.66	45	41	30
Great American	1.98	46	48	37
Interboro	2.40	47	10	4
Eagle	3.49	48	36	23
Leucadia	6.47	49	50	52
Clarendon	7.72	50	49	26
Merchants & Bus. Men's Mutual**	30.01	51	51	54

* Based on calendar year 2002 data.
** This company and its parent, Liberty Mutual, are listed separately in this report.

Complaint Ratios of Ten Largest Private Passenger Auto Insurers New York State, 2002

Company or Group	Complaint Ratio	Current Ranking	2001–2002 Average Premium (in millions)	Market Share
Allstate	0.49	40	$1,592.6	16.8%
State Farm	0.19	20	1,229.5	13.0
Berkshire-Hathaway (GEICO)	0.27	29	1,194.5	12.6
Travelers	0.18	19	598.1	6.3
Progressive	0.20	22	551.0	5.8
Liberty Mutual	0.31	31	409.8	4.3
Nationwide	0.20	23	364.0	3.8
AIG	0.66	41	355.9	3.8
White Mountains	0.18	16	331.0	3.5
New York Central Mutual	0.09	6	326.6	3.5
Top Ten			$6,953.0	73.5%
Total (all companies, incl. those with less than $10 million in premium)			$9,464.5	100.0%

* Based on calendar year 2002 data.

SOURCE: Adapted from New York State Insurance Department, *2003 Annual Ranking of Automobile Insurance Complaints,* December 2003.

■ *Greater efficiency*. It is argued that federal regulation would be more efficient. Insurers doing business nationally would deal with only one federal agency rather than with numerous insurance departments. Also, the federal agency would be less likely to yield to industry pressures, especially those reflecting the views of local insurers. Federal regulation would also be less expensive to administer.

■ *More competent regulators*. Federal regulation would attract higher-quality personnel who would do a superior job of regulating the insurance industry. The higher salaries and prestige would attract more highly talented and skilled individuals.

Advantages of State Regulation

Supporters of state regulation also offer convincing arguments for continued regulation of insurance by the states. The major advantages claimed for state regulation are as follows:

■ *Greater responsiveness to local needs*. Local needs vary widely and state regulators can respond more quickly to local needs. In contrast, under federal regulation, "red tape" and government bureaucracy would result in considerable delay in solving problems at the local level.

■ *Promotion of uniform laws by NAIC*. Proponents of state regulation argue that uniformity of laws can be achieved by the model laws and proposals of the NAIC. In addition, the NAIC has a plan called *A Reinforced Commitment: Insurance Regulatory Modernization Action Plan* that puts the states on a time deadline to modernize state regulation. The states would have to meet certain modernization goals that cover market regulation, consumer protection, producer licensing, company licensing, and solvency regulation by certain specified dates, ranging from December 31, 2003 to December 31, 2008.

■ *Greater opportunity for innovation*. State regulation provides greater opportunities for innovation in regulation. An individual state can experiment, and if the innovation fails, only that state is affected. In contrast, poor federal legislation would affect all states.

■ *Unknown consequences of federal regulation*. State regulation is already in existence, and its strengths and weaknesses are well known. In contrast, the consequences of federal regulation on consumers and the insurance industry are unknown.

■ *Decentralization of political power*. State regulation results in a decentralization of political power. Federal regulation would result in further encroachment of the federal government on the economy and a corresponding dilution of states' rights.

Shortcomings of State Regulation

Congressional committees and the General Accounting Office (GAO) have assessed the effectiveness of state regulation of insurance and have found serious shortcomings, including the following:[4]

■ *Inadequate protection against insolvency*. Because the insurance industry operates globally, existing state regulation is considered inadequate for supervising the solvency of insurers, which depend substantially on offshore companies to pay claims. State governments do not have sufficient resources, legal powers, or determination to protect policyowners from mismanagement and fraud by some insurers here and abroad. In addition, some property and liability insurers have been licensed to do business when they were undercapitalized, and state insurance departments have not carefully checked the background or monitored the activities of persons running the companies.

■ *Inadequate protection of consumers*. Critics argue that state insurance departments do not have systematic procedures for determining whether consumers are being treated properly with respect to claim payments, rate setting, and protection from unfair discrimination.

■ *Improvements needed in handling complaints*. Although many states prepare complaint ratios (ratio of complaints to premiums) for each company, the information may not be readily shared with the public.

■ *Inadequate market conduct examinations*. Market conduct examinations refer to insurance department examinations of consumer matters such as claims handling, underwriting, complaints, advertising, and other trade practices. Serious deficiencies have been found in many market conduct examination reports.

- *Insurance availability*. Many states have not conducted current studies to determine whether property and liability insurance availability is a serious problem in their states.
- *Regulators overly responsive to insurance industry*. State insurance departments are overly responsive to the insurance industry at the expense of consumers. Insurance regulation is not characterized by an "arm's-length" relationship between regulators and the regulated. Many state insurance commissioners were previously employed in the insurance industry, and many return to the industry after leaving office.

Repeal of the McCarran-Ferguson Act

As noted earlier, the McCarran-Ferguson Act gives the states primary responsibility for regulation of the insurance industry and also provides limited exemption from federal antitrust laws. Because of the shortcomings of state regulation, there is considerable public and political support for repeal of the McCarran-Ferguson Act. Because of the trend toward deregulation and greater price competition, critics also argue that insurers should not be exempt from federal antitrust laws that prohibit price fixing, collusion, and other activities harmful to consumers.

Critics of state regulation present several arguments for repeal of the McCarran-Ferguson Act. They include the following:

- *The insurance industry no longer needs broad antitrust exemption*. Critics argue that the "state action doctrine" has been fully developed and clarified by the Supreme Court. The state action doctrine defines certain activities required by state law that are exempt from federal antitrust activities. Because permissible actions of insurers have been clarified, exemption from the antitrust laws is no longer needed. In addition, it is argued that other industries are not exempt from antitrust laws, and the same should also be true for insurers.
- *Federal regulation is needed because of the defects in state regulation*. Critics argue that federal minimum standards are needed to ensure nondiscrimination in insurance pricing, full

availability of essential property and liability coverages, and elimination of unfair and excessive rate differentials among insureds.

The insurance industry, however, has generally opposed any legislation that would repeal the McCarran-Ferguson Act. The industry believes that substantial harm to both insurers and the public will result from repeal of the Act. The following arguments are presented in support of the industry's position:

- *The insurance industry is already competitive*. More than 3300 property and liability insurers and more than 1100 life insurers now compete for business.
- *Small insurers would be harmed*. Smaller insurers would be unable to compete because they cannot develop accurate rates based on their limited loss and expense experience. Thus, smaller insurers may go out of business or be taken over by larger insurers. Hence a small number of large insurers will ultimately control the business, a result exactly opposite of that intended by repeal of the McCarran-Ferguson Act.
- *Insurers may be prevented from developing common coverage forms*. This problem could lead to costly gaps in coverage for insurance buyers and increased litigation between insurers and policyowners. Also, it would be difficult for insureds to know what is covered and excluded if nonstandard forms are used.
- *Dual regulation may result from repeal of the McCarran-Ferguson Act*. However, the past record of federal regulation is poor. Federal regulators have done a poor job in regulating the savings and loan industry, which resulted in the insolvency of hundreds of thrifts with a cost to taxpayers of billions of dollars. Also, critics argue that federal regulation of railroads, airlines, and trucking has been destructive to competition. Federal regulation has also obstructed entry into an industry, entrenched the market power of large companies, and resulted in a cozy relationship between the regulators and the regulated.

Numerous federal proposals have been introduced during the past 20 years to repeal or modify the McCarran-Ferguson Act. In general, these proposals would prohibit certain activities of insurers, including price fixing, tying the sale of one product to another, attempting to monopolize, and dividing up territories with competitors.

CURRENT PROBLEMS AND ISSUES IN INSURANCE REGULATION

State insurance regulators face numerous problems and issues. Some important issues include the following:

- Optional federal charter
- Market conduct regulation
- Convergence of financial services
- Increase in mergers and acquisitions
- Insolvency of insurers
- Quality of insurance regulation
- Credit-based insurance score

Optional Federal Charter

The American Council of Life Insurers (ACLI), a life insurance trade association, has proposed an optional federal charter for life insurers. Under the proposal, life insurers would have the option of obtaining either a federal or state charter, depending on the insurer's specific needs and geographic scope of operations. Small local insurers may opt for a state charter, while large national insurers may prefer a federal charter. A major argument for a federal charter is that many new life insurance products sold today are investment products, and that life insurers are at a competitive disadvantage when they compete nationally with commercial banks and stock brokerage firms. Approval of new life insurance products may take as long as two years because of differences and inconsistencies in 50 state laws. In contrast, national commercial banks and stock brokerage firms can often develop and market new products in a shorter period. It is argued that a federal charter would enable large life insurers to speed up the development and approval of new products and make insurers more competitive at the national level.

Most industry trade associations and producer groups strongly oppose the ACLI proposal. Critics present two major arguments against a federal charter. First, there will be a dual system of insurance regulation, which will substantially increase the cost of insurance regulation. There will be at least two separate regulatory systems in each state—the present state system and a new federal system. The cost of regulation will increase because thousands of new federal employees must be hired; a mandatory federal charter may result in the loss of premium taxes to the states; and taxpayers and policyowners will have to pay more because of an additional layer of federal regulation.

Second, a new federal regulator would have the power to preempt state laws and may disagree with existing state laws that now affect policyowners and claimants under the present system. There are inconsistencies and differences in 50 state laws, which would make federal regulation difficult. Dual regulation may result in regulatory overlaps and confusion among policyowners and insurers as to which law should apply.

In addition, some consumer advocates believe that greater regulation of cash value products is needed at the state level to protect consumers, and that a federal charter may result in a "race to the bottom" to lower consumer protection standards if an insurer is chartered at the federal level.

Market Conduct Regulation

As stated earlier, market conduct regulation refers to regulation of insurers in areas that affect consumers, which include claims handling, underwriting, complaints, advertising, sales practices, and other trade practices. The U.S. General Accounting Office (GAO) found that two keys tools in market conduct regulation—market analysis and on-site examinations—are used inconsistently by the states or not at all. The result is inconsistent and spotty coverage in market conduct regulation among the states, which lead to potential gaps in the protection of consumers. *Market analysis* is the gathering of information to determine important issues and to identify insurers that need attention. *On-site examinations* refer to the frequency and breadth of insurance company examinations.

The GAO study found wide variation among the states with respect to how often the states use market analysis and market conduct examinations. The GAO made the following conclusions: (1) few states have formal programs for market analysis; (2) examinations are used inconsistently and infrequently in some cases; (3) the states use different criteria to select the insurers to examine; (4) most states limit the scope of their examinations by targeting certain areas, such as claim processing, and may not conduct broader and comprehensive market conduct examinations; and (5) the lack of coordination among the states results in multiple examinations that burden some insurers and leave others unexamined. With respect to the latter point, many insurers are subject to frequent and sometimes simultaneous market conduct examinations. For example, a GAO study of responses from 25 insurers for the years 1999–2001 showed that 19 insurers had been examined at their offices a total of 106 times over a three-year period; six insurers had been examined one or two times over the three-year period; and seven others had undergone three to five examinations. In contrast, six insurers, or nearly one quarter of those responding, had not been examined by any state during the period.[5] To attain greater uniformity, the GAO recommends that the states should identify and use a common set of market conduct standards that all states must follow. The recommendation would reduce the wide variation in market conduct examinations that now exists.

Convergence of Financial Services

Another important regulatory issue is the convergence of financial services. *A single financial institution can now sell a wide variety of financial products and services that were sold earlier by separate financial institutions.* Financial institutions include commercial banks, savings and loan institutions, insurance companies, stock brokerage firms, investment companies, real estate firms, and other financial institutions. In the past, because of legal and regulatory restrictions, the activities of financial institutions were limited to specific areas. For example, commercial banks provided banking services and generally did not sell insurance. In contrast, insurance companies sold insurance products and generally did not engage in banking. Investment firms sold investment products and generally did not engage in banking or insurance activities.

Because of court decisions, changes in banking laws and regulatory decisions, and new federal legislation, the distinction between banking, insurance, and investments has largely disappeared. Financial institutions can now provide banking services; sell life insurance, auto, homeowners, and other insurance contracts; offer annuities and other investments; and make real estate loans.

In particular, because of favorable court decisions, commercial banks are deeply entrenched in the insurance business and have become major competitors to traditional insurers. Commercial banks now sell term life insurance, universal life insurance, auto and homeowners insurance, long-term care insurance, disability insurance, group health insurance, annuities, and other investments. Likewise, several large insurers have acquired commercial banks or have announced plans to do so.

Financial Modernization Act of 1999 In 1999, Congress enacted the **Financial Modernization Act of 1999** (also called the Gramm-Leach-Bliley Act). The legislation changed federal law that prevented banks, insurers, and investment firms from making full entry into one another's financial markets. The legislation was considered necessary to allow financial institutions in the United States greater freedom to compete domestically and internationally in the financial markets and to provide better service to consumers. Insurers can now buy banks; banks can underwrite insurance and securities; and a company that wants to provide banking, insurance, and investment services through a single entity can form a new holding company for that purpose. As a result, the traditional lines that once separated types of financial institutions are disappearing.

Impact on State Insurance Regulation The legislation provides for several areas of regulation. State insurance departments regulate the insurance industry and insurance activities of other financial institutions. State and federal banking agencies regulate banks and thrifts, and the Securities and Exchange Commission regulates the sale of securities. The Federal Reserve has umbrella authority over bank affiliates that engage in risky activities such as underwriting insurance and developing real estate.

The legislation has an impact on state insurance regulation. Possible effects include the following:[6]

- *Competition between insurers and banks and other financial institutions may increase.*

- *State insurance departments will regulate the sale of insurance by noninsurance companies, such as banks.*
- *Mergers and acquisitions between insurers and other financial institutions will continue.*
- *Small insurers are more likely to be absorbed by large insurers.*
- *State insurance departments will be pressured to maintain a level playing field so that no financial institution will be disadvantaged in the sale of insurance.*
- *Some financial institutions may attempt to tie the sale of other financial products to the sale of insurance, which could harm insurers.*
- *Considerable coordination and cooperation between the different regulators of financial institutions will be required.*

The ability of state insurance departments to regulate effectively will be challenging, especially for departments with limited budgets. Conflicts between state insurance commissioners and federal banking regulators are also likely to occur.

Increase in Mergers and Acquisitions

In Chapter 25, we noted that mergers and acquisitions in the insurance industry have increased, especially among life insurers. However, in recent years, the number of mergers and acquisitions has tended to decline from the peak year of 1998 (see Exhibit 28.1).

The increase in mergers and acquisitions has both advantages and disadvantages for regulatory officials. On the positive side, regulators will be responsible for regulating a smaller group of larger and more sophisticated insurers, which should require less oversight and supervision.[7] Also, financially weaker insurers are more likely to be absorbed by stronger insurers, which should improve the regulatory environment.

On the negative side, mergers and acquisitions may result in highly leveraged insurers with complex financial structures; thus, the risk of insolvency will still be present.[8]

Also, regulators will have the additional burden of protecting existing policyowners if a mutual com-

EXHIBIT 28.1

Total Insurance-Related Reported Mergers and Acquisitions, 1991–2001[a]

[a] At least one of the companies involved in the transaction is a U.S.-domiciled insurer. Includes property/casualty, life, health/managed care, service and distribution companies.

SOURCE: *The I.I.I. Insurance Information Institute Fact Book 2003* (New York: Insurance Information Institute, 2003), p. 10.

pany demutualizes or forms a mutual holding company because of a possible conflict of interest between the policyowners and stockholders. For example, top-level management may receive company stock or stock options, which could reduce the company's operating profits. As a result, dividends to policyowners could decrease.

Finally, in the health insurance field, mergers and acquisitions may give health maintenance organizations (HMOs) too much power and leverage in dealing with patients and physicians.

Insolvency of Insurers

Insolvency of insurers continues to be an important regulatory problem. According to the National Association of Insurance Commissioners (NAIC), 238 property and casualty insurers and 116 life and health insurers became insolvent between 1991 through March 2004 (see Exhibit 28.2). Insolvency numbers for property and casualty insurers by the A. M. Best Company are higher because it counts separately each company in a group.

Reasons for Insolvencies Insurers fail for several reasons. Major causes of failure include charging of inadequate rates, inadequate reserves for claims, rapid growth and inadequate surplus, problems with affiliates, overstatement of assets, alleged fraud, failure of reinsurers to pay claims, mismanagement, and catastrophe losses.

When an insurer becomes insolvent or financially impaired, state regulators must take appropriate action. With proper management, the insurer may be rehabilitated. If rehabilitation is not feasible, the insurer may be involuntarily liquidated or acquired by a healthy insurer. Other possible regulatory actions include license revocation, cease-and-desist orders, and other actions that restrict an insurer's freedom to do business.

What happens to your policy or unpaid claim if your insurer becomes insolvent? Your policy may be sold to another insurer, and an unpaid claim may be paid by the state's guaranty fund. However, failure of a large insurer may result in delay of several years before all claims are paid.

Exhibit 28.2
Insurance Company Insolvencies 1991–2004

Year	NAIC (Property/Casualty)	A.M. Best Co. (Property/Casualty)	NAIC (Life/Health)
1991	19	46	25
1992	29	56	12
1993	15	43	11
1994	11	31	8
1995	4	15	2
1996	6	11	4
1997	14 (13)*	34	4 (1)*
1998	4 (5)	18	2 (4)
1999	3 (3)	7	7 (4)
2000	9 (9)	30	4 (6)
2001	17 (7)	30	0 (3)
2002	12 (9)	38	1 (1)
2003	23 (6)**	—	(4)
2004 to March	18 (2)**	—	11 (2)
Total	238	359	116

* Single state insurers are in parenthesis.
** Includes some insolvencies where single or multiple state is not identified.

Source: Insurance Information Institute, "Insolvencies/Guaranty Funds," *Hot Topics & Insurance Issues,* April 2004.

Methods of Ensuring Solvency The principal methods of ensuring solvency are the following:

- *Financial requirements.* Insurers must meet certain financial requirements that vary among the states, such as minimum capital and surplus requirements, restrictions on investments, and valuation of loss reserves.
- *Risk-based capital standards.* As noted earlier, insurers must meet the risk-based capital standards based on a model law developed by the NAIC. The increased capital requirements help to prevent insolvency.
- *Annual financial statements.* Certain annual financial statements must be submitted to state insurance departments in a prescribed manner to provide information on premiums written, expenses, losses, investments, and other information. The financial statements are then reviewed by regulatory officials.

EXHIBIT 28.3
IRIS Ratio Results: Life and Health Insurers

	Unusual Values Equal to or	
IRIS Ratio	Over	Under
1. Net change in capital and surplus	50	−10
2. Gross change in capital and surplus	50	−10
3. Net income to total income (including realized capital gains and losses)	—	0
4. Commissions and expenses to premiums and deposits (discontinued)		
5. Adequacy of investment income	900	125
6. Nonadmitted to admitted assets	10	—
7. Total real estate and total mortgage loans to cash and invested assets	30	—
8. Total affiliated investments to capital and surplus	100	—
9. Surplus relief (over $5 million capital and surplus)	30	−99
($5 million or less capital and surplus)	10	−10
10. Change in premium	50	−10
11. Change in product mix	5	—
12. Change in asset mix	5	—
13. Change in reserving ratio	20	−20

NOTE: The usual range of results for each ratio is shown as percentages.

SOURCE: National Association of Insurance Commissioners, NAIC Financial Analysis Solvency Tools, *Insurance Regulatory Information System (IRIS), 2002 Life/Health Edition*, 2002. Reprinted with permission. All rights reserved.

- *Field examinations.* State laws require that insurers generally must be examined every three to five years. The NAIC coordinates the examination of insurers that do business in several states.
- *Early warning system.* The NAIC administers an early warning system called the Insurance Regulatory Information System (IRIS). Financial ratios and other reports are developed based on information in the annual statement (see Exhibit 28.3 and Exhibit 28.4). Based on a review of this information, insurers may be designated for immediate review or targeted for regulatory attention. The system, however, is not perfect. The financial ratios may not identify all troubled insurers. The system also has identified an increasing number of insurers, some of which do not require immediate regulatory attention.
- *FAST system.* The NAIC employs a solvency screening system called FAST (Financial Analysis

Solvency Tracking) that prioritizes insurers for additional analysis. Different point values are assigned for the various ranges of financial ratio results. The points are then summed to determine a FAST score for each insurer. Based on their FAST scores, certain insurers are considered a priority for regulatory action.

Quality of Insurance Regulation

Improving the quality of insurance regulation remains an important issue. As noted earlier, studies by congressional committees and the U.S. General Accounting Office have pointed out numerous defects in state insurance regulation. More recently, consumer groups have criticized state insurance departments on the grounds that they provide inadequate insurance information to consumers.

The Consumer Federation of America has graded 51 jurisdictions on the types and usefulness

Exhibit 28.4
IRIS Ratio Results: Property and Casualty Insurers

IRIS Ratio	Unusual Values Equal to or	
	Over	Under
1. Gross premiums to policyholders' surplus	900	—
2. Net premiums to policyholders' surplus	300	—
3. Change in net writings	33	−33
4. Surplus aid to policyholders' surplus	15	—
5. Two-year overall operating ratio	100	—
6. Investment yield	10	4.5
7. Change in policyholders' surplus	50	−10
8. Liabilities to liquid assets	105	—
9. Agents' balances to policyholders' surplus	40	—
10. One-year reserve development to policyholders' surplus	20	—
11. Two-year reserve development to policyholder's surplus	20	—
12. Estimated current reserve deficiency to policyholders' surplus	25	—

NOTE: The usual range of results for each ratio is shown as percentages.
SOURCE: National Association of Insurance Commissioners, NAIC Financial Analysis Solvency Tools, *Insurance Regulatory Information System (IRIS), 2002 Property/Casualty Edition*, 2002. Reprinted with permission. All rights reserved.

of insurance information available to consumers, such as premium data, shopping guides, complaint data, and information on the major types of insurance consumers buy. The majority of jurisdictions received grades of "C" or higher (see Insight 28.2) However, seven jurisdictions received below-average grades of "D+" to "D−." Five jurisdictions received grades of "F." Seven jurisdictions received an incomplete (I) because they did not respond to requests for material. The NAIC blasted the study as flawed and incomplete because it presented a distorted picture of consumer activities and capabilities of state insurance departments. Nevertheless, it is clear that the negative perceptions of state insurance departments by consumer groups is likely to continue.

Improving the Efficiency of State Regulation State insurance regulators and the NAIC have identified several areas that require reexamination and review to promote greater competition and to protect consumers. Areas under review include company admission and licensing requirements, rate and form review, special deposit requirements, countersigna-

ture requirements, and regulation of commercial lines. In addition, some states have streamlined their insurance regulations by removing obsolete and unnecessary regulations.

Accreditation Program of NAIC To upgrade the quality of state regulation, the NAIC has also enacted certain financial regulation standards. States meeting those standards are accredited by the NAIC. At the time of this writing, virtually all states have been accredited.

Credit-Based Insurance Scores

Credit-based insurance scores are another important regulatory issue. An increasing number of insurers in auto and homeowners insurance are now using an applicant's credit record for purposes of underwriting and rating. As stated earlier in Chapters 8 and 11, the insurance score is derived from the applicant's credit history and is combined with other factors. Depending on the insurance score, the applicant may be denied insurance or placed in a higher rating class.

INSIGHT 28.2

Insurance Department Report Card

The Consumer Federation of America (CFA) has released a study grading each state's insurance department on the basis of informational brochures that each department has avail- able. After reviewing the materials, the CFA awarded each department a letter grade.

State	Grade	State	Grade
Alabama	I	Montana	C–
Alaska	B+	Nebraska	C+
Arizona	C+	Nevada	B+
Arkansas	I	New Hampshire	I
California	B+	New Jersey	D–
Colorado	A	New Mexico	D
Connecticut	B–	New York	B
Delaware	C+	North Carolina	D+
District of Columbia	I	North Dakota	D+
Florida	A	Ohio	A–
Georgia	F	Oklahoma	C–
Hawaii	C	Oregon	B–
Idaho	F	Pennsylvania	B–
Illinois	B+	Rhode Island	F
Indiana	C+	South Carolina	B–
Iowa	B–	South Dakota	F
Kansas	A	Tennessee	F
Kentucky	C+	Texas	A+
Louisiana	C	Utah	C
Maine	B	Vermont	C–
Maryland	I	Virginia	B
Massachusetts	D	Washington	C+
Michigan	I	West Virginia	D+
Minnesota	I	Wisconsin	A+
Mississippi	D+	Wyoming	C
Missouri	A		

SOURCE: Adapted from *Insurance Department Report Card*, Consumer Federation of America, March 24, 1999.

Insurance scoring based on the applicant's credit record is controversial. Proponents offer the following arguments:

- *There is a high correlation between an applicant's credit record and future claims experience.* Applicants with poor or marginal credit records are more likely to submit more auto or homeowners claims than applicants with good or superior credit records. Credit data enhances the ability of insurers to predict future claim experience with greater accuracy.
- *Insurers claim that underwriting and rating can be more objective and consistent.* Subjectivity

and human bias in underwriting can be removed by automated underwriting based on objective insurance scores.

- *Most consumers have good credit records and would be treated more equitably.* Consumers with good credit records may qualify for lower rates or obtain coverage that might otherwise have been difficult to obtain.

Critics of insurance scoring, however, present the following counterarguments:

- *The use of credit data in underwriting or rating discriminates against certain groups.* These groups include low-income people who are unable to obtain credit or have poor credit records, the unemployed who fall behind in paying their bills, the sick and disabled who are late with their monthly credit card payments, and female-headed families with children who do not receive child-support payments, or the payments are late. In addition, the system discriminates against applicants for insurance who do not use credit but pay cash for their purchases.
- *Credit reports are often wrong or contain errors that can harm insurance applicants.* Also, identity theft has increased, which could harm the ability of innocent victims to obtain insurance on favorable terms.

- *Insurance scoring is socially unacceptable.* An applicant for life insurance, for example, cannot be denied life insurance or charged higher premiums solely because of race. Some critics believe that the same argument should be applied to the use of credit records in underwriting.

To protect consumers, in early 2002, Washington passed legislation that places restrictions on credit-based scores in personal insurance. In 2003, some 40 states had considered some type of legislation, and more than 20 states enacted new laws.[9]

Washington's law is strict. Insurers cannot deny insurance coverage or determine rates for personal lines based on:

- The number of credit inquiries
- Credit histories based on collection accounts identified as coming from unpaid medical bills
- Use of a particular type of credit card, debit card, or charge card
- The total amount of credit available
- Absence of a credit history
- The initial purchase or financing of a vehicle or house

If the credit history is inaccurate, the insurer must reissue or rerate the policy retroactively to the effective date of the current policy term.

CASE APPLICATION

Ashley is an actuary who is employed by the Nebraska Department of Insurance. Her duties include monitoring the financial position of insurance companies doing business in Nebraska. Based on an analysis of annual financial statements that insurers are required to submit, she discovered that Mutual Life Insurance has a risk-based capital ratio of 175 percent. Based on this information, answer the following questions.

a. What is the purpose of requiring insurers to meet risk-based capital requirements?

b. What regulatory action, if any, should the Nebraska Department of Insurance take with respect to Mutual Life Insurance?

c. Would your answer to part (b) change if the risk-based capital ratio for Mutual Life Insurance fell to 65 percent? Explain your answer.

d. Mutual Life Insurance has 25 percent of its assets invested in common stocks. Assume the stocks are sold, and the proceeds are invested in U.S. government bonds. What effect, if any, will this investment change have on the risk-based capital ratio of Mutual Life Insurance? Explain your answer.

SUMMARY

- The insurance industry is regulated for several reasons:

    To maintain insurer solvency

    To compensate for inadequate consumer knowledge

    To ensure reasonable rates

    To make insurance available

- The insurance industry is regulated primarily by the states. The McCarran-Ferguson Act states that continued regulation and taxation of the insurance industry by the states are in the public interest.

- Three principal methods are used to regulate the insurance industry:

    Legislation

    Courts

    State insurance departments

- The principal areas that are regulated include the following:

    Formation and licensing of insurers

    Solvency regulation

    Rate regulation

    Policy forms

    Sales practices and consumer protection

- Property and casualty insurance rates must be adequate, reasonable (not excessive), and not unfairly discriminatory. The principal types of rating laws are as follows:

    Prior-approval laws

    File-and-use laws

    Open-competition laws

    Flex-rating laws

- Insurers must pay a state premium tax on gross premiums. The primary purpose is to raise revenues for the state, not to provide funds for insurance regulation.

- State versus federal regulation is an issue that has evoked considerable debate. The alleged advantages of federal regulation include the following:

    Uniformity of laws

    Greater efficiency

    More competent regulation

- The advantages of state regulation include the following:

    Greater responsiveness to local needs

    Promotion of uniform laws by the NAIC

    Greater opportunity for innovation

    Unknown consequences of federal regulation

    Decentralization of political power

- Critics argue that state regulation of insurance has serious shortcomings, including the following:

    Inadequate protection against insolvency

    Inadequate protection of consumers

    Improvements needed in handling complaints

    Inadequate market conduct examinations

    Insurance availability studies conducted only in a minority of states

    Regulators overly responsive to the insurance industry

- Several current issues in insurance regulation include the following:

    Optional federal charter market conduct regulation

    Convergence of financial services

    Increase in mergers and acquisitions

    Insolvency of insurers

    Quality of insurance regulation

    Credit-based insurance score

KEY CONCEPTS AND TERMS

Admitted assets
Alien insurer
Assessment method
Credit-based insurance score
Domestic insurer
File-and-use law
Flex-rating law
Financial Modernization Act of 1999
Foreign insurer
Guaranty funds
McCarran-Ferguson Act
National Association of Insurance Commissioners (NAIC)
Open-competition laws
Paul v. Virginia
Policyowners' surplus
Prior-approval law
Rebating
Reserves
Retaliatory tax laws
Risk-based capital (RBC)
South-Eastern Underwriters Association (SEUA)
Twisting
Use-and-file law

REVIEW QUESTIONS

1. Explain the reasons why the insurance industry is regulated.

2. Briefly explain the significance of the following legal cases with respect to insurance company regulation:
   a. Paul v. Virginia
   b. South-Eastern Underwriters Association Case
   c. McCarran-Ferguson Act

3. Explain the principal methods for regulating insurance companies.

4. Identify the principal areas of insurance company operations that are regulated by the states.

5. Briefly describe the following types of rating laws:
   a. Prior-approval laws
   b. File-and-use laws
   c. Open-competition laws
   d. Flex-rating laws

6. Explain the following actions by agents that are prohibited by state law:
   a. Twisting
   b. Rebating

7. a. Explain the major arguments for federal regulation of the insurance industry.
   b. Explain the major arguments in support of state regulation of the insurance industry.
   c. Describe the shortcomings of state regulation.

8. a. Explain the major arguments for repeal of the McCarran-Ferguson Act.
   b. Explain the major arguments against repeal of the McCarran-Ferguson Act.

9. Identify the major techniques that regulators use to ensure insurance company solvency.

10. Describe the risk-based capital standards that insurers must meet.

APPLICATION QUESTIONS

1. The Financial Services Company is a large life insurer that sells annuity products to retired people. Company actuaries have designed a new annuity contract that combines lifetime annuity benefits with long-term care in a skilled nursing home. Financial Services wants to market the new annuity nationally in all 50 states. The company faces competition from a national commercial bank that is trying to sell a similar product to Social Security beneficiaries. The CEO of Financial Services believes that the new annuity product could be marketed more efficiently if the company had a federal charter. Several members of the board of directors, however, believe that a federal charter would be undesirable.
   a. What major regulatory obstacle does Financial Services face in trying to market the new annuity product in each state under the present system of state regulation?
   b. Assume that Financial Services has the option of obtaining a federal charter. Explain the advantages, if any, of a federal charter to Financial Services in their efforts to market the new annuity product.
   c. Explain the major arguments against federal charters.

2. Opal, age 75, has a $100,000 ordinary life insurance policy that has a cash value of $35,000. Opal is concerned about the cost of long-term care in a nursing home. A new agent of a national life insurer persuaded her to transfer the $35,000 into a deferred annuity. The agent told Opal that the annuity pays lifetime income benefits and also allows her to withdraw the $35,000 without penalty if she should enter a nursing home. After the policy was issued, Opal had ten days to change her mind. During the free-look period, a friend of Opal examined the policy. Analysis of the policy showed that only 10 percent of the cash value could be withdrawn each year without penalty. A 7 percent surrender charge would apply to any excess amounts withdrawn. In addition, the income payments were scheduled to start in ten years when Opal attained age 85. Opal filed a complaint against the agent with the state insurance department. An investigation revealed that the agent had made similar misrepresentations to other clients.
   a. Based on the above facts, identify the illegal practice in which the agent engaged.
   b. What action can the state insurance department take against the dishonest agent?
   c. What action can the state insurance department take against the life insurer?

3. Although domiciled in Nebraska, Auto Insurance is licensed to sell auto insurance in ten states. In five states, prior approval of rates is required. Two states have a file-and-use law, and the remaining three states

have a flex-rating law. Auto Insurance has experienced poor underwriting results and needs to increase its rates.

    a. Explain how each of the above rating laws would apply to Auto Insurance.

    b. Describe some possible problems that Auto Insurance may experience in trying to get its rates increased in a prior-approval state.

4. Janet, age 35, is divorced and has two preschool children. Janet earns only the federal minimum wage, and money is tight. Her former husband failed to make child-support payments for the past three months because he lost his job in a company merger. As a result, Janet fell behind in the payment of her bills and received several threatening letters from collection agencies. Janet believes that she can save some money if she switched auto insurers. One auto insurer quoted her a rate that is substantially higher than the rates she is now paying. A company representative explained that Janet is being rated up because of a poor credit record. Janet is surprised because she has a good driving record and has not been involved in an accident within the last five years.

    a. Explain the rationale for charging Janet a higher premium for auto insurance because of a poor credit record.

    b. Explain the arguments against using credit-based insurance scores as a rating or underwriting factor in auto insurance.

INTERNET RESOURCES

■ The **Insurance Regulatory Examiners Society** is a non-profit professional and educational association for insurance company examiners and other professionals working in insurance regulation. Visit the site at

http://www.go-ires.org

■ The **National Association of Insurance Commissioners (NAIC)** is an organization of state insurance commissioners that promotes uniformity in state insurance laws and recommends legislation to state legislatures. The Web site for each state insurance department can be accessed through the NAIC Web site. Visit the site at

http://www.naic.org

■ The **National Association of Insurance Commissioners (NAIC)** also provides considerable information on complaints against individual insurers. Go to the NAIC Consumer Information Source, type in the company names, state, and business type. After locating the company, click on "Closed Complaints." Visit the site at

http://www.naic.org/cis

■ The **National Conference of Insurance Guaranty Funds** is an advisory organization to state guaranty funds. It gathers and disseminates information regarding insurer insolvencies. Visit the site at

http://www.ncigf.org

■ The **National Conference of Insurance Legislators** is an organization of state legislators whose main area of public policy concern is insurance regulation and legislation. Visit the site at

http://www.ncoil.org

SELECTED REFERENCES

American Council of Life Insurers. *ACLI Releases Working Draft Proposal on Optional Federal Chartering*, News Release, April 13, 2001.

Consumer Federation of America. *Many State Legislators Involved with National Insurance Organization Have Close Ties to Insurance Industry*, Press Release, July 9, 2003.

Insurance Information Institute. "Insolvencies/Guaranty Funds," *Hot Topics & Insurance Issues*. New York: Insurance Information Institute, April 2004.

Insurance Information Institute. "Optional Federal Charter," *Hot Topics & Insurance Issues*. New York: Insurance Information Institute, April 2004.

Insurance Information Institute. "Rates and Regulation," *Hot Topics & Insurance Issues*. New York: Insurance Information Institute, March 2004.

Klein, Robert W. *A Regulator's Introduction to the Insurance Industry*. Kansas City, MO: NAIC Education and Research Foundation, 1999.

National Association of Insurance Commissioners. *NAIC Annual Report 2003* at http://www.naic.org/about/annual_report.htm.

National Association of Insurance Commissioners. *NAIC Testifies on Recent Steps in Modernizing State Insurance Regulation*, News Release, October 22, 2003.

U.S. General Accounting Office. *Insurance Regulation, Common Standards and Improved Coordination Needed to Strengthen Market Regulation,* GAO-03-433, September 2003.

U.S. General Accounting Office. *Insurance Regulation, The NAIC Accreditation Can Be Improved,* GAO-01-948, August 2001.

NOTES

1. 8 Wall 168, 183 (1869).
2. 322 U.S. 533 (1944).
3. There are exceptions. Maximum credit life insurance rates are regulated by the states.
4. See U.S. General Accounting Office, *Insurance Regulation, Common Standards and Improved Coordination Needed to Strengthen Market Regulation,* GAO-03-433, September 2003; U.S. Congress, House, and Subcommittee on Oversight and Investigations of the Committee on Energy and Commerce, *Wishful Thinking, A World View of Insurance Solvency Regulation* (Washington, DC: U.S. Government Printing Office, 1994), and *Failed Promises: Insurance Company Insolvencies* (Washington, DC: U.S. Government Printing Office, 1990). See also United States General Accounting Office, *Health Insurance Regulation, Wide Variation in States' Authority, Oversight, and Resources* (Washington, DC: U.S. General Accounting Office, 1993); and Comptroller General of the United States, *Issues and Needed Improvements in State Regulation of the Insurance Business* (Executive Summary) (Washington, DC: U.S. General Accounting Office, 1979).
5. U.S. General Accounting Office, *Insurance Regulation, Common Standards and Improved Coordination Needed to Strengthen Market Regulation,* GAO-03-433, September 2003.
6. Robert W. Klein, *A Regulator's Introduction to the Insurance Industry* (Kansas City: MO: NAIC Education and Research Foundation, 1999), pp. 12-4, 12-5.
7. Ibid., p. 12-3.
8. Ibid.
9. Insurance Information Institute, "Automated Underwriting Tools: Credit & CLUE," *Hot Topics & Insurance Issues,* March 2004.

HOMEOWNERS 3 (SPECIAL FORM)

Homeowners Policy Declarations

POLICYHOLDER:
(Named Insured)

David M. and Joan G. Smith
216 Brookside Drive
Anytown, USA 40000

POLICY NUMBER: 296 H 578661

POLICY PERIOD: **Inception:**   March 30, 2004
Expiration: March 30, 2005

Policy period begins 12:01 A.M. standard time at the residence premises.

FIRST MORTGAGEE AND MAILING ADDRESS:

Federal National Mortgage Assn.
C/O Mortgagee, Inc.
P.O. Box 5000
Businesstown, USA 55000

We will provide the insurance described in this policy in return for the premium and compliance with all applicable policy provisions.

SECTION I COVERAGES   **LIMIT**

A—Dwelling	$ 200,000	**SECTION I DEDUCTIBLE:** $ 250
B—Other Structures	$ 20,000	(In case of loss under Section I, we cover
C—Personal Property	$ 100,000	only that part of the loss over the
D—Loss of Use	$ 60.000	deductible amount shown above.)

SECTION II COVERAGES   **LIMIT**

E—Personal Liability	$ 300,000	Each Occurrence
F—Medical Payments to Others	$ 1,000	Each Person

CONSTRUCTION: Masonry Veneer   **NO. FAMILIES:** One   **TYPE ROOF:** Approved

YEAR BUILT: 1970   **PROTECTION CLASS:** 7   **FIRE DISTRICT:** Cook Township

NOT MORE THAN 1000 FEET FROM HYDRANT

NOT MORE THAN 5 MILES FROM FIRE DEPT.

FORMS AND ENDORSEMENTS IN POLICY: HO 00 03, HO 04 61

POLICY PREMIUM: $650.00   **COUNTERSIGNATURE DATE:** March 1, 2004   **AGENT:** A.M. Abel

SAMPLE

655

HOMEOWNERS
HO 00 03 10 00

HOMEOWNERS 3 – SPECIAL FORM

AGREEMENT

We will provide the insurance described in this policy in return for the premium and compliance with all applicable provisions of this policy.

DEFINITIONS

A. In this policy, "you" and "your" refer to the "named insured" shown in the Declarations and the spouse if a resident of the same household. "We", "us" and "our" refer to the Company providing this insurance.

B. In addition, certain words and phrases are defined as follows:

1. "Aircraft Liability", "Hovercraft Liability", "Motor Vehicle Liability" and "Watercraft Liability", subject to the provisions in **b.** below, mean the following:

   a. Liability for "bodily injury" or "property damage" arising out of the:

   (1) Ownership of such vehicle or craft by an "insured";

   (2) Maintenance, occupancy, operation, use, loading or unloading of such vehicle or craft by any person;

   (3) Entrustment of such vehicle or craft by an "insured" to any person;

   (4) Failure to supervise or negligent supervision of any person involving such vehicle or craft by an "insured"; and

   (5) Vicarious liability, whether or not imposed by law, for the actions of a child or minor involving such vehicle or craft.

   b. For the purpose of this definition:

   (1) Aircraft means any contrivance used or designed for flight except model or hobby aircraft not used or designed to carry people or cargo;

   (2) Hovercraft means a self-propelled motorized ground effect vehicle and includes, but is not limited to, flarecraft and air cushion vehicles; and

   (3) Watercraft means a craft principally designed to be propelled on or in water by wind, engine power or electric motor.

   (4) Motor vehicle means a "motor vehicle" as defined in **7.** below.

2. "Bodily injury" means bodily harm, sickness or disease, including required care, loss of services and death that results.

3. "Business" means:

   a. A trade, profession or occupation engaged in on a full-time, part-time or occasional basis; or

   b. Any other activity engaged in for money or other compensation, except the following:

   (1) One or more activities, not described in (2) through (4) below, for which no "insured" receives more than $2,000 in total compensation for the 12 months before the inception date of the policy;

   (2) Volunteer activities for which no money is received other than payment for expenses incurred to perform the activity;

   (3) Providing home day care services for which no compensation is received, other than the mutual exchange of such services; or

   (4) The rendering of home day care services to a relative of an "insured".

4. "Employee" means an employee of an "insured", or an employee leased to an "insured" by a labor leasing firm under an agreement between an "insured" and the labor leasing firm, whose duties are other than those performed by a "residence employee".

5. "Insured" means:

   a. You and residents of your household who are:

   (1) Your relatives; or

   (2) Other persons under the age of 21 and in the care of any person named above;

   b. A student enrolled in school full time, as defined by the school, who was a resident of your household before moving out to attend school, provided the student is under the age of:

   (1) 24 and your relative; or

   (2) 21 and in your care or the care of a person described in **a.(1)** above; or

SAMPLE

c. Under Section II:

(1) With respect to animals or watercraft to which this policy applies, any person or organization legally responsible for these animals or watercraft which are owned by you or any person included in **a.** or **b.** above. "Insured" does not mean a person or organization using or having custody of these animals or watercraft in the course of any "business" or without consent of the owner; or

(2) With respect to a "motor vehicle" to which this policy applies:

(a) Persons while engaged in your employ or that of any person included in **a.** or **b.** above; or

(b) Other persons using the vehicle on an "insured location" with your consent.

Under both Sections I and II, when the word an immediately precedes the word "insured", the words an "insured" together mean one or more "insureds".

6. "Insured location" means:

a. The "residence premises";

b. The part of other premises, other structures and grounds used by you as a residence; and

(1) Which is shown in the Declarations; or

(2) Which is acquired by you during the policy period for your use as a residence;

c. Any premises used by you in connection with a premises described in **a.** and **b.** above;

d. Any part of a premises:

(1) Not owned by an "insured"; and

(2) Where an "insured" is temporarily residing;

e. Vacant land, other than farm land, owned by or rented to an "insured";

f. Land owned by or rented to an "insured" on which a one, two, three or four family dwelling is being built as a residence for an "insured";

g. Individual or family cemetery plots or burial vaults of an "insured"; or

h. Any part of a premises occasionally rented to an "insured" for other than "business" use.

7. "Motor vehicle" means:

a. A self-propelled land or amphibious vehicle; or

b. Any trailer or semitrailer which is being carried on, towed by or hitched for towing by a vehicle described in **a.** above.

8. "Occurrence" means an accident, including continuous or repeated exposure to substantially the same general harmful conditions, which results, during the policy period, in:

a. "Bodily injury"; or

b. "Property damage".

9. "Property damage" means physical injury to, destruction of, or loss of use of tangible property.

10. "Residence employee" means:

a. An employee of an "insured", or an employee leased to an "insured" by a labor leasing firm, under an agreement between an "insured" and the labor leasing firm, whose duties are related to the maintenance or use of the "residence premises", including household or domestic services; or

b. One who performs similar duties elsewhere not related to the "business" of an "insured".

A "residence employee" does not include a temporary employee who is furnished to an "insured" to substitute for a permanent "residence employee" on leave or to meet seasonal or short-term workload conditions.

11. "Residence premises" means:

a. The one family dwelling where you reside;

b. The two, three or four family dwelling where you reside in at least one of the family units; or

c. That part of any other building where you reside;

and which is shown as the "residence premises" in the Declarations.

"Residence premises" also includes other structures and grounds at that location.

HO 00 03 10 00

DEDUCTIBLE

Unless otherwise noted in this policy, the following deductible provision applies:

Subject to the policy limits that apply, we will pay only that part of the total of all loss payable under Section I that exceeds the deductible amount shown in the Declarations.

SECTION I – PROPERTY COVERAGES

A. Coverage A – Dwelling

1. We cover:

   a. The dwelling on the "residence premises" shown in the Declarations, including structures attached to the dwelling; and

   b. Materials and supplies located on or next to the "residence premises" used to construct, alter or repair the dwelling or other structures on the "residence premises".

2. We do not cover land, including land on which the dwelling is located.

B. Coverage B – Other Structures

1. We cover other structures on the "residence premises" set apart from the dwelling by clear space. This includes structures connected to the dwelling by only a fence, utility line, or similar connection.

2. We do not cover:

   a. Land, including land on which the other structures are located;

   b. Other structures rented or held for rental to any person not a tenant of the dwelling, unless used solely as a private garage;

   c. Other structures from which any "business" is conducted; or

   d. Other structures used to store "business" property. However, we do cover a structure that contains "business" property solely owned by an "insured" or a tenant of the dwelling provided that "business" property does not include gaseous or liquid fuel, other than fuel in a permanently installed fuel tank of a vehicle or craft parked or stored in the structure.

3. The limit of liability for this coverage will not be more than 10% of the limit of liability that applies to Coverage **A.** Use of this coverage does not reduce the Coverage **A** limit of liability.

C. Coverage C – Personal Property

1. **Covered Property**

   We cover personal property owned or used by an "insured" while it is anywhere in the world. After a loss and at your request, we will cover personal property owned by:

   a. Others while the property is on the part of the "residence premises" occupied by an "insured"; or

   b. A guest or a "residence employee", while the property is in any residence occupied by an "insured".

2. **Limit For Property At Other Residences**

   Our limit of liability for personal property usually located at an "insured's" residence, other than the "residence premises", is 10% of the limit of liability for Coverage **C,** or $1,000, whichever is greater. However, this limitation does not apply to personal property:

   a. Moved from the "residence premises" because it is being repaired, renovated or rebuilt and is not fit to live in or store property in; or

   b. In a newly acquired principal residence for 30 days from the time you begin to move the property there.

3. **Special Limits Of Liability**

   The special limit for each category shown below is the total limit for each loss for all property in that category. These special limits do not increase the Coverage **C** limit of liability.

   a. $200 on money, bank notes, bullion, gold other than goldware, silver other than silverware, platinum other than platinumware, coins, medals, scrip, stored value cards and smart cards.

   b. $1,500 on securities, accounts, deeds, evidences of debt, letters of credit, notes other than bank notes, manuscripts, personal records, passports, tickets and stamps. This dollar limit applies to these categories regardless of the medium (such as paper or computer software) on which the material exists.

   This limit includes the cost to research, replace or restore the information from the lost or damaged material.

SAMPLE

c. $1,500 on watercraft of all types, including their trailers, furnishings, equipment and outboard engines or motors.

d. $1,500 on trailers or semitrailers not used with watercraft of all types.

e. $1,500 for loss by theft of jewelry, watches, furs, precious and semiprecious stones.

f. $2,500 for loss by theft of firearms and related equipment.

g. $2,500 for loss by theft of silverware, silver-plated ware, goldware, gold-plated ware, platinumware, platinum-plated ware and pewterware. This includes flatware, hollow-ware, tea sets, trays and trophies made of or including silver, gold or pewter.

h. $2,500 on property, on the "residence premises", used primarily for "business" purposes.

i. $500 on property, away from the "residence premises", used primarily for "business" purposes. However, this limit does not apply to loss to electronic apparatus and other property described in Categories j. and k. below.

j. $1,500 on electronic apparatus and accessories, while in or upon a "motor vehicle", but only if the apparatus is equipped to be operated by power from the "motor vehicle's" electrical system while still capable of being operated by other power sources.

Accessories include antennas, tapes, wires, records, discs or other media that can be used with any apparatus described in this Category j.

k. $1,500 on electronic apparatus and accessories used primarily for "business" while away from the "residence premises" and not in or upon a "motor vehicle". The apparatus must be equipped to be operated by power from the "motor vehicle's" electrical system while still capable of being operated by other power sources.

Accessories include antennas, tapes, wires, records, discs or other media that can be used with any apparatus described in this Category k.

4. Property Not Covered

We do not cover:

a. Articles separately described and specifically insured, regardless of the limit for which they are insured, in this or other insurance;

b. Animals, birds or fish;

c. "Motor vehicles".

(1) This includes:

(a) Their accessories, equipment and parts; or

(b) Electronic apparatus and accessories designed to be operated solely by power from the electrical system of the "motor vehicle", but only while such property is in or upon the "motor vehicle". Accessories include antennas, tapes, wires, records, discs or other media that can be used with any apparatus described above, but only while such property is in or upon the "motor vehicle".

(2) We do cover "motor vehicles" not required to be registered for use on public roads or property which are:

(a) Used solely to service an "insured's" residence; or

(b) Designed to assist the handicapped;

d. Aircraft meaning any contrivance used or designed for flight including any parts whether or not attached to the aircraft;

We do cover model or hobby aircraft not used or designed to carry people or cargo;

e. Hovercraft and parts. Hovercraft means a self-propelled motorized ground effect vehicle and includes, but is not limited to, flare-craft and air cushion vehicles;

f. Property of roomers, boarders and other tenants, except property of roomers and boarders related to an "insured";

g. Property in an apartment regularly rented or held for rental to others by an "insured", except as provided in E.10. Landlord's Furnishings under Section I – Property Coverages;

h. Property rented or held for rental to others off the "residence premises";

i. "Business" data, including such data stored in:

(1) Books of account, drawings or other paper records; or

(2) Computers and related equipment.

We do cover the cost of blank recording or storage media, and of prerecorded computer programs available on the retail market;

Copyright, Insurance Services Office, Inc., 1999 HO 00 03 10 00

SAMPLE

j. Credit cards, electronic fund transfer cards or access devices used solely for deposit, withdrawal or transfer of funds except as provided in **E.6.** Credit Card, Electronic Fund Transfer Card Or Access Device, Forgery And Counterfeit Money under Section **I** – Property Coverages; or

k. Water or steam.

D. Coverage D – Loss Of Use

The limit of liability for Coverage **D** is the total limit for the coverages in **1.** Additional Living Expense, **2.** Fair Rental Value and **3.** Civil Authority Prohibits Use below.

1. Additional Living Expense

If a loss covered under Section **I** makes that part of the "residence premises" where you reside not fit to live in, we cover any necessary increase in living expenses incurred by you so that your household can maintain its normal standard of living.

Payment will be for the shortest time required to repair or replace the damage or, if you permanently relocate, the shortest time required for your household to settle elsewhere.

2. Fair Rental Value

If a loss covered under Section **I** makes that part of the "residence premises" rented to others or held for rental by you not fit to live in, we cover the fair rental value of such premises less any expenses that do not continue while it is not fit to live in.

Payment will be for the shortest time required to repair or replace that part of the premises rented or held for rental.

3. Civil Authority Prohibits Use

If a civil authority prohibits you from use of the "residence premises" as a result of direct damage to neighboring premises by a Peril Insured Against, we cover the loss as provided in **1.** Additional Living Expense and **2.** Fair Rental Value above for no more than two weeks.

4. Loss Or Expense Not Covered

We do not cover loss or expense due to cancellation of a lease or agreement.

The periods of time under **1.** Additional Living Expense, **2.** Fair Rental Value and **3.** Civil Authority Prohibits Use above are not limited by expiration of this policy.

E. Additional Coverages

1. Debris Removal

a. We will pay your reasonable expense for the removal of:

(1) Debris of covered property if a Peril Insured Against that applies to the damaged property causes the loss; or

(2) Ash, dust or particles from a volcanic eruption that has caused direct loss to a building or property contained in a building.

This expense is included in the limit of liability that applies to the damaged property. If the amount to be paid for the actual damage to the property plus the debris removal expense is more than the limit of liability for the damaged property, an additional 5% of that limit is available for such expense.

b. We will also pay your reasonable expense, up to $1,000, for the removal from the "residence premises" of:

(1) Your tree(s) felled by the peril of Windstorm or Hail or Weight of Ice, Snow or Sleet; or

(2) A neighbor's tree(s) felled by a Peril Insured Against under Coverage **C**;

provided the tree(s):

(3) Damage(s) a covered structure; or

(4) Does not damage a covered structure, but:

(a) Block(s) a driveway on the "residence premises" which prevent(s) a "motor vehicle", that is registered for use on public roads or property, from entering or leaving the "residence premises"; or

(b) Block(s) a ramp or other fixture designed to assist a handicapped person to enter or leave the dwelling building.

The $1,000 limit is the most we will pay in any one loss regardless of the number of fallen trees. No more than $500 of this limit will be paid for the removal of any one tree.

This coverage is additional insurance.

2. Reasonable Repairs

a. We will pay the reasonable cost incurred by you for the necessary measures taken solely to protect covered property that is damaged by a Peril Insured Against from further damage.

SAMPLE

b. If the measures taken involve repair to other damaged property, we will only pay if that property is covered under this policy and the damage is caused by a Peril Insured Against. This coverage does not:

(1) Increase the limit of liability that applies to the covered property; or

(2) Relieve you of your duties, in case of a loss to covered property, described in **B.4.** under Section I – Conditions.

3. Trees, Shrubs And Other Plants

We cover trees, shrubs, plants or lawns, on the "residence premises", for loss caused by the following Perils Insured Against:

a. Fire or Lightning;

b. Explosion;

c. Riot or Civil Commotion;

d. Aircraft;

e. Vehicles not owned or operated by a resident of the "residence premises";

f. Vandalism or Malicious Mischief; or

g. Theft.

We will pay up to 5% of the limit of liability that applies to the dwelling for all trees, shrubs, plants or lawns. No more than $500 of this limit will be paid for any one tree, shrub or plant. We do not cover property grown for "business" purposes.

This coverage is additional insurance.

4. Fire Department Service Charge

We will pay up to $500 for your liability assumed by contract or agreement for fire department charges incurred when the fire department is called to save or protect covered property from a Peril Insured Against. We do not cover fire department service charges if the property is located within the limits of the city, municipality or protection district furnishing the fire department response.

This coverage is additional insurance. No deductible applies to this coverage.

5. Property Removed

We insure covered property against direct loss from any cause while being removed from a premises endangered by a Peril Insured Against and for no more than 30 days while removed.

This coverage does not change the limit of liability that applies to the property being removed.

6. Credit Card, Electronic Fund Transfer Card Or Access Device, Forgery And Counterfeit Money

a. We will pay up to $500 for:

(1) The legal obligation of an "insured" to pay because of the theft or unauthorized use of credit cards issued to or registered in an "insured's" name;

(2) Loss resulting from theft or unauthorized use of an electronic fund transfer card or access device used for deposit, withdrawal or transfer of funds, issued to or registered in an "insured's" name;

(3) Loss to an "insured" caused by forgery or alteration of any check or negotiable instrument; and

(4) Loss to an "insured" through acceptance in good faith of counterfeit United States or Canadian paper currency.

All loss resulting from a series of acts committed by any one person or in which any one person is concerned or implicated is considered to be one loss.

This coverage is additional insurance. No deductible applies to this coverage.

b. We do not cover:

(1) Use of a credit card, electronic fund transfer card or access device:

(a) By a resident of your household;

(b) By a person who has been entrusted with either type of card or access device; or

(c) If an "insured" has not complied with all terms and conditions under which the cards are issued or the devices accessed; or

(2) Loss arising out of "business" use or dishonesty of an "insured".

c. If the coverage in **a.** above applies, the following defense provisions also apply:

(1) We may investigate and settle any claim or suit that we decide is appropriate. Our duty to defend a claim or suit ends when the amount we pay for the loss equals our limit of liability.

(2) If a suit is brought against an "insured" for liability under **a.(1)** or **(2)** above, we will provide a defense at our expense by counsel of our choice.

(3) We have the option to defend at our expense an "insured" or an "insured's" bank against any suit for the enforcement of payment under **a.(3)** above.

SAMPLE

7. Loss Assessment

a. We will pay up to $1,000 for your share of loss assessment charged during the policy period against you, as owner or tenant of the "residence premises", by a corporation or association of property owners. The assessment must be made as a result of direct loss to property, owned by all members collectively, of the type that would be covered by this policy if owned by you, caused by a Peril Insured Against under Coverage **A**, other than:

(1) Earthquake; or

(2) Land shock waves or tremors before, during or after a volcanic eruption.

The limit of $1,000 is the most we will pay with respect to any one loss, regardless of the number of assessments. We will only apply one deductible, per unit, to the total amount of any one loss to the property described above, regardless of the number of assessments.

b. We do not cover assessments charged against you or a corporation or association of property owners by any governmental body.

c. Paragraph **P.** Policy Period under Section **I** – Conditions does not apply to this coverage.

This coverage is additional insurance.

8. Collapse

a. With respect to this Additional Coverage:

(1) Collapse means an abrupt falling down or caving in of a building or any part of a building with the result that the building or part of the building cannot be occupied for its current intended purpose.

(2) A building or any part of a building that is in danger of falling down or caving in is not considered to be in a state of collapse.

(3) A part of a building that is standing is not considered to be in a state of collapse even if it has separated from another part of the building.

(4) A building or any part of a building that is standing is not considered to be in a state of collapse even if it shows evidence of cracking, bulging, sagging, bending, leaning, settling, shrinkage or expansion.

b. We insure for direct physical loss to covered property involving collapse of a building or any part of a building if the collapse was caused by one or more of the following:

(1) The Perils Insured Against named under Coverage **C**;

(2) Decay that is hidden from view, unless the presence of such decay is known to an "insured" prior to collapse;

(3) Insect or vermin damage that is hidden from view, unless the presence of such damage is known to an "insured" prior to collapse;

(4) Weight of contents, equipment, animals or people;

(5) Weight of rain which collects on a roof; or

(6) Use of defective material or methods in construction, remodeling or renovation if the collapse occurs during the course of the construction, remodeling or renovation.

c. Loss to an awning, fence, patio, deck, pavement, swimming pool, underground pipe, flue, drain, cesspool, septic tank, foundation, retaining wall, bulkhead, pier, wharf or dock is not included under **b.(2)** through **(6)** above, unless the loss is a direct result of the collapse of a building or any part of a building.

d. This coverage does not increase the limit of liability that applies to the damaged covered property.

9. Glass Or Safety Glazing Material

a. We cover:

(1) The breakage of glass or safety glazing material which is part of a covered building, storm door or storm window;

(2) The breakage of glass or safety glazing material which is part of a covered building, storm door or storm window when caused directly by earth movement; and

(3) The direct physical loss to covered property caused solely by the pieces, fragments or splinters of broken glass or safety glazing material which is part of a building, storm door or storm window.

SAMPLE

b. This coverage does not include loss:

(1) To covered property which results because the glass or safety glazing material has been broken, except as provided in **a.(3)** above; or

(2) On the "residence premises" if the dwelling has been vacant for more than 60 consecutive days immediately before the loss, except when the breakage results directly from earth movement as provided in **a.(2)** above. A dwelling being constructed is not considered vacant.

c. This coverage does not increase the limit of liability that applies to the damaged property.

10. Landlord's Furnishings

We will pay up to $2,500 for your appliances, carpeting and other household furnishings, in each apartment on the "residence premises" regularly rented or held for rental to others by an "insured", for loss caused by a Peril Insured Against in Coverage **C**, other than Theft.

This limit is the most we will pay in any one loss regardless of the number of appliances, carpeting or other household furnishings involved in the loss.

This coverage does not increase the limit of liability applying to the damaged property.

11. Ordinance Or Law

a. You may use up to 10% of the limit of liability that applies to Coverage **A** for the increased costs you incur due to the enforcement of any ordinance or law which requires or regulates:

(1) The construction, demolition, remodeling, renovation or repair of that part of a covered building or other structure damaged by a Peril Insured Against;

(2) The demolition and reconstruction of the undamaged part of a covered building or other structure, when that building or other structure must be totally demolished because of damage by a Peril Insured Against to another part of that covered building or other structure; or

(3) The remodeling, removal or replacement of the portion of the undamaged part of a covered building or other structure necessary to complete the remodeling, repair or replacement of that part of the covered building or other structure damaged by a Peril Insured Against.

b. You may use all or part of this ordinance or law coverage to pay for the increased costs you incur to remove debris resulting from the construction, demolition, remodeling, renovation, repair or replacement of property as stated in **a.** above.

c. We do not cover:

(1) The loss in value to any covered building or other structure due to the requirements of any ordinance or law; or

(2) The costs to comply with any ordinance or law which requires any "insured" or others to test for, monitor, clean up, remove, contain, treat, detoxify or neutralize, or in any way respond to, or assess the effects of, pollutants in or on any covered building or other structure.

Pollutants means any solid, liquid, gaseous or thermal irritant or contaminant, including smoke, vapor, soot, fumes, acids, alkalis, chemicals and waste. Waste includes materials to be recycled, reconditioned or reclaimed.

This coverage is additional insurance.

12. Grave Markers

We will pay up to $5,000 for grave markers, including mausoleums, on or away from the "residence premises" for loss caused by a Peril Insured Against under Coverage **C**.

This coverage does not increase the limits of liability that apply to the damaged covered property.

SECTION I – PERILS INSURED AGAINST

A. Coverage A – Dwelling And Coverage B – Other Structures

1. We insure against risk of direct physical loss to property described in Coverages **A** and **B**.

2. We do not insure, however, for loss:

a. Excluded under Section I – Exclusions;

b. Involving collapse, except as provided in **E.8.** Collapse under Section I – Property Coverages; and

c. Caused by:

(1) Freezing of a plumbing, heating, air conditioning or automatic fire protective sprinkler system or of a household appliance, or by discharge, leakage or overflow from within the system or appliance caused by freezing. This provision does not apply if you have used reasonable care to:

(a) Maintain heat in the building; or

SAMPLE

(b) Shut off the water supply and drain all systems and appliances of water.

However, if the building is protected by an automatic fire protective sprinkler system, you must use reasonable care to continue the water supply and maintain heat in the building for coverage to apply.

For purposes of this provision a plumbing system or household appliance does not include a sump, sump pump or related equipment or a roof drain, gutter, downspout or similar fixtures or equipment;

(2) Freezing, thawing, pressure or weight of water or ice, whether driven by wind or not, to a:

    (a) Fence, pavement, patio or swimming pool;

    (b) Footing, foundation, bulkhead, wall, or any other structure or device that supports all or part of a building, or other structure;

    (c) Retaining wall or bulkhead that does not support all or part of a building or other structure; or

    (d) Pier, wharf or dock;

(3) Theft in or to a dwelling under construction, or of materials and supplies for use in the construction until the dwelling is finished and occupied;

(4) Vandalism and malicious mischief, and any ensuing loss caused by any intentional and wrongful act committed in the course of the vandalism or malicious mischief, if the dwelling has been vacant for more than 60 consecutive days immediately before the loss. A dwelling being constructed is not considered vacant;

(5) Mold, fungus or wet rot. However, we do insure for loss caused by mold, fungus or wet rot that is hidden within the walls or ceilings or beneath the floors or above the ceilings of a structure if such loss results from the accidental discharge or overflow of water or steam from within:

    (a) A plumbing, heating, air conditioning or automatic fire protective sprinkler system, or a household appliance, on the "residence premises"; or

    (b) A storm drain, or water, steam or sewer pipes, off the "residence premises".

For purposes of this provision, a plumbing system or household appliance does not include a sump, sump pump or related equipment or a roof drain, gutter, downspout or similar fixtures or equipment; or

(6) Any of the following:

    (a) Wear and tear, marring, deterioration;

    (b) Mechanical breakdown, latent defect, inherent vice, or any quality in property that causes it to damage or destroy itself;

    (c) Smog, rust or other corrosion, or dry rot;

    (d) Smoke from agricultural smudging or industrial operations;

    (e) Discharge, dispersal, seepage, migration, release or escape of pollutants unless the discharge, dispersal, seepage, migration, release or escape is itself caused by a Peril Insured Against named under Coverage **C**.

Pollutants means any solid, liquid, gaseous or thermal irritant or contaminant, including smoke, vapor, soot, fumes, acids, alkalis, chemicals and waste. Waste includes materials to be recycled, reconditioned or reclaimed;

    (f) Settling, shrinking, bulging or expansion, including resultant cracking, of bulkheads, pavements, patios, footings, foundations, walls, floors, roofs or ceilings;

    (g) Birds, vermin, rodents, or insects; or

    (h) Animals owned or kept by an "insured".

Exception To c.(6)

Unless the loss is otherwise excluded, we cover loss to property covered under Coverage **A** or **B** resulting from an accidental discharge or overflow of water or steam from within a:

(i) Storm drain, or water, steam or sewer pipe, off the "residence premises"; or

SAMPLE

(ii) Plumbing, heating, air conditioning or automatic fire protective sprinkler system or household appliance on the "residence premises". This includes the cost to tear out and replace any part of a building, or other structure, on the "residence premises", but only when necessary to repair the system or appliance. However, such tear out and replacement coverage only applies to other structures if the water or steam causes actual damage to a building on the "residence premises".

We do not cover loss to the system or appliance from which this water or steam escaped.

For purposes of this provision, a plumbing system or household appliance does not include a sump, sump pump or related equipment or a roof drain, gutter, down spout or similar fixtures or equipment.

Section I – Exclusion **A.3.** Water Damage, Paragraphs **a.** and **c.** that apply to surface water and water below the surface of the ground do not apply to loss by water covered under **c.(5)** and **(6)** above.

Under **2.b.** and **c.** above, any ensuing loss to property described in Coverages **A** and **B** not precluded by any other provision in this policy is covered.

B. Coverage C – Personal Property

We insure for direct physical loss to the property described in Coverage **C** caused by any of the following perils unless the loss is excluded in Section I – Exclusions.

1. Fire Or Lightning

2. Windstorm Or Hail

This peril includes loss to watercraft of all types and their trailers, furnishings, equipment, and outboard engines or motors, only while inside a fully enclosed building.

This peril does not include loss to the property contained in a building caused by rain, snow, sleet, sand or dust unless the direct force of wind or hail damages the building causing an opening in a roof or wall and the rain, snow, sleet, sand or dust enters through this opening.

3. Explosion

4. Riot Or Civil Commotion

5. Aircraft

This peril includes self-propelled missiles and spacecraft.

6. Vehicles

7. Smoke

This peril means sudden and accidental damage from smoke, including the emission or puffback of smoke, soot, fumes or vapors from a boiler, furnace or related equipment.

This peril does not include loss caused by smoke from agricultural smudging or industrial operations.

8. Vandalism Or Malicious Mischief

9. Theft

a. This peril includes attempted theft and loss of property from a known place when it is likely that the property has been stolen.

b. This peril does not include loss caused by theft:

(1) Committed by an "insured";

(2) In or to a dwelling under construction, or of materials and supplies for use in the construction until the dwelling is finished and occupied;

(3) From that part of a "residence premises" rented by an "insured" to someone other than another "insured"; or

(4) That occurs off the "residence premises" of:

(a) Trailers, semitrailers and campers;

(b) Watercraft of all types, and their furnishings, equipment and outboard engines or motors; or

(c) Property while at any other residence owned by, rented to, or occupied by an "insured", except while an "insured" is temporarily living there. Property of an "insured" who is a student is covered while at the residence the student occupies to attend school as long as the student has been there at any time during the 60 days immediately before the loss.

10. Falling Objects

This peril does not include loss to property contained in a building unless the roof or an outside wall of the building is first damaged by a falling object. Damage to the falling object itself is not included.

11. Weight Of Ice, Snow Or Sleet

This peril means weight of ice, snow or sleet which causes damage to property contained in a building.

HO 00 03 10 00

SAMPLE

12. Accidental Discharge Or Overflow Of Water Or Steam

   a. This peril means accidental discharge or overflow of water or steam from within a plumbing, heating, air conditioning or automatic fire protective sprinkler system or from within a household appliance.

   b. This peril does not include loss:

   (1) To the system or appliance from which the water or steam escaped;

   (2) Caused by or resulting from freezing except as provided in Peril Insured Against **14.** Freezing;

   (3) On the "residence premises" caused by accidental discharge or overflow which occurs off the "residence premises"; or

   (4) Caused by mold, fungus or wet rot unless hidden within the walls or ceilings or beneath the floors or above the ceilings of a structure.

   c. In this peril, a plumbing system or household appliance does not include a sump, sump pump or related equipment or a roof drain, gutter, downspout or similar fixtures or equipment.

   d. Section I – Exclusion **A.3.** Water Damage, Paragraphs **a.** and **c.** that apply to surface water and water below the surface of the ground do not apply to loss by water covered under this peril.

13. Sudden And Accidental Tearing Apart, Cracking, Burning Or Bulging

   This peril means sudden and accidental tearing apart, cracking, burning or bulging of a steam or hot water heating system, an air conditioning or automatic fire protective sprinkler system, or an appliance for heating water.

   We do not cover loss caused by or resulting from freezing under this peril.

14. Freezing

   a. This peril means freezing of a plumbing, heating, air conditioning or automatic fire protective sprinkler system or of a household appliance but only if you have used reasonable care to:

   (1) Maintain heat in the building; or

   (2) Shut off the water supply and drain all systems and appliances of water.

   However, if the building is protected by an automatic fire protective sprinkler system, you must use reasonable care to continue the water supply and maintain heat in the building for coverage to apply.

   b. In this peril, a plumbing system or household appliance does not include a sump, sump pump or related equipment or a roof drain, gutter, downspout or similar fixtures or equipment.

15. Sudden And Accidental Damage From Artificially Generated Electrical Current

   This peril does not include loss to tubes, transistors, electronic components or circuitry that are a part of appliances, fixtures, computers, home entertainment units or other types of electronic apparatus.

16. Volcanic Eruption

   This peril does not include loss caused by earthquake, land shock waves or tremors.

SECTION I – EXCLUSIONS

A. We do not insure for loss caused directly or indirectly by any of the following. Such loss is excluded regardless of any other cause or event contributing concurrently or in any sequence to the loss. These exclusions apply whether or not the loss event results in widespread damage or affects a substantial area.

   1. Ordinance Or Law

   Ordinance Or Law means any ordinance or law:

   a. Requiring or regulating the construction, demolition, remodeling, renovation or repair of property, including removal of any resulting debris. This Exclusion **A.1.a.** does not apply to the amount of coverage that may be provided for in **E.11.** Ordinance Or Law under Section I – Property Coverages;

   b. The requirements of which result in a loss in value to property; or

   c. Requiring any "insured" or others to test for, monitor, clean up, remove, contain, treat, detoxify or neutralize, or in any way respond to, or assess the effects of, pollutants.

   Pollutants means any solid, liquid, gaseous or thermal irritant or contaminant, including smoke, vapor, soot, fumes, acids, alkalis, chemicals and waste. Waste includes materials to be recycled, reconditioned or reclaimed.

   This Exclusion **1.** applies whether or not the property has been physically damaged.

   2. Earth Movement

   Earth Movement means:

   a. Earthquake, including land shock waves or tremors before, during or after a volcanic eruption;

SAMPLE

b. Landslide, mudslide or mudflow;

c. Subsidence or sinkhole; or

d. Any other earth movement including earth sinking, rising or shifting;

caused by or resulting from human or animal forces or any act of nature unless direct loss by fire or explosion ensues and then we will pay only for the ensuing loss.

This Exclusion **2.** does not apply to loss by theft.

3. **Water Damage**

Water Damage means:

a. Flood, surface water, waves, tidal water, overflow of a body of water, or spray from any of these, whether or not driven by wind;

b. Water or water-borne material which backs up through sewers or drains or which overflows or is discharged from a sump, sump pump or related equipment; or

c. Water or water-borne material below the surface of the ground, including water which exerts pressure on or seeps or leaks through a building, sidewalk, driveway, foundation, swimming pool or other structure;

caused by or resulting from human or animal forces or any act of nature.

Direct loss by fire, explosion or theft resulting from water damage is covered.

4. **Power Failure**

Power Failure means the failure of power or other utility service if the failure takes place off the "residence premises". But if the failure results in a loss, from a Peril Insured Against on the "residence premises", we will pay for the loss caused by that peril.

5. **Neglect**

Neglect means neglect of an "insured" to use all reasonable means to save and preserve property at and after the time of a loss.

6. **War**

War includes the following and any consequence of any of the following:

a. Undeclared war, civil war, insurrection, rebellion or revolution;

b. Warlike act by a military force or military personnel; or

c. Destruction, seizure or use for a military purpose.

Discharge of a nuclear weapon will be deemed a warlike act even if accidental.

7. **Nuclear Hazard**

This Exclusion **7.** pertains to Nuclear Hazard to the extent set forth in **M.** Nuclear Hazard Clause under Section **I** – Conditions.

8. **Intentional Loss**

Intentional Loss means any loss arising out of any act an "insured" commits or conspires to commit with the intent to cause a loss.

In the event of such loss, no "insured" is entitled to coverage, even "insureds" who did not commit or conspire to commit the act causing the loss.

9. **Governmental Action**

Governmental Action means the destruction, confiscation or seizure of property described in Coverage **A, B** or **C** by order of any governmental or public authority.

This exclusion does not apply to such acts ordered by any governmental or public authority that are taken at the time of a fire to prevent its spread, if the loss caused by fire would be covered under this policy.

B. We do not insure for loss to property described in Coverages **A** and **B** caused by any of the following. However, any ensuing loss to property described in Coverages **A** and **B** not precluded by any other provision in this policy is covered.

1. Weather conditions. However, this exclusion only applies if weather conditions contribute in any way with a cause or event excluded in **A.** above to produce the loss.

2. Acts or decisions, including the failure to act or decide, of any person, group, organization or governmental body.

3. Faulty, inadequate or defective:

a. Planning, zoning, development, surveying, siting;

b. Design, specifications, workmanship, repair, construction, renovation, remodeling, grading, compaction;

c. Materials used in repair, construction, renovation or remodeling; or

d. Maintenance;

of part or all of any property whether on or off the "residence premises".

HO 00 03 10 00

SAMPLE

SECTION I – CONDITIONS

A. Insurable Interest And Limit Of Liability

Even if more than one person has an insurable interest in the property covered, we will not be liable in any one loss:

1. To an "insured" for more than the amount of such "insured's" interest at the time of loss; or

2. For more than the applicable limit of liability.

B. Duties After Loss

In case of a loss to covered property, we have no duty to provide coverage under this policy if the failure to comply with the following duties is prejudicial to us. These duties must be performed either by you, an "insured" seeking coverage, or a representative of either:

1. Give prompt notice to us or our agent;

2. Notify the police in case of loss by theft;

3. Notify the credit card or electronic fund transfer card or access device company in case of loss as provided for in E.6. Credit Card, Electronic Fund Transfer Card Or Access Device, Forgery And Counterfeit Money under Section I – Property Coverages;

4. Protect the property from further damage. If repairs to the property are required, you must:

   a. Make reasonable and necessary repairs to protect the property; and

   b. Keep an accurate record of repair expenses;

5. Cooperate with us in the investigation of a claim;

6. Prepare an inventory of damaged personal property showing the quantity, description, actual cash value and amount of loss. Attach all bills, receipts and related documents that justify the figures in the inventory;

7. As often as we reasonably require:

   a. Show the damaged property;

   b. Provide us with records and documents we request and permit us to make copies; and

   c. Submit to examination under oath, while not in the presence of another "insured", and sign the same;

8. Send to us, within 60 days after our request, your signed, sworn proof of loss which sets forth, to the best of your knowledge and belief:

   a. The time and cause of loss;

   b. The interests of all "insureds" and all others in the property involved and all liens on the property;

   c. Other insurance which may cover the loss;

   d. Changes in title or occupancy of the property during the term of the policy;

   e. Specifications of damaged buildings and detailed repair estimates;

   f. The inventory of damaged personal property described in 6. above;

   g. Receipts for additional living expenses incurred and records that support the fair rental value loss; and

   h. Evidence or affidavit that supports a claim under E.6. Credit Card, Electronic Fund Transfer Card Or Access Device, Forgery And Counterfeit Money under Section I – Property Coverages, stating the amount and cause of loss.

C. Loss Settlement

In this Condition C., the terms "cost to repair or replace" and "replacement cost" do not include the increased costs incurred to comply with the enforcement of any ordinance or law, except to the extent that coverage for these increased costs is provided in E.11. Ordinance Or Law under Section I – Property Coverages. Covered property losses are settled as follows:

1. Property of the following types:

   a. Personal property;

   b. Awnings, carpeting, household appliances, outdoor antennas and outdoor equipment, whether or not attached to buildings;

   c. Structures that are not buildings; and

   d. Grave markers, including mausoleums;

   at actual cash value at the time of loss but not more than the amount required to repair or replace.

2. Buildings covered under Coverage A or B at replacement cost without deduction for depreciation, subject to the following:

   a. If, at the time of loss, the amount of insurance in this policy on the damaged building is 80% or more of the full replacement cost of the building immediately before the loss, we will pay the cost to repair or replace, after application of any deductible and without deduction for depreciation, but not more than the least of the following amounts:

      (1) The limit of liability under this policy that applies to the building;

      (2) The replacement cost of that part of the building damaged with material of like kind and quality and for like use; or

      (3) The necessary amount actually spent to repair or replace the damaged building.

SAMPLE

If the building is rebuilt at a new premises, the cost described in **(2)** above is limited to the cost which would have been incurred if the building had been built at the original premises.

b. If, at the time of loss, the amount of insurance in this policy on the damaged building is less than 80% of the full replacement cost of the building immediately before the loss, we will pay the greater of the following amounts, but not more than the limit of liability under this policy that applies to the building:

(1) The actual cash value of that part of the building damaged; or

(2) That proportion of the cost to repair or replace, after application of any deductible and without deduction for depreciation, that part of the building damaged, which the total amount of insurance in this policy on the damaged building bears to 80% of the replacement cost of the building.

c. To determine the amount of insurance required to equal 80% of the full replacement cost of the building immediately before the loss, do not include the value of:

(1) Excavations, footings, foundations, piers, or any other structures or devices that support all or part of the building, which are below the undersurface of the lowest basement floor;

(2) Those supports described in **(1)** above which are below the surface of the ground inside the foundation walls, if there is no basement; and

(3) Underground flues, pipes, wiring and drains.

d. We will pay no more than the actual cash value of the damage until actual repair or replacement is complete. Once actual repair or replacement is complete, we will settle the loss as noted in **2.a.** and **b.** above.

However, if the cost to repair or replace the damage is both:

(1) Less than 5% of the amount of insurance in this policy on the building; and

(2) Less than $2,500;

we will settle the loss as noted in **2.a.** and **b.** above whether or not actual repair or replacement is complete.

e. You may disregard the replacement cost loss settlement provisions and make claim under this policy for loss to buildings on an actual cash value basis. You may then make claim for any additional liability according to the provisions of this Condition **C.** Loss Settlement, provided you notify us of your intent to do so within 180 days after the date of loss.

D. Loss To A Pair Or Set

In case of loss to a pair or set we may elect to:

1. Repair or replace any part to restore the pair or set to its value before the loss; or

2. Pay the difference between actual cash value of the property before and after the loss.

E. Appraisal

If you and we fail to agree on the amount of loss, either may demand an appraisal of the loss. In this event, each party will choose a competent and impartial appraiser within 20 days after receiving a written request from the other. The two appraisers will choose an umpire. If they cannot agree upon an umpire within 15 days, you or we may request that the choice be made by a judge of a court of record in the state where the "residence premises" is located. The appraisers will separately set the amount of loss. If the appraisers submit a written report of an agreement to us, the amount agreed upon will be the amount of loss. If they fail to agree, they will submit their differences to the umpire. A decision agreed to by any two will set the amount of loss.

Each party will:

1. Pay its own appraiser; and

2. Bear the other expenses of the appraisal and umpire equally.

F. Other Insurance And Service Agreement

If a loss covered by this policy is also covered by:

1. Other insurance, we will pay only the proportion of the loss that the limit of liability that applies under this policy bears to the total amount of insurance covering the loss; or

2. A service agreement, this insurance is excess over any amounts payable under any such agreement. Service agreement means a service plan, property restoration plan, home warranty or other similar service warranty agreement, even if it is characterized as insurance.

G. Suit Against Us

No action can be brought against us unless there has been full compliance with all of the terms under Section **I** of this policy and the action is started within two years after the date of loss.

   HO 00 03 10 00

SAMPLE

H. Our Option

If we give you written notice within 30 days after we receive your signed, sworn proof of loss, we may repair or replace any part of the damaged property with material or property of like kind and quality.

I. Loss Payment

We will adjust all losses with you. We will pay you unless some other person is named in the policy or is legally entitled to receive payment. Loss will be payable 60 days after we receive your proof of loss and:

1. Reach an agreement with you;

2. There is an entry of a final judgment; or

3. There is a filing of an appraisal award with us.

J. Abandonment Of Property

We need not accept any property abandoned by an "insured".

K. Mortgage Clause

1. If a mortgagee is named in this policy, any loss payable under Coverage **A** or **B** will be paid to the mortgagee and you, as interests appear. If more than one mortgagee is named, the order of payment will be the same as the order of precedence of the mortgages.

2. If we deny your claim, that denial will not apply to a valid claim of the mortgagee, if the mortgagee:

    a. Notifies us of any change in ownership, occupancy or substantial change in risk of which the mortgagee is aware;

    b. Pays any premium due under this policy on demand if you have neglected to pay the premium; and

    c. Submits a signed, sworn statement of loss within 60 days after receiving notice from us of your failure to do so. Paragraphs **E.** Appraisal, **G.** Suit Against Us and **I.** Loss Payment under Section I – Conditions also apply to the mortgagee.

3. If we decide to cancel or not to renew this policy, the mortgagee will be notified at least 10 days before the date cancellation or nonrenewal takes effect.

4. If we pay the mortgagee for any loss and deny payment to you:

    a. We are subrogated to all the rights of the mortgagee granted under the mortgage on the property; or

    b. At our option, we may pay to the mortgagee the whole principal on the mortgage plus any accrued interest. In this event, we will receive a full assignment and transfer of the mortgage and all securities held as collateral to the mortgage debt.

5. Subrogation will not impair the right of the mortgagee to recover the full amount of the mortgagee's claim.

L. No Benefit To Bailee

We will not recognize any assignment or grant any coverage that benefits a person or organization holding, storing or moving property for a fee regardless of any other provision of this policy.

M. Nuclear Hazard Clause

1. "Nuclear Hazard" means any nuclear reaction, radiation, or radioactive contamination, all whether controlled or uncontrolled or however caused, or any consequence of any of these.

2. Loss caused by the nuclear hazard will not be considered loss caused by fire, explosion, or smoke, whether these perils are specifically named in or otherwise included within the Perils Insured Against.

3. This policy does not apply under Section I to loss caused directly or indirectly by nuclear hazard, except that direct loss by fire resulting from the nuclear hazard is covered.

N. Recovered Property

If you or we recover any property for which we have made payment under this policy, you or we will notify the other of the recovery. At your option, the property will be returned to or retained by you or it will become our property. If the recovered property is returned to or retained by you, the loss payment will be adjusted based on the amount you received for the recovered property.

O. Volcanic Eruption Period

One or more volcanic eruptions that occur within a 72 hour period will be considered as one volcanic eruption.

P. Policy Period

This policy applies only to loss which occurs during the policy period.

Q. Concealment Or Fraud

We provide coverage to no "insureds" under this policy if, whether before or after a loss, an "insured" has:

1. Intentionally concealed or misrepresented any material fact or circumstance;

SAMPLE

2. Engaged in fraudulent conduct; or

3. Made false statements;

relating to this insurance.

R. Loss Payable Clause

If the Declarations show a loss payee for certain listed insured personal property, the definition of "insured" is changed to include that loss payee with respect to that property.

If we decide to cancel or not renew this policy, that loss payee will be notified in writing.

SECTION II – LIABILITY COVERAGES

A. Coverage E – Personal Liability

If a claim is made or a suit is brought against an "insured" for damages because of "bodily injury" or "property damage" caused by an "occurrence" to which this coverage applies, we will:

1. Pay up to our limit of liability for the damages for which an "insured" is legally liable. Damages include prejudgment interest awarded against an "insured"; and

2. Provide a defense at our expense by counsel of our choice, even if the suit is groundless, false or fraudulent. We may investigate and settle any claim or suit that we decide is appropriate. Our duty to settle or defend ends when our limit of liability for the "occurrence" has been exhausted by payment of a judgment or settlement.

B. Coverage F – Medical Payments To Others

We will pay the necessary medical expenses that are incurred or medically ascertained within three years from the date of an accident causing "bodily injury". Medical expenses means reasonable charges for medical, surgical, x-ray, dental, ambulance, hospital, professional nursing, prosthetic devices and funeral services. This coverage does not apply to you or regular residents of your household except "residence employees". As to others, this coverage applies only:

1. To a person on the "insured location" with the permission of an "insured"; or

2. To a person off the "insured location", if the "bodily injury":

a. Arises out of a condition on the "insured location" or the ways immediately adjoining;

b. Is caused by the activities of an "insured";

c. Is caused by a "residence employee" in the course of the "residence employee's" employment by an "insured"; or

d. Is caused by an animal owned by or in the care of an "insured".

SECTION II – EXCLUSIONS

A. "Motor Vehicle Liability"

1. Coverages **E** and **F** do not apply to any "motor vehicle liability" if, at the time and place of an "occurrence", the involved "motor vehicle":

a. Is registered for use on public roads or property;

b. Is not registered for use on public roads or property, but such registration is required by a law, or regulation issued by a government agency, for it to be used at the place of the "occurrence"; or

c. Is being:

(1) Operated in, or practicing for, any prearranged or organized race, speed contest or other competition;

(2) Rented to others;

(3) Used to carry persons or cargo for a charge; or

(4) Used for any "business" purpose except for a motorized golf cart while on a golfing facility.

2. If Exclusion **A.1.** does not apply, there is still no coverage for "motor vehicle liability" unless the "motor vehicle" is:

a. In dead storage on an "insured location";

b. Used solely to service an "insured's" residence;

c. Designed to assist the handicapped and, at the time of an "occurrence", it is:

(1) Being used to assist a handicapped person; or

(2) Parked on an "insured location";

d. Designed for recreational use off public roads and:

(1) Not owned by an "insured"; or

(2) Owned by an "insured" provided the "occurrence" takes place on an "insured location" as defined in Definitions **B. 6.a., b., d., e.** or **h.**; or

e. A motorized golf cart that is owned by an "insured", designed to carry up to 4 persons, not built or modified after manufacture to exceed a speed of 25 miles per hour on level ground and, at the time of an "occurrence", is within the legal boundaries of:

(1) A golfing facility and is parked or stored there, or being used by an "insured" to:

(a) Play the game of golf or for other recreational or leisure activity allowed by the facility;

Copyright, Insurance Services Office, Inc., 1999   HO 00 03 10 00

SAMPLE

(b) Travel to or from an area where "motor vehicles" or golf carts are parked or stored; or

(c) Cross public roads at designated points to access other parts of the golfing facility; or

(2) A private residential community, including its public roads upon which a motorized golf cart can legally travel, which is subject to the authority of a property owners association and contains an "insured's" residence.

B. "Watercraft Liability"

1. Coverages **E** and **F** do not apply to any "watercraft liability" if, at the time of an "occurrence", the involved watercraft is being:

   a. Operated in, or practicing for, any prearranged or organized race, speed contest or other competition. This exclusion does not apply to a sailing vessel or a predicted log cruise;

   b. Rented to others;

   c. Used to carry persons or cargo for a charge; or

   d. Used for any "business" purpose.

2. If Exclusion **B.1.** does not apply, there is still no coverage for "watercraft liability" unless, at the time of the "occurrence", the watercraft:

   a. Is stored;

   b. Is a sailing vessel, with or without auxiliary power that is:

      (1) Less than 26 feet in overall length; or

      (2) 26 feet or more in overall length and not owned by or rented to an "insured"; or

   c. Is not a sailing vessel and is powered by:

      (1) An inboard or inboard-outdrive engine or motor, including those that power a water jet pump, of:

         (a) 50 horsepower or less and not owned by an "insured"; or

         (b) More than 50 horsepower and not owned by or rented to an "insured"; or

      (2) One or more outboard engines or motors with:

         (a) 25 total horsepower or less;

         (b) More than 25 horsepower if the outboard engine or motor is not owned by an "insured";

         (c) More than 25 horsepower if the outboard engine or motor is owned by an "insured" who acquired it during the policy period; or

      (d) More than 25 horsepower if the outboard engine or motor is owned by an "insured" who acquired it before the policy period, but only if:

         (i) You declare them at policy inception; or

         (ii) Your intent to insure them is reported to us in writing within 45 days after you acquire them.

      The coverages in **(c)** and **(d)** above apply for the policy period.

      Horsepower means the maximum power rating assigned to the engine or motor by the manufacturer.

C. "Aircraft Liability"

This policy does not cover "aircraft liability".

D. "Hovercraft Liability"

This policy does not cover "hovercraft liability".

E. Coverage E – Personal Liability And Coverage F – Medical Payments To Others

Coverages **E** and **F** do not apply to the following:

1. **Expected Or Intended Injury**

   "Bodily injury" or "property damage" which is expected or intended by an "insured" even if the resulting "bodily injury" or "property damage":

   a. Is of a different kind, quality or degree than initially expected or intended; or

   b. Is sustained by a different person, entity, real or personal property, than initially expected or intended.

   However, this Exclusion **E.1.** does not apply to "bodily injury" resulting from the use of reasonable force by an "insured" to protect persons or property;

2. **"Business"**

   a. "Bodily injury" or "property damage" arising out of or in connection with a "business" conducted from an "insured location" or engaged in by an "insured", whether or not the "business" is owned or operated by an "insured" or employs an "insured".

   This Exclusion **E.2.** applies but is not limited to an act or omission, regardless of its nature or circumstance, involving a service or duty rendered, promised, owed, or implied to be provided because of the nature of the "business".

   b. This Exclusion **E.2.** does not apply to:

      (1) The rental or holding for rental of an "insured location";

SAMPLE

(a) On an occasional basis if used only as a residence;

(b) In part for use only as a residence, unless a single family unit is intended for use by the occupying family to lodge more than two roomers or boarders; or

(c) In part, as an office, school, studio or private garage; and

(2) An "insured" under the age of 21 years involved in a part-time or occasional, self-employed "business" with no employees;

3. Professional Services

"Bodily injury" or "property damage" arising out of the rendering of or failure to render professional services;

4. "Insured's" Premises Not An "Insured Location"

"Bodily injury" or "property damage" arising out of a premises:

a. Owned by an "insured";

b. Rented to an "insured"; or

c. Rented to others by an "insured";

that is not an "insured location";

5. War

"Bodily injury" or "property damage" caused directly or indirectly by war, including the following and any consequence of any of the following:

a. Undeclared war, civil war, insurrection, rebellion or revolution;

b. Warlike act by a military force or military personnel; or

c. Destruction, seizure or use for a military purpose.

Discharge of a nuclear weapon will be deemed a warlike act even if accidental;

6. Communicable Disease

"Bodily injury" or "property damage" which arises out of the transmission of a communicable disease by an "insured";

7. Sexual Molestation, Corporal Punishment Or Physical Or Mental Abuse

"Bodily injury" or "property damage" arising out of sexual molestation, corporal punishment or physical or mental abuse; or

8. Controlled Substance

"Bodily injury" or "property damage" arising out of the use, sale, manufacture, delivery, transfer or possession by any person of a Controlled Substance as defined by the Federal Food and Drug Law at 21 U.S.C.A. Sections 811 and 812. Controlled Substances include but are not limited to cocaine, LSD, marijuana and all narcotic drugs. However, this exclusion does not apply to the legitimate use of prescription drugs by a person following the orders of a licensed physician.

Exclusions **A.** "Motor Vehicle Liability", **B.** "Watercraft Liability", **C.** "Aircraft Liability", **D.** "Hovercraft Liability", and **E.4.** "Insured's" Premises Not An "Insured Location" do not apply to "bodily injury" to a "residence employee" arising out of and in the course of the "residence employee's" employment by an "insured".

F. Coverage E – Personal Liability

Coverage **E** does not apply to:

1. Liability:

a. For any loss assessment charged against you as a member of an association, corporation or community of property owners, except as provided in **D.** Loss Assessment under Section II – Additional Coverages;

b. Under any contract or agreement entered into by an "insured". However, this exclusion does not apply to written contracts:

(1) That directly relate to the ownership, maintenance or use of an "insured location"; or

(2) Where the liability of others is assumed by you prior to an "occurrence";

unless excluded in **a.** above or elsewhere in this policy;

2. "Property damage" to property owned by an "insured". This includes costs or expenses incurred by an "insured" or others to repair, replace, enhance, restore or maintain such property to prevent injury to a person or damage to property of others, whether on or away from an "insured location";

3. "Property damage" to property rented to, occupied or used by or in the care of an "insured". This exclusion does not apply to "property damage" caused by fire, smoke or explosion;

4. "Bodily injury" to any person eligible to receive any benefits voluntarily provided or required to be provided by an "insured" under any:

a. Workers' compensation law;

 HO 00 03 10 00

SAMPLE

b. Non-occupational disability law; or

c. Occupational disease law;

5. "Bodily injury" or "property damage" for which an "insured" under this policy:

  a. Is also an insured under a nuclear energy liability policy issued by the:

  (1) Nuclear Energy Liability Insurance Association;

  (2) Mutual Atomic Energy Liability Underwriters;

  (3) Nuclear Insurance Association of Canada;

  or any of their successors; or

  b. Would be an insured under such a policy but for the exhaustion of its limit of liability; or

6. "Bodily injury" to you or an "insured" as defined under Definitions **5.a.** or **b.**

  This exclusion also applies to any claim made or suit brought against you or an "insured":

  (1) To repay; or

  (2) Share damages with;

  another person who may be obligated to pay damages because of "bodily injury" to an "insured".

G. Coverage F – Medical Payments To Others

Coverage **F** does not apply to "bodily injury":

1. To a "residence employee" if the "bodily injury":

  a. Occurs off the "insured location"; and

  b. Does not arise out of or in the course of the "residence employee's" employment by an "insured";

2. To any person eligible to receive benefits voluntarily provided or required to be provided under any:

  a. Workers' compensation law;

  b. Non-occupational disability law; or

  c. Occupational disease law;

3. From any:

  a. Nuclear reaction;

  b. Nuclear radiation; or

  c. Radioactive contamination;

  all whether controlled or uncontrolled or however caused; or

  d. Any consequence of any of these; or

4. To any person, other than a "residence employee" of an "insured", regularly residing on any part of the "insured location".

SECTION II – ADDITIONAL COVERAGES

We cover the following in addition to the limits of liability:

A. Claim Expenses

We pay:

1. Expenses we incur and costs taxed against an "insured" in any suit we defend;

2. Premiums on bonds required in a suit we defend, but not for bond amounts more than the Coverage **E** limit of liability. We need not apply for or furnish any bond;

3. Reasonable expenses incurred by an "insured" at our request, including actual loss of earnings (but not loss of other income) up to $250 per day, for assisting us in the investigation or defense of a claim or suit; and

4. Interest on the entire judgment which accrues after entry of the judgment and before we pay or tender, or deposit in court that part of the judgment which does not exceed the limit of liability that applies.

B. First Aid Expenses

We will pay expenses for first aid to others incurred by an "insured" for "bodily injury" covered under this policy. We will not pay for first aid to an "insured".

C. Damage To Property Of Others

1. We will pay, at replacement cost, up to $1,000 per "occurrence" for "property damage" to property of others caused by an "insured".

2. We will not pay for "property damage":

  a. To the extent of any amount recoverable under Section **I**;

  b. Caused intentionally by an "insured" who is 13 years of age or older;

  c. To property owned by an "insured";

  d. To property owned by or rented to a tenant of an "insured" or a resident in your household; or

  e. Arising out of:

  (1) A "business" engaged in by an "insured";

  (2) Any act or omission in connection with a premises owned, rented or controlled by an "insured", other than the "insured location"; or

  (3) The ownership, maintenance, occupancy, operation, use, loading or unloading of aircraft, hovercraft, watercraft or "motor vehicles".

SAMPLE

This exclusion **e.(3)** does not apply to a "motor vehicle" that:

   (a) Is designed for recreational use off public roads;

   (b) Is not owned by an "insured"; and

   (c) At the time of the "occurrence", is not required by law, or regulation issued by a government agency, to have been registered for it to be used on public roads or property.

D. Loss Assessment

1. We will pay up to $1,000 for your share of loss assessment charged against you, as owner or tenant of the "residence premises", during the policy period by a corporation or association of property owners, when the assessment is made as a result of:

   a. "Bodily injury" or "property damage" not excluded from coverage under Section II – Exclusions; or

   b. Liability for an act of a director, officer or trustee in the capacity as a director, officer or trustee, provided such person:

     (1) Is elected by the members of a corporation or association of property owners; and

     (2) Serves without deriving any income from the exercise of duties which are solely on behalf of a corporation or association of property owners.

2. Paragraph I. Policy Period under Section II – Conditions does not apply to this Loss Assessment Coverage.

3. Regardless of the number of assessments, the limit of $1,000 is the most we will pay for loss arising out of:

   a. One accident, including continuous or repeated exposure to substantially the same general harmful condition; or

   b. A covered act of a director, officer or trustee. An act involving more than one director, officer or trustee is considered to be a single act.

4. We do not cover assessments charged against you or a corporation or association of property owners by any governmental body.

SECTION II – CONDITIONS

A. Limit Of Liability

Our total liability under Coverage **E** for all damages resulting from any one "occurrence" will not be more than the Coverage **E** limit of liability shown in the Declarations. This limit is the same regardless of the number of "insureds", claims made or persons injured. All "bodily injury" and "property damage" resulting from any one accident or from continuous or repeated exposure to substantially the same general harmful conditions shall be considered to be the result of one "occurrence".

Our total liability under Coverage **F** for all medical expense payable for "bodily injury" to one person as the result of one accident will not be more than the Coverage **F** limit of liability shown in the Declarations.

B. Severability Of Insurance

This insurance applies separately to each "insured". This condition will not increase our limit of liability for any one "occurrence".

C. Duties After "Occurrence"

In case of an "occurrence", you or another "insured" will perform the following duties that apply. We have no duty to provide coverage under this policy if your failure to comply with the following duties is prejudicial to us. You will help us by seeing that these duties are performed:

1. Give written notice to us or our agent as soon as is practical, which sets forth:

   a. The identity of the policy and the "named insured" shown in the Declarations;

   b. Reasonably available information on the time, place and circumstances of the "occurrence"; and

   c. Names and addresses of any claimants and witnesses;

2. Cooperate with us in the investigation, settlement or defense of any claim or suit;

3. Promptly forward to us every notice, demand, summons or other process relating to the "occurrence";

4. At our request, help us:

   a. To make settlement;

   b. To enforce any right of contribution or indemnity against any person or organization who may be liable to an "insured";

c. With the conduct of suits and attend hearings and trials; and

d. To secure and give evidence and obtain the attendance of witnesses;

5. With respect to **C.** Damage To Property Of Others under Section **II** – Additional Coverages, submit to us within 60 days after the loss, a sworn statement of loss and show the damaged property, if in an "insured's" control;

6. No "insured" shall, except at such "insured's" own cost, voluntarily make payment, assume obligation or incur expense other than for first aid to others at the time of the "bodily injury".

D. Duties Of An Injured Person – Coverage F – Medical Payments To Others

1. The injured person or someone acting for the injured person will:

a. Give us written proof of claim, under oath if required, as soon as is practical; and

b. Authorize us to obtain copies of medical reports and records.

2. The injured person will submit to a physical exam by a doctor of our choice when and as often as we reasonably require.

E. Payment Of Claim – Coverage F – Medical Payments To Others

Payment under this coverage is not an admission of liability by an "insured" or us.

F. Suit Against Us

1. No action can be brought against us unless there has been full compliance with all of the terms under this Section **II.**

2. No one will have the right to join us as a party to any action against an "insured".

3. Also, no action with respect to Coverage **E** can be brought against us until the obligation of such "insured" has been determined by final judgment or agreement signed by us.

G. Bankruptcy Of An "Insured"

Bankruptcy or insolvency of an "insured" will not relieve us of our obligations under this policy.

H. Other Insurance

This insurance is excess over other valid and collectible insurance except insurance written specifically to cover as excess over the limits of liability that apply in this policy.

I. Policy Period

This policy applies only to "bodily injury" or "property damage" which occurs during the policy period.

J. Concealment Or Fraud

We do not provide coverage to an "insured" who, whether before or after a loss, has:

1. Intentionally concealed or misrepresented any material fact or circumstance;

2. Engaged in fraudulent conduct; or

3. Made false statements;

relating to this insurance.

SECTIONS I AND II – CONDITIONS

A. Liberalization Clause

If we make a change which broadens coverage under this edition of our policy without additional premium charge, that change will automatically apply to your insurance as of the date we implement the change in your state, provided that this implementation date falls within 60 days prior to or during the policy period stated in the Declarations.

This Liberalization Clause does not apply to changes implemented with a general program revision that includes both broadenings and restrictions in coverage, whether that general program revision is implemented through introduction of:

1. A subsequent edition of this policy; or

2. An amendatory endorsement.

B. Waiver Or Change Of Policy Provisions

A waiver or change of a provision of this policy must be in writing by us to be valid. Our request for an appraisal or examination will not waive any of our rights.

C. Cancellation

1. You may cancel this policy at any time by returning it to us or by letting us know in writing of the date cancellation is to take effect.

2. We may cancel this policy only for the reasons stated below by letting you know in writing of the date cancellation takes effect. This cancellation notice may be delivered to you, or mailed to you at your mailing address shown in the Declarations. Proof of mailing will be sufficient proof of notice.

a. When you have not paid the premium, we may cancel at any time by letting you know at least 10 days before the date cancellation takes effect.

b. When this policy has been in effect for less than 60 days and is not a renewal with us, we may cancel for any reason by letting you know at least 10 days before the date cancellation takes effect.

SAMPLE

c. When this policy has been in effect for 60 days or more, or at any time if it is a renewal with us, we may cancel:

   (1) If there has been a material misrepresentation of fact which if known to us would have caused us not to issue the policy; or

   (2) If the risk has changed substantially since the policy was issued.

   This can be done by letting you know at least 30 days before the date cancellation takes effect.

d. When this policy is written for a period of more than one year, we may cancel for any reason at anniversary by letting you know at least 30 days before the date cancellation takes effect.

3. When this policy is canceled, the premium for the period from the date of cancellation to the expiration date will be refunded pro rata.

4. If the return premium is not refunded with the notice of cancellation or when this policy is returned to us, we will refund it within a reasonable time after the date cancellation takes effect.

D. Nonrenewal

We may elect not to renew this policy. We may do so by delivering to you, or mailing to you at your mailing address shown in the Declarations, written notice at least 30 days before the expiration date of this policy. Proof of mailing will be sufficient proof of notice.

E. Assignment

Assignment of this policy will not be valid unless we give our written consent.

F. Subrogation

An "insured" may waive in writing before a loss all rights of recovery against any person. If not waived, we may require an assignment of rights of recovery for a loss to the extent that payment is made by us.

If an assignment is sought, an "insured" must sign and deliver all related papers and cooperate with us.

Subrogation does not apply to Coverage **F** or Paragraph **C.** Damage To Property Of Others under Section **II** – Additional Coverages.

G. Death

If any person named in the Declarations or the spouse, if a resident of the same household, dies, the following apply:

1. We insure the legal representative of the deceased but only with respect to the premises and property of the deceased covered under the policy at the time of death; and

2. "Insured" includes:

   a. An "insured" who is a member of your household at the time of your death, but only while a resident of the "residence premises"; and

   b. With respect to your property, the person having proper temporary custody of the property until appointment and qualification of a legal representative.

PERSONAL AUTO POLICY

Personal Auto Policy Declarations

POLICYHOLDER:
(Named Insured)
Chris and Karen Swift
8110 lake Street
Lincoln, Nebraska 68506

POLICY NUMBER: 296 S 468211

POLICY PERIOD: **FROM:**   June 25, 2004
TO: December 25, 2004

But only if the required premium for this period has been paid, and for six-month renewal periods if renewal premiums are paid as required. Each period begins and ends at 12:01 A.M. standard time at the address of the policy-holder.

INSURED VEHICLES AND
SCHEDULE OF COVERAGES

VEHICLE	COVERAGES	LIMITS OF INSURANCE	PREMIUM
1	1999 Toyota Corolla	ID #JT2AL21E8B3306553	
	Coverage A—Liability:		
	Bodily Injury Liability	$100,000 **Each Person**	$ 72.00
		$300,000 **Each Accident**	
	Property Damage Liability	$ 50,000 **Each Accident**	$ 30.00
	Coverage B—Medical Payments	$ 5,000 **Each Person**	$ 18.00
	Coverage C—Uninsured Motorists:		
	Bodily Injury	$100,000 **Each Person**	$ 30.00
		$300,000 **Each Accident**	
		TOTAL	$150.00
2	2003 Ford Taurus	ID #1FABP3OU7GG212619	
	Coverage A—Liability:		
	Bodily Injury Liability	$100,000 **Each Person**	$ 72.00
		$300,000 **Each Accident**	
	Property Damage Liability	$ 50,000 **Each Accident**	$ 30.00
	Coverage B—Medical Payments	$ 5,000 **Each Person**	$ 18.00
	Coverage C—Uninsured Motorists:		
	Bodily Injury	$100,000 **Each Person**	$ 30.00
		$300,000 **Each Accident**	
	Coverage D—Other Than Collision	**Actual Cash Value Less** $250	$ 20.00
	—Collision	**Actual Cash Value Less** $500	$115.00
		TOTAL	$285.00

POLICY FORM AND ENDORSEMENTS: PP 00 01 06 98
COUNTERSIGNATURE DATE: June 1, 2004
AGENT: I.M. Abel

SAMPLE

PERSONAL AUTO POLICY
AGREEMENT

In return for payment of the premium and subject to all the terms of this policy, we agree with you as follows:

DEFINITIONS

A. Throughout this policy, "you" and "your" refer to:

1. The "named insured" shown in the Declarations; and

2. The spouse if a resident of the same household.

If the spouse ceases to be a resident of the same household during the policy period or prior to the inception of this policy, the spouse will be considered "you" and "your" under this policy but only until the earlier of:

1. The end of 90 days following the spouse's change of residency;

2. The effective date of another policy listing the spouse as a named insured; or

3. The end of the policy period.

B. "We", "us" and "our" refer to the Company providing this insurance.

C. For purposes of this policy, a private passenger type auto, pickup or van shall be deemed to be owned by a person if leased:

1. Under a written agreement to that person; and

2. For a continuous period of at least 6 months.

Other words and phrases are defined. They are in quotation marks when used.

D. "Bodily injury" means bodily harm, sickness or disease, including death that results.

E. "Business" includes trade, profession or occupation.

F. "Family member" means a person related to you by blood, marriage or adoption who is a resident of your household. This includes a ward or foster child.

G. "Occupying" means in, upon, getting in, on, out or off.

H. "Property damage" means physical injury to, destruction of or loss of use of tangible property.

I. "Trailer" means a vehicle designed to be pulled by a:

1. Private passenger auto; or

2. Pickup or van.

It also means a farm wagon or farm implement while towed by a vehicle listed in **1.** or **2.** above.

J. "Your covered auto" means:

1. Any vehicle shown in the Declarations.

2. A "newly acquired auto".

3. Any "trailer" you own.

4. Any auto or "trailer" you do not own while used as a temporary substitute for any other vehicle described in this definition which is out of normal use because of its:

   a. Breakdown;

   b. Repair;

   c. Servicing;

   d. Loss; or

   e. Destruction.

   This Provision (**J.4.**) does not apply to Coverage For Damage To Your Auto.

K. "Newly acquired auto":

1. "Newly acquired auto" means any of the following types of vehicles you become the owner of during the policy period:

   a. A private passenger auto; or

   b. A pickup or van, for which no other insurance policy provides coverage, that:

      (1) Has a Gross Vehicle Weight of less than 10,000 lbs.; and

      (2) Is not used for the delivery or transportation of goods and materials unless such use is:

         (a) Incidental to your "business" of installing, maintaining or repairing furnishings or equipment; or

         (b) For farming or ranching.

2. Coverage for a "newly acquired auto" is provided as described below. If you ask us to insure a "newly acquired auto" after a specified time period described below has elapsed, any coverage we provide for a "newly acquired auto" will begin at the time you request the coverage.

   a. For any coverage provided in this policy except Coverage For Damage To Your Auto, a "newly acquired auto" will have the broadest coverage we now provide for any vehicle shown in the Declarations. Coverage begins on the date you become the owner. However, for this coverage to apply to a "newly acquired auto" which is in addition to any vehicle shown in the Declarations, you must ask us to insure it within 14 days after you become the owner.

SAMPLE

If a "newly acquired auto" replaces a vehicle shown in the Declarations, coverage is provided for this vehicle without your having to ask us to insure it.

b. Collision Coverage for a "newly acquired auto" begins on the date you become the owner. However, for this coverage to apply, you must ask us to insure it within:

(1) 14 days after you become the owner if the Declarations indicate that Collision Coverage applies to at least one auto. In this case, the "newly acquired auto" will have the broadest coverage we now provide for any auto shown in the Declarations.

(2) Four days after you become the owner if the Declarations do not indicate that Collision Coverage applies to at least one auto. If you comply with the 4 day requirement and a loss occurred before you asked us to insure the "newly acquired auto", a Collision deductible of $500 will apply.

c. Other Than Collision Coverage for a "newly acquired auto" begins on the date you become the owner. However, for this coverage to apply, you must ask us to insure it within:

(1) 14 days after you become the owner if the Declarations indicate that Other Than Collision Coverage applies to at least one auto. In this case, the "newly acquired auto" will have the broadest coverage we now provide for any auto shown in the Declarations.

(2) Four days after you become the owner if the Declarations do not indicate that Other Than Collision Coverage applies to at least one auto. If you comply with the 4 day requirement and a loss occurred before you asked us to insure the "newly acquired auto", an Other Than Collision deductible of $500 will apply.

PART A – LIABILITY COVERAGE

INSURING AGREEMENT

A. We will pay damages for "bodily injury" or "property damage" for which any "insured" becomes legally responsible because of an auto accident. Damages include prejudgment interest awarded against the "insured". We will settle or defend, as we consider appropriate, any claim or suit asking for these damages. In addition to our limit of liability, we will pay all defense costs we incur. Our duty to settle or defend ends when our limit of liability for this coverage has been exhausted by payment of judgments or settlements. We have no duty to defend any suit or settle any claim for "bodily injury" or "property damage" not covered under this policy.

B. "Insured" as used in this Part means:

1. You or any "family member" for the ownership, maintenance or use of any auto or "trailer".

2. Any person using "your covered auto".

3. For "your covered auto", any person or organization but only with respect to legal responsibility for acts or omissions of a person for whom coverage is afforded under this Part.

4. For any auto or "trailer", other than "your covered auto", any other person or organization but only with respect to legal responsibility for acts or omissions of you or any "family member" for whom coverage is afforded under this Part. This Provision **(B.4.)** applies only if the person or organization does not own or hire the auto or "trailer".

SUPPLEMENTARY PAYMENTS

In addition to our limit of liability, we will pay on behalf of an "insured":

1. Up to $250 for the cost of bail bonds required because of an accident, including related traffic law violations. The accident must result in "bodily injury" or "property damage" covered under this policy.

2. Premiums on appeal bonds and bonds to release attachments in any suit we defend.

3. Interest accruing after a judgment is entered in any suit we defend. Our duty to pay interest ends when we offer to pay that part of the judgment which does not exceed our limit of liability for this coverage.

4. Up to $200 a day for loss of earnings, but not other income, because of attendance at hearings or trials at our request.

5. Other reasonable expenses incurred at our request.

EXCLUSIONS

A. We do not provide Liability Coverage for any "insured":

1. Who intentionally causes "bodily injury" or "property damage".

2. For "property damage" to property owned or being transported by that "insured".

Copyright, Insurance Services Office, Inc., 1997   **PP 00 01 06 98**

SAMPLE

3. For "property damage" to property:

   a. Rented to;

   b. Used by; or

   c. In the care of;

   that "insured".

   This Exclusion (A.3.) does not apply to "property damage" to a residence or private garage.

4. For "bodily injury" to an employee of that "insured" during the course of employment. This Exclusion (A.4.) does not apply to "bodily injury" to a domestic employee unless workers' compensation benefits are required or available for that domestic employee.

5. For that "insured's" liability arising out of the ownership or operation of a vehicle while it is being used as a public or livery conveyance. This Exclusion (A.5.) does not apply to a share-the-expense car pool.

6. While employed or otherwise engaged in the "business" of:

   a. Selling;

   b. Repairing;

   c. Servicing;

   d. Storing; or

   e. Parking;

   vehicles designed for use mainly on public highways. This includes road testing and delivery. This Exclusion (A.6.) does not apply to the ownership, maintenance or use of "your covered auto" by:

   a. You;

   b. Any "family member"; or

   c. Any partner, agent or employee of you or any "family member".

7. Maintaining or using any vehicle while that "insured" is employed or otherwise engaged in any "business" (other than farming or ranching) not described in Exclusion A.6.

   This Exclusion (A.7.) does not apply to the maintenance or use of a:

   a. Private passenger auto;

   b. Pickup or van; or

   c. "Trailer" used with a vehicle described in a. or b. above.

8. Using a vehicle without a reasonable belief that that "insured" is entitled to do so. This Exclusion (A.8.) does not apply to a "family member" using "your covered auto" which is owned by you.

9. For "bodily injury" or "property damage" for which that "insured":

   a. Is an insured under a nuclear energy liability policy; or

   b. Would be an insured under a nuclear energy liability policy but for its termination upon exhaustion of its limit of liability.

   A nuclear energy liability policy is a policy issued by any of the following or their successors:

   a. Nuclear Energy Liability Insurance Association;

   b. Mutual Atomic Energy Liability Underwriters; or

   c. Nuclear Insurance Association of Canada.

B. We do not provide Liability Coverage for the ownership, maintenance or use of:

1. Any vehicle which:

   a. Has fewer than four wheels; or

   b. Is designed mainly for use off public roads.

   This Exclusion (B.1.) does not apply:

   a. While such vehicle is being used by an "insured" in a medical emergency;

   b. To any "trailer"; or

   c. To any non-owned golf cart.

2. Any vehicle, other than "your covered auto", which is:

   a. Owned by you; or

   b. Furnished or available for your regular use.

3. Any vehicle, other than "your covered auto", which is:

   a. Owned by any "family member"; or

   b. Furnished or available for the regular use of any "family member".

   However, this Exclusion (B.3.) does not apply to you while you are maintaining or "occupying" any vehicle which is:

   a. Owned by a "family member"; or

   b. Furnished or available for the regular use of a "family member".

4. Any vehicle, located inside a facility designed for racing, for the purpose of:

   a. Competing in; or

   b. Practicing or preparing for;

   any prearranged or organized racing or speed contest.

SAMPLE

LIMIT OF LIABILITY

A. The limit of liability shown in the Declarations for each person for Bodily Injury Liability is our maximum limit of liability for all damages, including damages for care, loss of services or death, arising out of "bodily injury" sustained by any one person in any one auto accident. Subject to this limit for each person, the limit of liability shown in the Declarations for each accident for Bodily Injury Liability is our maximum limit of liability for all damages for "bodily injury" resulting from any one auto accident.

The limit of liability shown in the Declarations for each accident for Property Damage Liability is our maximum limit of liability for all "property damage" resulting from any one auto accident.

This is the most we will pay regardless of the number of:

1. "Insureds";
2. Claims made;
3. Vehicles or premiums shown in the Declarations; or
4. Vehicles involved in the auto accident.

B. No one will be entitled to receive duplicate payments for the same elements of loss under this coverage and:

1. Part **B** or Part **C** of this policy; or
2. Any Underinsured Motorists Coverage provided by this policy.

OUT OF STATE COVERAGE

If an auto accident to which this policy applies occurs in any state or province other than the one in which "your covered auto" is principally garaged, we will interpret your policy for that accident as follows:

A. If the state or province has:

1. A financial responsibility or similar law specifying limits of liability for "bodily injury" or "property damage" higher than the limit shown in the Declarations, your policy will provide the higher specified limit.
2. A compulsory insurance or similar law requiring a nonresident to maintain insurance whenever the nonresident uses a vehicle in that state or province, your policy will provide at least the required minimum amounts and types of coverage.

B. No one will be entitled to duplicate payments for the same elements of loss.

FINANCIAL RESPONSIBILITY

When this policy is certified as future proof of financial responsibility, this policy shall comply with the law to the extent required.

OTHER INSURANCE

If there is other applicable liability insurance we will pay only our share of the loss. Our share is the proportion that our limit of liability bears to the total of all applicable limits. However, any insurance we provide for a vehicle you do not own shall be excess over any other collectible insurance.

PART B – MEDICAL PAYMENTS COVERAGE

INSURING AGREEMENT

A. We will pay reasonable expenses incurred for necessary medical and funeral services because of "bodily injury":

1. Caused by accident; and
2. Sustained by an "insured".

We will pay only those expenses incurred for services rendered within 3 years from the date of the accident.

B. "Insured" as used in this Part means:

1. You or any "family member":
   a. While "occupying"; or
   b. As a pedestrian when struck by;

   a motor vehicle designed for use mainly on public roads or a trailer of any type.
2. Any other person while "occupying" "your covered auto".

EXCLUSIONS

We do not provide Medical Payments Coverage for any "insured" for "bodily injury":

1. Sustained while "occupying" any motorized vehicle having fewer than four wheels.

2. Sustained while "occupying" "your covered auto" when it is being used as a public or livery conveyance. This Exclusion (**2.**) does not apply to a share-the-expense car pool.
3. Sustained while "occupying" any vehicle located for use as a residence or premises.
4. Occurring during the course of employment if workers' compensation benefits are required or available for the "bodily injury".
5. Sustained while "occupying", or when struck by, any vehicle (other than "your covered auto") which is:
   a. Owned by you; or
   b. Furnished or available for your regular use.
6. Sustained while "occupying", or when struck by, any vehicle (other than "your covered auto") which is:
   a. Owned by any "family member"; or
   b. Furnished or available for the regular use of any "family member".

   However, this Exclusion (**6.**) does not apply to you.

Page 4 of 12   Copyright, Insurance Services Office, Inc., 1997   **PP 00 01 06 98**

SAMPLE

7. Sustained while "occupying" a vehicle without a reasonable belief that that "insured" is entitled to do so. This Exclusion **(7.)** does not apply to a "family member" using "your covered auto" which is owned by you.

8. Sustained while "occupying" a vehicle when it is being used in the "business" of an "insured". This Exclusion **(8.)** does not apply to "bodily injury" sustained while "occupying" a:

    a. Private passenger auto;

    b. Pickup or van that you own; or

    c. "Trailer" used with a vehicle described in **a.** or **b.** above.

9. Caused by or as a consequence of:

    a. Discharge of a nuclear weapon (even if accidental);

    b. War (declared or undeclared);

    c. Civil war;

    d. Insurrection; or

    e. Rebellion or revolution.

10. From or as a consequence of the following, whether controlled or uncontrolled or however caused:

    a. Nuclear reaction;

    b. Radiation; or

    c. Radioactive contamination.

11. Sustained while "occupying" any vehicle located inside a facility designed for racing, for the purpose of:

    a. Competing in; or

    b. Practicing or preparing for;

    any prearranged or organized racing or speed contest.

LIMIT OF LIABILITY

A. The limit of liability shown in the Declarations for this coverage is our maximum limit of liability for each person injured in any one accident. This is the most we will pay regardless of the number of:

    1. "Insureds";

    2. Claims made;

    3. Vehicles or premiums shown in the Declarations; or

    4. Vehicles involved in the accident.

B. No one will be entitled to receive duplicate payments for the same elements of loss under this coverage and:

    1. Part **A** or Part **C** of this policy; or

    2. Any Underinsured Motorists Coverage provided by this policy.

OTHER INSURANCE

If there is other applicable auto medical payments insurance we will pay only our share of the loss. Our share is the proportion that our limit of liability bears to the total of all applicable limits. However, any insurance we provide with respect to a vehicle you do not own shall be excess over any other collectible auto insurance providing payments for medical or funeral expenses.

PART C – UNINSURED MOTORISTS COVERAGE

INSURING AGREEMENT

A. We will pay compensatory damages which an "insured" is legally entitled to recover from the owner or operator of an "uninsured motor vehicle" because of "bodily injury":

    1. Sustained by an "insured"; and

    2. Caused by an accident.

    The owner's or operator's liability for these damages must arise out of the ownership, maintenance or use of the "uninsured motor vehicle".

    Any judgment for damages arising out of a suit brought without our written consent is not binding on us.

B. "Insured" as used in this Part means:

    1. You or any "family member".

    2. Any other person "occupying" "your covered auto".

3. Any person for damages that person is entitled to recover because of "bodily injury" to which this coverage applies sustained by a person described in **1.** or **2.** above.

C. "Uninsured motor vehicle" means a land motor vehicle or trailer of any type:

    1. To which no bodily injury liability bond or policy applies at the time of the accident.

    2. To which a bodily injury liability bond or policy applies at the time of the accident. In this case its limit for bodily injury liability must be less than the minimum limit for bodily injury liability specified by the financial responsibility law of the state in which "your covered auto" is principally garaged.

SAMPLE

3. Which is a hit-and-run vehicle whose operator or owner cannot be identified and which hits:

   a. You or any "family member";

   b. A vehicle which you or any "family member" are "occupying"; or

   c. "Your covered auto".

4. To which a bodily injury liability bond or policy applies at the time of the accident but the bonding or insuring company:

   a. Denies coverage; or

   b. Is or becomes insolvent.

However, "uninsured motor vehicle" does not include any vehicle or equipment:

1. Owned by or furnished or available for the regular use of you or any "family member".

2. Owned or operated by a self-insurer under any applicable motor vehicle law, except a self-insurer which is or becomes insolvent.

3. Owned by any governmental unit or agency.

4. Operated on rails or crawler treads.

5. Designed mainly for use off public roads while not on public roads.

6. While located for use as a residence or premises.

EXCLUSIONS

A. We do not provide Uninsured Motorists Coverage for "bodily injury" sustained:

   1. By an "insured" while "occupying", or when struck by, any motor vehicle owned by that "insured" which is not insured for this coverage under this policy. This includes a trailer of any type used with that vehicle.

   2. By any "family member" while "occupying", or when struck by, any motor vehicle you own which is insured for this coverage on a primary basis under any other policy.

B. We do not provide Uninsured Motorists Coverage for "bodily injury" sustained by any "insured":

   1. If that "insured" or the legal representative settles the "bodily injury" claim without our consent.

   2. While "occupying" "your covered auto" when it is being used as a public or livery conveyance. This Exclusion (B.2.) does not apply to a share-the-expense car pool.

   3. Using a vehicle without a reasonable belief that that "insured" is entitled to do so. This Exclusion (B.3.) does not apply to a "family member" using "your covered auto" which is owned by you.

C. This coverage shall not apply directly or indirectly to benefit any insurer or self-insurer under any of the following or similar law:

   1. Workers' compensation law; or

2. Disability benefits law.

D. We do not provide Uninsured Motorists Coverage for punitive or exemplary damages.

LIMIT OF LIABILITY

A. The limit of liability shown in the Declarations for each person for Uninsured Motorists Coverage is our maximum limit of liability for all damages, including damages for care, loss of services or death, arising out of "bodily injury" sustained by any one person in any one accident. Subject to this limit for each person, the limit of liability shown in the Declarations for each accident for Uninsured Motorists Coverage is our maximum limit of liability for all damages for "bodily injury" resulting from any one accident.

This is the most we will pay regardless of the number of:

1. "Insureds";

2. Claims made;

3. Vehicles or premiums shown in the Declarations; or

4. Vehicles involved in the accident.

B. No one will be entitled to receive duplicate payments for the same elements of loss under this coverage and:

   1. Part A. or Part B. of this policy; or

   2. Any Underinsured Motorists Coverage provided by this policy.

C. We will not make a duplicate payment under this coverage for any element of loss for which payment has been made by or on behalf of persons or organizations who may be legally responsible.

D. We will not pay for any element of loss if a person is entitled to receive payment for the same element of loss under any of the following or similar law:

   1. Workers' compensation law; or

   2. Disability benefits law.

OTHER INSURANCE

If there is other applicable insurance available under one or more policies or provisions of coverage that is similar to the insurance provided under this Part of the policy:

1. Any recovery for damages under all such policies or provisions of coverage may equal but not exceed the highest applicable limit for any one vehicle under any insurance providing coverage on either a primary or excess basis.

2. Any insurance we provide with respect to a vehicle you do not own shall be excess over any collectible insurance providing such coverage on a primary basis.

     PP 00 01 06 98

SAMPLE

3. If the coverage under this policy is provided:

  a. On a primary basis, we will pay only our share of the loss that must be paid under insurance providing coverage on a primary basis. Our share is the proportion that our limit of liability bears to the total of all applicable limits of liability for coverage provided on a primary basis.

  b. On an excess basis, we will pay only our share of the loss that must be paid under insurance providing coverage on an excess basis. Our share is the proportion that our limit of liability bears to the total of all applicable limits of liability for coverage provided on an excess basis.

ARBITRATION

A. If we and an "insured" do not agree:

1. Whether that "insured" is legally entitled to recover damages; or

2. As to the amount of damages which are recoverable by that "insured";

from the owner or operator of an "uninsured motor vehicle", then the matter may be arbitrated. However, disputes concerning coverage under this Part may not be arbitrated.

Both parties must agree to arbitration. If so agreed, each party will select an arbitrator. The two arbitrators will select a third. If they cannot agree within 30 days, either may request that selection be made by a judge of a court having jurisdiction.

B. Each party will:

1. Pay the expenses it incurs; and

2. Bear the expenses of the third arbitrator equally.

C. Unless both parties agree otherwise, arbitration will take place in the county in which the "insured" lives. Local rules of law as to procedure and evidence will apply. A decision agreed to by two of the arbitrators will be binding as to:

1. Whether the "insured" is legally entitled to recover damages; and

2. The amount of damages. This applies only if the amount does not exceed the minimum limit for bodily injury liability specified by the financial responsibility law of the state in which "your covered auto" is principally garaged. If the amount exceeds that limit, either party may demand the right to a trial. This demand must be made within 60 days of the arbitrators' decision. If this demand is not made, the amount of damages agreed to by the arbitrators will be binding.

PART D – COVERAGE FOR DAMAGE TO YOUR AUTO

INSURING AGREEMENT

A. We will pay for direct and accidental loss to "your covered auto" or any "non-owned auto", including their equipment, minus any applicable deductible shown in the Declarations. If loss to more than one "your covered auto" or "non-owned auto" results from the same "collision", only the highest applicable deductible will apply. We will pay for loss to "your covered auto" caused by:

1. Other than "collision" only if the Declarations indicate that Other Than Collision Coverage is provided for that auto.

2. "Collision" only if the Declarations indicate that Collision Coverage is provided for that auto.

If there is a loss to a "non-owned auto", we will provide the broadest coverage applicable to any "your covered auto" shown in the Declarations.

B. "Collision" means the upset of "your covered auto" or a "non-owned auto" or their impact with another vehicle or object.

Loss caused by the following is considered other than "collision":

1. Missiles or falling objects;

2. Fire;

3. Theft or larceny;

4. Explosion or earthquake;

5. Windstorm;

6. Hail, water or flood;

7. Malicious mischief or vandalism;

8. Riot or civil commotion;

9. Contact with bird or animal; or

10. Breakage of glass.

If breakage of glass is caused by a "collision", you may elect to have it considered a loss caused by "collision".

C. "Non-owned auto" means:

1. Any private passenger auto, pickup, van or "trailer" not owned by or furnished or available for the regular use of you or any "family member" while in the custody of or being operated by you or any "family member"; or

2. Any auto or "trailer" you do not own while used as a temporary substitute for "your covered auto" which is out of normal use because of its:

  a. Breakdown;

  b. Repair;

  c. Servicing;

  d. Loss; or

  e. Destruction.

TRANSPORTATION EXPENSES

A. In addition, we will pay, without application of a deductible, up to a maximum of $600 for:

SAMPLE

1. Temporary transportation expenses not exceeding $20 per day incurred by you in the event of a loss to "your covered auto". We will pay for such expenses if the loss is caused by:

   a. Other than "collision" only if the Declarations indicate that Other Than Collision Coverage is provided for that auto.

   b. "Collision" only if the Declarations indicate that Collision Coverage is provided for that auto.

2. Expenses for which you become legally responsible in the event of loss to a "non-owned auto". We will pay for such expenses if the loss is caused by:

   a. Other than "collision" only if the Declarations indicate that Other Than Collision Coverage is provided for any "your covered auto".

   b. "Collision" only if the Declarations indicate that Collision Coverage is provided for any "your covered auto".

   However, the most we will pay for any expenses for loss of use is $20 per day.

B. If the loss is caused by:

1. A total theft of "your covered auto" or a "non-owned auto", we will pay only expenses incurred during the period:

   a. Beginning 48 hours after the theft; and

   b. Ending when "your covered auto" or the "non-owned auto" is returned to use or we pay for its loss.

2. Other than theft of a "your covered auto" or a "non-owned auto", we will pay only expenses beginning when the auto is withdrawn from use for more than 24 hours.

C. Our payment will be limited to that period of time reasonably required to repair or replace the "your covered auto" or the "non-owned auto".

EXCLUSIONS

We will not pay for:

1. Loss to "your covered auto" or any "non-owned auto" which occurs while it is being used as a public or livery conveyance. This Exclusion (1.) does not apply to a share-the-expense car pool.

2. Damage due and confined to:

   a. Wear and tear;

   b. Freezing;

   c. Mechanical or electrical breakdown or failure; or

   d. Road damage to tires.

This Exclusion (2.) does not apply if the damage results from the total theft of "your covered auto" or any "non-owned auto".

3. Loss due to or as a consequence of:

   a. Radioactive contamination;

   b. Discharge of any nuclear weapon (even if accidental);

   c. War (declared or undeclared);

   d. Civil war;

   e. Insurrection; or

   f. Rebellion or revolution.

4. Loss to any electronic equipment designed for the reproduction of sound and any accessories used with such equipment. This includes but is not limited to:

   a. Radios and stereos;

   b. Tape decks; or

   c. Compact disc players.

This Exclusion (4.) does not apply to equipment designed solely for the reproduction of sound and accessories used with such equipment, provided:

   a. The equipment is permanently installed in "your covered auto" or any "non-owned auto"; or

   b. The equipment is:

      (1) Removable from a housing unit which is permanently installed in the auto;

      (2) Designed to be solely operated by use of the power from the auto's electrical system; and

      (3) In or upon "your covered auto" or any "non-owned auto" at the time of loss.

5. Loss to any electronic equipment that receives or transmits audio, visual or data signals and any accessories used with such equipment. This includes but is not limited to:

   a. Citizens band radios;

   b. Telephones;

   c. Two-way mobile radios;

   d. Scanning monitor receivers;

   e. Television monitor receivers;

   f. Video cassette recorders;

   g. Audio cassette recorders; or

   h. Personal computers.

This Exclusion (5.) does not apply to:

   a. Any electronic equipment that is necessary for the normal operation of the auto or the monitoring of the auto's operating systems; or

SAMPLE

b. A permanently installed telephone designed to be operated by use of the power from the auto's electrical system and any accessories used with the telephone.

6. Loss to tapes, records, discs or other media used with equipment described in Exclusions **4.** and **5.**

7. A total loss to "your covered auto" or any "non-owned auto" due to destruction or confiscation by governmental or civil authorities.

This Exclusion **(7.)** does not apply to the interests of Loss Payees in "your covered auto".

8. Loss to:

a. A "trailer", camper body, or motor home, which is not shown in the Declarations; or

b. Facilities or equipment used with such "trailer", camper body or motor home. Facilities or equipment include but are not limited to:

(1) Cooking, dining, plumbing or refrigeration facilities;

(2) Awnings or cabanas; or

(3) Any other facilities or equipment used with a "trailer", camper body, or motor home.

This Exclusion **(8.)** does not apply to a:

a. "Trailer", and its facilities or equipment, which you do not own; or

b. "Trailer", camper body, or the facilities or equipment in or attached to the "trailer" or camper body, which you:

(1) Acquire during the policy period; and

(2) Ask us to insure within 14 days after you become the owner.

9. Loss to any "non-owned auto" when used by you or any "family member" without a reasonable belief that you or that "family member" are entitled to do so.

10. Loss to equipment designed or used for the detection or location of radar or laser.

11. Loss to any custom furnishings or equipment in or upon any pickup or van. Custom furnishings or equipment include but are not limited to:

a. Special carpeting or insulation;

b. Furniture or bars;

c. Height-extending roofs; or

d. Custom murals, paintings or other decals or graphics.

This Exclusion **(11.)** does not apply to a cap, cover or bedliner in or upon any "your covered auto" which is a pickup.

12. Loss to any "non-owned auto" being maintained or used by any person while employed or otherwise engaged in the "business" of:

a. Selling;

b. Repairing;

c. Servicing;

d. Storing; or

e. Parking;

vehicles designed for use on public highways. This includes road testing and delivery.

13. Loss to "your covered auto" or any "non-owned auto", located inside a facility designed for racing, for the purpose of:

a. Competing in; or

b. Practicing or preparing for;

any prearranged or organized racing or speed contest.

14. Loss to, or loss of use of, a "non-owned auto" rented by:

a. You; or

b. Any "family member";

if a rental vehicle company is precluded from recovering such loss or loss of use, from you or that "family member", pursuant to the provisions of any applicable rental agreement or state law.

LIMIT OF LIABILITY

A. Our limit of liability for loss will be the lesser of the:

1. Actual cash value of the stolen or damaged property; or

2. Amount necessary to repair or replace the property with other property of like kind and quality.

However, the most we will pay for loss to:

1. Any "non-owned auto" which is a trailer is $500.

2. Equipment designed solely for the reproduction of sound, including any accessories used with such equipment, which is installed in locations not used by the auto manufacturer for installation of such equipment or accessories, is $1,000.

B. An adjustment for depreciation and physical condition will be made in determining actual cash value in the event of a total loss.

C. If a repair or replacement results in better than like kind or quality, we will not pay for the amount of the betterment.

SAMPLE

PAYMENT OF LOSS

We may pay for loss in money or repair or replace the damaged or stolen property. We may, at our expense, return any stolen property to:

1. You; or
2. The address shown in this policy.

If we return stolen property we will pay for any damage resulting from the theft. We may keep all or part of the property at an agreed or appraised value.

If we pay for loss in money, our payment will include the applicable sales tax for the damaged or stolen property.

NO BENEFIT TO BAILEE

This insurance shall not directly or indirectly benefit any carrier or other bailee for hire.

OTHER SOURCES OF RECOVERY

If other sources of recovery also cover the loss, we will pay only our share of the loss. Our share is the proportion that our limit of liability bears to the total of all applicable limits. However, any insurance we provide with respect to a "non-owned auto" shall be excess over any other collectible source of recovery including, but not limited to:

1. Any coverage provided by the owner of the "non-owned auto";
2. Any other applicable physical damage insurance;
3. Any other source of recovery applicable to the loss.

APPRAISAL

A. If we and you do not agree on the amount of loss, either may demand an appraisal of the loss. In this event, each party will select a competent appraiser. The two appraisers will select an umpire. The appraisers will state separately the actual cash value and the amount of loss. If they fail to agree, they will submit their differences to the umpire. A decision agreed to by any two will be binding. Each party will:

1. Pay its chosen appraiser; and
2. Bear the expenses of the appraisal and umpire equally.

B. We do not waive any of our rights under this policy by agreeing to an appraisal.

PART E – DUTIES AFTER AN ACCIDENT OR LOSS

We have no duty to provide coverage under this policy unless there has been full compliance with the following duties:

A. We must be notified promptly of how, when and where the accident or loss happened. Notice should also include the names and addresses of any injured persons and of any witnesses.

B. A person seeking any coverage must:

1. Cooperate with us in the investigation, settlement or defense of any claim or suit.
2. Promptly send us copies of any notices or legal papers received in connection with the accident or loss.
3. Submit, as often as we reasonably require:
   a. To physical exams by physicians we select. We will pay for these exams.
   b. To examination under oath and subscribe the same.
4. Authorize us to obtain:
   a. Medical reports; and

b. Other pertinent records.

5. Submit a proof of loss when required by us.

C. A person seeking Uninsured Motorists Coverage must also:

1. Promptly notify the police if a hit-and-run driver is involved.
2. Promptly send us copies of the legal papers if a suit is brought.

D. A person seeking Coverage For Damage To Your Auto must also:

1. Take reasonable steps after loss to protect "your covered auto" or any "non-owned auto" and their equipment from further loss. We will pay reasonable expenses incurred to do this.
2. Promptly notify the police if "your covered auto" or any "non-owned auto" is stolen.
3. Permit us to inspect and appraise the damaged property before its repair or disposal.

SAMPLE

PART F – GENERAL PROVISIONS

BANKRUPTCY

Bankruptcy or insolvency of the "insured" shall not relieve us of any obligations under this policy.

CHANGES

A. This policy contains all the agreements between you and us. Its terms may not be changed or waived except by endorsement issued by us.

B. If there is a change to the information used to develop the policy premium, we may adjust your premium. Changes during the policy term that may result in a premium increase or decrease include, but are not limited to, changes in:

1. The number, type or use classification of insured vehicles;

2. Operators using insured vehicles;

3. The place of principal garaging of insured vehicles;

4. Coverage, deductible or limits.

If a change resulting from **A.** or **B.** requires a premium adjustment, we will make the premium adjustment in accordance with our manual rules.

C. If we make a change which broadens coverage under this edition of your policy without additional premium charge, that change will automatically apply to your policy as of the date we implement the change in your state. This Paragraph (**C.**) does not apply to changes implemented with a general program revision that includes both broadenings and restrictions in coverage, whether that general program revision is implemented through introduction of:

1. A subsequent edition of your policy; or

2. An Amendatory Endorsement.

FRAUD

We do not provide coverage for any "insured" who has made fraudulent statements or engaged in fraudulent conduct in connection with any accident or loss for which coverage is sought under this policy.

LEGAL ACTION AGAINST US

A. No legal action may be brought against us until there has been full compliance with all the terms of this policy. In addition, under Part **A,** no legal action may be brought against us until:

1. We agree in writing that the "insured" has an obligation to pay; or

2. The amount of that obligation has been finally determined by judgment after trial.

B. No person or organization has any right under this policy to bring us into any action to determine the liability of an "insured".

OUR RIGHT TO RECOVER PAYMENT

A. If we make a payment under this policy and the person to or for whom payment was made has a right to recover damages from another we shall be subrogated to that right. That person shall do:

1. Whatever is necessary to enable us to exercise our rights; and

2. Nothing after loss to prejudice them.

However, our rights in this Paragraph (**A.**) do not apply under Part **D,** against any person using "your covered auto" with a reasonable belief that that person is entitled to do so.

B. If we make a payment under this policy and the person to or for whom payment is made recovers damages from another, that person shall:

1. Hold in trust for us the proceeds of the recovery; and

2. Reimburse us to the extent of our payment.

POLICY PERIOD AND TERRITORY

A. This policy applies only to accidents and losses which occur:

1. During the policy period as shown in the Declarations; and

2. Within the policy territory.

B. The policy territory is:

1. The United States of America, its territories or possessions;

2. Puerto Rico; or

3. Canada.

This policy also applies to loss to, or accidents involving, "your covered auto" while being transported between their ports.

TERMINATION

A. Cancellation

This policy may be cancelled during the policy period as follows:

1. The named insured shown in the Declarations may cancel by:

    a. Returning this policy to us; or

    b. Giving us advance written notice of the date cancellation is to take effect.

2. We may cancel by mailing to the named insured shown in the Declarations at the address shown in this policy:

    a. At least 10 days notice:

        (1) If cancellation is for nonpayment of premium; or

SAMPLE

(2) If notice is mailed during the first 60 days this policy is in effect and this is not a renewal or continuation policy; or

b. At least 20 days notice in all other cases.

3. After this policy is in effect for 60 days, or if this is a renewal or continuation policy, we will cancel only:

a. For nonpayment of premium; or

b. If your driver's license or that of:

(1) Any driver who lives with you; or

(2) Any driver who customarily uses "your covered auto";

has been suspended or revoked. This must have occurred:

(1) During the policy period; or

(2) Since the last anniversary of the original effective date if the policy period is other than 1 year; or

c. If the policy was obtained through material misrepresentation.

B. Nonrenewal

If we decide not to renew or continue this policy, we will mail notice to the named insured shown in the Declarations at the address shown in this policy. Notice will be mailed at least 20 days before the end of the policy period. Subject to this notice requirement, if the policy period is:

1. Less than 6 months, we will have the right not to renew or continue this policy every 6 months, beginning 6 months after its original effective date.

2. 6 months or longer, but less than one year, we will have the right not to renew or continue this policy at the end of the policy period.

3. 1 year or longer, we will have the right not to renew or continue this policy at each anniversary of its original effective date.

C. Automatic Termination

If we offer to renew or continue and you or your representative do not accept, this policy will automatically terminate at the end of the current policy period. Failure to pay the required renewal or continuation premium when due shall mean that you have not accepted our offer.

If you obtain other insurance on "your covered auto", any similar insurance provided by this policy will terminate as to that auto on the effective date of the other insurance.

D. Other Termination Provisions

1. We may deliver any notice instead of mailing it. Proof of mailing of any notice shall be sufficient proof of notice.

2. If this policy is cancelled, you may be entitled to a premium refund. If so, we will send you the refund. The premium refund, if any, will be computed according to our manuals. However, making or offering to make the refund is not a condition of cancellation.

3. The effective date of cancellation stated in the notice shall become the end of the policy period.

TRANSFER OF YOUR INTEREST IN THIS POLICY

A. Your rights and duties under this policy may not be assigned without our written consent. However, if a named insured shown in the Declarations dies, coverage will be provided for:

1. The surviving spouse if resident in the same household at the time of death. Coverage applies to the spouse as if a named insured shown in the Declarations; and

2. The legal representative of the deceased person as if a named insured shown in the Declarations. This applies only with respect to the representative's legal responsibility to maintain or use "your covered auto".

B. Coverage will only be provided until the end of the policy period.

TWO OR MORE AUTO POLICIES

If this policy and any other auto insurance policy issued to you by us apply to the same accident, the maximum limit of our liability under all the policies shall not exceed the highest applicable limit of liability under any one policy.

Copyright, Insurance Services Office, Inc., 1997   **PP 00 01 06 98**

SAMPLE

WHOLE LIFE INSURANCE POLICY WITH RIDERS

> INSURED – JOHN DOE
> POLICY NUMBER – 36 000 000
> POLICY DATE – AUGUST 8, 1999

ABC Life Insurance Company

123 Main Street, Anytown, USA

ABC Life Insurance Company will pay the benefits of this policy in accordance with its provisions. The pages which follow are also a part of this policy.

10 Day Right To Examine Policy. Please examine your policy. Within 10 days after delivery, you can return it to ABC Life Insurance Company or to the agent through whom it was purchased, with a written request for a full refund of premium. Upon such request, the policy will be void from the start, and a full premium refund will be made.

Premiums. The premiums for this policy are shown in the Premium Schedule on the Policy Data page. They are payable in accordance with the Premiums section.

This policy is executed as of the date of issue shown on the Policy Data page.

John Johnson
President

Mary Smith
Secretary

Whole Life Policy.

Life Insurance Proceeds Payable at Insured's Death.

Premiums Payable During Insured's Lifetime,　December 1, 2002
　as shown on the Policy Data page.

Policy is Eligible for Dividends.

SAMPLE

INSURED — JOHN DOE   AGE 37   MALE

POLICY NUMBER — 36000000   CLASS OF RISK - STANDARD
                                      (NON-SMOKER DISCOUNT)

POLICY DATE — AUGUST 8, 1999   DATE OF ISSUE
                                      AUGUST 15,1999

OWNER — INSURED

PLAN	WHOLE LIFE WITH
	OPTION TO PURCHASE PAID-UP ADDITIONS (OPP) AND
	ACCIDENTAL DEATH BENEFIT (ADB) AND
	DISABILITY WAIVER OF PREMIUM (WP) AND
	POLICY PURCHASE OPTION (PPO) - OPTION AMOUNT IS $50,000.00 AND
	ACCELERATION OF DEATH BENEFITS

AMOUNT	FACE AMOUNT	$100,000.00
	ACCIDENTAL DEATH BENEFIT	$100,000.00
	(ADB, WHEN PAYABLE, IS IN ADDITION TO	
	ANY OTHER INSURANCE BENEFIT)	

BENEFICIARY
(subject to change) FIRST - ESTATE OF THE INSURED

PREMIUM SCHEDULE
PREMIUMS PAYABLE AT MONTHLY INTERVALS, AS FOLLOWS (SEE ENDORSEMENT HEREON)
     (Premium includes the following amounts for any supplementary benefits)

BEGINNING AS OF			TOTAL			
MO.	DAY	YR.	PREMIUM			
8-	8-	1999	$144.00			
8-	8-	2008	$134.00			
8-	8-	2027	$130.00			
8-	8-	2032	$123.00	PAYABLE FOR REMAINDER OF INSURED'S LIFE.**		
			ADB	WP	PPO	
8-	8-	1999	$7.00	$5.50	$8.50	
8-	8-	2008	$7.00	$4.00		
8-	8-	2027	$7.00			
8-	8-	2032				

PREMIUM PAYING PERIOD MAY BE SHORTENED BY USING DIVIDEND VALUES TO MAKE POLICY FULLY PAID-UP.

THE EXPENSE CHARGE APPLIED TO ALL PAYMENTS MADE UNDER THE OPTION TO PURCHASE PAID-UP ADDITIONS (OPP) RIDER WILL NOT EXCEED 3%.

THE INTEREST RATES, REFERRED TO IN THE BASIS OF COMPUTATION SECTION, ARE AS FOLLOWS:

A) 6.25% PER YEAR FOR THE CALCULATION OF CASH VALUES, EXTENDED INSURANCE AND PAID-UP INSURANCE FOR THE FIRST 20 POLICY YEARS.

B) 5% PER YEAR FOR THE COMPUTATION OF ALL OTHER VALUES.

DIVIDENDS ARE NOT GUARANTEED. WE HAVE THE RIGHT TO CHANGE THE AMOUNT OF DIVIDENDS TO BE CREDITED TO THE POLICY WHICH MAY RESULT IN LOWER DIVIDEND VALUES, OR, IF APPLICABLE, MORE PREMIUMS TO BE PAID, THAN WERE ILLUSTRATED.

GAT111   Page 2

SAMPLE

TABLE OF GUARANTEED VALUES*

Alternatives to Cash Value

End of Policy Year	Cash Value	Paid-Up Insurance	or	Extended Insurance		End of Policy Year
				Years	Days	
1	*****	***		**	***	1
2	*****	***		**	***	2
3	$400.00	$2,400		1	18	3
4	1,400.00	7,900		3	114	4
5	2,400.00	12,900		5	62	5
6	3,500.00	17,900		6	328	6
7	4,500.00	22,000		8	55	7
8	5,600.00	26,200		9	109	8
9	6,800.00	30,400		10	121	9
10	8,000.00	34,300		11	50	10
11	9,300.00	38,100		11	321	11
12	11,000.00	43,200		12	325	12
13	12,900.00	48,500		13	323	13
14	14,800.00	53,300		14	239	14
15	16,700.00	57,700		15	91	15
16	18,700.00	61,900		15	287	16
17	20,700.00	65,800		16	73	17
18	22,700.00	69,300		16	187	18
19	24,800.00	72,800		16	291	19
20	26,900.00	75,900		16	358	20
AGE 60	32,300.00	69,400		14	319	AGE 60
AGE 65	41,700.00	77,300		13	198	AGE 65

*This table assumes premiums have been paid to the end of the policy year shown. These values do not include any dividend accumulations, paid-up additions, or policy loans.

POLICY DATA   ABC LIFE INSURANCE COMPANY

SAMPLE

WE & YOU
In this policy, the words "we," "our" or "us" refer to ABC Life Insurance Company, and the words "you" or "your" refer to the owner of this policy.

When you write to us, please include the policy number, the Insured's full name, and your current address.

——————— **CONTENTS** ———————

Note: This policy is a legal contract between the policyowner and the Company.
READ YOUR POLICY CAREFULLY FOR FULL DETAILS.

SAMPLE

LIFE INSURANCE PROCEEDS

Life Insurance Proceeds We will pay the life insurance proceeds to the beneficiary promptly when we have proof that the Insured died, if premiums have been paid as called for in the Premiums section. These proceeds will include the face amount and any other benefits from riders or dividends which are payable because of the Insured's death, all as stated in the policy. When we determine these proceeds, there may be an adjustment for the last premium. We will deduct any unpaid loan.

POLICY OWNERSHIP

Owner In this policy, the words "you" and "your" refer to the owner of this policy. As the owner, you have all rights of ownership in this policy while the Insured is living. To exercise these rights, you do not need the consent of any successor owner or beneficiary.

Successor Owner A successor owner can be named in the application, or in a notice you sign which gives us the facts that we need. The successor owner will become the new owner when you die, if you die before the Insured. If no successor owner survives you and you die before the Insured, your estate becomes the new owner.

Change of Ownership You can change the owner of this policy, from yourself to a new owner, in a notice you sign which gives us the facts that we need. When this change takes effect, all rights of ownership in this policy will pass to the new owner.

When we record a change of owner or successor owner, these changes will take effect as of the date you signed the notice, subject to any payment we made or action we took before recording these changes. We may require that these changes be endorsed in the policy. Changing the owner or naming a new successor owner cancels any prior choice of successor owner, but does not change the beneficiary.

BENEFICIARY

Naming of Beneficiary One or more beneficiaries for any life insurance proceeds can be named in the application, or in a notice you sign which gives us the facts that we need. If more than one beneficiary is named, they can be classed as first, second, and so on. If 2 or more are named in a class, their shares in the proceeds can be stated.

The stated shares of the proceeds will be paid to any first beneficiaries who survive the Insured. If no first beneficiaries survive, payment will be made to any beneficiary surviving in the second class, and so on. Beneficiaries who survive in the same class have an equal share in the proceeds, unless the shares are stated otherwise.

Change of Beneficiary While the Insured is living, you can change a beneficiary in a notice you sign which gives us the facts that we need. When we record a change, it will take effect as of the date you signed the notice, subject to any payment we made or action we took before recording the change.

Death of Beneficiary If no beneficiary for the life insurance proceeds, or for a stated share, survives the Insured, the right to these proceeds or this share will pass to you. If you are the Insured, this right will pass to your estate. Unless stated otherwise in the policy or in your signed notice which is in effect at the Insured's death, if any beneficiary dies at the same time as the Insured, or within 15 days after the Insured but before we receive proof of the Insured's death, we will pay the proceeds as though that beneficiary died first.

PREMIUMS

Payment of Premiums Each premium is payable, while the Insured is living, on or before its due date as shown in the Premium Schedule on the Policy Data page. Premiums are payable at our Home Office or at one of our service offices.

The premium for this policy can be paid at intervals of 3 months or 6 months, or once each year. The method we use to determine the premium rate for each of these intervals is the method that was in effect as of the policy date shown on the Policy Data page. The interval can be changed by paying the correct premium for the new interval. Premiums can be paid by any other method we make available.

Grace Period We allow 31 days from the due date for payment of a premium. All insurance coverage continues during this grace period.

Nonpayment of Premium If a premium is not paid by the end of the grace period, this policy will lapse. All insurance will end at the time of lapse, if the policy has no cash value and no dividend values. If the policy has cash value or dividend values, insurance can be continued only as stated in Options 1 or 2 of the Options Upon Lapse provision, but any insurance or benefits from riders or dividends will end at the time of lapse.

Options Upon Lapse If the policy has cash value or dividend values at the time of lapse, it will continue as extended insurance, if available. It may happen that the amount of extended insurance would be less than or equal to the amount of paid-up insurance available, or the Table of Guaranteed Values on the Policy Data page shows that extended insurance is not available. In these cases, the policy will continue under the paid-up insurance option instead.

Instead of extended insurance, paid-up insurance can be elected or you can surrender the policy for cash. The paid-up insurance option can be elected in the application or in your signed notice. We must receive this notice no later than 3 months after the due date of the overdue premium.

   1. **Extended Insurance** Extended insurance is level term insurance for which no more premiums are due. It is payable to the beneficiary when we

have proof that the Insured died after the end of the grace period and before the end of the term period. The amount of extended insurance will equal the face amount of this policy, plus the amount of any paid-up additions and dividend accumulations, less any unpaid loan. No insurance or benefits from riders or dividends will be provided after the end of the grace period.

We calculate the term period as of the due date of the overdue premium. We do this by applying the sum of the cash value and dividend values, less any unpaid loan, at the net single premium rate for term insurance for the Insured's age on that date. The term period is measured from that due date.

This insurance can be surrendered at any time for its cash value, but it has no loan value and is not eligible for dividends. All insurance will end when you send us your signed request for the cash value proceeds.

   2. **Paid-up Insurance** Paid-up life insurance begins as of the date we record your notice electing it, or begins at the end of the grace period if later. No more premiums are due for this insurance. It is payable to the beneficiary when we have proof that the Insured died while this paid-up insurance option was in effect.

We calculate the amount of paid-up insurance as of the due date of the overdue premium. We do this by applying the sum of the cash value and dividend values, less any unpaid loan, at the net single premium rate for the Insured's age on that date. In most cases, this amount will be less than the face amount of this policy. No insurance or benefits from riders will be provided after this paid-up insurance option goes into effect.

This insurance can be surrendered at any time. It has cash value and loan value, and is eligible for dividends. All insurance will end when you send us your signed request for the cash value proceeds.

   3. **Surrender for Cash** Instead of extended insurance or paid-up insurance, you can surrender this policy for its cash value and dividend values, less any unpaid loan, as stated in the Cash Value provision. All insurance will end when you send us your signed request for the cash value proceeds.

SAMPLE

PREMIUMS (continued)

Reinstatement Within 5 years after lapse, you may apply to reinstate the policy if you have not surrendered it. We must have evidence of insurability that is acceptable to us. All overdue premiums must be paid, with interest at 6% per year from each of their due dates, unless we declare a policy loan interest rate of less than 6%. In that case, the interest rate for all overdue premiums at the time of reinstatement will be the same as the policy loan interest rate, but not more than 6%. Any unpaid loan, and any loan deducted when we determined the extended or paid-up insurance, must also be repaid. Interest on the loan will be compounded once each year and will be based on the loan interest rate or rates that were in effect since the time of lapse.

All or part of these payments can be charged as a new unpaid loan if there is enough loan value.

We do not need evidence of insurability if we receive the required payment within 31 days after the end of the grace period, but the Insured must be living when we receive it.

Premium Adjustment at Death We will increase the life insurance proceeds by any part of a premium paid for the period after the policy month in which the Insured dies.

If the Insured dies during a grace period, we will reduce the proceeds by an amount equal to the premium for one policy month.

CASH VALUE AND LOANS

Cash Value Cash values for this policy at the end of selected policy years are as shown in the Table of Guaranteed Values on the Policy Data page, if premiums have been paid as called for in the Premiums section. These values do not include dividend values, and they do not reflect any unpaid loan. Cash values at other times depend on the date to which premiums have been paid, and on how much time has passed since the last policy anniversary. When you ask us, we will tell you how much cash value there is.

The cash value on the due date of an unpaid premium will not decrease during the 3 months after that date. Also, the cash value of any extended or paid-up insurance on a policy anniversary will not decrease during the next 31 days after that anniversary.

At any time after the policy has cash value or dividend values, you can surrender it for the sum of these values, less any unpaid loan. All insurance will end when you send us your signed request for these surrender proceeds.

We may defer paying these proceeds for up to 6 months after the date of surrender. Interest will be paid from the date of surrender on any payment deferred more than 10 days. We set the interest rate each year. This rate will be at least 3.5% per year or the rate required by law.

Loan Value You can borrow any amount up to the loan value, using this policy as sole security.

On a policy anniversary, on a premium due date, or during the grace period, the loan value is the cash value, plus any dividend values, less any unpaid loan and accrued interest. At any other time, the loan value is the amount which, with interest, will equal the loan value on the next anniversary or on the next premium due date, if earlier. Extended insurance has no loan value.

We may require that you sign a loan agreement. We may defer a loan, except to pay a premium due us for this policy, for as long as 6 months after we receive your loan request. Interest will be paid on any amount deferred if that amount is not mailed within 10 days after we receive the necessary information to complete the loan transaction. We will set the interest rate to be at least 3.5% per year or the rate required by law.

Loan Interest Loan interest accrues each day. Interest is due on each anniversary, or on the date of death, surrender, a lapse, a loan increase or loan repayment, or on any other date we specify. Interest not paid when due becomes part of the loan and will also bear interest.

Loan Interest Rate The loan interest rate for this policy may go up or down as described in this provision. However, the rate at any given time will apply to the entire amount of an unpaid loan. We will review this rate once every 3 months and, if necessary, adjust it.

SAMPLE

CASH VALUE AND LOANS (continued)

The loan interest rate will not be more than the Monthly Average Corporates yield shown in Moody's Corporate Bond Yield Averages published by Moody's Investors Services, Inc., or any successor to that service (the published monthly average), for the second calendar month prior to the date when we set an interest rate for this policy. If the rate, at this time, as determined by the published monthly average, is 0.5% or more above the current loan interest rate, we have the right to increase the loan interest rate to reflect this. However if the rate, at this time, as determined by the published monthly average, is 0.5% or more below the current loan interest rate, we will reduce the loan interest rate to reflect this. The loan interest rate will never be less than the interest rate shown on the Policy Data page plus 1%.

We will tell you the interest rate in effect when a loan, including an Automatic Premium Loan (APL), is made and when we send you notice of loan interest due. If a loan is outstanding 40 days or more before the effective date of an increase in the interest rate, we will notify you of that increase at least 30 days prior to its effective date. We will notify you of any increase in the interest rate when a loan is made during the 40 days before the effective date of the increase.

It may happen that the published monthly average ceases to be published. In this case, we will use a new basis approved by the insurance supervisory official of the state or district in which the policy is delivered.

Automatic Premium Loan (APL) If elected, APL provides an automatic loan which pays an overdue premium at the end of the grace period, subject to 2 conditions. First, the loan value must be enough to pay that premium.

Second, if premiums have been paid by APL for 2 years in a row, the next premium will not be paid by APL. After a premium is paid other than by APL, before the end of the grace period, premiums can again be paid by APL.

APL can be elected in the application. You can also elect APL in your signed notice which we must receive before the end of the grace period. You can cancel this election for future premiums by telling us in your signed notice.

Loan Repayment All or part of an unpaid loan and accrued interest can be repaid before the Insured's death or before you surrender the policy. We will deduct any unpaid loan when policy proceeds are payable.

If the policy is being continued as extended or paid-up insurance, any loan which we deducted in determining that insurance may be repaid only if the policy is reinstated. If that loan is not repaid, we will not deduct it again when policy proceeds are payable.

When Unpaid Loan Exceeds Loan Value In a given policy year it may happen that an unpaid loan and accrued interest will exceed the sum of the cash value and any dividend values. In this case, we will mail a notice to you at your last known address, and a copy to any assignee on our records. All insurance will end 31 days after the date on which we mail that notice, if the excess of the unpaid loan and accrued interest over the sum of the cash value and any dividend values is not paid within that 31 days.

We will not terminate this policy in a given policy year as the sole result of a change in the loan interest rate during that policy year.

SAMPLE

DIVIDENDS

Annual Dividend While this policy is in force, except as extended insurance, it is eligible to share in our divisible surplus. Each year we determine the policy's share, if any. This share is payable as a dividend on the policy anniversary, if all premiums due before then have been paid. We do not expect a dividend to be payable before the second anniversary.

Dividend Options Each dividend can be applied under one of the 4 options listed below. An option can be elected in the application. You can also elect or change the option for future dividends if you tell us in your signed notice.

1. Paid-up Addition Applied to provide paid-up life insurance at the net single premium rate for the Insured's age at that time. No more premiums are due for this insurance. It has cash value and is eligible for dividends. Before the Insured's death, you can surrender paid-up additions for their cash value that has not been borrowed against. The amount of this insurance in force at the Insured's death will be part of the life insurance proceeds.

2. Dividend Accumulation Left with us to accumulate at interest. On each policy anniversary, we credit interest at the rate we set each year. This rate will be at least 3.5% per year. Before the Insured's death, you can withdraw accumulations that have not been borrowed against, with interest to the date of withdrawal. Any accumulations which we still have at the Insured's death will be part of the life insurance proceeds.

3. Premium Payment Applied toward payment of a premium, provided any balance of that premium is also paid when due. Any part of the dividend not needed to pay the premium will be used to pay any loan interest due, unless you have asked to have that part paid in cash. Any part of the dividend not used to pay a premium or loan interest will be paid in cash.

4. Cash Paid in cash.

Automatic Dividend Option If no other option is in effect when a dividend becomes payable, we will apply it as a paid-up addition. If we pay a dividend in cash, and the dividend check is not cashed within one year after that dividend became payable, we will apply the dividend as a paid-up addition instead.

Dividend Values Dividend values are any dividend accumulations plus the cash value of any paid-up additions.

Fully Paid-up Policy You may shorten the premium paying period for this policy by having it made fully paid-up with no more premiums due. This may be done on any premium due date, if the sum of the cash value and dividend values equals the total single premium for the policy and any riders, based on the Insured's age on that date. We must receive your signed notice within 31 days of that date.

Dividend at Death The part of any annual dividend earned from the last policy anniversary to the end of the policy month in which the Insured dies will be part of the life insurance proceeds.

PAYMENT OF POLICY PROCEEDS

Payment We will pay the life insurance proceeds in one sum or, if elected, all or part of these proceeds may be placed under one or more of the options described in this section. If we agree, the proceeds may be placed under some other method of payment instead.

Any life insurance proceeds paid in one sum will bear interest compounded each year from the Insured's death to the date of payment. We set the interest rate each year. This rate will be at least 3.5% per year, and will not be less than required by law.

Election of Optional Method of Payment While the Insured is living, you can elect or change an option. You can also name or change one or more beneficiaries for the life insurance proceeds who will be the payee or payees under that option.

After the Insured dies, any person who is to receive proceeds in one sum (other than an assignee) can elect an option and name payees. The person who elects an option can also name one or more successor payees to receive any unpaid amount we have at the death of a payee. Naming these payees cancels any prior choice of successor payee.

SAMPLE

PAYMENT OF POLICY PROCEEDS (continued)

A payee who did not elect the option does not have the right to advance or assign payments, take the payments in one sum, or make any other change. However, the payee may be given the right to do one or more of these things if the person who elects the option tells us in writing and we agree.

Change of Option If we agree, a payee who elects Option 1A, 1B, 2A or 2B may later elect to have any unpaid amount we still have, or the present value of any elected payments, placed under some other option described in this section.

Payees Only individuals who are to receive payments in their own behalf may be named as payees or successor payees, unless we agree to some other payee. We may require proof of the age or the survival of a payee.

It may happen that when the last surviving payee dies, we still have an unpaid amount, or there are some payments which remain to be made. If so, we will pay the unpaid amount with interest to the date of payment, or pay the present value of the remaining payments, to that payee's estate in one sum. The present value of any remaining payments is based on the interest rate used to compute them, and is always less than their sum.

Minimum Payment When any payment under an option would be less than $20, we may pay any unpaid amount or present value in one sum.

Options 1 A and 1 B. Proceeds at Interest

The policy proceeds may be left with us at interest. We set the interest rate each year. This rate will be at least 3.5% per year.

1A. Interest Accumulation

We credit interest each year on the amount we still have. This amount can be withdrawn at any time in sums of $100 or more. We pay interest to the date of withdrawal on sums withdrawn.

1B. Interest Payment

We pay interest once each month, every 3 months or every 6 months, or once each year, as chosen, based on the amount we still have.

Options 2A and 2B. Elected Income

We make equal payments once each month, every 3 months or every 6 months, or once each year, as chosen, for an elected period of years or for an elected amount. We set the interest rate for these options each year. This rate will be at least 3.5% per year. If the rate is more than 3.5%, we will increase each payment to reflect this.

2A. Income for Elected Period

We make the payments for the number of years elected. Monthly payments based on 3.5% interest are shown in the Option 2A Table.

OPTION 2A TABLE
Minimum Monthly Payment per $1,000 of Proceeds

Years		Years		Years		Years	
1	$84.65	5	$18.12	9	$10.75	15	$7.10
2	43.05	6	15.35	10	9.83	20	5.75
3	29.19	7	13.38	11	9.09	25	4.96
4	22.27	8	11.90	12	8.46	30	4.45

When asked, we will state in writing what each payment would be, if made every 3 months or every 6 months, or once each year.

2B. Income of Elected Amount

We make payments of the elected amount until all proceeds and interest have been paid. The total payments made each year must be at least 5% of the proceeds placed under this option. Each year we credit interest of at least 3.5% on the amount we still have.

Options 3A, 3B, and 3C. Life Income

We make equal payments each month during the lifetime of the named payee or payees. We determine the amount of the monthly payment by applying the policy proceeds to purchase a corresponding single premium life annuity policy which is being issued when the first payment is due. Payments are based on the appropriately adjusted annuity premium rate in effect at that time, but will not be less than the corresponding minimum amount based on the tables for Options 3A, 3B, and 3C in this policy. The minimum amounts are based on the "1983 Table **a**" mortality table with projection, and with interest compounded each year at 4%.

SAMPLE

PAYMENT OF POLICY PROCEEDS (continued)

When asked, we will state in writing what the minimum amount of each monthly payment would be under these options. It is based on the sex and the adjusted age of the payee or payees in the year the first payment is due. To find the adjusted age, we increase or decrease the payee's age at that time, as follows:

1987–91	1992–98	1999–2006	2007–2013	2014–20	2021–28	2029+
+3	+2	+1	0	–1	–2	–3

3A.   Life Income–Guaranteed Period

We make a payment each month during the lifetime of the payee. Payments do not change, and are guaranteed for 5, 10, 15, or 20 years, as chosen, even if that payee dies sooner.

OPTION 3A TABLE
Minimum Monthly Payment per $1,000 of Proceeds

Payee's Adjusted Age	MALE Guaranteed Period 5 Yrs	10 Yrs	15 Yrs	20 Yrs	FEMALE Guaranteed Period 5 Yrs	10 Yrs	15 Yrs	20 Yrs
60	$5.14	$5.08	$4.98	$4.84	$4.68	$4.85	$4.61	$4.54
61	5.25	5.18	5.07	4.91	4.76	4.73	4.68	4.63
62	5.36	5.28	5.15	4.97	4.84	4.81	4.75	4.67
63	5.48	5.39	5.24	5.04	4.93	4.89	4.83	4.73
64	5.61	5.50	5.33	5.10	5.03	4.99	4.91	4.80
65	5.75	5.62	5.42	5.17	5.13	5.08	5.00	4.87
66	5.89	5.75	5.52	5.23	5.25	5.19	5.09	4.94
67	6.05	5.88	5.62	5.30	5.36	5.30	5.18	5.01
68	6.21	6.02	5.72	5.36	5.49	5.41	5.28	5.08
69	6.39	6.16	5.82	5.42	5.63	5.54	5.38	5.16
70	6.57	6.31	5.92	5.48	5.78	5.67	5.48	5.23
71	6.77	6.46	6.02	5.54	5.94	5.81	5.59	5.30
72	6.97	6.62	6.13	5.60	6.11	5.95	5.70	5.37
73	7.19	6.78	6.23	5.65	6.29	6.11	5.81	5.44
74	7.42	6.95	6.33	5.69	6.49	6.27	5.93	5.50
75	7.66	7.12	6.42	5.74	6.70	6.44	6.04	5.58
76	7.91	7.29	6.52	5.78	6.92	6.61	6.15	5.62
77	8.18	7.46	6.60	5.81	7.16	6.80	6.27	5.67
78	8.47	7.84	6.69	5.84	7.42	6.98	6.37	5.72
79	8.77	7.82	6.77	5.87	7.69	7.18	6.48	5.76
80	9.08	8.00	6.84	5.90	7.98	7.37	6.58	5.80
81	9.41	8.17	6.91	5.92	8.29	7.57	6.67	5.84
82	9.74	8.34	6.97	5.94	8.62	7.77	6.75	5.87
83	10.10	8.51	7.03	5.95	8.96	7.97	6.83	5.89
84	10.46	8.67	7.08	5.96	9.33	8.16	6.91	5.92
85 & over	10.84	8.82	7.13	5.97	9.71	8.34	6.97	5.94

3B. Life Income–Guaranteed Total Amount

We make a payment each month during the lifetime of the payee. Payments do not change, and are guaranteed until the total amount paid equals the amount placed under this option, even if that payee dies sooner.

OPTION 3B TABLE
Minimum Monthly Payment per $1,000 of Proceeds

Payee's Adjusted Age	Male	Female	Payee's Adjusted Age	Male	Female
60	$4.93	$4.57	73	$6.47	$5.87
61	5.02	4.64	74	6.84	6.01
62	5.11	4.71	75	6.81	6.17
63	5.20	4.79	76	7.00	6.34
64	5.30	4.87	77	7.19	6.51
65	5.40	4.96	78	7.40	6.70
66	5.52	5.05	79	7.62	6.90
67	5.63	5.14	80	7.85	7.11
68	5.75	5.25	81	8.09	7.33
69	5.88	5.36	82	8.35	7.57
70	6.02	5.47	83	8.61	7.81
71	6.16	5.60	84	8.89	8.07
72	6.31	5.73	85 & over	9.19	8.35

3C. Life Income–Joint and Survivor

We make a payment each month while both or one of the two payees are living. Payments do not change, and are guaranteed for 10 years, even if both payees die sooner.

OPTION 3C TABLE
10 YEAR GUARANTEED PERIOD
Minimum Monthly Payment per $1,000 of Proceeds

Male Payee's Adjusted Age	Female Payee's Adjusted Age 60	65	70	75	80
60	$4.32	$4.50	$4.67	$4.82	$4.93
65	4.42	4.66	4.91	5.15	5.34
70	4.81	4.81	5.14	5.49	5.80
75	4.57	4.92	5.34	5.81	6.27
80	4.61	4.99	5.49	6.07	6.69

SAMPLE

GENERAL PROVISIONS

Entire Contract The entire contract consists of this policy, any attached riders or endorsements and the attached copy of the application. Only our Chairman, President, Secretary, or one of our Vice Presidents can change the contract, and then only in writing. No change will be made in the contract without your consent. No agent is authorized to change this contract.

Application In issuing this policy, we have relied on the statements made in the application. All such statements are deemed to be representations and not warranties. We assume these statements are true and complete to the best of the knowledge and belief of those who made them.

No statement made in connection with the application will be used by us to void the policy or to deny a claim unless that statement is a material misrepresentation and is part of the application.

Incontestability We will not contest this policy after it has been in force during the lifetime of the Insured for 2 years from the date of issue.

Please refer to the Incontestability of Rider provision that may be in any rider or riders attached to this policy.

Suicide Exclusion Suicide of the Insured within one year of the date of issue, is not covered by this policy. In that event, this policy will end and the only amount payable will be the premiums paid to us, less any unpaid loan. **(SEE ENDORSEMENT HEREON)**

Dates Policy years, months, and anniversaries are measured from the policy date.

Age and Sex In this policy when we refer to a person's age on any date, we mean his or her age on the birthday which is nearest that date. If a date on the Policy Data page is based on an age that is not correct, we may change the date to reflect the correct age.

If the age or sex of an insured person is not correct as stated, any amount payable under this policy will be what the premiums paid would have purchased at the correct age and sex.

Policy Changes If we agree, you may have riders added to this policy, or have it changed to another plan or to a smaller amount of insurance.

Assignment While the Insured is living, you can assign this policy or any interest in it. If you do this, your interest, and anyone else's is subject to that of the assignee. As owner, you still have the rights of ownership that have not been assigned.

An assignee may not change the owner or the beneficiary, and may not elect or change an optional method of payment of proceeds. Any policy proceeds payable to the assignee will be paid in one sum.

We must have a copy of any assignment. We will not be responsible for the validity of an assignment. It will be subject to any payment we make or other action we take before we record it.

Protection Against Creditors Except as stated in the Assignment provision, payments we make under this policy are, to the extent the law permits, exempt from the claims, attachments, or levies of any creditors.

Payments to Company Any payment made to us by check or money order must be payable to ABC Life Insurance Company. When asked, we will give a counter-signed receipt, signed by our President or Secretary, for any premium paid to us.

Basis of Computation All cash values and net single premium rates referred to in this policy are based on the 1980 CSO Tables of Mortality. All extended insurance rates and cash values are based on the corresponding 1980 CET Insurance Tables. The interest rate is shown on the Policy Data page. Continuous functions are used.

At the end of each policy year not shown in the Table on the Policy Data page, the cash value is the reserve based on the Commissioner's Reserve Valuation Method. At any time, the cash value of any extended or paid-up insurance or paid-up additions is the reserve on each of these.

We have filed a statement with the insurance official in the state or district in which this policy is delivered. It describes, in detail, the method we used to compute these cash values. Each value is at least as much as the law requires.

Conformity with Law This policy is subject to all laws which apply.

Voting Rights Each year there is an election of persons to our Board of Directors. You have the right to vote in person or by mail if your policy is in force, and has been in force for at least one year after the date of issue. To find out more about this, write to the Secretary at our Home Office, 100 Ordinary Avenue, New York, New York 00000.

GAT111   Page 12

SAMPLE

RIDER

ACCIDENTAL DEATH BENEFIT (ADB)

Benefit We will pay this benefit to the beneficiary when we have proof that the Insured's death was caused directly, and apart from any other cause, by accidental bodily injury, and that death occurred within one year after that injury and while this rider was in effect.

When Benefit Not Payable We will not pay this benefit if death is caused or is contributed to by any of these items.

1. Disease or infirmity of mind or body.

2. Suicide.

3. Travel in or descent from an aircraft, if the Insured at any time during the aircraft's flight acted in any role other than as a passenger.

4. Any kind of war, declared or not, or by any act incident to a war or to an armed conflict involving the armed forces of one or more countries.

We will not pay this benefit if the Insured dies prior to his or her first birthday, or dies after the anniversary on which he or she is age 70.

Values This rider does not have cash or loan values.

Contract This rider, when paid for, is made a part of the policy, based on the application for the rider.

Incontestability of Rider We will not contest this rider after it has been in force during the lifetime of the Insured for 2 years from its date of issue.

Dates and Amounts When this rider is issued at the same time as the policy, we show the amount of ADB and the rider premium amount on the front page of the policy. The rider and the policy have the same date of issue.

When this rider is added to a policy which is already in force, we also put in an add-on rider. The add-on rider shows the date of issue and the amount of ADB. The rider premium amount is shown in a new Premium Schedule for the policy.

When Rider Ends You can cancel this rider as of the due date of a premium. To do this, you must send the policy and your signed notice to us within 31 days of that date. If this rider is still in effect on the anniversary on which the Insured is age 70, it will end on that date.

This rider ends if the policy ends or is surrendered. Also, this rider will not be in effect if the policy lapses or is in force as extended or paid-up insurance.

When this rider is part of an endowment policy, the rider will end on the day just before the endowment date, and will not be in effect if that date is deferred.

ABC LIFE INSURANCE COMPANY

Mary Smith
Secretary

John Johnson
President

SAMPLE

THIS PAGE INTENTIONALLY LEFT BLANK

SAMPLE

WHOLE LIFE INSURANCE POLICY WITH RIDERS   **705**

RIDER

DISABILITY WAIVER OF PREMIUM (WP)

Waiver of Premiums We will start to waive the premiums for this policy when proof is furnished that the Insured's total disability, as defined in this rider, has gone on for at least 6 months in a row.

If a total disability starts on or prior to the anniversary on which the Insured is age 60, we will waive all of the premiums which fall due during that total disability. If it goes on until the anniversary on which the Insured is age 65, we will make the policy fully paid-up as of that date, with no more premiums due.

If a total disability starts after the anniversary on which the Insured is age 60, we will waive only those premiums which fall due during that total disability, and prior to the anniversary on which the Insured is age 65.

Premiums are waived at the interval of payment in effect when the total disability started. While we waive premiums, all insurance goes on as if they had been paid. We will not deduct a waived premium from the policy proceeds.

Definition of Total Disability "Total Disability" means that, because of disease or bodily injury, the Insured can not do any of the essential acts and duties of his or her job, or of any other job for which he or she is suited based on schooling, training, or experience. If the Insured can do some but not all of these acts and duties, disability is not total and premiums will not be waived. If the Insured is a minor and is required by law to go to school, "Total Disability" means that, because of disease or bodily injury, he or she is not able to go to school.

"Total Disability" also means the Insured's total loss, starting while this rider is in effect, of the sight of both eyes or the use of both hands, both feet, or one hand and one foot.

Total Disabilities For Which Premiums Not Waived We will not waive premiums in connection with any of these total disabilities.

1. Those that start prior to the fifth birthday of the Insured, or start at a time when this rider is not in effect.

2. Those that are caused by an injury that is self-inflicted on purpose.

3. Those that are caused by any kind of war, declared or not, or by any act incident to a war or to an armed conflict involving the armed forces of one or more countries while the Insured is a member of those armed forces.

Proof of Total Disability Written notice and proof of this condition must be given to us, while the Insured is living and totally disabled, or as soon as it can reasonably be done. As long as we waive premiums, we may require proof from time to time. After we have waived premiums for 2 years in a row, we will not need to have this proof more than once each year. As part of the proof, we may have the Insured examined by doctors we approve.

Payment of Premiums Premiums must be paid when due, until we approve a claim under this rider. If a total disability starts during a grace period, the overdue premium must be paid before we will approve any claim.

Refund of Premiums If a total disability starts after a premium has been paid, and if it goes on for at least 6 months in a row, we will refund the part of that premium paid for the period after the policy month when that disability started. Any other premium paid and then waived will be refunded in full.

GAR012   Page 15

SAMPLE

DISABILITY WAIVER OF PREMIUM (WP)

(continued)

Values This rider does not have cash or loan values.

Contract This rider, when paid for, is made a part of the policy, based on the application for the rider.

Incontestability of Rider We have no right to contest this rider after it has been in force during the lifetime of the Insured for 2 years from its date of issue, unless the Insured is totally disabled at some time within 2 years of the date of issue.

Dates and Amounts When this rider is issued at the same time as the policy, we show the rider premium amount on the front page of the policy. The rider and the policy have the same date of issue.

When this rider is added to a policy which is already in force, we also put in an add-on rider. The add-on rider shows the date of issue. The rider premium amount is shown in a new Premium Schedule for the policy.

When Rider Ends You can cancel this rider as of the due date of a premium. To do this, you must send the policy and your signed notice to us within 31 days of that date. If this rider is still in effect on the anniversary on which the Insured is age 65, it will end on that date.

This rider ends if the policy ends or is surrendered. Also, this rider will not be in effect if the policy lapses or is in force as extended or paid-up insurance.

ABC LIFE INSURANCE COMPANY

Mary Smith
Secretary

John Johnson
President

SAMPLE

RIDER

POLICY PURCHASE OPTION (PPO)

Benefit The Owner can purchase a new policy on the Insured on each Scheduled Option Date or Special Option Date, without proof of insurability. The new policy will take effect as of the option date, with premiums based on the Insured's age and the Company's premium rates on that date. The face amount of the new policy may not be less than $10,000 or more than the Option Amount of the rider, except when a larger amount can be purchased on a Special Option Date.

During the 3 months prior to a Special Option Date, the Company provides term insurance on the Insured. The amount of this insurance is equal to the largest face amount of the new policy that can be purchased under this rider on that date.

Scheduled Option Dates The Scheduled Option Dates are the anniversaries on which the Insured is age 22, 25, 28, 31, 34, 37, 40, 43, and 46, and on which this rider is in effect. No new policy can be purchased on any Scheduled Option Date which has been cancelled by a prior Special Option Date purchase.

Special Option Dates A Special Option Date is the date 3 months after any of the events listed below.

1. The marriage of the Insured.
2. The birth of a living child to the Insured.
3. The legal adoption of a child by the Insured.

This rider must be in effect on the date the marriage, birth, or adoption takes place. Proof acceptable to the Company, that the event took place, may be required.

Each purchase of a new policy as of a Special Option Date cancels the next available Scheduled Option Date, except where 2 or more children are born or adopted on the same date. In this case, an amount of insurance can be purchased which equals the Option Amount times the number of these children.

The number of Scheduled Option Dates cancelled by this amount of purchase is equal to the number of these children.

Savings Allowance The Company provides a savings allowance when a new policy is purchased. The amount of this allowance is on file with the insurance official in the state or district in which the policy is delivered. This allowance is used to reduce premiums that are due during the first policy year of the new policy. At the time of purchase, the Company will tell the Owner how much the total allowance is for the new policy.

Purchase of Policy The Owner's application for the new policy must also be signed by the Insured. The application and the first premium for the new policy, less the savings allowance, may be submitted to the Company during the 60 days before or the 31 days after the option date. However, these must be received by the Company while the Insured is living.

On an option date, if the Owner does not have an insurable interest in the life of the Insured that is acceptable to the Company, the Insured may purchase the new policy instead.

If the Insured dies prior to the option date, any new policy which has been applied for will not take effect, and the Company will refund any premium paid for it.

New Policy The new policy may be on any life, term-life, or endowment plan offered on the option date, for the face amount being purchased.

The new policy may not be on a plan which provides only term insurance or provides an increasing amount of insurance. It will have the same provisions and be subject to the same limitations on the Company's liability as are generally in the series of policies being issued on that date. The Insured's class of risk will be the same as it was for the rider.

SAMPLE

POLICY PURCHASE OPTION (PPO)

(continued)

However, if this rider was issued with a policy in a preferred risk class, the new policy will be on a preferred risk basis only if it meets the Company's minimum amount and age limits for that class.

The time periods of the new policy, which relate to a suicide exclusion or to a contest of that policy, will start on the date of issue of this rider. However, in some cases the new policy may be issued with a rider or an additional amount of insurance which the Owner requested, and which required the Company's agreement. If this happens, the time periods for that rider or amount will start instead on the date of issue of the new policy.

Availability of Riders A waiver of premium rider can be made a part of the new policy if one is in effect under this policy on an option date. However, if the Insured has recovered from a total disability that had gone on for at least 6 months in a row, that rider can only be in a new policy for which premiums are payable for the rest of the Insured's life.

An accidental death benefit rider can be made a part of the new policy if one is in effect under this policy on an option date. The amount of that rider may not be more than the face amount of the new policy.

No other riders can be made a part of the new policy, unless the Company agrees.

Waiver of Premiums for New Policy If, on an option date, this policy has a waiver of premium rider in effect, and if the Insured is totally disabled and all conditions for waiver of premiums in that rider have been met, the Company will waive the premiums

for the new policy which fall due during that disability. The new policy must be on a plan with premiums payable for the rest of the Insured's life, and with the same premium interval as this policy.

Values This rider does not have cash or loan values.

Contract This rider, when paid for, is made a part of the policy, based on the application for the rider.

Incontestability of Rider The Company will not contest this rider after it has been in force during the lifetime of the Insured for 2 years from its date of issue.

Dates and Amounts When this rider is issued at the same time as the policy, the Company shows the Option Amount and the rider premium amount on the front page of the policy. The rider and the policy have the same date of issue.

When this rider is added to a policy which is already in force, the Company also puts in an add-on rider. The add-on rider shows the date of issue and the Option Amount. The rider premium amount is shown in a new Premium Schedule for the policy.

When Rider Ends The Owner can cancel this rider as of the due date of a premium. To do this, the policy and the Owner's signed notice must be sent to the Company within 31 days of that date. If this rider is still in effect on the anniversary on which the Insured is age 46, it will end on that date.

This rider ends if the policy ends or is surrendered. Also, this rider will not be in effect if the policy lapses or is in force as extended or reduced paid-up insurance.

ABC LIFE INSURANCE COMPANY

Mary Smith
Secretary

John Johnson
President

GAR013   Page 18

FLEXIBLE PREMIUM (UNIVERSAL) LIFE INSURANCE POLICY

ABC Life Insurance Company

An XYZ Company

123 Main Street, Anytown, USA 54321   (505) 555-1234   (800) 555-4321

WE PROMISE TO PAY THE Insurance Proceeds to the Beneficiary, subject to the provisions of this Contract, when We receive due proof of the Insured's death. Payment will be made only if this Contract is in force on the date of such Insured's death.

THE CONSIDERATION FOR THIS CONTRACT is the application hereof and the payment in advance of the premiums in accordance with the terms and conditions of this Contract. The first premium is payable on or before delivery of this contract; the amount of and the interval between planned premiums are shown in the Schedule.

Insured: John Q. Doe   **Face Amount: $ 75,000.00**   **Issue Date: July 3, 1999**

This is a legal Contract. Read Your Contract carefully.

20 DAY RIGHT TO EXAMINE CONTRACT.

It is important to Us that You are satisfied with this Contract. If You are not satisfied You may, within 20 days after this Contract is delivered to You, return it to Us or to Our agent. If You return the Contract within this time period We will refund all of the premium You have paid. The Contract will then be deemed void from the beginning.

SIGNED BY ABC LIFE INSURANCE COMPANY at Anytown, USA, its Home Office, 123 Main Street on the Contract Date of this Contract.

Mary Smith
Secretary

John Johnson
President

FLEXIBLE PREMIUM LIFE INSURANCE TO AGE 100

Life insurance payable if the Insured dies prior to age 100. Coverage continues provided Cash Value less indebtedness is sufficient to cover monthly deduction. Cash Value less indebtedness payable at Final Policy Date. Non-participating.

SAMPLE

POLICY CONTENTS

SAMPLE

SCHEDULE FOR CONTRACT NUMBER GA001

Form No.	Type of Coverage	Face Amount	Rate Class Numeral	Years Payable
XYZ-091	Flexible Premium Life Insurance to Attained Age 100	$75,000.00	Standard (1.0000)	65
XYZ-090	Endorsement			

Beneficiary - As stated in the application for this Contract unless changed in accordance with Contract provisions.

Owner .... John Q. Doe	Insured .... John Q. Doe
Issue Age 35	Issue Date .... July 3, 1999
Contract Date .... July 3, 1999	Final Policy Date .... July 3, 2064
Monthly Anniversary Date 3	Minimum Premium Due At Issue .... $ 36.00
Additional Initial Lump-Sum Premium .... $ 0.00	Planned Periodic Premium .... $ 1,004.31
Planned Payment Interval .... Annual	Permanent Monthly Flat Extra .... Amount $ 0.00
Monthly Secondary Guarantee Premium $36.00	Guaranteed Date† .... July 3, 2064

Temporary Monthly Flat Extra Amount ... $ 0.00 For all Contract Year(s).

Maximum Contract Loan Interest Rate 7.4% in advance

† The Guaranteed Date is the date to which coverage is guaranteed to continue provided We receive payment of the Additional Initial Lump-Sum Premium, if any, on the Issue Date plus the continuous timely, and uninterrupted monthly payment of a premium equal to the Monthly Secondary Guarantee Premium of $36.00 and no partial surrenders or indebtedness.

XYZ-091   Page 3   Contract GA001

SAMPLE

SCHEDULE FOR CONTRACT NUMBER GA001

PERCENT OF PREMIUM LOAD

A Maximum Premium Load of 10.00% will be deducted from each premium paid. We may from time to time, at Our sole discretion, charge a lesser Premium Load in a uniform manner based upon such factors as the rate class, the amount of cumulative premiums, Cash Value and number of Contract Years expired.

MONTHLY LIFE INSURANCE LOAD

A permanent monthly life insurance load of $2.70 will be included in the monthly deduction deducted from the Cash Value on the Issue Date and on each Monthly Anniversary Date.

A monthly life insurance load will be included in the monthly deduction deducted from the Cash Value on the Issue Date and on each Monthly Anniversary Date. The maximum monthly life insurance load per $1,000 of Face Amount is shown in Table A below. We may from time to time, at Our sole discretion, charge a lesser monthly life insurance load in a uniform manner based upon such factors as the rate class, amount of cumulative premiums paid, Cash Value and number of Contract Years expired.

TABLE A
TABLE OF MAXIMUM MONTHLY LOADS
(Per $1,000 of Face Amount)

Contract Year	Monthly Load	Contract Year	Monthly Load	Contract Year	Monthly Load	Contract Year	Monthly Load
1	0.2274	2	0.2158	3	0.2025	4	0.1875
5	0.1700	6 & Up	0.0000				

ACCELERATION OF FLAT EXTRA AND MONTHLY LOAD

Notwithstanding any other provision of this Contract to the contrary, if the Contract is surrendered during the first Contract Year then We reserve the right to deduct from the surrender value so many of the subsequent Monthly Life Insurance Loads and Permanent Monthly Flat Extra Amounts that otherwise would have been due for the first Contract Year as is equal to the remainder of full months (not less than zero) of (a) minus (b), where: (a) is the smaller of twelve (12), or the total premiums paid to date divided by the Minimum Premium Due At Issue; and, (b) is the number of Contract Months already expired.

SAMPLE

Definitions

To make this Contract easier to read, We have left out many cross-references and conditional statements. Therefore, the provisions of the Contract must be read as a whole.

In this Contract, the following words mean:

Attained Age - The Issue Age shown on page 3 increased by 1 on each succeeding Contract Anniversary Date. For example, if the Issue Age is 35, then the Attained Age on the 5th Contract Anniversary Date is 40 (35 plus 5).

Benchmark Cash Value - On each Monthly Anniverary Date the cash value that would have been produced pursuant to the terms of this Contract assuming: (a) the continuous, timely, and uninterrupted monthly payment of a premium equal to the Minimum Premium Due At Issue shown on page 3; (b) actual interest rates applied and actual cost of insurance rates used; and, (c) no prior Partial Surrenders. The Benchmark Cash Value will never be less than zero.

Beneficiary - The person, persons or entity named in writing by You to receive the Insurance Proceeds at the Insured's death while this Contract is in force

Contract Anniversary Date - The same day and month as the Issue Date shown on page 3 for each succeeding year.

Contract Month - The interval of time from the Issue Date to the Monthly Anniversary Date, and between consecutive Monthly Anniversary Dates.

Contract Year - The interval of time from the Issue Date to the first Contract Anniversary Date, and between consecutive Contract Anniversary Dates.

Cash Value - The amount in this Contract to which We credit interest.

Indebtedness - The sum of any unpaid Contract loans and any accrued and unpaid Contract loan interest.

Insurance Proceeds - The total amount of money We will pay the Beneficiary at the death of the Insured if this Contract is then in force.

Monthly Anniversary Date - The same day of each calendar month as shown on page 3.

Insured - The person whose life is insured under the terms of this Contract. See page 3.

You, Your - The owner of this Contract. The owner may be someone other than the Insured.

We, Our, Us - Texas Life Insurance Company at its Home Office.

Written Request - A writing to exercise any rights under this Contract, appropriately signed and received by Us at Our Home Office in Anytown, USA, on forms that We supply. We may also require that the Contract be sent to Us with any Written Request.

SAMPLE

TABLE OF GUARANTEED MAXIMUM MONTHLY COST
OF INSURANCE RATES PER $1,000

The table below is the guaranteed maximum monthly cost of insurance rates We will charge based on the Insured's Attained Age. These rates must be multiplied times the rate class numeral shown on page 3.

Attained Age	Male	Female	Attained Age	Male	Female
0	0.19417	0.19417	50	0.52083	0.52083
1	0.08000	0.08000	51	0.56417	0.56417
2	0.07667	0.07667	52	0.61333	0.61333
3	0.07417	0.07417	53	0.66833	0.66833
4	0.07167	0.07167	54	0.72833	0.72833
5	0.06917	0.06917	55	0.79083	0.79083
6	0.06583	0.06583	56	0.85667	0.85667
7	0.06250	0.06250	57	0.92417	0.92417
8	0.06083	0.06083	58	0.99500	0.99500
9	0.06000	0.06000	59	1.07333	1.07333
10	0.06000	0.06000	60	1.16000	1.16000
11	0.06417	0.06417	61	1.26083	1.26083
12	0.07000	0.07000	62	1.37833	1.37833
13	0.07917	0.07917	63	1.51250	1.51250
14	0.08917	0.08917	64	1.66167	1.66167
15	0.10000	0.10000	65	1.82083	1.82083
16	0.11000	0.11000	66	1.98833	1.98833
17	0.11833	0.11833	67	2.16333	2.16333
18	0.12417	0.12417	68	2.34667	2.34667
19	0.12833	0.12833	69	2.55000	2.55000
20	0.13083	0.13083	70	2.78250	2.78250
21	0.13167	0.13167	71	3.05083	3.05083
22	0.13083	0.13083	72	3.36583	3.36583
23	0.13000	0.13000	73	3.72833	3.72833
24	0.12833	0.12833	74	4.13083	4.13083
25	0.12750	0.12750	75	4.56667	4.56667
26	0.12667	0.12667	76	5.02707	5.02707
27	0.12667	0.12667	77	5.50750	5.50750
28	0.12750	0.12750	78	6.01333	6.01333
29	0.13000	0.13000	79	6.56167	6.56167
30	0.13333	0.13333	80	7.17417	7.17417
31	0.13750	0.13750	81	7.86917	7.86917
32	0.14250	0.14250	82	8.66333	8.66333
33	0.14917	0.14917	83	9.55250	9.55250
34	0.15667	0.15667	84	10.52000	10.52000
35	0.16500	0.16500	85	11.55167	11.55167
36	0.17667	0.17667	86	12.63583	12.63583
37	0.19000	0.19000	87	13.77083	13.77083
38	0.20500	0.20500	88	14.95917	14.95917
39	0.22250	0.22250	89	16.20917	16.20917
40	0.24167	0.24167	90	17.54000	17.54000
41	0.26333	0.26333	91	18.98667	18.98667
42	0.28500	0.28500	92	20.60917	20.60917
43	0.30833	0.30833	93	22.52417	22.52417
44	0.33250	0.33250	94	25.04500	25.04500
45	0.35917	0.35917	95	28.73917	28.73917
46	0.38667	0.38667	96	34.68083	34.68083
47	0.41583	0.41583	97	44.88917	44.88917
48	0.44750	0.44750	98	62.05500	62.05500
49	0.48250	0.48250	99	83.33333	83.33333

SAMPLE

Death Benefits

Insurance Proceeds

The Insurance Proceeds are the sum of (a) minus (b) where:

(a) is the death benefit as calculated below; and,

(b) is any Indebtedness.

The death benefit is the greater of (a) or (b), where:

(a) is the Face Amount shown on page 3 (or as reduced by the effect of a Partial Surrender); and,

(b) is the applicable percentage from Table B multiplied times the Cash Value on the date the Insured dies. The percentage is based upon the Insured's Attained Age and changes on each Contract Anniversary Date as shown in Table B below.

TABLE B

Attained Age	Percentage	Attained Age	Percentage	Attained Age	Percentage
0–40	250%	54	157%	68	117%
41	243	55	150	69	116
42	236	56	146	70	115
43	229	57	142	71	113
44	222	58	138	72	111
45	215	59	134	73	109
46	209	60	130	74	107
47	203	61	128	75–90	105
48	197	62	126	91	104
49	191	63	124	92	103
50	185	64	122	93	102
51	178	65	120	94 & Later	101
52	171	66	119		
53	164	67	118		

Payment of Insurance Proceeds

Subject to the provisions of this Contract, when the Insured dies We will pay the Insurance Proceeds to the Beneficiary, and this Contract will then terminate. We will pay the Insurance Proceeds to the Beneficiary only after We receive:

(a) this Contract;

(b) due proof that the Insured died while this Contract was in force;

(c) a properly completed claim form on a form which We will provide; and,

(d) an authorization on a form We supply, from the next of kin of the Insured, which allows Us to obtain and disclose information concerning the Insured.

SAMPLE

Effect of Partial Surrender on Insurance Proceeds

A partial surrender will decrease the Insurance Proceeds. If the death benefit is the Face Amount, We will reduce the Face Amount by the amount of the partial surrender. If the death benefit is not the Face Amount in calculating the new death benefit, We will reduce the Face Amount by the larger of zero, or (a) minus (b) plus (c) where:

(a)   is the amount of the partial surrender;

(b)   is the amount of death benefit prior to the partial surrender; and,

(c)   is the Face Amount.

Premiums And Reinstatement

Payment of Premiums

An initial premium equal to or greater than the Minimum Premium Due At Issue shown on page 3 is due on the Issue Date. This Contract is not in force until the initial premium has been paid. If premium payments cease, this Contract will continue in force, subject to the grace period provision. Subject to the provisions of this section, You can choose the amount and the frequency of any further premiums. Premiums are to be paid to Us at Our Home Office. You may request a receipt signed by one of Our officers.

Planned Periodic Premiums

Planned Periodic Premiums are shown on page 3. This is the amount and frequency of premiums You selected on the Issue Date. You may change the amount and frequency. You may choose only intervals of 1 month, 6 months (for a Planned Periodic Premium of $100 or more), or 12 months.

If You choose the monthly interval, payment must be:

(a)   by pre-authorized payment from a bank or institution that permits similar payment;

(b)   as a part of a billing involving five or more employees of a common employer; or,

(c)   by direct payment to Us, but only if premiums for this Contract were previously paid as a part of a billing involving a common employer. For this method of payment We will send You reminder notices each month, and to cover the added handling cost deduct from each premium so received a monthly direct billing fee not to exceed $2.00.

If You choose 6 or 12 month intervals, We will send You reminder notices at the planned payment interval.

Additional Premiums

You may pay additional premiums at any time while this Contract is in force, except that We may refuse to accept a premium if the death benefit is not the Face Amount.

We will not knowingly accept any premium which would result in the Internal Revenue Code not treating any of the Insurance Proceeds as life insurance. If We accept any premium in error, We will refund it to You with interest immediately after the error is discovered. The interest rate will be that credited to the Cash Value attributable to the premium refunded. Any premiums which We accept in error will not be considered premium paid under this Contract.

SAMPLE

Grace Period

On any Monthly Anniversary Date, if the Cash Value minus any Indebtedness is less than the monthly deduction this Contract will terminate 61 days after such date. These 61 days are called the grace period. We will notify You and any assignee recorded on Our records in writing of the Contract entering the grace period.

Reinstatement

Reinstatement means to place this Contract in force after it terminates because it reached the end of a grace period. We will reinstate this Contract if We receive:

(a) Your Written Request within five years after this Contract terminates at the end of a grace period;

(b) Satisfactory proof that the Insured is still insurable at the original rate class;

(c) Payment or reinstatement of any Indebtedness; and

(d) Payment of a premium which is equal to the result of multiplying the Minimum Premium Due At Issue times the sum of the number of Contract Months expired since termination plus three (the Cash Value and Indebtedness will not be less than they would have been had a premium equal to the Minimum Premium Due At Issue been paid each month during the period of termination).

If We approve Your Written Request for reinstatement on a Monthly Anniversary Date this Contract will again be in force on that day. If Our approval occurs on any other day this Contract will again be in force as of the preceding Monthly Anniversary Date.

Contract Values

Cash Value

On each Monthly Anniversary Date the Cash Value is the sum of (a) plus (b) plus (c) minus (d) minus (e), where:

(a) is the Cash Value on the preceding Monthly Anniversary Date;

(b) is the interest for one month on item (a);

(c) is all premiums received since the preceding Monthly Anniversary Date, less a premium load not to exceed the percent of premium load of such premiums, as shown on page 4;

(d) is the monthly deduction for the ensuing month; and

(e) is the sum of all partial surrenders since the preceding Monthly Anniversary Date.

On the Issue Date the Cash Value is (c) minus (d). On any other day the Cash Value is (a) plus (c) minus (e). The Cash Value will never be less than zero.

Interest Rate

We guarantee to credit interest at a rate not less than 0.46698% a month, compounded monthly, on that portion of the Cash Value up to the Benchmark Cash Value. This is equivalent to 5.75% a year, compounded yearly. On the balance of the Cash Value, if any, We guarantee to credit interest at a rate not less than 0.36748% a month, compounded monthly. This is equivalent to 4.50% a year, compounded yearly.

SAMPLE

We may, in Our discretion, use one or more higher interest rate(s) and credit each rate to different portions of Your Cash Value in such a manner as We determine. For example, We may credit a different interest rate to that portion of the Cash Value in excess of the Benchmark Cash Value. The monthly rate We will credit that portion of the Cash Value which equals any Indebtedness will be 0.36748% a month.

Monthly Deductions

The monthly deduction whether or not premium payments are received is (a) plus (b) plus (c) where:

(a) is the cost of insurance for this Contract and any riders attached to it;

(b) is the monthly life insurance load as described on page 4; and,

(c) is the Permanent and Temporary Monthly Flat Extra Amount(s), if any, for this Contract shown on page 3.

Continuation of Insurance

When the Cash Value minus Indebtedness is less than the monthly deduction this Contract will terminate according to the Grace Period provision.

Cost of Insurance

We calculate the cost of insurance for the ensuing month on the Issue Date and on each Monthly Anniversary Date. The cost of insurance is (a) multiplied times the quotient resulting from dividing the remainder of (b) minus (c) by 1,000 where:

(a) is the cost of insurance rate;

(b) is the amount of death benefit divided by 1.0036748; and

(c) is the Cash Value.

We calculate the cost of insurance for benefits provided by any riders attached to this Contract as provided in those riders.

Cost of Insurance Rates

The cost of insurance rate depends on the Issue Age, Contract Year and rate class. The guaranteed maximum monthly cost of insurance rates are found by multiplying (a) times (b) where:

(a) is the monthly cost of insurance rates shown on page 6; and

(b) is the rate class numeral shown on page 3. The monthly cost of insurance rates shown on page 6 are based on the 1980 CSO Mortality Table-C, Age Last Birthday. We can use cost of insurance rates that are lower than these guaranteed rates. The cost of insurance rates We will use will apply uniformly to all policies of the same class, Issue Age, and Contract Year. However, the guaranteed maximum cost of insurance rates will apply whenever the Cash Value is less than the Benchmark Cash Value.

Surrender

While the Insured is alive You may surrender this Contract for its Cash Value less any Indebtedness. We will pay You such amount in a lump sum after We receive Your Written Request to do so, subject to the "Deferment" provision. The amount will be determined as of the date the Written Request is received. If You request to surrender this Contract then all of Our obligations under it will end.

SAMPLE

In lieu of a lump sum payment, You may ask that the surrender amount be applied under one of the Optional Income Plans Upon surrender of this Contract during the grace period and within 30 days after a Contract Anniversary Date, the surrender amount will not be less than it would have been on such date. If the Insured is alive on the Final Policy Date shown on page 3 We will pay You the Cash Value minus any Indebtedness and this Contract and all of Our obligations under it will end.

Partial Surrender

On any Monthly Anniversary Date while the Insured is alive, You may make a partial surrender. The amount of the partial surrender must be for at least $500.00 but cannot exceed the amount You would receive if You surrendered this Contract.

Contract Loans

Contract Loan

By Written Request while this Contract is in force You may receive cash from Us by taking a Contract loan upon the assignment of this Contract to Us as sole security. If there is an existing loan You can increase it. The most You can borrow at any time is the Cash Value as of the date We receive Your Written Request. We will deduct the amount of any existing Indebtedness from the amount We send You. All or any part of the Indebtedness may be repaid at any time while this Contract is in force. However, this Contract will terminate when the total Indebtedness equals or exceeds the Cash Value. The effective date this Contract will so terminate will be 62 days after We mail a notice to the last known address of You and any assignee recorded on Our records.

Interest Rate Charged on Contract Loan

The maximum effective annual interest rate We charge on money You borrow under this Contract is shown on page 3. We can charge interest at a lower rate for any period of time. If We change the interest rate We charge We will notify You and any assignee recorded on Our records.

Interest to the next Contract Anniversary Date is due and payable on the date the loan is made. Thereafter interest is due and payable annually on each Contract Anniversary Date. If You do not pay the interest when it is due, any unpaid interest will be added to the amount You borrowed and will be charged the same interest rate.

General Provisions

Contract

This Contract, endorsements if any, and a copy of the application attached to it make up the entire Contract between You and Us. In the absence of fraud, all statements made in the application will be considered representations and not warranties. Also, We will not use any statement to void this Contract or defend against any claim made under it unless such statement is contained in the application. Only Our President or Our Secretary together with one of Our Vice Presidents have the authority to make any changes in this Contract. Any change must be in writing. We are not bound by any promise or representation made by any agent or person other than as specifically contained in this Contract. Any additional benefit rider attached to this Contract will become a part of this Contract and will be subject to all the terms and conditions of this Contract, unless We state otherwise in the rider.

SAMPLE

Your Rights

You can exercise Your rights under this Contract while the Insured is alive by making a Written Request. We will also require a Written Request from the assignee if Your Contract is assigned as collateral. We will also require a Written Request from the Beneficiary if You have not reserved the right to change the Beneficiary.

Misstatement Of Age

If the age of the Insured is misstated in the application, We will adjust the benefits of this Contract. The Face Amount shall be the amount the Minimum Premium Due At Issue would have then purchased if the Insured's age had been correctly stated. The Cash Value will be recalculated using the mortality rates actually charged for the correct age and the interest rates actually paid under this Contract.

Suicide

If the Insured commits suicide, while sane or insane, within two years from the Issue Date, this Contract will immediately terminate, and We will not pay the Insurance Proceeds. The amount We will pay shall be limited to the premiums We actually received for this Contract reduced by the amount of any Contract loan and accrued loan interest then outstanding, and by any prior partial surrenders.

Incontestability

Except for nonpayment of premiums, this Contract will be incontestable after it has been in force during the lifetime of the Insured for two years from the Issue Date. This provision does not apply to any rider providing benefits specifically for disability or death by accident.

If this Contract is reinstated, We will not contest the reinstatement after it is again in force during the lifetime of the Insured for two years from the effective date of the reinstatement. For this purpose, if We contest the reinstatement the contest will be based upon material statement(s) made only in the application for reinstatement.

Beneficiary

Unless You choose otherwise, any payment to beneficiaries will be paid based on the following order of priority. Payment will be made to:

(a) The Beneficiary. If more than one Beneficiary is then living, we will pay them in equal shares unless You specify otherwise.

(b) The contingent Beneficiary, if no Beneficiary is living when a payment is due. If more than one contingent Beneficiary is then living, we will pay them in equal shares unless You specify otherwise.

(c) The estate of the last Beneficiary or contingent Beneficiary to die, if no Beneficiary or contingent Beneficiary is living when payment is due. This payment will be in one sum.

You may change the Beneficiary by Written Request. Unless You specify otherwise, You will not need the permission of the Beneficiary to make another change in the future.

Computation of Values

We have filed in the state where this Contract is issued a detailed statement showing how Contract benefits and reserves are calculated. All values are at least as great as the values required by that state. We use the 1980 CSO Mortality Table-C, Age Last Birthday, to calculate minimum Cash Value and reserves. The interest rate used to calculate minimum Cash Values is 5.75% per annum on that portion created by the monthly payment of the Minimum Premium Due At Issue multiplied times the number of Contract Months expired and 4.5% per annum on the excess. Reserves are calculated by using a modified preliminary term method, but they are not less than the Commissioners Reserve Valuation Method reserves. Reserves held on this Contract will never be less than the Cash Value.

All computations assume that premiums are paid annually and that deaths during a Contract Year occur immediately. Any benefits provided by attached riders are excluded from these computations.

Ownership

As owner, You may by Written Request exercise all rights under Your Contract while the Insured is alive. You may name a contingent owner should You die before the death of the Insured.

Change of Ownership

By Written Request You may name a new owner at any time. If You designate a new owner, it will not change the Beneficiary or contingent Beneficiary, unless You specify otherwise. The new owner can exercise all the rights of ownership, unless You specify otherwise. No change is binding on Us until We record it. Once recorded, the change binds Us as of the date You signed it. The change will not apply to any payment made by Us before We record Your Written Request.

Collateral Assignment

Your Contract may be collaterally assigned. We are not bound by the assignment unless You make a Written Request. No assignment is binding on Us until We record it. We are not responsible for determining if Your assignment is valid or the extent of the assignee's interest.

Annual Report

We will send You a report shortly after each Contract Anniversary Date. This report will show: (a) premiums paid since the last report; (b) the Cash Value at the beginning of the period; (c) interest credited since the last report; (d) Monthly Deductions from the Cash Value since the last report; (e) Indebtedness activity; (f) the Cash Value at the end of the period; and, (g) Insurance Proceeds at the end of the period. Any time after the first Contract Anniversary Date We will provide a hypothetical illustration of future death benefits and Cash Values upon Written Request. We will charge a reasonable fee for this service not to exceed $25.00. We will make any necessary reasonable assumptions not otherwise prohibited by law.

Nonparticipating

This Contract does not participate in any distribution of surplus. No dividends are payable.

SAMPLE

Deferment

We may delay paying the Cash Value for up to 6 months from the date We receive Your Written Request for payment. If We delay for 30 days or more, interest will be paid from the date We receive the request at the rate We set from time to time. We also may delay making a Contract loan, except for a loan to pay a premium, for up to 6 months from the date We receive Your Written Request for the loan.

Right to Extend Final Policy Date

If the Insured is alive on the Final Policy Date shown on page 3 We will pay You the Cash Value minus any Indebtedness and this Contract and all of Our obligations under it will end. However, You may instead by Written Request extend the Contract during the life of Insured to a later alternative Final Policy Date, but not beyond Attained Age 110. Your Written Request must be received by Us within 60 days prior to the Final Policy Date shown on page 3.

If You elect an alternate Final Policy Date, the Cash Value at Attained Age 100 will therafter be credited interest at 0.36748% a month, compounded monthly. This is equivalent to 4.5% a year, compounded yearly. No monthly deduction will be deducted from the Cash Value after Attained Age 99.

> **NOTE**
>
> 1. **The policy may not qualify as life insurance after Attained Age 99;**
> 2. **The policy may be subject to tax consequences; and,**
> 3. **A tax advisor should be consulted prior to making any election.**

Tax Considerations

You are encouraged to consult a qualified tax advisor. Neither We nor Our agents are authorized to give tax or legal advice. The following is not intended as tax advice, and it is not a complete statement of what the effect of federal income taxes will be under all circumstances. Rather, it provides information about how We believe the tax law applies in the most common circumstances. There is no guarantee that the current federal income tax laws and regulations or interpretations will remain the same, and this provision should not be construed to mean that the Insurance Proceeds and/or other values will be exempt from the future actions of any tax authority.

We believe that We have taken adequate steps so that this Contract is considered life insurance for tax purposes, and that the Contract is designed to comply with Sections 7702 and 7702A of the Internal Revenue Code of 1986, or any other equivalent section of the Code. Your individual situation, or that of any Beneficiary, will determine the federal estate taxes and state and local estate, inheritance or other taxes due if You or the Insured die.

Governing Law

This Contract is subject to the laws of the state of Georgia. If any provision of the Contract does not conform to these laws, the Contract will be applied to conform to the law.

SAMPLE

Optional Income Plans

Unless otherwise requested, We may pay the Insurance Proceeds in one sum or by placing the amount in an account that earns interest. The payee will have immediate access to all or any part of the account. The Insurance Proceeds, instead of being paid in one sum, may be applied under one or more of the following Income Plans. Also, at any time while the Contract is in force and the Insured is alive, You may by Written Request ask that:

(a) all or a part of the Cash Value less any Indebtedness of this Contract be applied under a non-life income plan (a plan which provides a schedule of payments which is not dependent on the lifetime of the payee); or

(b) all or a part of the Cash Value less any Indebtedness of this Contract be applied under a life income plan (a plan which provides a schedule of payments which depends on the lifetime of one or more payees and which may guarantee that payments will be made for at least a specified number of years).

If only a part of the Cash Value is to be applied the balance of the value will be paid to You in a single sum. If only a part of the Insurance Proceeds is to be applied after the Insured dies, the balance of the Insurance Proceeds will be paid to the Beneficiary.

Non-Life Income Plans

Available with respect to the Insurance Proceeds or Cash Value less Indebtedness.

Option 1. Interest Income - The amount applied will earn interest which will be paid monthly. Withdrawals of at least $500 each may be made at any time by Written Request.

Option 2. Installment Income for a Stated Period - Monthly installment payments will be made so that the amount applied, with interest, will be paid over the period chosen (from 1 to 30 years). See Table 1.

Option 2A. Installment Income of a Stated Amount - Monthly installment payments of a chosen amount will be made until the entire amount applied, with interest, is paid

Life Income Plans

Available with respect to the Insurance Proceeds or Cash Value less Indebtedness.

Option 3. Single Life Income - With Guaranteed Payment Period - Monthly payments will be made during the lifetime of the payee with chosen guaranteed payment period of 10, 15 or 20 years. See Table 2.

Option 3A. Single Life Income - Installment Refund - Monthly payments will be made during the lifetime of the payee. If the payee dies before the total amount applied under this plan has been paid, the remainder will be paid in one sum as a death benefit. See Table 2.

Option 4. Joint and Survivor Life Income - Monthly payments will be made jointly to two persons during their lifetime and will continue during the remaining lifetime of the survivor. See Table 3.

Other Frequencies and Plans

Instead of monthly payments, You may choose to have payments made quarterly, semiannually or annually. Other Income Plans may be arranged which are mutually agreeable to You and Us.

SAMPLE

Choice of Income Plans

A choice of Income Plan for any Insurance Proceeds made by You while the Insured is alive will take effect when the Insured dies. All other choices of Income Plans will take effect when recorded by Us, or later, if requested. When an Income Plan starts, We will issue an agreement which will describe the terms of the plan. We may require that You send Us this Contract. We may also require proof of the payee's age.

Income Plans may be chosen:

    (a) By You during the lifetime of the Insured.

    (b) By the Beneficiary within one year after the date the Insured dies and before any payment has been made to the Beneficiary, if no election was in effect on the date of death.

A choice of an Income Plan will not become effective unless each payment under the plan would be at least $50.

Limitations

If the payee is not a natural person, the choice of an income plan will be subject to Our approval.

Income plan payments may not be assigned and, to the extent permitted by law, will not be subject to the claims of creditors.

Income Plan Rates

Amounts applied under the non-life income plans will earn interest at a rate We set from time to time. That rate will never be less than 3% a year.

Life income plan payments will be based on a rate set by Us and in effect on the date the Insurance Proceeds become payable or on the date the Cash Value less Indebtedness is applied. The minimum rates are shown in Tables 2 and 3 following, and are based upon the 1983 Table "a" for individual annuities and a guaranteed interest rate of 3.5% per annum.

Minimum Payments under Optional Income Plans

Monthly payments under Options 2, 3, and 4 for each $1,000 applied will not be less than the amount shown in the following Tables. Monthly life income payments will not be less than those that would be provided to a person in the same class as the Insured by a single payment immediate annuity bought with an equal amount at the time monthly payments start.

SAMPLE

TABLES

TABLE 1

Installment Income for a Stated Period
Monthly Payments for each $1,000 Applied

Years Payable	Monthly Payment	Years Payable	Monthly Payment	Years Payable	Monthly Payment
1	$84.47	11	$8.86	21	$5.32
2	42.86	12	8.24	22	5.15
3	28.99	13	7.71	23	4.99
4	22.06	14	7.26	24	4.84
5	17.91	15	6.87	25	4.71
6	15.14	16	6.53	26	4.59
7	13.16	17	6.23	27	4.47
8	11.68	18	5.96	28	4.37
9	10.53	19	5.73	29	4.27
10	9.61	20	5.51	30	4.18

Annual, semi-annual or quarterly payments will be determined by multiplying the monthly payment by 11.838, 5.963 or 2.991, respectively.

SAMPLE

TABLE 2

Single Life Income
Guaranteed Payment Period or Installment Refund

Age	Life Only	Guaranteed Period			Installment Refund
		10 Years	15 Years	20 Years	
35	3.57	3.56	3.56	3.55	3.54
36	3.60	3.59	3.59	3.58	3.57
37	3.63	3.62	3.62	3.61	3.60
38	3.66	3.65	3.65	3.64	3.63
39	3.69	3.69	3.68	3.67	3.66
40	3.73	3.72	3.71	3.70	3.69
41	3.76	3.76	3.75	3.73	3.72
42	3.80	3.80	3.78	3.77	3.76
43	3.84	3.84	3.82	3.81	3.80
44	3.89	3.88	3.86	3.84	3.83
45	3.93	3.92	3.91	3.88	3.87
46	3.98	3.97	3.95	3.92	3.92
47	4.03	4.02	4.00	3.97	3.96
48	4.08	4.07	4.05	4.01	4.01
49	4.14	4.12	4.10	4.06	4.06
50	4.20	4.18	4.15	4.11	4.11
51	4.26	4.24	4.21	4.16	4.16
52	4.32	4.30	4.26	4.21	4.22
53	4.39	4.36	4.33	4.27	4.27
54	4.46	4.43	4.39	4.32	4.34
55	4.54	4.51	4.46	4.38	4.40
56	4.62	4.58	4.53	4.44	4.47
57	4.71	4.66	4.60	4.51	4.54
58	4.80	4.75	4.68	4.57	4.62
59	4.90	4.84	4.76	4.64	4.70
60	5.00	4.93	4.84	4.70	4.78
61	5.11	5.03	4.93	4.77	4.87
62	5.23	5.14	5.02	4.84	4.96
63	5.36	5.25	5.12	4.91	5.06
64	5.49	5.37	5.21	4.98	5.17
65	5.64	5.50	5.31	5.05	5.28
66	5.79	5.63	5.42	5.12	5.39
67	5.95	5.77	5.53	5.19	5.52
68	6.13	5.91	5.63	5.25	5.65
69	6.32	6.07	5.74	5.32	5.79
70	6.53	6.23	5.86	5.37	5.94
71	6.75	6.40	5.97	5.43	6.09
72	6.99	6.58	6.08	5.48	6.26
73	7.26	6.76	6.18	5.52	6.44
74	7.54	6.95	6.29	5.57	6.63
75	7.85	7.14	6.39	5.60	6.83
76	8.18	7.34	6.48	5.63	7.04
77	8.54	7.54	6.57	5.66	7.26
78	8.94	7.74	6.65	5.68	7.51
79	9.36	7.94	6.72	5.70	7.76
80	9.82	8.13	6.79	5.71	8.03

Values for ages not shown will be furnished upon request.

SAMPLE

TABLE 3

Joint and Survivor Life Income
Minimum Amount of each Monthly Payment for each $1,000 Applied

| Age | - - - - - - - - - - - - Age of Second Participant - - - - - - - - - - - - | | | | | | | | |
	40	45	50	55	60	65	70	75	80
40	3.48	3.54	3.59	3.63	3.66	3.68	3.70	3.71	3.72
41	3.49	3.56	3.61	3.65	3.69	3.71	3.73	3.74	3.75
42	3.50	3.57	3.63	3.68	3.72	3.75	3.77	3.78	3.79
43	3.52	3.59	3.66	3.71	3.75	3.78	3.80	3.82	3.83
44	3.53	3.61	3.68	3.74	3.78	3.82	3.84	3.86	3.87
45	3.54	3.62	3.70	3.76	3.81	3.85	3.88	3.90	3.91
46	3.55	3.64	3.72	3.79	3.85	3.89	3.92	3.94	3.96
47	3.56	3.65	3.74	3.82	3.88	3.93	3.97	3.99	4.01
48	3.57	3.67	3.77	3.85	3.92	3.97	4.01	4.04	4.06
49	3.58	3.69	3.79	3.88	3.95	4.01	4.06	4.09	4.11
50	3.59	3.70	3.81	3.91	3.99	4.06	4.11	4.14	4.16
51	3.60	3.71	3.83	3.94	4.03	4.10	4.16	4.20	4.22
52	3.61	3.73	3.85	3.97	4.07	4.15	4.21	4.25	4.28
53	3.61	3.74	3.87	3.99	4.10	4.19	4.26	4.31	4.35
54	3.62	3.75	3.89	4.02	4.14	4.24	4.32	4.37	4.41
55	3.63	3.76	3.91	4.05	4.18	4.29	4.38	4.44	4.48
56	3.64	3.78	3.93	4.08	4.22	4.34	4.44	4.51	4.56
57	3.64	3.79	3.94	4.10	4.26	4.39	4.50	4.58	4.63
58	3.65	3.80	3.96	4.13	4.30	4.44	4.56	4.65	4.71
59	3.65	3.81	3.98	4.16	4.33	4.50	4.63	4.73	4.80
60	3.66	3.81	3.99	4.18	4.37	4.55	4.70	4.81	4.89
61	3.66	3.82	4.01	4.20	4.41	4.60	4.77	4.89	4.98
62	3.67	3.83	4.02	4.23	4.45	4.65	4.84	4.98	5.08
63	3.67	3.84	4.03	4.25	4.48	4.71	4.91	5.07	5.19
64	3.68	3.85	4.05	4.27	4.51	4.76	4.98	5.16	5.29
65	3.68	3.85	4.06	4.29	4.55	4.81	5.05	5.26	5.41
66	3.69	3.86	4.07	4.31	4.58	4.86	5.13	5.36	5.53
67	3.69	3.87	4.08	4.33	4.61	4.91	5.20	5.46	5.65
68	3.69	3.87	4.09	4.35	4.64	4.96	5.28	5.56	5.78
69	3.70	3.88	4.10	4.36	4.67	5.01	5.35	5.67	5.92
70	3.70	3.88	4.11	4.38	4.70	5.05	5.43	5.77	6.06
71	3.70	3.89	4.11	4.39	4.72	5.10	5.50	5.88	6.20
72	3.70	3.89	4.12	4.40	4.75	5.14	5.57	5.99	6.35
73	3.71	3.89	4.13	4.42	4.77	5.18	5.64	6.10	6.50
74	3.71	3.90	4.13	4.43	4.79	5.22	5.71	6.21	6.66
75	3.71	3.90	4.14	4.44	4.81	5.26	5.77	6.32	6.82
76	3.71	3.90	4.15	4.45	4.83	5.29	5.84	6.42	6.99
77	3.71	3.91	4.15	4.46	4.85	5.32	5.90	6.53	7.15
78	3.71	3.91	4.16	4.47	4.86	5.36	5.95	6.63	7.31
79	3.72	3.91	4.16	4.47	4.88	5.38	6.01	6.73	7.48
80	3.72	3.91	4.16	4.48	4.89	5.41	6.06	6.82	7.64

SAMPLE

ABC Life Insurance Company

An XYZ Company

ENDORSEMENT TO CONTRACT NUMBER GA001

Effective on the Issue Date, this endorsement is added to and made a part of the Contract referred to above.

Notwithstanding any other provision in this Contract to the contrary, this Contract will not terminate if for each Contract Month that the Contract has been in force, (a) equals or exceeds the sum of (b) plus (c), where:

(a)   is the total premiums paid less any partial surrenders and indebtedness;

(b)   is the Additional Initial Lump-Sum Premium (shown on page 3); and,

(c)   is the Monthly Secondary Guarantee Premium (shown on page 3) multiplied times the number of Contract Months elapsed since the Issue Date, including the current Contract Month.

Mary Smith
Secretary

John Johnson
President

Form: XYZ-090	Page 20	Contract GA001

APPENDIX E

IS YOUR LIFE INSURANCE REASONABLY PRICED? (HOW TO EVALUATE AN EXISTING LIFE INSURANCE POLICY)*

If you own a life insurance policy on which you have paid premiums for some years, and if you are wondering whether you are receiving fair value for your money, this appendix is aimed at you.

THE PLAYERS

Many of those in the life insurance business are legitimate and ethical salespeople; however, the business is plagued by a significant number of replacement artists and conservation artists. A replacement artist is a person who uses dubious methods to convince you—the owner of an existing life insurance policy—to replace your policy with a new one. Some replacement artists attempt to discredit the agent and the company from which you bought your existing policy. Some of what replacement artists say may be accurate, but some of it may be deceptive or even false. The problem is that most policyowners cannot determine what is accurate and what is not.

A conservation artist, on the other hand, is a person who uses dubious methods to convince you—the owner of an existing life insurance policy—that your policy should not be replaced. Some conservation artists attempt to discredit the replacement artist. Some of what conservation artists say may be accurate, but some of it may be deceptive or even false. The problem is that most policyowners cannot determine what is accurate and what is not.

In short, a war is going on between replacement artists and conservation artists. As the owner of an existing life insurance policy, you are caught in the middle. You probably do not know enough about life insurance to be able to distinguish accurate information from inaccurate information, and you probably do not know whom to believe. The purpose of this appendix is to arm you with the ability to find out for yourself whether the life insurance protection you own is reasonably priced.

THE GENERAL APPROACH

This appendix describes three steps you must follow to determine whether the life insurance protection you own is reasonably priced: (1) gather certain information about each policy you wish to evaluate; (2) perform certain calculations using the information gathered in the first step; and (3) compare the results of your calculations with certain benchmarks.

Gathering Information

The most difficult step is not the arithmetic, but rather assembling the necessary information. Some of what you need is in the policy itself, but you may find the information difficult to extract. And some of what you need may not be in the policy. It is suggested that you obtain the information by writing a carefully worded letter to the president of the life insurance company that issued the policy. A suggested letter is shown after the explanatory appendix.

*The material in this appendix was written by Joseph M. Belth, Ph.D., professor emeritus of insurance in the Kelley School of Business at Indiana University (Bloomington), and author of *Life Insurance: A Consumer's Handbook* (1985). It was first published in the June 1982 issue of *Insurance Forum*, of which Professor Belth is the editor, and was modified slightly in 2002 for purposes of this appendix. Copyright © 1982 by Insurance Forum, Inc., P.O. Box 245, Ellettsville, IN 47429. Used by permission.

You may find the address of the company on the policy itself, on a recent premium notice, or by calling your local library. You may find the policy number on the policy itself or on a recent premium notice. Your letter should request the following items of information:

1. The amount that the insurance company would have paid to your beneficiary if you had died at the end of the most recently completed policy year. This is the death benefit (*DB*) of your policy.
2. The amount that the insurance company would have paid to you if you had surrendered your policy at the end of the most recently completed policy year. This is the cash value (*CV*) of your policy. (Some policies do not have cash values, so the amount here could be zero.)
3. The amount that the insurance company would have paid to you if you had surrendered your policy at the end of the year preceding the most recently completed policy year. This (*CVP*) corresponds to item 2, but for one year earlier.
4. The annual premium (*P*) for the most recently completed policy year. (Policies that are "paid up" require no further premiums, so the amount here could be zero.)
5. The dividend (*D*) for the most recently completed policy year. (Some policies do not pay dividends, so the amount here could be zero.)
6. The date on which the most recently completed policy year began.
7. Your insurance age, in accordance with the company's method of determining age, on the date referred to in item 6.

It is recommended that you word the letter exactly as illustrated, and that you keep a copy of the letter. If you receive no response, or if you receive an inadequate response, you should file a written complaint with your state insurance commissioner. You may obtain the address of your state insurance commissioner from your local library.

The Calculations

Once you have acquired the information listed in the preceding section, you are ready to perform certain calculations, except for the choice of an interest rate

(*i*). It is suggested that you use an interest rate of 6 percent (0.06) in your calculations. (For comments concerning the interest rate, see the explanatory appendix.)

Now you are ready to perform certain calculations to arrive at a yearly price per $1000 of protection for the most recently completed policy year. The formula is as follows:

$$\frac{(P + CVP)(1 + i) - (CV + D)}{(DB - CV)(0.001)}$$

To illustrate, suppose the response to your letter provided the following information:

1. Death benefit (*DB*): $25,000
2. Cash value at end of most recently completed policy year (*CV*): $10,450
3. Cash value at end of year preceding most recently completed policy year (*CVP*): $10,000
4. Annual premium (*P*): $550
5. Dividend (*D*): $400
6. Date on which most recently completed policy year began: March 10, 2002
7. Your insurance age on March 10, 2002: 56

Your next step is to plug these figures into the formula. The calculations are as follows.

$$\frac{(550 + 10{,}000)(1 + 0.06) - (10{,}450 + 400)}{(25{,}000 - 10{,}450)(0.001)}$$

$$= \frac{(10{,}550)(1.06) - 10{,}850}{(14{,}550)(0.001)}$$

$$= \frac{11{,}183 - 10{,}850}{14.550}$$

$$= \frac{333}{14.550} = 22.89$$

In other words, the yearly price per $1000 of protection in the most recently completed policy year (which began on March 10, 2002) is $22.89, assuming 6 percent interest.

The Comparisions

The benchmarks against which to compare yearly prices per $1000 of protection are shown in the following table.

	Benchmarks
Age	*Price*
Under 30	$ 1.50
30–34	2.00
35–39	3.00
40–44	4.00
45–49	6.50
50–54	10.00
55–59	15.00
60–64	25.00
65–69	35.00
70–74	50.00
75–79	80.00
80–84	125.00

The suggested interpretations of the benchmark figures are as follows:

1. If the yearly price per $1000 of protection is less than the benchmark figure, the price of your protection is low, and you should not consider replacing your policy.
2. If the yearly price per $1000 of protection is more than the benchmark figure but less than double that figure, the price of your protection is moderate, and again you should not consider replacing your policy.
3. If the yearly price per $1000 of protection is more than double the benchmark figure, the price of your protection is high, and you should consider replacing your policy.

To illustrate, the benchmark figure for age 56 is $15, and the yearly price per $1000 of protection that came out of your calculations is $22.89. Because the latter is more than the benchmark figure but less than double that figure, the price of your protection is moderate, and you should not consider replacing your policy.

SEVERAL WARNINGS

Life insurance policies are complex financial instruments. In this appendix, we have tried to simplify the subject so that you can find out for yourself whether your life insurance protection is reasonably priced. The simplification process, however, makes it necessary to voice warnings in several areas.

1. If your policy carries an extra premium because of a health impairment or other problem, the analysis of such a policy is beyond the scope of this appendix.
2. If your policy covers more than one life, the analysis of such a policy is also beyond the scope of this appendix. Examples are family policies (in which husband, wife, and children are covered in one policy) and second-to-die policies (which cover two lives and pay the face amount on the second death).
3. It is possible that the year for which you perform the calculations—the most recently completed policy year—is not representative of other policy years. For example, the price of the protection in the first one or two policy years is often quite high, reflecting sales commissions and other expenses associated with the issuance of a life insurance policy. As another example, the price in a single isolated year may be quite low or quite high because of certain structural characteristics of the policy. For these reasons, you might wish to gather the information and perform the calculations for a few other years, especially if the figure for the most recently completed policy year is either very low or very high. The postscript of the suggested letter is optional; it is designed to help you obtain the information for a few other years, should you wish to perform the calculations.
4. You may obtain a negative result. This may arise because of an unusual year, as mentioned in the preceding paragraph, or because the price of the protection in your policy is extremely low. A negative figure does not mean the company is crazy—remember that you are using a modest interest rate of 6 percent in your calculations.
5. If the amount payable on surrender of your policy is equal to the amount payable on death, you have no life insurance protection, and the yearly price per $1000 of protection is without meaning. Under these circumstances, you should view your policy as a savings account. Calculate the yearly rate of return (expressed as a decimal) with the following formula:

$$\frac{CV + D}{P + CVP} - 1$$

You can then judge your policy by comparing the yearly rate of return with what you can earn on a savings account. In making such a comparison, however, you should consider the income-tax situation, as discussed in the explanatory appendix below.

6. If the amount payable on surrender of your policy is only slightly smaller than the amount payable on death (less than, say, 5 percent below the amount payable on death), you have very little life insurance protection, and the yearly price per $1000 of protection has very little meaning. Under these circumstances, you should view your policy as essentially a savings account. Use the above formula to approximate the yearly rate of return.

7. If yours is a small policy—less than, say, $3000 in face amount—the yearly price per $1000 of protection may be high because of the expenses associated with the maintenance of a small policy. It may not be worth the bother to replace a small policy; indeed, a small policy may not be worth keeping unless you have some emotional attachment to it.

8. We were careful to say that, if the price of the protection in your policy is high, you should *consider* replacing your policy. We did *not* say you should necessarily replace your policy. There are several reasons for you to proceed with caution: a replacement necessarily involves the purchase of a new policy, and the purchase of a new policy requires care if you wish to acquire low-priced protection; surrendering an existing policy may involve the sacrifice of certain valuable policy provisions; surrendering an existing policy may involve certain income-tax considerations; purchasing a new policy may involve significant expenses in the first one or two years, as mentioned earlier; and because of a health impairment or other problem, you may find it difficult to qualify for a new policy.

AN EXPLANATORY APPENDIX

Instead of following the suggestions in this appendix blindly, you may prefer to acquire some understanding of the formula and the benchmarks. The purpose of this section is to provide a brief explanation.

Let's consider the numerator of the formula. The first parenthetical expression $(P + CVP)$ is the amount that you would have had available to put into some other savings vehicle if you had decided to surrender the policy at the end of the year preceding the most recently completed policy year. You would have received the cash value (CVP) and you would have been relieved of the annual premium (P).

Multiplying this expression by $(1 + i)$ tells you what you would have had in that other savings vehicle by the end of the most recently completed policy year if you had invested the $(P + CVP)$ at an annual interest rate of i. This leads us to a discussion of the interest rate.

The interest rate you choose is not important if your policy has little or no cash value. However, the interest rate you choose is quite important if your policy has a substantial cash value. If your policy has a cash value, it probably has a loan clause that permits you to borrow against the policy up to approximately the cash value at a fixed interest rate of 5 to 8 percent or at a variable interest rate. If you believe you could put the money in some other savings vehicle at a much higher interest rate and with a high degree of safety, and if the amount available is substantial, you should consider borrowing against your policy and investing the proceeds of the loan. Bear in mind, however, that the savings vehicle you are thinking about may produce interest income that is subject to current income tax, and that the interest you pay on the policy loan is not deductible. The interest earnings built into cash-value life insurance, on the other hand, are income-tax deferred and eventually will be either partially or fully income-tax exempt. For simplicity, we suggested you use an interest rate of 6 percent in the calculations.

The last parenthetical expression in the numerator of the formula $(CV + D)$ is the amount that you had available at the end of the most recently completed policy year, having continued the policy for that year. The difference between the product of the first two expressions ($11,183 in the example) and the last expression ($10,850) is the price you paid ($333) for the life insurance protection in that year (assuming 6 percent interest).

Now let's consider the denominator of the formula. The cash value is the saving component of the policy, and is an asset from your point of view. Therefore, the life insurance protection you had ($14,550) is the difference between the death benefit

($25,000) and the cash value ($10,450). The other expression in the denominator moves the decimal point three places to the left, so that the denominator represents the amount of life insurance protection in thousands of dollars (14.550).

Since the price you paid for the protection (assuming 6 percent) was $333, and since the amount of protection in thousands of dollars was 14.550, the yearly price per $1000 of protection (assuming 6 percent) was $22.89.

Finally, the benchmarks were derived from certain U.S. population death rates. The benchmark figure for each five-year age bracket is slightly above the death rate per 1000 at the highest age in that bracket. What we are saying is that, if the price of your life insurance protection per $1000 is in the vicinity of the "raw material cost" (that is, the amount needed just to pay death claims based on population death rates), your life insurance protection is reasonably priced.

SUGGESTED LETTER

President
XYZ Life Insurance Company
Post Office Box 245
Ellettsville, IN 47429

Dear President:

Please furnish me with the following information concerning my policy number 1 234 567.

1. The amount that you would have paid in a single sum to my beneficiary if I had died at the end of the most recently completed policy year, including any supplemental term life insurance benefits. Please disregard any accidental death benefits, any dividends, and any loan against the policy.

2. The amount that you would have paid in a single sum to me if I had surrendered the policy at the end of the most recently completed policy year. Please disregard any dividends and any loan against the policy.

3. The amount that you would have paid in a single sum to me if I had surrendered the policy at the end of the year preceding the most recently completed policy year. Please disregard any dividends and any loan against the policy.

4. The premium for the most recently completed policy year, including the premiums for any supplemental term life insurance benefits. Please exclude the premiums for any accidental death benefits, disability benefits, or guaranteed insurability benefits. Please exclude the interest on any loan against the policy, and assume I paid the year's premium in full at the beginning of the year.

5. The dividend for the most recently completed policy year, including the dividends for any supplemental term life insurance benefits. Please exclude any dividends for any accidental death benefits or disability benefits. Please exclude any dividends credited to dividend accumulations or additions.

6. The date on which the most recently completed policy year began.

7. My age, according to your records, when the most recently completed policy year began.

Thank you for providing the information that I have requested.

Sincerely yours,

[Editor's note: The following postscript is optional. See the third point in the section entitled "Several Warnings."]

P.S.: Please furnish the above information for the two policy years preceding the most recently completed policy year, and for the two policy years following the most recently completed policy year. In the case of amounts payable in future years, please identify any nonguaranteed amounts and base the figures on your company's current scale.

Absolute liability Liability for damages even though fault or negligence cannot be proven, for example, in such situations as occupational injury of employees under a workers compensation law.

Accelerated death benefits rider A rider that allows insureds who are terminally ill or who suffer from certain catastrophic diseases to collect part or all of their life insurance benefits before they die, primarily to pay for the care they require.

Accident A loss-causing event that is sudden, unforeseen, and unintentional. *See also* Occurrence.

Accidental bodily injury Bodily injury resulting from an act whose result was accidental or unexpected.

Actual cash value Value of property at the time of its damage or loss, determined by subtracting depreciation of the item from its replacement cost.

Add-on plan Pays benefits to an accident victim without regard to fault, but the injured person still has the right to sue the negligent driver who caused the accident.

Adjustment bureau Organization for adjusting insurance claims that is supported by insurers using the bureau's services.

Advance funding Pension-funding method in which the employer systematically and periodically sets aside funds prior to the employee's retirement.

Advance premium mutual Mutual insurance company owned by the policyowners that does not issue assessable policies but charges premiums expected to be sufficient to pay all claims and expenses.

Adverse selection Tendency of persons with a higher-than-average chance of loss to seek insurance at standard (average) rates, which, if not controlled by underwriting, results in higher-than-expected loss levels.

Agency agreement Contract between an insurance agent and insurance comany that describess the powers, rights, and duties of the agent.

Agency building system Marketing system in life insurance by which an insurer builds its own agency force by recruiting, financing, training, and supervising new agents.

Agent Someone who legally represents the insurer, has the authority to act on the insurer's behalf, and can bind the principal by expressed powers, by implied powers, and by apparent authority.

Aggregate deductible Deductible in some property and health insurance contracts in which all covered losses during a year are added together and the insurer pays only when the aggregate deductible amount is exceeded.

Aleatory contract One in which the values exchanged may not be equal but depend on an uncertain event.

Alien insurer Insurance company chartered by a foreign country and meeting certain licensing requirements.

"All-risks" policy Coverage by an insurance contract that promises to cover all losses except those losses specifically excluded in the policy. Also called an **open perils policy** and a **special coverage policy.**

Alternative dispute resolution (ADR) techniques Techniques to resolve a legal dispute without litigation.

Annuitant Person who receives the periodic payment from an annuity.

Annuity Periodic payment to an individual that continues for a fixed period or for the duration of a designated life or lives.

Applicable credit amount Tax credit that can be used to reduce the amount of federal estate or gift tax; also known as **unified tax credit.**

Appraisal clause Used when the insured and insurer agree that the loss is covered, but the amount of the loss is in dispute.

Assessment mutual Mutual insurance company that has the right to assess policyowners for losses and expenses.

Assigned risk plan See Automobile insurance plan.

Assumption-of-risk Defense against a negligence claim that bars recovery for damages if a person understands and recognizes the danger inherent in a particular activity or occupation.

Attractive nuisance Condition that can attract and injure children. Occupants of land on which such a condition exists are liable for injuries to children.

Automatic premium loan Cash borrowed from a life insurance policy's cash value to pay an overdue premium after the grace period for paying the premium has expired.

Automobile insurance plan Formerly called **assigned risk plan.** Method for providing automobile insurance to persons considered to be high-risk drivers who cannot obtain protection in the voluntary markets. All automobile insurers in the state are assigned their share of such drivers based on the volume of automobile insurance business written in the state.

Average indexed monthly earnings (AIME) Under the OASDI program, the person's actual earnings are indexed to determine his or her primary insurance amount (PIA).

Avoidance *See* Loss avoidance.

Bailee's customer policy Policy that covers the loss or damage to property of customers regardless of a bailee's legal liability.

Basic form *See* Dwelling Property 1.

Benefit period A period of time, typically one to three years, during which major medical benefits are paid after the deductible is satisfied. When the benefit period ends, the insured must then satisfy a new deductible in order to establish a new benefit period.

Binder   Authorization of coverage by an agent given before the company has formally approved a policy. Provides evidence that the insurance is in force.

Blackout period   The period during which Social Security benefits are not paid to a surviving spouse—between the time the youngest child reaches age 16 and the surviving spouse's sixtieth birthday.

Blue Cross plans   Typically nonprofit, community-oriented prepayment plans that provide health insurance coverage primarily for hospital services.

Blue Shield plans   Typically nonprofit prepayment plans that provide health insurance coverage mainly for physicians's services.

Boat owners package policy   A special package policy for boat owners that combines physical damage insurance, medical expense insurance, liability insurance, and other coverages in one contract.

Broad form   *See* **Dwelling Property 2; Homeowners 2 policy.**

Broker   Someone who legally represents the insured, soliciting or accepting applications for insurance that are not in force until the company accepts the business.

Burglary   Taking of property from within the premises by someone who unlawfully enters or leaves the premises, with marks of forcible entry or exit.

Business income coverage form   Business income form drafted by the Insurance Services Office to cover the loss of business income regardless of whether the income is derived from retail or service operations, manufacturing, or rents.

Businessowners policy   Package policy specifically designed to meet the basic property and liability insurance needs of smaller business firms in one contract.

Cafeteria plan   Generic term for an employee benefit plan that allows employees to select among the various group life, medical expense, disability, dental, and other plans that best meet their specific needs. Also called flexible benefit plans.

Calendar-year deductible   Amount payable by an insured during a calendar year before a group or individual health insurance policy begins to pay for medical expenses.

Capacity   Term used in the property and liability insurance industry that refers to the relative level of surplus; the greater the industry's surplus position, the more willing underwriters will write new business or reduce premiums.

Capital budgeting   Method of determining which capital investment projects a company should undertake based on the time value of money.

Capital retention approach   A method used to estimate the amount of life insurance to own. Under this method, the insurance proceeds are retained and are not liquidated.

Capitation fee   A method of payment in managed care plans by which a physician or hospital receives a fixed annual payment for each plan member regardless of the frequency type or type of service provided.

Captive insurer   Insurance company established and owned by a parent firm in order to insure its loss exposures while reducing premium costs, providing easier access to a reinsurer, and perhaps easing tax burdens.

Cargo insurance   Type of ocean marine insurance that protects the shipper of the goods against financial loss if the goods are damaged or lost.

Cash refund annuity   The balance is paid in one lump sum to the beneficiary after the death of the annuitant, if total payments do not equal the annuity purchase price.

Cash surrender value   Amount payable to the owner of a cash-value life insurance policy should he or she decide it is no longer wanted. Calculated separately from the legal reserve.

Casualty insurance   Field of insurance that covers whatever is not covered by fire, marine, and life insurance. Includes auto, liability, burglary and theft, workers compensation, glass, and health insurance.

Catastrophe bonds   Corporate bonds that permit the issuer of the bond to skip or defer scheduled payments of principal or interest if a catastrophic loss occurs.

Causes-of-loss form   Form added to commercial property insurance policy that indicates the causes of loss that are covered. There are three causes-of-loss forms: basic, broad, and special.

Ceding company   Insurer that writes the policy initially and later shifts part or all of the coverage to a reinsurer.

Certified Financial Planner (CFP)   Professional who has attained a high degree of technical competency in financial planning and has passed a series of professional examinations.

Certified Insurance Counselor (CIC)   Professional in property and liability insurance who has passed a series of examinations sponsored by the Society of Certified Insurance Counselors.

Chance of loss   The probability that an event will occur.

Change-of-plan provision   Allows life insurance policyowners to exchange their present policies for different contracts, provides flexibility.

Chartered Financial Consultant (ChFC)   An individual who has attained a high degree of technical competency in the fields of financial planning, investments, and life and health insurance and has passed eight professional examinations administered by The American College.

Chartered Life Underwriter (CLU)   An individual who has attained a high degree of technical competency in the fields of life and health insurance and has passed eight professional examinations administered by The American College.

Chartered Property Casualty Underwriter (CPCU)   Professional who has attained a high degree of technical competency in property and liability insurance and has passed eight professional examinations administered by the American Institute for Chartered Property Casualty Underwriters.

Chief risk officer (CRO)   Person responsible for the treatment of pure and speculative risks faced by an organization.

Choice no-fault plans   Motorists can elect to be covered under the state's no-fault law with lower premiums or can retain the right to sue under the tort liability system with higher premiums.

Claims adjustor   Person who settles claims: an agent, company adjustor, independent adjustor, adjustment bureau, or public adjustor.

Claims-made policy   A liability insurance policy that only covers claims that are first reported during the policy period, provided the event occurred after the retroactive date (if any) stated in the policy.

Class rating   Rate-making method in which similar insureds are placed in the same underwriting class and each is charged the same rate. Also called manual rating.

CLU   *See* **Chartered Life Underwriter.**

Coinsurance provision   Common provision in commercial property insurance contracts that requires the insured to maintain insurance on the property at a stated percentage of its actual cash value or its replacement cost. Payment for a loss is determined by multiplying the amount of the loss by the fraction derived from the amount of insurance required. If the coinsurance requirement is not met at the time of loss, the insured will be penalized. Coinsurance is also used to refer to the percentage participation clause in health insurance. *See also* **Percentage participation clause.**

Collateral source rule   Under this rule, the defendant cannot introduce any evidence that shows the injured party has received compensation from other collateral sources.

Collision loss   Damages to an automobile caused by the upset of the automobile or its impact with another vehicle or object. Collision losses are paid by the insurer regardless of fault.

Commercial crime coverage form   ISO form that can be added to a package policy to cover crime exposures of business firms.

Commercial general liability policy (CGL)   Commercial liability policy drafted by the Insurance Services Office containing two coverage forms—an occurrence form and a claims-made form.

Commercial lines   Property and casualty coverages for business firms, nonprofit organizations, and government agencies.

Commercial package policy (CPP)   A commercial policy that can be designed to meet the specific insurance needs of business firms. Property and liability coverage forms are combined to form a single policy.

Commodity price risk   Risk of losing money if the price of a commodity changes.

Commutative contract   One in which the values exchanged by both parties are theoretically even.

Company adjustor   Claims adjustor who is a salaried employee representing only one company.

Comparative negligence laws   Laws enacted by many jurisdictions permitting an injured person to recover damages even though he or she may have contributed to the accident. The financial burden is shared by both parties according to their respective degrees of fault.

Completed operations   Liability arising out of faulty work performed away from the premises after the work or operations are completed; applicable to contractors, plumbers, electricians, repair shops, and similar firms.

Comprehensive major medical insurance   Type of group plan combining basic plan benefits and major medical insurance in one policy.

Compulsory insurance law   Law protecting accident victims against irresponsible motorists by requiring owners and operators of automobiles to carry certain amounts of liability insurance in order to license the vehicle and drive legally within the state.

Concealment   Deliberate failure of an applicant for insurance to reveal a material fact to the insurer.

Conditions   Provisions inserted in an insurance contract that qualify or place limitations on the insurer's promise to perform.

Consequential loss   Financial loss occurring as the consequence of some other loss. Often called an indirect loss.

Consolidation   Combining of business organizations through mergers and acquisitions.

Contingent beneficiary   Beneficiary of a life insurance policy who is entitled to receive the policy proceeds on the insured's

death if the primary beneficiary dies before the insured; or the beneficiary who receives the remaining payments if the primary beneficiary dies before receiving the guaranteed number of payments.

Contingent liability   Liability arising out of work done by independent contractors for a firm. A firm may be liable for the work done by an independent contractor if the activity is illegal, the situation does not permit delegation of authority, or the work is inherently dangerous.

Contract bond   Type of surety bond guaranteeing that the principal will fulfill all contractual obligations.

Contract of adhesion   The insured must accept the entire contract, with all of its terms and conditions.

Contractual liability   Legal liability of another party that the business firm agrees to assume by a written or oral contract.

Contribution by equal shares   Type of other-insurance provision often found in liability insurance contracts that requires each company to share equally in the loss until the share of each insurer equals the lowest limit of liability under any policy or until the full amount of loss is paid.

Contributory negligence   Common law defense blocking an injured person from recovering damages if he or she has contributed in any way to the accident.

Contributory plan   Group life, health, or pension plan in which the employees pay part of the premiums.

Coordination-of-benefits provision   Provision in a group medical expense plan that prevents over-insurance and duplication of benefits when one person is covered under more than one group plan.

Corridor deductible   Major medical plan deductible that integrates a basic plan with a supplemental group major medical expense policy.

Cost-of-living rider   Benefit that can be added to a life insurance policy under which the policyowner can purchase one-year term insurance equal to the cumulative percentage change in the consumer price index with no evidence of insurability.

Cost of risk   A risk management tool that measures certain costs in a risk management program, includdng premiums paid, retained losses, outide risk management services, financial guarantees, internal administrative costs, taxes and fees, and certain other expenses.

Coverage for damage to your auto   That part of the personal auto policy insuring payment for damage or theft of the insured automobile. This optional coverage can be used to insure both collision and other-than-collision losses.

CPCU   *See* **Chartered Property Casualty Underwriter.**

Currency exchange rate risk   Risk of loss of value caused by changes in exchange rates between countries.

Current assumption whole life insurance   Nonparticipating whole life policy in which the cash values are based on the insurer's current mortality, investment, and expense experience. An accumulation account is credited with a current interest rate that changes over time. Also called interest-sensitive whole life insurance.

Currently insured   Status of a covered person under the Old-Age, Survivors, and Disability Insurance (OASDI) program who has at least six credits out of the last thirteen quarters, ending with the quarter of death, disability, or entitlement to retirement benefits.

Damage to property of others   Damage covered up to $1000 per occurrence for an insured who damages another's property. Payment is made despite the lack of legal liability. Coverage is included in Section II of the homeowners policy.

Declarations   Statements in an insurance contract that provide information about the property to be insured and used for underwriting and rating purposes and identification of the property to be insured.

Deductible   A provision by which a specified amount is subtracted from the total loss payment that would otherwise be paid.

Deferred annuity   A retirement annuity that provides benefits at some future date.

Defined-benefit plan   Type of pension plan in which the retirement benefit is known in advance but the contributions vary depending on the amount necessary to fund the desired benefit.

Defined-contribution plan   Type of pension plan in which the contribution rate is fixed but the retirement benefit is variable.

Demutualization   A term to describe the conversion of a mutual insurer into a stock insurer.

Dependency period   Period of time following the readjustment period during which the surviving spouse's children are under eighteen and therefore dependent on the parent.

Deposit-administration plan   Type of pension plan in which all pension contributions are deposited in an unallocated fund. An annuity is purchased only when the employee retires.

Diagnosis-related groups (DRGs)   Method for reimbursing hospitals under the Medicare program. Under this system, a flat, uniform amount is paid to each hospital for the same type of medical care or treatment.

Difference in conditions insurance (DIC)   "All-risks" policy that covers other perils not insured by basic property insurance contracts, supplemental to and excluding the coverage provided by underlying contracts.

Direct loss   Financial loss that results directly from an insured peril.

Directors and officer liability (D&O)   A commercial liability coverage that provides financial protection for the directors, officers, and the corporation if the directors and officers are sued for mismanagement of the company's affairs.

Direct-response system   A marketing method where insurance is sold without the services of an agent. Potential customers are solicited by advertising in the mails, newspapers, magazines, television, radio, and other media.

Direct writer   Insurance company in which the salesperson is an employee of the insurer, not an independent contractor, and which pays all selling expenses, including salary.

Disability-insured   Status of an individual who is insured for disability benefits under the Old-Age, Survivors, and Disability Insurance (OASDI) program.

Dividend accumulations   A dividend option in a participating life insurance policy in which the dividend is retained by the insurer and accumulated at interest.

Domestic insurer   Insurance company domiciled and licensed in the state in which it does business.

Double indemnity rider   Benefit that can be added to a life insurance policy doubling the face amount of life insurance if death occurs as the result of an accident.

Dram shop law   Law that imputes negligence to the owner of a business that sells liquor in the event that an intoxicated customer causes injury or property damage to another person; usually excluded from general liability policies.

Driver education credit   Student discount or reduction in premium amount for which young drivers become eligible on completion of a driver education course.

Dwelling Property 1   Property insurance policy that insures the dwelling, structures, personal property, fair rental value, and certain other coverages; covers a limited number of perils.

Dwelling Property 2   Property insurance policy that insures the dwelling and other structures at replacement cost. It adds additional coverages and has a greater list of covered perils than the Dwelling Property 1 policy.

Dwelling Property 3   Property insurance policy that covers the dwelling and other structures against direct physical loss from any peril except for those perils otherwise excluded. However, personal property is covered on a named-perils basis.

Earnings test (retirement test)   Test under the Old-Age, Survivors, and Disability Insurance (OASDI) program that reduces monthly benefits to those persons who have annual earned income in excess of the maximum allowed.

Eligibility period   Brief period of time during which an employee can sign up for group insurance without furnishing evidence of insurability.

Elimination period (waiting period)   Waiting period in health insurance during which benefits are not paid. Also a period of time that must be met before disability benefits are payable.

Employee Retirement Income Security Act (ERISA)   Legislation passed in 1974 applying to most private pension and welfare plans that requires certain standards to protect participating employees.

Employers liability insurance   Covers employers against lawsuits by employees who are injured in the course of employment, but whose injuries (or disease) are not compensable under the state's workers compensation law.

Endorsement   Written provision that adds to, deletes, or modifies the provisions in the original contract. *See also* **Rider.**

Endowment insurance   Type of life insurance that pays the face amount of insurance to the beneficiary if the insured dies within a specified period or to the policyowner if the insured survives to the end of the period.

Enterprise risk   A term that encompasses all major risks faced by a business, including pure risk, speculative risk, strategic risk, operational risk, and financial risk.

Enterprise risk management   Comprehensive risk management program that considers an organization's pure risks, speculative risks, strategic risks, and operational risks.

Entire-contract clause   Provision in life insurance policies stating that the life insurance policy and attached application constitute the entire contract between the parties.

Equipment breakdown insurance   Insurance that covers losses due to accidental breakdown of covered equipment; also known as **boiler and machinery insurance.**

Equity in the unearned premium reserve   Amount by which an unearned premium reserve is overstated because it is established on the basis of gross premium rather than net premium.

Equity indexed annuity   A fixed, deferred annuity that allows participation in the stock market but guarantees the principal against loss if the contract is held to term.

ERISA   *See* **Employee Retirement Income Security Act.**

Errors and omissions insurance   Liability insurance policy that provides protection against loss incurred by a client because of some negligent act, error, or omission by the insured.

Estate planning   Process designed to conserve estate assets before and after death, distribute property according to the individual's wishes, minimize federal estate and state inheritance taxes, provide estate liquidity to meet costs of estate settlement, and provide for the family's financial needs.

Estoppel   Legal doctrine that prevents a person from denying the truth of a previous representation of fact, especially when such representation has been relied on by the one to whom the statement was made.

Excess insurance   Under an excess insurance plan, the insurer does not participate in the loss until the actual loss exceeds a certain amount.

Exclusion ratio   Calculation to determine the taxable and nontaxable portions of annuity payments, which is determined by dividing the investment in the contract by the expected return.

Exclusions   Provisions in an insurance contract that list the perils, losses, and property excluded from coverage.

Exclusive agency system   Type of insurance marketing system under which the agent represents only one company or group of companies under common ownership.

Exclusive provider organization (EPO)   A plan that does not cover medical care received outside of a network of preferred providers.

Exclusive remedy doctrine   Doctrine in workers compensation insurance that states that workers compensation benefits should be the exclusive or sole source of recovery for workers who have a job-related accident or disease; doctrine has been eroded by legal decisions.

Expense loading   *See* **Loading.**

Expense ratio   That proportion of the gross rate available for expenses and profit. Ratio of expenses incurred to premiums written.

Experience rating   (1) Method of rating group life and health insurance plans that uses the loss experience of the group to determine the premiums to be charged. (2) As applied to property and liability insurance, the class or manual rate is adjusted upward or downward based on past loss experience. (3) As applied to state unemployment insurance programs, firms with favorable employment records pay lower tax rates.

Exposure unit   Unit of measurement used in insurance pricing.

Extended nonowned coverage   Endorsement that can be added to an auto liability insurance policy that covers the insured while driving any nonowned automobile on a regular basis.

Extra expense coverage form   A separate form that can be used to cover the extra expenses incurred by a firm to continue operations during a period of restoration.

Factory mutual   Mutual insurance company insuring only properties that meet high underwriting standards; emphasizes loss prevention.

Facultative reinsurance   Optional, case-by-case method of reinsurance used when the ceding company receives an application for insurance that exceeds its retention limit.

Fair Access to Insurance Requirements (FAIR plan)   Property insurance plan that provides basic property insurance to property owners in areas where they are unable to obtain insurance in the normal markets. Each state with such a plan has a central placement facility.

Fair rental value   Amount payable to an insured homeowner for loss of rental income due to damage that makes the premises uninhabitable.

Family purpose doctrine   Concept that imputes negligence committed by immediate family members while operating a family car to the owner of the car.

Federal crop insurance   Various federal insurance programs that provides coverage for unavoidable crop losses, such as hail, wind, drought, and plant disease.

Federal surety bond   Type of surety bond required by federal agencies that regulates the actions of business firms. It guarantees that the bonded party will comply with federal standards, pay all taxes or duties accrued, or pay any penalty if the bondholder fails to pay.

File-and-use law   Law for regulating insurance rates under which companies are required only to file the rates with the state insurance department before putting them into effect.

Financial institution bond   Bond that covers crime loss exposures of commercial banks, savings and loan institutions, and other financial institutions; used to cover bank holdups, employee dishonesty, forgery, alteration of checks, armored car exposures, and other crime exposures of financial institutions.

Financial Modernization Act of 1999   A federal law that allows banks, insurers, investment firms, and other financial institutions to enter and compete in each other's financial markets.

Financial responsibility law   Law that requires persons involved in automobile accidents to furnish proof of financial responsibility up to a minimum dollar limit or face having driving privileges revoked or suspended.

Financial risk   A risk that business firms face because of adverse changes in commodity prices, interest rates, foreign exchange rates, and the value of money.

Fire legal liability   Liability of a firm or person for fire damage caused by negligence and damage to property of others.

Fixed-amount option   Life insurance settlement option in which the policy proceeds are paid out in fixed amounts.

Fixed annuity   Annuity whose periodic payment is a guaranteed fixed amount.

Fixed-period option   Life insurance settlement option in which the policy proceeds are paid out over a fixed period of time.

Flexible-premium annuity   An annuity contract that permits the owner to vary the size and frequency of premium payments. The amount of retirement income depends on the accumulated sum in the annuity at retirement.

Flexible-spending account   An arrangement by which the employee agrees to a salary reduction, which can be used to pay for plan benefits, unreimbursed medical and dental expenses, and other expenses permitted by the Internal Revenue Code.

Flex-rating law   Type of rating law in which prior approval of the rates is required only if the rates exceed a certain percentage above and below the rates previously filed.

Foreign insurer   Insurance company chartered by one state but licensed to do business in another.

Fortuitous loss   Unforeseen and unexpected loss that occurs as a result of chance.

Franchise deductible   Deductible found in some marine insurance contracts in which the insurer has no liability if the loss is under a certain percentage amount, but once this percentage is exceeded, the entire loss is paid in full.

Fraternal insurer   Mutual insurance company that provides life and health insurance to members of a social organization.

Fully insured   Insured status of a covered person under the Old-Age, Survivors, and Disability Insurance (OASDI) program. To be fully insured for retirement benefits, 40 credits are required.

Fundamental risk   A risk that affects the entire economy or large numbers of persons or groups within the economy.

Funding agency   A financial institution or individual that provides for the accumulation or administration of the pension contributions that will be used to pay pension benefits.

Funding instrument   An insurance contract or trust agreement that states the terms under which the funding agency will accumulate, administer, and disburse the pension funds.

General agency system   Type of life insurance marketing system in which the general agent is an independent businessperson who represents only one insurer, is in charge of a territory, and is responsible for hiring, training, and motivating new agents.

General aggregate limit   In the commercial general liability policy, it is the maximum amount the insurer will pay for the sum of the following—damages under Coverage A, B, and medical expenses under Coverage C.

General average   In ocean marine insurance, a loss incurred for the common good that is shared by all parties to the venture.

Good student discount   Reduction of automobile premium for a young driver at least sixteen who ranks in the upper 20 percent of his or her class, has a B or 3.0 average, or is on the Dean's list or honor roll. It is based on the premise that good students are better drivers.

Grace period   Period of time during which a policyowner may pay an overdue life insurance premium without causing the policy to lapse.

Gross estate   The value of the property that you own when you die. Also includes value of jointly-owned property, life insurance, death proceeds, and certain other items.

Gross premium   Amount paid by the insured, consisting of the gross rate multiplied by the number of exposure units.

Gross rate   The sum of the pure premium and a loading element.

Group deferred annuity   Type of allocated pension plan in which a single-premium deferred annuity is purchased each year and is equal to the retirement benefit for that year.

Group life insurance   Life insurance provided on a number of persons in a single master contract. Physical examinations are not required, and certificates of insurance are issued to members of the group as evidence of insurance.

Group term life insurance   Most common form of group life insurance. Yearly renewable term insurance on employees during their working careers.

Group universal life products (GULP)   Universal life insurance plans sold to members of a group, such as individual employees of an employer. There are some differences between GULP plans and individual universal life plans; for instance, GULP expense charges are generally lower than those assessed against individual policies.

Guaranteed investment contract   An investment contract with an insurer in which the insurer guarantees both principal and interest on a pension contribution.

Guaranteed purchase option   Benefit that can be added to a life insurance policy permitting the insured to purchase additional amounts of life insurance at specified times in the future without requiring evidence of insurability.

Guaranteed renewable   Continuance provision of a health insurance policy under which the company guarantees to renew the policy to a stated age, and whose renewal is at the insured's option. Premiums can be increased for broad classes of insureds.

Guaranteed replacement cost   In the event of a total loss, the insurer agrees to replace the home exactly as it was before the loss even though the replacement cost exceeds the amount of insurance stated in the policy.

Hard insurance market   A period in the underwriting cycle during which underwriting standards are strict and premiums are high. *See also* **soft insurance market** and **underwriting cycle**.

Hazard   Condition that creates or increases the chance of loss.

Health maintenance organization (HMO)   Organized system of health care that provides comprehensive health services to its members for a fixed prepaid fee.

Health savings account (HSA)   A tax-exempt trust or custodial account established exclusively for the purpose of paying qualified medical expenses of the account beneficiary who is covered under a high-deductible health insurance plan. HSAs receive favorable tax treatment.

Hedging   Technique for transferring the risk of unfavorable price fluctuations to a speculator by purchasing and selling options and futures contracts on an organized exchange.

HMO   See Health maintenance organization.

Hold-harmless clause   Clause written into a contract by which one party agrees to release another party from all legal liability, such as a retailer who agrees to release the manufacturer from legal liability if the product injures someone.

Home service life insurance   Industrial life insurance and monthly debit ordinary life insurance contracts that are serviced by agents who earlier called on the policyowners at their homes to collect the premiums.

Homeowners 2 policy (broad form)   Homeowners insurance policy that provides coverage on a named-perils basis on the dwelling, other structures, and personal property. Personal liability insurance is also provided.

Homeowners 3 policy (special form)   Homeowners insurance policy that covers the dwelling and other structures on a risk-of-direct-loss basis and personal property on a named-perils basis. Personal liability insurance is also provided.

Homeowners 4 policy (contents broad form)   Homeowners insurance policy that applies to tenants renting a home or apartment. Covers the tenant's personal property and provides personal liability insurance.

Homeowners 5 policy (comprehensive form)   Homeowners insurance policy that provides open perils coverage ("all risks coverage") on both the building and personal property. The dwelling, other structures, and personal property are insured against the risk of direct physical loss to property; all losses are covered except those losses specifically excluded.

Homeowners 6 policy (unit-owners form)   Homeowners insurance policy that covers personal property of insured owners of condominium units and cooperative apartments on a broad form, named-perils basis. Personal liability insurance is also provided.

Homeowners 8 policy (modified coverage form)   Homeowner policy that is designed for older homes. Dwelling and other structures are indemnified on the basis of repair cost using common construction materials and methods. Personal liability insurance is also provided.

Hospital expense insurance   Individual health insurance that pays for medical expenses incurred while in a hospital.

Hospital Insurance (Part A)   Part A of Medicare that covers in-patient hospital care, skilled nursing facility care, home health care services, and hospice care for Medicare beneficiaries.

Hospital-surgical insurance   Medical expense plan that provides hospital and surgical benefits and other ancillary benefits.

Hull insurance (1)   Class of ocean marine insurance that covers physical damage to the ship or vessel insured. Typically written on an "all-risks" basis. (2) Physical damage insurance on aircraft—similar to collision insurance in an auto policy.

Human life value   For purposes of life insurance, the present value of the family's share of the deceased breadwinner's future earnings.

Immediate annuity   An annuity where the first payment is due one payment interval from the date of purchase.

Immediate-participation guarantee plan (IPG)   Type of pension plan in which all pension contributions are deposited in an unallocated fund and used directly to pay benefits to retirees.

Imputed negligence   Case in which responsibility for damage can be transferred from the negligent party to another person, such as an employer.

Incontestable clause   Contractual provision in a life insurance policy stating that the insurer cannot contest the policy after it has been in force two years during the insured's lifetime.

Indemnification   Compensation to the victim of a loss, in whole or in part, by payment, repair, or replacement.

Independent adjustor   Claims adjustor who offers his or her services to insurance companies and is compensated by a fee.

Independent agency system   Type of property and liability insurance marketing system, sometimes called the American agency system, in which the agent is an independent businessperson representing several insurers. The agency owns the expirations or renewal rights to the business, and the agent is compensated by commissions that vary by line of insurance.

Indeterminate-premium whole life insurance   Nonparticipating whole life policy that permits the insurer to adjust premiums based on anticipated future experience. Initial premiums are guaranteed for a certain period. After the initial guaranteed period expires, the insurer can increase premiums up to some maximum limit.

Indirect loss   *See* **Consequential loss.**

Individual Retirement Account (IRA)   Individual retirement plan that can be established by a person with earned income. An IRA plan enjoys favorable income tax advantages.

Industrial life insurance   Type of life insurance in which policies are sold in small amounts and the premiums are collected weekly or monthly by a debit agent at the policyowner's home.

Inflation-guard endorsement   Endorsement added at the insured's request to a homeowners policy to increase periodically the face amount of insurance on the dwelling and other policy coverages by a specified percentage.

Initial reserve   In life insurance, the reserve at the beginning of any policy year.

Inland marine insurance   Transportation insurance that provides protection for goods shipped on land including imports, exports, domestic shipments, means of transportation, personal property floater risks, and commercial property floater risks.

Installment refund annuity   Pays the annuitant a lifetime income, but if death occurs before receiving payments equal to the purchase price, the income payments continue to the beneficiary.

Insurance   Pooling of fortuitous losses by transfer of risks to insurers who agree to indemnify insureds for such losses, to provide other pecuniary benefits on their occurrence, or to render services connected with the risk.

Insurance guaranty funds   State funds that provide for the payment of unpaid claims of insolvent insurers.

Insurance score   A credit-based score based on an individual's credit record and other factors that is highly predictive of future claim costs; insureds with low insurance scores generally file more homeowners and auto insurance claims than insureds with good credit and higher insurance scores.

Insurance Services Office (ISO)   Major rating organization in property and liability insurance that drafts policy forms for personal and commercial lines of insurance and provides rate data on loss costs for property and liability insurance lines.

Insuring agreement   That part of an insurance contract that states the promises of the insurer.

Integrated risk management   A risk management technique that combines coverage for pure and speculative risks in the same insurance contract.

Interest-adjusted method   Method of determining cost to an insured of a life insurance policy that considers the time cost of money by applying an interest factor to each element of cost. *See also* **Net payment cost index; Surrender cost index.**

Interest option   Life insurance settlement option in which the principal is retained by the insurer and interest is paid periodically.

Interest rate risk   Risk of loss caused by adverse interest rate movements.

Invitee   Someone who is invited onto the premises for the benefit of the occupant.

IPG plan   *See* **Immediate-participation guarantee plan.**

IRA   *See* **Individual Retirement Account.**

Irrevocable beneficiary   Beneficiary designation allowing no change to be made in the beneficiary of an insurance policy without the beneficiary's consent.

ISO   *See* **Insurance Services Office.**

Joint and several liability   Rule under which several people may be responsible for the injury, but a defendant who is only slightly responsible may be required to pay the full amount of damages.

Joint-and-survivor annuity   Annuity based on the lives of two or more annuitants. The annuity income (either the full amount of the original income or only two-thirds or one-half of the original income when the first annuitant dies) is paid until the death of the last annuitant.

Joint underwriting association (JUA)   Organization of auto insurers operating in a state that makes auto insurance available to high-risk drivers. All underwriting losses are proportionately shared by insurers on the basis of premiums written in the state.

Judgment rating   Rate-making method for which each exposure is individually evaluated and the rate is determined largely by the underwriter's judgment.

Judicial bond   Type of surety bond used for court proceedings and guaranteeing that the party bonded will fulfill certain obligations specified by law, for example, fiduciary responsibilities.

Juvenile insurance   Life insurance purchased by parents for children under a specified age.

Keogh plan for the self-employed   Retirement plan individually adopted by self-employed persons that allows a tax deductible contribution to a defined-contribution or defined-benefit plan.

Lapsed policy   One that is not in force because premiums have not been paid.

Last clear chance rule   Statutory modification of the contributory negligence law allowing the claimant endangered by his or her own negligence to recover damages from a defendant if the defendant has a last clear chance to avoid the accident but fails to do so.

Law of large numbers   Concept that the greater the number of exposures, the more closely will actual results approach the probable results expected from an infinite number of exposures.

Legal hazard   Characteristics of the legal system or regulatory environment that increase the frequency or severity of losses.

Legal reserve   Liability item on a life insurer's balance sheet representing the redundant or excessive premiums paid under the level-premium method during the early years. Assets must be accumulated to offset the legal reserve liability. Purpose of the legal reserve is to provide lifetime protection.

Liability coverage   That part of the personal auto policy that protects a covered person against a suit or claim for bodily injury or property damage arising out of negligent ownership or operation of an automobile. Liability coverage is also included in the homeowner's policy, which provides coverage for bodily injury and property damage liability.

Liability without fault   Principle on which workers compensation is based, holding the employer absolutely liable for occupa-tional injuries or disease suffered by workers, regardless of who is at fault.

License and permit bond   Type of surety bond guaranteeing that the person bonded will comply with all laws and regulations that govern his or her activities.

Licensee   Someone who enters or remains on the premises with the occupant's expressed or implied permission.

Life annuity with guaranteed payments   Pays a life income to the annuitant with a certain number of guaranteed payments.

Life income option   Life insurance settlement option in which the policy proceeds are paid during the lifetime of the beneficiary. A certain number of guaranteed payments may also be payable.

Life insurance planning   Systematic method of determining the insured's financial goals, which are translated into specific amounts of life insurance, then periodically reviewed for possible changes.

Limited-payment policy   Type of whole life insurance providing protection throughout the insured's lifetime and for which relatively high premiums are paid only for a limited period.

Liquor liability law   *See* **Dram shop law.**

Loading   The amount that must be added to the pure premium for expenses, profit, and a margin for contingencies.

Long-term-care insurance   A form of health insurance that pays a daily benefit for medical or custodial care received in a nursing facility or hospital.

Loss control   Risk management activities that reduce both the frequency and severity of losses for a firm or organization.

Loss exposure   Any situation or circumstance in which a loss is possible, regardless of whether a loss occurs.

Loss frequency   The probable number of losses that may occur during some given time period.

Loss ratio   The ratio of incurred losses and loss adjustment expenses to earned premiums.

Loss ratio method of rating   A rating system in property and casualty insurance by which the actual loss ratio is compared with the expected loss ratio, and the rate is adjusted accordingly.

Loss reserve   Amount set aside by property and liability insurers for claims reported and adjusted but not yet paid, claims reported and filed but not yet adjusted, and claims incurred but not yet reported to the insurer.

Loss severity   The probable size of the losses that may occur.

McCarran-Ferguson Act   Federal law passed in 1945 stating that continued regulation of the insurance industry by the states is in the public interest and that federal antitrust laws apply to insurance only to the extent that the industry is not regulated by state law.

Major medical insurance   Health insurance designed to pay a large proportion of the covered expenses of a catastrophic illness or injury.

Malpractice liability insurance   Covers acts of malpractice resulting in harm or injury to patients.

Managed care   A generic name for medical expense plans that provide covered services to the members in a cost-effective manner.

Manual rating   *See* **Class rating.**

Manuscript policy   Policy designed for a firm's specific needs and requirements.

Mass merchandising   Plan for insuring individual members of a group, such as employees of firms or members of labor unions, under a single program of insurance at reduced premiums. Property and liability insurance is sold to individual members using group insurance marketing methods.

Master contract   Formed between the insurer and group policyowner for the benefit of the individual members.

Maximum possible loss   Worst loss that could possibly happen to a firm during its lifetime.

Maximum probable loss   Worst loss that is likely to happen to a firm during its lifetime.

Mean reserve   In life insurance, the average of the terminal and initial reserves.

Medical Information Bureau (MIB)   Bureau whose purpose is to supply underwriting information in life insurance to member companies, which report any health impairments of an applicant for insurance.

Medical payments coverage   That part of the personal auto policy that pays all reasonable medical and funeral expenses incurred by a covered person within three years from the date of an accident.

Medical payments to others   Pays for medical expenses of others under the homeowners policy in the event that a person (not an insured) is accidentally injured on the premises, or by the activities of an insured, resident employee, or animal owned by or in the care of an insured.

Medicare   Part of the total Social Security program that covers the medical expenses of most people age 65 and older and certain disabled people under age 65.

Medicare Advantage   Formerly called Medicare + Choice. Medicare Advantage plans allow beneficiaries to choose alternatives to Parts A and B of Medicare, such as private managed care plans, private fee-for-service plans, preferred provider organizations, and Medicare specialty plans.

Merit rating   Rate-making method in which class rates are adjusted upward or downward based on individual loss experience.

MIB   *See* Medical Information Bureau.

Minimum coverage requirement   A test that must be met to prevent employers from establishing a qualified pension plan that covers only the highly compensated. *See also* **Ratio percentage test.**

Misstatement of age or sex clause   Contractual provision in a life insurance policy stating that if the insured's age or sex is misstated, the amount payable is the amount that the premium would have purchased at the correct age.

Mobile home insurance   A package policy that provides property insurance and personal liability insurance to mobil home owners. A special endorsement is added to HO-2 or HO-3.

Modified life policy   Whole life policy for which premiums are reduced for the first three to five years and are higher thereafter.

Modified no-fault plan   An injured person has the right to sue a negligent driver only if the bodily injury claim exceeds the dollar or verbal threshold.

Monetary threshold   An injured motorist would not be permitted to sue but would collect from his or her insurer, unless the claim exceeded the threshold amount.

Moral hazard   Dishonesty or character defects in an individual that increase the chance of loss.

Morale hazard   Carelessness or indifference to a loss because of the existence of insurance.

Multicar discount   Reduction in auto insurance premiums for an insured who owns two or more automobiles, on the assumption that two such autos owned by the same person will not be driven as frequently as only one.

Multiple distribution systems   Insurance marketing method that refers to the use of several distribution systems by an insurer; for example, a property and liability insurer may use the independent agency method and direct response system to sell insurance.

Multiple-line insurance   Type of insurance that combines several lines of insurance into one contract, for example, property insurance and casualty insurance.

Mutual insurer   Insurance corporation owned by the policyowners, who elect the board of directors. The board appoints managing executives, and the company may pay a dividend or give a rate reduction in advance to insureds.

NAIC   *See* National Association of Insurance Commissioners.

NALP   *See* Net annual level premium.

Named insured   The person or persons named in the declarations section of the policy, as opposed to someone who may have an interest in the policy but is not named as an insured.

Named-perils policy   Coverage by an insurance contract that promises to pay only for those losses caused by perils specifically listed in the policy.

National Association of Insurance Commissioners (NAIC)   Group founded in 1871 that meets periodically to discuss industry problems and draft model laws in various areas and recommends adoption of these proposals by state legislatures.

Needs approach   Method for estimating amount of life insurance appropriate for a family by analyzing various family needs that must be met if the family head should die and converting them into specific amounts of life insurance. Financial assets are considered in determining the amount of life insurance needed.

Negligence   Failure to exercise the standard of care required by law to protect others from harm.

Net amount at risk   Concept associated with a level-premium life insurance policy. Calculated as the difference between the face amount of the policy and the legal reserve.

Net annual level premium (NALP)   Annual level premium for a life insurance policy with no expense loading. Mathematically equivalent to the net single premium.

Net payment cost index   Method of measuring the cost of an insurance policy to an insured if death occurs at the end of some specified time period. The time value of money is taken into consideration.

Net present value   Used in capital budgeting and is the sum of the present values of the future cash flows minus the cost of the project. A positive net present value represents an increase in value for the firm.

Net retention   *See* Retention limit.

Net single premium (NSP)   Present value of the future death benefit of a life insurance policy.

No-fault insurance   A tort reform proposal in which the injured person would collect benefits from his or her insurer and would not have to sue a negligent third party who caused the accident and prove legal liability.

Nonbuilding agency system   Life insurance marketing system by which an insurer sells its products through established agents who are already engaged in selling life insurance.

Noncancellable   Continuance provision in a health insurance policy stipulating that the policy cannot be cancelled, that the renewal is guaranteed to a stated age, and that the premium rates cannot be increased.

Noncontributory plan   Employer pays the entire cost of a group insurance or private pension plan. All eligible employees are covered.

Nonforfeiture law   State law requiring insurance companies to provide at least a minimum nonforfeiture value to policy-owners who surrender their cash value life insurance policies.

Noninsurance transfers   Various methods other than insurance by which a pure risk and its potential financial consequences can be transferred to another party, for example, contracts, leases, and hold-harmless agreements.

Nonoccupational disability   The accident or illness must occur off the job.

Nonparticipating policy   Term used to describe a life insurance policy that does not pay dividends.

Objective risk   Relative variation of actual loss from expected loss, which varies inversely with the square root of the number of cases under observation.

Obligee   The party to a surety bond who is reimbursed for damages if the principal to the bond fails to perform.

Occurrence   An accident, including continuous or repeated exposure to substantially the same general, harmful conditions, which results in bodily injury or property damage during the policy period. *See also* **Accident.**

Occurrence policy   A liability insurance policy that covers claims arising out of occurrences that take place during the policy period, regardless of when the claim is made. *See also* **Claims-made policy.**

Ocean marine insurance   Type of insurance that provides protection for all types of oceangoing vessels and their cargoes as well as legal liability of owners and shippers.

Open-competition law   Law for regulating insurance rates under which insurers are not required to file rates at all with the state insurance department but may be required to furnish rate schedules and supporting data to state officials.

Open perils policy   See **"All-risks policy."**

Optionally renewable policy   The insurer has the right to terminate a policy on any anniversary date, or in some cases, on a premium date.

Ordinary life insurance   Type of whole life insurance providing protection throughout the insured's lifetime and for which premiums are paid throughout the insured's lifetime.

Other-insurance provisions   Provisions whose purpose is to prevent profiting from insurance and violation of the principle of indemnity.

Other-than-collision loss   Part of the coverage available under Part D: Coverage for Damage to Your Auto in the personal auto policy. All physical damage losses to an insured vehicle are covered except collision losses and those losses specifically excluded.

Ownership clause   Provision in life insurance policies under which the policyowner possesses all contractual rights in the policy while the insured is living. These rights can generally be exercised without the beneficiary's consent.

P&I Insurance   *See* **Protection and indemnity insurance.**

Package policy   Policy that combines two or more separate contracts of insurance in one policy, for example, homeowners insurance.

Partial disability   Inability of the insured to perform one or more important duties of his or her occupation.

Participating policy   Life insurance policy that pays dividends to the policyowners.

Particular average   An ocean marine loss that falls entirely on a particular interest as contrasted with a general average loss that falls on all parties to the voyage.

Particular risk   A risk that affects only individuals and not the entire community.

Past-service credits   Pension benefits awarded to employees based on service with the employer prior to the inception of the plan.

Paul v. Virginia   Landmark legal decision of 1869 establishing the right of the states, and not the federal government, to regulate insurance. Ruled that insurance was not interstate commerce.

Pension accrual benefit   A diability income benefit that makes a pension contribution so that the disabled employee's pension benefit remains intact.

Pension Benefit Guaranty Corporation (PBGC)   A federal corporation that guarantees the payment of vested or nonforfeitable benefits up to certain limits if a private defined benefit pension plan is terminated.

Percentage participation clause   Provision in a health insurance policy that requires the insured to pay a certain percentage of eligible medical expenses in excess of the deductible. Also called coinsurance.

Peril   Cause or source of loss.

Personal injury   Injury for which legal liability arises (such as for false arrest, detention or imprisonment, malicious prosecution, libel, slander, defamation of character, violation of the right of privacy, and unlawful entry or eviction) and which may be covered by an endorsement to the homeowners policy.

Personal liability insurance   Liability insurance that protects the insured for an amount up to policy limits against a claim or suit for damages because of bodily injury or property damage caused by the insured's negligence. This coverage is provided by Section II of the homeowners policy.

Personal lines   Property and liability insurance coverages that insure the home and personal property of individuals and families or provide protection against legal liability.

Personal-producing general agent   Term used to describe an above-average salesperson with a proven sales record who is hired primarily to sell life insurance under a contract that provides both direct and overriding commissions.

Personal umbrella policy liability   Policy designed to provide protection against a catastrophic lawsuit or judgment, whose coverage ranges generally from $1 million to $10 million and extends to the entire family. Insurance is excess over underlying coverages.

Physical hazard Physical condition that increases the chance of loss.

PIA *See* **Primary insurance amount.**

Point-of-service plan (POS) Establishes a network of preferred providers. If patients see a preferred provider, they pay little or nothing. Outside provider care is covered, but at a substantially higher deductible and copayment.

Policy loan Cash value of a life insurance policy that can be borrowed by the policyowner in lieu of surrendering the policy.

Policyowners' surplus Difference between an insurance company's assets and its liabilities.

Pooling Spreading of losses incurred by the few over the entire group, so that in the process, average loss is substituted for actual loss.

Preexisting condition Physical or mental condition of an insured that existed prior to issuance of a policy.

Preexisting-conditions clause Contractual provision in a health insurance policy stating that preexisting conditions are not covered or are covered only after the policy has been in force for a specified period.

Preferred risks Individuals whose mortality experience is expected to be lower than average.

Primary and excess insurance Type of other-insurance provision that requires the primary insurer to pay first in the case of a loss; when the policy limits under the primary policy are exhausted, the excess insurer pays.

Primary beneficiary Beneficiary of a life insurance policy who is first entitled to receive the policy proceeds on the insured's death.

Primary insurance amount (PIA) Monthly cash benefit paid to a retired worker at the full retirement age, or to a disabled worker eligible for benefits under the Old-Age, Survivors, and Disability Insurance (OASDI) program.

Principal The bonded party in the purchase of a surety bond who agrees to perform certain acts or fulfill certain obligations.

Principal of indemnity States that the insurer agrees to pay no more than the actual amount of the loss. The insured should not profit from a covered loss but should be restored to approximately the same financial position that existed prior to the loss.

Prior-approval law Law for regulating insurance rates under which the rates must be filed and approved by the state insurance department before they can be used.

Pro rata liability clause Clause in a property insurance policy that makes each company insuring the same interest in a property liable according to the proportion that its insurance bears to the total amount of insurance on the property.

Probationary period Waiting period of one to six months required of an employee before he or she is allowed to participate in a group insurance plan.

Products-completed operations hazard Liability losses that occur away from the premises and arise out of the insured's product or work after the insured has relinquished possession of the product, or the work has been completed.

Products liability The legal liability of manufacturers, wholesalers, and retailers to persons who are injured or who incur property damage from defective products.

Prospective reserve In life insurance, the difference between the present value of future benefits and the present value of future net premiums.

Protection and indemnity insurance (P&I) Coverage that can be added to an ocean marine insurance policy to provide broad, comprehensive liability insurance on an indemnity basis for property damage and bodily injury to third parties.

Proximate cause Factor causing damage to property for which there is an unbroken chain of events between the occurrence of an insured peril and damage or destruction of the property.

Public adjustor Claims adjustor who represents the insured rather than the insurance company and is paid a fee based on the amount of the claim settlement. A public adjustor may be employed in those cases where the insured and insurer cannot resolve a dispute over a claim, or if the insured needs technical assistance in a complex loss situation.

Public official bond Type of surety bond guaranteeing that public officials will faithfully perform their duties for the protection of the public.

Pure no-fault plan The injured person cannot sue at all, regardless of the seriousness of the claim, and no payments are made for pain and suffering.

Pure premium That portion of the insurance rate needed to pay losses and loss-adjustment expenses.

Pure premium method of rating A rating system in property and casualty insurance. The pure premium is determined by dividing the dollar amount of incurred losses and loss-adjustment expenses by the number of exposure units.

Pure risk Situation in which there are only the possibilities of loss or no loss.

Rate Price per unit of insurance.

Rate making Process by which insurance pricing or premium rates are determined for an insurance company.

Ratio percentage test A test that a qualified pension plan must meet to receive favorable income tax treatment. The pension plan must benefit a percentage of employees that is at least 70 percent of the highly compensated employees covered by the plan.

Readjustment period One- to two-year period immediately following the breadwinner's death during which time the family should receive approximately the same amount of income it received while the breadwinner was alive.

Reasonable and customary charges Payment of physicians' normal fees if they are reasonable and customary, such as a fee that does not exceed the 80th or 90th percentile for a similar procedure performed by physicians in the area.

Rebating A practice—illegal in virtually all states—of giving a premium reduction or some other financial advantage to an individual as an inducement to purchase the policy.

Reciprocal exchange Unincorporated mutual insuring organization in which insurance is exchanged among members and which is managed by an attorney-in-fact.

Regression analysis Method of characterizing the relationship between two or more variables, and then using this characterization as a predictor.

Reinstatement clause Contractual provision in a life insurance policy that permits the owner to reinstate a lapsed policy within five years if certain requirements are fulfilled; for example, evidence of insurability is required and overdue premiums plus interest must be paid.

Reinstatement provision   Provision of a health insurance policy that allows the insured to reinstate a lapsed policy by payment of premium either without an application or with an application.

Reinsurance   The shifting of part or all of the insurance originally written by one insurer to another insurer.

Reinsurance facility   Pool for placing high-risk automobile drivers that arranges for an insurer to accept all applicants for insurance. Underwriting losses are shared by all auto insurers in the state.

Replacement-cost insurance   Property insurance by which the insured is indemnified on the basis of replacement cost with no deduction for depreciation.

Reporting form   Coverage for commercial property insurance that requires the insured to report monthly or quarterly the value of the insured inventory, with automatic adjustment of insurance amount to cover the accurately reported inventory.

Representations   Statements made by an applicant for insurance, for example, in life insurance, occupation, state of health, and family history.

Residual disability   Residual disability means that a proportionate disability-income benefit is paid to an insured whose earned income is reduced because of an accident or illness.

Residual market   The residual market refers to plans in which auto insurers participate to make insurance available to high-risk drivers who are unable to obtain coverage in the standard markets. Examples include an automobile insurance plan, joint underwriting association, and reinsurance facility. Also called the **shared market.**

Res ipsa loquitur   Literally, the thing speaks for itself. Under this doctrine, the very fact that the event occurred establishes a presumption of negligence on behalf of the defendant.

Retained limit   Term found in an umbrella policy that refers to (1) the total limits of the underlying insurance or any other insurance available to the insured, or (2) the deductible stated in the declarations if the loss is covered by the umbrella policy but not by any underlying insurance or other insurance, whichever is applicable.

Retention   Risk management technique in which the firm retains part or all of the losses resulting from a given loss exposure. Used when no other method is available, the worst possible loss is not serious, and losses are highly predictable.

Retention limit   Amount of insurance retained by a ceding company for its own account in a reinsurance operation.

Retirement test   *See* **Earnings test.**

Retrocession   Process by which a reinsurer obtains reinsurance from another company.

Retrospective rating   Type of merit-rating method in which the insured's loss experience during the current policy period determines the actual premium paid for that period.

Retrospective reserve   In life insurance, the net premiums collected by the insurer for a particular block of policies, plus interest earnings at an assumed rate, less the amounts paid out as death claims.

Revocable beneficiary   Beneficiary designation allowing the policyowner the right to change the beneficiary without consent of the beneficiary.

Rider   Term used in insurance contracts to describe a document that amends or changes the original policy. *See also* **Endorsement.**

Risk   Uncertainty concerning the occurrence of a loss.

Risk-based capital   Under NAIC standards, insurers are required to have a certain amount of capital that is based on the riskiness of their investments and operations.

Risk control   Risk management techniques that reduce the frequency and severity of losses, such as avoidance, loss prevention, and an automatic sprinkler system.

Risk financing   Risk management techniques that provide for the funding of losses after they occur, such as retention, noninsurance transfers, and commercial insurance.

Risk management   Systematic process for the identification and evaluation of loss exposures faced by an organization or individual, and for the selection and implementation of the most appropriate techniques for treating such exposures.

Risk management information system   Computerized data base that permits the risk manager to store and analyze risk management data and to use such data to predict future loss levels.

Risk map   Map used in risk management that shows grids detailing the potential frequency and severity of risks faced by the organization.

Robbery   Taking of property from a person by someone who has (1) caused or threatens to cause bodily harm to that person, or (2) committed an obviously unlawful act witnessed by that person.

Roth IRA   An IRA in which the contributions are not income-tax deductible but distributions are received income-tax free if certain conditions are met.

Safe driver plan   Plan in which the automobile premiums paid are based on the insured's driving record and on the records of those living with the insured.

Savings bank life insurance   Life insurance originally sold by mutual savings banks in Massachusetts, New York, and Connecticut. Now sold in other states as well.

Scheduled personal property endorsement   Special coverage added at the insured's request to a homeowners policy to insure items specifically listed. Used to insure valuable property such as jewelry, furs, and paintings.

Schedule rating   Type of merit-rating method in which each exposure is individually rated and given a basis rate that is then modified by debits or credits for undesirable or desirable physical features.

Second-injury fund   State funds paying the excess amount of benefit awarded an employee for a second injury if the disability is greater than that caused by the second injury alone. Its purpose is to encourage employers to hire handicapped workers.

Section 401(k) plan   A qualified profit-sharing or thrift plan that allows participants the option of putting money into the plan or receiving the funds as cash. The employee can voluntarily elect to have his or her salary reduced up to some maximum annual limit, which is then invested in the employer's Section 401(k) plan.

Securitization of risk   Term to describe the transfer of an insurable risk to the capital markets through the creation of a financial instrument, such as a catastrophe bond, futures contract, options contract, or other financial instrument.

Self-insurance   Retention program in which the employer self-funds or pays part or all of its losses.

Self-insured retention   *See* **Retained limit.**

SEP   *See* **Simplified Employee Pension.**

Separate account   Variation of the deposit administration pension plan arrangement in which pension funds are segregated so that account assets are not commingled with insurance company's general assets and can be invested separately.

Service benefits   Health insurance benefits that pay hospital charges or payment for care received by the insured directly to the hospital or providers of care. The plan provides service rather than cash benefits to the insured.

Settlement options   Ways in which life insurance policy proceeds can be paid other than in a lump sum, including interest, fixed period, fixed amount, and life income options.

SEUA case   *See* **South-Eastern Underwriters Association (SEUA) case.**

Shared market   *See* **Residual market.**

SIMPLE retirement plan   A qualified retirement plan for smaller employers who are exempt from most nondiscrimination and administrative rules. Employees can elect to contribute up to certain annual limits. The employer has the option of (1) matching the employee's contribution on a dollar-for-dollar basis up to 3 percent of salary, or (2) making a nonelective contribution of 2 percent of salary for all eligible employees.

Simplified Employee Pension (SEP)   An employer-sponsored individual retirement account that meets certain requirements. Paperwork is reduced for employers who wish to cover employees in a retirement plan.

Single limit   The total amount of liability insurance that applies to the entire accident without a separate limit for each person. The total amount of insurance applies to both bodily injury liability and property damage liability.

Single-premium deferred annuity   A retirement annuity that is purchased with a single premium with benefits to start at some future date.

Single-premium whole life insurance   A whole life policy that provides lifetime protection with a single premium payment.

Social insurance   Government insurance programs with certain characteristics that distinguish them from other government insurance programs. Programs are generally compulsory; specific earmarked taxes fund the programs; benefits are heavily weighted in favor of low-income groups; and programs are designed to achieve certain social goals.

Soft insurance market   A period during which underwriting standards are more liberal and premiums are relatively low. *See also* **hard insurance market** and **underwriting cycle.**

South-Eastern Underwriters Association (SEUA) case   Legal landmark decision of 1944 overruling the Paul v. Virginia ruling and finding that insurance was interstate commerce when conducted across state lines and was subject to federal regulation.

Special coverage policy   See "**All-risks policy.**"

Speculative risk   Situation in which either profit or loss are clear possibilities.

Split limits   The amounts of insurance for bodily injury liability and property damage liability are stated separately.

Stop-loss limit   Modification of the coinsurance provision in major medical plans that places a dollar limit on the maximum amount that an individual must pay.

Straight deductible   Deductible in an insurance contract by which the insured must pay a certain number of dollars of loss before the insurer is required to make a payment.

Subjective risk   Uncertainty based on one's mental condition or state of mind.

Subrogation   Substitution of the insurer in place of the insured for the purpose of claiming indemnity from a negligent third party for a loss covered by insurance.

Suicide clause   Contractual provision in a life insurance policy stating that if the insured commits suicide within two years after the policy is issued, the face amount of insurance will not be paid; only premiums paid will be refunded.

Supplemental major medical insurance   Group health insurance plan that supplements the benefits provided by a basic medical expense plan. It provides more comprehensive benefits with higher limits and is designed for a catastrophic loss.

Supplementary Medical Insurance   Part B of the Medicare program that covers physicians' fees and other related medical services. Most eligible Medicare recipients are automatically included unless they voluntarily refuse this coverage.

Surety   Party who agrees to answer for the debt, default, or obligation of another in the purchase of a bond.

Surety bond   Bond that provides monetary compensation if the bonded party fails to perform certain acts.

Surgical expense insurance   Health insurance that provides for payment of physicians' fees for surgical operations performed in a hospital or elsewhere.

Surplus line broker   Specialized insurance broker licensed to place business with a nonadmitted insurer (a company not licensed to do business in the state).

Surrender cost index   Method of measuring the cost of an insurance policy to an insured if the policy is surrendered at the end of some specified time period. The time value of money is taken into consideration.

Term insurance   Type of life insurance that provides temporary protection for a specified number of years. It is usually renewable and convertible.

Terminal reserve   In life insurance, the reserve at the end of any given policy year.

Theft   Unlawful taking of money, securities, or other property to the deprivation of the insured; includes burglary, robbery. *See also* **Burglary; Robbery.**

Time limit on certain defenses provision   Provision in an individual health insurance policy that prohibits the company from canceling the policy or denying a claim on the basis of a preexisting condition or misstatement in the application after the policy has been in force for two or three years, with the exception of fraudulent misstatement.

Total disability   Condition of an insured that makes him or her completely unable to perform all duties of the insured's own occupation or unable to perform the duties of any occupation for which the insured is reasonably fitted by training, education, and experience.

Traditional IRA   An IRA that allows workers to deduct part or all of their IRA contributions if taxable compensation is under a certain limit. Distributions are taxed as ordinary income.

Traditional net cost method   Traditional method of determining cost to an insured of a life insurance policy, determined by subtracting the total dividends received and cash value at the end of a period from the total premiums paid during that period.

Treaty reinsurance   Type of reinsurance in which the primary company must cede insurance to the reinsurer and the reinsurer must accept. The ceding company is automatically reinsured according to the terms of the reinsurance contract.

Trespasser   A person who enters or remains on the owner's property without the owner's consent.

Trust   Arrangement in which property is legally transferred to a trustee who manages it for the benefit of named beneficiaries for their security and to insure competent management of estate property.

Trust-fund plan   Type of pension plan in which all pension contributions are deposited with a trustee who invests the funds according to a trust agreement between employer and trustee. Benefits are paid directly out of the trust fund.

Twisting   Illegal practice of inducing a policyowner to drop an existing policy in one company and take out a new policy in another through misrepresentation or incomplete information.

Ultimate net loss   The total amount that the insurer is legally obligated to pay in a commercial umbrella policy.

Underinsured motorists coverage   Coverage that can be added to the personal auto policy. Coverage pays damages for a bodily injury to an insured caused by the ownership or operation of an underinsured vehicle by another driver. The negligent driver may have insurance that meets the state's financial responsibility or compulsory insurance law requirement, but the amount carried is insufficient to cover the loss sustained by the insured.

Underwriting   The selection and classification of applicants for insurance through a clearly stated company policy consistent with company objectives.

Underwriting cycle   A term to describe the cyclical pattern in underwriting standards, premium levels, and profitability. *See also* **Hard insurance market; Soft insurance market.**

Unearned premium reserve   Liability reserve of an insurance company that represents the unearned part of gross premiums on all outstanding policies at the time of valuation.

Unified tax credit   Tax credit that can be used to reduce the amount of the federal estate or gift tax. Also called **applicable credit amount.**

Unilateral contract   Only one party makes a legally enforceable promise.

Uninsured motorists coverage   That part of the personal auto policy designed to insure against bodily injury caused by an uninsured motorist, a hit-and-run driver, or a driver whose company is insolvent.

Unisex rating   A rating system in which the pooled loss experience of both sexes is used to determine the rates charged.

Unit-owners form   *See* **Homeowners 6 policy.**

Universal life insurance   A flexible-premium whole life policy that provides lifetime protection under a contract that separates the protection and saving components. The contract is an interest-sensitive product that unbundles the protection, saving, and expense components.

Unsatisfied judgment fund   Fund established by a small number of states to compensate accident victims who have exhausted all other means of recovery.

Utmost good faith   That a higher degree of honesty is imposed on both parties to an insurance contract than is imposed on parties to other contracts.

Value at risk (VAR)   The value of the worst probable loss likely to occur in a given time period under regular market conditions at some level of confidence.

Valued policy   Policy that pays the face amount of insurance, regardless of actual cash value, if a total loss occurs.

Valued policy laws   Laws requiring payment to an insured of the face amount of insurance if a total loss to real property occurs from a peril specified in the law, even though the policy may state that only actual cash value will be paid.

Vanishing-premium policy   A whole life policy in which the premium vanishes or disappears after a number of years.

Variable annuity   Annuity whose periodic lifetime payments vary depending on the level of common stock prices (or other investments), based on the assumption that cost of living and common stock prices are correlated in the long run. Its purpose is to provide an inflation hedge.

Variable life insurance   Life insurance policy in which the death benefit and cash surrender values vary according to the investment experience of a separate account maintained by the insurer.

Verbal threshold   A suit for damages is allowed only in serious cases, such as those involving death, dismemberment, etc.

Vesting   Characteristic of pension plans guaranteeing the employee's right to part or all of the employer's contributions if employment terminates prior to retirement.

Vicarious liability   Responsibility for damage done by the driver of an automobile that is imputed to the vehicle's owner.

Waiver   Voluntary relinquishment of a known legal right.

Waiver-of-premium provision   Benefit that can be added to a life insurance policy providing for waiver of all premiums coming due during a period of total disability of the insured.

War clause   Restriction in a life insurance policy that excludes payment if the insured dies as a direct result of war.

Warranty   Statement of fact or a promise made by the insured, which is part of the insurance contract and which must be true if the insurer is to be liable under the contract.

Weather option   Provides a payment if a specified weather contingency (e.g. temperatures higher or lower than normal) occurs.

Workers compensation insurance   Insurance that covers payment of all workers compensation and other benefits that the employer must legally provide to covered employees who are occupationally disabled.

"Associate in Risk Management" (ARM)
designation, 80
Association captive, 48
Assumption-of-risk doctrine, 128, 143, 556
Attachment bond, 342
Attained-age method, 371
Attending physician's report, 589
Attorney fees, under no-fault laws, 237
Attractive nuisance doctrine, 129
Auctioneer's bond, 343
Automatic cost-of-living adjustment, Social
Security, 538
Automatic policy termination, under personal
auto policy, 222
Automatic premium loan, 401
Automatic reinsurance treaties, 603
Automobile accidents
damage from, 163
by driver age, 244
duties after, 221–222, 224, 225
staged, 31, 32
victims, compensating, 231–240
Automobile business vehicle exclusion, 207–208
Automobile coverage, misrepresentation in
application for, 96
Automobile damage coverage, 225
under Personal Auto Policy, 214–221
Automobile exclusion, commercial general
Liability policy, 307
Automobile insurance, 27, 202–229. *See also*
Personal auto policy (PAP)
commercial, 316–319
complaints, 638–639
cost of, 241–247
definition of insured person under, 112
discounts, 248–250
expenditures, by state, 243–244
for high-risk drivers, 240–241
no-fault, 235–240, 252
premiums, 253
saving on, 248
shopping for, 247–252, 253
society and, 230–255
Automobile insurance plan, 240–241
Automobile insurers, specialty, 241
Automobile owners and operators, 129–130
Automobile use, insurance cost and, 245
Average benefit test, 511
Average indexed monthly earnings (AIME), 538
Average value method, 620
Aviation exclusions, 399
Aviation insurance, 319–320, 328
Aviation market, 598
Avoidance, 46, 56, 58
as a method of handling risk, 13

B
Back-end surrender charge, 377–378
Bail bond, 342
Bailee forms, 295
Bailees, property held by, 293
Bailee's customers policy, 295, 320–321, 328
Bailee's liability policy, 295
"Balance sheet test," 49
Bankruptcies
asbestos, 141
medical bills and, 10

Basic medical expense insurance, 487–488
Belth, Joseph M., 370, 429
Benchmark prices, 424
Beneficiary designation, 398–399
Benefit formulas, retirement, 512–513
Benefit period, 462
under disability-income insurance, 468
Benefits
earnings-related, 534
limits on, 514, 524–525
prescribed by law, 534
Social Security, 536–545
unemployment insurance, 553
Bernstein, Peter L., 2, 42
Betterment, 217, 220
Bid bond, 343
Bierce, Ambrose, 19
Bilateral contracts, 99
Bill of rights, patients', 498
Binder, 98
Blackout period, 356
Blanket basis, 335
Blanket basis insurance, 260
Blended families, premature death and, 354
"Block" policies, inland marine, 293
Blue Cross and Blue Shield plans, 486, 507, 576
Boards of directors
directors and officers (D&O) liability
and, 327
lax governance by, 140–141, 144
Boat insurance, 270. *See also* Watercraft *entries*
Boat owners insurance, 27
Boat owners package policy, 260–261, 270
Bodily injury and property damage liability,
commercial umbrella policy exclusions, 322
Bodily injury claimants, net payment to, 238
Bodily injury coverage, commercial general
liability policy, 306–307
Bodily injury exclusion, 183, 207
Boiler and machinery insurance, 288
Boiler insurance, 28
BOP. *See* Businessowners policy (BOP)
Brands and labels coverage, 290
Breadwinner's death, readjustment period
after, 356
Breast cancer, 138
Broad coverage, under umbrella policy, 267
Broad evidence rule, 90
Brochures, state insurance department, 637
Brokers, 69, 577
licensing of, 636
Builders risk insurance, 287
Builders risk reporting form, 287
Building and personal property coverage form,
278–282, 298
Building collapse, coverage for, 159
Building construction, 611
Building coverage, under businessowners
policy, 296
Bulk reinsurance, 572
Burglary, safe, 335, 337, 344
Burglary insurance, 28
Burns, George, 509
Business, aviation insurance for, 320
Business activities exclusion, 180
Business auto coverage form, 317–318, 328

Business firms, incorporation of, 15
Business floaters, 295
Business income
from dependent properties, 287
extended, 285
insurance, 284–287
loss exposures, 45
loss of, 285
miscellaneous coverages, 287
Business income (and extra expense) coverage
form, 284–285, 298
Business income and extra expense-extra expense
only, 289
Business liability coverage form, 322
Business liability exclusion, ISO personal
umbrella policy, 269
Business liability insurance, 297
Businessowners policy (BOP), 295–297, 298, 328
liability insurance, 322–323
Business personal property, 280
coverage, under businessowners policy, 296
Business records, exclusion of, 157
Business risk, 633
Business vehicle exclusion, 208

C
Cafeteria plans, 502–503, 505
Calculable chance of loss, 23
Calculators on the Internet, interactive, 360
Calendar-year deductible, 114, 463, 489
Camera and musical instrument dealers coverage
form, 294
Cameras, 260
Camper exclusion, 163
Cancellation as to any employee provision, 339
Cancellation conditions, 170
Cancellation of personal auto policy, 222, 225
Cancer policy, 474
Cap, equity indexed annuity, 443
Capacity, insurance industry, 68
Capital budgeting, 75
Capital needs analysis, 359
Capital-raising transactions, 598–599
Capital retention approach, 359–360, 366
Capitation fee, 490
Captive.com, 60
Captive insurer, 48–49, 58
tax treatment of, 49
Care, custody, and control exclusion, ISO
personal umbrella policy, 269
Career-average earnings, 513
Cargo insurance, 291
Car number and type, insurance cost and, 246
Case, John, 333
Case reserves, 620
Cash-balance plans, 518–520, 528
Cash dividend, 401
Cash flows, analyzing, 78
Cash needs, life insurance and, 357, 358
Cash option, 437
Cash or deferred arrangement (CODA), 528
Cash refund option, 438
Cash surrender value, 373
Cash value(s), 364
actual, 89–90, 166
policy surrender for, 403